Lecture Notes in Computer Science　　13508

More information about this series at https://link.springer.com/bookseries/558

Yevgeniy Dodis · Thomas Shrimpton (Eds.)

Advances in Cryptology – CRYPTO 2022

42nd Annual International Cryptology Conference, CRYPTO 2022
Santa Barbara, CA, USA, August 15–18, 2022
Proceedings, Part II

Springer

Editors
Yevgeniy Dodis
New York University
New York, NY, USA

Thomas Shrimpton
University of Florida
Gainesville, FL, USA

ISSN 0302-9743   ISSN 1611-3349 (electronic)
Lecture Notes in Computer Science
ISBN 978-3-031-15978-7   ISBN 978-3-031-15979-4 (eBook)
https://doi.org/10.1007/978-3-031-15979-4

This Springer imprint is published by the registered company Springer Nature Switzerland AG
The registered company address is: Gewerbestrasse 11, 6330 Cham, Switzerland

Preface

The 42nd International Cryptology Conference (CRYPTO 2022) was held at the University of California, Santa Barbara, California, USA, during August 15–18, 2022. The conference had a hybrid format, with some presentations made in person, and some delivered virtually. CRYPTO 2022 was sponsored by the International Association for Cryptologic Research (IACR). The conference was preceded by two days of workshops on various topics.

The conference set new records for both submissions and publications: 455 papers were submitted, and 100 were accepted. Two papers were merged into a single joint paper. Three pairs of papers were soft-merged, meaning that they were written separately, but only one paper in each pair was given a presentation slot at the conference. This resulted in 96 presentations, a record by some margin for a non-virtual edition of Crypto. It took a Program Committee of 72 cryptography experts working with 435 external reviewers almost three months to select the accepted papers. We Chairs extend our heartfelt gratitude for the effort and professionalism displayed by the Program Committee; it was our pleasure to be your Chairs.

We experimented with some new policies and mechanisms this year. The most important had to do with the quality of reviewing, author feedback and interaction with the authors.

Shortly after the standard doubly-blind reviewing stage, we assigned a unique discussion leader (DL) to every paper. The DL's job was to make sure the paper received a thorough and fair treatment, and to moderate interactive communication between the reviewers and authors (described below). The DL also prepared a "Reviewers' consensus summary", which provided the authors with a concise summary of the discussion, the decision, and overall trajectory of the paper throughout the process. Many authors expressed gratitude for receiving the Reviewers' consensus summary, in addition to the usual reviews and scores. Overall, feedback on our DL experiment was quite positive, and we recommend it to future chairs to adopt this process as well.

We also experimented with an "interactive rebuttal" process. Traditionally, the rebuttal process has consisted of a single round: the authors were provided with the initial reviews, and had one opportunity to respond prior to the final decision. While better than no opportunity to rebut, our opinion is that the traditional process suffers from several important flaws. First, the authors were left to respond in (say) 750 words to multiple reviews that are, each, much longer. Too often, the authors are left to divine what are the *crucial* points to address; getting this wrong can lead to reviewers feeling that the rebuttal has missed (or dismissed) what mattered to them. In any case, the authors had no idea if their rebuttal was correctly focused, let alone convincing, until the decisions and final reviews were released. In many instances, the final reviews gave no signal that the rebuttal had been thoughtfully considered. In our view, and personal experience, the traditional rebuttal process led to frustration on both sides, with reviewers and authors feeling that their time had been wasted. Moreover, it had unclear benefits in terms of helping the PC to pick the best possible program.

To address this, we created a review form that required reviewers to make explicit what were their core concerns and criticisms; and we allowed for multiple, DL-moderated, rounds of communication between the reviewers and the authors.

Our review form had *exactly one* field visible to the authors during the initial rebuttal round. The field was called "Question/Clarifications for Authors", and reviewers were instructed to include *only* those things that had significant bearing upon the reviewer's accept/reject stance. We gave all reviewers detailed guidance on things that *must* be included. For example, any claimed errors, crucial prior work that was not cited, or other objective weaknesses that appeared in the detailed review comments. In addition, the reviewers were instructed to clearly state less objective concerns that factored into their initial score and disposition towards the paper. Thus, the authors should know exactly what to focus upon in their response. While not perfect, the new rebuttal format was a resounding success. Very strong/weak papers typically had very short rebuttals, allowing the PC to focus their time and energy on papers in need of extensive discussion or additional reviews.

In concert with the new review form and detailed review instructions, we also implemented *interactive discussions* between the reviewers and authors. The traditional rebuttal round became the first round of the interactive discussion. One round was enough for a fraction of the papers (primarily papers that were very strong or very weak), but the evaluation of most submissions benefited from numerous rounds: reviewers were able to sharpen their questions, authors were able to address points directly and in greater detail. The whole review process shifted more towards a collegial technical exchange. We did not encounter any problems that we initially feared, e.g., authors spamming the PC with comment. We believe that having the DLs moderate these interactions was important for keeping emotions and egos in check, and for encouraging reviewers to share any significant new concerns with the authors.

A few minor hiccups notwithstanding, the focused review forms and the "interactive rebuttal" mechanism received a lot of positive feedback, and we strongly encourage future chairs to adopt this tradition.

We also mention several smaller details which worked well. First, our review form included a "Brief Score Justification" field that remained reviewer-visible (only) for the entire process. This was a space for reviewers to speak freely, but concisely, about how they came to their scores. As Chairs, we found this extremely useful for getting a quick view of each paper's reviews. Second, we had an early rejection round roughly in the middle of our reviewing process. This allowed us to reject roughly half of submissions, i.e., those that clearly had no chance of being accepted to the final program. The process generally worked, and we tried to err on the side of caution, keeping papers alive if the PC was unsure of their seemingly negative views. For example, we allowed PC members to tag papers that they wanted to keep alive, even to the point of overturning a preliminary decision to early reject. However, we did feel slightly rushed in finalizing the early reject decisions, as we made them after less than two weeks after the initial reviewing round, and less than a week after the initial rebuttal round. Part of this rush was due to late reviews. Thus, we recommend that future chairs give themselves a bit more slack in the schedule, and perhaps add a second (less) early rejection round. Third, we experimented with allowing PC members to have a variable number of submissions, rather than the usual hard limits (e.g., at most one or two). Concretely, at most 4 papers could be submitted; the first paper was "free", but every subsequent paper submitted by the PC member resulted in this PC member getting roughly three more papers to review, and one additional DL appointment. We adopted this policy to make it easier for experts to accept our invitation to join the PC. (As always, the chairs were not allowed to submit papers.) Despite some unexpected difficulties and complaints about this system, most having to do with the logistic difficulty of assigning DLs to PC members with late initial reviews, many PC members told us that they appreciated the flexibility to submit more papers, especially when students were involved. We found no evidence that our system resulted in more accepted papers that were co-authored by the PC members, or any other biases and irregularities. Hence, we found it to be positive, overall.

The Program Committee recognized three papers and their authors for particularly outstanding work

- "Batch Arguments for NP and More from Standard Bilinear Group Assumptions," by Brent Waters and David Wu
- "Breaking Rainbow Takes a Weekend on a Laptop", by Ward Beullens
- "Some Easy Instances of Ideal-SVP and Implications to the Partial Vandermonde Knapsack Problem", by Katharina Boudgoust, Erell Gachon, and Alice Pellet-Mary

We were very pleased to have Yehuda Lindell as the Invited Speaker at CRYPTO 2022, who spoke about "The MPC journey from theoretical foundations to commercial success: a story of science and business".

We would like to express our sincere gratitude to all the reviewers for volunteering their time and knowledge in order to select a great program for 2022. Additionally, we are grateful to the following people for helping to make CRYPTO 2022 a success: Allison Bishop (General Chair, CRYPTO 2022), Kevin McCurley and Kay McKelly (IACR IT experts), Carmit Hazay (Workshops Chair), and Whitney Morris and her staff at UCSB conference services.

We would also like to thank the generous sponsors, all of the authors of the submissions, the rump session chair, the regular session chairs, and the speakers.

August 2022   Yevgeniy Dodis
                                                                   Thomas Shrimpton

Organization

General Chair

Allison Bishop   Proof Trading and City College, CUNY, USA

Program Committee Chairs

Yevgeniy Dodis   New York University, USA
Thomas Shrimpton   University of Florida, USA

Steering Committee

Helena Handschuh   Rambus Inc., USA
Anna Lysyanskaya   Brown University, USA

Program Committee

Shweta Agarwal	IIT Madras, India
Prabhanjan Ananth	University of California Santa Barbara, USA
Saikrishna Badrinarayanan	Visa Research, USA
Lejla Batina	Radboud University, Netherlands
Carsten Baum	Aarhus University, Denmark
Jeremiah Blocki	Purdue University, USA
Alexandra Boldyreva	Georgia Tech, USA
Elette Boyle	IDC Herzliya and NTT Research, Israel
David Cash	University of Chicago, USA
Itai Dinur	Ben-Gurion University, Israel
François Dupressoir	University of Bristol, UK
Nico Döttling	Helmholtz Center for Information Security (CISPA), Germany
Dario Fiore	IMDEA Software Institute, Spain
Ben Fisch	Stanford, USA
Marc Fischlin	TU Darmstadt, Germany
Rosario Gennaro	City College of New York, USA
Divya Gupta	Microsoft Research, India
Felix Günther	ETH Zurich, Switzerland
Mohammad Hajiabadi	University of Waterloo, Canada
Helena Handschuh	Rambus Inc., USA

Ni Trieu	Arizona State University, USA
Yiannis Tselekounis	Carnegie Mellon University, USA
Mayank Varia	Boston University, USA
Xiao Wang	Northwestern University, USA
Daniel Wichs	Northeastern University and NTT Research, USA
David Wu	UT Austin, USA
Shota Yamada	AIST, Japan
Kan Yasuda	NTT Labs, Japan
Kevin Yeo	Google and Columbia University, USA
Eylon Yogev	Bar-Ilan University, Israel
Vassilis Zikas	Purdue University, USA

Additional Reviewers

Masayuki Abe	Mihir Bellare
Calvin Abou Haidar	Adrien Benamira
Anasuya Acharya	Fabrice Benhamouda
Divesh Aggarwal	Huck Bennett
Shashank Agrawal	Ward Beullens
Gorjan Alagic	Tim Beyne
Navid Alamati	Rishabh Bhadauria
Martin R. Albrecht	Amit Singh Bhati
Nicolas Alhaddad	Ritam Bhaumik
Bar Alon	Sai Lakshmi Bhavana Obbattu
Estuardo Alpirez Bock	Jean-Francois Biasse
Jacob Alprerin-Shreiff	Alexander Bienstock
Joel Alwen	Nina Bindel
Ghous Amjad	Nir Bitansky
Kazumaro Aoki	Olivier Blazy
Gal Arnon	Alexander Block
Rotem Arnon-Friedman	Xavier Bonnetain
Arasu Arun	Jonathan Bootle
Thomas Attema	Katharina Boudgoust
Benedikt Auerbach	Christina Boura
Christian Badertscher	Pedro Branco
David Balbás	Konstantinos Brazitikos
Marco Baldi	Jacqueline Brendel
Gustavo Banegas	Marek Broll
Fabio Banfi	Chris Brzuska
Laaysa Bangalore	Ileana Buhan
James Bartusek	Benedikt Bunz
Andrea Basso	Bin-Bin Cai
Christof Beierle	Federico Canale
Amos Beimel	Ran Canetti

Ignacio Cascudo
Gaëtan Cassiers
Dario Catalano
Pyrros Chaidos
Suvradip Chakraborty
Jeff Champion
Benjamin Chan
Alishah Chator
Shan Chen
Weikeng Chen
Yilei Chen
Yu Long Chen
Nai-Hui Chia
Lukasz Chmielewski
Chongwon Cho
Arka Rai Choudhuri
Miranda Christ
Chitchanok Chuengsatiansup
Peter Chvojka
Michele Ciampi
Benoît Cogliati
Ran Cohen
Alex Cojocaru
Sandro Coretti-Drayton
Arjan Cornelissen
Henry Corrigan-Gibbs
Geoffroy Couteau
Elizabeth Crites
Jan Czajkwoski
Joan Daemen
Quang Dao
Pratish Datta
Bernardo David
Nicolas David
Hannah Davis
Koen de Boer
Leo de Castro
Luca De Feo
Gabrielle De Micheli
Jean Paul Degabriele
Patrick Derbez
Jesus Diaz
Jack Doerner
Jelle Don
Jesko Dujmovic

Sebastien Duval
Ted Eaton
Nadia El Mrabet
Reo Eriguchi
Llorenç Escolà Farràs
Daniel Escudero
Saba Eskandarian
Thomas Espitau
Antonio Faonio
Pooya Farshim
Serge Fehr
Peter Fenteany
Rex Fernando
Rune Fiedler
Matthias Fitzi
Nils Fleischhacker
Danilo Francati
Cody Freitag
Tommaso Gagliardoni
Chaya Ganesh
Rachit Garg
Lydia Garms
Luke Garratt
Adria Gascon
Romain Gay
Peter Gaži
Nicholas Genise
Marios Georgiou
Koustabh Ghosh
Ashrujit Ghoshal
Barbara Gigerl
Niv Gilboa
Emanuele Giunta
Aarushi Goel
Eli Goldin
Junqing Gong
Jesse Goodman
Lorenzo Grassi
Alex Grilo
Alex Bredariol Grilo
Aditya Gulati
Sam Gunn
Aldo Gunsing
Siyao Guo
Yue Guo

Chun Guo
Julie Ha
Ben Hamlin
Ariel Hamlin
Abida Haque
Patrick Harasser
Ben Harsha
Eduard Hauck
Julia Hesse
Clemens Hlauschek
Justin Holmgren
Alexander Hoover
Kai Hu
Yuval Ishai
Muhammad Ishaq
Takanori Isobe
Tetsu Iwata
Hakon Jacobsen
Aayush Jain
Ashwin Jha
Dingding Jia
Zhengzhong Jin
Nathan Ju
Fatih Kaleoglu
Daniel Kales
Simon Kamp
Daniel M. Kane
Dimitris Karakostas
Harish Karthikeyan
Shuichi Katsumata
Marcel Keller
Thomas Kerber
Mustafa Khairallah
Hamidreza Amini Khorasgani
Hamidreza Khoshakhlagh
Dakshita Khurana
Elena Kirshanova
Fuyuki Kitagawa
Susumu Kiyoshima
Dima Kogan
Lisa Kohl
Stefan Kolbl
Dimitris Kolonelos
Ilan Komargodski
Chelsea Komlo

Yashvanth Kondi
Venkata Koppula
Daniel Kuijsters
Mukul Kulkarni
Nishant Kumar
Fukang Liu
Norman Lahr
Russell W. F. Lai
Qiqi Lai
Baptiste Lambin
David Lanzenberger
Philip Lazos
Seunghoon Lee
Jooyoung Lee
Julia Len
Tancrède Lepoint
Gaëtan Leurent
Hanjun Li
Songsong Li
Baiyu Li
Xiao Liang
Yao-Ting Lin
Han-Hsuan Lin
Huijia Lin
Xiaoyuan Liu
Meicheng Liu
Jiahui Liu
Qipeng Liu
Zeyu Liu
Yanyi Liu
Chen-Da Liu-Zhang
Alex Lombardi
Sébastien Lord
Paul Lou
Donghang Lu
George Lu
Yun Lu
Reinhard Lüftenegger
Varun Madathil
Monosij Maitra
Giulio Malavolta
Mary Maller
Jasleen Malvai
Nathan Manohar
Deepak Maram

Lorenzo Martinico

Christian Matt

Sahar Mazloom

Kelsey Melissaris

Nicolas Meloni

Florian Mendel

Rebekah Mercer

Pierre Meyer

Charles Meyer-Hilfiger

Peihan Miao

Brice Minaud

Pratyush Mishra

Tarik Moataz

Victor Mollimard

Andrew Morgan

Tomoyuki Morimae

Travis Morrison

Fabrice Mouhartem

Tamer Mour

Pratyay Mukherjee

Marta Mularczyk

Marcel Nageler

Yusuke Naito

Kohei Nakagawa

Mridul Nandi

Varun Narayanan

Patrick Neumann

Gregory Neven

Samuel Neves

Ngoc Khanh Nguyen

Hai Nguyen

Luca Nizzardo

Ariel Nof

Adam O'Neill

Maciej Obremski

Kazuma Ohara

Miyako Ohkubo

Claudio Orlandi

Michele Orrù

Elisabeth Oswald

Morten Øygarden

Alex Ozdemir

Elena Pagnin

Tapas Pal

Jiaxin Pan

Giorgos Panagiotakos

Omer Paneth

Udaya Parampalli

Anat Paskin-Cherniavsky

Alain Passelègue

Sikhar Patranabis

Chris Peikert

Alice Pellet-Mary

Zachary Pepin

Leo Perrin

Giuseppe Persiano

Edoardo Persichetti

Peter Pessl

Thomas Peters

Stjepan Picek

Maxime Plancon

Bertram Poettering

Christian Porter

Eamonn Postlethwaite

Thomas Prest

Robert Primas

Luowen Qian

Willy Quach

Srinivasan Raghuraman

Samuel Ranellucci

Shahram Rasoolzadeh

Deevashwer Rathee

Mayank Rathee

Divya Ravi

Krijn Reijnders

Doreen Riepel

Peter Rindal

Guilherme Rito

Bhaskar Roberts

Felix Rohrbach

Leah Rosenbloom

Mike Rosulek

Adeline Roux-Langlois

Joe Rowell

Lawrence Roy

Tim Ruffing

Keegan Ryan

Yusuke Sakai

Louis Salvail

Simona Samardjiska

Katerina Samari
Olga Sanina
Amirreza Sarencheh
Pratik Sarkar
Yu Sasaki
Tobias Schmalz
Markus Schofnegger
Peter Scholl
Jan Schoone
Phillipp Schoppmann
André Schrottenloher
Jacob Schuldt
Sven Schäge
Gregor Seiler
Joon Young Seo
Karn Seth
Srinath Setty
Aria Shahverdi
Laura Shea
Yaobin Shen
Emily Shen
Sina Shiehian
Omri Shmueli
Ferdinand Sibleyras
Janno Siim
Jad Silbak
Luisa Siniscalchi
Daniel Slamanig
Yifan Song
Min Jae Song
Fang Song
Nicholas Spooner
Lukas Stennes
Igors Stepanovs
Christoph Striecks
Sathya Subramanian
Adam Suhl
George Sullivan
Mehrdad Tahmasbi
Akira Takahashi
Atsushi Takayasu
Abdul Rahman Taleb
Quan Quan Tan
Ewin Tang
Tianxin Tang

Stefano Tessaro
Justin Thaler
Emmanuel Thome
Søren Eller Thomsen
Mehdi Tibouchi
Radu Titiu
Yosuke Todo
Junichi Tomida
Monika Trimoska
Daniel Tschudi
Ida Tucker
Nirvan Tyagi
Rei Ueno
Dominique Unruh
David Urbanik
Wessel van Woerden
Prashant Vasudevan
Serge Vaudenay
Muthu Venkitasubramaniam
Damien Vergnaud
Thomas Vidick
Mikhail Volkhov
Satyanarayana Vusirikala
Riad Wahby
Roman Walch
Hendrik Waldner
Michael Walter
Qingju Wang
Han Wang
Haoyang Wang
Mingyuan Wang
Zhedong Wang
Geng Wang
Hoeteck Wee
Shiyi Wei
Mor Weiss
Chenkai Weng
Benjamin Wesolowski
Lichao Wu
Keita Xagawa
Jiayu Xu
Anshu Yadav
Sophia Yakoubov
Takashi Yamakawa
Trevor Yap Hong Eng

Xiuyu Ye
Albert Yu
Thomas Zacharias
Michal Zajac
Hadas Zeilberger

Mark Zhandry
Yupeng Zhang
Cong Zhang
Bingsheng Zhang
Dionysis Zindros

Sponsor Logos

Contents – Part II

Blockchain

Best Paper Awards

Coding Theory

Public Key Cryptography

Signatures

Secure Messaging

Universally Composable End-to-End Secure Messaging

Ran Canetti, Palak Jain(✉), Marika Swanberg, and Mayank Varia

Boston University, Boston, USA
{canetti,palakj,marikas,varia}@bu.edu

Abstract. We model and analyze the Signal end-to-end messaging protocol within the UC framework. In particular:

- We formulate an ideal functionality that captures end-to-end secure messaging, in a setting with PKI and an untrusted server, against an adversary that has full control over the network and can adaptively and momentarily compromise parties at any time and obtain their entire internal states. In particular our analysis captures the forward secrecy and recovery-of-security properties of Signal and the conditions under which they break.
- We model the main components of the Signal architecture (PKI and long-term keys, the backbone continuous-key-exchange or "asymmetric ratchet," epoch-level symmetric ratchets, authenticated encryption) as individual ideal functionalities that are realized and analyzed separately and then composed using the UC and Global-State UC theorems.
- We show how the ideal functionalities representing these components can be realized using standard cryptographic primitives under minimal hardness assumptions.

Our modeling introduces additional innovations that enable arguing about the security of Signal irrespective of the underlying communication medium, as well as secure composition of dynamically generated modules that share state. These features, together with the basic modularity of the UC framework, will hopefully facilitate the use of both Signal-as-a-whole and its individual components within cryptographic applications.

Two other features of our modeling are the treatment of fully adaptive corruptions, and making minimal use of random oracle abstractions. In particular, we show how to realize continuous key exchange in the plain model, while preserving security against adaptive corruptions.

1 Introduction

Secure communication, namely allowing Alice and Bob to exchange messages securely, over an untrusted communication channel, without having to trust any

This material is based upon work supported by the National Science Foundation under Grants No. 1718135, 1763786, 1801564, 1915763, and 1931714, by the DARPA SIEVE program under Agreement No. HR00112020021, by DARPA and the Naval Information Warfare Center (NIWC) under Contract No. N66001-15-C-4071, and by a Sloan Foundation Research Award.

Y. Dodis and T. Shrimpton (Eds.): CRYPTO 2022, LNCS 13508, pp. 3–33, 2022.
https://doi.org/10.1007/978-3-031-15979-4_1

intermediate component or party, is perhaps the quintessential cryptographic problem. Indeed, constructing and breaking secure communication protocols, as well as modeling security concerns and guarantees, providing a security analysis, and then breaking the modeling and analysis, has been a mainstay of cryptography since its early days.

Successful secure communication protocols have naturally been built to secure existing communication patterns. Indeed, IPSec has been designed to provide IP-layer end-to-end security for general peer-to-peer communication without the need to trust routers and other intermediaries, while SSL (which evolved into TLS) has been designed to secure client-server interactions, especially in the context of web browsing, and PGP has been designed to secure email communication.

Securing the communication over messaging applications poses a very different set of challenges, even for the case of pairwise communication (which is the focus of this work). First, the communicating parties do not typically have any direct communication connection and may not ever be online at the same time. Instead, they can communicate only via an untrusted server. Next, the communication may be intermittent and have large variability in volumes and level of interactivity. At the same time, a received message should be processed immediately and locally. Furthermore, connections may span very long periods of time, during which it is reasonable to assume that the endpoint devices would be periodically hacked or otherwise compromised – and hopefully later regain security.

The Signal protocol has been designed to give a response to these specific challenges of secure messaging, and in doing so it has revolutionized the concept of secure communication over the Internet in many ways. Built on top of predecessors like Off-The-Record [14], the Signal protocol is currently used to transmit hundreds of billions of messages per day [49].

Modeling the requirements of secure messaging in general, and analyzing the security properties of the Signal protocol in particular, has proved to be challenging and has inspired multiple analytical works [1–3,7,10,11,13,15,17,25–33,35–37,46–48,52–55,57]. Some of these works directly address the Signal architecture and realization, whereas others propose new cryptographic primitives that are inspired by Signal's various modules.

The Need for Composable Security Analysis. Standalone security analyses of the Signal protocol are not always sufficient to capture the security of an entire messaging ecosystem that includes (components of) the Signal protocol. People typically participate concurrently in several conversations spanning several multiplatform chat services (e.g., smartphone and web), and the subtleties between a chat service and the underlying messaging protocol have led to network and systems security issues (e.g., [31,32,40]). For example, the Signal protocol is combined with other cryptographic protocols in WhatsApp [56] to perform abuse reporting or Status [50] and Slyo [51] to perform cryptocurrency transactions and Tor-style onion routing.

Moreover, Signal isn't always employed as a single monolithic protocol. Rather, variations and subcomponents of the Signal protocol are used within the Noise protocol family [45], file sharing services like Keybase [38] (which performs less frequent ratcheting), and videoconferencing services like Zoom [39] (which isn't concerned with asynchrony).

This state of affairs seems to call for a security analysis within a framework that allows for modular analysis and composable security guarantees. First steps in this direction were taken by the work of Jost, Maurer, and Mularczyk [37] that defines an abstract ratcheting service within the Constructive Cryptography framework [41,42], and concurrent work by Bienstock et al. [12] that formulates an ideal functionality of the Signal protocol within the UC framework (see Sect. 1.5 for details). However, neither of these works give a modular decomposition of Signal into its basic components (as described in [44].)

The Apparent Non-modularity of Signal. One of the main sticking points when modeling and analyzing Signal in a composable fashion is that the protocol purposefully breaks away from the traditional structure of a short-lived "key exchange" module followed by a longer-lived module that primarily encrypts and decrypts messages using symmetric authenticated encryption. Instead, it features an intricate "continuous key exchange" module where shared keys are continually being updated, in an effort to provide forward security (i.e., preventing an attacker from learning past messages), as well as enabling the parties to quickly regain security as soon as the attacker loses access. Furthermore, Signal's process of updating the shared keys crucially depends on feedback from the "downstream" authenticated encryption module. This creates a seemingly inherent circularity between the key exchange and the authenticated encryption modules, and gets in the way of basing the security of Signal on traditional components such as authenticated symmetric encryption, authenticated key exchange, and key-derivation functions.

Security of Signal in Face of Adaptive Corruptions. Another potentially thorny aspect of the security of secure messaging protocols (Signal included) is the need to protect against an adversary that decides whom and when to corrupt, adaptively, based on all the communication seen so far. Indeed, not only is standard semantic security not known to imply security in this setting: there exist encryption schemes that are semantically secure (under reasonable intractability assumptions) but completely break in such a setting [34].

1.1 This Work

This work proposes a modular analysis of the Signal protocol and its components using the language of universally composable (UC) security [18,19]. We focus on modeling Signal at the level specified in their documentation [44] (i.e., not limited to any single choice, of cipher suite), taking care to adhere to the abstractions within the specification.

We provide an ideal functionality, $\mathcal{F}_{SM}$, for secure messaging along with individual ideal functionalities that capture each module within Signal's architecture. We then compose the modules to realize the top-level secure messaging functionality and demonstrate how to realize the modules in a manner consistent with the Signal specification [44]. Our instantiation achieves adaptive security against transient corruptions while making minimal use of the random oracle model. This combination of composability and modularity makes Signal and its components conveniently plug-and-play: future analyses can easily re-purpose or swap out instantiations of the modules in this work without needing to redo most of the security analysis.

In the process, we propose a new abstraction for Signal's continuous key derivation module, which we call a Cascaded PRF-PRG (CPRFG), and we show that it suffices for Signal's continuous key exchange module to achieve adaptive security. We also show how to construct CPRFGs from PRGs and puncturable PRFs. This may be of independent interest.

The rest of the Introduction is organized as follows. Section 1.2 presents and motivates our formulation of $\mathcal{F}_{SM}$. Section 1.3 presents and motivates the formulation of the individual modules, and describes how these modules can be realized. Section 1.5 discusses related work.

1.2 On the Ideal Secure Messaging Functionality, $\mathcal{F}_{SM}$

We provide an ideal functionality $\mathcal{F}_{SM}$ that captures end-to-end secure messaging, with some Signal-specific caveats. The goal here is to provide idealized security guarantees that will allow the analysis of existing protocols that use Signal, as well as enable Signal (or any protocol that realizes $\mathcal{F}_{SM}$) to be readily usable as a component within other protocols in security-preserving manner.

When a party asks to encrypt a message, $\mathcal{F}_{SM}$ returns a string to the party that represents the encapsulated message. When a party asks to decrypt (and provides the representative string), the functionality checks whether the provided string matches a prior encapsulation, and returns the original message in case of a match. The encapsulation string is generated via adversarially provided code that doesn't get any information about the encapsulated message, thereby guaranteeing secrecy.

Simple User Interface. The above encapsulation and decapsulation requests are the only ways that a parent protocol interacts with $\mathcal{F}_{SM}$. In particular, the parent protocol is not required to keep state related to the session, such as epoch-ids or sequence numbers. In addition to simplicity, this imparts the additional guarantee that a badly designed parent protocol cannot harm the security of a protocol realising $\mathcal{F}_{SM}$.

Abstracting Away Network Delivery. The fact that $\mathcal{F}_{SM}$ models a secure messaging scheme as a set of local algorithms (an encapsulation algorithm and a decapsulation one) substantially simplifies traditional UC modeling of secure communication, where the communication medium is modeled as part of the service provided by the protocol and the actual communication is abstracted away.

Furthermore, the fact that $\mathcal{F}_{SM}$ returns to the parent protocol an actual string (that represents an idealized encapsulated message) allows the parent protocol to further process the string as needed, similarly to what's done in existing systems.

Immediate Decryption. $\mathcal{F}_{SM}$ guarantees that message decapsulation requests are fulfilled locally on the receiver's machine, and are not susceptible to potential network delays. Furthermore, this holds even if only a subset of the messages arrive, and arrival is out of order (as formalized in [1]). To provide this guarantee within the UC framework, we introduce a mechanism that enables $\mathcal{F}_{SM}$ to execute adversarially provided code, without enabling the adversary to prevent immediate fulfillment of a decapsulation request. See more details in Sect. 2.

Modeling of PKI and Long Term Keys. We directly model Signal's specific design for the public keys and associated secret keys that are used to identify parties across multiple sessions. Specifically, we formulate a "PKI" functionality $\mathcal{F}_{DIR}$ that models a public "bulletin board," which stores the long-term, ephemeral, and one-time public keys associated with identities of parties. In addition, we model "long term private key" module $\mathcal{F}_{LTM}$ for each identity. This module stores the private keys associated with the public keys of the corresponding party. Both functionalities are modeled as *global,* namely they are used as subroutines by multiple instances of $\mathcal{F}_{SM}$. This modeling is what allows to tie the two participants of a session to long-term identities. Similarly to [16,24], we treat these modules as incorruptible. It is stressed, however, that, following the Signal architecture, our realization of $\mathcal{F}_{SM}$ calls the $\mathcal{F}_{LTM}$ module of each party exactly once, at the beginning of the session.

Modelling Corruptions. Resilience to recurring but transient break-ins is one of the main design goals of Signal. We facilitate the exposition of these properties as follows. First, we model corruption as an instantaneous event where the adversary learns the entire state of the corrupted party.

The security guarantees for corruption and recovery are then specified as follows. When the adversary instructs $\mathcal{F}_{SM}$ to corrupt a party, it is provided all the messages that have been sent to that party and were not yet received. In addition, the party is marked as compromised until a certain future point in the execution. While compromised, all the messages sent and received by the party are disclosed to the adversary, who can also instruct $\mathcal{F}_{SM}$ to decapsulate ciphertexts to any plaintext of its choice. This captures the fact that as long as any one of the parties is compromised, neither party can securely authenticate incoming messages.

Forward secrecy guarantees that the adversary learns nothing about any messages that have been sent and received by the party until the point of corruption. Furthermore, the adversary obtains no information on the history of the session such as its duration or the long term identity of the peer. In $\mathcal{F}_{SM}$, this is guaranteed because corruption does not provide the adversary with any messages that were previously sent and successfully received.

On the other hand, the specific point by which a compromised party regains its security is Signal-specific and described in more detail within. After this point, the adversary no longer obtains the messages the messages sent and received by the parties; furthermore, the adversary can no longer instruct $\mathcal{F}_{SM}$ to decapsulate forged ciphertexts.

Resilience to Adaptive Corruptions. All the security guarantees provided by $\mathcal{F}_{SM}$ hold in the presence of an adversary that has access to the entire communication among the parties and adaptively decides when and whom to corrupt based on all the communication seen so far. In particular, we do not impose any restrictions on when a party can be corrupted.

Signal-Specific Limitations. The properties discussed so far relate to the general task of secure messaging. In addition, $\mathcal{F}_{SM}$ incorporates the following two relaxations that represent known weaknesses that are specific to the Signal design.

First, Signal does not give parties a way to detect whether their peers have received forged messages in their name during corruption. (Such situations may occur when either party was corrupted in the past and then recovered.) This represents a known weakness of Signal [15,31]. Consequently, $\mathcal{F}_{SM}$ exhibits a similar behavior.

Second, as remarked in the Signal documentation [44], when one of the parties is compromised, an adversary can "fork" the messaging session. That is, the adversary can create a person-in-the-middle situation where both parties believe they are talking with each other in a joint session, and yet they are actually both talking with the adversary. Furthermore, this can remain the case indefinitely, even when no party is compromised anymore. (In fact, we know this situation is inherent in an unauthenticated network with transient attacks, at least without repeated use of a long-term uncompromised public key [20].) While such a situation is mentioned in the Signal design documents, pinpointing and analyzing the conditions under which forking occurs has not been formally done before our work and the concurrent work by Bienstock et al. [12]. In our modeling, $\mathcal{F}_{SM}$ forks when one of the parties is compromised, and at the same time the other party successfully decapsulates a forged incoming message with an "epoch ID" that is different than the one used by the sender. In that case, $\mathcal{F}_{SM}$ remains forked indefinitely, without any additional corruptions.

1.3 Realizing $\mathcal{F}_{SM}$, Modularly

Signal's strong forward secrecy and recovery from compromise guarantees are obtained via an intricate mechanism where shared keys are continually being updated, and each key is used to encapsulate at most a single message.

To help keep the parties in sync regarding which key to use for a given message, the conversation is logically partitioned into sending epochs, where each sending epoch is associated with one of the two parties, and consists of all the messages sent by that party from the end of its previous sending epoch until the first time this party successfully decapsulates an incoming message that belongs to the peer's latest sending epoch.

Within each sending epoch, the keys are pseudorandomly generated one after the other in a chain. The initial chaining key for each epoch is generated from a 'root chain' that ratchets forward every time a new sending epoch starts. Each ratcheting of the root chain involves a Diffie-Hellman key exchange; the resulting Diffe-Hellman secret is then used as input to the root ratchet (along with an existing chaining value). The public values of each such Diffie-Hellman exchange are piggybacked on the messages within the epoch and therefore authenticated using the same AEAD used for the data. Furthermore, these public values are used as unique identifiers of the sending epoch that each message is a part of. This mechanism allows the parties to keep in sync without storing any long-term information about the history of the session.

The Signal architecture document [44] de-composes the above mechanism into 3 main cryptographic modules, plus non-cryptographic code used to put these modules together. The modules are: (1) a symmetric authenticated encryption with associated data (AEAD) scheme that is applied to individual messages; (2) a symmetric key *ratcheting* mechanism to evolve the key between messages within an epoch; (3) an asymmetric key *ratcheting* (or "continuous key exchange") mechanism to evolve the "root chain." Since these modules are useful for applications beyond this particular protocol, we follow this partitioning and decompose Signal's protocol into similar components. (Our partitioning into components is also inspired by that of Alwen et al. [1].)

We model the security of each component as an ideal functionality within the UC framework. (These are $\mathcal{F}_{\mathsf{aead}}, \mathcal{F}_{\mathsf{mKE}}, \mathcal{F}_{\mathsf{eKE}}$, respectively.) This allows us to distill the properties provided by each module and demonstrate how they can be composed, along with the appropriate management code to obtain the desired functionality—namely to realize $\mathcal{F}_{\mathsf{SM}}$. The management code (specifically, protocols $\varPi_{\mathsf{fs\_aead}}$ and $\varPi_{\mathsf{SGNL}}$), does not directly access any keying material. Indeed, these protocols realise their respective specifications, namely $\mathcal{F}_{\mathsf{fs\_aead}}$ and $\mathcal{F}_{\mathsf{SM}}$, perfectly—see Theorems 1 and 2.

Before proceeding to describe the modules in more detail, we highlight the following apparent circularity in the security dependence between these modules: the messages in each sending epoch need to be authenticated (by the AEAD in use) using a key k *that's derived from the message itself*. Thus, modular security analysis along the above partitioning to modules might initially appear to be impossible.

The critical observation that allows us to proceed with modular decomposition is that the continuous key exchange module (which in our modeling corresponds to $\mathcal{F}_{\mathsf{eKE}}$) need not determine the authenticity of new epoch identifiers. Rather, this module is only tasked to assign a fresh pseudorandom secret key with each new epoch identifier, be it authentic or not. The determination of whether a new purported epoch identifier is authentic (or a forgery caused by an adversarially generated incoming message) is done elsewhere – specifically at the management level.

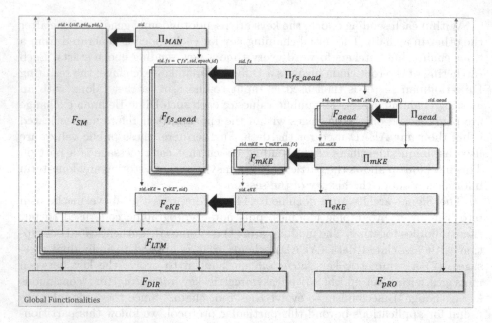

Fig. 1. Modeling and realizing secure messaging: The general subroutine structure. Ideal functionalities are denoted by F and protocols by Π. Thin vertical arrows denote subroutine calls, whereas thick horizontal arrows denote realization. Functionalities $\mathcal{F}_{DIR}, \mathcal{F}_{LTM}, \mathcal{F}_{pRO}$ are global with respect to $\mathcal{F}_{SM}$, whereas $\mathcal{F}_{eKE}$ (and Π_{eKE}) are global for $\mathcal{F}_{mKE}$, and each instance of $\mathcal{F}_{mKE}$ (and the corresponding instance of Π_{mKE}) are global for $\mathcal{F}_{aead}$. (Color figure online)

We proceed to provide a more detailed overview of our partitioning and the general protocol logic. See also Fig. 1.

$\mathcal{F}_{eKE}$. The core component of the protocol is the epoch key exchange functionality $\mathcal{F}_{eKE}$, which captures the generation of the initial shared secret key from the public information, as well as the continuous Diffie-Hellman protocol that generates the unique epoch identifiers and the "root chain" of secret keys. Whenever a party wishes to start a new epoch as a sender, it asks $\mathcal{F}_{eKE}$ for a new epoch identifier, as well as an associated secret key. The receiving party of an epoch must present an epoch identifier, and is then given the associated secret key.

As mentioned, we allow the receiving party of a new epoch to present multiple potential epoch identifiers, and obtain a secret epoch key associated with each one of these identifiers. Furthermore, while only one of these keys is the one used by the sender for this epoch, all the keys provided by $\mathcal{F}_{eKE}$ are guaranteed to appear random and independent to the adversary. In other words, $\mathcal{F}_{eKE}$ leaves it to the receiver to determine which of the candidate identifiers for the new epoch is the correct one. (If $\mathcal{F}_{eKE}$ recognizes, from observing the corruption activity and the generated epoch IDs, that the session has forked, then it exposes the secret keys to the adversary.) We postpone the discussion of realizing $\mathcal{F}_{\mathsf{eKE}}$ to the end of this section.

$\mathcal{F}_{\mathsf{mKE}}$. The per-epoch key chain is captured by an ideal functionality $\mathcal{F}_{\mathsf{mKE}}$ that is identified by an epoch-id, and generates, one at a time, a sequence of random symmetric keys associated with this epoch-id. The length of the chain is not a priori bounded; however, once $\mathcal{F}_{\mathsf{mKE}}$ receives an instruction to end the chain for a party, it complies. $\mathcal{F}_{\mathsf{mKE}}$ guarantees forward secrecy by making each key retrievable at most once by each party; that is, the key becomes inaccessible upon first retrieval, even for a corrupted party. However, it does not post-compromise security: once corrupted, all the future keys in the sequence are exposed to the adversary.

$\mathcal{F}_{\mathsf{mKE}}$ is realized by a protocol, Π_{mKE}, that first calls $\mathcal{F}_{\mathsf{eKE}}$ with its current epoch-id, to obtain the initial chaining key associated with that epoch-id. The rest of the keys in this epoch are derived using a generic length-doubling PRG (of which Signal's typical instantiation using HKDF is a special case).

Demonstrating that Π_{mKE} realizes $\mathcal{F}_{\mathsf{mKE}}$ is relatively straightforward, except for the need to address the fact that the same instance of $\mathcal{F}_{\mathsf{eKE}}$ is used by multiple instances of Π_{mKE}. Using the formalism of [5], we thus show that Π_{mKE} UC-realizes $\mathcal{F}_{\mathsf{mKE}}$ in the presence of a global $\mathcal{F}_{\mathsf{eKE}}$.

$\mathcal{F}_{\mathsf{aead}}$. Authenticated encryption with associated data is captured by ideal functionality $\mathcal{F}_{\mathsf{aead}}$, which provides a one-time ideal authenticated encryption service: the encrypting party calls $\mathcal{F}_{\mathsf{aead}}$ with a plaintext and a recipient identity, and obtains an opaque ciphertext. Once the recipient presents the ciphertext, $\mathcal{F}_{\mathsf{aead}}$ returns the plaintext. (The recipient is given the plaintext only once, even when corrupted.) The "associated data," namely the public part of the authenticated message, is captured via the session identifier of $\mathcal{F}_{\mathsf{aead}}$.

$\mathcal{F}_{\mathsf{aead}}$ is realized via protocol Π_{aead}, which employs an authenticated encryption algorithm using a key obtained from $\mathcal{F}_{\mathsf{mKE}}$. If we had opted to assert security against non-adaptive corruptions, any standard AEAD scheme would do. However, we strive to provide simulation-based security in the presence of fully adaptive corruptions, which is provably impossible in the plain model whenever the key is shorter than the plaintext [43]. We get around this issue by realizing $\mathcal{F}_{\mathsf{aead}}$ in the programmable random oracle model. While we provide a very simple AEAD protocol in this model, many common block cipher-based AEADs can also realize $\mathcal{F}_{\mathsf{aead}}$ provided we model the block cipher as a programmable random oracle. It is stressed however that the random oracle is used *only* in the case of short keys and adaptive corruptions. In particular, when corruptions are non-adaptive or the plaintext is sufficiently short, our protocol continues to UC-realize $\mathcal{F}_{\mathsf{aead}}$ even when the random oracle is replaced by the identity function.

Since each instance of $\mathcal{F}_{\mathsf{mKE}}$ is used by multiple instances of Π_{aead}, we treat $\mathcal{F}_{\mathsf{mKE}}$ as a global functionality with respect to Π_{aead}. That is, we show that Π_{aead} UC-realizes $\mathcal{F}_{\mathsf{aead}}$ in the presence of (a global) $\mathcal{F}_{\mathsf{mKE}}$.

$\mathcal{F}_{\text{fs\_aead}}$. Functionality $\mathcal{F}_{\text{fs\_aead}}$ is an abstraction of the management module that handles the encapsulation and decapsulation of all the messages within a single epoch. An instance of $\mathcal{F}_{\text{fs\_aead}}$ is created by the main module of Signal whenever a new epoch is created, with session ID that contains the identifier of this epoch. $\mathcal{F}_{\text{fs\_aead}}$ then provides encapsulation and decapsulation services, akin to those of $\mathcal{F}_{\text{aead}}$, for all the messages in its epoch. In addition, once instructed by the main module that its epoch has ended, $\mathcal{F}_{\text{aead}}$ no longer allows encapsulation of new messages—even when the party is corrupted.

$\mathcal{F}_{\text{fs\_aead}}$ is realized (perfectly, and in a straightforward way) by protocol $\Pi_{\text{fs\_aead}}$ that calls multiple instances of $\mathcal{F}_{\text{aead}}$, plus an instance of $\mathcal{F}_{\text{mKE}}$ for this epoch - where, again, the session ID of $\mathcal{F}_{\text{mKE}}$ contains the current epoch ID.

Π_{SGNL}. At the highest level of abstraction, we have each of the two parties run protocol Π_{SGNL}. When initiating a session, or starting a new epoch within a session, (i.e., when encapsulating the first message in an epoch), Π_{SGNL} first calls $\mathcal{F}_{\text{eKE}}$ to obtain the identifier of that epoch, then creates an instance of $\mathcal{F}_{\text{fs\_aead}}$ for that epoch ID and asks this instance to encapsulate the first message of the epoch. All subsequent messages of this epoch are encapsulated via the same instance of $\mathcal{F}_{\text{fs\_aead}}$.

On the receiver side, once Π_{SGNL} obtains an encapsulated message in a new epoch ID, it creates an instance of $\mathcal{F}_{\text{fs\_aead}}$ for that epoch ID and asks this instance to decapsulate the message. It is stressed that the epoch ID on the incoming message may well be a forgery; however in this case it is guaranteed that decapsulation will fail, since the peer has encapsulated this message with respect to a different epoch ID, namely a different instance of $\mathcal{F}_{\text{fs\_aead}}$. (This is where the circular dependence breaks: even though the environment may invoke Π_{SGNL} on arbitrary incoming encapsulated message, along with related epoch IDs, $\mathcal{F}_{\text{fs\_aead}}$ is guaranteed to reject unless the encapsulated message uses the same epoch ID as the as actual sender. Getting under the hood, this happens since the instances of $\mathcal{F}_{\text{mKE}}$ that correspond to different epoch IDs generate keys that are mutually pseudorandom.) IT is stressed that Π_{SGNL} is purely "management code" in the sense that it only handles idealized primitives and does not directly access cryptographic keying material. Commensurately, it UC-realizes $\mathcal{F}_{\text{SM}}$ perfectly.

Realizing $\mathcal{F}_{\text{eKE}}$. Recall that $\mathcal{F}_{\text{eKE}}$ is tasked to generate, at the beginning of each new epoch, multiple alternative keys for that epoch – a key for each potential epoch-id for that epoch. This should be done while preserving simulatability in the presence of adaptive corruptions.

Following the Signal architecture, the main component of the protocol that realizes $\mathcal{F}_{\text{eKE}}$ is a key derivation function (KDF) that combines existing secret state, with new public information (namely the public Diffie-Hellman exponents, which also double-up as an epoch-id), and a new shared key (the corresponding Diffie-Hellman secret), to obtains a new secret key associated with the given epoch-id, along with potential new local secret state for the KDF.

If the KDF is modeled as a random oracle then it is relatively straightforward to show that the resulting protocol UC-realizes $\mathcal{F}_{eKE}$.

On the other extreme, it can be seen that no plain-model instantiation of the KDF module, with bounded-size local state, can possibly realize $\mathcal{F}_{eKE}$ in our setting. Indeed, since the adversary can obtain unboundedly many alternative keys for a given epoch, where all keys are generated using the same bounded-size secret state, the Nielsen bound [43] applies.

We propose a middle-ground solution: we show how to instantiate the KDF via a plain-model primitive where the local state grows linearly with the number of keys requested from $\mathcal{F}_{eKE}$ at the beginning of a given epoch. Once the epoch advances, the state shrinks back to its original size. Our instantiation uses standard primitives: pseudorandom generators and puncturable pseudorandom functions. We also abstract the properties of our construction into a primitive which we call *cascaded pseudorandom function and generator (CPRFG)*, following a primitive of [1] that is used for a similar purpose. We stress however that technically the primitives are quite different; we elaborate in the related work section.

1.4   Streamlining UC Analysis

We highlight two additional modeling and analytical techniques that we used to simplify the overall analysis. We hope that these would be useful elsewhere.

Multiple Levels of Global State. Our analysis makes extensive use of universal composition with global state (UCGS) within the plain UC model, as formulated and proven in [5]. Specifically, we use UCGS to model a global directory that holds the public keys of parties, as well as the long-term storage, within each party, of the secret keys associated with said public keys. Similarly, we use UCGS to model the fact that a single instance of $\mathcal{F}_{eKE}$ is used by multiple instances of Π_{mKE}, and that a single instance of $\mathcal{F}_{mKE}$ is used by multiple instances of Π_{aead}. The random oracle is also modeled as a global functionality.

To facilitate our multi-layer use of the UCGS theorem we also prove a simple-but-useful lemma that allows us to get around the following difficulty. Recall that the UCGS theorem allows demonstrating that protocol π UC-realizes functionality $\mathcal{F}$ in the presence of some other 'global' functionality $\mathcal{G}$ that takes inputs from π, $\mathcal{F}$, and also potentially directly from the environment. Furthermore, we would like to use *multiple levels* of UCGS: after showing that π UC-realizes $\mathcal{F}$ in the presence of $\mathcal{G}$, we wish to argue that π UC-realizes $\mathcal{F}$ in the presence of protocol γ, where γ is some protocol that UC-realizes $\mathcal{G}$. However, such implication is not true in general [6,24].

Lemma 1 in Sect. 2 asserts that, if γ UC-realizes $\mathcal{G}$ via some simulator $\mathcal{S}$, then for any π that UC-realizes $\mathcal{F}$ in the presence of $\mathcal{G}$, it also holds that π UC-realizes $\mathcal{F}$ in the presence of $\mathcal{G}_{\mathcal{S}}$, where $\mathcal{G}_{\mathcal{S}}$ be the functionality that combines $\mathcal{G}$ and $\mathcal{S}$ in the natural way. We then show that, for the protocols in this work, having access to $\mathcal{G}_{\mathcal{S}}$ suffices.

Multiple Levels of Corruptions. The UC framework allows the adversary to adaptively and individually corrupt each party in each module within a composite protocol. While this is very general, it makes the handling of corruption events (where typically the internal states of multiple modules are exposed together) rather complex. We thus adopt a somewhat simpler modeling of party corruption: We let the environment directly corrupt parties and obtain their local states. Furthermore, a corrupted module forwards the corruption notice to all its subroutines and collects the local states of all to report to the environment. Ideal functionalities operate similarly, except that they ask their respective simulators for the appropriate simulated local states. In addition to being simpler, this modeling provide tighter correspondence between the real and ideal executions and is thus preferable whenever realizable (which is the case in this work).

1.5   Related Work

This section briefly surveys the state of the art for security analyses of the Signal architecture in particular and end-to-end secure messaging in general, highlighting the differences from and similarities to the present work.

There is a long line of research into the design and analysis of two-party Signal messaging, its subcomponents, and variants of the Signal architecture; this research builds upon decades of study into key exchange protocols (e.g., [8, 9, 22, 23]) and self-healing after corruption (e.g., [20, 28, 30]). Some of these secure messaging analyses purposely consider a limited notion of adaptive security in order to analyze instantiations of Signal based on standardized crypto primitives (e.g., [1, 10, 32, 36, 57]). Other works consider a strong threat model in which the adversary is malicious, fully adaptive, and can tamper with local state [4, 7, 35, 37, 46], which then intrinsically requires strong HIBE-like primitives that depart from the Signal specification. By contrast, we follow a middle ground in this work: our adversary is fully adaptive and has no restrictions on when it can corrupt a party, yet its corruptions are instantaneous and passive.

We stress that, while this work is inspired by the clear game-based modeling and analyses of Signal in works like Alwen et al. [1], our modeling differs in a number of significant ways. For one, our analysis provides a composable security guarantee. Furthermore, we directly model secrecy against a fully adaptive adversary that decides who and when to corrupt based on all the information seen so far. In contrast, Alwen et al. [1] guarantee secrecy only against a *selective* adversary that determines ahead of time who and when it will corrupt.

There are two prior works that perform composable analyses of Signal. In concurrent work to our own, Bienstock et al. [12] provide an alternative modeling of an ideal secure messaging within the UC framework and demonstrate how the Signal protocol can be modeled in a way that is shown to realize their formulation of ideal secure messaging. Like this work, they demonstrate several shortcomings of previous formulations, such as overlooking the effect of choosing keys too early or keeping them around for too long. They also propose and analyze an enhancement of the double ratchet structure that helps parties regain security faster following a compromise event. Additionally, Jost, Maurer, and Mularczyk

[37] conduct an analysis in the constructive cryptography framework. Their work provides a model for message transmission as well as one for ratcheting protocols.

That said, the ideal functionalities in [12] and [37] differ from our $\mathcal{F}_{\mathsf{SM}}$ in a number of ways. First, their modeling does not account for the session initiation process, nor the PKI and long-term key modules that are an integral part of any secure messaging application. Second, they include the communication medium as part of the protocol, which (a) makes it harder to argue about immediate decryption and (b) means that an instantiation of Signal would have to include an entire TCP/IP stack, which weakens modularity and inhibits the use of Signal as a sub-routine within larger functionalities.

Additionally, Bienstock et al. [12] models all key derivation modules as random oracles rather than formalizing the partition of continuous key exchange components within the UC framework as done in this work, and their modeling forces the "calling protocol" to keep track of—and ensure uniqueness for—the message IDs for the Secure Messaging functionality/protocol, which might create a security risk. On the other hand, [12] accounts for adversarial choice of randomness, which our modeling does not account for. Also, Jost et al. [37] requires explicit modeling of a global event history (a list of events having happened at each module), restricts the real-world adversary's events based on this global event history, and employs a HIBE-based implementation that is quite different than that of Signal (and ours) and requires heavier cryptographic primitives.

2 Universally Composable Security: New Capabilities

This work makes extensive use of UC with global subroutines, which allow analysis that a protocol Π UC-realizes functionality $\mathcal{F}$ in the presence of a global subroutine G that is not subroutine-respecting. Due to space constraints, we defer a primer of UC security (with global subroutines) to the full version of this work [21]. In this space, we describe two new modeling techniques that simplify our analysis, and may be of more general interest.

The first technique relates to applying the UC theorem to global functionalities. As stated in Sect. 1.4, the analysis in this work requires the ability to apply composition with global state across multiple layers of Fig. 1. We prove the following lemma in the full version of this work [21].

Lemma 1. *Let Π be a protocol that UC-realizes an ideal functionality $\mathcal{F}$, and let S be a simulator that demonstrates this fact, i.e. $\text{exec}_{\mathcal{E},\Pi} \approx \text{exec}_{\mathcal{E},\mathcal{F},S}$. Then protocols Π and $\mathcal{F}_S$ UC-emulate each other. Consequently, for any protocol ρ and ideal functionality Γ we have that ρ UC-realizes Γ in the presence of Π if and only if ρ UC-realizes Γ in the presence of $\mathcal{F}_S$*

The second technique is that, in order to model the immediate encryption and immediate decryption properties of secure messaging, we require the adversary to upload static code (which we call $\mathcal{I}$) to the global $\mathcal{F}_{\mathsf{lib}}$—shown in Fig. 2—that the relevant functionality will run in honest cases of the execution. This static code is specific to the protocol that realizes the functionality, and essentially it

$$\mathcal{F}_{\text{lib}}$$

Obtaining adversarial code: When receiving a message $(\tau, \alpha, \text{linking})$ from the adversary record it. //α represents the adversarial code, and τ represents the code of the target machines to obtain code α. The linking flag lets $\mathcal{F}_{\text{lib}}$ know whether the adversarial code calls adversarial code for other target machines.

Delivering adversarial code: When receiving input τ from a party, find the latest $(\tau, \alpha, \text{linking})$ that has been recorded. //This code runs for a bounded amount of time; if it exceeds its specified running time, then it outputs $\bot$.

1. If no such $(\tau, \alpha, \text{linking})$ was recorded, output $\bot$.
2. If linking $==$ *true* then:
   – Go through program α and link the program by doing the following for all calls to dependencies $(\tau', \mathcal{I})$:
     (a) Find the latest $(\tau', \alpha', \text{linking}')$ that has been recorded.
     (b) If no such record exists for a dependency, output $\bot$.
     (c) If linking$'$ $==$ *true* then run this compilation on α' starting at step 2.
     (d) Inline the code for the calls to α'.
     (e) If this is the last dependency, record $(\tau, \alpha, \text{linking} = \textit{false})$.
3. Output α.

Fig. 2. The code library functionality, $\mathcal{F}_{\text{lib}}$

acts as the ideal-world simulator during an honest execution. This ensures that the functionality does not need to wait for the adversary to encrypt or decrypt messages that are not corrupted. In cases where the message or ciphertext is corrupted, the fully adaptive adversary is called for input (for example, asking $\mathcal{A}$ to encrypt a message or decrypt a ciphertext). The state of the static code $\mathcal{I}$ is maintained across calls in a variable state$_\mathcal{I}$, and it is sent to the adversary upon corruption. $\mathcal{F}_{\text{lib}}$ is global because the static code must be defined at the time that the functionality is instantiated; however, the use of $\mathcal{F}_{\text{lib}}$ specifically is mainly a matter of plumbing rather than a topic of conceptual importance.

3   Formal Modeling and Analysis

In this section, we showcase our modular, iterative process for decomposing the ideal secure messaging functionality $\mathcal{F}_{\text{SM}}$ into a collection of functionalities and protocols that each address one specific purpose. After fully specifying $\mathcal{F}_{\text{SM}}$ itself, we present its realization at the "second level" of Fig. 1 by Π_{SGNL}, $\mathcal{F}_{\text{fs\_aead}}$, and $\mathcal{F}_{\text{eKE}}$, and at the "third level" by functionalities $\mathcal{F}_{\text{aead}}$ and $\mathcal{F}_{\text{mKE}}$.

Due to space constraints, we only give brief descriptions of these functionalities here and defer more exposition to the full version of this work [21]. The full version also contains rigorous specifications of the remaining protocols (on the far right of Fig. 1) and all underlying global functionalities (in blue at the bottom of Fig. 1), along with proofs of all theorems in this section.

Secure Messaging Functionality. Our top-level functionality $\mathcal{F}_{SM}$ can be found in Figs. 3 to 4. It takes two types of inputs: SendMessage is used to encapsulate a message for sending to the peer, whereas ReceiveMessage is used to decapsulate a received message. We also have a Corrupt input; this is a 'modeling input' that is used to capture party corruption. In addition, $\mathcal{F}_{SM}$ takes a number of 'side channel' messages from the adversary which are used to fine-tune the security guarantees. It relies on three global functionalities whose specifications are provided in the full version of this work [21]: $\mathcal{F}_{DIR}$ representing the directory of public keys, $\mathcal{F}_{LTM}$ representing the long-term key storage within a party, and a programmable random oracle $\mathcal{F}_{pRO}$.

The Double Ratchet. In our first layer, we decompose $\mathcal{F}_{SM}$ into two components that model the interconnected pieces of the double ratchet: a public key exchange component $\mathcal{F}_{eKE}$ and a symmetric key authenticated encryption component $\mathcal{F}_{fs\_aead}$. These components are 'glued' together with a manager protocol Π_{SGNL}.

There are three primary takeaways from the design of Π_{SGNL} (Fig. 5): it has the same input-output API as our ideal functionality $\mathcal{F}_{SM}$, it displays a idealized version of the double ratchet with clearly distinct roles for the two ratcheting subroutines, and finally it moves closer toward realism. Added features at this level of abstraction include key material stored within party states, explicit accounting for out-of-order messages by holding onto missed message keys, and epochs being identified directly by their epoch_id rather than an idealized epoch_num ordering.

The epoch key exchange functionality $\mathcal{F}_{eKE}$ (Figs. 6 to 7) comprises the public key "backbone" of the secure messaging continuous key agreement. The functionality is persistent during the entire session, mapping (epoch_id$_0$, epoch_id$_1$) pairs to sending and receiving chain keys for the symmetric ratchet. It also provides recovery from a state compromise (aka, post-compromise security).

The forward secure authenticated encryption functionality $\mathcal{F}_{fs\_aead}$ (Figs. 8 to 9) models the symmetric key ratchet for secure messaging. Each $\mathcal{F}_{fs\_aead}$ instance handles the encryption and decryption of messages for a single epoch. The protocol Π_{fs_aead} realizes $\mathcal{F}_{fs\_aead}$ by outsourcing authenticated encryption and decryption of each message to separate $\mathcal{F}_{aead}$ instances, described below.

Theorem 1. *Protocol Π_{SGNL} (perfectly) UC-realizes the ideal functionality $\mathcal{F}_{SM}$ in the presence of $\mathcal{F}_{DIR}$ and $\mathcal{F}_{LTM}$.*

The Symmetric Ratchet: Realizing $\mathcal{F}_{fs\_aead}$. Next, we decompose the symmetric key component of Signal into two smaller pieces: a one-time-use authenticated encryption routine $\mathcal{F}_{aead}$, and a message key exchange functionality $\mathcal{F}_{mKE}$ that interfaces with the epoch key exchange to produce the symmetric chain keys.

$\mathcal{F}_{\mathsf{SM}}$ **(Part 1)**

The local session ID is parsed as $\mathsf{sid} = (sid', \mathsf{pid}_0, \mathsf{pid}_1)$. Inputs arriving from machines whose identity is neither pid_0 nor pid_1 are ignored. //For notational simplicity we assume some fixed interpretation of pid_0 and pid_1 as complete identities of the two calling machines. It also has *internal adversary code* $\mathcal{I} = \mathcal{I}_{\mathsf{sm}}$. We initialize the state for $\mathcal{I}$ to be $\mathsf{state}_{\mathcal{I}} = \perp$.

Sending messages: On receiving $(\mathsf{SendMessage}, m)$ from pid do: //Here pid is an extended identity of a machine.

1. If initialized not set do: //initialization
   - If pid $\neq \mathsf{pid}_0$, end the activation. Otherwise, send $(\mathsf{ConfirmRegistration})$ to $(\mathcal{F}_{\mathsf{LTM}}, \mathsf{pid})$.
   - Upon output $(\mathsf{ConfirmRegistration}, t)$ from $\mathcal{F}_{\mathsf{LTM}}$, if $t = \mathtt{Fail}$ end the activation. Else input $(\mathsf{GetInitKeys})$ to $\mathcal{F}_{\mathsf{DIR}}$.
   - Upon output $(\mathsf{GetInitKeys}, \mathsf{pid}_1, \mathsf{ik}_1^{\mathsf{pk}}, \mathsf{rk}_1^{\mathsf{pk}}, \mathsf{ok}_1^{\mathsf{pk}})$ from $\mathcal{F}_{\mathsf{DIR}}$: if $\mathsf{ok}_1^{\mathsf{pk}} = \perp$, end the activation. Else:
     - Set initialized, $\mathsf{epoch\_num}_0 = 0$, $\mathsf{sent\_msgnum}_0 = 0$, $\mathsf{rcv\_msgnum}_0 = 0, N\_\mathsf{self}_0 = 0$, $\mathsf{diverge\_parties} = false$.
     - Create the dictionaries $\mathsf{advControl} = \{\}$, $\mathsf{id\_dict} = \{\}$, and $\mathsf{N\_dict} = \{\}$. Initialize $\mathsf{advControl}[\mathsf{epoch\_num}_0] = \perp$ and $\mathsf{advControl}[e] = \infty$ for all $e \geq 0$. //advControl will record which parties are adversarially controlled in each epoch, id_dict maps epoch id's to epoch numbers, and N_dict will hold the number of messages sent in each epoch.
   - Call $\mathcal{F}_{\mathsf{lib}}$ with input $\mathcal{F}_{\mathsf{SM}}$ to obtain the internal code $\mathcal{I}$.
2. Let i be such that $\mathsf{pid} = \mathsf{pid}_i$. Increment $\mathsf{sent\_msgnum}_i$ by 1.
3. If $\mathtt{leak} \in \mathsf{advControl}[\mathsf{epoch\_num}_i]$ or $\mathsf{diverge\_parties} = true$: Send a backdoor message $(\mathsf{state}_{\mathcal{I}}, \mathsf{SendMessage}, \mathsf{pid}, m)$ to $\mathcal{A}$.
4. Else $(\mathtt{leak} \notin \mathsf{advControl}[\mathsf{epoch\_num}_i]$ and $\mathsf{diverge\_parties} = false)$: Run $\mathcal{I}(\mathsf{state}_{\mathcal{I}}, \mathsf{SendMessage}, \mathsf{pid}, |m|)$
5. Upon obtaining $(\mathsf{state}'_{\mathcal{I}}, \mathsf{SendMessage}, \mathsf{pid}, \mathsf{epoch\_id}, c)$ from $\mathcal{A}$ or $\mathcal{I}$ do:
   - Update $\mathsf{state}_{\mathcal{I}} \leftarrow \mathsf{state}'_{\mathcal{I}}$.
   - If $\mathsf{sent\_msgnum}_i == 1$: If $\mathsf{epoch\_id}$ equals any of the keys in the dictionary id_dict then end the activation. Else record $\mathsf{id\_dict}[\mathsf{epoch\_id}] = \mathsf{epoch\_num}_i$.
   - Set $h = (\mathsf{epoch\_id}, \mathsf{sent\_msgnum}_i, N\_\mathsf{self}_i)$. //$N\_\mathsf{self}_i$ holds the # of messages sent by pid_i in its previous sending epoch.
   - If $\mathsf{diverge\_parties} = false$ then record (pid, h, c, m). //If the parties' states have diverged, then encrypted messages are no longer recorded.
   - Output $(\mathsf{SendMessage}, \mathsf{sid}, \mathsf{pid}, h, c)$ to pid.

Corrupt: On receiving a $(\mathsf{Corrupt}, \mathsf{pid}_i)$ request from Env for $\mathsf{pid}_i \in \{\mathsf{pid}_0, \mathsf{pid}_1\}$, do:

1. Append $(\mathsf{epoch\_num}_i, \mathsf{sent\_msg\_num}_i, \mathsf{received\_msg\_num}_i)$ to the list $\mathsf{corruptions}_i$.
2. For all epochs $e \leq \mathsf{epoch\_num}_i$, set $\mathsf{advControl}[e] = \{\mathtt{leak}, \mathtt{inject}\}$ to allow the adversary to influence messages still in transit.
3. Create a list pending_msgs with all records of the form $(\mathsf{pid}_{1-i}, h, c, m)$ corresponding to headers for which there is no record $(\mathsf{Authenticate}, \mathsf{pid}_{1-i}, h, \_, 1)$ (these are the messages that were not decrypted yet).
4. Send a request $(\mathsf{state}_{\mathcal{I}}, \mathsf{ReportState}, \mathsf{pid}_i, \mathsf{pending\_msgs})$ to $\mathcal{A}$.
5. On receiving a state $(\mathsf{ReportState}, \mathsf{pid}_i, S)$ from $\mathcal{A}$, send S to Env.

Fig. 3. The Secure Messaging Functionality $\mathcal{F}_{\mathsf{SM}}$

$\mathcal{F}_{\mathsf{SM}}$ (Part 2)

The local session ID is parsed as $\mathsf{sid} = (sid', \mathsf{pid}_0, \mathsf{pid}_1)$. Inputs arriving from machines whose identity is neither pid_0 nor pid_1 are ignored. //For notational simplicity we assume some fixed interpretation of pid_0 and pid_1 as complete identities of the two calling machines. It also has *internal adversary code* $\mathcal{I} = \mathcal{I}_{\mathsf{sm}}$. We initialize the state for $\mathcal{I}$ to be $\mathsf{state}_{\mathcal{I}} = \bot$.

Receiving messages: On receiving $(\mathtt{ReceiveMessage}, h = (\mathsf{epoch\_id}, \mathsf{msg\_num}, N), c)$ from pid, do:

1. Let i be such that $\mathsf{pid} = \mathsf{pid}_i$.
2. If this is the first $\mathtt{ReceiveMessage}$ request: If $i = 0$ then end the activation. Else ($\mathsf{pid} = \mathsf{pid}_1$), initialize the responder:
   - Send $(\mathtt{ConfirmRegistration})$ to $(\mathcal{F}_{\mathsf{LTM}}, \mathsf{pid})$.
   - Upon receiving the output $(\mathtt{ConfirmRegistration}, t)$ from $\mathcal{F}_{\mathsf{LTM}}$: If $t = \mathtt{Fail}$ then end activation. Else provide input $(\mathtt{GetResponseKeys}, \mathsf{pid}_0, \mathsf{pid}_1)$ to $\mathcal{F}_{\mathsf{DIR}}$.
   - Upon receiving output $(\mathtt{GetResponseKeys}, \mathsf{pid}_0, \mathsf{ik}_0^{\mathsf{pk}})$ from $\mathcal{F}_{\mathsf{DIR}}$, set $\mathsf{epoch\_num}_1 = 1$, $\mathsf{sent\_msgnum}_1 = 0$, and $\mathsf{rcv\_msgnum}_1 = 0$.
3. If there already was a successful $\mathtt{ReceiveMessage}$ for h (i.e there is a record $(\mathtt{Authenticate}, h, c', 1)$ for some c'), or this ciphertext previously failed to authenticate (i.e. a record $(\mathtt{Authenticate}, h, c, 0)$ exits), output $(\mathtt{ReceiveMessage}, h, c, \mathtt{Fail})$ to pid.
4. If $\mathsf{epoch\_id}$ appears as a key in $\mathsf{id\_dict}$, set $\mathsf{epoch\_num} = \mathsf{id\_dict}[\mathsf{epoch\_id}]$.
   Else: //this is a new epoch id that hasn't been generated within SendMessage
   - If $\mathsf{sent\_msgnum}_i = 0$, output $(\mathtt{ReceiveMessage}, h, c, \mathtt{Fail})$ to pid. //pid is in a receiving state and hasn't sent any messages in its current sending epoch, so it should not be accepting messages with a new epoch id
   - Otherwise set $\mathsf{epoch\_num} = \mathsf{epoch\_num}_i + 1$.
   //this temporary variable will never be made permanent if decryption is unsuccessful.
5. If $\mathsf{msg\_num} > \mathsf{N\_dict}[\mathsf{epoch\_num}]$, output $(\mathtt{ReceiveMessage}, h, c, \mathtt{Fail})$ to pid
   //For epoch_num's that are not finished yet, the N_dict returns a default value of ∞, so this check passes automatically.
6. If ($\mathsf{diverge\_parties} = false$ and $\mathsf{inject} \notin \mathsf{advControl}[\mathsf{epoch\_num}]$): Run $\mathcal{I}(\mathsf{state}_{\mathcal{I}}, \mathsf{inject}, \mathsf{pid}, h, c)$ //Honest Case
7. Else: send backdoor message $(\mathsf{state}_{\mathcal{I}}, \mathsf{inject}, \mathsf{pid}, h, c)$ to $\mathcal{A}$ // $\mathcal{F}_{\mathsf{SM}}$ is asking the adversary for advice on how to decrypt c.
8. On receiving $(\mathsf{state}'_{\mathcal{I}}, \mathsf{inject}, h, c, v)$ from $\mathcal{A}$ or $\mathcal{I}$ update $\mathsf{state}_{\mathcal{I}} \leftarrow \mathsf{state}'_{\mathcal{I}}$ and:
   If $(\mathsf{sender}, h, c, m)$ is recorded then record $(\mathtt{Authenticate}, \mathsf{pid}, h, c, 1)$ and set $m^* = m$. Else:
   - If $v = \bot$: record $(\mathtt{Authenticate}, \mathsf{pid}, h, c, 0)$ and output $(\mathtt{ReceiveMessage}, h, c, \mathtt{Fail})$.
   - If $v \neq \bot$ and $\mathsf{diverge\_parties} = false$ and $\mathsf{inject} \notin \mathsf{advControl}[\mathsf{epoch\_num}]$, then:
     - If there is no record $(\mathsf{sender}, h, c^*, m)$ for header h, output $(\mathtt{ReceiveMessage}, h, c, \mathtt{Fail})$. //since h contains N, this value will match the view of the sender if this check succeeds.
     - Else (there is such a record), record $(\mathtt{Authenticate}, h, c, 1)$ and set $m^* = m$.
     //allowing for authenticating a message with a different mac
   If $v \neq \bot$ and ($\mathsf{diverge\_parties} = true$ or $\mathsf{inject} \in \mathsf{advControl}[\mathsf{epoch\_num}]$)), then:
     - Record $(\mathtt{Authenticate}, h, c, 1)$, and set $m^* = v$.
     - If $\mathsf{epoch\_id}$ does not appear as a key in $\mathsf{id\_dict}$ then set $\mathsf{diverge\_parties} = true$.
     //diverge parties is being set here.
9. If $\mathsf{epoch\_num}_i < \mathsf{epoch\_num}$, do: //we only get to this step if decryption is successful
   - Set $\mathsf{N\_dict}[\mathsf{epoch\_num} - 2] = N$, $\mathsf{epoch\_num}_i \mathrel{+}= 2$, $\mathsf{N\_self}_i = \mathsf{sent\_msgnum}_i$, and $\mathsf{sent\_msgnum}_i = 0$.
   - if $\mathsf{diverge\_parties} = false$ then:
     - If $\mathsf{advControl}[\mathsf{epoch\_num} - 1] = \{\mathtt{leak}, \mathtt{inject}\}$ and $\mathsf{epoch\ num}_i \notin \mathsf{corruptions}_i$, then set $\mathsf{advControl}[\mathsf{epoch\_num}] = \{\mathtt{leak}\}$. //Corruption status is changed if this is the other party's first new sending epoch that involves a fresh epoch id generated after corruption.
     - If $\mathsf{advControl}[\mathsf{epoch\_num} - 1] = \{\mathtt{leak}\}$, then set $\mathsf{advControl}[\mathsf{epoch\_num}] = \bot$.
10. Output $(\mathtt{ReceiveMessage}, h, m^*)$ to pid.

Fig. 4. The Secure Messaging Functionality $\mathcal{F}_{\mathsf{SM}}$

$$\Pi_{\text{SGNL}}$$

SendMessage: Upon receiving input (SendMessage, m) from pid, do:

1. If this is the first activation do: //initialization for the initiator of the session
   - Parse the local session id sid to retrieve the party identifiers $(\text{pid}_0, \text{pid}_1)$ for the initiator and responder. If pid_0 is different from either the local party identifier pid, or the party identifier of pid, end the activation.
   - Initialize $\text{epoch\_id}_{\text{self}} = \bot$, $\text{epoch\_id}_{\text{partner}} = \bot$, $\text{sent\_msg\_num} = 0$, $N_{\text{last}} = 0$.
   - Provide input (ConfirmReceivingEpoch, $\bot$) to $(\mathcal{F}_{\text{eKE}}, \text{sid}.eKE)$.
   - On receiving (ConfirmReceivingEpoch, epoch_id) from $(\mathcal{F}_{\text{eKE}}, \text{sid}.eKE)$, set $\text{epoch_id}_{\text{self}} = $ epoch_id.
   - Initialize a list receiving_epochs $= []$.
2. Provide input (Encrypt, m, N_{last}) to $(\mathcal{F}_{\text{fs\_aead}}, \text{sid}.fs)$, where $\text{sid}.fs = (\text{sid}, \text{epoch\_id}_{\text{self}})$. //$\mathcal{F}_{\text{fs\_aead}}$ already knows epoch_id and msg_num
3. On receiving (Encrypt, c, N_{last}) from $(\mathcal{F}_{\text{fs\_aead}}, \text{sid}.fs)$, delete m, increment $\text{sent\_msg\_num} += 1$, output (SendMessage, sid, h, c) to pid, where $h = (\text{epoch\_id}_{\text{self}}, \text{sent\_msg\_num}, N_{\text{last}})$.

ReceiveMessage: Upon receiving (ReceiveMessage, $h = (\text{epoch\_id}, \text{msg\_num}, N)$, c) from pid:

1. If this is the first activation then do: //initialization for the responder of the session
   - Parse the local session identifier sid to retrieve the party identifiers $(\text{pid}_0, \text{pid}_1)$ for the initiator and responder. If pid_1 is different from either the local party identifier, or the party identifier for pid, then end the activation.
   - Initialize $\text{epoch\_id}_{\text{self}} = \bot$, $\text{epoch\_id}_{\text{partner}} = \bot$, $\text{sent\_msg\_num} = 0$ and $N_{\text{last}} = 0$, $\text{received\_msg\_num} = 0$.
   - Initialize a dictionary missed_msgs $= \{\}$ and a list receiving_epochs $= []$.
2. Provide input (Decrypt, c, msg_num, N) to $(\mathcal{F}_{\text{fs\_aead}}, \text{sid}.fs = (\text{sid}, \text{epoch\_id}))$.
3. Upon receiving (Decrypt, c, msg_num, N, v) from $(\mathcal{F}_{\text{fs\_aead}}, \text{sid}.fs)$: if $v = $ Fail then send (ReceiveMessage, h, ad, Fail) to pid. //Otherwise, v is the decrypted message
4. While msg_num > received_msg_num:
   //note down any expected messages
   - Append received_msg_num to the entry missed_msgs[epoch_id].
   - Increment $\text{received\_msg\_num} += 1$.
5. If msg_num is in the entry missed_msgs[epoch_id]:
   - remove it from the list.
   - If the entry missed_msgs[epoch_id] is now an empty list then remove epoch_id from missed_msgs.$keys$.
6. Else (msg_num $\notin$ missed_msgs[epoch_id]):
   - If $\text{epoch\_id} = \text{epoch\_id}_{\text{partner}}$ or $\text{sent\_msg\_num} = 0$, output (ReceiveMessage, h, c, $\bot$). Otherwise continue. //Starting new epoch–ratchet forward
   - Append the numbers received_msg_num, $\ldots$, N to the entry missed_msgs[epoch_id].
   - Send (StopDecrypting, N) to $(\mathcal{F}_{\text{fs\_aead}}, (\text{sid}, \text{epoch\_id}_{\text{partner}}))$. //'Closing' the $\mathcal{F}_{\text{fs\_aead}}$ for the last epoch.
   - On receiving (StopDecrypting, Success), update $\text{epoch_id}_{\text{partner}} = $ epoch_id, and send (StopEncrypting) to $(\mathcal{F}_{\text{fs\_aead}}, (\text{sid}, \text{epoch\_id}_{\text{self}}))$.
   - On receiving (StopEncrypting, Success), send (ConfirmReceivingEpoch, epoch_id) to $(\mathcal{F}_{\text{eKE}}, \text{sid}.eKE)$.
   - On receiving (ConfirmReceivingEpoch, epoch_id*), update $\text{epoch_id}_{\text{self}} = $ epoch_id*, $N_{\text{last}} = $ sent_msg_num, and sent_msg_num $= 0$.
7. Output (ReceiveMessage, h, c, v) to pid while deleting the decrypted message v.

Corruption: Upon receiving (Corrupt, pid) from Env:
//Note that the Corrupt interface is not part of the "real" protocol; it is only included for modelling purposes.

1. Initialize a list S and send (Corrupt) as input to $(\mathcal{F}_{\text{eKE}}, \text{sid}.eKE = \text{"}eKE\text{"}, \text{sid})$.
2. On receiving (Corrupt, S_{eKE}) from $(\mathcal{F}_{\text{eKE}}, \text{sid}.eKE = \text{"}eKE\text{"}, \text{sid})$, add it to S and continue. //now corrupt individual $\mathcal{F}_{\text{fs\_aead}}$ instances.
3. For epoch_id $\in$ missed_msgs.$keys$ do:
   - Send (Corrupt) as input to $(\mathcal{F}_{\text{fs\_aead}}, \text{sid}.fs = (\text{"}fs\_aead\text{"}, \text{sid}, \text{epoch\_id}))$.
   - On receiving $S_{\text{epoch\_id}}$, add it to S.
4. Output (Corrupt, pid_i, S) to Env.

Fig. 5. The Signal Protocol, Π_{SGNL}

$\mathcal{F}_{\mathsf{eKE}}$

This functionality has a session id sid.eKE that takes the following format: sid.eKE = ("eKE", sid). Inputs arriving from machines whose identity is neither pid_0 nor pid_1 are ignored. //For notational simplicity we assume some fixed interpertation of pid_0 and pid_1 as complete identities of the two calling machines.

ConfirmReceivingEpoch: On input (ConfirmReceivingEpoch, epoch_id*) from (Π_{SGNL}, sid, pid_i):

1. If this is the first activation:
   - Parse sid to retrieve two party ids (pid_0, pid_1) for the initiator and responder parties and store them. If $\mathsf{pid}_0 \neq \mathsf{pid}_i$, then end the activation.
   - Provide input (GetInitKeys, pid_1, pid_0) to ($\mathcal{F}_{\mathsf{DIR}}$).
   - Upon receiving output (GetInitKeys, $\mathsf{ik}_1^{\mathsf{pk}}$, $\mathsf{rk}_1^{\mathsf{pk}}$, $\mathsf{ok}_1^{\mathsf{pk}}$) from ($\mathcal{F}_{\mathsf{DIR}}$): if $\mathsf{ok}_{\mathsf{pid}_1}^{\mathsf{pk}} = \perp$ then output (ConfirmReceivingEpoch, Fail). Else, set epoch_id_partner$_0$ = epoch_id_self$_1$ = $\mathsf{ok}_{\mathsf{pid}_1}^{\mathsf{pk}}$, set epoch_num$_0$ = -2, epoch_num$_1$ = -1, initialize empty lists corruptions$_0$, corruptions$_1$, compromised_epochs, and send (ComputeSendingRootKey, $\mathsf{ik}_1^{\mathsf{pk}}$, $\mathsf{rk}_1^{\mathsf{pk}}$, $\mathsf{ok}_1^{\mathsf{pk}}$) to $\mathcal{F}_{\mathsf{LTM}}$.
   - On receiving (ComputeSendingRootKey, k, $\mathsf{ek}^{\mathsf{pk}}$), continue. //Don't start the conversation if the one time keys belonging to the other party have run out.
   - Call $\mathcal{F}_{\mathsf{lib}}$ to obtain internal code $\mathcal{I}$. Initialize the state for $\mathcal{I}$ to be state$_\mathcal{I} = \perp$.
2. If this is not the first activation, set epoch_id_partner$_i$ = epoch_id*. //save epoch_id_partner from input if this is not the first activation.
3. If epoch_id_partner$_i \neq$ epoch_id_self$_{1-i}$, then diverge_parties = $true$. //determine if the parties' views have diverged
4. If diverge_parties, send a backdoor message (state$_\mathcal{I}$, GenEpochId, i, epoch_id*) to $\mathcal{A}$.
5. Else, run $\mathcal{I}$(state$_\mathcal{I}$, GenEpochId, i, epoch_id*)
6. Upon receiving (state$'_\mathcal{I}$, GenEpochId, i, epoch_id) from $\mathcal{A}$ or from $\mathcal{I}$, update state$_\mathcal{I} \leftarrow$ state$'_\mathcal{I}$ and do the following:
   - If epoch_id is the same as the input to any previous invocation of ConfirmReceivingEpoch, end the activation.
   - Update epoch_num$_i$ += 2. Then set epoch_id_self$_i$ = epoch_id, epoch_num_dict[epoch_id] = epoch_num$_i$, and got_sending_key$_i$ = $false$.
7. Output (ConfirmReceivingEpoch, epoch_id_self$_i$) to (Π_{SGNL}, sid, pid_i).

(The rest of this functionality is in Fig. 7)

Fig. 6. The Epoch Key Exchange Functionality, $\mathcal{F}_{\mathsf{eKE}}$

Each authenticated encryption functionality instance $\mathcal{F}_{\mathsf{aead}}$ (Fig. 10) handles the encryption, decryption, and authentication of a particular message for a particular epoch. It hands the ciphertext or message back to $\Pi_{\mathsf{fs\_aead}}$.

Theorem 2. *Protocol* $\Pi_{\mathsf{fs\_aead}}$ *(perfectly) UC-realizes* $\mathcal{F}_{\mathsf{fs\_aead}}$*, in the presence of* $\mathcal{F}_{\mathsf{DIR}}, \mathcal{F}_{\mathsf{LTM}}, \mathcal{F}_{\mathsf{pRO}}$*, and* $\mathcal{F}_{\mathsf{eKE}}^{\Pi_{\mathsf{eKE}}} = (\mathcal{S}_{\mathsf{eKE}}, \mathcal{F}_{\mathsf{eKE}})$.

Note that the simulator $\mathcal{S}_{\mathsf{eKE}}$, along with a proof of this theorem, are deferred to the full version of this work [21].

Each instance of the message key exchange functionality $\mathcal{F}_{\mathsf{mKE}}$ (Fig. 11) handles the key derivation for the symmetric ratchet for a particular epoch. Specifically, it provides key_seed's to Π_{aead} instances that are then expanded to any length using the global random oracle $\mathcal{F}_{\mathsf{pRO}}$. When instructed, it also closes epochs at a certain message number N by generating all key_seed's up to N and later disallowing the generation of any further key seeds for its epoch.

$$\mathcal{F}_{\mathsf{eKE}} \text{ continued...}$$

GetSendingKey: On receiving input (GetSendingKey) from $(\Pi_{mKE}, \text{sid}.mKE, \text{pid})$:

1. Set i such that $\text{pid} = \text{pid}_i$.
2. If ConfirmReceivingEpoch has never been run successfully (i.e epoch_id_self$_0$ hasn't been initialized) or got_sending_key$_i$ = $true$, then end the activation.   //the functionality isn't initialized or the sending key for the current epoch has already been retrieved
3. Sample sending_chain_key$_i$ $\xleftarrow{\$} \mathcal{K}_{ep}$ from the key distribution.   //In the honest case, the key is not known to the adversary. Otherwise the key will get overwritten in the following step.
4. If diverge_parties = $true$, or epoch_num$_i \in$ compromised_epochs, then:
   - Send backdoor message (state$_{\mathcal{I}}$, GetSendingKey, i) to $\mathcal{A}$
   - On receiving backdoor message (state$'_{\mathcal{I}}$, GetSendingKey, i, K_{send}) from $\mathcal{A}$, update state$_{\mathcal{I}} \leftarrow$ state$'_{\mathcal{I}}$ and set sending_chain_key$_i$ = K_{send}.
5. Set got_sending_key$_i$ = $true$ and output (GetSendingKey, sending_chain_key$_i$).

GetReceivingKey: On receiving input (GetReceivingKey, epoch_id) from $(\Pi_{mKE}, \text{sid}, \text{pid})$:

1. If pid $\notin \{\text{pid}_0, \text{pid}_1\}$ then end this activation. Otherwise, set i such that pid = pid$_i$.
2. If ConfirmReceivingEpoch has never been run successfully (i.e epoch_id_self$_0$ hasn't been initialized) or sending_chain_key$_{1-i}$ has been deleted then end the activation.
3. If this is the first activation:
   - Initialize state variables root_key, epoch_id, epoch_key, sending_chain_key = $\perp$.
   - Parse epoch_id = (epoch_id$'$, ek$_j^{\mathsf{pk}}$, ok$_{i-j}^{\mathsf{pk}}$) and set temp_epoch_id_partner = epoch_id$'$
   - Send (GetResponseKeys, pid$_{1-i}$) to $\mathcal{F}_{\mathsf{DIR}}$.
   - Upon   receiving   (GetResponseKeys, ik$_j^{\mathsf{pk}}$),   send   input (ComputeReceivingRootKey, ik$_j^{\mathsf{pk}}$, ek$_j^{\mathsf{pk}}$, ok$_{i-j}^{\mathsf{pk}}$) to $\mathcal{F}_{\mathsf{LTM}}$.
   - Upon receiving (ComputeReceivingRootKey, k), call $\mathcal{F}_{\mathsf{lib}}$ to obtain internal code $\mathcal{I}$. Initialize the state for $\mathcal{I}$ to be state$_{\mathcal{I}} = \perp$.
4. If diverge_parties = $true$ or epoch_id $\neq$ epoch_id_self$_{1-i}$:   //Let $\mathcal{A}$ choose key
   - Send (state$_{\mathcal{I}}$, GetReceivingKey, i, epoch_id) to $\mathcal{A}$
   - Upon receiving (state$'_{\mathcal{I}}$, GetReceivingKey, i, epoch_id, recv_chain_key*) from $\mathcal{A}$, update state$_{\mathcal{I}} \leftarrow$ state$'_{\mathcal{I}}$.
   - If diverge_parties = $false$ and epoch_num$_i$ + 1 $\notin$ compromised_epochs, add epoch_id to receive_attempts[epoch_num].
5. Else (diverge_parties = $false$ and epoch_id = epoch_id_self$_{1-i}$), set recv_chain_key$_i$ = sending_chain_key$_{1-i}$ //Expected case
6. Output (GetReceivingKey, recv_chain_key$_i$) and erase recv_chain_key$_i$.

Corrupt: On receiving a (Corrupt) request from $(\Pi_{\mathsf{SGNL}}, \text{sid}, \text{pid}_i)$ for $i \in \{0, 1\}$ do:

- Add epoch_id_self$_i$ to the list corruptions$_i$.
- Add   epoch_num$_i$, epoch_num$_i$ + 1, epoch_num$_i$ + 2, epoch_num$_i$ + 3   to   the   list compromised_epochs.   //We need the compromise to go through the following stages: fully compromised, sender randomness updated, both parties' randomness updated.
- Initialize an empty list leak = [] and a variable recv_chain_key = $\perp$.
- If epoch_num$_{1-i}$ > epoch_num$_i$:
  - Set recv_chain_key = sending_chain_key$_{1-i}$.
  - If epoch_num$_{1-i} \in$ receive_attempts.$keys$ then set leak = receive_attempts[epoch_num$_{1-i}$]
- Send (ReportState, state$_{\mathcal{I}}$, i, recv_chain_key$_i$, leak) to $\mathcal{A}$.
- Upon receiving (ReportState, i, S) from $\mathcal{A}$, output (Corrupt, S) to $(\Pi_{\mathsf{SGNL}}, \text{sid}, \text{pid}_i)$.

Fig. 7. The Epoch Key Exchange Functionality, $\mathcal{F}_{\mathsf{eKE}}$ (continued)

$$\mathcal{F}_{\mathsf{fs\_aead}}$$

This functionality processes encryptions and decryptions for a *single* epoch and has session id sid.fs that takes the following format: sid.fs = ("*fs_aead*", sid = (sid', (pid$_0$, pid$_1$)), epoch_id). Inputs arriving from machines whose identity is neither pid$_0$ nor pid$_1$ are ignored. //For notational simplicity we assume some fixed interpertation of pid$_0$ and pid$_1$ as complete identities of the two calling machines. It also has *internal adversary code* $\mathcal{I} = \mathcal{I}_{\mathsf{fs}}$.

Encrypt: On receiving input (Encrypt, m, N) from (Π_{MAN}, sid, pid) do:

1. If this is the first activation then:
   – Let i be such that pid = pid$_i$ and initialize msg_num = 0 and state$_\mathcal{I}$ to empty, sender sender = i.
   – Call $\mathcal{F}_{\mathsf{lib}}$ with input $\mathcal{F}_{\mathsf{fs\_aead}}$ to obtain the internal code $\mathcal{I}$.
2. Verify that sid matches the one in the local state and pid = pid$_b$, otherwise end the activation.
3. If the sender has deleted the ability to encrypt messages, then end the activation.
4. Increment msg_num = msg_num + 1.
5. If IsCorrupt? = *false*: Run $\mathcal{I}$(state$_\mathcal{I}$, Encrypt, pid, msg_num, N, $|m|$). Obtain the updated state state$_\mathcal{I}$ and the output (Encrypt, pid, c, msg_num, N).
6. If IsCorrupt? = *true*: Send a backdoor message (state$_\mathcal{I}$, Encrypt, pid, msg_num, N, m) to $\mathcal{A}$. Upon receiving a response (state$_\mathcal{I}$, Encrypt, pid, c, msg_num, N), record the updated state state$_\mathcal{I}$.
7. Record (m, c, msg_num, N) and output (Encrypt, c) to (Π_{MAN}, sid, pid).

(The rest of this functionality is in Fig. 9)

Fig. 8. The Forward-Secure Encryption Functionality $\mathcal{F}_{\mathsf{fs\_aead}}$

Theorem 3. *Assume that* PRG *is a secure length-doubling pseudorandom generator. Then protocol* Π_{mKE} *UC-realizes* $\mathcal{F}_{\mathsf{mKE}}$ *in the presence of* $\mathcal{F}_{\mathsf{DIR}}, \mathcal{F}_{\mathsf{LTM}}$, *and* $\mathcal{F}_{\mathsf{eKE}}^{\Pi_{\mathsf{eKE}}} = (\mathcal{S}_{\mathsf{eKE}}, \mathcal{F}_{\mathsf{eKE}})$.

The Public Ratchet: Realizing $\mathcal{F}_{\mathsf{eKE}}$. By this point we have already described all of the functionalities in our model. As shown in Fig. 1, it only remains to construct real-world protocols that realize each of them. We defer a description of Π_{aead} to the full version [21] and show only the result here.

Theorem 4. *Assuming the unforgeability of* (MAC, Verify), *protocol* Π_{aead} *UC-realizes the ideal functionality* $\mathcal{F}_{\mathsf{aead}}$ *in the presence of* $\mathcal{F}_{\mathsf{pRO}}$, *as well as* $F_{mKE}^{\Pi} = (\mathcal{S}_{\mathsf{mKE}}, \mathcal{F}_{\mathsf{mKE}}), \mathcal{F}_{\mathsf{eKE}}^{\Pi_{\mathsf{eKE}}} = (\mathcal{S}_{\mathsf{eKE}}, \mathcal{F}_{\mathsf{eKE}}), \mathcal{F}_{\mathsf{DIR}}, \mathcal{F}_{\mathsf{LTM}}, \mathcal{F}_{\mathsf{lib}}$.

Instantiating $\mathcal{F}_{\mathsf{eKE}}$ via Π_{eKE} (Figs. 12 to 13) is subtle. The main challenge, as observed by Alwen et al. [1] and others, is that the key derivation module within the public ratchet must maintain security if either of the previous root key or the newly generated ephemeral keys are uncompromised. Alwen et al. formalized this guarantee by way of constructing a new primitive: a PRF PRG. In this work, we make two important improvements upon this construction. First, we contribute

$\mathcal{F}_{\text{fs\_aead}}$ **continued...**

Decrypt: On receiving $(\text{Decrypt}, c, \text{msg\_num}, N)$ from $(\Pi_{\text{SGNL}}, \text{sid}, \text{pid})$ do:

1. Verify that sid matches the one in the local state and $\text{pid} = \text{pid}_{1-\text{sender}}$, otherwise end the activation. //end the activation if the decrypt request is not from the receiving party
2. If msg_num is set as inaccessible, or there is a record $(\text{Authenticate}, c, \text{msg\_num}, N, 0)$, then output $(\text{Decrypt}, c, \text{msg\_num}, N, \text{Fail})$ to $(\Pi_{\text{SGNL}}, \text{sid}, \text{pid})$.
3. If IsCorrupt? $= \textit{false}$:
   - Run $\mathcal{I}(\text{state}_{\mathcal{I}}, \text{Authenticate}, \text{pid}, c, \text{msg\_num}, N)$ and obtain updated state $\text{state}_{\mathcal{I}}$ and output $(\text{Authenticate}, \text{pid}, c, \text{msg\_num}, N, v)$.
   - If $v = \perp$, then record $(\text{Authenticate}, c, \text{msg\_num}, N, 0)$ and output $(\text{Decrypt}, c, \text{msg\_num}, N, \text{Fail})$ to $(\Pi_{\text{SGNL}}, \text{sid}, \text{pid})$.
   - Otherwise, mark msg_num as inaccessible and output $(\text{Decrypt}, c, \text{msg\_num}, N, m)$ to $(\Pi_{\text{SGNL}}, \text{sid}, \text{pid})$.
4. Else (IsCorrupt? $= \textit{true}$):
   - Send $(\text{state}_{\mathcal{I}}, \text{inject}, \text{pid}, c, \text{msg\_num}, N)$ to $\mathcal{A}$.
   - On receiving the updated $\text{state}_{\mathcal{I}}$ and (inject, v) from $\mathcal{A}$, do:
     - If $v = \perp$, record $(\text{Authenticate}, c, \text{msg\_num}, N, 0)$ and output $(\text{Decrypt}, c, \text{msg\_num}, N, \text{Fail})$.
     - Else, then mark msg_num as inaccessible and output $(\text{Decrypt}, c, \text{msg\_num}, N, v)$ to $(\Pi_{\text{SGNL}}, \text{sid}, \text{pid})$.

StopEncrypting: On receiving (StopEncrypting) from $(\Pi_{\text{SGNL}}, \text{sid}, \text{pid})$ do:

1. If sid doesn't match the one in the local state, if $\text{pid} \neq \text{pid}_{\text{sender}}$, or if this is the first activation: end the activation.
2. Otherwise, note that pid_i has deleted the ability to encrypt future messages. Output $(\text{StopEncrypting}, \text{Success})$.

StopDecrypting: On receiving $(\text{StopDecrypting}, \text{msg\_num}^*)$ from $(\Pi_{\text{SGNL}}, \text{sid}, \text{pid})$ do:

1. If sid doesn't match the one in the local state, $\text{pid} \neq \text{pid}_{1-\text{sender}}$, or no messages have been successfully decrypted by pid_i: end the activation.
2. Mark all $\text{msg\_num} > \text{msg\_num}^*$ as inaccessible, and output $(\text{StopDecrypting}, \text{Success})$ to $(\Pi_{\text{SGNL}}, \text{sid}, \text{pid})$.

Corrupt: On receiving $(\text{Corrupt}, \text{pid})$ from $(\Pi_{\text{SGNL}}, \text{sid}, \text{pid})$:

1. Record $(\text{Corrupt}, \text{pid})$ and set IsCorrupt? $= \textit{true}$.
2. If $\text{pid} = \text{pid}_{1-\text{sender}}$ (pid is the receiver), let $\text{leak} = \{(\text{pid}_{\text{sender}}, h = (\text{epoch\_id}, \text{msg\_num}, N), c, m)\}$ be the set of all messages sent by $\text{pid}_{\text{sender}}$ which are not marked as inaccessible.
3. Otherwise (pid is the sender), set $\text{leak} = \emptyset$.
4. Send $(\text{ReportState}, \text{state}_{\mathcal{I}}, \text{pid}, \text{leak})$ to $\mathcal{A}$.
5. Upon receiving a response $(\text{ReportState}, \text{state}_{\mathcal{I}}, \text{pid}, S)$ from $\mathcal{A}$, send S to $(\Pi_{\text{SGNL}}, \text{sid}, \text{pid})$.

Fig. 9. The Forward-Secure Encryption Functionality $\mathcal{F}_{\text{fs\_aead}}$ (continued)

a new construction called a *Cascaded PRF-PRG* that allows for equivocation, in order to maintain security against adaptive adversaries. Second, we provide an instantiation in the plain model based on punctured PRFs.

$$\mathcal{F}_{\mathsf{aead}}$$

This functionality has a session id $\mathsf{sid}.aead$ = ("$aead$", $\mathsf{sid}.fs$, $\mathsf{msg\_num}$) where $\mathsf{sid}.fs$ = ("fs_aead", sid = (sid', pid_0, pid_1), $\mathsf{epoch\_id}$). It also has *internal adversary code* $\mathcal{I} = \mathcal{I}_{\mathsf{aead}}$.

We initialize the state for $\mathcal{I}$ to be $\mathsf{state}_\mathcal{I} = \bot$.

Encryption: On receiving (Encrypt, m, N) from ($\Pi_{\mathsf{fs\_aead}}$, $\mathsf{sid}.fs$, pid):

1. If this is not the first encryption request or $\mathsf{pid} \notin (\mathsf{pid}_0, \mathsf{pid}_1)$, end the activation. Let i be such that $\mathsf{pid} = \mathsf{pid}_i$.
2. Provide input (RetrieveKey, pid) to ($\mathcal{F}_{\mathsf{mKE}}$, $\mathsf{sid}.mKE$, pid)
3. Upon receiving output (RetrieveKey, pid, k) from ($\mathcal{F}_{\mathsf{mKE}}$, $\mathsf{sid}.mKE$, pid):
   - If $k = \bot$ then end the activation. //The key is not available.
   - Else if IsCorrupt? = *false*:
     • Call $\mathcal{F}_{\mathsf{lib}}$ with input $\mathcal{F}_{\mathsf{aead}}$ to obtain the internal code $\mathcal{I}$.
     • Run $\mathcal{I}(\mathsf{state}_\mathcal{I}, \mathsf{Encrypt}, \mathsf{pid}, |m|, N)$, obtain the updated state $\mathsf{state}_\mathcal{I}$, and the output (Encrypt, pid, c).
     • Record the tuple (c, k, m, N, 1), record i as the sender, and set $\mathsf{ready2decrypt} = $ *true*.
   - Else ($k \neq \bot$ and IsCorrupt? = *true*):
     • Send a backdoor message ($\mathsf{state}_\mathcal{I}$, Encrypt, pid, m, N) to $\mathcal{A}$.
     • Upon receiving a response ($\mathsf{state}_\mathcal{I}$, Encrypt, pid, c), record the updated state $\mathsf{state}_\mathcal{I}$, record the tuple ($c$, k, m, N, 1), record i as the sender, and set $\mathsf{ready2decrypt} = $ *true*.
   - Output (Encrypt, c) to ($\Pi_{\mathsf{fs\_aead}}$, $\mathsf{sid}.fs$, pid).

Decryption: On receiving (Decrypt, c, N) from ($\Pi_{\mathsf{fs\_aead}}$, $\mathsf{sid}.fs$, pid):

1. If there hasn't been a successful encryption request, if $\mathsf{pid} \neq \mathsf{pid}_{1-i}$, or if $\mathsf{ready2decrypt} = $ *false* then output (Decrypt, Fail) to ($\Pi_{\mathsf{fs\_aead}}$, $\mathsf{sid}.fs$, pid).
2. Provide input (RetrieveKey, pid) to ($\mathcal{F}_{\mathsf{mKE}}$, $\mathsf{sid}.mKE$, pid).
3. Upon obtaining a response (RetrieveKey, pid, k) from $\mathcal{F}_{\mathsf{mKE}}$: If $k = \bot$ then output (Decrypt, Fail). //Failure of decryption can occur for an honest receiver so we need an explicit failure notification.
4. If there is a record (c, k, m, N, 1), note $\mathsf{ready2decrypt} = $ *false* and output (Decrypt, m) to ($\Pi_{\mathsf{fs\_aead}}$, $\mathsf{sid}.fs$, pid).
5. If there is a record (c, N, 0), output (Decrypt, Fail) to ($\Pi_{\mathsf{fs\_aead}}$, $\mathsf{sid}.fs$, pid).
6. If IsCorrupt? = *false*
   - Run $\mathcal{I}(\mathsf{state}_\mathcal{I}, \mathsf{Authenticate}, \mathsf{pid}, c, N)$ and obtain updated state $\mathsf{state}_\mathcal{I}$ and a value v from $\mathcal{I}$.
   - If $v = \bot$ then record (c, N, 0), and output (Decrypt, Fail).
   - Otherwise, note $\mathsf{ready2decrypt} = $ *false*, and output (Decrypt, m).
7. Else (IsCorrupt? = *true*)
   - Send backdoor message ($\mathsf{state}_\mathcal{I}$, inject, pid, c, N) to $\mathcal{A}$.
   - Upon receiving response (inject, pid, c, N, v) from $\mathcal{A}$ continue.
   - If $v = \bot$ then record (c, N, 0), and output (Decrypt, Fail).
   - Else, note $\mathsf{ready2decrypt} = $ *false*, and output (Decrypt, v).

Corruption: On receiving (Corrupt) from ($\Pi_{\mathsf{fs\_aead}}$, $\mathsf{sid}.fs$, pid):

1. End the activation if $\mathsf{pid} \notin (\mathsf{pid}_0, \mathsf{pid}_1)$. Otherwise, let i be such that $\mathsf{pid} = \mathsf{pid}_i$. Else, set IsCorrupt? to *true*, and send (ReportState, $\mathsf{state}_\mathcal{I}$) to $\mathcal{A}$.
2. Upon receiving a response (ReportState, pid, S) from $\mathcal{A}$, send (Corrupt, S) to ($\Pi_{\mathsf{fs\_aead}}$, $\mathsf{sid}.fs$).

Fig. 10. The Authenticated Encryption with Associated Data Functionality, $\mathcal{F}_{\mathsf{aead}}$

$\mathcal{F}_{\mathsf{mKE}}$

This functionality has a session id sid.mKE that takes the following format: sid.mKE = ("mKE", sid.fs). Where sid.fs = ("fs_aead", sid, epoch_id). The local session ID is parsed as sid = (sid', pid_0, pid_1). Inputs arriving from machines whose identity is neither pid_0 nor pid_1 are ignored.

This functionality is parametrized by a seed length λ

RetrieveKey: On receiving (RetrieveKey, pid) from (Π_{aead}, sid.$aead$), where sid.$aead$ = ("$aead$", sid.fs, msg_num), or $\mathcal{F}_{\mathsf{aead}}$ if IsCorrupt? = $true$:

1. If this is the first activation,
   - Initialize dictionary key_dict and variables IsCorrupt? = $false$, msg_num$_0$, msg_num$_1$ = 0.
   - Parse sid to recover the two party ids (pid_0, pid_1).
2. If pid $\notin$ {pid_0, pid_1} then end this activation.
3. End the activation if there is record (Retrieved, i, msg_num) or a record (StopKeys, i, N) for $N <$ msg_num.
4. If IsCorrupt? = $false$:
   - If msg_num $\in$ key_dict.$keys$, set k = key_dict[msg_num].
   - Else (msg_num $\notin$ key_dict.$keys$), set $k \xleftarrow{\$} \{0,1\}^{\lambda}$.
5. Else (IsCorrupt? = $true$):
   - Send (RetrieveKey, pid, msg_num) to the the adversary.
   - Upon receiving (RetrieveKey, pid, k) from the adversary, continue.
6. Store key_dict[msg_num] = k.
7. If msg_num > msg_num$_i$, set msg_num$_i$ = msg_num.   //msg_num$_i$ is the largest successfully retrieved message by party i.
8. Record (Retrieved, i, msg_num) and output (RetrieveKey, pid, k) to (Π_{aead}, sid.$aead$).

StopKeys: On receiving (StopKeys, N) from (Π_{fs_aead}, sid.fs = ("fs_aead", sid, epoch_id, b), pid),

- Run steps 3-7 of RetrieveKey for all msg_num such that msg_num$_i$ < msg_num $\leq N$.
- Record (StopKeys, i, N) and output (StopKeys, Success).

Corruption: On receiving (Corrupt) from (Π_{fs_aead}, sid.fs = ("fs_aead", sid, epoch_id, b), pid):

1. Let i be such that pid = pid_i.
2. Set IsCorrupt? = $true$, create empty lists keys_in_transit, pending_msgs, and initialize chain_key $\xleftarrow{\$} \{0,1\}^{\lambda}$.
3. If msg_num$_i$ = 0 send (GetReceivingKey, epoch_id) to (Π_{eKE}, sid.eKE, pid).
   //The chain key is selected at random unless the receiver is corrupted before retrieving any keys for the epoch, this is because later chain keys should be unrelated to the initial one due to the PRG property. If the receiver has not retrieved any keys, we get the chain key from Π_{eKE} to provide to the simulator so that it matches the real world.
   //Also note that we only get corrupted if the sender has already initialized this box $\implies$ the sender's msg_num will never be 0.
4. On receiving (GetReceivingKey, recv_chain_key) set chain_key = recv_chain_key.
5. For all msg_num $\in$ key_dict.$keys$, if there is no record (Retrieved, i, msg_num) then append (msg_num, key_dict[msg_num]) to keys_in_transit and append msg_num to pending_msgs.
6. If there is a record (StopKeys, i, N) then let chain_key = $\bot$.
7. Send (ReportState, i, keys_in_transit, msg_num$_i$, chain_key) to $\mathcal{A}$.
8. On receiving a response (ReportState, i, S) from $\mathcal{A}$:
   - Output (Corrupt, pending_msgs, S) to ($\Pi_{\mathsf{fs\_aead}}$, sid.fs, pid_i).

Fig. 11. The Message Key Exchange Functionality $\mathcal{F}_{\mathsf{mKE}}$

$$\Pi_{\mathsf{eKE}}$$

This protocol has a party id pid and session id $\mathsf{sid}.eKE$ of the form: $\mathsf{sid}.eKE = (\text{``}eKE\text{''}, \mathsf{sid})$ where $\mathsf{sid} = (\mathsf{sid}', \mathsf{pid}_0, \mathsf{pid}_1)$.

keyGen chooses a random Diffie-Hellman exponent $\mathsf{epoch\_key} \xleftarrow{\$} |G|$ for a known group G and sets $\mathsf{epoch\_id} = g^{\mathsf{epoch\_key}}$.

ConfirmReceivingEpoch: On input $(\texttt{ConfirmReceivingEpoch}, \mathsf{epoch\_id}^*)$ from $(\Pi_{\mathsf{SGNL}}, \mathsf{sid}, \mathsf{pid}')$:

1. If $\mathsf{pid}' \neq \mathsf{pid}$, then end the activation. Let i be such that $\mathsf{pid} = \mathsf{pid}_i$.
2. Set $\mathsf{temp\_epoch\_id\_partner}_i = \mathsf{epoch\_id}^*$.
3. If this is the first activation:
   - Initialize state variables $\mathsf{root\_key}, \mathsf{epoch\_id}, \mathsf{epoch\_key}, \mathsf{sending\_chain\_key} = \bot$.
   - Send $(\texttt{GetInitKeys}, \mathsf{pid}_{1-i}, \mathsf{pid}_i)$ to $\mathcal{F}_{\mathsf{DIR}}$.
   - Upon receiving $(\texttt{GetInitKeys}, \mathsf{ik}_j^{\mathsf{pk}}, \mathsf{rk}_j^{\mathsf{pk}}, \mathsf{ok}_{j \leftarrow i}^{\mathsf{pk}})$, send input $(\texttt{ComputeSendingRootKey}, \mathsf{ik}_j^{\mathsf{pk}}, \mathsf{rk}_j^{\mathsf{pk}}, \mathsf{ok}_{j \leftarrow i}^{\mathsf{pk}})$ to $\mathcal{F}_{\mathsf{LTM}}$.
   - Upon receiving $(\texttt{ComputeSendingRootKey}, k, \mathsf{ek}_i^{\mathsf{pk}})$, set $\mathsf{root\_key} = k$.
   - Do steps 4-6 of **Compute Sending Chain Key**
   - Erase $\mathsf{ek}_i^{\mathsf{pk}}$ and output $(\texttt{ConfirmReceivingEpoch}, \mathsf{epoch\_id}_{\mathsf{self}} || \mathsf{ek}_i^{\mathsf{pk}} || \mathsf{ok}_{j \leftarrow i}^{\mathsf{pk}})$ to $(\Pi_{\mathsf{SGNL}}, \mathsf{sid}, \mathsf{pid}_i)$
4. Else (this is not the first activation):
   - **Compute Sending Chain Key.**
   - Output $(\texttt{ConfirmReceivingEpoch}, \mathsf{epoch\_id}_{\mathsf{self}})$ to $(\Pi_{\mathsf{SGNL}}, \mathsf{sid}, \mathsf{pid}_i)$.

GetSendingKey: On receiving input $(\texttt{GetSendingKey})$ from $(\Pi_{mKE}, \mathsf{sid}.mKE, \mathsf{pid}')$:

1. If $\mathsf{pid}' \neq \mathsf{pid}$, or if $\mathsf{sending\_chain\_key}$ has already been erased, end the activation.
2. Output $(\texttt{GetSendingKey}, \mathsf{sending\_chain\_key})$ and erase $\mathsf{sending\_chain\_key}$.

GetReceivingKey: On receiving input $(\texttt{GetReceivingKey}, \mathsf{epoch\_id})$ from $(\Pi_{mKE}, \mathsf{sid}, \mathsf{pid}')$:

1. If $\mathsf{pid}' \neq \mathsf{pid}$, then end the activation. Otherwise, let i be such that $\mathsf{pid} = \mathsf{pid}_i$.
2. Set $\mathsf{temp\_epoch\_id\_partner} = \mathsf{epoch\_id}$.
3. If this is the first activation:
   - Initialize state variables $\mathsf{root\_key}, \mathsf{epoch\_id}, \mathsf{epoch\_key}, \mathsf{sending\_chain\_key} = \bot$.
   - Parse $\mathsf{epoch\_id} = (\mathsf{epoch\_id}', \mathsf{ek}_j^{\mathsf{pk}}, \mathsf{ok}_{i \leftarrow j}^{\mathsf{pk}})$ and set $\mathsf{temp\_epoch\_id\_partner} = \mathsf{epoch\_id}'$
   - Send $(\texttt{GetResponseKeys}, \mathsf{pid}_{1-i})$ to $\mathcal{F}_{\mathsf{DIR}}$.
   - Upon receiving $(\texttt{GetResponseKeys}, \mathsf{ik}_j^{\mathsf{pk}})$, send input $(\texttt{ComputeReceivingRootKey}, \mathsf{ik}_j^{\mathsf{pk}}, \mathsf{ek}_j^{\mathsf{pk}}, \mathsf{ok}_{i \leftarrow j}^{\mathsf{pk}})$ to $\mathcal{F}_{\mathsf{LTM}}$.
   - Upon receiving $(\texttt{ComputeReceivingRootKey}, k)$, set $\mathsf{root\_key} = k$.
4. **Compute Receiving Chain Key.**
5. Output $(\texttt{GetReceivingKey}, \mathsf{temp\_recv\_chain\_key})$ and erase $\mathsf{temp\_recv\_chain\_key}$.

(The rest of this protocol is in Fig. 13)

Fig. 12. The Epoch Key Exchange Protocol Π_{eKE}

Π_{eKE} **continued...**

Corrupt: On   receiving   (Corrupt)   from   (Π_{SGNL}, sid, pid_i):   return
($\mathsf{epoch\_key}$, $\mathsf{epoch\_id}_{\mathsf{self}}$, $\mathsf{epoch\_id}_{\mathsf{partner}}$, $\mathsf{root\_key}$) to (Π_{SGNL}, sid, pid_i)

//Note that the Corrupt interface is not part of the "real" protocol; it is only included for UC-modelling purposes.

//Below are subroutines used in the interfaces above. The calls to Advance and Compute use Π_{KDF} that is a cascaded PRF − PRNG

Compute Sending Chain Key:

1. Compute $\mathsf{root\_input} = \mathsf{Exp}(\mathsf{temp\_epoch\_id}_{\mathsf{partner}}, \mathsf{epoch\_key}_{\mathsf{self}})$.
2. Compute ($\mathsf{root\_key}$) = $\Pi_{\mathsf{KDF}}.\mathsf{Advance}(\mathsf{root\_key}, \mathsf{root\_input})$.
3. Generate a key pair ($\mathsf{epoch\_key}_{\mathsf{self}}$, $\mathsf{epoch\_id}_{\mathsf{self}}$) ← keyGen().
4. Compute the next input $\mathsf{root\_input} = \mathsf{Exp}(\mathsf{temp\_epoch\_id}_{\mathsf{partner}}, \mathsf{epoch\_key}_{\mathsf{self}})$.
5. Compute ($\mathsf{root\_key}$, $\mathsf{sending\_chain\_key}$) = $\Pi_{\mathsf{KDF}}.\mathsf{Compute}(\mathsf{root\_key}, \mathsf{root\_input})$.
6. Finally, advance ($\mathsf{root\_key}$) = $\Pi_{\mathsf{KDF}}.\mathsf{Advance}(\mathsf{root\_key}, \mathsf{root\_input})$
7. Erase $\mathsf{root\_input}$. //The old root key is overwritten and therefore erased. The old sending chain key was already erased.

Compute Receiving Chain Key:

1. Compute $\mathsf{root\_input} = \mathsf{Exp}(\mathsf{temp\_epoch\_id}_{\mathsf{partner}}, \mathsf{epoch\_key}_{\mathsf{self}})$.
2. Compute ($\mathsf{root\_key}$, $\mathsf{temp\_recv\_chain\_key}$) = $\Pi_{\mathsf{KDF}}.\mathsf{Compute}(\mathsf{root\_key}, \mathsf{root\_input})$.
3. Erase $\mathsf{root\_input}$. //The old root key is overwritten and therefore already erased.

Fig. 13. The Epoch Key Exchange Protocol Π_{eKE} (continued)

Theorem 5. *Assume that* $KDF : \{0,1\}^n \to \{0,1\}^{2n}$ *is a CPRFG, that the DDH assumption holds in the group G. Then protocol Π_{eKE} UC-realizes the ideal functionality $\mathcal{F}_{\mathsf{eKE}}$ in the presence of global functionalities $\mathcal{F}_{\mathsf{DIR}}$ and $\mathcal{F}_{\mathsf{LTM}}$.*

Cascaded PRF-PRG. The goal of this primitive is to formalize the requirements required of a key derivation function (KDF) to adhere to the Signal specification [44] in the adaptive setting. We consider a stateful key derivation function (KDF) with two algorithms. Algorithm $\mathsf{Compute}(\mathsf{root\_key}, \mathsf{root\_input}) = (\mathsf{chain\_key}, \mathsf{root\_key}')$ is given a state $\mathsf{root\_key}$ and randomizer $\mathsf{root\_input}$, and computes a chaining key $\mathsf{chain\_key}$ and an updated state $\mathsf{root\_key}'$ (discarding the old state). Algorithm $\mathsf{Advance}(\mathsf{root\_key}, \mathsf{root\_input}) = \mathsf{root\_key}'$ is given a state $\mathsf{root\_key}$ and randomizer $\mathsf{root\_input}$, and updates the state for a new epoch.

Our *cascaded PRF-PRG* definition requires that the KDF be secure against an adversary who can repeatedly execute methods (Compute) and (Advance) at will, and who can also obtain the module's local state at any time. More specifically, we require existence of a simulator such that no adversary can distinguish an interaction with the scheme from an ideal interaction (Fig. 14) where the keys are truly random and the exposed state is generated by the simulator.

Cascaded PRF-PRG Security Game

Security game for a KDF (Compute, Advance) with domain $\{0,1\}^n$ for the initial secret state, domain $\{0,1\}^{m(n)}$ for the chaining keys and domain $\{R_n\}_{n \in N}$ for the randomizer, and a simulator S :

Real game:

– Oracle O is initialized with random state $s \leftarrow \{0,1\}^n$.
– On input (Compute, root_input): O runs Compute$(s, \text{root\_input}) = (\text{chain\_key}, \text{root\_key}')$, outputs chain_key and changes state $s = \text{root\_key}'$.
– On input (Advance): O chooses root_input$' \leftarrow R_n$ at random, runs Advance$(s, \text{root\_input}') = \text{root\_key}'$, and changes state $s = \text{root\_key}'$.
– On input (Expose–Advance): O outputs the old state s, chooses root_input$' \leftarrow R_n$ at random, computes Advance$(s, \text{root\_input}') = \text{root\_key}'$, and changes state $s = \text{root\_key}'$.

Ideal game:

– Oracle O is initialized with a state consisting of a random function $F : R_n \to \{0,1\}^m$.
– On input (Compute, root_input): O outputs $F(\text{root\_input}) = \text{chain\_key}$.
– On input (Advance): O updates its state to a new random function $F : R_n \to \{0,1\}^m$.
– On input (Expose–Advance): O outputs $S((\text{root\_input}_1, F(\text{root\_input}_1)), \ldots, (\text{root\_input}_k, F(\text{root\_input}_k)))$, where root_input$_1, \ldots,$ root_input$_k$ are all the queries made by A since the last Advance query and F is the currently used random function. Finally O updates its state to a new random function $F : R_n \to \{0,1\}^m$.

Fig. 14. Cascaded PRF-PRG Security Game

Definition 1 (Cascaded PRF-PRG (CPRFG)). *A KDF (Compute, Advance) is a cascaded PRF-PRG (CPRFG) if there exist polytime algorithm S such that any polytime oracle machine A can distinguish between the real and ideal interactions described in Fig. 14 only with advantage that is negligible in n.*

In the full version of this work [21], we show two constructions of a Cascaded PRF-PRG: a straightforward one based on a programmable random oracle, and a non-trivial construction in the plain model based on a puncturable PRF and a PRF-PRG (in the style of Alwen et al. [1]).

References

1. Alwen, J., Coretti, S., Dodis, Y.: The double ratchet: security notions, proofs, and modularization for the signal protocol. In: Ishai, Y., Rijmen, V. (eds.) EUROCRYPT 2019, Part I. LNCS, vol. 11476, pp. 129–158. Springer, Cham (2019). https://doi.org/10.1007/978-3-030-17653-2_5
2. Alwen, J., Coretti, S., Dodis, Y., Tselekounis, Y.: Security analysis and improvements for the IETF MLS standard for group messaging. In: Micciancio, D., Ristenpart, T. (eds.) CRYPTO 2020, Part I. LNCS, vol. 12170, pp. 248–277. Springer, Cham (2020). https://doi.org/10.1007/978-3-030-56784-2_9
3. Alwen, J., Coretti, S., Dodis, Y., Tselekounis, Y.: Modular design of secure group messaging protocols and the security of MLS. In: Vigna, G., Shi, E. (eds.) ACM CCS 2021, pp. 1463–1483. ACM Press, November 2021

4. Alwen, J., Coretti, S., Jost, D., Mularczyk, M.: Continuous group key agreement with active security. In: Pass, R., Pietrzak, K. (eds.) TCC 2020, Part II. LNCS, vol. 12551, pp. 261–290. Springer, Cham (2020). https://doi.org/10.1007/978-3-030-64378-2_10

5. Badertscher, C., Canetti, R., Hesse, J., Tackmann, B., Zikas, V.: Universal composition with global subroutines: capturing global setup within plain UC. In: Pass, R., Pietrzak, K. (eds.) TCC 2020, Part III. LNCS, vol. 12552, pp. 1–30. Springer, Cham (2020). https://doi.org/10.1007/978-3-030-64381-2_1

6. Badertscher, C., Hesse, J., Zikas, V.: On the (ir)replaceability of global setups, or how (not) to use a global ledger. In: Nissim, K., Waters, B. (eds.) TCC 2021, Part II. LNCS, vol. 13043, pp. 626–657. Springer, Cham (2021). https://doi.org/10.1007/978-3-030-90453-1_22

7. Balli, F., Rösler, P., Vaudenay, S.: Determining the core primitive for optimally secure ratcheting. In: Moriai, S., Wang, H. (eds.) ASIACRYPT 2020, Part III. LNCS, vol. 12493, pp. 621–650. Springer, Cham (2020). https://doi.org/10.1007/978-3-030-64840-4_21

8. Bellare, M., Rogaway, P.: Entity authentication and key distribution. In: Stinson, D.R. (ed.) CRYPTO 1993. LNCS, vol. 773, pp. 232–249. Springer, Heidelberg (1994). https://doi.org/10.1007/3-540-48329-2_21

9. Bellare, M., Rogaway, P.: Provably secure session key distribution: the three party case. In: 27th ACM STOC, pp. 57–66. ACM Press, May/June 1995

10. Bellare, M., Singh, A.C., Jaeger, J., Nyayapati, M., Stepanovs, I.: Ratcheted encryption and key exchange: the security of messaging. In: Katz, J., Shacham, H. (eds.) CRYPTO 2017, Part III. LNCS, vol. 10403, pp. 619–650. Springer, Cham (2017). https://doi.org/10.1007/978-3-319-63697-9_21

11. Bienstock, A., Dodis, Y., Rösler, P.: On the price of concurrency in group ratcheting protocols. In: Pass, R., Pietrzak, K. (eds.) TCC 2020, Part II. LNCS, vol. 12551, pp. 198–228. Springer, Cham (2020). https://doi.org/10.1007/978-3-030-64378-2_8

12. Bienstock, A., Fairoze, J., Garg, S., Mukherjee, P., Raghuraman, S.: A more complete analysis of the signal double ratchet algorithm. Cryptology ePrint Archive, Report 2022/355 (2022). https://eprint.iacr.org/2022/355

13. Blazy, O., Bossuat, A., Bultel, X., Fouque, P., Onete, C., Pagnin, E.: SAID: reshaping signal into an identity-based asynchronous messaging protocol with authenticated ratcheting. In: EuroS&P, pp. 294–309. IEEE (2019)

14. Borisov, N., Goldberg, I., Brewer, E.A.: Off-the-record communication, or, why not to use PGP. In: WPES, pp. 77–84. ACM (2004)

15. Caforio, A., Durak, F.B., Vaudenay, S.: Beyond security and efficiency: on-demand ratcheting with security awareness. In: Garay, J.A. (ed.) PKC 2021, Part II. LNCS, vol. 12711, pp. 649–677. Springer, Cham (2021). https://doi.org/10.1007/978-3-030-75248-4_23

16. Camenisch, J., Drijvers, M., Lehmann, A.: Universally composable direct anonymous attestation. In: Cheng, C.-M., Chung, K.-M., Persiano, G., Yang, B.-Y. (eds.) PKC 2016, Part II. LNCS, vol. 9615, pp. 234–264. Springer, Heidelberg (2016). https://doi.org/10.1007/978-3-662-49387-8_10

17. Campion, S., Devigne, J., Duguey, C., Fouque, P.-A.: Multi-device for signal. In: Conti, M., Zhou, J., Casalicchio, E., Spognardi, A. (eds.) ACNS 2020, Part II. LNCS, vol. 12147, pp. 167–187. Springer, Cham (2020). https://doi.org/10.1007/978-3-030-57878-7_9

18. Canetti, R.: Universally composable security: a new paradigm for cryptographic protocols. In: 42nd FOCS, pp. 136–145. IEEE Computer Society Press, October 2001

19. Canetti, R.: Universally composable security. J. ACM **67**(5), 28:1–28:94 (2020)
20. Canetti, R., Halevi, S., Herzberg, A.: Maintaining authenticated communication in the presence of break-ins. J. Cryptol. **13**(1), 61–105 (2000)
21. Canetti, R., Jain, P., Swanberg, M., Varia, M.: Universally composable end-to-end secure messaging. Cryptology ePrint Archive, Report 2022/376 (2022). https:// eprint.iacr.org/2022/376
22. Canetti, R., Krawczyk, H.: Analysis of key-exchange protocols and their use for building secure channels. In: Pfitzmann, B. (ed.) EUROCRYPT 2001. LNCS, vol. 2045, pp. 453–474. Springer, Heidelberg (2001). https://doi.org/10.1007/3-540-44987-6_28
23. Canetti, R., Krawczyk, H.: Universally composable notions of key exchange and secure channels. In: Knudsen, L.R. (ed.) EUROCRYPT 2002. LNCS, vol. 2332, pp. 337–351. Springer, Heidelberg (2002). https://doi.org/10.1007/3-540-46035-7_22
24. Canetti, R., Shahaf, D., Vald, M.: Universally composable authentication and key-exchange with global PKI. In: Cheng, C.-M., Chung, K.-M., Persiano, G., Yang, B.-Y. (eds.) PKC 2016, Part II. LNCS, vol. 9615, pp. 265–296. Springer, Heidelberg (2016). https://doi.org/10.1007/978-3-662-49387-8_11
25. Chase, M., Perrin, T., Zaverucha, G.: The signal private group system and anonymous credentials supporting efficient verifiable encryption. In: Ligatti, J., Ou, X., Katz, J., Vigna, G. (eds.) ACM CCS 2020, pp. 1445–1459. ACM Press, November 2020
26. Chen, K., Chen, J.: Anonymous end to end encryption group messaging protocol based on asynchronous ratchet tree. In: Meng, W., Gollmann, D., Jensen, C.D., Zhou, J. (eds.) ICICS 2020. LNCS, vol. 12282, pp. 588–605. Springer, Cham (2020). https://doi.org/10.1007/978-3-030-61078-4_33
27. Cohn-Gordon, K., Cremers, C., Dowling, B., Garratt, L., Stebila, D.: A formal security analysis of the signal messaging protocol. In: EuroS&P, pp. 451–466. IEEE (2017)
28. Cohn-Gordon, K., Cremers, C., Dowling, B., Garratt, L., Stebila, D.: A formal security analysis of the signal messaging protocol. J. Cryptol. **33**(4), 1914–1983 (2020)
29. Cohn-Gordon, K., Cremers, C., Garratt, L., Millican, J., Milner, K.: On ends-to-ends encryption: asynchronous group messaging with strong security guarantees. In: Lie, D., Mannan, M., Backes, M., Wang, X. (eds.) ACM CCS 2018, pp. 1802–1819. ACM Press, October 2018
30. Cohn-Gordon, K., Cremers, C.J.F., Garratt, L.: On post-compromise security. In: Hicks, M., Köpf, B. (eds.) CSF 2016 Computer Security Foundations Symposium, pp. 164–178. IEEE Computer Society Press (2016)
31. Cremers, C., Fairoze, J., Kiesl, B., Naska, A.: Clone detection in secure messaging: improving post-compromise security in practice. In: Ligatti, J., Ou, X., Katz, J., Vigna, G. (eds.) ACM CCS 2020, pp. 1481–1495. ACM Press, November 2020
32. Durak, F.B., Vaudenay, S.: Bidirectional asynchronous ratcheted key agreement with linear complexity. In: Attrapadung, N., Yagi, T. (eds.) IWSEC 2019. LNCS, vol. 11689, pp. 343–362. Springer, Cham (2019). https://doi.org/10.1007/978-3-030-26834-3_20
33. Hashimoto, K., Katsumata, S., Kwiatkowski, K., Prest, T.: An efficient and generic construction for signal's handshake (X3DH): post-quantum, state leakage secure, and deniable. In: Garay, J.A. (ed.) PKC 2021, Part II. LNCS, vol. 12711, pp. 410–440. Springer, Cham (2021). https://doi.org/10.1007/978-3-030-75248-4_15

34. Hofheinz, D., Rao, V., Wichs, D.: Standard security does not imply indistinguishability under selective opening. In: Hirt, M., Smith, A. (eds.) TCC 2016, Part II. LNCS, vol. 9986, pp. 121–145. Springer, Heidelberg (2016). https://doi.org/10.1007/978-3-662-53644-5_5

35. Jaeger, J., Stepanovs, I.: Optimal channel security against fine-grained state compromise: the safety of messaging. In: Shacham, H., Boldyreva, A. (eds.) CRYPTO 2018, Part I. LNCS, vol. 10991, pp. 33–62. Springer, Cham (2018). https://doi.org/10.1007/978-3-319-96884-1_2

36. Jost, D., Maurer, U., Mularczyk, M.: Efficient ratcheting: almost-optimal guarantees for secure messaging. In: Ishai, Y., Rijmen, V. (eds.) EUROCRYPT 2019, Part I. LNCS, vol. 11476, pp. 159–188. Springer, Cham (2019). https://doi.org/10.1007/978-3-030-17653-2_6

37. Jost, D., Maurer, U., Mularczyk, M.: A unified and composable take on ratcheting. In: Hofheinz, D., Rosen, A. (eds.) TCC 2019, Part II. LNCS, vol. 11892, pp. 180–210. Springer, Cham (2019). https://doi.org/10.1007/978-3-030-36033-7_7

38. Keybase blog: New cryptographic tools on keybase (2020). https://keybase.io/blog/crypto

39. Krohn, M.: Zoom rolling out end-to-end encryption offering (2020). https://blog.zoom.us/zoom-rolling-out-end-to-end-encryption-offering/

40. Martiny, I., Kaptchuk, G., Aviv, A.J., Roche, D.S., Wustrow, E.: Improving signal's sealed sender. In: NDSS. The Internet Society (2021)

41. Maurer, U.: Constructive cryptography – a primer. In: Sion, R. (ed.) FC 2010. LNCS, vol. 6052, p. 1. Springer, Heidelberg (2010). https://doi.org/10.1007/978-3-642-14577-3_1

42. Maurer, U.: Constructive cryptography – a new paradigm for security definitions and proofs. In: Mödersheim, S., Palamidessi, C. (eds.) TOSCA 2011. LNCS, vol. 6993, pp. 33–56. Springer, Heidelberg (2012). https://doi.org/10.1007/978-3-642-27375-9_3

43. Nielsen, J.B.: Separating random oracle proofs from complexity theoretic proofs: the non-committing encryption case. In: Yung, M. (ed.) CRYPTO 2002. LNCS, vol. 2442, pp. 111–126. Springer, Heidelberg (2002). https://doi.org/10.1007/3-540-45708-9_8

44. Open Whisper Systems: Technical information: Specifications and software libraries for developers (2016). https://signal.org/docs/

45. Perrin, T.: The noise protocol framework (2018). https://noiseprotocol.org/noise.html

46. Poettering, B., Rösler, P.: Towards bidirectional ratcheted key exchange. In: Shacham, H., Boldyreva, A. (eds.) CRYPTO 2018, Part I. LNCS, vol. 10991, pp. 3–32. Springer, Cham (2018). https://doi.org/10.1007/978-3-319-96884-1_1

47. Rösler, P., Mainka, C., Schwenk, J.: More is less: on the end-to-end security of group chats in signal, whatsapp, and threema. In: EuroS&P, pp. 415–429. IEEE (2018)

48. Rotem, L., Segev, G.: Out-of-band authentication in group messaging: computational, statistical, optimal. In: Shacham, H., Boldyreva, A. (eds.) CRYPTO 2018. LNCS, vol. 10991, pp. 63–89. Springer, Cham (2018). https://doi.org/10.1007/978-3-319-96884-1_3

49. Singh, M.: Whatsapp is now delivering roughly 100 billion messages a day (2020). https://techcrunch.com/2020/10/29/whatsapp-is-now-delivering-roughly-100-billion-messages-a-day/

50. Status: Private, secure communication (2022). https://status.im

51. Sylo: Comms for the metaverse (2022). https://sylo.io
52. Unger, N., et al.: SoK: secure messaging. In: 2015 IEEE Symposium on Security and Privacy, pp. 232–249. IEEE Computer Society Press, May 2015
53. Unger, N., Goldberg, I.: Deniable key exchanges for secure messaging. In: Ray, I., Li, N., Kruegel, C. (eds.) ACM CCS 2015, pp. 1211–1223. ACM Press, October 2015
54. Unger, N., Goldberg, I.: Improved strongly deniable authenticated key exchanges for secure messaging. PoPETs **2018**(1), 21–66 (2018)
55. Vatandas, N., Gennaro, R., Ithurburn, B., Krawczyk, H.: On the cryptographic deniability of the signal protocol. In: Conti, M., Zhou, J., Casalicchio, E., Spognardi, A. (eds.) ACNS 2020, Part II. LNCS, vol. 12147, pp. 188–209. Springer, Cham (2020). https://doi.org/10.1007/978-3-030-57878-7_10
56. WhatsApp LLC: About end-to-end encryption (2021). https://faq.whatsapp.com/general/security-and-privacy/end-to-end-encryption/
57. Yan, H., Vaudenay, S.: Symmetric asynchronous ratcheted communication with associated data. In: Aoki, K., Kanaoka, A. (eds.) IWSEC 2020. LNCS, vol. 12231, pp. 184–204. Springer, Cham (2020). https://doi.org/10.1007/978-3-030-58208-1_11

On the Insider Security of MLS

Joël Alwen[1], Daniel Jost[2(✉)] [iD], and Marta Mularczyk[1]

[1] AWS Wickr, New York, USA
{alwenjo,mulmarta}@amazon.com
[2] New York University, New York, USA
daniel.jost@cs.nyu.edu

Abstract. The *Messaging Layer Security* (MLS) protocol is an open standard for end-to-end (E2E) secure group messaging being developed by the IETF, poised for deployment to consumers, industry, and government. It is designed to provide E2E privacy and authenticity for messages in long-lived sessions whenever possible, despite the participation (at times) of malicious insiders that can adaptively interact with the PKI at will, actively deviate from the protocol, leak honest parties' states, and fully control the network. The core of the MLS protocol (from which it inherits essentially all of its efficiency and security properties) is a *Continuous Group Key Agreement* (CGKA) protocol. It provides asynchronous E2E *group management* by allowing group members to agree on a fresh independent symmetric key after every change to the group's state (e.g. when someone joins/leaves the group).

In this work, we make progress towards a precise understanding of the insider security of MLS (Draft 12). On the theory side, we overcome several subtleties to formulate the first notion of insider security for CGKA (or group messaging). Next, we isolate the core components of MLS to obtain a CGKA protocol we dub *Insider Secure TreeKEM* (ITK). Finally, we give a rigorous security proof for ITK. In particular, this work also initiates the study of insider secure CGKA and group messaging protocols. Along the way we give three new (very practical) attacks on MLS and corresponding fixes. (Those fixes have now been included into the standard.) We also describe a second attack against MLS-like CGKA protocols proven secure under all previously considered security notions (including those designed specifically to analyze MLS). These attacks highlight the pitfalls in simplifying security notions even in the name of tractability.

1 Introduction

1.1 Background and Motivation

A *Continuous Group Key Agreement* (CGKA) protocol allows an evolving group of parties to agree on a continuous sequence of shared symmetric keys. Most

D. Jost—Research supported by the Swiss National Science Foundation via Fellowship no. P2EZP2_195410. Work partially done while at ETH Zurich, Switzerland.

M. Mularczyk—Research supported by the Zurich Information Security and Privacy Center (ZISC). Work partially done while at ETH Zurich, Switzerland.

Y. Dodis and T. Shrimpton (Eds.): CRYPTO 2022, LNCS 13508, pp. 34–68, 2022.
https://doi.org/10.1007/978-3-031-15979-4_2

CGKA protocols are designed to be truly practical even when used over an adversarial network by large groups of uncoordinated parties with little, if any, common points of trust.

CGKA protocols should be end-to-end (E2E) secure and use *asynchronous* communication (in contrast to older, highly interactive, Dynamic Group Key Agreement protocols). That is, no assumptions are made about when or for how long parties are online. Instead, an (untrusted) network is expected only to buffer packets for each party until they come online again. As a consequence, all actions a party might wish to take must be performed non-interactively. Moreover, protocols cannot rely on specially designated parties (like the group managers in broadcast encryption). To achieve E2E security, protocols shouldn't rely on trusted third parties including the PKI that distributes long and short term public keys.[1]

Intuitively, CGKA protocols encapsulate the cryptographic core necessary to build higher-level distributed E2E secure group applications like secure messaging (not unlike how Key Encapsulation captures the core of Public Key Encryption). Any change to a group's state (e.g. parties joining/leaving) initiates a new *epoch* in a CGKA session. Each epoch E is equipped with its own uniform and independent epoch key k_E, called the *application secret* of E, which can be derived by all group members in E. The term "application secret" reflects the expectation that k_E will be used by a higher-level cryptographic application during E.[2] For example, k_E might seed a key schedule to derive (epoch specific) symmetric keys and nonces, allowing group members in E to use authenticated encryption for exchanging private and authenticated messages during E.

The Messaging Layer Security Protocol. Probably the most important family of CGKA protocols today is TreeKEM. An initial version was introduced in [34]. It was soon followed by a more precise description in [18] and the improved version [14]. Another major revision came with the introduction of the "propose-and-commit" paradigm [17]. The product of this evolution (implicitly) makes up most of the cryptographic core of the latest draft (Draft 12) of the *Messaging Layer Security* (MLS) protocol [13]. It is this most recent version which is the main focus of this work.

MLS is being developed under the auspices of the IETF. It aims to set an open standard for E2E secure group messaging; in particular, for very large groups (e.g. 50K users). MLS is being developed by an international collaboration of academic cryptographers and industry actors including Cisco, Cloudflare, Facebook, Google, Twitter, Wickr, and Wire. Together, these already provide messaging services to over 2 billion users across all sectors of society. The IETF is currently soliciting more feedback from the cryptographic community in hopes of finalizing the current draft.

---

[1] Concretely, the servers distributing keys are normally *not* trusted per se. Instead trust is established by, say, further equipping participants with tools to perform out-of-band audits of the responses they receive from the server.

[2] In the newest draft of MLS the term "application secret" has been changed to "encryption secret".

Insider Security. Intuitively, MLS is designed to provide security whenever possible in the face of a weak PKI and despite potential participation by malicious insiders with very powerful adaptive capabilities. These include full control of the network and repeatedly leaking the local states of honest users and even choosing their random coins[3]. However, thus far it has remained open how to formally capture (let alone analyze) such a security notion for CGKA/group messaging. Instead, simplified security models have been used to analyze (various versions of) TreeKEM. See Sect. 1.3 for a thorough discussion. Most critically, none of these models let the adversary deliver *arbitrary* packets; a very natural capability for a real-world attacker controlling the network. Further, they do not let the adversary register public keys in the PKI (let alone without proving knowledge of the corresponding secret keys) or choose all random coins of corrupt parties.

1.2   Our Contribution

New Security Model. To further our understanding of how MLS behaves against such insider attacks, we first precisely define insider security of CGKA. In our new model, the adversary has all above-mentioned capabilities available to malicious insiders. Our notion captures correctness as well as the following security goals: security of epoch secret keys, authenticity and agreement on group state. Formally, our model extends the notions in [8] to capture a more accurate and untrusted PKI (solving an open problem from [8]). E.g., in our model the adversary can register arbitrary (even long term) public keys on behalf of parties and without proving knowledge of corresponding secrets. Of course, security is degraded for epochs in which such keys are used but, crucially, only those.

We note that our notion can be used to analyze different CGKA protocols and compare their security guarantees. We believe that it should be directly applicable to (propose/commit versions of) protocols like [6,10,29]. Further, in a subsequent work [28] the authors use it (after small modification) to prove that their protocol enjoys the same security as TreeKEM.

Security of TreeKEM. Second, we isolate the core features of the full MLS protocol, Draft 12 (the most recent draft at the time of writing) sufficient for realizing an insider secure CGKA protocol. We call the result *Insider Secure TreeKEM* (ITK). Specifically, ITK augments TreeKEM with message authentication, tree-signing, confirmation keys and small parts of MLS's key schedule.

Third, we prove that ITK is secure in our model. Our analysis unveiled three new (and quite practical) attacks on MLS Draft 10. All attacks require the capabilities of malicious insiders, and hence they are outside the models used so far to analyze MLS, which explains why they went unnoticed until now. We proposed fixes for each of the three attacks. They have since been incorporated into to the IETF standard (in Draft 11) and are already reflected in ITK. In summary, the result of the attacks are as follows:

---

[3] We stress that adversarially chosen coins can lead to real-world attacks, see e.g. [22].

1. A malicious insider can invite a victim to an artificial group (that includes any number of other honest parties) such that the adversary can continue to derive epoch secrets in the group even after they were supposedly removed from the group by the victim.
2. A malicious insider can break agreement. That is, they can craft two packets delivering each to a different honest user with the result that they will both accept them, agree on their next epoch secret keys, but will in fact be out-of-sync and no longer accept each other's messages.
3. The mode of MLS where ITK packets are not encrypted provides weaker authenticity than intended.

The first attack is the most interesting, since it relies on the flawed design of the so-called tree-signing mechanism, adopted due to a lack of (even intuitive) clarity around what it *should* do (which lead to differing constructions being proposed and significant debate on the topic within the MLS working group, e.g. [1,32,35]). This work finally elucidates what is the goal of tree signing.

Justifying the New Model. Finally, to justify our model and the importance of formally capturing the *complete* adversarial capabilities against which CGKA protocols intend to defend, we formally prove the following: First, for each of the three fixes for the above mentioned attacks, ITK modified to undo the fix is *not* secure in our model. Second, we observe that all previous analyses of CGKA protocols (including TreeKEM and others) in simplified models assumed CPA security of the encryption schemes they use, implying that this is sufficient (see e.g. [6,7,10]). We show that this is an oversimplification by demonstrating a practical attack on ITK modified to use a particular (contrived) CPA secure scheme, resulting in malicious insiders being able to compute epoch secrets after having been removed from the group. Again, we show that the above modification of ITK is not secure in our model. (Fortunately, as implied by [5], the PKE used in MLS is indeed CCA secure which we show to be sufficient.)

1.3   Related Work

Analyses of MLS. A summary is given in Table 1. The research on CGKA was initiated with the introduction of the Asynchronous Ratcheting Tree (ART) protocol by Cohn-Gordon et al. in [24]. ART later was adopted as part of MLS Draft 1, before being replaced by TreeKEM as part of Draft 2. TreeKEM based MLS has been analyzed in the computational setting (using the game-based approach) in the works [6,7,21]. The work by [6] analyzed the TreeKEM portion of MLS and, to this end, coined the respective CGKA abstraction. On the other hand, [7] considers the full MLS protocol and, importantly, validates the soundness of the CGKA abstraction as an intermediate building block.

In contrast to this work, [6,7] however used simplified security models. In [6] the adversary is forced to deliver packets in the same order to all parties and learns nothing about the coins of parties she has compromised. Meanwhile, [7] permits arbitrary packet delivery scheduling and leaks the random coins of corrupt parties but still does not allow the adversary to choose corrupt parties'

Table 1. Related work: Analyses of MLS.

	MLS Version	Part Analyzed	Adversarial Model	Considers Group Splits	Framework
[24]	Draft 1 (ART)	CGKA in static groups	active	yes	part game-based, part symbolic
[6]	Draft 6	CGKA	passive	no	game-based
[19]	Draft 7	Messaging	insider	yes	symbolic
[7]	Draft 11	Messaging	semi-active	yes	game-based
[21]	Draft 11	Key derivation	insider	n/a	game-based
[25]	Draft 11	Multi-group messaging	n/a	n/a	n/a
this work	Draft 12	CGKA	insider	yes	UC

coins. Neither model allows fully active attacks. In [6], the adversary cannot modify/inject packets at all while in [7] she may only deliver modified/injected packets to an honest party if the party will reject the packet.

Further, [21] focuses exclusively on the pseudorandomness of secrets produced by the key derivation process in MLS. So, unlike other works, they do not consider the general effects malformed protocol packets can have (e.g. as part of an arbitrary active attack). Instead they focus only on a specific set of effects such packets could have on the key derivation mechanism in MLS. (So for example, they make no statements about authenticity.) In contrast to the other two works, they also only allow for a limited type of adaptivity where adversaries must leak secrets at the moment they are first derived and no later. On the other hand, [21] considers a more fine-grained leakage model where secrets can be individually leaked rather than the whole local state of the victim at once. Finally, the recent work of [25] considers the PCS guarantees provided by MLS in the multi-session setting. Surprisingly, they identify significant inefficiencies in terms of the amount of bandwidth (and computation) required by a multi-session MLS client to return to a fully secure state after a state compromise. They present intuitive deficiencies of MLS-style constructions but they do not define a formal security model.

Complementing the above line of work, the paper [19] analyzed the insider security of TreeKEM as of Draft 7 in the symbolic setting (in the sense of Dolev-Yao). Their model covers most intuitive adversary's abilities and security properties considered in this work. Actually, they even consider a slightly more fine-grained corruption model that allows the adversary to corrupt individual keys held by parties. It is noteworthy, however, that [19] analyze a version of TreeKEM that does not yet have any tree-signing mechanism. Consequently, they find an attack on TreeKEM Draft 7 (that would also appear in our insider security model) and proposes a strong version of tree signing (aka. "tree-hash based parent hash") that prevents it. Unfortunately, that scheme soon became unworkable (i.e. not correct) as it conflicts with new mechanisms in subsequent drafts of TreeKEM, namely truncation and unmerged leaves. Thus, Draft 9 TreeKEM/MLS adopted a different, more efficient version of tree signing. In this work, we show however that the latter version is too weak and propose a new tree-signing mechanism providing the desired security.

Table 2. Related work: Other CGKA protocols. Top: protocols that improve efficiency over TreeKEM. Bottom: protocols that improve security.

	Protocol	Approach to Improving Efficiency	Adversarial Model	Considers Group Splitting	Framework
[10]	Tainted TreeKEM	Geared to a setting with administrators	passive	yes	game-based
[36]	Causal TreeKEM	Concurrency (static groups, no PCS)	passive	yes	game-based
[20]	Concurrent Group Ratcheting	Concurrency (static groups)	passive synchronous	no	game-based
[4]	CoCoA	Concurrency and partial views of the group state (*)	passive	yes	game-based
[3]	DeCAF	Concurrency and partial views of the group state (faster PCS than CoCoA)	passive	yes	game-based
[28]	CmPKE	Server-aided CGKA: better bandwidth	insider	yes	UC
[9]	SAIK	Server-aided CGKA: better bandwidth	active	yes	UC
[2]	Grafting Key Trees	Utilize multiple overlapping groups	n/a	n/a	n/a

	Protocol	Security Goal	Adversarial Model	Considers Group Splitting	Framework
[6]	RTreeKEM	Stronger PCFS	passive	no	game-based
[8]	Optimally Secure	Best-possible security	active	yes	UC
[27]	Membership Private ART	Hiding group roster and message senders	n/a	n/a	n/a

(*) Partial views means that parties fetch parts of their state on demand from an untrusted server.

Other CGKA Protocols. Numerous alternative CGKA protocols have been considered, in various security models, as summarized in Table 2. First, the Tainted TreeKEM protocol [10] exhibits a different complexity profile than the TreeKEM protocol, optimized for groups with a small set of "administrators" (i.e., parties making changes to the group roster). It was shown to enjoy the same security as TreeKEM, Draft 7, at least with regards to adaptive but passive adversaries.

Another line of research aims for better efficiency than that of TreeKEM. First, the works [3,4,20,36] achieve this by supporting (to various degrees) concurrent changes to the group state. Further, the works [9,28] proposed a different communication model of CGKA: Instead of an untrusted broadcast channel, they consider a more general (untrusted) delivery service that processes the messages and delivers to each party only the part it needs, greatly improving bandwidth. We note that [9] uses a simplified security model based on [8], while [28] uses the model proposed in this work. Finally, the work [2] introduced new techniques to accommodate for multiple intersecting groups, which may enable to get better efficiency than running several CGKAs in parallel, partially remedying the issues uncovered by [25]. (They do not specify a CGKA protocol.)

From a different angle, various constructions aim to improve on the security guarantees of TreeKEM and MLS. First, the RTreeKEM construction of [6] improved on the forward secrecy properties of the TreeKEM family of protocols, albeit by making use of non-standard (but practically efficient) cryptographic components. Further, the three CGKA protocols in [8] eschew the constraint of practical efficiency to instead focus on exploring new mechanisms for achieving the increasingly stringent security notions introduced in that work. In particular, they introduce two notions of so-called robustness for CGKA. A *weakly robust* CGKA ensures that if a honest party in epoch E accepts an arbitrary packet p, then all other honest parties in epoch E either end up in the same state as that party or reject p. In a *strongly robust* CGKA it is further guaranteed that then all other parties currently in E will accept p. Note that neither ITK nor MLS (as a whole) are strongly robust.[4] A variant of strong robustness has also been considered by [26] who propose efficient zero-knowledge proofs with which a group member can prove to the delivery server that his message is well formed. They observe that in case the server behaves honestly, this allows the server to prevent group splitting attacks (a type of denial-of-service) caused by malicious insiders. Albeit, they do not introduce or analyze a full CGKA or messaging protocol. Finally, [27] presented CGKA with novel membership hiding properties. However, no security definitions are given.

1.4 Outline of the Rest of the Paper

We define insider secure CGKA in Sect. 3. In Sect. 4, we specify the ITK protocol. We then formalize the exact security properties achieved by ITK and sketch the respective security proof in Sect. 5. The four attacks are described in Sect. 6.

2 Preliminaries

2.1 Notation

We use $v \leftarrow x$ to denote assigning the value x to the variable v and $v \leftarrow\$ S$ to denote sampling an element u.a.r. from a set S. If V denotes a variable storing a set, then we write $V +\leftarrow x$ and $V -\leftarrow x$ as shorthands for $V \leftarrow V \cup \{x\}$ and $V \leftarrow V \setminus \{x\}$, respectively. We further make use of associative arrays and use $A[i] \leftarrow x$ and $y \leftarrow A[i]$ to denote assignment and retrieval of element i, respectively. Additionally, we denote by $A[*] \leftarrow v$ the initialization of the array to the default value v. Further, we use the following keywords: **req** *cond* denotes that if the condition *cond* is false, then the current function unwinds all state changes and returns $\bot$. **assert** *cond* is used in the description of functionalities to validate inputs of the simulator. It means that if *cond* is false, then the given functionality permanently halts, making the real and ideal worlds trivially distinguishable.

2.2 Universal Composability

We use the Universal Composability (UC) framework [23].

The Corruption Model. We use the—standard for CGKA/SGM but non-standard for UC—corruption model of continuous state leakage (transient passive corruptions) and adversarially chosen randomness of [8].[5] In a nutshell, this corruption model allows the adversary to repeatedly corrupt parties by sending

---

[4] E.g. a malformed (commit) packet can be constructed by an insider such that part of the group accepts it but the rest do not.

[5] Passive corruptions and full network control allow to emulate active corruptions.

them two types of corruption messages: (1) a message Expose causes the party to send its current state to the adversary (once), (2) a message (CorrRand, b) sets the party's rand-corrupted flag to b. If b is set, the party's randomness-sampling algorithm is replaced by the adversary providing the coins instead. Ideal functionalities are activated upon corruptions and can adjust their behavior accordingly.

Restricted Environments. In order to avoid the so-called commitment problem caused by adaptive corruptions in simulation-based frameworks, we restrict the environment not to corrupt parties at certain times. (This roughly corresponds to ruling out "trivial attacks" in game-based definitions. In simulation-based frameworks, such attacks are no longer trivial, but security against them requires strong cryptographic tools and is not achieved by most protocols.) To this end, we use the technique used in [8] (based on prior work by Backes et al. [12] and Jost et al. [30]) and consider a weakened variant of UC security that only quantifies over a restricted set of so-called admissible environments that do not exhibit the commitment problem. Whether an environment $\mathcal{Z}$ is admissible or not is defined as part of the ideal functionality $\mathcal{F}$: The functionality can specify certain boolean conditions, and $\mathcal{Z}$ is then called admissible (for $\mathcal{F}$), if it has negligible probability of violating any such condition when interacting with $\mathcal{F}$.

3   Insider-Secure Continuous Group Key Agreement

This section defines security of CGKA protocols. For better readability, we skip some less crucial details. We refer to the full version [11] for the precise definition.

3.1   Overview

Security via Idealized Services. We model security and correctness of CGKA in the Universal Composability (UC) framework [23]. At a high level, this means that a CGKA protocol is secure if no efficient environment $\mathcal{Z}$ can distinguish between the following two experiments: First, in the real world experiment, $\mathcal{Z}$ interacts with an instance of the CGKA protocol. It controls all parties, i.e., it chooses their inputs and receives their outputs and the adversary, i.e., it corrupts parties. Second, in the ideal world experiment, $\mathcal{Z}$ interacts with an ideal *CGKA functionality* $\mathcal{F}_{\text{CGKA}}$ and a simulator $\mathcal{S}$. $\mathcal{F}_{\text{CGKA}}$ represents the idealized "CGKA service" a CGKA protocol should provide and is secure by design (like a trusted third party). $\mathcal{S}$ translates the real-world adversary's actions into corresponding ones in the ideal world. Since $\mathcal{F}_{\text{CGKA}}$ is secure by definition, this implies that the real-world execution cannot exhibit any attacks either. Readers not familiar with UC should think of $\mathcal{Z}$ as the adversary attacking the protocol.

In our model, analogous to [8], whenever $\mathcal{Z}$ instructs a party to perform some group operation (e.g. adding a new member) $\mathcal{F}_{\text{CGKA}}$ simply hands back an idealized protocol message to that party—it is then up to $\mathcal{Z}$ to deliver those protocol messages to the other group members, thus not making any assumptions on the underlying network or the architecture of the delivery service.

The Attack Model. In this work, we consider a powerful adversary that (a) fully controls the network (i.e., the delivery service), and (b) potentially colludes with malicious insiders. The former is captured by having $\mathcal{Z}$ (i.e., the attacker) deliver packets. The latter is captured by giving the adversary the following abilities: to register arbitrary PKI keys on behalf of any party, to repeatedly leak parties' states and to choose randomness used by parties. The first attack vector is reflected in our PKI functionalities in Sect. 3.2. The latter two vectors are reflected in our choice of UC corruption model described in Sect. 2.

We remark that additionally considering a model with malicious insider attacker but an honest delivery infrastructure is an interesting open problem. It appears, however, that in case of MLS an honest delivery server cannot prevent most of a malicious insider's attacks such as group-splitting attacks (see below).

Security Guarantees. Our model captures the following security properties: consistency, confidentiality and authenticity. They are reflected in different aspects of the ideal functionality $\mathcal{F}_{\text{CGKA}}$. We note that $\mathcal{F}_{\text{CGKA}}$ maintains a symbolic representation of the group's evolution, including corruptions, in the form of a history graph [7], where nodes represent epochs.

Intuitively, consistency means that all parties in the same epoch agree on the group state, including e.g. the history of the group's evolution. This is formalized by $\mathcal{F}_{\text{CGKA}}$ outputting consistent information to all parties in the same node of the graph. $\mathcal{F}_{\text{CGKA}}$ is parameterized by a predicate **safe** which identifies confidential epochs, i.e., ones for which the adversary must have no information about its group secret, for a given CGKA protocol and graph. For each confidential epoch, $\mathcal{F}_{\text{CGKA}}$ chooses a random and independent secret (and outputs it to parties who decide to fetch it) while for other epochs the key is arbitrary, i.e., chosen by the simulator. Authenticity for a party A and epoch E holds if $\mathcal{Z}$ cannot inject messages on behalf of A in E. $\mathcal{F}_{\text{CGKA}}$ is parameterized by a predicate **inj-allowed** which decides whether messages can be injected on behalf of the party.

The PKI. In the real-world experiment, the parties execute the protocol that furthermore interacts with the (untrusted) PKI. The latter is modeled as two UC functionalities: Authentication Service (AS) which manages long-term identity keys and Key Service (KS) that allows parties to upload single-use key packages, used by group members to non-interactively add them to the group (see Sect. 3.2 for details). Our model is agnostic to how these functionalities are realized, as long as the behavior we describe is implemented.

The primary interaction with the PKI is not group specific and, thus, it is assumed to be handled by the higher-level protocol embedding CGKA. Intuitively, this means that the protocol requires that the environment registers all keys necessary for a given group operation before performing it. As the PKI management is exposed to the environment in the real world, those operations also need to be available in the ideal world. We achieve this by having "ideal-world variants" of the AS and KS, which should be thought of as part of $\mathcal{F}_{\text{CGKA}}$. The ideal AS records which keys have been exposed, which is then used to define the predicates. The actual keys in the ideal world do not convey any particular meaning beyond serving as identifiers.

Group-Splitting Attacks. The following attack is inherent to any CGKA protocol: A malicious delivery service selectively forwards different packets to different group members, causing them to have inconsistent views of the group's evolution. Such members will never end up in the same epoch again (and so they will not be able to communicate), as this would contradict the consistency property. Our ideal functionality $\mathcal{F}_{\mathrm{CGKA}}$ accounts for this with the history graph forming a tree, with different branches representing different partitions.

We remark that there is another type of splitting attack where (the delivery service may be honest but) a malicious insider creates a message that is accepted by some but not other members of the group. (Note that all parties accepting the commit will end up in a consistent state.) MLS does not prevent this attack, and this is reflected in our model. We note that the only way to prevent such attacks that we are aware of relies on zero-knowledge proofs [8,26] which are not widely implemented primitives MLS is constrained to use.

On the Choice of UC Security. First, the UC framework lends itself well to strong and comprehensive security definitions. Indeed, UC definitions naturally gravitate towards strongest possible guarantees. In fact, formalizing weak guarantees typically takes extra effort: Each of a protocol's weaknesses must be explicitly accounted for by providing the simulator all the necessary capabilities to emulate the effect when interacting with the ideal functionality. In contrast, game-based notions lend themselves well to simple definitions that focus on the core of a problem—potentially deliberately ignoring certain attack vectors (such as active attacks in many of the secure group-messaging work) for simplicity.

Second, the UC framework provides plenty of useful conventions and building blocks, such as the interaction with complex setup functionalities. Third, the UC framework allows us to directly formalize the *guarantees*, independent of the concrete scheme. For instance, when an active attacker can inject messages, we care about the potential effects and not so much about which exact bit-string the attacker might craft has which effect—which is handled by the simulator in our UC-based notion. (Game-based formalizations, such as [7], often circumvent this by augmenting the *primitive* to output additional information specially needed for formalizing the game, such as the interpretation of a given message.)

3.2   PKI Setup

In general, we model fully untrusted PKI, where the adversary can register arbitrary keys for any party (looking ahead, security guarantees degrade if such keys are used in the protocol). This especially models insider attacks.[6] All functionalities are formally defined in the full version [11].

---

[6] In particular, we do not assume so-called key-registration with knowledge. This is a significantly stronger assumption, typically not achieved by the heuristic checks deployed in reality, and it is not needed for security of ITK.

Authentication Service (AS). The AS provides an abstract credential mechanism that maps from user identities, e.g. phone numbers, to long-term identity keys of the given user. Different credential mechanisms of MLS are abstracted by the functionality $\mathcal{F}_{\mathrm{AS}}$, which maintains a set of registered pairs $(\mathsf{id}, \mathsf{spk})$, denoting that user id registered the key spk under their identity. It works as follows:

- A party id can check if a pair $(\mathsf{id}', \mathsf{spk}')$ is registered.
- id can register a new key. In this case, $\mathcal{F}_{\mathrm{AS}}$ generates a pair $(\mathsf{spk}, \mathsf{ssk})$ (the key-generation algorithm is a parameter), sends spk to id and registers $(\mathsf{id}, \mathsf{spk})$. spk can be later retrieved at any time and then deleted.[7] If id's randomness is corrupted, the adversary provides the key-generation randomness.
- The adversary can register an arbitrary pair $(\mathsf{id}, \mathsf{spk})$.
- When a party's state is exposed, all secret keys it has generated but not deleted yet are leaked to the adversary.

Key Service (KS). The KS allows parties to upload one-time key packages, used to add them to groups while they are offline. This is abstracted by the functionality $\mathcal{F}_{\mathrm{KS}}$. $\mathcal{F}_{\mathrm{KS}}$ maintains pairs $(\mathsf{id}, \mathsf{kp})$, denoting a user's identity and a registered key package. For each $(\mathsf{id}, \mathsf{kp})$, $\mathcal{F}_{\mathrm{KS}}$ stores id's long-term key spk which authenticates the package and for some $(\mathsf{id}, \mathsf{kp})$, it stores the secret key. $\mathcal{F}_{\mathrm{KS}}$ works as follows:

- A party id can request a key package for another party id'. $\mathcal{F}_{\mathrm{KS}}$ sends to id a kp chosen by the adversary in an arbitrary way, i.e. the KS is fully untrusted.
- id can register a new key package. To this end, id specifies a long-term key pair $(\mathsf{spk}, \mathsf{ssk})$ (reflecting that a key package may be signed), $\mathcal{F}_{\mathrm{KS}}$ generates a fresh package $(\mathsf{kp}, \mathsf{sk})$ for id (using a package-generation algorithm that takes as input $(\mathsf{spk}, \mathsf{ssk})$), sends kp to id and registers $(\mathsf{id}, \mathsf{kp})$ with spk.
- id can retrieve all its secret keys (this accounts for the protocol not a priori knowing which key package has been used to add it to the group).
- id can delete one of its secret keys. When its state is exposed, all secret keys it generated but not deleted are leaked to the adversary.

Note that the adversary does not need to register its own packages, since it already determines all retrieved packages.

Ideal-World Variants. The ideal-world variant of AS, $\mathcal{F}_{\mathrm{AS}}^{\mathrm{IW}}$, marks leaked and adversarially registered long-term keys as exposed. The ideal-world variant of KS, $\mathcal{F}_{\mathrm{KS}}^{\mathrm{IW}}$, stores the same mapping between key package and long-term key as $\mathcal{F}_{\mathrm{KS}}$. Intuitively, each key package for which the long-term key spk is exposed (according to AS) is considered exposed. (For simplicity, our ideal world abstracts away key packages. We believe this to be a good trade-off between abstraction and fine-grained guarantees.) Both $\mathcal{F}_{\mathrm{AS}}^{\mathrm{IW}}$ and $\mathcal{F}_{\mathrm{KS}}^{\mathrm{IW}}$ are not parameterized by key-generation algorithms. Instead, on key registration, the adversary is asked to provide a key pair.

---

[7] The secret key must be fetched separately, because the key is registered by the environment before the secret key is fetched by the protocol.

3.3   Interfaces of the CGKA Functionality

This section explains the inputs to $\mathcal{F}_{CGKA}$, which defines the syntax of CGKA.

Proposals and Commits. ITK is a so-called propose-and-commit variant of a CGKA, where current group members can propose to *add* new members, *remove* existing ones, or *update* their own key material (for PCS) by sending out a corresponding *proposal message*. The proposals do not affect the group state immediately. Rather, they (potentially) take effect upon transitioning to the next epoch: The party initiating the transition collects a list of proposals in a *commit message* broadcast to the group. Upon receiving such a message, each party applies the indicated proposals and transitions to the new epoch. For simplicity, we delegate the buffering of proposals to the higher-level protocol.

Identity Keys. In a real-world deployment, long-term identity keys maintained by the Authentication Service (AS) are likely to be shared across groups. Hence, we also delegate their handling to the higher-level messaging application invoking CGKA. In general, in each group a party uses one signing key at a time. Upon issuing an operation updating the CGKA secrets—i.e., proposing an update or committing—the higher-level may decide to update the signing key as well. Those operations, thus, explicitly take a signing public key spk as input.

Formal Syntax. The functionality accepts the following inputs (for simplicity, we treat the party's identity id as implicitly known to the protocol):

- **Group Creation:** $(\texttt{Create}, \text{spk})$ creates a new group with id being the single member, using the signing public key spk. (This input is only allowed once.)
- **Add, Remove Proposals:** $p \leftarrow (\texttt{Propose}, \text{add-id}_t)$ (resp., $p \leftarrow (\texttt{Propose}, \text{rem-id}_t)$) proposes to add (resp., remove) the party id_t. It outputs a proposal p, or $\perp$ if either id is not in or id_t already in (resp., not in) the group.
- **Update Proposal:** $p \leftarrow (\texttt{Propose}, \text{up-spk})$ proposes to update the member's key material, and optionally the long-term signature verification key spk. It outputs an update proposal message p (or $\perp$ if id is not in the group).
- **Commit:** $(c, w) \leftarrow (\texttt{Commit}, \vec{p}, \text{spk})$ commits the vector of proposals $\vec{p}$ and outputs the commit message c and the (optional) welcome message w. The operation optionally updates the signing public key of the committer.
- **Process:** $(\text{id}_c, \text{propSem}) \leftarrow (\texttt{Process}, c, \vec{p})$ processes the message c committing proposals $\vec{p}$ and advances id to the next epoch.[8] It outputs the committer id_c and a vector conveying the semantics of the applied proposals.
- **Join:** $(\text{roster}, \text{id}_c) \leftarrow (\texttt{Join}, w)$ allows id (who is not yet a group member) to join the group using the welcome message w. It outputs the roster, i.e. the set of identities and long-term keys of all group members, and the identity id_c of the member who committed the add proposal.
- **Key:** $K \leftarrow \texttt{Key}$ queries the current application secret. This can only be queried once per epoch by each group member (otherwise returning $\perp$).

---

[8] For simplicity, we require that the higher-level protocol that buffers proposals also finds the list p matching c. This is without loss of generality, since ITK uses MLSPlaintext for sending proposals, and c includes hashes of proposals in $\vec{p}$.

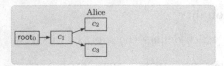

(a) The passive case. Alice processes c_1 and c_2.

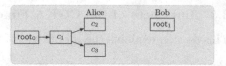

(b) Bob joins using injected w'. We don't know where to connect the detached root.

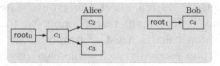

(c) Bob (honestly) commits, creating c_4 in detached tree.

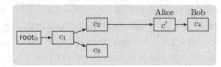

(d) Alice commits with bad randomness and re-computes c' corresponding to w'. We attach the root.

Fig. 1. An example execution with injections and bad randomness, and the corresponding history graph. For simplicity, proposal nodes are excluded.

3.4 History Graph

The functionality $\mathcal{F}_{\text{CGKA}}$ uses history graphs to symbolically represent a group's evolution. A history graph is a labeled directed graph. It has two types of nodes: *commit* and *proposal nodes*, representing all executed commit and propose operations, respectively. Note that each commit node represents an epoch. The nodes' labels, furthermore, keep track of all the additional information relevant for defining security. In particular, *all* nodes store the following values:

- orig: the party whose action created the node, i.e., the message sender;
- par: the parent commit node, representing the sender's current epoch;
- stat $\in \{\text{good}, \text{bad}, \text{adv}\}$: a status flag indicating whether secret information corresponding to the node is known to the adversary. Concretely, adv means that the adversary created this node by injecting the message, bad means that it was created using adversarial randomness (hence it is well-formed but the adversary knows the secrets), and good means that it is secure.

Proposal nodes further store the following value:

- act $\in \{\text{up-spk}, \text{add-id}_t\text{-spk}_t, \text{rem-id}_t\}$: the proposed action. The also keeps track of the signature keys: $\text{add-id}_t\text{-spk}_t$ means that id_t is added with the public key spk_t, and up-spk reflects the respective input to the update proposal.

Commit nodes further store the following values:

- pro: the ordered list of committed proposals;
- mem: the list of group members and their signature public keys;
- key: the group key;

– chall: a flag indicating whether the application secret has been challenged, i.e., chall is `true` if a random group key has been generated for this node, and `false` if the key was set by the adversary (or not generated);
– exp: a set keeping track of parties corrupted in this node, including whether only their secret state used to process the next commit message or also the current application secret leaked.

3.5 Details of the CGKA Functionality

This section presents a simplified version of $\mathcal{F}_{CGKA}$. Compared to the precise definition in the full version [11], we skip some less relevant border cases and details. A pseudo-code description is in Figs. 2, 3 and 4 and an example history graph built by $\mathcal{F}_{CGKA}$ is in Fig. 1. We next build some intuition about how $\mathcal{F}_{CGKA}$ works.

The Passive Case. For the start, consider environments that do not inject or corrupt randomness (this relates to parts of the functionality not marked by [Inj] or [RndCor]). Here, $\mathcal{F}_{CGKA}$ simply builds a history graph, where nodes are identified by messages, and the root is identified by the label $root_0$ (see Fig. 1a). Moreover, $\mathcal{F}_{CGKA}$ stores for each party id a pointer Ptr[id] to its current history-graph node. If, for example, id proposes to add id_t, $\mathcal{F}_{CGKA}$ creates a new proposal node identified by a message p chosen by the adversary, and hands p to id. Some other party can now commit p (having received it from the environment), which, analogously, creates a commit node identified by c. Then, if a party processes c, $\mathcal{F}_{CGKA}$ simply moves its pointer. The graph is initialized by a designated party $id_{creator}$, who creates the group with itself as a single member and can then invite additional members.

If a party id is exposed, $\mathcal{F}_{CGKA}$ records in the history graph which information inherently leaks from its state. This will be used by the predicate **safe** (recall that it determines if the epoch's key is random or arbitrary). In particular, two points are worth mentioning. First, we require that after outputting the group key, id removes it from its state (this is important for forward secrecy of the higher-level messaging protocol). $\mathcal{F}_{CGKA}$ uses the flag HasKey[id] to keep track of whether id outputted the key. Second, id has to store in its state key material for updates and commits it created in the current epoch. Accordingly, upon id's exposure $\mathcal{F}_{CGKA}$ sets the status **stat** of all such nodes to bad (note that leaking secrets has the same effect as choosing them with bad randomness).

Injections. The parts of $\mathcal{F}_{CGKA}$ related to injections are marked by comments containing [Inj]. As an example, say the environment makes id process a commit message c' not obtained from $\mathcal{F}_{CGKA}$, and hence not identifying any node. $\mathcal{F}_{CGKA}$ first asks the adversary if c' is simply malformed and, if this is the case, output $\perp$ to id. If the message is not malformed, the functionality creates the new commit node, allowing the adversary to interpret the sender $orig'$. We guarantee agreement—if any other party transitions to this node, it will output the same committer $orig'$, member set mem', group key etc. (recall that it is contained in

---

Functionality $\mathcal{F}_{\text{CGKA}}$: Initialization

Parameters: predicate **safe**(c) (are group secrets in c secure), predicate **inj-allowed**(c, id) (is injecting allegedly from id in c allowed), group creator's identity $\text{id}_{\text{creator}}$.

Initialization
// Pointers, commit nodes, proposal nodes
$\text{Ptr}[*], \text{Node}[*], \text{Prop}[*] \leftarrow \bot$
// Welcome message to commit message mapping
$\text{Wel}[*] \leftarrow \bot$
$\text{RndCor}[*] \leftarrow \text{good}; \text{HasKey}[*] \leftarrow \text{false}$
$\text{rootCtr} \leftarrow 0$

Input (Create, spk) **from** $\text{id}_{\text{creator}}$
// The group can be created only once.
req $\text{Node}[\text{root}_0] = \bot \wedge$ ***usable-spk**$(\text{id}_{\text{creator}}, \text{spk})$
// Create the root node and transition $\text{id}_{\text{creator}}$ there.
$\text{Node}[\text{root}_0] \leftarrow$ commit node with $\text{orig} = \text{id}_{\text{creator}}$,
$\quad \text{mem} = \{(\text{id}_{\text{creator}}, \text{spk})\}$ and $\text{stat} = \text{RndCor}[\text{id}_{\text{creator}}]$.
$\text{Ptr}[\text{id}_{\text{creator}}] \leftarrow \text{root}_0$
$\text{HasKey}[\text{id}_{\text{creator}}] \leftarrow \text{true}$

Functionality $\mathcal{F}_{\text{CGKA}}$: Propose and Commit

Input (Propose, act), act $\in$ {up-spk, add-id_t, rem-id_t}
$\hspace{6cm}$ **from** id
Send id and all inputs to the adv. and receive ack.
// Adv. can reject invalid inputs.
if ¬***require-correctness**('prop', id, act) **then**
$\quad$ **req** ack
// Compute the proposal node this action creates.
$P \leftarrow$ proposal node with $\text{par} = \text{Ptr}[\text{id}]$, $\text{orig} = \text{id}$,
$\hspace{3cm} \text{act} = \text{act}$, $\text{stat} = \text{RndCor}[\text{id}]$.
if act $=$ add **then**
$\quad$ // Adv. can choose the key package for adds.
$\quad$ Receive spk_t from the adversary
$\quad$ $P.\text{act} \leftarrow \text{add-spk}_t$
// Insert P into HG.
Receive p from the adversary.
if $\text{Prop}[p] = \bot$ **then**
$\quad$ // Passive case: created a new node.
$\quad$ $\text{Prop}[p] \leftarrow P$
else
$\quad$ // [Inj] [RndCor] Re-computing existing p.
$\quad$ **assert** ***consistent-nodes**$(\text{Prop}[p], P)$
if $\text{RndCor}[\text{id}]$ **then**
$\quad$ // [RndCor] Signed with bad randomness.
$\quad$ Notify $\mathcal{F}_{\text{AS}}^{\text{IW}}$ that id's spk is compromised.
return p

Input (Commit, $\boldsymbol{p}$, spk) **from** id
Send id and all inputs to the adv. and receive ack.
// Adv. can reject invalid inputs.
if ¬***require-correctness**('comm', id, $\boldsymbol{p}$, spk) **then**
$\quad$ **req** ack
// [Inj] Adv. interprets injected proposals.
for $p \in \boldsymbol{p}$ s.t. $\text{Prop}[p] = \bot$ **do**
$\quad$ $\text{Prop}[p] \leftarrow$ proposal node with $\text{par} = \text{Ptr}[\text{id}]$,
$\hspace{3cm}$ $\text{stat} = \text{adv}$, and orig and act chosen
$\hspace{3cm}$ by the adversary.
// Compute the commit node this action creates.
$C \leftarrow$ commit node with $\text{par} = \text{Ptr}[\text{id}]$, $\text{orig} = \text{id}$,
$\hspace{2cm}$ $\text{stat} = \text{RndCor}[\text{id}]$ $\text{pro} = \boldsymbol{p}$, and
$\hspace{2cm}$ $\text{mem} = $ ***members**$(\text{Ptr}[\text{id}], \text{id}, \boldsymbol{p}, \text{spk})$
// Insert C into HG.
Receive (c, rt) from the adversary.
if $\text{Node}[c] = \bot \wedge rt = \bot$ **then**
$\quad$ // Passive case: create new node.
$\quad$ $\text{Node}[c] \leftarrow C$
else if $\text{Node}[c] \neq \bot$ **then**
$\quad$ // [Inj] [RndCor] Re-computing injected c.
$\quad$ **assert** ***consistent-nodes**$(\text{Node}[c], C)$
else
$\quad$ // [Inj] [RndCor] c explains a detached root.
$\quad$ Set $\text{Node}[\text{root}_{rt}].\text{par} \leftarrow \text{Ptr}[\text{id}]$ and then replace
$\quad$ each occurrence of root_{rt} in the HG by c.
$\quad$ **assert** ***consistent-nodes**$(\text{Node}[c], C)$
// [Inj] Check that inserting C does not violate
authenticity and HG-consistency.
assert ***cons-invariant** $\wedge$ ***auth-invariant**
if $\text{RndCor}[\text{id}]$ **then**
$\quad$ // [RndCor] Commit signed with bad rand.
$\quad$ Notify $\mathcal{F}_{\text{AS}}^{\text{IW}}$ that id's current spk is compromised.
Receive w from the adversary.
if $\text{Wel}[w] \neq \bot$ **then**
$\quad$ **req** ***consistent-nodes**$(\text{Wel}[w], C)$
$\text{Wel}[w] \leftarrow c$.
return (c, w)

Fig. 2. $\mathcal{F}_{\text{CGKA}}$: initialization, propose and commit. Parts related to injections and randomness corruptions are marked by comments containing [Inj] and [RndCor], respectively.

Functionality $\mathcal{F}_{\text{CGKA}}$: Process and Join

Input (Process, c, p) **from** id
  Send id and all inputs to the adv. and receive *ack*.
  // Adv. can reject invalid inputs.
  if ¬*require-correctness*('proc', id, c, p) **then**
    req *ack*
  // [Inj] Adv. interprets injected proposals.
  for $p \in p$ s.t. Prop[p] = ⊥ **do**
    Prop[p] ← proposal node with par = Ptr[id],
           stat = adv, and orig and act chosen
           by the adversary.
  // Commit node id expects to transition to.
  Receive from the adversary (orig', spk').
  C ← commit node with par = Ptr[id], orig = orig',
         pro = p, mem = *members*(Ptr[id], id, p, spk')
  // [Inj] If c is injected, then assign a node to it.
  if Node[c] = ⊥ **then**
    // If c explains detached root, let adv. specify it.
    Receive rt from the adversary.
    if $rt \neq ⊥$ **then**
      Set Node[root$_{rt}$].par ← Ptr[id] and replace
      each occurrence of root$_{rt}$ in the HG by c.
    else
      Node[c] ← C
      Node[c].stat ← adv
  // Check that id transitions to expected node.
  assert consistent-nodes(Node[c], C)
  // Transition id.
  if $\exists p \in p$: Prop[p].act = rem-id **then**
    Ptr[id] ← ⊥
  else
    Ptr[id] ← c
    HasKey[id] ← true
  // Check that invariants are not violated.
  assert *cons-invariant* ∧ *auth-invariant*
  return *output-process*(C)

Input (Join, w) **from** id
  Send id and all inputs to the adv. and receive *ack*.
  req *ack*
  // [Inj] If w is injected, then assign a commit
  node to it.
  if Wel[w] = ⊥ **then**
    // If w leads to existing node, the adversary
    can specify it.
    Receive c from the adversary.
    if $c \neq ⊥$ **then**
      Wel[w] ← c
    else
      // Create detached root.
      rootCtr++
      Wel[w] ← root$_{\text{rootCtr}}$
      Node[root$_{\text{rootCtr}}$] ← commit node with
             par = ⊥, pro = ⊥, stat = adv, and
             orig and mem chosen by the adv.
  // Transition id.
  Ptr[id] ← Wel[w]
  HasKey[id] ← true
  // Check that joining id does not violate authen-
  ticity and HG-consistency.
  assert *cons-invariant* ∧ *auth-invariant*
  return *output-join*(Node[Wel[w]])

Functionality $\mathcal{F}_{\text{CGKA}}$: Corruptions and Group Key

Input (Expose, id) **from the adversary**
  // Record leaked information: if id is in the group, its
  state contains:
  if Ptr[id] = ⊥ **then**
    // 1) secrets needed to process other parties' mes-
    sages and potentially the group key
    Node[Ptr[id]].exp ++← (id, HasKey[id])
    // 2) secrets needed to process id's own messages
    For each commit or update-proposal node with
    orig = id and par = Ptr[id], set stat ← bad.
    // 3) the signing key
    Notify $\mathcal{F}_{\text{AS}}^{\text{iw}}$ that id's current spk is compromised.
  // Whether id is in the group or not, its state contains
  secrets needed to process welcome messages.
  for c s.t. *can-join*(Node[c], id) **do**
    Node[c].exp ++← (id, true)
  // Disallow adaptive corruptions in some cases.
  This input is not allowed if ∃c s.t Node[c].chall = true
  and ¬*safe*(c)

Input (CorrRand, id, b), $b \in$ {**good**, **bad**} **from** adv.
  RndCor[id] ← b

Input Key **from** id
  // Only possible if id has the key.
  req Ptr[id] $\neq$ ⊥ ∧ HasKey[id]
  // Set the key if id is the first party fetching it in
  its node. (Guarantees consistency across parties.)
  if Node[Ptr[id]].key = ⊥ **then**
    if *safe*(Ptr[id]) **then**
      Set key to a fresh random key and chall to
      true.
    else
      Let the adversary choose key and set chall
      to false.
  // id should remove the key from his state
  HasKey[id] ← false
  return Node[Ptr[id]].key

Fig. 3. $\mathcal{F}_{\text{CGKA}}$: inputs process, join, key and corruptions. Parts related to injections are marked by comments containing [Inj].

```
┌─ Functionality 𝓕_CGKA : Helpers ─────────────────────────────────┐
```

helper *require-correctness('comm', id, c, p)

  Returns true if a) c and each $p \in \boldsymbol{p}$ identifies a node with stat $\neq$ adv, and b) Ptr[id] = Node[c].par, and c) $\boldsymbol{p}$ = Node[c].pro.

helper *require-correctness('proc', id, $\boldsymbol{p}$, spk)

  Returns true if ***usable-spk**(id, spk) and $\forall p \in \boldsymbol{p}$: Prop[p] $\neq \perp$ and the vector can be committed by id (in its current node) according to MLS spec.

helper *require-correctness('prop', id, act)

  Returns true if act = up-spk and ***usable-spk**(id, spk) or if act = rem-id$_t$ and removing id$_t$ is allowed according to MLS spec.

helper *usable-spk(id, spk)

  Returns true if if either spk is id's current spk, or id has the secret key according to $\mathcal{F}_{AS}^{IW}$.

helper *members(C, id, $\boldsymbol{p}$, spk)

  Computes the member set after id, currently in C, calls commits with inputs $\boldsymbol{p}$ and spk, according to MLS spec. For each member, the set contains a tuples (id′, spk′), indicating the member's identity and his identity key.

helper *can-join(C, id)

  Returns true if C.pro adds id with spk and, according to $\mathcal{F}_{KS}^{IW}$, id has a secret key for some key-package registered together with spk.

helper *output-process(C)

  Computes committer id$_c$ and proposal semantics propSem, returned by Process when transitioning into C.

helper *output-join(C)

  Computes roster and committer id$_c$, returned when joining into C.

helper *consistent-nodes(N, N')

  Returns true if all values in proposal or commit nodes N and N' except status match.

helper *auth-invariant

  Returns true if there is no proposal or commit node s.t. stat = adv and **inj-allowed**(par, id) is false, where par is the node's parent.s

helper *cons-invariant

  Returns true if HG has no cycles, each id is in the member set of Ptr[id] and for each non-root c, the parent of each p in c's pro vector is c's parent.

Fig. 4. Additional helpers for $\mathcal{F}_{CGKA}$.

the output of process). Note that we also guarantee correctness—if the input of process is an honest message c generated by $\mathcal{F}_{CGKA}$, then the adversary cannot make the commit fail.

A more challenging scenario is when the environment injects a welcome message w'. Now there are two possibilities. First, w' could lead to an existing node. In this case, $\mathcal{F}_{CGKA}$ asks the adversary to provide the node c and records that w' leads to it. We require agreement—any party subsequently joining using w' transitions to c. However, in general, we cannot expect that the adversary (i.e., simulator), given an arbitrary w' computed by the environment, can come up with the whole commit message c' and its position in the history graph.[9] Therefore, in this case $\mathcal{F}_{CGKA}$ creates a detached root, identified by a unique label root$_{rootCtr}$, where rootCtr is a counter. If at some later point, e.g. after an additional commit by the newly joined party, the environment injects c' corresponding to w', then the root is attached and re-labeled as c'. This scenario is depicted in Figs. 1b to 1d. We require consistency—when creating a detached root, the adversary chooses the member set, but when it is attached, we check that it matches the new parent.

---

[9] For instance, say the environment computes a long chain of commits in its head and injects the last one. It is not clear how to construct a protocol for which it is possible to identify all ancestors, without including all their hashes in w.

Corrupted Randomness. The relevant parts of $\mathcal{F}_{\text{CGKA}}$ are marked by [RndCor]. Corrupted randomness leads to two adverse effects. First, the adversary can make parties re-compute existing messages, leading to the following scenarios:

- A party re-computes a message it already computed. In this case, $\mathcal{F}_{\text{CGKA}}$ only checks that the previous message was computed with the same inputs.
- A party re-computes a message previously injected by the environment. Here, $\mathcal{F}_{\text{CGKA}}$ verifies that the semantics of the existing node chosen by the adversary upon injection are consistent with the correct semantics computed using the party's inputs. (Technically, instead of creating a new node, $\mathcal{F}_{\text{CGKA}}$ checks that the node it would have created is consistent with the existing one.)
- A party re-computes a commit c' corresponding to an injected welcome message (see Fig. 1d). In this case, $\mathcal{F}_{\text{CGKA}}$ attaches the detached root, just like in case c' was injected into process.

Second, we note that each protocol message in MLS is signed, potentially using ECDSA, which reveals the secret key in case bad randomness is used. Therefore, every time a party id generates a message with bad randomness, $\mathcal{F}_{\text{CGKA}}$ notifies $\mathcal{F}_{\text{AS}}$, which marks all long-term keys of id as exposed.

Adaptive Corruptions. Adaptive corruptions become a problem if an exposure reveals secret keys that can be used to compute a key that has already been outputted by $\mathcal{F}_{\text{CGKA}}$ at random, i.e. a "challenge" key. Since fully adaptive security is not achieved by TreeKEM (without resorting to programmable random oracles), we restrict the environment not to corrupt if for some nodes with the flag chall set to true this would cause **safe** to switch to false.[10]

4   The Insider-Secure TreeKEM Protocol

This section provides a (high-level) description of the Insider-Secure TreeKEM (ITK) protocol. A formal description of the protocol can be found in the full version [11].

Distributed State. The primary object constituting the distributed state of the ITK protocol is the *ratchet tree* τ. The ratchet tree is a labeled binary tree (i.e., a binary tree where nodes have a number of named properties), where each group member is assigned to a leaf and each internal node represents the sub-group of parties whose leaves are part of the node's sub-tree.

To give a brief overview, each node has two (potentially empty) labels pk and sk, storing a key pair of a PKE scheme. Leaves have an additional label spk, storing a long-term signature public key of the leaf's owner. The root has a number of additional shared symmetric secret keys as labels (see below). See Fig. 5 for an example of a ratchet tree with the labels. The *public part* of τ

---

[10] In game based definitions, such corruptions are usually disallowed, as they allow to trivially distinguish. Our notion achieves the same level of adaptivity.

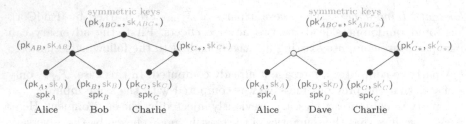

Fig. 5. (Left) An example ratchet tree τ for a group with three members. For Invariant (1), the public labels (green) are known to all parties. For Invariant (2), the secret labels (red) in a node v are only known to parties in v's subtree, e.g. Bob knows sk_B, sk_{AB} and sk_{ABC*}. (Right) the tree after Charlie commits removing Bob and adding Dave. The empty node ○ is blank. Messages to Alice and Dave are encrypted under its resolution $(\mathsf{pk}_A, \mathsf{pk}_D)$. (Color figure online)

consists of the tree structure, the leaf assignment, as well as all public labels, i.e., those storing public keys. The *secret part* consists of the labels storing secret keys and the symmetric keys. The ITK protocol maintains two invariants:

Invariant (1): The public part of τ is known to all parties.
Invariant (2): The secret labels in a node v are known only to the owners of leaves in the sub-tree rooted at v.

Evolving the Tree. Each epoch has one fixed ratchet tree τ. Proposals represent changes to τ, and a commit chooses which changes should be applied when advancing to the next epoch.

A *remove* proposal represents removing from τ all keys known to the removed party (see Fig. 5). That is, its leaf is cleared, and all keys in its *direct path*—i.e., the path from the party's leaf to the root—are *blanked*, meaning that all their labels are cleared. This is followed by shrinking the tree by removing unneeded leaves from the right side of the tree. Note that until a blanked node gets a new key pair assigned (as explained shortly), in order to encrypt to the respective subgroup one has to encrypt to the node's children instead (and recursing if either child is blanked as well). The minimal set of non-blanked nodes covering a given subgroup is called the subgroup's *resolution*.

An *update* proposes removing all keys currently known to the party (and hence possibly affected by state leakage), and replacing the public key in their leaf (and possibly the long-term verification key) by a fresh one, specified in the proposal. Hence, τ is modified as in a remove proposal, but instead of clearing the leaf, its key is replaced.

Finally, an *add* proposal indicates the new member's identity (defined on a higher application level), its long-term public key from the AS, and an ephemeral public key from KS. It represents the following modification: First, a leaf has to be assigned, with the public label set according to the public key from the proposal. If there exists a currently unused leaf, then this can be reused, otherwise a new leaf is added to the tree. In order to satisfy invariant (2), the party committing the add proposal would then have to communicate to the new member all secret keys on its direct path. Unfortunately, it can only communicate the keys for nodes above the least common ancestor of its and the new member's leaves. For all other nodes, the new member is added to a so-called *unmerged leaf set*, which can be accounted for when determining the node's resolution.

Re-keying. Whenever a party *commits* a sequence of proposals, they additionally replace their leaf key (providing an implicit update) and re-key their direct path. In order to maintain invariant (1) on the group state, the committer includes all new public keys in the commit message.

To minimize the number of secret keys needed to be communicated as part of the commit message, the committer samples the fresh key pairs along the path by "hashing up the tree". That is, the committer derives a sequence of *path secrets* s_i, one for each node on the path, where s_0 for the leaf is random and s_{i+1} is derived from s_i using the HKDF.Expand function. Then, each s_i is expanded again (with a different label) to derive random coins for the key generation. The secret s_n for the root, called the *commit secret*, is not used to generate a key pair, but instead used to derive the epoch's symmetric keys (see below). This implies that each other party only needs to be able to retrieve the path secret of the least common ancestor of their and the committer's leaves. Hence, invariant (2) can be maintained by including in the commit each path secret encrypted to (the resolution of) the node's child not on the direct path.

Note that for PCS, the new secret keys must not be computable using the committer's state from before sending the commit (we want that a commit heals the committer from a state). Hence, the committer simply stores all new secrets explicitly until the commit is confirmed.

Key Schedule. Each epoch has several associated symmetric keys, four of which are relevant for this paper: The *application secret* is the key exported to the higher-level protocol, the *membership key* is used for protecting message authenticity, the *init secret* is mixed into the next epoch's key schedule, and the *confirmation key* ensures agreement on the cryptographic material.

The epoch's keys are derived from the commit secret computed in the re-keying process, mixed with (some additional context and) the previous epoch's init secret. This ensures that only parties who knew the prior epoch's secrets can derive the new keys. One purpose of this is improving FS: corrupting a party in an epoch, say, 5 must not allow to derive the application secret for a prior epoch, say, 3. As, however, some internal nodes of the ratchet tree remain unchanged between epochs 3 and 5, it might be possible for the adversary to decrypt the commit secret of epoch 3, given the leakage from epoch 5. Mixing in the init secret of epoch 2 thus ensures that this is information is of no value per se (unless some party in epoch 2 was already corrupted.)

Welcoming Members. Whenever a commit adds new members to the group, the committer must send a *welcome message* to the new members, providing them with the necessary state. First, the welcome message contains the public group information, such as the public part of the ratchet tree. Second, it includes (encrypted) *joiner secret*, which combines current commit secret and previous init secret and allows the new members to execute the key schedule. Finally, it contains the seed to derive the secrets on the joint path, which the committer just re-keyed. (Recall that for the other nodes on the new party's direct path they are simply added to the unmerged leaves set, indicating that they do not know the corresponding secrets.) The above seeds, as well as the joiner secret, are encrypted under the public key (obtained from KS), specified in the add proposal (which thus serves dual purposes).

Security Mechanisms. All messages intended for existing group members— commit messages and proposals—are subject to *message framing*, which binds them to the group and epoch, indicates the sender, and protects the message's authenticity. The sender first signs the group identifier, the epoch, his leaf index, and the message using his private signing key. This in particular prevents imper- sonation by another (malicious) group member.

Since the signing key, however, is shared across groups and its replacement is also not tied to the PCS guarantees of the group, each package is additionally authenticated using shared key material. Proposals are MACed using the mem- bership key, while commit messages are protected using the confirmation tag (see below). Further, commit messages that include remove proposals are addi- tionally MACed using the membership key, since the confirmation tag cannot be verified by the removed members. In summary, to tamper or inject messages an adversary must both know at least the sender's signing key as well as the epoch's symmetric keys.

The protocol makes use of two (running) hashes on the communication tran- script to authenticate the group's history. For authentication purposes, it uses the *confirmed transcript hash*, which is computed by hashing the previous epoch's *interim transcript hash*, the content of the commit message, and its signature. The interim transcript hash is then computed by hashing the confirmed tran- script hash with the confirmation tag. Each commit message moreover contains a so-called confirmation tag that allows the receiving members to immediately verify whether they agree on the new epoch's key-schedule. To this end, the committer computes a MAC on the confirmed transcript hash under the new epoch's confirmation key.

Finally, ITK uses a mechanism called *tree signing* to achieve a certain level of insider security. We discuss this aspect in detail in Sect. 6.3.

Remark 1 (Simplifications and Deviations). While ITK closely follows the IETF MLS protocol draft, there are some small deviations as well as some omissions. In particular, our model assumes a fixed protocol version and ciphersuite, and omits features such as advanced meta-data protection, external proposals and commits, exporters, preshared keys, as well as extensions. We discuss those deviations and their implications on our results in more detail in the full version [11].

5   Security of ITK

Security of ITK is expressed by the predicates **safe**(c, id) and **inj-allowed**(c, id), where c is a commit message identifying a history graph node and id is a party. The predicates are formally stated in Fig. 6. They are defined using recursive deduction rules **know**(c, id) and **know**$(c, \text{'epoch'})$, indicating that the adversary knows id's secrets (such as the leaf secret), and that it knows the epoch secrets (such as the init secret), respectively. In more detail:

- **know**(c, id) consists of three conditions, the last two being recursive. Condition a) is true if id's secrets in c are known to the adversary because they leaked as part of an exposure or were injected by the adversary in id's name (due to many attack vectors, this can happen in many ways, see Fig. 6). The conditions b) and c) reflect that in ITK only commits sent by or affect id (id updates, is added, or removed) are guaranteed to modify all id's secrets. If c is not of this type, then **know**(c, id) is implied by **know**$(\text{Node}[c].\text{par}, \text{id})$ (condition b)). If a child c' of c is not of this type, then it is implied by **know**(c', id) (condition c)).
- **know**$(c, \text{'epoch'})$ takes into account the fact that ITK derives epoch secrets using the initSecret from the previous epoch, and hence achieves slightly better FS compared to parties' individual secrets.
  In particular, the adversary knows the epoch secrets in c only if it corrupted a party in c, or knows the epoch secrets in c's parent and knows individual secret of some party id in c. The latter condition allows the adversary to process c using id's protocol and is formalized by the ***can-traverse** predicate.
- The only difference between ¬**safe**(c) and **know**$(c, \text{'epoch'})$ is that the application secret is not leaked if id is exposed in c after outputting it.

With the predicates **safe** and **inj-allowed**, we can now state the following security statement for ITK.

Theorem 1. *Assuming that* PKE *is* IND-CCA *secure, and that* Sig *is* EUF-CMA *secure, then the* ITK *protocol securely realizes* $(\mathcal{F}_{\text{AS}}^{\text{IW}}, \mathcal{F}_{\text{KS}}^{\text{IW}}, \mathcal{F}_{\text{CGKA}})$ *in the* $(\mathcal{F}_{\text{AS}}, \mathcal{F}_{\text{KS}}, \mathcal{G}_{\text{RO}})$-*hybrid model, where* $\mathcal{F}_{\text{CGKA}}$ *uses the predicates* **safe** *and* **inj-allowed** *from Fig. 6 and calls to* HKDF.Expand, HKDF.Extract *and* MAC *functions are replaced by calls to the global random oracle* $\mathcal{G}_{\text{RO}}$.

Proof (Sketch). We here provide the high level proof idea; the complete proof is presented in the full version [11]. The proof proceeds in three steps. The first step is to show that various consistency mechanisms, such as MACing the group context, guarantee consistency of the distributed group state. More precisely, the real world (Hybrid 1) is indistinguishable from the following Hybrid 2: The experiment includes a modified CGKA functionality, $\mathcal{F}_{\text{CGKA}}^{\text{real}}$, which differs from $\mathcal{F}_{\text{CGKA}}$ in that it uses **safe** = false and **inj-allowed** = true. The functionality interacts with the trivial simulator who sets all keys and messages according to the protocol. The second step is to show that IND-CCA of the PKE scheme guarantees confidentiality: Hybrid 2 is indistinguishable from Hybrid 3 where

---

Predicate safe

Knowledge of parties' secrets.

$\textbf{know}(c, \text{id}) \iff$
  a) // id's state leaks directly e.g. via corruption (see below):
    *state-directly-leaks(c, id) $\vee$
  b) // know state in the parent:
    $(\text{Node}[c].\text{par} \neq \bot \wedge \neg$***secrets-replaced**$(c, \text{id}) \wedge \textbf{know}(\text{Node}[c].\text{par}, \text{id}))$ $\vee$
  c) // know state in a child:
    $\exists c' : (\text{Node}[c'].\text{par} = c \wedge \neg$***secrets-replaced**$(c', \text{id}) \wedge \textbf{know}(c', \text{id}))$

*state-directly-leaks$(c, \text{id}) \iff$
  a) // id has been exposed in c:
    $(\text{id}, *) \in \text{Node}[c].\text{exp}$ $\vee$
  b) // c is in a detached tree and id's spk is exposed
    $\exists rt : $***ancestor**$(\text{root}_{rt}, c) \wedge \exists \text{spk} : (\text{id}, \text{spk}) \in \text{Node}[c].\text{mem} \wedge \text{spk} \in \text{Exposed}$ $\vee$
  c) // id's secrets in c are injected by the adversary:
    $((\text{id}, \text{spk}) \in \text{Node}[c].\text{mem} \wedge $***secrets-injected**$(c, \text{id}))$

*secrets-injected$(c, \text{id}) \iff$
  a) // id is the sender of c and c was injected or generated with bad randomness
    $(\text{Node}[c].\text{orig} = \text{id} \wedge \text{Node}[c].\text{stat} \neq \text{good})$ $\vee$
  b) // c commits an update of id that is injected or generated with bad randomness
    $\exists p \in \text{Node}[c].\text{pro} : (\text{Prop}[p].\text{act} = \text{up-}* \wedge \text{Prop}[p].\text{orig} = \text{id} \wedge \text{Prop}[p].\text{stat} \neq \text{good})$ $\vee$
  c) // c adds id with corrupted spk
    $\exists p \in \text{Node}[c].\text{pro} : (\text{Prop}[p].\text{act} = \text{add-id-spk} \wedge \text{spk} \in \text{Exposed})$
*secrets-replaced$(c, \text{id}) \iff \text{Node}[c].\text{orig} = \text{id} \vee \exists p \in \text{Node}[c].\text{pro} :$
  $\text{Prop}[p].\text{act} \in \{\text{add-id-}*, \text{rem-id}\} \vee (\text{Prop}[p].\text{act} = \text{up-} * \wedge \text{Prop}[p].\text{orig} = \text{id})$

Knowledge of epoch secrets.

$\textbf{know}(c, \text{'epoch'}) \iff \text{Node}[c].\text{exp} \neq \varnothing \vee $***can-traverse**$(c)$

// Can the adversary process c using exposed individual secrets and parent's init secret?
*can-traverse$(c) \iff$
  a) // orphan root with a corrupted signature public key:
    $(\text{Node}[c].\text{par} = \bot \wedge (*, \text{spk}) \in \text{Node}[c].\text{mem} \wedge \text{spk} \in \text{Exposed})$ $\vee$
  b) // commit to an add proposal that uses an exposed key package:
    $(\exists p \in \text{Node}[c].\text{pro} : \text{Prop}[p].\text{act} = \text{add-id-spk} \wedge \text{spk} \in \text{Exposed})$ $\vee$
  c) // secrets encrypted in the welcome message under an exposed leaf key
    *leaf-welcome-key-reuse(c) $\vee$
  d) // know necessary info to traverse the edge:
    $(\textbf{know}(c, *) \wedge (c = \text{root}_* \vee \textbf{know}(\text{Node}[c].\text{par}, \text{'epoch'})))$

*leaf-welcome-key-reuse$(c) \iff \exists \text{id}, p \in \text{Node}[c].\text{pro} : \text{Prop}[p].\text{act} = \text{add-id-}*$
$\wedge \exists c_d : $***ancestor**$(c, c_d) \wedge (\text{id}, *) \in \text{Node}[c_d].\text{exp}$
$\wedge$ no node c_h with ***secrets-replaced**(c_h, id) on c-c_d path

Safe and can-inject.

$\textbf{safe}(c) \iff \neg((*, \text{true}) \in \text{Node}[c].\text{exp} \vee $***can-traverse**$(c))$

$\textbf{inj-allowed}(c, \text{id}) \iff \text{Node}[c].\text{mem}[\text{id}] \in \text{Exposed} \wedge \textbf{know}(c, \text{'epoch'})$

Fig. 6. The safety and injectability predicates for the CGKA functionality reflecting the sub-optimal security of the ITK protocol.

application and membership secrets in safe epochs are random, i.e. the original **safe** is restored. The final step is to show that unforgeability of the MAC and signature schemes implies that Hybrid 3 is indistinguishable from the ideal world, where the original **inj-allowed** is restored as well. (Considering confidentiality before integrity, while somewhat unusual, is necessary, because we must first argue secrecy of MAC keys. We note that IND-CPA would be anyway insufficient, because some injections are inherently possible.)

In this overview, we sketch the core of our proof, which is the second step concerning confidentiality. For simplicity, we do not consider randomness corruptions. We now proceed in two parts: first, we consider only passive environments, which do not inject messages. In the second part, we show how to modify the passive strategy to deal with active environments.

Part 1: Passive Security. For simplicity, consider $\mathcal{F}_{\text{CGKA}}^{\text{rand}}$, which uses the original **safe** only for the first (safe) key it sets (think of the first step in the hybrid argument). The goal is to show that *IND-CPA* security of the PKE scheme implies that $\mathcal{F}_{\text{CGKA}}^{\text{real}}$ and $\mathcal{F}_{\text{CGKA}}^{\text{rand}}$, both with the trivial simulator, are indistinguishable for *passive* environments.

Unfortunately, already the passive setting turns out challenging for the following reason: The path secrets in a (safe) commit c are encrypted under public keys created in another commit c', which contains encryptions of the corresponding secret keys under public keys created in another commit c'', and so on. Moreover, the keys are related by hash chains (of path secrets). Even worse, the environment can adaptively choose who to corrupt, revealing some subset of the secret keys, which mean that we cannot simply apply the hybrid argument to replace encryptions of secret keys by encryptions of zeros.[11]

To tackle adaptivity and related keys, we adapt the techniques of [10, 33]. Namely, we define a new security notion for PKE, called (modified) Generalized Selective Decryption (GSD),[12] which generalizes the way ITK uses PKE together with the hash function to derive its secrets. Roughly speaking, the GSD game creates a graph, where each node stores a secret seed. The adversary can instruct the game to 1) create a node with a random seed, 2) create a node v where the seed is a hash of the seed of another node u, 3) use a (different) hash of the seed in a node u to derive a key pair, use the public key to encrypt the seed in a node v and send the public key and ciphertext to the adversary. Each of the actions 2) and 3) creates an edge (u, v) to indicate their relation. Moreover, the adversary can adaptively corrupt nodes and receive their seeds. For the challenge of the game, she receives either a seed from a sink node or a random value. (See the full proof for a precise definition.)[13] It remains to be shown that 1) GSD security

---

[11] Observe that at the time a ciphertext is created we do not know if the key it contains will be used to create a safe epoch, or if some receiver will be corrupted.

[12] GSD was first defined for symmetric encryption [33] and then extended to prove security of TreeKEM [10]. Our notion is an extension of [10].

[13] The GSD game in the full proof is inherently more complex. For example, recall that joiner secret is a hash of init and commit secrets. Accordingly, the adversary is allowed to create nodes whose seeds are hashes of two other seeds.

implies secrecy of ITK keys, and 2) IND-CPA security implies GSD security. The latter proof is adapted from [10], so we now focus on 1).

To be a bit more concrete, assume an environment $\mathcal{Z}$ distinguighes between $\mathcal{F}_{\text{CGKA}}^{\text{real}}$ and $\mathcal{F}_{\text{CGKA}}^{\text{rand}}$ (each with the trivial simulator). We construct an adversary $\mathcal{A}$ against GSD security of the PKE scheme in the standard way: $\mathcal{A}$ executes the code of $\mathcal{F}_{\text{CGKA}}^{\text{real}}$ and the trivial simulator, except for all honest commits and updates, public keys and epoch keys are created using the GSD game. If a party is corrupted, $\mathcal{A}$ corrupts all GSD nodes needed to compute its state. Finally, $\mathcal{A}$ replaces the first key outputted by $\mathcal{F}_{\text{CGKA}}^{\text{real}}$ by its challenge.

Part 2: Injections. We sketch the main points of how the strategy from the passive setting can be adapted to show that IND-CCA security of PKE implies secrecy of keys in the presence of active environments. There are three types of messages $\mathcal{Z}$ can inject: proposals, commits and welcome messages. Proposals are the least problematic. Say $\mathcal{Z}$ injects an update proposal p' with public key pk' on behalf of Alice. Since Alice will never process a commit containing p', allegedly from her, that she did not send, all epochs created by such commits and their descendants are not safe until Alice is removed. This also removes pk' and any secrets encrypted to it. So, $\mathcal{A}$ can generate all secrets sent to pk' itself, as they don't matter for any safe epoch.

Now say $\mathcal{Z}$ makes Bob process an injected commit c' and assume Bob uses an honest key, i.e., one created in the GSD game for an uncorrupted node. Say Bob's ciphertext in c' is $\textit{ctxt}$. There are a few possible scenarios:

- $\mathcal{A}$ has never seen $\textit{ctxt}$ (e.g. because $\mathcal{Z}$ computed a commit in his head). Clearly, IND-CPA is not sufficient here. Hence, we extend the GSD game by a decrypt oracle (which does not work on ciphertexts that allow to trivially compute the challenge) and prove that the new notion is implied by IND-CCA.
- $\mathcal{A}$ generated $\textit{ctxt}$ using the GSD game, as part of a commit message c creating a safe epoch (note that c and c' may differ in places other than $\textit{ctxt}$). Now the decrypt oracle cannot be used, but fortunately the confirmation tag comes to the rescue. Indeed, any tag accepted by Bob allows $\mathcal{A}$ to extract the joiner in c from $\mathcal{Z}$'s RO queries (we soon explain how) and compute the application secret in c. Hence, $\mathcal{A}$ can request GSD challenge for this secret and win.
  For simplicity, assume c and c' are siblings, i.e., Bob is currently in c's parent (see the full proof for other cases). Recall that the tag is a MAC under the new epoch's confirmation key over the transcript hash, and that the transcript hash contains the whole commit message c or c' (except the tag). The MAC is modeled as an RO call on input (confirmation key, transcript hash), so the only way for $\mathcal{Z}$ to compute a valid tag for c' is to query the RO on input (confirmation key in c', transcript hash updated with c'). Moreover, the confirmation key is a hash of the joiner secret, so $\mathcal{A}$ can extract the joiner secret in c' as well (note that the joiner secret is never encrypted). Now observe that the joiner secret is a hash of the init and commit secrets. Moreover, the init secret is the same in c and c', since they are siblings, as is

the commit secret due to *ctxt* being the same. Hence, the joiner secret of c is the same as the one extracted from c'. □

6 Insider Attacks

We first discuss three insider attacks on the design of MLS Draft 10 (as it stood prior to applying the fixes proposed as part of this work). Each is practical, yet violates the design goals of MLS. Next, we present an insider attack on MLS made possible when its ciphersuite is replaced by a weaker one that still meets assumptions deemed sufficient in previous analyses. Together these attacks highlight the limitations of prior security notions.

6.1 An Attack on Authenticity in Certain Modes

MLS supports two wire formats for packets: MLSCiphertext, meant to provide extra metadata protection by applying an extra layer of authenticated symmetric encryption, and MLSPlaintext, allowing for additional server-assisted efficiency improvements. As part of our analysis, we realized that an MLSCiphertext (unintentionally) provides stronger authentication guarantees than an MLSPlaintext: Forging the latter requires only signature keys of a group member while the former also requires knowing the current epoch's key. This results in weaker than expected PCS since signature keys will be rotated much less frequently than epoch keys: Despite a party having issued an update proposal or a commit the adversary may, thus, still be able to forge certain types of messages, such as proposals.

Theorem 2. *The* $\mathsf{ITK}_{\mathsf{Atk\text{-}1}}$ *protocol, which behaves like the* ITK *protocol but does not include membership tags, does not securely realize* $(\mathcal{F}_{\mathrm{AS}}^{\mathrm{IW}}, \mathcal{F}_{\mathrm{KS}}^{\mathrm{IW}}, \mathcal{F}_{\mathrm{CGKA}})$ *in the* $(\mathcal{F}_{\mathrm{AS}}, \mathcal{F}_{\mathrm{KS}}, \mathcal{G}_{\mathrm{RO}})$*-hybrid model when* $\mathcal{F}_{\mathrm{CGKA}}$ *uses the predicates* **safe** *and* **inj-allowed** *from Fig. 6.*

Proof (Sketch). Let S be an arbitrary simulator and consider the following environment $\mathcal{Z}$ that initially sets up a group consisting of three parties A, B, and C in the same group state. In this state, $\mathcal{Z}$ then corrupts party A, hence learns its signing key ssk_A. Then, $\mathcal{Z}$ instructs A to issue a commit message c with an empty list of proposals and the old spk_A. (This causes A to update its ephemeral key and resample the compromised path in the ratchet tree, but keep its long-term signing key.) Now, $\mathcal{Z}$ crafts a proposal message p^* that removes C on behalf of A, according to the (modified) protocol $\mathsf{ITK}_{\mathsf{Atk\text{-}1}}$. Note that all the included values are public and thus known to the environment, and $\mathcal{Z}$ can sign the proposal using the leaked ssk_A. (Important: note that the environment does *not* instruct A do create such a proposal command, but forges it!) Finally, $\mathcal{Z}$ instructs B to commit to this proposal p^* and lets B process the respective commit message c^*. If B accepts and outputs the correct semantics for p^*, then $\mathcal{Z}$ returns 1, otherwise it returns 0.

It is easy to see that $\mathcal{Z}$ outputs 1 when interacting with the hybrid world as p^* is a valid proposal created identically to how the honest party A would. Now consider the ideal world functionality and observe that after A issues the commit c_2 all parties are in the same state, which is further marked as good, i.e., with stat = good for it is created by an honest party with good randomness. We now observe that functionality's authenticity invariant will fail at the end of B committing p^*, as **inj-allowed**(c, A) (whether the adversary can inject on behalf of A) in the parent state (the one created by A's second commit) as **know**$(c, \text{'epoch'})$ will return false indicating that the adversary does not know the symmetric key of said state. Hence, when interacting with the ideal functionality the authenticity invariant prevents B from successfully committing to the proposal p^*, causing $\mathcal{Z}$ to return 0. □

To bring the authenticity guarantees in line, we proposed adding a MAC to MLSPlaintexts [15].

6.2   Breaking Agreement

The way the transcript hash was computed and included in the confirmation tag in the original proposal of MLS lead to counter-intuitive behavior, where parties think they are in-sync and agree on all relevant state when they are not.

More concretely, the package's signature was not included into the confirmed transcript hash, but it was included into the interim transcript hash. Suppose that a malicious insider creates two valid commit messages c and c', which only differ in the signatures, and sends them to Alice and Bob respectively. If both signatures check out (which for most signatures an insider can achieve) then Alice and Bob both end up with the same confirmed transcript hash and, thus, with the same confirmation tag. Therefore, they both transition to the new epoch, agree on all epoch secrets and can exchange application messages. However, MLS messages Alice sends now include confirmation tags computed using the mismatching interim transcript hash, and hence are not accepted by Bob.

In our security model this shows up as a break on the notion of a group state, as formalized by the history graph nodes. That is, in our model each history graph node is supposed to correspond to a well-defined and consistent group state. The way the transcript hash used to be computed violated this property, as on the one hand parties had the same key and could exchange messages (same state) while on the other hand parties would no longer be able to process each other's commit messages (different states). In particular, when processing two such related commit messages c and c' that only differ in the signature, in the ideal functionality $\mathcal{F}_{\text{CGKA}}$ the parties end up in two distinct states. Yet, in the real world execution the parties would still accept each other's proposals, which in $\mathcal{F}_{\text{CGKA}}$ is ruled out by the consistency invariant.

Theorem 3. *Assume the signature scheme* Sig *does not have unique signatures (this strong property is not achieved by the schemes used by MLS). Then, the* ITK$_{\text{Atk-2}}$ *protocol, which behaves like* ITK *using* Sig *but does not include the* *package's signature into the confirmed transcript hash, does not securely realize* $(\mathcal{F}_{AS}^{IW}, \mathcal{F}_{KS}^{IW}, \mathcal{F}_{CGKA})$ *in the* $(\mathcal{F}_{AS}, \mathcal{F}_{KS}, \mathcal{G}_{RO})$*-hybrid model when* $\mathcal{F}_{CGKA}$ *uses the predicates* **safe** *and* **inj-allowed** *from Fig. 6.*

Proof (Sketch). Let $\mathcal{S}$ be an arbitrary simulator and consider the following environment $\mathcal{Z}$ that initially sets up a group consisting of parties A, B, and C that are in the same consistent state, as in the previous proof. Then, the environment acts as a malicious insider A sending semi-inconsistent commit messages to B and C. To this end, it corrupts party A and learns ssk_A. Afterwards it computes a commit message c_1 (to an empty proposal list) and another one c_1' by first copying c_1 and then replacing the signature by a different valid one. It delivers c_1 to B and c_1' to C. Finally, $\mathcal{Z}$ instructs B to create a proposal p that removes A from the group. Moreover, instruct both B and C to first commit to this proposal (creating commit messages c_2 and c_2', respectively) and have each of the parties process their own commit message. If both parties successfully process their commit messages, $\mathcal{Z}$ outputs 1, and 0 otherwise.

It is easy to see that when interacting with the hybrid world both B and C successfully process their own commits, as the interim transcript hash does not affect the proposal p, making it valid for both B and C whose views agree in everything but the interim transcript hash. In the ideal world, however, p is associated with B's node and as a result cannot be committed to by C, as enforced by the consistency invariant. (In our model two different ciphertexts c_1 and c_1' cannot point to the same node.) As a result, $\mathcal{Z}$ outputs 0 when interacting with the ideal world.   □

Our fix that moves the signature into the confirmed transcript hash has been incorporated into MLS [16].

6.3   Inadequate Joiner Security (Tree-Signing)

The role of the tree-signing mechanism of MLS is to provide additional guarantees for joiners by leveraging the long-term signature keys distributed by the PKI. Intuitively, we may hope for the following guarantee: A joiner (potentially invited by a malicious insider to a non-existing group) ends up in a secure epoch once all malicious parties have been removed. A bit more precisely, a key is corrupt if the secret key is registered by or leaked to a malicious actor.

Surprisingly, we can show that the initial tree signing mechanism introduced in MLS Draft 9 does not achieve this guarantee. Rather, it achieves something much weaker: A joiner ends up in a secure epoch once all members with the following types of long-term signature keys have been removed: (a) corrupt keys and (b) keys used in a different epoch that includes a key of type (a). We believe this to be an unexpectedly weak guarantee. In particular, it means that malicious insiders can read messages after being removed.[14]

---

[14] It also seems to contradict the (informal) notion of the "tree-invariant" often cited on the MLS mailing list.

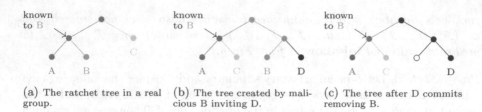

(a) The ratchet tree in a real group.

(b) The tree created by malicious B inviting D.

(c) The tree after D commits removing B.

Fig. 7. The attack on the tree signing of $\mathsf{ITK}_{\mathsf{Atk-3}}$. (Color figure online)

The Attack on Tree-Signing. We call ITK using the tree-signing mechanism from MLS Draft 9 $\mathsf{ITK}_{\mathsf{Atk-3}}$. We next present a simple and highly practical attack against $\mathsf{ITK}_{\mathsf{Atk-3}}$. It results in groups with epochs containing no keys of type A) yet for which the epoch key is easy to compute by the malicious insiders.

We first recall the tree signing of $\mathsf{ITK}_{\mathsf{Atk-3}}$. It works by storing in each ratchet-tree node v a value $v.\mathsf{parentHash}$ computed as follows.

> **if** $v.\mathsf{isroot}$ **then** $v.\mathsf{parentHash} \leftarrow \epsilon$
> **else** $v.\mathsf{parentHash} \leftarrow \mathsf{Hash}(v.\mathsf{parent.pk}, v.\mathsf{parent.parentHash})$

Further, each leaf contains a signature over its content, including its parentHash, under the long-term key of its owner. This means that during each commit the committer signs the new parentHash of their leaf, which binds all new PKE public keys they generated. We say that the committer's signature attests to the new PKE keys. Now joiners can verify that each public key in the ratchet tree they receive in the welcome message is attested to by some group member who generated it. (The joiners check the validity of the long-term keys in the PKI.)

Intuitively, the issue is, however, that committers only attest to the key pairs they (honestly) generated, but *not* to which parties they informed of the secret keys. This allows a malicious insider to create his own ratchet tree, where they knows secrets of nodes that are not on his direct path. Therefore, removing them from the fake group doesn't cause removal of every key they know, breaking Invariant (2) of the protocol.

Theorem 4. *The* $\mathsf{ITK}_{\mathsf{Atk-3}}$ *protocol, that behaves like* ITK *but with the MLS Draft 9 tree-signing mechanism, does not securely realize* $(\mathcal{F}_{\mathrm{AS}}^{\mathrm{IW}}, \mathcal{F}_{\mathrm{KS}}^{\mathrm{IW}}, \mathcal{F}_{\mathrm{CGKA}})$ *in the* $(\mathcal{F}_{\mathrm{AS}}, \mathcal{F}_{\mathrm{KS}}, \mathcal{G}_{\mathrm{RO}})$-*hybrid model when* $\mathcal{F}_{\mathrm{CGKA}}$ *uses the predicates* **safe** *and* **inj-allowed** *from Fig. 6.*

Proof (Sketch). The attack is illustrated in Fig. 7. Assume that the environment $\mathcal{Z}$ sets up a group with a group creator A adding parties B and C (in this order), leading in the hybrid world to ratchet tree depicted in Fig. 7a. In this state, the adversary corrupts party B, which henceforth is assumed to be malicious, while A and C are never corrupted and, thus, honest. In the following $\mathcal{Z}$ acts on behalf of the corrupted B and builds the fake ratchet tree from Fig. 7b, meaning $\mathcal{Z}$ swaps parties B and C (their public keys), then adds party D on behalf of B to the group, outputting a respective welcome message w using B's leaked signing key. Crucially, we observe that the ratchet tree from Fig. 7b represents a valid one that D will accept: In Fig. 7a C's leaf signature only attested to C's leaf key (the green one) as the parent hash field is empty. Second, A's leaf signature does not attests to B's leaf key (but only the blue ones) as the parent hash only includes the nodes on A's direct path to the root. Third, $\mathcal{Z}$ can re-key B's new path and attest to the fresh keys (the red ones) using the leaked signing key.

The environment then delivers w to D, joining them to the fake group, and afterwards $\mathcal{Z}$ instructs D remove B, i.e., to propose, commit, and then process the respective commit message c'. Finally, $\mathcal{Z}$ queries D's group key key and also computes the expected group key key$'$ by taking D's commit message and using the secret key known to $\mathcal{Z}$ marked in Fig. 7c and perform the same computation C would in the $\mathsf{ITK}_{\mathsf{Atk}\text{-}3}$ protocol. If key $=$ key$'$, then $\mathcal{Z}$ outputs 1 and 0 otherwise.

It remains to convince ourselves that $\mathcal{Z}$ distinguishes with non-negligible probability for any simulator $\mathcal{S}$. It is easy to see that when interacting with the hybrid world $\mathcal{Z}$ outputs 1. Finally, consider the ideal-world. We argue that safe(c') $=$ true meaning that the functionality outputs an independent and u.a.r. key and, thus, $\mathcal{Z}$ outputs 0 with overwhelming probability. First, it is easy to see that $\mathcal{S}$ has to join D to a detached root as no other group state matches, e.g., none has D as a member. Next, observe that D has not been corrupted implying that the node created by D's commit is marked with Node[c'].stat $=$ good and has no direct exposures, i.e., Node[c'].exp $= \varnothing$. As a result, we have safe(c') $= \neg$*can-traverse(c') while *can-traverse(c') $=$ false as clearly only case (d) might apply but know(c', id) $=$ false for all id $\in \{A, B, C, D\}$ for the following reasons: First, A, C, and D have never been corrupted, in particular implying *state-directly-leaks(c', id) $=$ false and know(root$_1$, id) $=$ false, where root$_1$ denotes the detached root to which D joined. Second, for B, observe that *state-directly-leaks(c', B) $=$ false as $B \notin$ Node[c'].mem and $B \notin$ Node[c'].exp while *secrets-replaced(c', B) $=$ true as B has been removed from that state. Thus, we can deduce that safe(c') $=$ true, concluding the proof. $\square$

Fixing Tree Signing. In essence, we can prevent the attack by modifying the parent hash such that committers attest to the key pairs they generated *and* to which parties were informed about the secret keys. We can achieve this by computing the parent hash v.parentHash as Hash(w.pk, w.parentHash, w.memberCert) where w is v's parent and memberCert attests to the set of parties informed about the w.sk. It is left to find a good candidate for memberCert; one that is secure and easy to compute. We next discuss 3 candidates for memberCert.

The first candidate is called *the leaf parent hash.* This is the most direct solution which simply sets w.memberCert to the list of all leaves in the subtree of v.sibling that are not unmerged at w. Observe that, by Invariant (2) of ITK, the owners of these leaves, and only they, were informed about w.sk (recall that the unmerged leaves are defined as those that do not know w.sk). One disadvantage of the leaf hash is that it is not very implementation-friendly.

The second candidate, called *the tree parent hash,* has been initially considered for MLS [35]. It basically sets w.memberCert to the tree hash of v.sibling with the unmerged leaves omitted (recall that ITK computes the tree hash as the

Merkle hash of the ratchet tree). Observe that the tree hash binds strictly more than the leaf hash. The tree hash would be more straightforward to compute. Unfortunately, it is not workable due to other mechanisms of MLS.[15]

Therefore, we propose a new candidate called *the resolution parent hash*. It improves upon the leaf hash in 2 ways: it is more implementation-friendly and it has slightly better deniability properties.[16] The resolution hash sets memberCert to the PKE public keys of nodes in u.origChildResolution where u.origChildResolution is the resolution of u with the unmerged leaves of u.parent omitted. Observe that u.origChildResolution is the resolution of u at the time the last committer in the subtree of v generated the key pair of w.

The reason this works is less direct than in the case of leaf and tree hashes. Intuitively, assume all long-term keys in the subtree of w are uncorrupted. The honest committer who generated w's key pair attests to w.pk and all PKE keys in u.origChildResolution, i.e. those they encrypted w.sk to. These PKE keys are in turn attested to by the honest members in their subtrees who generated them. Applying this argument recursively and relying on the security of the encryption scheme, we can conclude that all key pairs in the ratchet tree remain secure.

6.4 IND-CPA Security Is Insufficient

Many prior analysis of MLS only assume IND-CPA security of the PKE scheme it uses. However, there are PKE schemes that are IND-CPA secure but that make MLS clearly insecure against active attackers—despite MLS employing signatures and MACs to protect authenticity—highlighting the inadequacies of those works' simplified security models to account for all relevant aspects (and the danger of analyzing too piecemeal protocols without considering their composition in general).

Consider the protocol $\mathsf{ITK_{cpa}}$ which behaves like ITK but replaces its PKE scheme with PKE^*. PKE^* is IND-CPA secure and has the following property: a ciphertext ctx containing a message m can be modified into ctx_i, s.t. decrypting ctx_i outputs $\perp$ if and only if the i-th bit of m is 0, and otherwise decrypting ctx_i outputs m.[17] The following attack shows that $\mathsf{ITK_{cpa}}$ is clearly insecure in the setting with active attackers. In particular, a malicious insider can decrypt messages after being removed from the group. Let κ denote the length of a path secret used by MLS. The attack proceeds as follows:

1. An honest execution leads to an epoch E_1 where the group has $N = 4\kappa$ members $P_1, \dots, P_N$, ordered according to their leaves from left to right. Further, the ratchet tree has no blanks.

---

[15] With adds and removes, the subtree of v can grow or shrink since the last commit, changing the tree hash. It is not clear how to revert these changes.

[16] With the leaf hash, members sign each other's credentials, thus attesting to being in a group together. The resolution hash gets rid of this side effect.

[17] PKE^* can be easily obtained as a straightforward adaptation of the artificial symmetric encryption scheme by Krawczyk [31] (used to show that the authenticate-then-encrypt paradigm is not secure in general) to the public key setting.

2. The adversary corrupts P_1 and P_N.
3. P_1 (honestly) sends a commit c_1, creating an epoch E_2. P_{N-1} transitions to E_2, and sends a commit c_2 that removes P_N, creating epoch E_3.
   The expectation is that E_3 is secure due to PCS and removing all corrupted members. The adversary will next compute group key in E_3.
4. The adversary has the following information: P_1's signing key ssk_1 (the same in all epochs), the secret key sk of the right child of the root in E_1 (corrupted P_N knows sk), the init secret in E_1 and the ciphertexts $ctxRoot$ and $ctxLchild$ encrypting P_1's two last path secrets in c_1.
   The adversary shouldn't know the path secret s encrypted in $ctxLchild$, since this breaks the tree invariant. He will next learn s it bit by bit.
5. The members who will decrypt $ctxLchild$ are $P_{\kappa+1}$ to $P_{2\kappa}$. For $i = 1$ to κ, the adversary injects to $P_{\kappa+i}$ the packet c_1 modified as follows:
   (a) Replace $ctxLchild$ by $ctxLchild_i$ obtained using the PKE^* property.
   (b) Update the confirmation tag accordingly: 1) Decrypt $ctxRoot$ using sk. The result is the next path secret s' after s. 2) Use s' to compute the commit secret. 3) Compute the new key schedule using the init secret in E_1 and the commit secret from 2). 4) Compute the tag.
   (c) Update the signature using ssk_1.
6. Clearly, if $P_{\kappa+i}$ accepts, then the i-th bit of s is 0, else 1.
   Now the adversary uses s to compute the key in E_3.
7. Using s, the adversary derives the secret key for the left child of the root in E_2. Since this node is in the copath of P_{N-1}, the adversary can use it to decrypt the commit secret from c_2. The adversary then computes the init secret in E_2 by honestly running P_N's protocol and mixes it with the commit to derive the key schedule in E_3.

Clearly, however, the **safe** predicate of our $\mathcal{F}_{\mathrm{CGKA}}$ functionality considers the resulting key from epoch E_3 as secure. Hence, we get the following result.

Theorem 5. *The $\mathsf{ITK}_{\mathsf{cpa}}$ protocol that behaves like ITK does not securely realize $(\mathcal{F}_{\mathrm{AS}}^{\mathrm{IW}}, \mathcal{F}_{\mathrm{KS}}^{\mathrm{IW}}, \mathcal{F}_{\mathrm{CGKA}})$ in the $(\mathcal{F}_{\mathrm{AS}}, \mathcal{F}_{\mathrm{KS}}, \mathcal{G}_{\mathrm{RO}})$-hybrid model when $\mathcal{F}_{\mathrm{CGKA}}$ uses the predicates* **safe** *and* **inj-allowed** *from Fig. 6.*

Proof. We show that for every simulator $\mathcal{S}$, there exists an environment $\mathcal{Z}$ that has non-negligible advantage in distinguishing the ideal world from the real world with $\mathsf{ITK}_{\mathsf{cpa}}$. Let $\mathcal{S}$ be any simulator. The environment $\mathcal{Z}$ executes the attack described above, i.e., it gives appropriate instructions to honest parties and performs the adversary's attacks. Let key' denote the group key computed at the end by the adversary. $\mathcal{Z}$ fetches the group key key in E_3 (via the Key query to say P_5). If $\mathsf{key} = \mathsf{key}'$, it outputs 1 else 0.

We will show that **safe** is true in E_3. Given this, we can conclude the proof with the following observations: Clearly, in the real world, $\mathcal{Z}$ always outputs 1 (for simplicity we assume perfect correctness). In the ideal world, since **safe** is true, key is chosen by $\mathcal{F}_{\mathrm{CGKA}}$ random and independent of $\mathcal{S}$. Since key' is computed by $\mathcal{Z}$ only from information given to $\mathcal{S}$, this means that with overwhelming probability $\mathsf{key} \neq \mathsf{key}'$, and hence $\mathcal{Z}$ outputs 0.

It remains to show that **safe** is true. Informally, the only corruptions are of P_1 and P_N in E_1. Transitioning to E_1 "heals" from P_1's corruption, since this is an honest commit from them, and transitioning to E_3 heals from P_N's corruption, since they are removed.

Formally, we will show that **know** is false for all parties in E_3. This will mean that ***can-traverse**$(c_2) = \texttt{false}$ (by inspection, all other conditions that can make it true do not occur). Hence, **safe** is true in E_3.

Observe that **know** can only be true for P_1 and P_N, as ***state-directly-leaks** is only true for these parties in E_1. First, ***secrets-replaced**(c_1, P_1) is true, since $\mathsf{None}[c_1].\mathsf{orig} = P_1$. Therefore, **know**$(c_1, P_1) = \texttt{false}$ and by recursion **know**$(c_2, P_1) = \texttt{false}$. Second, ***secrets-replaced**(c_2, P_2) is true, since it includes a proposal with $\mathsf{act} = \mathsf{rem}\text{-}P_N$. Therefore, **know**$(c_1, P_1) = \texttt{false}$.   □

References

1. Messagying layer security (MLS) WG - meeting minutes for interim 2020-1, January 2020. https://datatracker.ietf.org/doc/minutes-interim-2020-mls-01-202001110900/

2. Alwen, J., et al.: Grafting key trees: efficient key management for overlapping groups. In: Nissim, K., Waters, B. (eds.) TCC 2021, Part III. LNCS, vol. 13044, pp. 222–253. Springer, Cham (2021). https://doi.org/10.1007/978-3-030-90456-2_8

3. Alwen, J., Auerbach, B., Noval, M.C., Klein, K., Pascual-Perez, G., Pietrzak, K.: DeCAF: decentralizable continuous group key agreement with fast healing. Cryptology ePrint Archive, Report 2022/559 (2022). https://eprint.iacr.org/2022/559

4. Alwen, J., et al.: CoCoA: concurrent continuous group key agreement. In: Dunkelman, O., Dziembowski, S. (eds.) EUROCRYPT 2022, Part II. LNCS, vol. 13276, pp. 815–844. Springer, Heidelberg (2022). https://doi.org/10.1007/978-3-031-07085-3_28

5. Alwen, J., Blanchet, B., Hauck, E., Kiltz, E., Lipp, B., Riepel, D.: Analysing the HPKE standard. In: Canteaut, A., Standaert, F.-X. (eds.) EUROCRYPT 2021. LNCS, vol. 12696, pp. 87–116. Springer, Cham (2021). https://doi.org/10.1007/978-3-030-77870-5_4

6. Alwen, J., Coretti, S., Dodis, Y., Tselekounis, Y.: Security analysis and improvements for the IETF MLS standard for group messaging. In: Micciancio, D., Ristenpart, T. (eds.) CRYPTO 2020, Part I. LNCS, vol. 12170, pp. 248–277. Springer, Cham (2020). https://doi.org/10.1007/978-3-030-56784-2_9

7. Alwen, J., Coretti, S., Dodis, Y., Tselekounis, Y.: Modular design of secure group messaging protocols and the security of MLS. In: Vigna, G., Shi, E. (eds.) ACM CCS 2021, pp. 1463–1483. ACM Press, November 2021. https://doi.org/10.1145/3460120.3484820

8. Alwen, J., Coretti, S., Jost, D., Mularczyk, M.: Continuous group key agreement with active security. In: Pass, R., Pietrzak, K. (eds.) TCC 2020, Part II. LNCS, vol. 12551, pp. 261–290. Springer, Cham (2020). https://doi.org/10.1007/978-3-030-64378-2_10

9. Alwen, J., Hartmann, D., Kiltz, E., Mularczyk, M.: Server-aided continuous group key agreement. Cryptology ePrint Archive, Report 2021/1456 (2021). https://eprint.iacr.org/2021/1456

10. Alwen, J., et al.: Keep the dirt: tainted treekem, adaptively and actively secure continuous group key agreement. In: 2021 IEEE Symposium on Security and Privacy, S&P, pp. 268–284 (2021). https://doi.org/10.1109/SP40001.2021.00035. Full version: https://eprint.iacr.org/2019/1489

11. Alwen, J., Jost, D., Mularczyk, M.: On the insider security of MLS. Cryptology ePrint Archive, Paper 2020/1327 (2020). https://eprint.iacr.org/2020/1327. Full version of this paper

12. Backes, M., Dürmuth, M., Hofheinz, D., Küsters, R.: Conditional reactive simulatability. In: Gollmann, D., Meier, J., Sabelfeld, A. (eds.) ESORICS 2006. LNCS, vol. 4189, pp. 424–443. Springer, Heidelberg (2006). https://doi.org/10. 1007/11863908_26

13. Barnes, R., Beurdouche, B., Millican, J., Omara, E., Cohn-Gordon, K., Robert, R.: The messaging layer security (MLS) protocol (draft-ietf-mls-protocol-12). Technical report, IETF, March 2020. https://datatracker.ietf.org/doc/draft-ietf-mls-protocol/12/

14. Barnes, R.: Subject: [MLS] Remove without double-join (in TreeKEM). MLS Mailing List, 06 August 2018. https://mailarchive.ietf.org/arch/msg/mls/Zzw2tqZC1FCbVZA9LKERsMIQXik

15. Barnes, R.: MLS Protocol Pull Requests #396: Authenticate group membership in MLSPlaintext, 18 August 2020. https://github.com/mlswg/mls-protocol/pull/396

16. Barnes, R.: MLS Protocol Pull Requests #416: Inlclude the signature in the confirmation tag, 18 August 2020. https://github.com/mlswg/mls-protocol/pull/416

17. Barnes, R.: Subject: [MLS] Proposal: Proposals (was: Laziness). MLS Mailing List, 22 August 2019. https://mailarchive.ietf.org/arch/msg/mls/5dmrkULQeyvNu5k3MV_sXreybj0/

18. Bhargavan, K., Barnes, R., Rescorla, E.: TreeKEM: Asynchronous Decentralized Key Management for Large Dynamic Groups, May 2018. https://prosecco.inria. fr/personal/karthik/pubs/treekem.pdf. Published at https://mailarchive.ietf.org/arch/msg/mls/e3ZKNzPC7Gxrm3Wf0q96dsLZoD8

19. Bhargavan, K., Beurdouche, B., Naldurg, P.: Formal Models and Verified Protocols for Group Messaging: Attacks and Proofs for IETF MLS. Research report, Inria Paris, December 2019. https://hal.inria.fr/hal-02425229

20. Bienstock, A., Dodis, Y., Rösler, P.: On the price of concurrency in group ratcheting protocols. In: Pass, R., Pietrzak, K. (eds.) TCC 2020, Part II. LNCS, vol. 12551, pp. 198–228. Springer, Cham (2020). https://doi.org/10.1007/978-3-030-64378-2_8

21. Brzuska, C., Cornelissen, E., Kohbrok, K.: Security analysis of the MLS key derivation. In: 2022 IEEE Symposium on Security and Privacy, S&P, pp. 595–613. IEEE Computer Society, Los Alamitos, May 2022. https://doi.org/10.1109/SP46214. 2022.00035. https://doi.ieeecomputersociety.org/10.1109/SP46214.2022.00035

22. Bushing, Marcan, Segher, Sven: Console hacking 2010 – PS3 epic fail. In: 27th Chaos Communication Congress – 27C3 (2010). https://fahrplan.events.ccc.de/congress/2010/Fahrplan/events/4087.en.html

23. Canetti, R.: Universally composable security: a new paradigm for cryptographic protocols. In: 42nd FOCS, pp. 136–145. IEEE Computer Society Press, October 2001. https://doi.org/10.1109/SFCS.2001.959888

24. Cohn-Gordon, K., Cremers, C., Garratt, L., Millican, J., Milner, K.: On ends-to-ends encryption: asynchronous group messaging with strong security guarantees. In: Lie, D., Mannan, M., Backes, M., Wang, X. (eds.) ACM CCS 2018, pp. 1802–1819. ACM Press, October 2018. https://doi.org/10.1145/3243734.3243747

25. Cremers, C., Hale, B., Kohbrok, K.: The complexities of healing in secure group messaging: why cross-group effects matter. In: Bailey, M., Greenstadt, R. (eds.) USENIX Security 2021, pp. 1847–1864. USENIX Association, August 2021

26. Devigne, J., Duguey, C., Fouque, P.-A.: MLS group messaging: how zero-knowledge can secure updates. In: Bertino, E., Shulman, H., Waidner, M. (eds.) ESORICS 2021, Part II. LNCS, vol. 12973, pp. 587–607. Springer, Cham (2021). https://doi.org/10.1007/978-3-030-88428-4_29

27. Emura, K., Kajita, K., Nojima, R., Ogawa, K., Ohtake, G.: Membership privacy for asynchronous group messaging. Cryptology ePrint Archive, Report 2022/046 (2022). https://eprint.iacr.org/2022/046

28. Hashimoto, K., Katsumata, S., Postlethwaite, E., Prest, T., Westerbaan, B.: A concrete treatment of efficient continuous group key agreement via multi-recipient PKEs. In: Proceedings of the 2021 ACM SIGSAC Conference on Computer and Communications Security, pp. 1441–1462 (2021)

29. Jost, D., Maurer, U., Mularczyk, M.: Efficient ratcheting: almost-optimal guarantees for secure messaging. In: Ishai, Y., Rijmen, V. (eds.) EUROCRYPT 2019, Part I. LNCS, vol. 11476, pp. 159–188. Springer, Cham (2019). https://doi.org/10.1007/978-3-030-17653-2_6

30. Jost, D., Maurer, U., Mularczyk, M.: A unified and composable take on ratcheting. In: Hofheinz, D., Rosen, A. (eds.) TCC 2019, Part II. LNCS, vol. 11892, pp. 180–210. Springer, Cham (2019). https://doi.org/10.1007/978-3-030-36033-7_7

31. Krawczyk, H.: The order of encryption and authentication for protecting communications (or: how secure is SSL?). In: Kilian, J. (ed.) CRYPTO 2001. LNCS, vol. 2139, pp. 310–331. Springer, Heidelberg (2001). https://doi.org/10.1007/3-540-44647-8_19

32. Miller, M.A.: Messaging layer security (MLS) WG - meeting minutes for IETF105, August 2019. https://datatracker.ietf.org/doc/minutes-105-mls/

33. Panjwani, S.: Tackling adaptive corruptions in multicast encryption protocols. In: Vadhan, S.P. (ed.) TCC 2007. LNCS, vol. 4392, pp. 21–40. Springer, Heidelberg (2007). https://doi.org/10.1007/978-3-540-70936-7_2

34. Rescorla, E.: Subject: [MLS] TreeKEM: An alternative to ART. MLS Mailing List, 03 May 2018. https://mailarchive.ietf.org/arch/msg/mls/WRdXVr8iUwibaQu0tH6sDnqU1no

35. Sullivan, N.: Subject: [MLS] Virtual interim minutes. MLS Mailing List, 29 January 2020. https://mailarchive.ietf.org/arch/msg/mls/ZZAz6tXj-jQ8nccf7SyIwSnhivQ/

36. Weidner, M.: Group messaging for secure asynchronous collaboration. MPhil dissertation, 2019. Advisors: A. Beresford and M. Kleppmann (2019). https://mattweidner.com/acs-dissertation.pdf

Lattice-Based Zero Knowledge

Lattice-Based Zero-Knowledge Proofs and Applications: Shorter, Simpler, and More General

Vadim Lyubashevsky[1], Ngoc Khanh Nguyen[1,2][✉] [ID], and Maxime Plançon[1,2]

[1] IBM Research Europe, Ruschlikon, Switzerland
nkn@zurich.ibm.com
[2] ETH Zurich, Zurich, Switzerland

Abstract. We present a much-improved practical protocol, based on the hardness of Module-SIS and Module-LWE problems, for proving knowledge of a short vector $\vec{s}$ satisfying $A\vec{s} = \vec{t} \bmod q$. The currently most-efficient technique for constructing such a proof works by showing that the ℓ_∞ norm of $\vec{s}$ is small. It creates a commitment to a polynomial vector $\mathbf{m}$ whose CRT coefficients are the coefficients of $\vec{s}$ and then shows that (1) $A \cdot \mathsf{CRT}(\mathbf{m}) = \vec{t} \bmod q$ and (2) in the case that we want to prove that the ℓ_∞ norm is at most 1, the polynomial product $(\mathbf{m} - \mathbf{1}) \cdot \mathbf{m} \cdot (\mathbf{m} + \mathbf{1})$ equals to 0. While these schemes are already quite practical, the requirement of using the CRT embedding and only being naturally adapted to proving the ℓ_∞-norm, somewhat hinders the efficiency of this approach.

In this work, we show that there is a more direct and more efficient way to prove that the coefficients of $\vec{s}$ have a small ℓ_2 norm which does not require an equivocation with the ℓ_∞ norm, nor any conversion to the CRT representation. We observe that the inner product between two vectors $\vec{r}$ and $\vec{s}$ can be made to appear as a coefficient of a product (or sum of products) between polynomials which are functions of $\vec{r}$ and $\vec{s}$. Thus, by using a polynomial product proof system and hiding all but one coefficient, we are able to prove knowledge of the inner product of two vectors (or of a vector with itself) modulo q. Using a cheap, "approximate range proof", one can then lift the proof to be over $\mathbb{Z}$ instead of $\mathbb{Z}_q$. Our protocols for proving short norms work over all (interesting) polynomial rings, but are particularly efficient for rings like $\mathbb{Z}[X]/(X^n + 1)$ in which the function relating the inner product of vectors and polynomial products happens to be a "nice" automorphism.

The new proof system can be plugged into constructions of various lattice-based privacy primitives in a black-box manner. As examples, we instantiate a verifiable encryption scheme and a group signature scheme which are more than twice as compact as the previously best solutions.

1 Introduction

The fundamental hardness assumption upon which lattice-based cryptography rests is that it is computationally difficult to find a low-norm vector $\mathbf{s}$ satisfying

$$\mathbf{A}\mathbf{s} = \mathbf{t} \bmod q. \tag{1}$$

© International Association for Cryptologic Research 2022
Y. Dodis and T. Shrimpton (Eds.): CRYPTO 2022, LNCS 13508, pp. 71–101, 2022.
https://doi.org/10.1007/978-3-031-15979-4_3

It is then natural that for creating privacy-preserving protocols based on the hardness of lattice problems, one is usually required to prove the knowledge of an $\mathbf{s}$ satisfying the above, or a related, equality. Unlike in the analogous case of discrete logarithms, where proving knowledge of a secret s satisfying $g^s = t$ turns out to have a very simple and efficient solution [36], the added requirement of showing that $\|\mathbf{s}\|$ is small turns out to be a major complication for *practical* lattice cryptography.

Over polynomial rings (i.e. rings of the form $\mathbb{Z}[X]/(f(X))$, where $f(X)$ is a monic, irreducible polynomial), one can give a fairly-efficient zero-knowledge proof of knowledge of a vector $\bar{\mathbf{s}}$ and a polynomial c with small coefficients satisfying

$$\mathbf{A}\bar{\mathbf{s}} = c\mathbf{t} \bmod q, \qquad (2)$$

where $\|\bar{\mathbf{s}}\|$ is some factor (depending on the dimension of $\mathbf{s}$) larger than $\|\mathbf{s}\|$ [24,25]. While such proofs are good enough for constructing fairly efficient basic protocols (e.g. signature schemes [4,15,24,25]), the fact that the norm of the extracted $\bar{\mathbf{s}}$ is noticeably larger than that of $\mathbf{s}$, along with the presence of the extra multiplicand c, makes these proofs awkward to use in many other situations. This very often results in the protocols employing these proofs being less efficient than necessary, or in not giving the resulting scheme the desired functionality.

As simple examples of inefficiencies that may creep up when only being able to prove (2), consider Regev-style lattice-based encryption schemes (e.g. [32,35]) where $\mathbf{s}$ is the randomness (including the message) and $\mathbf{t}$ is the ciphertext. In order to decrypt, it is necessary for $\mathbf{t}$ to have a short pre-image, and so being able to only prove knowledge of (2) is not enough to guarantee that the ciphertext $\mathbf{t}$ can be decrypted because it is $c\mathbf{t}$ that has a short pre-image, not $\mathbf{t}$ (and c is not known to the decryptor). A consequence of this is that the currently most-efficient lattice-based verifiable encryption scheme [26] has the undesirable property that the expected decryption time is equal to the adversary's running time because the decryptor needs to essentially guess c. Employing this scheme in the real world would thus require setting up a scenario where the adversary cannot use too much time to construct the proof. Other lattice-based constructions (e.g. group signature schemes [28]) were required to select much larger parameters than needed in order to accommodate the presence of the multiplicand c and the "slack" between the length of the known solution $\mathbf{s}$ and the solution $\bar{\mathbf{s}}$ that one can prove.

1.1   Prior Art for Proofs of (1)

Early protocols for exactly proving (1) used the combinatorial algorithm of Stern [37] to prove that the ℓ_∞ norm of $\mathbf{s}$ is bounded by revealing a random permutation of $\mathbf{s}$. The main problem with these protocols was that their soundness error was $2/3$, and so they had to be repeated around 200 times to achieve an acceptably small (i.e. 2^{-128}) soundness error. This resulted in proofs for even basic statements[1] being more than 1MB in size [23], while more interesting constructions required outputs on the order of dozens of Megabytes (e.g. [22]). A noticeable improvement was achieved in [9] by generically combining Stern's protocol with a "cut-and-choose" technique to noticeably decrease the soundness error of each protocol run (at the expense of higher running times). This allowed proofs for basic statements to be around 200 KB in size.

A very different, more algebraic, approach for proving (1) utilized lattice-based commitments and zero-knowledge proofs about committed values to prove relations between the coefficients of s and also prove a bound on its ℓ_∞ norm. The first such protocols [11,17,38] had proof sizes that were on the order of several hundred kilobytes. These schemes were greatly improved in [3,16], where it was shown how to very efficiently prove products of polynomial products over a ring and then linear relations over the CRT coefficients of committed values. Optimizations of these techniques [31] decreased the proof size for the basic example to around 33 KB.

The high level idea for these proofs, when s has coefficients in the set $\{-1, 0, 1\}$, is to create a BDLOP commitment [6] to a polynomial m whose CRT coefficients are the coefficients of s, prove this (linear) relationship as well as the one in (1) [16], and then prove that $(m - 1) \cdot m \cdot (m + 1) = 0$ [3].

There are a few intrinsic elements of this approach which hinder its efficiency, especially in certain situations. The first is that m consists of large polynomial coefficients, and so committing to it requires using a more expensive commitment scheme, which is especially costly when s is long[2] (we discuss this in more detail when talking about various commitments in Sect. 1.3). Another downside is that for vectors s with somewhat-large coefficients, such as ones that are obtained from trapdoor sampling (e.g. [1,34]), proving the smallness of the ℓ_∞-norm becomes significantly costlier because the degree of the polynomial product increases. There is also an incompatibility between the requirement that the underlying ring has a lot of CRT slots and negligible soundness error of the protocol – thus a part of the protocol needs to be repeated for soundness amplification. And finally, proving the ℓ_2 norm, rather than the ℓ_∞ one, is very often what one would like to do when constructing proofs for lattice-based primitives. This is because efficient trapdoor-sampling used in many lattice primitives produces vectors of (tightly) bounded ℓ_2 norm, and noise also generation generally results in tight ℓ_2-norm bounds.

---

[1] A standard example that has been used for comparison-purposes in several works is 1024×2048 integer matrix A, a 32-bit modulus q, and s having coefficients in $\{-1, 0, 1\}$ (or $\|s\| \leqslant \sqrt{2048}$).

[2] The aforementioned framework was most appropriate for committing to small-dimensional messages (e.g. in protocols related to anonymous transactions (e.g. [18,19,31]) and proving various relationships between them.

1.2   Our Results

We propose a simpler, more efficient, and more direct approach for proving a tight bound on the ℓ_2 norm of s satisfying (1). Unlike in the previous approach, we do not need to recommit to s in CRT form, and therefore don't have a ring algebra requirement which had a negative effect on the protocol soundness. Furthermore, not needing to create a BDLOP commitment to s noticeably shrinks the proof size. In particular, we define a commitment scheme which combines the Ajtai [2] and BDLOP [6] commitments into one, and then put the long commitment to s into the "Ajtai" part of the commitment scheme, which does not increase the commitment size.[3]

We then observe that the inner product of two vectors over $\mathbb{Z}$ can be made to appear as the constant coefficient of a polynomial product, or as a coefficient in a sum of polynomial products. Our protocol for proving the ℓ_2-norm of s is then a specific application of a more general protocol that can prove knowledge of constant coefficients of quadratic relations over polynomial rings for messages that are committed in the "Ajtai" and "BDLOP" parts of our new commitment. Our protocols are built up in a black-box manner from basic building blocks, and can then also be used in a black box manner for implementing the zero-knowledge proof parts of various lattice-based primitives. As examples, the ZK proof of the basic relation from (1) is $\approx 2.5X$ shorter than in previous works, a verifiable encryption scheme can be as short as the one from [26] without the constraint that the decryption time is proportional to the adversary's attack time, and we give a group signature scheme whose signatures are more than $2X$ smaller than the currently most compact one.

Our proof system for the basic equality from (1) is around 14 KB, and approximately 8 KB of that consists of just the "minimum" commitment (i.e. a commitment to just one element in $\mathcal{R}_q$ that doesn't include s) and its opening proof. This shows that our construction is quite close to being optimal for any approach that requires creating a commitment to s using known lattice-based commitment schemes. Since all zero-knowledge proofs that we're aware of for showing that a secret s satisfies $f(s)$ work by first committing to s, it appears that any significant improvement to this proof system (e.g. another factor of 2) would require noticeable improvements in fundamental lattice primitives, basing security on stronger assumptions, or a noticeable departure from the current approach.

We now give a detailed overview of the techniques and results in this work, and then sketch how our framework can be used to construct lattice-based privacy protocols.

1.3   Techniques Overview

Throughout most of the introduction and paper, we will concentrate on the ring $\mathcal{R}_q = \mathbb{Z}_q[X]/(X^d + 1)$, as our constructions are most efficient here because

---

[3] The BDLOP part of the commitment scheme is then used for low-dimensional auxiliary elements that will need to be committed to later in the protocol.

they can utilize a specific automorphism in this ring. Towards the end of this section and in the full version of the paper [27], we describe how to adapt our construction, and most applications, to other rings that do not have this algebraic structure. All our constructions will be based on the hardness of the Module-SIS and Module-LWE problems and one should think of the degree of the underlying ring d to be something small like 64 or 128 (we use 128 for all our instantiations).

Commitment Schemes. In the original Ajtai commitment scheme, implicit in [2], one commits to a message s_1 using randomness s_2, where $\|s_i\|$ are small, as

$$A_1 s_1 + A_2 s_2 = t \bmod q. \tag{3}$$

It's easy to see that creating a second valid opening (s_1', s_2') for the same commitment value t is equivalent to solving the SIS problem over $\mathcal{R}_q$, and the hiding aspect of the commitment scheme is based on the indistinguishability of $(A_2, A_2 s_2)$ from uniform. A useful feature of the above commitment scheme is that the dimension of the message s_1 does not increase the commitment size. And since the hardness of SIS does not really depend on the dimension of the solution, increasing the dimension of s_1 does not negatively impact the security either. On the other hand, one does need the coefficients of s_1 to be small.

A different commitment scheme, called the BDLOP scheme [6], commits to a message m using randomness s as

$$\begin{bmatrix} A \\ B \end{bmatrix} \cdot s + \begin{bmatrix} 0 \\ m \end{bmatrix} = \begin{bmatrix} t_A \\ t_B \end{bmatrix} \bmod q, \tag{4}$$

where only the randomness s needs to have a small norm. An opening of this commitment is just s since it uniquely determines m, and so it is again easy to see that two different openings lead to a solution to SIS for the matrix A. The hiding property of this commitment is based on the indistinguishability from uniform of $\left(\begin{bmatrix} A \\ B \end{bmatrix}, \begin{bmatrix} A \\ B \end{bmatrix} \cdot s \right)$.

This scheme has two advantages and one disadvantage over the one in (3). The disadvantage is that both the commitment size and the opening size grow linearly with the dimension of the message vector m. An advantage is that the coefficients of m can be arbitrarily large modulo q. The other advantage is that if one plans ahead and sets the dimension of s large enough, one can very cheaply append commitments of new elements in $\mathcal{R}_q$. For example, if we have already created a commitment to m as in (4) and would like to commit to another polynomial vector m', we can compute $B's \mid m' - t_B' \bmod q$, where B' is some public randomness. If $\left(\begin{bmatrix} A \\ B \\ B' \end{bmatrix}, \begin{bmatrix} A \\ B \\ B' \end{bmatrix} \cdot s \right)$ is indistinguishable from uniform, then (t_A, t_B, t_B') is a commitment to m, m'. Note that committing to k extra $\mathcal{R}_q$ elements requires growing the commitment size by only k $\mathcal{R}_q$ elements, something that cannot be done using the scheme from (3).

For optimality, our construction will require features from both of these schemes, and it actually turns out to be possible to combine the two of them into one. So to commit to a message s_1 with a small norm, and a message m with unrestricted coefficients (modulo q), one can create a commitment

$$\begin{bmatrix} A_1 \\ 0 \end{bmatrix} \cdot s_1 + \begin{bmatrix} A_2 \\ B \end{bmatrix} \cdot s_2 + \begin{bmatrix} 0 \\ m \end{bmatrix} = \begin{bmatrix} t_A \\ t_B \end{bmatrix} \bmod q, \tag{5}$$

where the randomness is s_2. We will call this combination of the Ajtai and BDLOP commitment scheme, the ABDLOP commitment. The savings over creating two separate commitments is that instead of needing the t term from (3) and the t_A term from (4), we only have the t_A term. So we get an Ajtai commitment to s_1 for free! And similarly, the opening does not require both s_2 from (3) and s from (4).

One can show that (5) is indeed a commitment scheme and has an efficient zero-knowledge opening proof.[4] Furthermore, there is also an efficient zero-knowledge proof (much like in [6]) which allows one to efficiently show that the committed values s_1, m satisfy a relation over $\mathcal{R}_q$

$$R_1 s_1 + R_m m = u \bmod q, \tag{6}$$

where the matrices R_1, R_m, and the vector u are public. This proof system is given in Fig. 4, and we just mention that the proof size is not affected by the sizes of R_1 and R_m. In other words, the proof size for proving linear relations over $\mathcal{R}_q$ is the same as the proof size of just proving knowledge of the committed values. The only way in which this proof puts a restriction on the underlying ring is that the modulus q must be large enough so that the extracted SIS solution is hard, and that the challenge set $\mathcal{C}$ is such that the difference of challenges is (with high probability) invertible. This can be done by choosing the modulus q in a way that $X^d + 1$ splits into very few irreducible factors of the form $X^k - r_i$ modulo q (or the prime factors of q), which in turn implies that all elements of $\mathcal{R}_q$ with small coefficients are invertible [33].

The way this commitment scheme will be used in our protocols is that we will put high-dimensional messages with small coefficients into s_1, while putting small-dimensional values with large coefficients – generally auxiliary "garbage terms" that we will need to commit to during the protocol which aid in proving relations among the elements in s_1 – into m.

Inner Products over $\mathbb{Z}_q$. Suppose that instead of just wanting to prove linear relations over $\mathcal{R}_q$, as above, we wanted to prove linear relations over $\mathbb{Z}_q$. That is, if we let R_1, R_m be integer matrices, and we write $\vec{s}_1$ and $\vec{m}$ to be integer vectors whose coefficients are the integer coefficients of the polynomial vectors s_1 and m, then we would like to prove that $R_1 \vec{s}_1 + R_m \vec{m} = \vec{u} \bmod q$.

---

[4] As for the Ajtai and BDLOP commitments, the opening needs to be carefully defined because the ZK proof only proves approximate relations as in (2). The details are in Sect. 3.1.

An important observation is the following: if $\vec{r} = (r_0, r_1, \ldots, r_{d-1}), \vec{s} = (s_0, s_1, \ldots, s_{d-1}) \in \mathbb{Z}_q^d$ are vectors and $r(X) = \sum_i r_i X^i, s(X) = \sum_i s_i X^i \in \mathcal{R}_q$ are the corresponding polynomials, then $\langle \vec{r}, \vec{s} \rangle \bmod q$ is equal to the constant coefficient of the polynomial product $r(X^{-1}) \cdot s(X)$ over $\mathcal{R}_q$.[5] Similarly, for $\vec{r}, \vec{s} \in \mathbb{Z}_q^{kd}$, one can define the corresponding polynomial vectors $\mathbf{r} = (r_1, \ldots, r_k), \mathbf{s} = (s_1, \ldots, s_k) \in \mathcal{R}_q^k$ to have the same coefficients as $\vec{r}, \vec{s}$ in the straightforward manner, then $\langle \vec{r}, \vec{s} \rangle \bmod q$ is equal to the constant coefficient of $\sum_i r_i(X^{-1}) \cdot s_i(X)$, where the multiplication is performed over $\mathcal{R}_q$.

For a polynomial $h = h_0 + h_1 X + \ldots + h_{d-1} X^{d-1} \in \mathcal{R}_q$, we will write $\tilde{h}$ to mean the constant coefficient h_0. The procedure to prove that $\langle \vec{r}, \vec{s} \rangle \bmod q = \alpha$ is then to create polynomial vectors $\mathbf{r}, \mathbf{s}$ such that $\widetilde{\langle \mathbf{r}, \mathbf{s} \rangle}$ (where the inner product is over $\mathcal{R}_q$) is equal to $\langle \vec{r}, \vec{s} \rangle$. One can hope to use the protocol from Fig. 4 to prove the linear relation over $\mathcal{R}_q$, which would imply the linear relation over $\mathbb{Z}_q$. The problem is that naively proving the relation over $\mathcal{R}_q$ would necessarily require the prover to reveal all the coefficients of $\langle \mathbf{r}, \mathbf{s} \rangle$ instead of just the constant one, which implies giving out extra information about the committed vector $\vec{s}$, and so is clearly not zero-knowledge.

We now outline the solution to this problem for general linear functions. For a linear function $f : \mathcal{R}_q^k \to \mathcal{R}_q$, we would like to prove that the committed values $\mathbf{s}_1, \mathbf{m}$ in the ABDLOP commitment satisfy $\tilde{f}(\mathbf{s}_1, \mathbf{m}) = 0$ (for aesthetics, we will write $\tilde{f}(x)$ to mean $\widetilde{f(x)}$). In order to mask all but the constant coefficient, we use a masking technique from [16], where the prover first creates a commitment to a polynomial $g \in \mathcal{R}_q$ such that $\tilde{g} = 0$ and all of its other coefficients are chosen uniformly at random. In our proof system, he commits to this polynomial in the "BDLOP part" of (5) by outputting $t_g = \langle \mathbf{b}, \mathbf{s}_2 \rangle + g$, where $\mathbf{b}$ is some random public polynomial vector. The verifier then sends a random challenge $\gamma \in \mathbb{Z}_q$, and the prover computes

$$h = \gamma \cdot f(\mathbf{s}_1, \mathbf{m}) + g. \tag{7}$$

The prover then creates a proof, as in Fig. 4, that the committed values $\mathbf{s}_1, \mathbf{m}$, and g satisfy this linear relation, and sends h along with this proof to the verifier. The verifier simply checks the validity of the linear proof, and also that $\tilde{h} = 0 \bmod q$.

The proof leaks no information about all but the constant coefficient of $f(\mathbf{s}_1, \mathbf{m})$ because they are masked by the completely random coefficients of g. To see that this proof is sound, note that for all g, if $\tilde{f}(\mathbf{s}_1, \mathbf{m}) \neq 0$, then $\Pr_\gamma[\gamma \cdot \tilde{f}(\mathbf{s}_1, \mathbf{m}) + \tilde{g} = 0] \leqslant 1/q_1$, where q_1 is the smallest prime factor of q. In order to reduce the soundness error down to ϵ, the prover would need to create a commitment to λ different g_i, where $(1/q_1)^\lambda = \epsilon$ and then reply to λ different challenges γ_i by creating λ different h_i as in (7). Since the g_i are just one polynomial in $\mathcal{R}_q$, the h_i are also just one polynomial each, and so amplifying the proof requires sending just 2λ extra elements in $\mathcal{R}_q$.

---

[5] For a polynomial $r(X) = \sum_{i=0}^{d-1} r_i X^i \in \mathcal{R}_q$, $r(X^{-1}) = r_0 - \sum_{i=1}^{d-1} r_i X^{d-i}$.

The above shows that proving one relation $\tilde{f}(\mathbf{s}_1, \mathbf{m}) = 0$ requires a small number λ of extra polynomials g and h. Usually, we will want to prove many such linear equations, and so it would be quite inefficient if our proof size grew linearly in their number. But, just like in the basic protocol in Fig. 4, we can show that the number of equations that we need to prove does not affect the size of the proof. If we would like to prove k equations $\tilde{f}_i(\mathbf{s}_1, \mathbf{m}) = 0$, the prover still sends the term g in the first round (let's ignore the amplification for now), but this time instead of sending just one random challenge $\gamma \in \mathbb{Z}_q$, the verifier sends k random challenges γ_i. The prover then creates the equation

$$h = \sum_i \gamma_i \cdot f_i(\mathbf{s}_1, \mathbf{m}) + g, \qquad (8)$$

and sends h along with a proof that the $\mathbf{s}_1, \mathbf{m}$, and g satisfy the above. The verifier checks the proof and that $\tilde{h} = 0 \bmod q$. Hence, the fact that this proof leaks no information and that the soundness error is again $1/q_1$ is virtually identical as for (7).

Quadratic Relations and Norms. In the above, we saw an overview of how one can prove knowledge of inner products over $\mathcal{R}_q$ and $\mathbb{Z}_q$ when one of the values is committed to and the other is public. We now show how to do the same thing when both values are in the commitment – in other words, how to prove quadratic relations over committed values.

The most efficient protocol for proving quadratic relations between committed polynomials in $\mathcal{R}_q$ is given in [3]. That protocol assumes that the elements were committed using the BDLOP commitment scheme, and one can show that a similar approach works for the ABDLOP scheme as well. And so one can prove arbitrary quadratic relations over $\mathcal{R}_q$ between the committed polynomials in the polynomial vector $\mathbf{s}_1$ and $\mathbf{m}$ in (5). We will now explain how to use this proof system, together with the ideas presented above, to construct a proof that the $\mathbf{s}$ satisfying (1) has small ℓ_2-norm. For simplicity of this description, let's just suppose that we would like to prove that $\|\mathbf{s}\| = \beta$ instead of $\|\mathbf{s}\| \leqslant \beta$.[6] The idea is to first commit to $\mathbf{s}$ as part of the $\mathbf{s}_1$ part of (5) (i.e. in the "Ajtai part" of the ABDLOP scheme). Then we use the observation from the previous section that notes that if $\mathbf{s}_1 = (s_1, \ldots, s_k) \in \mathcal{R}_q^k$, then $\|\mathbf{s}\|^2$ is the constant coefficient of $\sum_i s_i(X^{-1}) \cdot s_i(X)$. We cannot directly use the proof system for linear proofs because that one assumed that one of the multiplicands was public. We thus need to extend the protocol from [3] to prove knowledge of $\sum_i s_i(X^{-1}) \cdot s_i(X)$ when having a commitment to $\mathbf{s}$.

Let us recall the main ideas from [3] and then see how they can be applied to the ABDLOP commitment. Suppose, for example, that we wanted to prove that

---

[6] To prove the latter, one would commit to a vector $\vec{b}$ which is the binary representation of the integer $\beta^2 - \|\mathbf{s}\|^2$ and then prove that it is indeed binary and that $\langle \vec{b}, (1, 2, 2^2, \ldots 0, \ldots, 0) \rangle$ is $\beta^2 - \|\mathbf{s}\|^2$; which implies that the latter is positive. Note that it is still a quadratic relation in the committed values $\mathbf{s}$ and $\vec{b}$.

$s_1 s_2 - s_3 = 0$, and we had commitments to s_i in the Ajtai part of the ABDLOP commitment (i.e. the s_i are part of the $\mathbf{s}_1$ in (5)). If one looks at the protocol in Fig. 4 for proving knowledge of committed values in the ABDLOP protocol, then we note that the prover sends the vector $\mathbf{z}_1 = c\mathbf{s}_1 + \mathbf{y}_1$. This $\mathbf{z}_1$ consists of terms $z_i = s_i c + y_i$, where c is a polynomial challenge (with small coefficients) and y_i is a masking polynomial whose job is to hide s_i.

The high level idea in which the protocol from [3] (and some that preceded it [11,17,38]) proves quadratic relations is by having the verifier create a quadratic equation (in c) out of the linear equations $z_i = cs_i + y_i$. That is, the verifier computes

$$z_1 z_2 - cz_3 = (s_1 s_2 - s_3)c^2 + g_1 c + g_0, \tag{9}$$

where g_1 and g_0 are some terms which depend on y_i and s_i and are committed to by the prover prior to receiving the challenge c.[7] The above is a quadratic equation in the variable c (since all the other terms are already committed to), and so if the prover shows that $z_1 z_2 - cz_3 = g_1 c + g_0$ (i.e. it's actually a linear equation) it will imply that with high probability the quadratic coefficient, $s_1 s_2 - s_3$ is equal to 0.

To prove that the constant coefficient of $s(X^{-1}) \cdot s(X)$ is some value β, one can try to do something similar. Here, it becomes important that the function mapping s to $s(X^{-1})$ is an automorphism (call it σ) for $\mathcal{R}_q$. Given the term $z = sc + y$, the verifier is able to compute

$$\sigma(z) \cdot z - \sigma(c) \cdot c \cdot \beta^2 = (\sigma(s) \cdot s - \beta^2) \cdot \sigma(c) \cdot c + \sigma(s) \cdot y \cdot \sigma(c) + s \cdot \sigma(y) \cdot c + \sigma(y) \cdot y, \tag{10}$$

and, if the above is equal to $g_2 \cdot \sigma(c) + g_1 \cdot c + g_0$, would like to conclude that the coefficients in front of $\sigma(c) \cdot c$ is 0. Unfortunately, we can't conclude this because the c and $\sigma(c)$ are not independent. What we instead do is choose the challenges c from a set that is fixed under this automorphism – that is, $\sigma(c) = c$. Then (10) becomes

$$\sigma(z) \cdot z - c^2 \beta^2 = (\sigma(s) \cdot s - \beta^2) \cdot c^2 + (\sigma(s) \cdot y + s \cdot \sigma(y)) \cdot c + \sigma(y) \cdot y, \tag{11}$$

and we again have a quadratic equation in c. Luckily, the requirement that $\sigma(c) = c$ does not restrict the challenge set too much. In particular, if we choose $c \in \mathcal{R}_q$ to be of the form $c = c_0 + \sum_{i=1}^{d/2-1} c_i \cdot (X^i - X^{d-i})$, where $c_i \in \mathbb{Z}_q$, then $c = \sigma(c)$.[8] So we are free to set $d/2$ coefficients of the challenge polynomial instead of the usual d. So obtaining the same soundness requires the coefficients to be a little larger, but this has a rather small effect on the proof size.

The protocol in Fig. 5 is a very general protocol for proving that a quadratic function in the coefficients of $\mathbf{s}_1$ and $\mathbf{m}$, and the automorphisms of $\mathbf{s}_1$ and $\mathbf{m}$,

---

[7] [3] showed that the y_i were already implicitly committed to by the first part of the protocol.

[8] This is easy to see because $\sigma(X^i - X^{d-i}) = X^{-i} - X^{i-d}$, and multiplying by $-X^d = 1$, we obtain $\sigma(X^i - X^{d-i}) = -X^{d-i} + X^i$.

is satisfied as long as the challenge set is fixed under the particular automorphism. If we only want to prove the ℓ_2 norm, then we do not want to prove a quadratic function over $\mathcal{R}_q$, but rather we just want to prove something about the *constant coefficient* of a quadratic relation over $\mathcal{R}_q$. To do this, we employ the same masking technique as in (7) that we used for our linear proofs over $\mathbb{Z}_q$. Furthermore, just like in the linear proofs setting, if we need to prove multiple quadratic relations, we can first combine them into one equation, and then the proof size does not increase. Also note that we can clearly combine linear and quadratic equations together into one quadratic equation. The full protocol is presented in Fig. 7.

We are almost done, except for the fact that all of our proofs are modulo q. That is, the protocol only proves that $\|s\|^2 = \beta^2 \bmod q$, which is not the same as proving $\|s\|^2 = \beta^2$. In order to prove that there is no "wraparound" modulo q, we employ a version of the "approximate range proof" technique to show that the coefficients of s are all small-enough. We do not need a sharp bound on these coefficients, but just need to show that they are small-enough that no wraparound occurs. For this, we use the technique [7,8,20,29] of committing to a masking vector $\vec{y}$ (in the BDLOP part of (5)), receiving a $-1/0/1$ challenge matrix R, and outputting $\vec{z} = R\vec{s} + \vec{y}$ (and doing a rejection sampling to hide $\vec{s}$). It can be shown that if $\|\vec{z}\|$ is small, then $\|\vec{s}\|$ is also small. The dimension of $\vec{y}$ and $\vec{z}$ is small (between 128 and 256), and so the extra commitment to $\vec{y}$ and the revealing of $\vec{z}$ is inexpensive. The protocol for the approximate range proof, and the general protocol proving these approximate range proofs in combination with other quadratic functions are given in the full version of the paper [27].

Putting Everything Together. The structure for proving (1) involves creating an ABDLOP commitment as in (5) with $s_1 = s$ and making the randomness s_2 long enough to accommodate future commitments to a few intermediate terms necessary in the proof. One then uses the aforementioned proofs to show that $\|s_1\|$ is small, and that the linear equation in (1) is satisfied. Notice that we don't really need any ring structure on the equation in (1); if it is over $\mathbb{Z}_q$, we can simply prove it using the linear proofs over $\mathbb{Z}_q$. This is computationally more expensive than if the equation were over $\mathcal{R}_q$, because for every multiplication over $\mathbb{Z}_q$, we have to compute one multiplication over $\mathcal{R}_q$, but the proof size will be the same.

We also note that the modulus in (1) does not have to be the same as in the commitment scheme. In fact, it will often be necessary to use a larger modulus in the commitment scheme because it has to be larger than $\|s\|^2$. For example, we can set the commitment scheme modulus to $p \cdot q$ and then simply lift the equation in (1) to this modulus by multiplying both sides of it by p. As long as the challenge differences are invertible in the ring $\mathcal{R}_q$ and $\mathcal{R}_p$, all the protocols go through unchanged.

Another possibility is, instead of proving $\mathbf{As} = \mathbf{t} \bmod q$, one proves that

$$\mathbf{As} - \mathbf{t} = \mathbf{r} \cdot q \tag{12}$$

over the integers. If each row of $\mathbf{A}$ consists of m integer coefficients, then each coefficient of $\mathbf{r}$ has magnitude at most mq. One can then do the proof system using a larger modulus p, and also prove that each coefficient of $q^{-1}(\mathbf{As} - \mathbf{t}) \bmod p$ is small using the approximate range proof. The advantage of this method over using pq as the modulus for the commitment scheme, as above, is that it allows the commitment scheme modulus p to be a prime, and so one needs fewer terms for coefficient masking (see the discussion after (7)), which could save a few kilobytes in the complete proof. A disadvantage is that there is now the extra secret $\mathbf{r}$ term that needs to be dealt with.

Useful Extensions. While we concentrated on proving the smallness of the ℓ_2-norm of a vector $\vec{s}$ (or more generally the knowledge of the inner product between two vectors), it is also possible to use our techniques to prove many other inter-vector relations. In particular, a useful relation (e.g. if dealing with general functions/circuits) is proving the knowledge of the component-wise product $\vec{r} \circ \vec{s}$. This can be generally accomplished by proving a polynomial product over a ring $\mathcal{R}_p$ of two vectors $\mathbf{r}$ and $\mathbf{s}$ whose CRT coefficients are $\vec{r}$ and $\vec{s}$. The important thing is to choose a prime p such that the polynomial $X^d + 1$ factors into linear factors modulo p. As mentioned above, by simply subtracting off the remainder as in (12), one can use different moduli for the commitment scheme for the relations that we would like to prove. Thus one can choose a "CRT-friendly" modulus for the underlying relation, while using a modulus that allows the polynomial differences to be invertible (so not a CRT-friendly one) for the commitment scheme.

We also point out that proving inner products can be directly used to prove another very natural function – showing that all the coefficients of a vector are from the set $\{0, 1\}$. For this, one uses the observation that $\vec{s}$ has coefficients in $\{0, 1\}$ if and only if $\langle \vec{s}, \vec{1} - \vec{s} \rangle = 0$. And since given a commitment for $\vec{s}$, one can maul it into a commitment to $\vec{1} - \vec{s}$, one can generically apply the aforementioned protocol in Fig. 7.

Using Other Rings. In proving that the norm of a polynomial s was small, we exploited the fact that in the ring $\mathcal{R}$, $s(\widetilde{X^{-1}}) \cdot s = \|s\|^2$ and that $s(X^{-1})$ was an automorphism. In the full version of the paper, we show that the same high level ideas can also be made to work for rings that don't have this algebraic structure. Specifically, for all rings $R = \mathbb{Z}[X]/(X^d + f_{d-1}X^{d-1} + \ldots + f_1 X \pm 1)$, there exists a linear function $g : R \to R$ such that $\widetilde{g(r)} \cdot s$ is equal to $\langle \vec{r}, \vec{s} \rangle$. If g is not an automorphism, then proving knowledge of $\|s\|^2 = g(s) \cdot s$ would require the prover to commit to both s and $g(s)$, and then also prove the linear relationship between the commitments of s and $g(s)$. Opening two commitments instead of one will increase the proof size, but this is slightly mitigated by the fact that the challenges no longer need to be restricted to be fixed under any automorphism.

Sample Constructions. In the full version of the paper, we present various instantiations of lattice-based primitives that can be constructed using our zero-knowledge proof system. We now give a very high-level description of a group signature scheme. In a group signature scheme, the Setup Authority uses a master secret keys to distribute member secret keys to the members of the group. The members can then use their secret keys to sign messages on behalf of the group. An entity known as the Opener (or group manager) also has a special secret key that allows him to obtain the identity of the signer of any message. The privacy criterion states that it should be impossible, for everyone but the Opener, to trace back a signature to the particular user, nor link that two signatures were signed by the same user. Conversely, the traceability requirement states that every message signed by a user with identity μ will get traced back to him by the Opener. Group signatures are an interesting primitive in their own right, but are particularly useful in determining the practicality of zero-knowledge proofs as they contain some ingredients which are prevalent throughout privacy-based cryptography.

We show how we can use our improved ZK proof to construct a lattice-based group signature following the framework of [13,28]. The master public key is $[\mathbf{A} \mid \mathbf{B}], \mathbf{u}$, and the secret key of a group member with identity μ is a short vector $\begin{bmatrix} \mathbf{s}_1 \\ \mathbf{s}_2 \end{bmatrix}$ such that

$$[\mathbf{A} \mid \mathbf{B} + \mu\mathbf{G}] \cdot \begin{bmatrix} \mathbf{s}_1 \\ \mathbf{s}_2 \end{bmatrix} = \mathbf{u} \bmod q. \tag{13}$$

The setup authority with a trapdoor for the lattice $\mathcal{L} = \{\mathbf{x} : [\mathbf{A} \mid \mathbf{B}] \cdot \mathbf{x} = \mathbf{0} \bmod q\}$ can create such short vectors which are distributed according to a discrete Gaussian distribution [1,34].

The group member's signature of a message consists of a Module-LWE encryption of his identity μ as

$$\begin{bmatrix} \mathbf{A}' \\ \mathbf{b} \end{bmatrix} \cdot \mathbf{r} + \begin{bmatrix} 0 \\ \lceil p/2 \rceil \mu \end{bmatrix} = \mathbf{t} \bmod p, \tag{14}$$

where $\mathbf{A}', \mathbf{b}$ is the public key (of the Opener) and $\mathbf{r}$ is the randomness, together with a ZKPoK that he knows $\mu, \mathbf{r}$, and $\begin{bmatrix} \mathbf{s}_1 \\ \mathbf{s}_2 \end{bmatrix}$ satisfying (13) and (14). The message that the user is signing is, as usual, put into the input of the hash function used in the Fiat-Shamir transform of the ZKPoK.

To create this signature, the user commits to $\mathbf{s}_1, \mathbf{s}_2, \mathbf{r}, \mu$ in the "Ajtai" part of the ABDLOP commitment (5). He then proves that the norms of $\mathbf{s}_1, \mathbf{s}_2, \mathbf{r}$ are small, that μ has 0/1 coefficients, and that (14) and (13) hold. Notice that (14) is just a linear equation and proving (13) is proving the quadratic relation $\mathbf{A}\mathbf{s}_1 + \mathbf{B}\mathbf{s}_2 + \mathbf{G}\mu\mathbf{s}_2 = \mathbf{u} \bmod q$. All of these proofs fit into the appropriate quadratic functions and the full description of the group signature is given in the full version of the paper.

The security of the scheme rests on the fact that creating a valid proof on a μ that is not the user's identity implies having a solution to (13) on a new identity, which is directly equivalent to breaking the ABB signature scheme [1,34], which in turn implies breaking the Module-SIS problem. Prior to this work, proving tight bounds on the ℓ_2 norm of polynomial vectors with somewhat large coefficients was not very efficient, and so constructions of group signature schemes using this approach [13,28] did not prove (13), but rather proved an approximate version of it as in (2) – i.e. they proved knowledge of $\bar{s}_1, \bar{s}_2, c$ satisfying

$$[\mathbf{A} \mid \mathbf{B} + \mu\mathbf{G}] \cdot \begin{bmatrix} \bar{s}_1 \\ \bar{s}_2 \end{bmatrix} = cu \bmod q, \tag{15}$$

where $\|\bar{s}_i\| \gg \|s_i\|$.

A consequence of being only able to prove the above is a vicious cycle of the larger norms and the presence of c resulting in a larger extracted solution to the Module-SIS problem, which in turn requires having a larger modulus for SIS security, which then also requires a larger lattice dimension for LWE security. Furthermore, because these schemes relied on the verifiable encryption scheme of [26], they also did not prove (14), but rather an approximate version of it as in (2). The implication is that in order to decrypt, the Opener needed to guess the unknown c, which in expectation requires the same number of guesses as the adversary's number of calls to the random oracle during the proof. Thus special care would be needed to instantiate the scheme in an environment that would not allow the adversary to be able to have too much time to try and forge a signature. We believe that efficiently eliminating this requirement in all lattice-based schemes requiring a verifiable encryption scheme is a notable improvement on the state of affairs.

Table 1. Our group signature and that of [28].

	Public Key Size	Signature Size	Opening Time Independent of Adversary's Forgery Time
[28]	96 KB	203 KB	✗
This Work	48 KB	92 KB	✓

We compare the instantiation of the group signature from this paper to the previously most efficient one from [28] in Table 1. We mention that there are also tree-based group signatures (e.g. [10,18]) which have shorter outputs for small group sizes, but have the disadvantage that the signing time, verification time, and public key size are linear in the group size. The signature length of these schemes also grows slightly with the group size, and for groups having more than $\approx 2^{21}$ members, our scheme has a comparable signature size (in addition to a much smaller public key and signing/verification times).

Table 2. The table on the left compares the difference in proof size of proving knowledge of short $\vec{s}, \vec{e}$ satisfying $A\vec{s} + \vec{e} = \vec{t} \bmod q$, where $A \in \mathbb{Z}_q^{1024 \times 1024}$ and $q \approx 2^{32}$, and $\|(\vec{s}, \vec{e})\| \leqslant \sqrt{2048}$. The protocol from [30] needs to make the additional restriction that all the coefficients in $\vec{s}, \vec{e}$ are from $\{-1, 0, 1\}$. The table on the right compares our instantiation of a verifiable encryption scheme from this paper with [26] and [30].

	Proof Size
[30]	33 KB
This Work	14 KB

	Ciphertext Size	Proof Size	Decryption Time Independent of Forgery Time
[26]	9 KB	9 KB	✗
[30][a]	4 KB	33–44 KB	✓
This Work	1 KB	19 KB	✓

[a] This paper presents a verifiable *decryption* scheme, but the proof size for a verifiable encryption scheme constructed in the same manner would be similar. At the very least, it needs to be as large as the proof of the basic equation in (1).

Part of the group signature includes a verifiable encryption scheme, in which the encryptor proves that the encryption is valid. When looked at separately, this scheme has a similar size to the one from [26], but with the noticeable advantage of not having a dependency between the decryption time and the adversary's forgery time. We also give a comparison of the proof size for the basic system in (1) between our proof system and the prior best one from [30] that followed the framework of [3] and [16]. The comparisons for the verifiable encryption scheme and the basic proof system are in Table 2 and detailed descriptions of the proofs can be found in the full version of the paper.

2 Preliminaries

2.1 Notation

Denote $\mathbb{Z}_p$ to be the ring of integers modulo p. Let $q = q_1, \ldots, q_n$ be a product of n odd primes where $q_1 < q_2 < \ldots < q_n$. Usually, we pick $n = 1$ or $n = 2$. We write $\vec{v} \in \mathbb{Z}_q^m$ to denote vectors over a ring $\mathbb{Z}_q$. Matrices over $\mathbb{Z}_q$ will be written as regular capital letters R. By default, all vectors are column vectors. We write $\vec{v} \| \vec{w}$ for a usual concatenation of $\vec{v}$ and $\vec{w}$ (which is still a column vector). For $\vec{v}, \vec{w} \in \mathbb{Z}_q^k$, $\vec{v} \circ \vec{w}$ is the usual component-wise multiplication. For simplicity, we denote $\vec{u}^2 = \vec{u} \circ \vec{u}$. We write $x \leftarrow S$ when $x \in S$ is sampled uniformly at random from the finite set S and similarly $x \leftarrow D$ when x is sampled according to the distribution D. Let $[n] := \{1, \ldots, n\}$.

For a power of two d and a positive integer p, denote $\mathcal{R}$ and $\mathcal{R}_p$ respectively to be the rings $\mathbb{Z}[X]/(X^d + 1)$ and $\mathbb{Z}_p[X]/(X^d + 1)$. Lower-case letters denote elements in $\mathcal{R}$ or $\mathcal{R}_p$ and bold lower-case (resp. upper-case) letters represent column vectors (resp. matrices) with coefficients in $\mathcal{R}$ or $\mathcal{R}_p$. For a polynomial $f \in \mathcal{R}_p$, denote $\vec{f} \in \mathbb{Z}_q^d$ to be the coefficient vector of f. By default, we write its

i-th coefficient as its corresponding regular font letter subscript i, e.g. $f_{d/2} \in \mathbb{Z}_p$ is the coefficient corresponding to $X^{d/2}$ of $f \in \mathcal{R}_p$. For the constant coefficient, however, we will denote $\tilde{f} := f_0 \in \mathbb{Z}_p$. The ring $\mathcal{R}$ has a group of automorphisms $\mathsf{Aut}(\mathcal{R})$ that is isomorphic to $\mathbb{Z}_{2d}^\times$. Let $\sigma_i \in \mathsf{Aut}(\mathcal{R}_q)$ be defined by $\sigma_i(X) = X^i$. For readability, we denote for an arbitrary vector $\mathbf{m} \in \mathcal{R}^k$:

$$\sigma_i(\mathbf{m}) := (\sigma_i(m_1), \ldots, \sigma_i(m_k))$$

and similarly $\sigma_i(\mathbf{R})$ for any matrix $\mathbf{R}$. When we write $\langle \mathbf{u}, \mathbf{v} \rangle \in \mathbb{Z}$ for $\mathbf{u}, \mathbf{v} \in \mathcal{R}^k$, we mean the inner product of their corresponding coefficient vectors.

For an element $w \in \mathbb{Z}_q$, we write $\|w\|_\infty$ to mean $|w \bmod^\pm q|$. Define the ℓ_∞ and ℓ_p norms for $w = w_0 + w_1 X + \ldots + w_{d-1} X^{d-1} \in \mathcal{R}$ as follows:

$$\|w\|_\infty = \max_j \|w_j\|_\infty, \quad \|w\|_p = \sqrt[p]{\|w_0\|_\infty^p + \ldots + \|w_{d-1}\|_\infty^p}.$$

If $\mathbf{w} = (w_1, \ldots, w_m) \in \mathcal{R}^k$, then

$$\|\mathbf{w}\|_\infty = \max_j \|w_j\|_\infty, \quad \|\mathbf{w}\|_p = \sqrt[p]{\|w_1\|^p + \ldots + \|w_k\|^p}.$$

By default, $\|\mathbf{w}\| := \|\mathbf{w}\|_2$. Similarly, we define the norms for vectors over $\mathbb{Z}_q$. Denote $S_\gamma = \{x \in \mathcal{R}_q : \|x\|_\infty \leqslant \gamma\}$.

2.2 Probability Distributions

We first define the discrete Gaussian distribution used for the rejection sampling.

Definition 1. *The discrete Gaussian distribution on $\mathcal{R}^\ell$ centered around $\mathbf{v} \in \mathcal{R}^\ell$ with standard deviation $\mathfrak{s} > 0$ is given by*

$$D_{\mathbf{v}, \mathfrak{s}}^\ell(\mathbf{z}) = \frac{e^{-\|\mathbf{z}-\mathbf{v}\|^2/2\mathfrak{s}^2}}{\sum_{\mathbf{z}' \in \mathcal{R}^\ell} e^{-\|\mathbf{z}'\|^2/2\mathfrak{s}^2}}.$$

When it is centered around $\mathbf{0} \in \mathcal{R}^\ell$ we write $D_\mathfrak{s}^\ell = D_{\mathbf{0},\mathfrak{s}}^\ell$.

We will use the following tail bound, which follows from [5, Lemma 1.5(i)].

Lemma 1. *Let $\mathbf{z} \leftarrow D_\mathfrak{s}^m$. Then $\Pr\left[\|\mathbf{z}\| > t \cdot \mathfrak{s}\sqrt{md} \right] < \left(te^{\frac{1-t^2}{2}} \right)^{md}$.*

Next, we recall the binomial distribution.

Definition 2. *The binomial distribution with a positive integer parameter κ, written as Bin_κ is the distribution $\sum_{i=1}^\kappa (a_i - b_i)$, where $a_i, b_i \leftarrow \{0,1\}$. The variance of this distribution is $\kappa/2$ and it holds that $\mathsf{Bin}_{\kappa_1} \pm \mathsf{Bin}_{\kappa_2} = \mathsf{Bin}_{\kappa_1+\kappa_2}$.*

2.3   Module-SIS and Module-LWE Problems

Security of the [6] commitment scheme used in our protocols relies on the well-known computational lattice problems, namely Module-LWE (MLWE) and Module-SIS (MSIS) [15,21]. Both problems are defined over $\mathcal{R}_q$.

Definition 3 (MSIS$_{\kappa,m,B}$). *Given* $\mathbf{A} \leftarrow \mathcal{R}_q^{\kappa \times m}$, *the* Module-SIS *problem with parameters* $\kappa, m > 0$ *and* $0 < B < q$ *asks to find* $\mathbf{z} \in \mathcal{R}_q^m$ *such that* $\mathbf{Az} = \mathbf{0}$ *over* $\mathcal{R}_q$ *and* $0 < \|\mathbf{z}\| \leqslant B$. *An algorithm* $\mathcal{A}$ *is said to have advantage* ϵ *in solving* MSIS$_{\kappa,m,B}$ *if*

$$\Pr\left[0 < \|\mathbf{z}\|_\infty \leqslant B \wedge \mathbf{Az} = \mathbf{0} \,\middle|\, \mathbf{A} \leftarrow \mathcal{R}_q^{\kappa \times m}; \mathbf{z} \leftarrow \mathcal{A}(\mathbf{A})\right] \geqslant \epsilon.$$

Definition 4 (MLWE$_{m,\lambda,\chi}$). *The* Module-LWE *problem with parameters* $m, \lambda > 0$ *and an error distribution* χ *over* $\mathcal{R}$ *asks the adversary* $\mathcal{A}$ *to distinguish between the following two cases: 1)* $(\mathbf{A}, \mathbf{As} + \mathbf{e})$ *for* $\mathbf{A} \leftarrow \mathcal{R}_q^{m \times \lambda}$, *a secret vector* $\mathbf{s} \leftarrow \chi^\lambda$ *and error vector* $\mathbf{e} \leftarrow \chi^m$, *and 2)* $(\mathbf{A}, \mathbf{b}) \leftarrow \mathcal{R}_q^{m \times \lambda} \times \mathcal{R}_q^m$. *Then,* $\mathcal{A}$ *is said to have advantage* ϵ *in solving* MLWE$_{m,\lambda,\chi}$ *if*

$$\left|\Pr\left[b = 1 \,\middle|\, \mathbf{A} \leftarrow \mathcal{R}_q^{m \times \lambda}; \mathbf{s} \leftarrow \chi^\lambda; \mathbf{e} \leftarrow \chi^m; b \leftarrow \mathcal{A}(\mathbf{A}, \mathbf{As} + \mathbf{e})\right] \right. \tag{16}$$
$$\left. - \Pr\left[b = 1 \,\middle|\, \mathbf{A} \leftarrow \mathcal{R}_q^{m \times \lambda}; \mathbf{b} \leftarrow \mathcal{R}_q^m; b \leftarrow \mathcal{A}(\mathbf{A}, \mathbf{b})\right]\right| \geqslant \epsilon.$$

We also recall the (simplified) Extended Module-LWE problem [30].

Definition 5 (Extended-MLWE$_{m,\lambda,\chi,\mathcal{C},\mathfrak{s}}$). *The* Extended Module-LWE *problem with parameters* $m, \lambda > 0$, *probability distribution* χ *over* $\mathcal{R}_q$, *challenge space* $\mathcal{C} \subseteq \mathcal{R}_q$ *and the standard deviation* $\mathfrak{s}$ *asks the adversary* $\mathcal{A}$ *to distinguish between the following two cases:*

1. $(\mathbf{B}, \mathbf{Br}, c, \mathbf{z}, \mathsf{sign}\,(\langle \mathbf{z}, c\mathbf{r} \rangle))$ *for* $\mathbf{B} \leftarrow \mathcal{R}_q^{m \times (m+\lambda)}$, *a secret vector* $\mathbf{r} \leftarrow \chi^{m+\lambda}$ *and* $\mathbf{z} \leftarrow D_\mathfrak{s}^{(m+\lambda)}, c \leftarrow \mathcal{C}$
2. $(\mathbf{B}, \mathbf{u}, c, \mathbf{z}, \mathsf{sign}\,(\langle \mathbf{z}, c\mathbf{r} \rangle))$ *for* $\mathbf{B} \leftarrow \mathcal{R}_q^{m \times (m+\lambda)}, \mathbf{u} \leftarrow \mathcal{R}_q^m, \mathbf{z} \leftarrow D_\mathfrak{s}^{(m+\lambda)}, c \leftarrow \mathcal{C}$,

where $\mathsf{sign}(a) = 1$ *if* $a \geqslant 0$ *and 0 otherwise. Then,* $\mathcal{A}$ *is said to have advantage* ϵ *in solving Extended-MLWE$_{m,\lambda,\chi,\mathcal{C},\mathfrak{s}}$ if*

$$\left|\Pr\left[b = 1 \,\middle|\, \mathbf{B} \leftarrow \mathcal{R}_q^{m \times (m+\lambda)}; \mathbf{r} \leftarrow \chi^{m+\lambda}; \mathbf{z} \leftarrow D_\mathfrak{s}^{(m+\lambda)}; c \leftarrow \mathcal{C}; b \leftarrow \mathcal{A}(\mathbf{B}, \mathbf{Br}, \mathbf{z}, c, s)\right] \right.$$
$$\left. - \Pr\left[b = 1 \,\middle|\, \mathbf{B} \leftarrow \mathcal{R}_q^{m \times \lambda}; \mathbf{u} \leftarrow \mathcal{R}_q^m; \mathbf{z} \leftarrow D_\mathfrak{s}^{(m+\lambda)}; c \leftarrow \mathcal{C}; b \leftarrow \mathcal{A}(\mathbf{B}, \mathbf{u}, \mathbf{z}, c, s)\right]\right| \geqslant \epsilon.$$

where $s = \mathsf{sign}\,(\langle \mathbf{z}, c\mathbf{r} \rangle)$.

2.4   Rejection Sampling

In lattice-based zero-knowledge proofs, the prover will want to output a vector $\mathbf{z}$ whose distribution should be independent of a secret message/randomness vector $\mathbf{r}$, so that $\mathbf{z}$ cannot be used to gain any information on the prover's secret. During the protocol, the prover computes $\mathbf{z} = \mathbf{y} + c\mathbf{r}$ where $\mathbf{r}$ is either a secret vector or randomness used to commit to the prover's secret, $c \leftarrow \mathcal{C}$ is a challenge polynomial, and $\mathbf{y}$ is a "masking" vector. In order to remove the dependency of $\mathbf{z}$ on $\mathbf{r}$, one applies *rejection sampling* [25].

Lemma 2 (Rejection Sampling [14, 25, 30]). *Let $V \subseteq \mathcal{R}^\ell$ be a set of polynomials with norm at most T and $\rho\colon V \to [0,1]$ be a probability distribution. Fix the standard deviation $\mathfrak{s} = \gamma T$. Then, the following statements hold.*

1. *Let $M = \exp(14/\gamma + 1/(2\gamma^2))$. Now, sample $\mathbf{v} \leftarrow \rho$ and $\mathbf{y} \leftarrow D_\mathfrak{s}^\ell$, set $\mathbf{z} = \mathbf{y} + \mathbf{v}$, and run $b \leftarrow \mathrm{Rej}_1(\mathbf{z}, \mathbf{v}, \mathfrak{s})$ as defined in Fig. 1. Then, the probability that $b = 0$ is at least $(1 - 2^{-128})/M$ and the distribution of $(\mathbf{v}, \mathbf{z})$, conditioned on $b = 0$, is within statistical distance of 2^{-128} of the product distribution $\rho \times D_\mathfrak{s}^\ell$.*
2. *Let $M = \exp(1/(2\gamma^2))$. Now, sample $\mathbf{v} \leftarrow \rho$ and $\mathbf{y} \leftarrow D_\mathfrak{s}^\ell$, set $\mathbf{z} = \mathbf{y} + \mathbf{v}$, and run $b \leftarrow \mathrm{Rej}_2(\mathbf{z}, \mathbf{v}, \mathfrak{s})$ as defined in Fig. 1. Then, the probability that $b = 0$ is at least $1/(2M)$ and the distribution of $(\mathbf{v}, \mathbf{z})$, conditioned on $b = 0$, is identical to the distribution $\mathcal{F}$ where $\mathcal{F}$ is defined as follows: sample $\mathbf{v} \leftarrow \rho$, $\mathbf{z} \leftarrow D_\mathfrak{s}^{ld}$ conditioned on $\langle \mathbf{v}, \mathbf{z} \rangle \geqslant 0$ and output $(\mathbf{v}, \mathbf{z})$.*
3. *Let $M = \exp(1/(2\gamma^2))$. Now, sample $\mathbf{v} \leftarrow \rho, \beta \leftarrow \{0,1\}$ and $\mathbf{y} \leftarrow D_\mathfrak{s}^\ell$, set $\mathbf{z} = \mathbf{y} + (-1)^\beta \mathbf{v}$, and run $b \leftarrow \mathrm{Rej}_0(\mathbf{z}, \mathbf{v}, \mathfrak{s})$ as defined in Fig. 2. Then, the probability that $b = 0$ is at least $1/M$ and the distribution of $(\mathbf{v}, \mathbf{z})$, conditioned on $b = 0$, is identical to the product distribution $\rho \times D_\mathfrak{s}^\ell$.*

$\mathrm{Rej}_1(\vec{z}, \vec{v}, \mathfrak{s})$	$\mathrm{Rej}_2(\vec{z}, \vec{v}, \mathfrak{s})$
01 $u \leftarrow [0, 1)$	01 If $\langle \vec{z}, \vec{v} \rangle < 0$
02 If $u > \frac{1}{M} \cdot \exp\left(\frac{-2\langle \vec{z}, \vec{v} \rangle + \|\vec{v}\|^2}{2\mathfrak{s}^2}\right)$	02 $\quad$ return 1 (i.e. *reject*)
03 $\quad$ return 1 (i.e. *reject*)	03 $u \leftarrow [0, 1)$
04 Else	04 If $u > \frac{1}{M} \cdot \exp\left(\frac{-2\langle \vec{z}, \vec{v} \rangle + \|\vec{v}\|^2}{2\mathfrak{s}^2}\right)$
05 $\quad$ return 0 (i.e. *accept*)	05 $\quad$ return 1 (i.e. *reject*)
	06 Else
	07 $\quad$ return 0 (i.e. *accept*)

Fig. 1. Two rejection sampling algorithms: the one used generally in previous works [25] (left) and the one proposed recently in [30] (right).

We recall how parameters $\mathfrak{s}$ and M in the first statement Lemma 2 are selected. Concretely, the repetition rate M is chosen to be an upper-bound on:

$$\frac{D_\mathfrak{s}^\ell(\mathbf{z})}{D_{\mathbf{v}, \mathfrak{s}}^\ell(\mathbf{z})} = \exp\left(\frac{-2\langle \mathbf{z}, \mathbf{v} \rangle + \|\mathbf{v}\|^2}{2\mathfrak{s}^2}\right) \leqslant \exp\left(\frac{28\mathfrak{s}\|\mathbf{v}\| + \|\mathbf{v}\|^2}{2\mathfrak{s}^2}\right) = M. \quad (17)$$

For the inequality we used the which says that with probability at least $1 - 2^{128}$ we have $|\langle \mathbf{z}, \mathbf{v} \rangle| < 14\mathfrak{s}\|\mathbf{v}\|$ for $\mathbf{z} \leftarrow D_\mathfrak{s}^\ell$ [5, 25]. Hence, by setting $\mathfrak{s} = 13\|\mathbf{v}\|$ we obtain $M \approx 3$.

Recently, Lyubashevsky et al. [30] proposed a modified rejection sampling algorithm (see $\mathrm{Rej}_2(\mathbf{z}, \mathbf{v}, \mathfrak{s})$ in Fig. 1) where it forces $\mathbf{z}$ to satisfy $\langle \mathbf{z}, \mathbf{v} \rangle \geqslant 0$, otherwise it aborts. With this additional assumption, we can set M in the following way:

$$\exp\left(\frac{-2\langle \mathbf{z}, \mathbf{v} \rangle + \|\mathbf{v}\|^2}{2\mathfrak{s}^2}\right) \leqslant \exp\left(\frac{\|\mathbf{v}\|^2}{2\mathfrak{s}^2}\right) = M. \quad (18)$$

Hence, for $M \approx 3$ one would select $\mathfrak{s} = 0.675 \cdot \|\mathbf{v}\|$. Note that the probability for $\mathbf{z} \leftarrow D_{\mathfrak{s}}^{\ell}$ that $\langle \mathbf{z}, \mathbf{v} \rangle \geqslant 0$ is at least $1/2$. Hence, the expected number of rejections would be at most $2M = 6$. On the other hand, if one aims for $M = 6$ repetitions using (17), then $\mathfrak{s} = 8 \cdot \|\mathbf{v}\|$. Thus, [30] manages to reduce the standard deviation by more than a factor of 10. Further, we remark that this method is still not as efficient as using bimodal Gaussians [14], since even though the value M is calculated exactly as in (18), the expected number of rejections is at most M and not $2M$. We summarise the results from [14, 30] in the latter two statements of Lemma 2.

$$
\begin{array}{|l|}
\hline
\mathrm{Rej}_0(\vec{z}, \vec{v}, \mathfrak{s}) \\
\hline
01 \quad u \leftarrow [0, 1) \\
02 \quad \text{If } u > \dfrac{1}{M \exp\left(-\frac{\|\vec{v}\|^2}{2\mathfrak{s}^2}\right) \cosh\left(\frac{\langle \vec{z}, \vec{v} \rangle}{\sigma^2}\right)} \\
03 \qquad \text{return } 1 \text{ (i.e. } reject) \\
04 \quad \text{Else} \\
05 \qquad \text{return } 0 \text{ (i.e. } accept) \\
\hline
\end{array}
$$

Fig. 2. Bimodal rejection sampling [14].

Finally, we highlight that the procedure in the second statement of Lemma 2 reveals the sign of $\langle \mathbf{z}, \mathbf{v} \rangle$. This is still fine when working with "one-time commitments" [30] since we only leak one bit of information if $\mathbf{v}$ is a randomness vector which is generated every execution. However, secure signature schemes cannot be produced using this method because each generation of a signature reveals some information about the secret key.

By using this technique, zero-knowledge property (or rather commit-and-prove simulatability as described in later sections) of our protocols relies on the (simplified) Extended-MLWE problem [30] where the adversary is given the additional one bit of information about the secret. We describe this problem in Sect. 2.3.

2.5 Challenge Space

In our applications, the set $V \subseteq \mathcal{R}^{\ell}$ will consist of vectors of the form $c\mathbf{r}$ where $c \in \mathcal{R}_q$ is sampled from a challenge space $\mathcal{C}$ and $\mathbf{r} \in \mathcal{R}_q^{\ell}$ comes from a set of secret (either randomness or message) vectors. In order to set the standard deviation for rejection sampling, we need to bound the norm of such vectors. Here, we present a new way to bound $\|c\mathbf{r}\|$.

Lemma 3. *Let* $\mathbf{r} \in \mathcal{R}_q^{\ell}$ *and* $c \in \mathcal{R}_q$. *Then, for any power-of-two* k, *we have* $\|c\mathbf{r}\| \leqslant \sqrt[2k]{\|\sigma_{-1}(c^k) c^k\|_1} \cdot \|\mathbf{r}\|$.

We provide the proof in the full version of the paper. In order to apply this lemma, we fix a power-of-two k and set the challenge space $\mathcal{C}$ as:

$$
\mathcal{C} := \left\{ c \in S_{\kappa}^{\sigma} : \sqrt[2k]{\|\sigma_{-1}(c^k) c^k\|_1} \leqslant \eta \right\} \tag{19}
$$

where

$$S_\kappa^\sigma := \{c \in S_\kappa : \sigma(c) = c\}. \tag{20}$$

and the $\sigma \in \mathsf{Aut}(\mathcal{R}_q)$ will be specified in our protocols. Also, we denote $\bar{\mathcal{C}} := \{c - c' : c, c' \in \mathcal{C} \text{ and } c \neq c'\}$ to be the set of differences of any two distinct elements in $\mathcal{C}$. In practice, $\sigma \in \{\sigma_1, \sigma_{-1}\}$. We will choose the constants η such that (experimentally) the probability for $c \leftarrow S_\kappa^\sigma$ to satisfy $\sqrt[2k]{\|\sigma_{-1}(c^k) c^k\|_1} \leqslant \eta$ is at least 99%. In our experiments, we observe that the bounds in Lemma 3 are about $4 - 6X$ larger than the actual norms $\|cr\|$.

For security of our protocols, we need $\kappa < \frac{1}{2\sqrt{2}} q_1^{1/2}$ to ensure the invertibility property of the challenge space $\mathcal{C}$, i.e. the difference of any two distinct elements of $\mathcal{C}$ is invertible over $\mathcal{R}_q$. Indeed, this property follows from [33]. However, if we set $\sigma := \sigma_{-1}$ then we can apply our new result in the full version of the paper and thus we only need $\kappa < q_1/2$. Secondly, to achieve negligible soundness error under the MSIS assumption, we will need $|\mathcal{C}|$ to be exponentially large. In Fig. 3 we propose example parameters to instantiate the challenge space $\mathcal{C}$ for different automorphisms σ. Finally, for implementation purposes, in order to sample from $\mathcal{C}$, we simply generate $c \leftarrow S_\kappa^\sigma$ and check whether $\sqrt[2k]{\|\sigma_{-1}(c^k) c^k\|_1} \leqslant \eta$. Hence, we cannot choose k to be too large.

σ	d	κ	η	$|S_\kappa^\sigma|$	$|\mathcal{C}|$
σ_1	128	1	27	2^{202}	2^{201}
σ_{-1}	128	2	59	2^{148}	2^{147}

Fig. 3. Example parameters to instantiate the challenge space $\mathcal{C} := \{c \in S_\kappa : \sigma(c) = c \wedge \sqrt[2k]{\|\sigma_{-1}(c^k) c^k\|_1} \leqslant \eta\}$ for a modulus q such that its smallest prime divisor q_1 is greater than 8. In our examples we picked $k = 32$.

Setting the Standard Deviation. By definition of the challenge space $\mathcal{C}$ and Lemma 3, if we know that $\|\mathbf{r}\| \leqslant \alpha$, then we can set the standard deviation $\mathfrak{s} := \gamma\eta\alpha$ where $\gamma > 0$ defines the repetition rate M. On the other hand, if $\|\mathbf{r}\|_\infty \leqslant \nu$, e.g. because $\mathbf{r} \leftarrow S_\nu^\ell$, then we can set $\mathfrak{s} := \gamma\nu\eta\sqrt{\ell n}$.

3 The ABDLOP Commitment Scheme and Proofs of Linear Relations

In this section we formally present the ABDLOP commitment scheme together with ZKPoK of the committed messages. In the same protocol, we also include a proof of knowledge that the committed messages satisfy some arbitrary linear relations over $\mathcal{R}_q$ (Fig. 4). In the full version of the paper, we also show how one can use this commitment scheme and proof of knowledge to prove knowledge of linear relations over $\mathbb{Z}_q$. This latter proof is best modelled as a commit-and-prove protocol because it will be creating some intermediate commitments under the same randomness, which cannot be simulated. In particular, what we prove is that the view, for all possible committed messages, is computationally indistinguishable from commitments to 0.

3.1   The ABDLOP Commitment Scheme

Figure 4 presents the ABDLOP commitment scheme, which commits to messages $\mathbf{s}_1$ and $\mathbf{m}$, using randomness $\mathbf{s}_2$, and then proves knowledge of these messages and that they satisfy the relation $\mathbf{R}_1\mathbf{s}_1 + \mathbf{R}_m\mathbf{m} = \mathbf{u}$. The challenge space $\mathcal{C}$ is as in (19). The standard deviations $\mathfrak{s}_1$ and $\mathfrak{s}_2$ are set as in Sect. 2.4 so as to provide a balance between the running time of the algorithm (the lower the values, the higher the probability that the protocol will need to be repeated) and the security of the commitment scheme based on the hardness of the MSIS problem (the higher the values, the easier the problem becomes). Because the most common way in which our commitment scheme will be used involves committing to some values, proving that they satisfy some relations, and then never using the commitment again, we use a more efficient rejection sampling (Rej$_2$ in Fig. 1) from [30], which ends up leaking one bit of the secret, on the *randomness* part of the commitment (i.e. $\mathbf{s}_2$). If one will not be throwing out this commitment, then one should use Rej$_1$ for everything.

The hiding property of the commitment scheme follows from the MLWE problem when $\mathbf{s}_2$ is chosen from some distribution such that $\left(\begin{bmatrix} \mathbf{A}_2 \\ \mathbf{B} \end{bmatrix}, \begin{bmatrix} \mathbf{A}_2 \\ \mathbf{B} \end{bmatrix} \cdot \mathbf{s}_2 \right)$ is indistinguishable from uniform. The zero-knowledge property of the protocol follows from the standard argument from [25,30] showing that $\mathbf{z}_1, \mathbf{z}_2$ are distributed according to $D_{\mathfrak{s}_1}^{m_1}$ and $D_{\mathfrak{s}_2}^{m_2}$ (possibly with 1 bit of leakage for the latter) independent of $\mathbf{s}_1$ and $\mathbf{s}_2$. The correctness of the protocol then follows due to the fact that $m_i d$-dimensional integer vectors sampled from a discrete Gaussian with standard deviation $\mathfrak{s}_i$ has norm at most $\mathfrak{s}_i \sqrt{2 m_i d}$ with overwhelming probability [5].

The commitment opening needs to be defined to be whatever one can extract from the protocol. Since the protocol is an approximate proof of knowledge, it does not prove knowledge of $\mathbf{s}_1, \mathbf{s}_2$ satisfying $\mathbf{A}_1\mathbf{s}_1 + \mathbf{A}_2\mathbf{s}_2 = \mathbf{t}_A$, but instead an approximate proof as in (2). Lemma 4 states that under the assumption that the Module-SIS problem is hard, the extracted values $(\bar{\mathbf{s}}_1, \bar{\mathbf{s}}_2)$ are unique and they satisfy the desired linear equation $\mathbf{R}_1\bar{\mathbf{s}}_1 + \mathbf{R}_m(\mathbf{t}_B - \mathbf{B}\bar{\mathbf{s}}_2) = \mathbf{u}$, where $\mathbf{m}$ is implicitly defined as $\mathbf{t}_B - \mathbf{B}\bar{\mathbf{s}}_2$. The last statement proved in the Lemma shows, as in [3], that not only are the extracted commitments $\mathbf{s}_i$, unique but also $\mathbf{z}_i - c\bar{\mathbf{s}}_i$ is uniquely determined by the first two moves of the protocol. This is crucial to efficiently proving knowledge of polynomial products later in the paper.

As far as the communication complexity of the protocol, it is important to note that in the real protocol, one would not actually send $\mathbf{w}$ and $\mathbf{v}$, but instead send their hash. Then one would verify the hash of the equalities. Therefore proving linear relations over $\mathcal{R}_q$ is not any more costly, communication-wise, than just proving knowledge of the committed values. We don't write the hashes in our protocols because when they eventually get converted to non-interactive ones using the Fiat-Shamir transform, the hashes will naturally enter the picture.

We will refer to the protocol in Fig. 4 as $\Pi_{\mathsf{many}}^{(1)}\left((\mathbf{s}_2, \mathbf{s}_1, \mathbf{m}), (f_1, f_2, \ldots, f_N)\right)$, where the f_i are linear functions mapping $(\mathbf{s}_1, \mathbf{m})$ to $\mathcal{R}_q$ such that $f_i(\mathbf{s}_1, \mathbf{m}) = 0$, represented by the rows of $\mathbf{R}_1, \mathbf{R}_m$, and $\mathbf{u}$.

Lemma 4. *The protocol in Fig. 4 is a proof of knowledge of* $(\bar{\mathbf{s}}_1, \bar{\mathbf{s}}_2, \bar{c}) \in \mathcal{R}_q^{m_1} \times \mathcal{R}_q^{m_2} \times \bar{\mathcal{C}}$ *satisfying*

1. $\mathbf{A}_1 \bar{\mathbf{s}}_1 + \mathbf{A}_2 \bar{\mathbf{s}}_2 = \mathbf{t}_A$
2. $\|\bar{\mathbf{s}}_i \bar{c}\| \leqslant 2\mathfrak{s}_i \sqrt{2m_i d}$ *for* $i = 1, 2$
3. $\mathbf{R}_1 \bar{\mathbf{s}}_1 + \mathbf{R}_m(\mathbf{t}_B - \mathbf{B}\bar{\mathbf{s}}_2) = \mathbf{u}$

   Furthermore, under the assumption that $\mathsf{MSIS}_{n,m_1+m_2,B}$ *is hard for* $B = 8\eta\sqrt{(\mathfrak{s}_1\sqrt{2m_1 d})^2 + (\mathfrak{s}_2\sqrt{2m_2 d})^2}$,

4. *This* $(\bar{\mathbf{s}}_1, \bar{\mathbf{s}}_2)$ *is unique*
5. *For any two valid transcripts* $(\mathbf{w}, \mathbf{v}, c, \mathbf{z}_1, \mathbf{z}_2)$ *and* $(\mathbf{w}, \mathbf{v}, c', \mathbf{z}_1', \mathbf{z}_2')$, *it holds that* $\mathbf{z}_i - c\bar{\mathbf{s}}_i = \mathbf{z}_i' - c'\bar{\mathbf{s}}_i$.

We present the proof of Lemma 4 in the full version of the paper.

4 Proofs of Quadratic Relations

In this section we show how to prove various quadratic equations between committed messages using the ABDLOP commitment. More concretely, suppose we have message vectors $\mathbf{s}_1 \in \mathcal{R}_q^{m_1}$ and $\mathbf{m} \in \mathcal{R}_q^{\ell}$ such that $\|\mathbf{s}_1\| \leqslant \alpha$. Let $\sigma \in \mathsf{Aut}(\mathcal{R}_q)$ be a public automorphism over $\mathcal{R}$ of degree k and for presentation purposes define:

$$(\sigma^i(\mathbf{x}))_{i \in [k]} := (\mathbf{x}, \sigma(\mathbf{x}), \ldots, \sigma^{k-1}(\mathbf{x})) \in \mathcal{R}_q^{ka}$$

for arbitrary vector $\mathbf{x} \in \mathcal{R}_q^a$. Then, we consider the following statements:

- *Single quadratic equation with automorphisms.* For a public $k(m_1 + \ell)$-variate quadratic function f over $\mathcal{R}_q$,

$$f\left((\sigma^i(\mathbf{s}_1))_{i \in [k]}, (\sigma^i(\mathbf{m}))_{i \in [k]}\right) = 0.$$

- *Many quadratic equations with automorphisms.* For N public $k(m_1 + \ell)$-variate quadratic functions $f_1, \ldots, f_N$ over $\mathcal{R}_q$,

$$f_j\left((\sigma^i(\mathbf{s}_1))_{i \in [k]}, (\sigma^i(\mathbf{m}))_{i \in [k]}\right) = 0 \text{ for } j \in [N].$$

- *Many quadratic equations with automorphisms and a proof that polynomial evaluations have no constant coefficients.* For $N + M$ public $k(m_1 + \ell)$-variate quadratic functions $f_1, \ldots, f_N$ and $F_1, \ldots, F_M$ over $\mathcal{R}_q$, the following hold:
  - $f_j\left((\sigma^i(\mathbf{s}_1))_{i \in [k]}, (\sigma^i(\mathbf{m}))_{i \in [k]}\right) = 0$ for $j \in [N]$,
  - let $x_j := F_j\left((\sigma^i(\mathbf{s}_1))_{i \in [k]}, (\sigma^i(\mathbf{m}))_{i \in [k]}\right) \in \mathcal{R}_q$ for $j \in [M]$. Then $\tilde{x}_1 = \ldots = \tilde{x}_M = 0$.

Remark 1. Similarly as for [3], our techniques can be easily generalized to prove higher degree relations. Concretely, if we want to prove degree k equations, we end up committing to $k - 1$ additional garbage terms. Throughout this paper, however, we will only consider quadratic relations.

Private information: $(\mathbf{s}_1, \mathbf{m}, \mathbf{s}_2) \in \mathcal{R}_q^{m_1+m_2+\ell}$ so that $\|\mathbf{s}_1\| \leqslant \alpha$ and $\|\mathbf{s}_2\|_\infty \leqslant \nu$
Public information: $\mathbf{A}_1 \in \mathcal{R}_q^{n \times m_1}, \mathbf{A}_2 \in \mathcal{R}_q^{n \times m_2}, \mathbf{B} \in \mathcal{R}_q^{\ell \times m_2}, \mathbf{R}_1 \in \mathcal{R}_q^{N \times m_1}$,
$\mathbf{R}_m \in \mathcal{R}_q^{N \times \ell}$,
$$\begin{bmatrix} \mathbf{t}_A \\ \mathbf{t}_B \end{bmatrix} = \begin{bmatrix} \mathbf{A}_1 \\ \mathbf{0} \end{bmatrix} \cdot \mathbf{s}_1 + \begin{bmatrix} \mathbf{A}_2 \\ \mathbf{B} \end{bmatrix} \cdot \mathbf{s}_2 + \begin{bmatrix} \mathbf{0} \\ \mathbf{m} \end{bmatrix}, \mathbf{u} = \mathbf{R}_1 \mathbf{s}_1 + \mathbf{R}_m \mathbf{m}$$

Prover	Verifier

Prover

$\mathbf{y}_1 \leftarrow D_{\mathfrak{s}_1}^{m_1}$
$\mathbf{y}_2 \leftarrow D_{\mathfrak{s}_2}^{m_2}$
$\mathbf{w} := \mathbf{A}_1 \mathbf{y}_1 + \mathbf{A}_2 \mathbf{y}_2$
$\mathbf{v} := \mathbf{R}_1 \mathbf{y}_1 - \mathbf{R}_m \mathbf{B} \mathbf{y}_2$

$\xrightarrow{\quad \mathbf{w}, \mathbf{v} \quad}$

$c \leftarrow \mathcal{C}$

$\xleftarrow{\quad c \quad}$

$\mathbf{z}_1 := c\mathbf{s}_1 + \mathbf{y}_1$
$\mathbf{z}_2 := c\mathbf{s}_2 + \mathbf{y}_2$
for $i = 1, 2$:
  if $\mathsf{Rej}_i(\mathbf{z}_i, c\mathbf{s}_i, \mathfrak{s}_i) = 1$
    then $\mathbf{z}_1, \mathbf{z}_2 := \bot$

$\xrightarrow{\quad \mathbf{z}_1, \mathbf{z}_2 \quad}$

Accept iff:

1. $\|\mathbf{z}_1\| \leqslant \mathfrak{s}_1 \sqrt{2m_1 d}, \|\mathbf{z}_2\| \leqslant \mathfrak{s}_2 \sqrt{2m_2 d}$
2. $\mathbf{A}_1 \mathbf{z}_1 + \mathbf{A}_2 \mathbf{z}_2 - c\mathbf{t}_A = \mathbf{w}$
3. $\mathbf{R}_1 \mathbf{z}_1 + \mathbf{R}_m(c\mathbf{t}_B - \mathbf{B}\mathbf{z}_2) - c\mathbf{u} = \mathbf{v}$

Fig. 4. Proof of knowledge $\Pi_{\text{many}}^{(1)}((\mathbf{s}_2, \mathbf{s}_1, \mathbf{m}), (f_1, f_2, \ldots, f_N))$ of $(\mathbf{s}_1, \mathbf{s}_2, \bar{c}) \in \mathcal{R}_q^{m_1} \times \mathcal{R}_q^{m_2} \times \bar{\mathcal{C}}$ satisfying (i) $\mathbf{A}_1 \mathbf{s}_1 + \mathbf{A}_2 \mathbf{s}_2 = \mathbf{t}_A$, $\mathbf{B}\mathbf{s}_2 + \mathbf{m} = \mathbf{t}_B$ (ii) $\|\mathbf{s}_i \bar{c}\| \leqslant 2\mathfrak{s}_i \sqrt{2m_i d}$ for $i = 1, 2$ and (iii) $f_i(\mathbf{s}_1, \mathbf{m}) = 0$ for $i \in [N]$ where each $f_1, \ldots, f_N : \mathcal{R}_q^{m_1+\ell} \to \mathcal{R}_q$ is a linear function. The linear functions f_i are represented by the corresponding rows of matrices $\mathbf{u}, \mathbf{R}_1, \mathbf{R}_m$ and prove $\mathbf{u} = \mathbf{R}_1 \mathbf{s}_1 + \mathbf{R}_m \mathbf{m}$ where $\mathbf{R}_1^{N \times m_1}, \mathbf{R}_m^{N \times \ell}, \mathbf{u} \in \mathcal{R}_q^N$ are public.

4.1 Single Quadratic Equation with Automorphisms

Let $(\mathbf{t}_A, \mathbf{t}_B)$ be the commitment to the message pair $(\mathbf{s}_1, \mathbf{m})$ under randomness $\mathbf{s}_2$, i.e.

$$\begin{bmatrix} \mathbf{t}_A \\ \mathbf{t}_B \end{bmatrix} = \begin{bmatrix} \mathbf{A}_1 \\ \mathbf{0} \end{bmatrix} \cdot \mathbf{s}_1 + \begin{bmatrix} \mathbf{A}_2 \\ \mathbf{B} \end{bmatrix} \cdot \mathbf{s}_2 + \begin{bmatrix} \mathbf{0} \\ \mathbf{m} \end{bmatrix}.$$

Suppose the prover wants to prove knowledge of the message

$$\mathbf{s} = \begin{bmatrix} (\sigma^i(\mathbf{s}_1))_{i \in [k]} \\ (\sigma^i(\mathbf{m}))_{i \in [k]} \end{bmatrix} \in \mathcal{R}_q^{k(m_1+\ell)}$$

such that $f(\mathbf{s}) = 0$ where f is a $k(m_1 + \ell)$-variate quadratic function over $\mathcal{R}_q$. Note that each function f can be written explicitly as:

$$f(\mathbf{s}) = \mathbf{s}^T \mathbf{R}_2 \mathbf{s} + \mathbf{r}_1^T \mathbf{s} + r_0$$

where $r_0 \in \mathcal{R}_q, \mathbf{r}_1 \in \mathcal{R}_q^{k(m_1+\ell)}$ and $\mathbf{R}_2 \in \mathcal{R}_q^{k(m_1+\ell) \times k(m_1+\ell)}$.

In order to prove this relation, let us consider the protocol for proving linear equations over $\mathcal{R}_q$ in Fig. 4. In the last round, the honest prover sends the *masked openings* $\mathbf{z}_i = c\mathbf{s}_i + \mathbf{y}_i$ of $\mathbf{s}_i$ for $i = 1, 2$ where the challenge space $\mathcal{C}$ is defined as in (19) with the σ automorphism. Even though this is not the case for $\mathbf{m}$, we can define the masked opening of $\mathbf{m}$ as

$$\mathbf{z}_m := c\mathbf{t}_B - \mathbf{B}\mathbf{z}_2 = c\mathbf{m} - \mathbf{B}\mathbf{y}_2.$$

By construction, $\mathbf{z}_m$ can be computed by the verifier.

Define the following vectors $\mathbf{y}$ and $\mathbf{z}$:

$$\mathbf{y} := \begin{bmatrix} (\sigma^i(\mathbf{y}_1))_{i \in [k]} \\ -(\sigma^i(\mathbf{B}\mathbf{y}_2))_{i \in [k]} \end{bmatrix} \in \mathcal{R}_q^{k(m_1+\ell)} \tag{21}$$

and

$$\mathbf{z} := \begin{bmatrix} (\sigma^i(\mathbf{z}_1))_{i \in [k]} \\ (\sigma^i(\mathbf{z}_m))_{i \in [k]} \end{bmatrix} = c \begin{bmatrix} (\sigma^i(\mathbf{s}_1))_{i \in [k]} \\ (\sigma^i(\mathbf{m}))_{i \in [k]} \end{bmatrix} + \begin{bmatrix} (\sigma^i(\mathbf{y}_1))_{i \in [k]} \\ -(\sigma^i(\mathbf{B}\mathbf{y}_2))_{i \in [k]} \end{bmatrix} = c\mathbf{s} + \mathbf{y}. \tag{22}$$

Here we used the fact that for $c \in \mathcal{C}, \sigma(c) = c$. Then, we have

$$\mathbf{z}^T \mathbf{R}_2 \mathbf{z} + c\mathbf{r}_1^T \mathbf{z} + c^2 r_0 = c^2 \left(\mathbf{s}^T \mathbf{R}_2 \mathbf{s} + \mathbf{r}_1^T \mathbf{s} + r_0 \right) + c g_1 + g_0 \tag{23}$$

where polynomials g_1 and g_0 are defined as:

$$g_1 = \mathbf{s}^T \mathbf{R}_2 \mathbf{y} + \mathbf{y}^T \mathbf{R}_2 \mathbf{s} + \mathbf{r}_1^T \mathbf{y}, \quad g_0 = \mathbf{y}^T \mathbf{R}_2 \mathbf{y}.$$

Hence, we want to prove that the quadratic term in the expression $\mathbf{z}^T \mathbf{R}_2 \mathbf{z} + c\mathbf{r}_1^T \mathbf{z} + c^2 r_0$ vanishes. This is done by first sending a commitment t to the polynomial g_1, i.e. $t = \mathbf{b}^T \mathbf{s}_2 + g_1$ as well as $v := g_0 + \mathbf{b}^T \mathbf{y}_2$ in the clear. Then, given t and the masked opening $\mathbf{z}_2$ of $\mathbf{s}_2$, the verifier can compute $f = ct - \mathbf{b}^T \mathbf{z}_2 = cg_1 - \mathbf{b}^T \mathbf{y}_2$. Finally, it checks whether

$$\mathbf{z}^T \mathbf{R}_2 \mathbf{z} + c\mathbf{r}_1^T \mathbf{z} + c^2 r_0 - f \stackrel{?}{=} v$$

which is a simple transformation of (23) when $\mathbf{s}^T \mathbf{R}_2 \mathbf{s} + \mathbf{r}_1^T \mathbf{s} + r_0 = 0$.

We present the full protocol in Fig. 5 which follows the commit-and-prove paradigm [12,30]. Namely, we assume the prover has already sent the commitments $\mathbf{t}_A \mathbf{t}_B$ to the verifier using fresh randomness $\mathbf{s}_2 \leftarrow \chi^{m_2}$. Prover starts by sampling masking vectors $\mathbf{y}_1 \leftarrow D_{\mathfrak{s}_1}^{m_1}, \mathbf{y}_2 \leftarrow D_{\mathfrak{s}}^{m_2}$ and computing $\mathbf{w} = \mathbf{A}_1 \mathbf{y}_1 + \mathbf{A}_2 \mathbf{y}_2$. Then, it calculates $g_1 = \mathbf{s}^T \mathbf{R}_2 \mathbf{y} + \mathbf{y}^T \mathbf{R}_2 \mathbf{s} + \mathbf{r}_1^T \mathbf{y}$, where $\mathbf{y}$ is defined in (21), and the commitment $t = \mathbf{b}^T \mathbf{s}_2 + g_1$ to g_1. Finally, the prover sets $v = \mathbf{y}^T \mathbf{R}_2 \mathbf{y} + \mathbf{b}^T \mathbf{y}_2$ and sends $\mathbf{w}, t, v$ to the verifier.

Next, given a challenge $c \in \mathcal{C}$, the prover computes $\mathbf{z}_i = c\mathbf{s}_i + \mathbf{y}_i$ for $i = 1, 2$ and applies rejection sampling. If it does not abort, the prover outputs $\mathbf{z}_1, \mathbf{z}_2$.

Eventually, the verifier checks whether $\mathbf{z}_1$ and $\mathbf{z}_2$ have small norms, $\mathbf{A}_1 \mathbf{z}_1 + \mathbf{A}_2 \mathbf{z}_2 = \mathbf{w} + c\mathbf{t}_A$ and $\mathbf{z}^T \mathbf{R}_2 \mathbf{z} + c\mathbf{r}_1^T \mathbf{z} + c^2 r_0 - f = v$ where $\mathbf{z}$ is defined in (22) and f is defined as $f = ct - \mathbf{b}^T \mathbf{z}_2$.

We summarise security properties of the protocol in Fig. 5 in the full version of the paper.

Private information: $(\mathbf{s}_1, \mathbf{m}) \in \mathcal{R}_q^{m_1+\ell}$ so that $\|\mathbf{s}_1\| \leq \alpha$, $\mathbf{s}_2 \leftarrow \chi^{m_2}$

Public information: $\mathbf{A}_1 \in \mathcal{R}_q^{n \times m_1}, \mathbf{A}_2 \in \mathcal{R}_q^{n \times m_2}, \mathbf{B} \in \mathcal{R}_q^{\ell \times m_2}, \mathbf{b} \in \mathcal{R}_q^{m_2}$

$$\begin{bmatrix} \mathbf{t}_A \\ \mathbf{t}_B \end{bmatrix} = \begin{bmatrix} \mathbf{A}_1 \\ 0 \end{bmatrix} \cdot \mathbf{s}_1 + \begin{bmatrix} \mathbf{A}_2 \\ \mathbf{B} \end{bmatrix} \cdot \mathbf{s}_2 + \begin{bmatrix} 0 \\ \mathbf{m} \end{bmatrix},$$

$r_0 \in \mathcal{R}_q, \mathbf{r}_1 \in \mathcal{R}_q^{k(m_1+\ell)}, \mathbf{R}_2 \in \mathcal{R}_q^{k(m_1+\ell) \times k(m_1+\ell)}, \sigma \in \mathsf{Aut}(\mathcal{R}_q)$

$\mathbf{s}^T \mathbf{R}_2 \mathbf{s} + \mathbf{r}_1^T \mathbf{s} + r_0 = 0$

Prover	Verifier

Prover:

$\mathbf{s} := \begin{bmatrix} (\sigma^i(\mathbf{s}_1))_{i \in [k]} \\ (\sigma^i(\mathbf{m}))_{i \in [k]} \end{bmatrix}$

$\mathbf{y}_1 \leftarrow D_{\mathfrak{s}_1}^{m_1}$

$\mathbf{y}_2 \leftarrow D_{\mathfrak{s}_2}^{m_2}$

$\mathbf{w} := \mathbf{A}_1 \mathbf{y}_1 + \mathbf{A}_2 \mathbf{y}_2$

$\mathbf{y} := \begin{bmatrix} (\sigma^i(\mathbf{y}_1))_{i \in [k]} \\ -(\sigma^i(\mathbf{B}\mathbf{y}_2))_{i \in [k]} \end{bmatrix}$

$g_1 := \mathbf{s}^T \mathbf{R}_2 \mathbf{y} + \mathbf{y}^T \mathbf{R}_2 \mathbf{s} + \mathbf{r}_1^T \mathbf{y}$

$t := \mathbf{b}^T \mathbf{s}_2 + g_1$

$v := \mathbf{y}^T \mathbf{R}_2 \mathbf{y} + \mathbf{b}^T \mathbf{y}_2$

$\xrightarrow{\quad \mathbf{w}, t, v \quad}$

$\xleftarrow{\quad c \quad} \qquad c \leftarrow \mathcal{C}$

$\mathbf{z}_1 := c\mathbf{s}_1 + \mathbf{y}_1$

$\mathbf{z}_2 := c\mathbf{s}_2 + \mathbf{y}_2$

for $i = 1, 2$:

    if $\mathsf{Rej}_i(\mathbf{z}_i, c\mathbf{s}_i, \mathfrak{s}_i) = 1$

        then $\mathbf{z}_1, \mathbf{z}_2 := \bot$

$\xrightarrow{\quad \mathbf{z}_1, \mathbf{z}_2 \quad}$

$\mathbf{z} := \begin{bmatrix} (\sigma^i(\mathbf{z}_1))_{i \in [k]} \\ (\sigma^i(c\mathbf{t}_B - \mathbf{B}\mathbf{z}_2))_{i \in [k]} \end{bmatrix}$

$f := ct - \mathbf{b}^T \mathbf{z}_2$

Accept iff

    $\|\mathbf{z}_1\| \leq \mathfrak{s}_1 \sqrt{2m_1 d}$ and

    $\|\mathbf{z}_2\| \leq \mathfrak{s}_2 \sqrt{2m_2 d}$ and

    $\mathbf{A}_1 \mathbf{z}_1 + \mathbf{A}_2 \mathbf{z}_2 = \mathbf{w} + c\mathbf{t}_A$ and

    $\mathbf{z}^T \mathbf{R}_2 \mathbf{z} + c\mathbf{r}_1^T \mathbf{z} + c^2 r_0 - f = v$

Fig. 5. Commit-and-prove protocol $\Pi^{(2)}((\mathbf{s}_2, \mathbf{s}_1, \mathbf{m}), \sigma, f)$ for messages $(\mathbf{s}_1, \mathbf{m}) \in \mathcal{R}_q^{m_1+\ell}$, randomness $\mathbf{s}_2 \in \mathcal{R}_q^{m_2}$ and $\bar{c} \in \bar{\mathcal{C}}$ which satisfy: $\mathbf{A}_1 \mathbf{s}_1 + \mathbf{A}_2 \mathbf{s}_2 = \mathbf{t}_A$, $\mathbf{B}\mathbf{s}_2 + \mathbf{m} = \mathbf{t}_B$ (ii) $\|\mathbf{s}_i \bar{c}\| \leq 2\mathfrak{s}_i \sqrt{2m_i d}$ for $i = 1, 2$ and (iii) $f((\sigma^i(\mathbf{s}_1))_{i \in [k]}, (\sigma^i(\mathbf{m}))_{i \in [k]}) = 0$ where function $f : \mathcal{R}_q^{k(m_1+\ell)} \to \mathcal{R}_q$ is defined as $f(\mathbf{x}) := \mathbf{x}^T \mathbf{R}_2 \mathbf{x} + \mathbf{r}_1^T \mathbf{x} + r_0$. Here, we assume that the commitment $(\mathbf{t}_A, \mathbf{t}_B)$ was generated honestly and already sent by the prover. In particular, $\mathbf{s}_2 \leftarrow \chi^{m_2}$.

Private information: $(\mathbf{s}_1, \mathbf{m}) \in \mathcal{R}_q^{m_1+\ell}$ so that $\|\mathbf{s}_1\| \leqslant \alpha$, $\mathbf{s}_2 \leftarrow \chi^{m_2}$
Public information: $\mathbf{A}_1 \in \mathcal{R}_q^{n \times m_1}, \mathbf{A}_2 \in \mathcal{R}_q^{n \times m_2}, \mathbf{B} \in \mathcal{R}_q^{\ell \times m_2}, \mathbf{b} \in \mathcal{R}_q^{m_2}$

$$\begin{bmatrix} \mathbf{t}_A \\ \mathbf{t}_B \end{bmatrix} = \begin{bmatrix} \mathbf{A}_1 \\ \mathbf{0} \end{bmatrix} \cdot \mathbf{s}_1 + \begin{bmatrix} \mathbf{A}_2 \\ \mathbf{B} \end{bmatrix} \cdot \mathbf{s}_2 + \begin{bmatrix} \mathbf{0} \\ \mathbf{m} \end{bmatrix},$$

$f_1, \ldots, f_N : \mathcal{R}_q^{k(m_1+\ell)} \to \mathcal{R}_q, \sigma \in \mathsf{Aut}(\mathcal{R}_q)$

<u>Prover</u>   <u>Verifier</u>

$$\mu_1, \ldots, \mu_N \leftarrow \mathcal{R}_q$$

$$\xleftarrow{\quad \mu_1, \ldots, \mu_N \quad}$$

$f := \sum_{j=1}^N \mu_j f_j$
Run $\Pi^{(2)}\left((\mathbf{s}_2, \mathbf{s}_1, \mathbf{m}), \sigma, f\right)$

Fig. 6. Commit-and-prove protocol $\Pi^{(2)}_{\mathsf{many}}\left((\mathbf{s}_2, \mathbf{s}_1, \mathbf{m}), \sigma, (f_1, f_2, \ldots, f_N)\right)$ for messages $(\mathbf{s}_1, \mathbf{m}) \in \mathcal{R}_q^{m_1+\ell}$, randomness $\mathbf{s}_2 \in \mathcal{R}_q^{m_2}$ and $\bar{c} \in \bar{\mathcal{C}}$ which satisfy: $\mathbf{A}_1\mathbf{s}_1 + \mathbf{A}_2\mathbf{s}_2 = \mathbf{t}_A$, $\mathbf{B}\mathbf{s}_2 + \mathbf{m} = \mathbf{t}_B$ (ii) $\|\mathfrak{s}_i\bar{c}\| \leqslant 2\mathfrak{s}_i\sqrt{2m_i d}$ for $i = 1, 2$ (where $\mathfrak{s}_i$ are used in Fig. 5) and (iii) $f_j\left((\sigma^i(\mathbf{s}_1))_{i \in [k]}, (\sigma^i(\mathbf{m}))_{i \in [k]}\right) = 0$ for $j \in [N]$. Vector $\mathbf{b}$ is used in the sub-protocol $\Pi^{(2)}$.

4.2 Many Quadratic Equations with Automorphisms

We consider a scenario when the prover wants to simultaneously prove N quadratic relations. Clearly, if one were to prove them separately using the approach from Sect. 4.1, one would end up committing to N garbage polynomials g. Here, we circumvent this issue by linear-combining the N equations into one quadratic equation and prove it using the protocol in Fig. 5. This results in committing to only one garbage polynomials at the cost of reducing the soundness error by a negligible additive factor.

More precisely, suppose that we want to prove for N public $k(m_1+\ell)$-variate quadratic functions $f_1, \ldots, f_N$ over $\mathcal{R}_q$ that

$$f_j\left((\sigma^i(\mathbf{s}_1))_{i \in [k]}, (\sigma^i(\mathbf{m}))_{i \in [k]}\right) = 0 \text{ for } i \in [N]. \tag{24}$$

We let the verifier begin by sending challenges $\mu_1, \ldots, \mu_N \leftarrow \mathcal{R}_q$. Then, we define a single quadratic function

$$f := \sum_{i=j}^N \mu_j f_j$$

and prove that

$$f\left((\sigma^i(\mathbf{s}_1))_{i \in [k]}, (\sigma^i(\mathbf{m}))_{i \in [k]}\right) = 0 \tag{25}$$

using the protocol from Fig. 5. Now, we observe that if one of the conditions in (24) does not hold, then Eq. 25 is satisfied with probability at most $q_1^{-d/2}$ (recall that $X^d + 1$ splits into two irreducible factors modulo each q_i).

The protocol is provided in Fig. 6. We skip the full security analysis since it will be implicitly included in the more general case in the next subsection.

4.3   Polynomial Evaluations with Vanishing Constant Coefficients

Suppose we want to prove simultaneously N quadratic relations (i.e. (24)) and *additionally* prove that for quadratic $k(m_1 + \ell)$-variate polynomials $F_1, \ldots, F_M$, evaluations $F_j\left((\sigma^i(\mathbf{s}_1))_{i \in [k]}, (\sigma^i(\mathbf{m}))_{i \in [k]}\right)$ have the constant coefficient equal to zero. Concretely, if we denote

$$x_j := F_j\left((\sigma^i(\mathbf{s}_1))_{i \in [k]}, (\sigma^i(\mathbf{m}))_{i \in [k]}\right) \in \mathcal{R}_q$$

then $\widetilde{x}_j = 0$ for $j \in [M]$.

For simplicity we first present an approach with soundness error $1/q_1$. We apply the strategy from [16] and first commit to a random masking polynomial $g \leftarrow \{x \in \mathcal{R}_q : \widetilde{x} = 0\}$. Then, given random challenges $\gamma_1, \ldots, \gamma_M \leftarrow \mathbb{Z}_q$, we send

$$h := g + \sum_{j=1}^{M} \gamma_j F_j\left((\sigma^i(\mathbf{s}_1))_{i \in [k]}, (\sigma^i(\mathbf{m}))_{i \in [k]}\right) \tag{26}$$

to the verifier. Then, it simply checks whether the constant coefficient of h is indeed equal to zero. What is left to prove is that h is well-formed, i.e. (26) holds. This is done by defining the quadratic function $f_{N+1} : \mathcal{R}_q^{k(m_1+\ell+1)} \to \mathcal{R}_q$ as follows.

Let $\mathbf{x}_1 \in \mathcal{R}_q^{km_1}$, $\mathbf{x}_2 = (\mathbf{x}_{2,1}, \ldots, \mathbf{x}_{2,k}) \in \mathcal{R}_q^{k(\ell+1)}$ and denote

$$\mathbf{x}_{2,j} := \mathbf{x}_{2,j}^{(m)} \,\|\, x_{2,j}^{(g)} \in \mathcal{R}_q^{\ell+1} \text{ for } j \in [k], \quad \mathbf{x}_2^{(m)} := \left(\mathbf{x}_{2,1}^{(m)}, \ldots, \mathbf{x}_{2,k}^{(m)}\right).$$

Then,

$$f_{N+1}(\mathbf{x}_1, \mathbf{x}_2) := x_{2,1}^{(g)} + \sum_{j=1}^{M} \gamma_j F_j\left(\mathbf{x}_1, \mathbf{x}_2^{(m)}\right) - h.$$

By construction, if $(\mathbf{x}_1, \mathbf{x}_2) = (\sigma^i(\mathbf{s}_1))_{i \in [k]}, (\sigma^i(\mathbf{m} \,\|\, g))_{i \in [k]}$ then

$$\mathbf{x}_1 = \sigma^i(\mathbf{s}_1))_{i \in [k]}, \quad \mathbf{x}_2^{(m)} = (\sigma^i(\mathbf{m}))_{i \in [k]} \quad \text{and} \quad x_{2,1}^{(g)} = g.$$

Moreover, (26) holds if and only if

$$f_{N+1}\left((\sigma^i(\mathbf{s}_1))_{i \in [k]}, (\sigma^i(\mathbf{m} \,\|\, g))_{i \in [k]}\right) = 0.$$

Recall that we also want to prove (24). We can define analogous polynomials $f_1, \ldots, f_N : \mathcal{R}_q^{k(m_1+\ell+1)} \to \mathcal{R}_q$ as:

$$f_j(\mathbf{x}_1, \mathbf{x}_2) := f_j\left(\mathbf{x}_1, \mathbf{x}_2^{(m)}\right).$$

Hence, we simply want to prove that for every $j = 1, 2, \ldots, N+1$:

$$f_j\left((\sigma^i(\mathbf{s}_1))_{i \in [k]}, (\sigma^i(\mathbf{m} \,\|\, g))_{i \in [k]}\right) = 0.$$

Finally, this can then be directly done using the protocol

$$\Pi_{\text{many}}^{(2)}\left((\mathbf{s}_2, \mathbf{s}_1, \mathbf{m}, g), \sigma, (f_1, f_2, \ldots, f_{N+1})\right)$$

Private information: $(\mathbf{s}_1, \mathbf{m}) \in \mathcal{R}_q^{m_1+\ell}$ so that $\|\mathbf{s}_1\| \leqslant \alpha$, $\mathbf{s}_2 \leftarrow \chi^{m_2}$

Public information: $\mathbf{A}_1 \in \mathcal{R}_q^{n \times m_1}, \mathbf{A}_2 \in \mathcal{R}_q^{n \times m_2}, \mathbf{B} \in \mathcal{R}_q^{\ell \times m_2}, \mathbf{B}_g \in \mathcal{R}_q^{\lambda \times m_2}, \mathbf{b} \in \mathcal{R}_q^{m_2}$

$$\begin{bmatrix} \mathbf{t}_A \\ \mathbf{t}_B \end{bmatrix} = \begin{bmatrix} \mathbf{A}_1 \\ \mathbf{0} \end{bmatrix} \cdot \mathbf{s}_1 + \begin{bmatrix} \mathbf{A}_2 \\ \mathbf{B} \end{bmatrix} \cdot \mathbf{s}_2 + \begin{bmatrix} \mathbf{0} \\ \mathbf{m} \end{bmatrix},$$

$f_1, \ldots, f_N, F_1, \ldots, F_M : \mathcal{R}_q^{k(m_1+\ell)} \to \mathcal{R}_q, \sigma \in \mathsf{Aut}(\mathcal{R}_q)$

<u>Prover</u>   <u>Verifier</u>

$\mathbf{s} := \begin{bmatrix} (\sigma^i(\mathbf{s}_1))_{i \in [k]} \\ (\sigma^i(\mathbf{m}))_{i \in [k]} \end{bmatrix}$

$\mathbf{g} := (g_1, \ldots, g_\lambda) \leftarrow \{x : \mathcal{R}_q : \tilde{x} = 0\}^\lambda$

$\mathbf{t}_g := \mathbf{B}_g \mathbf{s}_2 + \mathbf{g}$

$\xrightarrow{\quad \mathbf{t}_g \quad}$

$\Gamma = (\gamma_{i,j}) \leftarrow \mathbb{Z}_q^{\lambda \times M}$

$\xleftarrow{\quad (\gamma_{i,j})_{i \in [\lambda], j \in [M]} \quad}$

for $i \in [\lambda]$:

$\quad h_i := g_i + \sum_{j=1}^{M} \gamma_{i,j} F_j(\mathbf{s})$

$\xrightarrow{\quad h_1, \ldots, h_\lambda \quad}$

define $f_1, \ldots, f_{N+\lambda}$ as in (28) and (29)

run $\Pi_{\mathsf{many}}^{(2)} ((\mathbf{s}_2, \mathbf{s}_1, \mathbf{m} \parallel \mathbf{g}), \sigma, (f_i)_{i \in [N+\lambda]})$

Accept iff

$\Pi_{\mathsf{many}}^{(2)}$ verifies and

$\tilde{h}_1 = \ldots = \tilde{h}_\lambda = 0$

Fig. 7. Commit-and-prove protocol $\Pi_{\mathsf{eval}}^{(2)} ((\mathbf{s}_2, \mathbf{s}_1, \mathbf{m}), \sigma, (f_1, \ldots, f_N), (F_1, \ldots, F_M))$ for messages $(\mathbf{s}_1, \mathbf{m}) \in \mathcal{R}_q^{m_1+\ell}$, randomness $\mathbf{s}_2 \in \mathcal{R}_q^{m_2}$ and $\bar{c} \in \bar{\mathcal{C}}$ which satisfy: $\mathbf{A}_1 \mathbf{s}_1 + \mathbf{A}_2 \mathbf{s}_2 = \mathbf{t}_A$, $\mathbf{B}\mathbf{s}_2 + \mathbf{m} = \mathbf{t}_B$ (ii) $\|\mathbf{s}_i \bar{c}\| \leqslant 2\mathfrak{s}_i \sqrt{2 m_i d}$ for $i = 1, 2$, (iii) $f_j ((\sigma^i(\mathbf{s}_1))_{i \in [k]}, (\sigma^i(\mathbf{m}))_{i \in [k]}) = 0$ for $j \in [N]$ (where $\mathfrak{s}_i$ are used in Fig. 5) and (iv) all the evaluations $F_j ((\sigma^i(\mathbf{s}_1))_{i \in [k]}, (\sigma^i(\mathbf{m}))_{i \in [k]})$, where $j \in [M]$, have constant coefficients equal to zero. Vector $\mathbf{b}$ is used in the sub-protocol $\Pi_{\mathsf{many}}^{(2)}$.

in Fig. 6.

We provide intuition for the soundness argument. Assume that the verifier is convinced that h is of the correct form (26) and $\tilde{h} = 0$. Also, note that a cheating prover committed to g before seeing the challenges $\gamma_1, \ldots, \gamma_M$. Hence, if for some $j \in [M]$, the constant coefficient of $F_j ((\sigma^i(\mathbf{s}_1))_{i \in [k]}, (\sigma^i(\mathbf{m}))_{i \in [k]})$ is non-zero, then the cheating prover has probability at most $1/q_1$ of guessing the constant coefficient of $\sum_{j=1}^{M} \gamma_j F_j ((\sigma^i(\mathbf{s}_1))_{i \in [k]}, (\sigma^i(\mathbf{m}))_{i \in [k]})$.

Boosting Soundness. We exponentially decrease the soundness error by parallel repetition. Namely, in order to obtain $q_1^{-\lambda}$ soundness error, we commit to λ random masking polynomials $\mathbf{g} = (g_1, \ldots, g_\lambda) \leftarrow \{x : \mathcal{R}_q : \tilde{x} = 0\}^\lambda$ as follows:

$$\mathbf{t}_g := \mathbf{B}_g \mathbf{s}_2 + \mathbf{g}.$$

Then, we send $\mathbf{t}_g$ to the verifier which in return outputs the challenge matrix $(\gamma_{i,j})_{i \in [\lambda], j \in [M]} \leftarrow \mathbb{Z}_q^{\lambda \times M}$. Then, we compute the vector $\mathbf{h} = (h_1, \ldots, h_\lambda)$ as follows:

$$\begin{bmatrix} h_1 \\ h_2 \\ \vdots \\ h_\lambda \end{bmatrix} = \begin{bmatrix} g_1 \\ g_2 \\ \vdots \\ g_\lambda \end{bmatrix} + \begin{bmatrix} \gamma_{1,1} & \gamma_{1,2} & \cdots & \gamma_{1,M} \\ \vdots & \vdots & \cdots & \vdots \\ \gamma_{\lambda,1} & \gamma_{\lambda,2} & \cdots & \gamma_{\lambda,M} \end{bmatrix} \begin{bmatrix} F_1\left((\sigma^i(\mathbf{s}_1))_{i\in[k]}, (\sigma^i(\mathbf{m}))_{i\in[k]}\right) \\ F_2\left((\sigma^i(\mathbf{s}_1))_{i\in[k]}, (\sigma^i(\mathbf{m}))_{i\in[k]}\right) \\ \vdots \\ F_M\left((\sigma^i(\mathbf{s}_1))_{i\in[k]}, (\sigma^i(\mathbf{m}))_{i\in[k]}\right) \end{bmatrix} \quad (27)$$

and send it to the verifier. It directly checks if all polynomials $h_1, \dots, h_\lambda \in \mathcal{R}_q$ have constant coefficients equal to zero.

As before, we still need to prove that vector $\mathbf{h}$ was constructed correctly. We reduce this problem to proving quadratic relations. Namely, we define polynomials $f_{N+1}, \dots, f_{N+\lambda} : \mathcal{R}_q^{k(m_1+\ell+\lambda)} \to \mathcal{R}_q$ as follows.

Let $\mathbf{x}_1 \in \mathcal{R}_q^{km_1}$, $\mathbf{x}_2 = (\mathbf{x}_{2,1}, \dots, \mathbf{x}_{2,k}) \in \mathcal{R}_q^{k(\ell+\lambda)}$ and denote

$$\mathbf{x}_{2,j} := \left(\mathbf{x}_{2,j}^{(m)}, \mathbf{x}_{2,j}^{(g)}\right) \in \mathcal{R}_q^{\ell+\lambda} \text{ for } j \in [k],$$

$$\mathbf{x}_2^{(m)} := \left(\mathbf{x}_{2,1}^{(m)}, \dots, \mathbf{x}_{2,k}^{(m)}\right), \quad \mathbf{x}_{2,1}^{(g)} := \left(x_{2,1,1}^{(g)}, \dots, x_{2,1,\lambda}^{(g)}\right).$$

Then,

$$f_{N+i}(\mathbf{x}_1, \mathbf{x}_2) := x_{2,1,i}^{(g)} + \sum_{j=1}^{M} \gamma_{i,j} F_j\left(\mathbf{x}_1, \mathbf{x}_2^{(m)}\right) - h_i \text{ for } i \in [\lambda]. \quad (28)$$

By construction, if $(\mathbf{x}_1, \mathbf{x}_2) = (\sigma^i(\mathbf{s}_1))_{i\in[k]}, (\sigma^i(\mathbf{m} \parallel \mathbf{g}))_{i\in[k]}$ then

$$\mathbf{x}_1 = (\sigma^i(\mathbf{s}_1))_{i\in[k]}, \quad \mathbf{x}_2^{(m)} = (\sigma^i(\mathbf{m}))_{i\in[k]} \quad \text{and} \quad x_{2,1,i}^{(g)} = g_i.$$

Furthermore, Eq. (27) is true if and only if for all $j \in [\lambda]$ we have:

$$f_{N+j}\left((\sigma^i(\mathbf{s}_1))_{i\in[k]}, (\sigma^i(\mathbf{m} \parallel \mathbf{g}))_{i\in[k]}\right) = 0.$$

Since we also need to prove (24), for convenience we define polynomials $f_1, \dots, f_N : \mathcal{R}_q^{k(m_1+\ell+\lambda)} \to \mathcal{R}_q$ as:

$$f_j(\mathbf{x}_1, \mathbf{x}_2) := f_j\left(\mathbf{x}_1, \mathbf{x}_2^{(m)}\right). \quad (29)$$

Finally, we simply run $\Pi_{\text{quad-many}}\left((\mathbf{s}_2, \mathbf{s}_1, \mathbf{m}, \mathbf{g}), \sigma, (f_j)_{j\in[N+\lambda]}\right)$ from Fig. 6. We summarise the protocol in Fig. 7 and provide commitment and proof size analysis in the full version of the paper.

Note that with this approach we need to commit to additional λ garbage polynomials. In the full version of the paper we describe an optimisation which reduces the number of garbage polynomials by a factor of two in a scenario for $\sigma := \sigma_{-1}$. As discussed in the introduction, this will indeed be the automorphism that is going to be used throughout the paper.

Acknowledgements. We would like to thank Ward Beullens for generalising Lemma 3 for all powers-of-two k (initially, the lemma only covered $k = 1$) and also Damien Stehlé and Elena Kirshanova for their very useful feedback. This work is supported by the EU H2020 ERC Project 101002845 PLAZA.

References

1. Agrawal, S., Boneh, D., Boyen, X.: Efficient lattice (H)IBE in the standard model. In: Gilbert, H. (ed.) EUROCRYPT 2010. LNCS, vol. 6110, pp. 553–572. Springer, Heidelberg (2010). https://doi.org/10.1007/978-3-642-13190-5_28
2. Ajtai, M.: Generating hard instances of lattice problems (extended abstract). In: STOC, pp. 99–108 (1996)
3. Attema, T., Lyubashevsky, V., Seiler, G.: Practical product proofs for lattice commitments. In: Micciancio, D., Ristenpart, T. (eds.) CRYPTO 2020. LNCS, vol. 12171, pp. 470–499. Springer, Cham (2020). https://doi.org/10.1007/978-3-030-56880-1_17
4. Bai, S., Galbraith, S.D.: An improved compression technique for signatures based on learning with errors. In: Benaloh, J. (ed.) CT-RSA 2014. LNCS, vol. 8366, pp. 28–47. Springer, Cham (2014). https://doi.org/10.1007/978-3-319-04852-9_2
5. Banaszczyk, W.: New bounds in some transference theorems in the geometry of numbers. Math. Ann. **296**(1), 625–635 (1993)
6. Baum, C., Damgård, I., Lyubashevsky, V., Oechsner, S., Peikert, C.: More efficient commitments from structured lattice assumptions. In: Catalano, D., De Prisco, R. (eds.) SCN 2018. LNCS, vol. 11035, pp. 368–385. Springer, Cham (2018). https://doi.org/10.1007/978-3-319-98113-0_20
7. Baum, C., Lyubashevsky, V.: Simple amortized proofs of shortness for linear relations over polynomial rings. IACR Cryptology ePrint Archive, 2017:759 (2017)
8. Baum, C., Nof, A.: Concretely-efficient zero-knowledge arguments for arithmetic circuits and their application to lattice-based cryptography. In: Kiayias, A., Kohlweiss, M., Wallden, P., Zikas, V. (eds.) PKC 2020. LNCS, vol. 12110, pp. 495–526. Springer, Cham (2020). https://doi.org/10.1007/978-3-030-45374-9_17
9. Beullens, W.: Sigma protocols for MQ, PKP and SIS, and fishy signature schemes. In: Canteaut, A., Ishai, Y. (eds.) EUROCRYPT 2020. LNCS, vol. 12107, pp. 183–211. Springer, Cham (2020). https://doi.org/10.1007/978-3-030-45727-3_7
10. Beullens, W., Dobson, S., Katsumata, S., Lai, Y., Pintore, F.: Group signatures and more from isogenies and lattices: generic, simple, and efficient. IACR Cryptology ePrint Archive, p. 1366 (2021)
11. Bootle, J., Lyubashevsky, V., Seiler, G.: Algebraic techniques for short(er) exact lattice-based zero-knowledge proofs. In: Boldyreva, A., Micciancio, D. (eds.) CRYPTO 2019. LNCS, vol. 11692, pp. 176–202. Springer, Cham (2019). https://doi.org/10.1007/978-3-030-26948-7_7
12. Canetti, R., Lindell, Y., Ostrovsky, R., Sahai, A.: Universally composable two-party and multi-party secure computation. In: STOC, pp. 494–503. ACM (2002)
13. del Pino, R., Lyubashevsky, V., Seiler, G.: Lattice-based group signatures and zero-knowledge proofs of automorphism stability. In: ACM Conference on Computer and Communications Security, pp. 574–591. ACM (2018)
14. Ducas, L., Durmus, A., Lepoint, T., Lyubashevsky, V.: Lattice signatures and bimodal gaussians. In: Canetti, R., Garay, J.A. (eds.) CRYPTO 2013. LNCS, vol. 8042, pp. 40–56. Springer, Heidelberg (2013). https://doi.org/10.1007/978-3-642-40041-4_3

15. Ducas, L., et al.: Crystals-dilithium: a lattice-based digital signature scheme. IACR Trans. Cryptogr. Hardw. Embed. Syst. **2018**(1), 238–268 (2018)
16. Esgin, M.F., Nguyen, N.K., Seiler, G.: Practical exact proofs from lattices: new techniques to exploit fully-splitting rings. In: Moriai, S., Wang, H. (eds.) ASIACRYPT 2020. LNCS, vol. 12492, pp. 259–288. Springer, Cham (2020). https://doi.org/10.1007/978-3-030-64834-3_9
17. Esgin, M.F., Steinfeld, R., Liu, J.K., Liu, D.: Lattice-based zero-knowledge proofs: new techniques for shorter and faster constructions and applications. In: Boldyreva, A., Micciancio, D. (eds.) CRYPTO 2019. LNCS, vol. 11692, pp. 115–146. Springer, Cham (2019). https://doi.org/10.1007/978-3-030-26948-7_5
18. Esgin, M.F., Steinfeld, R., Zhao, R.K.: Matrict+: more efficient post-quantum private blockchain payments. IACR Cryptology ePrint Archive, p. 545 (2021)
19. Esgin, M.F., Zhao, R.K., Steinfeld, R., Liu, J.K., Liu, D.: Matrict: efficient, scalable and post-quantum blockchain confidential transactions protocol. In: CCS, pp. 567–584. ACM (2019)
20. Gentry, C., Halevi, S., Lyubashevsky, V.: Practical non-interactive publicly verifiable secret sharing with thousands of parties. IACR Cryptology ePrint Archive, p. 1397 (2021)
21. Langlois, A., Stehlé, D.: Worst-case to average-case reductions for module lattices. Des. Codes Crypt. **75**(3), 565–599 (2014). https://doi.org/10.1007/s10623-014-9938-4
22. Libert, B., Ling, S., Nguyen, K., Wang, H.: Zero-knowledge arguments for lattice-based accumulators: logarithmic-size ring signatures and group signatures without trapdoors. In: Fischlin, M., Coron, J.-S. (eds.) EUROCRYPT 2016. LNCS, vol. 9666, pp. 1–31. Springer, Heidelberg (2016). https://doi.org/10.1007/978-3-662-49896-5_1
23. Ling, S., Nguyen, K., Stehlé, D., Wang, H.: Improved zero-knowledge proofs of knowledge for the ISIS problem, and applications. In: Kurosawa, K., Hanaoka, G. (eds.) PKC 2013. LNCS, vol. 7778, pp. 107–124. Springer, Heidelberg (2013). https://doi.org/10.1007/978-3-642-36362-7_8
24. Lyubashevsky, V.: Fiat-Shamir with aborts: applications to lattice and factoring-based signatures. In: Matsui, M. (ed.) ASIACRYPT 2009. LNCS, vol. 5912, pp. 598–616. Springer, Heidelberg (2009). https://doi.org/10.1007/978-3-642-10366-7_35
25. Lyubashevsky, V.: Lattice signatures without trapdoors. In: Pointcheval, D., Johansson, T. (eds.) EUROCRYPT 2012. LNCS, vol. 7237, pp. 738–755. Springer, Heidelberg (2012). https://doi.org/10.1007/978-3-642-29011-4_43
26. Lyubashevsky, V., Neven, G.: One-shot verifiable encryption from lattices. In: Coron, J.-S., Nielsen, J.B. (eds.) EUROCRYPT 2017. LNCS, vol. 10210, pp. 293–323. Springer, Cham (2017). https://doi.org/10.1007/978-3-319-56620-7_11
27. Lyubashevsky, V., Nguyen, N.K., Plancon, M.: Lattice-based zero-knowledge proofs and applications: shorter, simpler, and more general. IACR Cryptology ePrint Archive, p. 284 (2022)
28. Lyubashevsky, V., Nguyen, N.K., Plancon, M., Seiler, G.: Shorter lattice-based group signatures via "almost free" encryption and other optimizations. In: Tibouchi, M., Wang, H. (eds.) ASIACRYPT 2021. LNCS, vol. 13093, pp. 218–248. Springer, Cham (2021). https://doi.org/10.1007/978-3-030-92068-5_8
29. Lyubashevsky, V., Nguyen, N.K., Seiler, G.: Practical lattice-based zero-knowledge proofs for integer relations. In: CCS, pp. 1051–1070. ACM (2020)

30. Lyubashevsky, V., Nguyen, N.K., Seiler, G.: Shorter lattice-based zero-knowledge proofs via one-time commitments. In: Garay, J.A. (ed.) PKC 2021. LNCS, vol. 12710, pp. 215–241. Springer, Cham (2021). https://doi.org/10.1007/978-3-030-75245-3_9

31. Lyubashevsky, V., Nguyen, N.K., Seiler, G.: SMILE: set membership from ideal lattices with applications to ring signatures and confidential transactions. In: Malkin, T., Peikert, C. (eds.) CRYPTO 2021. LNCS, vol. 12826, pp. 611–640. Springer, Cham (2021). https://doi.org/10.1007/978-3-030-84245-1_21

32. Lyubashevsky, V., Peikert, C., Regev, O.: On ideal lattices and learning with errors over rings. In: Gilbert, H. (ed.) EUROCRYPT 2010. LNCS, vol. 6110, pp. 1–23. Springer, Heidelberg (2010). https://doi.org/10.1007/978-3-642-13190-5_1

33. Lyubashevsky, V., Seiler, G.: Short, invertible elements in partially splitting cyclotomic rings and applications to lattice-based zero-knowledge proofs. In: Nielsen, J.B., Rijmen, V. (eds.) EUROCRYPT 2018. LNCS, vol. 10820, pp. 204–224. Springer, Cham (2018). https://doi.org/10.1007/978-3-319-78381-9_8

34. Micciancio, D., Peikert, C.: Trapdoors for lattices: simpler, tighter, faster, smaller. In: Pointcheval, D., Johansson, T. (eds.) EUROCRYPT 2012. LNCS, vol. 7237, pp. 700–718. Springer, Heidelberg (2012). https://doi.org/10.1007/978-3-642-29011-4_41

35. Regev, O.: On lattices, learning with errors, random linear codes, and cryptography. J. ACM **56**(6), 1–40 (2009)

36. Schnorr, C.P.: Efficient identification and signatures for smart cards. In: Brassard, G. (ed.) CRYPTO 1989. LNCS, vol. 435, pp. 239–252. Springer, New York (1990). https://doi.org/10.1007/0-387-34805-0_22

37. Stern, J.: A new identification scheme based on syndrome decoding. In: Stinson, D.R. (ed.) CRYPTO 1993. LNCS, vol. 773, pp. 13–21. Springer, Heidelberg (1994). https://doi.org/10.1007/3-540-48329-2_2

38. Yang, R., Au, M.H., Zhang, Z., Xu, Q., Yu, Z., Whyte, W.: Efficient lattice-based zero-knowledge arguments with standard soundness: construction and applications. In: Boldyreva, A., Micciancio, D. (eds.) CRYPTO 2019. LNCS, vol. 11692, pp. 147–175. Springer, Cham (2019). https://doi.org/10.1007/978-3-030-26948-7_6

Lattice-Based SNARKs: Publicly Verifiable, Preprocessing, and Recursively Composable

(Extended Abstract)

Martin R. Albrecht[1], Valerio Cini[2(✉)], Russell W. F. Lai[3], Giulio Malavolta[4], and Sri AravindaKrishnan Thyagarajan[5]

[1] Royal Holloway, University of London, Egham, UK
[2] AIT Austrian Institute of Technology, Seibersdorf, Austria
valerio.cini@ait.ac.at
[3] Aalto University, Espoo, Finland
[4] Max Planck Institute for Security and Privacy, Bochum, Germany
[5] Carnegie Mellon University, Pittsburgh, USA

Abstract. A succinct non-interactive argument of knowledge (SNARK) allows a prover to produce a short proof that certifies the veracity of a certain NP-statement. In the last decade, a large body of work has studied candidate constructions that are secure against quantum attackers. Unfortunately, no known candidate matches the efficiency and desirable features of (pre-quantum) constructions based on bilinear pairings.

In this work, we make progress on this question. We propose the first lattice-based SNARK that simultaneously satisfies many desirable properties: It (i) is tentatively post-quantum secure, (ii) is publicly-verifiable, (iii) has a logarithmic-time verifier and (iv) has a purely algebraic structure making it amenable to efficient recursive composition. Our construction stems from a general technical toolkit that we develop to translate pairing-based schemes to lattice-based ones. At the heart of our SNARK

M. R. Albrecht—The research of MA was supported by EPSRC grants EP/S020330/1, EP/S02087X/1 and by the European Union Horizon 2020 Research and Innovation Program Grant 780701.

M. R. Albrecht, V. Cini, R. W. F. Lai, G. Malavolta, S. A. Thyagarajan—This work was supported by Protocol Labs under PL-RGP1-2021-050.

V. Cini—This work was in part done while visiting Max Planck Institute for Security and Privacy. The research of VC was in part funded by the European Union's Horizon 2020 research and innovation programme under grant agreement No. 830929 (CyberSec4Europe), No. 871473 (KRAKEN), and by the Austrian Science Fund (FWF) and netidee SCIENCE grant P31621-N38 (PROFET).

R. W. F. Lai—This work was done at Friedrich-Alexander-Universität Erlangen-Nürnberg.

G. Malavolta—This work has been partially supported by the German Federal Ministry of Education and Research BMBF (grant 16K15K042, project 6GEM).

Supplementary Information The online version contains supplementary material available at https://doi.org/10.1007/978-3-031-15979-4_4.

Y. Dodis and T. Shrimpton (Eds.): CRYPTO 2022, LNCS 13508, pp. 102–132, 2022.
https://doi.org/10.1007/978-3-031-15979-4_4

is a new lattice-based vector commitment (VC) scheme supporting openings to constant-degree multivariate polynomial maps, which is a candidate solution for the open problem of constructing VC schemes with openings to beyond linear functions. However, the security of our constructions is based on a new family of lattice-based computational assumptions which naturally generalises the standard Short Integer Solution (SIS) assumption.

1   Introduction

A succinct non-interactive argument of knowledge (SNARK) [45,58] allows a prover to convince a verifier that they know a witness to an NP statement. The succinctness property demands that the size of the proof and, after preprocessing, the work of the verifier are sublinear in (ideally independent of) the time needed to check the validity of the witness. Over the last decade, SNARKs have witnessed a meteoric rise in their efficiency and applicability [9,11,13,22,30,62]. More recently, SNARKs have found their way into real-world systems in the context of blockchain-based cryptocurrencies [10,15,18,20,47].

The looming threat of quantum computers has given rise to a movement in the cryptographic community to investigate cryptographic constructions from assumptions that would plausibly withstand the presence of a quantum attacker. Unfortunately, present SNARKs based on post-quantum assumptions are in many ways inferior to pre-quantum constructions based on bilinear pairings. The goal of this work is to make progress in this area.

1.1   The Seascape of SNARKs

To put our work into context, we give a brief outline of the current seascape of SNARK constructions[1]. We split the schemes depending on the underlying cryptographic assumptions used as the source of hardness.

Bilinear Pairings. To date, the most efficient and feature-rich SNARKs are constructed over bilinear pairing groups (e.g. [42]) with a trusted setup. Typically, a pairing-based SNARK proof consists of only a small constant number of base group elements and is also publicly verifiable. Furthermore, offline preprocessing can often be performed, such that the online verification time is sublinear in the size of the statement being proved and the corresponding witness. Moreover, pairing-based SNARKs are favourable because of their algebraic structures that is known to enable proof batching [21,50] and efficient recursive composition [12]. However, due to their reliance on the hardness of problems related to discrete logarithms, pairing-based SNARKs are not sound against a cheating quantum prover.

Random Oracles. Promising post-quantum candidate for SNARKs are constructions based on Micali's CS proofs paradigm: They are obtained by first building an interactive argument using (generalisations of) probabilistically checkable proofs (PCP) [45], then compiling it into a non-interactive one using the Fiat-Shamir transformation [27] in the random oracle (RO) model.

A major difference between pairing-based and RO-based SNARKs, from both theoretical and practical perspectives, is the algebraic structure of the

---

[1] It can be succinctly verified that SNARKs, like sharks, are creatures of the sea.

verification algorithm. In RO-based SNARKs, the verification algorithms query the RO, which is a combinatorial object. This is especially important when recursively composing the SNARK: On the theoretical side, proving the knowledge of a valid RO-based SNARK proof requires specifying the circuit computing the RO. This makes it challenging to formally argue about soundness, even in the RO model. From a practical perspective, the RO is instantiated with cryptographic hash functions, which typically have high multiplicative degree.[2] Since the multiplicative degree of the relation being proven often dominates the prover computation complexity in SNARKs, proving the satisfiability of a cryptographic hash function becomes computationally expensive.

Lattices. A prominent source of hardness for post-quantum security are computational problems over lattices. Not only do lattice-based assumptions allow us to build most standard cryptographic primitives, e.g. [34,66], but also enable new powerful primitives [33,38,39,72], which are currently out of the reach of group-based assumptions. Unfortunately, in the context of SNARKs, lattices have yet to be established as competitive alternatives to group-based constructions. So far, lattice-based SNARKs either require designated verifiers [32,43] or linear-time verification [6,19].

Beyond their theoretical appeal, one additional motivation for constructing lattice-based SNARKs is that they are potentially more compatible with other basic lattice-based primitives when composing them to construct more advanced systems. More concretely, consider the task of proving the satisfiability of certain algebraic relations over a ring $\mathcal{R}$ by a solution vector of norm bounded by some δ, a language which arises naturally when composing lattice-based building blocks. Using an argument system for proving algebraic relations over a finite field without norm constraints, arithmetisation would be needed to express certain witness component in, say, binary representation and translate the bounded-norm condition to the satisfiability of a potentially-high-degree polynomial, depending on the choice of the norm and the norm bound δ. In contrast, the bounded-norm constraint could be proven natively if we have an argument system which supports proving the satisfiability of algebraic relations over $\mathcal{R}$ by solutions of norm bounded by some $\alpha \leq \delta$. This is done by expressing the solution vector in a likely more compact $O(\alpha)$-ary representation such that, if the representation has norm bounded by α, then the original solution has norm bounded by δ.

1.2   Our Contributions

In this work, we construct the first lattice-based SNARK for an NP-complete language defined over a ring $\mathcal{R}$. Specifically, the language being supported is the satisfiability of polynomial maps over $\mathcal{R}$ by bounded-norm solutions. Our construction qualitatively matches pairing-based SNARKs, i.e. it is publicly verifiable and can achieve sublinear verification time given preprocessing, while requiring a trusted setup. In addition, it is tentatively post-quantum secure. Furthermore, our construction uses only algebraic operations over a ring $\mathcal{R}$, and is therefore friendly to recursive composition. The soundness of our scheme is

---

[2] Though we mention that there is recent progress [5,40] in crafting hash functions that are friendlier to multiparty computation and argument systems.

based on new lattice-based (knowledge) assumptions. The introduction of new knowledge assumptions is, to some extent, necessary: The work of Gentry and Wichs [35] shows that the soundness of any SNARK cannot be based on falsifiable assumptions in a black-box manner. We summarise the main steps of our work in the following.

(1) **Translation Technique.** We put forward a new paradigm for translating pairing-based constructions to the lattice world. Our constructions stem from techniques from the literature on pairing-based cryptography [53], while simultaneously exploiting the ring structure offered by the lattice setting. We develop the necessary technical toolkit that helps us mimic operations of pairing-based VC constructions in the lattice setting. We view this translation strategy as a major conceptual contribution of our work and we expect it to be instrumental in enabling new applications of lattice-based cryptography.

(2) **Vector Commitments for Constant-Degree Polynomials.** A vector commitment (VC) allows a committer to commit to a vector of w values $\mathbf{x} := (x_0, \ldots, x_{w-1}) \in \mathcal{R}^w$ and then reveal selected portions of the input vector, or more generically a function $f : \mathcal{R}^w \to \mathcal{R}^t$ over the input vector, along with a proof π that can be publicly verified. We require both the commitment and the opening proof to be *compact*. In terms of security, we want to ensure an adversary cannot output a valid opening proof for an incorrect function evaluation of the input vector. VCs have been established as a central primitive in cryptography [23,24,29,37,49,52]. As a central technical contribution, we present the first (lattice-based) VC that supports openings beyond linear functions. Specifically, our VC commits to short vectors of ring elements $\mathbf{x} \in \mathcal{R}^w$ and supports openings to constant-degree d multivariate polynomial maps. We then show how this VC is sufficient to construct SNARKs for the satisfiability of degree-d polynomial maps (which is NP-complete for $d \geq 2$) by bounded-norm solutions.

(3) **New Assumptions and Analysis.** Our translation techniques (and consequently the resulting cryptographic schemes) rely on a new family of assumptions that we refer to as the k-*Ring-Inhomogenous Short Integer Solution* (or k-R-ISIS for short) assumptions. Roughly, a k-R-ISIS assumption says that it is hard to find a short preimage $\mathbf{u}_{g^*}$ satisfying $\langle \mathbf{a}, \mathbf{u}_{g^*} \rangle = g^*(\mathbf{v}) \bmod q$, where g^* is a Laurent monomial[3] and $\mathbf{v}$ is a random point, given short preimages of other Laurent monomials $\mathcal{G}$ evaluated on the same random point. Our new assumptions can be viewed as inhomogenous ring variants of the k-SIS assumption [17,54] (where the rational functions are zeros). The key difference to k-SIS is that we allow to hand out more preimages than the dimension of $\mathbf{a}$ but these preimages are all of different images.

In fact, the assumptions we introduce, k-M-ISIS, are slightly more general in being defined over modules rather than rings. Our generalisation to modules

---

[3] A Laurent monomial is a monomial where negative powers are allowed. Generally, one could consider k-R-ISIS problems for rational functions.

is motivated by the knowledge assumptions that we also introduce. In the knowledge assumptions images live in a moderately sized submodule.

We consider the introduction and study of the k-R-ISIS assumptions as a contribution to the programme of charting the territory between LWE and multilinear maps assumptions called for in [1].

To gain confidence in our newly introduced assumptions, we initiate their study. We show that certain subclasses of the k-R-ISIS problems (parameterised by the algebraic structure on the k-R-ISIS images) are as hard as the R-SIS problem. We show that, as expected, the k-M-ISIS problems are as hard as their k-R-ISIS counterparts, although the former have slightly skewed parameters. We also show that certain k-M-ISIS problems are as hard as the k-M-SIS problem, the natural module variant of the k-SIS problem, where the former have higher module ranks. Furthermore, we show that the k-M-ISIS problems for $(\mathcal{G}, g^*)$ is as hard as those for $(\mathcal{G}, 0)$, and that the hardness is preserved when scaling both $\mathcal{G}$ and g^* multiplicatively by any non-zero Laurent monomial.

However, since none of the reductions from well-established problems cover the case we rely upon in our constructions, we perform cryptanalysis to assess the hardness of general k-M-ISIS problems. While we did not identify any structural weaknesses, we encourage independent analysis to gain confidence in or invalidate our assumptions.

(4) **Post-Quantum Security.** As a contribution of independent interest, we show that our VC satisfies a strong notion of binding known as *collapsing* (as an ordinary commitment, not with respect to functional openings), a recently introduced security notion in the quantum setting [70]. For this, we introduce a new technique of embedding NTRU ciphertexts into the public parameters of our VC. To the best of our knowledge, this is the first VC not based on Merkle trees that is shown to satisfy such a notion.

(5) **New Applications.** Our SNARK supports proving the satisfiability of polynomial maps over $\mathcal{R}$ by bounded-norm solutions, a language which directly captures those statements which naturally arise in lattice-based cryptographic constructions. We highlight two native applications of our SNARK which do not rely on expensive conversions between different NP-complete languages.

The first application is the recursive composition of our SNARK, which refers to the process of using the SNARK to prove knowledge of another SNARK proof and the satisfiability of a polynomial map; for details see the full version. This is natively supported because the verification algorithm of our SNARK construction is itself checking the satisfiability of certain algebraic relations over $\mathcal{R}$ by a bounded-norm solution. Recursive composition of SNARKs is a general purpose technique for aggregating proofs or proving complex statements in a piece-by-piece fashion. The technique is also useful for constructing incremental verifiable computation [71] and verifiable delay functions [14,41].

The second application is the aggregation of GPV signatures [34]. While it is folklore that any signatures can be aggregated by a SNARK for an NP-complete language, we stress that the GPV verification algorithm, again, checks the satisfiability of certain algebraic relations over $\mathcal{R}$ by a bounded-norm solution which our SNARK natively supports. We discuss how to handle relations in $\mathcal{R}_q$ in the full version of this work. Apart from obtaining short aggregated GPV signatures, in the setting where a set of n signers are signing a common message at a time, the verification of the aggregated signatures could be preprocessed, resulting in an online verification time *sublinear* in n. As a bonus result on GPV signatures, we further show how to construct lattice-based adaptor signatures [7] based on the GPV paradigm. Combining the two results, we obtain the first aggregatable adaptor signatures from any assumption.

Open Problems. Our work paves the way for what we believe to be an exciting line of research. As we initiate the study of inhomogenous variants of the k-SIS assumptions, we ask whether better (possibly quantum) algorithms can be found for solving this problem that exploit the additional algebraic structure. We also presume that for further families of rational functions the k-R-ISIS assumption can be shown to be as hard as standard hard lattice problems. Another compelling question is to study new cryptographic applications of the k-R-ISIS family. We expect that such an abstraction will be useful in transferring techniques from pairing-based cryptography into the lattice world.

1.3   Technical Overview

We give a concise overview of the process of obtaining our lattice-based SNARK. **From Vector Commitments to SNARKs.** In this work, we are interested in VCs supporting openings to constant-degree-d w-variate t-output polynomial maps with bounded coefficients. The standard properties of interest for VCs are:

Compactness. Commitments and opening proofs are of size $\mathsf{poly}(\lambda, \log w, \log t)$.

Binding. It is infeasible to produce a commitment c and proofs for polynomials maps, such that the system of equations induced by them is not satisfiable.[4]

In addition, we require the following stronger notion of binding.

Extractability. To produce a commitment c and a proof that the image of a polynomial map f at the committed vector is $\mathbf{y}$, one must know a preimage $\mathbf{x}$ such that c is a commitment of $\mathbf{x}$ and $f(\mathbf{x}) = \mathbf{y}$.

It is well known that one can construct SNARKs from VCs supporting linear openings in the RO model [49]. However, in this work we take a different route and adopt a more structured approach to construct SNARKs. Specifically, recall that the satisfiability of systems of degree-d polynomials is NP-complete for any constant $d \geq 2$. As such, a SNARK can be trivially constructed from a compact and extractable VC for degree-d polynomials: The prover simply commits to the root of the system $(f, \mathbf{y})$ and immediately produces an opening proof for $(f, \mathbf{y})$. As a concrete example, a popular NP-complete language supported by existing SNARKs is rank-1 constraint satisfiability (R1CS). An R1CS instance consists of three matrices $(\mathbf{A}, \mathbf{B}, \mathbf{C})$ over a field or in general a ring. The instance

---

[4] This generalises position binding.

is satisfied by a vector $\mathbf{x}$ if $(\mathbf{A} \cdot (1, \mathbf{x})) \circ (\mathbf{B} \cdot (1, \mathbf{x})) = (\mathbf{C} \cdot (1, \mathbf{x}))$, where $\circ$ denotes the Hardamard product. It is easy to see that an R1CS instance is a special case of an instance $(f, \mathbf{y})$ of degree-2 polynomial satisfiability where $f(\mathbf{X}) := (\mathbf{A} \cdot (1, \mathbf{X})) \circ (\mathbf{B} \cdot (1, \mathbf{X})) - (\mathbf{C} \cdot (1, \mathbf{X}))$ and $\mathbf{y} = \mathbf{0}$. For a full description of our SNARK we refer the reader to the full version of the paper.

Throughout the rest of this overview, we therefore focus on constructing lattice-based VCs supporting degree-d openings. Since known constructions are restricted to positional openings, we turn our attention to pairing-based schemes (which support linear openings) and develop a new strategy to translate them into lattice-based VCs and simultaneously to extend the degree to $d > 1$.

General Translation Strategy. Our strategy for constructing a lattice-based VC is a novel translation technique that lets us port techniques from the pairing-land to the lattice-land. We describe a general translation strategy for translating not only VC but also potentially other pairing-based constructions to the lattice setting. For the group setting, we adopt the implicit notation for bilinear groups $\mathbb{G}_1$, $\mathbb{G}_2$, and $\mathbb{G}_t$ of prime order q, i.e. the vector of elements in $\mathbb{G}_i$ with (entry-wise) discrete logarithm $\mathbf{x} \in \mathbb{Z}_q$ base an arbitrary fixed generator of $\mathbb{G}_i$ is denoted by $[\mathbf{x}]_i$, with group operations written additively, and the pairing product between $[\mathbf{x}]_1$ and $[\mathbf{y}]_2$ is written as $\langle [\mathbf{x}]_1, [\mathbf{y}]_2 \rangle$. For the lattice setting, we let $\mathcal{R}$ be a cyclotomic ring, $q \in \mathbb{N}$ be a large enough rational prime such that random elements in $\mathcal{R}_q := \mathcal{R}/q\mathcal{R}$ are invertible with non-negligible probability.

Consider a pairing-based construction where the elements $\{[1]_1, [g(\mathbf{v})]_t\}_{g \in \mathcal{G}}$ are publicly available to all parties, where $\mathcal{G}$ is a set of linearly-independent rational functions and $\mathbf{v}$ is a vector of secret exponents. An authority, knowing the secret exponents $\mathbf{v}$, is responsible for giving out secret elements $\{[g(\mathbf{v})]_2\}_{g \in \mathcal{G}}$ to user A. In turn, user A can compute $[u]_2 := \sum_{g \in \mathcal{G}} c_g \cdot [g(\mathbf{v})]_2$ and present it to user B, who can then check the correctness of $[u]_2$ by checking

$$\langle [1]_1, [u]_2 \rangle \overset{?}{=} \sum_{g \in \mathcal{G}} c_g \cdot [g(\mathbf{v})]_t.$$

Note that in this check one side of the pairing (i.e. $[1]_1$) is public, while the other side (i.e. $[u]_2$) is computed from secrets delegated by the authority to user A. This property will be crucial for our translation technique to apply.

The above structure can be seen in many pairing-based constructions. For example, the secret vector $\mathbf{v}$ could be a trapdoor, a master secret key of an identity-based encryption scheme, or a signing key; the delegated secrets $\{[g(\mathbf{v})]_2\}_{g \in \mathcal{G}}$ could be hints given alongside the public parameters of a VC, an identity-based secret key, or a signature; and the pairing-product check could be for opening proof verification, decryption, or signature verification.

Our strategy of translating the above to a lattice-based construction is as follows. First, the public elements $\{[1]_1, [g(\mathbf{v})]_t\}_{g \in \mathcal{G}}$ over $\mathbb{G}_1$ and $\mathbb{G}_t$ are translated to the public vector and elements $\{\mathbf{a}, g(\mathbf{v})\}_{g \in \mathcal{G}}$, where $\mathbf{a}$ and $\mathbf{v}$ are random vectors over $\mathcal{R}_q$ and $\mathcal{R}_q^\times$ respectively. Since $\{g(\mathbf{v})\}_{g \in \mathcal{G}}$ does not necessarily hide $\mathbf{v}$ in the lattice setting (e.g. when $\mathcal{G}$ consists of many linear functions), the authority might as well publicly hand out the vectors $\{\mathbf{a}, \mathbf{v}\}$ directly. Next, the secret elements $\{[g(\mathbf{v})]_2\}_{g \in \mathcal{G}}$ are translated to the *short* secret vectors $\{\mathbf{u}_g\}_{g \in \mathcal{G}}$ satisfying

$\langle \mathbf{a}, \mathbf{u}_g \rangle = g(\mathbf{v}) \bmod q$. These short preimages can be sampled given a trapdoor of $\mathbf{a}$, which the authority should have generated alongside $\mathbf{a}$. Given $\{\mathbf{u}_g\}_{g \in \mathcal{G}}$, user A can similarly compute $\mathbf{u} := \sum_{g \in \mathcal{G}} c_g \cdot \mathbf{u}_g$, although the coefficients c_g are now required to be short. The pairing-product check is then translated to checking

$$\langle \mathbf{a}, \mathbf{u} \rangle \overset{?}{\equiv} \sum_{g \in \mathcal{G}} c_g \cdot g(\mathbf{v}) \bmod q \qquad \text{and} \qquad \mathbf{u} \text{ is short.}$$

The same strategy can also be used to translate (conjectured-)hard computational problems over bilinear groups to the lattice setting to obtain also seemingly-hard problems. For example, consider a variant of the ℓ-Diffie-Hellman Exponent problem, which asks to find $[v^\ell]_2$ given $([1]_1, [1]_2, [v]_2, \ldots, [v^{\ell-1}]_2)$. A natural lattice-counterpart of the problem is to find a short preimage $\mathbf{u}_\ell$ satisfying $\langle \mathbf{a}, \mathbf{u}_\ell \rangle \equiv v^\ell \bmod q$ given short preimages $(\mathbf{u}_i)_{i \in \mathbb{Z}_\ell}$ each satisfying $\langle \mathbf{a}, \mathbf{u}_i \rangle = v^i \bmod q$.

We remark that a direct translation of pairing-based constructions does not necessarily yield the most efficient lattice-based scheme. For this reason, it will be useful to generalise pairing-based constructions into a family parameterised by the function class $\mathcal{G}$. We will then have the freedom to pick $\mathcal{G}$ to optimise the efficiency of translated lattice-based scheme.

Translating Vector Commitments. We next demonstrate how the above translation strategy can be applied to translate pairing-based VCs, using the following pairing-based VC with openings to linear forms $f : \mathbb{Z}_q^w \to \mathbb{Z}_q$ adapted from [24,49,52] as an example.

- Public parameters: $\Big([1]_1, [1]_2, ([v_i]_1)_{i \in \mathbb{Z}_w}, ([\bar{v}_j]_2)_{j \in \mathbb{Z}_w}, ([v_i \cdot \bar{v}_j]_2)_{i,j \in \mathbb{Z}_w : i \neq j},$
  $[\bar{v}]_t \Big)$ where $\bar{v} - \prod_{k \in \mathbb{Z}_w} v_k$ and $\bar{v}_j = \bar{v}/v_j$.
- Committing $\mathbf{x} \in \mathbb{Z}_q$: $[c]_1 := \sum_{i \in \mathbb{Z}_w} x_i \cdot [v_i]_1 = \langle [\mathbf{v}]_1, \mathbf{x} \rangle$
- Opening f: $[u]_2 := \sum_{i,j \in \mathbb{Z}_w : i \neq j} f_j \cdot x_i \cdot [v_i \cdot \bar{v}_j]_2$
- Verifying (f, y): $\langle [1]_1, [u]_2 \rangle \overset{?}{=} \Big\langle [c]_1, \sum_{j \in \mathbb{Z}_w} f_j \cdot [\bar{v}_j]_2 \Big\rangle - y \cdot [\bar{v}]_t$

The weak binding property of the scheme, i.e. the infeasibility of opening a commitment c to both (f, y) and (f, y') with $y \neq y'$, relies on the hardness of computing $[v]_2$, whose exponent corresponds to evaluating the "target monomial" $\prod_{k \in \mathbb{Z}_w} X_k$ at $\mathbf{v}$. Notice that the target monomial is set up in such a way that $[\bar{v}]_t = [v_i]_1 \cdot [\bar{v}_i]_2$ holds for all $i \in \mathbb{Z}_w$, where $[\bar{v}_i]_2$ can be viewed as a "complement" of $[v_i]_1$. Consequently, the value $y = \langle \mathbf{f}, \mathbf{x} \rangle$ appears as the coefficient of $[v]_t$ in the inner product $\Big\langle \sum_{i \in \mathbb{Z}_w} x_i \cdot [v_i]_1, \sum_{j \in \mathbb{Z}_w} f_j \cdot [\bar{v}_j]_2 \Big\rangle$.

While the above pairing-based scheme is ready to be translated to the lattice setting using our translation strategy, to prepare for our generalised scheme for higher-degree polynomials, we divide the target and complement monomials by $\prod_{k \in \mathbb{Z}_w} X_k$. The complement of X_i becomes X_i^{-1} and the target monomial becomes the constant 1. Concretely, we divide the opening and the verification equation by $\bar{v}$ to obtain

$$[u']_2 := \sum_{i,j \in \mathbb{Z}_w : i \neq j} f_j \cdot x_i \cdot [v_i/v_j]_2$$

$$\langle [1]_1, [u']_2 \rangle \overset{?}{=} \left\langle [c]_1, \sum_{j \in \mathbb{Z}_w} f_j \cdot [v_j^{-1}]_2 \right\rangle - y \cdot [1]_t.$$

Recall that in the VC construction above we relied on the hardness of computing $[\bar{v}]_2$. What we have done here might seem absurd, since the element $[1]_2$ now is given in the group setting, but finding a short pre-image of a fixed image, say 1, is seemingly hard in the lattice setting. Indeed, translating the modified scheme, we derive the following lattice-based scheme.

- Public Parameters: $\left(\mathbf{a}, \mathbf{v}, (\mathbf{u}_{i,j})_{i \neq j \in \mathbb{Z}_w} \right)$ where $\langle \mathbf{a}, \mathbf{u}_{i,j} \rangle \equiv v_i/v_j$, $\mathbf{u}_{i,j}$ are short
- Committing $\mathbf{x} \in \mathcal{R}^w$: $c := \langle \mathbf{v}, \mathbf{x} \rangle \bmod q$
- Opening f: $\mathbf{u} := \sum_{i,j \in \mathbb{Z}_w : i \neq j} f_j \cdot x_i \cdot \mathbf{u}_{i,j}$
- Verifying (f, y): $\langle \mathbf{a}, \mathbf{u} \rangle \overset{?}{\equiv} \left(\sum_{j \in \mathbb{Z}_w} f_j \cdot v_j^{-1} \right) \cdot c - y \bmod q$ and $\mathbf{u}$ is short

For correctness, we require that the committed vector $\mathbf{x}$ and the function f both have short coefficients.

The weak binding property of the translated lattice-based scheme relies on the hardness of finding a short preimage of (a small multiple of) 1 given short preimages of v_i/v_j for all $i, j \in \mathbb{Z}_w$ with $i \neq j$ – a new computational assumption obtained by translating its pairing-counterpart, which belongs to a new family of assumptions called the k-R-ISIS assumption family.

Furthermore, the computation of $\sum_{j \in \mathbb{Z}_w} f_j \cdot v_j^{-1}$ in the verification equation can be preprocessed before knowing the commitment c and the opening proof $\mathbf{u}$, such that the online verification can be performed in time sublinear in w.

Supporting Higher-Degree Polynomials. Notice that in the group setting the (modified) verification algorithm can be seen as evaluating the linear form f at $([v_0^{-1}]_2 \cdot [c]_1, \dots, [v_{w-1}^{-1}]_2 \cdot [c]_1)$ where $[c]_1$ supposedly encodes $\mathbf{x}$. In the group setting, f has to be linear since we cannot multiply two $\mathbb{G}_1$ elements together to get an encoding of the Kronecker product $\mathbf{x} \otimes \mathbf{x}$.

In the lattice setting, however, the commitment c is a ring element and thus we can evaluate a non-linear polynomial f at $(v_0^{-1} \cdot c, \dots, v_{w-1}^{-1} \cdot c)$. Moreover, we notice that each degree-d monomial $\mathbf{x}^\mathbf{e}$ is encoded in c^d as (a factor of) the coefficient of $\mathbf{v}^\mathbf{e}$, which has a natural complement $\mathbf{v}^{-\mathbf{e}}$ satisfying $(\mathbf{v}^\mathbf{e}) \cdot (\mathbf{v}^{-\mathbf{e}}) = 1$, our modified target monomial. This suggests the possibility of generalising the translated lattice-based scheme above to support openings to higher-degree polynomials. Indeed, this technique allows us to generalise the scheme to support bounded-coefficient polynomials of degrees up to a constant, whose weak binding property is now based on another member of the k-R-ISIS assumption family.

Achieving Compactness and Extractability. The VC scheme obtained above achieves succinctness, i.e. commitments and opening proofs are of size sublinear in w (not t), and weak binding, which fall short of the compactness and extractability required to construct a SNARK. Indeed, a black-box construction of SNARK using this VC is unlikely since, so far, we are only relying on falsifiable assumptions. To resolve this problem, we propose a knowledge version of the k-R-ISIS assumptions. For concreteness, we will use the following member of the knowledge k-R-ISIS assumption family:

Let $\mathbf{a}' \leftarrow_{\$} \mathcal{R}_q^{\ell}$ and $\mathbf{v} \leftarrow_{\$} \mathcal{R}_q^w$ be random vectors and $t \leftarrow_{\$} \mathcal{R}_q$ be a random element such that $|t \cdot \mathcal{R}_q|$ is super-polynomial in λ and $|t \cdot \mathcal{R}_q|/|\mathcal{R}_q|$ is negligible in λ. If there exists an efficient algorithm $\mathcal{A}$ which, given short vectors $\mathbf{u}'_i$ satisfying $\langle \mathbf{a}', \mathbf{u}'_i \rangle = v_i \cdot t \bmod q$ for all $i \in \mathbb{Z}_w$, produces $(c, \mathbf{u}')$ such that $\mathbf{u}'$ is a short vector satisfying $\langle \mathbf{a}', \mathbf{u}' \rangle = c \cdot t \bmod q$, then there exists an efficient extractor $\mathcal{E}_{\mathcal{A}}$ which extracts a short vector $\mathbf{x} \in \mathcal{R}^w$ such that $\langle \mathbf{v}, \mathbf{x} \rangle = c \bmod q$.

Equipped with this k-R-ISIS of knowledge assumption, we can upgrade our VC construction to achieve extractability as follows. First, we let the public parameters to additionally include $(\mathbf{a}', (\mathbf{u}'_i)_{i \in \mathbb{Z}_w}, t)$. Here t generates an ideal that is small enough for random elements in $\mathcal{R}_q$ not to be contained within it, but big enough to provide sufficient entropy. Next, we let the committer also include $\mathbf{u}' = \sum_{i \in \mathbb{Z}_w} x_i \cdot \mathbf{u}'_i$ in an opening proof. Finally, we let the verifier additionally check that $\mathbf{u}'$ is short and $\langle \mathbf{a}', \mathbf{u}' \rangle = c \cdot t \bmod q$.

To see why the modified scheme is extractable, suppose an adversary is able to produce a commitment c and a valid opening proof for (f, y). By the k-R-ISIS of knowledge assumption, we can extract a short vector $\mathbf{x} \in \mathcal{R}^w$ such that $\langle \mathbf{v}, \mathbf{x} \rangle = c \bmod q$. Now, if $f(\mathbf{x}) = y' \neq y$, we can use the extracted $\mathbf{x}$ to compute a valid opening proof for (f, y'). However, being able to produce valid opening proofs for both (f, y) and (f, y') with $y \neq y'$ violates the weak binding property. We therefore conclude that $f(\mathbf{x}) = y$.

It remains to show how we can achieve compactness. Since our lattice-based VC schemes preserve the property of the original pairing-based schemes that the verification algorithm is linearly-homomorphic in the opening proofs, a natural strategy towards compactness is to aggregate multiple opening proofs into one using a random linear combination, with coefficients generated using a random oracle. The binding property of an aggregated opening proof can be proven using a classic rewinding argument which involves inverting a Vandermode matrix defined by the randomness used for aggregation. This strategy works particularly well in the prime-order group setting since scalars are field elements and Vandermonde matrices defined by distinct field elements are always invertible. In the lattice setting, however, the coefficients used for aggregation have to be chosen from a set where the difference between any pair of elements is (almost) invertible (over $\mathcal{R}$) for an analogous argument to go through. This is a severe limitation since sets satisfying this property cannot be too large [4].

To achieve compactness in the lattice setting, we are forced to use a different strategy. Specifically, the coefficients $\mathbf{h} = (h_i)_{i \in \mathbb{Z}_t} \in \mathcal{R}$ that we use to aggregate opening proofs are given by an instance of the R-SIS problem over $\mathcal{R}_p$ (taking

smallest $\mathcal{R}$-representatives of $\mathcal{R}_p$ elements) sampled as part of the public parameters, where p is chosen such that the R-SIS assumption is believed to hold over
$\mathcal{R}_p$ while p is small relative to q.

To see why extractability still holds, suppose an adversary is able to produce
a commitment c and a valid opening proof for (f, y) where $f = \sum_{i \in \mathbb{Z}_t} h_i \cdot f_i$ and
$y = \sum_{i \in \mathbb{Z}_t} h_i \cdot y_i$. By our previous argument, we can extract $\mathbf{x}$ satisfying $f(\mathbf{x}) = y$.
Suppose it is not the case that $f_i(\mathbf{x}) = y_i$ for all $i \in \mathbb{Z}_t$, then $(f_i(\mathbf{x}) - y_i)_{i \in \mathbb{Z}_t}$
is a short vector satisfying $\sum_{i \in \mathbb{Z}_t} h_i \cdot (f_i(\mathbf{x}) - y_i) = 0$ over $\mathcal{R}$, which implies
$\sum_{i \in \mathbb{Z}_t} h_i \cdot (f_i(\mathbf{x}) - y_i) = 0 \bmod p$, breaking the R-SIS assumption over $\mathcal{R}_p$.

Discussion and Generalisations. We discuss the resulting VC scheme obtained through the aforementioned series of transformations. Our VC scheme supports openings to w-variate t-output constant-degree polynomial maps with
bounded coefficients. The scheme achieves compactness and extractability, where
the latter is based on the standard R-SIS assumption over $\mathcal{R}_p$ and our two new
assumptions: k-R-ISIS and the k-R-ISIS of knowledge assumption over $\mathcal{R}_q$, where
p is short relative to q. The construction uses only algebraic operations over $\mathcal{R}$
and $\mathcal{R}_q$. Furthermore, a major part of the verification equation can be precomputed, so that the online verification time is sublinear in w and t.

Our construction and the k-R-ISIS (of knowledge) assumption families admit
natural generalisations to the module setting, where the vector $\mathbf{a}$ is replaced by a
matrix $\mathbf{A}$ and other components are modified accordingly. Expectedly, we show
that the module versions of the k-R-ISIS assumptions are at least as hard as the
ring versions for certain parameter choices.

In many applications (e.g. aggregating signatures), often only a main part
(e.g. a set of signature verification keys) of the function-image tuple (f, y) is
known in advance, while the remaining small part (e.g. a message signed by all
parties) is known when it comes the time to perform verification. It is desirable
to preprocess the main part of (f, y) offline, so that the online verification cost
is only dependent on the size of the small part. In our formal construction,
we capture this flexibility by considering y itself to be a polynomial map, and
allowing f and y to take an (additional, for f) public input $\mathbf{z}$. This allows the
maps (f, y) to be preprocessed, such that the online cost depends mostly on $\mathbf{z}$.

1.4   Application

We highlight an application of interest of our VC, and in particular of the resulting SNARK, in aggregating GPV signatures [34]. As a bonus result, we also show
how to build adaptor signatures [7] based on GPV signatures while preserving
aggregatability. For more comprehensive details we refer the reader to the full
version of the paper.

Aggregate GPV Signatures. GPV signatures [34] are a lattice-based signature scheme paradigm of which an instantiation is a finalist in the NIST
Post-Quantum Process (Falcon [65]). On a high level, a GPV signature on a
message m is a short vector $\mathbf{u}$ such that $\mathbf{A} \cdot \mathbf{u} \equiv \mathbf{v} \bmod q$, where $\mathbf{A}$ is the public key, $\mathbf{v} = H(m)$ with the hash function H modelled as a random oracle in

the security analysis. The verification is simply the check of the linear relation $\mathbf{A} \cdot \mathbf{u} \equiv \mathbf{v} \bmod q$ and that $\mathbf{u}$ is short.

Our SNARK can be used to prove knowledge of GPV signatures natively given the signature verification involves algebraic operations only. For instance, to aggregate n signatures $(\mathbf{u}_i)_{i \in \mathbb{Z}_n}$ on the same message m (a scenario that arises in a PoS consensus protocol [26]), the aggregator can compute a SNARK proof of knowledge of short $(\mathbf{u}_i)_{i \in \mathbb{Z}_n}$ satisfying $\mathbf{A}_i \cdot \mathbf{u}_i = \mathbf{v} \bmod q$, where $\mathbf{A}_i$ is the public key of the i-th signer. The aggregated signature i.e. the SNARK proof, can be verified in time sublinear in the number of signers and signatures n by first preprocessing the part of the verification equation depending on $(\mathbf{A}_i)_{i \in \mathbb{Z}_n}$. In fact, this preprocessing step is one-time for the given set of signers, and the online verification after knowing m is only logarithmic in n. If the signers sign different messages, a similar SNARK but now over the different messages results in a compact proof, but with verification time linear in n (similar to the case of BLS signatures [16]). Such aggregation can result in compact blocks in a blockchain as shown for the case of BLS signatures [16], but now with post-quantum security.

Aggregate Adaptor Signatures. Adaptor signatures [7] let a user generate an encryption $\hat{\sigma}$ of a signature σ on a message m with respect to an instance Y of a hard language $\mathcal{L}$. Here $\hat{\sigma}$ is also referred to as a *pre-signature*. Given the public key, it is efficient to verify if a given pre-signature $\hat{\sigma}$ is indeed valid with respect to the instance and the message. One can *adapt* the pre-signature $\hat{\sigma}$ into a valid signature σ given the witness y for the instance Y, and given $\hat{\sigma}$ and σ one can efficiently *extract* the witness y. The primitive has found itself useful in enhancing efficiency and privacy of conditional payments in cryptocurrencies [7], and aggregation of signatures adds clear benefits to this primitive. In the following we discuss how GPV signatures can be turned into adaptor signatures, which consequently implies that they can be aggregated via our newly constructed SNARK.

We consider the lattice trapdoor from [61] for our GPV signatures, and view the GPV signatures as follows. The public parameters are given by a uniformly random matrix $\mathbf{A}$, the signing key is $\mathsf{sk} := \mathbf{X}$, where $\mathbf{X}$ is a short norm matrix such that the public key, $\mathbf{Y} := \mathbf{A} \cdot \mathbf{X}$, is distributed statistically close to random. The signature is simply $(\mathbf{z}, \mathbf{c})$ such that during verification we have $[\mathbf{A}|\mathbf{G} + \mathbf{Y}] \cdot [\mathbf{z}|\mathbf{c}]^{\mathsf{T}} = H(m)$ and $\|(\mathbf{c}, \mathbf{z})\|$ is small as stipulated by GPV signatures. Here $\mathbf{G}$ is the gadget matrix. We choose the hard language

$$\mathcal{L} := \{(\mathbf{A}, \mathbf{v}') : \exists\ \mathbf{u}'\ s.t.\ \mathbf{A} \cdot \mathbf{u}' = \mathbf{v}' \wedge \|\mathbf{u}'\| \leq \beta^*\},$$

where $\mathbf{A} \in \mathcal{R}_q^{\eta \times \ell}$, $\mathbf{v}' \in \mathcal{R}_q^{\eta}$. A pre-signature $\hat{\sigma}$ is simply $(\mathbf{c}, \hat{\mathbf{z}})$ with $\mathbf{v}'$ as the hard instance, such that during pre-signature verification, it holds that $[\mathbf{A}|\mathbf{G} + \mathbf{Y}] \cdot [\hat{\mathbf{z}}|\mathbf{c}]^{\mathsf{T}} = H(m) - \mathbf{v}'$ and $\|(\mathbf{c}, \hat{\mathbf{z}})\|$ is small. It is easy to adapt $\hat{\sigma}$ given the witness $\mathbf{u}'$ by setting $\mathbf{z} := \hat{\mathbf{z}} + \mathbf{u}'$ and $\sigma := (\mathbf{c}, \mathbf{z})$. To extract a witness one can simply compute $\mathbf{u}' := \mathbf{z} - \mathbf{z}'$. We have that the extracted $\mathbf{u}'$ has a slightly higher norm than that was used to adapt the pre-signature. The security of our scheme only relies on the M-SIS problem and the RO model.

1.5   Related Work

Apart from applications to succinct arguments [49], VCs have found numerous applications, such as verifiable databases [24], verifiable decentralized storage [23], updatable zero-knowledge sets [55,59], keyless Proofs of Retrievability (PoR) [28,29], pseudonymous credentials [44], and cryptocurrencies with stateless transaction validation [25]. Several works have studied various extensions to VC, with updatable commitments and proofs [24], aggregatable opening proofs for different commitments [37], and incremental aggregatable proofs [23].

Libert, Ramanna, and Yung [52] showed that a VC for linear functions over $\mathbb{Z}_q$ implies a polynomial commitment for polynomials over $\mathbb{Z}_q$. The result was obtained by VC-committing to the coefficient vector of the polynomial and opening it to a linear function whose coefficients are evaluations of monomials at the evaluation point. Since our VC only allows committing to a short vector $\mathbf{x} \in \mathcal{R}^w$ and opening to a polynomial map f with short coefficients, we need to suitably tune the norm bound α of f and $\mathbf{x}$ to obtain similar applications. Concretely, by setting $\alpha \approx \delta^{d+1} \cdot \gamma_{\mathcal{R}}^d$ where $\gamma_{\mathcal{R}}$ is the ring expansion factor of $\mathcal{R}$, we obtain a polynomial commitment for degree-d multivariate polynomials with coefficients bounded by δ which supports evaluations at vectors of norm also bounded by δ. Note that only constant-degree polynomials are supported by our polynomial commitment since α depends exponentially on d.

In the same work [52], Libert, Ramanna, and Yung also showed that the polynomial commitment constructed from a VC for linear functions over $\mathbb{Z}_q$ implies an accumulator for $\mathbb{Z}_q$ elements, the construction requires committing to the polynomial $p(X) = \prod_{a \in A}(X - a)$ encoding the set A of elements to be accumulated. The polynomial commitment obtained via our VC unfortunately does not support committing to $p(X)$ since its degree is as large as $|A|$.

In a recent work [63], Peikert, Pepin, and Sharp proposed a VC for positional openings based on the standard SIS assumption. Relative to our construction outlined in Sect. 1.3, their construction can be interpreted as follows. Instead of handing out preimages $\mathbf{u}_{i,j}$ with $\langle \mathbf{a}, \mathbf{u}_{i,j} \rangle = v_j/v_i \bmod q$, they sample multiple $\mathbf{a}_i$ for $i \in \mathbb{Z}_w$ and let $\mathbf{u}_{i,j}$ satisfy $\langle \mathbf{a}_i, \mathbf{u}_{i,j} \rangle = v_j \bmod q$. To verify an opening to position i, the vector $\mathbf{a}_i$ is used. The removal of the non-linear term v_j/v_i allows proving security from the SIS assumption. On the flip side, using a different vector $\mathbf{a}_i$ to verify openings to different positions i forbids the standard technique of aggregating openings using a random linear combination. Furthermore, there seems to be no natural way of generalising their construction to support functional openings without significantly changing the VC model, e.g. introducing an authority responsible for issuing functional opening keys [63]. Even if we consider the model with an authority, the resulting VC only satisfies *weak binding* (using the terminology of our work) making it unsuitable to be transformed into a SNARG: There is in fact an explicit attack when compiling their VC (with authority) into a SNARG.[5]

---

[5] We stress that this does not contradict any of the claims made in [63], but rather exemplifies the difference between their approach and ours.

Prior to our work, all lattice-based SNARKs were in the designated-verifier setting. These constructions [32,43] are based on "linear-only" assumptions which are similar in spirit to the knowledge k-M-ISIS assumptions introduced in this work but with a key difference: While linear-only assumptions are with respect to specific encryption schemes, our assumptions are with respect to general rings. In terms of applications, linear-only encryption has always been used to construct designated-verifier primitives. In contrast, knowledge k-M-ISIS naturally leads to constructions of publicly verifiable primitives.

2   Preliminaries

Let $\lambda \in \mathbb{N}$ denote the security parameter. Define $\mathbb{N}_0 := \mathbb{N} \cup \{0\}$. Let $\mathcal{R}$ be a ring. We write $\mathcal{R}[\mathbf{X}]$ for the (multivariate) polynomial ring over $\mathcal{R}$ and $\mathcal{R}(\mathbf{X})$ for the ring of (multivariate) rational functions over $\mathcal{R}$ with intermediates $\mathbf{X} = (X_i : i \in \mathbb{Z}_w)$. We write $\langle \mathcal{G} \rangle$ for the ideal resp. module spanned by the elements of the set $\mathcal{G} \subset \mathcal{R}^\eta$ for $\eta \in \mathbb{N}$. When $\mathcal{G}$ is a singleton set we may suppress the $\{\cdot\}$ notation. We write $|\langle \mathcal{G} \rangle|$ for size of the ideal $\langle \mathcal{G} \rangle$ as a set.

For $m \in \mathbb{N}$, let $\zeta_m \in \mathbb{C}$ be any fixed primitive m-th root of unity. Denote by $\mathcal{K} = \mathbb{Q}(\zeta_m)$ the cyclotomic field of order $m \geq 2$ and degree $n = \varphi(m)$, and by $\mathcal{R} = \mathbb{Z}[\zeta_m]$ its ring of integers, called a cyclotomic ring for short. We have $\mathcal{R} \cong \mathbb{Z}[x]/\langle \Phi_m(x) \rangle$, where $\Phi_m(x)$ is the m-th cyclotomic polynomial. If m is a power of 2, we call $\mathcal{R}$ a power-of-2 cyclotomic ring. If m is a prime-power, we call $\mathcal{R}$ a prime-power cyclotomic ring. Let $q \in \mathbb{N}$ be prime, we write $\mathcal{R}_q := \mathcal{R}/q\mathcal{R}$ and $\mathcal{R}_q^\times$ for all invertible elements in $\mathcal{R}_q$. We have that $\mathcal{R}_q$ splits into f fields of degree $\phi(m)/f$. We write $\text{vec}(r) \in \mathbb{Z}^n$ for the coefficient vector of r (with the powerful basis). For any $r \in \mathcal{R}$ there exists a matrix $\text{rot}(r) \in \mathbb{Z}^{n \times n}$ s.t. $\forall s \in \mathcal{R}$ we have $\text{vec}(r \cdot s) = \text{rot}(r) \cdot \text{vec}(s)$. For elements $x \in \mathcal{R}$ we denote the infinity norm of its coefficient vector as $\|x\| := \|\text{vec}(x)\|$. If $\mathbf{x} \in \mathcal{R}^\ell$ we write $\|\mathbf{x}\|$ for the infinity norm of $\mathbf{x}$. We write $\|\cdot\|_p$ for the ℓ_p-norm, e.g. $\|\cdot\|_2$ for the Euclidean norm. We write $\mathcal{M}_{\mathcal{G}}(\cdot)$ for a function that takes vectors indexed by $\mathcal{G}$ and returns a matrix where each column corresponds to one such vector. We write $\mathbf{I}_n$ for the identity matrix of dimension n over whatever ring is clear from context.

For $w \in \mathbb{N}$, $\mathbf{x} = (x_i : i \in \mathbb{Z}_w) \in \mathcal{R}^w$, and $\mathbf{e} = (e_i : i \in \mathbb{Z}_w) \in \mathbb{Z}^w$, we write $\mathbf{x}^{\mathbf{e}} := \prod_{i \in \mathbb{Z}_w} x_i^{e_i}$ whenever it is defined. For $\mathbf{v} = (v_i : i \in \mathbb{Z}_w) \in (\mathcal{R}_q^\times)^w$, we write $\bar{\mathbf{v}} := (v_i^{-1} : i \in \mathbb{Z}_w)$ for the entry-wise inverse of $\mathbf{v}$. A Laurent monomial $g(\mathbf{X}) \in \mathcal{R}(\mathbf{X})$ is an expression $g(\mathbf{X}) = \mathbf{X}^{\mathbf{e}} := \prod_{i \in \mathbb{Z}_w} X_i^{e_i}$ with exponent vector $\mathbf{e} = (e_i : i \in \mathbb{Z}_w) \in \mathbb{Z}^w$.

We may suppress arbitrary subscripts and superscripts from problem and advantage notations when those are clear from context. We write $x \leftarrow \mathcal{D}$ for sampling from the distribution $\mathcal{D}$ and $x \leftarrow\!\!\$ \ S$ to sample an element from the finite space S uniformly at random. We write $U(S)$ for the uniform distribution over S and $\{\mathbf{u}_{\mathcal{G}}\} := \{\mathbf{u}_g\}_{g \in \mathcal{G}}$.

Definition 1 (Ring Expansion Factor). *Let $\mathcal{R}$ be a ring. The expansion factor of $\mathcal{R}$, denoted by $\gamma_{\mathcal{R}}$, is $\gamma_{\mathcal{R}} := \max_{a,b \in \mathcal{R}} \frac{\|a \cdot b\|}{\|a\| \cdot \|b\|}$.*

Proposition 1 ([4]). *If $\mathcal{R} = \mathbb{Z}[\zeta_m]$ is a prime-power cyclotomic ring, then $\gamma_{\mathcal{R}} \leq 2n$. If $\mathcal{R} = \mathbb{Z}[\zeta_m]$ is a power-of-2 cyclotomic ring, then $\gamma_{\mathcal{R}} \leq n$.*

Proposition 2. *Let $q = \omega((w \cdot f)^{f/\phi(m)})$ be a rational prime such that $\mathcal{R}_q$ splits into f fields each of size $q^{\varphi(m)/f}$. For $\mathbf{v} \leftarrow\!\!\$\ \mathcal{R}_q^w$, we have $\mathbf{v} \in (\mathcal{R}_q^\times)^w$ with non-negligible probability.*

Proof. The probability that $\mathbf{v} \in (\mathcal{R}_q^\times)^w$ is $(1 - 1/q^{\varphi(m)/f})^{w \cdot f} \geq 1 - (w \cdot f)/q^{\varphi(m)/f}$ which is non-negligible. $\qquad\square$

For the rest of this work, we implicitly assume q is large enough so that a uniformly random $\mathbf{v} \leftarrow\!\!\$\ \mathcal{R}_q^w$ satisfies $\mathbf{v} \in (\mathcal{R}_q^\times)^w$ with non-negligible probability.

2.1 Lattices

We write $\Lambda(\mathbf{B})$ for the Euclidean lattice generated by the columns of $\mathbf{B} \in \mathbb{Z}^{n \times d} = [\mathbf{b}_0| \ldots \mathbf{b}_{d-1}]$, i.e. $\{z_i \cdot \mathbf{b}_i \mid z_i \in \mathbb{Z}\}$. When $\mathbf{B}$ has full rank we call it a basis and when $n = d$ we say that $\Lambda(\mathbf{B})$ has full rank. The determinant of a full rank lattice is the absolute value of the determinant of any of its bases. Minkowski's theorem implies that there is a vector $\mathbf{x} \in \Lambda \subset \mathbb{R}^d$ of (infinity) norm $\|\mathbf{x}\| \leq \det(\Lambda)^{1/d}$ when Λ has full rank. The Gaussian heuristic predicts that a random full-rank lattice Λ contains a shortest vector of (Euclidean) norm $\approx \sqrt{\frac{d}{2\pi e}} \cdot \det(\Lambda)^{1/d}$.

For any $\mathbf{c} \in \mathbb{R}^n$ and any real $\sigma > 0$, the (spherical) Gaussian function with standard deviation parameter σ and centre $\mathbf{c}$ is:

$$\forall \mathbf{x} \in \mathbb{R}^n, \rho_{\sigma,\mathbf{c}}(\mathbf{x}) = \exp\left(-\frac{\pi \cdot \|\mathbf{x} - \mathbf{c}\|_2^2}{\sigma^2}\right).$$

The Gaussian distribution is $\mathcal{D}_{\sigma,\mathbf{c}}(\mathbf{x}) = \rho_{\sigma,\mathbf{c}}(\mathbf{x})/\sigma^n$. The (spherical) discrete Gaussian distribution over a lattice $\Lambda \in \mathbb{R}^n$, with standard deviation parameter $\sigma > 0$ and centre $\mathbf{c}$ is:

$$\forall \mathbf{x} \in \Lambda, \mathcal{D}_{\Lambda,\sigma,\mathbf{c}} = \frac{\rho_{\sigma,\mathbf{c}}(\mathbf{x})}{\rho_{\sigma,\mathbf{c}}(\Lambda)},$$

where $\rho_{\sigma,\mathbf{c}}(\Lambda) := \sum_{\mathbf{x} \in \Lambda} \rho_{\sigma,\mathbf{c}}(\mathbf{x})$. When $\mathbf{c} = \mathbf{0}$ we omit the subscript $\mathbf{c}$. We may write $\mathcal{D}_{\mathcal{R},\sigma}$ where we interpret $\mathcal{R}$ to be the lattice spanned by $\mathcal{R}$.

The dual of a lattice Λ is defined by $\Lambda^* = \{\mathbf{y} \in \mathbb{R}^n : \mathbf{y}^T \cdot \Lambda \subseteq \mathbb{Z}\}$. The smoothing parameter of an n-dimensional lattice Λ with respect to $\epsilon > 0$, denoted $\eta_\epsilon(\Lambda)$, is the smallest $\sigma > 0$, such that $\rho_{1/\sigma}(\Lambda^* \setminus \{\mathbf{0}\}) \leq \epsilon$.

Lattice reduction with parameter κ returns a vector of Euclidean norm $\approx \delta^{d-1} \cdot \det(\Lambda)^{1/d}$ where δ is the root Hermite factor δ and a function of κ.[6] A root Hermite factor $\delta \approx \left(\frac{\kappa}{2\pi e}\right)^{1/(2\kappa)}$ can be achieved in time $2^{0.292\,\kappa + o(\kappa)}$ classically using the BKZ algorithm [67] with block size κ and sieving as the SVP oracle [8] (quantum algorithms do not promise a sufficiently substantial speed-up [3,48]). Concretely, for $\lambda = 128$ we require $\kappa \geq 484$ and thus $\delta \leq 1.0034$.

---

[6] The literature routinely simplifies the first expression to $\approx \delta^d \cdot \det(\Lambda)^{1/d}$.

2.2 Sampling Algorithms

The following relies on analogues of the Leftover Hash Lemma over rings attesting that given $\mathbf{a}_i \leftarrow_\$ U(\mathcal{R}_q^\eta)$ and $r_i \leftarrow_\$ \mathcal{D}$ where $\mathcal{D}$ is a small uniform [60, 69] or discrete Gaussian distribution [57, 68], we have that $\left(\mathbf{a}_0, \ldots, \mathbf{a}_{\ell-1}, \sum_{0 \le i < \ell} \mathbf{a}_i \cdot r_i\right)$ is close to uniform. In what follows, we will write $\mathsf{lhl}(\mathcal{R}, \eta, q, \mathcal{D})$ for an algorithm that outputs a minimal $\ell \in \mathbb{N}$ ensuring that the resulting distribution is within $\mathsf{negl}(\lambda)$ to uniform. We may also write $\mathsf{lhl}(\mathcal{R}, \eta, q, \beta)$ for some $\mathcal{D}$ outputting elements bounded by β (with overwhelming probability). In many cases the reader may think $\ell \in O(\eta \log_\beta(q))$. Let $(\mathsf{TrapGen}, \mathsf{SampD}, \mathsf{SampPre})$ be PPT algorithms with the following syntax and properties [31, 34, 61]:

- $(\mathbf{A}, \mathsf{td}) \leftarrow \mathsf{TrapGen}(1^\eta, 1^\ell, q, \mathcal{R}, \beta)$ takes dimensions $\eta, \ell \in \mathbb{N}$, a modulus $q \in \mathbb{N}$, a ring $\mathcal{R}$, and a norm bound $\beta \in \mathbb{R}$. It generates a matrix $\mathbf{A} \in \mathcal{R}_q^{\eta \times \ell}$ and a trapdoor td. For any $n \in \mathsf{poly}(\lambda)$ and $\ell \ge \mathsf{lhl}(\mathcal{R}, \eta, q, \beta)$, the distribution of $\mathbf{A}$ is within $\mathsf{negl}(\lambda)$ statistical distance of $U(\mathcal{R}_q^{\eta \times \ell})$.
- $\mathbf{u} \leftarrow \mathsf{SampD}(1^\eta, 1^\ell, \mathcal{R}, \beta')$ with $\ell \ge \mathsf{lhl}(\mathcal{R}, \eta, q, \beta)$ outputs an element in $\mathbf{u} \in \mathcal{R}^\ell$ with norm bound $\beta' \ge \beta$. We have that $\mathbf{v} := \mathbf{A} \cdot \mathbf{u} \bmod q$ is within $\mathsf{negl}(\lambda)$ statistical distance to $U(\mathcal{R}_q^\eta)$.
- $\mathbf{u} \leftarrow \mathsf{SampPre}(\mathsf{td}, \mathbf{v}, \beta')$ with $\ell \ge \mathsf{lhl}(\mathcal{R}, \eta, q, \beta)$ takes a trapdoor td, a vector $\mathbf{v} \in \mathcal{R}_q^\eta$, and a norm bound $\beta' \ge \beta$. It samples $\mathbf{u} \in \mathcal{R}^\ell$ satisfying $\mathbf{A} \cdot \mathbf{u} \equiv \mathbf{v} \bmod q$ and $\|\mathbf{u}\| \le \beta'$. Furthermore, $\mathbf{u}$ is within $\mathsf{negl}(\lambda)$ statistical distance to $\mathbf{u} \leftarrow \mathsf{SampD}(1^\eta, 1^\ell, \mathcal{R}, \beta')$ conditioned on $\mathbf{v} \equiv \mathbf{A} \cdot \mathbf{u} \bmod q$. The syntax can be extended in the natural way for $\mathsf{SampPre}$ to take a matrix $\mathbf{V}$ as input, in which case $\mathsf{SampPre}$ is run on each column of $\mathbf{V}$ and the output vectors are concatenated column-wise to form a matrix.

For all algorithms we may replace β by $\mathcal{D}$ where it is understood that $\mathcal{D}$ outputs samples bounded by β (with overwhelming probability).

2.3 Hard Problems

The Short Integer Solution problem was introduced in the seminal work of Ajtai [2]. It asks to find a short element (of Euclidean norm β_2) in the kernel of a random matrix mod q. An inhomogeneous version, asking to find a short solution to a linear algebra problem mod q was formalised later [60].

For both problems, it was shown [34] that solving the problem for $q \ge \beta_2 \cdot \omega(\sqrt{n \cdot \log n})$ implies solving certain presumed hard lattice problems (finding a short basis) to within approximation factor $\beta_2 \cdot \tilde{O}(\sqrt{n})$. Thus, since $\beta_2 \ge \beta_\infty$, an appropriate choice of parameters is $n = \mathsf{poly}(\lambda)$, $q \ge \beta_\infty \cdot n \cdot \log n$ and $\ell \gtrsim 2n \log_{\beta_\infty} q$. An algorithm solving ISIS can be used to solve SIS (by making one of the columns of $\mathbf{A}$ the target) and solving ISIS twice allows to solve SIS by considering the difference of these solutions. Ring variants were introduced in [56, 60, 64]; module variants in [51].

Definition 2 (*M*-SIS, adapted from [51]). *Let* $\mathcal{R}, \eta, q, \ell, \beta$ *depend on* λ. *The Module-SIS (or M-SIS) problem, denoted* $M\text{-}SIS_{\mathcal{R}_q, \eta, \ell, \beta^*}$, *is: Given a uniform* $\mathbf{A} \leftarrow_\$ \mathcal{R}_q^{\eta \times \ell}$, $\mathbf{t} \equiv 0 \bmod q$ *find some* $\mathbf{u} \ne \mathbf{0} \in \mathcal{R}^\ell$ *such that* $\|\mathbf{u}\|_\infty \le \beta^*$ *and* $\mathbf{A} \cdot$

$\mathbf{u} \equiv \mathbf{t} \bmod q$. We write $\mathsf{Adv}^{\text{m-sis}}_{\mathcal{R}_q,\eta,\ell,\beta^*}(\lambda)$ for the advantage of any algorithm $\mathcal{A}$ in solving $M\text{-SIS}_{\mathcal{R}_q,\eta,\ell,\beta^*}$. We assume $\mathsf{Adv}^{\text{m-sis}}_{\mathcal{R}_q,\eta,\ell,\beta^*,\mathcal{A}}(\lambda) \leq \mathsf{negl}(\lambda)$ for appropriately chosen $\mathcal{R}_q, \eta, \ell, \beta^*$ and PPT $\mathcal{A}$. When $\mathbf{t} \neq 0$ we speak of the Module-ISIS or M-ISIS problem, denoted $M\text{-ISIS}_{\mathcal{R}_q,\eta,\ell,\beta^*}$. When $\eta = 1$ we speak of Ring-(I)SIS or R-(I)SIS, denoted $R\text{-SIS}_{\mathcal{R}_q,\ell,\beta^*}$ or $R\text{-ISIS}_{\mathcal{R}_q,\ell,\beta^*}$.

In [51] it was shown that solving Module-SIS is as hard as finding a short basis in modules. In [56,64] it was shown that solving Ring-SIS is as hard as find a short vector in any ideal in $\mathcal{R}$. A similar result was established for Ring-ISIS [60]. From a cryptanalytic perspective, no known algorithm solves Ring/Module-(I)SIS significantly faster than those solving (I)SIS. Our assumption is a generalisation and adaptation to more general rings of the k-SIS assumption.

Definition 3 (k-M-SIS, **generalised from** [17,54]). *For any integer $k \geq 0$, an instance of the k-M-SIS$_{\mathcal{R}_q,\eta,\ell,\beta,\beta^*}$ problem is a matrix $\mathbf{A} \in \mathcal{R}_q^{\eta \times \ell}$ and a set of k vectors $\mathbf{u}_0, \ldots \mathbf{u}_{k-1}$ s.t. $\mathbf{A} \cdot \mathbf{u}_i \equiv 0 \bmod q$. A solution to the problem is a nonzero vector $\mathbf{u} \in \mathcal{R}^\ell$ such that*

$$\|\mathbf{u}\|_\infty \leq \beta, \quad \mathbf{A} \cdot \mathbf{u} \equiv 0, \quad and \quad \mathbf{u} \notin \mathcal{K}\text{-span}(\{\mathbf{u}_i\}_{0 \leq i < k}).$$

If $\mathcal{B}$ is an algorithms that takes as input a matrix $\mathbf{A} \in \mathcal{R}_q^{\eta \times \ell}$ and vectors $\mathbf{u}_i \in \mathcal{R}^\ell$ for $0 \leq i < k$, we define $\mathsf{Adv}^{\text{k-m-sis}}_{\mathcal{R}_q,\eta,\ell,\beta,\beta^*,\mathcal{B}}(\lambda)$ to be the probability that $\mathcal{B}$ outputs a solution to the k-M-SIS$_{\mathcal{R}_q,\eta,\ell,\beta,\beta^*}$ problem instance $\mathbf{A}, \mathbf{u}_0, \ldots, \mathbf{u}_{k-1}$ over uniformly random $\mathbf{A} \in \mathcal{R}_q^{\eta \times \ell}$ and $\mathbf{u}_i$ drawn from $\mathsf{SampD}(1^\eta, 1^\ell, \mathcal{R}, \beta)$ conditioned on $\mathbf{A} \cdot \mathbf{u}_i \equiv 0 \bmod q$.

In [17,54] it is shown that if SIS is hard for $\mathbb{Z}_q^{n \times (\ell-k)}$ and norm bound β then k-M-SIS$_{\mathbb{Z}_q,n,\ell,\beta',\beta''}$ is hard for any $k < \ell$, and certain $\beta', \beta'' \in \mathsf{poly}(\beta)$. Looking ahead, here we are interested in k-R-SIS$_{\mathcal{R}_q,\ell,\beta,\beta^*} := k$-$M$-SIS$_{\mathcal{R}_q,1,\ell,\beta,\beta^*}$.

3   The k-M-ISIS Assumption

We first introduce a family of assumptions over modules – k-M-ISIS – which we then specialise to rings to obtain k-R-ISIS mentioned above.

We note that the most immediate candidate notion for k-ISIS, i.e. generalising k-SIS, is to simply hand out short preimages of random images and then ask the adversary to solve ISIS. This notion is trivially equivalent to ISIS since short preimages of random images can be efficiently sampled by sampling short $\mathbf{u} \in \mathbb{Z}^\ell$ and computing $\mathbf{t} := \mathbf{A} \cdot \mathbf{u}$. The same reasoning can be lifted to $\mathcal{R}$. On the other hand, k-SIS is trivially insecure when $k \geq \ell$ in the intuitive sence since then $\{\mathbf{u}_i\}$ constitutes a trapdoor for $\mathbf{A}$ when the $\mathbf{u}_i$ are linearly independent [34]. Formally, the problem as stated is impossible to solve since all vectors will be in $\mathbb{Q}\text{-span}(\{\mathbf{u}_i\}_{0 \leq i < k})$, i.e. there are no valid solutions.

Our variants are neither trivially equivalent to M-ISIS nor immediately broken when $k > \ell$ by imposing on the images an algebraic structure which is independent of the challenge matrix $\mathbf{A}$. Before stating our family of assumptions, we define a notion of admissibility to formally rule out trivial wins.

Definition 4 (k-M-ISIS-**Admissible**). *Let $g(\mathbf{X}) \in \mathcal{R}(\mathbf{X})$ be a Laurent monomial, i.e. $g(\mathbf{X}) = \mathbf{X}^{\mathbf{e}} := \prod_{i \in \mathbb{Z}_w} X_i^{e_i}$ for some exponent vector $\mathbf{e} = (e_i : i \in \mathbb{Z}_w) \in \mathbb{Z}^w$. Let $\mathcal{G} \subset \mathcal{R}(\mathbf{X})$ be a set of Laurent monomials with $k := |\mathcal{G}|$ and let $\mathbf{\mathcal{G}}$ be a vector of those monomials. Let $g^* \in \mathcal{R}(\mathbf{X})$ be a target Laurent monomial. We call a family $\mathcal{G}$ k-M-ISIS-admissible if (i) all $g \in \mathcal{G}$ have constant degree, i.e. $\|\mathbf{e}\|_1 \in O(1)$; (ii) all $g \in \mathcal{G}$ are distinct, i.e. $\mathcal{G}$ is not a multiset; and (iii) $0 \notin \mathcal{G}$. We call a family $(\mathcal{G}, g^*)$ k-M-ISIS-admissible if $\mathcal{G}$ is k-M-ISIS-admissible, g^* has constant degree, and $g^* \notin \mathcal{G}$.*

Remark 1. Condition (i) rules out monomials that depend on the ring $\mathcal{R}$, such as $X^{\phi(m)}$. Condition (ii) rules out that trivial linear combinations of known preimages produce a preimage for the target. Condition (iii) rules out trivially producing multiple preimages of the same image. On the other hand, we do not target full generality here but restrict ourselves to a slight generalisation of what we require in this work. It is plausible that we can replace Laurent monomials by Laurent "terms", i.e. with coefficients $\neq 1$ in $\mathcal{R}_q$, or rational functions.

Definition 5 (k-M-ISIS **Assumptions**). *Let $\ell, \eta \in \mathbb{N}$. Let q be a rational prime, $\mathcal{R}$ the m-th cyclotomic ring, and $\mathcal{R}_q := \mathcal{R}/q\mathcal{R}$. Let $\mathcal{T} \subset \mathcal{R}_q^\eta$ be such that, for any $\mathbf{t} = (t_i)_{i \in \mathbb{Z}_\eta} \in \mathcal{T}$, $\langle\{t_i\}\rangle = \mathcal{R}_q$. Let $\mathcal{G} \subset \mathcal{R}(\mathbf{X})$ be a set of w-variate Laurent monomial. Let $g^* \in \mathcal{R}(\mathbf{X})$ be a target Laurent monomial. Let $(\mathcal{G}, g^*)$ be k-M-ISIS-admissible. Let $\bar{\mathcal{G}} := \mathcal{G} \cup \{g^*\}$. Let $\beta \geq 1$ and $\beta^* > 1$ be reals. For $\eta, \ell \in \mathbb{N}$, $g \in \bar{\mathcal{G}}$, $\ell \geq \mathsf{lhl}(\mathcal{R}, \eta, q, \beta)$, $\mathbf{A} \in \mathcal{R}_q^{\eta \times \ell}$, $\mathbf{t} \in \mathcal{T}$, and $\mathbf{v} \in (\mathcal{R}_q^\times)^w$, let $\mathcal{D}_{g,\mathbf{A},\mathbf{t},\mathbf{v}}$ be a distribution over*

$$\{\mathbf{u}_g \in \mathcal{R}^\ell : \mathbf{A} \cdot \mathbf{u}_g \equiv g(\mathbf{v}) \cdot \mathbf{t} \bmod q, \|\mathbf{u}_g\| \leq \beta\}.$$

Let $\mathcal{D} := \{\mathcal{D}_{g,\mathbf{A},\mathbf{t},\mathbf{v}} : \eta, \ell \in \mathbb{N}, g \in \bar{\mathcal{G}}, \mathbf{A} \in \mathcal{R}_q^{\eta \times \ell}, \mathbf{v} \in (\mathcal{R}_q^\times)^w\}$ be the family of these distributions. Write $\mathsf{pp} := (\mathcal{R}_q, \eta, \ell, w, \mathcal{G}, g^*, \mathcal{D}, \mathcal{T}, \beta, \beta^*)$. The k-M-ISIS$_{\mathsf{pp}}$ assumption states that for any PPT adversary $\mathcal{A}$ we have $\mathsf{Adv}_{\mathsf{pp},\mathcal{A}}^{k\text{-}r\text{-}isis}(\lambda) \leq \mathsf{negl}(\lambda)$, where

$$\mathsf{Adv}_{\mathsf{pp},\mathcal{A}}^{k\text{-}m\text{-}isis}(\lambda) := \Pr\left[\begin{array}{c} \mathbf{A} \cdot \mathbf{u}_{g^*} \equiv s^* \cdot g^*(\mathbf{v}) \cdot \mathbf{t} \\ \wedge\ 0 < \|s^*\| \leq \beta^* \\ \wedge\ \|\mathbf{u}_{g^*}\| \leq \beta^* \\ \wedge\ (g^*, \mathbf{u}_{g^*}) \neq (0, \mathbf{0}) \end{array} \middle| \begin{array}{l} \mathbf{A} \leftarrow_\$ \mathcal{R}_q^{\eta \times \ell} \bmod q \\ \mathbf{t} \leftarrow_\$ \mathcal{T};\ \mathbf{v} \leftarrow_\$ (\mathcal{R}_q^\times)^w \\ \mathbf{u}_g \leftarrow_\$ \mathcal{D}_{g,\mathbf{A},\mathbf{t},\mathbf{v}},\ \forall\ g \in \mathcal{G} \\ (s^*, \mathbf{u}_{g^*}) \leftarrow \mathcal{A}(\mathbf{A}, \mathbf{t}, \{\mathbf{u}_{\mathcal{G}}\}, \mathbf{v}) \end{array} \right].$$

Remark 2. Since for any $\mathbf{t}' \in \mathcal{T}$ there exist matrices $\mathbf{X}, \mathbf{Y}$ s.t. $\mathbf{X} \cdot \mathbf{Y} \equiv \mathbf{I}$, $\mathbf{X} \cdot \mathbf{t}' \equiv (1, 0, \ldots, 0)^{\mathsf{T}} \bmod q$ and $\mathbf{Y} \cdot (1, 0, \ldots, 0)^{\mathsf{T}} \equiv \mathbf{t}' \bmod q$, we can assume that $\mathcal{T} = \{(1, 0, \ldots, 0)^{\mathsf{T}}\}$ without loss of generality.

Definition 6 (k-R-ISIS). *When $\eta = 1$ we may write*

$$k\text{-}R\text{-}\mathsf{ISIS}_{\mathcal{R}_q, \ell, w, \mathcal{G}, g^*, \mathcal{D}, \mathcal{T}, \beta, \beta^*} := k\text{-}M\text{-}\mathsf{ISIS}_{\mathcal{R}_q, 1, \ell, w, \mathcal{G}, g^*, \mathcal{D}, \mathcal{T}, \beta, \beta^*}.$$

Remark 3. Analogous to the ℓ-Diffie-Hellman exponent assumption, an example of $(w, \mathcal{G}, g^*)$ is $w = 1$, $\mathcal{G} = \{1, X, \ldots, X^\ell, X^{\ell+2}, \ldots, X^{2\ell}\}$, and $g^*(X) = X^{\ell+1}$ for some $\ell \in \mathbb{N}$.

As written above we have a separate assumption for each family of $(\mathcal{G}, g^*)$ which are application dependent. As we will show below, there are $(\mathcal{G}, g^*)$ that are as hard as M-ISIS and our discussion of admissibility indicates that some $(\mathcal{G}, g^*)$ are trivially insecure. However, to encourage analysis and to avoid "bodacious assumptions" [46] we make the following, strong, meta assumption.

Definition 7 (k-M-ISIS Meta Assumption). *For any k-M-ISIS-admissible $(\mathcal{G}, g^*)$, k-M-ISIS$_{pp}$ is hard.*

3.1 Knowledge Variants

We next propose a "knowledge" version of the k-M-ISIS assumption. It captures the intuition that if the images are restricted to scalar multiples of $\mathbf{t}$ then the only way to produce preimages of them under $\mathbf{A}$ is to perform a linear combination of the given preimages under $\mathbf{A}$ with small coefficients.

Definition 8 (Knowledge k-M-ISIS Assumption). *Adopt the notation from Definition 5, but let* $\text{pp} := (\mathcal{R}_q, \eta, \ell, w, \mathcal{G}, \mathcal{D}, \mathcal{T}, \alpha, \beta, \beta^*)$ *where $\alpha \geq 1$ is real and $\eta > 1$. The knowledge k-M-ISIS$_{pp}$ assumption states that for any PPT adversary $\mathcal{A}$ there exists a PPT extractor $\mathcal{E}_{\mathcal{A}}$ such that* $\text{Adv}_{pp,\mathcal{A}}^{k\text{-m-isis}}(\lambda) \leq \text{negl}(\lambda)$, *where*

$$\text{Adv}_{pp,\mathcal{A}}^{k\text{-m-isis}}(\lambda) := \Pr\left[\begin{array}{c|c} \begin{array}{c} \mathbf{A} \cdot \mathbf{u} \equiv c \cdot \mathbf{t} \bmod q \\ \wedge \ \|\mathbf{u}\| \leq \beta^* \\ \wedge \ \neg \left(\begin{array}{c} c \equiv \sum_{g \in \mathcal{G}} x_g \cdot g(\mathbf{v}) \\ \wedge \ \|(x_g)_{g \in \mathcal{G}}\| \leq \alpha \end{array}\right) \end{array} & \begin{array}{c} \mathbf{A} \leftarrow_{\$} \mathcal{R}_q^{\eta \times \ell} \\ \mathbf{t} \leftarrow_{\$} \mathcal{T}; \ \mathbf{v} \leftarrow_{\$} (\mathcal{R}_q^{\times})^w \\ \mathbf{u}_g \leftarrow_{\$} \mathcal{D}_{g,\mathbf{A},\mathbf{t},\mathbf{v}}, \ \forall \ g \in \mathcal{G} \\ \left((c,\mathbf{u}), (x_g)_{g \in \mathcal{G}}\right) \\ \leftarrow (\mathcal{A}\|\mathcal{E}_{\mathcal{A}})(\mathbf{A}, \mathbf{t}, \{\mathbf{u}_{\mathcal{G}}\}, \mathbf{v}) \end{array} \end{array}\right]$$

where the notation $(\mathcal{A}\|\mathcal{E}_{\mathcal{A}})$ means that $\mathcal{A}$ and $\mathcal{E}_{\mathcal{A}}$ are run on the same input including the randomness, and $(c, \mathbf{u})$ and $(x_g)_{g \in \mathcal{G}}$ are the outputs of $\mathcal{A}$ and $\mathcal{E}_{\mathcal{A}}$ respectively.

The knowledge k-M-ISIS assumption, as stated, only makes sense for $\eta \geq 2$, i.e. not for k-R-ISIS. To see this, consider an adversary $\mathcal{A}$ which does the following: First, it samples random short $\mathbf{u}$ and checks whether $\mathbf{A} \cdot \mathbf{u}$ is in the submodule of $\mathcal{R}_q^\eta$ generated by $\mathbf{t}$. If not, $\mathcal{A}$ aborts. If so, it finds c such that $\mathbf{A} \cdot \mathbf{u} = c \cdot \mathbf{t} \bmod q$ and outputs $(c, \mathbf{u})$. When $\eta = 1$ and assuming without loss of generality that $\mathcal{T} = \{(1, 0, \ldots, 0)^\intercal\}$, we observe that $t = 1$ generates $\mathcal{R}_q$, which means $\mathcal{A}$ never aborts. Clearly, when $\mathcal{A}$ does not abort, it has no "knowledge" of how c can be expressed as a linear combination of $\{g(\mathbf{v})\}_{g \in \mathcal{G}}$. Note that when $\eta \geq 2$ the adversary $\mathcal{A}$ aborts with overwhelming probability since $\mathbf{A} \cdot \mathbf{u}$ is close to uniform over $\mathcal{R}_q^\eta$ but the submodule generated by $\mathbf{t}$ is only a negligible faction of $\mathcal{R}_q^\eta$. However, in order to be able to pun about "crises of knowledge", we also define a ring version of the knowledge assumption. In the ring setting, we consider proper ideals rather than submodules.

Definition 9 (Knowledge k-R-ISIS Assumption). *Let the parameters* pp *be as in Definition 5 except that $\eta = 1$ and $\mathcal{T}$ contains elements $t \in \mathcal{R}_q$ s.t. $1/|\langle t \rangle| = \mathsf{negl}(\lambda)$ and $|\langle t \rangle|/|\mathcal{R}_q| = \mathsf{negl}(\lambda)$.[7] The knowledge k-R-ISIS$_{\mathsf{pp}}$ assumption states that for any PPT adversary $\mathcal{A}$ there exists a PPT extractor $\mathcal{E}_{\mathcal{A}}$ such that $\mathsf{Adv}_{\mathsf{pp},\mathcal{A}}^{\text{k-r-isis}}(\lambda) \leq \mathsf{negl}(\lambda)$, where*

$$\mathsf{Adv}_{\mathsf{pp},\mathcal{A}}^{\text{k-r-isis}}(\lambda) := \Pr\left[\begin{array}{c} \langle \mathbf{a}, \mathbf{u} \rangle \equiv c \cdot t \bmod q \\ \wedge \; \|\mathbf{u}\| \leq \beta^* \\ \wedge \; \neg \left(\begin{array}{c} c \equiv \sum_{g \in \mathcal{G}} x_g \cdot g(\mathbf{v}) \\ \wedge \; \|(x_g)_{g \in \mathcal{G}}\| \leq \alpha \end{array} \right) \end{array} \middle| \begin{array}{c} \mathbf{a} \leftarrow_{\$} \mathcal{R}_q^{\ell} \\ t \leftarrow_{\$} \mathcal{T}; \; \mathbf{v} \leftarrow_{\$} (\mathcal{R}_q^{\times})^w \\ \mathbf{u}_g \leftarrow_{\$} \mathcal{D}_{g,\mathbf{a},t,\mathbf{v}}, \; \forall \, g \in \mathcal{G} \\ \left((c, \mathbf{u}), (x_g)_{g \in \mathcal{G}} \right) \\ \leftarrow (\mathcal{A} \| \mathcal{E}_{\mathcal{A}}) \, (\mathbf{a}, t, \{\mathbf{u}_{\mathcal{G}}\}, \mathbf{v}) \end{array} \right].$$

Definition 10 (k-M-ISIS Meta Knowledge Assumption). *For any k-M-ISIS-admissible $\mathcal{G}$, the knowledge k-M-ISIS$_{\mathsf{pp}}$ assumption holds.*

We provide reductions for some parameter regimes and some preliminary cryptanalysis of our assumption in the full version of this work.

4   Compact Extractable Vector Commitments

We construct compact extractable vector commitments with openings to constant-degree multivariate polynomial maps from the knowledge k-M-ISIS assumption.

4.1   Definitions

We define a non-interactive variant of vector commitments with preprocessing.

Definition 11 (Vector Commitments (VC)). *A (preprocessing non-interactive) vector commitment (VC) scheme is parameterised by the families*

$$\mathcal{F} = \{\mathcal{F}_{s,w,t} \subseteq \{f : \mathcal{R}^s \times \mathcal{R}^w \to \mathcal{R}^t\}\}_{s,w,t \in \mathbb{N}} \; and$$
$$\mathcal{Y} = \{\mathcal{Y}_{s,t} \subseteq \{y : \mathcal{R}^s \to \mathcal{R}^t\}\}_{s,t \in \mathbb{N}}$$

of functions over $\mathcal{R}$ and an input alphabet $\mathcal{X} \subseteq \mathcal{R}$. The parameters $s, w,$ and t are the dimensions of public inputs, secret inputs, and outputs of f respectively. The VC scheme consists of the PPT algorithms (Setup, Com, Open, PreVerify, Verify) *defined as follows.*

- pp $\leftarrow$ Setup$(1^\lambda, 1^s, 1^w, 1^t)$: *The setup algorithm generates the public parameters on input the security parameter $\lambda \in \mathbb{N}$ and the size parameters $s, w, t \in \mathbb{N}$.*

---

[7] Concretely, let $\mathcal{T}$ be the set of all $\mathcal{R}_q$ elements t where half of the components of t in the Chinese remainder theorem (CRT) representation are zero and the other half are non-zero. Note that this is well-defined only when $\langle q \rangle$ is not a prime ideal in $\mathcal{R}$.

- $(c, \mathsf{aux}) \leftarrow \mathsf{Com}(\mathsf{pp}, \mathbf{x})$: *The commitment algorithm generates a commitment c of a given vector $\mathbf{x} \in \mathcal{X}^w$ with some auxiliary opening information aux.*
- $\pi \leftarrow \mathsf{Open}(\mathsf{pp}, f, \mathbf{z}, \mathsf{aux})$: *The opening algorithm generates a proof π for $f(\mathbf{z}, \cdot)$ for the public input $\mathbf{z} \in \mathcal{X}^s$ and function $f \in \mathcal{F}_{s,w,t}$.*
- $\mathsf{pp}_{f,y} \leftarrow \mathsf{PreVerify}(\mathsf{pp}, (f, y))$: *Given functions $f \in \mathcal{F}_{s,w,t}$ and $y \in \mathcal{Y}_{s,t}$, the verification preprocessing algorithm generates the preprocessed public parameters $\mathsf{pp}_{f,y}$ for verifying proofs for (f, y).*
- $b \leftarrow \mathsf{Verify}(\mathsf{pp}_{f,y}, \mathbf{z}, c, \pi)$: *The verification algorithm inputs a preprocessed public parameters $\mathsf{pp}_{f,y}$, a public input $\mathbf{z} \in \mathcal{X}^s$, a commitment c, and an opening proof π. It outputs a bit b deciding whether to accept or reject that the vector $\mathbf{x}$ committed in c satisfies $f(\mathbf{z}, \mathbf{x}) = y(\mathbf{z})$.*

Definition 12 (Correctness). *A VC scheme for $(\mathcal{F}, \mathcal{X}, \mathcal{Y})$ is said to be correct if for any $\lambda, s, w, t \in \mathbb{N}$, any $\mathsf{pp} \in \mathsf{Setup}(1^\lambda, 1^s, 1^w, 1^t)$, any $(f, \mathbf{z}, \mathbf{x}, y) \in \mathcal{F}_{s,w,t} \times \mathcal{X}^s \times \mathcal{X}^w \times \mathcal{Y}_{s,t}$ satisfying $f(\mathbf{z}, \mathbf{x}) = y(\mathbf{z})$, any $(c, \mathsf{aux}) \in, (\mathsf{pp}, \mathbf{x})$, any $\pi \in \mathsf{Open}(\mathsf{pp}, f, \mathbf{z}, \mathsf{aux})$, and any $\mathsf{pp}_{f,y} \in \mathsf{PreVerify}(\mathsf{pp}, (f, y))$, it holds that $\mathsf{Verify}(\mathsf{pp}_{f,y}, \mathbf{z}, c, \pi) = 1$.*

Informally, a VC scheme is extractable if, whenever an adversary $\mathcal{A}$ is able to produce a commitment c and a valid opening proof π for some $(f(\mathbf{z}, \cdot), y(\mathbf{z}))$, then it must "know" a preimage $\mathbf{x}$ which is committed in c and satisfies $f(\mathbf{z}, \mathbf{x}) = y(\mathbf{z})$. Clearly, an extractable VC must also be binding, i.e. it is infeasible to open a commitment c to a set $\{(f_i(\mathbf{z}_i, \cdot), y_i(\mathbf{z}_i))\}_i$ of inconsistent function-image tuples.

Definition 13 (Extractability). *Let $\kappa : \mathbb{N}^4 \to [0, 1]$. A VC scheme for $(\mathcal{F}, \mathcal{X}, \mathcal{Y})$ is said to be κ-extractable if for any PPT adversary $\mathcal{A}$ there exists a PPT extractor $\mathcal{E}_\mathcal{A}$ such that the following probability is at most $\kappa(\lambda, s, w, t)$:*

$$\Pr\left[\begin{array}{l} (\mathsf{Verify}(\mathsf{pp}_{f,y}, \mathbf{z}, c, \pi) = 1) \\ \wedge \; ((f, \mathbf{z}, \mathbf{x}, y) \notin \mathcal{F}_{s,w,t} \times \mathcal{X}^s \times \mathcal{X}^w \times \mathcal{Y}_{s,t} \\ \vee \; c' \neq c \vee f(\mathbf{z}, \mathbf{x}) \neq y(\mathbf{z})) \end{array} \middle| \begin{array}{l} \mathsf{pp} \leftarrow \mathsf{Setup}(1^\lambda, 1^s, 1^w, 1^t) \\ (f, y, \mathbf{z}, c, \pi) \leftarrow \mathcal{A}(\mathsf{pp}; r_\mathcal{A}) \\ (\mathbf{x}, r) \leftarrow \mathcal{E}_\mathcal{A}(\mathsf{pp}; r_\mathcal{A}) \\ (c', \mathsf{aux}') \leftarrow \mathsf{Com}(\mathsf{pp}, \mathbf{x}; r) \\ \mathsf{pp}_{f,y} \leftarrow \mathsf{PreVerify}(\mathsf{pp}, (f, y)) \end{array}\right].$$

In case Com is deterministic, we suppress the output r of $\mathcal{E}_\mathcal{A}$. We say that the scheme is extractable if it is κ-extractable and $\kappa(\lambda, s, w, t)$ is negligible in λ for any $s, w, t \in \mathsf{poly}(\lambda)$.

Definition 14 (Compactness). *A VC scheme for $(\mathcal{F}, \mathcal{X}, \mathcal{Y})$ is said to be compact if there exists $p(\lambda, s, w, t) \in \mathsf{poly}(\lambda, \log s, \log w, \log t)$ such that for any $\lambda, s, w, t \in \mathbb{N}$, any $\mathsf{pp} \in \mathsf{Setup}(1^\lambda, 1^s, 1^w, 1^t)$, any $(f, \mathbf{z}, \mathbf{x}, y) \in \mathcal{F}_{s,w,t} \times \mathcal{X}^s \times \mathcal{X}^w \times \mathcal{Y}_{s,t}$, any $(c, \mathsf{aux}) \in \mathsf{Com}(\mathsf{pp}, \mathbf{x})$, and any $\pi \in \mathsf{Open}(\mathsf{pp}, f, \mathbf{z}, \mathsf{aux})$, it holds that $\max\{|c|, |\pi|\} \leq p(\lambda, s, w, t)$, where $|\cdot|$ denotes the description size.*

4.2 Construction

A formal description of our VC construction is in Fig. 1 where important parameters and shorthands are listed and explained in Table 1.

Table 1. Parameters and shorthands with λ as security parameter.

$s \in \mathbb{N}$		Dimension of public input $\mathbf{z}$
$w \in \mathbb{N}$		Dimension of $\mathbf{v}$ and secret input $\mathbf{x}$
$t \in \mathbb{N}$		Number of outputs
$d \in \mathbb{N}$	$O(1)$	Degree of polynomial maps
$n \in \mathbb{N}$	$\mathrm{poly}(\lambda)$	Degree of $\mathcal{R}$
$\alpha \in \mathbb{R}$	$\mathrm{poly}(\lambda)$	Norm bound for f and $\mathbf{x}$
$\beta \in \mathbb{R}$	$\mathrm{poly}(\lambda)$	Norm bound for public preimages
$\delta_i \in \mathbb{R}$	$\mathrm{poly}(\lambda, s, w, t)$ (Theorem 1)	Norm bound for opening proof $\mathbf{u}_i$
$\delta_p \in \mathbb{R}$	$(s + w + d)^d \, \alpha^{d+1} \, \gamma^d \, n$	Norm bound of evaluation of a degree-d $(s + w)$-variate polynomial with coefficients of norm bounded by α at a point of norm bounded by α
$p \in \mathbb{N}$	$\geq \delta_p \, n \log n$	Moduli for $\mathcal{R}_p$
$q \in \mathbb{N}$	$\geq \max\{\delta_0, \delta_1\} \cdot n \log n$	Moduli for $\mathcal{R}_q$
$\eta_i \in \mathbb{N}$	$O(1)$	Number of rows of $\mathbf{A}_i$
$\ell_i \in \mathbb{N}$	$\geq \mathsf{lhl}(\mathcal{R}, \eta_i, q, \beta)$	Number of columns of $\mathbf{A}_i$
$\mathcal{X} \subseteq \mathcal{R}$	$\{x \in \mathcal{R} : \|x\| \leq \alpha\}$	$\mathcal{R}$ elements with norm bound α
$\mathcal{F}_{s,w,t}$		Degree-d $(s + w)$-variate t-output homogeneous polynomial maps over $\mathcal{X}$
$\mathcal{Y}_{s,t}$		s-variate t-output polynomial maps over $\mathcal{X}$
$\mathcal{E}_k \subseteq \mathbb{N}_0^w$	$\{\mathbf{e} \in \mathbb{N}_0^w : \|\mathbf{e}\|_1 = k\}$	Non-negative integer vectors of 1-norm k, for $k \in [d]$
$\mathcal{G}_0 \subseteq \mathcal{R}(\mathbf{X})$	$\bigcup_{k=1}^d \{\mathbf{X}^{\mathbf{e}'-\mathbf{e}} : \mathbf{e}' \neq \mathbf{e} \in \mathcal{E}_k\}$	Laurent monomials expressible as ratios of distinct degree-k monomials, for $k \in [d]$
$\mathcal{G}_1 \subseteq \mathcal{R}(\mathbf{X})$	$\{X_i : i \in \mathbb{Z}_w\}$	Degree-1 monomials
$\binom{k}{\mathbf{e}}$	$\binom{k}{e_0, \ldots, e_{w-1}}$	Multinomial coefficient, for $\mathbf{e} \in \mathcal{E}_k$ and $k \in [d]$
$\mathcal{T}_i$		Subset of $\mathcal{R}_q^{\eta_i}$ (Definition 5)
$f_{i,\mathbf{e}}$		For $f(\mathbf{Z}, \mathbf{X}) \in \mathcal{F}_{s,w,t}$, $f_{i,\mathbf{e}}(\mathbf{Z})$ is the coefficient of the monomial $\mathbf{X}^{\mathbf{e}}$ of the i-th output

The public parameters consists of a k-M-ISIS instance $(\mathbf{A}_0, \mathbf{t}_0, \mathbf{v}, (\mathbf{u}_{0,g})_{g \in \mathcal{G}_0})$ over $\mathcal{R}_q$, a correlated k-M-ISIS of knowledge instance $(\mathbf{A}_1, \mathbf{t}_1, \mathbf{v}, (\mathbf{u}_{1,g})_{g \in \mathcal{G}_1})$ over $\mathcal{R}_q$ sharing the same $\mathbf{v}$ as the k-M-ISIS instance, and a R-SIS instance $\mathbf{h}$ over $\mathcal{R}_p$, where p is short relative to q. Intuitively, the k-M-ISIS instance is for weak binding, the knowledge k-M-ISIS instance is for upgrading weak binding to extractability, and the R-SIS instance is for compactness. The commitment c to a vector $\mathbf{x}$ is simply $c := \langle \mathbf{v}, \mathbf{x} \rangle \bmod q$.

We next explain the opening and verification mechanism. Suppose for the moment that $f(\mathbf{z}, \cdot)$ is a single-output polynomial, i.e. $t = 1$. Consider the commitment c of $\mathbf{x}$ and the evaluation of $f(\mathbf{z}, \cdot)$ at $(v_0^{-1} \cdot c, \ldots, v_w^{-1} \cdot c)$ as polynomials in $\mathbf{v}$. The value $f(\mathbf{z}, \mathbf{x})$ is encoded as the constant term in the evaluation polynomial. To open the commitment c of $\mathbf{x}$ to a function $f(\mathbf{z}, \cdot)$, the committer computes the coefficient of each non-zero Laurent monomial $g \in \mathcal{G}_0$ in the evaluation polynomial, and use these coefficients to compute a linear combination

$\mathsf{Setup}(1^\lambda, 1^s, 1^w, 1^t)$

$\mathbf{v} \leftarrow\!\!\$ \, (\mathcal{R}_q^\times)^w$

$\mathbf{h} \leftarrow\!\!\$ \, \mathcal{R}_p^t$

for $i \in \{0,1\}$ **do**

$\quad (\mathbf{A}_i, \mathsf{td}_i) \leftarrow \mathsf{TrapGen}(1^{n_i}, 1^{\ell_i}, q, \mathcal{R}, \beta)$

$\quad \mathbf{t}_i \leftarrow\!\!\$ \, \mathcal{T}_i$

$\quad \mathbf{u}_{i,g} \leftarrow \mathsf{SampPre}(\mathsf{td}_i, g(\mathbf{v}) \cdot \mathbf{t}_i, \beta), \; \forall g \in \mathcal{G}_i$

$\mathbf{return} \; \mathsf{pp} := \begin{pmatrix} \mathbf{A}_0, \mathbf{t}_0, (\mathbf{u}_{0,g})_{g \in \mathcal{G}_0}, \\ \mathbf{A}_1, \mathbf{t}_1, (\mathbf{u}_{1,g})_{g \in \mathcal{G}_1}, \\ \mathbf{v}, \qquad \mathbf{h} \end{pmatrix}$

$\mathsf{Com}(\mathsf{pp}, \mathbf{x})$

$c := \langle \mathbf{v}, \mathbf{x} \rangle \bmod q; \quad \mathbf{u}_1 := \sum_{X_i \in \mathcal{G}_1} x_i \cdot \mathbf{u}_{1,X_i}$

$\mathbf{for} \; e \in \bigcup_{k \in [d]} \mathcal{E}_k \; \mathbf{do} \quad \mathbf{u}_{0,e} := d! \cdot \sum_{e' \in \mathcal{E}_k \setminus \{e\}} \frac{\binom{k}{e'}}{\binom{k}{e}} \cdot \mathbf{x}^{e'} \cdot \mathbf{u}_{0,\mathbf{x}^{e'-e}}$

$\mathsf{aux} := \left((\mathbf{u}_{0,e})_{e \in \bigcup_{k \in [d]} \mathcal{E}_k}, \mathbf{u}_1 \right)$

$\mathbf{return} \; (c, \mathsf{aux})$

$\mathsf{PreVerify}(\mathsf{pp}, (f, y))$

if $(f, y) \notin \mathcal{F}_{s,w,t} \times \mathcal{Y}_{s,t}$ **then return** $\perp$

$\hat{f}_y(\mathbf{Z}, C) := d! \cdot \left(\sum_{i \in \mathbb{Z}_t} h_i \cdot \left(\sum_{k=1}^d \sum_{e \in \mathcal{E}_k} \binom{k}{e}^{-1} \cdot f_{i,e}(\mathbf{Z}) \cdot \mathbf{v}^{-e} \cdot C^k - y_i(\mathbf{Z}) \right) \right)$

$\mathsf{pp}_{f,y} := (\mathbf{A}_0, \mathbf{t}_0, \mathbf{A}_1, \mathbf{t}_1, \hat{f}_y)$

$\mathbf{return} \; \mathsf{pp}_{f,y}$

$\mathsf{Open}(\mathsf{pp}, f, \mathbf{z}, \mathsf{aux})$

$\mathbf{u}_0 := \sum_{i \in \mathbb{Z}_t} \sum_{k=1}^d \sum_{e \in \mathcal{E}_k} h_i \cdot f_{i,e}(\mathbf{z}) \cdot \mathbf{u}_{0,e}$

$\mathbf{return} \; \pi := (\mathbf{u}_0, \mathbf{u}_1)$

$\mathsf{Verify}(\mathsf{pp}_{f,y}, \mathbf{z}, c, \pi)$

$b_0 := \left(\mathbf{A}_0 \cdot \mathbf{u}_0 \stackrel{?}{\equiv} \hat{f}_y(\mathbf{z}, c) \cdot \mathbf{t}_0 \bmod q \right)$

$b_1 := \left(\mathbf{A}_1 \cdot \mathbf{u}_1 \stackrel{?}{\equiv} c \cdot \mathbf{t}_1 \bmod q \right)$

$b_2 := \left(\|\mathbf{u}_0\| \stackrel{?}{\leq} \delta_0 \right); b_3 := \left(\|\mathbf{u}_1\| \stackrel{?}{\leq} \delta_1 \right)$

$\mathbf{return} \; b_0 \wedge b_1 \wedge b_2 \wedge b_3$

Fig. 1. Our VC Construction.

of $(\mathbf{u}_{0,g})_{g \in \mathcal{G}_0}$ to produce $\mathbf{u}_0$. In general, for $t \geq 1$, the committer further compresses the multiple instances of $\mathbf{u}_0$ into a single one using a linear combination with coefficients given by $\mathbf{h}$. To enable extraction (in the security proof), the committer also provides $\mathbf{u}_1$ which is a linear combination of $(\mathbf{u}_{1,g})_{g \in \mathcal{G}_1}$ using $\mathbf{x}$ as coefficients. Given the above, the meaning behind the verification algorithm is immediate.

Finally, we explain the choice of p and q in Table 1. First, p is chosen such that the element $f(\mathbf{z}, \mathbf{x}) - y(\mathbf{z})$ is considered short (in the context of R-SIS problems) relative to p for all $f \in \mathcal{F}_{s,w,t}$, $y \in \mathcal{Y}_{s,t}$, $\mathbf{z} \in \mathcal{X}^s$, and $\mathbf{x} \in \mathcal{X}^w$. By some routine calculations, we can see that for such choice of $(f, \mathbf{z}, \mathbf{x}, y)$, we have $\|f(\mathbf{z}, \mathbf{x}) - y(\mathbf{z})\| \le (s + w + d)^d \cdot \alpha^{d+1} \cdot \gamma_{\mathcal{R}}^d$. A standard choice for R-SIS problems over $\mathcal{R}_p$ is for p to be at least $n \log n$ times the norm bound; we thus simply pick this. Similarly, q is chosen such that δ_0 and δ_1 are both considered short relative to q, concretely by setting q to be $n \log n$ times the maximum among them.[8]

Remark 4 (Updating Commitments and Opening Proofs). We discuss the cost of updating a commitment of $\mathbf{x}$ to that of $\mathbf{x}'$, and an opening proof for $f(\mathbf{z}, \mathbf{x})$ to that of $f'(\mathbf{z}', \mathbf{x}')$, omitting fixed $\mathsf{poly}(\lambda)$ factors. Due to the linearity of the commitment $c = \langle \mathbf{v}, \mathbf{x} \rangle \bmod q$ and opening proof component $\mathbf{u}_1 = \sum_{i \in \mathbb{Z}_w} x_i \cdot \mathbf{u}_{1,X_i}$ in the committed vector $\mathbf{x}$, they can be updated for a new committed vector $\mathbf{x}'$ easily by adding $\langle \mathbf{v}, \mathbf{x}' - \mathbf{x} \rangle \bmod q$ and $\sum_{i \in \mathbb{Z}_w} (x_i' - x_i) \cdot \mathbf{u}_{1,X_i}$ respectively. The computation complexity of the update is $O(\Delta)$, where Δ is the Hamming distance between $\mathbf{x}$ and $\mathbf{x}'$. Updating the $\mathbf{u}_{0,\mathbf{e}}$ terms is more computationally expensive due to its non-linearity in $\mathbf{x}$. The cost of computing the difference term for $\mathbf{u}_{0,\mathbf{e}}$ is linear in $\binom{w}{k} - \binom{w-\Delta}{k} = O(\Delta^k)$ for each $\mathbf{e} \in \mathcal{E}_k$ and each $k \in [d]$. The total work needed for updating $\{\mathbf{u}_{0,\mathbf{e}}\}_{\mathbf{e} \in \mathcal{E}_k, k \in [d]}$ is thus $O(w^d \cdot \Delta^d)$. For fixed $\mathbf{x}$ and hence fixed $\{\mathbf{u}_{0,\mathbf{e}}\}_{\mathbf{e} \in \mathcal{E}_k, k \in [d]}$, updating $\mathbf{u}_0$ by the same method costs computation linear in the Hamming distance between the coefficient vector of $f(\mathbf{z}, \cdot)$ and that of $f'(\mathbf{z}', \cdot)$.

We show that our VC construction is correct, extractable under a knowledge k-M-ISIS assumption, and compact. The formal analysis of the theorems are deferred to the full version.

Theorem 1. *For $d = O(1)$, $\ell_0 := \ell_1 := \mathsf{lhl}(\mathcal{R}, \eta, q, \beta)$,*

$$\delta_0 = 2 \cdot p \cdot t \cdot (s + d)^d \cdot (w + d)^{2d} \cdot \alpha^{2d+1} \cdot \beta \cdot \gamma_{\mathcal{R}}^{2d+2} \quad and \quad \delta_1 = w \cdot \alpha \cdot \beta \cdot \gamma_{\mathcal{R}},$$

our VC construction in Fig. 1 is correct.

Theorem 2. *Our VC construction for $(\mathcal{F}, \mathcal{X}, \mathcal{Y})$ is extractable if it is correct, $\beta \ge \alpha$, $\ell_i \ge \mathsf{lhl}(\mathcal{R}, \eta_i, q, \beta)$ for $i \in \{0, 1\}$, and the k-M-$\mathsf{ISIS}_{\mathcal{R}_q, \eta_0, \ell_0, w, \mathcal{G}_0, 1, \mathcal{D}_0, \mathcal{T}_0, \beta, 2\delta_0}$ assumption, the knowledge version k-M-$\mathsf{ISIS}_{\mathcal{R}_q, \eta_1, \ell_1, w, \mathcal{G}_1, \mathcal{D}_1, \mathcal{T}_1, \alpha, \beta, \delta_1}$ assumption, and the R-$\mathsf{SIS}_{\mathcal{R}_p, t, 2\delta_p}$ assumption hold, where $\mathcal{D}_i$ is such that the distribution*

$$\left\{ (\mathbf{A}_i, \mathbf{t}_i, \{\mathbf{u}_{\mathcal{G}_i}\}, \mathbf{v}) \,\middle|\, \begin{array}{l} \mathbf{A}_i \leftarrow_{\$} \mathcal{R}_q^{\eta_i \times \ell_i}; \ \mathbf{t}_i \leftarrow_{\$} \mathcal{T}_i; \ \mathbf{v} \leftarrow_{\$} (\mathcal{R}_q^{\times})^w \\ \mathbf{u}_g \leftarrow_{\$} \mathcal{D}_{0,g,\mathbf{A}_i,\mathbf{t}_i,\mathbf{v}}, \ \forall g \in \mathcal{G}_i \end{array} \right\}$$

is statistically close to the distribution

$$\left\{ (\mathbf{A}_i, \mathbf{t}_i, \{\mathbf{u}_{\mathcal{G}_i}\}, \mathbf{v}) \,\middle|\, \begin{array}{l} \mathbf{A}_i \leftarrow_{\$} \mathcal{R}_q^{\eta_i \times \ell_i}; \ \mathbf{t}_i \leftarrow_{\$} \mathcal{T}_i; \ \mathbf{v} \leftarrow_{\$} (\mathcal{R}_q^{\times})^w \\ \mathbf{u}_g \leftarrow_{\$} \mathsf{SampD}(1^{\eta_i}, 1^{\ell_i}, \mathcal{R}, \beta) : \mathbf{A}_i \cdot \mathbf{u}_g \equiv g(\mathbf{v}) \cdot \mathbf{t}_i \bmod q, \ \forall g \in \mathcal{G}_i \end{array} \right\}.$$

---

[8] In practice the gap may be smaller or larger and when picking parameters we optimise over these gaps.

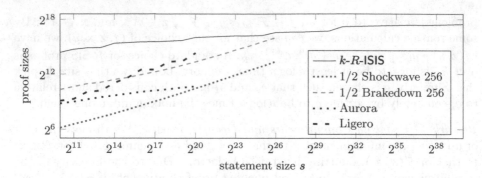

Fig. 2. Combined size (in KB) of a commitment and an opening proof for the concrete parameters chosen in Theorem 3, setting $\lambda = 128$, optimising for ρ and comparing with SNARK proof sizes in prior works [36, Fig. 5]. We picked $\alpha = s$.

Theorem 3. *For $n \in \mathsf{poly}(\lambda)$, $q, \delta_0, \delta_1 \in \mathsf{poly}(\lambda, s, w, t)$, and $\ell_0, \ell_1 \in \Theta(\log q) = \mathsf{polylog}(\lambda, s, w, t)$, covering the choices of parameters in Theorems 1 and 2, the VC construction in Fig. 1 is compact.*

Concretely, let $\mathcal{R}$ be a power-of-2 cyclotomic ring so that $\gamma_{\mathcal{R}} = n$. For $s = w = t \geq n$ and for the following choices of parameters,

$$d, \eta_0, \eta_1 = O(1), \quad \beta \geq \alpha$$
$$\delta_0 = 2 \cdot p \cdot t \cdot (s + d)^d \cdot (w + d)^{2d} \cdot \alpha^{2d+1} \cdot \beta \cdot \gamma_{\mathcal{R}}^{2d+2},$$
$$\delta_1 = w \cdot \alpha \cdot \beta \cdot \gamma_{\mathcal{R}},$$
$$p \approx \delta_p \cdot n \cdot \log n, \quad q \approx \delta_0 \cdot n \cdot \log n, \text{ and}$$
$$\ell_0 = \ell_1 = \mathsf{lhl}(\mathcal{R}, 1, q, \beta) \approx 2 \log_\beta q,$$

a commitment and openings are of size $O(n \log s)$, and $O(n \cdot (\log s + \log \beta)^2 / \log \beta)$, respectively. The minimum is attained at $\beta = \Theta(s)$, where an opening proof is of size $O(n \log s)$.

To translate these into concrete sizes we need to pick n such that solving k-R-ISIS and R-SIS costs $\approx 2^\lambda$ operations. Here it can be beneficial to set $q = \delta_0^\rho \cdot n \cdot \log n$ for some parameter $\rho \in \mathbb{N}$. Specifically, we require that $R\text{-SIS}_{\mathcal{R}_q, \ell_0, 2 \cdot \sqrt{n} \cdot \delta_0}$, $R\text{-SIS}_{\mathcal{R}_q, \ell_1, 2 \cdot \sqrt{n} \cdot \delta_1}$ and $R\text{-SIS}_{\mathcal{R}_p, t, 2 \cdot \sqrt{n} \cdot \delta_p}$ are hard where $\delta_p := (s + w + d)^d \cdot \alpha^{d+1} \cdot \gamma_{\mathcal{R}}^d$. The factor of two arises from our reduction and the factor $\sqrt{n}$ translates between ℓ_∞ and ℓ_2. In Fig. 2 we report the concrete combined size (in KB) of a commitment and an opening proof for the concrete parameters chosen in Theorem 3, specifically setting $d = 2$, $\eta_0 = \eta_1 = 1$, and $\beta = s = w = t \in \{2^{10}, 2^{11}, \ldots, 2^{40}\}$.

To analyse computation complexity, we assume the concrete parameter choices in Theorem 3 with the exception that s, w, t are treated as free vari-

Table 2. Computation complexities (in number of $\mathcal{R}$ or $\mathcal{R}_q$ operations) of our VC.

Com	$O(w^{2d} \cdot (\log s + \log w + \log t + \log \beta) / \log \beta)$
Open	$O(t \cdot (s + w)^d \cdot (\log s + \log w + \log t + \log \beta) / \log \beta)$
PreVerify	$O(t \cdot (s + w)^d)$
Verify	$O(s^d + (\log s + \log w + \log t + \log \beta) / \log \beta)$

ables for more fine-grained complexity measures and to highlight the benefits of preprocessing. For simplicity, we assume $\max\{s, w, t\} \geq n$. The computation complexities (in number of $\mathcal{R}$ or $\mathcal{R}_q$ operations) of Com, Open, PreVerify, and Verify are reported in Table 2. Note that each $\mathcal{R}$ or $\mathcal{R}_q$ operation takes at most $\mathsf{poly}(\lambda, \log s, \log w, \log t)$ time. In summary, the combined time needed to commit to $\mathbf{x}$ and open to $f(\mathbf{z}, \cdot)$ is quasi-quadratic in the time needed to compute $f(\mathbf{z}, \mathbf{x})$, and the time needed to pre-verify (f, y) is quasi-linear in the time needed to compute $f(\mathbf{z}, \mathbf{x})$. We highlight that the online verification cost, i.e. the computation complexity of Verify, is dominated additively by s^d where s is the dimension of the public input. In applications where $s^d = O(\log w + \log t)$ and setting $\beta = \Theta(w + t)$, the online verification cost (in number of bit operations) is $O(n \log w + n \log t)$.

References

1. Agrawal, S.: Unlikely friendships: the fruitful interplay of cryptography assumptions. Invited talk at ASIACRYPT 2020, December 2020. https://youtu.be/Owz8UuWTsqg
2. Ajtai, M.: Generating hard instances of lattice problems (extended abstract). In: 28th ACM STOC, pp. 99–108. ACM Press, May 1996. https://doi.org/10.1145/237814.237838
3. Albrecht, M.R., Gheorghiu, V., Postlethwaite, E.W., Schanck, J.M.: Estimating quantum speedups for lattice sieves. In: Moriai, S., Wang, H. (eds.) ASIACRYPT 2020, Part II. LNCS, vol. 12492, pp. 583–613. Springer, Cham (2020). https://doi.org/10.1007/978-3-030-64834-3_20
4. Albrecht, M.R., Lai, R.W.F.: Subtractive sets over cyclotomic rings. In: Malkin, T., Peikert, C. (eds.) CRYPTO 2021, Part II. LNCS, vol. 12826, pp. 519–548. Springer, Cham (2021). https://doi.org/10.1007/978-3-030-84245-1_18
5. Albrecht, M.R., Rechberger, C., Schneider, T., Tiessen, T., Zohner, M.: Ciphers for MPC and FHE. In: Oswald, E., Fischlin, M. (eds.) EUROCRYPT 2015, Part I. LNCS, vol. 9056, pp. 430–454. Springer, Heidelberg (2015). https://doi.org/10.1007/978-3-662-46800-5_17
6. Attema, T., Cramer, R., Kohl, L.: A compressed Σ-protocol theory for lattices. In: Malkin, T., Peikert, C. (eds.) CRYPTO 2021, Part II. LNCS, vol. 12826, pp. 549–579. Springer, Cham (2021). https://doi.org/10.1007/978-3-030-84245-1_19
7. Aumayr, L., et al.: Generalized channels from limited blockchain scripts and adaptor signatures. In: Tibouchi, M., Wang, H. (eds.) ASIACRYPT 2021. LNCS, vol. 13091, pp. 635–664. Springer, Cham (2021). https://doi.org/10.1007/978-3-030-92075-3_22

8. Becker, A., Ducas, L., Gama, N., Laarhoven, T.: New directions in nearest neighbor searching with applications to lattice sieving. In: Krauthgamer, R. (ed.) 27th SODA, pp. 10–24. ACM-SIAM, January 2016. https://doi.org/10.1137/1.9781611974331.ch2

9. Belenkiy, M., Camenisch, J., Chase, M., Kohlweiss, M., Lysyanskaya, A., Shacham, H.: Randomizable proofs and delegatable anonymous credentials. In: Halevi, S. (ed.) CRYPTO 2009. LNCS, vol. 5677, pp. 108–125. Springer, Heidelberg (2009). https://doi.org/10.1007/978-3-642-03356-8_7

10. Ben-Sasson, E., et al.: Zerocash: decentralized anonymous payments from bitcoin. In: 2014 IEEE Symposium on Security and Privacy, pp. 459–474. IEEE Computer Society Press, May 2014. https://doi.org/10.1109/SP.2014.36

11. Ben-Sasson, E., Chiesa, A., Genkin, D., Tromer, E., Virza, M.: SNARKs for C: verifying program executions succinctly and in zero knowledge. In: Canetti, R., Garay, J.A. (eds.) CRYPTO 2013, Part II. LNCS, vol. 8043, pp. 90–108. Springer, Heidelberg (2013). https://doi.org/10.1007/978-3-642-40084-1_6

12. Ben-Sasson, E., Chiesa, A., Tromer, E., Virza, M.: Scalable zero knowledge via cycles of elliptic curves. In: Garay, J.A., Gennaro, R. (eds.) CRYPTO 2014, Part II. LNCS, vol. 8617, pp. 276–294. Springer, Heidelberg (2014). https://doi.org/10.1007/978-3-662-44381-1_16

13. Ben-Sasson, E., Chiesa, A., Tromer, E., Virza, M.: Succinct non-interactive zero knowledge for a von neumann architecture. In: Fu, K., Jung, J. (eds.) USENIX Security 2014, pp. 781–796. USENIX Association, August 2014

14. Boneh, D., Bonneau, J., Bünz, B., Fisch, B.: Verifiable delay functions. In: Shacham, H., Boldyreva, A. (eds.) CRYPTO 2018, Part I. LNCS, vol. 10991, pp. 757–788. Springer, Cham (2018). https://doi.org/10.1007/978-3-319-96884-1_25

15. Boneh, D., Drake, J., Fisch, B., Gabizon, A.: Halo Infinite: proof-carrying data from additive polynomial commitments. In: Malkin, T., Peikert, C. (eds.) CRYPTO 2021, Part I. LNCS, vol. 12825, pp. 649–680. Springer, Cham (2021). https://doi.org/10.1007/978-3-030-84242-0_23

16. Boneh, D., Drijvers, M., Neven, G.: Compact multi-signatures for smaller blockchains. In: Peyrin, T., Galbraith, S. (eds.) ASIACRYPT 2018, Part II. LNCS, vol. 11273, pp. 435–464. Springer, Cham (2018). https://doi.org/10.1007/978-3-030-03329-3_15

17. Boneh, D., Freeman, D.M.: Linearly homomorphic signatures over binary fields and new tools for lattice-based signatures. In: Catalano, D., Fazio, N., Gennaro, R., Nicolosi, A. (eds.) PKC 2011. LNCS, vol. 6571, pp. 1–16. Springer, Heidelberg (2011). https://doi.org/10.1007/978-3-642-19379-8_1

18. Bonneau, J., Meckler, I., Rao, V., Shapiro, E.: Coda: decentralized cryptocurrency at scale. Cryptology ePrint Archive (2020)

19. Bootle, J., Chiesa, A., Sotiraki, K.: Sumcheck arguments and their applications. In: Malkin, T., Peikert, C. (eds.) CRYPTO 2021, Part I. LNCS, vol. 12825, pp. 742–773. Springer, Cham (2021). https://doi.org/10.1007/978-3-030-84242-0_26

20. Bowe, S., Grigg, J., Hopwood, D.: Halo: recursive proof composition without a trusted setup. Cryptology ePrint Archive, Report 2019/1021 (2019). https://eprint.iacr.org/2019/1021

21. Bünz, B., Maller, M., Mishra, P., Tyagi, N., Vesely, P.: Proofs for inner pairing products and applications. In: Tibouchi, M., Wang, H. (eds.) ASIACRYPT 2021, Part III. LNCS, vol. 13092, pp. 65–97. Springer, Cham (2021). https://doi.org/10.1007/978-3-030-92078-4_3

22. Camenisch, J., Groß, T.: Efficient attributes for anonymous credentials. In: Ning, P., Syverson, P.F., Jha, S. (eds.) ACM CCS 2008, pp. 345–356. ACM Press, October 2008. https://doi.org/10.1145/1455770.1455814

23. Campanelli, M., Fiore, D., Greco, N., Kolonelos, D., Nizzardo, L.: Incrementally aggregatable vector commitments and applications to verifiable decentralized storage. In: Moriai, S., Wang, H. (eds.) ASIACRYPT 2020. LNCS, vol. 12492, pp. 3–35. Springer, Cham (2020). https://doi.org/10.1007/978-3-030-64834-3_1

24. Catalano, D., Fiore, D.: Vector commitments and their applications. In: Kurosawa, K., Hanaoka, G. (eds.) PKC 2013. LNCS, vol. 7778, pp. 55–72. Springer, Heidelberg (2013). https://doi.org/10.1007/978-3-642-36362-7_5

25. Chepurnoy, A., Papamanthou, C., Zhang, Y.: Edrax: a cryptocurrency with stateless transaction validation. Cryptology ePrint Archive, Report 2018/968 (2018). https://eprint.iacr.org/2018/968

26. Drijvers, M., Gorbunov, S., Neven, G., Wee, H.: Pixel: multi-signatures for consensus. In: 29th USENIX Security Symposium (USENIX Security 2020), pp. 2093–2110. USENIX Association, August 2020. https://www.usenix.org/conference/usenixsecurity20/presentation/drijvers

27. Fiat, A., Shamir, A.: How to prove yourself: practical solutions to identification and signature problems. In: Odlyzko, A.M. (ed.) CRYPTO 1986. LNCS, vol. 263, pp. 186–194. Springer, Heidelberg (1987). https://doi.org/10.1007/3-540-47721-7_12

28. Fisch, B.: PoReps: proofs of space on useful data. Cryptology ePrint Archive, Report 2018/678 (2018). https://eprint.iacr.org/2018/678

29. Fisch, B.: Tight proofs of space and replication. In: Ishai, Y., Rijmen, V. (eds.) EUROCRYPT 2019, Part II. LNCS, vol. 11477, pp. 324–348. Springer, Cham (2019). https://doi.org/10.1007/978-3-030-17656-3_12

30. Garman, C., Green, M., Miers, I.: Decentralized anonymous credentials. In: NDSS 2014. The Internet Society, February 2014

31. Genise, N., Micciancio, D.: Faster gaussian sampling for trapdoor lattices with arbitrary modulus. In: Nielsen, J.B., Rijmen, V. (eds.) EUROCRYPT 2018, Part I. LNCS, vol. 10820, pp. 174–203. Springer, Cham (2018). https://doi.org/10.1007/978-3-319-78381-9_7

32. Gennaro, R., Minelli, M., Nitulescu, A., Orrù, M.: Lattice-based zk-SNARKs from square span programs. In: Lie, D., Mannan, M., Backes, M., Wang, X. (eds.) ACM CCS 2018, pp. 556–573. ACM Press, October 2018. https://doi.org/10.1145/3243734.3243845

33. Gentry, C.: Fully homomorphic encryption using ideal lattices. In: Mitzenmacher, M. (ed.) 41st ACM STOC, pp. 169–178. ACM Press, May/June 2009. https://doi.org/10.1145/1536414.1536440

34. Gentry, C., Peikert, C., Vaikuntanathan, V.: Trapdoors for hard lattices and new cryptographic constructions. In: Ladner, R.E., Dwork, C. (eds.) 40th ACM STOC, pp. 197–206. ACM Press, May 2008. https://doi.org/10.1145/1374376.1374407

35. Gentry, C., Wichs, D.: Separating succinct non-interactive arguments from all falsifiable assumptions. In: Fortnow, L., Vadhan, S.P. (eds.) 43rd ACM STOC, pp. 99–108. ACM Press, June 2011. https://doi.org/10.1145/1993636.1993651

36. Golovnev, A., Lee, J., Setty, S., Thaler, J., Wahby, R.S.: Brakedown: linear-time and post-quantum SNARKs for R1CS. Cryptology ePrint Archive, Report 2021/1043 (2021). https://eprint.iacr.org/2021/1043

37. Gorbunov, S., Reyzin, L., Wee, H., Zhang, Z.: Pointproofs: aggregating proofs for multiple vector commitments. In: Ligatti, J., Ou, X., Katz, J., Vigna, G. (eds.) ACM CCS 2020, pp. 2007–2023. ACM Press, November 2020. https://doi.org/10.1145/3372297.3417244

38. Gorbunov, S., Vaikuntanathan, V., Wee, H.: Predicate encryption for circuits from LWE. In: Gennaro, R., Robshaw, M. (eds.) CRYPTO 2015, Part II. LNCS, vol. 9216, pp. 503–523. Springer, Heidelberg (2015). https://doi.org/10.1007/978-3-662-48000-7_25

39. Goyal, R., Koppula, V., Waters, B.: Lockable obfuscation. In: Umans, C. (ed.) 58th FOCS, pp. 612–621. IEEE Computer Society Press, October 2017. https://doi.org/10.1109/FOCS.2017.62

40. Grassi, L., Kales, D., Khovratovich, D., Roy, A., Rechberger, C., Schofnegger, M.: Starkad and Poseidon: New hash functions for zero knowledge proof systems. Cryptology ePrint Archive, Report 2019/458 (2019). https://eprint.iacr.org/2019/458

41. Gross, J.: Practical SNARK based VDF (2021). https://zkproof.org/2021/11/24/practical-snark-based-vdf/

42. Groth, J.: On the size of pairing-based non-interactive arguments. In: Fischlin, M., Coron, J.-S. (eds.) EUROCRYPT 2016, Part II. LNCS, vol. 9666, pp. 305–326. Springer, Heidelberg (2016). https://doi.org/10.1007/978-3-662-49896-5_11

43. Ishai, Y., Su, H., Wu, D.J.: Shorter and faster post-quantum designated-verifier zkSNARKs from lattices. In: Vigna, G., Shi, E. (eds.) ACM CCS 2021, pp. 212–234. ACM Press, November 2021. https://doi.org/10.1145/3460120.3484572

44. Kate, A., Zaverucha, G.M., Goldberg, I.: Constant-size commitments to polynomials and their applications. In: Abe, M. (ed.) ASIACRYPT 2010. LNCS, vol. 6477, pp. 177–194. Springer, Heidelberg (2010). https://doi.org/10.1007/978-3-642-17373-8_11

45. Kilian, J.: A note on efficient zero-knowledge proofs and arguments (extended abstract). In: 24th ACM STOC, pp. 723–732. ACM Press, May 1992. https://doi.org/10.1145/129712.129782

46. Koblitz, N., Menezes, A.: The brave new world of bodacious assumptions in cryptography. Not. Am. Math. Soc. **57**(3), 357–365 (2010)

47. Kosba, A.E., Miller, A., Shi, E., Wen, Z., Papamanthou, C.: Hawk: the blockchain model of cryptography and privacy-preserving smart contracts. In: 2016 IEEE Symposium on Security and Privacy, pp. 839–858. IEEE Computer Society Press, May 2016. https://doi.org/10.1109/SP.2016.55

48. Laarhoven, T.: Search problems in cryptography: from fingerprinting to lattice sieving. Ph.D. thesis, Eindhoven University of Technology (2015)

49. Lai, R.W.F., Malavolta, G.: Subvector commitments with application to succinct arguments. In: Boldyreva, A., Micciancio, D. (eds.) CRYPTO 2019, Part I. LNCS, vol. 11692, pp. 530–560. Springer, Cham (2019). https://doi.org/10.1007/978-3-030-26948-7_19

50. Lai, R.W.F., Malavolta, G., Ronge, V.: Succinct arguments for bilinear group arithmetic: Practical structure-preserving cryptography. In: Cavallaro, L., Kinder, J., Wang, X., Katz, J. (eds.) ACM CCS 2019, pp. 2057–2074. ACM Press, November 2019. https://doi.org/10.1145/3319535.3354262

51. Langlois, A., Stehlé, D.: Worst-case to average-case reductions for module lattices. Des. Codes Crypt. **75**(3), 565–599 (2014). https://doi.org/10.1007/s10623-014-9938-4

52. Libert, B., Ramanna, S.C., Yung, M.: Functional commitment schemes: from polynomial commitments to pairing-based accumulators from simple assumptions. In: Chatzigiannakis, I., Mitzenmacher, M., Rabani, Y., Sangiorgi, D. (eds.) ICALP 2016. LIPIcs, vol. 55, pp. 30:1–30:14. Schloss Dagstuhl, July 2016. https://doi.org/10.4230/LIPIcs.ICALP.2016.30

53. Libert, B., Yung, M.: Concise mercurial vector commitments and independent zero-knowledge sets with short proofs. In: Micciancio, D. (ed.) TCC 2010. LNCS, vol. 5978, pp. 499–517. Springer, Heidelberg (2010). https://doi.org/10.1007/978-3-642-11799-2_30

54. Ling, S., Phan, D.H., Stehlé, D., Steinfeld, R.: Hardness of k-LWE and applications in traitor tracing. In: Garay, J.A., Gennaro, R. (eds.) CRYPTO 2014, Part I. LNCS, vol. 8616, pp. 315–334. Springer, Heidelberg (2014). https://doi.org/10.1007/978-3-662-44371-2_18

55. Liskov, M.: Updatable zero-knowledge databases. In: Roy, B. (ed.) ASIACRYPT 2005. LNCS, vol. 3788, pp. 174–198. Springer, Heidelberg (2005). https://doi.org/10.1007/11593447_10

56. Lyubashevsky, V., Micciancio, D.: Generalized compact knapsacks are collision resistant. In: Bugliesi, M., Preneel, B., Sassone, V., Wegener, I. (eds.) ICALP 2006, Part II. LNCS, vol. 4052, pp. 144–155. Springer, Heidelberg (2006). https://doi.org/10.1007/11787006_13

57. Lyubashevsky, V., Peikert, C., Regev, O.: A toolkit for ring-LWE cryptography. In: Johansson, T., Nguyen, P.Q. (eds.) EUROCRYPT 2013. LNCS, vol. 7881, pp. 35–54. Springer, Heidelberg (2013). https://doi.org/10.1007/978-3-642-38348-9_3

58. Micali, S.: CS proofs (extended abstracts). In: 35th FOCS, pp. 436–453. IEEE Computer Society Press, November 1994. https://doi.org/10.1109/SFCS.1994.365746

59. Micali, S., Rabin, M.O., Kilian, J.: Zero-knowledge sets. In: 44th FOCS, pp. 80–91. IEEE Computer Society Press, October 2003. https://doi.org/10.1109/SFCS.2003.1238183

60. Micciancio, D.: Generalized compact knapsacks, cyclic lattices, and efficient one-way functions. Comput. Complex. **16**(4), 365–411 (2007)

61. Micciancio, D., Peikert, C.: Trapdoors for lattices: simpler, tighter, faster, smaller. In: Pointcheval, D., Johansson, T. (eds.) EUROCRYPT 2012. LNCS, vol. 7237, pp. 700–718. Springer, Heidelberg (2012). https://doi.org/10.1007/978-3-642-29011-4_41

62. Parno, B., Howell, J., Gentry, C., Raykova, M.: Pinocchio: nearly practical verifiable computation. In: 2013 IEEE Symposium on Security and Privacy, pp. 238–252. IEEE Computer Society Press, May 2013. https://doi.org/10.1109/SP.2013.47

63. Peikert, C., Pepin, Z., Sharp, C.: Vector and functional commitments from lattices. Cryptology ePrint Archive, Report 2021/1254 (2021). https://ia.cr/2021/1254

64. Peikert, C., Rosen, A.: Efficient collision-resistant hashing from worst-case assumptions on cyclic lattices. In: Halevi, S., Rabin, T. (eds.) TCC 2006. LNCS, vol. 3876, pp. 145–166. Springer, Heidelberg (2006). https://doi.org/10.1007/11681878_8

65. Prest, T., et al.: FALCON. Technical report, National Institute of Standards and Technology (2020). https://csrc.nist.gov/projects/post-quantum-cryptography/round-3-submissions

66. Regev, O.: On lattices, learning with errors, random linear codes, and cryptography. In: Gabow, H.N., Fagin, R. (eds.) 37th ACM STOC, pp. 84–93. ACM Press, May 2005. https://doi.org/10.1145/1060590.1060603

67. Schnorr, C., Euchner, M.: Lattice basis reduction: improved practical algorithms and solving subset sum problems. Math. Program. **66**, 181–199 (1994)

68. Stehlé, D., Steinfeld, R.: Making NTRU as secure as worst-case problems over ideal lattices. In: Paterson, K.G. (ed.) EUROCRYPT 2011. LNCS, vol. 6632, pp. 27–47. Springer, Heidelberg (2011). https://doi.org/10.1007/978-3-642-20465-4_4

69. Stehlé, D., Steinfeld, R., Tanaka, K., Xagawa, K.: Efficient public key encryption based on ideal lattices. In: Matsui, M. (ed.) ASIACRYPT 2009. LNCS, vol. 5912, pp. 617–635. Springer, Heidelberg (2009). https://doi.org/10.1007/978-3-642-10366-7_36

70. Unruh, D.: Computationally binding quantum commitments. In: Fischlin, M., Coron, J.-S. (eds.) EUROCRYPT 2016, Part II. LNCS, vol. 9666, pp. 497–527. Springer, Heidelberg (2016). https://doi.org/10.1007/978-3-662-49896-5_18

71. Valiant, P.: Incrementally verifiable computation or proofs of knowledge imply time/space efficiency. In: Canetti, R. (ed.) TCC 2008. LNCS, vol. 4948, pp. 1–18. Springer, Heidelberg (2008). https://doi.org/10.1007/978-3-540-78524-8_1

72. Wichs, D., Zirdelis, G.: Obfuscating compute-and-compare programs under LWE. In: Umans, C. (ed.) 58th FOCS, pp. 600–611. IEEE Computer Society Press, October 2017. https://doi.org/10.1109/FOCS.2017.61

Practical Sublinear Proofs for R1CS from Lattices

Ngoc Khanh Nguyen[1,2] and Gregor Seiler[1(✉)]

[1] IBM Research Europe, Rüschlikon, Switzerland
gseiler@inf.ethz.ch
[2] ETH Zurich, Zürich, Switzerland

Abstract. We propose a practical sublinear-size zero-knowledge proof system for Rank-1 Constraint Satisfaction (R1CS) based on lattices. The proof size scales asymptotically with the square root of the witness size. Concretely, the size becomes 2–3 times smaller than Ligero (ACM CCS 2017), which also exhibits square root scaling, for large instances of R1CS. At the core lies an interactive variant of the Schwartz-Zippel Lemma that might be of independent interest.

1 Introduction

Zero-Knowledge proof systems are an important tool in the construction of many cryptographic protocols, especially in the area of privacy-preserving cryptography. This paper is about zero-knowledge proof systems based on techniques and hardness assumptions from lattice cryptography. In recent years there has been a lot of progress in the construction of lattice-based proof systems whose proof sizes scale linearly with the statement size [ESS+19, EZS+19, ALS20, ENS20, LNS20]. The concrete proof sizes for typical statements have been reduced by a factor of about 100 over earlier proof systems. This in turn has made it possible to construct efficient advanced quantum-safe privacy-preserving schemes, for example group and ring signature schemes, that achieve or get near to practically acceptable bandwidth requirements [ESLL19, LNPS21, LNS21b].

On the other hand, the linear scaling of the proof systems implies that they are only practical for proving relatively small statements and great care needs to be taken to minimize the statement sizes when using them in the construction of advanced schemes. For example, the linear-size proof systems can not be used to construct efficient group signature schemes on top of vetted lattice-based basic signature schemes such as the NIST PQC finalists Dilithium [DKL+18] and Falcon [FHK+18]. Dilithium and Falcon involve a hash function that is modeled as a random oracle and proving a preimage to such a hash function would lead to a very large proof size.

For solving this problem and more generally for being able to prove arbitrary circuit satisfaction with lattice-based proof systems, practically efficient sublinear-size proof systems are needed. There are several proposals of asymptotically sublinear lattice-based proof systems in the literature [BBC+18, BLNS20,

---

This work is supported by the EU H2020 ERC Project 101002845 PLAZA.

Y. Dodis and T. Shrimpton (Eds.): CRYPTO 2022, LNCS 13508, pp. 133–162, 2022.
https://doi.org/10.1007/978-3-031-15979-4_5

ACK21, AL21], but their concrete proof sizes are not analyzed in the papers and they are not practically efficient. These sublinear-size lattice-based proof systems use adaptations and extensions of techniques from discrete-log-based proof systems. In particular several forms of "folding" stemming from the two-tiered commitment scheme [Gro11] and Bulletproofs [BBB+18]. While folding techniques are very effective in the discrete-log setting and retain asymptotic efficiency in the lattice setting, they do not play nicely with the shortness requirement in lattice cryptography. This leads to a concrete blow-up of the proof size. We exemplify this in the case of lattice-based Bulletproofs. On a high level, it must be possible to invert the folding in the extraction such that the extracted solution vector is still short. For general (short) challenges this will not be the case. In [BLNS20, ACK21] monomial challenges X^i are used that result in a large soundness error which can not be boosted [AF21]. But even when ignoring this problem, the length of the extracted solution vector grows by a factor of $12d^3$ for every level of folding where d is the dimension of the polynomial ring. Then the parameters must be chosen such that the Module Short Integer Solution problem (Module-SIS) is hard with respect to the length of the extracted solution vector, resulting in the need for large integer moduli q. It follows that the length of the extracted solution becomes prohibitively large for less than 10 foldings. When choosing an optimal number of foldings the required modulus q still needs to be in the order of several hundred bits and the proof size turns out to be in excess of 100 Megabytes for typical example applications.

In light of these problems, we construct the first concretely efficient sublinear-size lattice-base zero-knowledge proof system in this paper. Our proof system uses new techniques that avoid any folding and the proof size scales with the square root of the statement size. We apply it for proving R1CS [BCG+13] where it is most efficient and achieves optimal sizes for numbers of constraints above 2^{20}. Because of the square root scaling, we compare our proof system to the PCP-type Ligero proof system [AHIV17], and more specifically to the straightforward extension Ligero-R1CS from [BCR+19] to the R1CS language, which also exhibits square root scaling and is faster and less memory-demanding than other PCP-type proof systems. In the setting over a finite field of size 128 bits our system results in a proof size of 10.79 Megabytes for 2^{24} constraints, whereas Ligero results in 31.83 Megabytes, for the same field size, number of constraints, and comparable soundness error around 2^{-110}.

Outside of lattice-based cryptography there has been tremendous progress in the construction of practical zero-knowledge proof systems and they have progressed to the point where they can be used routinely to prove relatively large arithmetic circuits with practical costs. When restricting to (plausibly) quantum-safe protocols, the PCP-type systems like Ligero++ [BFH+20] or Aurora [BCR+19] achieve proof sizes that scale poly-logarithmically with the witness size and have small concrete base sizes in the order of 100 Kilobytes. Moreover, these systems only rely on unstructured quantum-safe hardness assumptions (hash functions). It is clear that the polylogarithmic proof systems with small concrete costs like e.g. Aurora offer much smaller proof sizes for large statements than our square-root sized proof system. We use the comparison with Ligero to be able to claim practicality of our proof system. Namely, that our proof system has very small constants for a proof system that asymptotically scales with the square root of the witness size. It is an important and interesting open research question whether it will be possible to improve upon the polylogarithmic PCP-type systems by relying on structured quantum-safe assumptions as for example lattice-based assumptions, which for example has been achieved for basic signature schemes where lattice-based signatures are more efficient than hash-based ones.

Next to the conventional publicly verifiable proof systems this paper is about, there has recently been much work on (lattice-based) proof systems in the designated verifier preprocessing model. For example, [GMNO18], MAC'n'Cheese [BMRS21], Wolverine [WYKW21], QuickSilver [YSWW21], and [ISW21]. These proof systems achieve very practical sizes but are not directly comparable to publicly verifiable protocols.

1.1 Technical Overview

Our proof system from this paper is constructed in two stages and uses the protocols from [ALS20,ENS20] as a building block. First, we construct an exact binary amortized opening proof for many lattice-based hashes. Then we use this proof to prove an opening to a Merkle hash tree via induction over the levels of the tree. Both proofs can be amended to also prove linear and product relations among the preimage coefficients. We now give some more details about the techniques.

Our sublinear-size proof system is presented as a protocol for proving preimages to many collision-resistant hashes $\vec{u}_i = A\vec{s}_i$ over a cyclotomic polynomial ring, typically $\mathcal{R}_q = \mathbb{Z}_q[X]/(X^{128} + 1)$ with fully splitting prime $q \approx 2^{128}$. The preimages $\vec{s}_i$ are binary and lie in $\{0,1\}^m \subset \mathcal{R}_q^{m/128}$ where m is a multiple of 128. The hashes can be commitments if parts of the $\vec{s}_i$ are random, but our proof system does not rely on this. Concretely, there are n hashes to m bits each, and we want $m \approx n$ and a proof size that is linear in n. Then our proof system scales with the square root of the witness size. We start from an amortized approximate opening proof for all the hashes that is a variant of the protocol in [LNS21a]. In the protocol the prover sends an amortized masked opening

$$\vec{z} = \vec{y} + x_1\vec{s}_1 + \cdots + x_n\vec{s}_n,$$

where $\vec{y}$ is the masking vector and $x_i \in \mathbb{Z}_q$ are integer challenges. We forget the polynomial structure and let $\vec{s}_i$ be the coefficient vectors corresponding to the $\vec{s}_i$. We then enhance the protocol with a binary proof that shows that all the $\vec{s}_i$ are binary vectors $\vec{s}_i \in \{0,1\}^m$. To this end, we construct the polynomial (in the x_i)

$$f(x_1, \ldots, x_n) = \langle \vec{\varphi}, \vec{z} \circ ((x_1 + \cdots + x_n)\vec{1} - \vec{z}) \rangle$$

for a challenge vector $\vec{\varphi}$. Here $\circ$ denotes the componentwise product. The terms divisible by x_i^2 for $i \in \{1, \ldots, n\}$ are given by $\langle \vec{\varphi}, \vec{s}_i \circ (\vec{1} - \vec{s}_i) \rangle$ and vanish when

$\vec{s}_i$ is binary, which we want to prove. There are now two problems that we need to overcome to make this work. First, there is a quadratic number $(n^2+n+2)/2$ of terms that we would need to commit to in order to prove that the interesting terms divisible by x_i^2 vanish. These are called garbage commitments and they would be very expensive and not result in a sublinear-size proof system. Secondly, it is not clear how to prove hat $\vec{z}$ is always of the same form with fixed masking vector $\vec{y}$ so that the polynomial f is really independent of the challenges. We solve the first problem with a technique that can be seen as a multi-round interactive variant of the Schwartz-Zippel lemma. The high-level idea is that we prove

$$f(x_1,\ldots,x_n) = f_0 + f_1(x_1) + f_2^{(x_1)}(x_2) + \cdots + f_n^{(x_1,\ldots,x_{n-1})}(x_n), \qquad (1)$$

where $f_0 \in \mathbb{Z}_q$ and $f_i^{(x_1,\ldots,x_{i-1})} \in \mathbb{Z}_q[x_i]$ is a degree-one polynomial in x_i with zero constant coefficient, depending on $x_1,\ldots,x_{i-1}$. More precisely, we do not prove that the $f_i^{(x_1,\ldots,x_{i-1})}(x_i)$ are in fact multivariate polynomials in $x_1,\ldots,x_i$ of degree 2 whose terms x_i^2 vanish. It suffices to prove that they are arbitrary functions from $\mathbb{Z}_q^{i-1}$ to $\mathbb{Z}_q[x_i]$ given by $(x_1,\ldots,x_{i-1}) \mapsto f^{(x_1,\ldots,x_{i-1})}(x_i)$ where the image polynomials are of the form $\gamma_i x_i$ for all $(x_1,\ldots,x_{i-1})$. The important information is that $f_i^{(x_1,\ldots,x_{i-1})}$ does not depend on $x_i,\ldots,x_n$. This can be proven in a protocol with $2n$ rounds where the prover has to commit to the coefficient γ_i for $f^{(x_1,\ldots,x_{i-1})}$ after he has received the challenges $x_1,\ldots,x_{i-1}$ but before getting the challenges $x_i,\ldots,x_n$. Then, intuitively, if $\vec{s}_i$ is not binary, the prover can not use $\gamma_i x_i$ to make Eq. (1) true for all $(x_1,\ldots,x_n)$ because the left-hand side contains the non-zero term $\langle \vec{\varphi}, \vec{s}_i \circ (\vec{1} - \vec{s}_i)\rangle x_i^2$ that is quadratic in x_i. He can also not use the later γ_j because they all get multiplied by later challenges x_j that the prover does not know when making the commitments. A precise analysis shows that this argument has soundness error $2n/q$ for uniformly random challenges x_i.

So our protocol will have many rounds but we do not consider this to be a problem as we are only interested in the non-interactive variant where the number of rounds has no direct impact on the performance of the proof system. The interactive variant only serves as a convenient intermediate representation that is easy to reason about. From a theoretical point of view our multi round protocol is simple in that the extraction algorithm is relatively straight-forward compared to for example Bulletproofs where a complicated tree extraction algorithm is needed.

For the second problem we do not know how to prove that $\vec{z}$ must follow the fixed form from using the approximate opening proof protocol alone. But in conjunction with the binary proof protocol it turns out to be provable. The argument proceeds along the following lines. Let $\vec{s}_i^*$ be the bound weak openings to the hashes $\vec{u}_i$ that we can extract from the approximate proof. If they are not all binary, then there is a last non-binary vector $\vec{s}_{i_0}^*$. We can write $\vec{z} - x_{i_0+1}\vec{s}_{i_0+1}^* - \cdots - x_n\vec{s}_n^* = \vec{y}^* + x_{i_0}\vec{s}_{i_0}^*$ in any accepting transcript where $A\vec{y}^* = \vec{w} + x_1\vec{u}_1 + \cdots + x_{i_0-1}\vec{u}_{i_0-1}$. So this can be viewed as a masked opening of the single secret vector $\vec{s}_{i_0}^*$ because the left hand side is short. Then we can use the argument for the non-amortized case to argue that the prover is bound to the

$\vec{y}^*$ in all interactions with fixed first challenges $x_1, \ldots, x_{i_0-1}$. Indeed, if in an accepting transcript $\vec{z}' = \vec{y}^{**} + x'_{i_0}\vec{s}^*_{i_0} + \cdots + x'_n\vec{s}^*_n$ with $\vec{y}^{**} \neq \vec{y}^{**}$, then we can compute a short Module-SIS solution

$$\bar{x}(\vec{y}^* - \vec{y}^{**}) = \bar{x}(\vec{z} - \vec{z}' - (x_{i_0+1} - x'_{i_0+1})\vec{s}^*_{i_0+1} - \cdots - (x_n - x'_n)\vec{s}^*_n) - (x_{i_0} - x'_{i_0})\bar{x}\vec{s}^*_{i_0}$$

for A, where $\bar{x}$ is a difference of two challenges such that $\bar{x}\vec{s}^*_{i_0}$ is short. This in turn suffices to show that the prover has small success probability in the binary proof restricted to the vectors $\vec{s}_{i_0}, \ldots, \vec{s}_n$.

Given this exact amortized binary opening proof, we extend it to be also able to prove linear and product relations on the secret vectors. This already provides a sublinear-size proof system even when the size of the commitments $\vec{u}_i$ is counted as part of the proof size. There are n hashes, each of essentially constant size. Unfortunately, this simple sublinear-size proof system is only competitive in a small regime of parameters. We achieve competitive proof sizes for larger parameters in a further protocol where we use the previous exact amortized binary opening proof as a building block to prove knowledge of a Merkle tree opening by induction over the levels of the tree when only the root hash is given (see Sect. 5 and the full version of the paper.).

So we use a Merkle tree with hashes $\vec{u}_i = A\vec{s}_i$ for $i = 1, \ldots, 2^a - 1$, where $\vec{u}_1$ is the root hash and $\vec{u}_{2^{a-1}}, \ldots, \vec{u}_{2^a-1}$ are the leaves. The binary preimages $\vec{s}_i$ are the expansions of the two children $\vec{u}_{2i}$ and $\vec{u}_{2i+1}$; that is, $\vec{s}_i = \vec{s}_{i,l} \parallel \vec{s}_{i,r}$ and $\vec{u}_{2i} = G\vec{s}_{i,l}$, $\vec{u}_{2i+1} = G\vec{s}_{i,r}$. Here G is the power-of-two gadget matrix $G = I \otimes (1, 2, \ldots, 2^{\lceil \log q \rceil})$, i.e. the identity matrix tensored with the two-power vector.

Now, in the protocol the prover sends an amortized masked opening of all the preimages,

$$\vec{z} = \vec{y} + \sum_{i=1}^{2^a-1} x_i\vec{s}_i.$$

The main idea is that all the terms $x_i\vec{s}_i$ for $i > 1$ can be absorbed into the masking vector so that we have $\vec{z} = \vec{y}_0 + x_1\vec{s}_1$. This is just a masked opening of $\vec{s}_1$ and the verifier checks that

$$A\vec{z} = \vec{w}_0 + x_1\vec{u}_1$$

using the vector $\vec{w}_0 = A\vec{y}_0 = A\vec{y} + \sum_{i=2}^{2^a-1} s_i\vec{u}_i$ that he has received from the prover before the challenge x_1. Next, from this opening proof we can extract $\vec{s}_1$. Moreover the prover also proves the linear relation

$$\vec{w}_0 = \vec{w}_1 + x_2G\vec{s}_{1,l} + x_3G\vec{s}_{1,r}$$

for a vector $\vec{w}_1 = A\vec{y}_1 = A\vec{y} + \sum_{i=4}^{2^a-1} x_i\vec{u}_i$ that he has sent before the challenges x_2 and x_3. So, this implies

$$A\vec{z} = \vec{w}_1 + x_1\vec{u}_1 + x_2\vec{u}_2 + x_3\vec{u}_3.$$

In other words the extracted $\vec{s}_1$ defines the hashes in the first level of the tree and there is a proof for the verification equation of an amortized opening proof for this level. So we can continue recursively and extract level by level from the prover until we have an opening for the full tree. Our protocol can be seen as a sequence of exact amortized binary opening proofs, one for each level for the tree, that use the linear proof technique to prove the verification equation for the proof for the next level. The proof also shows that all the preimages $\vec{s}_i$ are binary as this is needed for the approach to work, as explained.

We use our Merkle tree opening protocol that can also prove linear and product relations on the preimages of the leaves to prove instances of Rank-1 Constraint Satisfaction (R1CS) [BCG+13] which is an NP-complete problem. Recall that in the (simplified) R1CS setting, the prover $\mathcal{P}$ wants to convince the verifier $\mathcal{V}$ that it knows a vector $\vec{s} \in \mathbb{Z}_q^k$ such that

$$(A\vec{s}) \circ (B\vec{s}) = C\vec{s} \tag{2}$$

where $A, B, C \in \mathbb{Z}_q^{k \times k}$ are public matrices and $\circ$ denotes the component-wise product. The usual way to prove such a relation is to first commit to $\vec{s}$ as well as to the vectors

$$\vec{a} = A\vec{s}, \vec{b} = B\vec{s}, \vec{c} = C\vec{s}. \tag{3}$$

Then, $\mathcal{P}$ only needs to prove the linear relations described in (3) and the multiplicative relation $\vec{a} \circ \vec{b} = \vec{c}$. This method requires us to commit to three additional vectors over $\mathbb{Z}_q$ of length k.

Table 1 contains a comparison of our proof system for R1CS to Ligero. We chose a range of constraints above 2^{20} as our proof system is most effective for such large numbers of constraints. In particular, we observe that for large instances, e.g. $k \geq 2^{24}$, our system achieves 2–3 times smaller proof sizes than Ligero. The proof sizes for Ligero were directly measured by running the implementation from https://github.com/scipr-lab/libiop. For both proof systems we used a field size of about 128 bits and comparable soundness errors.

2   Preliminaries

2.1   Notation

Let q be an odd prime, and $\mathbb{Z}_q$ denote the ring of integers modulo q. For $r \in \mathbb{Z}$, we define $r \bmod q$ to be the unique element in the interval $[-\frac{q-1}{2}, \frac{q-1}{2}]$ that is congruent to r modulo q. We write $\vec{v} \in \mathbb{Z}_q^m$ to denote vectors over $\mathbb{Z}_q$ and matrices over $\mathbb{Z}_q$ will be written as regular capital letters M. By default, all vectors are column vectors. We write $\vec{v} \parallel \vec{w}$ for the concatenation of $\vec{v}$ and $\vec{w}$ (which is still a column vector). We write $x \xleftarrow{\$} S$ when $x \in S$ is sampled uniformly at random from the finite set S and similarly $x \xleftarrow{\$} D$ when x is sampled according to the distribution D.

Let d be a power of two and denote $\mathcal{R}$ and $\mathcal{R}_q$ to be the rings $\mathbb{Z}[X]/(X^d+1)$ and $\mathbb{Z}_q[X]/(X^d+1)$, respectively. Bold lower-case letters $\boldsymbol{p}$ denote elements in

Table 1. Comparison of proof sizes between our proof system for R1CS over $\mathbb{Z}_q$ with $q \approx 2^{128}$, and Ligero.

		Proof Size	
Number of constraints	Soundness error	Ligero	Our System
2^{19}	2^{-115}	4.58 MB	**4.53 MB**
2^{20}	2^{-114}	8.35 MB	**5.22 MB**
2^{21}	2^{-113}	8.90 MB	**6.08 MB**
2^{22}	2^{-112}	16.23 MB	**7.19 MB**
2^{23}	2^{-111}	17.39 MB	**10.79 MB**
2^{24}	2^{-110}	31.83 MB	**13.21 MB**
2^{25}	2^{-109}	34.15 MB	**16.59 MB**
2^{26}	2^{-108}	62.14 MB	**21.68 MB**
2^{27}	2^{-107}	66.03 MB	**29.04 MB**
2^{28}	2^{-106}	121.90 MB	**42.42 MB**

$\mathcal{R}$ or $\mathcal{R}_q$ and bold lower-case letters with arrows $\vec{b}$ represent column vectors with components in $\mathcal{R}$ or $\mathcal{R}_q$. We also use bold upper-case letters for matrices $\boldsymbol{B}$ over $\mathcal{R}$ or $\mathcal{R}_q$. The ring $\mathcal{R}_q$ is a $\mathbb{Z}_q$-module spanned by the power basis $\{1, X, \ldots, X^{d-1}\}$. The multiplication homomorphism $x \mapsto ax$ for an $a = a_0 + \cdots + a_{d-1}X^{d-1} \in \mathcal{R}_q$ is represented by the negacyclic rotation matrix

$$\mathsf{Rot}(\boldsymbol{a}) = \begin{pmatrix} a_0 & -a_{d-1} & \ldots & -a_1 \\ a_1 & a_0 & \ldots & -a_2 \\ \vdots & \vdots & \ddots & \vdots \\ a_{d-1} & a_{d-2} & \ldots & a_0 \end{pmatrix} \in \mathbb{Z}_q^{d \times d}.$$

This extends to $\mathcal{R}_q$-module homomorphisms given by $\boldsymbol{A} \in \mathcal{R}^{m \times n}$ in a block-wise fashion. They are represented by $\mathsf{Rot}(\boldsymbol{A}) \in \mathbb{Z}_q^{md \times nd}$.

In this paper we choose prime q such that $\mathbb{Z}_q$ contains a primitive $2d$-th root of unity $\zeta \in \mathbb{Z}_q$ but no elements whose order is a higher power of two, i.e. $q - 1 \equiv 2d \pmod{4d}$. Therefore, we have

$$X^d + 1 \equiv \prod_{j=0}^{d-1} \left(X - \zeta^{2j+1} \right) \pmod{q} \tag{4}$$

where ζ^{2j+1} $(j \in \mathbb{Z}_d)$ ranges over all the d primitive $2d$-th roots of unity. We define the Number Theoretic Transform (NTT) of a polynomial $\boldsymbol{p} \in \mathcal{R}_q$ as follows:

$$\mathsf{NTT}(\boldsymbol{p}) := \begin{bmatrix} \hat{\boldsymbol{p}}_0 \\ \vdots \\ \hat{\boldsymbol{p}}_{d-1} \end{bmatrix} \in \mathbb{Z}_q^d \text{ where } \hat{\boldsymbol{p}}_j = \boldsymbol{p} \bmod (X - \zeta^{2j+1}),$$

We will use the property that for any polynomials $\boldsymbol{f}, \boldsymbol{g} \in \mathcal{R}_q$, we have $\mathsf{NTT}(\boldsymbol{f}) \circ \mathsf{NTT}(\boldsymbol{g}) = \mathsf{NTT}(\boldsymbol{fg})$ where $\circ$ is the component-wise vector multiplication.

We also define the inverse NTT operation. Namely, for a vector $\vec{v} \in \mathbb{Z}_q^d$, $\mathsf{NTT}^{-1}(\vec{v})$ is the polynomial $\boldsymbol{p} \in \mathcal{R}_q$ such that $\mathsf{NTT}(\boldsymbol{p}) = \vec{v}$.

Norms and Sizes. For an element $w \in \mathbb{Z}_q$, we write $|w|$ to mean $|w \bmod q|$. Define the ℓ_∞ and ℓ_2 norms for $\boldsymbol{w} \in \mathcal{R}_q$ as follows,

$$\|\boldsymbol{w}\|_\infty = \max_i |w_i| \quad \text{and} \quad \|\boldsymbol{w}\|_2 = \sqrt{|w_0|^2 + \ldots + |w_{d-1}|^2}.$$

Similarly, for $\vec{\boldsymbol{w}} = (\boldsymbol{w}_1, \ldots, \boldsymbol{w}_k) \in \mathcal{R}^k$, we define

$$\|\vec{\boldsymbol{w}}\|_\infty = \max_i \|\boldsymbol{w}_i\|_\infty \quad \text{and} \quad \|\vec{\boldsymbol{w}}\|_2 = \sqrt{\|\boldsymbol{w}_1\|_2^2 + \ldots + \|\boldsymbol{w}_k\|_2^2}.$$

2.2 Module-SIS and Module-LWE Problems

We employ the computationally binding and computationally hiding commitment scheme from [BDL+18] in our protocols, and rely on the well-known Module-LWE (MLWE) and Module-SIS (MSIS) problems [LPR10, Din12, LS15, Mic02, LM06, PR06] problems to prove the security of our constructions. Both problems are defined over a ring $\mathcal{R}_q$ for a positive modulus $q \in \mathbb{Z}^+$.

Definition 1 (MSIS$_{\kappa,\beta}$). *In the Module-SIS problem with parameters $\kappa, \lambda > 0$ and $\beta < q$ a uniformly random matrix $\boldsymbol{A} \overset{\$}{\leftarrow} \mathcal{R}_q^{\kappa \times (\kappa + \lambda)}$ is given. Then the goal is to find a vector $\vec{\boldsymbol{s}} \in \mathcal{R}_q^{\kappa + \lambda}$ such that $\boldsymbol{A}\vec{\boldsymbol{s}} = \vec{\boldsymbol{0}}$ and $0 < \|\vec{\boldsymbol{s}}\|_2 \leq \beta$. We say that an adversary $\mathcal{A}$ has advantage ϵ in solving MSIS$_{\kappa,\beta}$ if*

$$\Pr\left[\boldsymbol{A}\vec{\boldsymbol{s}} = \vec{\boldsymbol{0}} \text{ and } 0 < \|\vec{\boldsymbol{s}}\|_2 \leq \beta \;\middle|\; \boldsymbol{A} \overset{\$}{\leftarrow} \mathcal{R}_q^{\kappa \times (\kappa + \lambda)}; \vec{\boldsymbol{s}} \leftarrow \mathcal{A}(\boldsymbol{A})\right] \geq \epsilon.$$

Definition 2 (MLWE$_{\lambda,\chi}$). *In the Module-LWE problem with parameters $\kappa, \lambda > 0$ and χ an "error" distribution over $\mathbb{Z}_q$, a pair $(\boldsymbol{A}, \vec{\boldsymbol{t}}) \in \mathcal{R}_q^{\kappa \times (\kappa + \lambda)} \times \mathcal{R}_q^\kappa$ is given where $\boldsymbol{A}$ is uniformly random. Then the goal is to distinguish between the two cases where either $\vec{\boldsymbol{t}}$ is given by $\vec{\boldsymbol{t}} = \boldsymbol{A}\vec{\boldsymbol{s}}$ for a secret vector $\vec{\boldsymbol{s}} \overset{\$}{\leftarrow} \chi^{(\kappa + \lambda)d}$ sampled from the error distribution, or $\vec{\boldsymbol{t}}$ is independently uniformly random. We say that an adversary $\mathcal{A}$ has advantage ϵ in distinguishing MLWE$_{\lambda,\chi}$ if*

$$\left| \Pr\left[b = 1 \;\middle|\; \boldsymbol{A} \overset{\$}{\leftarrow} \mathcal{R}_q^{\kappa \times (\kappa + \lambda)}; \vec{\boldsymbol{s}} \overset{\$}{\leftarrow} \chi^{(\kappa + \lambda)d}; \vec{\boldsymbol{t}} = \boldsymbol{A}\vec{\boldsymbol{s}}; b \leftarrow \mathcal{A}(\boldsymbol{A}, t)\right] \right.$$
$$\left. - \Pr\left[b = 1 \;\middle|\; \boldsymbol{A} \overset{\$}{\leftarrow} \mathcal{R}_q^{\kappa \times (\kappa + \lambda)}; \vec{\boldsymbol{t}} \overset{\$}{\leftarrow} \mathcal{R}_q^\kappa; b \leftarrow \mathcal{A}(\boldsymbol{A}, \vec{\boldsymbol{t}})\right] \right| \geq \epsilon.$$

For our practical security estimations of these two problems against known attacks, the parameter κ in the Module-LWE problem and the parameter λ in the Module-SIS problem do not play a crucial role. Therefore, we omit then in the notations MSIS$_{\kappa,\beta}$ and MLWE$_{\lambda,\chi}$.

2.3 Challenge Space

Let $C := \{-1, 0, 1\}^d \subset \mathcal{R}_q$ be the challenge set of ternary polynomials with coefficients $-1, 0, 1$. We define the following probability distribution $\mathcal{C} : C \to [0, 1]$.

The coefficients of a challenge $c \xleftarrow{\$} \mathcal{C}$ are independently identically distributed with $P(0) = 1/2$ and $\Pr(1) = \Pr(-1) = 1/4$.

Consider the coefficients of the polynomial $c \bmod (X - \zeta^{2j+1})$ for $c \leftarrow \mathcal{C}$. Then, all coefficients follow the same distribution over $\mathbb{Z}_q$. Let us write Y for the random variable over $\mathbb{Z}_q$ that follows this distribution. Attema et al. [ALS20] give an upper bound on the maximum probability of Y.

Lemma 1. *Let the random variable* Y *over* $\mathbb{Z}_q$ *be defined as above. Then for all* $x \in \mathbb{Z}_q$,

$$\Pr[Y = x] \leq \frac{1}{q} + \frac{2d}{q} \sum_{j \in \mathbb{Z}_q^\times / \langle \zeta \rangle} \prod_{i=0}^{d-1} \left| \frac{1}{2} + \frac{1}{2} \cos(2\pi j y \zeta^i / q) \right|. \tag{5}$$

One observes that computing the sum on the right-hand side would take essentially $O(q)$ time. Hence, computing the upper-bound for $\Pr[Y = x]$ is infeasible for large primes q. However, based on experiments for smaller primes[1], we assume that the probability is very close to $1/q$. In fact, this process exhibits a phase-shift behaviour, where the probability very rapidly drops to values close to $1/q$ as soon as the entropy of c is slightly higher than $\log q$.

2.4 BDLOP Commitment Scheme

We use a variant of the commitment scheme from [BDL+18], which allows to commit to a vector of polynomials in $\mathcal{R}_q$[2]. Suppose that we want to commit to $\vec{m} = (m_1, \ldots, m_\mu)^T \in \mathcal{R}_q^\mu$. Then, in the commitment parameter generation, a uniformly random matrix $\boldsymbol{B}_0 \xleftarrow{\$} \mathcal{R}_q^{\kappa \times (\kappa + \lambda + \mu)}$ and vectors $\vec{b}_1, \ldots, \vec{b}_\mu \xleftarrow{\$} \mathcal{R}_q^{\kappa + \lambda + \mu}$ are generated and output as public parameters. In practice they never have to be stored because they can be expanded from a short seed. One may choose to generate $\boldsymbol{B}_0, \vec{b}_1, \ldots, \vec{b}_\mu$ in a more structured way as in [BDL+18] since it saves some computation.

To commit to $\vec{m}$, we first sample $\vec{r} \xleftarrow{\$} \chi^{(\kappa + \lambda + \mu)d}$. Now, there are two parts of the commitment scheme; the binding part and the message encoding part. We compute

$$\vec{t}_0 = \boldsymbol{B}_0 \vec{r},$$
$$t_i = \langle \vec{b}_i, \vec{r} \rangle + m_i \quad \text{for } i = 1, \ldots, \mu,$$

where $\vec{t}_0$ forms the binding part and each t_i encodes a message polynomial m_i. The commitment $\vec{t} = \vec{t}_0 \parallel t_1 \parallel \cdots \parallel t_\mu$ is computationally hiding under the $\mathsf{MLWE}_{\lambda, \chi}$ assumption and computationally binding under the $\mathsf{MSIS}_{\kappa, \beta}$ assumption for some $q > \beta > 2\sqrt{(\kappa + \lambda + \mu)d}$; see [BDL+18].

---

[1] In particular, [ALS20,ENS20] computed that for $q \approx 2^{32}$, the maximum probability for each coefficient of $c \bmod X^4 - \zeta^{8j+4}$ is around $2^{-31.4}$.

[2] We provide more background on commitment schemes in the full version.

Moreover, the scheme is not only binding for the opening $(\vec{m}, \vec{r})$ known by the prover, but also binding with respect to a relaxed opening $(\vec{m}^*, \bar{c}, \vec{r}^*)$. The relaxed opening also includes a short invertible polynomial $\bar{c}$ and the randomness vector $\vec{r}^*$ is longer than $\vec{r}$. Attema et al. [ALS20] further reduce the requirements of an opening and define the notion of a weak opening (see the full version).

3   Interactive Schwartz-Zippel

The Schwartz-Zippel Lemma [Sch80, Zip79] (first proven by Ore [Ore22]) is an important tool in the construction of many zero-knowledge proof systems. It says that for a non-zero polynomial $f \in \mathbb{Z}_q[X_1, \ldots, X_n]$ of total degree d, the probability that $f(x_1, \ldots, x_n) = 0$ for independently uniformly random $x_1, \ldots, x_n \in \mathbb{Z}_q$ is at most d/q. Note that the probability does not depend on the number n of variables. This is used in zero-knowledge proof systems by committing to the coefficients c_α of f, where $\alpha = (\alpha_1, \ldots, \alpha_n) \in \mathbb{N}^n$ is a multi-index, and then proving

$$f(x_1, \ldots, x_n) = \sum_{|\alpha| \leq d} c_\alpha x_1^{\alpha_1} \ldots x_n^{\alpha_n}$$

for uniformly random challenges $x_1, \ldots, x_n \in \mathbb{Z}_q$ from the verifier. Then, if the coefficient commitments where made before the challenges x_i were known by the prover, it is clear that the coefficients must be independent from the x_i. So, this implies that $f = \sum_{|\alpha| \leq d} c_\alpha X_1^{\alpha_1} \ldots X_n^{\alpha_n}$ with soundness error d/q. Now, one is usually only interested in a few of the coefficients c_α, typically the n coefficients of the pure highest-degree terms divisible by X_i^d for some i. The rest are called garbage coefficients. But since the total number of coefficients, and hence commitments, is equal to $\binom{n+d}{d}$, this gets impractical already for small n and therefore the multivariate case with $n > 1$ is not often used in practical zero-knowledge proof systems.

In this section we develop a new proof technique that only needs a number of garbage commitments that is linear in n while having a modest cost of a linear loss in soundness. First, we decompose the polynomial f such that

$$f(X_1, \ldots, X_n) = f_0 + f_1(X_1) + \cdots + f_n(X_1, \ldots, X_n), \tag{6}$$

where $f_0 \in \mathbb{Z}_q$ is the constant coefficient of f and $f_i \in \mathbb{Z}_q[X_1, \ldots, X_i]$, $i \geq 1$, consist of the monomials $c_\alpha X_1^{\alpha_1} \ldots X_n^{\alpha_n}$ of f with $\alpha_i \geq 1$ and $\alpha_{i+1} = \cdots = \alpha_n = 0$, i.e. the monomials that are divisible by X_i but not by any X_j for $j > i$. Next, note that every polynomial f_i can be viewed as a univariate polynomial in X_i over the ring $\mathbb{Z}_q[X_1, \ldots, X_{i-1}]$, divisible by X_i. More precisely, $f_i = f_{i,1} X_i + \cdots + f_{i,d-1} X_i^{d-1} + l_i X_i^d$ where $f_{i,j} \in \mathbb{Z}_q[X_1, \ldots, X_{i-1}]$ and $l_i \in \mathbb{Z}_q$ since f is of total degree d. Now, we are only really interested in the coefficients l_i, and it turns out there is no need to prove that the other coefficients are actually polynomials in $X_1, \ldots, X_{i-1}$ of degree at most $d - 1$. Indeed, we have the following lemma.

Lemma 2. *Let $f \colon \mathbb{Z}_q^n \to \mathbb{Z}_q$ be a function of the form*

$$f(x_1, \ldots, x_n) = f_0 + f_1(x_1) + f_2^{(x_1)}(x_2) + \cdots + f_n^{(x_1, \ldots, x_{n-1})}(x_n),$$

where $f_0 \in \mathbb{Z}_q$, $f_1 \in \mathbb{Z}_q[X_1]$, and, for $i \geq 2$, $f_i \in (\mathbb{Z}_q[X_i])^{\mathbb{Z}_q^{i-1}}$, i.e. f_i is a function from $\mathbb{Z}_q^{i-1}$ to $\mathbb{Z}_q[X_i]$, given by $(x_1, \ldots, x_{i-1}) \mapsto f_i^{(x_1, \ldots, x_{i-1})}$. Suppose that $f_i^{(x_1, \ldots, x_{i-1})}$ is divisible by X_i (i.e. has zero constant coefficient) and of degree at most d for all $(x_1, \ldots, x_{i-1}) \in \mathbb{Z}_q^{i-1}$, $i \geq 1$. Moreover, suppose that there exists a $j \geq 1$ such that $f_j^{(x_1, \ldots, x_{j-1})} \neq 0$ for all $(x_1, \ldots, x_{j-1}) \in \mathbb{Z}_q^{j-1}$. Then, for uniformly random $(x_1, \ldots, x_n) \in \mathbb{Z}_q^n$, the probability that $f(x_1, \ldots, x_n) = 0$ is at most $(n + 1 - j)d/q$. That is,

$$\Pr[f(x_1, \ldots, x_n) = 0] \leq \frac{(n + 1 - j)d}{q}.$$

Proof. We write $f_{\leq i}$ for the partial function

$$f_{\leq i}(x_1, \ldots, x_i) = f_0 + f_1(x_1) + f_2^{(x_1)}(x_2) + \cdots + f_i^{(x_1, \ldots, x_{i-1})}(x_i)$$

that only includes the functions up to f_i. In particular, $f_{\leq n} = f$. Then we find

$$
\begin{aligned}
&\Pr[f(x_1, \ldots, x_n) = 0] \\
={}& \Pr[f_{\leq n-1}(x_1, \ldots, x_{n-1}) = 0] \\
&\quad \cdot \Pr[f(x_1, \ldots, x_n) = 0 \mid f_{\leq n-1}(x_1, \ldots, x_{n-1}) = 0] \\
&\quad + \Pr[f_{\leq n-1}(x_1, \ldots, x_{n-1}) \neq 0] \\
&\quad\quad \cdot \Pr[f(x_1, \ldots, x_n) = 0 \mid f_{\leq n-1}(x_1, \ldots, x_{n-1}) \neq 0] \\
\leq{}& \Pr[f_{\leq n-1}(x_1, \ldots, x_{n-1}) = 0] \\
&\quad + \Pr[f(x_1, \ldots, x_n) = 0 \mid f_{\leq n-1}(x_1, \ldots, x_{n-1}) \neq 0] \\
\leq{}& \Pr[f_{\leq n-2}(x_1, \ldots, x_{n-2}) = 0] \\
&\quad + \Pr[f_{\leq n-1}(x_1, \ldots, x_{n-1}) = 0 \mid f_{\leq n-2}(x_1, \ldots, x_{n-2}) \neq 0] \\
&\quad + \Pr[f(x_1, \ldots, x_n) = 0 \mid f_{\leq n-1}(x_1, \ldots, x_{n-1}) \neq 0] \\
\leq{}& \ldots \\
\leq{}& \Pr[f_{\leq j}(x_1, \ldots, x_j) = 0] \\
&\quad + \Pr[f_{\leq j+1}(x_1, \ldots, x_{j+1}) = 0 \mid f_{\leq j}(x_1, \ldots, x_j) \neq 0] \\
&\quad + \ldots \\
&\quad + \Pr[f(x_1, \ldots, x_n) = 0 \mid f_{\leq n-1}(x_1, \ldots, x_{n-1}) \neq 0].
\end{aligned}
$$

Consider the first probability $\Pr[f_{\leq j}(x_1, \ldots, x_j) = 0]$ after the last inequality. For every choice $(x_1', \ldots, x_{j-1}') \in \mathbb{Z}_q^{j-1}$, the function

$$f_{\leq j}(x_1', \ldots, x_{j-1}', x_j) = f_{\leq j-1}(x_1', \ldots, x_{j-1}') + f_j^{(x_1', \ldots, x_{j-1}')}(x_j)$$

is a fixed univariate polynomial in x_j of degree at most d and the random variable x_j is independent from it. Moreover, we know from the assumption in the lemma that the polynomial is non-zero since f_j is non-zero and divisible by x_j; that is, f_j is never constant. Therefore,

$$\Pr\left[f_{\leq j}(x_1,\ldots,x_j) = 0\right]$$

$$= \sum_{x'_1,\ldots,x'_{j-1}\in\mathbb{Z}_q} \Pr\left[x_1 = x'_1 \wedge \cdots \wedge x_{j-1} = x'_{j-1}\right] \Pr\left[f_{\leq j}(x'_1,\ldots,x'_{j-1},x_j) = 0\right]$$

$$\leq \sum_{x'_1,\ldots,x'_{j-1}\in\mathbb{Z}_q} \left(\frac{1}{q}\right)^{j-1} \frac{d}{q} = \frac{d}{q}.$$

Similarly, for the other probabilities $\Pr\left[f_{\leq i}(x_1,\ldots,x_i) = 0 \mid f_{\leq i-1}(x_1,\ldots,x_{i-1}) \neq 0\right]$ we interpret $f_{\leq i}(x_1,\ldots,x_i)$ as the evaluation of a polynomial of degree at most d at the independently uniformly random point x_i. This time we condition on the event that the constant coefficient of the polynomial, which is given by $f_{\leq i-1}(x_1,\ldots,x_{i-1})$, is non-zero. Hence,

$$\Pr\left[f_{\leq i}(x_1,\ldots,x_i) = 0 \mid f_{\leq i-1}(x_1,\ldots,x_{i-1}) \neq 0\right] \leq d/q$$

for all $i = j+1,\ldots,n$.   □

3.1   Making Use of Lemma 2 in Zero-Knowledge Protocols

Suppose we want to prove that the polynomial $f \in \mathbb{Z}_q[X_1,\ldots,X_n]$ of total degree d does not contain any terms divisible by X_i^d for any i; that is, f is of degree at most $d-1$ in each X_i. Then decompose f as in Eq. (6), and define the functions $\mathbb{Z}_q^{i-1} \to \mathbb{Z}_q[X_i]$, $(x_1,\ldots,x_{i-1}) \mapsto f_i^{(x_1,\ldots,x_{i-1})}(X_i) = f_i(x_1,\ldots,x_{i-1},X_i)$, that forget the polynomial structure of f_i in the variables $X_1,\ldots,X_i$. Now, in a multi-round protocol where the uniformly random challenges x_i are spread-out over $2n$ rounds we can commit to the $d-1$ coefficients $\gamma_{i,k}$ of $f_i^{(x_1,\ldots,x_{i-1})}(X_i) = \gamma_{i,1}X_i + \cdots + \gamma_{i,d-1}X_i^{d-1}$ immediately after seeing $x_1,\ldots,x_{i-1}$ but before knowing $x_i,\ldots,x_n$. Then we show

$$f(x_1,\ldots,x_n) - \left(\gamma_0 + \sum_{k=1}^{d-1}\gamma_{1,k}x_1^k + \cdots + \sum_{k=1}^{d-1}\gamma_{n,k}x_n^k\right) = 0.$$

Here we assume that we know how to prove that some element of $\mathbb{Z}_q$ is the evaluation $f(x_1,\ldots,x_n)$ of the fixed polynomial f of degree d. The fact that the commitments to the coefficients $\gamma_{i,k}$ were produced before $x_i,\ldots,x_n$ were known shows that they can only be functions of $x_1,\ldots,x_{i-1}$. So, we have effectively proven

$$g_0 + g_1(x_1) + g_2^{(x_1)}(x_2) + \cdots + g_n^{(x_1,\ldots,x_{n-1})}(x_n) = 0,$$

for uniformly random $(x_1,\ldots,x_n) \in \mathbb{Z}_q^n$ and functions g_i as in Lemma 2 that fulfill the requirements that they have zero constant coefficient and are of degree at most d. Furthermore, for each $i \in \{1,\ldots,n\}$ and all $(x'_1,\ldots,x'_{i-1}) \in \mathbb{Z}_q^{i-1}$, the coefficient for X_i^d of $g_i^{(x'_1,\ldots,x'_{i-1})}$ is given by the corresponding coefficient in

f. It follows that we proven f to be of degree $d - 1$ in all X_i with soundness error nd/q. Note that we only needed $n(d - 1) + 1$ garbage commitments.

As an example, in our lattice-based protocols we let the prover ultimately send amortized masked openings $\vec{z}(x_1, \ldots, x_n) = \vec{y} + x_1 \vec{s}_1 + \cdots + x_n \vec{s}_n$ of secret vectors $\vec{s}_i \in \mathbb{Z}_q^m$ with challenges $x_i \in \mathbb{Z}_q$, and we want to be able to prove that all secret vectors are binary. So, using another uniformly random challenge vector $\vec{\varphi} \in \mathbb{Z}_q^m$, we want to show that the quadratic ($d = 2$) polynomial

$$f(x_1, \ldots, x_n) = \langle \vec{z} \circ ((x_1 + \cdots + x_n) \vec{1} - \vec{z}), \vec{\varphi} \rangle \tag{7}$$

does not contain terms of the form x_i^2. Here each of the polynomials $f_i^{(x_1, \ldots, x_{i-1})}$ involves only one garbage coefficient and is of the form $f_i^{(x_1, \ldots, x_{i-1})}(X_i) = \gamma_i X_i$. So we end up only needing $n + 1$ garbage commitments to the coefficients γ_i. The protocol proceeds as follows. The prover receives the challenge vector $\vec{\varphi}$ and commits to the first garbage coefficient $\gamma_0 = -\langle \vec{y} \circ \vec{y}, \vec{\varphi} \rangle$. Then, over the course of the next $2n$ rounds, the protocol alternates between the prover committing to the next garbage coefficient

$$\gamma_i = \left\langle \vec{y} \circ (1 - 2\vec{s}_i) + \sum_{j=1}^{i-1} x_j (\vec{s}_j \circ (\vec{1} - \vec{s}_i) + \vec{s}_i \circ (\vec{1} - \vec{s}_j)), \vec{\varphi} \right\rangle,$$

and the verifier sending the next challenge x_i, for $i = 1, \ldots, n$. Afterwards, the protocol is finished by proving the linear relation (in the garbage coefficients)

$$\langle \vec{z} \circ ((x_1 + \cdots + x_n) \vec{1} - \vec{z}), \vec{\varphi} \rangle - (\gamma_0 + \gamma_1 x_1 + \cdots + \gamma_n x_n) = 0. \tag{8}$$

In the PCP literature, when proving such pointwise multiplicative relations on many vectors, a different technique is used to keep the number of garbage coefficients linear in the number of vectors. Namely, instead of multivariate masked openings of degree one, univariate openings of degree n are used where the different vectors are separated as the basis coefficients with respect to a basis given by Lagrange interpolation polynomials. See [GGPR13] for details. This technique does not seem to be compatible with our lattice-based setting. Concretely, we will later need to conclude from SIS hardness that the prover is bound to the vectors in the masked opening and our approach for achieving this requires multivariate openings.

Moreover, the so-called sum check protocols for multivariate polynomials from [LFKN92, Sha92] have similarities with our protocol. These protocols also have n rounds and in each round the polynomial is reduced to a univariate polynomial.

We don't consider it a problem that our protocol has many rounds. We don't view the number of rounds to be of practical importance that needs to be optimized. The interactive variants of our protocols only serve as a convenient intermediate representation that is easy to reason about. But in practice only the non-interactive variants will ever be used and there the number of rounds only has an indirect effect on for example the prover and verifier runtime and the soundness error but no independent relevance. If the protocol can achieve negligible soundness error and still has acceptable runtimes and proof sizes, then the number of rounds doesn't matter.

4   Exact Amortized Binary Opening Proof

The aim of this section is to present a protocol for proving knowledge of (exactly) binary preimages $\vec{s}_i \in \{0,1\}^m \subset \mathcal{R}_q^{m/d}$ to n collision-resistant hashes $\vec{u}_i = A\vec{s}_i$. Our starting point is the approximate amortized proof that goes back to [BBC+18]. There the prover samples a short masking vector $\vec{y}$ and commits to it by sending $\vec{w} = A\vec{y}$. The verifier then sends n short challenge polynomials $c_1, \ldots, c_n$ and the prover replies by sending the amortized masked opening $\vec{z} = \vec{y} + c_1\vec{s}_1 + \cdots + c_n\vec{s}_n$. The verifier accepts if $\vec{z}$ is short and a preimage of $\vec{w} + c_1\vec{u}_1 + \cdots + c_n\vec{u}_n$. This protocol is sound, because, for every $i = 1, \ldots, n$, the prover must be able to answer two challenge tuples successfully that differ only in the one challenge c_i. Then the difference of the two corresponding masked openings yields the approximate solution $A(\vec{z} - \vec{z}') = (c_i - c_i')\vec{u}_i$.

Next, we want to get rid of the perturbation factors $\bar{c}_i = c_i - c_i'$. In general and for efficient parameters they are not invertible so we can not simply divide through, but it is possible to use the strategy from [ALS20] where one pieces together many extractions from potentially several parallel repetitions of the protocol in order to get so-called weak openings $\vec{s}_i^*$ such that $A\vec{s}_i^* = \vec{u}_i$ (c.f. [ALS20, Definition 4.2]). The weak openings are not necessarily short but the prover is still bound to them; see [ALS20, Lemma 4.3].

Now, to extend the proof and show that the $\vec{s}_i^*$ are in fact binary, the amortized masked opening $\vec{z}$ from above with polynomial challenges is not of much help. The problem is that the polynomial product effectively intermingles all the secret coefficients and then it seems inefficient to prove all the quadratic relations about individual coefficients that we need for proving that each and every coefficient is binary. Therefore, our protocol has a second stage with integer challenges $x_i \in \mathbb{Z}_q$ and masked opening

$$\vec{z} = \vec{y} + x_1\vec{s}_1 + \cdots + x_n\vec{s}_n.$$

To get as much soundness as possible, and at the same time not increase q more than necessary, we want the challenges x_i to be uniformly random modulo q. But since we are relying on MSIS hardness we can not send $\vec{z}$ directly. Instead, we compose it from l short $\vec{z}_j$ with short integer challenges $x_{i,j} \in \mathbb{Z}$, $j = 0, \ldots, l-1$. More precisely, we set $\delta = \lceil q^{1/l} \rceil$, and $x_i \bmod q = x_{i,0} + \cdots + x_{i,l-1}\delta^{l-1}$ (non-negative standard representative), where $0 \le x_{i,j} < \delta$. Then, the prover sends the polynomial vectors

$$\vec{z}_j = \vec{y}_j + x_{1,j}\vec{s}_1 + \cdots + x_{n,j}\vec{s}_n.$$

In principle the second stage with integer challenges $x_{i,j}$ alone would allow to extract the weak openings $\vec{s}_i^*$, but we still include the first stage with polynomial challenges as it turns out that the final norm bound for which we need Module-SIS to be hard depends on the norm of the product of two challenges. Hence, when one of the challenges can be a shorter polynomial challenge, this results in a smaller Module-SIS norm bound and ultimately smaller proof sizes.

Next, for the actual binary proof we work with the composed $\vec{z} = \vec{z}_0 + \cdots + \vec{z}_{l-1}\delta^{l-1}$. We forget the polynomial structure and let $\vec{z} = \vec{y} + x_1\vec{s}_1 + \cdots + x_n\vec{s}_n \in \mathbb{Z}_q^m$ be given by the coefficient vectors that correspond to the polynomial vectors. This allows for the approach from Sect. 3.1 for proving that all secret coefficients are binary. Let $\vec{\varphi} \in \mathbb{Z}_q^m$ be a uniformly random challenge vector from the verifier. Eventually we need to prove Eq. (8) with garbage coefficients γ_i that are from commitments produced interactively with increasing dependence on the challenges x_i as explained. We use the BDLOP commitment scheme and apply the linear proof from [ENS20], which we call the *auxiliary proof* in this protocol. Since our binary proof has a soundness error bigger than $1/q$, there is no need to apply the soundness boosting techniques for the linear proof. That is, we use the simpler proof without automorphisms. So, after the initial approximate proof, at the beginning of the second stage, the prover initializes the BDLOP commitment scheme. He samples a randomness vector $\vec{r}^{(t)} \in \mathcal{R}_q^{\kappa_2+\lambda+\mu}$ and commits to it in the top part $\vec{t}_0 = B_0\vec{r} \in \mathcal{R}_q^{\kappa_2}$. Here κ_2, λ, and $\mu = \lceil(n+1)/d\rceil + 1$ are the BDLOP MSIS rank, MLWE rank, and message rank, respectively. Since the prover needs to commit to only one $\mathbb{Z}_q$-element at a time and not a full $\mathcal{R}_q$-polynomial, he is going to send individual NTT coefficients of the low part of the BDLOP commitment scheme. More precisely, the prover precomputes the NTT vector $\vec{e} = \mathsf{NTT}(B_1\vec{r}^{(t)}) \in \mathbb{Z}_q^{\lceil(n+1)/d\rceil d}$. Then, when he wants to commit to $\gamma_i \in \mathbb{Z}_q$, he sends $\tau_i = e_i + \gamma_i$, $i = 0, \ldots, n$. In the end the verifier has the full commitment polynomial vector $\vec{t}_2 = \mathsf{NTT}^{-1}(\vec{\tau}) = B_2\vec{r} + \mathsf{NTT}^{-1}(\vec{\gamma})$.

After the initialization of BDLOP, the prover samples l masking vectors $\vec{y}_j$ for the short shares $\vec{z}_j$ of $\vec{z}$ and sends the commitments $\vec{w}_j = A\vec{y}_j$, together with $\vec{t}_0$. The verifier follows by sending the challenge vector $\vec{\varphi}$ for the binary proof. Next, the core subprotocol with $2n+2$ rounds starts. Here the prover and verifier alternate between garbage commitments to the parts $f_i = \gamma_i x_i$ of the polynomial $f(x_1, \ldots, x_n)$ in Eq. (7), and the challenges x_i. Finally, the prover computes the shares $\vec{z}_j$, performs rejection sampling on them, and sends them if there was no rejection. This concludes the second stage and main part of the protocol. Finally, the protocol is finished with the auxiliary proof for Eq. (8), exactly as in [ENS20].

Before we spell-out the protocol in detail in Fig. 1 and then analyze its security, we mention a technical problem that we have to overcome in the security proof of the protocol. When we sketched the binary proof in Sect. 3.1, we assumed that $\vec{z}$ is the evaluation of a fixed polynomial in the challenges $x_1, \ldots, x_n$. In other words for the extraction this means that we must be sure that

$$\vec{z} = \vec{y}^* + x_1\vec{s}_1^* + \cdots + x_n\vec{s}_n^*$$

in (almost all) accepting transcripts with always the same weak openings $\vec{y}^*$ and $\vec{s}_i^*$. The problem is that this is harder to prove in our amortized setting. Let us recall the argument for the single-secret case with $\vec{z} = \vec{y}^* + x\vec{s}^*$, which was presented in [ALS20]. If we find some accepting transcript where the masked opening $\vec{z}'$ is given by $\vec{z}' = \vec{y}^{**} + x'\vec{s}^*$ with a different $\vec{y}^{**} \neq \vec{y}^*$, then we know a challenge difference $\bar{x}$ such that $\bar{x}\vec{s}^*$ is short and $\bar{x}(\vec{z} - \vec{z}') - (x - x')\bar{x}\vec{s}^* = \bar{x}(\vec{y}^* - \vec{y}^{**}) \neq 0$ is a Module-SIS solution. This argument can not be extended to the amortized setting since we would need to multiply by many different $\bar{x}_i$ and not find a sufficiently short Module-SIS solution. But it turns out we can turn the whole argument around and proceed via the contraposition. Concretely, if one of the weak openings $\vec{s}_i^*$ is not binary, then we must be able to find accepting transcripts with different $\vec{y}^{**}$ that results in a SIS solution. See the proof of Theorem 1 for the details (Fig. 3).

Theorem 1. *The protocol in Fig. 1 is correct, computationally honest verifier zero-knowledge under the Module-LWE assumption and computationally knowledge-sound under the Module-SIS assumption. More precisely, let p be the maximum probability of $\mathbf{c} \bmod X - \zeta$ as in Lemma 1. Let ω be a bound on the ℓ_1-norm of the $\mathbf{c}_i$.*

Then, for correctness, unless the honest prover $\mathcal{P}$ aborts due to rejection sampling, it convinces the honest verifier $\mathcal{V}$ with overwhelming probability.

For zero-knowledge, there exists an efficient simulator $\mathcal{S}$, that, without access to the secret $\vec{s}_i$, outputs a simulation of a non-aborting transcript of the protocol between $\mathcal{P}$ and $\mathcal{V}$ for every statement $\vec{u}_i = \mathbf{A}\vec{s}_i$. An algorithm that can distinguish the simulation from the real transcript with advantage ε can distinguish $\mathsf{MLWE}_{\lambda,\chi}$ with advantage $\varepsilon - 2^{100}$ in the same running time.

For knowledge-soundness, there is an extractor $\mathcal{E}$ with the following properties. When given resettable black-box access to a deterministic prover $\mathcal{P}^*$ that convinces $\mathcal{V}$ with probability $\varepsilon > (2n + 2)/q + p$, $\mathcal{E}$ either outputs binary preimages $\vec{s}_i^* \in \{0,1\}^m$ for all hashes $\vec{u}_i$, an $\mathsf{MSIS}_{\kappa,B}$ solution for $\mathbf{A}$ with $B = 4(\omega\beta_2 + \delta\beta_1 + n\omega\delta\sqrt{m})$, or an $\mathsf{MSIS}_{\kappa_2,8\omega\beta_3}$ solution for $\mathbf{B}_0$.

The proof of Theorem 1 is contained in the full version of the paper.

Remark. In the interest of simplicity, we have chosen to present the protocol for binary secret vectors only. It should be clear that the protocol can easily be adapted to prove knowledge of secret preimages that have coefficients from a larger interval, for example ternary coefficients in $\{-1, 0, 1\}$. Then the prover would send two garbage commitments before each challenge x_i.

4.1   Extending the Proof to Linear and Product Relations

In applications of our exact opening proof one usually also wants to prove linear and product relations on the preimage (coefficient) vectors $\vec{s}_i$. We now show that our protocol can easily be extended to include such relations with little additional cost.

Prover $\mathcal{P}$	Verifier $\mathcal{V}$

Inputs:

$B_0 \in \mathcal{R}_q^{\kappa_2 \times (\kappa_2 + \lambda + \mu)}$

$B_1 \in \mathcal{R}_q^{(\mu-1) \times (\kappa_2 + \lambda + \mu)}$

$\vec{b}_2 \in \mathcal{R}_q^{\kappa_2 + \lambda + \mu}$

$A \in \mathcal{R}_q^{\kappa \times m/d}$

For $i = 1, \ldots, n$:

$\quad \vec{s}_i \in \{0,1\}^m \subset \mathcal{R}_q^{m/d}$

$\quad \vec{u}_i = A\vec{s}_i$

Verifier inputs: $B_0, B_1, \vec{b}_2$ and $A, \vec{u}_i$

The prover and verifier run the approximate amortized opening proof from Figure 2, $\langle \mathcal{P}_{\mathsf{approx}}(A, \vec{s}_i), \mathcal{V}_{\mathsf{approx}}(A, \vec{u}_i) \rangle$. The verifier rejects if $\mathcal{V}_{\mathsf{approx}}$ rejects.

$(\vec{r}^{(t)}, \vec{t}_0, \vec{e}) = \mathsf{AUXINIT}(B_0, B_1)$

For $j = 0, \ldots, l-1$:

$\quad \vec{y}_j \xleftarrow{\$} D_{\mathfrak{s}_2}^m$

$\quad \vec{w}_j = A\vec{y}_j$ $\qquad \xrightarrow{\vec{t}_0, \vec{w}_j}$

$\qquad \xleftarrow{\vec{\varphi}} \qquad \vec{\varphi} \xleftarrow{\$} \mathbb{Z}_q^m$

$\vec{y} = \sum_{j=0}^{l-1} \vec{y}_j \delta^j$

$\gamma_0 = -\langle \vec{y} \circ \vec{y}, \vec{\varphi} \rangle$

$\tau_0 = e_0 + \gamma_0$ $\qquad \xrightarrow{\tau_0}$

The prover and verifier run the core protocol from Figure 4, $(\tau_1, x_1, \ldots, \tau_n, x_n) = \langle \mathcal{P}_{\mathsf{core}}(\vec{e}, \vec{y}, \vec{\varphi}, \vec{s}_i), \mathcal{V}_{\mathsf{core}}() \rangle$. Then they set $\vec{\tau} = (\tau_0, \ldots, \tau_n)^T$, $\vec{x} = (1, x_1, \ldots, x_n)^T$ and $\vec{t}_1 = \mathsf{NTT}^{-1}(\vec{\tau})$, and decompose $x_i = x_{i,0} + \cdots + x_{i,l-1}\delta^{l-1}$ for $i = 1, \ldots, n$. The prover keeps the garbage coefficients γ_i from $\mathcal{P}_{\mathsf{core}}$ and sets $\vec{\gamma} = (\gamma_0, \ldots, \gamma_n)^T$.

For $j = 0, \ldots, l-1$:

$\quad \vec{z}_j = \vec{y}_j + \sum_{i=1}^{n} x_{i,j} \vec{s}_i$

If $\mathsf{Rej}\left((\vec{z}_j), (\vec{y}_j), \mathfrak{s}_2 \right) = 1$, abort $\qquad \xrightarrow{\vec{z}_j}$

$\qquad \mathsf{VERIFY}(A, \vec{u}_i, \vec{w}_j, x_{i,j}, \vec{z}_j)$

The prover and verifier run the auxiliary linear proof from Figure 5, $\langle \mathcal{P}_{\mathsf{aux}}(B, \vec{r}^{(t)}, \vec{t}, \vec{\gamma}, \vec{x}), \mathcal{V}_{\mathsf{aux}}(B, \vec{t}, p, \vec{x}) \rangle$, where $p = \langle \vec{z} \circ ((x_1 + \cdots + x_n)\vec{1} - \vec{z}), \vec{\varphi} \rangle$ for $\vec{z} = \sum_{j=0}^{l-1} \vec{z}_j \delta^j$. The verifier accepts if $\mathcal{V}_{\mathsf{aux}}$ accepts.

Fig. 1. Exact amortized opening proof for lattice-based hashes.

$$
\begin{array}{ll}
\textbf{Prover } \mathcal{P}_{\mathsf{approx}} & \textbf{Verifier } \mathcal{V}_{\mathsf{approx}} \\
\text{Inputs:} & \\
\boldsymbol{A} \in \mathcal{R}_q^{\kappa \times m/d} & \boldsymbol{A}, \vec{\boldsymbol{u}}_i \\
\text{For } i = 1, \ldots, n: & \\
\quad \vec{\boldsymbol{s}}_i \in \{0,1\}^m \subset \mathcal{R}_q^{m/d} & \\
\quad \vec{\boldsymbol{u}}_i = \boldsymbol{A}\vec{\boldsymbol{s}}_i &
\end{array}
$$

$$
\begin{array}{ll}
\vec{\boldsymbol{y}}^{(c)} \xleftarrow{\$} D_{\mathfrak{s}_1}^m & \\
\vec{\boldsymbol{w}}^{(c)} = \boldsymbol{A}\vec{\boldsymbol{y}}^{(c)} & \xrightarrow{\ \vec{\boldsymbol{w}}^{(c)}\ } \\
& \xleftarrow{\ \boldsymbol{c}_i\ } \quad \boldsymbol{c}_i \xleftarrow{\$} \mathcal{C}\ \forall i \in [n] \\
\vec{\boldsymbol{z}}^{(c)} = \vec{\boldsymbol{w}}^{(c)} + \displaystyle\sum_{i=1}^{n} \boldsymbol{c}_i \vec{\boldsymbol{s}}_i & \\
\text{If } \mathsf{Rej}\left(\vec{\boldsymbol{z}}^{(c)}, \vec{\boldsymbol{y}}^{(c)}, \mathfrak{s}_1\right) = 1,\ \text{abort} & \xrightarrow{\ \vec{\boldsymbol{z}}^{(c)}\ } \\
& \|\vec{\boldsymbol{z}}^{(c)}\| \overset{?}{\leq} \mathfrak{s}_1\sqrt{2m} = \beta_1 \\
& \boldsymbol{A}\vec{\boldsymbol{z}}^{(c)} \overset{?}{=} \vec{\boldsymbol{w}}^{(c)} + \displaystyle\sum_{i=1}^{n} \boldsymbol{c}_i \vec{\boldsymbol{u}}_i
\end{array}
$$

Fig. 2. Approximate amortized opening proof for lattice-based hashes. Used for bootstrapping the exact amortized proof in Fig. 1.

$\mathsf{VERIFY}(\boldsymbol{A}, \vec{\boldsymbol{u}}_i, \vec{\boldsymbol{w}}_j, x_{i,j}, \vec{\boldsymbol{z}}_j)$

01 For $j = 0, \ldots, l-1$:

02 $\quad \|\vec{\boldsymbol{z}}_j\| \overset{?}{\leq} \mathfrak{s}_2\sqrt{2m} = \beta_2$

03 $\quad \boldsymbol{A}\vec{\boldsymbol{z}}_j \overset{?}{=} \vec{\boldsymbol{w}}_j + \sum_{i=1}^n x_{i,j}\vec{\boldsymbol{u}}_i$

$\mathsf{AUXINIT}(\boldsymbol{B}_0, \boldsymbol{B}_1)$

01 $\vec{\boldsymbol{r}}^{(t)} \xleftarrow{\$} \chi^{(\kappa_2 + \lambda + \mu)d}$

02 $\vec{\boldsymbol{t}}_0 = \boldsymbol{B}_0 \vec{\boldsymbol{r}}^{(t)}$

03 $\vec{\boldsymbol{e}} = \mathsf{NTT}(\boldsymbol{B}_1 \vec{\boldsymbol{r}}^{(t)})$

04 return $(\vec{\boldsymbol{r}}^{(t)}, \vec{\boldsymbol{t}}_0, \vec{\boldsymbol{e}})$

$\mathsf{VERFYAUX}(\boldsymbol{B}, \vec{\boldsymbol{t}}, \vec{\boldsymbol{w}}^{(t)}, \boldsymbol{c}^{(t)}, \vec{\boldsymbol{z}}^{(t)}, \theta, \boldsymbol{h}, \boldsymbol{v}, p, \vec{\boldsymbol{x}})$

01 $h_0 \overset{?}{=} 0$

02 $\|\vec{\boldsymbol{z}}^{(t)}\| \overset{?}{\leq} \mathfrak{s}_3\sqrt{2(\kappa_2 + \lambda + \mu)d} = \beta_3$

03 $\boldsymbol{B}_0 \vec{\boldsymbol{z}}^{(t)} \overset{?}{=} \vec{\boldsymbol{w}}^{(t)} + \boldsymbol{c}^{(t)} \vec{\boldsymbol{t}}_0$

04 $\langle \vec{\boldsymbol{b}}_2, \vec{\boldsymbol{z}}^{(t)} \rangle + \langle \mathsf{NTT}^{-1}(d\theta\vec{\boldsymbol{x}}), \boldsymbol{B}_1 \vec{\boldsymbol{z}}^{(t)} \rangle$
$\quad \overset{?}{=} \boldsymbol{v} + \boldsymbol{c}^{(t)}(\boldsymbol{t}_2 + \langle \mathsf{NTT}^{-1}(d\theta\vec{\boldsymbol{x}}), \vec{\boldsymbol{t}}_1 \rangle) - \theta p - \boldsymbol{h}$

Fig. 3. Helper functions $\mathsf{VERIFY}()$, $\mathsf{AUXINIT}()$ and $\mathsf{VERIFYAUX}()$ used by exact amortized opening proof in Fig. 1. They check the verification equations, initialize the auxiliary commitment, and check the verification equations of the auxiliary linear proof, respectively.

Prover $\mathcal{P}_{core}$ Verifier $\mathcal{V}_{core}$

Inputs:

$\vec{e} \in \mathbb{Z}_q^{n+1}$

$\vec{y}, \vec{\varphi} \in \mathbb{Z}_q^m$

$\vec{s}_1, \ldots, \vec{s}_n \in \mathbb{Z}_q^m$

$\gamma_1 = \langle \vec{y} \circ (\vec{1} - 2\vec{s}_1), \vec{\varphi} \rangle$

$\tau_1 = e_1 + \gamma_1$

$\xrightarrow{\quad \tau_1 \quad}$

$\xleftarrow{\quad x_1 \quad}$ $\qquad x_1 \xleftarrow{\$} \mathbb{Z}_q^\times$

$\gamma_2 = \langle \vec{y} \circ (\vec{1} - 2\vec{s}_2), \vec{\varphi} \rangle$

$\qquad + x_1 \langle \vec{s}_1 \circ (\vec{1} - \vec{s}_2) + \vec{s}_2 \circ (\vec{1} - \vec{s}_1), \vec{\varphi} \rangle$

$\tau_2 = e_2 + \gamma_2$

$\xrightarrow{\quad \tau_2 \quad}$

$\xleftarrow{\quad x_2 \quad}$ $\qquad x_2 \xleftarrow{\$} \mathbb{Z}_q^\times$

$\vdots$

$\gamma_n = \langle \vec{y} \circ (\vec{1} - 2\vec{s}_n), \vec{\varphi} \rangle$

$\qquad + \sum_{i=1}^{n-1} x_i \langle \vec{s}_i \circ (\vec{1} - \vec{s}_n) + \vec{s}_n \circ (\vec{1} - \vec{s}_i), \vec{\varphi} \rangle$

$\tau_n = e_n + \gamma_n$

$\xrightarrow{\quad \tau_n \quad}$

$\xleftarrow{\quad x_n \quad}$ $\qquad x_n \xleftarrow{\$} \mathbb{Z}_q^\times$

Fig. 4. Core protocol for exact amortized opening proof in Fig. 1

Prover $\mathcal{P}_{\mathsf{aux}}$ Verifier $\mathcal{V}_{\mathsf{aux}}$

Inputs:

$\boldsymbol{B}_0 \in \mathcal{R}_q^{\kappa_2 \times (\kappa_2+\lambda+\mu)}$ $\boldsymbol{B}_0, \boldsymbol{B}_1, \vec{\boldsymbol{b}}_2$

$\boldsymbol{B}_1 \in \mathcal{R}_q^{(\mu-1) \times (\kappa_2+\lambda+\mu)}$ $\vec{\boldsymbol{t}}_0, \vec{\boldsymbol{t}}_1$

$\vec{\boldsymbol{b}}_2 \in \mathcal{R}_q^{\kappa_2+\lambda+\mu}$ $p \in \mathbb{Z}_q$

$\vec{\boldsymbol{r}}^{(t)} \in \{-1,0,1\}^{(\kappa_2+\lambda+\mu)d} \subset \mathcal{R}_q^{\kappa_2+\lambda+\mu}$ $\vec{x} \in \mathbb{Z}_q^{(\mu-1)d}$

$\vec{\boldsymbol{t}}_0 = \boldsymbol{B}_0 \vec{\boldsymbol{r}}^{(t)}$

$\vec{\boldsymbol{t}}_1 = \boldsymbol{B}_1 \vec{\boldsymbol{r}}^{(t)} + \mathsf{NTT}^{-1}(\vec{\gamma})$

$\vec{\gamma}, \vec{x} \in \mathbb{Z}_q^{(\mu-1)d}$

$g \overset{\$}{\leftarrow} \{g \in \mathcal{R}_q \mid g_0 = 0\}$

$t_2 = \langle \vec{\boldsymbol{b}}_2, \vec{\boldsymbol{r}}^{(t)} \rangle + g$

$\vec{\boldsymbol{y}}^{(t)} \overset{\$}{\leftarrow} D_{\mathfrak{s}_3}^{(\kappa_2+\lambda+\mu)d}$

$\vec{\boldsymbol{w}}^{(t)} = \boldsymbol{B}_0 \vec{\boldsymbol{y}}^{(t)}$ $\xrightarrow{\quad t_2, \vec{\boldsymbol{w}}^{(t)} \quad}$

                                             $\xleftarrow{\quad \theta \quad}$ $\theta \overset{\$}{\leftarrow} \mathbb{Z}_q$

$h = g + \langle \mathsf{NTT}^{-1}(d\theta\vec{x}), \mathsf{NTT}^{-1}(\vec{\gamma})\rangle - \theta\langle \vec{x}, \vec{\gamma}\rangle$

$v = \langle \vec{\boldsymbol{b}}_2, \vec{\boldsymbol{y}}^{(t)} \rangle + \langle \mathsf{NTT}^{-1}(d\theta\vec{x}), \boldsymbol{B}_1 \vec{\boldsymbol{y}}^{(t)}\rangle$ $\xrightarrow{\quad h, v \quad}$

                                             $\xleftarrow{\quad \boldsymbol{c}^{(t)} \quad}$ $\boldsymbol{c}^{(t)} \overset{\$}{\leftarrow} \mathcal{C}$

$\vec{\boldsymbol{z}}^{(t)} = \vec{\boldsymbol{y}}^{(t)} + \boldsymbol{c}^{(t)} \vec{\boldsymbol{r}}^{(t)}$

If $\mathsf{Rej}\left(\vec{\boldsymbol{z}}^{(t)}, \vec{\boldsymbol{y}}^{(t)}, \mathfrak{s}_3\right) = 1$, abort $\xrightarrow{\quad \vec{\boldsymbol{z}}^{(t)} \quad}$

                                                           $\mathsf{VERIFYAUX}(\boldsymbol{B}, \vec{\boldsymbol{t}},$
                                                             $\vec{\boldsymbol{w}}^{(t)}, \boldsymbol{c}^{(t)}, \vec{\boldsymbol{z}}^{(t)},$
                                                             $\theta, h, v, p, \vec{x})$

Fig. 5. Auxiliary linear proof needed in our exact amortized opening proof in Fig. 1 and in the tree opening proof.

Linear Relations. Let $\vec{s} = \vec{s}_1 \parallel \cdots \parallel \vec{s}_n$ be the concatenation of all the binary $\vec{s}_i$ and $M = (M_1, \ldots, M_n) \in \mathbb{Z}_q^{\nu \times nm}$ with $M_i \in \mathbb{Z}_q^{\nu \times m}$ be a public matrix. Now suppose in full generality that we want to prove the linear equation

$$M\vec{s} = M_1\vec{s}_1 + \cdots + M_n\vec{s}_n = \vec{v}$$

for some public vector $\vec{v} \in \mathcal{R}_q^\nu$. So this is an "unstructured" linear equation not necessarily compatible with the polynomial structure. As usual, the equation can be proven by probabilistically reducing it to a scalar product first. So we prove

$$\langle M\vec{s} - \vec{v}, \vec{\psi} \rangle = \langle \vec{s}, M^T\vec{\psi} \rangle - \langle \vec{v}, \vec{\psi} \rangle = \sum_{i=1}^{n} \langle \vec{s}_i, M_i^T\vec{\psi} \rangle - \langle \vec{v}, \vec{\psi} \rangle = 0$$

for a uniformly random challenge vector $\vec{\psi} \in \mathbb{Z}_q^\nu$ that is given to the prover after the hashes $\vec{u}_i = A\vec{s}_i$ are known.

Now, we use a very similar approach to the one from Sect. 3.1. Concretely, let $\vec{\rho} = x_1^{-1}\vec{\rho}_1 + \cdots + x_n^{-1}\vec{\rho}_n$ where $\vec{\rho}_i = M_i^T\vec{\psi}$. Then we want to show that in the multivariate quadratic polynomial

$$f_{\mathsf{lin}}(x_1, \ldots, x_n) = \langle \vec{z}, \vec{\rho} \rangle - \langle \vec{v}, \vec{\psi} \rangle$$

the constant coefficient vanishes. More precisely, we want to prove the relation

$$\langle \vec{z}, \vec{\rho} \rangle - \langle \vec{v}, \vec{\psi} \rangle - \sum_{i=1}^{n} (\gamma_{2i-1}x_i^{-1} + \gamma_{2i}x_i) = 0$$

with garbage coefficients

$$\gamma_{2i-1}^{(\mathsf{lin})} = \langle \vec{y}, \vec{\rho}_i \rangle + \sum_{i=1}^{i-1} x_j \langle \vec{s}_j, \vec{\rho}_i \rangle,$$

$$\gamma_{2i}^{(\mathsf{lin})} = \sum_{j=1}^{i-1} x_j^{-1} \langle \vec{s}_i, \vec{\rho}_j \rangle.$$

We can share the garbage commitments between the linear and binary proofs by simply adding f_{lin} to f from Eq. (7). That is, we finally prove

$$\langle \vec{z} \circ ((x_1 + \cdots + x_n)\vec{1} - \vec{z}), \vec{\varphi} \rangle + \langle \vec{z}, \vec{\rho} \rangle - \langle \vec{v}, \vec{\psi} \rangle$$
$$- \left(\gamma_0 + \sum_{i=1}^{n} (\gamma_{2i-1}x_i^{-1} + \gamma_{2i}x_i) \right) = 0.$$

This is sufficient although the equation now contains the constant garbage coefficient γ_0 so that it is not immediately clear why the contribution from the linear proof to the constant term vanishes. The reason is that the prover can commit to $\gamma_0 = -\langle \vec{y} \circ \vec{y}, \vec{\varphi} \rangle$ before the challenge $\vec{\psi}$ is known. Then, if the linear equation $M\vec{s} = \vec{v}$ were false, there would be a uniformly random contribution to the constant term that is independent from γ_0.

Product Relations. By product relations we mean multiplicative relations of the form $s_1 s_2 = s_3$ between coefficients s_1, s_2, s_3 of the secret vectors $\vec{s}_i$. For simplicity we restrict to the case where the coefficients s_1, s_2, s_3 are from the same vector $\vec{s}_i$ and the relation holds in all vectors $\vec{s}_i$. More precisely, we consider relations $s_{i,j_1} s_{i,j_2} = s_{i,j_3}$ for a triple $(j_1, j_2, j_3) \in \{0, \ldots, m-1\}^3$ and all i. This is sufficient for many applications by packing the $\vec{s}_i$ in a suitable manner. For example, if we want to hash three binary vectors $\vec{a}, \vec{b}, \vec{c} \in \{0,1\}^{kn}$ for some $k \geq 1$, and prove that $\vec{a} \circ \vec{b} = \vec{c}$, then we write $\vec{a} = \vec{a}_1 \| \cdots \| \vec{a}_k$ with $\vec{a}_i \in \{0,1\}^n$, and let $\vec{s}_i$ be the columns of the matrix with rows $\vec{a}_i^T, \vec{b}_i^T, \vec{c}_i^T$,

$$\left(\vec{s}_1 \ldots \vec{s}_n \right) = \left(\vec{a}_1 \cdots \vec{a}_k \; \vec{b}_1 \cdots \vec{b}_k \; \vec{c}_1 \cdots \vec{c}_k \right)^T.$$

Now to prove the above relation we need to show that $s_{i,j} s_{i,j+k} = s_{i,j+2k}$ for all $i = 1, \ldots, n$ and $j = 0, \ldots, k-1$. Note that such relations are only a very slight generalisation of the relations $s_{i,j}(1 - s_{i,j}) = 0$ that we already prove in the binary proof. More general product relations are possible, but they come with a cost of more garbage commitments.

In the protocol, for every product relation $s_{i,j_1} s_{i,j_2} = s_{i,j_3}$ we add the polynomial

$$f_{\mathsf{prod}}(x_1, \ldots, x_n) = (z_{j_1} z_{j_2} - (x_1 + \cdots + x_n) z_{j_3})\theta$$

for a uniformly random challenge $\theta \in \mathbb{Z}_q$ to the previous $f + f_{\mathsf{lin}}$ that we prove. Similarly as f from the binary proof, the polynomial f_{prod} is a quadratic polynomial that has no terms divisible by x_i^2 if the product relation is true.

4.2   Proof Size

We study the size of the proof that is output by the non-interactive version of the protocol in this section. The non-interactive version is obtained by applying the Fiat-Shamir transform. We handle the slightly more general case where the secret vectors $\vec{s}_i$ are not necessarily binary but have coefficients in the range $\{-\lfloor b/2 \rfloor, \ldots, \lfloor (b-1)/2 \rfloor\}$. Then there are $(b-1)n + 1$ garbage coefficients. The masking vector commitments $\vec{w}^{(c)}$, $\vec{w}_j$ and $\vec{w}^{(t)}$ do not need to be included in the proof since they can be computed from the verification equations and then verified with the random oracle when the challenges are included in the proof. For $\vec{w}^{(c)}$ and $\vec{w}^{(t)}$ this is always efficient. Whether it is also efficient for the $\vec{w}_j$ depends on n. For large n the cost of the n challenges x_i becomes bigger than the cost of the $\vec{w}_j$. The polynomial v in the auxiliary proof does not need to be transmitted either. Hence a complete proof amounts to the objects $\vec{c}, \vec{z}^{(c)}$ for the approximate amortized proof; $\vec{t}_0, \vec{\varphi}, \vec{t}_1, \vec{x}, \vec{z}_j$ for the main part; and $\vec{t}_2, \theta, \boldsymbol{h}, \boldsymbol{c}^{(t)}, \vec{z}^{(t)}$ for the auxiliary proof. The actual size of the challenges as (vectors of) polynomials or $\mathbb{Z}_q$-integers does not contribute to the proof size since they can be expanded from small seeds by using a PRG. For the security level we are aiming for, 16 bytes suffice for each challenge seed. The full-size elements $\vec{t}_0, \vec{t}_1, \boldsymbol{t}_2, \boldsymbol{h}$ have a total size of $(\kappa_2 + \mu + 1)d\lceil \log q \rceil = (\kappa_2 + \lceil ((b-1)n+1)/d \rceil + 2)d\lceil \log q \rceil$ bits. Next, the short vectors $\vec{z}^{(c)}, \vec{z}_j, \vec{z}^{(t)}$ have size $m \log 12\mathfrak{s}_1 + lm \log 12\mathfrak{s}_2 + (\kappa_2 + \lambda + \mu)d \log 12\mathfrak{s}_3$ bits. Here we assume that the coefficients of the short vectors are bounded by $6\mathfrak{s}_i$ in absolute value, which can be ensured by the prover. Finally, the challenges $\vec{c}, \vec{\varphi}, \vec{x}, \theta, c^{(t)}$ need $4 + n$ seeds of total size $128(4 + n)$ bits.

We now compute the required standard deviations $\mathfrak{s}_1, \mathfrak{s}_2, \mathfrak{s}_3$ for the Gaussian masking vectors $\vec{y}^{(c)}, \vec{y}_j$ and $\vec{y}^{(t)}$. So, we need to bound the ℓ_2 norms of the secrets vectors $c_1\vec{s}_1 + \cdots + c_n\vec{s}_n$, $x_{1,j}\vec{s}_1 + \cdots + x_{n,j}\vec{s}_n$, and $c^{(t)}\vec{r}$. For the rejection sampling we use the improved algorithm from [LNS21a] that leaks one bit of information about the secret. In usual applications of the proof system the prover will only ever compute one or at most very few proofs about a particular set of hashes $\vec{u}_i$. We assume that the challenge polynomial distribution $\mathcal{C}$ for c_i and $c^{(t)}$ is such that the polynomial coefficients are independently identically distributed in $\{-1, 0, 1\}$ with probabilities $1/4, 1/2, 1/4$, respectively. So the challenge polynomials have $3d/2$ bits of entropy. In particular, for ring rank $d = 128$ and fully splitting q of length around 128 bits, the NTT coefficients of c_i will have maximum probability p close to $1/q$. Then, a coefficient of a polynomial in $c_i\vec{s}_i$ is the weighted sum of d independent coefficients of c_i, where the weights are given by the coefficients of the corresponding polynomial in $\vec{s}_i$ (up to signs). Moreover, a coefficient of $c_1\vec{s}_1 + \cdots + c_n\vec{s}_n$ is the sum of dn such coefficients. Write S_n for this random variable. Its distribution is centered and has standard deviation $\mathfrak{s}_n \leq \lfloor b/2 \rfloor \sqrt{dn/2}$. By the central limit theorem, the distribution of the standardization $\frac{S_n}{\mathfrak{s}_n}$ converges to the standard normal distribution for $n \to \infty$. This is also true for the random variable S_n' that is distributed according to the discrete Gaussian Distribution $D_{\mathfrak{s}_n}$ with the same standard deviation as S_n. So, for all $x \in \mathbb{Z}$,

$$\lim_{n \to \infty} |\Pr[S_n \leq x\mathfrak{s}_n] - \Pr[S_n' \leq x\mathfrak{s}_n]| = 0,$$

and $D_{\mathfrak{s}_n}$ is a good model for the distribution of the coefficients of $c_1\vec{s}_1 + \cdots + c_n\vec{s}_n$. By the tail bound, a coefficient is smaller than $14\lfloor b/2 \rfloor \sqrt{dn/2}$ in absolute value with probability bigger than $1 - 2^{-140}$. Then, using the union bound we conclude that no coefficient is bigger than that. Therefore, we have

$$\|c_1\vec{s}_1 + \cdots + c_n\vec{s}_n\|_2 \leq 14 \left\lfloor \frac{b}{2} \right\rfloor \sqrt{\frac{dmn}{2}} = \mathfrak{s}_1,$$

and similarly,

$$\|x_{1,j}\vec{s}_1 + \cdots + x_{n,j}\vec{s}_n\|_2 \leq 14 \left\lfloor \frac{b}{2} \right\rfloor \sqrt{\frac{(\delta^2 - 1)dmn}{12}} = \mathfrak{s}_2.$$

In the second inequality we have used that the discrete uniform distribution on $[-\delta/2, \delta/2 - 1]$ has standard deviation $\sqrt{(\delta^2 - 1)/12}$. For $c^{(t)}\vec{r}^{(t)}$ we make use of the fact that also $\vec{r}^{(t)}$ is random with polynomial coefficients distributed according to the centered binomial distribution χ_2 modulo 3. It follows that every coefficient has standard deviation $\sqrt{5d/16}$, and, again by the tail and union bounds, no coefficient is bigger than $14\sqrt{5d/16}$ with large probability. So,

$$\left\|c^{(t)}\vec{r}^{(t)}\right\|_2 \leq 14\sqrt{5d^2(\kappa_2 + \lambda + \mu)/16} = \mathfrak{s}_3.$$

Example. As an example we compute concrete sizes for proving $n = 1024$ hashes $\vec{u}_i = A\vec{s}_i$ of binary vectors $\vec{s}_i$ of length $m = 2048$ over the ring $\mathcal{R}_q$ of rank $d = 128$ modulo a 128-bit fully-splitting prime q. We choose $l = 4$ so that $\delta \approx 2^{32}$. For the Module-SIS rank κ_2 and the Module-LWE rank λ of the BDLOP commitments scheme we use $\kappa_2 = 2$ and $\lambda = 32$. Then $\mathsf{MSIS}_{\kappa_2, 8d\beta_3}$ has a classical Core-SVP cost of 2^{100} when using the BDGL16 sieve, and $\mathsf{MLWE}_{\lambda, \chi_2}$ has a classical Core-SVP cost of 2^{108}. The height κ of A, i.e. the hash rank for the $\vec{u}_i$, does not influence the proof size of our protocol, but we need Module-SIS to be hard for vectors of length $B = 4(d\beta_2 + \delta\beta_1/2 + dn\delta b\sqrt{m}/4)$. This is for example the case with $\kappa = 7$, where $\mathsf{MSIS}_{\kappa, B}$ has classical Core-SVP cost of 2^{213}. With these parameters we find that the proof size as explained above is 108.5 kilobytes. This translates to an amortized size of 108.6 bytes per equation.

One application of our amortized exact proof system is for proving statement about the plaintexts in FHE ciphertexts. The FHE ciphertexts have a purpose outside of the proof system and therefore their size does not count towards the proof size. Moreover, they can not be compressed because otherwise one could decrypt them anymore. Our proof system now allows to proof many such ciphertexts with a small amortized cost.

5   Induction

In many applications the public input hashes $\vec{u}_i$ to our exact binary opening proof from Sect. 4 are in fact produced as part of a larger zero-knowledge proof system and their size counts towards the proof size. In the opening proof the two dominating terms in the proof size are of order $n \log q$ for the garbage commitments, and $m \log q$ for the masked openings, for a total of mn secret coefficients. On the other hand, the hashes $\vec{u}_i$ are of size $n\kappa d \log q$. So we see that their size is very significant for the overall bandwidth efficiency. In fact, the hashes are about two orders of magnitude larger than their proof and it would be good if we did not need to transmit all the $\vec{u}_i$. In this section we show how this can in fact be achieved by hashing them up in a Merkle hash tree and using our opening proof as a building block to prove by induction an opening to the hash tree when only the root hash is given.

Tree Construction. In our lattice-based hash tree, the hash input vector for an inner node consists of the binary expansions of the hash output vectors from the two children of the node. So the number of input bits m of the hash function must be twice the number of output bits, i.e. $m = 2\kappa d \lceil \log q \rceil$. Then we define the *gadget matrix*

$$G = I_\kappa \otimes \left(1\ 2 \cdots 2^{\lceil \log q \rceil - 1}\right) \in \mathcal{R}_q^{\kappa \times \kappa \lceil \log q \rceil}$$

that we use to reconstruct the hashes from their binary expansions. Now, the hash tree is constructed as follows. Let a be the depth of the tree. Then, the inner nodes are given by

$$\vec{u}_i = A\vec{s}_i, \quad \vec{s}_i = \begin{pmatrix} \vec{s}_{i,l} \\ \vec{s}_{i,r} \end{pmatrix} \in \{0,1\}^m \subset \mathcal{R}_q^{m/d},$$

$$G\vec{s}_{i,l} = \vec{u}_{2i},$$

$$G\vec{s}_{i,r} = \vec{u}_{2i+1} \tag{9}$$

for $i = 1, \ldots, 2^{a-1} - 1$. In particular $\vec{u}_1$ is the root of the tree. The leafs are $\vec{u}_{2^{a-1}+j} = A\vec{s}_{2^{a-1}+j}$ for $j = 0, \ldots, 2^{a-1} - 1$. More generally, the nodes $\vec{u}_{2^k}, \ldots, \vec{u}_{2^{k+1}-1}$ form level k of the tree, where $0 \leq k \leq a - 1$.

Proof by Induction. So we have a total of $n = 2^a - 1$ binary vectors $\vec{s}_i$ that recursively hash to $\vec{u}_1$ and that we want to prove knowledge of. Our protocol is easiest to understand as a sequence $\pi_{a-1}, \pi_{a-2}, \ldots, \pi_0$ of $a = \lceil \log n \rceil$ subproofs that are essentially instances of our binary opening proof from Sect. 4. There is one subproof for each level of the tree in the order from the leaves to the root, and the subproofs are indexed by the corresponding level. More precisely, π_k proves knowledge of the level-k binary vectors $\vec{s}_{2^k}, \ldots, \vec{s}_{2^{k+1}-1}$.

All the π_k share one amortized masked opening of all the vectors $\vec{s}_i$. Hence, in the very end the prover sends

$$\vec{z} = \vec{y} + \sum_{i=1}^{2^a-1} x_i \vec{s}_i.$$

Actually, the prover sends the short shares $\vec{z}_j = \vec{y}_j + \sum_i x_{i,j} \vec{s}_i$ that compose to $\vec{z}$ but we explain the protocol in terms of the single vector $\vec{z}$ as this simplifies the presentation. The 2^k challenges $x_{2^k}, \ldots, x_{2^{k+1}-1}$ for the level-k binary vectors are from the subproof π_k. Therefore and because of the reverse ordering of the subproofs, at the beginning of π_k the prover knows all the challenges $x_{2^{k+1}}, \ldots, x_{2^a-1}$ from deeper levels. We can thus absorb the terms $x_i \vec{s}_i$, $i \geq 2^{k+1}$, in $\vec{z}$ into the masking vector and use

$$\vec{y}_k = \vec{y} + \sum_{i=2^{k+1}}^{2^a-1} x_i \vec{s}_i$$

as the masking vector in π_k. So unlike in isolated instances of the binary opening proof, π_k inherits the mask from previous parts of the overall protocol instead of sampling a fresh mask. The prover then sends the commitment $\vec{w}_k = A\vec{y}_k$ (composed from $\vec{w}_{k,j} = A\vec{y}_{k,j}$). Next, he engages in the 2^{k+1}-round interaction where he produces the garbage commitments and receives the challenges x_{2^k+j} for proving exactly as before that the vectors $\vec{s}_{2^k+j}$ are binary. Furthermore, the verifier only knows the root hash $\vec{u}_1$ and can check the verification equation

$$A\vec{z} = \vec{w}_0 + x_1 \vec{u}_1.$$

for the last subproof π_0 at the end of the protocol. So, to connect the subproofs with each other and prove the verification equations for the π_k, $k \geq 1$, the prover proves the following linear relations,

$$\sum_{i=2^k}^{2^{k+1}-1} (x_{2i} \boldsymbol{G} \vec{s}_{i,l} + x_{2i+1} \boldsymbol{G} \vec{s}_{i,r}) = \vec{w}_k - \vec{w}_{k+1}. \tag{10}$$

The challenges x_{2i}, x_{2i+1}, and the vectors $\vec{w}_k$, $\vec{w}_{k+1}$ are known by both the prover and the verifier at the start of π_k so this relation can be proven with the linear proof technique from Sect. 4.1. Concretely, for each $k = 0, \ldots, a - 2$ let $\vec{\psi}_k \in \mathbb{Z}_q^{\kappa d}$ be a challenge and define

$$\vec{\rho}_i = \mathsf{Rot} \begin{pmatrix} x_{2i} \boldsymbol{G}^\dagger \\ x_{2i+1} \boldsymbol{G}^\dagger \end{pmatrix} \vec{\psi}_k$$

for all $i = 2^k, \ldots, 2^{k+1}$ with the multiplication matrix $\mathsf{Rot}(\boldsymbol{G}^\dagger)$ associated to the conjugate transpose of the polynomial matrix $\boldsymbol{G}$. Then in π_k the prover commits to the garbage coefficients

$$\gamma_{2i-1}^{(\mathsf{lin})} = \left\langle \vec{y}_k + \sum_{j=i+1}^{2^{k+1}-1} x_j \vec{s}_j, \vec{\rho}_i \right\rangle,$$

$$\gamma_{2i}^{(\mathsf{lin})} = \left\langle \vec{s}_i, \sum_{j=i+1}^{2^{a-1}-1} x_j^{-1} \vec{\rho}_j \right\rangle$$

for $i = 2^k, \ldots, 2^{k+1} - 1$. Finally, the following linear relation is proven in the auxiliary proof at the end of the protocol,

$$\left\langle \vec{z}, \sum_{i=1}^{2^{a-1}-1} x_i^{-1} \vec{\rho}_i \right\rangle - \sum_{k=0}^{a-2} \left\langle \vec{w}_k - \vec{w}_{k+1}, \vec{\psi}_k \right\rangle$$

$$= \sum_{i=1}^{2^{a-1}-1} \left(x_i^{-1} \gamma_{2i-1}^{(\mathsf{lin})} + x_i \gamma_{2i}^{(\mathsf{lin})} \right).$$

We now explain at a high level why this protocol suffices for proving the hash tree. For $0 \leq k \leq a - 2$, consider the statement S_k that the prover knows binary vectors $\vec{s}_1, \ldots, \vec{s}_{2^k-1}$ and corresponding $\vec{u}_1, \ldots, \vec{u}_{2^{k+1}-1}$ as in Eq. (9), and that

$$\boldsymbol{A} \vec{z} = \vec{w}_{k'} + \sum_{i=1}^{2^{k'+1}-1} x_i \vec{u}_i \tag{11}$$

is true for all $0 \leq k' \leq k$ in (almost) all accepting interactions. The statement is trivially true for $k = 0$ because the list of known vectors is empty in this case and (11) is directly checked by the verifier.

Now, we argue that the subproof π_k proves the statement S_{k+1} if S_k holds true. We rewrite (11) and have

$$A \left(\vec{z} - \sum_{i=1}^{2^k-1} x_i \vec{s}_i \right) = \vec{w}_k + \sum_{i=2^k}^{2^{k+1}-1} x_i \vec{u}_i.$$

Here the preimage on the left hand side is short since $\vec{z}$ is short and all the $\vec{s}_i$ are binary. So, for every accepting transcript we can compute a short vector $\vec{z}_k = \vec{z} - \sum_{i=1}^{2^k-1} x_i \vec{s}_i$ that fulfills the main verification equation for the binary opening proof π_k for level k. Conceptually this means any prover for the protocol in this section can be converted to a prover for the level-k hashes exactly as in Sect. 4. Therefore we can use the extractor for our exact opening proof from Sect. 4 and compute binary preimages $\vec{s}_{2^k}, \ldots, \vec{s}_{2^{k+1}-1}$ for the hashes $\vec{u}_{2^k}, \ldots, \vec{u}_{2^{k+1}-1}$. Moreover the newly extracted binary preimages define the level-$(k+1)$ hashes $\vec{u}_{2^{k+1}}, \ldots, \vec{u}_{2^{k+2}-1}$, and from the linear proof for (10) included in π_k it follows that

$$A\vec{z} = \vec{w}_k + \sum_{i=1}^{2^{k+1}-1} x_i u_i = \vec{w}_{k+1} + \sum_{i=1}^{2^{k+2}-1} x_i \vec{u}_i.$$

Therefore we have established that statement S_{k+1} is true.

It then follows by induction that the statement S_{a-1} is true. And a very similar argument for the last-level proof π_{a-1}, just without the linear proof connecting to a previous level, shows that the prover also knows preimages for the tree leaves, which completes the proof of the full hash tree.

Note that there is no problem with zero-knowledge associated with sending all the $\vec{w}_k$ since they differ from $\vec{w}_{a-1} = A\vec{y}$ only by terms of the form $x_i \vec{u}_i$ that we would send in the clear if we directly used the proof from Sect. 4. Finally note that the size of the $\vec{w}_k$ is small—we have effectively traded the $n + 1 = 2^a$ uniformly random vectors $\vec{u}_i, \vec{w}$ for the only $a + 1$ vectors $\vec{u}_1$ and $\vec{w}_k$.

As before we want to use the approximate amortized opening proof with polynomial challenges to bootstrap our protocol in order to benefit from smaller SIS norm bounds. Therefore, the prover also samples an additional masking vector $\vec{y}^{(c)}$ at the beginning of the protocol. Then, in each subproof π_k, he first sends $\vec{w}_k^{(c)} = A\vec{y}^{(c)} + \sum_{i=2^{k+1}}^{2^a-1} c_i \vec{u}_i$, and then receives the next challenge polynomials $c_{2^k}, \ldots, c_{2^{k+1}-1}$. Finally, at the end of the protocol the prover sends $\vec{z}^{(c)} = \vec{y}^{(c)} + \sum_{i=1}^{2^a-1} c_i \vec{s}_i$. The verifier checks that $\vec{z}^{(c)}$ is short and a preimage of $\vec{w}_0^{(c)} + c_1 \vec{u}_1$.

We defer the specification of the protocol and its security analysis to the full version of the paper. There we also describe how to apply it for proving R1CS, and discuss the comparison of the protocol to Ligero.

References

[ACK21] Attema, T., Cramer, R., Kohl, L.: A compressed ς-protocol theory for lattices. In: Malkin, T., Peikert, C. (eds.) CRYPTO 2021. LNCS, vol. 12826, pp. 549–579. Springer, Cham (2021). https://doi.org/10.1007/978-3-030-84245-1_19

[AF21]   Attema, T., Fehr, S.: Parallel repetition of $(k_{1,\text{dots},k_\mu})$-special-sound multi-round interactive proofs. IACR Cryptology ePrint Archive, p. 1259 (2021)

[AHIV17] Ames, S., Hazay, C., Ishai, Y., Venkitasubramaniam, M.: Ligero: lightweight sublinear arguments without a trusted setup. In: CCS, pp. 2087–2104. ACM (2017)

[AL21]   Albrecht, M.R., Lai, R.W.F.: Subtractive sets over cyclotomic rings. In: Malkin, T., Peikert, C. (eds.) CRYPTO 2021. LNCS, vol. 12826, pp. 519–548. Springer, Cham (2021). https://doi.org/10.1007/978-3-030-84245-1_18

[ALS20]   Attema, T., Lyubashevsky, V., Seiler, G.: Practical product proofs for lattice commitments. In: Micciancio, D., Ristenpart, T. (eds.) CRYPTO 2020. LNCS, vol. 12171, pp. 470–499. Springer, Cham (2020). https://doi.org/10.1007/978-3-030-56880-1_17

[BBB+18] Bünz, B., Bootle, J., Boneh, D., Poelstra, A., Wuille, P., Maxwell, G.: Bulletproofs: short proofs for confidential transactions and more. In: IEEE Symposium on Security and Privacy, pp. 315–334. IEEE Computer Society (2018)

[BBC+18] Baum, C., Bootle, J., Cerulli, A., del Pino, R., Groth, J., Lyubashevsky, V.: Sub-linear lattice-based zero-knowledge arguments for arithmetic circuits. In: Shacham, H., Boldyreva, A. (eds.) CRYPTO 2018. LNCS, vol. 10992, pp. 669–699. Springer, Cham (2018). https://doi.org/10.1007/978-3-319-96881-0_23

[BCG+13] Ben-Sasson, E., Chiesa, A., Genkin, D., Tromer, E., Virza, M.: SNARKs for C: verifying program executions succinctly and in zero knowledge. In: Canetti, R., Garay, J.A. (eds.) CRYPTO 2013. LNCS, vol. 8043, pp. 90–108. Springer, Heidelberg (2013). https://doi.org/10.1007/978-3-642-40084-1_6

[BCR+19] Ben-Sasson, E., Chiesa, A., Riabzev, M., Spooner, N., Virza, M., Ward, N.P.: Aurora: transparent succinct arguments for R1CS. In: Ishai, Y., Rijmen, V. (eds.) EUROCRYPT 2019. LNCS, vol. 11476, pp. 103–128. Springer, Cham (2019). https://doi.org/10.1007/978-3-030-17653-2_4

[BDL+18] Baum, C., Damgård, I., Lyubashevsky, V., Oechsner, S., Peikert, C.: More efficient commitments from structured lattice assumptions. In: Catalano, D., De Prisco, R. (eds.) SCN 2018. LNCS, vol. 11035, pp. 368–385. Springer, Cham (2018). https://doi.org/10.1007/978-3-319-98113-0_20

[BFH+20] Bhadauria, R., Fang, Z., Hazay, C., Venkitasubramaniam, M., Xie, T., Zhang, Y.: Ligero++: a new optimized sublinear IOP. In: CCS, pp. 2025–2038. ACM (2020)

[BLNS20] Bootle, J., Lyubashevsky, V., Nguyen, N.K., Seiler, G.: A non-PCP approach to succinct quantum-safe zero-knowledge. In: Micciancio, D., Ristenpart, T. (eds.) CRYPTO 2020. LNCS, vol. 12171, pp. 441–469. Springer, Cham (2020). https://doi.org/10.1007/978-3-030-56880-1_16

[BMRS21] Baum, C., Malozemoff, A.J., Rosen, M.B., Scholl, P.: Mac'n'Cheese: zero-knowledge proofs for boolean and arithmetic circuits with nested disjunctions. In: Malkin, T., Peikert, C. (eds.) CRYPTO 2021. LNCS, vol. 12828, pp. 92–122. Springer, Cham (2021). https://doi.org/10.1007/978-3-030-84259-8_4

[Din12]   Ding, J.: New cryptographic constructions using generalized learning with errors problem. IACR Cryptology ePrint Archive, p. 387 (2012)

[DKL+18]   Ducas, L., et al.: Crystals-dilithium: a lattice-based digital signature scheme. IACR Trans. Cryptogr. Hardw. Embed. Syst. **2018**(1), 238–268 (2018)

[ENS20]   Esgin, M.F., Nguyen, N.K., Seiler, G.: Practical exact proofs from lattices: new techniques to exploit fully-splitting rings. In: Moriai, S., Wang, H. (eds.) ASIACRYPT 2020. LNCS, vol. 12492, pp. 259–288. Springer, Cham (2020). https://doi.org/10.1007/978-3-030-64834-3_9

[ESLL19]   Esgin, M.F., Steinfeld, R., Liu, J.K., Liu, D.: Lattice-based zero-knowledge proofs: new techniques for shorter and faster constructions and applications. In: Boldyreva, A., Micciancio, D. (eds.) CRYPTO 2019. LNCS, vol. 11692, pp. 115–146. Springer, Cham (2019). https://doi.org/10.1007/978-3-030-26948-7_5

[ESS+19]   Esgin, M.F., Steinfeld, R., Sakzad, A., Liu, J.K., Liu, D.: Short lattice-based one-out-of-many proofs and applications to ring signatures. In: Deng, R.H., Gauthier-Umaña, V., Ochoa, M., Yung, M. (eds.) ACNS 2019. LNCS, vol. 11464, pp. 67–88. Springer, Cham (2019). https://doi.org/10.1007/978-3-030-21568-2_4

[EZS+19]   Esgin, M.F., Zhao, R.K., Steinfeld, R., Liu, J.K., Liu, D.: MatRiCT: efficient, scalable and post-quantum blockchain confidential transactions protocol. In: CCS, pp. 567–584. ACM (2019)

[FHK+18]   Fouque, P.-A., et al.: Falcon: fast-fourier lattice-based compact signatures over NTRU. Submission to the NIST's Post-quantum Cryptography Standardization Process, vol. 36 (2018)

[GGPR13]   Gennaro, R., Gentry, C., Parno, B., Raykova, M.: Quadratic span programs and succinct NIZKs without PCPs. In: Johansson, T., Nguyen, P.Q. (eds.) EUROCRYPT 2013. LNCS, vol. 7881, pp. 626–645. Springer, Heidelberg (2013). https://doi.org/10.1007/978-3-642-38348-9_37

[GMNO18]   Gennaro, R., Minelli, M., Nitulescu, A., Orrù, M.: Lattice-based zk-SNARKs from square span programs. In: CCS, pp. 556–573. ACM (2018)

[Gro11]   Groth, J.: Efficient zero-knowledge arguments from two-tiered homomorphic commitments. In: Lee, D.H., Wang, X. (eds.) ASIACRYPT 2011. LNCS, vol. 7073, pp. 431–448. Springer, Heidelberg (2011). https://doi.org/10.1007/978-3-642-25385-0_23

[ISW21]   Ishai, Y., Su, H., Wu, D.J.: Shorter and faster post-quantum designated-verifier zkSNARK from lattices. In: CCS, pp. 212–234. ACM (2021)

[LFKN92]   Lund, C., Fortnow, L., Karloff, H.J., Nisan, N.: Algebraic methods for interactive proof systems. J. ACM **39**(4), 859–868 (1992)

[LM06]   Lyubashevsky, V., Micciancio, D.: Generalized compact knapsacks are collision resistant. In: Bugliesi, M., Preneel, B., Sassone, V., Wegener, I. (eds.) ICALP 2006. LNCS, vol. 4052, pp. 144–155. Springer, Heidelberg (2006). https://doi.org/10.1007/11787006_13

[LNPS21]   Lyubashevsky, V., Nguyen, N.K., Plancon, M., Seiler, G.: Shorter lattice-based group signatures via "almost free" encryption and other optimizations. In: Tibouchi, M., Wang, H. (eds.) ASIACRYPT 2021. LNCS, vol. 13093, pp. 218–248. Springer, Cham (2021). https://doi.org/10.1007/978-3-030-92068-5_8

[LNS20]   Lyubashevsky, V., Nguyen, N.K., Seiler, G.: Practical lattice-based zero-knowledge proofs for integer relations. In: CCS, pp. 1051–1070. ACM (2020)

[LNS21a] Lyubashevsky, V., Nguyen, N.K., Seiler, G.: Shorter lattice-based zero-knowledge proofs via one-time commitments. In: Garay, J.A. (ed.) PKC 2021. LNCS, vol. 12710, pp. 215–241. Springer, Cham (2021). https://doi.org/10.1007/978-3-030-75245-3_9

[LNS21b] Lyubashevsky, V., Nguyen, N.K., Seiler, G.: SMILE: set membership from ideal lattices with applications to ring signatures and confidential transactions. In: Malkin, T., Peikert, C. (eds.) CRYPTO 2021. LNCS, vol. 12826, pp. 611–640. Springer, Cham (2021). https://doi.org/10.1007/978-3-030-84245-1_21

[LPR10] Lyubashevsky, V., Peikert, C., Regev, O.: On ideal lattices and learning with errors over rings. In: Gilbert, H. (ed.) EUROCRYPT 2010. LNCS, vol. 6110, pp. 1–23. Springer, Heidelberg (2010). https://doi.org/10.1007/978-3-642-13190-5_1

[LS15] Langlois, A., Stehlé, D.: Worst-case to average-case reductions for module lattices. Des. Codes Crypt. **75**(3), 565–599 (2014). https://doi.org/10.1007/s10623-014-9938-4

[Mic02] Micciancio, D.: Generalized compact knapsacks, cyclic lattices, and efficient one-way functions from worst-case complexity assumptions. In: FOCS, pp. 356–365. IEEE Computer Society (2002)

[Ore22] Ore, Ø.: Über höhere kongruenzen. Norsk Mat. Forenings Skrifter **1**(7), 15 (1922)

[PR06] Peikert, C., Rosen, A.: Efficient collision-resistant hashing from worst-case assumptions on cyclic lattices. In: Halevi, S., Rabin, T. (eds.) TCC 2006. LNCS, vol. 3876, pp. 145–166. Springer, Heidelberg (2006). https://doi.org/10.1007/11681878_8

[Sch80] Schwartz, J.T.: Fast probabilistic algorithms for verification of polynomial identities. J. ACM **27**(4), 701–717 (1980)

[Sha92] Shamir, A.: IP = PSPACE. J. ACM **39**(4), 869–877 (1992)

[WYKW21] Weng, C., Yang, K., Katz, J., Wang, X.: Wolverine: fast, scalable, and communication-efficient zero-knowledge proofs for boolean and arithmetic circuits. In: IEEE Symposium on Security and Privacy, pp. 1074–1091. IEEE (2021)

[YSWW21] Yang, K., Sarkar, P., Weng, C., Wang, X.: Quicksilver: efficient and affordable zero-knowledge proofs for circuits and polynomials over any field. In: CCS, pp. 2986–3001. ACM (2021)

[Zip79] Zippel, R.: Probabilistic algorithms for sparse polynomials. In: Ng, E.W. (ed.) Symbolic and Algebraic Computation. LNCS, vol. 72, pp. 216–226. Springer, Heidelberg (1979). https://doi.org/10.1007/3-540-09519-5_73

Quantum Cryptography II

On the Impossibility of Key Agreements from Quantum Random Oracles

Per Austrin[1], Hao Chung[2], Kai-Min Chung[3], Shiuan Fu[3], Yao-Ting Lin[3(✉)],
and Mohammad Mahmoody[4]

[1] KTH Royal Institute of Technology, Stockholm, Sweden
austrin@kth.se
[2] Carnegie Mellon University, Pittsburgh, USA
haochung@andrew.cmu.edu
[3] Academia Sinica, Taipei, Taiwan
kmchung@iis.sinica.edu.tw, rubik.sf@gmail.com,
1213tonylin@gmail.com
[4] University of Virginia, Charlottesville, USA
mohammad@virginia.edu

Abstract. We study the following question, first publicly posed by Hosoyamada and Yamakawa in 2018. Can parties A, B with quantum computing power and classical communication rely only on a random oracle (that can be queried in quantum superposition) to agree on a key that is private from eavesdroppers?

We make the first progress on the question above and prove the following.

- When only *one* of the parties A is classical and the other party B is quantum powered, as long as they ask a total of d oracle queries and agree on a key with probability 1, then there is always a way to break the key agreement by asking $O(d^2)$ number of *classical* oracle queries.

- When both parties can make quantum queries to the random oracle, we introduce a natural conjecture, which if true would imply attacks with poly(d) *classical* queries to the random oracle. Our conjecture, roughly speaking, states that the multiplication of any two degree-d real-valued polynomials over the Boolean hypercube of influence at most $\delta = 1/\text{poly}(d)$ is nonzero. We then prove our conjecture for exponentially small influences, which leads to an (unconditional) classical $2^{O(md)}$-query attack on any such key agreement protocol, where m is the oracle's output length.

- Since our attacks are classical, we then ask whether it is always possible to find classical attacks on key agreements with imperfect completeness in the quantum random oracle model. We prove a barrier for this approach, by showing that if the folklore "Simulation Conjecture" (first formally stated by Aaronson and Ambainis in 2009) about the possibility of

H. Chung—Supported by Packard Fellowship and NSF award 2044679. Part of the work was done when working at Academia Sinica.

K.-M. Chung—Partially supported by the 2021 Academia Sinica Investigator Award (AS-IA-110-M02) and Executive Yuan Data Safety and Talent Cultivation Project (AS-KPQ-110-DSTCP).

M. Mahmoody—Supported by NSF grants CCF-1910681 and CNS1936799.

Y. Dodis and T. Shrimpton (Eds.): CRYPTO 2022, LNCS 13508, pp. 165–194, 2022.
https://doi.org/10.1007/978-3-031-15979-4_6

simulating efficient-query quantum algorithms using efficient-query classical algorithms is false, then there is in fact such a secure key agreement in the quantum random oracle model that cannot be broken classically.

1   Introduction

In a course project, now known as "Merkle Puzzles", Merkle [Mer74] proposed the first ever nontrivial key agreement protocol between two parties using an ideal hash function. This protocol can be formally analyzed in the random oracle model (ROM) to prove that Alice and Bob can ask d queries to a random oracle h and agree on a key, while an eavesdropper Eve, who can see the exchanged messages t, needs $\Omega(d^2)$ queries to h to find the key. Shortly after, seminal works [DH76, RSA78] showed how to achieve a super-polynomially secure key agreement protocol by relying on number theoretic assumptions. In comparison, Merkle's protocol suffers from only offering polynomial security. However, after all the years of research and newly developed candidate constructions for public-key encryption and key agreements (see the survey [Bar17] for such works), Merkle's protocol enjoys a qualitative advantage: it only relies on an idealized *symmetric primitive*, namely a random function without any structure. Indeed, basing public-key encryption or key agreement on symmetric key primitives is still one of the most fundamental open questions in cryptography.

Merkle's protocol led to the following natural question (also attributed to Merkle by [IR89]). Is there any d-query key agreement protocol in the ROM with larger security $\omega(d^2)$, or is the $O(d^2)$ bound optimal?[1] Impagliazzo and Rudich were the first to prove an upper bound on the security of key agreement protocols in the ROM. They showed that all such protocols can be broken by an attacker who asks $\tilde{O}(dr)^3$ queries, where r is the round complexity of the protocol. This result, in particular, showed that there is no "black-box" way of obtaining key agreements from one-way functions, because roughly speaking a random oracle is one-way with high probability. Finally, Barak and Mahmoody [BM17] showed that every key agreement in the ROM can be broken by $O(d^2)$ queries, showing that Merkle's protocol was indeed optimal.

Key Agreement in a Quantum World. Merkle's protocol and attacks of [IR89, BM17] are all classical. With the growing interest in understanding the power and limitations of quantum computation, this brings up the following natural question. What if parties can perform quantum computation? Bennett and Brassard [BB84] showed that when parties can communicate quantum bits, then there is an information-theoretically secure key agreement protocol. This still leaves out the case of protocols with classical communication, which is the focus of our work. Classical-communication protocols are particularly attractive as they can be used over the current infrastructure (e.g., the Internet). In this model, all the quantum computation is done locally by the parties who exchange classical messages and aim to establish a private key. We refer to this model as the quantum-computation classical-communication (QCCC) model.

---

[1] Note that a sufficiently large *polynomial gap* could still be a meaningful fine-grained security, particularly because this cap can only mean *more* security when the CPU clocks get shorter. In particular, with faster computers, Alice and Bob can pick a *larger* d, while running in the same time as before, while Eve now needs d times more running time than Alice and Bob.

Quantum Random Oracle. A QCCC protocol in the quantum random oracle model (QROM) allows a quantum-powered party to ask superposition queries to the oracle. This party could be the honest parties or the attacker. Brassard and Salvail [BS08] and Biham, Goren and Ishai [BGI08] revisited the security of Merkle's protocol against quantum adversaries and showed that Merkle's protocol can be broken by a quantum eavesdropper (essentially, Grover's search [Gro96]) that asks $O(d)$ number of quantum queries to the random oracle. This showed that Merkle's protocol gives no super-linear security over d against quantum attackers. Brassard and Salvail [BS08] then showed how to regain a super-linear gap by having Alice and Bob also leverage quantum queries to the oracle. Their protocol had the extra property that only *one* of the parties Alice and Bob needs to run a quantum algorithm.[2] Brassard et al. [BHK+15] further improved this result and showed that a quantum Alice and Bob can agree on a key by d queries, while even a quantum attacker would require $\approx d^2$ number of queries to break it.

All of these works seek lower bounds on the gap between the query complexity of quantum algorithms Alice/Bob and the adversary Eve. However, no previous work has shown an *upper* bound on the achievable security. In fact, our current knowledge about the limitations of security in the QROM is consistent with the possibility that QCCC protocols can establish a key agreement over a *classical* channel, while it would take exponentially many queries to the oracle (even by a quantum attacker) to find the key. This brings up the main question of this work, which was also posed by Hosoyamada and Yamakawa [HY20].[3]

> Is there a key agreement protocol using classical communication, in which Alice and Bob ask d quantum queries to a random oracle, while the eavesdropper needs a super-polynomial $d^{\omega(1)}$ number of queries to find the key?

1.1 Our Results

In this work, we present the first barriers against obtaining super-polynomially secure QCCC key agreement protocols in the QROM model.

Classical Alice Quantum Bob (CAQB). Our first result shows that when one of the parties Alice is classical, the quadratic gap achieved by Merkle is optimal, *even against classical* adversaries. This is an interesting setting on its own, as it can model unbalanced parties. For example, suppose Google wants to agree on a key with a typical user, who does not have any quantum computing power, over the Internet. Then, our result shows that there is a limit to how much security such protocols can achieve.

Theorem 1.1 (Attacking CAQB protocols – informal). *Suppose Π is a QCCC d-query key agreement protocol with perfect completeness in the QROM. If Alice is classical and only Bob uses quantum queries to the random oracle, then there is a classical adversary who can find the key by asking $O(d^2)$ classical queries to the oracle.*

---

[2] In comparison, Theorem 1.1 shows that such protocols (with a classical party and a quantum party) cannot offer more than quadratic security when the protocol has perfect completeness.

[3] To the best of our knowledge, the question was first asked in 2018 [HY18].

Note that the above result assumes that the two parties agree on a key with probability one, and this is the case for all of our attacks in this work; extending them to allow imperfect completeness is an intriguing question for future work.

Quantum Alice and Quantum Bob (QAQB). We then turn to study protocols in which Alice and Bob both have quantum access to the oracle. For this more general setting, we show a *conditional result* based on a conjecture about multilinear polynomials, which will also prove for some extreme cases.

Some Basic Notions. We first recall some basic notions about polynomials. Suppose

$$f = \sum_{S \subseteq [N]} \alpha_S \prod_{i \in S} x_i$$

is a multilinear polynomial over binary variables $x_i \in \{\pm 1\}, i \in [N]$ and real coefficients $\alpha_S \in \mathbb{R}, S \subseteq [N]$. The degree of f is $\max_{\alpha_S \neq 0} |S|$ and the ℓ_2 norm of f is $\|f\|_2 = \mathbb{E}_{\mathbf{x} \leftarrow \{\pm 1\}^N}[f(\mathbf{x})^2]$. The influence of x_i on f is defined as $\mathrm{Inf}_i(f) = \sum_{i \in S} \alpha_S^2$, and more generally for a distribution F over such multilinear polynomials, we let $\mathrm{Inf}_i(F) = \mathbb{E}_{f \leftarrow F}[\mathrm{Inf}_i(f)]$ denote the *expected* influence.

Conjecture 1.2 (Polynomial Compatibility). *There is a function $\delta(d) = 1/\mathrm{poly}(d)$, such that the following holds for all $d \in \mathbb{N}$. Suppose F, G are distributions over multilinear polynomials of degree d with variables $x_1, \dots, x_N \in \{\pm 1\}$ and ℓ_2-norm 1 and bounded influences $\mathrm{Inf}_i(F), \mathrm{Inf}_i(G) \leq \delta(d)$ for all $i \in [N]$. Then, there exist $f \in \mathrm{supp}(F), g \in \mathrm{supp}(G)$ and $\mathbf{x} \in \{\pm 1\}^N$ such that $f(\mathbf{x}) \cdot g(\mathbf{x}) \neq 0$.*

All Assumptions are Needed. In Appendix B of the full version [ACC+22] we show, through constructive examples, that for Conjecture 1.2 to be true one needs *both* F, G to have *both* of the low-degree and low-influence conditions. Furthermore, we give an example showing that relation between δ and the degree d must satisfy $\delta < \frac{1}{2d}$, otherwise the conjecture is false.

We then prove the following conditional result. We state the group structure $\mathbb{Z}_2^m$ to clarify how the answers are read by the quantum algorithm. In particular, the oracle answers are added (in $\mathbb{Z}_2^m$) to the answer registers.

Theorem 1.3 (Attacking QAQB protocols – informal). *If Alice and Bob ask a total of d quantum queries to a random oracle $h \colon [N] \to \mathbb{Z}_2^m$ and agree on a key k with probability 1, and if Conjecture 1.2 holds, then there is an attacker who asks $\mathrm{poly}(d, m)$ classical queries to h and finds the key k with probability 0.9.*

More generally, we show that if the Polynomial Compatibility Conjecture holds with respect to an influence δ, then for any d-query key agreement protocol using the random oracle $h : [N] \to \{0, 1\}^m$, there is an attacker who asks $\mathrm{poly}(dm/\delta)$ number of queries and finds the key with high probability. Thus while we are unable to prove Conjecture 1.2 as stated, this motivates trying to prove it for some smaller influence δ which is independent of the size of the input space $N = 2^\kappa$ for security parameter κ.

Random Oracles Using Other Groups for Answers. Random oracles can be defined with an arbitrary Abelian group G (other than $\mathbb{Z}_2^m$). We further extend Theorem 1.3 in two directions. We first generalize the Polynomial Compatibility Conjecture (see Conjecture 5.5) that is parameterized by an Abelian group G_1, such that when $G_1 = \mathbb{Z}_2$, then this becomes Conjecture 1.2. We then show (see Lemma 4.8) that if this conjecture holds for any constant-size Abelian group G_1, then for all Abelian groups G_2 we can get $\mathrm{poly}(d, \log |G_2|)$-query (classical) attacks on perfectly complete key agreement protocols that use a random oracle $h \colon [N] \to G_2$. Note that this reduction allows the size of the group elements in G_2 to grow polynomially with the security parameter κ, while we still get a $\mathrm{poly}(\kappa)$-query (classical) attack.

Proving the Conjecture for Exponentially Small Influence. We then prove (a variant of) Conjecture 1.2 where δ is exponentially small $\delta(d) < O(2^{-d}/d)$ as a function of d instead of polynomially small. As a result, we obtain an $O(2^{dm} \cdot d^2)$-query (classical) attack on any key agreement in the QROM. Note that this is a nontrivial upper bound on the security, only when the input length n is sufficiently larger than m (e.g., when $n = m^2$, or that the input space is $\{0, 1\}^*$, while the outputs have fixed length m).

Learning Heavy Queries for Quantum Protocols. One of the major contributions of our work in proving Theorem 1.3 is to generalize the "heavy-queries learner" of Barak and Mahmoody [BMG09a] to the quantum setting. In fact, doing so is crucial for us even to come up with *any candidate attack* in the QAQB model, regardless of proving it to be successful. Our quantum-heavy query learner could pave the way for proving more separations in the quantum random oracle model.

Implications to Quantum Black-Box Separations. The $\mathrm{poly}(d)$-query attacks of [IR89, BM17] were used to obtain black-box separations for key agreement from one-way functions. The same argument extends to the case of QCCC key agreements with perfect completeness. Our Theorem 1.1 also leads to a $\mathrm{poly}(d, m) \le \mathrm{poly}(\kappa)$-query attack, and hence can be used to obtain similar separations with respect to "quantum black-box" constructions, for the case of perfect completeness and classical Alice. In a quantum black-box construction [HY20] the reductions (to implement the primitive and prove its security) can have quantum superposition access to the oracles they use. Our Theorem 1.3 implies a similar separation for QCCC key agreement protocols from one-way functions, but based on the assumption that Polynomial Compatibility Conjecture holds. See Theorem 6.3 of the full version [ACC+22] for a formalization.

Attacking Other Primitives. Once we obtain polynomial-query attacks on QCCC key agreement in the QROM model, we also immediately obtain further corollaries about the impossibility of using quantum random oracles for realizing other primitives such as public-key encryption and oblivious transfer, or more generally, any primitive $\mathcal{P}$ that implies key agreement in a black-box way, when the communication and the inputs are classical. For example, since oblivious transfer implies key agreement [GKM+00], our Theorems 1.1 and 1.3 also extend to rules out the possibility of OT protocols with perfect completeness in the QCCC model using random oracles. Similarly, our separations extend to similar separations from other primitives, such as Oblivious Transfer, that imply key agreements in a black-box way.

Connection to the Simulation Conjecture. Since our attacks on perfectly complete key agreement protocols in the QROM model are classical, it is natural to ask if such classical attacks can be extended to all such protocols, even against protocols with imperfect completeness. We show that obtaining such attacks would resolve a basic and long-standing open question about the power of quantum vs. classical algorithms. That means obtaining such classical attacks *unconditionally* might be quite challenging. More specifically, a folklore conjecture, which we refer to as the "Simulation Conjecture", states that for any $\text{poly}(\kappa)$-query quantum algorithm Q^h using a random oracle h, and for any $\varepsilon = 1/\text{poly}(\kappa)$, there is another $\text{poly}(\kappa)$-query *classical* algorithm S^h that can approximate the acceptance probability $\Pr[Q^h = 1]$ with $\pm\varepsilon$ additive error, for $1 - \varepsilon$ fraction of oracles h. Aaronson and Ambainis (see Conjecture 4 in [AA09]) formalized this conjecture and showed that it is implied by a Fourier-analytic conjecture, now known as the Aaronson-Ambainis conjecture, that has some resemblance to our Polynomial Compatibility Conjecture but also with key differences (see Sect. 1.3).

In this work, we observe that the Simulation Conjecture is in fact necessary for extending classical attacks on key agreement protocols in the QCCC model using quantum random oracles and with negligible completeness error. Doing so shows that proving an unconditional classical attack of $\text{poly}(\kappa)$ query complexity on QCCC key agreements in the QROM are not possible, unless one resolves the Simulation Conjecture positively.

Theorem 1.4 (QCCC key agreement against classical adversaries – informal). *If the Simulation Conjecture is false, then there is a key agreement in the QCCC model in which quantum powered parties Alice and Bob use a random oracle to agree on a bit b with probability $1 - \text{negl}(\kappa)$, while for an infinite set of security parameters κ, the protocol is secure against all classical $\text{poly}(\kappa)$-query eavesdropping algorithms.*

See Theorem 7.6 of the full version [ACC+22] for a formalization of the theorem above, and see the next section below for a highlight of the ideas behind its proof.

1.2 Technical Overview

In this section, we highlight the ideas behind Theorems 1.1, 1.3, and 1.4.

Our starting point is the work of Brakerski et al. [BKSY11] that showed a simpler attack and analysis than that of [IR89, BM17], to break any key agreement *with perfect completeness* in the ROM using $O(d^2)$ queries. To obtain our results, we start by modifying the attack of [BKSY11] to a version that is more robust so that it can be adapted to the quantum setting. We start by describing this attack for the setting that *both* Alice and Bob are *classical*. We then discuss, step by step, the new ideas that are introduced to extend the attack to the case of quantum parties.

Case of Classical Alice and Classical Bob. Let $h : [N] \to \{0,1\}^m$ be the random oracle. Suppose t is the (classical) transcript of the protocol, and P_A (resp. P_B) is the partial function that defines the set of queries asked by Alice (resp. Bob) and their answers. Let $Q_A = \text{dom}(P_A)$ (resp. $Q_B = \text{dom}(P_B)$) be the set of queries asked by Alice (resp. Bob). Also, let k be the key that Alice and Bob agree upon.

Attacking CACB Protocols. The adversary Eve E is given the transcript t and wants to find out the key k. Our simple attack follows the "heavy query learning" approach of [IR89, BM17]. Eve maintains a partial function L that defines the answers to the queries Q_L that are asked by Eve has asked so far. (At the beginning $L = \emptyset$.) During the attack, Eve asks any query $x \notin Q_L$ that is "ε-heavy for being in Q_A" conditioned on what Eve knows so far: (L, t). More formally, x is called ε-heavy if $\Pr[x \in Q_A | L, t] \geq \varepsilon$. Whenever Eve reaches a point that there is no heavy query left to ask, Eve simply samples a full (fake) view V'_A for Alice in her head and outputs the key k'_A that is implied by V'_A. We claim that the attack is both efficient and successful. Namely, Eve asks an expected number of at most d/ε queries, and that it finds the key $k'_A = k$ with probability at least $1 - \varepsilon d$. Then, by taking $\varepsilon \approx 1/d$ we obtain the desired result.

Efficiency of the Attack. It is easy to prove, using the linearity of expectation, that $\mathbb{E}[|L|] \leq d/\varepsilon$. This is roughly because every query asked by Eve has at least ε-chance of being in Q_A, and that there are a limited $|Q_A| \leq d$ possible queries in Q_A.

Success of the Attack. Perhaps the more interesting aspect is the success of the attack, which is argued based on two facts.

- Independence: For every fixed oracle h and transcript t, the random variables V_A and V_B that describe the views of Alice and Bob conditioned on h and t are independent random variables (i.e., they have a product distribution).
- Consistency: If (1) the views V_A and V_B are each consistent with the transcript t, and (2) their partial functions P_A, P_B are also consistent partial functions, then one can conclude that there is an oracle h that is consistent with each of the views V_A, V_B. The second condition is equivalent to saying that there is a partial function L such (1) L is consistent with both P_A, P_B, and (2) $(Q_A \setminus Q_L) \cap (Q_B \setminus Q_L) = \emptyset$.[4]

The above two facts can be used to argue the success of the attack as follows. Let us fix Bob's (real) view V_B. Let $x \in Q_B$ be any particular query asked by Bob that is *not* in Q_L, and hence not learned by Eve. Any such query shall be ε-light (otherwise it was learned by Eve and hence in Q_L). Therefore, the probability that x is in Q'_A, where Q'_A is the set of queries in the fake view V'_A sampled by Eve, is at most ε. By a union bound, with probability at least $1 - d\varepsilon$, it holds that P'_A and P_B are consistent (where P'_A is the partial function of the view of the fake Alice V'_A sampled by Eve). This means that there is a full oracle h that is consistent with both of V'_A, V_B. Then, by perfect completeness, this means the key $k = k_B$ for Bob should match the key $k_E = k'_A$ output by Eve.

Case of Classical Alice and Quantum Bob. Here we describe what steps would be different when attacking protocols with a quantum Bob (but still classical Alice). Interestingly, the attack description remains exactly the same as before. First note that, because Alice is classical it is well-defined to talk about whether $x \in Q_A$ or not at the end of the protocol as once a query is asked by Alice it would belong to Q_A forever.[5] The efficiency analysis of the attack also remains the same as the CACB case above. Below, we describe the key differences in the analysis of the success of the attack.

Success of the Attack. At a high level, we prove quantum variants for both of the Independence and Consistency properties.

- Independence: We show that, even if Alice and Bob are both quantum, then their "views" (i.e., the measurement of their registers) would be independent conditioned on the fixed classical transcript t and oracle h. More generally, we show that the *joint quantum state* of Alice and Bob, conditioned on h, t is a *product state*.

---

[4] In [IR89,BM17], this condition is referred to as having no "intersection queries" outside L.
[5] One cannot say the same thing for quantum algorithm Bob, as it might choose to "forget" things about oracle as it proceeds.

– Consistency: Again, we first prove a result that applies to the more general case of *two* quantum parties. We start by using two ideas that were popularized following the breakthrough work of Zhandry [Zha19]. First, we use a purified quantum random oracle h that is in the uniform superposition over all possible classical oracles (which is equivalent to using a classical random oracle). Second, we represent the oracle's answers in the Fourier domain, and denote the oracle $\hat{h}$.

We show that if parties ask a total of d queries to the oracle, then the joint quantum state $|\phi\rangle$ that describes both Alice's and Bob's registers W and the oracle $\hat{h}$ (using registers H) is "d-sparse" over its oracle part H, in the sense that $\hat{h}$ can be represented with a degree d multi-linear polynomial f with variables $x_i, i \in [2^n]$.

Finally, we show that in the case when Alice is classical, then if Alice's fake queries Q'_A do not intersect with the "queries" in $\mathcal{S}$, where $\mathcal{S}$ is a (maximal) monomial $\prod_{i \in \mathcal{S}} x_i$ in f of $\deg(f)$, then there exists an oracle h such that (1) h is consistent with the real views $|\phi\rangle$, and (2) h is also consistent with Alice's fake view V'_A.

The above generalization of the Consistency condition allows us to now basically apply the same argument used in the CACB case by treating the variables in the maximal monomial $\mathcal{S}$ as Bob's queries. In particular, once $Q'_A \cap \mathcal{S} = \emptyset$, then we conclude that there is an oracle h that is consistent with each of V'_A and the real (quantum) Alice and Bob. Then, by the Independence property, h is consistent with V'_A and real Bob *at the same time*, and hence by perfect completeness the key implied by Alice's fake view V'_A sampled by Eve shall match that of the real Bob.

Case of Quantum Alice and Quantum Bob. When it comes to the case of quantum Alice and Bob, we can no longer use the classical attack of the CACB setting, as both Alice and Bob can now ask *superposition* queries to the oracle (e.g., all of their queries might have non-zero amplitude for *all* possible oracle queries). Hence, we need to change the attack and its analysis. In this case, without loss of generality, we focus on the simpler case that the key k is a bit.

Description of the Attack. In the previous case of CAQB, we described how we choose to represent the (now quantum) random oracle $\hat{h}$ in the Fourier domain. Roughly speaking, in the Fourier domain, an oracle answer $\hat{0}$ to a query x, means that it has uniform distribution (when measured in the computational basis), and any other answer $\hat{y} \neq \hat{0}$ refers to non-uniform answers. Therefore, a "non-uniform" $\hat{y} \neq \hat{0}$ answer here means that either Alice or Bob have (at least partially) "read" the answer to x at some point. More precisely, conditioned on all Eve knows, let p_x be the probability that after measuring the answer to the query x in the Fourier basis, we obtain an answer other than $\hat{0}$. Then, informally speaking, we interpret p_x as the "probability that either Alice or Bob has read x from the oracle". In that case, if $p_x \geq \varepsilon$, then Eve will call x *quantum ε-heavy*. In the new attack, Eve goes ahead and asks any (classical query) x that is quantum ε-heavy (under the new definition) and updates L as before. When no "quantum ε-heavy query" is left, Eve outputs the more likely key $k \in \{0, 1\}$.

Efficiency. We generalize the efficiency argument for the classical case to the quantum regime. Namely, if Alice and Bob ask a total of d queries to the oracle, then the quantum ε-heavy learner Eve will stop after asking $|L|$ queries, where we have $\mathbb{E}[|L|] \leq d/\varepsilon$.

Success of the Attack. Our goal is to show that once no quantum ε-heavy query is left, then conditioned on Eve's knowledge (t, L), at least one of the possible keys $k \in \{0, 1\}$

is much more likely to be the key chosen by Alice and bob. In that case, Eve will indeed succeed in finding the true key with high probability. For sake of contradiction, suppose after learning L and conditioned on (t, L) both values of $k \in \{0, 1\}$ have probabilities $\approx 1/2$. We would like to show that this situation violates perfect completeness. As explained in the previous case of CAQB, once we view the oracle $\hat{h}$ in the Fourier domain, after Alice and Bob ask d oracle queries, the joint state of the oracle and the registers of Alice and Bob corresponds to a *distribution* F over degree-d multi-linear polynomials like f. The distribution is obtained by measuring the work registers of Alice and Bob.[6] Below, we further analyze this distribution over low-degree polynomials, while for simplicity we assume that we deal with *one* fixed polynomial f.

Because at the end of the attack Eve has learned all the quantum ε-heavy queries of the oracle, it can be shown that any unlearned query x, which corresponds to a variable in the polynomial f, has influence (as defined prior to Conjecture 1.2) at most ε. Putting things together, the polynomial f has the following properties: (1) f has ℓ_2 norm 1, because of representing a quantum state, (2) f has degree d, and (3) the influence of every variable in f is bounded by ε. Furthermore, if we let f_b be the polynomials that represent the "conditional states" of the oracle and Alice-Bob registers *conditioned* on the key being $k = b$, then by the fact that the key k is still unbiased (in Eve's view) we can conclude that f_0, f_1 both essentially inherit all the properties of f (the only difference being that the influences increase to $\approx 2\varepsilon$ instead of ε).

Our Conjecture 1.2 states that when ε is sufficiently small, any two polynomials f_0, f_1 with properties stated above would have a nonzero product. This implies that there exists an oracle h that is consistent with two very different executions with two outcomes for the final key. By the Independence property, we can now choose Alice's view from the execution leading to the key 0 and choose Bob's view from the execution leading to key 1, but this violates the perfect completeness.

Obtaining Exponentially Small Influences. To prove the weaker variant of Conjecture 1.2 where the influences are less than $2^{-d}/d$ rather than the desired $1/\operatorname{poly}(d)$, the high level idea is as follows. Take any maximum-degree term appearing in f, and consider what happens when we fix all variables except the $\leq d$ ones in the term. Clearly, the resulting restriction of f is not a constant function so there is always some assignment to the remaining d variables that makes f non-zero, regardless of how the first variables were fixed. We show that, if g has all influences less than $2^{-d}/d$ then there is some assignment to the variables outside the term such that g is non-zero for all assignments to the remaining d variables, yielding an $\mathbf{x}$ such that $f(\mathbf{x}) \cdot g(\mathbf{x}) \neq 0$. To prove this property of g, we show that in expectation over a random assignment of the variables outside the term, the resulting restriction of g has a constant term that dominates all the non-constant terms. The exponential loss of 2^d essentially comes from the fact that there are 2^d non-constant terms in this restriction of g.

Ideas behind Theorem 1.4. We now sketch some of the ideas behind the proof of Theorem 1.4. We start by assuming that Q is a quantum algorithm accessing a random oracle h that asks $\operatorname{poly}(\kappa)$ queries, while there is $\varepsilon = 1/\operatorname{poly}(\kappa)$ such that any $\operatorname{poly}(\kappa)$-query

---

[6] As expected, the formulation of our Polynomial Compatibility Conjecture is such that, to use the conjecture for obtaining attacks, it does not matter in which basis the work registers of Alice and Bob are measured.

classical algorithm will fail to approximate $\Pr[Q^h = 1]$ within $\pm\varepsilon$ additive error for *at least ε* fraction of the sampled random oracles h. Note that even though a classical algorithm cannot do so, a quantum algorithm (e.g., Alice or Bob) can indeed approximate $\Pr[Q^h]$ within an arbitrarily small additive error $\delta = 1/\operatorname{poly}(\kappa)$. As a result, quantum Alice and Bob can access the "same" number (approximately) that is, at least sometimes, not as accessible by the classical Eve. Therefore, roughly speaking, the quantum parties can leverage on this "source of shared unpredictable" numbers and bootstrap it to a full fledged key agreement that is secure against classical Eve in the QROM.

In more detail, we first show that the above argument leads to a "weak" key agreement such that the key cannot be guessed with probability $1-\delta$ for some $\delta = 1/\operatorname{poly}(\kappa)$. We then use a careful number of repetitions to agree on a longer key that is much harder for the adversary to guess. The proof of this steps relies on the fact that *concurrent* composition of interactive *proofs* (rather than arguments) decrease the soundness error optimally. Then, one approach is to use the Goldreich-Levin technique to extract a uniform key from the "unpredictable key", and then bootstrap the completeness to $1 - \operatorname{negl}(\kappa)$ using the amplification technique of Holenstein [Hol05]. More conveniently, we use a tool from the recent work of Haitner et al. [HMST21] that combines the last two steps.

Complexity of Our Attacks. When one aims to use *only* a random oracle for security, then it means that the security is defined based on the number of adversary queries, regardless of how computationally hard it is to run such attacks. Indeed, if one adds computational intractability assumptions, one can ignore the random oracle all together and run a computationally secure protocol. In this work, we also primarily focus on studying the feasibility of key agreements from quantum random oracles in the QCCC model, while the implications to *fully* black-box separations are also discussed in Sect. 6 of the full version [ACC+22]. For sake of completeness, here we also comment on the computational complexity of our attack. In the classical setting, an **NP** oracle can be used to "uniformly invert" efficient processes that do not use an **NP** oracle themselves [BGP00]. This allows the adversary Eve to find the heavy queries, as needed in the attack of [BMG09a], through repeated sampling of the views conditioned on the transcript.[7]). In the quantum setting, we can use a "post-selection" gate [Aar05] to do the same thing. More formally, first we observe that Zhandry's compressed oracle lets us efficiently simulate the quantum random oracle while we maintain the "sampled oracle answers" in the Fourier basis using a list of polynomial size. Then, using post-selection one can sample oracle queries that are queried conditioned on the given transcript. Finally, by repeated sampling, we can again efficiently find the heavy queries.

1.3 Related Work

Black-Box Separations. Impagliazzo and Rudich [IR89] initiated the field of "black-box separations" by proving the existence of an oracle relative which one-way functions exist but secure key agreement protocols do not. The notions of black-box reductions, in various forms, were later formalized by Reingold, Trevisan, and Vadhan [RTV04].

Quantum Black-Box Separations. The work of Hosoyamada and Yamakawa [HY20] initiated the study of "quantum black-box" separations by formalizing the notion

---

[7] See Remark 3.2 in https://www.boazbarak.org/Papers/merkle.pdf.

of quantum black-box constructions (for primitives with non-interactive adversaries) and showing that even quantum black-box constructions cannot base collision resistant hash functions on one-way functions. Their work extended the previous result of Haitner et al. [HHRS07] about classical constructions to the quantum setting. Cao and Xue [CX21] proved quantum black-box separation of one-way permutations from one-way functions. Their work extended the previous result of Rudich [Rud88] and Kahn et al. [KSS00] about classical constructions and classical security proofs, to the setting of allowing quantum reductions of security.

The QCCC Model. The model of classical communication and quantum-powered parties is also used in other lines of work. One such recent body of work aims to classically verify a quantum computation [Mah18, CCY20, ACGH20, BKVV20, Zha21, Bar21]. More generally, an active line of work aims for designing on post-quantum security (e.g., see the recent works [BS20, BKS21, ABG+21, ACP21]) in which we deal with quantum powered adversaries, while the honest parties are fully classical. However, in our setting, honest parties are also quantum powered.

Limitations of Random Oracles. Haitner et al. [HOZ16], and Mahmoody et al. [MMP14] studied the limitations of using random oracles for *secure multiparty computation*. It was shown in [HOZ16] that inputless functionalities cannot rely on ROM to get security (unless they are trivially possible). [MMP14] showed that non-trivial and non-complete two-party functionalities cannot be based on random oracles. The work of Haitner et al. [HMO+21] studies the *communication* complexity of key agreement from random oracles. It is interesting to see whether similar lower bounds on the communication complexity of key agreement hold in the QROM model.

Comparison with the Aaronson-Ambainis Conjecture. As mentioned above, Aaronson Ambainis [AA09] proved that if a Fourier-theoretic conjecture, with resemblance to our Polynomial Compatibility Conjecture holds, then the Simulation Conjecture holds as well. The AA Conjecture states that any *bounded* degree d polynomial $f : \{-1, 1\}^n \to [0, 1]$ with variance ε has a variable with influence at least $\text{poly}(\varepsilon/d)$. In a language closer to our Polynomial Compatibility Conjecture, the contrapositive of the AA Conjecture says that for any degree d polynomial f with constant variance and polynomially small influences $\text{poly}(\text{Var}[f]/d)$, there must exist an $\mathbf{x} \in \{0, 1\}^n$ such that $|f(\mathbf{x})| > 1$. One interesting similarity is that both conjectures hold, when we assume *exponentially* small influences [DFKO06]. Despite that, our conjecture and the AA conjecture do not seem to be directly comparable, and it would be interesting to prove implications in either direction between them. For the application to key agreements, the implications of the two conjectures also seem incomparable. Our conjecture is tailored for perfect completeness and can be applied when there *is* communication. On the contrary, the AA conjecture can be applied to give an attack in the setting of imperfect completeness, but (as far as we can see) it is limited to the case of no communication. Furthermore, the "intersection" of these, i.e., the case of no communication and perfect completeness, can be proved without a conjecture [OSSS05].

2   Preliminaries and Notation

2.1   Quantum Computation

Let Σ be a finite and nonempty set of classical states. The finite dimensional Hilbert space associated with a *register* X is defined to be $\mathbb{C}^{|\Sigma|}$ for Σ being the state set of X. A *quantum state* of a register X is a unit vector in $\mathbb{C}^{|\Sigma|}$. We use standard bra-ket notation for vectors and their adjoint. That is, we can write $|\psi\rangle_X \in \mathbb{C}^{|\Sigma|}$ as a vector

$$|\psi\rangle_X = \sum_{i \in \Sigma} \alpha_i |i\rangle_X,$$

where $\sum_{i \in \Sigma} |\alpha_i|^2 = 1$, and $\{|i\rangle\}_{i \in \Sigma}$ is an orthonormal basis of $\mathbb{C}^{|\Sigma|}$. We define $\langle\psi|_X$ as the row vector that is conjugate to $|\psi\rangle_X$. The inner product between $|\phi\rangle_X$ and $|\psi\rangle_X$ is denoted by $\langle\phi|\psi\rangle_X$. We sometimes neglect the subscripts when the corresponding registers are clear form the context.

For combined registers $Y = (X_1, \ldots, X_n)$, where Σ_i is the state set for each X_i, the state set of Y is defined as $\Sigma = \Sigma_1 \times \cdots \times \Sigma_n$. The finite dimensional Hilbert space associated with Y is defined to be $\mathbb{C}^{|\Sigma_1|} \otimes \cdots \otimes \mathbb{C}^{|\Sigma_n|}$. Since every register is labeled by a distinct name, we sometimes permute the order of tensor product for ease of expression. A quantum state $|\psi\rangle_{AB}$ over registers A, B is called a *product state* if and only if it can be written as $|\psi\rangle_{AB} = |\phi_1\rangle_A \otimes |\phi_2\rangle_B$.

The evolution of a quantum state $|\psi\rangle \in \mathbb{C}^{|\Sigma|}$ is governed by a unitary operator $U : \mathbb{C}^{|\Sigma|} \to \mathbb{C}^{|\Sigma|}$. The state becomes $|\psi'\rangle = U|\psi\rangle$. The measurement operator corresponding to a finite nonempty set of outcomes Γ is a set of operators $\{M_i\}_{i \in \Gamma}$ which satisfies $\sum_{i \in \Gamma} M_i^\dagger M_i = I$, where $(\cdot)^\dagger$ denotes Hermitian conjugation and I is the identity operator. The probability of obtaining i by measuring $|\psi\rangle$ is $\|M_i|\psi\rangle\|_2^2$, and the post-measurement state then collapses to $\frac{M_i|\psi\rangle}{\|M_i|\psi\rangle\|_2}$, where $\|\cdot\|_2$ denotes the Euclidean norm. An operator $\Pi_X : \mathbb{C}^{|\Sigma|} \to \mathbb{C}^{|\Sigma|}$ is called a projection operator (or projector) if it satisfies $\Pi_X^2 = \Pi_X$. For projection operators acting on multiple registers of the form $\Pi_{X_1 X_2} = \Pi_{X_1} \otimes I_{X_2}$, we write only the non-trivial part Π_{X_1} for convenience. We say an operator A commutes with another operator B if $AB = BA$.

A quantum circuit consists of registers, unitary gates and measurements. By the deferred measurement principle, all intermediate measurements can be delayed at the end of the circuit by introducing ancillary registers. Without loss of generality, we assume that at the end all the registers are measured in the computational basis. Indeed (efficient) classical algorithms can be simulated using quantum circuits (efficiently).

Some of the components of our analysis rely on ideas inspired by the Compressed Oracle technique of Zhandry [Zha19]. The following preliminary follows closely to the formalization in Sect. 3 of [CFHL21].

The Computational and the Fourier Bases. Let $\mathcal{Y}$ be a finite Abelian group of cardinality $|\mathcal{Y}|$. Let $\{|y\rangle\}_{y \in \mathcal{Y}}$ be an orthonormal basis of $\mathbb{C}^{|\mathcal{Y}|}$, where the basis vectors are labeled by the elements of $\mathcal{Y}$. We refer to this basis as the *computational basis*. Let $\hat{y}$ be the dual group of $\mathcal{Y}$, which consists of all group homomorphisms $\mathcal{Y} \to \{\omega \in \mathbb{C} \mid |\omega| = 1\}$ and is known to be isomorphic to $\mathcal{Y}$, and thus to have cardinality $|\mathcal{Y}|$ as well.[8] We consider

---

[8] We do not rely on $\hat{y}$ and $\mathcal{Y}$ being isomorphic and think of them simply as disjoint sets.

$\hat{\mathcal{Y}}$ to be an additive group; the neutral element is denoted $\hat{0}$. The *Fourier basis* $\{|\hat{y}\rangle\}_{\hat{y}\in\hat{y}}$ of $\mathbb{C}^{|\mathcal{Y}|}$ is defined by the transformations below, where $(\cdot)^*$ is complex conjugation.

$$|\hat{y}\rangle = \frac{1}{\sqrt{|\mathcal{Y}|}} \sum_{y\in\mathcal{Y}} \hat{y}(y)^* |y\rangle \qquad\qquad |y\rangle = \frac{1}{\sqrt{|\mathcal{Y}|}} \sum_{\hat{y}\in\hat{y}} \hat{y}(y)|\hat{y}\rangle.$$

An elementary property of the Fourier basis is the following.

Fact 2.1. *The operator defined by* $|y\rangle|y'\rangle \mapsto |y + y'\rangle|y'\rangle$ *for all* $y, y' \in \mathcal{Y}$ *is the same as the operator defined by* $|\hat{y}\rangle|\hat{y}'\rangle \mapsto |\hat{y}\rangle|\hat{y}' - \hat{y}\rangle$ *for all* $\hat{y}, \hat{y}' \in \hat{y}$.

Functions and Their (Quantum) Representations. Let $\mathcal{H}$ be the set of all functions $h : \mathcal{X} \to \mathcal{Y}$ and $\hat{\mathcal{H}}$ be the set of all functions $\hat{h} : \mathcal{X} \to \hat{y}$. For any $h \in \mathcal{H}$, we define its *quantum representation* to be $|h\rangle_H := \bigotimes_{x\in\mathcal{X}} |h(x)\rangle_{H_x}$ in the computational basis, where the register H_x is associated with $\mathbb{C}^{|\mathcal{Y}|}$ for all $x \in \mathcal{X}$, and the register H is compounded of all H_x. One can view $|h\rangle_H$ as the vector representing the truth table of h. Similarly, for any $\hat{h} \in \hat{\mathcal{H}}$ we define $|\hat{h}\rangle_H := \bigotimes_{x\in\mathcal{X}} |\hat{h}(x)\rangle_{H_x}$ in the Fourier basis. Both $\{|h\rangle_H\}_{h\in\mathcal{H}}$ and $\{|\hat{h}\rangle_H\}_{\hat{h}\in\hat{\mathcal{H}}}$ are orthonormal bases of $\mathbb{C}^{|\mathcal{Y}|^{|\mathcal{X}|}}$.

Superposition Oracle. In the quantum random oracle model, an oracle-aided quantum algorithm A consists of the *query* register X, the *answer* register Y and ancillary register Z. For convenience, we let $W := (X, Y, Z)$ denote the *internal registers* of A. Initially, a function $h : \mathcal{X} \to \mathcal{Y}$ is sampled from $\mathcal{H}$ uniformly at random, and A begins with the state $|0\rangle_W$. The algorithm A is able to ask adaptive quantum queries. Between the queries, A can apply unitaries and perform measurements on its registers. The query operation O is defined as the following unitary mapping in the computational basis.

$$|x\rangle_X |y\rangle_Y |h\rangle_H \mapsto |x\rangle_X |y + h(x)\rangle_Y |h\rangle_H$$

Since quantum operators are reversible, we assume the algorithm has access to $O^\dagger$ as well. By default, O acts as identity on registers other than X, Y and H.

We define the quantum state $|\Phi_0\rangle_H$ to be a uniform superposition over all $h \in \mathcal{H}$

$$|\Phi_0\rangle_H := \sum_{h\in\mathcal{H}} \frac{1}{\sqrt{|\mathcal{H}|}} |h\rangle_H = \bigotimes_{x\in\mathcal{X}} |\hat{0}\rangle_{H_x}. \tag{1}$$

The sampling of h is equivalent to measuring $|\Phi_0\rangle_H$ in the computational basis. Since the unitary operators and measurements performed by A commute with the measurement on $|\Phi_0\rangle_H$, and the fact that registers in H are used only as control-bits for O, we can delay the measurement on $|\Phi_0\rangle_H$ to the end of the computation.

Now, we analyze the behavior of the superposition oracle in the Fourier basis. By Fact 2.1, O becomes

$$|x\rangle_X |\hat{y}\rangle_Y |\hat{h}\rangle_H \mapsto |x\rangle_X |\hat{y}\rangle_Y \bigotimes_{x'\in\mathcal{X}} |\hat{h}(x') - \hat{y} \cdot \delta_{x,x'}\rangle_{H_{x'}}, \tag{2}$$

in the Fourier basis, where $\delta_{x,x'} = 1$ when $x = x'$ and $\delta_{x,x'} = 0$ otherwise.

2.2   Key Agreement Using Quantum Computation and Classical Communication

A key agreement protocol in the Quantum-Computation Classical-Computation (QCCC) model is a protocol in which two quantum algorithms, Alice and Bob, can query the oracle, apply quantum operation on their internal registers, and send classical strings over the public channel to the other party. We also refer to this model as the *Quantum-Alice Quantum-Bob* model. The sequence of the strings sent during the protocol is called the *transcript* of the protocol. Let W_A and W_B be Alice's and Bob's internal registers, respectively. Before the protocol starts, an oracle function h is chosen from $\mathcal{H}$ uniformly at random, and query operation O_h given the oracle h is defined as

$$O_h : |x\rangle|y\rangle \mapsto |x\rangle|y + h(x)\rangle.$$

When we consider the case that Alice and Bob are both quantum algorithms, they start with a product state $|0\rangle_{W_A} \otimes |0\rangle_{W_B}$. When Alice is a classical algorithm and Bob is a quantum algorithm, Alice is given a random tape at the beginning. That is, Alice and Bob start with a product state $|r_A\rangle_{W_A} \otimes |0\rangle_{W_B}$, where $r_A \in \{0,1\}^*$ is uniform.

Apart from the *real* execution, we can take not only W_A, W_B but also the oracle register H initialized as $|\Phi_0\rangle_H$ into account. As we mentioned, the sampling of h can be postponed at the end. Additionally, by the deferred measurement principle, all the intermediate measurements can be delayed as well. Now, the joint state of W_A, W_B and H remains as a *pure* state during the protocol. Importantly, such a switching of viewpoints could display several non-trivial properties providing better leverage while still being perfectly indistinguishable from the previous one. Therefore, the analysis will be done in the so-called *purified view* in the following sections. In other word, whenever any classical information appears, the joint state collapses to the corresponding post-measurement state and stays pure. For any key agreement protocol, we define its *purified version* as follows:

- Start with $|0\rangle_{W_A}|0\rangle_{W_B}|\Phi_0\rangle_H$.
- Alice and Bob runs the protocol in superposition, that is, all the measurements (including those used for generating the transcript[9]) are delayed and the query operator O_h is replaced by O.
- Let $|\Psi\rangle_{W_A W_B H}$ denote the state at the end of the protocol and $|\Psi_t\rangle_{W_A W_B H}$ be its post-measurement that is consistent with the transcript t.

Definition 2.2 (Nonzero queries in Fourier basis). *For any $\hat{h} \in \hat{\mathcal{H}}$, we define the set*

$$Q_{\hat{h}} := \{x : x \in \mathcal{X}, \hat{h}(x) \neq \hat{0}\}$$

and the size of $\hat{h}$ by

$$|\hat{h}| := |\{x : x \in \mathcal{X}, \hat{h}(x) \neq \hat{0}\}| = |Q_{\hat{h}}|.$$

---

[9] By delaying the measurement for the transcript, one can view it as applying an CNOT gate, where the controlled bit is the register that supposed to sent and the target bit is an ancilla. Then, one sends the ancilla bit, and in the rest of the computation, the ancilla bits are served only as control bits for Alice's and Bob's computation. The ancilla bits (transcript) remain unchanged throughout the computation. Thus, it is equivalent to sending classical information, and it is consistent with QCCC model.

Definition 2.3 (Oracle support). *For any vector* $|\phi\rangle_{WH} = \sum_{w,\hat{h}\in\hat{\mathcal{H}}} \alpha_{w,\hat{h}}|w\rangle_W|\hat{h}\rangle_{\hat{H}}$, *we define the* oracle support in the Fourier basis *of* $|\phi\rangle$ *as*

$$\widehat{\mathrm{supp}}^H(|\phi\rangle) := \{\hat{h} : \exists w \ s.t. \ \alpha_{w,\hat{h}} \neq 0\}.$$

We denote the largest $\hat{h}$ *in* $\widehat{\mathrm{supp}}^H(|\phi\rangle)$ *as*

$$\hat{h}_{\max}^H(|\phi\rangle) := \underset{\hat{h}\in\widehat{\mathrm{supp}}^H(|\phi\rangle)}{\arg\max} \ |\hat{h}|.$$

(If the choice is not unique, then choose the alphabetically first one.) When the oracle registers H are clear, we simply denote this by $\hat{h}_{\max}(|\phi\rangle)$. Similarly, if we write the oracle part in the computational basis $|\phi\rangle_{WH} = \sum_{w,h\in\mathcal{H}} \beta_{w,h}|w\rangle_W|h\rangle_H$*, then we define the* oracle support in the computational basis *of* $|\phi\rangle$ *as*

$$\mathrm{supp}^H(|\phi\rangle) := \{h : \exists w \ s.t. \ \beta_{w,h} \neq 0\}.$$

Lemma 2.4 (Sparse representation). *If* A *asks at most d queries to the superposition oracle, then for all possible outcomes of* A*'s intermediate measurements, the joint state* $|\psi\rangle_{WH}$ *conditioned on the outcome satisfies* $|\hat{h}_{\max}(|\psi\rangle)| \leq d$.

Proof. We prove the lemma by induction on the number of queries asked by A, denoted by q. For the base case $q = 0$, the joint state $|\psi_0\rangle_{WH} = |0\rangle_W|\Phi_0\rangle_H$ satisfies the statement. Assume that the joint state $|\psi_k\rangle_{WH}$ satisfies $|\hat{h}_{\max}(|\psi_k\rangle)| \leq k$ for some k.

For the induction step, since the unitaries and measurements act only on W, the size of the state never increases. Moreover, for every $x \in \mathcal{X}, \hat{y} \in \hat{\mathcal{Y}}$ and $\hat{h} \in \hat{\mathcal{H}}$, by the observation in Eq. (2), the size of $\hat{h}$ increases at most by one after the query operation. Therefore, the size of the state increases at most by one. By induction hypothesis the resulting state $|\psi_{k+1}\rangle_{WH}$ satisfies $|\hat{h}_{\max}(|\psi_{k+1}\rangle)| \leq k + 1$. □

Definition 2.5. *A partial oracle L is a partial function from $\mathcal{X}$ to $\mathcal{Y}$. The domain of L is denoted by $Q_L = \mathrm{dom}(L)$. Equivalently, we view L as a finite set of pairs $(x, y_x) \in \mathcal{X} \times \mathcal{Y}$ such that for all $(x, y_x), (x', y'_x) \in L$, $x \neq x'$.*

Note that our partial oracles are always in the computational basis. We say a partial oracle L is consistent with $h : \mathcal{X} \rightarrow \mathcal{Y}$ if and only if $h(x) = y_x$ holds for all $x \in Q_L$.

Definition 2.6. *For any partial oracle L, we define the associated projector Π_L by*

$$\Pi_L := \bigotimes_{x\in Q_L} |y_x\rangle\langle y_x|_{H_x} \bigotimes_{x\notin Q_L} I_{H_x},$$

where I_{H_x} is the identity operator acting on H_x. It holds that $\Pi_L|h\rangle_H = |h\rangle_H$ if h is consistent with L, and $\Pi_L|h\rangle_H = 0$ otherwise.

Lemma 2.7. *Given a state $|\psi\rangle_{WH}$ and a partial oracle L, the state $\Pi_L|\psi\rangle_{WH}$ can be written as*

$$\Pi_L|\psi\rangle_{WH} = \sum_{w\in\mathcal{W},\hat{h}\in\hat{\mathcal{H}}'} \alpha'_{w,\hat{h}}|w\rangle_W \bigotimes_{x\notin Q_L} |\hat{h}(x)\rangle_{H_x} \bigotimes_{x\in Q_L} |y_x\rangle_{H_x},$$

where $\hat{\mathcal{H}}'$ is the set of functions from $\mathcal{X}\setminus Q_L$ to $\hat{\mathcal{Y}}$. Furthermore, if $|\hat{h}_{\max}^H(|\psi\rangle)| \leq d$, then $|\hat{h}_{\max}^{H'}(\Pi_L|\psi\rangle)| \leq d$, where H' is the set of registers corresponding to $\mathcal{X}\setminus Q_L$.

3   Attacking Classical-Alice Quantum-Bob Protocols

In this section, we consider the case where A is a classical algorithm and B is a quantum algorithm and prove the following theorem.

Theorem 3.1 (Breaking CAQB protocols). *Let* (A, B) *be a two-party protocol in which algorithm classical A communicates with a quantum algorithm B and they both have access to a random oracle* $h: \mathcal{X} \rightarrow \mathcal{Y}$, *and at the end they agree on a key* k *with probability 1. Suppose Alice asks at most* d_A *classical oracle queries, while Bob asks at most* d_B *quantum oracle queries. Then, there is an eavesdropper E who, after receiving the transcript* t, *asks at most* $d_A \cdot d_B / \lambda$ *queries to* h *after receiving the classical transcript* t *and finds the key* k *with probability* $1 - \lambda$.

Note that in the above theorem, the adversary's query complexity is $d_A \cdot d_B / \lambda$ rather than the simpler (still correct) bound of d^2 / λ where $d = d_A + d_B$. Even though, when $d_A = \Theta(d_B)$, it also holds that $d_A \cdot d_B = \Theta(d^2)$, when the query complexity of the parties are unbalanced, e.g., when $d_A = \sqrt{\kappa}, d = \kappa$ for security parameter κ, our attacker's query complexity will be $O(\kappa^{1.5})$ rather than $O(\kappa^2)$. This is particularly a natural scenario when the quantum-powered party is more powerful and can ask many more queries. Later on, we will give a concrete construction of the adversary (Theorem 3.5) in the proof. Notice that the adversary is actually a classical algorithm, where it only makes classical queries.

The rest of this section will be dedicated to proving the theorem. Before constructing the attacker and analyzing it, we introduce some useful lemmas.

3.1   Useful Lemmas

Lemma 3.2 (Independence of quantum views in the QCCC model). *Suppose two quantum algorithms A and B interact classically in the quantum random oracle model. Let* W_A *and* W_B *denote their registers respectively. Then, at any time during the protocol, conditioned on the transcript* t *and the fixed oracle* $h \in \mathcal{H}$, *the joint state of the registers* W_A *and* W_B *conditioned on* t *and* h *is a product state.*

Proof. We prove the lemma by induction on the round index r. For the base case $r = 0$, A and B's joint state $|0\rangle_{W_A} \otimes |0\rangle_{W_B}$. Suppose for some k, A and B's joint state after k rounds is a product state conditioned on the transcript t and oracle h. For the induction step, in the $(k + 1)$-th round, one of them will apply "deterministic" local unitaries and query operators O_h conditioned on t and h. Therefore, further conditioned on the message generated in this round, the resulting joint state is still a product state.   □

Lemma 3.3 (Consistency). *Given a state* $|\psi\rangle_H$, *if* L *is a partial oracle such that* $Q_{\hat{h}_{\max}(|\psi\rangle)} \cap Q_L = \emptyset$, *then* $\|\Pi_L |\psi\rangle\|_2^2 > 0$. *Equivalently, there exists at least one oracle* $h \in \mathcal{H}$ *such that (i)* h *is consistent with* L *and (ii)* $h \in \mathrm{supp}^H(|\psi\rangle)$.

Proof. For convenience, we write $\hat{h}_{\max}$ to denote $\hat{h}_{\max}(|\psi\rangle)$, and we represent $|\psi\rangle_H = \sum_{\hat{h}} \gamma_{\hat{h}} |\hat{h}\rangle$ in the Fourier basis. The proof directly comes from the following two claims:

Claim. $\gamma_{\hat{h}_{\max}} \Pi_L |\hat{h}_{\max}\rangle$ is not a zero vector.

Proof of Section 3.1. Since $Q_{\hat{h}_{\max}} \cap Q_L = \emptyset$ and $\gamma_{\hat{h}_{\max}} \neq 0$ by definition, we have

$$\gamma_{\hat{h}_{\max}} \Pi_L |\hat{h}_{\max}\rangle = \frac{\gamma_{\hat{h}_{\max}}}{\sqrt{|\mathcal{Y}|^{|Q_L|}}} \bigotimes_{x \in Q_L} |y_x\rangle_{H_x} \bigotimes_{x \notin Q_L} |\hat{h}_{\max}(x)\rangle_{H_x},$$

which is not a zero vector. $\qquad \square$

Claim. For all $\hat{h} \in \widehat{\mathrm{supp}}^H(|\psi\rangle) \setminus \{\hat{h}_{\max}\}$, it holds that $\Pi_L|\hat{h}_{\max}\rangle$ is orthogonal to $\Pi_L|\hat{h}\rangle$. As a corollary, we have that $\gamma_{\hat{h}_{\max}} \Pi_L|\hat{h}_{\max}\rangle$ is orthogonal to $\sum_{\hat{h} \neq \hat{h}_{\max}} \gamma_{\hat{h}} \Pi_L|\hat{h}\rangle$ since the latter is a linear combination of vectors which are orthogonal to the former.

Proof of Section 3.1. Since $\hat{h}_{\max}$ is maximal and $Q_{\hat{h}_{\max}} \cap Q_L = \emptyset$, for all $\hat{h} \in \widehat{\mathrm{supp}}^H(|\psi\rangle) \setminus \{\hat{h}_{\max}\}$, it holds that

$$|\{x : x \in \mathcal{X} \setminus Q_L, \hat{h}_{\max}(x) \neq \hat{0}\}| \geq |\{x : x \in \mathcal{X} \setminus Q_L, \hat{h}(x) \neq \hat{0}\}|.$$

For the case of $|\{x : x \in \mathcal{X} \setminus Q_L, \hat{h}_{\max}(x) \neq \hat{0}\}| > |\{x : x \in \mathcal{X} \setminus Q_L, \hat{h}(x) \neq \hat{0}\}|$, there exist an $x' \in \mathcal{X} \setminus Q_L$ such that $\hat{h}(x') = \hat{0}$ and $\hat{h}_{\max}(x') \neq \hat{0}$. Therefore, we have

$$\langle \hat{h}|\Pi_L|\hat{h}_{\max}\rangle = \bigotimes_{x \in Q_L} \langle \hat{h}(x)|y_x\rangle\langle y_x|\hat{h}(x)\rangle \bigotimes_{x \notin Q_L} \langle \hat{h}(x)|\hat{h}_{\max}(x)\rangle = 0,$$

since $\langle \hat{h}(x')|\hat{h}_{\max}(x')\rangle = 0$.

For the case of $|\{x : x \in \mathcal{X} \setminus Q_L, \hat{h}_{\max}(x) \neq \hat{0}\}| = |\{x : x \in \mathcal{X} \setminus Q_L, \hat{h}(x) \neq \hat{0}\}|$, suppose there exists an $\hat{h}$ such that $\hat{h}(x) = \hat{h}_{\max}(x)$ holds for all $x \in \mathcal{X} \setminus Q_L$. There are two possible cases. First, For all $x \in Q_L$, it holds that $\hat{h}(x) = \hat{0}$. Because $Q_{\hat{h}_{\max}} \cap Q_L = \emptyset$, we have $\hat{h}_{\max}(x) = 0$ for all $x \in Q_L$. Consequently, we have $\hat{h} = \hat{h}_{\max}$ which contradicts to $\hat{h} \neq \hat{h}_{\max}$. Second, there exists $x \in Q_L$ such that $\hat{h}(x) \neq \hat{0}$. It implies $|\hat{h}| > |\hat{h}_{\max}|$ which contradicts to the maximal size of $\hat{h}_{\max}$. Therefore, for all $\hat{h}$ of the second case, there exists an $x' \in \mathcal{X} \setminus Q_L$ such that $\hat{h}(x') \neq \hat{h}_{\max}(x')$. It implies $\langle \hat{h}|\Pi_L|\hat{h}_{\max}\rangle = 0$. $\qquad \square$

Finally, by Sect. 3.1 and Sect. 3.1 we can conclude that

$$\|\Pi_L|\psi\rangle\|_2^2 = \|\gamma_{\hat{h}_{\max}} \Pi_L|\hat{h}_{\max}\rangle\|_2^2 + \left\| \sum_{\hat{h} \neq \hat{h}_{\max}} \gamma_{\hat{h}} \Pi_L|\hat{h}\rangle \right\|_2^2 \geq \|\gamma_{\hat{h}_{\max}} \Pi_L|\hat{h}_{\max}\rangle\|_2^2 > 0.$$

$\qquad \square$

The proof of the following lemma could be found in the full version [ACC+22].

Lemma 3.4 (Bounding the classical heavy queries). *Let Q be a random variable over subsets of universe $\mathcal{U}$. Suppose $z_1, x_1, z_2, x_2, \ldots$ is a finite sequence of random variables that are correlated with Q, and we have $x_i \in \mathcal{U} \cup \{\perp\}$ for all i. Suppose $x_i = x_j$ for $i \neq j$, then $x_i = x_j = \perp$. (Namely, no nontrivial x_i gets repeated). For a full sample $z_1, x_1, z_2, x_2, \ldots$, call x_i ε-heavy (conditioned on $z_1, x_1, \ldots, z_i$) if $\Pr[x_i \in Q \mid z_1, x_1, \ldots, z_i] \geq \varepsilon$, and for the same sequence, define $\mathcal{S} = \{x_i \mid x_i \text{ is } \varepsilon\text{-heavy}\}$. (Note that $\mathcal{S}$ is also a random variable correlated with Q.) Then, $\mathbb{E}[|\mathcal{S}|] \leq \mathbb{E}[|Q|]/\varepsilon$.*

3.2 The Attack and Its Analysis

Notation and Basic Notions. For a classical algorithm A (perhaps in a multi-party proto-col) in an oracle model, we use $V_A = (r_A, t, P)$ to denote Alice's view in an execution, which consists of Alice's randomness r_A, the transcript t, and the partial oracle P of query-answer pairs that Alice encounters during her execution. By f_A we denote the function which takes V_A as input and outputs A's key k_A. We use $Q_A = Q_P$ to refer to the set of queries asked by A. Given transcript t and some partial knowledge about the oracle h encoded by a partial oracle L, we call x an ε-heavy query for Alice (con-ditioned on (t, L)) if $\Pr[x \in Q_A \mid t, L] \geq \varepsilon$, where the probability is over Alice's randomness and the oracle answers outside L.

Construction 3.5 (Attacking Classical-Alice Quantum-Bob protocols). *Let* (A, B) *be a key agreement protocol in which* A *(Alice) is classical and* B *(Bob) is quantum and they both have access to a random oracle* h. *Given the transcript* t, *the attacking algorithm* E *(Eve) is parameterized by* ε *and works as follows.*

- *Let* $L = \emptyset$.
- *While there is any* ε-*heavy query for Alice conditioned on* (t, L), *do the following.*
  - *Ask the lexicographically first* ε-*heavy query for Alice from the oracle* h.
  - *Update* L *by adding* $(x, h(x))$ *to* L.
- *Sample Alice's view* V_A' *conditioned on* (t, L), *and output the key* $k_A' = f_A(V_A')$.

Lemma 3.6 (Efficiency). *The expected number of queries asked by Eve in Construc-tion 3.5 is at most* d_A/ε, *where* d_A *is the maximum number of queries asked by Alice.*

Proof. The proof is identical to the efficiency argument of the attack from [BM17]. More formally, we can use the abstract Lemma 3.4 to derive the claim by letting Q model Alice's set of queries, x_i be the ith query asked by E, and letting z_i be the information E receives about Q after asking x_{i-1}. In particular z_1 is the transcript, and z_i is the oracle answer to the query x_{i-1}, in case it is asked, and $x_j = \bot$ if no heavy query is left after asking x_i for $i < j$. In this case, all the queries Q_L asked by Eve E are ε-likely to be in Q_A conditioned on the transcript and the previously revealed information encoded in L, and so at the end we have $\mathbb{E}[|L|] \leq |d_A|/\varepsilon$.   □

Lemma 3.7 (Success). *If Alice and Bob, respectively, ask a total of* d_A, d_B *oracle queries (where Bob's queries can be quantum queries) and agree on a key with proba-bility 1, then Eve of Construction 3.5 outputs a key* k_E *such that* $\Pr[k_E = k] \geq 1 - \varepsilon d_B$, *where* k *is the key agreed by Alice and Bob.*

Proof. For the proof, we need to define a "quantum extension" of Alice's algorithm, which is denoted by QA. QA basically runs A by making "pure" quantum queries to the oracle h, and measuring Alice's quantum registers W_A would reveal the answers to the oracles queries of the original Alice who is emulated by QA.

Let QAB be the combined party of QA and B. Let W be all the registers of QA and B. Let $\mathcal{W}$ be the set of all possible outcomes of measuring registers W in the computational basis. Below, let $d = d_A + d_B$ be the total number of oracle queries.

For simplicity of presentation, we first give a proof with a looser probability $1 - \varepsilon d$ of finding the key. See the full version for the full proof for the tighter bound.

Loose Analysis. Consider the purified version of the protocol execution, let $|\Psi_t\rangle_{WH}$ be the state conditioned on the transcript t. Since there is at most d queries in total, it holds that $|\hat{h}_{\max}^H(|\Psi_t\rangle)| \le d$ by Lemma 2.4. Suppose the attacker E asks her queries from the oracle, starting from the transcript t, and obtains the partial oracle L where for every x asked by E we have $(x, y_x) \in L$. After she learns the first (x, y_x), the state becomes the post-measurement state corresponding to measuring $|\Psi_t\rangle_{WH}$ on register H_x with the outcome y_x. In this sense, for any t and L we can define the state conditioned on them, denoted by $|\Psi_{t,L}\rangle_{WH}$. Similarly, by Lemma 2.7 it holds that $|\hat{h}_{\max}^{H'}(|\Psi_{t,L}\rangle)| \le d$. Since the oracle registers corresponding to Q_L are now measured, we can consider the "truncated" version of $|\Psi_{t,L}\rangle_{WH}$ by discarding those registers. Let H' be the set of remaining registers, that is, $H' = \{H_x\}_{x \in \mathcal{X} \setminus Q_L}$. By $|\Psi_{t,L}\rangle_{WH'}$ we denote the truncated $|\Psi_{t,L}\rangle_{WH}$. In the following analysis, we further assume that QAB measure the internal registers $W = (W_A, W_B)$ at the end of the protocol and then obtain the outcome w in the computational basis. The resulting state is denoted by $|\Psi_{t,L,w}\rangle_{WH'}$. By Lemma 2.7, for any w it holds that $|\hat{h}_{\max}^{H'}(|\Psi_{t,L,w}\rangle)| \le d$. In the following proof, we will show that for every (t, L, w), E will find the correct key in (t, L, w) with probability at least $1 - \varepsilon d$. From now on, we fix an arbitrary (t, L, w) and define $Q_{\max} := Q_{\hat{h}_{\max}^{H'}(|\Psi_{t,L,w}\rangle)}$.

Recall that Alice A was a classical algorithm and all the ε-heavy queries of A were already learned by the attacker E, and hence for any $x \notin Q_L$ we have $\Pr[x \in Q_A \mid t, L] \le \varepsilon$. In particular, this holds for every $x \in Q_{\max}$. Therefore, by a union bound, with probability at least $1 - \varepsilon|Q_{\max}| \ge 1 - \varepsilon d$, it holds that $Q'_A \cap Q_{\max} = \emptyset$, where Q'_A is the set of queries in the fake view V'_A of Alice sampled by Eve. All we have to show is that for any Q'_A such that $Q'_A \cap Q_{\max} = \emptyset$, it holds that Eve finds Bob's key: $f_A(V'_A) = k_B$. (By perfect completeness, it also holds that $k_B = k_A$.)

Let P'_A be the set of query-answer pairs in the view V'_A. We now apply Lemma 3.3 with L and H in Lemma 3.3 set to be P'_A and H', respectively. Then, Lemma 3.3 shows that there exists an oracle $|h\rangle$ in the computational basis that is simultaneously consistent with L, t, P'_A (and hence Alice's fake view V'_A) and the measurements w of real Alice and Bob. Hence, we have the following:

- The probability of obtaining h as the oracle and V'_A as Alice's view is nonzero.
- The probability of obtaining h as the oracle and $w = w_A, w_B$ as the views of Alice and Bob is nonzero. In particular, the probably of obtaining (h, w_B) is nonzero.

By Lemma 3.2, we conclude that the probability of obtaining (V'_A, h, w_B) is nonzero. Then, by the perfect completeness, the key output by V'_A and w_B should be equal, and this finishes the proof of the weak bound, showing that Eve finds the key with probability $1 - \varepsilon d = 1 - \varepsilon(d_A + d_B)$.   □

4   Attacking Quantum-Alice Quantum-Bob Protocols

In this section, we consider the case where both A and B are quantum algorithms in the QCCC model. In this general setting, we show a *conditional result* based on a conjecture, that any QCCC key agreement protocol with perfect completeness can be broken with an expected polynomial number of queries. While we have so far been unable to prove the conjecture, we can prove a weaker version of the conjecture with exponentially worse parameters, which still leads to a non-trivial attack on QCCC key agreement protocols. We present the conjecture and the variant that we can prove in Sect. 4.1. In Sect. 4.2, we state the main result, which gives an efficient attack when combined with the conjecture and a non-trivial attack when combined with the weak variant we can prove. In Sect. 4.3, we prove the necessary lemma for our main result.

4.1 Main Conjecture and Related Notions

Let $\mathcal{Y}$ be an Abelian group of order $|\mathcal{Y}|$ and $\hat{\mathcal{Y}}$ be the dual group. Let $\mathcal{H}$ be the set of all functions $h : \mathcal{X} \to \mathcal{Y}$ and $\hat{\mathcal{H}}$ be the set of all functions $\hat{h} : \mathcal{X} \to \hat{\mathcal{Y}}$.

Definition 4.1 $((\mathcal{Y}, \delta, d, N)$**-state**$)$. *Let H be a register over the Hilbert space $\mathcal{Y}^N$. A quantum state $|\psi\rangle$ over registers W and H is a $(\mathcal{Y}, \delta, d, N)$-state if it satisfies the following two conditions:*

- *d-sparsity: $|\hat{h}^H_{\max}(|\psi\rangle)| \leq d$.*
- *δ-lightness: For every $x \in \mathcal{X}$, if we measure the H_x register of $|\psi\rangle$ in the Fourier basis, the probability of getting $\hat{0}$ is at least $1 - \delta$.*

The first item above is equivalent to saying that for any measurement of registers H in the Fourier basis, and W in any basis, the oracle support in the Fourier basis (as defined in Definition 2.3) is at most d. Also, looking ahead, the second property above is equivalent to saying that $|\psi\rangle$ has no δ-heavy queries as defined in Definition 4.9.

Definition 4.2 (Compatibility). *Two quantum states $|\psi\rangle$ and $|\phi\rangle$ over registers W and H are compatible if $\operatorname{supp}^H(|\psi\rangle) \cap \operatorname{supp}^H(|\phi\rangle) \neq \emptyset$, i.e., if their oracle supports in the computational basis (as defined in Definition 2.3) have non-empty intersection.*

In general, we pose the following question. *How small should δ be, as a function of $|\mathcal{Y}|$ and d, in order to guarantee that any two $(\mathcal{Y}, \delta, d, N)$-states are compatible?* Our main conjecture is as follows.

Conjecture 4.3. *There exists a finite Abelian group $\mathcal{Y}$ and $\delta = 1/\operatorname{poly}(d)$ such that for any $d, N \in \mathbb{N}$, it holds that any two $(\mathcal{Y}, \delta(d), d, N)$-states $|\psi\rangle$ and $|\phi\rangle$ are compatible.*

Readers may notice that we introduce Conjecture 1.2 in terms of polynomials, while Conjecture 4.3 is formulated in terms of quantum states. In Sect. 5.1, we will show that two formulations are equivalent. We found that the one in quantum states is more natural to use, while the one in polynomials has a clearer mathematical statement.

While we do not have a proof of Conjecture 4.3, we can prove the following theorem when the influences are exponentially small. The proof is deferred to Sect. 5.2.

Theorem 4.4. *For all groups $\mathcal{Y}$, $d, N \in \mathbb{N}$, and $\delta < |\mathcal{Y}|^{-d}/d$, it holds that any two $(\mathcal{Y}, \delta, d, N)$-states $|\psi\rangle$ and $|\phi\rangle$ are compatible.*

4.2 Attacking Quantum-Alice Quantum-Bob Protocols

Now we are ready to state our main result in this section, which states that if Conjecture 4.3 holds for parameter δ, then any QCCC key agreement protocols can be broken in roughly $1/\operatorname{poly}(\delta)$ queries. Additionally, by applying Theorem 4.4, we obtain an attack by using exponentially-many queries without resorting to any conjecture. Out results are formulated as the following two theorems.

Theorem 4.5 (Polynomial-query attacks). *Let* (A, B) *be a two-party QCCC protocol where Alice and Bob asks at most d queries to a random oracle h whose range is $\mathcal{Y}$. If Conjecture 4.3 is true, then, there exists an attacker that breaks* (A, B) *by asking* $\text{poly}(d, \log |\mathcal{Y}|)$ *many* classical *queries to h and finds the key with probability ≥ 0.8.*

Theorem 4.6 (Exponential-query attacks). *Let* (A, B) *be a two-party QCCC protocol with a total of d queries to a random oracle h whose range is $\mathcal{Y}$. Then, there is an attacker who asks an expected number of $|\mathcal{Y}|^d d^2 / \lambda$ classical queries to h and finds the key with probability at least $1 - \lambda$.*

The rest of this section dedicates to proving Theorem 4.5 and Theorem 4.6. In a nutshell, the proof consists of the following steps.

- In Lemma 4.7, we show that once any two $(\mathcal{Y}, \delta = \varepsilon/\lambda, d, N)$-states are compatible, then any QCCC key agreement protocols can be broken in roughly $1/\text{poly}(\delta)$ queries. The exponential-query attack follows from Theorem 4.4 and Lemma 4.7.
- In Lemma 4.8, we show that if there exists a group $\mathcal{Y}$ such that any key agreement using the oracle with the range $\mathcal{Y}$ is broken by polynomial-query attacks, then any key agreements with a different group $\mathcal{Y}'$ can also be broken by such attacks.

In this section, Alice and Bob always output the same key $k \in \{0, 1\}$ with probability 1. Notice that assuming the output is just a bit only makes our impossibility stronger. Besides, we say a key agreement protocol (A^h, B^h) using the random oracle h is (τ, s)-broken, if there exists an attacker that finds the key in (A^h, B^h) with probability at least τ after asking s many queries to h in expectation. We call the scheme (τ, s)-classically broken, if the same thing holds using only classical queries in the attack.

Lemma 4.7 ((Conditionally) breaking QCCC protocols in the QROM). *Let $\mathcal{Y}$ be any finite Abelian group. Let (A, B) be a key agreement protocol with at most d quantum queries to the random oracle h whose range is $\mathcal{Y}$. If it holds that any two $(\mathcal{Y}, \delta = \varepsilon/\lambda, d, N)$-states are compatible, then (A, B) is $(1 - \lambda, d/\varepsilon)$-classically broken.*

The proof of Lemma 4.7 is given in Sect. 4.3.

Lemma 4.8 (Group equivalence). *Suppose there exists a finite Abelian group $\mathcal{Y}$, a constant $\tau > 0$ and a function $s(\cdot)$ such that for all $d \in \mathbb{N}$ and any single-bit key agreement protocol $(A_1^{h_1}, B_1^{h_1})$ where Alice and Bob asks d queries to random oracles h_1 whose range is $\mathcal{Y}$, it holds that $(A_1^{h_1}, B_1^{h_1})$ is $(\tau, s(d))$-broken. Then, for any finite Abelian group $\mathcal{Y}'$, any $d' \in \mathbb{N}$, $\delta > 0$ and any single-bit key agreement protocol $(A'^{h'}, B'^{h'})$ where Alice and Bob asks d' queries to random oracles h' whose range is $\mathcal{Y}'$, $(A'^{h'}, B'^{h'})$ can be $(\tau - \delta, 4s(md'))$-broken, where $m = \lceil \log_{|\mathcal{Y}|}(d'^3 |\mathcal{Y}'| / 4\delta^2) \rceil$.*

The proof of Lemma 4.8 is given in Sect. 8.2 of the full version [ACC+22].

Proof of Theorem 4.5. Because Conjecture 4.3 is true, there exists a finite Abelian group $\mathcal{Y}$ such that for any $d, N \in \mathbb{N}$, any sufficiently small $\delta = 1/\text{poly}(d)$, it holds that any two $(\mathcal{Y}, \delta, d, N)$-states $|\psi\rangle$ and $|\phi\rangle$ are compatible. Then, Lemma 4.7 guarantees that for any key agreement protocol (A, B) where Alice and Bob asks at most d queries to an oracle h whose range is $\mathcal{Y}$, there exists an attacker that breaks (A, B) by asking $\text{poly}(d)$ many queries to h in expectation and finds the key with probability at least 0.9.

Next, by Lemma 4.8, for any finite Abelian group $\mathcal{Y}'$, $d' \in \mathbb{N}$, $\delta > 0$ and single-bit key agreement $(\mathsf{A}'^{h'}, \mathsf{B}'^{h'})$ where Alice and Bob asks d' queries to random oracles h' with range $\mathcal{Y}'$, $(\mathsf{A}'^{h'}, \mathsf{B}'^{h'})$ can be $(0.9 - \delta, \text{poly}(md'))$-classically broken, where

$$m = \lceil \log_{|\mathcal{Y}|}(d'^3 |\mathcal{Y}'| / 4\delta^2) \rceil.$$

Choosing $\delta = 0.1$, we obtain a $\text{poly}(d', |\mathcal{Y}'|)$-query attack which finds the key with probability 0.8. Moreover, since $d', \log |\mathcal{Y}'|$ are both at most $\text{poly}(\kappa)$, where κ is the security parameter (as Alice and Bob both run in time $\text{poly}(\kappa)$), this would lead to a $\text{poly}(\kappa)$-query attack. $\square$

Proof of Theorem 4.6. The proof follows from Theorem 4.4 and Lemma 4.7 with $\varepsilon/\lambda = \delta = |\mathcal{Y}|^{-d}/d$. $\square$

4.3   Proof of Lemma 4.7

The rest of this section will be dedicated to proving Lemma 4.7.

Definition 4.9 (Quantum ε-heavy queries). *For $x \in \mathcal{X}$, let $\Pi_x := \sum_{\hat{y} \in \hat{\mathcal{Y}} \setminus \{\hat{0}\}} |\hat{y}\rangle\langle\hat{y}|_{H_x}$. Given a quantum state $|\psi\rangle_{W_A W_B H}$, the weight of any $x \in \mathcal{X}$ is defined as*

$$w(x) := \| \Pi_x |\psi\rangle \|_2^2.$$

We call $x \in \mathcal{X}$ a quantum ε-heavy query if $w(x) \geq \varepsilon$.

Construction 4.10 (Attack). *Suppose (A, B) is a quantum-Alice quantum-Bob key agreement protocol using the random oracle h. Given the transcript t, attacking algorithm E' is parameterized by ε and works as follows.*

1. *Prepare $L = \emptyset$ and the classical description of the state*

$$|\psi\rangle_{W_A' W_B' H'} = |0\rangle_{W_A'} |0\rangle_{W_B'} |\Phi_0\rangle_{H'},$$

   where W_A', W_B' and H' are the simulated registers for Alice, Bob and the oracle prepared by E'.[10]
2. *Simulate the state evolution during the protocol. Concretely, E' calculates the state in $W_A' W_B' H'$ after each round in the protocol. Whenever E' encounters the moments in which Alice (Bob) send their messages, E' calculates the post-measurement state that is consistent with t.*
3. *While there is any query $x \notin L$ that is quantum ε-heavy conditioned on (t, L), do the following.*
   (a) *Ask the lexicographically first quantum ε-heavy query x from the real oracle h.*
   (b) *Update the state in $W_A' W_B' H'$ to the post-measurement state that is consistent with $(x, h(x))$.*
   (c) *Update L by adding $(x, h(x))$ to L.*
4. *When there is no quantum ε-heavy query left to ask, E' obtains distributions of Alice's and Bob's final keys conditioned on (L, t), and it outputs the key $k \in \{0, 1\}$ that has the highest probability of being Alice's key in this distribution.*

---

[10] Recall that $|\Phi_0\rangle$ is a uniform superposition over all $h \in \mathcal{H}$, defined as Eq. (1).

Remark 4.11. The attacking algorithm E′ is purely classical. It does not need to actually prepare quantum states and apply quantum operation to them. Instead, at each round, the entire protocol, including the sampling of the oracle, can be represented as a pure quantum state. The classical algorithm E′ only needs to query the real oracle h classically and simulate how that pure state evolves conditioned on the classical information (t, L) that E′ has so far, and all of that is done in Eve's head.

Lemma 4.12 (Efficiency). *Let L be the final list of Eve's algorithm in Construction 4.10. Then $\mathbb{E}[|L|] \leq d/\varepsilon$, where the probability is over the measurement outcomes.*

Proof. By asking queries, Eve gradually gathers a set of query-answer pairs. It naturally introduces a tree where each node corresponds to an intermediate state of L during the procedure. At each node, Eve deterministically chooses the next query q based on t and L and each of its children corresponds to different possible $h(q)$ answered by the oracle. Similar to the proof of Lemma 3.7, in the purified view we denote the state conditioned on t and L by $|\Psi_{t,L}\rangle$. Formally, each node v of the tree consists of the following:

- A label (t, L).
- A quantum state $|\Psi_v\rangle_{W_A'W_B'H'} := |\Psi_{t,L}\rangle_{W_A'W_B'H'}$.
- A non-negative real number *total weight* $\mathbf{W}(v)$ defined as

$$\mathbf{W}(v) := \sum_{x \in \mathcal{X} \backslash Q_{L'}} \|\Pi_x|\Psi_{t,L'}\rangle\|_2^2.$$

- A Boolean feature $stop(v) \in \{0, 1\}$. If there is no quantum ε-heavy query, then $stop(v) = 1$. In particular, $\mathbf{W}(v) < \varepsilon$ implies $stop(v) = 1$.

The random walk on this tree can start from any node. Whenever $stop(v) = 0$, it moves to of one of its children u according the distribution of measuring the register H_q of $|\Psi_v\rangle$ in the computational basis, where q is Eve's next query at v. Actually, this distribution, denoted by $\Gamma(v)$, is equivalent to the distribution of Eve's query-answer from h conditioned on t and L. By $u \leftarrow \Gamma(v)$ we denote the step from v to its child u. Observes that the depth of the tree is finite since $|L|$ is at most $|\mathcal{X}|$.

For any v and its children u, we have the following property

$$\mathbb{E}_{u \leftarrow \Gamma(v)}[\mathbf{W}(u)] = \sum_{x \in \mathcal{X} \backslash Q_{L'}} \sum_{y \in \mathcal{Y}} \|\Pi_x|y\rangle\langle y|_{H_q'}|\Psi_v\rangle\|_2^2$$

$$= \sum_{x \in \mathcal{X} \backslash Q_{L'}} \sum_{y \in \mathcal{Y}} \||y\rangle\langle y|_{H_q'}\Pi_x|\Psi_v\rangle\|_2^2 = \sum_{x \in \mathcal{X} \backslash Q_{L'}} \|\Pi_x|\Psi_v\rangle\|_2^2 \tag{3}$$

$$= \sum_{x \in \mathcal{X} \backslash Q_L} \|\Pi_x|\Psi_v\rangle\|_2^2 - \|\Pi_q|\Psi_v\rangle\|_2^2 \leq \mathbf{W}(v) - \varepsilon,$$

where q is Eve's next query at v, L is the partial oracle of v, and $Q_{L'} := Q_L \cup \{q\}$. The second equality holds since $|y\rangle\langle y|_{H_q'}$ commutes with Π_x for all $x \in \mathcal{X} \backslash Q_{L'}$, and the inequality is due to the heaviness of q.

We claim the following inequality holds for every v

$$\mathbb{E}[|S(v)|] \leq \frac{\mathbf{W}(v)}{\varepsilon}, \tag{4}$$

where by $S(v)$ we denote the total number of steps that the random walk takes when starting form v. We prove it by induction on the depth of the starting node. By D we denote the depth of the tree. For v in depth D we shall have $stop(v) = 1$, in which case $|S(v)| = 0 \leq \mathbf{W}(v)/\varepsilon$, and so the claim follows. Now suppose the inequality holds for depth i nodes and we move to v in depth $i - 1$. If $stop(v) = 0$, again we have $|S(v)| = 0 \leq \mathbf{W}(v)/\varepsilon$ which is what we need. Otherwise, by induction and the linearity of expectation,

$$
\begin{aligned}
\mathbb{E}[|S(v)|] &= 1 + \mathop{\mathbb{E}}_{u \leftarrow \Gamma(v)} [\mathbb{E}[|S(u)|]] \\
&\leq 1 + \mathop{\mathbb{E}}_{u \leftarrow \Gamma(v)} [\mathbf{W}(u)/\varepsilon] \\
&= 1 + \frac{\mathbb{E}_{u \leftarrow \Gamma(v)}[\mathbf{W}(u)]}{\varepsilon} \\
&\leq 1 + \frac{\mathbf{W}(v) - \varepsilon}{\varepsilon} = \frac{\mathbf{W}(v)}{\varepsilon},
\end{aligned}
$$

where the first inequality is due to induction hypothesis and the second inequality follows by Eq. 3. By Lemma 2.4, the total weight of the root R (where the state is $|\Psi_t\rangle$ in the purified view) is at most d since

$$
\mathbf{W}(R) = \sum_{x \in \mathcal{X}} \left\| \sum_{\hat{h} \in \hat{\mathcal{H}}} \alpha_{\hat{h}} |\psi_{\hat{h}}\rangle_{W_A' W_B'} \Pi_x |\hat{h}\rangle_{H'} \right\|_2^2 = \sum_{\hat{h} \in \hat{\mathcal{H}}} |\hat{h}| \cdot |\alpha_{\hat{h}}|^2 \leq d \cdot \sum_{\hat{h} \in \hat{\mathcal{H}}} |\alpha_{\hat{h}}|^2 = d,
$$

where we represent the attached state as $|\Psi_t\rangle_{W_A' W_B' H'} = \sum_{\hat{h}} \alpha_{\hat{h}} |\psi_{\hat{h}}\rangle_{W_A' W_B'} |\hat{h}\rangle_{H'}$. Therefore, starting from the root we have $\mathbb{E}[|L|] \leq d/\varepsilon$ by Eq. 4. $\qquad \square$

Lemma 4.13 (Success). *Suppose that Alice and Bob ask a total of d quantum queries. If any two $(|\mathcal{Y}|, \delta = \varepsilon/\lambda, d, N)$-states are compatible, then there is an eavesdropper E who finds the key k with probability at least $1 - \lambda$.*

Proof. Consider the purified version of the protocol. Let $|\Psi_t\rangle_{WH}$ be the joint state after the protocol finishes, conditioned on the transcript t. By Lemma 2.4 it holds that $|\hat{h}_{\max}^H(|\Psi_t\rangle)| \leq d$. After E' learns the heavy queries, the resulting state becomes $|\Psi_{t,L}\rangle$ conditioned on L. Similarly, by Lemma 2.7 it holds that $|\hat{h}_{\max}^{H'}(|\Psi_{t,L}\rangle)| \leq d$. Since the oracle registers corresponding to Q_L are now measured, we can consider the "truncated" version of $|\Psi_{t,L}\rangle_{WH}$ by discarding those registers. Let $H' = \{H_x\}_{x \in \mathcal{X} \setminus Q_L}$ be the set of remaining registers. By $|\Psi_{t,L}\rangle_{WH'}$ we denote the truncated $|\Psi_{t,L}\rangle_{WH}$.

Now, set the register H in Definition 4.1 to be H'. The state $|\Psi_{t,L}\rangle$ is d-sparse and ε-light by definition, so $|\Psi_{t,L}\rangle$ is a $(|\mathcal{Y}|, \varepsilon, d)$-state. Recall that at the end of the attack, E' learns all the heavy queries, calculates the key distribution of $|\Psi_{t,L}\rangle$ among the remaining oracles and outputs the key with the highest probability to be outputted. We are going to show that there exist a key $k = b \in \{0, 1\}$ such that the probability of the key b in the key distribution of $|\Psi_{t,L}\rangle$, denoted by $\Pr[k = b \text{ in } |\Psi_{t,L}\rangle]$, is larger than $1 - \lambda$. We will prove this by contradiction. Namely, in the following, suppose $\Pr[k = b \text{ in } |\Psi_{t,L}\rangle] \geq \lambda$ for both $b = 0$ and $b = 1$.

Let $|\Psi_{t,L,k=b}\rangle$ be the residual state of $|\Psi_{t,L}\rangle$ conditioned on $k = b$. Observe that $|\Psi_{t,L,k=b}\rangle$ is a $(C, \varepsilon/\lambda, d)$-state for both $k \in \{0, 1\}$. In addition, $|\Psi_{t,L,k=b}\rangle$ is d-sparse since $|\Psi_{t,L}\rangle$ is d-sparse and conditioning on k is a process acting on A and B's registers and will not affect the sparsity of the oracle. $|\Psi_{t,L,k=b}\rangle$ is ε/λ-light because $|\Psi_{t,L}\rangle$ is ε-light and $\Pr[k = b \text{ in } |\Psi_{t,L}\rangle] \geq \lambda$. By the premise in the lemma statement, $|\Psi_{t,L,k=0}\rangle$ and $|\Psi_{t,L,k=1}\rangle$ are compatible, which means that there exists an oracle h, a state $w_A \in W_A$ which outputs the key $k = 0$, and a state $w_B \in W_B$ outputs the key $k = 1$ such that h is consistent with both w_A and w_B with nonzero probability, that is, there is a nonzero chance that in a real execution of the protocol, A outputs the key 0 and B outputs the key 1, which violates the perfect completeness of the protocol.   □

Proof of Theorem 4.7. We use the Eve of Construction 4.10 with parameter ε. Then, by Lemma 4.12, the expected number of queries of Eve is at most d/ε, and by Lemma 4.13, it finds the key with probability $1 - \lambda$.   □

5 Case of Exponentially Small Influences: Proving Theorem 4.4

Before proving Theorem 4.4, we describe a connection between $(|\mathcal{Y}|, \delta, d, N)$-states and distributions of polynomials with bounded degree and influence, giving an alternative formulation of Conjecture 4.3.

5.1 The Polynomial Formulation

As in the rest of the paper, we let $\mathcal{Y}$ be an Abelian group of order $|\mathcal{Y}|$ and $\hat{\mathcal{Y}}$ be its dual group having $\hat{0}$ as the identity element. Recall that we are working with quantum states over a register H whose basis states are all functions $h : \mathcal{X} \to \mathcal{Y}$ for some $|\mathcal{X}| = N$. To keep the notation clean in this section, we identify $\mathcal{X}$ with $[N]$ and view functions $h : \mathcal{X} \to \mathcal{Y}$ as vectors in $\mathcal{Y}^N$ (i.e., we write h_i rather than $h(x)$ for a typical value).

We recall that any $f : \mathcal{Y}^N \to \mathbb{C}$ can be written in terms of its Fourier transform

$$f(\mathbf{x}) = \sum_{\chi \in \hat{\mathcal{Y}}^N} \hat{f}(\chi) \prod_{i=1}^N \chi_i(\mathbf{x}_i)$$

The *degree* of a character $\chi \in \hat{\mathcal{Y}}^N$ is $\deg(\chi) = |\{i \,|\, \chi_i \neq \hat{0}\}|$, and the degree of f is $\deg(f) = \max\{\deg(\chi) \,|\, \hat{f}(\chi) \neq 0\}$. The *influence* of variable i on f is $\text{Inf}_i(f) = \sum_{\substack{\chi \in \hat{\mathcal{Y}}^N \\ \chi_i \neq \hat{0}}} |\hat{f}(\chi)|^2$. We denote by $\max \text{Inf}(f) = \max_{i=1...N} \text{Inf}_i(f)$ the maximum influence of f.

Definition 5.1 (State polynomial). *For a quantum state $|\psi\rangle$ over the register H, the state polynomial of $|\psi\rangle$ is the function $f_\psi : \mathcal{Y}^N \to \mathbb{C}$ defined by*

$$f_\psi(h) = |\mathcal{Y}|^{N/2} \cdot \langle \psi | h \rangle = \sum_{\chi \in \hat{\mathcal{Y}}^N} \langle \psi | \chi \rangle \prod_{i=1}^N \chi_i(h_i). \tag{5}$$

Lemma 5.2 (Sparsity vs. degree, heaviness vs. influence). *For a quantum state $|\psi\rangle$ over register H, f_ψ has the following properties.*

1. f_ψ has ℓ_2-norm equal to 1, i.e., $\mathbb{E}_{\mathbf{x} \leftarrow \mathcal{Y}^N} |f_\psi(\mathbf{x})|^2 = 1$.
2. $|\psi\rangle$ is d-sparse if and only if $\deg(f_\psi) \leq d$.
3. $|\psi\rangle$ has no δ-heavy queries if and only if $\max \mathrm{Inf}(f_\psi) \leq \delta$.

Proof. For Item 1, we have by definition $\mathbb{E}_{\mathbf{x} \leftarrow \mathcal{H}}[|f_\psi(\mathbf{x})|^2 = \sum_h |\langle \psi | h \rangle|^2 = 1$ (since the set of h form a basis for the space). For Item 2, recall from Definition 4.1 that $|\psi\rangle$ is d-sparse if and only if $|\hat{h}_{\max}^H(|\psi\rangle)| \leq d$, i.e., if for $\chi \in \hat{\mathcal{Y}}$, we have $\langle \psi | \chi \rangle \neq 0$ only if $d \geq |\{i \,|\, \chi_i \neq \hat{0}\}| = \deg(\chi)$. Equivalently, the non-zero terms in the right hand side of (5) are those where $\deg(\chi) \leq d$, i.e., $\deg(f_\psi) \leq d$. Finally, for Item 3, recall from Definition 4.9 that $|\psi\rangle$ has no δ-heavy queries if and only if $\| \Pi_i |\psi\rangle \|_2^2 \leq \delta$ for all $i \in [N]$, where $\Pi_i = \sum_{\chi_i \in \hat{Y} \backslash \hat{0}} |\chi_i\rangle \langle \chi_i|_{H_i}$. Expanding, we see that

$$\| \Pi_i |\psi\rangle \|_2^2 = \sum_{\substack{\chi \in \hat{Y}^N \\ \chi_i \neq \hat{0}}} |\langle \psi | \chi \rangle|^2 = \mathrm{Inf}_i(f_\psi).$$

$\square$

Definition 5.3 (State polynomial distribution). *For a quantum state $|\psi\rangle$ over registers W, H, the state polynomial distribution of $|\psi\rangle$ is the distribution F_ψ over polynomials $f : \mathcal{Y} \rightarrow \mathbb{C}$ which is sampled by measuring W in some fixed basis and taking the resulting state polynomial for H.*

Observation 5.4. *Two quantum states $|\psi\rangle$ and $|\phi\rangle$ over registers W, H are compatible if and only if there exist $f \in \mathrm{supp}(F_\psi)$, $g \in \mathrm{supp}(F_\phi)$ and an $\mathbf{x} \in \mathcal{Y}^N$ such that $f(\mathbf{x}) \cdot g(\mathbf{x}) \neq 0$.*

The observations above motivate us to formulate our main conjecture in terms of polynomials. Notice that, in the following formulation, we focus on the distributions of functions whose range is $\mathbb{R}$ instead of $\mathbb{C}$. Later on, in Theorem 5.6, we will show that it suffices to consider real functions.

Conjecture 5.5. *There exists a finite Abelian group $\mathcal{Y}$ and a function $\delta(d) = 1/\mathrm{poly}(\cdot)$ such that the following holds for all d. Let F and G be two distributions of functions from $\mathcal{Y}^N$ to $\mathbb{R}$ such that the following holds for all $f \in \mathrm{supp}(F)$ and $g \in \mathrm{supp}(G)$.*

- **Unit ℓ_2 norm:** *f and g have ℓ_2-norm 1.*
- *d-degrees: $\deg(f) \leq d$ and $\deg(g) \leq d$.*
- *δ-influences on average: For all $i \in [N]$, we have $\mathbb{E}_{f \leftarrow F}[\mathrm{Inf}_i(f)] \leq \delta$ and $\mathbb{E}_{g \leftarrow G}[\mathrm{Inf}_i(g)] \leq \delta$, where $\delta = \delta(d)$.*

Then, there is an $f \in \mathrm{supp}(F)$, $g \in \mathrm{supp}(G)$, and $\mathbf{x} \in \mathcal{Y}^N$ such that $f(\mathbf{x}) \cdot g(\mathbf{x}) \neq 0$.

Theorem 5.6. *Conjecture 5.5 is true if and only if Conjecture 4.3 is true.*

The proof is given in Appendix A of the full version [ACC+22].

5.2 Proving Theorem 4.4

In this subsection, we prove Theorem 4.4, using the polynomial formulation explained in the previous subsection. In other words, we prove a weaker version of Conjecture 5.5 where we set $\delta < |\mathcal{Y}|^{-d}/d$. Interestingly, the theorem holds without any influence condition on F, and without any degree restriction on G. I.e., we only use that there is an $f \in \text{supp}(F)$ of degree $\leq d$, and that $\mathbb{E}_{g \leftarrow G}[\text{Inf}_i(g)] \leq \delta$ for all $i \in [N]$.

For any $f \in \text{supp}(F)$, let $f(\mathbf{x}) = \sum_{\chi \in \hat{\mathcal{Y}}^x} \hat{f}(\chi)\chi(\mathbf{x})$ and $\chi^* \in \hat{\mathcal{Y}}^N$ be a character for which $\hat{f}(\chi) \neq 0$ and $\deg(\chi) = \deg(f)$. Since $\deg(f) \leq d$ we can without loss of generality assume that $\chi_i^* = \hat{0}$ for $i = d+1, \ldots, N$ by reordering the coordinates.

Note that for any partial assignment $\mathbf{x}_{>d} = (x_{d+1}, \ldots, x_N)$, the restricted function $f|_{\mathbf{x}_{>d}}$ is non-constant and in particular there exists a $\mathbf{x}_{\leq d}$ such that $f(\mathbf{x}_{\leq d}, \mathbf{x}_{>d}) \neq 0$.

For any function $g : \mathcal{Y}^N \to \mathbb{C}$, decompose it as

$$g(\mathbf{x}) = \sum_{\chi \in \hat{\mathcal{Y}}^d} g_\chi(\mathbf{x}_{>d})\chi(\mathbf{x}_{\leq d})$$

for $|\mathcal{Y}|^d$ functions $\{g_\chi\}_{\chi \in \hat{\mathcal{Y}}^d}$ on $\mathbf{x}_{>d}$. Writing $\hat{\mathbf{0}} = (\hat{0}, \ldots, \hat{0}) \in \mathcal{Y}^d$ we then have

$$\sum_{\chi \neq \hat{\mathbf{0}}} \mathbb{E}_{\mathbf{x}_{>d}}\left[|g_\chi(\mathbf{x}_{>d})|^2\right] \leq \sum_{i=1}^{d} \sum_{\chi_i \neq \hat{0}} \mathbb{E}_{\mathbf{x}_{>d}}\left[|g_\chi(\mathbf{x}_{>d})|^2\right] = \sum_{i=1}^{d} \text{Inf}_i(g)$$

and $\mathbb{E}_{\mathbf{x}_{>d}}\left[|g_{\hat{\mathbf{0}}}(\mathbf{x}_{>d})|^2\right] \geq \|g\|_2^2 - \sum_{i=1}^{d} \text{Inf}_i(g)$. Thus, we have

$$\mathbb{E}_{\mathbf{x}_{>d}}\left[|g_{\hat{\mathbf{0}}}(\mathbf{x}_{>d})|^2 - (|\mathcal{Y}|^d - 1)\sum_{\chi \neq \hat{\mathbf{0}}}|g_\chi(\mathbf{x}_{>d})|^2\right] \geq \|g\|_2^2 - |\mathcal{Y}|^d \sum_{i=1}^{d} \text{Inf}_i(g)$$

Taking the expectation over $g \leftarrow G$ and using the condition $\mathbb{E}_{g \leftarrow G}[\text{Inf}_i(g)] \leq \delta < |\mathcal{Y}|^{-d}/d$ on the influences of G we thus conclude

$$\mathbb{E}_{g \leftarrow G} \mathbb{E}_{\mathbf{x}_{>d}}\left[|g_{\hat{\mathbf{0}}}(\mathbf{x}_{>d})|^2 - (|\mathcal{Y}|^d - 1)\sum_{\chi \neq \hat{\mathbf{0}}}|g_\chi(\mathbf{x}_{>d})|^2\right] > 0.$$

In particular there exists a $g \in \text{supp}(G)$ such that

$$\mathbb{E}_{\mathbf{x}_{>d}}\left[|g_{\hat{\mathbf{0}}}(\mathbf{x}_{>d})|^2\right] > \mathbb{E}_{\mathbf{x}_{>d}}\left[(|\mathcal{Y}|^d - 1)\sum_{\chi \neq \hat{\mathbf{0}}}|g_\chi(\mathbf{x}_{>d})|^2\right] \geq \mathbb{E}_{\mathbf{x}_{>d}}\left[\left(\sum_{\chi \neq \hat{\mathbf{0}}}|g_\chi(\mathbf{x}_{>d})|\right)^2\right],$$

where the second inequality is Cauchy-Schwarz. It follows that there is $\mathbf{x}_{>d}$ such that

$$|g_{\hat{\mathbf{0}}}(\mathbf{x}_{>d})| > \sum_{\chi \neq \hat{\mathbf{0}}}|g_\chi(\mathbf{x}_{>d})|.$$

As observed above, for this $\mathbf{x}_{>d}$ there must exist some $\mathbf{x}_{\leq d}$ such that $f(\mathbf{x}_{\leq d}, \mathbf{x}_{>d}) \neq 0$. But, that means we obtain the following as desired.

$$|g(\mathbf{x}_{\leq d}, \mathbf{x}_{>d})| = \left| \sum_{\chi \in \hat{\mathcal{Y}}^d} g_\chi(\mathbf{x}_{>d}) \chi(\mathbf{x}_{\leq d}) \right| \geq |g_{\hat{0}}(\mathbf{x}_{>d})| - \sum_{\chi \neq \hat{0}} |g_\chi(\mathbf{x}_{>d})| > 0.$$

References

[AA09]   Aaronson, S., Ambainis, A.: The need for structure in quantum speedups. arXiv preprint arXiv:0911.0996 (2009)

[Aar05] Aaronson, S.: Quantum computing, postselection, and probabilistic polynomial-time. Proc. R. Soc. A Math. Phys. Eng. Sci. **461**(2063), 3473–3482 (2005)

[ABG+21] Agarwal, A., Bartusek, J., Goyal, V., Khurana, D., Malavolta, G.: Post-quantum multi-party computation. In: Canteaut, A., Standaert, F.-X. (eds.) EUROCRYPT 2021. LNCS, vol. 12696, pp. 435–464. Springer, Cham (2021). https://doi.org/10.1007/978-3-030-77870-5_16

[ACC+22] Austrin, P., Chung, H., Chung, K.-M., Fu, S., Lin, Y.-T., Mahmoody, M.: On the impossibility of key agreements from quantum random oracles. Cryptology ePrint Archive, Paper 2022/218 (2022). https://eprint.iacr.org/2022/218

[ACGH20] Alagic, G., Childs, A.M., Grilo, A.B., Hung, S.-H.: Non-interactive classical verification of quantum computation. In: Pass, R., Pietrzak, K. (eds.) TCC 2020. LNCS, vol. 12552, pp. 153–180. Springer, Cham (2020). https://doi.org/10.1007/978-3-030-64381-2_6

[ACP21] Ananth, P., Chung, K.-M., Placa, R.L.L.: On the concurrent composition of quantum zero-knowledge. In: Malkin, T., Peikert, C. (eds.) CRYPTO 2021. LNCS, vol. 12825, pp. 346–374. Springer, Cham (2021). https://doi.org/10.1007/978-3-030-84242-0_13

[Bar17] Barak, B.: The complexity of public-key cryptography. In: Tutorials on the Foundations of Cryptography. ISC, pp. 45–77. Springer, Cham (2017). https://doi.org/10.1007/978-3-319-57048-8_2

[Bar21] Bartusek, J.: Secure quantum computation with classical communication. Cryptology ePrint Archive, Report 2021/964 (2021). https://ia.cr/2021/964

[BB84]   Bennett, C.H., Brassard, G.: Quantum cryptography: public key distribution and coin tossing. In: Proceedings of IEEE International Conference on Computers, Systems, and Signal Processing, pp. 175–179 (1984)

[BGI08] Biham, E., Goren, Y.J., Ishai, Y.: Basing weak public-key cryptography on strong one-way functions. In: Canetti, R. (ed.) TCC 2008. LNCS, vol. 4948, pp. 55–72. Springer, Heidelberg (2008). https://doi.org/10.1007/978-3-540-78524-8_4

[BGP00] Bellare, M., Goldreich, O., Petrank, E.: Uniform generation of NP-witnesses using an NP-oracle. Inf. Comput. **163**(2), 510–526 (2000)

[BHK+15] Brassard, G., Hoyer, P., Kalach, K., Kaplan, M., Laplante, S., Salvail, L.: Key establishment à la merkle in a quantum world (2015)

[BKS21] Bitansky, N., Kellner, M., Shmueli, O.: Post-quantum resettably-sound zero knowledge. In: Nissim, K., Waters, B. (eds.) TCC 2021. LNCS, vol. 13042, pp. 62–89. Springer, Cham (2021). https://doi.org/10.1007/978-3-030-90459-3_3

[BKSY11] Brakerski, Z., Katz, J., Segev, G., Yerukhimovich, A.: Limits on the power of zero-knowledge proofs in cryptographic constructions. In: Ishai, Y. (ed.) TCC 2011. LNCS, vol. 6597, pp. 559–578. Springer, Heidelberg (2011). https://doi.org/10.1007/978-3-642-19571-6_34

[BKVV20] Brakerski, Z., Koppula, V., Vazirani, U., Vidick, T.: Simpler proofs of quantumness. arXiv preprint arXiv:2005.04826 (2020)

[BM17] Barak, B., Mahmoody, M.: Merkle's key agreement protocol is optimal: an $O(n^2)$ attack on any key agreement from random oracles. J. Cryptol. **30**(3), 699–734 (2017)

[BMG09a] Barak, B., Mahmoody-Ghidary, M.: Merkle puzzles are optimal — an $O(n^2)$-query attack on any key exchange from a random oracle. In: Halevi, S. (ed.) CRYPTO 2009. LNCS, vol. 5677, pp. 374–390. Springer, Heidelberg (2009). https://doi.org/10.1007/978-3-642-03356-8_22

[BS08] Brassard, G., Salvail, L.: Quantum Merkle puzzles. In: International Conference on Quantum, Nano and Micro Technologies (ICQNM), pp. 76–79. IEEE Computer Society (2008)

[BS20] Bitansky, N., Shmueli, O.: Post-quantum zero knowledge in constant rounds. In: Proceedings of the 52nd Annual ACM SIGACT Symposium on Theory of Computing, pp. 269–279 (2020)

[CCY20] Chia, N.-H., Chung, K.-M., Yamakawa, T.: Classical verification of quantum computations with efficient verifier. In: Pass, R., Pietrzak, K. (eds.) TCC 2020. LNCS, vol. 12552, pp. 181–206. Springer, Cham (2020). https://doi.org/10.1007/978-3-030-64381-2_7

[CFHL21] Chung, K.-M., Fehr, S., Huang, Y.-H., Liao, T.-N.: On the compressed-oracle technique, and post-quantum security of proofs of sequential work. In: Canteaut, A., Standaert, F.-X. (eds.) EUROCRYPT 2021. LNCS, vol. 12697, pp. 598–629. Springer, Cham (2021). https://doi.org/10.1007/978-3-030-77886-6_21

[CX21] Cao, S., Xue, R.: Being a permutation is also orthogonal to one-wayness in quantum world: impossibilities of quantum one-way permutations from one-wayness primitives. Theor. Comput. Sci. **855**, 16–42 (2021)

[DFKO06] Dinur, I., Friedgut, E., Kindler, G., O'Donnell, R.: On the Fourier tails of bounded functions over the discrete cube. In: Proceedings of the Thirty-Eighth Annual ACM Symposium on Theory of Computing, pp. 437–446 (2006)

[DH76] Diffie, W., Hellman, M.E.: New directions in cryptography. IEEE Trans. Inf. Theory **22**(6), 644–654 (1976)

[GKM+00] Gertner, Y., Kannan, S., Malkin, T., Reingold, O., Viswanathan, M.: The relationship between public key encryption and oblivious transfer. In: Proceedings 41st Annual Symposium on Foundations of Computer Science, pp. 325–335. IEEE (2000)

[Gro96] Grover, L.K.: A fast quantum mechanical algorithm for database search. In: Proceedings of the Twenty-Eighth Annual ACM Symposium on Theory of Computing, pp. 212–219 (1996)

[HHRS07] Haitner, I., Hoch, J.J., Reingold, O., Segev, G.: Finding collisions in interactive protocols - a tight lower bound on the round complexity of statistically-hiding commitments. In: Proceedings of the 48th Annual IEEE Symposium on Foundations of Computer Science (FOCS 2007), Providence, RI, USA, 20–23 October 2007, pp. 669–679 (2007)

[HMO+21] Haitner, I., Mazor, N., Oshman, R., Reingold, O., Yehudayoff, A.: On the communication complexity of key-agreement protocols. arXiv preprint arXiv:2105.01958 (2021)

[HMST21] Haitner, I., Mazor, N., Silbak, J., Tsfadia, E.: On the complexity of two-party differential privacy (2021)

[Hol05] Holenstein, T.: Key agreement from weak bit agreement. In: Proceedings of the Thirty-Seventh Annual ACM Symposium on Theory of Computing, pp. 664–673 (2005)

[HOZ16] Haitner, I., Omri, E., Zarosim, H.: Limits on the usefulness of random oracles. J. Cryptol. **29**(2), 283–335 (2016)

[HY18] Hosoyamada, A., Yamakawa, T.: Finding collisions in a quantum world: quantum black-box separation of collision-resistance and one-wayness. Cryptology ePrint Archive, Report 2018/1066 (2018). http://ia.cr/2018/1066

[HY20] Hosoyamada, A., Yamakawa, T.: Finding collisions in a quantum world: quantum black-box separation of collision-resistance and one-wayness. In: Moriai, S., Wang, H. (eds.) ASIACRYPT 2020. LNCS, vol. 12491, pp. 3–32. Springer, Cham (2020). https://doi.org/10.1007/978-3-030-64837-4_1

[IR89] Impagliazzo, R., Rudich, S.: Limits on the provable consequences of one-way permutations. In: Proceedings of the 21st Annual ACM Symposium on Theory of Computing (STOC), pp. 44–61. ACM Press (1989)

[KSS00] Kahn, J., Saks, M., Smyth, C.: A dual version of Reimer's inequality and a proof of Rudich's conjecture. In: Proceedings 15th Annual IEEE Conference on Computational Complexity, pp. 98–103. IEEE (2000)

[Mah18] Mahadev, U.: Classical verification of quantum computations. In: 2018 IEEE 59th Annual Symposium on Foundations of Computer Science (FOCS), pp. 259–267. IEEE (2018)

[Mer74] Merkle, R.: C.s. 244 project proposal (1974). Facsimile http://www.merkle.com/1974

[MMP14] Mahmoody, M., Maji, H.K., Prabhakaran, M.: Limits of random oracles in secure computation. In: Proceedings of the 5th Conference on Innovations in Theoretical Computer Science, pp. 23–34 (2014)

[OSSS05] O'Donnell, R., Saks, M., Schramm, O., Servedio, R.A.: Every decision tree has an influential variable. In: 46th Annual IEEE Symposium on Foundations of Computer Science (FOCS 2005), pp. 31–39. IEEE (2005)

[RSA78] Rivest, R.L., Shamir, A., Adleman, L.M.: A method for obtaining digital signatures and public-key cryptosystems. Commun. ACM 21(2), 120–126 (1978)

[RTV04] Reingold, O., Trevisan, L., Vadhan, S.: Notions of reducibility between cryptographic primitives. In: Naor, M. (ed.) TCC 2004. LNCS, vol. 2951, pp. 1–20. Springer, Heidelberg (2004). https://doi.org/10.1007/978-3-540-24638-1_1

[Rud88] Rudich, S.: Limits on the provable consequences of one-way functions. Ph.D. thesis, University of California (1988)

[Zha19] Zhandry, M.: How to record quantum queries, and applications to quantum indifferentiability. In: Boldyreva, A., Micciancio, D. (eds.) CRYPTO 2019. LNCS, vol. 11693, pp. 239–268. Springer, Cham (2019). https://doi.org/10.1007/978-3-030-26951-7_9

[Zha21] Zhang, J.: Succinct blind quantum computation using a random oracle. In: STOC 2021: 53rd Annual ACM SIGACT Symposium on Theory of Computing, Virtual Event, Italy, 21–25 June 2021, pp. 1370–1383 (2021)

Succinct Classical Verification of Quantum Computation

James Bartusek[1], Yael Tauman Kalai[2], Alex Lombardi[3(✉)], Fermi Ma[1,4],
Giulio Malavolta[5], Vinod Vaikuntanathan[3], Thomas Vidick[6], and Lisa Yang[3]

[1] UC Berkeley, Berkeley, USA
bartusek.james@gmail.com
[2] Microsoft Research and MIT, Cambridge, USA
yael@microsoft.com
[3] MIT, Cambridge, USA
{alexjl,vinodv,lisayang}@mit.edu
[4] Simons Institute, Berkeley, USA
fermima@alum.mit.edu
[5] MPI-SP, Bochum, Germany
giulio.malavolta@hotmail.it
[6] Caltech, Pasadena, USA
vidick@caltech.edu

Abstract. We construct a classically verifiable *succinct* interactive argument for quantum computation (BQP) with communication complexity and verifier runtime that are poly-logarithmic in the runtime of the BQP computation (and polynomial in the security parameter). Our protocol is secure assuming the post-quantum security of indistinguishability obfuscation (iO) and Learning with Errors (LWE). This is the first succinct argument for quantum computation *in the plain model*; prior work (Chia-Chung-Yamakawa, TCC '20) requires both a long common reference string and non-black-box use of a hash function modeled as a random oracle.

At a technical level, we revisit the framework for constructing classically verifiable quantum computation (Mahadev, FOCS '18). We give a self-contained, modular proof of security for Mahadev's protocol, which we believe is of independent interest. Our proof readily generalizes to a setting in which the verifier's first message (which consists of many public keys) is *compressed*. Next, we formalize this notion of compressed public keys; we view the object as a generalization of constrained/programmable PRFs and instantiate it based on indistinguishability obfuscation. Finally, we compile the above protocol into a fully succinct argument using a (sufficiently composable) succinct argument of knowledge for NP. Using our framework, we achieve several additional results, including

- Succinct arguments for QMA (given multiple copies of the witness),
- Succinct *non-interactive* arguments for BQP (or QMA) in the quantum random oracle model, and
- Succinct batch arguments for BQP (or QMA) assuming post-quantum LWE (without iO).

© International Association for Cryptologic Research 2022
Y. Dodis and T. Shrimpton (Eds.): CRYPTO 2022, LNCS 13508, pp. 195–211, 2022.
https://doi.org/10.1007/978-3-031-15979-4_7

1   Introduction

Efficient verification of computation is one of the most fundamental and intriguing concepts in computer science, and lies at the heart of the P vs. NP question. It has been studied in the classical setting for over three decades, giving rise to beautiful notions such as interactive proofs [GMR85], multi-prover interactive proofs [BGKW88], probabilistically checkable proofs [BFL90, ALM+92, AS92], and culminating with the notion of a *succinct* (interactive and non-interactive) *argument* [Kil92, Mic94]. Roughly speaking, a succinct argument for a T-time computation enables a prover running in $\mathsf{poly}(T)$ time to convince a $\mathsf{polylog}(T)$-time verifier of the correctness of the computation using only $\mathsf{polylog}(T)$ bits of communication, with soundness against all polynomial-time cheating provers.

In a breakthrough result in 2018, Mahadev [Mah18] presented an interactive argument system that enables a classical verifier to check the correctness of an arbitrary *quantum* computation. Mahadev's protocol represents a different kind of interactive argument—unlike the traditional setting in which the prover simply has more *computational resources* (i.e., running time) than the verifier, the prover in Mahadev's protocol works in a qualitatively more powerful *computational model*. More precisely, for any T-time quantum computation, Mahadev's protocol enables a quantum prover running in time $\mathsf{poly}(T)$ to convince a classical $\mathsf{poly}(T)$-time verifier with $\mathsf{poly}(T)$ bits of classical communication. Soundness holds against all quantum polynomial-time cheating provers under the post-quantum hardness of the learning with errors (LWE) problem.

A fundamental question is whether we can get the best of both worlds: can the prover have *both* a more powerful computational model *and* significantly greater computational resources? Namely, we want an interactive argument system for T-time quantum computation in which the quantum prover runs in $\mathsf{poly}(T)$ time and convinces a $\mathsf{polylog}(T)$-time classical verifier with $\mathsf{polylog}(T)$ bits of classical communication.

We answer this question affirmatively, both for $\mathsf{poly}(T)$-time quantum computations, corresponding to the complexity class **BQP**, and also for the nondeterministic analog **QMA**.

Theorem 1.1 (Succinct Arguments for BQP). *Let λ be a security parameter. Assuming the existence of a post-quantum secure indistinguishability obfuscation scheme (iO) and the post-quantum hardness of the learning with errors problem (LWE), there is an interactive argument system for any T-time quantum computation on input x,[1] where*

- *the prover is quantum and runs in time $\mathsf{poly}(T, \lambda)$,*
- *the verifier is classical and runs in time $\mathsf{poly}(\log T, \lambda) + \tilde{O}(|x|)$,[2] and*
- *the protocol uses $\mathsf{poly}(\log T, \lambda)$ bits of classical communication.*

---

[1] A T-time quantum computation is a *language L* decidable by a bounded-error T-time quantum Turing machine [BV97]. We leave it to future work to address more complex tasks such as *sampling* problems (as in [CLLW20]).

[2] As in the classical setting, some dependence on $|x|$ is necessary at least to read the input; as in [Kil92], we achieve a fairly minimal $|x|$-dependence.

Theorem 1.2 (Succinct Arguments for QMA). *Assuming the existence of a post-quantum secure indistinguishability obfuscation scheme* (iO) *and the post-quantum hardness of the learning with errors problem* (LWE), *there is an interactive argument system for any T-time quantum computation on input x and a* poly(T)*-qubit witness, where*

- *the prover is quantum and runs in time* poly(T, λ), *using polynomially many copies of the witness,*[3]
- *the verifier is classical and runs in time* poly$(\log T, \lambda) + \tilde{O}(x)$, *and*
- *the protocol uses* poly$(\log T, \lambda)$ *bits of classical communication.*

A New Proof of Security for the [Mah18] *Protocol.* One might hope to prove Theorems 1.1 and 1.2 by treating the Mahadev result as a "black box" and showing that *any* (classical) interactive argument for quantum computations can be compressed into a succinct protocol via a suitable cryptographic compiler. This is especially appealing given the extremely technical nature of Mahadev's security proof. Unfortunately, for reasons that will become clear in the technical overview, this kind of generic compilation seems unlikely to be achievable in our setting. Even worse, there does not appear to be any easily formalized property of the Mahadev protocol that would enable such a compilation.

Instead, our solution consists of two steps.

(1) We build a modified variant of the [Mah18] protocol and give an entirely self-contained proof of security. This modified protocol satisfies a few technical conditions that the original [Mah18] does not; most prominently, the *first verifier message* of our modified protocol is already succinct.

(2) We give a generic compiler that converts the protocol from Step (1) into a succinct argument system.

Our Step (1) also results in a self-contained proof of security of the original [Mah18] protocol that is more modular and amenable to further modification and generalization, which we believe will be useful for future work. Our analysis builds upon [Mah18] itself as well as an alternative approach described in Vidick's (unpublished) lecture notes [Vid20]. A concrete consequence of our new proof is that one of the two "hardcore bit" security requirements of the main building block primitive ("extended noisy trapdoor claw-free functions") in [Mah18] is not necessary.

Additional Results. Beyond our main result of succinct arguments for **BQP** and **QMA**, we explore a number of extensions and obtain various new protocols with additional properties.

---

[3] We inherit the need for polynomially-many copies of the witness from prior works. This is a feature common to all previous classical verification protocols, and even to the quantum verification protocol of [FHM18].

- *Non-Interactive*: Although our protocols are not public-coin, we show how to modify them in order to apply the Fiat-Shamir transformation and round-collapse our protocols. As a result, we obtain designated-verifier non-interactive arguments for **BQP** (and the non-deterministic analog **QMA**) with security in the quantum random oracle model (QROM).
- *Zero-Knowledge*: We show how to lift both variants of our protocol (interactive and non-interactive) to achieve zero-knowledge. We show a generic transformation based on classical two-party computation for reactive functionalities that makes our protocols simulatable. This transformation does not add any new computational assumption to the starting protocol.
- *Batch Arguments from LWE*: For the case of batch arguments, i.e., where the parties engage in the parallel verification of n statements, we show a succinct protocol that only assumes the post-quantum hardness of LWE (without iO). In this context, succinctness requires that the verifier's complexity scales with the size of a *single instance*, but is independent of n.

Prior Work. As discussed above, Mahadev [Mah18] constructs a *non-succinct* argument system for **BQP**/**QMA** under LWE. The only prior work addressing *succinct* classical arguments for quantum computation is the recent work of Chia, Chung and Yamakawa [CCY20]. [CCY20] constructs a classically verifiable argument system for quantum computation in the following setting:

- The prover and verifier share a $\mathsf{poly}(T)$-bits long, structured reference string (which requires a trusted setup to instantiate) along with a hash function h (e.g. SHA-3).
- The "online communication" of the protocol is succinct ($\mathsf{poly}(\log T)$).
- Security is heuristic: it can be proved when h is modeled as a random oracle, but the *protocol description itself* explicitly requires the code of h (i.e. uses h in a non-black-box way).

We specifically note that when viewed in the *plain model* (i.e., without setup), the verifier must send the structured reference string to the prover, resulting in a protocol that is *not succinct*. We note that [CCY20] was specifically optimizing for a *two-message* protocol, but their approach seems incapable of achieving succinctness in the plain model even if further interaction is allowed.

By contrast, our succinct interactive arguments are in the plain model and are secure based on well-formed cryptographic assumptions, and our succinct 2-message arguments are proved secure in the QROM (and do not require a long common reference string).

Finally, we remark that our approach to achieving succinct arguments fundamentally (and likely necessarily) differs from [CCY20] because we manipulate the "inner workings" of the [Mah18] protocol; by contrast [CCY20] makes "black-box" use of a specific soundness property of the [Mah18] protocol (referred to as "computational orthogonality" by [ACGH20]) and is otherwise agnostic to how the protocol is constructed.

2   Technical Overview

Our starting point is Mahadev's protocol for classical verification of quantum computation [Mah18], the core ingredient of which is a *measurement protocol*.

2.1   Recap: Mahadev's Measurement Protocol

We begin by reviewing Mahadev's N-qubit measurement protocol. In Mahadev's protocol, a quantum prover holding an N-qubit quantum state ρ interacts with a classical verifier, who wants to obtain the result of measuring ρ according to measurement bases $h \in \{0,1\}^N$ (h_i specifies a basis choice for the ith qubit, with $h_i = 1$ corresponding to the Hadamard basis and $h_i = 0$ corresponding to the standard basis).

Trapdoor Claw-Free Functions. At the heart of the protocol is a cryptographic primitive known as an *injective/claw-free trapdoor function* (a variant of lossy trapdoor functions [PW08, PVW08, GVW15]), which consists of two trapdoor function families Inj (for injective) and Cf (for claw-free), with the following syntactic requirements:[4]

- Each function in $\mathsf{Cf} \cup \mathsf{Inj}$ is indexed by a public-key pk, where functions $f_{\mathsf{pk}} \in \mathsf{Inj}$ are injective and functions $f_{\mathsf{pk}} \in \mathsf{Cf}$ are two-to-one. Moreover, pk can be sampled along with a secret key sk that enables computing f_{pk}^{-1} (i.e., $f_{\mathsf{pk}}^{-1}(y)$ consists of a single pre-image if $f_{\mathsf{pk}} \in \mathsf{Inj}$, and two pre-images if $f_{\mathsf{pk}} \in \mathsf{Cf}$).
- All functions in Inj and Cf have domain $\{0,1\}^{\ell+1}$ (for some ℓ) and the two pre-images of y under $f_{\mathsf{pk}} \in \mathsf{Cf}$ are of the form $(0, x_0)$ and $(1, x_1)$ for some $x_0, x_1 \in \{0,1\}^\ell$.

An injective/claw-free trapdoor function must satisfy the following security properties:[5]

1. **Claw-Free/Injective Indistinguishability.** A random function in $f_{\mathsf{pk}} \leftarrow \mathsf{Cf}$ is computationally indistinguishable from a random function $f_{\mathsf{pk}} \leftarrow \mathsf{Inj}$.
2. **Adaptive Hardcore Bit.** Given $f_{\mathsf{pk}} \leftarrow \mathsf{Cf}$, it is computationally infeasible to output both (1) a pair (x, y) satisfying $f_{\mathsf{pk}}(x) = y$ and (2) a non-zero string $d \in \{0,1\}^{\ell+1}$ such that $d \cdot (1, x_0 \oplus x_1) = 0$, where $(0, x_0)$ and $(1, x_1)$ are the two preimages of y.[6]

To build some intuition about the usefulness of such function families, notice that they can be used to commit to a single classical bit quite easily. The

---

[4] The actual syntactic requirements are somewhat more complex due to the fact that the functions in question are probabilistic.

[5] In fact, Mahadev's proof relies on two different hardcore bit properties, but we show in this work that only the adaptive hardcore bit property is needed.

[6] The full definition places a slightly stronger restriction on d than simply being non-zero. However, this simplified version will suffice for this overview.

commitment key is a function $f_{\mathsf{pk}} \in \mathsf{Inj}$, and commitment to a bit b is $y = f_{\mathsf{pk}}(b, x)$ for a random $x \in \{0,1\}^n$. It is not hard to verify that this is a statistically binding and computationally hiding commitment of b. On the other hand, if $f_{\mathsf{pk}} \in \mathsf{Cf}$, it is a statistically hiding and computationally binding commitment of b.[7]

Protocol Description. With this intuition in mind, we now describe a (slightly simplified version of) the Mahadev measurement protocol. Mahadev's protocol is a many-fold sequential repetition of the following one-bit challenge protocol.

V $\to$ P : The verifier samples N pairs of functions and their trapdoors: for every $i \in [\ell]$, he samples $(\mathsf{pk}_i, \mathsf{sk}_i) \leftarrow \mathsf{Inj}$ if $h_i = 0$ and $(\mathsf{pk}_i, \mathsf{sk}_i) \leftarrow \mathsf{Cf}$ if $h_i = 1$. He sends the N-tuple of public keys (function descriptions) $\underline{(\mathsf{pk}_1, \ldots, \mathsf{pk}_N)}$ to the prover.

P $\to$ V : The prover holds an N-qubit state ρ on register $\mathcal{B} = \mathcal{B}_1 \otimes \cdots \mathcal{B}_N$. She initializes registers $\mathcal{X} = \mathcal{X}_1 \otimes \cdots \mathcal{X}_N$ so that each $\mathcal{X}_i$ is an ℓ-qubit register in uniform superposition. Then she evaluates each f_{pk_i} on the $\ell+1$ qubit register $\mathcal{B}_i \otimes \mathcal{X}_i$ and measures the output to obtain y_i. Finally, she sends $\underline{(y_1, \ldots, y_N)}$ to the verifier, keeping the registers $\mathcal{B}, \mathcal{X}$ for herself.

V $\to$ P : The verifier picks a random challenge bit $c \leftarrow \{0,1\}$ and sends it to the prover. $c = 0$ indicates a "test round" and $c = 1$ indicates a "measurement round".

P $\to$ V : If $c = 0$ ("test"), the prover measures each $\mathcal{B}_i \otimes \mathcal{X}_i$ in the standard basis, obtaining $(b_i, x_i) \in \{0,1\} \times \{0,1\}^\ell$, and sends $\underline{(b_i, x_i)_{i=1}^N}$ to the verifier. If $c = 1$ ("measure"), she measures each $\mathcal{B}_i \otimes \mathcal{X}_i$ in the Hadamard basis (i.e., she applies the Hadamard gate H on each qubit and then measures in the standard basis), obtaining $d_i \in \{0,1\}^{\ell+1}$, and sends $\underline{(d_i)_{i=1}^N}$ to the verifier.

V (output): If $c = 0$ ("test"), **V** either accepts or rejects the interaction but outputs nothing. In particular, **V** checks that $f_{\mathsf{pk}_i}(b_i, x_i) = y_i$. If any of the checks fail, reject.

If $c = 1$ ("measure"), proceed as follows. Let $R \subseteq [N]$ be the set of indices where $h_i = 1$, corresponding to Hadamard basis measurements, and let $S = [N] \setminus R$ be the set of indices corresponding to standard basis measurements. For each $i \in R$, **V** computes the two inverses $(0, x_{i,0})$ and $(1, x_{i,1})$ of y_i (which are guaranteed to exist since $f_{\mathsf{pk},i} \in \mathsf{Cf}$) using sk_i. **V** sets $u_i := d \cdot (1, x_{i,0} \oplus x_{i,1})$ as the ith measurement outcome. For every $i \in S$, **V** ignores d_i, and sets v_i to be the first bit of $f_{\mathsf{pk},i}^{-1}(y_i)$, computed using the trapdoor sk_i (this is well-defined since $f_{\mathsf{pk},i} \in \mathsf{Inj}$). Finally **V** outputs the N-bit string $(u, v) \in \{0,1\}^R \times \{0,1\}^S$.

Mahadev [Mah18] proves that if a malicious prover **P*** passes the test round with probability 1, then there exists an N-qubit quantum state ρ^*—*independent* of the verifier's measurement basis h—such that the result of measuring ρ^* according to h is computationally indistinguishable from the verifier's N-bit

---

[7] In particular, $f_{\mathsf{pk}} \in \mathsf{Cf}$ satisfies Unruh's definition of *collapse-binding* [Unr16].

output distribution in the measurement round.[8] While her definition requires that such a ρ^* *exists*, Vidick and Zhang [VZ21] showed that Mahadev's proof steps implicitly define an extractor that efficiently produces ρ^* using black-box access to $\mathbf{P}^*$.

2.2   Defining a (Succinct) Measurement Protocol

Our first (straightforward but helpful) step is to give an explicit definition of a *commit-and-measure protocol* that abstracts the completeness and soundness properties of Mahadev's measurement protocol as established in [Mah18, VZ21]. Roughly speaking, a commit-and-measure protocol is sound if, for any malicious prover $\mathbf{P}^*$ that passes the test round with probability 1 and any basis choice h, there exists an efficient extractor that (without knowledge of h) interacts with prover and outputs an extracted state τ such that the following are indistinguishable:

- the distribution of verifier outputs obtained in the measurement round from interacting with $\mathbf{P}^*$ using basis choice h, and
- the distribution of measurement outcomes obtained from measuring τ according to h.

This abstraction will be particularly helpful for reasoning about our eventual *succinct* measurement protocols, which will necessitate modifying Mahadev's original protocol.

Can a Measurement Protocol be Succinct? Given the definition of a measurement protocol, an immediate concern arises with respect to obtaining succinct arguments: the verifier's *input* to the measurement protocol – the basis vector h – is inherently non-succinct. Since the number of qubits N grows with the runtime of the BQP computation when used to obtain quantum verification [FHM18], this poses an immediate problem.

   Our solution to this problem is to only consider basis vectors h that are *succinct*; our formalization is that h must be the truth table of an efficiently computable function $f : [\log N] \to \{0, 1\}$. For any such h, we can represent the verifier's input as a circuit C that computes h, removing the above obstacle.

   However, in order for there to be any hope of this idea working, it must be the case that measurement protocols for bases with succinct representations are still useful for constructing delegation for BQP. Fortunately, it has been shown [ACGH20] that classically verifiable (non-succinct) arguments for BQP can be constructed by invoking Mahadev's measurement protocol (and, by inspection of the proof, any measurement protocol satisfying our definition) on a *uniformly*

---

[8] This can be extended to provers that pass the test round with probability $1 - \varepsilon$ by the gentle measurement lemma. In particular, an efficient distinguisher can only distinguish the verifier's output distribution from the result of measuring some ρ^* with advantage $\mathsf{poly}(\varepsilon)$.

random basis string $h \leftarrow \{0,1\}^N$. Then, by computational indistinguishability, it is also possible to use a *pseudorandom* string h that has a succinct representation, i.e., $h = (\mathsf{PRF}_s(1), ..., \mathsf{PRF}_s(N))$ for some (post-quantum) pseudorandom function PRF.

Thus, we focus for the moment on constructing a succinct measurement protocol for h with succinct representation, and return to the full delegation problem later.

2.3 Constructing a Verifier-Succinct Measurement Protocol

Inspecting the description of the [Mah18] protocol, there are three distinct reasons that the protocol is not succinct:

1. The verifier's first message, which consists of N TCF public keys, is non-succinct.
2. The prover's two messages, consisting of the commitments y_i and openings z_i respectively, are non-succinct.
3. The verifier's decision predicate, as it is a function of these commitments and openings, requires $\mathsf{poly}(N)$ time to evaluate.

The latter two issues turn out to be not too difficult to resolve (although there is an important subtlety that we discuss later); for now, we focus on resolving (1), which is our main technical contribution. Concretely, we want to construct a measurement protocol for succinct bases h where the verifier's first message is succinct.

Idea: Compress the Verifier's Message with iO. Given the problem formulation, a natural idea presents itself: instead of having V send over N i.i.d. public keys pk_i, perhaps V can send a succinct program PK that contains the description of N public keys pk_i that are in some sense "pseudoindependent!" Using the machinery of obfuscation and the "punctured programs" technique [SW14], it is straightforward to write down a candidate program for this task: simply obfuscate the following code.

Here, C is an efficient circuit with truth table h, and $\mathsf{Gen}(1^\lambda, \mathsf{mode})$ indicates sampling either from Inj or Cf depending on whether $h_i = C(i) = 0$ or $h_i = C(i) = 1$.

Letting PK denote an obfuscation of the above program, V could send PK to P and allow the prover to compute each $\mathsf{pk}_i = \mathsf{PK}(i)$ on its own, and the protocol could essentially proceed as before, except that the verifier will have to expand its PRF seed s into $(\mathsf{sk}_1, ..., \mathsf{sk}_N)$ in order to compute its final output.

Input: index $i \leq N$
Hardwired Values: Puncturable PRF seed s. Circuit C.

- Compute mode $= C(i)$ and $r = \mathsf{PRF}_s(i)$.
- Compute $(\mathsf{pk}_i, \mathsf{sk}_i) \leftarrow \mathsf{Gen}(1^\lambda, \mathsf{mode}; r)$.
- Output pk_i.

Problem: Proving Soundness. While it is not hard to describe this plausible modification to the [Mah18] protocol that compresses the verifier's message, it is very unclear how to argue that the modified protocol is sound. The obfuscation literature has no shortage of proof techniques developed over the last 10 years, but since we have made a "non-black-box" modification of the [Mah18] protocol, a deep understanding of the [Mah18] proof of soundness is required in order to understand to what extent these techniques are compatible with the application at hand.

We believe it *should* be possible to incorporate punctured programming techniques into Mahadev's proof of soundness in [Mah18] and conclude the desired soundness property of the new protocol. However, doing so would result in an extremely complex proof that would require the reader to verify the entirety of the [Mah18] (already very complicated) original security proof with our modifications in mind.

2.4 Proof of Soundness

Given the complicated nature of the [Mah18] proof of soundness, we instead give a *simpler* and *more modular* proof of soundness for the [Mah18] measurement protocol. Moreover, we give this proof for a generic variant of the [Mah18] protocol where the prover is given an arbitrary representation PK of N TCF public keys and show that precisely two properties of this representation PK are required in order for the proof to go through:

- An appropriate generalization of the "dual-mode" property of individual TCFs must hold for PK: for any two circuits C_1, C_2, it should be that PK_1 generated from basis C_1 is computationally indistinguishable from PK_2 generated from basis C_2. In fact, a stronger variant of this indistinguishability must hold: it should be the case that $\mathsf{PK}_1 \approx_c \mathsf{PK}_2$ even if the distinguisher is given all secret keys sk_j such that $C_1(j) = C_2(j)$.
- For every i, the adaptive hardcore bit property of f_{pk_i} should hold *even given* sk_j for all $j \neq i$.

Since these two properties are (essentially) all that is required for our proof to go through, in order to obtain a verifier-succinct protocol, it suffices to show that the obfuscated program PK above satisfies these two properties, which follows from standard techniques.

Thus, we proceed by describing our new soundness proof for the [Mah18] measurement protocol, which transparently generalizes to the verifier-succinct setting.

The "Operational Qubits" Approach. Let P^* denote a prover that passes the test round (i.e., makes the verifier accept on the 0 challenge) with probability 1. Our goal is to show that the prover in some sense "has an N-qubit state" such that measuring this state in the h-bases produces the same (or an indistinguishable) distribution as the verifier's protocol output, which we will denote $D_{P^*,\text{Out}}$. This N-qubit state should be efficiently computable from the prover's internal state $|\psi\rangle$; specifically, we use $|\psi\rangle$ to denote the prover's state after its first message y has been sent.

In order to show this, taking inspiration from [Vid20],[9] we will proceed in two steps:

1. Identify N "operational qubits" within $|\psi\rangle$. That is, we will identify a set of $2N$ observables $Z_1, ..., Z_N, X_1, ..., X_N$ (analogous to the "Pauli observables" $\sigma_{z,1}, ..., \sigma_{z,N}, \sigma_{x,1}, ... \sigma_{x,N}$) such that measuring $|\psi\rangle$ with these observables gives the outcome distribution $D_{P^*,\text{Out}}$.

   Provided that these $2N$ observables roughly "behave like" Pauli observables with respect to $|\psi\rangle$ (e.g. satisfy the X/Z uncertainty principle), one could then hope to:
2. Extract a related state $|\psi'\rangle$ such that measuring $|\psi'\rangle$ in the *actual* standard/Hadamard bases matches the "pseudo-Pauli" $\{Z_j\}, \{X_i\}$, measurements of $|\psi\rangle$ (and therefore $D_{P^*,\text{Out}}$).

Relating the Verifier's Output to Measuring $|\psi\rangle$. Our current goal is to achieve Step (1) above. Let $|\psi\rangle$ denote P^*'s post-commitment state and let U denote the unitary such that P^*'s opening is a measurement of $U|\psi\rangle$ in the Hadamard basis.

Now, let us consider the verifier's output distribution. The ith bit of the verifier's output when $h_i = 1$ is defined to be $d \cdot (x_{0,i} \oplus x_{1,i})$ (where d is the opening sent by the prover) of $U|\psi\rangle$ in the Hadamard basis. For each such i, we can define an observable X_i characterizing this measurement, that *roughly* takes the form

$$X_i \approx U^\dagger (H_{\mathcal{Z}_i} \otimes \text{Id}) \left(\sum_d (-1)^{d \cdot (1, x_{0,i} \oplus x_{1,i})} |d\rangle\langle d|_{\mathcal{Z}_i} \otimes \text{Id}_{\mathcal{I}, \{\mathcal{Z}_j\}_{j \neq i}} \right) (H_{\mathcal{Z}_i} \otimes \text{Id})U.$$

---

[9] [Vid20] gives a soundness proof for a variant of the [Mah18] protocol, but in a qualitatively weaker setting. [Vid20] only proves indistinguishability of N-qubit measurements that are either *all* in the standard basis or *all* in the Hadamard basis, and only proves indistinguishability with respect to *linear* tests of the distribution (that is, [Vid20] proves small-bias rather than full indistinguishability). Both of these relaxations are unacceptable in our setting, and achieving the latter specifically requires a different proof strategy.

Here we have slightly simplified the expression for X_i for the sake of presentation; the correct definition of X_i (see the full version) must account for the case where d is rejected by the verifier. To reiterate, the observable X_i is a syntactic interpretation of the verifier's output m_i as a function of $|\psi\rangle$.

On the other hand, when $h_i = 0$, the verifier's output m_i is not *a priori* a measurement of $|\psi\rangle$; indeed, the verifier ignores the prover's second message and just inverts y_i. However, under the assumption that the prover P^* passes the test round with probability $1 - \mathsf{negl}(\lambda)$, making use of the fact that f_{pk_i} is injective, this y_i-inverse must be equal to what the prover *would* have sent in the test round. This defines another observable on $|\psi\rangle$ that we call Z_i:

$$Z_i = \sum_{b,x}(-1)^b |b,x\rangle\langle b,x|_{\mathcal{Z}_i} \otimes \mathsf{Id}_{\mathcal{I},\{\mathcal{Z}_j\}_{j \neq i}}.$$

Finally, note that the operator Z_i syntactically makes sense even when $h_i = 1$. However, X_i cannot even be *defined* when f_{pk_i} is injective, corresponding to $h_i = 0$, since X_i explicitly requires *two* inverses of y_i. Therefore, from now on, we sample all $(\mathsf{pk}_i, \mathsf{sk}_i) \leftarrow \mathsf{Cf}$ (forcing all TCFs to be 2-to-1).

This brings us to the punchline of this step: by invoking a computational assumption (the indistinguishability of Cf and Inj), we can define observables (X_i, Z_i) for all $i \in [N]$ such that for *every* i and *every* basis choice h, the distribution resulting from measuring $|\psi\rangle$ with X_i (resp. Z_i) matches the ith bit of the verifier's output distribution.

With a little more work, one can actually show that the verifier's *entire* output distribution in the h-basis is computationally indistinguishable from the following distribution $D_{P^*,\text{2-to-1}}$:

- Sample keys $(\mathsf{pk}_i, \mathsf{sk}_i) \leftarrow \mathsf{Cf}$. Run P^* to obtain $y, |\psi\rangle$.
- For each i such that $h_i = 0$, measure the first bit of the prover's ith response register in the standard basis to obtain (and output) a bit b_i.
- Measure $U|\psi\rangle$ in the Hadamard basis, obtaining strings $(d_1,...,d_N)$.
- For each i such that $h_i = 1$, compute (and output) $d_i \cdot (1, x_{0,i} \oplus x_{1,i})$.

Aside: Why Are These Z_j and X_i Helpful? As alluded to earlier, this approach is inspired by *operational* definitions of "having an N-qubit state," which consists of a state $|\psi\rangle$ and $2N$ "pseudo-Pauli" observables $Z_1, ..., Z_N, X_1, ...X_N$ that behave "like Pauli observables" on $|\psi\rangle$. For example, it is possible to prove that many of the "Pauli group relations" hold *approximately* on these X_i, Z_j with respect to $|\psi\rangle$, meaning that (for example)

$$\langle\psi| Z_iX_iZ_i + X_i |\psi\rangle = \mathsf{negl}(\lambda)$$

and

$$\langle\psi| Z_jX_iZ_j - X_i |\psi\rangle = \mathsf{negl}(\lambda)$$

for $i \neq j$. In fact, these relations turn out to *encode* the two basic properties of the TCF f_{pk_i}: the adaptive hardcore bit property (encoded in the first relation) and that f_{pk_i} is indistinguishable from injective[10] (encoded in the second relation)! We will not directly prove the relations here, but they are implicit in our full security proof and are the motivation for this proof strategy.

The Extracted State. Given these protocol observables $Z_1, ..., Z_N, X_1, ..., X_N$, it remains to implement Step (2) of our overall proof strategy: extracting a state $|\psi'\rangle$ whose standard/Hadamard measurement outcomes match $D_{P^*,\mathrm{Out}}$. At a high level, this is achieved by "teleporting" the state $|\psi\rangle$ onto a fresh N-qubit register in a way that *transforms* the "pseudo-Paulis" $\{X_i\}, \{Z_j\}$ into *real* Pauli observables $\{\sigma_{x,i}\}, \{\sigma_{z,j}\}$.

Fix a choice of $\{X_i, Z_i\}, |\psi\rangle \leftarrow \mathsf{Samp}$. For ease of notation, write $\mathcal{H} = \mathcal{Z} \otimes \mathcal{I} \otimes \mathcal{U}$ so that $|\psi\rangle \in \mathcal{H}$. We would like an efficient extraction procedure that takes as input $|\psi\rangle \in \mathcal{H}$ and generates an N-qubit state τ such that, roughly speaking, measuring $|\psi\rangle$ with X/Z and measuring τ with σ_X/σ_Z produce indistinguishable outcomes.

Intuition for the Extractor. Before we describe our extractor, we first provide some underlying intuition. For an arbitrary N-qubit Hilbert space, let $\sigma_{x,i}/\sigma_{z,i}$ denote the Pauli σ_x/σ_z observable acting on the ith qubit. For each $r, s \in \{0,1\}^N$, define the N-qubit Pauli "parity" observables

$$\sigma_x(r) := \prod_{i:r_i=1} \sigma_{x,i} \, , \, \sigma_z(s) := \prod_{i:r_i=1} \sigma_{z,i}.$$

Suppose for a moment that $|\psi\rangle \in \mathcal{H}$ is *already* an N-qubit state (i.e., $\mathcal{H}$ is an N-qubit Hilbert space) and moreover, that each X_i/Z_i observable is simply the corresponding Pauli observable $\sigma_{x,i}/\sigma_{z,i}$. While these assumptions technically trivialize the task (the state already has the form we want from the extracted state), it will be instructive to **write down an extractor that "teleports" this state into another N-qubit external register**.

We can do this by initializing two N-qubit registers $\mathcal{A}_1 \otimes \mathcal{A}_2$ to $|\phi^+\rangle^{\otimes N}$ where $|\phi^+\rangle$ is the EPR state $(|00\rangle + |11\rangle)/\sqrt{2}$ (the ith EPR pair lives on the ith qubit of $\mathcal{A}_1$ and $\mathcal{A}_2$). Now consider the following steps, which are inspired by the (N-qubit) quantum teleportation protocol

1. Initialize a $2N$-qubit ancilla $\mathcal{W}$ to $|0^{2N}\rangle$, and apply $H^{\otimes 2N}$ to obtain the uniform superposition.
2. Apply a "controlled-Pauli" unitary, which does the following for all $r, s \in \{0,1\}^N$ and all $|\phi\rangle \in \mathcal{H} \otimes \mathcal{A}_1$:

$$|r,s\rangle_{\mathcal{W}} |\phi\rangle_{\mathcal{H},\mathcal{A}_1} \rightarrow |r,s\rangle_{\mathcal{W}} (\sigma_x(r)\sigma_z(s)_{\mathcal{H}} \otimes \sigma_x(r)\sigma_z(s)_{\mathcal{A}_1}) |\phi\rangle_{\mathcal{H},\mathcal{A}_1}$$

3. Apply the unitary that XORs onto $\mathcal{W}$ the outcome of performing N Bell-basis measurements[11] on $\mathcal{A}_1 \otimes \mathcal{A}_2$ onto $\mathcal{W}$, i.e., for all $u, v, r, s \in \{0,1\}^N$:

$$|u,v\rangle_{\mathcal{W}} (\sigma_x(r)\sigma_z(s) \otimes \mathsf{Id})_{\mathcal{A}_1,\mathcal{A}_2} |\phi^+\rangle^{\otimes N}_{\mathcal{A}_1,\mathcal{A}_2}$$

---

[10] Technically, the property encoded is the *collapsing* of f_{pk_i}, which is implied by (but not equivalent to) being indistinguishable from injective.

[11] The Bell basis consists of the 4 states $(\sigma_x^a \sigma_z^b \otimes \mathsf{Id}) |\phi^+\rangle$ for $a, b \in \{0,1\}$ on 2 qubits.

$$\mapsto |u \oplus r, v \oplus s\rangle_{\mathcal{W}} (\sigma_x(r)\sigma_z(s) \otimes \mathsf{Id})_{\mathcal{A}_1,\mathcal{A}_2} |\phi^+\rangle_{\mathcal{A}_1,\mathcal{A}_2}^{\otimes N}.$$

Finally, discard $\mathcal{W}$.

One can show that the resulting state is

$$\frac{1}{2^N} \sum_{r,s \in \{0,1\}^N} (\sigma_x(r)\sigma_z(s) \otimes \sigma_x(r)\sigma_z(s) \otimes \mathsf{Id}) |\psi\rangle_{\mathcal{H}} |\phi^+\rangle_{\mathcal{A}_1,\mathcal{A}_2} = |\phi^+\rangle_{\mathcal{H},\mathcal{A}_1} |\psi\rangle_{\mathcal{A}_2},$$

(1)

where $|\psi\rangle$ is now "teleported" into the $\mathcal{A}_2$ register.

The Full Extractor. To generalize this idea to the setting where $|\psi\rangle \in \mathcal{H}$ is an arbitrary quantum state and $\{X_i, Z_i\}_i$ are an arbitrary collection of $2N$ observables, we simply replace each $\sigma_x(r)$ and $\sigma_z(s)$ acting on $\mathcal{H}$ above with the corresponding parity observables $X(r)$, $Z(s)$, defined analogously (for $r, s \in \{0,1\}^N$ as

$$Z(s) = \prod_{i=1}^{N} Z_i^{s_i} \quad \text{and} \quad X(r) = \prod_{i=1}^{N} X_i^{r_i}.$$

The rough intuition is that as long as the $\{X_i\}$ and $\{Z_i\}$ observables "behave like" Pauli observables with respect to $|\psi\rangle$, the resulting procedure will "teleport" $|\psi\rangle$ into the N-qubit register $\mathcal{A}_2$.

Relating Extracted State Measurements to Verifier Outputs. With the extracted state defined to be the state on $\mathcal{A}_2$ after performing the "generalized teleportation" described above, it remains to prove that the distribution $D_{P^*,\text{Ext}}$ resulting from measuring the extracted state on $\mathcal{A}_2$ in the h bases is indistinguishable from $D_{P^*,\text{2-to-1}}$.

One can show (by a calculation) that $D_{P^*,\text{Ext}}$ is the following distribution (differences from $D_{P^*,\text{2-to-1}}$ in red)

1. Sample keys $(\mathsf{pk}_i, \mathsf{sk}_i) \leftarrow$ Cf. Run P^* to obtain $y, |\psi\rangle$.
2. For each i such that $h_i = 0$, measure the first bit of the prover's ith response register in the standard basis to obtain (and output) a bit b_i.
3. For each i such that $h_i = 1$, flip a random bit w_i and apply the unitary $Z_i^{w_i}$.
4. Measure $U|\psi\rangle$ in the Hadamard basis, obtaining strings $(d_1, ..., d_N)$.
5. For each i such that $h_i = 1$, compute (and output) $d_i \cdot (1, x_{0,i} \oplus x_{1,i}) \oplus w_i$.

We prove indistinguishability between the N-bit distributions $D_{P^*,\text{Ext}}$ and $D_{P^*,\text{2 to 1}}$ by considering N hybrid distributions, where the difference between Hybrid $j - 1$ and Hybrid j is:

- an additional application of the unitary Z_j in Item 3, and
- an additional XOR of e_j (the jth standard basis vector) in Item 5.

To conclude the soundness proof, we show that Hybrid $j - 1$ and Hybrid j in the following three steps.

- First, we prove that the marginal distributions of Hybrid $(j-1)$ and Hybrid j on $N \setminus \{j\}$ are indistinguishable due to the collapsing property of f_{pk_j}. Intuitively this holds because the marginal distributions on $N \setminus \{j\}$ only differ by the application of Z_j, which is undetectable by collapsing.
- By invoking an elementary lemma about N-bit indistinguishability, the task reduces to proving a 1-bit indistinguishability of the jth bit of Hybrid $(j-1)$ and Hybrid j, conditioned on an efficiently computable property of the marginal distributions on $N \setminus \{j\}$.
- Finally, we show that the indistinguishability of the jth bit holds due to the adaptive hardcore bit property of f_{pk_j}. At a very high level, the above jth bit property involves a measurement of X_j, and the two hybrids differ in whether a random Z_j^b is applied before X_j is measured; in words, this exactly captures the adaptive hardcore bit security game.

We refer the reader to the full version for a complete proof of indistinguishability.

2.5   From a Verifier-Succinct Measurement Protocol to Succinct Arguments for BQP

Using Sects. 2.3 and 2.4, we have constructed a *verifier-succinct* measurement protocol, for succinctly represented basis strings, with a single bit verifier challenge. What remains is to convert this into a (fully) succinct argument system for BQP (or QMA). This is accomplished via the following transformations:

- Converting a measurement protocol into a quantum verification protocol. As described earlier, this is achieved by combining the [FHM18] protocol for BQP verification with a limited quantum verifier (as modified by [ACGH20]) with our measurement protocol, using a PRF to generate a pseudorandom basis choice instead of a uniformly random basis choice for the [FHM18, ACGH20] verifier. This results in a verifier-succinct argument system for BQP/QMA with constant soundness error.
- Parallel repetition to reduce the soundness error. This follows from the "computational orthogonal projectors" property of the 1-bit challenge protocol and follows from [ACGH20] (we give a somewhat more abstract formulation of their idea in the full version). This results in a verifier-succinct argument system for BQP/QMA with negligible soundness error.
- Converting a verifier-succinct argument system into a fully succinct argument system. We elaborate on this last transformation below, as a few difficulties come up in this step.

Assume that we are given a (for simplicity, 4-message) verifier-succinct argument system for BQP/QMA. Let m_1, m_2, m_3, m_4 denote the four messages in such an argument system. In order to obtain a fully succinct argument system, we must reduce (1) the prover communication complexity $|m_2| + |m_4|$, and (2) the runtime of the verifier's decision predicate.

The first idea that comes to mind is to ask the prover to send short (e.g. Merkle tree) commitments σ_2 and σ_4 of m_2 and m_4, respectively, instead of sending m_2 and m_4 directly. At the end of the interaction, the prover and verifier could then engage in a succinct interactive argument (of knowledge) for a (classical) NP statement that "the verifier would have accepted the committed messages underlying σ_2 and σ_4". One could potentially employ Kilian's succinct interactive argument of knowledge for NP which was recently shown to be post-quantum secure under the post-quantum LWE assumption [CMSZ21].

There are a few issues with this naive idea. First of all, the verifier's decision predicate is *private* (it depends on the secret key SK in the measurement protocol and the PRF seed for its basis), so the NP statement above is not well-formed. One reasonable solution to this issue is to simply have the verifier send this secret information st after the verifier-succinct protocol emulation has occurred and before the NP-succinct argument has started. For certain applications (e.g. obtaining a non-interactive protocol in the QROM) we would like to have a *public-coin* protocol; this can be achieved by using fully homomorphic encryption to encrypt this secret information in the *first* round rather than sending it in the clear in a later round. For this overview, we focus on the private-coin variant of the protocol.

Now, we can indeed write down the appropriate NP relation[12]

$$\mathcal{R}_V = \{((h, m_1, \sigma_2, m_3, \sigma_4, \mathsf{st}), (m_2, m_4)) : \sigma_2 = h(m_2) \text{ and}$$
$$\sigma_4 = h(m_4) \text{ and } V(\mathsf{st}, m_1, m_2, c, m_4) = \mathsf{accept}\}$$

and execute the aforementioned strategy. However, this construction turns out not to work. Specifically, it does not seem possible to *convert* a cheating prover P^* in the above fully succinct protocol into a cheating prover P^{**} for the verifier-succinct protocol; for example, P^{**} needs to be able to produce a message m_2 given only m_1 from the verifier; meanwhile, the message m_1 can only be extracted from P^* by repeatedly rewinding P^*'s *last* message algorithm, which requires the verifier's secret information st as input! This does not correspond to a valid P^{**}, who does not have access to st when computing m_2.

Our refined compiler is to execute several arguments of knowledge: one right after the prover sends σ_2, proving knowledge of m_2; another one right after she sends σ_4, proving knowledge of m_4 (both before receiving the secret state st from the verifier); and a third one for the relation $\mathcal{R}_V$ described above. The first two arguments of knowledge are for the relation

$$\mathcal{R}_H = \{(h, \sigma), m) : h(m) = \sigma\}$$

This allows for *immediate extraction* of m_2 and m_3 and appears to clear the way for a reduction between the verifier-succinct and fully succinct protocol soundness properties.

However, there is one remaining problem: the argument-of-knowledge property of Kilian's protocol proved by [CMSZ21] is *insufficiently composable* to be used in our compiler. They demonstrate an extractor for Kilian's protocol that

---

[12] Note that the verifier also takes as input the QMA instance, but we suppress it here for clarity.

takes any quantum cheating prover that convinces the verifier and extracts a witness from them. However, their post-quantum extractor might significantly disturb the prover's state, meaning that once we extract m_2 above, we may not be able to continue the prover execution in our reduction.

Fortunately, a recent work [LMS21] shows that a slight variant of Kilian's protocol is a succinct argument of knowledge for NP satisfying a composable extraction property called "state-preservation." This security property is exactly what is required for our compiler to extract a valid cheating prover strategy P^{**} for the verifier-succinct argument given a cheating prover P^* for the compiled protocol. A complete discussion of this is given in the full version.

This completes our construction of a succinct argument system for BQP (and QMA). We discuss additional results (2-message protocols, zero knowledge, batch arguments) in the full version of this paper.

Acknowledgment. AL is supported in part by a Charles M. Vest fellowship. GM is partially supported by the German Federal Ministry of Education and Research BMBF (grant 16K15K042, project 6GEM). TV is supported by AFOSR YIP award number FA9550-16-1-0495, a grant from the Simons Foundation (828076, TV), MURI Grant FA9550-18-1-0161, the NSF QLCI program through grant number OMA-2016245 and the IQIM, an NSF Physics Frontiers Center (NSF Grant PHY-1125565) with support of the Gordon and Betty Moore Foundation (GBMF-12500028). AL, VV, and LY are supported in part by DARPA under Agreement No. HR00112020023, a grant from the MIT-IBM Watson AI, a grant from Analog Devices and a Microsoft Trustworthy AI grant. Any opinions, findings and conclusions or recommendations expressed in this material are those of the author(s) and do not necessarily reflect the views of the United States Government or DARPA. LY was supported in part by an NSF graduate research fellowship.

References

[ACGH20] Alagic, G., Childs, A.M., Grilo, A.B., Hung, S.-H.: Non-interactive classical verification of quantum computation. In: Pass, R., Pietrzak, K. (eds.) TCC 2020, Part III. LNCS, vol. 12552, pp. 153–180. Springer, Cham (2020). https://doi.org/10.1007/978-3-030-64381-2_6

[ALM+92] Arora, S., Lund, C., Motwani, R., Sudan, M., Szegedy, M.: Proof verification and hardness of approximation problems, pp. 14–23 (1992)

[AS92] Arora, S., Safra, S.: Probabilistic checking of proofs: a new characterization of NP, pp. 2–13 (1992)

[BFL90] Babai, L., Fortnow, L., Lund, C.: Non-deterministic exponential time has two-prover interactive protocols, 16–25 (1990)

[BGKW88] Ben-Or, M., Goldwasser, S., Kilian, J., Wigderson, A.: Multi-prover interactive proofs: how to remove intractability assumptions, pp. 113–131 (1988)

[BV97] Bernstein, E., Vazirani, U.: Quantum complexity theory. SIAM J. Comput. **26**(5), 1411–1473 (1997)

[CCY20] Chia, N.-H., Chung, K.-M., Yamakawa, T.: Classical verification of quantum computations with efficient verifier. In: Pass, R., Pietrzak, K. (eds.) TCC 2020, Part III. LNCS, vol. 12552, pp. 181–206. Springer, Cham (2020). https://doi.org/10.1007/978-3-030-64381-2_7

[CLLW20] Chung, K.-M., Lee, Y., Lin, H.-H., Wu, X.: Constant-round blind classical verification of quantum sampling. arXiv preprint arXiv:2012.04848 (2020)

[CMSZ21] Chiesa, A., Ma, F., Spooner, N., Zhandry, M.: Post-quantum succinct arguments: breaking the quantum rewinding barrier. In: FOCS 2021 (2021)

[FHM18] Fitzsimons, J.F., Hajdusek, M., Morimae, T.: Post hoc verification of quantum computation. Phys. Rev. Lett. **120**, 040501 (2018)

[GMR85] Goldwasser, S., Micali, S., Rackoff, C.: The knowledge complexity of interactive proof-systems (extended abstract), pp. 291–304 (1985)

[GVW15] Gorbunov, S., Vaikuntanathan, V., Wichs, D.: Leveled fully homomorphic signatures from standard lattices, pp. 469–477 (2015)

[Kil92] Kilian, J.: A note on efficient zero-knowledge proofs and arguments (extended abstract), pp. 723–732 (1992)

[LMS21] Lombardi, A., Ma, F., Spooner, N.: Post-quantum zero knowledge, revisited (or: how to do quantum rewinding undetectably). Cryptology ePrint Archive, Report 2021/1543 (2021). https://eprint.iacr.org/2021/1543

[Mah18] Mahadev, U.: Classical verification of quantum computations, pp. 259–267 (2018)

[Mic94] Micali, S.: A secure and efficient digital signature algorithm. Technical Memo MIT/LCS/TM-501b, Massachusetts Institute of Technology, Laboratory for Computer Science, April 1994

[PVW08] Peikert, C., Vaikuntanathan, V., Waters, B.: A framework for efficient and composable oblivious transfer. In: Wagner, D. (ed.) CRYPTO 2008. LNCS, vol. 5157, pp. 554–571. Springer, Heidelberg (2008). https://doi.org/10.1007/978-3-540-85174-5_31

[PW08] Peikert, C., Waters, B.: Lossy trapdoor functions and their applications, pp. 187–196 (2008)

[SW14] Sahai, A., Waters, B.: How to use indistinguishability obfuscation: deniable encryption, and more, pp. 475–484 (2014)

[Unr16] Unruh, D.: Computationally binding quantum commitments. In: Fischlin, M., Coron, J.-S. (eds.) EUROCRYPT 2016, Part II. LNCS, vol. 9666, pp. 497–527. Springer, Heidelberg (2016). https://doi.org/10.1007/978-3-662-49896-5_18

[Vid20] Vidick, T.: Interactions with quantum devices (course) (2020). http://users.cms.caltech.edu/~vidick/teaching/fsmp/fsmp.pdf

[VZ21] Vidick, T., Zhang, T.: Classical proofs of quantum knowledge. In: Canteaut, A., Standaert, F.-X. (eds.) EUROCRYPT 2021, Part II. LNCS, vol. 12697, pp. 630–660. Springer, Cham (2021). https://doi.org/10.1007/978-3-030-77886-6_22

On the Feasibility of Unclonable
Encryption, and More

Prabhanjan Ananth[1], Fatih Kaleoglu[1], Xingjian Li[2], Qipeng Liu[3(✉)],
and Mark Zhandry[4,5]

[1] University of California, Santa Barbara, CA, USA
prabhanjan@cs.ucsb.edu, kaleoglu@ucsb.edu
[2] Tsinghua University, Beijing, China
lixj18@mails.tsinghua.edu.cn
[3] Simons Institute for the Theory of Computing, Berkeley, CA, USA
qipengliu0@gmail.com
[4] NTT Research, Palo Alto, CA, USA
[5] Princeton University, Princeton, NJ, USA
https://www.users/~iekeland/web/welcome.html

Abstract. Unclonable encryption, first introduced by Broadbent and
Lord (TQC'20), is a one-time encryption scheme with the following
security guarantee: any non-local adversary $(\mathcal{A}, \mathcal{B}, \mathcal{C})$ cannot simultaneously distinguish encryptions of two equal length messages. This notion
is termed as unclonable indistinguishability. Prior works focused on
achieving a weaker notion of unclonable encryption, where we required
that any non-local adversary $(\mathcal{A}, \mathcal{B}, \mathcal{C})$ cannot simultaneously recover the
entire message m. Seemingly innocuous, understanding the feasibility of
encryption schemes satisfying unclonable indistinguishability (even for
1-bit messages) has remained elusive.

We make progress towards establishing the feasibility of unclonable
encryption.

- We show that encryption schemes satisfying unclonable indistinguishability exist unconditionally in the quantum random oracle
  model.
- Towards understanding the necessity of oracles, we present a negative result stipulating that a large class of encryption schemes cannot
  satisfy unclonable indistinguishability.
- Finally, we also establish the feasibility of another closely related
  primitive: copy-protection for single-bit output point functions. Prior
  works only established the feasibility of copy-protection for multi-bit
  output point functions or they achieved constant security error for
  single-bit output point functions.

1 Introduction

Quantum information ushers in a new era for cryptography. Cryptographic constructs that are impossible to achieve classically can be realized using quantum
information. In particular, the no-cloning principle of quantum mechanics has
given rise to many wonderful primitives such as quantum money [24] and its

© International Association for Cryptologic Research 2022
Y. Dodis and T. Shrimpton (Eds.): CRYPTO 2022, LNCS 13508, pp. 212–241, 2022.
https://doi.org/10.1007/978-3-031-15979-4_8

variants [2,18,25], tamper detection [14], quantum copy-protection [1], one-shot signatures [4], single-decryptor encryption [10,13], secure software leasing [6], copy-detection [3] and many more.

Unclonable Encryption. Of particular interest is a primitive called unclonable encryption, introduced by Broadbent and Lord [9]. Roughly speaking, unclonable encryption is a one-time secure encryption scheme with *quantum* ciphertexts having the following security guarantee: any adversary given a ciphertext, modeled as a quantum state, cannot produce two (possibly entangled) states that both encode some information about the original message. This is formalized in terms of a splitting game.

A splitting adversary $(\mathcal{A}, \mathcal{B}, \mathcal{C})$ first has $\mathcal{A}$ receive as input an encryption of m_b, for two messages m_0 and m_1. $\mathcal{A}$ then outputs a bipartite state to $\mathcal{B}$ and $\mathcal{C}$. $\mathcal{B}$ and $\mathcal{C}$ additionally receive as input the classical decryption key and respectively output b_B and b_C. They win if $b = b_B = b_C$. Clearly, $\mathcal{A}$ could give $\mathcal{B}$ the entire ciphertext and $\mathcal{C}$ nothing, in which case $b_B = b$ but b_C would be independent of b, giving an overall winning probability of $1/2$. Security therefore requires that the splitting adversary wins with probability only negligibly larger than $1/2$. This security property, introduced by [9], is called *unclonable indistinguishability*. Unclonable indistinguishability clearly implies plain semantic security, as $\mathcal{A}$ could use any semantic security adversary to make a guess b_A for b, and then simply send b_A to $\mathcal{B}$ and $\mathcal{C}$, who set $b_B = b_C := b_A$.

Unclonable encryption is motivated by a few interesting applications. Firstly, unclonable encryption implies private-key quantum money. It is also useful for preventing storage attacks where malicious entities steal ciphertexts in the hope that they can decrypt them when the decryption key is compromised later. Recently, the works of [5,11] showed that unclonable encryption implies copy-protection for a restricted class of functions with computational correctness guarantees.

Despite being a natural primitive, actually constructing unclonable encryption (even for 1-bit messages!) and justifying its security has remained elusive. Prior works [5,9] established the feasibility of unclonable encryption satisfying a weaker property simply called *unclonability*: this is modeled similar to unclonable indistinguishability, except that the message m encrypted is sampled uniformly at random and both $\mathcal{B}$ and $\mathcal{C}$ are expected to guess the entire message m. This weaker property is far less useful, and both applications listed above – preventing storage attacks and copy-protection – crucially rely on indistinguishability security. Moreover, unclonability does not on its own even imply plain semantic security, meaning the prior works must separately posit semantic security.

The following question has been left open from prior works:

Q1. Do encryption schemes satisfying unclonable indistinguishability, exist?

Copy-Protection for Point Functions. Copy-protection, first introduced by Aaronson [1], is another important primitive closely related to unclonable encryption. Copy-protection is a compiler that converts a program into a quantum state that not only retains the original functionality but also satisfies the following property: a splitting adversary $(\mathcal{A}, \mathcal{B}, \mathcal{C})$ first has $\mathcal{A}$ receive as input a copy-protected state that can be used to compute a function f. $\mathcal{A}$ then outputs a bipartite state to $\mathcal{B}$ and $\mathcal{C}$. As part of the security guarantee, we require that both $\mathcal{B}$ and $\mathcal{C}$ should not be able to simultaneously compute f.

While copy-protection is known to be impossible for general unlearnable functions [6], we could still hope to achieve it for simple classes of functions. Of particular interest to us is the class of point functions. A single-bit output point function is of the form $f_y(\cdot)$: it takes as input x and outputs 1 if and only if $x = y$. One could also consider the notion of multi-bit output point functions, where the function outputs a large string, rather than 0 or 1.

Prior works [5,11] either focus on constructing copy-protection for *multi*-bit output point functions or they construct copy-protection for single-bit output point functions with constant security, rather than optimal security, where the adversary can only do negligibly better than a trivial guess.

Yet another important question that has been left open from prior works is the following:

Q2. Does copy-protection for single-bit output point functions, with optimal security, exist?

As we will see later, the techniques used in resolving Q1 will shed light on resolving Q2. Hence, we focus on highlighting challenges in resolving Q1. The reader familiar with the challenges involved in constructing unclonable encryption could skip Sect. 1.1 and directly go to Sect. 1.2.

1.1   Achieving Unclonable Indistinguishability: Challenges

We need to achieve a *one-time* secure encryption scheme for *1-bit* messages satisfying unclonable indistinguishability: *how hard can this problem be?* Indeed one might be tempted to conclude that going from the weaker unclonability property to the stronger unclonable indistinguishability notion is a small step. The former is a search problem while the latter is a decision problem, and could hope to apply known search-to-decision reductions. As we will now explain, unfortunately this intuition is false, due both to the effects of quantum information and also to the fact that unclonable encryption involves multiple interacting adversaries.

– Recall that in an unclonable encryption scheme, the secret key is revealed to both $\mathcal{B}$ and $\mathcal{C}$. As a consequence, the secret information of any underlying cryptographic tool we use to build unclonable encryption could be revealed. For example, consider the following construction: to encrypt $m \in \{0,1\}$, compute $(r, \mathsf{PRF}(k, r) \oplus m)$, where $k \xleftarrow{\$} \{0,1\}^\lambda$ is the pseudorandom function key and $r \xleftarrow{\$} \{0,1\}^\lambda$ is a random tag. In the security experiment, the secret key, namely k, will be revealed to both $\mathcal{B}$ and $\mathcal{C}$. This restricts the type of cryptographic tools we can use to build unclonable encryption.

- Another challenge is to perform security reductions. Typically, we use the adversary to come up with a reduction that breaks a cryptographic game that is either conjectured to be or provably hard. However, this is tricky when there are two adversaries, $\mathcal{B}$ and $\mathcal{C}$. Which of the two adversaries do we use to break the underlying game? Suppose we decide to use $\mathcal{B}$ to break the game. For all we know, $\mathcal{A}$ could have simply handed over the ciphertext it received to $\mathcal{B}$ and clearly, $\mathcal{B}$ cannot be used to break the underlying game. Even worse, Alice can send a superposition of $\mathcal{B}$ getting the ciphertext and $\mathcal{C}$ receiving nothing v.s. $\mathcal{C}$ receiving the ciphertext and $\mathcal{B}$ getting nothing.
- Even if we somehow manage to achieve unclonable indistinguishability for 1-bit messages, it is a priori unclear how to achieve unclonable indistinguishability for multi-bit messages. In classical cryptography, the standard transformation goes from encryption of 1-bit messages to encryption of multi-bit messages via a hybrid argument. This type of argument fails in the setting of unclonable encryption. Let us illustrate why: suppose we encrypt a 2-bit message $m = m_1 \| m_2$ by encrypting 1-bit messages m_1 and m_2, denoted respectively by ρ_1 and ρ_2. This scheme is unfortunately insecure. An encryption of 11 can be (simultaneously) distinguished from an encryption of 00 by a non-local adversary $(\mathcal{A}, \mathcal{B}, \mathcal{C})$: $\mathcal{A}$ can send ρ_1 to $\mathcal{B}$ and ρ_2 to $\mathcal{C}$. Since, both $\mathcal{B}$ and $\mathcal{C}$ receive the secret key, they can check whether the underlying message was 1 or 0.
- A recent result by Majenz, Schaffner and Tahmasbi [16] explores the difficulties in constructing unclonable encryption schemes. They show that any unclonable encryption scheme satisfying indistinguishability property needs to have ciphertexts, when represented as density matrices, with sufficiently large eigenvalues. As a consequence, it was shown that [9] did not satisfy unclonable-indistinguishability property. Any unclonable encryption scheme we come up with needs to overcome the hurdles set by [16].

We take an example below that concretely highlights some of the challenges explained above.

Example: Issues with Using Extractors. For instance, we could hope to use randomness extractors. To encrypt a message m, we output $(\rho_x, c_r, \mathsf{Ext}(r, x) \oplus m)$, where ρ_x is an unclonable encryption of x satisfying the weaker unclonability property, c_r is a classical encryption of a random seed r, and Ext is an extractor using seed r. The intuition for this construction is that unclonable security implies that at least one of the two parties, say $\mathcal{B}$ cannot predict x, and therefore x has min-entropy conditioned on $\mathcal{B}$'s view. Therefore, $\mathsf{Ext}(r, x)$ extracts bits that are statistically random against $\mathcal{B}$, and thus completely hides m.

There are a few problems with this proposal. First, since $\mathcal{A}$ generates $\mathcal{B}$'s state and has access to the entire ciphertext, the conditional distribution of x given Bob's view will depend on c_r. This breaks the extractor application, since it requires r to be independent. One could hope to perform a hybrid argument to replace c_r with a random ciphertext, but this is not possible: $\mathcal{B}$ eventually learns the decryption key for c_r and would be able to distinguish such a hybrid. This example already begins to show how the usual intuition fails.

A deeper problem is that extractor definitions deal with a single party, whereas unclonable encryption has two recipient parties. To illustrate the issue, note that it is actually *not* the case that x has min-entropy against one of the parties: if $\mathcal{A}$ randomly sends the ciphertext to $\mathcal{B}$ or $\mathcal{C}$, each one of them can predict x with probability $1/2$, so the min-entropy is only 1. In such a case the extractor guarantee is meaningless. Now, in this example one can condition on the message $\mathcal{A}$ sends to $\mathcal{B}, \mathcal{C}$, and once conditioned it will in fact be the case that one of the two parties has high min-entropy. But other strategies are possible which break such a conditioning argument. For example, $\mathcal{A}$ could send messages that are *superposition* v.s. $\mathcal{B}$ getting the ciphertext (and $\mathcal{C}$ nothing) v.s. $\mathcal{C}$ getting the ciphertext (and $\mathcal{B}$ nothing). By being in superposition, we can no longer condition on which party receives the ciphertext.

1.2   Our Results

We overcome the aforementioned challenges and make progress on addressing both questions Q1 and Q2. We start with our results on unclonable encryption before moving onto copy-protection.

Unclonable Encryption. For the first time, we establish the feasibility of unclonable encryption. Our result is in the quantum random oracle model. Specifically, we prove the following.

Theorem 1 (Informal).   *There exists an unconditionally secure one-time encryption scheme satisfying unclonable indistinguishability in the quantum random oracle model.*

Our construction is simple: we make novel use of coset states considered in recent works [10]. However, our analysis is quite involved: among many other things, we make use of threshold projective implementation introduced by Zhandry [25].

A recent work [5] showed a generic transformation from one-time unclonable encryption to public-key unclonable encryption[1]. By combining the above theorem with the generic transformation of [5], we obtain a public-key unclonable encryption satisfying the unclonable indistinguishability property.

Theorem 2 (Informal). *Assuming the existence of post-quantum public-key encryption, there exists a post-quantum public-key encryption scheme satisfying the unclonable indistinguishability property in the quantum random oracle model.*

It is natural to understand whether we can achieve unclonable encryption in the plain model. Towards understanding this question, we show that a class of

---

[1] While their result demonstrates that the generic transformation preserves the unclonability property, we note that the same transformation preserves unclonable indistinguishability.

unclonable encryption schemes, that we call *deterministic* schemes, are impossible to achieve. By 'deterministic', we mean that the encryptor is a unitary U and the decryptor is $U^\dagger$. Moreover, the impossibility holds even if the encryptor and the decryptor are allowed to run in exponential time!

In more detail, we show the following.

Theorem 3 (Informal). *There do not exist unconditionally secure deterministic one-time encryption schemes satisfying the unclonable indistinguishability property.*

In light of the fact that any classical one-time encryption scheme can be made deterministic without loss of generality[2], we find the above result to be surprising. An interesting consequence of the above result is an alternate proof that the conjugate encryption scheme of [9] does not satisfy unclonable indistiguishability[3]. This was originally proven by [16].

We can overcome the impossibility result by either devising an encryption algorithm that traces out part of the output register (in other words, performs non-unitary operations) or the encryption scheme is based on computational assumptions.

Copy-Protection for Point Functions. We also make progress on Q2. We show that there exists copy-protection for single-bit output functions with optimal security. Prior work by Coladangelo, Majenz and Poremba [11] achieved a copy-protection scheme for single-bit output point functions that only achieved constant security.

We show the following.

Theorem 4 (Informal). *There exists a copy-protection scheme for single-bit output point functions in the quantum random oracle model.*

While there are generic transformations from unclonable encryption to copy-protection for point functions explored in the prior works [5,11], the transformations only work for multi-bit point functions. Our construction extensively makes use of the techniques for achieving unclonable encryption (Theorem 1). Our result takes a step closer in understanding the classes of functions for which the feasibility of copy-protection can be established in the plain model.

1.3 Organization

The rest of the paper is organized as follows. In Sect. 2, we cover all the necessary preliminaries, including Jordan's lemma, measuring success probability of a quantum adversary and the definitions of unclonable encryption schemes. Followed by Sect. 3, we recall coset states and their properties. We introduce a new game called "strengthened MOE games in the QROM" and prove security

---

[2] We can always include the randomness used in the encryption as part of the secret key.

[3] It is easy to see why conjugate encryption of multi-bit messages is insecure. The insecurity of conjugate encryption of 1-bit messages was first established by [16].

in this game. This part is our main result and consists of most technique novelties. In Sect. 4, we build our unclonable encryption on the new property. In the final section (Sect. 5), we present our construction for copy-protection of single-output point functions Similar techniques as in Sect. 3 are used. Most details are omitted and can be found in the full version, as well as our impossibility result.

1.4   Technical Overview

Attempts Based on Wiesner States. We start by recalling the unclonable encryption scheme proposed by Broadbent and Lord [9]. The core idea is to encrypt a message m under a randomly chosen secret key x and encode x into an unclonable quantum state ρ_x. Intuitively, for any splitting adversary $(\mathcal{A}, \mathcal{B}, \mathcal{C})$, there is no way for $\mathcal{A}$ to split ρ_x into two quantum states, such that no-communicating $\mathcal{B}$ and $\mathcal{C}$ can both recover enough information about x to decrypt $\mathsf{Enc}(x, m)$.

A well-known choice of no-cloning states is the famous Wiesner conjugate coding [24]. For a string $x = x_1 x_2 \cdots x_\lambda \in \{0,1\}^\lambda$, λ bases are chosen uniformly at random, one for each x_i. Let θ_i denote the basis for x_i. If θ_i is 0, x_i is encoded under the computational basis $\{|0\rangle, |1\rangle\}$; otherwise, x_i is encoded under the Hadamard basis $\{|+\rangle, |-\rangle\}$. The conjugate coding of x under basis θ is then denoted by $|x^\theta\rangle$. By knowing θ, one can easily recover x from the Wiesner state.

The unclonability of Wiesner conjugate coding (or Wiesner states for short) is well understood and characterized by *monogamy-of-entanglement games* (MOE games) in [9,20]. In the same paper, Broadbent and Lord show that no strategy wins the following MOE game[4] with probability more than 0.85^λ.

- A challenger samples uniformly at random $x, \theta \in \{0,1\}^\lambda$ and sends $|x^\theta\rangle$ to $\mathcal{A}$.
- $\mathcal{A}$ taking the input from the challenger, produces a bipartite state to $\mathcal{B}$ and $\mathcal{C}$.
- The non-communicating $\mathcal{B}$ and $\mathcal{C}$ then additionally receive the secret basis information θ and make a guess $x_\mathcal{B}, x_\mathcal{C}$ for x respectively.
- The splitting adversary $(\mathcal{A}, \mathcal{B}, \mathcal{C})$ wins the game if and only if $x_\mathcal{B} = x_\mathcal{C} = x$.

Fig. 1. MOE Games for Wiesner States.

A natural attempt to construct unclonable encryption schemes is by composing one-time pad with Wiesner states. A secret key is the basis information $\theta \in \{0,1\}^n$. An encryption algorithm takes the secret key θ and a plaintext m,

---

[4] This is a variant of MOE games discussed in [20]. We will be using this notation throughout the paper.

it samples a $x \in \{0,1\}^n$ and outputs $m \oplus x$ together with the Wiesner conjugate coding of x, i.e. $|x^\theta\rangle$. However, such scheme can never satisfy unclonable indistinguishability. Recall that unclonable indistinguishability requires either $\mathcal{B}$ or $\mathcal{C}$ can not distinguish whether the ciphertext is an encryption of message m_0 or m_1. Broadbent and Lord observe that although it is hard for $\mathcal{B}$ and $\mathcal{C}$ to completely recover the message, they can still recover half of the message and hence simultaneously distinguish with probability 1.

Towards unclonable indistinguishability, they introduce a random oracle $H : \{0,1\}^\lambda \times \{0,1\}^\lambda \rightarrow \{0,1\}^n$ in their construction (Fig. 2). If an adversary can distinguish between $m_0 \oplus H(\alpha, x)$ and $m_1 \oplus H(\alpha, x)$, it must query $H(\alpha, x)$ at some point; hence, one can extract x from this adversary by measuring a random query. Following the same reasoning, one may hope to base the security (of Fig. 2) on the MOE games (Fig. 1), by extracting x from both parties.

Gen(1^λ): on input λ, outputs uniformly random $(\alpha, \theta) \in \{0,1\}^{2\lambda}$.
Enc$^H((\alpha, \theta), m)$: samples $x \in \{0,1\}^\lambda$, outputs $(|x^\theta\rangle, m \oplus H(\alpha, x))$.
Dec$^H((\alpha, \theta), (|x^\theta\rangle, c))$: recovers x from $|x^\theta\rangle$, outputs $c \oplus H(\alpha, x)$.

Fig. 2. Unclonable Encryption by Broadbent and Lord.

The above idea, thought intuitive, is hard to instantiate. It will require simultaneous extraction of the secret x from both $\mathcal{B}$ and $\mathcal{C}$. Since $\mathcal{B}$ and $\mathcal{C}$ can be highly entangled with each other, a successful extraction of x on $\mathcal{B}$'s register may always result in an extraction failure on the other register. Broadbent and Lord use a "simultaneous" variant of the so called "O2H" (one-way-to-hiding) lemma [21] to prove their scheme satisfy unclonable indistinguishability for un-entangled adversaries $\mathcal{B}, \mathcal{C}$, or for messages with constant length. The unclonable indistinguishability for general adversaries and message spaces remains quite unknown.

Even worse, Majenz, Schaffner and Tahmasbi [16] show that there is an inherent limitation to this simultaneous variant of O2H lemma. They give an explicit example that shatters the hope of proving unclonable indistinguishability of the construction in [9] using this lemma.

Instantiating [9] *Using Coset States.* Facing with the above barrier, we may resort to other states that possess some forms of unclonability. One candidate is the so called "coset states", first proposed by Vidick and Zhang [23] in the context of proofs of quantum knowledge and later studied by Coladangelo et al. [10] for copy-protection schemes.

A coset state is described by three parameters: a subspace $A \subseteq \mathbb{F}_2^\lambda$ of dimension $\lambda/2$ and two vectors $s, s' \in \mathbb{F}_2^\lambda$ denoting two cosets $A + s$ and $A^\perp + s'$[5]; we write the state as $|A_{s,s'}\rangle$. Coset states have many nice properties, among those we only need the followings:

1. Given $|A_{s,s'}\rangle$ and a classical description of subspace A, an efficient quantum algorithm can compute both s and s'.
2. No adversary can win the MOE game (Fig. 3) for coset states with probability more than $\sqrt{e} \cdot (\cos(\pi/8))^\lambda$ (first proved in [10] and later improved by Culf and Vidick [12]).

- A challenger samples uniformly at random a subspace $A \subseteq \mathbb{F}_2^\lambda$ of dimension $\lambda/2$ $s, s' \in \mathbb{F}_2^\lambda$ and sends $|A_{s,s'}\rangle$ to $\mathcal{A}$.
- $\mathcal{A}$ taking the input from the challenger, produces a bipartite state to $\mathcal{B}$ and $\mathcal{C}$.
- The non-communicating $\mathcal{B}$ and $\mathcal{C}$ then additionally receive a classical description of the subspace A and make a guess $s_\mathcal{B}, s'_\mathcal{B}, s_\mathcal{C}, s'_\mathcal{C}$ for s, s' respectively.
- The splitting adversary $(\mathcal{A}, \mathcal{B}, \mathcal{C})$ wins the game if and only if $s_\mathcal{B} = s_\mathcal{C} = s, s'_\mathcal{B} = s'_\mathcal{C} = s'$.

Fig. 3. MOE Games for Coset States.

Readers may already notice the similarity between Wiesner states and coset states. If we substitute the basis information θ with A and the secret x with $s\|s'$, we get coset states and their corresponding MOE games. Hence, we can translate the construction in [9] using the languages of coset states. A question naturally rises: if these two kinds of states are very similar, why replacing Wiesner states with coset states even matters?

Indeed, they differ on one crucial place. Let us come back to Wiesner states. As shown by [15] in the setting of private key quantum money, given $|x^\theta\rangle$ together with an oracle P_x that outputs 1 only if input $y = x$, there exists an efficient quantum adversary that learns x without knowing θ. This further applies to the MOE games for Wiesner states: if $\mathcal{A}$ additionally gets oracle access to P_x, the MOE game is no longer secure.

MOE games for coset states remain secure if oracles for checking s and s' are given. More formally, let P_{A+s} be an oracle that outputs 1 only if the input $y \in A + s$, similarly for $P_{A^\perp + s'}$. No adversary $(\mathcal{A}, \mathcal{B}, \mathcal{C})$ can win the MOE games for coset states with more than some exponentially small probability in λ, even if

---

[5] There are many vectors in $A + s$. In the rest of the discussion, we assume s is the lexicographically smallest vector in $A + s$. Similarly for s'.

$\mathcal{A}, \mathcal{B}, \mathcal{C}$ all query P_{A+s} and $P_{A^{\perp}+s'}$ polynomially many times. We call this game *MOE game for coset states with membership checking oracles*.

We now give our construction of unclonable encryption that satisfies unclonable indistinguishability in Fig. 4. In our construction, we get rid of the extra input α in [9] construction. We believe α can be similarly removed in their construction as well. Also note that in our construction, we only require coset states and random oracles. The membership checking oracles will only be given to the adversary when we prove its security. We indeed prove a stronger security guarantee. Due to this, we can not prove the security of their construction using Wiesner states following the same idea; nonetheless, we do not know how to disprove it. We leave it as an interesting open question.

$\mathsf{Gen}(1^{\lambda})$: on input λ, outputs uniformly random subspace $A \subseteq \mathbb{F}_2^{\lambda}$ of
dimension $\lambda/2$.
$\mathsf{Enc}^H(A, m)$: samples $s, s' \in \mathbb{F}_2^{\lambda\,a}$, outputs $(|A_{s,s'}\rangle, m \oplus H(s, s'))$.
$\mathsf{Dec}^H(A, (|A_{s,s'}\rangle, c))$: recovers s, s' from the coset state, outputs $c \oplus$
$H(s, s')$.

---

^{a} We again require s, s' to be the lexicographically smallest vector in $A+s$
and $A^{\perp} + s'$.

Fig. 4. Our Unclonable Encryption Scheme.

Basing Security on Reprogram Games. Now we look at what property we require for coset states to establish unclonable indistinguishability. We will focus on the case $n = 1$ for length-1 messages in this section. By a sequence of standard variable substitution, unclonable indistinguishability of our scheme can be based on the following security game (Fig. 5) in the identical challenge mode, where each of $\mathcal{B}, \mathcal{C}$ tries to identify whether the oracle has been reprogrammed or not. We want to show any adversary $(\mathcal{A}, \mathcal{B}, \mathcal{C})$ only achieves successful probability $1/2 + \mathsf{negl}$; when $\mathcal{B}$ gets the coset state and $\mathcal{C}$ makes a random guess, they win with probability $1/2$.

Note that in the above reprogram game (Fig. 5), $\mathcal{A}$ has no access to H. This is different from unclonable indistinguishability games or MOE games. Nevertheless, we show the oracle access to H does not help $\mathcal{A}$ and thus can be safely removed by introducing a small loss.

The security of the reprogram games in the identical challenge mode can be reduced to the security in the independent challenge mode. A careful analysis of Jordan's lemma (Sect. 2.3) is required to show such a reduction. We believe that this reduction is highly non-trivial. However, since it is not the place that highlights the difference between Wiesner states and coset states, we leave it to the main body (Sect. 3.3).

- H be a random oracle with binary range, $H : \mathbb{F}_2^\lambda \times \mathbb{F}_2^\lambda \to \{0,1\}$.
  Additionally, $\mathcal{A}, \mathcal{B}, \mathcal{C}$ get oracle access to P_{A+s} and $P_{A^\perp+s'}$.
- A challenger samples a coset state $|A_{s,s'}\rangle$ and sends $(|A_{s,s'}\rangle, H(s,s'))$
  to $\mathcal{A}$.
- $\mathcal{A}$ (having *no access* to the random oracle H) taking the input from the
  challenger, produces a bipartite state to $\mathcal{B}$ and $\mathcal{C}$.
- The non-communicating $\mathcal{B}$ and $\mathcal{C}$ then receive a classical description of
  the subspace A:
  - Let $H_0 := H$ be the original random oracle.
  - Let H_1 be identical to H, except the outcome on (s,s') is flipped.
  - (Identical Challenge Mode): Flip a coin b, both $\mathcal{B}$ and $\mathcal{C}$ get oracle
    access to H_b.
  - (Independent Challenge Mode): Flip two coins $b_\mathcal{B}, b_\mathcal{C}$, $\mathcal{B}$ has oracle
    access to $H_{b_\mathcal{B}}$ and $\mathcal{C}$ gets oracle access to $H_{b_\mathcal{C}}$.
- $\mathcal{B}, \mathcal{C}$ makes a guess b', b'' respectively.
- The adversary $(\mathcal{A}, \mathcal{B}, \mathcal{C})$ wins the game if and only if $b' = b'' = b$ (in the
  identical challenge mode), or $b' = b_\mathcal{B}$ and $b'' = b_\mathcal{C}$ (in the independent
  challenge mode).

Fig. 5. Reprogram Games for Coset States in the QROM

The remaining is to show the security of the game in the independent challenge mode. Inspired by the work of [26] which initiates the study of measuring success probability of a quantum program, we show there is an efficient procedure that operates locally on both the entangled adversaries $(\mathcal{B}, \mathcal{C})$ and outputs $(\mathcal{B}', p_\mathcal{B})$, $(\mathcal{C}', p_\mathcal{C})$ such that: informally,

- $\mathcal{B}'$ and $\mathcal{C}'$ are un-entangled[6].
- The success probability of $\mathcal{B}'$ on guessing H_0 or H_1 is $p_\mathcal{B}$.
- The success probability of $\mathcal{C}'$ on guessing H_0 or H_1 is $p_\mathcal{C}$.
- The expectation of $p_\mathcal{B} \cdot p_\mathcal{C}$ is equal to $(\mathcal{B}, \mathcal{C})$'s success probability in the reprogram game in the independent challenge mode.

The above procedure requires to run $\mathcal{B}'$ and $\mathcal{C}'$ on H and $H_{s,s'}$. In other words, the procedure should be able to reprogram H on the input (s,s'). Since the procedure will be used in the reduction for breaking MOE games for coset states, it should not know s or s', but only knows A and $P_{A+s}, P_{A^\perp+s'}$. Nonetheless, we show with the membership checking oracle, such reprogramming is possible:

$$H_1 = \begin{cases} \neg H(z,z') & Q_s(z) = 1 \text{ and } Q_{s'}(z') = 1 \\ H(z,z') & \text{Otherwise} \end{cases},$$

---

[6] Indeed, $\mathcal{B}'$ and $\mathcal{C}'$ satisfy a weaker guarantee than being un-entangled. They can still be entangled but the same analysis we discuss applies to this weaker guarantee. For ease of presentation, we assume that they are un-entangled.

where Q_s is the point function that only outputs 1 on s, similarly for $Q_{s'}$. The remaining is to show Q_s (or $Q_{s'}$) can be instantiated by the classical description of A and P_{A+s} (or $P_{A^\perp+s'}$ respectively). Q_s can be implemented by (1) check if the input z is in $A + s$, (2) check if the input z is the lexicographically smallest in $A + s$. Step (1) can be done via P_{A+s}. Step (2) can be done by knowing A and some $z \in A + s$ (which is known from step (1)): one can check if there exists some lexicographically smaller z^* such that $(z - z^*) \in \operatorname{span}(A)$; this can be done efficiently by enumerating each coordinate and Gaussian elimination. Thus, both Q_s and $Q_{s'}$ can be implemented.

Without membership checking oracle, we do not know how to reprogram a random oracle, or run the above procedure. Thus the proof fails for Wiesner states.

Finally, we prove the security of reprogram games in the independent challenge mode. If $(\mathcal{A}, \mathcal{B}, \mathcal{C})$ has non-trivial success probability $1/2 + \gamma$ for some large γ, the above procedure must output large $p_\mathcal{B}, p_\mathcal{C} > 1/2 + \gamma/2$ with non-negligible probability. If $\mathcal{B}'$ never queries H_0 or H_1 on (s, s'), the best probability it can achieve is $1/2$. Thus, by measuring a random query of $\mathcal{B}'$, we can extract s, s' with non-negligible probability. Similarly for $\mathcal{C}'$. This violates the MOE games for coset states with membership checking oracles, a contradiction. Therefore, the security of the reprogram in the independent mode is established.

1.5 Related Work

Unclonable Encryption. Broadbent and Lord [9] demonstrated the feasibility of unclonable encryption satisfying the weaker unclonability property. They present two constructions. The first construction based on Wiesner states achieve 0.85^n-security (i.e., the probability that both $\mathcal{B}$ and $\mathcal{C}$ simultaneously guess the message is at most 0.85^n), where n is the length of the message being encrypted. Their second construction, in the quantum random oracle model, achieves $\frac{9}{2^n} + \operatorname{negl}(\lambda)$-security. In the same work, they show that any construction satisfying 2^{-n}-unclonability implies unclonable indistinguishability property. Following Broadbent and Lord, Ananth and Kaleoglu [5] construct public-key and private-key unclonable encryption schemes from computational assumptions. Even [5] only achieve unclonable encryption with the weaker unclonability guarantees.

Majenz, Schaffner and Tahmasbi [16] explore the difficulties in constructing unclonable encryption schemes. In particular, they show that any scheme achieving unclonable indistinguishability should have ciphertexts with large eigenvalues. Towards demonstrating a better bound for unclonability, they also showed inherent limitations in the proof technique of Broadbent and Lord.

Copy-Protection. Copy-protection was first introduced by Aaronson [1]. Recently, Aaronson, Liu, Liu, Zhandry and Zhang [3] demonstrated the existence of copy-protection in the presence of classical oracles. Coladangelo, Majenz and Poremba [11] showed that copy-protection for multi-bit output point functions exists in the quantum random oracle model. They also showed that copy-protection for single-bit output point functions exists in the quantum random oracle model with constant security.

Ananth and La Placa [6] showed a conditional result that copy-protection for arbitrary unlearnable functions, without the use of any oracles, does not exist. Recently, Coladangelo, Liu, Liu and Zhandry [10], assuming post-quantum indistinguishability obfuscation and one-way functions, demonstrated the first feasibility of copy-protection for a non-trivial class of functions (namely, pseudorandom functions) in the plain model. Another recent work by Broadbent, Jeffrey, Lord, Podder and Sundaram [8] studies copy-protection for a novel (but weaker) variant of copy-protection.

2   Preliminaries

2.1   Basics

We will briefly introduce some basic notations in our work and some preliminaries on quantum computing in this section.

We denote by λ the security parameter. We write $\mathsf{poly}(\cdot)$ to denote an arbitrary polynomial and $\mathsf{negl}(\cdot)$ to denote an arbitrary negligible function. We say that an event happens with *overwhelming probability* if the probability is at least $1 - \mathsf{negl}(\lambda)$.

Readers unfamiliar with quantum computation and quantum information could refer to [17] for a comprehensive introduction.

Given Hilbert space $\mathcal{H}$, we write $\mathcal{S}(\mathcal{H})$ for the unit sphere set $\{x : ||x||_2 = 1\}$ in $\mathcal{H}$, $\mathcal{U}(\mathcal{H})$ for the set of unitaries acting on Hilbert space $\mathcal{H}$, $\mathcal{D}(\mathcal{H})$ for the set of density operators on $\mathcal{H}$. We write $\mathcal{H}_X$ to denote the Hilbert space associated with a quantum register X. Given two quantum states ρ, σ, we denote the (normalized) trace distance between them by

$$\mathsf{TD}(\rho, \sigma) := \frac{1}{2} ||\rho - \sigma||_{\mathsf{tr}}.$$

We say that two states ρ, σ are δ-*close* if $\mathsf{TD}(\rho, \sigma) \leq \delta$.

A positive operator-valued measurement (POVM) on the Hilbert space $\mathcal{H}$ is defined as a set of positive semidefinite operators $\{E_i\}$ on $\mathcal{H}$ that satisfies $\sum_i E_i = I$. A projective measurement means the case that E_is are projectors.

A common technique in quantum computation is uncomputing [7]. A quantum algorithm could be modeled as a unitary U acting on some hilbert space $\mathcal{H}$, then perform measurement on output registers on without loss of generality. By uncomputation we mean that acting $U^\dagger$ on the same hilbert space after the measurement. It is easy to examine that if the measurement outputs same result with overwhelming probability, the trace distance between the final state and the original state is negligible.

Quantum Oracle Algorithms. A quantum oracle for a function f is defined as the controlled unitary O_f: $O_f |x\rangle |y\rangle = |x\rangle |y \oplus f(x)\rangle$. We define a query to the quantum oracle as applying O_f on the given quantum state once.

We say that a quantum adversary $\mathcal{A}$ with access to oracle(s) is *query-bounded* if it makes at most $p(\lambda)$ queries to each oracle for some polynomial $p(\cdot)$.

2.2 Quantum Random Oracle Model (QROM)

This is the quantum analogue of Random Oracle Model, where we model a hash function H as a random classical function, and it can be accessed by an adversary in superposition, modeled by the unitary O_H.

The following theorem, paraphrased from [7], will be used for reprogramming oracles without adversarial detection on inputs which are not queried with large weight:

Theorem 5 ([7]). *Let $\mathcal{A}$ be an adversary with oracle access to $H : \{0,1\}^m \to \{0,1\}^n$ that makes at most T queries. Define $|\phi_i\rangle$ as the global state after $\mathcal{A}$ makes i queries, and $W_y(|\phi_i\rangle)$ as the sum of squared amplitudes in $|\phi_i\rangle$ of terms in which $\mathcal{A}$ queries H on input y. Let $\epsilon > 0$ and let $F \subseteq [0, T-1] \times \{0,1\}^m$ be a set of time-string pairs such that $\sum_{(i,y)\in F} W_y(|\phi_i\rangle) \leq \epsilon^2/T$.*

Let H' be an oracle obtained by reprogramming H on inputs $(i,y) \in F$ to arbitrary outputs. Define $|\phi'_i\rangle$ as above for H'. Then, $\mathsf{TD}(|\phi_T\rangle, |\phi'_T\rangle) \leq \epsilon/2$.

Note that the theorem can be straightforwardly generalized to mixed states by convexity.

2.3 More on Jordan's Lemma

We first recall the following version of Jordan's lemma, adapted from [19] and [22]:

Lemma 1. *Let $\mathcal{H}$ be a finite-dimensional Hilbert space and let Π_0, Π_1 be any two projectors in $\mathcal{H}$, then there exists an orthogonal decomposition of $\mathcal{H}$ into one-dimensional and two dimensional subspaces $\mathcal{H} = \oplus_i S_i$ that are invariant under both Π_0 and Π_1; each S_i is spanned by one or two eigenvectors of $(\Pi_0 + \Pi_1)/2$.*

Whenever S_i is 2-dimensional, there is a basis for it in which Π_0 and Π_1 (restricting on S_i) take the form:

$$\Pi_{0,S_i} = \begin{pmatrix} 1 & 0 \\ 0 & 0 \end{pmatrix} \quad and \quad \Pi_{1,S_i} = \begin{pmatrix} c_i^2 & c_i s_i \\ c_i s_i & s_i^2 \end{pmatrix},$$

where $c_i = \cos\theta_i$ and $s_i = \sin\theta_i$ for some principal angle $\theta_i \in [0, \pi/2]$.

Proof. The proof can be found in the references above.

We additionally show a relation between two eigenvalues in the same Jordan block.

Lemma 2. *For any two projectors Π_0, Π_1, let S_i be a 2-dimensional subspace in the above decomposition. Let $|\phi_0\rangle, |\phi_1\rangle$ be two eigenvectors of $(\Pi_0 + \Pi_1)/2$ that span S_i and λ_0, λ_1 be their eigenvalues. We have $\lambda_0 + \lambda_1 = 1$.*

Proof. Restricting on S_i, we have:

$$\lambda_0 + \lambda_1 = \mathrm{Tr}\left[(\Pi_{0,S_i} + \Pi_{1,S_i})/2\right] = (1 + c_i^2 + s_i^2)/2 = 1.$$

Corollary 1. *For any two projectors Π_0, Π_1, let $|\phi_0\rangle$ and $|\phi_1\rangle$ be two eigenvectors of $(\Pi_0 + \Pi_1)/2$ with eigenvalues λ_0, λ_1. If $\lambda_0 + \lambda_1 \neq 1$, then*

$$\langle\phi_0|\Pi_0|\phi_1\rangle = \langle\phi_0|\Pi_1|\phi_1\rangle = 0.$$

Proof. If $\lambda_0 + \lambda_1 \neq 1$, by Lemma 2, $|\phi_0\rangle$ and $|\phi_1\rangle$ can not be in the same Jordan block. Because $|\phi_0\rangle$ still belongs to the corresponding subspace S_0 of its Jordan block after the action of Π_0, $\Pi_0|\phi_0\rangle$ is orthogonal to $|\phi_1\rangle$. Similarly, $\Pi_1|\phi_0\rangle$ is orthogonal to $|\phi_1\rangle$.

2.4 Measuring Success Probability

In this section we list theorems about simultaneously approximating the eigenvalues of a bipartite quantum program which are crucial tools in our security proofs.

Theorem 6 (Inefficient Measurement). *Let $\mathcal{P} = (P, Q)$ be a binary outcome POVM. Let $\mathcal{D}$ be the set of eigenvalues of P. There exists a projective measurement $\mathcal{E} = \{E_p\}_{p \in \mathcal{D}}$ with index set $\mathcal{D}$ that satisfies the following: for every quantum state ρ, let ρ_p be the sub-normalized post-measurement state obtained after measuring ρ with respect to E_p. That is, $\rho_p = E_p \rho E_p$. We have,*

(1) For every $p \in \mathcal{D}$, ρ_p is an eigenvector of P with eigenvalue p;
(2) The probability of ρ when measured with respect to P is $\mathrm{Tr}[P\rho] = \sum_{p \in \mathcal{D}} \mathrm{Tr}[P\rho_p]$.

A measurement $\mathcal{E}$ which satisfies these properties is the measurement in the common eigenbasis of P and $Q = I - P$ (due to simultaneous diagonalization theorem, such common eigenbasis exists since P and Q commute). Let P have eigenbasis $\{|\psi_i\rangle\}$ with eigenvalues $\{\lambda_i\}$. Without loss of generality, let us assume ρ is a pure state $|\psi\rangle\langle\psi|$ and $\{\lambda_i\}$ has no duplicated eigenvalues. We write $|\psi\rangle$ in the eigenbasis of P: $|\psi\rangle = \sum_i \alpha_i |\psi_i\rangle$. Applying $\mathcal{E}$ will result in an outcome λ_i and a leftover state $|\psi_i\rangle$ with probability $|\alpha_i|^2$.

Looking ahead, we will write a quantum program under the eigenbasis of P in the proof of the strengthened MOE game.

Theorem 7 (Inefficient Threshold Measurement). *Let $\mathcal{P} = (P, Q)$ be a binary outcome POVM. Let P have eigenbasis $\{|\psi_i\rangle\}$ with eigenvalues $\{\lambda_i\}$. Then, for every $\gamma \in (0, 1)$ there exists a projective measurement $\mathcal{E}_\gamma = (E_{\leq\gamma}, E_{>\gamma})$ such that:*

(1) $E_{\leq\gamma}$ projects a quantum state into the subspace spanned by $\{|\psi_i\rangle\}$ whose eigenvalues λ_i satisfy $\lambda_i \leq \gamma$;

(2) $E_{>\gamma}$ projects a quantum state into the subspace spanned by $\{|\psi_i\rangle\}$ whose eigenvalues λ_i satisfy $\lambda_i > \gamma$.

Similarly, for every $\gamma \in (0, 1/2)$, there exists a projective measurement $\mathcal{E}'_\gamma = (\widetilde{E}_{\leq \gamma}, \widetilde{E}_{>\gamma})$ such that:

(1) $\widetilde{E}_{\leq \gamma}$ projects a quantum state into the subspace spanned by $\{|\psi_i\rangle\}$ whose eigenvalues λ_i satisfy $|\lambda_i - \frac{1}{2}| \leq \gamma$;
(2) $\widetilde{E}_{>\gamma}$ projects a quantum state into the subspace spanned by $\{|\psi_i\rangle\}$ whose eigenvalues λ_i satisfy $|\lambda_i - \frac{1}{2}| > \gamma$.

It is easy to see how to construct $\mathcal{E}_\gamma, \mathcal{E}'_\gamma$ from $\mathcal{E}$, e.g. by setting

$$\widetilde{E}_{\leq \gamma} = \sum_{i:|\lambda_i - 1/2| \leq \gamma} E_{\lambda_i}.$$

Note that for any quantum state ρ, $\mathrm{Tr}[\widetilde{E}_{>\gamma}\rho]$ is the weight over eigenvectors with eigenvalues λ that are γ away from $1/2$.

Below, we give the formal theorem statement about efficient approximated threshold measurement, which is adapted from Theorem 6.2 in [26] and Lemma 3 in [3].

Theorem 8 (Efficient Threshold Measurement). *Let $\mathcal{P}_b = (P_b, Q_b)$ be a binary outcome POVM over Hilbert space $\mathcal{H}_b$ that is a mixture of projective measurements for $b \in \{1, 2\}$. Let P_b have eigenbasis $\{|\psi_i^b\rangle\}$ with eigenvalues $\{\lambda_i^b\}$. For every $\gamma_1, \gamma_2 \in (0, 1), 0 < \epsilon < \min(\gamma_1/2, \gamma_2/2, 1 - \gamma_1, 1 - \gamma_2)$ and $\delta > 0$, there exist efficient binary-outcome quantum algorithms, interpreted as the POVM element corresponding to outcome 1, $\mathsf{ATI}_{\mathcal{P}_b, \gamma}^{\epsilon, \delta}$ such that for every quantum program $\rho \in \mathcal{D}(\mathcal{H}_1) \otimes \mathcal{D}(\mathcal{H}_2)$ the following are true about the product algorithm $\mathsf{ATI}_{\mathcal{P}_1, \gamma_1}^{\epsilon, \delta} \otimes \mathsf{ATI}_{\mathcal{P}_2, \gamma_2}^{\epsilon, \delta}$:*

(0) *Let $(E_{\leq \gamma}^b, E_{>\gamma}^b)$ be the inefficient threshold measurement in Theorem 7 for $\mathcal{H}_b$.*
(1) *The probability of measuring 1 on both registers satisfies*

$$\mathrm{Tr}\left[\left(\mathsf{ATI}_{\mathcal{P}_1, \gamma_1}^{\epsilon, \delta} \otimes \mathsf{ATI}_{\mathcal{P}_2, \gamma_2}^{\epsilon, \delta}\right) \rho\right] \geq \mathrm{Tr}\left[\left(E_{>\gamma_1 + \epsilon}^1 \otimes E_{>\gamma_2 + \epsilon}^2\right) \cdot \rho\right] - 2\delta.$$

(2) *The post-measurement state ρ' after getting outcome $(1, 1)$ is 4δ-close to a state in the support of $\{|\psi_i^1\rangle |\psi_j^2\rangle\}$ such that $\lambda_i^1 > \gamma_1 - 2\epsilon$ and $\lambda_j^2 > \gamma_2 - 2\epsilon$.*
(3) *The running time of the algorithm is polynomial in the running time of $P_1, P_2, 1/\epsilon$ and $\log(1/\delta)$.*

Intuitively the theorem says that if a quantum state ρ has weight p on eigenvectors of (P_1, P_2) with eigenvalues greater than $(\gamma_1 + \epsilon, \gamma_2 + \epsilon)$, then the quantum algorithm will produce (with probability at least $p - 2\delta$) a post-measurement state which has weight $1 - 4\delta$ on eigenvectors with eigenvalues greater than $(\gamma_1 - 2\epsilon, \gamma_2 - 2\epsilon)$.

In this paper, we will work with indistinguishability games. Therefore, we will particularly be interested in the projective measurement that projects onto eigenvectors with eigenvalues away from $1/2$ (meaning its behavior is more than random guessing). For this reason, we will need the following symmetric version of Theorem 8:

Theorem 9 (Efficient Symmetric Threshold Measurement). *Let $\mathcal{P}_b = (P_b, Q_b)$ be a binary outcome POVM over Hilbert space $\mathcal{H}_b$ that is a mixture of projective measurements for $b \in \{1, 2\}$. Let P_b have eigenbasis $\{|\psi_i^b\rangle\}$ with eigenvalues $\{\lambda_i^b\}$. For every $\gamma_1, \gamma_2 \in (0, 1/2), 0 < \epsilon < \min(\gamma_1/2, \gamma_2/2)$, and $\delta > 0$, there exist efficient binary-outcome quantum algorithms, interpreted as the POVM element corresponding to outcome 1, $\mathsf{SATI}_{\mathcal{P}_b, \gamma}^{\epsilon, \delta}$ such that for every quantum program $\rho \in \mathcal{D}(\mathcal{H}_1) \otimes \mathcal{D}(\mathcal{H}_2)$ the following are true about the product algorithm $\mathsf{SATI}_{\mathcal{P}_1, \gamma_1}^{\epsilon, \delta} \otimes \mathsf{SATI}_{\mathcal{P}_2, \gamma_2}^{\epsilon, \delta}$:*

(0) Let $(\widetilde{E}_{\leq \gamma_b}^b, \widetilde{E}_{>\gamma_b}^b)$ be the inefficient threshold measurement in Theorem 7 for $\mathcal{H}_b$.

(1) The probability of measuring 1 on both registers satisfies

$$\mathrm{Tr}\left[\left(\mathsf{SATI}_{\mathcal{P}_1, \gamma_1}^{\epsilon, \delta} \otimes \mathsf{SATI}_{\mathcal{P}_2, \gamma_2}^{\epsilon, \delta}\right) \rho\right] \geq \mathrm{Tr}\left[\left(\widetilde{E}_{>\gamma_1+\epsilon}^1 \otimes \widetilde{E}_{>\gamma_2+\epsilon}^2\right) \cdot \rho\right] - 2\delta.$$

(2) The post-measurement state ρ' after getting outcome (1,1) is 4δ-close to a state in the support of $\{|\psi_i^1\rangle |\psi_j^2\rangle\}$ such that $|\lambda_i^1 - 1/2| > \gamma_1 - 2\epsilon$ and $|\lambda_j^2 - 1/2| > \gamma_2 - 2\epsilon$.

(3) The running time of the algorithm is polynomial in the running time of P_1, P_2, $1/\epsilon$ and $\log(1/\delta)$.

2.5 Unclonable Encryption

In this subsection, we provide the definition of unclonable encryption schemes. By unclonable encryption, we are referring to the security defined in [5]. This is a variant of the original security definition in [9], which forces one of m_0, m_1 to be uniformly random. We would remark that our security is stronger than the original one in [9], since in our definition m_0, m_1 can be arbitrarily chosen.

Definition 1. *An unclonable encryption scheme is a triple of efficient quantum algorithms* (Gen, Enc, Dec) *with the following interface:*

- Gen(1^λ) : sk *on input a security parameter 1^λ, returns a classical key* sk.
- Enc(sk, $|m\rangle \langle m|$) : ρ_{ct} *takes the key* sk *and the message $|m\rangle \langle m|$ for $m \in \{0, 1\}^{\mathrm{poly}(\lambda)}$, outputs a quantum ciphertext ρ_{ct}.*
- Dec(sk, ρ_{ct}) : ρ_m *takes the key* sk *and the quantum ciphertext ρ_{ct}, outputs a message in the form of quantum states ρ_m.*

Correctness. The following must hold for the encryption scheme. For sk $\leftarrow$ Gen(1^λ), *we must have* $\mathrm{Tr}[|m\rangle \langle m| \mathsf{Dec}(\mathsf{sk}, \mathsf{Enc}(\mathsf{sk}, |m\rangle \langle m|))] \geq 1 - \mathsf{negl}(\lambda)$.

Unclonability. In the following sections, we focus on unclonable IND-CPA security. To define our unclonable security, we introduce the following security game.

Definition 2 (Unclonable IND-CPA game). *Let $\lambda \in \mathbb{N}^+$. Given encryption scheme $\mathcal{S}$, consider the following game against the adversary $(\mathcal{A}, \mathcal{B}, \mathcal{C})$.*

- *The adversary $\mathcal{A}$ generates $m_0, m_1 \in \{0,1\}^{n(\lambda)}$ and sends to the challenger as the chosen plaintext.*
- *The challenger randomly chooses a bit $b \in \{0,1\}$ and returns $\mathsf{Enc}(\mathsf{sk}, m_b)$ to $\mathcal{A}$. $\mathcal{A}$ produces a quantum state ρ_{BC} in register B and C, and sends corresponding registers to $\mathcal{B}$ and $\mathcal{C}$.*
- *$\mathcal{B}$ and $\mathcal{C}$ receive the key sk, and output bits $b_{\mathcal{B}}$ and $b_{\mathcal{C}}$ respectively*

and the adversary wins if $b_{\mathcal{B}} = b_{\mathcal{C}} = b$.

We denote the advantage (success probability) of above game by $\mathsf{adv}_{\mathcal{G},\mathcal{A},\mathcal{B},\mathcal{C}}(\lambda)$. We say that scheme $\mathcal{S}$ is informational (computational) secure if for all(efficient) adversaries $(\mathcal{G}, \mathcal{A}, \mathcal{B}, \mathcal{C})$,

$$\mathsf{adv}_{\mathcal{G},\mathcal{A},\mathcal{B},\mathcal{C}}(\lambda) \le \frac{1}{2} + \mathsf{negl}(\lambda).$$

3 More on Coset States

In this section, we will recall the basic properties of coset states. We will then introduce a strengthened unclonable game in the quantum random oracle model (QROM), upon which we will build our unclonable encryption scheme. The last subsection is devoted to prove the security of this strengthened game.

3.1 Preliminaries

In this subsection, we recall the basic definitions and properties of coset states in [10]. Let $A \subseteq \mathbb{F}_2^n$ be a subspace. Define its orthogonal complement of A as $A^\perp = \{b \in \mathbb{F}_2^n \mid \langle a, b \rangle \bmod 2 = 0, \forall a \in A\}$. It satisfies $\dim(A) + \dim(A^\perp) = n$. We also let $|A| = 2^{\dim(A)}$ denote the size of A.

Definition 3 (Coset States). *For any subspace $A \subseteq \mathbb{F}_2^n$ and vectors $s, s' \in \mathbb{F}_2^n$, the coset state $|A_{s,s'}\rangle$ is defined as:*

$$|A_{s,s'}\rangle = \frac{1}{\sqrt{|A|}} \sum_{a \in A} (-1)^{\langle s', a \rangle} |a + s\rangle.$$

By applying $H^{\otimes n}$ to the state $|A_{s,s'}\rangle$, one obtains exactly $|A_{s',s}^\perp\rangle$. Given A, s, s', the coset state is efficiently constructable.

For a subspace A and vectors s, s', we define $A + s = \{v + s : v \in A\}$, and $A^\perp + s' = \{v + s' : v \in A^\perp\}$. We define P_{A+s} and $P_{A^\perp+s'}$ as the membership checking oracle for both cosets.

It is also convenient for later sections to define a canonical representation of a coset $A + s$, with respect to subspace A,

Definition 4 (Canonical Representative of a Coset). *For a subspace A, we define the function $\mathsf{Can}_A(\cdot)$ such that $\mathsf{Can}_A(s)$ is the lexicographically smallest vector contained in $A + s$. We call this the canonical representative of coset $A + s$.*

If $\tilde{s} \in A + s$, then $\mathsf{Can}_A(s) = \mathsf{Can}_A(\tilde{s})$. We also note that $\mathsf{Can}_A(\cdot)$ is polynomial-time computable given the description of A. Accordingly, we can efficiently sample from $\mathsf{CS}(A) := \{\mathsf{Can}_A(s) : s \in \mathbb{F}_2^n\}$, which denotes the set of canonical representatives for A.

For a fixed subspace A, the coset states $\{|A_{s,s'}\rangle\}_{s \in \mathsf{CS}(A), s' \in \mathsf{CS}(A^\perp)}$ form an orthonormal basis. (See Lemma C.2 in [10])

Next, we recall the regular direct product and MOE properties of coset states. These properties will be used to prove the strengthened unclonable property.

Direct Product Hardness

Theorem 10 (Theorem 4.5, 4.6 in [10]). *Let $A \subseteq \mathbb{F}_2^\lambda$ be a uniformly random subspace of dimension $\frac{\lambda}{2}$, and s, s' be two uniformly random vectors from $\mathbb{F}_2^\lambda$. Let $\epsilon > 0$ such that $1/\epsilon = o(2^{n/2})$. Given one copy of $|A_{s,s'}\rangle$ and oracle access to P_{A+s} and $P_{A^\perp+s'}$, an adversary needs $\Omega(\sqrt{\epsilon}2^{\lambda/2})$ queries to output a pair (v, w) that $v \in A + s$ and $w \in A^\perp + s'$ with probability at least ϵ.*

An important corollary immediately follows.

Corollary 2. *There exists an exponential function exp such that, for any query-bounded (polynomially many queries to $P_{A+s}, P_{A^\perp+s'}$) adversary, its probability to output a pair (v, w) that $v \in A + s$ and $w \in A^\perp + s'$ is smaller than $1/\exp(\lambda)$.*

Monogamy-of-Entanglement (with Membership Checking Oracles).

Definition 5. *Let $\lambda \in \mathbb{N}^+$. Consider the following game between a challenger and an adversary $(\mathcal{A}, \mathcal{B}, \mathcal{C})$.*

- *The challenger picks a uniformly random subspace $A \subseteq \mathbb{F}_2^\lambda$ of dimension $\frac{\lambda}{2}$, and uniformly random vectors $(s, s') \in \mathsf{CS}(A) \times \mathsf{CS}(A^\perp)$. It sends $|A_{s,s'}\rangle$ to $\mathcal{A}$.*
- *$\mathcal{A}, \mathcal{B}, \mathcal{C}$ get (quantum) oracle access to P_{A+s} and $P_{A^\perp+s'}$.*
- *$\mathcal{A}$ creates a bipartite state on registers B and C. Then, $\mathcal{A}$ sends register B to $\mathcal{B}$, and C to $\mathcal{C}$.*
- *The description of A is then sent to both $\mathcal{B}, \mathcal{C}$.*
- *$\mathcal{B}$ and $\mathcal{C}$ return respectively (s_1, s'_1) and (s_2, s'_2).*

$(\mathcal{A}, \mathcal{B}, \mathcal{C})$ wins if and only if for $i \in \{1, 2\}$, $s_i = s$ and $s'_i = s'$.

We denote the advantage (success probability) of the above game by $\mathsf{adv}_{\mathcal{A}, \mathcal{B}, \mathcal{C}}(\lambda)$. We have the following theorem.

Theorem 11 (Theorem 4.14, 4.15 in [10]). *There exists an exponential function exp such that, for every $\lambda \in \mathbb{N}^+$, for any query-bounded (polynomially many queries to $P_{A+s}, P_{A^\perp+s'}$) adversary $(\mathcal{A}, \mathcal{B}, \mathcal{C})$,*

$$\mathsf{adv}_{\mathcal{A}, \mathcal{B}, \mathcal{C}}(\lambda) \leq 1/\exp(\lambda).$$

Note that in [10], the authors only proved the above theorem for a sub-exponential function and membership checking oracles are given in the form of indistinguishability obfuscation (iO). The proof trivially holds if we replace iO with VBB obfuscation (quantum access to these oracles). Culf and Vidick [12] further proved the theorem holds for an exponential function.

3.2 Strengthened MOE Game in the QROM

In this subsection, we will introduce the strengthened MOE game in the QROM and state our main theorem. We present the proof in the next section.

Definition 6. *Let $\lambda \in \mathbb{N}^+$. Consider the following security game between a challenger and an adversary $(\mathcal{A}, \mathcal{B}, \mathcal{C})$ with a random oracle $H : \mathbb{F}_2^\lambda \times \mathbb{F}_2^\lambda \to \{0,1\}^{n(\lambda)}$.*

- *The adversary $\mathcal{A}$ generates $\Delta \in \{0,1\}^{n(\lambda)}$ and sends Δ to the challenger.*
- *The challenger samples a random subspace $A \subseteq \mathbb{F}_2^\lambda$ of dimension $\lambda/2$ and two random vectors $(s, s') \in \mathsf{CS}(A) \times \mathsf{CS}(A^\perp)$. The challenger also randomly chooses a bit $b \in \{0,1\}$ and calculates $w = H(s, s') \oplus (b \cdot \Delta)$. It gives $|A_{s,s'}\rangle$ and w to $\mathcal{A}$.*
- *$\mathcal{A}, \mathcal{B}, \mathcal{C}$ get (quantum) oracle access to P_{A+s} and $P_{A^\perp + s'}$.*
- *$\mathcal{A}$ produces a quantum state over registers BC and sends B to $\mathcal{B}$ and C to $\mathcal{C}$.*
- *$\mathcal{B}, \mathcal{C}$ are given the description of A, they try to produce bits $b_\mathcal{B}, b_\mathcal{C}$.*

$(\mathcal{A}, \mathcal{B}, \mathcal{C})$ win if and only if $b_\mathcal{B} = b_\mathcal{C} = b$.

We denote the advantage of the above game by $\mathsf{adv}_{\mathcal{A},\mathcal{B},\mathcal{C}}(\lambda)$. Note that since s, s' is defined as the canonical vector of both cosets, they are uniquely defined; similarly, $H(s, s')$ is also uniquely defined.

We show the following theorem:

Theorem 12. *Let $n = \Omega(\lambda)$, then for every $\lambda \in \mathbb{N}^+$ and all query-bounded algorithms $(\mathcal{A}, \mathcal{B}, \mathcal{C})$, $\mathsf{adv}_{\mathcal{A},\mathcal{B},\mathcal{C}}(\lambda) \leq \frac{1}{2} + \mathsf{negl}(\lambda)$.*

3.3 Proof for Theorem 12

Proof. We prove the theorem by following hybrid arguments.

Hybrid 0 *This hybrid is the original game.*

Hybrid 1 *This hybrid follows Hybrid 0, but the oracle of $\mathcal{A}$ will be reprogrammed as $H_{s,s'}$ defined as follows:*

$$H_{s,s'}(z, z') = \begin{cases} u & \text{if } z = s, z' = s' \\ H(z, z') & \text{otherwise} \end{cases},$$

where $u \in \{0,1\}^n$ is chosen uniformly at random.

Hybrid 2 *This hybrid will modify the access to random oracle of $\mathcal{B}$ and $\mathcal{C}$.*

- *The adversary $\mathcal{A}$ generates $\Delta \in \{0,1\}^{n(\lambda)}$ and sends Δ to the challenger.*

- *The challenger samples a random subspace $A \subseteq \mathbb{F}_2^\lambda$ of dimension $\lambda/2$ and two random vectors $(s, s') \in \mathsf{CS}(A) \times \mathsf{CS}(A^\perp)$. The challenger uniform randomly samples a bit $b \in \{0, 1\}$ and $r \in \{0, 1\}^{n(\lambda)}$, and defines the oracle $H_{s,s'}^b$ as follows:*

$$H_{s,s'}^b(z, z') = \begin{cases} r \oplus (b \cdot \Delta) & \text{if } z = s, z' = s' \\ H(z, z') & \text{otherwise} \end{cases},$$

  It gives $|A_{s,s'}\rangle$ and r to $\mathcal{A}$.
- *$\mathcal{A}, \mathcal{B}, \mathcal{C}$ get (quantum) oracle access to P_{A+s} and $P_{A^\perp + s'}$.*
- *With access to quantum random oracle $H_{s,s'}$, $\mathcal{A}$ produces a quantum state over registers BC and sends B to $\mathcal{B}$ and C to $\mathcal{C}$.*
- *With access to quantum random oracle $H_{s,s'}^b$, $\mathcal{B}, \mathcal{C}$ are given the description of A, they try to produce bits $b_\mathcal{B}, b_\mathcal{C}$.*

$(\mathcal{A}, \mathcal{B}, \mathcal{C})$ win if and only if $b_\mathcal{B} = b_\mathcal{C} = b$.

We denote by p_i the optimal success probability of the game in **Hybrid i**. For the relations between different p_i, we have following lemmas:

Lemma 3. $|p_0 - p_1| \leq \mathsf{negl}(\lambda)$.

Lemma 4. $p_1 = p_2$.

Lemma 5. $p_2 \leq \frac{1}{2} + \mathsf{negl}(\lambda)$.

Combining the three lemmas, we have completed the proof of Theorem 12.
    Now we provide proofs for lemmas beyond.

Proof for Lemma 3. We prove by contradiction. Suppose $p_0 \geq p_1 + 1/q(\lambda)$ for some polynomial $q(\lambda)$, then we can construct an adversary $\mathcal{A}'$ that violates the direct product hardness of coset states. $\mathcal{A}'$ will perform as follows:

- *$\mathcal{A}'$ samples a random oracle $H : \mathbb{F}_2^\lambda \times \mathbb{F}_2^\lambda \to \{0, 1\}^{n(\lambda)}$.*
- *$\mathcal{A}'$ simulates $\mathcal{A}$ using H and applies computational basis measurement on a random quantum query made by $\mathcal{A}$ to the random oracle.*

By Theorem 5, assuming $\mathcal{A}$ makes at most T queries, then $\mathcal{A}'$ gets (s, s') with probability at least $4/(q^2 T)$, a contradiction to Corollary 2.

Proof for Lemma 4. Fixing Δ and b, the two games are identical by renaming the $w = H(s, s') \oplus (b \cdot \Delta)$ to r. Since $H(s, s')$ is uniformly random, its distribution is identical to r.

Proof for Lemma 5. Fixing A, r, Δ, two canonical vectors s, s', let $H_{-s,s'}$ be a partial random oracle that is defined on every input except (s, s'). Fix any partial random oracle $H_{-s,s'}$,
    we define two *projectors* Π_0^B, Π_1^B over register B as:

- Π_0^B: runs $\mathcal{B}$ on input A with oracle access to $H_{s,s'}^0$ where $H_{s,s'}^0$ is the same as $H_{-s,s'}$ except on input (s, s') it outputs r; it measures if the outcome is r; then it undoes all the computation.
- Π_1^B: similar to Π_0^B except on input (s, s'), the random oracle $H_{s,s'}^1$ outputs $r \oplus \Delta$ and it checks if the outcome is $r \oplus \Delta$.

Let $\{|\phi_i\rangle\}_i$ be a set of the eigenvectors of $(\Pi_0^B + \Pi_1^B)/2$ with eigenvalues $\{\lambda_i\}_i$.

Fixing the same A, s, s', r and $H_{-s,s'}$, we can similarly define Π_0^C, Π_1^C for $\mathcal{C}$. Let $\{|\psi_j\rangle\}_j$ be a set of the eigenvectors of $(\Pi_0^C + \Pi_1^C)/2$ with eigenvalues $\{\mu_j\}_j$.

Let $|\phi_{\mathsf{BC}}\rangle$ be the state prepared by $\mathcal{A}$. Without loss of generality, we can assume the state is pure. We write the state under the basis $\{|\phi_i\rangle\}_i$ and $\{|\psi_j\rangle\}_j$:

$$|\phi_{\mathsf{BC}}\rangle = \sum_{i,j} \alpha_{i,j} |\phi_i\rangle_{\mathsf{B}} \otimes |\psi_j\rangle_{\mathsf{C}}.$$

Lemma 6. *Taken the randomness of A, s, s' and $H_{-s,s'}$, for every polynomial $p(\cdot)$, there exists a negligible function negl such that with overwhelming probability the following weight is bounded:*

$$\sum_{\substack{i:\, |\lambda_i - 1/2| > 1/p \\ j:\, |\mu_j - 1/2| > 1/p}} |\alpha_{i,j}|^2 \leq \mathsf{negl}(n).$$

The proof for this lemma is given at the end of this section.

With the above lemma, we can claim that over the randomness of A, s, s' and $H_{-s,s'}$, for every polynomial $p(\cdot)$, $|\phi_{\mathsf{BC}}\rangle$ is negligibly close to the following state $|\phi_{\mathsf{BC}}'\rangle$:

$$\sum_{i:\, |\lambda_i - 1/2| \leq 1/p} \alpha_{i,j} |\phi_i\rangle_{\mathsf{B}} \otimes |\psi_j\rangle_{\mathsf{C}} + \sum_{\substack{i:\, |\lambda_i - 1/2| > 1/p \\ j:\, |\mu_j - 1/2| \leq 1/p}} \alpha_{i,j} |\phi_i\rangle_{\mathsf{B}} \otimes |\psi_j\rangle_{\mathsf{C}}.$$

For convenience, we name the left part as $|\phi_{\mathcal{B}}'\rangle$ (indicating $\mathcal{B}$ can not win) and the right part as $|\phi_{\mathcal{C}}'\rangle$ (indicating $\mathcal{C}$ can not win). Thus, for every polynomial $p(\cdot)$, there exists a negligible function $\mathsf{negl}(\cdot)$, $||\phi_{\mathsf{BC}}\rangle - (|\phi_{\mathcal{B}}'\rangle + |\phi_{\mathcal{C}}'\rangle)||_1$ is at most $\mathsf{negl}(\cdot)$ (in expectation, taken the randomness of A, s, s', r and $H_{-s,s'}$).

The probability that $(\mathcal{A}, \mathcal{B}, \mathcal{C})$ wins is at most:

$$(|(\Pi_0^B \otimes \Pi_0^C) |\phi_{\mathsf{BC}}'\rangle|^2 + |(\Pi_1^B \otimes \Pi_1^C) |\phi_{\mathsf{BC}}'\rangle|^2)/2.$$

$\Pi_0^B \otimes \Pi_0^C$ is the case that they both get access to H_0 and $\Pi_1^B \otimes \Pi_1^C$ for H_1.

The probability is at most

$$\left(\left|(\Pi_0^B \otimes \Pi_0^C)(|\phi_{\mathcal{B}}'\rangle + |\phi_{\mathcal{C}}'\rangle)\right|^2 + \left|(\Pi_1^B \otimes \Pi_1^C)(|\phi_{\mathcal{B}}'\rangle + |\phi_{\mathcal{C}}'\rangle)\right|^2\right)/2$$

$$= \frac{1}{2} \cdot \left(\langle\phi_{\mathcal{B}}'|(\Pi_0^B \otimes \Pi_0^C)|\phi_{\mathcal{B}}'\rangle + \langle\phi_{\mathcal{B}}'|(\Pi_1^B \otimes \Pi_1^C)|\phi_{\mathcal{B}}'\rangle + \langle\phi_{\mathcal{C}}'|(\Pi_0^B \otimes \Pi_0^C)|\phi_{\mathcal{C}}'\rangle\right.$$

$$\left. + \langle\phi_{\mathcal{C}}'|(\Pi_1^B \otimes \Pi_1^C)|\phi_{\mathcal{C}}'\rangle\right) + \mathsf{Re}\left(\langle\phi_{\mathcal{B}}'|(\Pi_0^B \otimes \Pi_0^C)|\phi_{\mathcal{C}}'\rangle + \langle\phi_{\mathcal{B}}'|(\Pi_1^B \otimes \Pi_1^C)|\phi_{\mathcal{C}}'\rangle\right)$$

$$\leq \frac{1}{2} \cdot \left(\langle\phi_{\mathcal{B}}'|(\Pi_0^B \otimes I)|\phi_{\mathcal{B}}'\rangle + \langle\phi_{\mathcal{B}}'|(\Pi_1^B \otimes I)|\phi_{\mathcal{B}}'\rangle + \langle\phi_{\mathcal{C}}'|(I \otimes \Pi_0^C)|\phi_{\mathcal{C}}'\rangle\right.$$

$$\left. + \langle\phi_{\mathcal{C}}'|(I \otimes \Pi_1^C)|\phi_{\mathcal{C}}'\rangle\right) + \mathsf{Re}\left(\langle\phi_{\mathcal{B}}'|(\Pi_0^B \otimes \Pi_0^C)|\phi_{\mathcal{C}}'\rangle + \langle\phi_{\mathcal{B}}'|(\Pi_1^B \otimes \Pi_1^C)|\phi_{\mathcal{C}}'\rangle\right).$$

We bound each term separately.

- $\frac{1}{2}\left(\langle\phi_{\mathcal{B}}'|(\Pi_0^B \otimes I)|\phi_{\mathcal{B}}'\rangle + \langle\phi_{\mathcal{B}}'|(\Pi_1^B \otimes I)|\phi_{\mathcal{B}}'\rangle\right)$. It is equal to $\langle\phi_{\mathcal{B}}'|(\Pi_0^B + \Pi_1^B)/2 \otimes I|\phi_{\mathcal{B}}'\rangle$; by the definition of $|\phi_{\mathcal{B}}'\rangle$, it will be at most $(\frac{1}{2} + \frac{1}{p})|\,|\phi_{\mathcal{B}}'\rangle\,|^2$.
- $\frac{1}{2}\left(\langle\phi_{\mathcal{C}}'|(I \otimes \Pi_0^C)|\phi_{\mathcal{C}}'\rangle + \langle\phi_{\mathcal{C}}'|(I \otimes \Pi_1^C)|\phi_{\mathcal{C}}'\rangle\right)$. Similar to the above case, it is at most $(\frac{1}{2} + \frac{1}{p})|\,|\phi_{\mathcal{C}}'\rangle\,|^2$.
- $\mathsf{Re}\left(\langle\phi_{\mathcal{B}}'|(\Pi_0^B \otimes \Pi_0^C)|\phi_{\mathcal{C}}'\rangle\right)$. By Corollary 1, the inner product will be 0:

$$\langle\phi_{\mathcal{B}}'|(\Pi_0^B \otimes \Pi_0^C)|\phi_{\mathcal{C}}'\rangle$$
$$= \sum_{\substack{i:|\lambda_i - 1/2| \leq 1/p}} \sum_{\substack{i':|\lambda_{i'} - 1/2| > 1/p \\ j':|\mu_{j'} - 1/2| \leq 1/p}} \alpha_{i,j}^\dagger \alpha_{i',j'} \langle\phi_i|\Pi_0^B|\phi_{i'}\rangle \langle\psi_j|\Pi_0^C|\psi_{j'}\rangle;$$

since every possible i, i' satisfy $\lambda_i + \lambda_{i'} \neq 1$, we have $\langle\phi_i|\Pi_0^B|\phi_{i'}\rangle = 0$.
- $\mathsf{Re}\left(\langle\phi_{\mathcal{B}}'|(\Pi_1^B \otimes \Pi_1^C)|\phi_{\mathcal{C}}'\rangle\right)$. By Corollary 1, the inner product will be 0 as well.

Therefore, the total probability will be at most $\left(\frac{1}{2} + \frac{1}{p}\right)(|\,|\phi_{\mathcal{B}}'\rangle\,|^2 + |\,|\phi_{\mathcal{C}}'\rangle\,|^2) +$ $\mathsf{negl}(n) \leq \frac{1}{2} + \frac{1}{p} + \mathsf{negl}(n)$.

Since the above statement holds for every polynomial $p(\cdot)$, it finishes the proof for Theorem 12.

Finally, we give the proof for Lemma 6.

Proof of Lemma 6. We prove by contradiction: suppose there exists an adversary $(\mathcal{A}, \mathcal{B}, \mathcal{C})$ such that the weight, which we call W, is non-negligible, i.e. $W > 1/q(\lambda)$ for some polynomial $q(\cdot)$, with some non-negligible probability $\eta(\lambda)$. For convenience, we will omit λ in the proof when it is clear from the context.

We construct the following adversary $(\mathcal{A}', \mathcal{B}', \mathcal{C}')$ that breaks the regular MOE game in Definition 5:

1. $\mathcal{A}', \mathcal{B}', \mathcal{C}'$ get (quantum) oracle access to P_{A+s} and $P_{A^\perp + s'}$.
2. $\mathcal{A}'$ first receives Δ from simulated $\mathcal{A}$, it samples $r \in \{0,1\}^{n(\lambda)}$ and a random oracle H. Given $|A_{s,s'}\rangle$, r and two membership checking oracles, it simulates $\mathcal{A}$ via reprogrammed $H_{s,s'}$, and produces $|\phi_{BC}\rangle$; it gives B to $\mathcal{B}'$ and C to $\mathcal{C}'$. Note that, although H is a total random oracle, we will later reprogram H at the input (s, s'). Thus, H will only serve as $H_{-s,s'}$. Since $\mathcal{A}'$ does not know (s, s'), it is hard for $\mathcal{A}'$ to only sample $H_{-s,s'}$.

3. Define two projectors Π_0^B, Π_1^B over register B as what we have described at the beginning of the proof, with the random oracle $H_{s,s'}^0$ and $H_{s,s'}^1$ is defined as:

$$H_{s,s'}^0(z,z') = \begin{cases} r & \text{if } z = s, z' = s' \\ H(z,z') & \text{otherwise} \end{cases},$$

and

$$H_{s,s'}^1(z,z') = \begin{cases} r \oplus \Delta & \text{if } z = s, z' = s' \\ H(z,z') & \text{otherwise} \end{cases}.$$

Given $P_{A+s}, P_{A^\perp+s'}$ and the description of A, one can efficiently implement point functions that check the canonical vectors s and s'; thus, additionally given H, $H_{s,s'}^0$ and $H_{s,s'}^1$ can also be efficiently simulated. Therefore, $\mathcal{B}'$ can implement both Π_0^B, Π_1^B efficiently.

$\mathcal{B}'$ gets B, it applies the efficient approximate threshold measurement $\mathsf{SATI}_{(P,Q),\gamma}^{\epsilon,\delta}$ in Theorem 9 with $P = (\Pi_0^B + \Pi_1^B)/2$, $Q = I - P$, $\gamma = 3/4p$, $\epsilon = 1/4p$ and $\delta = 2^{-\lambda}$.

If the outcome is 1, $\mathcal{B}'$ then runs $\mathcal{B}$ on the leftover state with H_0 or H_1 picked uniformly at random. It measures and outputs a random query $\mathcal{B}$ makes to the random oracle.

4. Similarly define Π_0^C, Π_1^C as above on register C. $\mathcal{C}'$ gets C, it applies the efficient approximated threshold measurement $\mathsf{SATI}_{(P,Q),\gamma}^{\epsilon,\delta}$ with $P = (\Pi_0^C + \Pi_1^C)/2$, $Q = I - P$, $\gamma = 3/4p$, $\epsilon = 1/2p$, and $\delta = 2^{-\lambda}$.

When the outcome is 1, $\mathcal{C}'$ runs $\mathcal{C}$ on the leftover state with H_0 or H_1 picked uniformly at random. It measures and outputs a random query to the random oracle.

By Theorem 9 bullet (1), conditioned on $W \geq 1/q$, both $\mathcal{B}'$ and $\mathcal{C}'$ will get outcome 1 with probability $1/q - 2\delta = O(1/q)$. When both outcomes are 1, by bullet (2) of Theorem 9, the leftover state is 4δ-close to the the following state:

$$\sum_{\substack{i:|\lambda_i - 1/2| > 1/4p \\ j:|\mu_j - 1/2| > 1/4p}} \beta_{i,j} |\phi_i\rangle_B \otimes |\psi_j\rangle_C.$$

Observe that when $\mathcal{B}$ does not query (s,s'), it will succeed with probability exactly $1/2$. Therefore, by Theorem 5, the query weight of $\mathcal{B}$ on (s,s') is at least $1/4p^2 T - \mathsf{negl}(\lambda)$, where T is an upper-bound on the number of queries made by $\mathcal{B}$. Arguing similarly for $\mathcal{C}$, we conclude that the adversary $(\mathcal{A}', \mathcal{B}', \mathcal{C}')$ wins with probability at least $O(\eta/(qp^4 T^2))$, which is non-negligible.

4 Unclonable Encryption in the QROM

The following is the unclonable encryption scheme for a single bit:

1. $\mathsf{sk} = A$ where A is a random subspace $A \subseteq \mathbb{F}_2^n$ of dimension $n/2$;
2. $\mathsf{Enc}^H(\mathsf{sk}, m)$: it samples $s \leftarrow \mathsf{CS}(A)$ and $s' \leftarrow \mathsf{CS}(A^\perp)$ uniformly at random; it outputs $|A_{s,s'}\rangle$, $c = H(s, s') \oplus m$;
3. $\mathsf{Dec}^H(\mathsf{sk} = A, (|A_{s,s'}\rangle, c))$:
   - It first computes s in superposition. We know that there is a classical algorithm that on any vector in $A + s$ and the description of A, outputs the canonical vector of $A + s$ (which is s in this case). See [10] Definition 4.3 for more references.
     We can run this classical algorithm coherently on $|A_{s,s'}\rangle$ to learn s.
   - Since the algorithm on any vector in $A + s$ outputs the same vector, the quantum state stays intact. We can run the same algorithms coherently on the Hadamard basis and the description of $A^\perp$ to learn s'.
   - Output $c \oplus H(s, s')$.

With Theorem 12, we can show the scheme satisfy the unclonable IND-CPA security.

Proof. If we have some adversary $(\mathcal{A}, \mathcal{B}, \mathcal{C})$ for the scheme beyond, we can construct an adversary $(\mathcal{A}', \mathcal{B}', \mathcal{C}')$ for the strengthened MOE game with the same advantage.

- The adversary $\mathcal{A}'$ gets $(m_0, m_1) \leftarrow \mathcal{A}$ and sends $\Delta = m_0 \oplus m_1$ to the challenger.
- After receiving $|A_{s,s'}\rangle$ and w from the challenger, $\mathcal{A}'$ calculates $c = w \oplus m_0$, and sends $(|A_{s,s'}\rangle, c)$ to $\mathcal{A}$. The output registers B, C of $\mathcal{A}$ are sent to $\mathcal{B}', \mathcal{C}'$ respectively.
- $\mathcal{B}', \mathcal{C}'$ exactly run the algorithm of $\mathcal{B}, \mathcal{C}$, and output their output respectively.

Thus we have concluded the unclonable IND-CPA security of our game.

Remark 1. Notice that compared to the strengthened MOE game, our construction does not provide additional membership checking oracles.

5   Copy-Protection for Point Functions in QROM

5.1   Copy-Protection Preliminaries

Below we present the definition of a copy-protection scheme.

Definition 7 (Copy-Protection Scheme). *Let $\mathcal{F} = \mathcal{F}(\lambda)$ be a class of efficiently computable functions of the form $f : X \rightarrow Y$. A copy protection scheme for $\mathcal{F}$ is a pair of QPT algorithms $(\mathsf{CopyProtect}, \mathsf{Eval})$ such that:*

- *Copy Protected State Generation: $\mathsf{CopyProtect}(1^\lambda, d_f)$ takes as input the security parameter 1^λ and a classical description d_f of a function $f \in \mathcal{F}$ (that efficiently computes f). It outputs a mixed state $\rho_f \in \mathcal{D}(\mathcal{H}_Z)$, where Z is the output register.*
- *Evaluation: $\mathsf{Eval}(1^\lambda, \rho, x)$ takes as input the security parameter 1^λ, a mixed state $\rho \in \mathcal{D}(\mathcal{H}_Z)$, and an input value $x \in X$. It outputs a bipartite state $\rho' \otimes |y\rangle\langle y| \in \mathcal{D}(\mathcal{H}_Z) \otimes \mathcal{D}(\mathcal{H}_Y)$.*

We will sometimes abuse the notation and write $\mathsf{Eval}(1^\lambda, \rho, x)$ to denote the classical output $y \in Y$ when the residual state ρ' is not significant.

Definition 8 (Correctness). *A copy-protection scheme* $(\mathsf{CopyProtect}, \mathsf{Eval})$ *for* $\mathcal{F}$ *is* δ-**correct** *if the following holds: for every* $x \in X$, $f \in \mathcal{F}$,

$$\Pr\left[f(x) \leftarrow \mathsf{Eval}(1^\lambda, \rho_f, x) \;:\; \rho_f \leftarrow \mathsf{CopyProtect}(1^\lambda, d_f)\right] \geq \delta.$$

If $\delta \geq 1 - \mathsf{negl}(\lambda)$, *we simply say that the scheme is* **correct**.

Remark 2. When δ is negligibly close to 1, the evaluation algorithm Eval can be implemented so that it does not disturb the state ρ_f. This ensures that ρ_f can be reused polynomially many times with arbitrary inputs.

We define security via a piracy experiment.

Definition 9 (Piracy Experiment). *A* **piracy experiment** *is a security game defined by a copy-protection scheme* $(\mathsf{CopyProtect}, \mathsf{Eval})$ *for a class of functions* $\mathcal{F}$ *of the form* $f : X \rightarrow Y$, *a distribution* $\mathcal{D}_\mathcal{F}$ *over* $\mathcal{F}$, *and a class of distributions* $\mathfrak{D}_X = \{\mathfrak{D}_X(f)\}_{f \in \mathcal{F}}$ *over* $X \times X$. *It is the following game between a challenger and an adversary, which is a triplet of algorithms* $(\mathcal{A}, \mathcal{B}, \mathcal{C})$:

- **Setup Phase:** *The challenger samples a function* $f \leftarrow \mathcal{D}_\mathcal{F}$ *and sends* $\rho_f \leftarrow \mathsf{CopyProtect}(1^\lambda, d_f)$ *to* $\mathcal{A}$.
- **Splitting Phase:** $\mathcal{A}$ *applies a CPTP map to split* ρ_f *into a bipartite state* ρ_{BC}; *it sends the* B *register to* $\mathcal{B}$ *and the* C *register to* $\mathcal{C}$. *No communication is allowed between* $\mathcal{B}$ *and* $\mathcal{C}$ *after this phase.*
- **Challenge Phase:** *The challenger samples* $(x_B, x_C) \leftarrow \mathfrak{D}_X(f)$ *and sends* x_B, x_C *to* $\mathcal{B}, \mathcal{C}$, *respectively.*
- **Output Phase:** $\mathcal{B}$ *and* $\mathcal{C}$ *output* $y_B \in Y$ *and* $y_C \in Y$, *respectively, and send to the challenger. The challenger outputs 1 if* $y_B = f(x_B)$ *and* $y_C = f(x_C)$, *indicating that the adversary has succeeded, and 0 otherwise.*

The bit output by the challenger is denoted by $\mathsf{PirExp}_{\mathcal{D}_\mathcal{F}, \mathfrak{D}_X}^{\mathsf{CopyProtect}, \mathsf{Eval}}(1^\lambda, (\mathcal{A}, \mathcal{B}, \mathcal{C}))$.

As noted by [11], the adversary can always succeed in this game with probability negligibly close to

$$p^{\mathsf{triv}}(\mathcal{D}_\mathcal{F}, \mathfrak{D}_X) := \max_{E \in \{B,C\}} \mathop{\mathbb{E}}_{\substack{f \leftarrow \mathcal{D}_\mathcal{F} \\ (x_B, x_C) \leftarrow \mathfrak{D}_X(f)}} \max_{y \in Y} \Pr\left[y \mid x_E\right]$$

by sending ρ_f to $\mathcal{B}$ and have $\mathcal{C}$ guess the most likely output y given input x_C (or vice versa). In other words, p^{triv} is the success probability of optimal guessing strategy for one party $E \in \{B, C\}$ given only the test input x_E.

Bounding the success probability of the adversary is bounded by p^{triv} captures the intuition that ρ_f is no more helpful for simultaneous evaluation than a black-box program that could only be given to one party.

Definition 10 (Copy-Protection Security). *Let* (CopyProtect, Eval) *be a copy-protection scheme for a class* $\mathcal{F}$ *of functions* $f : X \rightarrow Y$. *Let* $\mathcal{D}_\mathcal{F}$ *be a distribution over* $\mathcal{F}$ *and* $\mathfrak{D}_X = \{\mathfrak{D}_X(f)\}_{f \in \mathcal{F}}$ *a class of distributions over* X. *Then,* (CopyProtect, Eval) *is called* $(\mathcal{D}_\mathcal{F}, \mathfrak{D}_X)$*-secure if there exists a negligible function* negl *such that any QPT adversary* $(\mathcal{A}, \mathcal{B}, \mathcal{C})$ *satisfies*

$$\Pr\left[b = 1 \ : \ b \leftarrow \mathsf{PirExp}_{\mathcal{D}_\mathcal{F}, \mathfrak{D}_X}^{\mathsf{CopyProtect}, \mathsf{Eval}} \left(1^\lambda, (\mathcal{A}, \mathcal{B}, \mathcal{C})\right)\right] \leq p^{\mathsf{triv}}(\mathcal{D}_\mathcal{F}, \mathfrak{D}_X) + \mathsf{negl}(\lambda).$$

Copy Protection for Point Functions. A *point function* $f_y : \{0,1\}^m \rightarrow \{0,1\}$ *is of the form*

$$f_y(x) = \begin{cases} 1, & x = y \\ 0, & x \neq y \end{cases}.$$

When dealing with point functions, the classical description of f_y will simply be y, and accordingly the distribution $\mathcal{D}_\mathcal{F}$ over point functions will be represented by a distribution $\mathcal{D} = \mathcal{D}_\lambda$ over $\{0,1\}^m$. Since copy protection is trivially impossible for a learnable distribution $\mathcal{D}$, we are going to restrict our attention to unlearnable distributions.

Definition 11. *A distribution* $\mathcal{D}_\lambda$ *over* $\{0,1\}^m$, *with* $m = \mathsf{poly}(\lambda)$, *is called unlearnable if for any query-bounded adversary* $\mathcal{A}^{f_y(\cdot)}$ *with oracle access to* $f_y(\cdot)$, *we have*

$$\Pr\left[y' = y : \begin{smallmatrix} y \leftarrow \mathcal{D}_\lambda \\ y' \leftarrow \mathcal{A}^{f_y(\cdot)}(1^\lambda) \end{smallmatrix}\right] \leq \mathsf{negl}(\lambda).$$

Definition 12 (Copy-Protection Security for Point Functions). *Let* $m = \mathsf{poly}(\lambda)$ *and* $\mathcal{F}$ *be the class of point functions* $f_y : \{0,1\}^m \rightarrow \{0,1\}$. *Let* $\mathfrak{D}_X = \{\mathfrak{D}_X(f)\}_{f \in \mathcal{F}}$ *be a class of input distributions over* $\{0,1\}^m \times \{0,1\}^m$. *A copy protection scheme* (CopyProtect, Eval) *for* $\mathcal{F}$ *is called* $\mathfrak{D}_X$*-secure if there exists a negligible function* negl *such that* (CopyProtect, Eval) *is* $(\mathcal{D}_\lambda, \mathfrak{D}_X)$*-secure for all unlearnable distributions* $\mathcal{D}_\lambda$ *over* $\{0,1\}^m$.

5.2   Construction

In this section, we design copy-protection for a class of point functions. We set $n = 2\lambda$ and $d = \lambda$ throughout the section. Our construction will use two hash functions: (a) $G : \{0,1\}^\lambda \rightarrow \{0,1\}^{n \cdot d}$ and (b) $H : \mathbb{F}_2^n \times \mathbb{F}_2^n \rightarrow \{0,1\}^{4n+\lambda}$. In the security proof, we will treat G and H as random oracles. We will use $\mathbb{F}_2^n$ and $\{0,1\}^n$ interchangeably.

We denote the set of all d-dimensional subspaces of $\mathbb{F}_2^n$ by $\mathcal{S}_d$.

We describe the copy-protection scheme (CopyProtect, Eval) for a class of point functions $\mathcal{F} = \{f_y(\cdot)\}_{y \in \{0,1\}^\lambda}$ as follows:

- CopyProtect $(1^\lambda, y)$: it takes as input λ in unary notation, $y \in \{0,1\}^\lambda$ and does the following:

1. Compute $\mathbf{v} = G(y)$. Parse $\mathbf{v}$ as a concatenation of d vectors $v_1, \ldots, v_d$, where each v_i has dimension n. Abort if the vectors $\{v_1, \ldots, v_d\}$ are not linearly independent.
2. Let $A = \text{Span}(v_1, \ldots, v_d)$.
3. Sample $s \leftarrow \text{CS}(A)$ and $s' \leftarrow \text{CS}(A^\perp)$ uniformly at random.
4. Output   the   copy-protected   state
   $\sigma = |A_{s,s'}\rangle\langle A_{s,s'}|\mathbf{X} \otimes |H(s,s')\rangle\langle H(s,s')|\mathbf{Y}$.

- Eval(σ, x): on input the copy-protected state $\sigma \in \mathcal{D}(\mathcal{H}_\mathbf{X} \otimes \mathcal{H}_\mathbf{Y})$, input $x \in \{0,1\}^\lambda$, it does the following:
  1. Measure the register $\mathbf{Y}$ of σ to obtain the value θ. Call the resulting state σ'.
  2. Compute $\mathbf{v} = G(x)$. Parse $\mathbf{v}$ as a concatenation of d vectors $v_1, \ldots, v_d$, where each v_i has dimension n. Abort if the vectors $\{v_1, \ldots, v_d\}$ are not linearly independent.
  3. Let $A = \text{Span}(v_1, \ldots, v_d)$.
  4. Apply U_A coherently on
     $\sigma' \otimes |0^{2n}\rangle\langle 0^{2n}|\mathbf{Z} \otimes |0^{\text{poly}(\lambda)}\rangle\langle 0^{\text{poly}(\lambda)}|\text{anc}$ to obtain the state σ'', where U_A is a unitary that computes (s, s') given $|A_{s,s'}\rangle$.
  5. Query H on the register $\mathbf{Z}$ and store the answer in a new register **out**.
  6. Measure the register **out** in the computational basis. Denote the post-measurement state by $\sigma_\mathbf{out}$ and the measurement outcome by θ'.
  7. If $\theta = \theta'$, output $\sigma_\mathbf{out} \otimes |1\rangle\langle 1|$. Otherwise, output $\sigma_\mathbf{out} \otimes |0\rangle\langle 0|$.

We first discuss at a high level why this construction works. Regarding correctness, we argue that Eval on input $x \neq y$ computes a random subspace A', such that $|A'_{s,s'}\rangle$ is nearly orthogonal to $|A_{s,s'}\rangle$. As a result, Eval recovers (s, s') incorrectly. Since as a sufficiently expanding hash function H is injective with high probability, Eval fails.

As for security, first we show that it is hard for $\mathcal{A}$ to query the oracles G, H on inputs $y, (s, s')$. Next, we argue that $\mathcal{B}$ and $\mathcal{C}$ cannot both recover (s, s'), otherwise they break the MOE game in Theorem 11.

We give the formal statements below. Detailed proofs can be found in the full version.

Lemma 7. (CopyProtect, Eval) *satisfies correctness.*

Lemma 8. (CopyProtect, Eval) *is a $\mathfrak{D}_X$-secure copy-protection scheme for point functions with input length λ, where $\mathfrak{D}_X(y) = \mathfrak{D}_y^B \times \mathfrak{D}_y^C$ is a product distribution.*

Remark 3. In our security proof, the adversary can run in unbounded time as long as it is query-bounded.

Remark 4. Using techniques from the proof of Theorem 12, our scheme can also be shown to be secure for the case when $\mathfrak{D}_X(y)$ samples correlated test inputs, i.e. the case when either $x_B = x_C = y$ or x_B, x_C are both random.

References

1. Aaronson, S.: Quantum copy-protection and quantum money. In: 2009 24th Annual IEEE Conference on Computational Complexity, pp. 229–242. IEEE (2009)
2. Aaronson, S., Christiano, P.: Quantum money from hidden subspaces. In: Proceedings of the Forty-Fourth Annual ACM Symposium on Theory of Computing, pp. 41–60 (2012)
3. Aaronson, S., Liu, J., Liu, Q., Zhandry, M., Zhang, R.: New approaches for quantum copy-protection. In: Malkin, T., Peikert, C. (eds.) CRYPTO 2021. LNCS, vol. 12825, pp. 526–555. Springer, Cham (2021). https://doi.org/10.1007/978-3-030-84242-0_19
4. Amos, R., Georgiou, M., Kiayias, A., Zhandry, M.: One-shot signatures and applications to hybrid quantum/classical authentication. In: Proceedings of the 52nd Annual ACM SIGACT Symposium on Theory of Computing, pp. 255–268 (2020)
5. Ananth, P., Kaleoglu, F.: Unclonable encryption, revisited. In: Nissim, K., Waters, B. (eds.) TCC 2021. LNCS, vol. 13042, pp. 299–329. Springer, Cham (2021). https://doi.org/10.1007/978-3-030-90459-3_11
6. Ananth, P., La Placa, R.L.: Secure software leasing. In: Canteaut, A., Standaert, F.-X. (eds.) EUROCRYPT 2021. LNCS, vol. 12697, pp. 501–530. Springer, Cham (2021). https://doi.org/10.1007/978-3-030-77886-6_17
7. Bennett, C.H., Bernstein, E., Brassard, G., Vazirani, U.: Strengths and weaknesses of quantum computing. SIAM J. Comput. **26**(5), 1510–1523 (1997)
8. Broadbent, A., Jeffery, S., Lord, S., Podder, S., Sundaram, A.: Secure software leasing without assumptions. In: Nissim, K., Waters, B. (eds.) TCC 2021. LNCS, vol. 13042, pp. 90–120. Springer, Cham (2021). https://doi.org/10.1007/978-3-030-90459-3_4
9. Broadbent, A., Lord, S.: Uncloneable quantum encryption via oracles. In: Flammia, S.T. (ed.) 15th Conference on the Theory of Quantum Computation, Communication and Cryptography (TQC 2020). Leibniz International Proceedings in Informatics (LIPIcs), vol. 158, pp. 4:1–4:22, Dagstuhl, Germany. Schloss Dagstuhl-Leibniz-Zentrum für Informatik (2020). https://doi.org/10.4230/LIPIcs.TQC.2020.4
10. Coladangelo, A., Liu, J., Liu, Q., Zhandry, M.: Hidden cosets and applications to unclonable cryptography. In: Malkin, T., Peikert, C. (eds.) CRYPTO 2021. LNCS, vol. 12825, pp. 556–584. Springer, Cham (2021). https://doi.org/10.1007/978-3-030-84242-0_20
11. Coladangelo, A., Majenz, C., Poremba, A.: Quantum copy-protection of compute-and-compare programs in the quantum random oracle model (2020)
12. Culf, E., Vidick, T.: A monogamy-of-entanglement game for subspace coset states. arXiv preprint arXiv:2107.13324 (2021)
13. Georgiou, M., Zhandry, M.: Unclonable decryption keys. IACR Cryptol. ePrint Arch. **877**, 3 (2020)
14. Gottesman, D.: Uncloneable encryption. arXiv preprint arXiv:quant-ph/0210062 (2002)
15. Lutomirski, A.: An online attack against Wiesner's quantum money. arXiv preprint arXiv:1010.0256 (2010)
16. Majenz, C., Schaffner, C., Tahmasbi, M.: Limitations on uncloneable encryption and simultaneous one-way-to-hiding, November 2021
17. Nielsen, M.A., Chuang, I.L.: Quantum Computation and Quantum Information: 10th Anniversary Edition. Cambridge University Press, Cambridge (2010). https://doi.org/10.1017/CBO9780511976667

18. Radian, R., Sattath, O.: Semi-quantum money. J. Cryptol. **35**(2), 1–70 (2022)
19. Oded Regev. Witness-preserving amplification of qma, 2005. https://cims.nyu.edu/~regev/teaching/quantum_fall_2005/ln/qma.pdf
20. Tomamichel, M., Fehr, S., Kaniewski, J., Wehner, S.: A monogamy-of-entanglement game with applications to device independent-quantum cryptography. New J. Phys. **15**(10), 103002 (2013). https://doi.org/10.1088/1367-2630/15/10/103002
21. Unruh, D.: Revocable quantum timed-release encryption. J. ACM **62**(6), December 2015. https://doi.org/10.1145/2817206. ISSN 0004-5411
22. Vidick, T.: Lecture notes on interactive proofs with quantum devices (2021). https://users.cms.caltech.edu/~vidick/teaching/fsmp/lecture1.pdf
23. Vidick, T., Zhang, T.: Classical proofs of quantum knowledge. In: Canteaut, A., Standaert, F.-X. (eds.) EUROCRYPT 2021. LNCS, vol. 12697, pp. 630–660. Springer, Cham (2021). https://doi.org/10.1007/978-3-030-77886-6_22
24. Wiesner, S.: Conjugate coding. ACM SIGACT News **15**(1), 78–88 (1983)
25. Zhandry, M.: Quantum lightning never strikes the same state twice or: quantum money from cryptographic assumptions. J. Cryptol. **34**(1), 1–56 (2021)
26. Zhandry, M.: Schrödinger's pirate: how to trace a quantum decoder. In: Pass, R., Pietrzak, K. (eds.) TCC 2020. LNCS, vol. 12552, pp. 61–91. Springer, Cham (2020). https://doi.org/10.1007/978-3-030-64381-2_3

Lattice-Based Signatures

Shorter Hash-and-Sign Lattice-Based Signatures

Thomas Espitau[1] , Mehdi Tibouchi[1] , Alexandre Wallet[2] ,
and Yang Yu[3,4](✉)

[1] NTT Corporation, Tokyo, Japan
thomas.espitau.ax@hco.ntt.co.jp, mehdi.tibouchi.br@hco.ntt.co.jp
[2] IRISA, Univ Rennes 1, Inria, Bretagne-Atlantique Center, Rennes, France
alexandre.wallet@inria.fr
[3] BNRist, Tsinghua University, Beijing, China
yu-yang@mail.tsinghua.edu.cn
[4] National Financial Cryptography Research Center, Beijing, China

Abstract. Lattice-based digital signature schemes following the hash-and-sign design paradigm of Gentry, Peikert and Vaikuntanathan (GPV) tend to offer an attractive level of efficiency, particularly when instantiated with structured compact trapdoors. In particular, NIST postquantum finalist FALCON is both quite fast for signing and verification and quite compact: NIST notes that it has the smallest bandwidth (as measured in combined size of public key and signature) of all round 2 digital signature candidates. Nevertheless, while FALCON–512, for instance, compares favorably to ECDSA–384 in terms of speed, its signatures are well over 10 times larger. For applications that store large number of signatures, or that require signatures to fit in prescribed packet sizes, this can be a critical limitation.

In this paper, we explore several approaches to further improve the size of hash-and-sign lattice-based signatures, particularly instantiated over NTRU lattices like FALCON and its recent variant MITAKA. In particular, while GPV signatures are usually obtained by sampling lattice points according to some *spherical* discrete Gaussian distribution, we show that it can be beneficial to sample instead according to a suitably chosen *ellipsoidal* discrete Gaussian: this is because only half of the sampled Gaussian vector is actually output as the signature, while the other half is recovered during verification. Making the half that actually occurs in signatures shorter reduces signature size at essentially no security loss (in a suitable range of parameters). Similarly, we show that reducing the modulus q with respect to which signatures are computed can improve signature size as well as verification key size almost "for free"; this is particularly true for constructions like FALCON and MITAKA that do not make substantial use of NTT-based multiplication (and rely instead on transcendental FFT). Finally, we show that the Gaussian vectors in signatures can be represented in a more compact way with appropriate coding-theoretic techniques, improving signature size by an additional 7 to 14%. All in all, we manage to reduce the size of, e.g., FALCON signatures by 30–40% at the cost of only 4–6 bits of Core-SVP security.

© International Association for Cryptologic Research 2022
Y. Dodis and T. Shrimpton (Eds.): CRYPTO 2022, LNCS 13508, pp. 245–275, 2022.
https://doi.org/10.1007/978-3-031-15979-4_9

1   Introduction

Currently deployed public-key cryptography is, to a large extent, vulnerable to general-purpose quantum computers. As the likelihood increases that such computers may be built in the coming decades, it appears important to prepare the transition to quantum-secure primitives instead. Doing so, however, requires postquantum schemes that are not far below currently deployed ones in terms of efficiency. Selecting and recommending such schemes is the main goal of the ongoing NIST standardization effort for postquantum cryptography. As part of that effort, primitives based on algebraic lattices have generally been strong contenders, with good performance and conservative security analyses: many of the finalists are in that category.

For digital signatures in particular, two of the three NIST round 3 finalists are lattice-based: Dilithium [11,29] and FALCON [37]. The third finalist, Rainbow [9], is a multivariate scheme that boasts very short signatures and fast signing and verification, but suffers from very large keys and has seen its security substantially reduced by recent attacks [3]; as a result, NIST has leaned towards the lattice candidates. Indeed, the lattice-based signatures are the only "TLS-ready" candidates, in the sense that they are reasonably efficient and have a relatively small bandwidth requirement (the sum of public key size and signature size, which is the relevant size metric for TLS and other protocols relying on public key certificates). Recently, isogeny-based signatures [8] have also emerged as possible options with even better bandwidth requirements (although they were developed too late for the current NIST process), but they are considerably slower than lattice-based schemes, and thus limited in terms of possible applications.

Dilithium and FALCON represent each of the two main paradigms for the construction of lattice-based signatures: Dilithium follows Lyubashevsky's Fiat–Shamir with aborts framework [27,28], while FALCON uses the hash-and-sign framework of Gentry, Peikert and Vaikuntanathan [21]. Due to this and several other design choices (such as the deliberate avoidance of Gaussian sampling), Dilithium is substantially simpler and easier to implement. FALCON on the other hand, is the strongest contender in terms of performance: it has signing times on par with Dilithium or better, faster verification times, and its public key and signature sizes are significantly smaller (by a factor of ≈ 1.5 for public keys and ≈ 3.5 for signatures at equivalent security levels). In fact, NIST mentions that FALCON had the best bandwidth requirements of all nine round 2 candidates for signatures.

In terms of speed, at least on larger CPU architectures, both Dilithium and FALCON could replace currently deployed schemes without much trouble: for example, FALCON–512 outperforms OpenSSL's implementation of ECDSA (as of version 1.1.11) for all supported curve parameters in terms of verification time (by far), and all parameters except nistp224 and nistp256 for signing. Key and signature sizes, however, are a different story. While ECDSA over a 256-bit curve has 32-byte verification keys and 64-byte signatures those numbers are 897 and 666 respectively for FALCON–512, and 1312 and 2420 respectively for the smallest round 3 parameters of Dilithium: bandwidth requirements are thus ≈ 16 times larger with FALCON and ≈ 39 times larger with Dilithium.

These larger key and signature sizes can be a serious impediment for numerous applications. For example, the DNSSEC protocols transmits verification keys as well as signatures on DNS records for signed DNS zones, and this information has to fit within a single TCP DNS packet. ICANN has pointed out [38] how this could cause difficulties for the transition to postquantum signatures. Similarly, TLS handshakes involve the transmission of multiple signatures and verification keys, and larger keys and signatures lead to more data transmission at handshake stage. CloudFlare observed [41] that this caused the handshake to exceed the initial TCP congestion window of most network infrastructure, leading to substantial slowdown. DNSSEC and TLS (or routers worldwide) could in principle be updated to mitigate those issues, but the massive coordination needed to do so makes that unlikely even in the medium term. Finally, some protocols like blockchains also require storing considerable amounts of digital signatures, and are therefore directly affected by signature size in terms of storage requirements and communication cost.

In view of these challenges, exploring ways of making lattice-based signatures and keys shorter is of clear importance.

1.1 Hash-and-Sign Signatures over Lattices

In this paper, we propose several approaches to reduce the size of lattice-based signatures, with particular emphasis on hash-and-sign signatures over NTRU lattices: we mainly have FALCON in mind, but our techniques also apply to its recent variant MITAKA [17], as well as to the earlier scheme of Ducas, Lyubashevsky and Prest [12]. In order to describe these approaches, it is useful to briefly recall the structure of these schemes.

First, following the framework of Gentry, Peikert and Vaikuntanathan, hash-and-sign signatures over lattices are constructed as follows: they are defined with respect to a certain lattice $\mathscr{L}$ (a subgroup of $\mathbb{Z}^d$, say), which is usually chosen q-ary (i.e., such that $q\mathbb{Z}^d \subset \mathscr{L}$ for some integer modulus q). The signing key is a good basis, or *trapdoor*, for the lattice $\mathscr{L}$, the knowledge of which makes it possible to solve the approximate closest vector problem for $\mathscr{L}$ within a relatively small factor. In other words, given an arbitrary vector $\mathbf{c} \in \mathbb{Z}^d$, the trapdoor makes it possible to find $\mathbf{x} \in \mathscr{L}$ such that the distance $\|\mathbf{x} - \mathbf{c}\|$ is relatively small. By carefully randomizing this operation, it also becomes possible to do *discrete Gaussian sampling*: sample a lattice point $\mathbf{x} \in \mathscr{L}$ according to a distribution statistically close to the discrete Gaussian $D_{\mathscr{L},\sigma,\mathbf{c}}$ over $\mathscr{L}$ centered at $\mathbf{c}$ with relatively small standard deviation σ. On the other hand, the verification key is a "bad" basis of $\mathscr{L}$, with which one can decide membership to the lattice, but that is not good enough to enable finding close vectors or sample discrete Gaussians with small standard deviation.

Then, the signing algorithm proceeds as follows. The message to be signed is hashed to a certain point $\mathbf{c} \in \mathbb{Z}_q^d$, and the signer uses its discrete Gaussian sampling algorithm to sample a vector $\mathbf{x} \in \mathscr{L}$ according to $D_{\mathscr{L},\sigma,\mathbf{c}}$. The signature is then the vector $\mathbf{s} = \mathbf{x} - \mathbf{c}$, which is relatively short: $\|\mathbf{s}\| \approx \sigma\sqrt{d}$ (it can also be seen as a sample from the Gaussian distribution $D_{\mathscr{L}-\mathbf{c},\sigma}$ supported over the lattice coset $\mathscr{L} - \mathbf{c}$). To verify the signature, one recomputes $\mathbf{c}$ by hashing the message, checks that $\mathbf{x} = \mathbf{s} + \mathbf{c}$ belongs to the lattice $\mathscr{L}$ and that $\mathbf{s}$ is indeed short. Security relies in a crucial way on the discrete Gaussian sampling, which ensures that signatures follow a distribution that depend only on the lattice $\mathscr{L}$ and the message, and *not* on the specific trapdoor used by the signer (contrary to what happened in early insecure hash-and-sign constructions like NTRUSign and GGH, in which signatures would leak information on the trapdoor, and therefore ultimately allow key recovery [13,34,42]).[1]

A standard optimization is the following. Since the lattice $\mathscr{L}$ is q-ary, it can be described by a parity-check matrix $\mathbf{A} \in \mathbb{Z}_q^{k \times d}$ such that $\mathbf{x} \in \mathscr{L}$ if and only if $\mathbf{A}\mathbf{x} \equiv \mathbf{0} \bmod q$. One can assume without loss of generality (at least for prime q) that $\mathbf{A} = [\mathbf{A}_0|\mathbf{I}_k]$ for some $\mathbf{A}_0 \in \mathbb{Z}_q^{k \times (d-k)}$. Thus, for any $\mathbf{x} = (\mathbf{x}_0, \mathbf{x}_1) \in \mathbb{Z}^{d-k} \times \mathbb{Z}^k$, we have $\mathbf{x} \in \mathscr{L}$ if and only if $\mathbf{A}_0\mathbf{x}_0 + \mathbf{x}_1 \equiv \mathbf{0} \bmod q$. In that setting, if the signature $\mathbf{s}$ computed above is written as $(\mathbf{s}_0, \mathbf{s}_1) \in \mathbb{Z}^{d-k} \times \mathbb{Z}^k$, one can simply transmit the compressed signature $\mathbf{s}_0$. Indeed, the verifier can then recover $\mathbf{s}_1$ using the relation:

$$\mathbf{0} \equiv \mathbf{A}\mathbf{x} \equiv \mathbf{A}(\mathbf{s} + \mathbf{c}) \equiv \mathbf{A}_0\mathbf{s}_0 + \mathbf{s}_1 + \mathbf{A}\mathbf{c} \bmod q$$

and hence $\mathbf{s}_1 \equiv -\mathbf{A}_0\mathbf{s}_0 - \mathbf{A}\mathbf{c} \bmod q$. Signature verification then consists in recovering the $\mathbf{s}_1$ component and checking that $\mathbf{s}$ is small as expected (if it is, it is a valid signature with respect to the uncompressed verification algorithm by construction, so compression does not weaken security).

A further optimization used in practical schemes is as regards to the representation of the signature vector $\mathbf{s}_0$. By construction, it follows a discrete Gaussian distribution: therefore, its coefficients are far from uniform. They lie in an interval $[-B, B]$ with $B = \Theta(\sigma\sqrt{\log(d - k)})$, but concentrate around 0. Therefore, simply representing them as numbers in $[-B, B]$ is suboptimal: while the vector $\mathbf{s}_0$ has $\Theta((d - k)\log\sigma)$ bits of entropy, this naive representation would use $\Theta((d - k)\log\log(d - k))$ more bits. This can be addressed by coding-theoretic compression techniques: for example, FALCON (following the Gaussian-sampling based Fiat–Shamir signature scheme BLISS [10]) uses Huffman coding to reduce the representation size.

1.2   Our Contributions

Using the two techniques described above, it may seem that all the available information on $\mathbf{s}$ is used to make the signature smaller: by transmitting only $\mathbf{s}_0$, we fully use the fact that $\mathbf{s}$ is in a known lattice coset, and by carrying out Huffman coding, we also take advantage of its Gaussian distribution. Since those two properties basically describe the distribution, it does not seem easy to do better.

In this paper, we explore and analyze three further strategies to reduce signature size (and, in one case, verification key size as well): one on the coding-theoretic side, and two on the lattice side.

---

[1] This independence of the distribution on the trapdoor could in principle be achieved by distributions other than Gaussians, and it was recently shown to be feasible [30], albeit with much worse parameters than can be achieved with Gaussian sampling.

Improved Coding of Gaussian Vectors. Our first observation (although it is presented last in the paper) is that the Huffman coding technique used in FALCON is fairly suboptimal: in particular, it represents the sign bit of Gaussian samples separately, and carries out a unary encoding of the absolute value, which follows a folded Gaussian distribution. Instead, we show that we can represent the whole Gaussian sample more compactly using batch Golomb-Rice coding with ANS (Asymmetric Numeral System), and achieve a representation size for the full vector very close to the entropy bound without any computationally expensive technique like arithmetic coding. This allows us to reduce the size of signatures for FALCON by 7–14% essentially for free, and applies to all Gaussian sampling techniques in a black-box way.

Ellipsoidal Gaussians. Our second idea is based on the observation that the hardness of the approximate closest vector problem that underlies the security of a hash-and-sign based signature is, roughly speaking, determined by the volume of the decoding domain (the domain around the hashed point c that contains lattice vectors x corresponding to valid signatures $s = x - c$). When transmitting the entire vector s, it is thus optimal to choose the decoding radius as a ball around c, and hence sample x according to a spherical Gaussian around c, so as to minimize the length of s for a fixed decoding volume. However, as we have seen, we actually only transmit s_0. Therefore, one can try to make the actually transmitted signature shorter by choosing a different decoding domain making the transmitted part s_0 shorter, and the recovered part s_1 longer, while maintaining the overall decoding volume constant.

This intuition can be realized by sampling x according to an *ellipsoidal* discrete Gaussian distribution instead of a spherical one. Indeed, existing lattice Gaussian samplers either support ellipsoidal Gaussians out-of-the-box (as is the case for the Klein–GPV [21] and Peikert [35] samplers) or can be fairly easily adapted to do so for our ellipsoids of interest (as is the case for Prest's hybrid sampler [17,36] and the fast Fourier orthogonalization-based sampler [14] used in FALCON).

There are of course substantial technical difficulties to address in order to fully make this idea work. To begin with, one needs to verify that it is possible to construct trapdoors for these ellipsoidal Gaussian samplers that achieve the same decoding volume as the one we started from; this is experimentally validated in our case. Moreover, while preserving the decoding volume is a rule of thumb to maintain security, extensive analysis is needed to evaluate the actual security level of the resulting scheme, at least for practical constructions like DLP, FALCON and MITAKA whose security is heuristic in nature (it provably reduces to, e.g., approximate CVP in a certain family of lattices, but the concrete parameters are too aggressive to support worst-case to average-case reductions in the style of [39,40]). As a matter of fact, we find that this approach does cause a mild security loss of a 3–4 bits for typical parameters, when reducing signature size by 20–30%. Given the comfortable security margin of lattice-based constructions, this is likely to be an acceptable trade-off in many contexts.

Using a Smaller Modulus q. A simpler idea of the same flavor as the previous one is to simply reduce the modulus q with respect to which the q-ary lattice $\mathscr{L}$ is defined. We focus on NTRU lattices in what follows. The security analysis already carried out for the NTRU-based schemes DLP, FALCON and MITAKA shows that, at the proposed parameters for those schemes (and unlike other schemes like MODFALCON [6]), the best attacks are actually independent of q. As a result, it is possible to increase or decrease q in a certain range at no security loss, up to the point where other q-dependent attacks start to kick in.

For those lattices, the trapdoor makes it possible to sample signatures $\mathbf{s} \sim D_{\mathscr{L}-\mathbf{c},\sigma}$ with parameter $\sigma = \Theta(\sqrt{q})$: the transmitted vector $\mathbf{s}_0 \in \mathbb{Z}^{d/2}$ then has coefficients of magnitude $\approx \sqrt{q}$ (and can be represented by $\Theta(\log(d\sqrt{q}))$ bits after encoding). Moreover, the module structure reduces the parity-check matrix (i.e., the verification key of the signature scheme) to a single ring element $\mathbf{h}$ which can be seen as a uniform-looking element of $\mathbb{Z}_q^{d/2}$. As a result, a very simple way to reduce both signature size and verification key size is to choose a smaller q: reducing q by a factor of γ should reduce signature size by roughly $\frac{d}{4} \log_2 \gamma$ bits and verification key by $\frac{d}{2} \log_2 \gamma$ bits.

FALCON parameters (like BLISS, DLP, and MITAKA in the power-of-two setting) are chosen for the modulus $q = 12289$, which is the smallest prime with the property that $q \equiv 1 \bmod 2^{12}$, making it number theoretic transform-friendly for power-of-two cyclotomics up to dimension 2048 (and in particular also 512 and 1024). Reducing q loses this property, and therefore can be seen as a trade-off. Practically speaking, however, this is a fairly minor trade-off as far as larger CPU architectures are concerned, because FALCON mostly relies on transcendental FFT instead of NTT for multiplication. NTT is only used for simplicity in signature verification and a small part of key generation, but it is easy to replace it by FFT followed by reduction modulo q everywhere, at little performance cost. And the same holds for variants like MITAKA.

An obvious question, however, is how far we can go. Certainly, arbitrarily small values of q should be impossible, if only for the fact that signatures would not "fit" anymore (in the sense that $\|\mathbf{s}\|_\infty$ would exceed $q/2$). But even before that, one encounters q-dependent attacks that slightly reduce security with respect to forgeries, as well as an issue with the generation of trapdoors. Normally, the NTRU trapdoor consists of a pair of ring elements $(\mathbf{f}, \mathbf{g})$ such that $\mathbf{h} = \mathbf{g}/\mathbf{f} \bmod q$ over the ring. Moreover, $\mathbf{f}$ and $\mathbf{g}$ have to be sampled such that $\|(\mathbf{f}, \mathbf{g})\| \approx \sqrt{q}$. As a result, $\mathbf{f}$ and $\mathbf{g}$ are normally sampled as discrete Gaussians with parameter $\approx \sqrt{q/d}$. However, when q becomes small, $\sqrt{q/d}$ can go below 1 (or more precisely, below the so-called "smoothing parameter" of $\mathbb{Z}^d$), at which point the discrete Gaussian vector $(\mathbf{f}, \mathbf{g})$ stops "behaving like" a continuous Gaussian. It becomes ternary and sparse, with abnormally high probability of very low Hamming weight, giving rise to weak keys with non-negligible probability.

The correct approach is then to generate $(\mathbf{f}, \mathbf{g})$ directly as sparse ternary vectors of prescribed Hamming weight in order to reach to target length $\approx \sqrt{q}$ (and this observation also applies to the ellipsoidal case for very skewed ellipsoids). This eliminates the abnormal behavior of sub-smoothing discrete Gaussians, but still

Table 1. Parameters and classical bit security estimates for FALCON and MITAKA with $q = 257$ and ellipsoidal Gaussians with factor $\gamma = 8$ compared to the original schemes, in dimension 512 and 1024.

	FALCON–512			MITAKA–512		
	Security	Sig Size	Key Size	Security	Sig Size	Key Size
Original	123	666	896	102	710	896
Small $q = 257$	118	425	576	94	475	576
Ellipsoidal $\gamma = 8$	116	410	896	92	460	896
	FALCON–1024			MITAKA–1024		
	Security	Sig Size	Key Size	Security	Sig Size	Key Size
Original	272	1280	1792	233	1405	1792
Small $q = 257$	264	805	1152	209	935	1152
Ellipsoidal $\gamma = 8$	261	780	1792	204	905	1792

opens up the possibility of additional attacks exploiting the small, sparse secret keys. We therefore carefully analyze those attacks, and find that they allow us to reduce q down to values like $q = 257$ at little security loss, and for very substantial gains in terms of key and signature size!

Security Analysis. As was apparent from the previous discussion, the security analysis of our new compression techniques relies on extensive cryptanalytic work. Since there is no simple way of relating the security of a scheme like FALCON between different values of q, or between different choices of Gaussian covariance matrices, one has to estimate the best attacks in each setting and parameter range. As usual, this is done separately for forgery (which follows a fairly standard methodology, but with appropriate twists for the ellipsoidal setting) and key recovery (where more subtle attacks come into play).

We in particular identify several parameter regimes relevant to the key recovery analysis, and carefully evaluate possible attacks in each of them. For ellipsoidal sampling, we distinguish between a range where both components $(\mathbf{f}, \mathbf{g})$ of the trapdoor are Gaussian, and a range where the smaller component becomes ternary and sparse (and is therefore chosen with fixed Hamming weight). Similarly, for the small q case, while the security analysis of FALCON and MITAKA applies directly for Gaussian $(\mathbf{f}, \mathbf{g})$, other attacks become relevant in the sparse ternary regime.

As part of this analysis, we propose several new lattice-based attacks that may be of independent interest.

Resulting Parameters. Example parameters achievable with our approaches, including signature size, verification key size and classical bit security, are presented in Table 1. More complete numbers can be found in Table 2. As we can see, our techniques lead to a gain of 30–40% in signature size for FALCON, for example, at the cost of only a few bits of Core-SVP security. Using small q also leads to a considerable improvement in key size, of around 35%.

1.3 Related Works

Chuengsatiansup et al. extended the FALCON design to NTRU lattices of larger (module) ranks and proposed MODFALCON [6]. This relaxation of constraints lead to additional parameters sets for intermediate security level. We note that our techniques can apply to MODFALCON as well.

In [5], Chen, Genise and Mukherjee introduce the notion of approximate trapdoors to construct smaller hash-and-sign signatures based on LWE and SIS. The size of such signatures is then further reduced using elliptic Gaussian sampling in [23]. However, we stress that these constructions rely on Micciancio-Peikert "gadget trapdoors" [31], and that adapting their techniques to the NTRU setting that is the focus of our paper seems far from being straightforward. On the other hand, some of our analysis and techniques could be used in Micciancio-Peikert schemes. efficient than NTRU-trapdoor based signatures.

Asymmetric variants of LWE and SIS were studied in [43] and used to design lattice-based cryptosystems. The asymmetry allows to reduce the bandwidth at no cost on the security level, and the flavour reminds of the elliptic Gaussian sampling of our work. We note that [43] focuses on lattice-based KEM and Fiat-Shamir signatures, which have constraints and challenges quite different from our setting.

Lastly, some efforts have been made to design lattice schemes with a small modulus. By using error correcting codes, the modulus in LWE-based KEMs can be reduced to byte-level [26]. Fouque et al. designed BAT–KEM, also based on optimal NTRU trapdoors combined with a new decryption approach to work with small moduli [20]. While the underlying objects in there schemes and ours are similar, the cryptanalysis of KEM and signatures are significantly different problems. modulus size affects the security of the signature scheme.

2 Background

When f is a real-valued function over a countable set S, we note $f(S) = \sum_{s \in S} f(s)$ assuming that this sum is absolutely convergent. Write $\mathbf{A}^t$ for the transpose of any matrix $\mathbf{A}$. Let $Q \in \mathbb{R}^{n \times n}$ be a symmetric matrix. We write $Q \succ 0$ when Q is *positive definite*, i.e. $\mathbf{x}^t Q \mathbf{x} > 0$ for all non-zero $\mathbf{x} \in \mathbb{R}^n$. We also write $Q_1 \succ Q_2$ when $Q_1 - Q_2 \succ 0$. It holds that $Q \succ 0$ if and only if $Q^{-1} \succ 0$ and that $Q_1 \succ Q_2 \succ 0$ if and only if $Q_2^{-1} \succ Q_1^{-1} \succ 0$. A positive definite matrix Q defines a norm as $\|\mathbf{x}\|_Q = \sqrt{\mathbf{x}^t Q \mathbf{x}}$, and corresponds uniquely to a bilinear form $\langle \mathbf{x}, \mathbf{y} \rangle_Q = \mathbf{x}^t Q \mathbf{y}$. Let $s_{1,Q}(\mathbf{A}) = \max_{\mathbf{x} \neq 0} \frac{\|\mathbf{A}\mathbf{x}\|_Q}{\|\mathbf{x}\|_Q}$.

A lattice $\mathscr{L}$ is a discrete additive subgroup in a Euclidean space. When the space is $\mathbb{R}^m$, and if it is generated by (the columns of) $\mathbf{B} \in \mathbb{R}^{m \times d}$, we also write $\mathscr{L}(\mathbf{B}) = \{\mathbf{B}\mathbf{x} \mid \mathbf{x} \in \mathbb{Z}^d\}$. If $\mathbf{B}$ has full column rank, then we call $\mathbf{B}$ a basis and d the rank of $\mathscr{L}$. When the ambient space is equipped with a norm $\|\cdot\|_Q$, the volume of $\mathscr{L}$ is $\mathrm{Vol}_Q(\mathscr{L}) = \det(\mathbf{B}^t Q \mathbf{B})^{\frac{1}{2}} = |\det(\mathbf{B})|\sqrt{\det(Q)}$ for any basis $\mathbf{B}$.

Power-of-Two Cyclotomic Fields. Let $d = 2^\ell$ for some integer $\ell \geqslant 1$ and ζ_d to be a $2d$-th primitive root of 1. Then for a fixed d, $\mathscr{K} := \mathbb{Q}(\zeta_d)$ is the d-th power-of-two cyclotomic field, and its ring of algebraic integers is $\mathscr{R} := \mathbb{Z}[\zeta_d]$. The field automorphism $\zeta_d \mapsto \zeta_d^{-1} = \overline{\zeta_d}$ corresponds to the complex conjugation, and we write the image f^* of f under this automorphism. We have $\mathcal{K} \simeq \mathbb{Q}[x]/(x^d + 1)$ and $\mathcal{R} \simeq \mathbb{Z}[x]/(x^d + 1)$, and both are contained in $\mathcal{K}_{\mathbb{R}} := \mathcal{K} \otimes \mathbb{R} \simeq \mathbb{R}[x]/(x^d + 1)$. Each $f = \sum_{i=0}^{d-1} f_i \zeta_d^i \in \mathcal{K}_{\mathbb{R}}$ can be identified[2] with its coefficient vector $(f_0, \ldots, f_{d-1}) \in \mathbb{R}^d$. The adjoint operation extends naturally to $\mathcal{K}_{\mathbb{R}}$, and $\mathcal{K}_{\mathbb{R}}^+$ is the subspace of elements satisfying $f^* = f$.

The cyclotomic field $\mathcal{K}$ comes with d complex field embeddings $\varphi_i : \mathcal{K} \to \mathbb{C}$ which map f seen as a polynomial to its evaluations at the odd powers of ζ_d. This defines the so-called *canonical embedding* $\varphi(f) := (\varphi_1(f), \ldots, \varphi_d(f))$. It extends straightforwardly to $\mathcal{K}_{\mathbb{R}}$ and identifies it to the space $\mathcal{H} = \{\mathbf{v} \in \mathbb{C}^d : v_i = \overline{v_{d/2+i}}, 1 \leqslant i \leqslant d/2\}$. For notational simplicity, we sometimes identify an element $x \in \mathcal{K}_{\mathbb{R}}$ as $\varphi(x) \in \mathcal{H}$ and denote by $\varphi_i(x)$ its i-th coordinate. Note that $\varphi(fg) = (\varphi_i(f)\varphi_i(g))_{i \leqslant d}$. When needed, this embedding extends entry-wise to vectors or matrices over $\mathcal{K}_{\mathbb{R}}$. We let $\mathcal{K}_{\mathbb{R}}^{++}$ be the subset of $\mathcal{K}_{\mathbb{R}}^+$ which have all positive coordinates in the canonical embedding. We have a partial ordering over $\mathcal{K}_{\mathbb{R}}^+$ by $f \succ g$ if and only if $f - g \in \mathcal{K}_{\mathbb{R}}^{++}$. The algebra $\mathcal{K}_{\mathbb{R}}$ is also equipped with a norm $\mathrm{N}(x) = \prod_i \varphi_i(x)$, which extends the standard field norm.

$\mathcal{K}_{\mathbb{R}}$-Valued Matrices. For $Q \in \mathcal{K}_{\mathbb{R}}^{2 \times 2}$, we write Q^* its conjugate-transpose, where $*$ is the conjugation in $\mathcal{K}_{\mathbb{R}}$. Positive definiteness extends to such matrices: we say Q is *totally* positive definite when $Q = Q^*$ and all the d matrices $\varphi_i(Q)$ induced by the field embeddings are hermitian positive definite. We then write $Q \succ 0$. For example, $\mathbf{B}^*\mathbf{B} \succ 0$ for all $\mathbf{B} \in \mathcal{K}_{\mathbb{R}}^{2 \times 2}$. A positive definite form over $\mathcal{K}_{\mathbb{R}}$ corresponds uniquely to a $\mathcal{K}_{\mathbb{R}}$-bilinear form $\langle \mathbf{x}, \mathbf{y} \rangle_Q = \mathbf{x}^* Q \mathbf{y}$.[3] Under the canonical embedding, it induces a euclidean norm on $\mathcal{H}$ as $\|\varphi(\mathbf{x})\|_Q^2 = \sum_i \varphi_i(\langle \mathbf{x}, \mathbf{x} \rangle_Q)$. Such forms come with a corresponding notion of orthogonality. In particular, the well-known Gram-Schmidt orthogonalization procedure for a pair of linearly independent vectors $\mathbf{b}_1, \mathbf{b}_2 \in \mathcal{K}^2$ is defined as $\widetilde{\mathbf{b}}_1 := \mathbf{b}_1$, $\widetilde{\mathbf{b}}_2 := \mathbf{b}_2 - \frac{\langle \mathbf{b}_1, \mathbf{b}_2 \rangle_Q}{\langle \mathbf{b}_1, \mathbf{b}_1 \rangle_Q} \cdot \widetilde{\mathbf{b}}_1$. One readily checks that $\langle \widetilde{\mathbf{b}}_1, \widetilde{\mathbf{b}}_2 \rangle_Q = 0$. The Gram-Schmidt matrix with columns $\widetilde{\mathbf{b}}_1, \widetilde{\mathbf{b}}_2$ is denoted by $\widetilde{\mathbf{B}}$ and we have $\det \widetilde{\mathbf{B}} = \det \mathbf{B}$. For a given form Q, we let $|\mathbf{B}|_{\mathcal{K}, Q} = \max(\|\varphi(\langle \widetilde{\mathbf{b}}_1, \widetilde{\mathbf{b}}_1 \rangle_Q)\|_\infty, \|\varphi(\langle \widetilde{\mathbf{b}}_2, \widetilde{\mathbf{b}}_2 \rangle_Q)\|_\infty)^{1/2}$.

NTRU Lattices. This work deals with free $\mathcal{R}$-modules of rank 2 in $\mathcal{K}^2$, or in other words, groups of the form $\mathcal{M} = \mathcal{R}\mathbf{x} + \mathcal{R}\mathbf{y}$ where $\mathbf{x} = (x_1, x_2), \mathbf{y} = (y_1, y_2)$ span $\mathcal{K}^2$. A mild change compared to previous works on the subject is that we equip the ambient space $\mathcal{K}_{\mathbb{R}}^2$ with a totally positive definite form Q and its corresponding inner product. If we write $\mathbf{B}$ the basis matrix for $\mathcal{M}$, the volume of the associated lattice is $\mathrm{Vol}_Q(\mathcal{M}) = \mathrm{N}(\det(\mathbf{B}^* Q \mathbf{B}))^{1/2}$. If $\widetilde{\mathbf{B}}$ is the Gram-Schmidt orthogonalization of $\mathbf{B}$ with respect to Q, then we also have $\mathrm{Vol}_Q(\mathcal{M})^2 = \prod_i \mathrm{N}(\langle \mathbf{b}_i, \widetilde{\mathbf{b}}_i \rangle_Q)$.

Given $f, g \in \mathcal{R}$ such that f is invertible modulo some prime $q \in \mathbb{Z}$, we let $h = f^{-1}g \bmod q$. The NTRU module determined by h is $\mathscr{L}_{\mathrm{NTRU}} = \{(u, v) \in \mathcal{R}^2 :$

---

[2] This is the so-called coefficient embedding.

[3] We keep the same notation as in the common real case, since in the context of our work it will causes no confusion.

$uh - v = 0 \bmod q\}$. Two bases of this free module are of particular interest:

$$\mathbf{B}_h = \begin{bmatrix} 1 & 0 \\ h & q \end{bmatrix} \text{ and } \mathbf{B}_{f,g} = \begin{bmatrix} f & F \\ g & G \end{bmatrix},$$

where $F, G \in \mathscr{R}$ are such that $fG - gF = q$, and $\|(F, G)\|$ should be relatively small. This module is usually seen as a lattice of volume $q^d \, \mathrm{N}(\det Q)^{1/2}$ in $(\mathbb{R}^{2d}, Q)$ in the coefficient embedding.

Lemma 1 ([17,36], **adapted**). *Let* $\mathbf{B}_{f,g}$ *be a basis of an NTRU module and* $\mathbf{b}_1 = (f, g)$. *We have* $\sqrt{q} \, \mathrm{N}(\det Q)^{1/(4d)} \leqslant |\mathbf{B}_{f,g}|_{\mathscr{K},Q}$ *and*

$$|\mathbf{B}_{f,g}|^2_{\mathscr{K},Q} = \max\left(\|\varphi(\langle \mathbf{b}_1, \mathbf{b}_1 \rangle_Q)\|_\infty, \left\| \frac{q^2 \cdot \det Q}{\varphi(\langle \mathbf{b}_1, \mathbf{b}_1 \rangle_Q)} \right\|_\infty \right).$$

Gaussians Measures and Module Lattices. For a positive definite matrix $Q \in \mathbb{R}^{d \times d}$, the Gaussian function with standard deviation σ is $\rho_{Q,\sigma}(\mathbf{x}) = \exp(-\frac{1}{2}\|\mathbf{x}\|^2_Q / \sigma^2)$. The standard (spherical) Gaussian function corresponds to $Q = \mathbf{I}$. Then, for a full rank lattice $\mathscr{L}$ in $\mathbb{R}^d$ and a given $\mathbf{t} \in \mathbb{R}^d$, the discrete Gaussian probability with parameters $\mathbf{t}$ and σ with respect to the form Q is defined as $D_{\mathscr{L},Q,\sigma,\mathbf{t}}(\mathbf{x}) = \frac{\rho_{Q,\sigma}(\mathbf{x}-\mathbf{t})}{\rho_{Q,\sigma}(\mathscr{L}-\mathbf{t})}$, where $\mathbf{x}$ ranges in $\mathscr{L}$. When $\mathbf{t} = 0$, we omit it. When given a totally positive definite Q over $\mathscr{K}_\mathbb{R}$ and representing $\mathscr{R}$-modules with any embedding of $\mathscr{K}$, we keep the same notation, that is, we omit writing the embedding in formulas, as the context will always be clear.

For any positive definite form Q, there are always matrices $\mathbf{T} \in \mathbb{R}^{d \times d}$ such that $Q = \mathbf{T}^t \mathbf{T}$ (one example is given by the Cholesky decomposition). One checks that $\rho_{Q,\sigma}(\mathbf{x}) = \rho_{\mathbf{I},\sigma}(\mathbf{T}\mathbf{x})$ for any such $\mathbf{T}$, and well-known results about lattice Gaussian measures then extend to any form Q. The smoothing parameter of a lattice $\mathscr{L}$ for a given $\varepsilon > 0$ is $\eta_{Q,\varepsilon}(\mathscr{L}) = \min\{s > 0 : \rho_{Q^{-1},1/s}(\mathscr{L}^\vee) \leqslant 1 + \varepsilon\}$. Here, $\mathscr{L}^\vee$ refers to the dual lattice, and its exact definition is not needed: in this work, it is enough to know that for a full rank lattice $\mathscr{L}(\mathbf{B}) \subset \mathbb{R}^d$, it is encoded by $\mathbf{B}^{-t}$. The next lemma says that above the smoothing parameter, a discrete Gaussian measure does not "see" cosets of a lattice (hence the name).

Lemma 2 (Adapted from [32]). *Let* Q *be a positive definite form over* $\mathbb{R}^d$, $\mathbf{t} \in \mathbb{R}^d$ *and* $\varepsilon > 0$. *Let* $\mathscr{L} \subset \mathbb{R}^d$ *be a full rank lattice. If* $\sigma \geqslant \eta_{Q,\varepsilon}(\mathscr{L})$, *we have* $\rho_{Q,\sigma}(\mathscr{L} - \mathbf{t}) \in [\frac{1-\varepsilon}{1+\varepsilon}, 1] \cdot \rho_{Q,\sigma}(\mathscr{L})$.

We will also use standard tail bounds for elliptic discrete Gaussians.

Lemma 3 (Adapted from [28]). *Let* Q *be a positive definite form over* $\mathbb{R}^d$, $\mathbf{t} \in \mathbb{R}^d$ *and* $\varepsilon > 0$. *Let* $\mathscr{L} \subset \mathbb{R}^d$ *be a full rank lattice and* $\mathbf{x} \leftarrow D_{\mathscr{L},Q,\sigma,\mathbf{t}}$, *where* $\sigma > \eta_{Q,\varepsilon}(\mathscr{L})$. *For any* $\tau > 1$, *we have* $\mathbb{P}[\|\mathbf{x}-\mathbf{t}\|_Q > \tau \cdot \sigma \sqrt{d}] \leqslant 2 \cdot \frac{1+\varepsilon}{1-\varepsilon} \cdot \tau^d \exp((1-\tau^2)d/2)$.

Lastly, we give the following upper bound on the smoothing parameter.

Lemma 4 (Adapted from [17,21]). *Let* $\mathbf{B}\mathscr{R}^2$ *be a free* $\mathscr{R}$-*module, and* $[\mathbf{b}_1, \dots, \mathbf{b}_{2d}]$ *the basis of the associated lattice* $\mathscr{L}$ *in* $\mathbb{R}^{2d}$. *Let* $\varepsilon > 0$. *For all totally positive definite* $\mathscr{Q} \in \mathscr{K}_\mathbb{R}^{2 \times 2}$, *we have* $\eta_{\mathscr{Q},\varepsilon}(\mathscr{L}) \leqslant |\mathbf{B}|_{\mathscr{Q},\mathscr{K}} \cdot \eta_\varepsilon(\mathbb{Z}^d)$.

Algorithm 1: Ring sampler

Input: A target center $t \in \mathscr{K}_{\mathbb{R}}$, parameters $\sigma \in \mathscr{K}_{\mathbb{R}}^{\times}$ and a real $r > 0$.
Result: y with distribution close to $D_{\mathscr{R},(\sigma\sigma^*+r^2)^{-1}\mathbf{I},1,t}$

1   $x \leftarrow \sigma \cdot \mathcal{N}_{\mathscr{K}_{\mathbb{R}}}$
2   **return** $\lfloor t - x \rceil_r$

Algorithm 2: Module Elliptic Gaussian sampler

Input: A target center $\mathbf{t} \in \mathscr{K}_{\mathbb{R}}^2$, a totally positive matrix $Q \in \mathscr{K}_{\mathbb{R}}^{2\times2}$, a
     basis $\mathbf{B} = [\mathbf{b}_1, \mathbf{b}_2]$ of a free $\mathscr{R}$-module $\mathscr{M}$ and its GSO $[\widetilde{\mathbf{b}_1}, \widetilde{\mathbf{b}_2}]$ with
     respect to Q, and a parameter $\sigma \in \mathscr{K}_{\mathbb{R}}$.
Result: $\mathbf{z}$ with distribution negligibly far from $D_{\mathscr{M},(\sigma\sigma^*)^{-1}Q,1,\mathbf{c}}$.

1   *Precomputed:* $\tau_i := \sqrt{\frac{\sigma\sigma^*}{\langle \widetilde{\mathbf{b}_i}, \widetilde{\mathbf{b}_i}\rangle_Q} - r^2} \in \mathscr{K}_{\mathbb{R}}^{++}$.
2   $\mathbf{s} \leftarrow 0$
3   $\widetilde{t_2} \leftarrow \frac{\langle \widetilde{\mathbf{b}_2}, \mathbf{t}\rangle_Q}{\langle \widetilde{\mathbf{b}_2}, \widetilde{\mathbf{b}_2}\rangle_Q}$
4   $x_2 \leftarrow$ Algorithm $1(\widetilde{t_2}, \tau_2, r)$
5   $\mathbf{t}' \leftarrow \mathbf{t} - x_2\mathbf{b}_2, \mathbf{s} \leftarrow x_2\mathbf{b}_2$
6   $\widetilde{t_1} \leftarrow \frac{\langle \widetilde{\mathbf{b}_1}, \mathbf{t}'\rangle_Q}{\langle \widetilde{\mathbf{b}_1}, \widetilde{\mathbf{b}_1}\rangle_Q}$
7   $x_1 \leftarrow$ Algorithm $1(\widetilde{t_1}, \tau_1, r)$
8   $\mathbf{s} \leftarrow \mathbf{s} + x_1\mathbf{b}_1$
9   **return** $\mathbf{s}$

For any positive definite form $Q \in \mathbb{R}^{2d\times 2d}$, we have $\eta_{Q,\varepsilon}(\mathscr{L}) \leqslant \max \|\widetilde{\mathbf{b}}_i\|_Q \cdot \eta_\varepsilon(\mathbb{Z})$, where $\widetilde{\mathbf{b}}_1, \ldots, \widetilde{\mathbf{b}}_{2d}$ is the Gram-Schmidt orthogonalization of the $\mathbf{b}_i$'s with respect to Q. For any integer $n > 0$, we have $\eta_\varepsilon(\mathbb{Z}^n) \leqslant \frac{1}{\pi}\sqrt{\frac{\log(2n(1+1/\varepsilon))}{2}}$.

Some Gaussian Samplers. Algorithm 1 is a subcase of [35] and inspired of [17,36]. It allows to sample spherical discrete Gaussians in $\mathscr{R}$ for adequate parameters, as long as a discrete Gaussian sampler *over the integer* is given.

Proposition 1 (Adapted from [17,35]). *Let $\mathscr{D}$ be the output distribution of Algorithm 1. If $\varepsilon < \frac{1}{2}$ and $r \geqslant \eta_\varepsilon(\mathscr{R})$, then the statistical distance between $\mathscr{D}$ and $D_{\mathscr{R},1,\sigma\sigma^*+r^2,t}$ is bounded by 2ε and we have $\sup_{y\in\mathscr{R}} \left| \frac{\mathscr{D}(y)}{D_{\mathscr{R},(\sigma\sigma^*+r^2)^{-1}\mathbf{I},1,t}(y)} - 1\right| \leqslant 4\varepsilon$.*

We observe that equivalently, Algorithm 1 can reach any covariance parameter $\tau \in \mathscr{K}_{\mathbb{R}}^{++}$ as long as $\tau - r^2 \in \mathscr{K}_{\mathbb{R}}^{++}$. Algorithm 2 is a generalization of the so-called *hybrid sampler* of [17,36] to obtain Gaussian ring elements with elliptic covariances.

Proposition 2. *Let $\mathscr{D}$ be the output distribution of Algorithm 2. If $\varepsilon < \frac{1}{2}$ and $\sigma\sigma^* \succ (|\mathbf{B}|_{\mathscr{K},Q} \cdot \eta_\varepsilon(\mathscr{R}))^2$, then the statistical distance between $\mathscr{D}$ and $D_{\mathscr{M},(\sigma\sigma^*)^{-1}Q,1,\mathbf{t}}$ is bounded by 7ε and we have $\sup_{\mathbf{y}\in\mathscr{M}} \left| \frac{\mathscr{D}(\mathbf{y})}{D_{\mathscr{M},(\sigma\sigma^*)^{-1}Q,1,\mathbf{t}}(\mathbf{y})} - 1\right| \leqslant 14\varepsilon$.*

As already observed, sampling elliptically amounts to sampling spherically but changing the form defining the metric. It is thus no surprise that the well-known Klein sampler [21] can be extended identically by simply computing the initial Gram-Schmidt orthogonalization with respect to the adequate form: this change is purely syntactic. In particular, there is no obstruction either to extending FALCON's *fast Fourier sampler* [14]: its core mechanic relies on the underlying tower of cyclotomic field and an adequate representation of the Cholesky factor for the lattice basis. The proof and description would be tedious and uneventful, yet for the sake of modularity, we restrict ourselves to a statement in this article.

Proposition 3 (Adapted from [21,36]). *The fast Fourier sampler of [37] can be extended to a Gaussian sampler over a module lattice $\mathscr{L}(\mathbf{B}) \in (\mathbb{R}^{2d}, Q)$. Let $\mathscr{D}$ be its output distribution. Let also $\widetilde{\mathbf{b}}_1, \ldots, \widetilde{\mathbf{b}}_{2d}$ be the Gram-Schmidt of $\mathbf{B}$ with respect to Q, $\varepsilon < 1/2$ and $\mathbf{t} \in \mathbb{R}^{2d}$. When $\sigma > \eta_\varepsilon(\mathbb{Z}) \cdot \max_{i \leqslant 2d} \|\widetilde{\mathbf{b}}_i\|_Q$, the statistical distance between $\mathscr{D}$ and $D_{\mathscr{L}(\mathbf{B}),Q,\sigma,\mathbf{t}}$ is bounded by $(2d+1)\varepsilon$ and we have $\sup_{\mathbf{y} \in \mathscr{L}(\mathbf{B})} \left| \frac{\mathscr{D}(\mathbf{y})}{D_{\mathscr{L}(\mathbf{B}),Q,\sigma,\mathbf{t}}(\mathbf{y})} - 1 \right| \leqslant (4d+1)\varepsilon.$*

3   New Hash-and-Sign Tradeoffs

3.1   Shorter Signatures by Elliptic Sampling

In hash-and-sign over NTRU lattices, it is well-known that only one of the components of a signature $(s_1, s_2) \in \mathscr{L}_{\text{NTRU}}$ is needed as input to the verification algorithm. This comes from the algebraic definition of such lattices, as we always have $s_1 h = s_2 \bmod q$ when h is the corresponding public key. To compress signatures, it, therefore, makes sense to try to minimize the magnitude of the coefficients in the component that is sent. To this end, we let $\gamma \succ 1$ (in $\mathscr{K}_\mathbb{R}$) and consider the totally positive form

$$Q = \begin{pmatrix} \gamma^2 & 0 \\ 0 & \gamma^{-2} \end{pmatrix},$$

and keep the same notation for its version in the coefficient embedding. Note that the resulting lattice volumes are preserved, as $\det Q = 1$. Following Algorithm 3, a signature is an elliptic Gaussian in $\mathscr{L}_{\text{NTRU}}$ centered at $\mathbf{c} = (0, c)$, where c is the (hash of the) message. Such random vectors can be sampled with Algorithm 2 or implicit in Proposition 3, for an input basis $\mathbf{B}_{f,g}$ reaching a good quality (as conditioned by Lemma 1). the smallest $|\mathbf{B}_{f,g}|_{Q,\mathscr{K}}$ is, the shortest the signatures are.

Now, since Q "favors" vectors with smaller first components, we send s_1 as the signature. Indeed, we can show that the first component of elliptic signatures has an expected length shorter by a factor γ compared to "regular" spherical ones. We however keep our discussion at an informal level for the sake of clarity, as the arguments are standard. Note first that saying $\mathbf{s} \leftarrow D_{\mathscr{L},Q,\sigma,\mathbf{c}}$ is equivalent to saying $\mathbf{Ts} \leftarrow D_{\mathbf{T}\mathscr{L},\mathbf{I},\sigma,\mathbf{Tc}}$ for any $\mathbf{T}$ such that $\mathbf{T}^t\mathbf{T} = Q$. Taking $\mathbf{T} = \text{diag}(\gamma, \gamma^{-1})$, the first coordinates of $\mathbf{Tc}$ in the signing algorithm are 0. Therefore, the first component of $\mathbf{Ts}$, i.e. γs_1, closely follows a Gaussian of covariance $\sigma^2\mathbf{I}_d$, which shows that the signature s_1 has an expected length of essentially $\frac{\sigma\sqrt{d}}{\gamma}$.

Algorithm 3: Hash-and-sign

Input: an NTRU trapdoor $\mathbf{B}_{f,g}$ and message m; a parameter $\sigma > 0$, a quadratic form Q and an acceptance bound $B > 0$
Result: a signature $s \in \mathscr{R}$.

1 $c := \text{hash}(m) \in \mathscr{R}$, $\mathbf{c} := \begin{pmatrix} 0 \\ c \end{pmatrix}$
2 Sample $\mathbf{s} = (s_1, s_2)$ from $D_{\mathscr{L}(\mathbf{B}_{f,g}),Q,\sigma,\mathbf{c}}$ with Algorithm 2
3 **if** $\|\mathbf{s} - \mathbf{c}\|_Q > B$ **then**
4 $\quad$ Restart
5 **end if**
6 **return** s_1

Algorithm 4: Verification

Input: an NTRU public key h and a signature s for a message m; a quadratic form Q and and acceptance bound $B > 0$
Result: Accept or Reject.

1 $c := \text{hash}(m) \in \mathscr{R}$
2 $s' = hs - c \bmod q$
3 **if** $\|(s, s')\|_Q > B$ **then**
4 $\quad$ Reject
5 **end if**
6 Accept

3.2 Parameters Selection

The resilience of hash-and-sign over lattices against forgery requires signatures to be short. Getting short signatures is achieved thanks to a *trapdoor* for $\mathscr{L}_{\text{NTRU}}$, that is, a basis composed of short vectors with good properties with respect to a selected sampling algorithm. We consider two instantiations of the framework, namely, FALCON [37] and the recent MITAKA [17]. Each of these schemes find good trapdoors with the following method. First, candidates f and g are sampled according to a fixed distribution. Because the resulting lattice is morally a 2 dimensional object with prescribed volume q, it is possible to deduce the quality $\mathcal{Q}(\mathbf{B}_{f,g}) = \alpha\sqrt{q}$ of the basis before computing it, so that if the expected quality is good, the basis is completed, else another pair f, g is sampled. We first deal with the value of α depending on the scheme, then discuss the distribution of f, g.

In our work, we sometimes consider different norms on the ambient space. This could have an impact on the quality that the key generation algorithm achieves; our experiments however suggested that it has no impact on the trapdoors we could find. Additionally, FALCON relies on the algebraic structure of power-of-two cyclotomic fields, while MITAKA allow for more number field choices. However, here, we will restrict to the power-two-cyclotomic case.

3.2.1 Quality of Gaussian Samplers

FALCON uses the so-called fast Fourier sampler [14], while MITAKA relies on the so-called hybrid sampler [36] to sample signatures. If $\mathbf{b}_1, \mathbf{b}_2$ is the module basis of $\mathscr{L}_{\text{NTRU}}$ and $\mathbf{b}_1^{\mathbb{Z}}, \ldots, \mathbf{b}_{2d}^{\mathbb{Z}}$ its corresponding lattice basis, the requirements are:

- $\mathcal{Q}_{\text{FALCON}} = \max_{i \leqslant 2d} \|\widetilde{\mathbf{b}}_i^{\mathbb{Z}}\|_Q = \alpha_{\text{FALCON}} \cdot \sqrt{q}$ where $\alpha_{\text{FALCON}} = 1.17$;
- $\mathcal{Q}_{d,\text{MITAKA}} = |\mathbf{B}_{f,g}|_{Q,\mathscr{K}} = \alpha_{d,\text{MITAKA}} \cdot \sqrt{q}$, where $\alpha_{512,\text{MITAKA}} = 2.04$ and $\alpha_{1024,\text{MITAKA}} = 2.33$.

The standard deviation parameters for our signatures are set with Lemma 4 as $\sigma = r\mathcal{Q}_*$ where:

- we want $\sigma_{\text{FALCON}} \geqslant \eta_\varepsilon(\mathbb{Z}) \cdot \alpha_{\text{FALCON}} \sqrt{q}$, so we take $r = \frac{1}{\pi}\sqrt{\frac{\log(2(1+1/\varepsilon))}{2}}$;
- we want $\sigma_{d,\text{MITAKA}} \geqslant \eta_\varepsilon(\mathbb{Z}^d) \cdot \alpha_{\text{MITAKA}} \sqrt{q}$, so we take $r = \frac{1}{\pi}\sqrt{\frac{\log(2d(1+1/\varepsilon))}{2}}$.

These parameters combined give us the tailcut rate of the used sampler. We set the rejection bound as

$$\rho = \tau \cdot \sigma \sqrt{2d}, \tag{1}$$

where $\tau = 1.04$ is enough to guarantee that 90% of samples might be too long, thanks to Lemma 3. Lastly, the analyses in [17] states that $\varepsilon_{\text{MITAKA}} = 2^{-41}$, while FALCON claims $\varepsilon_{\text{FALCON}} = 2^{-36}$.

3.2.2 On the Distribution of Secret Keys

The standard choice [12,37] for FALCON is to sample f, g as independent discrete Gaussians in $\mathscr{R}$ to satisfy

$$\mathbb{E}[\|(f,g)\|_Q^2] = \alpha_{\text{FALCON}}^2 q, \tag{2}$$

which means the standard deviation parameter is $\sigma_{\text{FALCON}} = r_{\text{FALCON}}\alpha_{\text{FALCON}}\sqrt{q}$. On top of several tricks to speed up the key-generation algorithm, MITAKA uses a different strategy. The approach is to look for good trapdoors among those which could already be used by FALCON. This also means that the expected behavior of f, g for the Euclidean norm is the same. We now distinguish the regime where the norm is changed and an elliptic signature is sampled, from the regime where q is reduced and the signature are regular spherical samples.

Selection in Twisted Norm: To simplify the exposition, we take $\gamma \in \mathbb{R}$. Condition (2) becomes

$$\gamma^2 \mathbb{E}[\|f\|^2] + \frac{1}{\gamma^2}\mathbb{E}[\|g\|^2] = \alpha^2 q. \tag{3}$$

If we want to keep f, g as discrete Gaussians, Eq. (2) shows that we can select $\sigma_f = \frac{\alpha}{\gamma}\sqrt{q/2d}$ and $\sigma_g = \gamma\alpha\sqrt{q/2d}$, where γ remains *a priori* arbitrary. This choice[4] has expectedly a large impact on the security, and γ should not be too large either.

---

[4] In particular, we could have selected a variable Hamming weight; our analyses suggest that it is a suboptimal choice for security.

In any case, when γ grows, there is a parameter window where f looks essentially sparse and ternary, and the target standard deviation may be below the smoothing parameter of $\mathbb{Z}$. Since we can no longer predict the behavior of Gaussians in that regime, it is then natural to sample it directly as a uniform ternary vector of small (fixed) Hamming weight κ, and we now have $\mathbb{E}[\|f\|^2] = \kappa$. This change also enables different attacks exploiting the sparseness of f, see also Sect. 4. The next step is simplified by balancing the terms in Eq. (3), asking

$$\frac{1}{\gamma^2}\mathbb{E}[\|g\|^2] = \gamma^2\kappa = \frac{\alpha^2 q}{2}. \tag{4}$$

The distortion factor can then be as large as $\gamma = \alpha\sqrt{\frac{q}{2\kappa}}$, and we can keep g sampled as a spherical discrete Gaussian with $\sigma_g^2 = (\alpha\gamma)^2 \frac{q}{2d}$.

Selection for Small q's: The ambient norm corresponds here to $Q = \mathbf{I}$, and the situation is simplified by taking the same distribution for f, g. As q is now close to d, the standard deviation of secret keys in the usual setting makes them again behave essentially like ternary and sparse vectors. This prompts us to sample directly f, g uniform in the set of ternary vectors of hamming weight κ, which translates in the following constraint:

$$\kappa = \frac{\alpha^2 q}{2}. \tag{5}$$

This implies in particular that q should be slightly smaller than $2d$, and may open the road for combinatoric and hybrid attacks against the secret keys.

4 Security Analysis

To assess the concrete security of our methods, we proceed using the usual cryptanalytic methodology of estimating the complexity of the best attacks against *key recovery attacks* on the one hand, and *signature forgery* on the other. For the rest of this section, we consider that the ambient norm over our lattices is given by

$$\|\mathbf{x}\|_\gamma^2 = \mathbf{x}^t Q_\gamma \mathbf{x} \quad \text{with} \quad Q_\gamma = \mathbf{T}_\gamma^t \mathbf{T}_\gamma \quad \text{and} \quad \mathbf{T}_\gamma := \begin{bmatrix} \gamma\mathbf{I}_d & \\ & \gamma^{-1}\mathbf{I}_d \end{bmatrix}, \tag{6}$$

for some *real* $\gamma \geqslant 1$. To better reflect the impact of this distortion factor, we propose a parameterized security analysis, and instantiate it depending on our use case (either elliptic sampling, or "small q" regime with $\gamma = 1$).

Lattice Reduction Setting. In all of the following, we follow the so-called *Geometric series assumption* (GSA), asserting that a reduced basis sees its Gram-Schmidt vectors' norm decrease with geometric decay. More formally, it can be instantiated as follows for self-dual BKZ (DBKZ) reduction algorithm of Micciancio and Walter [33]: an output basis $(\mathbf{b}_1, \ldots, \mathbf{b}_n)$ yielded by DBKZ algorithm with block size β on a lattice $\mathscr{L}$ of rank n satisfies the following relation on the length of its Gram-Schmidt vectors:

$$\|\widetilde{\mathbf{b}}_i\| = \delta_\beta^{n-2(i-1)} \mathrm{Vol}_Q(\mathscr{L})^{\frac{1}{n}}, \quad \text{where} \quad \delta_\beta = \left(\frac{(\pi\beta)^{\frac{1}{\beta}} \cdot \beta}{2\pi e}\right)^{\frac{1}{2(\beta-1)}}. \tag{7}$$

4.1 Forging Signatures

In the hash-and-sign paradigm signature, forging a signature boils down to finding a point $\mathbf{v} \in \mathscr{L}_{\mathrm{NTRU}}$ at distance at most ρ from a random space point $\mathbf{x}$. Since we are quite above $\lambda_1(\mathscr{L}_{\mathrm{NTRU}})/2$, this is an instance of the Approximate Closest Vector Problem (APPROXCVP). This problem can be solved using the so-called *Nearest-Cospace* framework developed by Espitau and Kirchner in [18]. Under the Geometric Series assumption, Theorem 3.3 of [18] states that the decoding can be done in time $\mathrm{Poly}(d)$ calls to a CVP oracle in dimension β under the condition

$$\|\mathbf{x} - \mathbf{v}\|_\gamma \leqslant \delta_\beta^{2d} \mathrm{Vol}_{Q_\gamma}(\mathscr{L}_{\mathrm{NTRU}})^{\frac{1}{2d}}.$$

Equivalently, an adversary can consider the lattice spanned by $\mathbf{T}_\gamma \mathbf{B}_h$ and decode $\mathbf{T}_\gamma \mathbf{x}$ in the usual ℓ_2 norm $\| \cdot \|$, where $\mathbf{B}_h = \begin{bmatrix} \mathbf{I}_d & \mathbf{0}_d \\ \mathbf{H} & q\mathbf{I}_d \end{bmatrix}$, and $\mathbf{H}$ is the matrix of multiplication by h in the power basis of $\mathscr{R}$.

While this change with regards to the classical situation of FALCON and MITAKA [17,37] seems purely syntactic, it can have an impact on the best approach to decoding, and some care must be taken in the details. Indeed, as mentioned in [6], a standard optimization of this attack consists in only considering the lattice spanned by a subset of the vectors of the public basis and performing the decoding within this sublattice. The only interesting subset seems to remove only the $k \leqslant d$ first vectors. The dimension is of course reduced by k, at the cost of working with a lattice with of relatively bigger *normalized* covolume.

Let $S \subset [d]$ a set of k indices. Write $\mathbf{H}_S$ as the submatrix with column indices outside of S, and $\mathbf{I}_S$ the analogous submatrix of $\mathbf{I}_d$. Let also $\mathbf{B}_S$ be the corresponding submatrix of $\mathbf{B}_h$ while keeping all the "q vectors". We then have

$$(\mathbf{T}_\gamma \mathbf{B}_S)^t (\mathbf{T}_\gamma \mathbf{B}_S) = \begin{pmatrix} \gamma^2 \mathbf{I}_{d-k} + \frac{1}{\gamma^2}\mathbf{H}_S^t \mathbf{H}_S & \frac{q}{\gamma^2}\mathbf{H}_S^t \\ \frac{q}{\gamma^2}\mathbf{H}_S & \frac{q^2}{\gamma^2}\mathbf{I}_d \end{pmatrix}.$$

By Shur's complement formula, we find

$$\mathrm{Vol}_{Q_\gamma}(\mathscr{L}(\mathbf{B}_S))^2 = (q/\gamma)^{2d} \cdot \det(\gamma^2 \mathbf{I}_{d-k}) = q^{2d}\gamma^{-2k}.$$

As such, we need to enforce the following condition on the blocksize β with respect to the rejection bound:

$$\rho \geqslant \min_{k \leqslant d} \left(\delta_\beta^{2d-k} q^{\frac{d}{2d-k}} \gamma^{-\frac{k}{2d-k}} \right). \tag{8}$$

From Sect. 3.2.1 and Eq. (1), we know that ρ is proportional to $\sqrt{q}$ once other parameters are fixed. Then Eq. (8) is equivalent to

$$\tau \cdot \alpha \cdot \eta_\varepsilon \cdot \sqrt{2d} \geqslant \min_{k \leqslant d} \left(\delta_\beta^{2d-k} \left(\frac{\sqrt{q}}{\gamma} \right)^{\frac{k}{2d-k}} \right), \tag{9}$$

where α and η_ε depends on whether FALCON or MITAKA parameters are considered.

There are three noteworthy observations about Condition (9). In the previous security analysis for FALCON and MITAKA, saturating the bound showed that $k = 0$ was the best case[5] from an attacker's point of view. A first and immediate observation is that the distortion of the norm directly impacts the hardness of the forgery. For fixed q, larger distortion factors γ, we observed that $\gamma \geqslant 2.3$ for $d = 512$ and $\gamma \geqslant 1.7$ for $d = 1024$ made forgetting vectors interesting for the attacker. The second one is more subtle. Note that the regime of schemes such FALCON or MITAKA always assumes that q is fixed in advance. In our work, we tolerate smaller q, and it turns out that when q gets smaller, an attacker finds it advantageous to forget some of the vectors. Experimentally[6] we found that the phase transition happens when $q \leqslant 2434$ for $d = 512$ and $q \leqslant 4820$ when $d = 1024$. Lastly, Condition (9) reveals that tolerating smaller q's with the standard norm, or keeping usual (larger) choices but twisting the norm by γ has essentially an identical effect on the forgery. One can indeed think of q/γ^2 as a "reduced modulus", or in other words, designing a signature scheme with $q' = \lfloor q/\gamma^2 \rfloor$. Hence from the point of view of forgery, our compression techniques can be seen as equivalent. However, they differ notably when we enter the domain of key recovery.

4.2   Key-Recovery Attacks

As advertised in Sect. 3.2, there are three distinct regimes to consider:

– in the **twisted Gaussian** regime, we twist the norm by $\gamma > 1$ and have imbalanced Gaussian secret keys;
– the **twisted-mixed** regime, the norm is also twisted by a larger γ, so the first half f of the secret key is now sparse ternary with Hamming weight κ;
– and in the **small q** regime, we keep the standard norm, but $q \leqslant 2d/\alpha^2$ so that both f and g are sparse, ternary with Hamming weight $\kappa = \alpha^2 q/2$.

A direct approach to key recovery is to do lattice reduction on the public basis, aiming at finding a relatively short vector in the spanned lattice: such attacks are addressed in Sect. 4.2.1. Whenever (a part of) the key becomes sparse ternary, combinatorics and more importantly *hybrid* attacks (combining lattice reduction and meet-in-the-middle approach) can be considered as a potential threat. In particular, in our mixed setting, we propose in Sect. 4.2.2 a new hybrid approach, of a slightly different flavor than the well-known Howgrave-Graham approach [22].

We also identify a new attack exploiting the sparsity of the secret keys in Sect. 4.2.3 The core idea is that when at least f is sparse, the number of "modulo turns" $k := (fh - g)/q$ is expected to be small too. This leads to another lattice reduction attack in a suitable orthogonal lattice (of rank $2d$ in a $3d$ dimensional space), that can also be improved by the "hybridization" approach. We also consider different metric choices for the ambient space of the lattice. Finally, we deal with algebraic, combinatoric, and classic hybrid attacks in Sect. 4.2.4.

---

[5] But this does not hold for MODFALCON, as observed in [6].
[6] It is of course possible to *calculate* the local maximum of the function, but an experiment confirmation seems enough for the purpose of this work.

4.2.1 Projection onto the Tail of the Reduced Basis

The key recovery consists in finding the private secret key (i.e. $f, g \in \mathcal{R}^2$) from the sole data of the public elements q and h. The most powerful attacks are up-to-our-knowledge realized through lattice reduction. It consists in constructing the algebraic lattice over $\mathcal{R}$ spanned by the vectors $(q, 0)$ and $(h, 1)$ (i.e. the public basis of the NTRU key) and retrieve the lattice vector $\mathbf{s} = (f, g)$ among all possible lattice vectors of norm bounded by $\|\mathbf{s}\|_\gamma = \sigma\sqrt{2d}$ (or a functionally equivalent vector, for instance $(\mu g, \mu f)$ for any unit μ of the number field). We make use of the so-called *projection trick* to avoid enumerating over all the sphere of radius $\sigma\sqrt{2d}$ (which contains around $\left(\frac{2d\sigma^2}{q}\right)^d$ vectors under the Gaussian heuristic).

More precisely we proceed as follows. Set β to be the block size parameter of the DBKZ algorithm and start by reducing the public basis with this latter algorithm. Call $\mathbf{b}_1, \dots, \mathbf{b}_{2d}$ the resulting vectors. Then, if we can recover the *projection* of the secret key onto the orthogonal space $\mathcal{P}$ to $\mathrm{Span}(\mathbf{b}_1, \dots, \mathbf{b}_{2d-\beta-1})$, then we can retrieve in polynomial time the full key by *Babai nearest plane* algorithm to lift it to a lattice vector of the desired norm. Hence it is enough to find the projection of the secret key among the shortest vectors of the lattice generated by the last β vectors projected onto $\mathcal{P}$.

Classically, sieving on this projected lattice will recover all vectors of norm smaller than $\sqrt{4/3} \cdot \ell$, where ℓ is the norm of the $2d - \beta$-th Gram-Schmidt vector $\tilde{\mathbf{b}}_{2d-\beta}$ of the reduced basis. Under the GSA (7), we therefore have:

$$\ell = \sqrt{q}\delta_\beta^{-2d+2\beta+2} \approx \left(\frac{\beta}{2\pi e}\right)^{1-\frac{d}{\beta}}.$$

Moreover, considering that $\mathbf{s}$ behaves as a random vector of norm $\sigma\sqrt{2d}$, and using the GSA again, the expected norm of its projection over $\mathcal{P}$ is $\sqrt{\beta/(2d)}\|\mathbf{s}\|_\gamma = \beta^{\frac{1}{2}}\sigma$. Hence, we will retrieve the projection among the sieved vectors if $\beta^{\frac{1}{2}}\sigma \leqslant \sqrt{4/3}\ell$, that is if the following condition is fulfilled:

$$\sigma^2 \leqslant \frac{4q}{3\beta} \cdot \delta_\beta^{4(\beta+1-d)} \tag{10}$$

Remark 1. This approach is similar to the one used in the security evaluation of [1], but we use all the vectors given by the last step of sieving, resulting in a slightly stronger attack and as such more conservative parameters choices.

Finding Short Vectors in Tweaked-Norm Setting: As our scheme suggests the use of different (Euclidean) norms, when it comes to the analysis of key recovery, it is also legitimate to wonder which norm is indeed the best to mount lattice attacks. Let us assume that we take an inner product matrix G and split in blocks of size $d \times d$ as $G = \begin{pmatrix} A & B \\ B^T & C \end{pmatrix}$ with $A, C \in \mathrm{Sym}^+(\mathbb{R}, d)$. By homogeneity, we can restrict the study to the case where the determinant of G is 1. Hence, the squared norm of (f, g) (viewed as a vector over $\mathbb{Z}^{2d}$) for this norm is $\langle Af, f\rangle + \langle Cg, g\rangle + 2\langle f, Bg\rangle$. Observe that since f, g (and thereof f, Bg) are *centered* independent vectors, the expected value of the inner product $\langle f, Bg\rangle$

is zero. Thus, we have by (bi)linearity:

$$\mathcal{E} := \mathbb{E}\left[\|(f,g)\|_G^2\right] = \mathbb{E}\left[\langle Af, f\rangle\right] + \mathbb{E}\left[\langle Cg, g\rangle\right] + 2\mathbb{E}\left[\langle f, Bg\rangle\right]$$
$$= \mathrm{Tr}(A\mathrm{Cov}(f)) + \mathrm{Tr}(C\mathrm{Cov}(g)). \tag{11}$$

Following Sect. 3.2.2, we have:

- in the twisted Gaussian regime, $\sigma_f^2 = (\frac{\alpha}{\gamma})^2 \cdot \frac{q}{2d}$ and $\sigma_g^2 = (\alpha\gamma)^2 \cdot \frac{q}{2d}$;
- in twisted-mixed f has scalar covariance[7] with parameter $\frac{\kappa}{d} = \sigma_f^2$;
- in the small q regime, we have $\gamma = 1$ and $\mathrm{Cov}(f) = \mathrm{Cov}(g) = \frac{\alpha^2 q}{2d}$.

In all cases, Eq. (11) becomes $\mathcal{E} = \frac{\alpha^2 q}{2d} \cdot \left(\frac{1}{\gamma^2}\mathrm{Tr}(A) + \gamma^2\mathrm{Tr}(C)\right)$. To favor lattice attacks, the used norm defined by G should minimize $\mathcal{E}$. By the arithmetic-geometric inequality and Fischer's inequality, we have

$$\frac{1}{\gamma^2}\mathrm{Tr}(A) + \gamma^2\mathrm{Tr}(C) \geqslant \frac{d}{\gamma^2}\det(A)^{\frac{1}{d}} + d\gamma^2\det(C)^{\frac{1}{d}} \geqslant 2d \cdot (\det(A)\det(C))^{\frac{1}{2d}} \geqslant 2d.$$

Hence $\mathcal{E}$ achieves a minimum $\alpha^2 q$ at $\mathrm{Tr}(A) = \gamma^2 d, \mathrm{Tr}(C) = \frac{d}{\gamma^2}$, which proves the optimality of Q_γ (Eq. (6)) whatever the regime.

4.2.2 An Hybrid Attack on Half-Sparse Vectors

We now show that we can improve this attack by exploiting the sparsity of the f part of the secret key. Indeed, if its sparsity level is low, then with a reasonable probability we can guess the positions of some zeros of the vector. If such a guess of positions, say $\mathcal{I} \subseteq \{1, \cdots, 2d\}$ appears to be correct, we can intersect the NTRU lattice with $\mathbb{Z}^{\overline{\mathcal{I}}}$. (where $\overline{\mathcal{I}}$ refers to the complement of the set $\mathcal{I}$ in the overset $\{1, \cdots, 2d\}$) In this lattice, we can apply readily the methodology of Sect. 4.2.1 to retrieve the intersected secret and as such the secret itself. This new lattice has dimension $2d - |\mathcal{I}|$ and its covolume is likely to be q^d (see infra for a discussion of this phenomena). As a result, the normalized covolume of the intersection lattice is bigger than previously, and its dimension of course smaller. As such, this final lattice reduction part is now easier and thus faster. Hence, there exists a trade-off between the probability of right guessing (the more zeroes to guess, the harder it becomes to correctly guess their positions) and the time required by the lattice reduction.

Estimation of the Cost of the Attack

Good Guess Probability Estimation [Fixed Hamming Weight]. We now derive an estimation of the probability of making a successful guess of the zero coefficients. Suppose that the sparsity of f is $0 < \kappa < d$ and that $|\mathcal{I}| = k$. Then, over the randomness of f, the probability of getting a correct guess is equal to the probability of f having its non-zero coefficient outside the k positions of $\mathcal{I}$, i.e. is $\binom{d-k}{\kappa}\binom{d}{\kappa}$.

---

[7] Indeed, $\mathbb{E}[f_i f_j] = 0$ for $i \neq j$ and by invariance of the distribution by permutation, all the diagonal elements are equal.

Remark now that we can enhance this probability by remarking that it suffices that a *conjugate* of f has is zero on $\mathcal{I}$. It seems however difficult to estimate such a probability explicitly as it depends on the pattern of $\mathcal{I}$. An underestimate of this probability consists in assuming that the event of right guessing for each of the conjugates are independent. Using this heuristic, the average number of conjugates with zeroes on $\mathcal{I}$ is $d\binom{d-k}{\kappa}\binom{d}{\kappa}^{-1}$. This heuristic is in practice precise enough for the simulation: we simulated the behavior, in cryptographically relevant parameters, of this expectation by repeating the counting on 2^{19} trials and report a relative error of at most 0.5% for results greater than 2^{-12}.

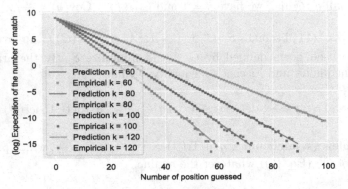

Volume of Intersection. Suppose now that a good guess was performed. We intersect the whole NTRU $\mathcal{L}$ lattice with $\mathbb{Z}^{\overline{\mathcal{I}}}$ and claim that with high probability this lattice has volume in ℓ_2 norm equal to $q^{d/2}$. First, remark that it necessarily q-ary and as such that it is sufficient to study the rank of $\mathcal{L}$ with $\mathbb{Z}^{\mathcal{I}}$, which will be full rank with overwhelming probability, according to [7]. As such the volume of the intersection is expected to be $q^{\frac{1}{2}}$. We can now compute the volume in the twisted norm $\|.\|_\gamma$. Remember that we obtained the intersection by removing d rows coordinates over f, which are all scaled by the parameter γ in $\|.\|_\gamma$. Hence, the volume is now scaled by the determinant of the intersected Gram matrix $G = \mathrm{Diag}(\overline{\mathcal{I}})Q_\gamma\mathrm{Diag}(\overline{\mathcal{I}})$, which is exactly γ^k. All in all the (normalized) volume of the intersected lattice for the twisted norm is $q^{\frac{d}{2d-k}}\gamma^{\frac{k}{2d-k}}$.

Remark 2. The normalized covolume of the intersection is now bigger than the original normalized covolume (which is $\sqrt{q}$), making the lattice reduction attack slightly easier. However this normalized covolume is not large enough to enter the *overstretched NTRU* regime (see [15] for recent developments on this matter).

Remark 3 (On non-fixed Hamming weight secrets). It could seem natural to let the small secret vectors be sampled with ternary distribution and no restriction on the Hamming weight (as a limit case of a tail cut Gaussian for instance).

However this choice is suboptimal security-wise. Indeed in this case, a simple estimation reveals that the probability of getting abnormally short vectors (i.e. with shorter weight than expected) is sufficiently high to reduce the whole security of the scheme: in other words, the fraction of generable weak keys is too high. Fixing in advance the Hamming weight avoids this phenomenon and has zero drawback on the key generation nor the scheme itself.

4.2.3 A New Attack Using the Small Number of Modulus Rounds

First of all, we stress that this attack only concerns the **twisted-mixed** and **small q** regimes, as it exploits the sparseness of f. In the twisted Gaussian regime, little can be said about the Hamming weight, and as the standard deviation parameter is still above the smoothing of $\mathbb{Z}$, it is also likely that the vector is not "so ternary", that is, it has enough coefficients of magnitude at least 2 so that the enumerating part of the attack becomes too costly anyway. As f is small, we can give a closer look at the size of the polynomial $hf - g$ which vanishes mod q by the construction of the NTRU basis (Sect. 2). It appears that $k := \frac{1}{q}(hf - g)$ has a norm closely related to the Hamming weight of f as it grows proportionally to $\sqrt{\kappa}$ (see infra. for an analysis of this fact). For small κ, this quantity is sufficiently small to be exploited in the lattice reduction. Indeed, instead of working modulo q as in the previous attack to recover directly f and g, we can aim at recovering directly the vector (f, g, k) in a rank two module, embedded in a $\mathscr{K}$-vector space of dimension 3. Since $fh - g = kq$, this module is nothing else than the orthogonal module to the vector $(h, -1, q)$. A public basis of this module (in rows) is $\mathbf{B} = \begin{pmatrix} 1 & h & 0 \\ 0 & q & 1 \end{pmatrix}$. On the space containing f, g the metric is given by Q_γ as defined in (6), and the "q part" is rescaled to take into account the expected length of k. Equivalently, this metric is described over $\mathscr{K}$ by the matrix $D = \mathrm{diag}(\gamma^2, \gamma^{-2}, \delta^2)$, for a parameter δ to be discussed later. The corresponding Gram matrix is then $G = \mathbf{B}D\mathbf{B}^* = \begin{pmatrix} \gamma^2 + \frac{hh^*}{\gamma^2} & \frac{qh}{\gamma^2} \\ \frac{qh^*}{\gamma^2} & \delta^2 + \frac{q^2}{\gamma^2} \end{pmatrix}$, and it follows that $\mathrm{N}_{\mathscr{K}/\mathbb{Q}}(\det(G)) = \mathrm{N}_{\mathscr{K}/\mathbb{Q}}\left(q^2 + (\gamma\delta)^2 + \frac{\delta^2}{\gamma^2}hh^*\right)$. We now estimate the expected normalized volume $\mathcal{V} = \mathrm{N}_{\mathscr{K}/\mathbb{Q}}(\det G)^{1/4d}$ of $\mathscr{L}(\mathbf{B})$. The intuition guiding the calculation is that q^2 will be the dominating term in the expansion and that we want δ to be a "balancing parameter" for the expected norm of k. Ultimately, its choice will make $\gamma\delta$ to be a small fraction of q, and δ/γ to be constant, see the full version [19] for details about the calculation:

$$\mathbb{E}|\mathcal{V}| \leqslant \sqrt{q} \cdot \left(1 + \frac{(\gamma\delta)^2}{q^2} + \frac{\delta^2}{\gamma^2} \cdot \frac{d}{12}\right)^{1/4}. \tag{12}$$

On the Expected Size of k: We now give a model of the distribution of the euclidean norm k in our setting, in the sense that its approximations match accurately our experimental results. Let f be uniform among the set of ternary polynomials of degree d with weight κ. Recall that we already assumed that h is uniform in $\mathscr{R}/q\mathscr{R}$. Then, we model the coefficients of fh as a sum of κ

independent discrete uniform random variables in $[-q/2, q/2] \cap \mathbb{Z}$. Such a sum as expected value 0 and variance $\frac{\kappa(q^2-1)}{12}$. Assuming that the coefficients of hf behaves independently, then the (squared) expected norm of the vector hf/q is then $\frac{d\kappa(q^2-1)}{12q^2} \approx \frac{d\kappa}{12}$. In the twisted–mixed regime, as seen in Sect. 3.2.2, the vector g is a discrete Gaussian distributed with standard deviation $\sigma_g = \gamma\alpha\sqrt{q/2d}$, and thus the expected squared norm of g/q is $\frac{\alpha^4 q^2}{\kappa q^2} = \frac{\alpha^4}{\kappa}$. When q is small, Sect. 3.2.2 says $\|g\|^2 = \kappa$ so that $(fh - g)/q$ has a squared norm of $\kappa(\frac{d}{12} + \frac{1}{q})$, which is still reasonably close to $\frac{d\kappa}{12}$. Therefore, a reasonable approximation for the expected squared norm of k is

$$\mathbb{E}[\|k\|^2] = \frac{d\kappa}{12}.$$

With that additional estimation in our arsenal, we can now see concrete values for the parameters. We chose δ so that the vector (f, g, k) has balanced coordinates in the given norm. Since we have $\mathbb{E}[\|(f, g, k)\|_D^2] = \alpha^2 q + \delta^2 \mathbb{E}[\|k\|^2]$, we set $\delta^2 = \frac{\alpha^2 q}{2\mathbb{E}[\|k\|^2]}$, and our attack has to find a short vector of expected length $\alpha(\frac{3q}{2})^{1/2}$. Now, in the twisted–mixed regime, we have $(\gamma\delta)^2 = \frac{3\alpha^4}{2\kappa^2 d}q^2$ and $\frac{\delta^2}{\gamma^2} = \frac{12}{d}$, and in the small q regime, $\gamma = 1$ and $\delta^2 = \frac{\kappa}{\mathbb{E}[\|k\|^2]} = \frac{12}{d}$. In any case, Inequality (12) becomes:

$$\mathbb{E}[\mathcal{V}] \leqslant \begin{cases} \alpha\sqrt{q} \cdot \left(\frac{2}{\alpha^4} + \frac{3}{2\kappa^2 d}\right)^{1/4} & \text{in the twisted-mixed regime,} \\ \sqrt{q} \cdot \left(2 + \frac{12}{dq^2}\right)^{1/4} & \text{in the small } q \text{ regime.} \end{cases}$$

For our smallest considered Hamming weight, we observe that $\mathbb{E}[\mathcal{V}] \leqslant 1.19 \cdot \sqrt{q}$ in the twisted–mixed regime. This was in turn confirmed by our experiments: we computed the average of these normalized volumes for several classes of parameters and found that the ratio $\mathcal{V}/\sqrt{q}$ never exceeded $\alpha = 1.17$. In the small q regime, the experiments showed that $\mathcal{V}/\sqrt{q} \leqslant 1.19$ on average too. As in the previous attack, the vector f is sparse so we hybridize the lattice reduction attack with the guessing technique. The whole attack is algorithmically depicted in the full version [19].

4.2.4 Combinatorial and Hybrid Attacks
In this section, we list the other possible type of attacks on signatures, which are nonetheless not the most effective for the parameters we consider.

Exploiting the Algebraic Structure. The schemes we consider are defined over algebraic lattices, which have a rich structure that could in principle lead to improved attacks. However, there is no known way to improve all the algorithms previously mentioned for their general lattice equivalent by more than polynomial factors in an asymptotic sense (see for instance the speedup on lattice reduction of [24]), and they do not affect our concrete security levels.

Overstretched NTRU. As observed in [25] and reanalysed in [15], when the modulus q is significantly larger than the magnitudes of the NTRU secret key coefficients, the attack on the key based on lattice reduction recovers the secret key better than the results presented above. This so-called "overstretched NTRU" parameters occurs when $q > n^{2.484}$ for binary secrets, implying that, as it is the case for FALCON and other NTRU-based NIST candidates, that even *very* significant improvements to this attack would still be irrelevant to the security of our proposed parameters: in fact, we are even further away from the fatigue point when reducing q!

Combinatorial and Hybrid Attacks. Odlyzko's meet-in-the-middle attack, and its recent improvements by May and Kirshanova–May, are a priori very relevant to our ternary sparse settings, particularly in the small-q case (and although non-ternary errors has not been analyzed in the literature, the Kirshanova–May improvements do in principle extend to that setting as well, and hence could affect our ternary regime even for distortion). However, running bit security estimator for the state-of-the-art attack of this type shows that it is very far from competing with the lattice attacks considered earlier in this section. At best, they yield time complexities over 2^{180} in dimension 512, for example.

The hybrid attack of Howgrave-Graham [22], and its improved analysis by Wunderer, appears to be more of a threat in principle. However, again using the available estimator (adapted to use the Core-SVP metric for BKZ cost) reveals that attacks reach at best 2^{138} complexity in dimension 512, again not competing with tailor-made lattice approaches.

4.3   Concrete Security Estimates

Under the heuristics we explicited, we can estimate the concrete bit security of our techniques on the FALCON and MITAKA NTRU based hash and sign signatures schemes. The analysis translates into concrete bit-security estimates following the methodology of NEWHOPE [1], sometimes called "core-SVP methodology". In this model [2], the bit complexity of lattice sieving (which is asymptotically the best SVP oracle) is taken as $\lfloor 0.292\beta \rfloor$ in the classical setting and $\lfloor 0.2570\beta \rfloor$ in the quantum setting in dimension β (using the recent progress of [4]).

4.3.1   Example Parameters

We now present the concrete data obtained for our new tradeoffs. In Table 2 we gathered several options for $d \in \{512, 1024\}$, and choices for moduli q and distortion factor γ, for both FALCON and MITAKA. The bit-security was obtained by taking into account our new attacks (impacting the more extremal ranges of parameters) and the last quantum sieving exponent for the core-SVP hardness, using updated versions of the scripts from the FALCON and MITAKA team. In Figs. 1 and 2, we also provide curves representing the security level in function of the main compression parameter.

Table 2. Bit security estimates for FALCON and MITAKA with small q and ellipsoidal Gaussians (compared to the original schemes), in dimension 512 and 1024. Security levels are given in pairs Classical/Quantum.

	FALCON-512				MITAKA-512			
	KeyRec	Forgery	Sig Size	Key Size	KeyRec	Forgery	Sig Size	Key Size
Original	133/117	123/108	666	896	133/117	102/89	710	896
Small $q = 1031$	132/116	122/108	490	704	132/116	99/87	540	704
Small $q = 521$	132/116	121/106	455	640	132/116	97/85	505	640
Small $q = 257$	130/114	118/104	425	576	130/114	94/82	475	576
Distortion $\gamma = 2$	132/116	123/108	540	896	132/116	101/89	590	896
Distortion $\gamma = 4$	132/116	122/107	475	896	132/116	98/87	525	896
Distortion $\gamma = 6$	131/115	119/105	440	896	131/115	95/84	490	896
Distortion $\gamma = 8$	128/113	116/102	410	896	128/113	92/81	460	896
Distortion $\gamma = 10$	125/110	113/99	390	896	125/110	88/78	441	896
	FALCON-1024				MITAKA-1024			
Original	272/239	284/250	1280	1792	272/239	233/205	1405	1792
Small $q = 1031$	272/239	280/246	932	1408	272/239	224/197	1160	1408
Small $q = 521$	269/237	275/242	870	1280	269/237	218/191	1000	1280
Small $q = 257$	264/233	268/235	805	1152	264/233	209/184	935	1152
Distortion $\gamma = 2$	271/239	284/250	1033	1792	271/239	230/202	1160	1792
Distortion $\gamma = 4$	270/237	278/245	905	1792	270/237	221/195	1035	1792
Distortion $\gamma = 6$	267/235	271/239	830	1792	267/235	213/187	960	1792
Distortion $\gamma = 8$	261/229	263/232	780	1792	261/229	204/180	905	1792

5 Batch Compressing Gaussian Vectors

In this section, we deal with the problem of efficient and lossless compression of a batch of random discrete Gaussian variables. Our goal is to further compress the s_1 part of the signature before outputting it. Of course, arithmetic coding would reach almost perfect entropic coding at the cost of requiring arithmetic computations of high precision floating-point numbers. We thus want to exploit the specificities of Gaussian variables to design a near entropic compression while retaining maximal efficiency.

5.1 Preliminary Information-Theoretical Analysis

Let n be a positive integer and $X = (X_i)_{1 \leqslant i \leqslant n}$ be a sequence of independent variables drawn under the discrete Gaussian distribution of standard deviation σ (assumed to be larger than the smoothing parameter of $\mathbb{Z}$). The entropy of this random vector is (close to) $\mathscr{H} = \frac{n}{2} \left(1 + \log_2(2\pi\sigma^2)\right)$ Therefore for a given sample $\mathbf{x}$, an entropic code for this distribution should have a codeword of length:

$$L(\mathbf{x}) = \mathscr{H} - n\log_2\left(e^{-\frac{\|\mathbf{x}\|^2}{2\sigma^2}}\right) = \underbrace{\frac{n}{2}\left(1 + \log_2(2\pi) + \frac{\|\mathbf{x}\|^2}{\sigma^2\log(2)}\right)}_{:=H} + \underbrace{n\log_2(\sigma)}_{:=T}$$

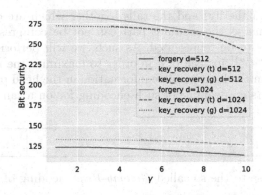

Fig. 1. Bit-security in function of the Hamming weight, $q = 12289$

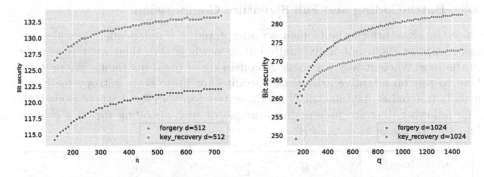

Fig. 2. Bit-security in function of q, for $d = 512$ (left) and $d = 1024$ (right).

The decomposition of this expression in the two main terms H, T (which we will refer to by *Head* and *Tail*) indicates two contributions, of different geometrical interpretations. The H part can be thought of as the σ-quantile where x landed, whereas the T part demonstrates that the $\log(\sigma)$ least significant bits of each coefficient behave as uniform variables in $[0, 2^\sigma]$, giving the position of x inside the quantile. This rough analysis invites us to work modulo σ: we can not compress the $\log_2(\sigma)$-lower-order bits, but we can work on the most significant bits.

5.2 Golomb-Rice Style Coding of a Single Variable

This preliminary observation leads to a first natural algorithm, working coefficient-wise: we can not compress the reminder modulo σ, which remains in binary form. If the quotient behaves roughly like a discrete normal distribution of unit standard deviation, then we can encode its values using a Huffman encoding. We then stack the coded heads (as the Huffman code is prefix, we can decode the heads on the fly) and the tails together which are chunks of equal lengths. Remark that as the modulus part can not be compressed it will take up to $\lceil \log_2(\sigma) \rceil$-bits to be represented. As such, we will perform the euclidean division by $k = 2^{\lceil \log_2(\sigma) \rceil}$ instead of σ in order to maximize the information put in the tail and retain the least possible information in the head part. The following diagram presents an example of such encoding for on a sample (x_1, x_2, x_3), where $x_i = t_i + h_i k$:

$H(h_1)$	$H(h_2)$	$H(h_3)$	t_1	t_2	t_3

This is very close to the so-called *Golomb-Rice* encoding of each coefficient with split at k.

5.3   Batch-Coding and Full Signature Compression

Since the signature can be (somehow) interpreted as d independent samples, we can compress them not individually but as a whole. We then want to encode in the most efficient way the message consisting of the d quotients. We propose here to rely on adaptive arithmetic encoding (or finite state entropy method), usually referred as Asymmetric Numeral system (or ANS for short) of Duda [16]. The following diagram presents an example of such encoding for on a sample (x_1, x_2, x_3), where $x_i = t_i + h_i k$:

$ANS(h_1 \| h_2 \| h_3)$	t_1	t_2	t_3

5.3.1   Ranged Arithmetic Encoding

Adapting the ranged version to our contexts, works as follow. Suppose that the distribution of the quotient part is a discrete Gaussian of standard deviation σ_q, denoted by $\mathcal{G}$ and of probability density function (pdf for short) ρ. As the size of signature is itself bounded by construction, we can truncate this distribution as well by a certain threshold T^8.

We also choose an *integral quantization factor* $p > 0$, and denote by f the quantized quotient distribution of $\mathcal{G}_{\leqslant T}$, that is to say its approximation at p bits of precision. More formally, we construct the distribution $\mathcal{G}_{\leqslant T}^{(p)}$ as the distribution of support $\{-T, \ldots, T\}$ and of pdf $\tilde{\rho}$ proportional to $x \mapsto \lceil 2^p \rho_{\leqslant T}(x) \rceil 2^{-p}$.

Then denoting by $R(x) = \sum_0^x \tilde{\rho}(x)$ its cumulative distribution function, we define the symbol encoding function to be

$$s : \begin{vmatrix} [0; 2^{p-1}] \longrightarrow [0, 2T] \\ x \longmapsto \operatorname{argmin}_s \{F(s) \leqslant x < F(s+1)\}. \end{vmatrix}$$

The coding function is now:

---

[8] By truncating a discrete distribution $\mathcal{D}$ over $\mathbb{Z}$ of pdf p, we mean constructing the distribution $\mathcal{D}_{\leqslant T}$ of support $\{-T, \ldots, T\} \cap \operatorname{Supp}(\mathcal{D})$ and of pdf $p_{\leqslant T}(x) = p(x) \left(\sum_{u=-T}^{T} p(u) \right)^{-1}$.

$C(x, s) = \left\lfloor \frac{x}{f(s)2^p} \ll n \right\rfloor + (x \mod f[s]) + F(s)$, The encoding of the (head) of the signature is then performed iteratively by (left)-folding the function C: for a sequence of integers $[s_1, \ldots, s_n]$, define inductively $x_0 := 0$ and $x_{i+1} = C(x_i, s_i)$. The encoded sequence is then the integer x_n.

With this construction, the decoding function is now, denoting by & the bitwise and operator, $D(x) = (f(s)(x \gg n) + (x \& (2^n - 1))) - F(s), s)$, used again by left folding: given a compressed sequence represented as the integer x, we stream out the sequence $(s_i)_i$ defined inductively by $x_0 = x$, $(x_{i+1}, s_{i+1}) = D(x_i)$.

5.3.2   ANS on the Raw Input

As the distribution of the signature coefficient is public, we could use ANS encoding directly on the coefficients. This is of course possible and naturally would offer the best compression rates, but it would require to multiply larger numbers. Indeed, using the aforementioned separation only requires handling the head, which is encoded on a small integer, whereas a direct ANS would require to handle arithmetic with numbers of around $n/2 \log(2\pi\sigma^2)$ bits.

In addition, as the standard deviation of the quotients is small, the alphabet will be very limited and we also can use a *tabulated variant* to completely avoid arithmetic computations (or so-called finite-state-entropy methods).

5.4   Nearly Optimal Encoding for Hash-and-Sign Signatures

5.4.1   Encoding of Falcon Signatures

For completeness, we recall the compression process used in the FALCON. The outline of the compression is quite similar to the one of Sect. 5.2, but the sign is taken out of the coefficient and encoded as a separated bit. As such, the quotient by σ is now following a folded-normal distribution. A careful study of this distribution reveals that the corresponding Huffman coding corresponds to the unary encoding of the variable. The following diagram presents an example of such encoding for on a sample (x_1, x_2), where $|x_i| = t_i + h_i k$ and $s_i = \mathrm{sgn}(x_i)$

0^{h_1}	1	s_1	t_1	0^{h_2}	1	s_2	t_2

5.4.2   Practical Comparison with Our Method

We exhibit a practical comparison of the compression performances between our encoding and Falcon's, together with the entropy lower bound. The experiments reveal that our technique is nearly optimal (standing at *at most* 3 bytes to the entropic limit). For dimension 512, we can save between 45 and 65 bytes compared to FALCON's Huffman-based coefficient-wise compression. In dimension 1024, the gaps now lie in between 80 and 130 bytes, which represents a total gain of 7%–14% on the signature size (Fig. 3).

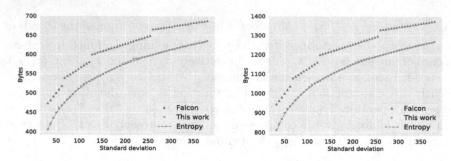

Fig. 3. Comparison between FALCON and our encoding. The left figure is for $d = 512$, the right one is for $d = 1024$. They are computed using a quantization factor of $f = 16$ (i.e. 16-bits approximation of the density function of the distribution).

Acknowledgements. We thank the anonymous reviewers for their helpful comments. Yang Yu is supported by the National Natural Science Foundation of China (No. 62102216), the National Key Research and Development Program of China (Grant No. 2018YFA0704701), the Major Program of Guangdong Basic and Applied Research (Grant No. 2019B030302008) and Major Scientific and Technological Innovation Project of Shandong Province, China (Grant No. 2019JZZY010133).

References

1. Alkim, E., Ducas, L., Pöppelmann, T., Schwabe, P.: Post-quantum key exchange - a new hope. In: Holz, T., Savage, S. (eds.) USENIX Security 2016, pp. 327–343. USENIX Association, August 2016
2. Becker, A., Ducas, L., Gama, N., Laarhoven, T.: New directions in nearest neighbor searching with applications to lattice sieving. In: Krauthgamer, R. (ed.) 27th SODA, pp. 10–24. ACM-SIAM, January 2016. https://doi.org/10.1137/1.9781611974331.ch2
3. Beullens, W.: Improved cryptanalysis of UOV and rainbow. In: Canteaut, A., Standaert, F.-X. (eds.) EUROCRYPT 2021. LNCS, vol. 12696, pp. 348–373. Springer, Cham (2021). https://doi.org/10.1007/978-3-030-77870-5_13
4. Chailloux, A., Loyer, J.: Lattice sieving via quantum random walks. In: Tibouchi, M., Wang, H. (eds.) ASIACRYPT 2021, Part IV. LNCS, vol. 13093, pp. 63–91. Springer, Cham (2021). https://doi.org/10.1007/978-3-030-92068-5_3
5. Chen, Y., Genise, N., Mukherjee, P.: Approximate trapdoors for lattices and smaller hash-and-sign signatures. In: Galbraith, S.D., Moriai, S. (eds.) ASIACRYPT 2019, Part III. LNCS, vol. 11923, pp. 3–32. Springer, Cham (2019). https://doi.org/10.1007/978-3-030-34618-8_1
6. Chuengsatiansup, C., Prest, T., Stehlé, D., Wallet, A., Xagawa, K.: ModFalcon: compact signatures based on module-NTRU lattices. In: Sun, H.M., Shieh, S.P., Gu, G., Ateniese, G. (eds.) ASIACCS 2020, pp. 853–866. ACM Press, October 2020. https://doi.org/10.1145/3320269.3384758
7. Coja-Oghlan, A., Ergür, A.A., Gao, P., Hetterich, S., Rolvien, M.: The rank of sparse random matrices. In: Proceedings of the Thirty-First Annual ACM-SIAM Symposium on Discrete Algorithms, SODA 2020, pp. 579–591. Society for Industrial and Applied Mathematics, USA (2020)

8. De Feo, L., Kohel, D., Leroux, A., Petit, C., Wesolowski, B.: SQISign: compact post-quantum signatures from quaternions and isogenies. In: Moriai, S., Wang, H. (eds.) ASIACRYPT 2020, Part I. LNCS, vol. 12491, pp. 64–93. Springer, Cham (2020). https://doi.org/10.1007/978-3-030-64837-4_3

9. Ding, J., et al.: Rainbow: submission to the NIST's post-quantum cryptography standardization process. https://csrc.nist.gov/Projects/post-quantum-cryptography/round-3-submissions

10. Ducas, L., Durmus, A., Lepoint, T., Lyubashevsky, V.: Lattice signatures and bimodal Gaussians. In: Canetti, R., Garay, J.A. (eds.) CRYPTO 2013, Part I. LNCS, vol. 8042, pp. 40–56. Springer, Heidelberg (2013). https://doi.org/10.1007/978-3-642-40041-4_3

11. Ducas, L., et al.: Crystals-dilithium: a lattice-based digital signature scheme. IACR Trans. Cryptogr. Hardw. Embed. Syst. 238–268 (2018)

12. Ducas, L., Lyubashevsky, V., Prest, T.: Efficient identity-based encryption over NTRU lattices. In: Sarkar, P., Iwata, T. (eds.) ASIACRYPT 2014. LNCS, vol. 8874, pp. 22–41. Springer, Heidelberg (2014). https://doi.org/10.1007/978-3-662-45608-8_2

13. Ducas, L., Nguyen, P.Q.: Learning a zonotope and more: cryptanalysis of NTRUSign countermeasures. In: Wang, X., Sako, K. (eds.) ASIACRYPT 2012. LNCS, vol. 7658, pp. 433–450. Springer, Heidelberg (2012). https://doi.org/10.1007/978-3-642-34961-4_27

14. Ducas, L., Prest, T.: Fast Fourier orthogonalization. In: ISSAC 2016, pp. 191–198 (2016)

15. Ducas, L., van Woerden, W.: NTRU fatigue: how stretched is overstretched? In: Tibouchi, M., Wang, H. (eds.) ASIACRYPT 2021, Part IV. LNCS, vol. 13093, pp. 3–32. Springer, Cham (2021). https://doi.org/10.1007/978-3-030-92068-5_1

16. Duda, J., Tahboub, K., Gadgil, N.J., Delp, E.J.: The use of asymmetric numeral systems as an accurate replacement for Huffman coding. In: 2015 Picture Coding Symposium (PCS) (2015)

17. Espitau, T., et al.: Mitaka: a simpler, parallelizable, maskable variant of falcon. In: Dunkelman, O., Dziembowski, S. (eds.) EUROCRYPT 2022, Part III. LNCS, vol. 13277, pp. 222–253. Springer, Heidelberg (2022). https://doi.org/10.1007/978-3-031-07082-2_9

18. Espitau, T., Kirchner, P.: The nearest-colattice algorithm: time-approximation tradeoff for approx-CVP. In: ANTS XIV, p. 251 (2020)

19. Espitau, T., Tibouchi, M., Wallet, A., Yu, Y.: Shorter hash-and-sign lattice-based signatures. Cryptology ePrint Archive, Paper 2022/785 (2022). https://eprint.iacr.org/2022/785

20. Fouque, P.A., Kirchner, P., Pornin, T., Yu, Y.: Bat: small and fast KEM over NTRU lattices. IACR Trans. Cryptogr. Hardw. Embed. Syst. **2022**(2), 240–265 (2022)

21. Gentry, C., Peikert, C., Vaikuntanathan, V.: Trapdoors for hard lattices and new cryptographic constructions. In: STOC 2008, pp. 197–206 (2008)

22. Howgrave-Graham, N.: A hybrid lattice-reduction and meet-in-the-middle attack against NTRU. In: Menezes, A. (ed.) CRYPTO 2007. LNCS, vol. 4622, pp. 150–169. Springer, Heidelberg (2007). https://doi.org/10.1007/978-3-540-74143-5_9

23. Jia, H., Hu, Y., Tang, C.: Lattice-based hash-and-sign signatures using approximate trapdoor, revisited. IET Inf. Secur. **16**(1), 41–50 (2022)

24. Kirchner, P., Espitau, T., Fouque, P.-A.: Fast reduction of algebraic lattices over cyclotomic fields. In: Micciancio, D., Ristenpart, T. (eds.) CRYPTO 2020, Part II. LNCS, vol. 12171, pp. 155–185. Springer, Cham (2020). https://doi.org/10.1007/978-3-030-56880-1_6

25. Kirchner, P., Fouque, P.-A.: Revisiting lattice attacks on overstretched NTRU parameters. In: Coron, J.-S., Nielsen, J.B. (eds.) EUROCRYPT 2017, Part I. LNCS, vol. 10210, pp. 3–26. Springer, Cham (2017). https://doi.org/10.1007/978-3-319-56620-7_1

26. Lu, X., et al.: LAC: practical ring-LWE based public-key encryption with byte-level modulus. Cryptology ePrint Archive, Paper 2018/1009 (2018). https://eprint.iacr.org/2018/1009

27. Lyubashevsky, V.: Fiat-Shamir with aborts: applications to lattice and factoring-based signatures. In: Matsui, M. (ed.) ASIACRYPT 2009. LNCS, vol. 5912, pp. 598–616. Springer, Heidelberg (2009). https://doi.org/10.1007/978-3-642-10366-7_35

28. Lyubashevsky, V.: Lattice signatures without trapdoors. In: Pointcheval, D., Johansson, T. (eds.) EUROCRYPT 2012. LNCS, vol. 7237, pp. 738–755. Springer, Heidelberg (2012). https://doi.org/10.1007/978-3-642-29011-4_43

29. Lyubashevsky, V., et al.: Dilithium: submission to the NIST's post-quantum cryptography standardization process. https://csrc.nist.gov/Projects/post-quantum-cryptography/round-3-submissions

30. Lyubashevsky, V., Wichs, D.: Simple lattice trapdoor sampling from a broad class of distributions. In: Katz, J. (ed.) PKC 2015. LNCS, vol. 9020, pp. 716–730. Springer, Heidelberg (2015). https://doi.org/10.1007/978-3-662-46447-2_32

31. Micciancio, D., Peikert, C.: Trapdoors for lattices: simpler, tighter, faster, smaller. In: Pointcheval, D., Johansson, T. (eds.) EUROCRYPT 2012. LNCS, vol. 7237, pp. 700–718. Springer, Heidelberg (2012). https://doi.org/10.1007/978-3-642-29011-4_41

32. Micciancio, D., Regev, O.: Worst-case to average-case reductions based on Gaussian measures. SIAM J. Comput. **37**(1), 267–302 (2007)

33. Micciancio, D., Walter, M.: Practical, predictable lattice basis reduction. In: Fischlin, M., Coron, J.-S. (eds.) EUROCRYPT 2016, Part I. LNCS, vol. 9665, pp. 820–849. Springer, Heidelberg (2016). https://doi.org/10.1007/978-3-662-49890-3_31

34. Nguyen, P.Q., Regev, O.: Learning a parallelepiped: cryptanalysis of GGH and NTRU signatures. In: Vaudenay, S. (ed.) EUROCRYPT 2006. LNCS, vol. 4004, pp. 271–288. Springer, Heidelberg (2006). https://doi.org/10.1007/11761679_17

35. Peikert, C.: An efficient and parallel Gaussian sampler for lattices. In: Rabin, T. (ed.) CRYPTO 2010. LNCS, vol. 6223, pp. 80–97. Springer, Heidelberg (2010). https://doi.org/10.1007/978-3-642-14623-7_5

36. Prest, T.: Gaussian sampling in lattice-based cryptography. Ph.D. thesis, École Normale Supérieure, Paris, France (2015)

37. Prest, T., et al.: Falcon: submission to the NIST's post-quantum cryptography standardization process. https://csrc.nist.gov/Projects/post-quantum-cryptography/round-3-submissions

38. Rasmussen, R.: ICANN SSAC comment to NIST on quantum cryptography algorithms. Technical report, December 2019. https://www.icann.org/en/system/files/files/sac-107-en.pdf

39. Regev, O.: On lattices, learning with errors, random linear codes, and cryptography. In: Gabow, H.N., Fagin, R. (eds.) 37th ACM STOC, pp. 84–93. ACM Press, May 2005. https://doi.org/10.1145/1060590.1060603

40. Stehlé, D., Steinfeld, R.: Making NTRU as secure as worst-case problems over ideal lattices. In: Paterson, K.G. (ed.) EUROCRYPT 2011. LNCS, vol. 6632, pp. 27–47. Springer, Heidelberg (2011). https://doi.org/10.1007/978-3-642-20465-4_4

41. Westerbaan, B.: Sizing up post-quantum signatures, September 2021. https://blog. cloudflare.com/sizing-up-post-quantum-signatures/
42. Yu, Y., Ducas, L.: Learning strikes again: the case of the DRS signature scheme. In: Peyrin, T., Galbraith, S. (eds.) ASIACRYPT 2018, Part II. LNCS, vol. 11273, pp. 525–543. Springer, Cham (2018). https://doi.org/10.1007/978-3-030-03329-3_18
43. Zhang, J., Yu, Yu., Fan, S., Zhang, Z., Yang, K.: Tweaking the asymmetry of asymmetric-key cryptography on lattices: KEMs and signatures of smaller sizes. In: Kiayias, A., Kohlweiss, M., Wallden, P., Zikas, V. (eds.) PKC 2020, Part II. LNCS, vol. 12111, pp. 37–65. Springer, Cham (2020). https://doi.org/10.1007/978-3-030-45388-6_2

MuSig-L: Lattice-Based Multi-signature with Single-Round Online Phase

Cecilia Boschini[1,2], Akira Takahashi[3]($\boxtimes$), and Mehdi Tibouchi[4]

[1] Technion, Haifa, Israel
cecilia.bo@cs.technion.ac.il
[2] Reichman University, Herzliya, Israel
[3] Aarhus University, Aarhus, Denmark
takahashi@cs.au.dk
[4] NTT Corporation, Tokyo, Japan
mehdi.tibouchi.br@hco.ntt.co.jp

Abstract. Multi-signatures are protocols that allow a group of signers to jointly produce a single signature on the same message. In recent years, a number of practical multi-signature schemes have been proposed in the discrete-log setting, such as MuSig2 (CRYPTO'21) and DWMS (CRYPTO'21). The main technical challenge in constructing a multi-signature scheme is to achieve a set of several desirable properties, such as (1) security in the plain public-key (PPK) model, (2) concurrent security, (3) low online round complexity, and (4) key aggregation. However, previous lattice-based, post-quantum counterparts to Schnorr multi-signatures fail to satisfy these properties.

In this paper, we introduce MuSig-L, a lattice-based multi-signature scheme simultaneously achieving these design goals for the first time. Unlike the recent, round-efficient proposal of Damgård et al. (PKC'21), which had to rely on lattice-based trapdoor commitments, we do not require any additional primitive in the protocol, while being able to prove security from the standard module-SIS and LWE assumptions. The resulting output signature of our scheme therefore looks closer to the usual Fiat–Shamir-with-abort signatures.

1 Introduction

A multi-signature is a primitive that allows a group of signers holding individual key pairs $(\mathsf{sk}_1, \mathsf{pk}_1), \ldots, (\mathsf{sk}_n, \mathsf{pk}_n)$ to jointly produce a signature on a message μ of their choice. A number of multi-signatures have been proposed in recent years, mainly motivated by several new real-world applications such as cryptocurrencies. Recent developments in the discrete log setting particularly garnered renewed attention among practitioners, since some of them even serve as a drop-in replacement for ordinary signatures already deployed in practice [36].

The main technical challenge when constructing a new multi-signature scheme is to achieve a set of desirable properties, such as (1) security in the plain public-key (PPK) model, (2) concurrent security, (3) low online round complexity, and (4) key aggregation. The PPK model requires that each signer publishes its public key in the clear without any dedicated interactive key generation protocol,

Y. Dodis and T. Shrimpton (Eds.): CRYPTO 2022, LNCS 13508, pp. 276–305, 2022.
https://doi.org/10.1007/978-3-031-15979-4_10

and that no adversaries be able to convince a verifier that an honest party P_1[1] participated in signing any messages, unless P_1 has ever agreed on it. This is essentially to prevent the well-known rogue-key attacks (e.g., [32]) in a plain way (i.e., without requiring *proof of possession* wherein each party must submit a proof to prove knowledge of their secret key [39]). Thus proving security under the PPK model is often considered ideal in the literature.

Several round-efficient Schnorr-based proposals with proof in the PPK model appeared in the literature. However, the seminal work of Drijvers et al. [18] pointed out subtle pitfalls of many existing interactive schemes, by presenting an adversarial strategy that exploits many *concurrent sessions*. The adversary in this scenario may launch multiple instances of the signing protocol with an honest party, and forge a signature on a new message by carefully combining signature shares from different sessions. Benhamouda et al. [9] recently improved the attack and proved that those schemes can be broken even in polynomial time. Given such devastating attacks, it is crucial to prove security of the scheme in the model where concurrent sign queries are allowed.

Although some previous schemes, such as BN [7], MuSig [31], MuSig-DN [37], mBCJ [18], and HBMS [6], are indeed provably secure against concurrent attacks, they all require (at least) two rounds of interaction during the *online phase*, i.e., after parties receive the message to sign. On the other hand, it is desirable in practice to *preprocess* part of the interaction and computation without knowledge of the message to be signed, so that participants can minimize round-/-communication complexity later. Such an offline-online trick has become increasingly common in context of general-purpose multi-party computation (e.g., [17]), and therefore it is also another important design goal when constructing a multi-signature. Recently, Nick, Ruffing, and Seurin [36], and Alper and Burdges [4] concurrently proposed near-optimal Schnorr-based multi-signatures in this paradigm. One remarkable feature of these schemes – MuSig2 and DWMS– is that they only require a *single round* of interaction in the online phase while retaining security against concurrent attacks. They also support *key aggregation*, an additional optimization technique that takes a set of public keys to produce a single combined Schnorr public key. It is crucial for a multi-signature scheme to support key aggregation, because it allows verifiers to verify a signature with an ordinary Schnorr public key and thus makes the scheme interoperable with the existing verification algorithms.

State-of-the-Art in the Lattice Setting. As Schnorr-based constructions do not withstand quantum attacks, it is an interesting question how to construct post-quantum alternatives. Indeed, several lattice-based counterparts to the aforementioned schemes exist in the literature [16,20,21,30]. All of these schemes follow the so-called *Fiat-Shamir with aborts (FSwA)* paradigm [26], which shares the basic structure with Schnorr. Hence, it is well-known that many observations in the DLog setting can be reused to construct similar FSwA-based instantiations, e.g., ES, MJ, and FH follow the ideas of BN three-round Schnorr

---

[1] Note in multi-signature every honest party behaves identically and thinks of themselves as "P_1" [7]. Other parties $P_2, \ldots, P_n$ are called *co-signers*.

multi-signature, and the most recent scheme due to Damgård et al. [16] closely follows the mBCJ two-round scheme. There are however several subtle issues that only arise in the lattice world. For example, one inherent issue with the Fiat-Shamir "with aborts" multi-signature is simulation of the honest sign oracle. The basic idea of these schemes is to take the sum of usual FSwA signatures produced by different parties as follows: party P_1 first starts a protocol by sending "commit" messages $\mathbf{w}_1$ of the underlying Σ-protocol, and then upon receiving $\mathbf{w}_2, \ldots, \mathbf{w}_n$ from others, P_1 locally derives challenge c by hashing $\mathbf{w} := \sum_{i=1}^{n} \mathbf{w}_i$, together with the message μ to be signed. It then performs rejection sampling on the response $\mathbf{z}_1$, and the protocol must restart as long as there exists a party who rejected their response. This means that $\mathbf{w}_1$ is always revealed, whether P_1 aborts or not. However, there is currently no known way to simulate $(\mathbf{w}_1, c)$ for rejected instances, and thus publicly available proofs of ES and MJ are incomplete, and FH had to rely on a non-standard assumption (which they call "rejected" LWE). Although DOTT managed to circumvent the issue by having P_1 send a [5]-based *trapdoor homomorphic commitment* Commit($\mathbf{w}_1$) to keep $\mathbf{w}_1$ secret until rejection sampling is successful, their approach inevitably makes the scheme incompatible with preprocessing: because each $\mathbf{w}_1$ must be committed using *message-dependent commitment keys*, two rounds of interaction must always happen online. Moreover, since their scheme has to output combined commitments or randomness as part of the signature, the verifier also needs to check an aggregated commitment is opened correctly. These are in fact limitations inherited from mBCJ, and thus it is an interesting open question whether lattice-based multi-signature can be securely improved while benefiting from the latest tricks in the DL setting.

1.1   Our Contributions

In this paper, we introduce MuSig-L, a lattice-based multi-signature scheme simultaneously achieving the aforementioned design goals for the first time: concurrent security in the PPK model, single-round online phase, and key aggregation. In Table 1 we compare ours to previous schemes following the same paradigm. Just as MuSig2 and DWMS, our MuSig-L allows parties to preprocess the first-round "commit" messages before receiving the message to be signed. Thus all they have to communicate during the online phase is the final response value $\mathbf{z}_i$. Although the protocol must abort if there is one party that fails in rejection sampling (which is also the case with other FSwA distributed/multi-signatures), we can mitigate by executing sufficiently many parallel instances of the protocol at once. Since security against concurrent attackers is crucial in this setting, we provide detailed security proofs in a suitable model.

Our scheme does not require any additional primitive for instantiating the protocol, unlike the two-round, provably secure scheme of Damgård et al. This was made possible by our generalized rejection sampling lemma in combination with trapdoor preimage sampling of [34] and several technical lemmas, as we sketch below. The resulting output signature of our scheme therefore looks much closer to the usual Fiat–Shamir-with-abort signatures.

Table 1. Comparison with previous DLog/FSwA-based multi-signatures with concurrent security in the plain-public key model. The column "#Off" indicates the number of rounds that can be preprocessed in the offline phase (Although ES, MJ, and FH do not explicitly support offline-online paradigm, we conjecture the first round of these schemes can be securely preprocessed since they all follow the same blueprint of BN). "#On" indicates the number of rounds that must occur online after receiving a signature to sign. The total number of rounds is thus given as "#Off + #On". The column "Agg." indicates whether a scheme supports key aggregation or not.

	Assumption	#Off	#On	Agg.	Note
BN [7]	DL	1	2	N	
MuSig [31]	DL	1	2	Y	
mBCJ [18]	DL	0	2	Y	
MuSig-DN [37]	DL & DDH	0	2	Y	
MuSig2 [36]	AOMDL	1	1	Y	
DWMS [4]	AGM	1	1	Y	
HBMS [6]	DL	0	2	Y	
ES [20]	DCK	1	2	N	Proof incomplete
MJ [30]	RSIS	1	2	Y	Proof incomplete
FH [21]	MLWE & rMLWE	1	2	N	Proof in QROM
DOTT [16]	MLWE & MSIS	0	2	N	TD Commitment
Our MuSig-L	MLWE & MSIS	1	1	Y	L must be a set[a]

[a]This is because in our scheme each signer explicitly prohibits duplicate keys in the key list L so that the security proof goes through in the *offline-online* security model. The rationale behind this choice will be detailed in Sect. 4.5.

Although our MuSig-L partially follows tricks present in MuSig2 and DWMS, the resulting scheme and our new proof techniques (outlined below) are significantly different from theirs. As a consequence, we are able to prove security solely based on the standard SIS and LWE assumptions in the ring setting and in the (classical) random oracle model, while MuSig2 and DWMS are proven secure either under the "one-more" DL assumption or in the algebraic group model.

1.2   Our Techniques

Scheme Overview. Figure 1 describes overview of our scheme, executed by Γ_1. In Sect. 3.1 we will provide more formal algorithm specifications. In MuSig-L, a key pair is the same as in the usual FSwA: $sk_i = s_i$ and $pk_i = t_i = \bar{A}s_i$, where s_i consists of small elements in a ring $R_q = \mathbb{Z}_q[X]/(F(X))$. On receiving public keys from the other parties, P_1 derives "aggregation coefficients" by hashing a set of keys and each public key held by P_i. Here the hash function is instantiated by the random oracle $H_{agg} : \{0,1\}^* \to C$, where C is the same as the challenge space used by the underlying FSwA Σ-protocol. It then constructs an aggregated key $\tilde{t}$ by taking the linear combination of all keys. This is similar to the key aggregation technique introduced in MuSig [31] (where they choose a_i to be *uniform in* $\mathbb{Z}_q$), but we must carefully choose the size of aggregation coefficients so that it enables security reduction to the Module-SIS assumption.

In the offline phase, parties exchange a bunch of "commit" messages $\mathbf{w}_i^{(1)}, \ldots,$ $\mathbf{w}_i^{(m)}$. We then use the "random linear combination" trick similar to MuSig2 and DWMS, to aggregate the "commit" messages coming from the offline phase. That is, we force everyone to derive the "nonce" coefficients $b^{(j)}$'s through another random oracle H_{non}, and these nonces are used for computing a single aggregate commit $\tilde{\mathbf{w}}$. This operation essentially prevents malicious parties from adaptively influencing inputs to the next random oracle H_{sig} deriving "joint challenge" $c \in C$ that all parties must agree on. Finally, P_1 locally performs rejection sampling on a potential response value $\mathbf{z}_1$, such that the distribution of revealed $\mathbf{z}_1$ is always independent of the secret $\mathbf{s}_1$.

Generalized Rejection Sampling. Not relying on a commitment scheme has a major drawback: we need to deal with possible leakage, due to both sending the first messages in the clear, and with aggregating them using random coefficients.

As the $\mathbf{w}_i^{(j)}$ are sent in the clear, the adversary $\mathcal{A}$ knows *before receiving* $\mathbf{z}_i$ that the response will be sampled from the coset $\Lambda_{\tilde{\mathbf{u}}}^{\perp}(\bar{\mathbf{A}})$, where $\tilde{\mathbf{u}} := \sum_j b^{(j)} \mathbf{w}_1^{(j)} + c \cdot a_1 \cdot \mathbf{t}_1$. This information does not give $\mathcal{A}$ any advantage in case the signing protocol succeeds. However, in case of abort $\mathcal{A}$ has gained some information on $\mathbf{z}_1$, that is, it knows that some element of $\Lambda_{\tilde{\mathbf{u}}}^{\perp}(\bar{\mathbf{A}})$ has been rejected. This could potentially leak information about the secret key, a subtle issue avoided in [16] by opening the commitment to the first message only in case of a success.

The second issue is related to efficiency. Aggregating the "commit" messages using some random coefficients implies that the distribution of the response $\mathbf{z}_1$ depends on those coefficients. In particular, the distributions of $\mathbf{z}_1$ is a Gaussian with parameter Σ that changes with different choices of the $b^{(j)}$'s. This is not just a nuisance: Σ leaks information about the $b^{(j)}$'s. It is not immediate to see why this is concerning, as it only becomes an issue when simulating honest signers in the security proof. Essentially, this requires to generate $\mathbf{z}_1$ *after* generating $\mathbf{w}_1^{(1)}, \ldots, \mathbf{w}_1^{(m)}$ with a trapdoor and sampling the $b^{(j)}$'s *using such a trapdoor*. Thus, the distribution of $\mathbf{z}_1$ has to be independent of the $b^{(j)}$'s.

Perhaps unsurprisingly, rejection sampling can take care of all the leakage. In particular, we show that the rejection sampling technique is secure even if: (1) $\mathcal{A}$ knows the lattice coset, (2) the secret and public Gaussian distributions have different centers, and covariance matrices (obviously, for this to make sense neither difference can be too large). In fact, we prove a more general result than what the security of MuSig-L needs, allowing not only spherical, but ellipsoidal discrete Gaussians (i.e., Gaussians whose covariance matrix Σ is not diagonal). The proof of this result required quite the effort: while we could follow the structure of the proof of the original rejection sampling theorem, the intermediate steps required to extend many existing results, either to the case of ellipsoidal

Gaussians, or to sampling from lattice cosets, or both. Proofs were simplified by relying on the canonical representation of ring elements, even though the rest of the algorithms will use the coefficient representation. This is not an issue per se, as these embeddings are isometric in power-of-2 cyclotomics. The result is a rather powerful extension of the rejection sampling technique, that we believe of independent interest.

Exploiting Trapdoor Sampling for Simulation. As usual, the main technical challenge in proving security of multi-signature is to simulate the behaviors of an honest party P_1 without knowledge of the actual secret key. Although our rejection sampling lemma allows to simulate the distribution of $\mathbf{z}_1$ and thus the aggregated offline outputs $\tilde{\mathbf{w}}_1 = \bar{\mathbf{A}}\mathbf{z}_1 - c \cdot a_1 \cdot \mathbf{t}_1$, it is not immediately clear how one can make sure $\tilde{\mathbf{w}}_1$ is consistent with the offline messages $\mathbf{w}_1^{(j)}$ and nonces $b^{(j)}$. One naive approach would be to mimic the security proof for MuSig2: they essentially avoid the issue with simulation by relying on hardness of the *one-more* DL problem, a stronger assumption that solving DL is still hard even after making a limited number of queries to a DL solver oracle. Although a similar lattice-based problem was recently introduced by Agrawal et al. [2] and it might make an interesting alternative approach to proving our scheme, it is not a well-studied assumption yet and we're thus motivated to propose an entirely different proof strategy.

One crucial observation in this work is that, in the lattice world, a simulator can secretly produce a *trapdoor* when creating the offline messages $\mathbf{W} := [\mathbf{w}_1^{(1)}, \dots, \mathbf{w}_1^{(m)}]$, using the gadget-based trapdoor generation algorithm of Micciancio and Peikert [34] with $m = O(k \log q)$. Once the corresponding trapdoor is known, the simulator can now sample $\mathbf{b} = [b^{(1)}, \dots, b^{(m)}]$ from a coset $\Lambda_{\tilde{\mathbf{w}}_1}^{\perp}(\mathbf{W})$ using a Gaussian preimage sampling for the SIS function $f_{\mathbf{W}}$. In this way, our simulator can successfully output a simulated signature, offline messages, and nonces $b^{(j)}$ that are all statistically indistinguishable with actual outputs of the honest party. In Sect. 4.4 we realize this idea in the form of *oracle simulation lemma*, which is proven by combining the utility lemma in Sect. 4.2 and instantiation of the trapdoor in Sect. 4.3. Finally, Sect. 4.5 formally states CMA security of our scheme.

Supporting Technical Lemmas. Our analysis and the security proof of our protocol rely on a number of technical facts related to discrete Gaussian distributions over module lattices, sometimes with general covariance matrices. Most of those facts are simple extensions and generalizations of well-known results in the literature, while others are less easy to come up with. Since a number of them may be of independent interest, we have tried to state them in a relatively high level of generality, and to provide relatively self-contained proofs either way.

1.3   Other Related Work

Multi-signatures belong to a larger family of signatures that support aggregation, its closest relatives being aggregate signatures and threshold signatures.

$P_1(\bar{\mathbf{A}} = [\mathbf{A}|\mathbb{I}_k], \mathsf{sk}_1 = \mathbf{s}_1, \mathsf{pk}_1 = \mathbf{t}_1 = \bar{\mathbf{A}} \cdot \mathbf{s}_1, \mu)$

// Key aggregation phase

$\xrightarrow{\quad\quad\quad\quad\mathbf{t}_1\quad\quad\quad\quad}$

$\xleftarrow{\quad\quad(\mathbf{t}_i)_{i \in [2,n]}\quad\quad}$

//Derive aggregation coefficients

For $i \in [n] : a_i := \mathsf{H}_{\mathsf{agg}}((\mathbf{t}_i)_{i \in [n]}, \mathbf{t}_i)$

$\bar{\mathbf{t}} := \sum_{i=1}^{n} a_i \mathbf{t}_i \bmod q$

// Offline phase

$\mathbf{y}_1^{(1)} \leftarrow \mathscr{D}_{\sigma_1}^{\ell+k}$

For $j \in [2,m] : \mathbf{y}_1^{(j)} \leftarrow \mathscr{D}_{\sigma_y}^{\ell+k}$

For $j \in [1,m] : \mathbf{w}_1^{(j)} := \bar{\mathbf{A}} \mathbf{y}_1^{(j)} \bmod q$

$\mathsf{com}_1 := (\mathbf{w}_1^{(j)})_{j \in [m]}$

$\xrightarrow{\quad\quad\quad\mathsf{pk}_1 || \mathsf{com}_1\quad\quad\quad}$

$\xleftarrow{\quad(\mathsf{pk}_i || \mathsf{com}_i)_{i \in [2,n]}\quad}$

// Online phase

If $\exists i \geq 2 : \mathsf{pk}_i = \mathsf{pk}_1$: Abort

$(r^{(j)})_{j \in [2,m]} := \mathsf{H}_{\mathsf{non}}((\mathsf{pk}_i || \mathsf{com}_i)_{i \in [n]}, \mu, \bar{\mathbf{t}})$

$b^{(1)} := 1$

For $j \in [2,m]$: sample $b^{(j)} \sim \mathscr{D}_{\sigma_b}$ using randomness $r^{(j)}$

$\tilde{\mathbf{w}} := \sum_{j=1}^{m} b^{(j)} \cdot \left(\sum_{i=1}^{n} \mathbf{w}_i^{(j)} \right) \bmod q$

$\tilde{\mathbf{y}}_1 := \sum_{j=1}^{m} b^{(j)} \cdot \mathbf{y}_1^{(j)}$

$c := \mathsf{H}_{\mathsf{sig}}(\tilde{\mathbf{w}}, \mu, \bar{\mathbf{t}})$

$\mathbf{z}_1 := c \cdot a_1 \cdot \mathbf{s}_1 + \tilde{\mathbf{y}}_1$

If $\mathsf{RejSamp}(c \cdot a_1 \cdot \mathbf{s}_1, \mathbf{z}_1, (b^{(j)})_{j \in [m]}) = 0$:

$\quad \mathbf{z}_1 := \bot$

$\xrightarrow{\quad\quad\quad\quad\mathbf{z}_1\quad\quad\quad\quad}$

If $\mathbf{z}_i = \bot$ for some i, abort

$\xleftarrow{\quad\quad(\mathbf{z}_i)_{i \in [2,n]}\quad\quad}$

Otherwise, compute $\tilde{\mathbf{z}} := \sum_{i=1}^{n} \mathbf{z}_i$

Output $(\tilde{\mathbf{w}}, \tilde{\mathbf{z}})$

Fig. 1. Stylized overview of our two-round lattice-based multi-signature

There have been a number of results on threshold Schnorr-style signatures [22,23,38,40]. However, to the best of our knowledge the most recent *two-round* schemes all rely on non-standard assumptions. For example, the modular approach to proving security of threshold and multi-signatures based on Schnorr signatures in [15] strongly relies on the AGM, while the threshold signature FROST [25] is proven secure in a non-standard heuristic which models the hash function (a public primitive) used for deriving the coefficients for the linear combination as a one-time VRF (a primitive with a secret key) in the security proof.

Threshold signatures can be instantiated from lattices, but the existing t-out-of-n constructions require either to threshold secret share the signing key of GPV signature [8], or FHE [3,11]. The multi-signature of [16] also gives rise to the n-out-of-n threshold signature, and they in fact showed that essentially the same tricks work under both security models. We therefore highlight adapting our techniques in the threshold setting as an interesting direction for future work. The panorama of aggregate signature from lattices is similar. A three-round construction by Boneh and Kim [12] requires interactive aggregation, which again closely follows the BN Schnorr-based scheme. The recent aggregate signature by Boudgoust and Roux-Langlois [13] requires no interaction between signers although the asymptotic signature size grows linearly in the number of signers.

2 Preliminaries

Notations. For positive integers a and b such that $a < b$ we use the integer interval notation $[a, b]$ to denote $\{a, a+1, \ldots, b\}$. We also use $[b]$ as shorthand for $[1, b]$. We denote by $\mathbf{y}[j]$ the j-th component of vector $\mathbf{y}$, and by $\mathbb{I}_n$ the identity matrix of dimension n. If S is a set we write $s \leftarrow\!\!\$\ S$ to indicate sampling s from the uniform distribution defined over S; if $\mathscr{D}$ is a probability distribution we write $s \leftarrow \mathscr{D}$ to indicate sampling s from $\mathscr{D}$; if $\mathcal{A}$ is a randomized (resp. deterministic) algorithm we write $s \leftarrow \mathcal{A}$ (resp. $s := \mathcal{A}$) to indicate assigning an output from $\mathcal{A}$ to s. For a set S, $\langle S \rangle$ denotes a unique encoding of S (e.g., the sequence of strings in lexicographic order). Throughout, the security parameter is denoted by λ.

Power-of-Two Cyclotomics and Norms. We instantiate the scheme over power-of-two cyclotomics. Let N be a power of two and ζ be a primitive $2N$th root of unity. The $2N$th cyclotomic number field is denoted by $K := \mathbb{Q}(\zeta) \cong \mathbb{Q}[X]/(X^N + 1)$ and the corresponding ring of algebraic integers is $R := \mathbb{Z}[\zeta] \cong \mathbb{Z}[X]/(X^N + 1)$. Both are contained in $K_\mathbb{R} := K \otimes \mathbb{R} \cong \mathbb{R}[X]/(X^N + 1)$. Throughout the paper, we fix q to be a prime satisfying $q = 5 \bmod 8$ and let $R_q := \mathbb{Z}_q[X]/(X^N + 1)$. An L^p-norm for a module element $\mathbf{v} \in R^m$ is given by the coefficient embedding: for $\mathbf{v} = (\sum_{i=0}^{N-1} v_{i,1} X^i, \ldots, \sum_{i=0}^{N-1} v_{i,m} X^i)^T$, we define

$$\|\mathbf{v}\|_p := \|(v_{0,1}, \ldots, v_{N-1,1}, \ldots, v_{0,m}, \ldots, v_{N-1,m})^T\|_p.$$

The Euclidean norm of a vector $\mathbf{v} = (v_1, \ldots, v_m)^T \in R^m$ in the canonical representation is defined as

$$\|\varphi(\mathbf{v})\|_2 := \frac{1}{\sqrt{N}} \cdot \sqrt{\sum_{i \in [n], j \in \mathbb{Z}_{2N}^*} |\varphi_j(v_i)|^2},$$

where the scaling factor is needed to ensure that $\|\varphi(1)\| = 1$. For power-of-2 cyclotomics, this choice of norm yields that the coefficient embedding and the canonical embedding are isometric, thus we denote the L^2-norm by $\|\cdot\|$ for both representations.

We will need the following results on invertibility.

Lemma 1 ([29, **Corollary 1.2**]). *Let $N \geq k > 1$ be powers of 2 and $q = 2k+1$ mod $4k$ be a prime. Then any y in R_q that satisfies either $0 < \|y\|_\infty < \frac{1}{\sqrt{k}} \cdot q^{1/k}$ or $0 < \|y\| < q^1/k$ has an inverse in R_q.*

Lemma 2 ([27, **Lemma 2.2**]). *Let $N > 1$ be a power of 2 and q a prime congruent to 5 mod 8. The ring R_q has exactly $2q^{N/2} - 1$ elements without an inverse. Moreover, every non-zero polynomial a in R_q with $\|a\|_\infty < \sqrt{q}/2$ has an inverse.*

Singular Values. Given a matrix $B \in K_{\mathbb{R}}^{n \times m}$, let $s_1(B)$ (resp., $s_m(B)$) be the *largest* (resp., *least*) *singular value* of B, i.e., $s_1(B) = \sup\{\|B\mathbf{v}\| : \mathbf{v} \in K_{\mathbb{R}}^m \wedge \|\mathbf{v}\| = 1\}$ (resp., $s_m(B) = \inf\{\|B\mathbf{v}\| : \mathbf{v} \in K_{\mathbb{R}}^m \wedge \|\mathbf{v}\| = 1\}$). For all $\mathbf{v}$, $s_m(B)\|\mathbf{v}\| \leq \|B\mathbf{v}\| \leq s_1(B)\|\mathbf{v}\|$. If B is a diagonal matrix, i.e., $B = \sigma_i \mathbb{I}_m$ for some $\sigma_i \in K_{\mathbb{R}}$, we have that $s_1(B) = \max_i \|\sigma_i\|$ and $s_m(B) \leq \min_i \|\sigma_i\|$ (the proof trivially follows from standard bounds, cf. [33]).

Lemma 3. *Given a symmetric positive definite matrix $B \in K_{\mathbb{R}}^{m \times m}$, and a nonsingular matrix $\sqrt{B} \in K_{\mathbb{R}}^{m \times m}$ such that $B = \sqrt{B}\sqrt{B}^*$, it holds that $s_i(B) = (s_i(\sqrt{B}))^2$ for $i = 1, m$, and $s_1(B^{-1}) = (s_m(B))^{-1}$.*

Discrete Gaussian Distribution. Let $\Sigma \in K_{\mathbb{R}}^{m \times m}$ be a symmetric positive definite matrix, and let $\sqrt{\Sigma} \in K_{\mathbb{R}}^{m \times m}$ be a nonsingular matrix such that $\Sigma = \sqrt{\Sigma}\sqrt{\Sigma}^*$. The discrete Gaussian distribution $\mathscr{D}_{\Sigma, \mathbf{c}, \Lambda}$ over a lattice $\Lambda \subseteq R^m$ with parameters $\mathbf{c}$ and Σ is defined as

$$\rho_{\sqrt{\Sigma}, \mathbf{c}}(\mathbf{z}) := \exp\left(-\pi \|\sqrt{\Sigma}^{-1}(\mathbf{z} - \mathbf{c})\|^2\right) \quad \text{and} \quad \mathscr{D}_{\sqrt{\Sigma}, \mathbf{c}, \Lambda}^m(\mathbf{z}) := \frac{\rho_{\sqrt{\Sigma}, \mathbf{c}}(\mathbf{z})}{\sum_{\mathbf{x} \in \Lambda} \rho_{\sqrt{\Sigma}}(\mathbf{x})}.$$

We denote by $\mathscr{D}_{\Sigma, \mathbf{c}}^m$ the discrete Gaussian over R^m, and omit $\mathbf{c}$ when $\mathbf{c} = 0$. For technical reasons, *Gaussian sampling will be always be done w.r.t. the canonical representation*, even though the rest of the algorithms will use the coefficient representation. This is not an issue per se, as the canonical and coefficient embeddings are isometric, and our generalized rejection sampling technique holds for the canonical representation. One should only be careful to use the canonical embedding whenever sampling from a Gaussian, and to immediately convert a fresh sample to the coefficient embedding.

The *smoothing parameter* $\eta_\varepsilon(\Lambda)$ of a lattice for $\varepsilon > 0$ is the smallest $s > 0$ such that $\rho_{1/s\mathbb{I}_m}(\Lambda^* \setminus \{0\}) \leq \varepsilon$. For a positive definite matrix $\sqrt{\Sigma}$, we say that $\Sigma \geq \eta_\varepsilon(\Lambda)$ (i.e., $s_m(\Sigma) \geq \eta_\varepsilon(\Lambda)$) if $\eta_\varepsilon(\sqrt{\Sigma}^{-1}\Lambda) \leq 1$, i.e., if $\rho_{\sqrt{\Sigma}^{-1}}(\Lambda) \leq \varepsilon$. The full version of the paper contains an upper bound on the smoothing parameter of a uniformly random lattice. Throughout the paper we assume $\varepsilon = 2^{-N}$.

The next lemma extends the classical bound on the norm of a sample from a discrete ellipsoid Gaussian over the cosets. Its proof is analogous to the original; it essentially follows observing that $\mathscr{D}_{\Lambda+\mathbf{u},\sqrt{\Sigma}}(\mathbf{z}) = \rho_{\sqrt{\Sigma}}(\mathbf{z})/\rho_{\sqrt{\Sigma}}(\Lambda+\mathbf{u}) \propto \rho_{\sqrt{\Sigma}}(\mathbf{z})$.

Lemma 4 ([1, Lemma 3] adapted to rings and sampling from cosets). *For any $0 < \varepsilon < 1$, lattice $\Lambda \subseteq R^m$, $\mathbf{u} \in R^m$, and symmetric positive definite matrix $\Sigma \in K_\mathbb{R}^{m \times m}$ such that $s_m(\Sigma) \geq \eta_\varepsilon(\Lambda)$,*

$$\Pr\left[\|\mathbf{z}\| \geq s_1(\sqrt{\Sigma})\sqrt{mN} \; : \; \mathbf{z} \xleftarrow{\$} \mathscr{D}_{\sqrt{\Sigma},\Lambda+\mathbf{u}}^m\right] < \frac{1+\varepsilon}{1-\varepsilon}2^{-mN} .$$

The following result is a direct generalization of [35, Theorem 3.3] to the ring setting. The proof is identical, but we include it in the full version for the sake of completeness.

Lemma 5. *Let $\Lambda \subset R^n$ be a full-rank module lattice, $z_1, \ldots, z_m \in R$ arbitrary elements, and $\sigma_1, \ldots, \sigma_m \in K_\mathbb{R}^{++}$ satisfying $\sigma_i \succ \sqrt{2}\eta_\varepsilon(\Lambda) \cdot \max_j \|\sqrt{z_j z_j^*}\|$ for all i. Pick $\mathbf{y}_1, \ldots, \mathbf{y}_m \in K_\mathbb{R}^n$ independently with distributions $\mathbf{y}_i \sim \mathscr{D}_{\Lambda+\mathbf{c}_i,\sigma_i}$ for some centers $\mathbf{c}_i \in K_\mathbb{R}^n$, and let $\mathbf{y} = \sum_i z_i \cdot \mathbf{y}_i$. Then, the distribution of $\mathbf{y}$ is statistically close to $\mathscr{D}_{\mathscr{I} \cdot \Lambda + \mathbf{c},\sigma}$ where $\mathscr{I}$ is the ideal generated by the z_i's, $\mathbf{c} = \sum_i z_i \cdot \mathbf{c}_i$ and*

$$\sigma = \sqrt{\sum_i z_i z_i^* \cdot \sigma_i^2}.$$

In particular, if the z_i's are coprime (i.e., $\mathscr{I} = R$), the distribution of $\mathbf{y}$ statistically close to $\mathscr{D}_{\Lambda+\mathbf{c},\sigma}$.

2.1 Assumptions

We restate the two lattice problems over a module that are standard in the literature: module short integer solution (MSIS) and learning with errors (MLWE). Note that the latter k elements of $\mathbf{s}$ correspond to the error term of MLWE. The set S_η is defined in Table 2.

Definition 1 (MSIS$_{q,k,\ell,\beta}$ assumption). *Let $\lambda \in \mathbb{N}$ be a security parameter. For a prime $q(\lambda)$, a bound $\beta = \beta(\lambda) > 0$ and positive integers $k = k(\lambda)$, $\ell = \ell(\lambda)$, the MSIS$_{q,k,\ell,\beta}$ assumption holds if for any probabilistic polynomial-time algorithm $\mathcal{A}$, the following advantage is negligible in λ.*

$$\mathsf{Adv}_{q,k,\ell,\beta}^{\mathsf{MSIS}}(\mathcal{A}) := \Pr\left[0 < \|\mathbf{x}\| \leq \beta \wedge [\mathbf{A}|\mathbb{I}_k] \cdot \mathbf{x} = \mathbf{0} \bmod q \; : \; \mathbf{A} \xleftarrow{\$} R_q^{k \times \ell}; \mathbf{x} \leftarrow \mathcal{A}(\mathbf{A})\right].$$

Definition 2 (MLWE$_{q,k,\ell,\eta}$ assumption). *Let $\lambda \in \mathbb{N}$ be a security parameter. For a prime $q(\lambda)$, and positive integers $k = k(\lambda)$, $\ell = \ell(\lambda)$, $\eta = \eta(\lambda)$, the MLWE$_{q,k,\ell,\eta}$ assumption holds if for any probabilistic polynomial-time algorithm $\mathcal{D}$, the following advantage is negligible in λ.*

$$\mathsf{Adv}^{\mathsf{MLWE}}_{q,k,\ell,\eta}(\mathcal{D}) := |\Pr\left[b = 1 :\ \mathbf{A} \leftarrow_\$ R_q^{k \times \ell}; \mathbf{s} \leftarrow_\$ S_\eta^{\ell+k}; \mathbf{t} := [\mathbf{A}|\mathbb{I}_k] \cdot \mathbf{s} \bmod q; b \leftarrow \mathcal{D}(\mathbf{A}, \mathbf{t})\right]$$
$$\Pr\left[b = 1 :\ \mathbf{A} \leftarrow_\$ R_q^{k \times \ell}; \mathbf{s} \leftarrow_\$ S_\eta^{\ell+k}; \mathbf{t} \leftarrow_\$ R_q^k; b \leftarrow \mathcal{D}(\mathbf{A}, \mathbf{t})\right]|.$$

2.2 Offline-Online Multi-signature

Following [36], we define a two-round multi-signature scheme tailored to the offline-online paradigm. A multi-signature MS consists of a tuple of algorithms (Setup, Gen, KAgg, SignOff, SignOn, Agg, Ver).

- Setup(1^λ) outputs public parameters pp. Throughout, we assume that pp is given as implicit input to all other algorithms.
- Gen() outputs a key pair (pk, sk)
- KAgg(L) takes a set of public keys $L = \{\mathsf{pk}_1, \ldots, \mathsf{pk}_n\}$ and deterministically outputs an aggregated public key $\tilde{\mathsf{pk}}$.
- SignOff(sk) is an offline signing algorithm that can be run independently of the message μ to sign. It outputs an offline message off and some state information st.
- SignOn(st, msgs, sk, μ, $\{\mathsf{pk}_2, \ldots, \mathsf{pk}_n\}$) is an online signing algorithm that takes as input the state information passed on to by SignOff, offline messages msgs $= \{\mathsf{off}_2, \ldots, \mathsf{off}_n\}$ from cosigners, a secret key sk, a message to sign μ, and cosigner's public keys $\{\mathsf{pk}_2, \ldots, \mathsf{pk}_n\}$. It outputs an online message on. Following the convention introduced in [7], each signer assign indices $1, \ldots, n$ to the signers, with itself being signer 1. In particular, these indices are merely local references to each signer and thus they are not identities.
- Agg($\mathsf{on}_1, \ldots, \mathsf{on}_n$) takes online messages as input, and outputs an aggregated signature σ, which might potentially contain $\perp$.
- Ver($\tilde{\mathsf{pk}}$, μ, σ) takes an aggregated key $\tilde{\mathsf{pk}}$, a message μ, and a signature σ as input. It outputs 1 or 0.

Remark 1. Nick et al. [36] additionally defines "an aggregator node" in their syntax to further optimize communication complexity of the protocol. We omit this optimization because as we shall see later, our security proof relies on each signer's ability to check individual outputs from co-signers.

In this work, we propose a scheme where cosigners may *abort* (indicated by on $= \perp$ after running SignOn), which is inherent in the FSwA-based interactive multi-signature [16,20,21]. Hence, a single run of the protocol fails to output a valid signature with certain probability. To reduce such a correctness error, we define correctness so that it explicitly handles τ parallel repetitions of the signing protocol.

Game 1: MS-COR$_{MS}$(λ)

1: pp $\leftarrow$ Setup(1^λ)
2: for $i \in [1,n]$ do
3:      (pk$_i$,sk$_i$) $\leftarrow$ Gen()
4:      for $j \in [1,\tau]$ do
5:          (off$_{i,j}$,st$_{i,j}$) $\leftarrow$ SignOff(sk$_i$)
6: msgs$_j$:= (off$_{1,j}$,...,off$_{n,j}$)
7: L := $\{$pk$_1$,...,pk$_n\}$

8: for $j \in [1,\tau]$ do
9:      for $i \in [1,n]$ do
10:         on$_{i,j}$ $\leftarrow$ SignOn(st$_{i,j}$, msgs$_j \setminus \{$off$_{i,j}\}$, sk$_i$, μ, $L \setminus \{$pk$_i\}$)
11:     σ_j $\leftarrow$ Agg(on$_{1,j}$,...,on$_{n,j}$)
12: if $\exists j \in [1,\tau] : \sigma_j \neq \bot$ then
13:     return Ver(KAgg(L), μ, σ_j)
14: else
15:     return 0

Definition 3 (MS-COR). *A two-round multi-signature scheme MS has correctness error δ if*

$$\Pr[0 \leftarrow \textit{MS-COR}_{MS}(\lambda, n, \tau)] \leq \delta$$

where the game MS-COR$_{MS}$ is described in Game 1.

The following definition guarantees unforgeability of a multi-signature scheme with two rounds of interactions. Note that we explicitly allow the adversary to launch many signing sessions in parallel rather than forcing them to finish every signing attempt before starting the next one. This models real-world adversarial behaviors that exploit concurrent attacks as observed in Drijvers et al. [18] It is also crucial for the offline sign oracle OSignOff to not take any message as inputs, and instead a pair (μ, L) only gets included in the query set $\mathcal{Q}$ once queried to OSignOn.

Definition 4 (MS-UF-CMA). *A two-round multi-signature scheme MS is said to be MS-UF-CMA secure in the random oracle model, if for any PPT adversary $\mathcal{A}$*

$$\mathsf{Adv}_{MS}^{MS\text{-}UF\text{-}CMA}(\mathcal{A}, \lambda) := \Pr[1 \leftarrow \textit{MS-UF-CMA}_{MS}(\mathcal{A}, \lambda)] \leq \mathsf{negl}(\lambda)$$

where the game MS-UF-CMA$_{MS}$ is described in Game 2 and $\mathcal{H}$ denotes the random oracle.

As a special case, if the adversary makes no queries to the sign oracles OSignOff and OSignOn in Game 2 and its advantage is negligible, a scheme MS is said to be MS-UF-KOA (*unforgeable against key only attacks*).

3   Our MuSig-L Scheme

3.1   Definition of the Scheme

See Protocol 1 for detailed specifications. The basic algorithms, such as Setup, Gen and Ver closely follow non-optimized version of the Dilithium-G signature [19]. In the offline phase each party outputs m individual "commit" messages, followed by their own public key.

Game 2: MS-UF-CMA$_{MS}(\mathcal{A}, \lambda)$

1: $pp \leftarrow Setup(1^\lambda)$
2: $(pk_1, sk_1) \leftarrow Gen()$
3: $ctr := 0$
4: $S := \varnothing; \mathcal{Q} := \varnothing$
5: $(L^*, \mu^*, \sigma^*) \leftarrow \mathcal{A}^{OSignOn, OSignOff, \mathcal{H}}(pp, pk_1)$
6: **if** $(pk_1 \notin L^*) \vee ((L^*, \mu^*) \in \mathcal{Q})$ **then**
7:    **return** 0
8: **return** $Ver(KAgg(L^*), \mu^*, \sigma^*)$

OSignOff
1: $ctr := ctr + 1$
2: $sid := ctr; S := S \cup \{sid\}$
3: $(off, st_{sid}) \leftarrow SignOff(sk_1)$
4: **return** off

OSignOn$(sid, msgs, \mu, \{pk_2, \ldots, pk_n\})$
1: **if** $sid \notin S$ **then return** $\perp$
2: $on \leftarrow SignOn(st_{sid}, msgs, sk_1, \mu, \{pk_2, \ldots, pk_n\})$
3: $L := \{pk_1, \ldots, pk_n\}$
4: $\mathcal{Q} := \mathcal{Q} \cup \{(L, \mu)\}$
5: $S := S \setminus \{sid\}$
6: **return** on

At the beginning of the online phase, a party P_1 performs a few sanity checks on the inputs. First, it checks that the offline messages from other parties do contain a correct set of co-signer's public keys. It then checks that its own public key t_1 does not appear in the received messages. As we shall see in the next section, this is crucial for our security proof to go through, although we are not aware of any attacks in case duplicates are allowed. Finally, it verifies the sum of the mth commit messages $\mathbf{w}^{(m)}$ has an invertible element. This is to prevent the adversary from maliciously choosing their shares of commits so that the final sum $\tilde{\mathbf{w}} = \sum_{j=1}^m b^{(j)} \cdot \mathbf{w}^{(j)}$ completely cancels out.

If the inputs look reasonable, P_1 proceeds by hashing encoded offline messages to derive randomness used for sampling Gaussian nonces $b^{(j)}$'s. Since these are generated from spherical Gaussian, the algorithm Samp can be efficiently instantiated with existing samplers such as [24]. It then performs our generalized rejection sampling detailed in Sect. 3.2.

3.1.1 Parameters

Each element of the secret signing key is chosen from $S_\eta \subseteq R$ parameterized by $\eta \geq 0$ consisting of small polynomials: $S_\eta = \{x \in R : \|x\|_\infty \leq \eta\}$. As our scheme is defined over a module of dimension $\ell + k$ every signing key belongs to $S_\eta^{\ell+k}$.

Moreover the *challenge set* $C \subseteq R$ parameterized by $\kappa \geq 0$ consists of small and sparse polynomials, which will be used as the image of random oracles H_{sig} and H_{agg}: $C = \{c \in R : \|c\|_\infty = 1 \wedge \|c\|_1 = \kappa\}$. In particular, a set of differences $\bar{C} := \{c - c' : c, c' \in C \wedge c \neq c'\}$ consists of invertible elements thanks to Lemma 1.

Finally, correctness requires $q > 16\sigma_1 n$ (where n is the number of parties, cf. Theorem 1) and $\alpha\eta\kappa^2 < \sigma_1$ (cf. Lemma 6), and $2k\lceil \log_2 q \rceil + 1 > \ell + k$ is required by security (cf. Sect. 4.3).

Protocol 1: MuSig-L

The random oracles $H_{agg} : \{0,1\}^* \to C$, $H_{sig} : \{0,1\}^* \to C$, $H_{non} : \{0,1\}^* \to \{0,1\}^l$. $\langle S \rangle$ denotes unique encoding of a set S, e.g., lexicographical ordering. $||$ denotes concatenation of two strings.

$\text{Setup}(1^\lambda)$
1: $\mathbf{A} \leftarrow\!\!\$ R_q^{k \times \ell}$
2: $\bar{\mathbf{A}} := [\mathbf{A}\|\mathbb{I}_k]$
3: $\text{pp} := \bar{\mathbf{A}}$
4: **return** pp

$\text{Gen}()$
1: $\mathbf{s}_1 \leftarrow\!\!\$ S_\eta^{\ell+k}$
2: $\mathbf{t}_1 := \bar{\mathbf{A}}\mathbf{s}_1 \bmod q$
3: $(\text{pk}, \text{sk}) := (\mathbf{t}_1, \mathbf{s}_1)$
4: **return** (pk, sk)

$\text{Agg}(\text{on}_1, \ldots, \text{on}_n)$
1: **if** $\exists i \in [1, n] : \mathbf{z}_i = \bot$ **then**
2:     **return** $\bot$
3: $\mathbf{z} := \sum_{i=1}^n \mathbf{z}_i$
4: $\sigma := (\tilde{\mathbf{w}}, \mathbf{z})$
5: **return** σ

$\text{KAgg}(L)$
1: $\{\mathbf{t}_1, \ldots, \mathbf{t}_n\} := L$
2: **for** $i \in [1, n]$ **do**
3:     $a_i := H_{agg}(\langle L \rangle, \mathbf{t}_i)$
4: $\tilde{\mathbf{t}} := \sum_{i=1}^n a_i \mathbf{t}_i \bmod q$
5: **return** t

$\text{Ver}(\text{pk}, \sigma, \mu)$
1: $(\tilde{\mathbf{w}}, \mathbf{z}) := \sigma$
2: $\tilde{\mathbf{t}} := \text{pk}$
3: $c := H_{sig}(\tilde{\mathbf{w}}, \mu, \tilde{\mathbf{t}})$
4: **if** $\bar{\mathbf{A}}\mathbf{z} - c\tilde{\mathbf{t}} = \tilde{\mathbf{w}} \bmod q \wedge \|\mathbf{z}\|_2 \leq B_n$ **then**
5:     **return** 1
6: **else**
7:     **return** 0

$\text{Samp}(r)$
1: Sample $b \sim \mathscr{D}_{\sigma_b}$ using randomness r
2: **return** b

$\text{RejSamp}(\mathbf{v}, \mathbf{z}, (b^{(j)})_{j \in [m]})$
1: $\Sigma := (\sigma_1^2 + \sigma_y^2 \sum_{j=2}^m (b^{(j)})^* b^{(j)}) \cdot \mathbb{I}_{\ell+k}$
2: $\rho \leftarrow\!\!\$ [0, 1]$
3: **if** $\rho \geq \min\left(\dfrac{\mathscr{D}_{\sqrt{\Sigma}}^{\ell+k}(\mathbf{z})}{M \cdot \mathscr{D}_{\sqrt{\Sigma}, \mathbf{v}}^{\ell+k}(\mathbf{z})}, 1 \right)$ **then**
4:     **return** 0
5: **return** 1

$\text{SignOff}(\text{sk}_1)$
1: $\mathbf{s}_1 := \text{sk}_1$
2: $\mathbf{y}_1^{(1)} \leftarrow \mathscr{D}_{\sigma_1}^{\ell+k}$
3: **For** $j \in [2, m] : \mathbf{y}_1^{(j)} \leftarrow \mathscr{D}_{\sigma_y}^{\ell+k}$
4: **For** $j \in [1, m] : \mathbf{w}_1^{(j)} := \bar{\mathbf{A}}\mathbf{y}_1^{(j)} \bmod q$
5: $_{,1} := (\mathbf{w}_1^{(1)}, \ldots, \mathbf{w}_1^{(m)})$
6: $\text{off}_1 := (\mathbf{t}_1, _{,1})$
7: $\text{st}_1 := (\mathbf{y}_1^{(1)}, \ldots, \mathbf{y}_1^{(m)}, _{,1})$
8: **return** $(\text{off}_1, \text{st}_1)$

$\text{SignOn}(\text{st}_1, \text{msgs}, \text{sk}_1, \mu, (\text{pk}_2, \ldots, \text{pk}_n))$
1: $(\mathbf{t}_i, _{,i})_{i \in [2,n]} := \text{msgs}$
2: **if** $\langle (\mathbf{t}_i)_{i \in [2,n]} \rangle \neq \langle (\text{pk}_i)_{i \in [2,n]} \rangle$ **then**
3:     **return** $\bot$
4: **if** $\exists i \geq 2 : \mathbf{t}_i = \mathbf{t}_1$ **then**
5:     **return** $\bot$
6: $L := \{\mathbf{t}_1, \ldots, \mathbf{t}_n\}$
7: $a_1 := H_{agg}(\langle L \rangle, \mathbf{t}_1)$
8: $\tilde{\mathbf{t}} := \text{KAgg}(L)$
9: $W := \{\mathbf{t}_i\|_{,i}\}_{i \in [n]}$
10: $(r^{(j)})_{j \in [2,m]} := H_{non}(\langle W \rangle, \mu, \tilde{\mathbf{t}})$
11: $b^{(1)} := 1$
12: **For** $j \in [2, m] : b^{(j)} := \text{Samp}(r^{(j)})$
13: **For** $j \in [1, m] : \mathbf{w}^{(j)} := \sum_{i=1}^n \mathbf{w}_i^{(j)}$
14: $[w_1^{(m)}, \ldots, w_k^{(m)}]^T := \mathbf{w}^{(m)}$
15: **if** $w_1^{(m)} \notin R_q^\times$ **then**
16:     **return** $\bot$
17: $\tilde{\mathbf{w}} := \sum_{j=1}^m b^{(j)} \cdot \mathbf{w}^{(j)} \bmod q$
18: $\tilde{\mathbf{y}}_1 := \sum_{j=1}^m b^{(j)} \cdot \mathbf{y}_1^{(j)}$
19: $c := H_{sig}(\tilde{\mathbf{w}}, \mu, \tilde{\mathbf{t}})$
20: $\mathbf{v} := c \cdot a_1 \cdot \mathbf{s}_1$
21: $\mathbf{z}_1 := \mathbf{v} + \tilde{\mathbf{y}}_1$
22: **if** $\text{RejSamp}(\mathbf{v}, \mathbf{z}_1, (b^{(j)})_{j \in [m]}) = 0 :$ **then**
23:     $\mathbf{z}_1 := \bot$
24: $\text{on}_1 := (\mathbf{z}_1, \tilde{\mathbf{w}})$
25: **return** on_1

Table 2. Parameters for our multi-signature. Further details can be found in the full version.

Parameter	Description
n	Number of parties
τ	Number of parallel repetitions
$N = \mathsf{poly}(\lambda)$	A power of two defining the degree of $f(X)$
$f(X) = X^N + 1$	The $2N$-th cyclotomic polynomial
$q = 5 \mod 8$	Prime modulus
$w = \lceil \log_2 q \rceil$	Logarithm of the modulus
$R = \mathbb{Z}[X]/(f(X))$	Cyclotomic ring
$R_q = \mathbb{Z}_q[X]/(f(X))$	Ring
k	The height of random matrix $\mathbf{A}$
ℓ	The width of random matrix $\mathbf{A}$
$B = \sigma_1 \sqrt{N(\ell+k)}$	The maximum L^2-norm of signature share $\mathbf{z}_i \in R^{\ell+k}$
$B_n = \sqrt{n} B$	The maximum L^2-norm of combined signature $\mathbf{z} \in R^{\ell+k}$
κ	The maximum L^1-norm of challenge vector c
$C = \{c \in R : \|c\|_\infty = 1 \wedge \|c\|_1 = \kappa\}$	Challenge space where $|C| = \binom{N}{\kappa} 2^\kappa$
η	The maximum L^∞-norm of the secret $\mathbf{s}$
$S_\eta = \{\mathbf{s} \in R : \|\mathbf{s}\|_\infty \leq \eta\}$	Set of small secrets
$T = \kappa^2 \eta \sqrt{N(\ell+k)}$	Chosen to satisfy the hypotheses of Lemma 6
$\sigma_1 = \sigma_b \sigma_y \sqrt{N(2kw+1)(\ell+k)}$	Standard deviation of the Gaussian distribution
$\sigma_y = \frac{2^9}{\sqrt{\pi}} 2^{\frac{1}{2k}} q^{\frac{k}{\ell+k}} N^2 \sqrt{(kw+1)} \left(2 + N + \log\left((\ell+k)N\right)\right)$	Standard deviation of the Gaussian distribution
$\sigma_b = \frac{2^{5/2}}{\sqrt{\pi}} \cdot 2^{\frac{1}{2k}} N^{3/2} \sqrt{kw+1}$	Standard deviation of the Gaussian distribution
$\hat{\Sigma} = diag(\sigma_1, \dots, \sigma_1)$	Covariance matrix of the target Gaussian distribution
$\alpha = \frac{\sigma_1 - 1}{\kappa}$	Parameter defining M
$t = \sqrt{\frac{N}{(\pi-1)\log_2 e}}$	Parameter defining M
$M = e^{t/\alpha + 1/(2\alpha^2)}$	The expected number of restarts until a single party can proceed
$M_n = M^n$	The expected number of restarts until all n parties proceed simultaneously
l	Output bit lengths of the random oracle $\mathsf{H}_{\mathrm{non}}$

3.2   Rejection Sampling

We now describe the rejection sampling algorithm used in the generation of a partial signature. For the sake of exposition, in this section *we ignore the subscript index i* indicating which signer generated a given vector or element, as we consider the view of only one signer.

To understand the distribution of the response $\mathbf{z}$, we start from analyzing the distribution of the masking vector $\tilde{\mathbf{y}} = \sum_{j=1}^{m} b^{(j)} \cdot \mathbf{y}^{(j)}$. The vectors $\mathbf{y}^{(j)}$ and the elements $b^{(j)}$ are sampled according different Gaussian distributions:

- The vectors $\mathbf{y}^{(j)} \in R^{\ell+k}$ are sampled from two discrete Gaussians with parameters $\sigma_1 > \sigma_y > 0$ so that $\mathbf{y}^{(1)}$ has higher entropy:

$$\mathbf{y}^{(1)} \xleftarrow{\$} \mathscr{D}_{\sigma_1}^{\ell+k} \quad \wedge \quad \mathbf{y}^{(j)} \xleftarrow{\$} \mathscr{D}_{\sigma_y}^{\ell+k} \text{ for all } 1 < j \leq m .$$

- The elements $b^{(j)} \in R$, $j = 1, \dots, m$ are all sampled from a discrete Gaussian with parameter $\sigma_b > 0$ but the first, which is constant:

$$b^{(1)} \leftarrow 1, \quad b^{(j)} \xleftarrow{\$} \mathscr{D}_{\sigma_b} \text{ for all } 1 < j \leq m .$$

Applying Lemma 5 with $b^{(j)}$ in the place of the z_i and $\mathbf{y}^{(j)}$ of y_i yields that the masking vector $\tilde{\mathbf{y}} = \mathbf{y}^{(1)} + \sum_{j=2}^{m} b^{(j)} \cdot \mathbf{y}^{(j)}$ is distributed according to a discrete Gaussian with parameter

$$\Sigma = s \cdot \mathbb{I}_{\ell+k} \in K_{\mathbb{R}}^{(\ell+k)\times(\ell+k)}, \text{ where } s = \sigma_1^2 + \sigma_y^2 \cdot \sum_{j=2}^{m} {b^{(j)}}^* b^{(j)} \qquad (1)$$

As the products $b^{(j)*}b^{(j)}$ are small and $\sigma_1 \gg \sigma_y$, we have that $\Sigma \approx \sigma_1^2 \cdot \mathbb{I}_{\ell+k}$. Generalizing the rejection sampling lemma to the case of sampling from ellipsoid discrete Gaussians allows to ensure that the distribution of $\mathbf{z}$ does not depend on the $b^{(j)}$, but it is always statistically close to a spherical Gaussian with parameter σ_1. However, as the first message of the protocol is sent in the clear instead of being committed to like in [16], we also need to make sure that in case of aborts this message does not leak information about the secret. In such a case, an adversary knows that the rejected instance was sampled from the coset $\Lambda_{\tilde{\mathbf{u}}}^{\perp}(\bar{\mathbf{A}})$, where $\tilde{\mathbf{u}} := \bar{\mathbf{A}}\left(\sum_j b^{(j)}\mathbf{y}^{(j)}\right) + c \cdot a \cdot \mathbf{t}$. Thus we need to further generalize the rejection sampling technique, to the case in which the adversary always knows from which coset the response has beet sampled.

Lemma 6 summarizes the rejection sampling technique used in MuSig-L; the general result can be found in the full version. Its proof is similar to the proof of the original rejection sampling lemma, but relies on a new result about the concentration of the squared norm of ellipsoidal Gaussians. Essentially, we first show that the behavior of the two distributions is not that different when restricted to Gaussian samples from cosets. Finally, we extend the original generalized rejection sampling lemma [26, Lemma 4.7] to consider the case of the behavior of a pair of distributions over a subset of their domain . Observe that the latter requires that the measure of the coset does not change significantly. All results are proved w.r.t. the canonical embedding.

Lemma 6 (Rejection Sampling Algorithm). *Let $\Lambda \in R^{\ell+k}$ be a lattice. Let $\alpha, T, m > 0$, $\varepsilon \leq 1/2$. Define $\sigma_1, \sigma_b, \sigma_y > 0$ such that $\sigma_y > \eta_\varepsilon(\Lambda^{\perp})$, $\sigma_b > \eta_\varepsilon(R)$, and $\sigma_1 \geq \max\{\alpha T, \sigma_y\sigma_b\sqrt{Nm(\ell+k)}\}$.*

Consider a set $V \subseteq R^{1\times m} \times R^k \times R^{\ell+k}$. Let $h : V \to [0,1]$ be the composition of three probability distributions $h := \mathscr{D}_b \times \mathscr{D}_u \times \mathscr{D}_v$, where $\mathscr{D}_b$ returns $\{1, b^{(2)}, \ldots, b^{(m)}\}$ for $b^{(j)} \xleftarrow{\$} \mathscr{D}_{\sigma_b}$, $\mathscr{D}_u$ returns a vector $\mathbf{u} \in R^k$, and $\mathscr{D}_v$ returns a vector $\mathbf{v} \in R^{\ell+k}$ such that $\|\mathbf{v}\| \leq T$.

Let $\Sigma = (\sigma_1^2 + \sigma_y^2\sum_{j=2}^m b^{(j)*}b^{(j)}) \cdot \mathbb{I}_{\ell+k}$, and $\widehat{\Sigma} = diag(\sigma_1^2, \ldots, \sigma_1^2)$. Then, for any $t > 0$, $M := \exp(\pi/\alpha^2 + \pi t/\alpha)$, and $\epsilon := 2(1+\varepsilon)/(1-\varepsilon)\exp(-t^2(pi-1))$ the distribution of the following algorithm

RejSamp:
 - $(b^{(1)}, \ldots, b^{(m)}, \mathbf{u}, \mathbf{v}) \xleftarrow{\$} h$
 - $\mathbf{z} \xleftarrow{\$} \mathscr{D}_{\sqrt{\Sigma}, \mathbf{v}, \Lambda_{\mathbf{u}}^{\perp}}^{\ell+k}$
 - *with probability* $1 - \min\left(1, \dfrac{\mathscr{D}_{\sqrt{\widehat{\Sigma}}}^{\ell+k}(\mathbf{z})}{M \cdot \mathscr{D}_{\sqrt{\Sigma}, \mathbf{v}}^{\ell+k}(\mathbf{z})}\right)$, *set* $\mathbf{z} := \perp$
 - *output* $(\mathbf{z}, b^{(1)}, \ldots, b^{(m)}, \mathbf{u}, \mathbf{v})$

is within statistical distance $\frac{\epsilon}{2M} + \frac{2\varepsilon}{M}$ of the distribution of:
SimRS:
 - $(b^{(1)}, \ldots, b^{(m)}, \mathbf{u}, \mathbf{v}) \xleftarrow{\$} h$

- $\mathbf{z} \xleftarrow{\$} \mathcal{D}^{\ell+k}_{\sqrt{\widehat{\Sigma}}, \Lambda_{\mathbf{u}}^{\perp}}$
- with probability $1 - 1/M$, set $\mathbf{z} := \perp$
- output $(\mathbf{z}, b^{(1)}, \ldots, b^{(m)}, \mathbf{u}, \mathbf{v})$

Moreover, RejSamp outputs something with probability larger than $\frac{1-\varepsilon}{M}(1 - \frac{4\varepsilon}{(1+\varepsilon)^2})$.

Observe that efficient sampling from cosets requires a trapdoor for $\mathbf{A}$, which is not compatible with a reduction from MSIS with the matrix $\mathbf{A}$. However, we only use this lemma in the security reduction to prove that honest signing can be simulated, thus this sampling does not have to be efficient.

Lemma 7. *The definition of the signing algorithm of MuSig-L in Protocol 1 with the parameters in Table 2 satisfies the hypotheses of Lemma 6.*

The proof of Lemma 7 is a routine calculation, thus we defer it to the full version of the paper. Observe that the statistical distance is negligible, and the probability of returning something is larger than $1/M(1 - \mathsf{negl}(\lambda))$ as $\varepsilon = 2^{-N}$ and t is set so that $\exp(-t(\pi - 1)) = 2^{-N} = \mathsf{negl}(\lambda)$.

3.3 Correctness and Efficiency Analysis

Theorem 1. *MuSig-L has correctness error $\delta = \left(1 - \frac{1}{M^n}\right)^{\tau}(1 + \mathsf{negl}(\lambda))$ when defined with the parameters in Table 2, i.e.,*

$$\Pr\left[0 \leftarrow \mathsf{MS\text{-}COR_{MS}}(\lambda, n, \tau)\right] \leq \delta$$

where the game $\mathsf{MS\text{-}COR_{MS}}$ is described in Game 1.

Proof. The correctness game $\mathsf{MS\text{-}COR_{MS}}$ returns 0 if for every $j \in [1, \tau]$ one of the following five events occurs:

1. The public keys have not been encoded correctly:

$$\mathsf{bad}_1 := (\langle(\mathbf{t}_i)_{i \in [2,n]}\rangle \neq \langle(\mathsf{pk}_i)_{i \in [2,n]}\rangle).$$

By definition of correctness, $\Pr[\mathsf{bad}_1] = 0$.

2. There is a collision on the public keys:

$$\mathsf{bad}_2 := (\exists i_1, i_2 \in [1, n] : \mathbf{t}_{i_1} = \mathbf{t}_{1_2}).$$

The vectors $\mathbf{t}_i$ are generated as the product of the public matrix $\bar{\mathbf{A}}$ times a secret vector sampled uniformly at random in the set $S_\eta^{\ell+k}$. As $\bar{\mathbf{A}} = [\mathbf{A}|\mathbb{I}_k]$, multiplication by $\bar{\mathbf{A}}$ is injective over the last k coefficients, and by the birthday argument we obtain the bound $\Pr[\mathsf{bad}_2] \leq \frac{n(n-1)}{|S_\eta^k|^2} = \frac{n(n-1)}{\eta^{kN}} \leq 2^{-\mathsf{poly}(\lambda)}$.

3. The invertibility condition is not satisfied:

$$\mathsf{bad}_3 := (\exists i \in [1, n] : w_1^{(m)} \notin R_q^\times).$$

Again, the vector $w_1^{(m)}$ is the product of the first row of $\bar{A}$ times $\bar{y} := \sum_{i=1}^{n} y_i^{(m)}$. As $\sigma_y \geq \eta_\varepsilon(R)\sqrt{2}$, Lemma 5 applied component-wise to $\bar{y}$ guarantees that each of its components is statistically close to a Gaussian with parameter $n\sigma_y$. Thus, by [28, Corollary 7.5] (i.e., Lemma 8) $w_1^{(m)}$ is statistically close to uniform over the entire ring, (and the same for all the signers) and Lemma 2 ensures that: $\Pr[\mathsf{bad}_3] = \frac{2}{q^{N/2}} - \frac{1}{q^N} = 2^{-\mathsf{poly}(\lambda)}$.

4. One of the signers aborts during the RS step:

$$\mathsf{bad}_4 := (\exists i \in [1,n] : \mathsf{RejSamp}(\mathbf{v}, \mathbf{z}_1, (b^{(j)})_{j\in[m]}) = 0) .$$

Lemma 7 shows that the hypotheses of Lemma 6 are satisfied, thus we have:
$\Pr[\mathsf{bad}_4] \leq 1 - [\frac{1}{M} + \frac{\varepsilon+\delta_2-\varepsilon\delta_2}{M}]^n = 1 - \frac{1}{M^n} + \mathsf{negl}(\lambda)$.

5. The aggregated signature does not pass verification:

$$\mathsf{bad}_5 := (\mathsf{Ver}(\mathsf{KAgg}(L), \mu, \sigma_j) = 0) .$$

The verification includes two checks, the linear relation and the norm bound. The former is trivially always satisfied, as the output of the hashes is the same for all signers once the ordering of the components of the input to each hash is set (e.g., to the lexicographical ordering). Analogously, the sampling of the $b^{(j)}$'s is deterministic once the nonces are computed, thus all the signers get the same $\tilde{\mathbf{w}}$. One only needs to estimate the probability that a honestly generated $\mathbf{z}$ does not satisfy the norm bound.

By Lemma 6 $\mathbf{z}_i$ is statistically close to a Gaussian with parameter $\hat{\Sigma} = \sigma_1 \mathbb{I}_{\ell+k}$. Hence by Lemma 4 we can bound the norm of $\mathbf{z}_i$ as: $\|\mathbf{z}_i\| \leq s_1(\sqrt{\Sigma})\sqrt{N(\ell+k)} = \sigma_1\sqrt{N(\ell+k)} =: B$. Since the sum of n independent Gaussian samples with parameter σ_1 is statistically close to Gaussian with $\sqrt{n} \cdot \sigma_1$ (Lemma 5), the norm of the aggregate signature can be bound by $B_n = \sqrt{n} \cdot B$. Finally, we need to ensure that there is no wrap around when aggregating signatures, i.e., that $q/2 > n\|\mathbf{z}\|_\infty$. The norm of $\mathbf{z}$ can be bounded as $\|\mathbf{z}\|_\infty \leq 8\sigma_1$ by substituting $m = 1$, $\mathbf{c} = 1$, and $r = 8\sigma_b$ in Lemma B.6 of the full version. The bound holds with probability smaller than 2^{-195}. Hence, $q > 16n\sigma_1$ is enough to avoid the wrap around in the aggregation. The bound holds with probability greater than $1 - 2^{-195}$. Thus $\Pr[\mathsf{bad}_5] \leq n2^{-195}$.

Putting everything together we get that

$$\Pr[0 \leftarrow \mathsf{MS\text{-}COR}_{\mathsf{MS}}(\lambda, n, \tau)] = \prod_{j=1}^{\tau} \sum_{i=1}^{5} \Pr[\mathsf{bad}_i] = \left(1 - \frac{1}{M^n} + n2^{-195} + \mathsf{negl}(\lambda)\right)^\tau .$$

$\square$

3.3.1 Number of Aborts, Round Complexity, and Signature Length

In its standard form, this protocol requires some repetitions to deal with possible aborts in order to produce a signature. As the probability that a single signer outputs something is essentially $\frac{1}{M}$ (cf. Sect. 3.2), successful signing requires around M^n rounds, where $M = \exp(1/(2\alpha^2) + t/(2\alpha))$. Analogously to [16], having a small M^n requires $\alpha \propto n$. However, as long as $n = o(N^{-4})$ this does not imply an increase in the norm of each signature share, as $\sigma_1 = O(N^4\sqrt{N})$. Larger values of n yield an increase of roughly[2] $O(\log(n))$ in the signature size when comparing with Dilithium-G. Standard optimizations are possible. For example, running parallel executions of the same protocol at once yields at least one instance in which no signer aborts, thus the protocol is exactly 2-rounds. To this aim $\lambda \cdot \log\left(\frac{M_n}{M_n-1}\right)$ parallel instances suffice.

The length of the signature only depends on B_n, as a standard optimization is for signatures to be composed by $(c, \mathbf{z})$ instead of $(\tilde{\mathbf{w}}, \mathbf{z})$. Verification in this case amounts to checking $c = \mathsf{H}_{\mathrm{sig}}(\bar{\mathbf{A}}\mathbf{z} - c\bar{\mathbf{t}}, \mu, \tilde{\mathbf{t}})$ instead of $\bar{\mathbf{A}}\mathbf{z} - c\bar{\mathbf{t}} = \tilde{\mathbf{w}}$ in addition to the norm check. With this optimization, signatures output by our scheme are $O(N(\ell + k)\log(\sigma_1\sqrt{n}))$ bits long. Relying on a trapdoor to simulate the signing oracle in the security proof affects the length of the signature, as it yields $\sigma_y = O(N^2\sqrt{N})$ and $\sigma_b = O(N^2)$ (cf. Sect. 4.3). Moreover, our rejection sampling technique requires σ_1 to be larger than $\sigma_y \cdot \sigma_b$, i.e., $\sigma_1 = O(N^4\sqrt{N})$. This implies that signature length is in fact $O(N(\ell + k)\log(N\sqrt{n}))$, i.e., larger than a non-optimized, single-user version of Dilithium-G by a factor $O(\log(N\sqrt{n}))$, but equal to [16][3].

4   Security Proofs

4.1   Reduction to LWE and SIS

For simplicity, we first consider a situation where the adversary does not make any sign oracle queries, i.e., $Q_s = 0$. Our proof closely follows "the double forking technique" of [31], except that in our scheme the aggregation coefficients a_i's are picked from the challenge space C consisting of small and sparse ring elements. Full security proof is deferred to the full version.

---

[2] Observe that to avoid rejecting valid signatures due to arithmetic overflow q has to be larger than the size of the coefficients in the aggregated signature, i.e., the size of the ring has to grow linearly with $\sqrt{n}$ too. This is inherent to additively aggregating signatures. As observed in [16], having a larger q makes MSIS harder, but MLWE easier. Compensating for it requires increasing N by a factor $O\left(1 + \frac{\log n}{\log q_0}\right)$, where q_0 is the modulus used in the single party case. However, one usually sets $q > 2^{20}$, which makes $\frac{\log n}{\log q_0}$ less than 2 even for billions of users, and allows to neglect this factor in the signature size estimates.

[3] This is not immediately evident from their analysis of the signature length. In fact, verifiability requires a signature to include the randomness used to generate the commitments. Such randomness is sampled from a discrete Gaussian of parameter s, which has to be large enough to be sampled using a trapdoor, i.e., linear in N (cf. [16, Theorem 2]) times square root of the number of parties (since the *sum* of n Gaussian randomness is output as a signature). This adds a factor $O(\log(N\sqrt{n}))$ to their signature length, making it equivalent to ours.

Theorem 2. *MuSig-L is MS-UF-KOA-secure under* $\text{MSIS}_{q,k,\ell+1,\beta}$ *and* $\text{MLWE}_{q,k,\ell,\eta}$ *assumptions with* $\beta = 8\kappa\sqrt{B_n^2 + \kappa^3}$. *Concretely, for any PPT adversary* $\mathcal{A}$ *against MS-UF-KOA that makes at most* Q *queries to the random oracles, there exist PPT adversaries* $\mathcal{B}'$ *and* $\mathcal{D}$ *such that*

$$\text{Adv}^{\text{MS-UF-KOA}}_{\text{MuSig-L}}(\mathcal{A}) \leq \frac{Q(2Q+3)}{|C|} + \frac{2^{k+1}}{q^{kN/2}} + \text{Adv}^{\text{MLWE}}_{q,k,\ell,\eta}(\mathcal{B}') + \sqrt{\frac{Q^2}{|C|} + Q\sqrt{Q \cdot \text{Adv}^{\text{MSIS}}_{q,k,\ell+1,\beta}(\mathcal{D})}}$$

$$(2)$$

Proof Sketch. We first sketch the high-level ideas of proof. The complete reduction algorithms are described in the full version. First, we construct a "wrapper" $\mathcal{B}$ that internally invokes $\mathcal{A}$ to obtain a forged signature. The wrapper makes sure that a crucial query to H_{sig} with input $\tilde{t}^*$ is only made *after* the corresponding query to H_{agg}, and aborts otherwise (indicated by the bad_{agg} flag). Moreover, it guarantees that no aggregated keys collide with each other, and aborts otherwise (indicated by the bad_{kcol} flag). By the $\text{MLWE}_{q,k,\ell,\eta}$ assumption, an honestly generated public key $\mathbf{t}_1 := \mathbf{t}^* = \bar{\mathbf{A}}\mathbf{s}^* \bmod q$ is indistinguishable with a uniformly random element in R_q. Hence, one can regard the input $(\mathbf{A}, \mathbf{t}^*)$ as an instance of the $\text{MSIS}_{q,k,\ell+1,\beta}$ problem.

We then invoke the general forking lemma [7] twice. The first fork happens at the return value of $\mathsf{H}_{\text{agg}} : \{0,1\}^* \to C$ (handled by the algorithm $\mathcal{D}$, internally running C); the second fork happens at the return value of $\mathsf{H}_{\text{sig}} : \{0,1\}^* \to C$ (handled by C, internally running $\mathcal{B}$). Hence, after running the wrapper $\mathcal{B}$ in total 4 times, we get four forgeries satisfying the equations

$$\tilde{\mathbf{w}}_1 = \bar{\mathbf{A}}\mathbf{z}_1^* - c_1^* \sum_{i \neq 1} a_i \mathbf{t}_i - c_1^* a_{1,1} \mathbf{t}^* = \bar{\mathbf{A}}\hat{\mathbf{z}}_1^* - \hat{c}_1^* \sum_{i \neq 1} a_i \mathbf{t}_i - \hat{c}_1^* a_{1,1} \mathbf{t}^* \bmod q \quad (3)$$

$$\tilde{\mathbf{w}}_2 = \bar{\mathbf{A}}\mathbf{z}_2^* - c_2^* \sum_{i \neq 1} a_i \mathbf{t}_i - c_2^* a_{2,1} \mathbf{t}^* = \bar{\mathbf{A}}\hat{\mathbf{z}}_2^* - \hat{c}_2^* \sum_{i \neq 1} a_i \mathbf{t}_i - \hat{c}_2^* a_{2,1} \mathbf{t}^* \bmod q \quad (4)$$

where, in particular, $c_1^* \neq \hat{c}_1^*$, $c_2^* \neq \hat{c}_2^*$, and $a_{1,1} \neq a_{2,1}$ thanks to the forker algorithms $\mathcal{F}_{\mathcal{B}}$ and $\mathcal{F}_{\mathcal{C}}$, respectively. Rearranging the above equations, we get that

$$\bar{\mathbf{A}}\bar{\mathbf{z}}_1 - \bar{c}_1 \sum_{i \neq 1} a_i \mathbf{t}_i - \bar{c}_1 a_{1,1} \mathbf{t}^* = \mathbf{0} \bmod q \quad (5)$$

$$\bar{\mathbf{A}}\bar{\mathbf{z}}_2 - \bar{c}_2 \sum_{i \neq 1} a_i \mathbf{t}_i - \bar{c}_2 a_{2,1} \mathbf{t}^* = \mathbf{0} \bmod q \quad (6)$$

where $\bar{\mathbf{z}}_i = \mathbf{z}_i^* - \hat{\mathbf{z}}_i^*$ and $\bar{c}_i = c_i^* - \hat{c}_i^*$ for $i = 1, 2$, respectively. By multiplying the first equation by $\bar{c}_2$ and the second by $\bar{c}_1$, the second terms cancel out. This gives us

$$\bar{\mathbf{A}}(\bar{c}_2\bar{\mathbf{z}}_1 - \bar{c}_1\bar{\mathbf{z}}_2) - \bar{c}_1\bar{c}_2\bar{a}\mathbf{t}^* = 0. \quad (7)$$

where $\bar{a} = a_{1,1} - a_{2,1}$. Since $\bar{c}_1$, $\bar{c}_2$, and $\bar{a}$ are all non-zero and none of them are zero-divisors thanks to Lemma 1, $\bar{c}_1\bar{c}_2\bar{a}$ is guaranteed to be non-zero. Moreover, both $\bar{c}_2\bar{\mathbf{z}}_1 - \bar{c}_1\bar{\mathbf{z}}_2$ and $\bar{c}_1\bar{c}_2\bar{a}$ have relatively small L^2-norms. Thus we obtain a valid solution to SIS w.r.t. the instance matrix $[\mathbf{A}|\mathbb{I}_k|\mathbf{t}^*]$.

4.2   Switching Lemma

Before sketching our CMA security proof, we first prove a simple yet very powerful technical lemma. Let us first recall a regularity lemma in the ring setting.

Lemma 8 (Corollary 7.5 of [28]). *Let $F(X)$ be the $2N$-th cyclotomic polynomial and let $R = \mathbb{Z}[X]/(F(X))$ and $R_q = R/qR$. For positive integers $k \le n \le \mathsf{poly}(N)$, let $\bar{\mathbf{A}} = [\mathbf{A}|\mathbb{I}_k] \in R_q^{k \times n}$, where $\mathbb{I}_k \in R_q^{k \times k}$ is the identity matrix and $\mathbf{A} \in R_q^{k \times (n-k)}$ is uniformly random. Then with probability $1 - 2^{-\Omega(N)}$ over the choice of $\mathbf{A}$, the distribution of $\bar{\mathbf{A}}\mathbf{x} \in R_q^k$, where $\mathbf{x} \leftarrow_\$ \mathscr{D}_\sigma^n$ with parameter $\sigma > 2N \cdot q^{k/n+2/(Nn)}$, satisfies that the probability of each of the q^{Nk} possible outcomes is in the interval $(1 \pm 2^{-\Omega(N)})q^{-Nk}$. In particular, it is within statistical distance $2^{-\Omega(N)}$ of the uniform distribution over R_q^k.*

As a consequence, we obtain the following switching lemma. This will make the hybrid arguments for simulation significantly modular as we shall see soon.

Lemma 9 (Switching lemma). *Let R, N, q, k, n and σ be as in Lemma 8. Consider the following two algorithms:*

$\mathcal{A}_0$: $\mathbf{A} \leftarrow_\$ R_q^{k \times (n-k)}$; $\mathbf{x} \leftarrow \mathscr{D}_\sigma^n$; $\mathbf{u} = [\mathbf{A}|\mathbb{I}_k] \cdot \mathbf{x} \bmod q$; *output* $(\mathbf{A}, \mathbf{x}, \mathbf{u})$.
$\mathcal{A}_1$: $\mathbf{A} \leftarrow_\$ R_q^{k \times (n-k)}$; $\mathbf{u} \leftarrow_\$ R_q^k$; $\mathbf{x} \leftarrow \mathscr{D}_{\Lambda_{\mathbf{u}}^\perp(\bar{\mathbf{A}}),\sigma}^n$; *output* $(\mathbf{A}, \mathbf{x}, \mathbf{u})$.

Then $\Delta(\mathcal{A}_0, \mathcal{A}_1) = 2^{-\Omega(N)}$.

Proof. Let (A_i, X_i, U_i) be random variables corresponding to outputs of $\mathcal{A}_i$. For any fixed $\mathbf{A} \in R_q^{k \times (n-k)}$, $\mathbf{x} \in R_q^n$ and $\mathbf{u} \in R_q^k$, we have

$$\Pr\left[(A_0, X_0, U_0) = (\mathbf{A}, \mathbf{x}, \mathbf{u})\right] = \Pr[A_0 = \mathbf{A}] \cdot \Pr[X_0 = \mathbf{x}] \cdot \left[\mathbf{u} = \bar{\mathbf{A}}\mathbf{x} \bmod q\right]$$

$$= \frac{1}{|R_q^{k \times (n-k)}|} \cdot \mathscr{D}_\sigma^n(\mathbf{x}) \cdot \left[\mathbf{x} \in \Lambda_{\mathbf{u}}^\perp(\bar{\mathbf{A}})\right]$$

where we have let $\bar{\mathbf{A}} = [\mathbf{A}|\mathbb{I}_k]$, and $\left[\mathbf{u} = \bar{\mathbf{A}}\mathbf{x} \bmod q\right] = \left[\mathbf{x} \in \Lambda_{\mathbf{u}}^\perp(\bar{\mathbf{A}})\right]$ is the Iverson bracket notation: it has value 1 if the condition is met and 0 otherwise. Thus, the probability is 0 if $\mathbf{x} \notin \Lambda_{\mathbf{u}}^\perp(\bar{\mathbf{A}})$, and for $\mathbf{x} \in \Lambda_{\mathbf{u}}^\perp(\bar{\mathbf{A}})$, we have:

$$\Pr\left[(A_0, X_0, U_0) = (\mathbf{A}, \mathbf{x}, \mathbf{u})\right] = \frac{1}{|R_q^{k \times (n-k)}|} \cdot \frac{\rho_\sigma(\mathbf{x})}{\rho_\sigma(R^n)}$$

$$= \frac{1}{q^{Nk(n-k)}} \cdot \frac{\rho_\sigma(\mathbf{x})}{\rho_\sigma(\Lambda_{\mathbf{u}}^\perp)} \cdot \frac{\rho_\sigma(\Lambda_{\mathbf{u}}^\perp)}{\rho_\sigma(R^n)}$$

$$= \frac{1}{q^{Nk(n-k)}} \cdot \mathscr{D}_{\Lambda_{\mathbf{u}}^\perp(\bar{\mathbf{A}}),\sigma}(\mathbf{x}) \cdot \frac{\rho_\sigma(\Lambda_{\mathbf{u}}^\perp)}{\rho_\sigma(R^n)}.$$

In particular, summing over all possible choices of $\mathbf{x}$ for a fixed $\mathbf{A}$, we see that:

$$\frac{\rho_\sigma(\Lambda_{\mathbf{u}}^\perp)}{\rho_\sigma(R^n)} = \Pr_{\mathbf{x} \sim \mathscr{D}_\sigma^n}\left[\mathbf{u} = \bar{\mathbf{A}}\mathbf{x} \bmod q\right].$$

We denote this probability $H_{\mathbf{A},\sigma}(\mathbf{u})$. In other words, $H_{\mathbf{A},\sigma}$ is the probability distribution over R_q^k given by $\bar{\mathbf{A}} \cdot \mathscr{D}_\sigma^n \bmod q$. To sum up, we have shown that for all $(\mathbf{A}, \mathbf{x}, \mathbf{u})$:

$$
\Pr\left[(A_0, X_0, U_0) = (\mathbf{A}, \mathbf{x}, \mathbf{u})\right] =
\begin{cases}
\mathscr{D}_{\Lambda_{\mathbf{u}}^\perp(\bar{\mathbf{A}}),\sigma}^n(\mathbf{x}) \cdot \dfrac{H_{\mathbf{A},\sigma}(\mathbf{u})}{q^{Nk(n-k)}} & \text{if } \mathbf{x} \in \Lambda_{\mathbf{u}}^\perp(\bar{\mathbf{A}}), \\
0 & \text{if } \mathbf{x} \notin \Lambda_{\mathbf{u}}^\perp(\bar{\mathbf{A}}).
\end{cases}
$$

On the other hand, still for fixed $\mathbf{A}, \mathbf{u}, \mathbf{x}$, we have:

$$
\begin{aligned}
\Pr\left[(A_1, X_1, U_1) = (\mathbf{A}, \mathbf{x}, \mathbf{u})\right] &= \frac{1}{|R_q^{k \times (n-k)}|} \cdot \frac{1}{|R_q^k|} \cdot \mathscr{D}_{\Lambda_{\mathbf{u}}^\perp(\bar{\mathbf{A}}),\sigma}^n(\mathbf{x}) \\
&= \frac{1}{q^{Nk(n-k)}} \cdot \frac{1}{q^{Nk}} \cdot \mathscr{D}_{\Lambda_{\mathbf{u}}^\perp(\bar{\mathbf{A}}),\sigma}^n(\mathbf{x}),
\end{aligned}
$$

and in particular this probability is non zero only for vectors $\mathbf{x} \in \Lambda_{\mathbf{u}}^\perp(\bar{\mathbf{A}})$. Therefore, the statistical distance $\Delta(\mathcal{A}_0, \mathcal{A}_1)$ can be written as:

$$
\begin{aligned}
\Delta(\mathcal{A}_0, \mathcal{A}_1) &= \sum_{\mathbf{A},\mathbf{u},\mathbf{x}} \left| \Pr\left[(A_0, X_0, U_0) = (\mathbf{A}, \mathbf{x}, \mathbf{u})\right] - \Pr\left[(A_1, X_1, U_1) = (\mathbf{A}, \mathbf{x}, \mathbf{u})\right] \right| \\
&= \sum_{\mathbf{A} \in R_q^{k \times (n-k)}, \mathbf{u} \in R_q^k} \frac{1}{q^{Nk(n-k)}} \sum_{\mathbf{x} \in \Lambda_{\mathbf{u}}^\perp(\bar{\mathbf{A}})} \mathscr{D}_{\Lambda_{\mathbf{u}}^\perp(\bar{\mathbf{A}}),\sigma}^n(\mathbf{x}) \cdot \left| H_{\mathbf{A},\sigma}(\mathbf{u}) - \frac{1}{q^{Nk}} \right| \\
&= \sum_{\mathbf{A} \in R_q^{k \times (n-k)}} \frac{1}{q^{Nk(n-k)}} \sum_{\mathbf{u} \in R_q^k} \left| H_{\mathbf{A},\sigma}(\mathbf{u}) - \frac{1}{q^{Nk}} \right| \\
&= \sum_{\mathbf{A} \in R_q^{k \times (n-k)}} \frac{1}{q^{Nk(n-k)}} \Delta(H_{\mathbf{A},\sigma}, \mathscr{U}_{R_q^k}),
\end{aligned}
$$

for $\mathscr{U}_{R_q^k}$ the uniform distribution on R_q^k. Now Lemma 8 says that there exists a subset $S \subset R_q^{k \times (n-k)}$ of cardinality at most $2^{-\Omega(N)} |R_q^{k \times (n-k)}|$ such that for all $\mathbf{A} \notin S$, we have $\Delta(H_{\mathbf{A},\sigma(\mathbf{u})}, \mathscr{U}_{R_q^k}) = 2^{-\Omega(N)}$. As a result:

$$
\begin{aligned}
\Delta(\mathcal{A}_0, \mathcal{A}_1) &= \sum_{\mathbf{A} \in S} \frac{1}{q^{Nk(n-k)}} \Delta(H_{\mathbf{A},\sigma}, \mathscr{U}_{R_q^k}) + \sum_{\mathbf{A} \notin S} \frac{1}{q^{Nk(n-k)}} \Delta(H_{\mathbf{A},\sigma}, \mathscr{U}_{R_q^k}) \\
&\leq \frac{|S|}{q^{Nk(n-k)}} \cdot 1 + 1 \cdot 2^{-\Omega(N)} \leq 2^{-\Omega(N)}
\end{aligned}
$$

as required. $\qquad\square$

4.3 Simulating Nonces via Trapdoor Sampling

As a first step towards CMA security, recall that our goal is to simulate the view of the adversary interacting with an honest singer P_1. This essentially amounts to simulating the distribution of the offline messages $(\mathbf{w}_1^{(j)})_{j \in [m]}$, nonces $(b^{(j)})_{j \in [m]}$, challenge c, and $\mathbf{z}_1$, such that they satisfy the condition:

$$\bar{\mathbf{A}}\mathbf{z}_1 - c \cdot a_1 \cdot \mathbf{t}_1 = \sum_{j=1}^{m} b^{(j)} \mathbf{w}_1^{(j)} \bmod q. \tag{8}$$

From our rejection sampling lemma (Lemma 6), we can indeed simulate c and $\mathbf{z}_1$, and thus they already determine the sum $\tilde{\mathbf{w}}_1 := \sum_{j=1}^{m} b^{(j)} \mathbf{w}_1^{(j)} \bmod q$. However, since the offline commit messages $\mathbf{w}_1^{(j)}$ must be handed over to the adversary *before* the simulator sees adversary's commitments $\mathbf{w}_i^{(j)}$, we are restricted to generating $b^{(j)}$'s such that they "explain" the above constraint for already fixed $(\mathbf{w}_1^{(j)})_{j \in [m]}$ and $\tilde{\mathbf{w}}_1$.

More concretely, after OSignOff outputs $\mathbf{w}_1^{(j)}$, whenever the simulator receives a query to $\mathsf{H}_{\mathrm{non}}$ or the online oracle OSignOn with adversarially chosen $\mathbf{w}_i^{(j)}$ and μ as inputs, the simulator already has to prepare $c, \mathbf{z}_1$ as well as $b^{(j)}$ satisfying (8), and then program the random oracles $\mathsf{H}_{\mathrm{non}}$ and $\mathsf{H}_{\mathrm{sig}}$ such that they output $b^{(j)}$'s and c, respectively.[4] We overcome this technical hurdle by making use of lattice-based trapdoor sampling. For readability we will drop the party index "1" for the rest of this subsection.

Recall that the first "commit" messages are computed as $\mathbf{w}^{(j)} := \bar{\mathbf{A}}\mathbf{y}^{(j)}$ for $j = 1, \ldots, m$. From the regularity result (Lemma 8), they are statistically indistinguishable with matrices uniformly sampled from $R_q^{k \times m}$. Now let us define suitable trapdoor generator and sampling algorithms to perform sign oracle simulation. To sample the vector $\mathbf{b} := [b^{(2)}, \ldots, b^{(m)}]$, we take advantage of the gadget-based trapdoor (Ring-)SIS inversion algorithm of [34]. (Recall that $b^{(1)} = 1$ so we only need to sample $m - 1$ elements.) Let $\mathbf{W} := [\mathbf{w}^{(2)}, \ldots, \mathbf{w}^{(m)}]$ be the parity check matrix for which we would like to obtain a trapdoor. For integers $k, w = \lceil \log_2 q \rceil, m' = kw + 1$, let $m = 2kw + 1$. Let $\mathbf{g}^T = [1, 2, 4, \ldots, 2^{w-1}]$ be a gadget vector and $\mathbf{G} = \mathbb{I}_k \otimes \mathbf{g} \in R^{k \times kw}$ be the corresponding gadget matrix. Then the Micciancio-Peikert trapdoor can be directly applied as follows.

- TrapGen(1^λ): It samples a uniformly random matrix $[\mathbf{w}^{(2)}, \ldots, \mathbf{w}^{(kw+1)}] \in R_q^{k \times kw}$. It sets $\bar{\mathbf{W}} = [\mathbf{w}^{(2)}, \ldots, \mathbf{w}^{(kw+1)}]$ and samples the trapdoor matrix $\mathbf{R} \in R^{kw \times kw}$ following the Gaussian $\mathscr{D}_{\bar{s}}^{kw \times kw}$ with parameter $\bar{s}$. Then the parity check matrix is defined as

$$\mathbf{W} = [\bar{\mathbf{W}} | \mathbf{G} - \bar{\mathbf{W}}\mathbf{R}] \in R_q^{k \times 2kw}. \tag{9}$$

It outputs $(\mathbf{W}, \mathbf{R})$.
- TrapSamp$(\mathbf{R}, \mathbf{w}', \sigma_b)$: Given a target vector $\mathbf{w}' \in R^k$, it samples a vector $\mathbf{b} \in R^{2kw} = R^{m-1}$, whose distribution is statistically close the discrete Gaussian $\mathscr{D}_{\Lambda_{\mathbf{w}'}^{\perp}(\mathbf{W}), \sigma_b}^{m-1}$ supported on the lattice coset

---

[4] Note that once $b^{(j)}$'s are simulated, finding corresponding uniform randomness $r^{(j)}$'s are easy assuming that the Samp algorithm is "sampleable" [14]. Such a property can be for example satisfied by simple CDT-based samplers.

$$\Lambda_{\mathbf{w}'}^{\perp}(\mathbf{W}) := \{\mathbf{x} \in R^{2kw} : \mathbf{W} \cdot \mathbf{x} = \mathbf{w}' \mod q\}. \tag{10}$$

This can be instantiated with [34, Alg. 3] or its adaptation in the module setting [10]. Note that efficiency of the sampler does not matter here, since trapdoor Gaussian sampling operations are only required by simulation, and parties in the actual protocol are never asked to do so.

4.3.1 Indistinguishability of W Output by TrapGen

We show that m columns of the parity check matrix $\mathbf{W}$ generated as above is indistinguishable with $[\mathbf{w}^{(2)}, \ldots, \mathbf{w}^{(m)}]$ in the actual protocol. We apply the regularity lemma twice to argue that $\mathbf{w}^{(2)}, \ldots, \mathbf{w}^{(m)}$ are uniform both in the actual protocol and in TrapGen, up to an negligible error.

– In the actual protocol, the distribution of $\mathbf{w}^{(2)} = \bar{\mathbf{A}}\mathbf{y}^{(2)}, \ldots, \mathbf{w}^{(m)} = \bar{\mathbf{A}}\mathbf{y}^{(m)}$ is statistically close to uniform over $R_q^{k \times 2kw}$ if

$$\sigma_y > 2N \cdot q^{k/(\ell+k)+2/(N(\ell+k))} \tag{11}$$

as required by Lemma 8. Note that, since the matrix $\bar{\mathbf{A}}$ is reused, the statistical distance grows linearly in m. The same remark applies to $\bar{\mathbf{W}}\mathbf{R}$ below.
– We now check the distribution of $\mathbf{W}$ output by TrapGen. By construction, the distribution of kw columns $\bar{\mathbf{W}} = [\mathbf{w}^{(2)}, \ldots, \mathbf{w}^{(kw+1)}]$ are uniform over $R_q^{k \times kw}$. As Lemma 8 requires a matrix to contain an identity submatrix, we need to bound the probability that $\bar{\mathbf{W}}$ contains no invertible submatrix, i.e., $\bar{\mathbf{W}}$ is not full rank. As our scheme assumes $q = 5 \mod 8$, we can use Lemma 2 to argue this only happens with negligible probability (see full version for formal analysis). Hence, we can indeed apply Lemma 8 to guarantee the distribution of $\bar{\mathbf{W}} \cdot \mathbf{R}$ is statistically close to uniform over $R_q^{k \times kw}$ if

$$\bar{s} > 2N \cdot q^{1/w+2/(Nkw)}. \tag{12}$$

4.3.2 Indistinguishability of $b^{(j)}$'s Output by TrapSamp

To sample from spherical Guassian with parameter σ_b, the gadget-based TrapSamp algorithm requires $\sigma_b \approx s_1(\mathbf{R}) \cdot s_1(\sqrt{\Sigma_{\mathbf{G}}})$ [34, §5.4] where $\sqrt{\Sigma_{\mathbf{G}}}$ is a parameter used when performing Gaussian sampling from a coset $\Lambda_{\mathbf{w}'}^{\perp}(\mathbf{G})$. As $\Sigma_{\mathbf{G}}$ is a constant, we only need to evaluate $s_1(\mathbf{R})$, which is $\bar{s} \cdot O(\sqrt{Nkw} + \sqrt{Nk\log_2 q})$ from [34, §5.2]. Together with the condition (12) on $\bar{s}$ required by regularity, one can bound the parameter σ_b.

4.4 Oracle Simulation Lemma

Now let us turn to our main goal: security against adversaries that make concurrent chosen-message queries. For our honest party oracle simulator to succeed,

---

Algorithm 1: Simulation of honest signing algorithm

$\mathcal{T}(\bar{\mathbf{A}}, a, \mathbf{s}, \mathbf{t})$

    // Offline

1: **for** $j \in [1, m]$ **do**

2:      **if** $j = 1$ **then**

3:          $\mathbf{y}^{(1)} \leftarrow \mathscr{D}_{\sigma_1}^{\ell+k}$

4:          $b^{(1)} := 1$

5:      **else**

6:          $\mathbf{y}^{(j)} \leftarrow \mathscr{D}_{\sigma_y}^{\ell+k}$

7:          $b^{(j)} \leftarrow \mathscr{D}_{\sigma_b}$

8:      $\mathbf{w}^{(j)} := \bar{\mathbf{A}}\mathbf{y}^{(j)} \bmod q$

9: $\tilde{\mathbf{y}} := \sum_{j=1}^{m} b^{(j)}\mathbf{y}^{(j)}$

    // Online

10: $c \leftarrow_\$ C$

11: $\mathbf{v} := c \cdot a \cdot \mathbf{s}$

12: $\mathbf{z} := \mathbf{v} + \tilde{\mathbf{y}}$

13: $\rho \leftarrow_\$ [0, 1)$

14: **if** $\rho > \min\left(\dfrac{\mathscr{D}_{\sqrt{\widehat{\Sigma}}}^{\ell+k}(\mathbf{z})}{M \cdot \mathscr{D}_{\sqrt{\Sigma}, \mathbf{v}}^{\ell+k}(\mathbf{z})}, 1\right)$ **then**

15:      $\mathbf{z} := \bot$

16: **return** $(\bar{\mathbf{A}}, a, \mathbf{t}, (\mathbf{w}^{(j)}, b^{(j)})_{j \in [m]}, c, \mathbf{z})$

$\mathcal{S}(\bar{\mathbf{A}}, a, \mathbf{t})$

1: $\mathbf{w}^{(1)} \leftarrow_\$ R_q^k$

2: $([\mathbf{w}^{(2)}, \ldots, \mathbf{w}^{(m)}], \mathbf{R}) \leftarrow \mathsf{TrapGen}(1^\lambda)$

3: $\mathbf{z} \leftarrow \mathscr{D}_{\sqrt{\widehat{\Sigma}}}^{\ell+k}$

4: $c \leftarrow_\$ C$

5: $\mathbf{w}' := \bar{\mathbf{A}}\mathbf{z} - c \cdot a \cdot \mathbf{t} - \mathbf{w}^{(1)}$

6: $b^{(1)} := 1$

7: $(b^{(2)}, \ldots, b^{(m)}) \leftarrow \mathsf{TrapSamp}(\mathbf{R}, \mathbf{w}', \sigma_b)$

8: $\rho \leftarrow_\$ [0, 1)$

9: **if** $\rho > 1/M$ **then**

10:      $\mathbf{z} := \bot$

11: **return** $(\bar{\mathbf{A}}, a, \mathbf{t}, (\mathbf{w}^{(j)}, b^{(j)})_{j \in [m]}, c, \mathbf{z})$

---

we need the following lemma. It can proved via standard hybrid arguments, by invoking the switching lemma multiple times, indistinguishability of TrapGen and TrapSamp as stated above, and our generalized rejection sampling lemma (Lemma 6). Conditions on the parameters are detailed in the full version.

Lemma 10. *Let* $\sigma_1, \sigma_y, \sigma_b, \Sigma, \widehat{\Sigma}, M$ *be parameters satisfying conditions in Lemma 6 and Sect. 4.3. Suppose* $q = 5 \bmod 8$ *as in Lemma 2. Let* $\mathbf{A} \leftarrow_\$ R^{k \times \ell}$, $\bar{\mathbf{A}} := [\mathbf{A} | \mathbb{I}_k]$, $\mathbf{s} \in S_\eta^{\ell+k}$, $\mathbf{t} := \bar{\mathbf{A}}\mathbf{s}$, $a \in C$. *The output distributions of* $\mathcal{T}$ *and* $\mathcal{S}$ *in Algorithm 1 are statistically indistinguishable.*

Proof. We prove via standard hybrid arguments. Each hybrid is detailed in the full version.

– Hyb_0 is identical to $\mathcal{T}$.
– Hyb_1 is identical to Hyb_0, except that $\mathbf{w}^{(j)}$'s are sampled uniformly and $\mathbf{y}^{(j)}$'s are sampled from Gaussian defined over a coset $\Lambda_{\mathbf{w}^{(j)}}^\perp(\bar{\mathbf{A}}) = \{\mathbf{x} \in R^{k+\ell} : \bar{\mathbf{A}}\mathbf{x} = \mathbf{w}^{(j)} \bmod q\}$. From Lemma 9, Hyb_0 and Hyb_1 are statistically close.
– Hyb_2 is identical to Hyb_1, except that $\tilde{\mathbf{y}}$, a linear combination of $\mathbf{y}^{(j)}$'s, is directly sampled from Gaussian over a coset $\Lambda_{\tilde{\mathbf{w}}}^\perp(\bar{\mathbf{A}})$, where $\tilde{\mathbf{w}} = \sum_j b^{(j)}\mathbf{w}^{(j)}$ $\bmod q$. From Lemma 5, Hyb_1 and Hyb_2 are statistically close.
– Hyb_3 is identical to Hyb_2, except that $\mathbf{z}$ is sampled from Gaussian over a coset $\Lambda_{\mathbf{u}}^\perp$ centered at $\mathbf{v}$, where $\mathbf{u} = \tilde{\mathbf{w}} + c \cdot a \cdot \mathbf{t}$ and $\mathbf{v} = c \cdot a \cdot \mathbf{s}$. Clearly, the output distributions of Hyb_2 and Hyb_3 are equivalent.

- Hyb_4 is identical to Hyb_3, except that $\mathbf{z}$ is sampled from Gaussian over a coset $\Lambda_{\mathbf{u}}^{\perp}$ centered at 0 and it is output with constant probability $1/M$. From Lemma 6, Hyb_3 and Hyb_4 are statistically close.
- Hyb_5 is identical to Hyb_4, except that $\mathbf{w}' = \tilde{\mathbf{w}} - \mathbf{w}^{(1)}$ is uniformly sampled from R_q^k and a vector $[b^{(2)}, \ldots, b^{(m)}]$ is sampled from spherical Gaussian over a coset $\Lambda_{\mathbf{w}'}^{\perp}(\mathbf{W})$, where $\mathbf{W} = [\mathbf{w}^{(2)}, \ldots, \mathbf{w}^{(m)}]$. From Lemma 9, Hyb_4 and Hyb_5 are statistically close.
- Hyb_6 is identical to Hyb_5, except that $\mathbf{z}$ is sampled from Gaussian over $R_q^{\ell+k}$ and $\tilde{\mathbf{w}}$ is defined as $\tilde{\mathbf{w}} = \bar{\mathbf{A}}\mathbf{z} - c \cdot a \cdot \mathbf{t}$. From Lemma 9, Hyb_5 and Hyb_6 are statistically close.
- Hyb_7 is identical to Hyb_6, except that a matrix $[\mathbf{w}^{(2)}, \ldots, \mathbf{w}^{(m)}]$ is generated with the corresponding trapdoor $\mathbf{R}$. From indistinguishability of the TrapGen algorithm, Hyb_6 and Hyb_7 are statistically close.
- Hyb_8 is identical to Hyb_7, except that a vector $[b^{(2)}, \ldots, b^{(m)}]$ is sampled using the trapdoor sampling algorithm. From indistinguishability of the TrapSamp algorithm, Hyb_7 and Hyb_8 are statistically close.

Note that the distribution output by Hyb_8 is identical to one by $\mathcal{S}$. This concludes the proof. □

4.5 MS-UF-CMA Security of MuSig-L

Given the oracle simulation lemma, we are finally ready to conclude with our main theorem.

Theorem 3. *If MuSig-L is MS-UF-KOA-secure, then it is MS-UF-CMA-secure. Concretely, for any PPT adversary $\mathcal{X}$ against MS-UF-KOA that makes at most Q_h queries to the random oracles and in total Q_s queries to OSignOff and OSignOn, there exists PPT adversary $\mathcal{A}$ such that*

$$\mathsf{Adv}_{MuSig\text{-}L}^{MS\text{-}UF\text{-}CMA}(\mathcal{X}) \leq 2(Q_h + Q_s)^2 \cdot \left(\frac{1 + 2^{-\Omega(N)}}{q^{kN}} \right)^m + \frac{(2Q_h + Q_s)^2}{\rho_{\sigma_b}(R)}$$
$$+ e \cdot (Q_s + 1) \cdot \left(Q_s \cdot \epsilon_s + \mathsf{Adv}_{MuSig\text{-}L}^{MS\text{-}UF\text{-}KOA}(\mathcal{A}) \right)$$

where ϵ_s is determined by the statistical distance of Lemma 10.

Proof Sketch. We sketch the high-level ideas. Full security proof is deferred to the full version. We denote by $\mathsf{H}'_{\mathsf{agg}}, \mathsf{H}'_{\mathsf{non}}, \mathsf{H}'_{\mathsf{sig}}$ (resp. $\mathsf{H}_{\mathsf{agg}}, \mathsf{H}_{\mathsf{non}}, \mathsf{H}_{\mathsf{sig}}$) the random oracles in the MS-UF-CMA game (resp. MS-UF-KOA game), respectively. On a high-level, we simulate the adversary's view by first producing a trapdoor for the outputs of OSignOff, and then answer every query to OSignOn and $\mathsf{H}_{\mathsf{non}}$ using a known trapdoor. In a bit more detail:

- OSignOff: For every concurrent session launched by the adversary, it stores in table WT party 1's commit messages $[\mathbf{w}_1^{(j)}, \ldots, \mathbf{w}_1^{(m)}]$ with a known trapdoor $\mathbf{R}$ produced by the TrapGen algorithm.

- H'_{non}: Whenever it receives a query of the form $(\{t_i \| \text{com}_i\}_{i \in [n]}, \mu, \tilde{t})$, it first makes sure that (1) there is no duplicate honest keys in the input, (2) the mth sum of commit message contains an invertible element, and (3) $\text{com}_1 = [\mathbf{w}_1^{(j)}, \ldots, \mathbf{w}_1^{(m)}]$ (i.e., a commit message appended to the honest party's key t_1) has been previously produced by OSignOff. It does (3) by looking up the table WT, and if it finds a suitable trapdoor $\mathbf{R}$ associated with the corresponding session ID, H'_{non} internally performs simulation following the procedures of Algorithm 1, and then programs outputs of the random oracles H'_{sig} and H'_{non} accordingly. A simulated signature is finally stored in the table ST.

- OSignOn: When the online oracle is queried, it always invokes H'_{non} first and checks whether a simulated signature is recorded in ST. The simulation succeeds if that is the case, and aborts otherwise. The reason for aborts is that H'_{non} must *not* produce simulated signatures for all queries, because it might be that the adversary will later submit a forgery based on the challenge c programmed inside H'_{non}. If that happens, the output of the external RO H_{sig} is not consistent with that of H'_{sig} anymore, and thus the reduction cannot win the MS-UF-KOA game. However, this issue can be handled by having H'_{non} perform simulation only probabilistically, a proof technique similar to [18] and [16]. Such "bad challenges" are then kept in the table CT, and we evaluate the probability that the adversary does not use bad challenge to create a forgery.

- Note that this is exactly where appended public keys come in to play, and interestingly, they are crucial for proving security in the offline-online paradigm. Consider a modified scheme where H'_{non} does not take individual public keys, i.e., it simply derives randomness via $H'_{\text{non}}(\langle \text{com}_i \rangle_{i \in [n]}, \mu, \tilde{t})$. It is easy to see that the simulator would have a hard time looking up the right trapdoor to perform simulation: say OSignOff has produced $(\text{com}_1, \mathbf{R})$ in session 1 and $(\text{com}'_1, \mathbf{R}')$ in session 2, respectively. Now, if the adversary queries H'_{non} with input $((\text{com}_1, \text{com}'_1), \mu, \tilde{t})$ there is no way for the simulator to determine which trapdoor should be used for performing simulation to sign a queried message μ. E.g. if the simulator uses a trapdoor $\mathbf{R}$, and the adversary later queries OSignOn in session 2 with μ and com_1 (by maliciously claiming com_1 to be adversary's offline commit), a signature previously simulated by H'_{non} is clearly invalid. Essentially the same issue happens if t_1 occurs multiple times in the key list L.

Acknowledgment. The authors are grateful to Claudio Orlandi for discussions in the earlier stages of this work. We thank Carsten Baum, Katharina Boudgoust, and Mark Simkin for helpful comments and discussions. Cecilia Boschini has been supported by the Università della Svizzera Italiana under the SNSF project number 182452, and by the Postdoc. Mobility grant No. P500PT_203075. Akira Takahashi has been supported by the Carlsberg Foundation under the Semper Ardens Research Project CF18-112 (BCM); the European Research Council (ERC) under the European Unions's Horizon 2020 research and innovation programme under grant agreement No. 803096 (SPEC).

References

1. Agrawal, S., Gentry, C., Halevi, S., Sahai, A.: Discrete gaussian leftover hash lemma over infinite domains. In: Sako, K., Sarkar, P. (eds.) ASIACRYPT 2013, Part I. LNCS, vol. 8269, pp. 97–116. Springer, Heidelberg (2013). https://doi.org/10.1007/978-3-642-42033-7_6
2. Agrawal, S., Kirshanova, E., Stehlé, D., Yadav, A.: Can round-optimal lattice-based blind signatures be practical? IACR Cryptology ePrint Archive, p. 1565 (2021)
3. Agrawal, S., Stehle, D., Yadav, A.: Round-optimal lattice-based threshold signatures, revisited. Cryptology ePrint Archive, Paper 2022/634 (2022)
4. Alper, H.K., Burdges, J.: Two-round trip schnorr multi-signatures via delinearized witnesses. In: Malkin, T., Peikert, C. (eds.) CRYPTO 2021, Part I. LNCS, vol. 12825, pp. 157–188. Springer, Cham (2021). https://doi.org/10.1007/978-3-030-84242-0_7
5. Baum, C., Damgård, I., Lyubashevsky, V., Oechsner, S., Peikert, C.: More efficient commitments from structured lattice assumptions. In: Catalano, D., De Prisco, R. (eds.) SCN 2018. LNCS, vol. 11035, pp. 368–385. Springer, Cham (2018). https://doi.org/10.1007/978-3-319-98113-0_20
6. Bellare, M., Dai, W.: Chain reductions for multi-signatures and the HBMS scheme. In: Tibouchi, M., Wang, H. (eds.) ASIACRYPT 2021, Part IV. LNCS, vol. 13093, pp. 650–678. Springer, Cham (2021). https://doi.org/10.1007/978-3-030-92068-5_22
7. Bellare, M., Neven, G.: Multi-signatures in the plain public-key model and a general forking lemma. In: ACM CCS 2006, pp. 390–399. ACM Press (2006)
8. Bendlin, R., Krehbiel, S., Peikert, C.: How to share a lattice trapdoor: threshold protocols for signatures and (H)IBE. In: Jacobson, M., Locasto, M., Mohassel, P., Safavi-Naini, R. (eds.) ACNS 2013. LNCS, vol. 7954, pp. 218–236. Springer, Heidelberg (2013). https://doi.org/10.1007/978-3-642-38980-1_14
9. Benhamouda, F., Lepoint, T., Loss, J., Orrù, M., Raykova, M.: On the (in)security of ROS. In: Canteaut, A., Standaert, F.-X. (eds.) EUROCRYPT 2021, Part I. LNCS, vol. 12696, pp. 33–53. Springer, Cham (2021). https://doi.org/10.1007/978-3-030-77870-5_2
10. Bert, P., Eberhart, G., Prabel, L., Roux-Langlois, A., Sabt, M.: Implementation of lattice trapdoors on modules and applications. In: Cheon, J.H., Tillich, J.-P. (eds.) PQCrypto 2021 2021. LNCS, vol. 12841, pp. 195–214. Springer, Cham (2021). https://doi.org/10.1007/978-3-030-81293-5_11
11. Boneh, D., et al.: Threshold cryptosystems from threshold fully homomorphic encryption. In: Shacham, H., Boldyreva, A. (eds.) CRYPTO 2018, Part I. LNCS, vol. 10991, pp. 565–596. Springer, Cham (2018). https://doi.org/10.1007/978-3-319-96884-1_19
12. Boneh, D., Kim, S.: One-time and interactive aggregate signatures from lattices. preprint (2020)
13. Boudgoust, K., Roux-Langlois, A.: Compressed linear aggregate signatures based on module lattices. IACR Cryptology ePrint Archive, p. 263 (2021)
14. Brier, E., Coron, J.-S., Icart, T., Madore, D., Randriam, H., Tibouchi, M.: Efficient indifferentiable hashing into ordinary elliptic curves. In: Rabin, T. (ed.) CRYPTO 2010. LNCS, vol. 6223, pp. 237–254. Springer, Heidelberg (2010). https://doi.org/10.1007/978-3-642-14623-7_13
15. Crites, E.C., Komlo, C., Maller, M.: How to prove schnorr assuming schnorr: security of multi- and threshold signatures. IACR Cryptology ePrint Archive, p. 1375 (2021)

16. Damgård, I., Orlandi, C., Takahashi, A., Tibouchi, M.: Two-round n-out-of-n and multi-signatures and trapdoor commitment from lattices. In: Garay, J.A. (ed.) PKC 2021, Part I. LNCS, vol. 12710, pp. 99–130. Springer, Cham (2021). https://doi.org/10.1007/978-3-030-75245-3_5

17. Damgård, I., Pastro, V., Smart, N., Zakarias, S.: Multiparty computation from somewhat homomorphic encryption. In: Safavi-Naini, R., Canetti, R. (eds.) CRYPTO 2012. LNCS, vol. 7417, pp. 643–662. Springer, Heidelberg (2012). https://doi.org/10.1007/978-3-642-32009-5_38

18. Drijvers, M., et al.: On the security of two-round multi-signatures. In: 2019 IEEE Symposium on Security and Privacy, pp. 1084–1101. IEEE Computer Society Press (2019)

19. Ducas, L., Lepoint, T., Lyubashevsky, V., Schwabe, P., Seiler, G., Stehlé, D.: CRYSTALS - dilithium: digital signatures from module lattices. IACR Cryptology ePrint Archive, p. 633 (2018)

20. El Bansarkhani, R., Sturm, J.: An efficient lattice-based multisignature scheme with applications to bitcoins. In: Foresti, S., Persiano, G. (eds.) CANS 2016. LNCS, vol. 10052, pp. 140–155. Springer, Cham (2016). https://doi.org/10.1007/978-3-319-48965-0_9

21. Fukumitsu, M., Hasegawa, S.: A lattice-based provably secure multisignature scheme in quantum random oracle model. In: Nguyen, K., Wu, W., Lam, K.Y., Wang, H. (eds.) ProvSec 2020. LNCS, vol. 12505, pp. 45–64. Springer, Cham (2020). https://doi.org/10.1007/978-3-030-62576-4_3

22. Garillot, F., Kondi, Y., Mohassel, P., Nikolaenko, V.: Threshold schnorr with stateless deterministic signing from standard assumptions. In: Malkin, T., Peikert, C. (eds.) CRYPTO 2021, Part I. LNCS, vol. 12825, pp. 127–156. Springer, Cham (2021). https://doi.org/10.1007/978-3-030-84242-0_6

23. Gennaro, R., Jarecki, S., Krawczyk, H., Rabin, T.: Secure distributed key generation for discrete-log based cryptosystems. J. Cryptol. **20**(1), 51–83 (2007)

24. Howe, J., Prest, T., Ricosset, T., Rossi, M.: Isochronous gaussian sampling: from inception to implementation. In: Ding, J., Tillich, J.-P. (eds.) PQCrypto 2020. LNCS, vol. 12100, pp. 53–71. Springer, Cham (2020). https://doi.org/10.1007/978-3-030-44223-1_4

25. Komlo, C., Goldberg, I.: FROST: flexible round-optimized schnorr threshold signatures. In: Dunkelman, O., Jacobson, Jr., M.J., O'Flynn, C. (eds.) SAC 2020. LNCS, vol. 12804, pp. 34–65. Springer, Cham (2021). https://doi.org/10.1007/978-3-030-81652-0_2

26. Lyubashevsky, V.: Lattice signatures without trapdoors. In: Pointcheval, D., Johansson, T. (eds.) EUROCRYPT 2012. LNCS, vol. 7237, pp. 738–755. Springer, Heidelberg (2012). https://doi.org/10.1007/978-3-642-29011-4_43

27. Lyubashevsky, V., Neven, G.: One-shot verifiable encryption from lattices. In: Coron, J.-S., Nielsen, J.B. (eds.) EUROCRYPT 2017, Part I. LNCS, vol. 10210, pp. 293–323. Springer, Cham (2017). https://doi.org/10.1007/978-3-319-56620-7_11

28. Lyubashevsky, V., Peikert, C., Regev, O.: A toolkit for ring-LWE cryptography. In: Johansson, T., Nguyen, P.Q. (eds.) EUROCRYPT 2013. LNCS, vol. 7881, pp. 35–54. Springer, Heidelberg (2013). https://doi.org/10.1007/978-3-642-38348-9_3

29. Lyubashevsky, V., Seiler, G.: Short, invertible elements in partially splitting cyclotomic rings and applications to lattice-based zero-knowledge proofs. In: Nielsen, J.B., Rijmen, V. (eds.) EUROCRYPT 2018, Part I. LNCS, vol. 10820, pp. 204–224. Springer, Cham (2018). https://doi.org/10.1007/978-3-319-78381-9_8

30. Ma, C., Jiang, M.: Practical lattice-based multisignature schemes for blockchains. IEEE Access **7**, 179765–179778 (2019)

31. Maxwell, G., Poelstra, A., Seurin, Y., Wuille, P.: Simple schnorr multi-signatures with applications to bitcoin. Des. Codes Cryptogr. **87**(9), 2139–2164 (2019)
32. Micali, S., Ohta, K., Reyzin, L.: Accountable-subgroup multisignatures: extended abstract. In: ACM CCS 2001, pp. 245–254. ACM Press (2001)
33. Micciancio, D.: Generalized compact knapsacks, cyclic lattices, and efficient one-way functions from worst-case complexity assumptions. In: 43rd FOCS, pp. 356–365. IEEE Computer Society Press (2002)
34. Micciancio, D., Peikert, C.: Trapdoors for lattices: simpler, tighter, faster, smaller. In: Pointcheval, D., Johansson, T. (eds.) EUROCRYPT 2012. LNCS, vol. 7237, pp. 700–718. Springer, Heidelberg (2012). https://doi.org/10.1007/978-3-642-29011-4_41
35. Micciancio, D., Peikert, C.: Hardness of SIS and LWE with small parameters. In: Canetti, R., Garay, J.A. (eds.) CRYPTO 2013, Part I. LNCS, vol. 8042, pp. 21–39. Springer, Heidelberg (2013). https://doi.org/10.1007/978-3-642-40041-4_2
36. Nick, J., Ruffing, T., Seurin, Y.: MuSig2: simple two-round schnorr multi-signatures. In: Malkin, T., Peikert, C. (eds.) CRYPTO 2021, Part I. LNCS, vol. 12825, pp. 189–221. Springer, Cham (2021). https://doi.org/10.1007/978-3-030-84242-0_8
37. Nick, J., Ruffing, T., Seurin, Y., Wuille, P.: MuSig-DN: schnorr multi-signatures with verifiably deterministic nonces. In: ACM CCS 2020, pp. 1717–1731. ACM Press (2020)
38. Nicolosi, A., Krohn, M.N., Dodis, Y., Mazières, D.: Proactive two-party signatures for user authentication. In: NDSS 2003. The Internet Society (2003)
39. Ristenpart, T., Yilek, S.: The power of proofs-of-possession: securing multiparty signatures against rogue-key attacks. In: Naor, M. (ed.) EUROCRYPT 2007. LNCS, vol. 4515, pp. 228–245. Springer, Heidelberg (2007). https://doi.org/10.1007/978-3-540-72540-4_13
40. Stinson, D.R., Strobl, R.: Provably secure distributed schnorr signatures and a (t, n) threshold scheme for implicit certificates. In: Varadharajan, V., Mu, Y. (eds.) ACISP 2001. LNCS, vol. 2119, pp. 417–434. Springer, Heidelberg (2001). https://doi.org/10.1007/3-540-47719-5_33

A New Framework for More Efficient Round-Optimal Lattice-Based (Partially) Blind Signature via Trapdoor Sampling

Rafael del Pino[1] and Shuichi Katsumata[2,3(✉)]

[1] PQShield SAS, Paris, France
rafael.del.pino@pqshield.com
[2] AIST, Tokyo, Japan
shuichi.katsumata@aist.go.jp
[3] PQShield Ltd., Oxford, UK

Abstract. Blind signatures, proposed by Chaum (CRYPTO'82), are interactive protocols between a signer and a user, where a user can obtain a signature without revealing the message to be signed. Recently, Hauck et al. (EUROCRYPT'20) observed that all efficient lattice-based blind signatures following the blueprint of the original blind signature by Rükert (ASIACRYPT'10) have a flawed security proof. This puts us in a situation where all known lattice-based blind signatures have at least two of the following drawbacks: heuristic security; 1 MB or more signature size; only supporting bounded polynomially many signatures, or being based on non-standard assumptions.

In this work, we construct the first *round-optimal* (i.e., two-round) lattice-based blind signature with a signature size roughly 100 KB that supports unbounded polynomially many signatures and is provably secure under standard assumptions. Even if we allow non-standard assumptions and more rounds, ours provide the shortest signature size while simultaneously supporting unbounded polynomially many signatures. The main idea of our work is revisiting the generic blind signature construction by Fischlin (CRYPTO'06) and optimizing the *commit-then-open* proof using techniques tailored to lattices. Our blind signature is also the first construction to have a formal security proof in the *quantum* random oracle model. Finally, our blind signature extends naturally to *partially* blind signatures, where the user and signer can include an agreed-upon public string in the message.

1 Introduction

1.1 Background

Blind signatures, originally proposed by Chaum [23], are interactive protocols between a signer and a user, where a user can obtain a signature without revealing the message to be signed to the signer. Blind signatures satisfy two security notions: *one-more unforgeability* and *blindness*. One-more unforgeability states that if a malicious user engages only in at most ℓ (possibly concurrent) signing

© International Association for Cryptologic Research 2022
Y. Dodis and T. Shrimpton (Eds.): CRYPTO 2022, LNCS 13508, pp. 306–336, 2022.
https://doi.org/10.1007/978-3-031-15979-4_11

sessions with the signer, then it cannot output more than ℓ signatures. Blindness states that a malicious signer can neither learn the message during the signing session nor link a particular message-signature pair to a particular signing session. The typical applications of blind signatures include e-cash [23,25,43], anonymous credentials [19,21], e-voting [24,32], and so on, and more recently, it has found exciting applications in the context of adding privacy features to blockchains [50] and privacy-preserving authentication tokens [1].

In this paper, we focus on one class of blind signatures that has recently attracted a lot of attention: *lattice-based* blind signatures; currently the only known class of blind signatures believed to withstand quantum attacks for other related works). The first lattice-based blind signature was proposed by Rükert [47], who followed a design paradigm similar to the classical Schnorr or Okamoto-Schnorr blind signatures [45,48]. The blind signature consists of three rounds and supports poly-logarithmically many signatures (in the security parameter λ) before having to regenerate the verification key. This general approach has been extended and optimized in subsequent works [8–10,36,44], where BLAZE+ by Alkadri et al. [10] currently stands as the most efficient proposal. However, recently, Hauck et al. [34] showed that all constructions following the blueprint of Rükert's blind signature contain the same bug in their security proof[1], consequently leaving them only heuristically secure at best. Building on Rükert's blind signature and optimizations employed by BLAZE+, Hauck et al. managed to construct the first provably secure lattice-based blind signature. Unfortunately, the security proof required very large parameter sets, and their proposal resulted in a signature size of roughly 7.9 MB with a communication cost of 34 MB and supported only 7 signatures per verification key. Thus, the work of Hauck et al. [34] reopened the question of building efficient *and* provably secure lattice-based blind signatures.

Very recently, two works aimed at solving this. One by Agrawal et al. [5]. Instead of following the three-move structure seen in Schnorr's blind signature [48], Agrawal et al. builds on Fischlin [31] and Garg et al. [33] that provide a generic construction of a two-move (i.e., *round-optimal*) blind signatures. Concretely, they propose two constructions. One produces a short signature in the range of a few KB with a communication cost of around 50 MB but comes with several caveats: the scheme can support only bounded polynomially many signatures; blindness only holds against *very honest* signers (i.e. the public key must be generated honestly and the signer cannot deviate from the protocol), and the scheme is only heuristically secure as it needs to homomorphically evaluate a standard signature scheme that internally uses a hash function modeled as a random oracle. The second can support unbounded polynomially many signatures and blindness holds against *honest* signers (i.e. the public key must be generated honestly but the signer can deviate from the protocol) but it requires a new non-standard hardness assumption called the *one-more*-inhomogeneous

---

[1] Alkadri et al. [8] claims to have fixed the bug of BLAZE+ (and thus by Rükert) but we have found several errors in their security proof. This has been confirmed by the authors through personal communication.

SIS assumption. Moreover, the signature size becomes as large as 1 MB[2,3], while the communication cost is lowered to a few KB. The other work is by Lyubashevsky et al. [39]. They propose a round-optimal blind signature based on a new approach using one-time signatures and OR-proofs. Unlike [5], the security of their blind signature is based on the standard hardness of the MSIS and MLWE assumptions. However, the scheme only supports bounded polynomially many signatures with a signature size of roughly 150 KB. The communication cost is around 16 MB and the signer running time scales linearly in the maximum number of signatures that can be signed.

In summary, all known lattice-based blind signatures have at least two of the following drawbacks: heuristic security; 1 MB or more signature size; only supporting bounded polynomially many signatures, or based on non-standard assumptions. This leaves open the following natural question:

Can we construct an efficient and provably secure lattice-based blind signature supporting unbounded polynomially many signatures based on standard assumptions?

As an independent interest, we also note that all provably secure lattice-based blind signatures mentioned above are only proven secure against classical adversaries in the classical random oracle model (ROM). Indeed, most strategies used to prove security completely break down when handling quantum adversaries in the quantum ROM (QROM). Although we do not imagine all previous constructions can be broken using quantum adversaries, considering that one of the main appeals of lattice-based cryptography is their resilience against quantum adversaries, we believe any formal post-quantum security guarantee is highly desirable.

1.2 Our Contribution

In this work, we answer the above question in the affirmative. We construct the first round-optimal lattice-based blind signature with a signature size roughly 100 KB that supports unbounded many signatures and is provably secure under standard assumptions. Even if we allow non-standard assumptions and more rounds, ours provide the shortest signature size while also supporting unbounded many signatures. The communication cost currently sits at 850 KB, but as we explain later, we believe by using the right non-interactive zero-knowledge

---

[2] Agrawal et al. provide an informal estimate of 30 KB to 100 KB and states to use the NIZK by [29,41]. However, considering that their security proof relies on an *exact* proof for a relation $\mathbf{C}s = u$ for a large matrix $\mathbf{C}$ (since the authors argue that $\mathbf{C}$ is indistinguishable from uniform with the leftover hash lemma) and a witness s with entries as large as $\Omega(\sqrt{q})$, even an optimistic estimate gives a lower bound of 1 MB with current lattice-based NIZKs.

[3] After submission of this paper, Agrawal et al. updated their paper to use the NIZK by Lyubashevsky et al. [40] appearing at CRYPTO 2022. See [6] work for more detail.

(NIZK) proofs, we could cut this down to roughly 100 KB while maintaining the same signature size. The security of our blind signature is established both in the classical ROM and QROM. It is secure against *malicious* signers, where blindness holds even when the signer can register malicious keys and deviate from the protocol. Moreover, our scheme can be easily transformed into a *partially* blind signature [2]. This allows the user and signer to include a common agreed-upon message into the signature and has proven to be useful in applications such as e-cash [23,25,43] and e-voting [24,32].

We obtain our blind signature by a new generic construction tailored to lattices. The starting point of our work is the generic round-optimal blind signature construction by Fischlin [31]. The signature in Fischlin's blind signature consists of a complex NIZK proof that informally proves possession of two things: a signature from a standard signature scheme and an opening to a commitment. At the heart of our generic construction is a technique inspired by del Pino et al. [27] that allows us to transform such complex statement into a simple lattice statement consisting only of proving possession of a short vector. Consequently, we can rely on well-known efficient lattice-based NIZKs such as those by Lyubashevsky [37,38] to generate the signature.

One tool required by our generic construction is a *multi-proof straight-line extractable* NIZK [16],[4] which is used by the user to prove the well-formedness of its first message sent to the signer. Informally, such an NIZK guarantees the existence of an extractor that, on input a simulation trapdoor and any adaptively chosen proofs, outputs the corresponding witnesses. This is in sharp contrast to standard NIZKs in the (Q)ROM where witness extraction is performed via rewinding [14,45]. If we were to rely on rewinding-based extractions, our security proof would incur an exponential security loss in the number of signing sessions, and result in a scheme that can only support poly-logarithmically many signatures. Similar issues crop up in the context of IND-CCA secure public key encryptions [15,49] and group signatures [16]. In this work, to construct such strong NIZKs for relatively complex lattice-based statements, we rely on the recent technique of *extractable linear homomorphic commitments* proposed by Katsumata [35].

Finally, we highlight that due to the modularity of our generic construction, any future improvements in lattice-based NIZKs may lead to more efficient blind signatures. For instance, if we were able to combine the technique of Katsumata with the recent efficient lattice-based NIZKs [11,29], then we could potentially reduce the communication cost from 850 KB to roughly 100 KB. We leave further optimized instantiations of our generic construction as an interesting future work.

1.3 Technical Overview

We give an overview of our techniques in two parts. In Part 1, we explain the high level idea of our generic construction and in Part 2, we explain how to instantiate the building blocks.

---

[4] This notion is also called *online* extractable in the literature.

Part 1. We first explain our generic construction tailored to lattices.

Blind Signature by Fischlin. Our starting point is the generic construction of blind signatures by Fischlin [31]. The blind signature is round optimal and supports polynomially many signatures. His generic construction relies on general NIZKs for a complex statement and the proof overhead (i.e. signature size) becomes prohibitively large when instantiated using known lattice-based NIZKs. Our goal is to replace this complex statement with a lattice-friendly statement.

We first recall Fischlin's construction. In his construction, the signer publishes verification key of a standard signature scheme as the verification key vk of the blind signature and keeps the corresponding signing key sk secret. If a user wants the signer to blindly sign on message M, it submits a commitment com ← Com(M; rand) to the signer and obtains a signature $\sigma \overset{\$}{\leftarrow}$ Sig(sk, com). The user then constructs a ciphertext ct ← Enc(ek, com‖rand‖σ; rand′) using a PKE scheme and constructs an NIZK proof π that proves

$$\text{com} = \text{Com}(M; \text{rand}) \land \text{Verify}(\text{vk}, \sigma, \text{com}) = \top$$
$$\land\ \text{ct} = \text{Enc}(\text{ek}, \text{com}\|\text{rand}\|\sigma; \text{rand}'), \tag{1}$$

where the statement is (vk, ek, ct, M) and the witness is (com, rand, σ, rand′). Finally, the user outputs $\Sigma = (\pi, \text{ct})$ as the blind signature. Here, we assume ek is pseudorandom and is generated as an output of the random oracle. This ensures that nobody, including a malicious signer, knows the corresponding decryption key dk of the PKE scheme in the real-world. dk is only used during the security proof of one-more unforgeability, where the reduction uses dk to decrypt com‖rand‖σ from ct.

Although it is theoretically possible to instantiate Fischlin's generic construction from lattices, the main bottleneck is constructing an efficient lattice-based NIZK for Eq. (1). Agrawal et al. [5] attempts to heuristically[5] instantiate Fischlin's generic construction based on Dilithium [28], one of the most efficient lattice-based signatures, but they estimated the signature to require at least 100 KB with prover complexity approaching 1 h.

Lattice-Friendly Enc-then-Prove by del Pino et al. The main complexity of Eq. (1) comes from the need to show possession of a valid signature on a hidden message (i.e. com). Roughly, this is because we do not have a lattice-based signature whose verification algorithm is compatible with known efficient lattice-based NIZKs. Now, although not exactly what we require, we observe that a technique used by del Pino et al. [27] for constructing efficient group signatures comes close to what we need.

A group signature allows a user to anonymously sign on behalf of a group, while a special entity called a group manager can deanonymize the signer should the need arise. A typical recipe for constructing a group signature is the _enc-then-prove_ paradigm [20]. Each group user is assigned an identity $I \in [N]$, where

---

[5] Their NIZK requires evaluating a hash function used by Dilithium which is modeled as a random oracle. Considering that a random oracle does not have a function description in the ROM, this approach fails to provide any form of provable security.

$N = \mathsf{poly}(\lambda)$ is the size of the group, and the group manager provides a signature $\sigma \xleftarrow{\$} \mathsf{Sign}(\mathsf{sk}, I)$; this serves as a certificate for user I belonging to the group. To sign on behalf of the group, user I constructs a ciphertext $\mathsf{ct} \leftarrow \mathsf{Enc}(\mathsf{ek}, I; \mathsf{rand}')$ using a PKE scheme and constructs an NIZK proof π that proves

$$\mathsf{Verify}(\mathsf{vk}, \sigma, I) = \top \ \wedge \ \mathsf{ct} = \mathsf{Enc}(\mathsf{ek}, I; \mathsf{rand}'), \tag{2}$$

where the statement X_{GS} is $(\mathsf{vk}, \mathsf{ek}, \mathsf{ct})$ and the witness W_{GS} is $(\sigma, I, \mathsf{rand}')$. Note that NIZKs based on the Fiat-Shamir paradigm allows to bind any message M to a proof π so π indeed serves as a signature for M. Although Eq. (2) seems simpler than Eq. (1), it serves our purpose since it still includes the most complex component, which is proving a valid signature on a hidden message (i.e. I).

We briefly go over the group signature by del Pino et al. [27]. They use Boyen's lattice-based signature [4,18] as the underlying signature scheme. In Boyen's signature, the verification key consists of a random element $u \in R_q$ and vectors $(\mathbf{a}_1, \mathbf{a}_2) \in R_q^k \times R_q^k$, where R_q is the polynomial ring $\mathbb{Z}_q[X]/(X^d + 1)$. The signing key sk is a short basis $\mathbf{T}_{\mathbf{a}_1} \in R^{k \times k}$ such that $\mathbf{a}_1 \mathbf{T}_{\mathbf{a}_1} = \mathbf{0} \mod q$. To give out a credential for user $I \in [N]$, the group manager views I as a message and samples, using sk, a short vector $\mathbf{e} \in R^{2k}$ satisfying

$$[\mathbf{a}_1 | \mathbf{a}_2 + I \cdot \mathbf{g}]\mathbf{e}^\top = u, \tag{3}$$

where $\mathbf{g}$ is the so-called gadget matrix [42]. It outputs $\mathbf{e}$ as the certificate for user I belonging to the group. If I can be made public, then a user can simply use a standard lattice-based NIZK for proving MSIS/MLWE relations to prove possession of the certificate $\mathbf{e}$. That is, relations of the form $\overline{\mathbf{a}} \, \overline{\mathbf{e}}^\top = \overline{u}$, where $(\overline{\mathbf{a}}, \overline{u})$ is the statement and $\overline{\mathbf{e}}$ is the witness. On the other hand, if I needs to be kept private, which is the case for group signatures, then Eq. (3) becomes a quadratic relation over the witness and we no longer know how to prove it efficiently using lattice-based NIZKs.

The technical novelty of del Pino et al. was to linearize Eq. (3) by using the commitment scheme by Baum et al. [13], a.k.a., the BDLOP commitment. The BDLOP commitment is of the form $\mathsf{com} = \begin{bmatrix} \mathbf{t}_0 \\ \mathbf{t}_1 \end{bmatrix} = \begin{bmatrix} \mathbf{b}_0 \\ \mathbf{b}_1 \end{bmatrix} \mathbf{R} + \begin{bmatrix} \mathbf{0} \\ I \cdot \mathbf{g} \end{bmatrix}$, where $\mathbf{b}_0, \mathbf{b}_1 \in R_q^k$ is the commitment key, $\mathbf{R} \in R^{k \times k}$ is the commitment randomness, and $I \cdot \mathbf{g}$ is the message. This commitment satisfies binding and hiding based on the MSIS and MLWE assumptions. Using the lower half of the commitment $\mathbf{t}_1$, we can rewrite the left hand side of Eq. (3) as

$$[\mathbf{a}_1 | \mathbf{a}_2 + I \cdot \mathbf{g}]\mathbf{e}^\top = [\mathbf{a}_1 | \mathbf{a}_2 + \mathbf{b}_1 \mathbf{R} + I \cdot \mathbf{g}] \, \mathbf{e}^\top - \mathbf{b}_1 \mathbf{R} \mathbf{e}_2^\top$$

$$= [\mathbf{a}_1 | \mathbf{a}_2 + \mathbf{t}_1 | \mathbf{b}_1] \begin{bmatrix} \mathbf{e}^\top \\ -\mathbf{R} \mathbf{e}_2^\top \end{bmatrix}, \tag{4}$$

where $\mathbf{e} = [\mathbf{e}_1 | \mathbf{e}_2] \in R^{2k}$. Notice that $[\mathbf{a}_1 | \mathbf{a}_2 + \mathbf{t}_1 | \mathbf{b}_1]$ consists only of public elements included in the statement X_{GS}. Specifically, Eq. (3) can now be expressed as an MSIS relation where the statement is $[\mathbf{a}_1 | \mathbf{a}_2 + \mathbf{t}_1 | \mathbf{b}_1]$ and the witness vector is $[\mathbf{e}| - \mathbf{e}_2 \mathbf{R}^\top] \in R^{3k}$. Thus, the user transforms Eq. (3) into Eq. (4), constructs an efficient NIZK proof π for Eq. (4), and finally outputs the group signature $\Sigma = (\pi, \mathsf{com}).$[6]

Reversing the Order for Blind Signatures. The technique of del Pino et al. [27] can be seen as transforming a Boyen signature on message M into a signature on a commitment com of M. This is a good fit for the group signature functionality; a group authority signs the message $\mathsf{M} = I$ in the clear and the user can later prove possession of the signature while hiding its identity I by planting a commitment com.

Our idea is to turn this technique around and use it for blind signatures. Blind signature has an opposite functionality; the signer signs the message blindly through a commitment and the user later unblinds the commitment to prove possession of a signature. Concretely, a user first constructs a BDLOP commitment com for a message $I \in [N]$ and sends it to the signer.[7] The signer then pulls out $\mathbf{t}_1 \in R_q^k$ included in com and signs $\mathbf{t}_1$ with the Boyen signature. Specifically, the signer samples a short vector $\mathbf{e} \in R^{2k}$ satisfying

$$[\mathbf{a}_1|\mathbf{a}_2 + \mathbf{t}_1]\mathbf{e}^\top = u.$$

The user then reverses the transformation in Eq. (4) to obtain

$$[\mathbf{a}_1|\mathbf{a}_2 + \mathbf{t}_1]\mathbf{e}^\top = [\mathbf{a}_1|\mathbf{a}_2 + \mathbf{b}_1\mathbf{R} + I \cdot \mathbf{g}]\mathbf{e}^\top = [\mathbf{a}_1|\mathbf{a}_2 + I \cdot \mathbf{g}|\mathbf{b}_1]\begin{bmatrix}\mathbf{e}^\top \\ \mathbf{R}\mathbf{e}_2^\top\end{bmatrix}, \quad (5)$$

where notice the right hand side has the desired form of a public vector being multiplied by a short secret vector. Therefore, the signature output by the user can be a standard NIZK proof π for the MSIS relation, where the statement is $[\mathbf{a}_1|\mathbf{a}_2 + I \cdot \mathbf{g}|\mathbf{b}_1]$ and the witness vector is $[\mathbf{e}|\mathbf{e}_2\mathbf{R}^\top] \in R^{3k}$.

While the above construction satisfies correctness and blindness, it is not clear how to prove one-more unforgeability. To explain why, let us first see how del Pino et al. showed the unforgeability of their group signature. The reduction simulates the group manager by sampling $\mathbf{a}_1 \xleftarrow{\$} R_q^k$ and programming $\mathbf{a}_2$ as $\mathbf{a}_2 = \mathbf{a}_1\mathbf{R}^* - I^* \cdot \mathbf{g}$ for a random short matrix $\mathbf{R}^*$, where $I^* \in [N]$ is a guess for the user on which the adversary forges on. When the adversary queries the certificate for some user $I \neq I^*$, the reduction can use standard techniques [3,22] to sample a short vector for $[\mathbf{a}_1|\mathbf{a}_2 + I \cdot \mathbf{g}] = [\mathbf{a}_1|\mathbf{a}_1\mathbf{R}^* + (I - I^*) \cdot \mathbf{g}]$ using the simulation trapdoor $\mathbf{R}^*$ and the fact that $(I - I^*)$ is invertible over R_q. Once the adversary outputs a forgery, which consists of a proof π and commitment $\mathbf{t}_1$ satisfying Eq. (4), the reduction (roughly) extracts a witness $(I', \mathbf{R}', \mathbf{e}')$ via rewinding the

---

[6] To be precise, the user also needs to prove additional relations, e.g., com is a commitment to some $I \in [N]$. Since these details are not relevant to the core idea, we omit them.

[7] A keen reader may notice that the message space (i.e. group size) $[N]$ has to be polynomial large for the security proof of [27] to work. We later show how to support an exponentially large message space as required for blind signatures. .

adversary. By soundness of the NIZK, the witness satisfies $\mathbf{t}_1 = \mathbf{b}_1\mathbf{R}' + I' \cdot \mathbf{g}$ (i.e. a valid BDLOP commitment) and

$$[\mathbf{a}_1|\mathbf{a}_2 + \mathbf{t}_1|\mathbf{b}_1]\,\mathbf{e}'^\top = [\mathbf{a}_1|\mathbf{a}_1\mathbf{R}^* - I^* \cdot \mathbf{g} + \mathbf{b}_1\mathbf{R}' + I' \cdot \mathbf{g}|\mathbf{b}_1]\,\mathbf{e}'^\top = [\mathbf{a}_1|\mathbf{b}_1]\begin{bmatrix} \mathbf{e}_1'^\top + \mathbf{R}^*\mathbf{e}_2'^\top \\ \mathbf{R}'\mathbf{e}_2'^\top + \mathbf{e}_3'^\top \end{bmatrix},$$

where $\mathbf{e}' = [\mathbf{e}_1'|\mathbf{e}_2'|\mathbf{e}_3'] \in R^{3k}$ and we assume the guess made by the reduction is correct, i.e. $I^* = I'$, which happens with non-negligible probability when $N = \mathsf{poly}(\lambda)$. Thus, the reduction can break the MSIS problem with respect to the public vector $[\mathbf{a}_1|\mathbf{b}_1]$ if the adversary breaks unforgeability.

Unfortunately, this proof strategy fails in the blind signature setting. In the group signature setting, the reduction only had to sample from the vector $[\mathbf{a}_1|\mathbf{a}_2 + I \cdot \mathbf{g}] = [\mathbf{a}_1|\mathbf{a}_1\mathbf{R}^* + (I - I^*) \cdot \mathbf{g}]$, where $I \in [N]$ was the only component controlled by the adversary. However, in the blind signature setting, the reduction must be able to sample from the vector $[\mathbf{a}_1|\mathbf{a}_2 + \mathbf{t}_1] = [\mathbf{a}_1|\mathbf{a}_1\mathbf{R}^* - I^* \cdot \mathbf{g} + \mathbf{t}_1]$ for an arbitrary $\mathbf{t}_1$. This change no longer allows the reduction to rely on prior trapdoor sampling techniques [3,22] and it is not obvious anymore how to simulate the real-world signer without the full trapdoor $\mathbf{T}_{\mathbf{a}_1}$.

Adding Proof of Wellformedness. To fix the above idea, we modify the user to also include an NIZK proof π_{com} of the fact that com is well-formed, which in particular implies that $\mathbf{t}_1 = \mathbf{b}_1\mathbf{R}' + I' \cdot \mathbf{g}$ for some short $\mathbf{R}'$ and $I' \in [N]$. However, this cannot be just any standard NIZK. When the reduction is given the proof π_{com} and com from the adversary, it must extract $(\mathbf{R}', I')$ from it without interrupting the simulation. This is in contrast to rewinding-type extractions [14,45], where the reduction performs extraction only after the adversary finished playing the security game. For example, recall above to see how the reduction extracted an MSIS solution from the adversary's forgery in the unforgeability proof of the group signature. To this end, as we have already pointed to in Sect. 1.2, we rely on a stronger type of *multi-proof straight-line extractable* NIZK [16]. Such NIZK allows the reduction to directly extract $(\mathbf{R}', I')$ from the adversary without altering its behavior.

In summary, the high level description of our blind signature is as follows. The user first constructs a BDLOP commitment com for the message M and adds a multi-proof straight-line extractable NIZK proof π_{com} of its well-formedness. The signer receives $(\pi_{\mathsf{com}}, \mathsf{com})$ from the user and then samples a short vector $\mathbf{e}$ such that $[\mathbf{a}_1|\mathbf{a}_2 + \mathbf{t}_1|\mathbf{b}_1]\mathbf{e}^\top = u$, where notice that we modify the public vector to also include $\mathbf{b}_1$. Given $\mathbf{e}$ from the signer, the user transforms the signature verification equation into an MSIS relation following almost the same computation as in Eq. (5), and outputs a standard NIZK proof π for the MSIS relation as its signature.

In the security proof, the reduction uses the multi-proof straight-line extractable NIZK to extract $(\mathbf{R}', I')$ such that $\mathbf{t}_1 = \mathbf{b}_1\mathbf{R}' + I' \cdot \mathbf{g}$ without rewinding the adversary. Then, it can rewrite $[\mathbf{a}_1|\mathbf{a}_2 + \mathbf{t}_1|\mathbf{b}_1]$ as $[\mathbf{a}_1|\mathbf{a}_1\mathbf{R}^* + \mathbf{b}_1\mathbf{R}' + (I' - I^*) \cdot \mathbf{g}|\mathbf{b}_1]$. Since $(\mathbf{R}^*, \mathbf{R}')$ serves as a simulation trapdoor for $[\mathbf{a}_1|\mathbf{b}_1]$, the reduction is able to sample a short vector using prior techniques [3,22] when $I' \neq I^*$. If the adversary outputs a forgery on message I^*, the reduction can obtain an MSIS solution following an argument similar to that of del Pino et al. This completes the high-level description of our blind signature.

Omitted Details. As we briefly mentioned in Footnote 7, the above proof only works when the message space $[N]$ is polynomially large, which was the only case required in the context of group signatures. Here, if N was larger than polynomial, the probability that the reduction guesses the message I^* output by the adversary becomes negligible. To support an exponential message space, we hash the message I onto a carefully chosen exponential-sized set and sign the hashed message instead. If the hash function is modeled as a random oracle, then the reduction will be able to guess the *hash* of the message used in the forgery with non-negligible probability. Although this simple idea no longer works in the QROM since the adversary can query the entire input space in superposition, we rely on the programming technique of Zhandry [51] to prove security.

Another subtle yet important detail we glossed over is the fact that typical lattice-based NIZKs do not allow for *exact* extraction/soundness. Namely, the reduction may only be able to extract a witness $(\mathbf{R}', I')$ such that $\widehat{c} \cdot \mathbf{t}_1 = \mathbf{b}_1 \mathbf{R}' + I' \cdot \mathbf{g}$ from the malicious user, where $\widehat{c}$ is some small invertible element in R_q. In this case, $[\mathbf{a}_1|\mathbf{a}_2 + \mathbf{t}_1|\mathbf{b}_1]$ can only be rewritten as $[\mathbf{a}_1|\mathbf{a}_1\mathbf{R}^* + \mathbf{b}_1(\mathbf{R}'/\widehat{c}) + (I'/\widehat{c} - I^*) \cdot \mathbf{g}|\mathbf{b}_1]$, where $\widehat{c}^{-1}$ is in general not small. Then, since the trapdoor $(\mathbf{R}^*, \mathbf{R}'/\widehat{c})$ is not necessarily small, it no longer fits the description required by prior trapdoor sampling techniques [3, 22]. We show that prior sampling techniques can be naturally extended to work for this setting.

Part 2. Our generic construction relies on two NIZKs for different statements. One is a multi-proof straight-line extractable NIZK used by the user to prove the well-formedness of the first message, i.e. BDLOP commitment. The other is a standard NIZK for the MSIS relation that only needs to be single-proof extractable via rewinding, which is used by the user to construct the final blind signature. We only explain the former as it is the more technically challenging NIZK to construct.

To construct a multi-proof straight-line extractable NIZK, we rely on the recent Katsumata transform [35]. At a high level, it provides a generic method to upgrade many of the known lattice-based NIZKs proven to be secure in the classical ROM to NIZKs secure in the QROM. More precisely, this transform can be seen as a technique to upgrade a single-proof *rewinding*-extractable lattice-based NIZK in the classical ROM into a single-proof *straight-line* extractable NIZK in the QROM. We show that using a more fine-grained analysis, we can further upgrade this transform to provide the desired *multi-proof* straight-line extractable NIZK in the QROM. Thus, the question boils down to constructing a lattice-based NIZK in the classical ROM that is compatible with the Katsumata transform.

Recall the statement we need to prove was roughly $\mathbf{t}_1 = \mathbf{b}_1 \mathbf{R} + \mathsf{M} \cdot \mathbf{g}$ with witness $(\mathbf{R}, \mathsf{M})$, where $(\mathbf{R}, \mathsf{M})$ are short/small elements over R_q. A standard way to prove such relation is to first decompose the statement into $(t_{1,i} = \mathbf{b}_1 \mathbf{r}_i^\top + \mathsf{M} \cdot g_i)_{i \in [k]}$, where $t_{1,i}, g_i$ and $\mathbf{r}_i$ are the i-th elements and column of $\mathbf{t}_1, \mathbf{g}$, and $\mathbf{R}$, respectively. By rewriting each $\mathbf{b}_1 \mathbf{r}_i^\top + \mathsf{M} \cdot g_i$ into an MSIS relation as $\begin{bmatrix} \mathbf{b}_1 | 0 \\ 0 | g_i \end{bmatrix} \begin{bmatrix} \mathbf{r}_i^\top \\ \mathsf{M} \end{bmatrix}$, we can prove that $t_{1,i}$ has the correct form for some small $(\mathbf{r}_i', \mathsf{M}_i')$ using standard NIZKs for MSIS relations. We can then further prove that $\mathsf{M}_i' = \mathsf{M}_{i+1}'$ for all $i \in [k-1]$ by proving linear relations between $t_{1,i}$ and $t_{1,i+1}$.

It turns out that for concrete efficiency, the extraction/soundness slack on $\mathbf{R}$ has a very large impact on the final signature size. For instance, if we use Lyubashevsky's NIZK [37,38] to prove the MSIS relation, we are only able to extract a witness $(\mathbf{R}', I')$ such that $\widehat{c} \cdot \mathbf{t}_1 = \mathbf{b}_1 \mathbf{R}' + I' \cdot \mathbf{g}$ for some small and invertible $\widehat{c}$. Although $\widehat{c}$ is relatively small, this negatively impacts the size of the short vector sampled by the signer, which then negatively impacts the witness size used by the user to construct the final blind signature. Due to the way the slackness propagates in each step, the blow-up in the parameter accumulates and the final blind signature can become quite large.

To this end, we use the exact proof by Bootle et al. [17] to prove the MSIS relation and glue the proof of linear relation together. This allows the reduction to extract an *exact* witness with regards to $\mathbf{R}'$ but a *relaxed* witness with regards to the message I'. This idea is somewhat similar to the very recent "hybrid exact/relaxed" lattice proofs introduced in an independent and concurrent work by Esgin et al. [30]. We finish by showing that we can apply the Katsumata transform to this new protocol to obtain the desired multi-proof straight-line extractable NIZK. Here, we highlight that while using a more complex NIZK has a positive impact on the final blind signature size, it harms the communication cost from the user to the signer. This is because the exact proof of Bootle et al. [17] has a larger proof size compared to the standard NIZK for MSIS/MLWE relations. If we wanted to minimize the sum of the communication cost and signature size, then other NIZKs could be a better fit. We believe one of the benefits of our generic construction is that one can choose different instantiations of the NIZKs to optimize the scheme concerning their specific metric. We also note that we were not able to use the more recent efficient exact-proof NIZKs [11,29] since it was non-trivial to apply the Katsumata transform. We leave it as an interesting open question to extend the Katsumata transform to these efficient NIZKs.

Finally, the above NIZK gives us full straight-line extraction capability but we show that we can relax this when considering the concrete proof of one-more unforgeability of our blind signature (in the classical ROM). This allows us to reduce the proof size of our NIZK by roughly 40 folds (i.e. from 34 MB to 851 KB). At a very high level, the Katsumata transform applied to the proof of the linear relation already allows us to straight-line extract a *relaxed* relation with regards to $\mathbf{R}'$ as well. If $\mathbf{R}'$ is not the same as the $\mathbf{R}''$ extracted from the *exact* relation of the proof of Bootle et al., then it turns out that we can solve the MSIS problem. In other words, unless the adversary against the one-more unforgeability breaks the MSIS assumption, the $\mathbf{R}'$ that the reduction straight-line extracts from the linear relation are exact, rather than being relaxed. Hence, the reduction tries to straight-line extract from the linear proof, and if it fails to extract an exact witness $\mathbf{R}'$, then it can quit the simulation of the one-more unforgeability game. It then simply resorts to rewinding the adversary to extract $\mathbf{R}''$ from the exact proof of Bootle et al. aiming to break the MSIS problem. Thus, we can reduce the proof size by removing the Katsumata transform applied the exact proof of Bootle et al.

2 Preliminaries

2.1 Blind Signature

We provide the definition of blind signatures. For simplicity, we give a definition focusing on round-optimal (i.e. two-round) blind signatures.

Definition 2.1 (Blind Signature). *A round-optimal blind signature scheme Π_{BS} with a message space $\mathcal{M}$ consists of PPT algorithms $(\mathsf{BSGen}, \mathcal{U}_1, \mathcal{S}_2, \mathcal{U}_{\mathsf{der}}, \mathsf{BSVerify})$ defined as follows:*

$\mathsf{BSGen}(1^\lambda) \to (\mathsf{vk}, \mathsf{sk})$: *The key generation algorithm takes as input the security parameter 1^λ and outputs a verification key vk and a signing key sk.*

$\mathcal{U}_1(\mathsf{vk}, \mathsf{M}) \to (\rho_1, \mathsf{st}_{\mathcal{U}})$: *This is the user's first message generation algorithm that takes as input a verification key vk and a message $\mathsf{M} \in \mathcal{M}$ and outputs a first message ρ_1 and a state $\mathsf{st}_{\mathcal{U}}$.*

$\mathcal{S}_2(\mathsf{sk}, \rho_1) \to \rho_2$: *This is the signer's second message generation algorithm that takes as input a signing key sk and a first message ρ_1 as input and outputs a second message ρ_2.*

$\mathcal{U}_{\mathsf{der}}(\mathsf{st}_{\mathcal{U}}, \rho_2) \to \Sigma$: *This is the user's signature derivation algorithm that takes as input a state $\mathsf{st}_{\mathcal{U}}$ and a second message ρ_2 as input and outputs a signature Σ.*

$\mathsf{BSVerify}(\mathsf{vk}, \mathsf{M}, \Sigma) \to \top \text{ or } \bot$: *This is a deterministic verification algorithm that takes as input a verification key vk, a message $\mathsf{M} \in \mathcal{M}$, and a signature Σ, and outputs $\top$ to indicate acceptance or $\bot$ to indicate rejection.*

Definition 2.2 (Correctness). *A blind signature is* correct *if for any $\lambda \in \mathbb{N}$ and $\mathsf{M} \in \mathcal{M}$, we have $\mathsf{BSVerify}(\mathsf{vk}, \mathsf{M}, \Sigma) = \top$ with overwhelming probability when $(\mathsf{vk}, \mathsf{sk}) \xleftarrow{\$} \mathsf{BSGen}(1^\lambda)$, $(\rho_1, \mathsf{st}_{\mathcal{U}}) \xleftarrow{\$} \mathcal{U}_1(\mathsf{vk}, \mathsf{M})$, $\rho_2 \xleftarrow{\$} \mathcal{S}_2(\mathsf{sk}, \rho_1)$, and $\Sigma \xleftarrow{\$} \mathcal{U}_{\mathsf{der}}(\mathsf{st}_{\mathcal{U}}, \rho_2)$.*

Definition 2.3 (One-More Unforgeability). *A blind signature is classically (resp. quantumly)* one-more unforgeable *if for any $\mathsf{Q} = \mathsf{poly}(\lambda)$ and PPT (resp. QPT) adversary $\mathcal{A}$ that makes at most Q classical queries, $\mathsf{Adv}_{\Pi_{\mathsf{BS}}}^{\mathsf{OMU}}(\mathcal{A})$ defined as*

$$\Pr\left[\begin{array}{l} (\mathsf{vk}, \mathsf{sk}) \xleftarrow{\$} \mathsf{BSGen}(1^\lambda) \\ \{(\mathsf{M}_i, \Sigma_i)\}_{i \in [\mathsf{Q}+1]} \xleftarrow{\$} \mathcal{A}^{\mathcal{S}_2(\mathsf{sk}, \cdot)}(\mathsf{vk}) \end{array} : \begin{array}{l} \mathsf{BSVerify}(\mathsf{vk}, \mathsf{M}_i, \Sigma_i) = \top \text{ for all } i \in [\mathsf{Q}+1] \\ \wedge \{\mathsf{M}_i\}_{i \in [\mathsf{Q}+1]} \text{ is pairwise distinct} \end{array} \right],$$

is $\mathsf{negl}(\lambda)$, where we say that $\{\mathsf{M}_i\}_{i \in [\mathsf{Q}+1]}$ is pairwise distinct if we have $\mathsf{M}_i \neq \mathsf{M}_j$ for all $i \neq j$.

Definition 2.4 (Blindness Under Malicious Keys). *To define* blindness, *we consider the following game between an adversary $\mathcal{A}$ and a challenger.*

Setup. $\mathcal{A}$ *is given as input the security parameter* 1^λ, *and sends a verification key* vk *and a pair of messages* $(\mathsf{M}_0, \mathsf{M}_1)$ *to the challenger.*

First Message. *The challenger generates* $(\rho_{1,b}, \mathsf{st}_{\mathcal{U},b}) \overset{\$}{\leftarrow} \mathcal{U}_1(\mathsf{vk}, \mathsf{M}_b)$ *for each* $b \in \{0,1\}$, *picks* coin $\overset{\$}{\leftarrow} \{0,1\}$, *and gives* $(\rho_{1,\mathsf{coin}}, \rho_{1,1-\mathsf{coin}})$ *to* $\mathcal{A}$.

Second Message. *The adversary sends* $(\rho_{2,\mathsf{coin}}, \rho_{2,1-\mathsf{coin}})$ *to the challenger.*

Signature Derivation. *The challenger generates* $\Sigma_b \overset{\$}{\leftarrow} \mathcal{U}_{\mathsf{der}}(\mathsf{st}_{\mathcal{U},b}, \rho_{2,b})$ *for each* $b \in \{0,1\}$. *If* $\mathsf{BSVerify}(\mathsf{vk}, \mathsf{M}_b, \Sigma_b) = \bot$ *for either* $b = 0$ *or* 1, *then the challenger gives* $(\bot, \bot)$ *to* $\mathcal{A}$. *Otherwise, it gives* (Σ_0, Σ_1) *to* $\mathcal{A}$.

Guess. $\mathcal{A}$ *outputs its guess* coin$'$.

We say that $\mathcal{A}$ *wins if* coin $=$ coin$'$. *We say that a blind signature is classically (resp. quantumly) blind against malicious senders if for any PPT (resp. QPT) adversary* $\mathcal{A}$, *we have* $\mathsf{Adv}_{\Pi_{\mathsf{BS}}}^{\mathsf{blind}}(\mathcal{A}) := |\Pr[\mathcal{A} \ wins] - 1/2| = \mathsf{negl}(\lambda)$.

2.2 Non-interactive Zero-Knowledge Proofs in the (Q)ROM

We consider a non-interactive zero-knowledge proof of knowledge (or simply NIZK) in the (Q)ROM. We assume that the prover and verifier are provided with a common *random* string crs. Looking ahead, our blind signature generates this crs as the output of another random oracle so it does not rely on any trusted setup, thus making the blind signature also blind against malicious senders.

Definition 2.5 (NIZK Proof System). *A non-interactive zero-knowledge (NIZK) proof system* Π_{NIZK} *for the relations* $\mathcal{R}$ *and* $\mathcal{R}_{\mathsf{gap}}$ *(which are implicitly parameterized by the security parameter* λ*)[8] and a common random string* crs *with length* $\ell(\lambda)$ *consists of oracle-calling PPT algorithms* (Prove, Verify) *defined as follows:*

Prove$^{\mathcal{O}}$(crs, X, W) $\to \pi/\bot$: *The prover algorithm takes as inputs a common random string* crs $\in \{0,1\}^\ell$, *statement and witness pair* $(\mathsf{X}, \mathsf{W}) \in \mathcal{R}$, *and outputs a proof* π *or a special symbol* $\bot$ *denoting abort.*

Verify$^{\mathcal{O}}$(crs, X, π) $\to \top/\bot$: *The verifier algorithm takes as inputs a* crs, *a statement* X *and a proof* π, *and outputs either* $\top$ *(accept) or* $\bot$ *(reject).*

We denote by $\mathcal{L}_{\mathcal{R}} := \{\mathsf{X} \mid \exists \mathsf{W}, (\mathsf{X}, \mathsf{W}) \in \mathcal{R}\}$ *the language induced by* $\mathcal{R}$. *Moreover, we may omit* crs *when they are not required.*

We rely on the standard notions of correctness, zero-knowledge, and *single-proof extractable* NIZKs, which is typically defined as a specific type of *proof of knowledge* in the literature. Below, we define a strong type of proof of knowledge where we can directly extract from multiple statement and proof pairs output by the adversary.

---

[8] Unlike conventional definition of "gap" soundness, we do not require $\mathcal{R} \subseteq \mathcal{R}_{\mathsf{gap}}$ to hold. The NIZK is useful as long as $\mathcal{R}_{\mathsf{gap}}$ defines a hard language.

Definition 2.6 (Multi-Proof Extractability). *An* NIZK *proof system* Π_{NIZK} *is classically (resp. quantumly) multi-proof extractable if there exists a PPT (resp. QPT) oracle simulator* S_{crs} *and a PPT (resp. QPT) extractor* Multi-Extract *with the following properties:*

CRS Indistinguishability. *For any PPT (resp. QPT) adversary* $\mathcal{A}$*, the following advantage* $\mathsf{Adv}^{\mathsf{crs}}_{\Pi_{\mathsf{NIZK}}}(\mathcal{A})$ *is* $\mathsf{negl}(\lambda)$*:*

$$\left| \Pr[\mathsf{crs} \xleftarrow{\$} \{0,1\}^{\ell} : \mathcal{A}^{|\mathcal{O}\rangle}(\mathsf{crs}) = 1] - \Pr[(\widetilde{\mathsf{crs}}, \tau) \xleftarrow{\$} S_{\mathsf{crs}}(1^{\lambda}) : \mathcal{A}^{|\mathcal{O}\rangle}(\widetilde{\mathsf{crs}}) = 1] \right|.$$

Straight-Line Extractability. *There exists constants* c, e_1, e_2 *and polynomial* $p(\lambda)$ *such that for any* $\mathsf{Q_H} = \mathsf{poly}(\lambda)$ *and PPT (resp. QPT) adversary* $\mathcal{A}$ *that makes at most* $\mathsf{Q_H}$ *random oracle queries with*

$$\Pr\left[\begin{array}{c} (\widetilde{\mathsf{crs}}, \tau) \xleftarrow{\$} S_{\mathsf{crs}}(1^{\lambda}), \\ \{(\mathsf{X}_i, \pi_i)\}_{i \in [\mathsf{Q_S}]} \xleftarrow{\$} \mathcal{A}^{|\mathcal{O}\rangle}(\widetilde{\mathsf{crs}}) \end{array} : \forall i \in [\mathsf{Q_S}], \mathsf{Verify}^{\mathcal{O}}(\widetilde{\mathsf{crs}}, \mathsf{X}_i, \pi_i) = \top \right] \geq \mu(\lambda),$$

we have,

$$\Pr\left[\begin{array}{c} (\widetilde{\mathsf{crs}}, \tau) \xleftarrow{\$} S_{\mathsf{crs}}(1^{\lambda}), \{(\mathsf{X}_i, \pi_i)\}_{i \in [\mathsf{Q_S}]} \xleftarrow{\$} \mathcal{A}^{|\mathcal{O}\rangle}(\widetilde{\mathsf{crs}}), \\ \{\mathsf{W}_i \xleftarrow{\$} \mathsf{Multi\text{-}Extract}(1^{\lambda}, \mathsf{Q_H}, \mathsf{Q_S}, 1/\mu, \tau, \mathsf{X}_i, \pi_i)\}_{i \in [\mathsf{Q_S}]} \end{array} : \begin{array}{c} \forall i \in [\mathsf{Q_S}], (\mathsf{X}_i, \mathsf{W}_i) \in \mathcal{R}_{\mathsf{gap}} \\ \land \mathsf{Verify}^{\mathcal{O}}(\widetilde{\mathsf{crs}}, \mathsf{X}_i, \pi_i) = \top \end{array} \right]$$

is larger than $\mu(\lambda)/2 - \mathsf{negl}(\lambda)$*. Moreover, the runtime of* Multi-Extract *is upper bounded by* $\mathsf{Q_H}^{e_1} \cdot \mathsf{Q_S}^{e_2} \cdot \frac{1}{\mu^c} \cdot p(\lambda)$*.*

We show that for our NIZK, we have $(c, e_1, e_2) = (1, 1, 0)$ in the classical setting where $p(\lambda)$ is roughly the time it takes to perform a standard PKE decryption. In the quantum setting, we instead have $(c, e_1, e_2) = (1, 2, 1)$.

3   Lattice-Based Blind Signature from Compatible Commitments

In this section, we provide our generic construction of a blind signature tailored to lattices. A high level overview of our construction is provided in Sect. 1.3.

3.1   Trapdoor-Sampling-Compatible Commitments

We first explain the type of lattice-based commitments applicable to our generic construction, which we call *trapdoor-sampling-compatible* commitments. For instance, the BDLOP commitment by Baum et al. [13] is one specific instantiation. We keep this layer of abstraction as we believe this captures the essential properties required by our generic construction and allows drop-in of different types of commitments.

Definition 3.1 (Trapdoor-Sampling-Compatibility). *Let* L *and* ℓ_{com} *be positive integers. Let* Π_{Com} *be a commitment scheme with message space*

$\mathcal{M} := R_q^L$ and an ℓ_{com}-bit common random string crs. Π_{Com} is (k, δ)-trapdoor-sampling-compatible *if there exists accompanying deterministic PT algorithms* (ParseCom, ParseRand) *such that for any* crs $\in \{0,1\}^{\ell_{com}}$, rand $\in \mathcal{R}$, $\mathbf{M} \in \mathcal{M}$, *and* com $= Com(\text{crs}, \mathbf{M}; \text{rand})$, *we have the following:*

- $(\mathbf{b}_i)_{i \in [L]} \subseteq \text{crs}^9$, $\mathbf{t} = \text{ParseCom(com)}$, *and* $(\mathbf{r}_i)_{i \in [L]} = \text{ParseRand(rand)}$, *where* $\mathbf{b}_i \in R_q^k$, $\mathbf{t} \in R_q^L$, *and* $\mathbf{r}_i \in R^k$;
- *for each* $i \in [L]$, $t_i = \mathbf{b}_i \mathbf{r}_i^\top + M_i \in R_q$, *where* t_i *is the i-th entry of* $\mathbf{t}$, M_i *is the i-th entry of* $\mathbf{M}$, *and* $\mathbf{r}_i$ *satisfies* $s_1([\mathbf{r}_1^\top | \dots | \mathbf{r}_L^\top]) \leq \delta$;
- *finally, the concatenated vector* $[\mathbf{b}_1 | \dots | \mathbf{b}_L] \in R_q^{Lk}$ *consists of elements in* $\{0,1\} \subset R_q$ *or uniform random elements in* R_q, *where the probability is taken over the randomness of* crs $\xleftarrow{\$} \{0,1\}^{\ell_{com}}$. *Note that when* $\mathbf{b}_i$ *and* $\mathbf{b}_j$ *contain duplicate entries, say the first entry of* $\mathbf{b}_i$ *and* $\mathbf{b}_j$ *are defined identically, then we only consider randomness over one of them.*

Roughly, δ dictates the "quality" of the randomness used to hide the message. The choice of the spectral norm $s_1(\cdot)$ is arbitrary, and for instance, we can use the two-norm.

3.2   Construction of Blind Signature

Parameters. For reference, we provide in Table 1 the parameters used in the scheme and in the security proof. The main parameters to keep in mind are (q, d, k_1, k_2, k_3): q and d define the polynomial ring R_q; k_1 is the lattice dimension used to perform trapdoor sampling; k_2 is the dimension of the message space $\mathcal{M}$ of the commitment scheme Π_{Com}; and k_3 is the length of $(\mathbf{b}_i)_{i \in [L = k_2]}$ of Π_{Com}. For those only interested in the asymptotic, one can safely assume k_1, k_2, k_3 are the same value.

Building Blocks. Our blind signature Π_{BS} relies on the following building blocks. The norm bounds on vectors and matrices are chosen with the later concrete parameter selection in mind. For the asymptotic result, we could have simply used the two-norm.

- A commitment scheme Π_{Com} with message space $\mathcal{M} = R_q^{k_2}$ (i.e., $L := k_2$ in Definition 3.1), randomness space $\mathcal{R}$, and an ℓ_{com}-bit common random string crs_{com} that satisfies hiding and (k_3, δ)-*trapdoor-sampling-compatiblity*.
- A NIZK proof system Π_{NIZK}^s (without a common random string) for the relations $\mathcal{R}^s$ and $\mathcal{R}_{gap}^s$ that satisfies correctness, zero-knowledge and *single-proof* extractability, where $\mathcal{R}^s$ and $\mathcal{R}_{gap}^s$ are defined as follows:[10]

$$\bullet \ \mathcal{R}^s := \left\{ \begin{array}{l} \mathsf{X} = (\mathbf{a}_1, \mathbf{a}_0, \\ \quad (\mathbf{b}_i)_{i \in [k_2]}, u, h), \\ \mathsf{W} = \tilde{\mathbf{e}} \end{array} \middle| \begin{array}{l} (\tilde{\mathbf{e}}_1, \tilde{\mathbf{e}}_2, \tilde{\mathbf{e}}_0) := \tilde{\mathbf{o}} \subset R^{k_1 + k_2 + k_2 \cdot k_3}, \\ \quad \forall i \in [3], \|\tilde{\mathbf{e}}_i\|_2 \leq B_{\Sigma, i}^{\mathcal{U}} \\ \wedge \ [\mathbf{a}_1 | \mathbf{a}_2 + h \cdot \mathbf{g} | \mathbf{b}_1 | \dots | \mathbf{b}_{k_2}]\tilde{\mathbf{e}}^\top = u \end{array} \right\};$$

---

[9] That is, we assume the bit-representation of each $\mathbf{b}_i$ is included in crs. Without loss of generality, we can think instead that crs lives in $(R_q^k)^L \times \{0,1\}^\ell$.

[10] With an abuse of notation, when we write $(\tilde{\mathbf{e}}_1, \tilde{\mathbf{e}}_2, \tilde{\mathbf{e}}_3) = \tilde{\mathbf{e}} \in R^{k_1 + k_2 + k_2 \cdot k_3}$, we assume $(\tilde{\mathbf{e}}_1, \tilde{\mathbf{e}}_2, \tilde{\mathbf{e}}_3) \in R^{k_1} \times R^{k_2} \times R^{k_2 \cdot k_3}$.

Table 1. Overview of parameters and notations. The rows following the second double horizontal line are parameters mainly used in the security proof.

Parameter	Explanation
R_q	Polynomial ring $R_q = \mathbb{Z}[X]/(q, X^d + 1)$
B_{inv}	Any $a \in R_q$ s.t. $\|a\|_2 \le B_{\mathsf{inv}}$ is invertible
k_1	Size of lattice trapdoor $\mathbf{T} \in R^{k_1 \times k_1}$
k_2	Size of the message space $\mathcal{M} = R_q^{k_2}$ for Π_{Com}
(k_3, δ)	Parameters for the trapdoor-sampling-compatible Π_{Com}
σ	Gaussian parameter for trapdoor sampling
$(\ell_{\mathsf{NIZK}}^{\mathsf{m}}, \ell_,)$	Length of crs for $\Pi_{\mathsf{NIZK}}^{\mathsf{m}}$ and Π_{Com}
δ^{gap}	Spectral norm bound on the extracted com. rand.
$B_{\Sigma,i}^{\mathcal{S}},\ i \in [3]$	Two-norm bound on $(\mathbf{e}_1, \mathbf{e}_2, \mathbf{e}_3) := \mathbf{e}$ sampled by the signer
$B_{\Sigma,i}^{\mathcal{U}},\ i \in [3]$	Two-norm bound on real secret $(\tilde{\mathbf{e}}_1, \tilde{\mathbf{e}}_2, \tilde{\mathbf{e}}_3) := \tilde{\mathbf{e}}$
$B_{\Sigma,i}^{\mathcal{U},\mathsf{gap}},\ i \in [3]$	Two-norm bound on extracted $(\tilde{\mathbf{e}}_1, \tilde{\mathbf{e}}_2, \tilde{\mathbf{e}}_3) := \tilde{\mathbf{e}}$
$S_{\mathsf{chal}} \subset R_q$	Challenge set of the interactive proof sys. implicit in $\Pi_{\mathsf{NIZK}}^{\mathsf{m}}$
B_c	One-norm bound on $c \in S_{\mathsf{chal}}$
$S_{\mathsf{hash}} \subset R_q$	Hashed message set with size $> 2^\lambda$ s.t. $\forall (c, h) \in S_{\mathsf{chal}} \times S_{\mathsf{hash}}, \|c \cdot h\|_2 \le B_{\mathsf{inv}}/2$
Δ_{MLWE}	Bound s.t. *search* MLWE has non-unique solution
$(\chi_{\mathsf{MLWE}}, B_{\mathsf{MLWE}})$	Noise distribution for *decision* MLWE, where $\mathbf{R} \xleftarrow{\$} \chi_{\mathsf{MLWE}}^{k_1 \times k_2} \Rightarrow s_1(\mathbf{R}) \le B_{\mathsf{MLWE}}$ w.o.p
$(\chi_{\mathsf{DSMR}}, B_{\mathsf{DSMR}})$	Noise distribution $\chi_{\mathsf{DSMR}} := D_{\mathbb{Z}, B_{\mathsf{DSMR}}}$ for DSMR
B_{MSIS}	Two-norm bound on the solution for MSIS

- $\mathcal{R}_{\mathsf{gap}}^{\mathsf{s}} := \left\{ \begin{array}{l} \mathsf{X} = (\mathbf{a}_1, \mathbf{a}_2, \\ (\mathbf{b}_i)_{i \in [k_2]}, u, h), \\ \mathsf{W} = (\tilde{\mathbf{e}}, c) \end{array} \middle| \begin{array}{l} (\tilde{\mathbf{e}}_1, \tilde{\mathbf{e}}_2, \tilde{\mathbf{e}}_3) := \tilde{\mathbf{e}} \in R^{k_1 + k_2 + k_2 \cdot k_3}, \\ \forall i \in [3], \|\tilde{\mathbf{e}}_i\|_2 \le B_{\Sigma,i}^{\mathcal{U},\mathsf{gap}} \wedge \|c\|_1 \le B_c \\ \wedge [\mathbf{a}_1 \mid \mathbf{a}_2 + h \cdot \mathbf{g} \mid \mathbf{b}_1 \mid \cdots \mid \mathbf{b}_{k_2}]\,\tilde{\mathbf{e}}^\top = c \cdot u \end{array} \right\}.$

- A NIZK proof system $\Pi_{\mathsf{NIZK}}^{\mathsf{m}}$ (with a common random string $\mathsf{com}_{\mathsf{NIZK}}^{\mathsf{m}}$) for the relations $\mathcal{R}^{\mathsf{m}}$ and $\mathcal{R}_{\mathsf{gap}}^{\mathsf{m}}$ that satisfies correctness, zero-knowledge and *multi-proof* extractability, where $\mathcal{R}^{\mathsf{m}}$ and $\mathcal{R}_{\mathsf{gap}}^{\mathsf{m}}$ are defined as follows:

  - $\mathcal{R}^{\mathsf{m}} := \left\{ \begin{array}{l} \mathsf{X} = (\mathsf{crs}_{\mathsf{com}}, \mathsf{com}), \\ \mathsf{W} = (h, \mathsf{rand}) \end{array} \middle| \begin{array}{l} (h, \mathsf{rand}) \in S_{\mathsf{hash}} \times \mathcal{R}, \\ \wedge\ \mathsf{com} = \mathsf{Com}(\mathsf{crs}_{\mathsf{com}}, h \cdot \mathbf{g}; \mathsf{rand}) \end{array} \right\};$

  - $\mathcal{R}_{\mathsf{gap}}^{\mathsf{m}} := \left\{ \begin{array}{l} \mathsf{X} = (\mathsf{crs}_{\mathsf{com}}, \mathsf{com}), \\ \mathsf{W} = (h', c', c, (\mathbf{r}_i)_{i \in [k_2]}) \end{array} \middle| \begin{array}{l} \|h'\|_2 \le B_{\mathsf{inv}}/2 \wedge \|c'\|_1, \|c\|_1 \le B_c \\ \wedge\ s_1([\mathbf{r}_1^\top \mid \cdots \mid \mathbf{r}_{k_2}^\top]) \le \delta^{\mathsf{gap}} \\ \wedge\ t_i = \mathbf{b}_i(\mathbf{r}_i/c)^\top + (h'/c') \cdot g_i \end{array} \right\},$

  where $\mathbf{t} = \mathsf{ParseCom}(\mathsf{com})$, $(\mathbf{b}_i)_{i \in [k_2]} \subseteq \mathsf{crs}_{\mathsf{com}}$, $\mathbf{g} = [1 \mid b \mid \cdots \mid b^{k_2-1}] \in R_q^{k_2}$ is the gadget matrix with $k_2 = \lceil \log_b(q) \rceil$, and g_i is the i-th element of $\mathbf{g}$.

- Four hash functions $\mathsf{H}_{\mathsf{crs}}$, H_{M}, H_{m}, and H_{s} modeled as a random oracle in the security proof. The latter two H_{m} and H_{s} are hash functions used by the NIZK proof systems $\Pi_{\mathsf{NIZK}}^{\mathsf{m}}$ and $\Pi_{\mathsf{NIZK}}^{\mathsf{s}}$, respectively. $\mathsf{H}_{\mathsf{M}} : \{0,1\}^* \to R_q$ is a hash function used to map messages to ring elements. $\mathsf{H}_{\mathsf{crs}}$ is a special hash function, for which we only use the input 0. Specifically, $\mathsf{H}_{\mathsf{crs}}(0) = (\mathsf{crs}_{\mathsf{NIZK}}^{\mathsf{m}}, \mathsf{crs}_{\mathsf{com}}, \mathbf{a}_2)$

contains the common random strings $\mathsf{crs}^{\mathsf{m}}_{\mathsf{NIZK}}$ and $\mathsf{crs}_{\mathsf{com}}$ used by $\Pi^{\mathsf{m}}_{\mathsf{NIZK}}$ and Π_{Com}, respectively, and a random vector $\mathbf{a}_2 \in R^{k_2}_q$.

Construction. The construction of our blind signature Π_{BS} is provided below. We assume $\mathsf{H}_{\mathsf{crs}}(0) = (\mathsf{crs}^{\mathsf{m}}_{\mathsf{NIZK}}, \mathsf{crs}_{\mathsf{com}}, \mathbf{a}_2)$ and $(\mathbf{b}_i)_{i \in [k_2]} \subseteq \mathsf{crs}_{\mathsf{com}}$ are derived correctly by all the algorithms and omit the process of generating them.

$\mathsf{BSGen}(1^\lambda)$: It runs $(\mathbf{a}_1, \mathbf{T}_{\mathbf{a}_1}) \xleftarrow{\$} \mathsf{TrapGen}(1^{k_1 d}, q)$, samples $\mathbf{s} \xleftarrow{\$} [-\Delta_{\mathsf{MLWE}}, \Delta_{\mathsf{MLWE}}]^{(k_1+k_2 k_3)11}_{\mathsf{coeff}}$ and sets $u = [\mathbf{a}_1 \mid \mathbf{b}_1 \mid \cdots \mid \mathbf{b}_{k_2}] \cdot \mathbf{s}^\top \in R_q$, where recall $\mathbf{a}_1 \in R^{k_1}_q$, $\mathbf{b}_i \in R^{k_3}_q$ for $i \in [k_2]$. It then outputs $(\mathsf{vk}, \mathsf{sk}) = ((\mathbf{a}_1, u), \mathbf{T}_{\mathbf{a}_1})$.

$\mathcal{U}_1(\mathsf{vk}, \mathsf{M})$: It hashes $h = \mathsf{H}_{\mathsf{M}}(\mathsf{M})$, samples $\mathsf{rand} \xleftarrow{\$} \mathcal{R}$, and computes $\mathsf{com} = \mathsf{Com}(\mathsf{crs}_{\mathsf{com}}, h \cdot \mathbf{g}; \mathsf{rand})$. It then creates a proof $\pi^{\mathsf{m}} \xleftarrow{\$} \mathsf{Prove}^{\mathsf{H}_{\mathsf{m}}}(\mathsf{crs}^{\mathsf{m}}_{\mathsf{NIZK}}, (\mathsf{crs}_{\mathsf{com}}, \mathsf{com}), (h, \mathsf{rand}))$ that proves the wellformedness of the commitment com, and outputs the first message $\rho_1 = (\mathsf{com}, \pi^{\mathsf{m}})$. Finally, it sets its state as $\mathsf{st}_{\mathcal{U}} = \mathsf{rand}$.

$\mathcal{S}_2(\mathsf{sk}, \rho_1)$: It parses $(\mathsf{com}, \pi^{\mathsf{m}}) \leftarrow \rho_1$ and outputs $\bot$ if $\mathsf{Verify}^{\mathsf{H}_{\mathsf{m}}}(\mathsf{crs}^{\mathsf{m}}_{\mathsf{NIZK}}, (\mathsf{crs}_{\mathsf{com}}, \mathsf{com}), \pi^{\mathsf{m}}) = \bot$. Otherwise, it computes $\mathbf{t} \leftarrow \mathsf{ParseCom}(\mathsf{com})$ and samples a short vector $\mathbf{e} \in R^{k_1+k_2+k_2 k_3}$ such that

$$[\mathbf{a}_1 \mid \mathbf{a}_2 + \mathbf{t} \mid \mathbf{b}_1 \mid \cdots \mid \mathbf{b}_{k_2}] \cdot \mathbf{e}^\top = u, \tag{6}$$

using $\mathbf{e} \xleftarrow{\$} \mathsf{SampleLeft}(\mathbf{a}_1, [\mathbf{a}_2 + \mathbf{t} \mid \mathbf{b}_1 \mid \cdots \mid \mathbf{b}_{k_2}], u, \mathbf{T}_{\mathbf{a}_1}, \sigma)$. It outputs the second message $\rho_2 = \mathbf{e}$.

$\mathcal{U}_{\mathsf{der}}(\mathsf{st}_{\mathcal{U}}, \rho_2)$: It parses $(\mathbf{e}_1, \mathbf{e}_2, \mathbf{e}_3) := \mathbf{e} \leftarrow \rho_2$, $\mathsf{rand} \leftarrow \mathsf{st}_{\mathcal{U}}$, and outputs $\bot$ if either $\exists i \in [3], \|\mathbf{e}_i\|_2 > B^{\mathcal{S}}_{\Sigma, i}$ or Eq. (6) does not hold. Otherwise, it computes $\mathbf{t} \leftarrow \mathsf{ParseCom}(\mathsf{com}_{\mathsf{crs}})$ and $(\mathbf{r}_i)_{i \in [k_2]} \leftarrow \mathsf{ParseRand}(\mathsf{rand})$, where $h = \mathsf{H}_{\mathsf{M}}(\mathsf{M})$, $t_i = \mathbf{b}_i \mathbf{r}^\top_i + h \cdot g_i \in R_q$, and t_i and g_i are the i-th entries of $\mathbf{t}$ and $\mathbf{g}$, respectively. It then rewrites the left hand side of Eq. (6) as follows:

$$[\mathbf{a}_1 \mid \mathbf{a}_2 + \mathbf{t} \mid \mathbf{b}_1 \mid \cdots \mid \mathbf{b}_{k_2}] \cdot \mathbf{e}^\top$$

$$= [\mathbf{a}_1 \mid \mathbf{a}_2 + [\mathbf{b}_1 \mathbf{r}^\top_1 + h \cdot g_1 \mid \cdots \mid \mathbf{b}_{k_2} \mathbf{r}^\top_{k_2} + h \cdot g_{k_2}] \mid \mathbf{b}_1 \mid \cdots \mid \mathbf{b}_{k_2}] \cdot \mathbf{e}^\top$$

$$= [\mathbf{a}_1 \mid \mathbf{a}_2 + h \cdot \mathbf{g} \mid \mathbf{b}_1 \mid \cdots \mid \mathbf{b}_{k_2}] \underbrace{\begin{bmatrix} \mathbf{e}^\top_1 \\ \mathbf{e}^\top_2 \\ e_{2,1} \cdot \mathbf{r}^\top_1 + \mathbf{e}^\top_{3,1} \\ \cdots \\ e_{2,k_2} \cdot \mathbf{r}^\top_{k_2} + \mathbf{e}^\top_{3,k_2} \end{bmatrix}}_{=: \tilde{\mathbf{e}} \in R^{k_1+k_2+k_2 k_3}},$$

where $\mathbf{e}_3 = [\mathbf{e}_{3,1} \mid \cdots \mid \mathbf{e}_{3,k_2}] \in R^{k_2 k_3}$ and $\mathbf{e}_2 = [e_{2,1} \mid \cdots \mid e_{2,k_2}] \in R^{k_2}$ are parsed into appropriate sizes. It then creates a proof $\pi^{\mathsf{s}} \xleftarrow{\$} \mathsf{Prove}^{\mathsf{H}_{\mathsf{s}}}((\mathbf{a}_1, \mathbf{a}_2, (\mathbf{b}_i)_{i \in [k_2]}, u, h), \tilde{\mathbf{e}})$ that proves knowledge of a short vector $\tilde{\mathbf{e}}$. If $\bot \leftarrow \mathsf{Verify}^{\mathsf{H}_{\mathsf{s}}}((\mathbf{a}_1, \mathbf{a}_2, (\mathbf{b}_i)_{i \in [k_2]}, u, h), \pi^{\mathsf{s}})$, then it outputs $\Sigma = \bot$. Otherwise, it outputs $\Sigma = \pi^{\mathsf{s}}$ as the signature.

---

[11] For integers a and b such that $a < b$, $[a, b]_{\mathsf{coeff}} \subset R_q$ denotes the set of all polynomials in R_q with coefficients in $[a, b]$.

BSVerify(vk, M, Σ) : It parses $\pi^s \leftarrow \Sigma$, sets $h = H_M(M)$, and returns the output of Verify$^{H_s}((\mathbf{a}_1, \mathbf{a}_2, (\mathbf{b}_i)_{i \in [k_2]}, u, h), \pi^s)$.

Remark 3.1 (Variations of the Construction). We can consider slight variations of the above construction. For instance, in case the commitment vectors satisfy $\mathbf{b}_1 = \cdots = \mathbf{b}_{k_2}$, which is the case for our concrete instantiation in Sect. 4.1, the signer can alternatively sample $\mathbf{e}$ such that $[\mathbf{a}_1 \mid \mathbf{a}_2 + \mathbf{t} \mid \mathbf{b}_1] \cdot \mathbf{e}^\top = u$ instead of Eq. (6). Which variation offers the "best" blind signature highly depends on many factors: the criteria that we wish to optimize (e.g., minimize the signature size, minimize the total communication cost); the concrete choice of NIZKs and commitments we use; and other implicit parameter selections.

The proof of correctness consists of a routine check. Blindness under malicious keys follows from a standard proof using the zero-knowledge and hiding of the underlying NIZKs and commitment.

3.3 Proof of One-More Unforgeability

The following establishes that our blind signature is one-more unforgeable even against quantum adversaries in the QROM.

Theorem 3.1. *The blind signature Π_{BS} is quantumly one-more unforgeable if the two NIZKs Π_{NIZK}^s for $(\mathcal{R}^s, \mathcal{R}_{gap}^s)$ and Π_{NIZK}^m for $(\mathcal{R}^m, \mathcal{R}_{gap}^m)$ are quantumly single-proof and multi-proof extractable, respectively, and the $\mathsf{MSIS}_{d,1,k_1+k_2k_3,B_{MSIS},q}$, $\mathsf{MLWE}_{d,1,k_1-1,\chi_{MLWE},q}$, $\mathsf{DSMR}_{d,k_1-1,\chi_{DSMR},q,1}$ and $\mathsf{DSMR}_{d,k_2k_3-1,\chi_{DSMR},q,1}$ problems are hard.*

Proof Sketch. Assume there exists a QPT adversary $\mathcal{A}$ with non-negligible advantage ϵ against the one-more unforgeability game that makes at most Q_S (classical) signature queries. Further assume $\mathcal{A}$ makes at most Q_{H_M} (resp. $Q_{H_{crs}}$, Q_{H_m}, Q_{H_s}) (quantum) random oracle queries to H_M (resp. H_{crs}, H_m, H_s). We consider a sequence of games, where we denote E_i as the event $\mathcal{A}$ wins in Game$_i$. Game$_1$ is the real one-more unforgeability game.

Game$_2$: The challenger simulates all the QRO's by using $2Q_{H_{crs}}/2Q_{H_M}/2Q_{H_s}/2Q_{H_m}$-wise independent hash functions. This allows the challenger to *efficiently* simulate the QROs.

Game$_3$: The challenger programs $H_{crs}(0)$ to use the simulated CRS $\widetilde{crs}_{NIZK}^m$ output by the CRS simulator $\mathcal{S}_{crs}$ of Π_{NIZK}^m.

Game$_4$: When $\mathcal{A}$ submits $\rho_{j,1} = (com_j, \pi_j^m)$ to the challenger as its j-th ($j \in [Q_S]$) first message, the challenger runs $W_j \leftarrow$ Multi-Extract$(1^\lambda, Q_{H_m}, Q_S, 1/\mu, \tau, X_j, \pi_j^m)$, where $\mu = \Pr[E_3]$ and $X_j = (crs_{com}, com_j)$. Due to the definition of the multi-proof extractor Multi-Extract (see Definition 2.6), the challenger succeeds in extracting a witness in $\mathcal{R}_{gap}^m$ with non-negligible probability and runs in time proportional to $Q_{H_m}^{e_1} \cdot Q_S^{e_2+1} \cdot \frac{1}{\mu^c} \cdot p(\lambda)$, which is a polynomial.

Game_5 : The challenger replaces the function $\mathsf{H_M} : \mathcal{M} \to \mathcal{S}_{\mathsf{hash}} \subset R_q$ by a *small-range distribution*. Specifically, it sets $r = 2 \cdot C_0 \cdot \mathsf{Q}^3_{\mathsf{H_M}}/\mu'$, where $\mu' = \Pr[\mathsf{E}_4]$ and C_0 is some universal constant. It then samples $\mathbf{h} = (h_1, \cdots, h_r) \xleftarrow{\$} (\mathcal{S}_{\mathsf{hash}})^r$ and $P \xleftarrow{\$} \mathsf{Func}(\mathcal{M}, [r])$, and defines $\mathsf{H_M}$ as $\mathsf{H_M}(x) = h_{P(x)}$.

Game_6 : The challenger samples a uniformly random index $j^* \xleftarrow{\$} [r]$ at the beginning of the game and performs two types of checks. First, when the challenger extracts $\mathsf{W}_j = (h'_j, c'_j, c_j, (\mathbf{r}_{j,i})_{i \in [k_2]}) \in \mathcal{R}^m_{\mathsf{gap}}$ from the first message $\rho_{j,1}$ submitted to by $\mathcal{A}$, the challenger checks if $h'_j/c'_j \neq h_{j^*}$. Moreover, at the end of the game, when $\mathcal{A}$ outputs the forgery $\{(\mathsf{M}_i, \Sigma_i)\}_{i \in [\mathsf{Q_s}+1]}$, the challenger checks if $\mathsf{M}'_{j^*} \in \{\mathsf{M}_i\}_{i \in [\mathsf{Q_s}+1]}$ and if $\{\mathsf{H_M}(\mathsf{M}_i)\}_{i \in [\mathsf{Q_s}+1]}$ are pairwise distinct.

Game_7 : After it samples $j^* \xleftarrow{\$} [r]$ at the beginning of the game, the challenger sets $\mathbf{a}_2 = \widetilde{\mathbf{a}}_2 - h_{j^*} \cdot \mathbf{g}$ where $\widetilde{\mathbf{a}}_2 \xleftarrow{\$} R^k_q$, and programs $\mathsf{H_{crs}}(0)$ to use this $\mathbf{a}_2$.

Game_8 : The challenger gets rid of the trapdoor $\mathbf{T}_{\mathbf{a}_1}$ included in the secret key sk. In particular, the challenger samples $\mathbf{a}_1 \xleftarrow{\$} R^{k_1}_q$, $\mathbf{R} \xleftarrow{\$} \chi^{k_1 \times k_2}_{\mathsf{MLWE}}$, and sets $\widetilde{\mathbf{a}}_2 = \mathbf{a}_1 \mathbf{R}$. On input the first message $\rho_1 = (\mathsf{com}, \pi^m)$ from $\mathcal{A}$, it extracts $\mathsf{W} = (h', c', c, (\mathbf{r}_i)_{i \in [k_2]}) \in \mathcal{R}^m_{\mathsf{gap}}$ and computes

$$[\mathbf{a}_1 \mid \mathbf{a}_2 + \mathbf{t} \mid \mathbf{b}_1 \mid \cdots \mid \mathbf{b}_{k_2}]$$

$$= \left[\mathbf{a}_1 \mid \mathbf{a}_1 \mathbf{R} - h_{j^*} \cdot \mathbf{g} + \left[\frac{\mathbf{b}_1 \mathbf{r}_1^\top}{c} + \frac{h'}{c'} \cdot g_1 \mid \cdots \mid \frac{\mathbf{b}_{k_2} \mathbf{r}_{k_2}^\top}{c} + \frac{h'}{c'} \cdot g_{k_2}\right] \mid \mathbf{b}_1 \mid \cdots \mid \mathbf{b}_{k_2}\right]$$

$$= \left[\mathbf{a}_1 \mid \widehat{\mathbf{b}} \mid \left[\mathbf{a}_1 \mid \widehat{\mathbf{b}}\right] \mathbf{R}' + \left(\frac{h'}{c'} - h_{j^*}\right) \cdot \mathbf{g}\right] \cdot \mathbf{P}_{\mathsf{perm}},$$

where $\widehat{\mathbf{b}} = [\mathbf{b}_1 \mid \cdots \mid \mathbf{b}_{k_2}] \in R^{k_2 k_3}_q$, $\widehat{\mathbf{R}} = \mathbf{I}_{k_2} \otimes [\mathbf{r}_1^\top \mid \cdots \mid \mathbf{r}_{k_2}^\top] \in R^{k_2 k_3 \times k_2}$, $\mathbf{R}' = \begin{bmatrix} \mathbf{R} \\ \frac{1}{c}\widehat{\mathbf{R}} \end{bmatrix} \in R^{k_2(k_3+1) \times k_2}$, and $\mathbf{P}_{\mathsf{perm}}$ is a permutation matrix that appropriately reorders the columns. It then samples a short vector $\mathbf{e}' \in R^{k_1+k_2+k_2 k_3}$ such that $\left[\mathbf{a}_1 \mid \widehat{\mathbf{b}} \mid \left[\mathbf{a}_1 \mid \widehat{\mathbf{b}}\right] \mathbf{R}' + \left(\frac{h'}{c'} - h_{j^*}\right) \cdot \mathbf{g}\right] \cdot \mathbf{e}'^\top = u$, using the algorithm $\mathsf{SampleRight}$. By setting the parameters correctly, we have invertibility of $h'/c' - h_{j^*}$ as required by the sampling algorithm. The signer algorithm $\mathcal{S}_2$ finally outputs the second message $\rho_2 = \mathbf{e}'(\mathbf{P}_{\mathsf{perm}}^{-1})^\top$.

At this point, the challenger in Game_8 no longer relies on a trapdoor for $\mathbf{a}_1$. Using the single-proof extractability of $\Pi^{\$}_{\mathsf{NIZK}}$, the challenger will be able to extract an MSIS solution with respect to $[\mathbf{a}_1 | \widehat{\mathbf{b}}]$. $\qquad\square$

3.4 Extension: Partially Blind Signatures

We are able to obtain a *partially* blind signature [2] with a simple modification to our blind signature without increasing the signature size. To bind the signature to a specific common message γ, the signer shifts the public syndrome $u \in R_q$ to $u - \mathsf{H_{Mc}}(\gamma)$, where $\mathsf{H_{Mc}}$ is a newly introduced hash function that is modeled as a random oracle in the security proof.

4 Instantiating Our Generic Construction

In this section, we instantiate our generic construction of blind signature, which in particular involves concretizing the building blocks laid out in Sect. 3.2: the trapdoor-sampling-compatible commitment scheme Π_{Com}, the single-proof extractable NIZK proof system $\Pi_{\mathsf{NIZK}}^{\mathsf{s}}$, and the multi-proof extractable NIZK proof system $\Pi_{\mathsf{NIZK}}^{\mathsf{m}}$. In Sect. 4.3 we provide a concrete set of parameters for our resulting blind signature scheme.

4.1 Concrete Choices for Trapdoor-Sampling-Compatible Commitments and Single-Proof Extractable NIZK

For the trapdoor-sampling-compatible commitment, we rely on (a slight variant of) the BDLOP commitment by Baum et al. [13]. The common random string is of the form $\mathsf{crs}_{\mathsf{com}} := (\mathbf{b}_0, \mathbf{b}_1) := \left([1|\mathbf{b}_0'], [0|1|\mathbf{b}_1'] \right) \in R_{q'}^{k_3} \times R_{q'}^{k_3}$, where we use two different moduli q' and q, and q is the modulus that explicitly showed up in the blind signature construction in the previous section. The commitment to a message $\mathbf{M} = (\mathsf{M}_1, \cdots, \mathsf{M}_L) \in R_q^L$ is

$$\mathsf{com} := [\mathbf{t}_1 // \mathbf{t}_2] = \left(\begin{bmatrix} \mathbf{b}_0 \\ \mathbf{b}_1 \end{bmatrix} \mathbf{R} + \begin{bmatrix} \mathbf{0} \\ \mathsf{M}_1 \mid \cdots \mid \mathsf{M}_L \end{bmatrix} \begin{array}{c} \bmod q' \\ \bmod q \end{array} \right) \in R_{q'}^L \times R_q^L.$$

The single-proof extractable NIZK is based on the basic Lyubashevsky's sigma protocol [37,38], where soundness is argued through rewinding (or the forking lemma [14,45] to be precise). One minor difference is that we take advantage of the fact that the witness vector $\tilde{\mathbf{e}} \in R^{k_1+k_2+k_3}$ has unbalanced size; the first $(k_1 + k_2)$-entries are smaller than the last k_3 entries.

4.2 Concrete Choice for Multi-proof Extractable NIZK

Preparation. Let us prepare some notations. Let $R_{q'} = \mathbb{Z}_{q'}[X]/(X^d + 1)$ be a ring that fully splits and consider the NTT over the ring $R_{q'}$ with $\mathsf{NTT} : R_{q'} \to (\mathbb{Z}_{q'}^d)^\top$, and $\mathsf{NTT}^{-1} : (\mathbb{Z}_{q'}^d)^\top \to R_{q'}$. Here, we make it explicit that NTT and NTT^{-1} operates over column vectors. These notions extend naturally to matrices over $R_{q'}$, where NTT^{-1} is only well-defined when the column length of the matrix is divisible by d. We define $\Phi : R_{q'} \mapsto (\mathbb{Z}_{q'}^d)^\top$ to be the map that sends a polynomial to its (column) coefficient vector. We define $\mathsf{Rot} : R_{q'} \mapsto \mathbb{Z}_{q'}^{d \times d}$ to be the map that sends a polynomial $a \in R_{q'}$ to a matrix whose i-th column is $\Phi(a \cdot X^i \bmod (X^d + 1))$. It can be checked that for $a, b \in R_{q'}$, we have $\mathsf{Rot}(a)\Phi(b) = \Phi(a \cdot b)$. We extend the definition of Rot to vectors in $R_{q'}$, where we have $\mathsf{Rot}(\mathbf{b})\Phi(a) = \Phi(a \cdot \mathbf{b})$ for $(a, \mathbf{b}) \in R_{q'} \times R_{q'}^n$. Here, note that $\mathsf{Rot}(\mathbf{b}) \in \mathbb{Z}_{q'}^{dn \times d}$ and $\Phi(a) \in \mathbb{Z}_{q'}^{d}{}^\top$. We use $\circ$ for the component-wise product of matrices over $R_{q'}$. Finally, we define the matrix $\Delta \in R_q^{L \times L}$ such that the first column of Δ is $\mathbf{g}$ and all the diagonal entries except for the $(1, 1)$-th entry is -1. Specifically, Δ is invertible over R_q and we have $\mathbf{g}\Delta = [1|0|\cdots|0]$.

Construction. We consider the relations $(\mathcal{R}^{\mathsf{m}}, \mathcal{R}_{\mathsf{gap}}^{\mathsf{m}})$ defined as follows:

$$-\mathcal{R}^m := \left\{ \begin{array}{l} X = (\mathsf{crs}_{\mathsf{com}} := (\mathbf{b}_0, \mathbf{b}_1), \mathsf{com}), \\ W = (h, \mathsf{rand} := \mathbf{R}) \end{array} \middle| \begin{array}{l} h \in S_{\mathsf{hash}} \wedge \mathbf{R} \in [-1,1]^{k_3 \times L}_{\mathsf{coeff}}, \\ \wedge \ \mathsf{com} = \left(\begin{bmatrix} \mathbf{b}_0 \\ \mathbf{b}_1 \end{bmatrix} \mathbf{R} + \begin{bmatrix} \mathbf{0} \\ h \cdot \mathbf{g} \end{bmatrix} \begin{array}{l} \bmod q' \\ \bmod q \end{array} \right) \end{array} \right\};$$

$$-\mathcal{R}^m_{\mathsf{gap}} := \left\{ \begin{array}{l} X = (\mathsf{crs}_{\mathsf{com}} := (\mathbf{b}_0, \mathbf{b}_1), \mathsf{com}), \\ W = (h', c, (\mathbf{r}_i)_{i \in [L]}) \end{array} \middle| \begin{array}{l} \|h'\|_2 \le B_{\mathsf{inv}}/2 \ \wedge \ \|c\|_1 \le B_c \\ \wedge \ \mathbf{t} = \mathsf{ParseCom}(\mathsf{com}) \\ \wedge \mathbf{R} \in [-1,1]^{k_3 \times L}_{\mathsf{coeff}} \\ \wedge \ \forall i \in [L], t_i = \mathbf{b}_1 \mathbf{r}_i^\top + (h'/c) \cdot q^{\frac{i-1}{L}} \end{array} \right\},$$

Notice the gap relation $\mathcal{R}^m_{\mathsf{gap}}$ has no slack for the commitment randomness. We recover $\mathcal{R}^m_{\mathsf{gap}}$ in Sect. 3.2 by setting $\delta^{\mathsf{gap}} = \sqrt{k_3 L} \cdot d$.

The prove and verify algorithms of Π^m_{NIZK} for the relations $(\mathcal{R}^m, \mathcal{R}^m_{\mathsf{gap}})$ are provided in Figs. 1 and 2, respectively. The texts in gray are used by the exact proof of [17], the texts in black without highlight are used to prove linear relations, and finally the texts highlighted in gray are used for multi-proof straight-line extractability as in [35]. The crs for Π^m_{NIZK} consists of a random element H (used for extraction) and random matrices $(\mathbf{a}_0, (\mathbf{A}_k)_{k \in [4]})$ (used for committing), and the crs for Π_{Com} is a random tuple $(\mathbf{b}_0, \mathbf{b}_1)$. Following prior conventions [17,35], we prove that $\mathbf{R} \in [0,2]^{k_3 \times L}_{\mathsf{coeff}}$ instead, i.e., $\mathbf{R}$ consists of $\{0,1,2\}$-coefficient polynomials. This is without loss of generality since we can add the all one matrix $\mathbb{1}$ to any $\mathbf{R} \in [-1,1]^{k_3 \times L}_{\mathsf{coeff}}$ to obtain a matrix in $[0,2]^{k_3 \times L}_{\mathsf{coeff}}$.

The protocol uses three polynomial rings: $R_{q'} = \mathbb{Z}_{q'}[X]/(X^d + 1)$ is a fully splitting ring used by Bootle et al.'s [17] exact proof; $R_q = \mathbb{Z}_q[X]/(X^d + 1)$ is a ring where any small element is invertible and is used by the linear proof; $R_Q = \mathbb{Z}_Q[X]/(X^d + 1)$ is used by the the multi-proof straight-line extractability as in [35], and in particular, we require the NTRU assumption to hold over this ring. The interactive protocol implicit in our NIZK is defined with respect to two challenge spaces. The challenge space used in the second (resp. fourth) flow is $\mathbb{Z}^\tau_{q'}$ (resp. $C^{\tau\tau'}_X \times C_{\mathsf{ham}}$, where $C_X := \{X^i \mid i \in [2d]\}$ and C_{ham} is the set of $\{0,1\}$-coefficient polynomials in R_q with Hamming weight smaller than B_c). Specifically, we require any element with two-norm smaller than $2B_c$ to be invertible over R_q. Here, τ and τ' are set so that $q^\tau \approx (2d)^{\tau\tau'} \approx 2^{128}$ or asymptotically $1/q^\tau \approx 1/(2d)^{\tau\tau'} = \mathsf{negl}(\lambda)$. Our protocol also relies on several different Gaussian distributions. They are used either to perform rejection sampling or to invoke the MLWE and DSMR assumptions. The concrete parameter selection is provided in Sect. 4.3.

Security. Below, we provide the proof sketch of the *classical* multi-proof extractability.

Theorem 4.1. *The* NIZK Π^m_{NIZK} *in Figs. 1 and 2 is classically multi-proof extractable with* $(c_1, e_1, e_2) = (1, 1, 0)$ *and* $p(\lambda) = \mathsf{poly}(\lambda)$ *if the* $\mathsf{DSMR}_{d,1,\chi_{\mathsf{DSMR}},Q,p}$, $\mathsf{MSIS}_{d,1,k_4,16B_z,q'}$, *and* $\mathsf{MSIS}_{d,1,k_3,2(B_{z'}+B_c\delta^{\mathsf{gap}}),q'}$ *problems are hard.*

Proof. CRS indistinguishability is a simple consequence of the $\mathsf{DSMR}_{d,1,\chi_{\mathsf{DSMR}},Q,p}$ assumption. The proof of straight-line extractability, which is the most technical proof of this work, consists of three parts. We first show in Lemma 4.1 that (roughly) if the adversary $\mathcal{A}$ outputs a valid proof, then $\mathcal{A}$ must have been able

$\Pi_{\mathsf{NIZK}}^{\mathsf{m}} : \mathsf{Prove}^{\mathsf{H_m}}(\mathsf{crs}_{\mathsf{NIZK}}^{\mathsf{m}}, X, W)$

$\mathsf{crs}_{\mathsf{NIZK}}^{\mathsf{m}} = (H, \mathbf{a}_0, (\mathbf{A}_k)_{k \in [4]}) \in R_Q \times R_{q'}^{k_4} \times \left(R_{q'}^{k_3 \times k_4}\right)^4$

$X := (\mathsf{crs}_{\mathsf{com}} := (\mathbf{b}_0, \mathbf{b}_1), \mathsf{com} := \mathbf{T}) \in R_{q'}^{k_3} \times R_{q}^{k_3} \times (R_{q'}^L \times R_q^L),$

$W := (h, \mathsf{rand} := \mathbf{R}) \in S_{\mathsf{hash}} \times [0,2]_{\mathsf{coeff}}^{k_3 \times L}$ s.t $\mathbf{T} = \begin{bmatrix} \mathbf{b}_0 \\ \mathbf{b}_1 \end{bmatrix} \mathbf{R} + \begin{bmatrix} 0 \\ h \cdot \mathbf{g} \end{bmatrix} \begin{array}{l} \bmod q' \\ \bmod q \end{array}$

For $i \in [\tau]$:

$(\mathbf{Y}_i, \mathbf{E}_i) \xleftarrow{\$} R_{q'}^{k_3 \times L} \times D_{\gamma_E}^{k_4 \times L}$

$\mathbf{u}_{0,i} := \mathbf{a}_0 \mathbf{E}_i$

$\mathbf{U}_{1,i} := \mathbf{A}_1 \mathbf{E}_i + \mathbf{Y}_i$

$\mathbf{U}_{2,i} := \mathbf{A}_2 \mathbf{E}_i + \mathsf{NTT}^{-1}(\Phi(\mathbf{R}))$

$\mathbf{U}_{3,i} := \mathbf{A}_3 \mathbf{E}_i + \mathbf{Y}_i \circ (2\mathsf{NTT}^{-1}(\Phi(\mathbf{R})) - 3)$

$\mathbf{U}_{4,i} := \mathbf{A}_4 \mathbf{E}_i + \mathbf{Y}_i \circ \mathbf{Y}_i \circ (\mathsf{NTT}^{-1}(\Phi(\mathbf{R})) - 3)$

$\mathbf{W}_i := \mathsf{Rot}(\mathbf{b}_0)\mathsf{NTT}\left(\mathbf{Y}_i\right) \in \mathbb{Z}_{q'}^{d \times L}$

$(\mathbf{D}_{1,i}, \mathbf{D}_{2,i}) \xleftarrow{\$} \left(D_{\gamma_D}^{k_4 \times L}\right)^2$

$\mathbf{V}_i := H\mathbf{D}_{1,i} + p\mathbf{D}_{2,i} + \mathbf{E}_i \in R_Q^{k_4 \times L}$

For $j \in [\tau']$:

  $\mathbf{S}_{i,j} \leftarrow D_{\gamma_S}^{k_4 \times L}$

  $(\bar{\mathbf{D}}_{1,i,j}, \bar{\mathbf{D}}_{2,i,j}) \leftarrow \left(D_{\gamma_{\bar{D}}}^{k_4 \times L}\right)^2$

  $\bar{\mathbf{V}}_{i,j} := H\bar{\mathbf{D}}_{1,i,j} + p\bar{\mathbf{D}}_{2,i,j} + \mathbf{S}_{i,j} \in R_Q^{k_4 \times L}$

$(h', \mathbf{Y}') \xleftarrow{\$} D_{\gamma_{h'}} \times D_{\gamma_{\mathbf{Y}'}}^{k_3 \times L}$

$(w_1', w_2') := (\mathbf{b}_0 \mathbf{Y}', \mathbf{b}_1 \mathbf{Y}' \Delta + [h' | 0 | \dots | 0]) \in R_q^L \times R_q^L$

$(d_1', d_2', \bar{d}_1', \bar{d}_2') \xleftarrow{\$} \left(D_{\gamma_{d'}}\right)^2 \times \left(D_{\gamma_{\bar{d}'}}\right)^2$

$(\mathbf{D}_1', \mathbf{D}_2', \bar{\mathbf{D}}_1', \bar{\mathbf{D}}_2') \xleftarrow{\$} \left(D_{\gamma_{\mathbf{D}'}}^{k_3 \times L}\right)^2 \times \left(D_{\gamma_{\bar{\mathbf{D}}'}}^{k_3 \times L}\right)^2$

$v' := Hd_1' + pd_2' + h \in R_Q$

$\bar{v}' := H\bar{d}_1' + p\bar{d}_2' + h' \in R_Q$

$\mathbf{V}' := H\mathbf{D}_1' + p\mathbf{D}_2' + \mathbf{R} \in R_Q^{k_3 \times L}$

$\bar{\mathbf{V}}' := H\bar{\mathbf{D}}_1' + p\bar{\mathbf{D}}_2' + \mathbf{Y}' \in R_Q^{k_3 \times L}$

$a_1 := \begin{pmatrix} \mathbf{u}_{0,i}, \mathbf{U}_{1,i}, \mathbf{U}_{2,i}, \\ \mathbf{U}_{3,i}, \mathbf{U}_{4,i}, \mathbf{W}_i, \\ \mathbf{V}_i, \bar{\mathbf{V}}_{i,j}, \\ w_1', w_2', \\ v', \bar{v}', \mathbf{V}', \bar{\mathbf{V}}', \end{pmatrix}_{i,j}$

$c_1 := (c_i)_{i \in [\tau]} := \mathsf{H_m}(X, 1, a_1) \in \mathbb{Z}_{q'}^{\tau}$

For $i \in [\tau]$:

$\mathbf{Z}_{0,i} := c_i \cdot \mathsf{NTT}^{-1}(\Phi(\mathbf{R})) + \mathbf{Y}_i$

For $j \in [\tau']$:

  $\mathbf{x}_{0,i,j} := \mathbf{a}_0 \mathbf{S}_{i,j}$

  $\mathbf{X}_{1,i,j} := (\mathbf{A}_1 + c_i \cdot \mathbf{A}_2)\mathbf{S}_{i,j}$

  $\mathbf{X}_{2,i,j} := (\mathbf{Z}_{0,i} - c_i) \circ (\mathbf{Z}_{0,i} - 2c_i) \circ (\mathbf{A}_2 \mathbf{S}_{i,j})$

    $- \mathbf{Z}_{0,i} \circ (\mathbf{A}_3 \mathbf{S}_{i,j}) + \mathbf{A}_4 \mathbf{S}_{i,j}$

$a_2 := \begin{pmatrix} \mathbf{Z}_{0,i}, \mathbf{x}_{0,i,j}, \\ \mathbf{X}_{1,i,j}, \mathbf{X}_{2,i,j} \end{pmatrix}_{i,j}$

$c_2 := (\beta := (\beta_{i,j})_{(i,j) \in [\tau] \times [\tau']}, \beta')$
$:= \mathsf{H_m}(X, 2, a_1, c_1, a_2) \in C_X^{\tau \cdot \tau'} \times C_{\mathsf{ham}}$

For $i \in [\tau]$:

For $j \in [\tau']$:

$\mathbf{Z}_{i,j} := \beta_{i,j} \cdot \mathbf{E}_i + \mathbf{S}_{i,j}$

$\mathbf{F}_{1,i,j} := \beta_{i,j} \cdot \mathbf{D}_{1,i} + \bar{\mathbf{D}}_{1,i,j}$

$\mathbf{F}_{2,i,j} := \beta_{i,j} \cdot \mathbf{D}_{2,i} + \bar{\mathbf{D}}_{2,i,j}$

$(\zeta, \mathbf{Z}') := (\beta' \cdot h + h', \beta' \cdot \mathbf{R} + \mathbf{Y}')$

$(f_1', f_2') := (\beta' \cdot d_1' + \bar{d}_1', \beta' \cdot d_2' + \bar{d}_2')$

$(\mathbf{F}_1', \mathbf{F}_2') := (\beta' \cdot \mathbf{D}_1' + \bar{\mathbf{D}}_1', \beta' \cdot \mathbf{D}_2' + \bar{\mathbf{D}}_2')$

If $\mathsf{Rej}((\mathbf{Z}_{i,j})_{i,j}, (\beta_{i,j} \cdot \mathbf{E}_i)_{i,j}, \phi, B_{\tau, \mathbf{Z}}, \mathsf{err}) = \bot$

$\lor \mathsf{Rej}(\mathbf{Z}', \beta' \cdot \mathbf{R}, \phi, B_{\tau, \mathbf{Z}'}, \mathsf{err}) = \bot$

$\lor \mathsf{Rej}(\zeta, \beta' \cdot h, \phi, B_{\tau, \zeta}, \mathsf{err}) = \bot$

$\lor \mathsf{Rej}((\mathbf{F}_{1,i,j}, \mathbf{F}_{2,i,j})_{i,j},$
$\quad (\beta_{i,j} \cdot \mathbf{D}_{1,i}, \beta_{i,j} \cdot \mathbf{D}_{2,i})_{i,j}, \phi, B_{\tau, \mathbf{F}}, \mathsf{err}) = \bot$

$\lor \mathsf{Rej}((f_b', \mathbf{F}_b')_{b \in [2]}, (\beta' \cdot d_b', \beta' \cdot \mathbf{D}_b')_{b \in [2]}, \phi, B_{\tau, \mathbf{F}'}, \mathsf{err}) = \bot$

then restart

$\pi^{\mathsf{m}} := ((\mathbf{u}_{0,i}, (\mathbf{U}_{k,i})_{k \in [4]}, \mathbf{V}_i)_{i \in [\tau]}, v', \mathbf{V}', c_1, (\mathbf{Z}_{0,i})_{i \in [\tau]},$

$c_2, (\mathbf{Z}_{i,j}, \mathbf{F}_{1,i,j}, \mathbf{F}_{2,i,j})_{(i,j) \in [\tau] \times [\tau']}, \zeta, \mathbf{Z}', (f_b', \mathbf{F}_b')_{b \in [2]})$

π^{m}

Fig. 1. Prove algorithm for the multi-proof NIZK $\Pi_{\mathsf{NIZK}}^{\mathsf{m}}$ for the relations $(\mathcal{R}^{\mathsf{m}}, \mathcal{R}_{\mathsf{gap}}^{\mathsf{m}})$. We illustrate the 5-round interactive protocol that implicitly underlies the NIZK.

$\Pi_{\mathsf{NIZK}}^m : \mathsf{Verify}^{H_m}(\mathsf{crs}_{\mathsf{NIZK}}^m, X, \pi^m)$

$\mathsf{crs}_{\mathsf{NIZK}}^m = (H, \mathbf{a}_0, (\mathbf{A}_k)_{k\in[4]}) \in R_Q \times R_{q'}^{k_4} \times \left(R_{q'}^{k_3 \times k_4}\right)^4$

$X := (\mathsf{crs}_{\mathsf{com}} := (\mathbf{b}_0, \mathbf{b}_1), \mathsf{com} := \mathbf{T}) \in R_q^{k_3} \times R_q^{k_3} \times (R_{q'}^L \times R_q^L),$

$\pi^m := ((\mathbf{u}_{0,i}, (\mathbf{U}_{k,i})_{k\in[4]}, \mathbf{V}_i)_{i\in[\tau]}, v', \mathbf{V}', c_1,$

$\qquad (\mathbf{Z}_{0,i})_{i\in[\tau]}, c_2, (\mathbf{Z}_{i,j}, \mathbf{F}_{1,i,j}, \mathbf{F}_{2,i,j})_{(i,j)\in[\tau]\times[\tau']}, \mathbf{Z}', \zeta, (f_b', \mathbf{F}_b')_{b\in[2]})$

$\begin{bmatrix} \mathbf{t}_1 \\ \mathbf{t}_2 \end{bmatrix} := \mathbf{T} \in R_{q'}^L \times R_q^L$

For $i \in [\tau]$:

$\quad \mathbf{W}_i := \mathsf{Rot}(\mathbf{b}_0)\mathsf{NTT}(\mathbf{Z}_{0,i}) - c_i \cdot \Phi(\mathbf{t}_1) \in \mathbb{Z}_{q'}^{d \times L}$

$\quad$ **For** $j \in [\tau']$:

$\qquad \bar{\mathbf{V}}_{i,j} := H\mathbf{F}_{1,i,j} + p\mathbf{F}_{2,i,j} + \mathbf{Z}_{i,j} - \beta_{i,j} \cdot \mathbf{V}_i \in R_Q^{k_4 \times L}$

$\qquad \mathbf{x}_{0,i,j} := \mathbf{a}_0 \mathbf{Z}_{i,j} - \beta_{i,j} \cdot \mathbf{u}_{0,i} \in R_{q'}^L$

$\qquad \mathbf{X}_{1,i,j} := (\mathbf{A}_1 + c_i \cdot \mathbf{A}_2)\mathbf{Z}_{i,j} + \beta_{i,j} \cdot (\mathbf{Z}_{0,i} - (\mathbf{U}_{1,i} + c_i \cdot \mathbf{U}_{2,i})) \in R_{q'}^{k_4 \times L}$

$\qquad \mathbf{X}_{2,i,j} := (\mathbf{Z}_{0,i} - c_i) \circ (\mathbf{Z}_{0,i} - 2c_i) \circ (\mathbf{A}_2 \mathbf{Z}_{i,j}) - \mathbf{Z}_{0,i} \circ (\mathbf{A}_3 \mathbf{Z}_{i,j}) + \mathbf{A}_4 \mathbf{Z}_{i,j}$

$\qquad\qquad - \beta_{i,j} \cdot \left((\mathbf{Z}_{0,i} - c_i) \circ (\mathbf{Z}_{0,i} - 2c_i) \circ \mathbf{U}_{2,i} - \mathbf{Z}_{0,i} \circ \mathbf{U}_{3,i} + \mathbf{U}_{4,i}\right) \in R_{q'}^{k_4 \times L}$

$\mathbf{w}_1' := \mathbf{b}_0 \mathbf{Z}' - \beta' \cdot \mathbf{t}_1 \in \mathbb{Z}_{q'}^L$

$\mathbf{w}_2' := \mathbf{b}_1 \mathbf{Z}' \Delta + [\zeta|0|\dots|0] - \beta' \cdot \mathbf{t}_2 \Delta \in \mathbb{Z}_{q'}^L$

$\bar{v}' := H f_1' + p f_2' + \zeta - \beta' \cdot v' \in R_Q$

$\bar{\mathbf{V}}' := H\mathbf{F}_1' + p\mathbf{F}_2' + \mathbf{Z}' - \beta' \cdot \mathbf{V}' \in R_Q^{k_3 \times L}$

$a_1 := \left((\mathbf{u}_{0,i}, \mathbf{U}_{1,i}, \mathbf{U}_{2,i}, \mathbf{U}_{3,i}, \mathbf{U}_{4,i}, \mathbf{W}_i, \mathbf{V}_i, (\bar{\mathbf{V}}_{i,j})_{j\in[\tau']})_{i\in[\tau]}, \mathbf{w}_1', \mathbf{w}_2', v', \bar{v}', \mathbf{V}', \bar{\mathbf{V}}'\right)$

$a_2 := \left(\mathbf{Z}_{0,i}, (\mathbf{x}_{0,i,j}, \mathbf{X}_{1,i,j}, \mathbf{X}_{2,i,j})_{j\in\times[\tau']}\right)_{i\in[\tau]}$

If $\begin{cases} \|\zeta\|_2 \geq B \\ \vee \; \|\mathbf{Z}'\|_2 \geq B_{\mathbf{Z}'} \\ \vee \; \exists(i,j) \in [\tau] \times [\tau'], \|\mathbf{Z}_{i,j}\|_2 \geq B_{\mathbf{Z}} \\ \vee \; \|\mathbf{F}_1'\|_\infty \geq B_{1,\mathbf{F}'} \\ \vee \; \|\mathbf{F}_2'\|_\infty \geq B_{2,\mathbf{F}'} \\ \vee \; \exists(i,j) \in [\tau] \times [\tau'], \|\mathbf{F}_{1,i,j}\|_\infty \geq B_{1,\mathbf{F}} \\ \vee \; \exists(i,j) \in [\tau] \times [\tau'], \|\mathbf{F}_{2,i,j}\|_\infty \geq B_{2,\mathbf{F}} \\ \vee \; c_1 \neq H_m(X, 1, a_1) \\ \vee \; c_2 \neq H_m(X, 2, a_1, c_1, a_2) \end{cases}$ **then return** $\perp$

return $\top$

Fig. 2. Verify algorithm for the multi-proof NIZK for the relations $(\mathcal{R}^m, \mathcal{R}_{\mathsf{gap}}^m)$.

to succeed on many challenges. That is, the probability that $\mathcal{A}$ succeeds in forging a proof without a witness by guessing the output of the random oracle is at most $\frac{\mu}{2} - \mathsf{negl}(\lambda)$, where μ is the advantage of $\mathcal{A}$ outputting a valid proof. We then show in Lemma 4.2 a specific form of special soundness where an extractor $\mathsf{Extract}_{\mathsf{ss}}$ given the purported proof output by $\mathcal{A}$ along with several specific challenges, extracts a witness in $\mathcal{R}_{\mathsf{gap}}^{\mathsf{m}}$. We finally provide the description of our straight-line extractor $\mathsf{Multi\text{-}Extract}$ that internally runs $\mathsf{Extract}_{\mathsf{ss}}$ and bound its success probability.

We present our first lemma which shows that if $\mathcal{A}$ outputs a valid proof, then there must have been multiple challenges for which it could have succeeded on. Formally, we define the sets $\{\Gamma_{1,i}\}_{i \in [\tau]}$ and Γ_2 that count for how many challenges there exists a valid response, and argue that they cannot be too small. More specifically, $\Gamma_{1,i}$ counts the number of second flow challenges c_i for which there exists at least two distinct $\beta_{i,j}$'s included in the fourth flow challenge with a corresponding valid response. Γ_2 on the other hand counts the number of β' included in the fourth flow challenge with a corresponding valid response. Roughly, the former (resp. latter) set is the set of challenges for which $\mathcal{A}$ was able to complete the exact proof of Bootle et al. (resp. proof of linear relation).

Lemma 4.1. *Consider an interactive protocol as defined implicitly in Fig. 1. That is, the transcript is $(a_1, \mathbf{c}_1, a_2, \mathbf{c}_2, \mathsf{resp})$, where $\mathbf{c}_1, \mathbf{c}_2$ are the challenges the (honest) verifier samples uniformly at random and resp is the response $((\mathbf{Z}_{i,j}, \mathbf{F}_{1,i,j}, \mathbf{F}_{2,i,j})_{(i,j) \in [\tau] \times [\tau']}, \mathbf{Z}', \zeta, f_1', f_2', \mathbf{F}_1', \mathbf{F}_2')$ sent by the prover. For any statement X, first, second, third, and fourth flows $a_1, \mathbf{c}_1, a_2,$ and $\mathbf{c}_2$, respectively, we define the following sets for all $i \in [\tau]$:*

$$\Gamma_{1,i}(a_1, \mathbf{c}_1, a_2, \mathbf{c}_2)$$

$$:= \left\{ \overline{c}_i \in \mathbb{Z}_{q'} \middle| \begin{array}{l} (c_{i'})_{i' \in [\tau]} \leftarrow \mathbf{c}_1, \overline{\mathbf{c}}_1 := (\overline{c}_i) \cup (c_{i'})_{i' \in [\tau] \setminus \{i\}}, \\ (\boldsymbol{\beta} = (\beta_{i',j'})_{(i',j') \in [\tau] \times [\tau']}, \beta') \leftarrow \mathbf{c}_2 \\ \exists j \in [\tau'], \text{ distinct } (\overline{\beta}_{i,j}, \overline{\beta}'_{i,j}) \in (C_{\mathsf{X}})^2, \\ \overline{\boldsymbol{\beta}} := (\overline{\beta}_{i,j}) \cup (\beta_{i',j'})_{(i',j') \neq (i,j)}, \overline{\boldsymbol{\beta}}' := (\overline{\beta}'_{i,j}) \cup (\beta_{i',j'})_{(i',j') \neq (i,j)}, \\ \exists (\overline{a}_2, \overline{a}'_2), (\overline{\mathsf{resp}}, \overline{\mathsf{resp}}') \text{ s.t. } (a_1, \overline{\mathbf{c}}_1, \overline{a}_2, \mathbf{c}_2 := (\overline{\boldsymbol{\beta}}, \beta'), \overline{\mathsf{resp}}) \text{ and} \\ (a_1, \overline{\mathbf{c}}_1, \overline{a}'_2, \overline{\mathbf{c}}_2 := (\overline{\boldsymbol{\beta}}', \beta'), \overline{\mathsf{resp}}') \text{ are valid} \end{array} \right\}$$

$$\Gamma_2(\mathsf{X}, a_1, \mathbf{c}_1, a_2, \mathbf{c}_2)$$

$$:= \left\{ \overline{\beta}' \in C_{\mathsf{ham}} \mid (\boldsymbol{\beta}, \beta') \leftarrow \mathbf{c}_2, \exists \overline{\mathsf{resp}} \text{ s.t. } (a_1, \mathbf{c}_1, a_2, \mathbf{c}_2 := (\boldsymbol{\beta}, \overline{\beta}'), \overline{\mathsf{resp}}) \text{ is valid} \right\},$$

where we say a transcript $(a_1, \mathbf{c}_1, a_2, \mathbf{c}_2, \mathsf{resp})$ is valid if the proof π^{m} implicitly defined by $(a_1, \mathbf{c}_1, a_2, \mathbf{c}_2, \mathsf{resp})$ is valid for statement X.

Then, for any $\mathsf{Q}_\mathsf{H} = \mathsf{poly}(\lambda)$ and PPT adversary $\mathcal{A}$ that makes at most Q_H random oracle queries with

$$\Pr\left[\begin{array}{c} (\widetilde{\mathsf{crs}}_{\mathsf{NIZK}}^{\mathsf{m}}, \tau) \xleftarrow{\$} \mathcal{S}_{\mathsf{crs}}(1^\lambda), \\ \{(\mathsf{X}_k, \pi_k^{\mathsf{m}})\}_{k \in [\mathsf{Q}_\mathsf{S}]} \xleftarrow{\$} \mathcal{A}^{\mathsf{H}_\mathsf{m}}(1^\lambda, \widetilde{\mathsf{crs}}_{\mathsf{NIZK}}^{\mathsf{m}}), \end{array} : \forall k \in [\mathsf{Q}_\mathsf{S}], \mathsf{Verify}^{\mathsf{H}_\mathsf{m}}(\widetilde{\mathsf{crs}}, \mathsf{X}_k, \pi_k^{\mathsf{m}}) = \top \right] \geq \mu(\lambda),$$

we have,

$$\Pr\left[\begin{array}{cc}(\widetilde{\mathsf{crs}}_{\mathsf{NIZK}}^{\mathsf{m}},\tau)\overset{\$}{\leftarrow}\mathcal{S}_{\mathsf{crs}}(1^{\lambda}), & \forall k\in[\mathsf{Q}_{\mathsf{S}}],\mathsf{Verify}^{\mathsf{H}_{\mathsf{m}}}(\widetilde{\mathsf{crs}}_{\mathsf{NIZK}}^{\mathsf{m}},\mathsf{X}_k,\pi_k^{\mathsf{m}})=\top\\ \{(\mathsf{X}_k,\pi_k^{\mathsf{m}})\}_{k\in[\mathsf{Q}_{\mathsf{S}}]}\overset{\$}{\leftarrow}\mathcal{A}^{\mathsf{H}_{\mathsf{m}}}(1^{\lambda},\widetilde{\mathsf{crs}}_{\mathsf{NIZK}}^{\mathsf{m}}), & :\wedge\exists i\in[\tau],|\varGamma_{1,i}(\mathsf{X}_k,a_{1,k},\mathbf{c}_{1,k},a_{2,k},\mathbf{c}_{2,k})|\geq 3\\ & \wedge|\varGamma_2(\mathsf{X}_k,a_{1,k},\mathbf{c}_{1,k},a_{2,k},\mathbf{c}_{2,k})|\geq\frac{\mu}{2\mathsf{Q}_{\mathsf{H}}}|\mathcal{C}_{\mathsf{ham}}|\end{array}\right]$$

is at least $\mu(\lambda)/2-\mathsf{negl}(\lambda)$

Proof Sketch. For simplicity, denote $\varGamma_{1,i}^{(k)}:=\varGamma_{1,i}(\mathsf{X}_k,a_{1,k},\mathbf{c}_{1,k},a_{2,k},\mathbf{c}_{2,k})$ and $\varGamma_2^{(k)}:=\varGamma_2(\mathsf{X}_k,a_{1,k},\mathbf{c}_{1,k},a_{2,k},\mathbf{c}_{2,k})$ for each $(k,i)\in[\mathsf{Q}_{\mathsf{S}}]\times[\tau]$. We denote by ValidProofs the event that $\mathsf{Verify}^{\mathsf{H}_{\mathsf{m}}}(\widetilde{\mathsf{crs}}_{\mathsf{NIZK}}^{\mathsf{m}},\mathsf{X}_k,\pi_k^{\mathsf{m}})=\top$ for all $k\in[\mathsf{Q}_{\mathsf{S}}]$. Then, to lower bound the desired probability, it suffices to upper bound $\sum_{k\in[\mathsf{Q}_{\mathsf{S}}]}\Pr[\mathsf{ValidProofs}\wedge\forall i\in[\tau],|\varGamma_{1,i}^{(k)}|<3|]$ and $\sum_{k\in[\mathsf{Q}_{\mathsf{S}}]}\Pr[\mathsf{ValidProofs}\wedge|\varGamma_2^{(k)}|<\frac{\mu}{2\mathsf{Q}_{\mathsf{H}}}\cdot|\mathcal{C}_{\mathsf{ham}}|]$. To obtain the bound on the later, observe that if $\varGamma_2^{(k)}$ has size at most T, then even a computationally unbounded (classical) adversary can find an input that hashes to $\varGamma_2^{(k)}$ with probability at most T/C_{ham} for every RO query. We can tune the size of T to get the desired bound. The bound on the former requires more work since at a high level the adversary can cheat twice; once for the second flow challenge and once for the fourth flow challenge. We show that if it cheats with respect to the second (resp. fourth) flow challenge then even a computationally unbounded (classical) adversary cannot cheat in the fourth (resp. second) flow challenge. □

We note that the main differences of the proof in the classical ROM and QROM is the bound in the statement of Lemma 4.1 and how it is proven. Informally, the reason why the above proof fails is because a quantum adversary can query the random oracle on all the input space in super position. To this end, we rely on (roughly) the optimality of the Grover's search to bound the success probability of the adversary.

We next show a restricted notion of the standard *special soundness* for interactive protocols. Typically, an extractor for special soundness is provided multiple valid transcripts containing the same commitments and is asked to extract a witness from them. Below, we show that for our particular interactive protocol, the extractor only requires one valid transcript along with several challenges for which existence of a valid response is guaranteed. Put differently, rather than taking multiple valid transcripts as input, our extractor only requires one transcript and the challenges included in the remaining valid transcripts. As explained in the overview of [6], the crux of the proof is that given a valid challenge, the extractor can extract parts of the response by using the trapdoor τ (i.e., NTRU decryption key).

Lemma 4.2. *Consider the following 7 valid transcripts for a statement* X*:*

- *For* $(\eta,b)\in[3]\times[2]$, $\mathsf{trans}^{(\eta,b)}:=(a_1,\mathbf{c}_1^{(\eta)}:=(c_i^{(\eta)})_{i\in[\tau]},a_2^{(\eta)},\mathbf{c}_2^{(\eta,b)}:=(\boldsymbol{\beta}^{(\eta,b)}:=(\beta_{i,j}^{(\eta,b)})_{(i,j)\in[\tau]\times[\tau']},\beta'),\mathsf{resp}^{(\eta,b)})$,
- $\widehat{\mathsf{trans}}^{(1,0)}:=(a_1,\mathbf{c}_1^{(1)},a_2^{(1)},\widehat{\mathbf{c}}_2^{(1,0)}:=(\boldsymbol{\beta}^{(1,0)},\widehat{\beta}'),\widehat{\mathsf{resp}}^{(1,0)})$,

such that there exists $(i^*, j_1^*, j_2^*, j_3^*) \in [\tau] \times [\tau']^3$ that $(c_{i^*}^{(1)}, c_{i^*}^{(2)}, c_{i^*}^{(3)})$ are pairwise distinct, $(\beta_{i^*, j_1^*}^{(1,0)}, \beta_{i^*, j_1^*}^{(1,1)})$, $(\beta_{i^*, j_2^*}^{(2,0)}, \beta_{i^*, j_2^*}^{(2,1)})$, and $(\beta_{i^*, j_3^*}^{(3,0)}, \beta_{i^*, j_3^*}^{(3,1)})$ are each pairwise distinct, and $\beta' \neq \widehat{\beta}'$.

Then, there exists a deterministic PT special sound extractor $\mathsf{Extract_{ss}}$ such that given a trapdoor τ to $\widetilde{\mathsf{crs}}_{\mathsf{NIZK}}^{\mathsf{m}}$, any statement X and $\left(\mathsf{trans}^{(1,0)}, (\beta_{i^*, j_\eta^*}^{(\eta,0)}, \beta_{i^*, j_\eta^*}^{(\eta,1)})_{\eta \in [3]}, (\beta', \widehat{\beta}')\right)$ included in any of the 7 valid transcripts of the above form, $\mathsf{Extract_{ss}}$ outputs a witness W such that $(\mathsf{X}, \mathsf{W}) \in \mathcal{R}_{\mathsf{gap}}^{\mathsf{m}}$ or a solution to the $\mathsf{MSIS}_{d,1,k_4,16B_{\mathbf{Z}},q'}$ problem with respect to $\mathbf{a}_0 \in R_{q'}^{k_4}$ included in $\widetilde{\mathsf{crs}}_{\mathsf{NIZK}}^{\mathsf{m}}$ or a solution to the $\mathsf{MSIS}_{d,1,k_3,2(B_{\mathbf{Z}'}+B_c\delta^{\mathsf{gap}}),q'}$ problem with respect to $\mathbf{b}_0 \in R_{q'}^{k_3}$ included in $\mathsf{crs_{com}}$.

Proof Sketch. The proof consists of three parts: in Part (A), we extract a witness that proves the linear relation (i.e., $\begin{bmatrix} \mathbf{t}_1 \\ \mathbf{t}_2 \end{bmatrix} = \begin{bmatrix} \mathbf{b}_0 \\ \mathbf{b}_1 \end{bmatrix} \mathbf{R}' + \begin{bmatrix} 0 \\ h\mathbf{g} \end{bmatrix}$); in Part (B), if the extracted witness from Part (A) is not in $\mathcal{R}_{\mathsf{gap}}^{\mathsf{m}}$, then we further extract a different witness that proves the exact relation for $\mathbf{t}_1$ (i.e., $\mathbf{t}_1 = \mathbf{b}_0 \mathbf{R}''$); in Part (C), we show that given two different openings to $\mathbf{t}_1$, we can extract a solution to an MSIS problem. Looking ahead, if $\mathsf{Extract_{ss}}$ does not succeed in outputting a valid witness for $\mathcal{R}_{\mathsf{gap}}^{\mathsf{m}}$ in Part (A), then it will only output a solution to the MSIS solution in the following Parts (B) and (C). This subtle observation will be used to optimize the proof size of our multi-proof extractable NIZK in the classical ROM.

Part (A). First observe that from $\mathsf{trans}^{(1,0)}$, we have

$$\bar{\mathbf{V}}' + \beta' \cdot \mathbf{V}' = H\mathbf{F}_1^{(1,0)'} + p\mathbf{F}_2^{(1,0)'} + \mathbf{Z}^{(1,0)'} \text{ (over } R_Q).$$

Notice the right hand side is a valid NTRU ciphertext. Namely, by using the trapdoor $\tau = (f, v)$ such that $H = p \cdot v \cdot f^{-1}$ (i.e., secret key for the NTRU encryption scheme), $\mathsf{Extract_{ss}}$ can decrypt $\bar{\mathbf{V}}' + \beta' \cdot \mathbf{V}'$ to recover the "message" $\mathbf{Z}^{(1,0)'}$. Formally, $\mathbf{Z}^{(1,0)'} = f^{-1} \cdot (f \cdot (\bar{\mathbf{V}}' + \beta' \cdot \mathbf{V}') \mod Q) \mod p$. Moreover, by setting the parameters appropriately, the NTRU encryption scheme will have no decryption error. Thus, if $\bar{\mathbf{V}}' + \beta' \cdot \mathbf{V}'$ is guaranteed to be in the above form, then the possible $\mathbf{Z}^{(1,0)'}$ that can be included in $\mathsf{resp}^{(1,0)}$ is unique. In other words, there can not exist a distinct $\hat{\mathbf{Z}}^{(1,0)'}$ in $\mathsf{resp}^{(1,0)}$ such that verification still holds. The same argument holds for the $\zeta^{(1,0)}$ component since we have $\bar{v}' + \beta' \cdot v' = Hf_1^{(1,0)'} + pf_2^{(1,0)'} + \zeta^{(1,0)}$.

With this observation in mind, given $\mathsf{trans}^{(1,0)}$ and $\widehat{\beta}'$, $\mathsf{Extract_{ss}}$ first performs NTRU decryption as follows, which is guaranteed to succeed by assumption:

$$\widehat{\mathbf{Z}}^{(1,0)'} := f^{-1} \cdot (f \cdot (\bar{\mathbf{V}}' + \widehat{\beta}' \cdot \mathbf{V}') \mod Q) \mod p,$$
$$\widehat{\zeta}^{(1,0)} := f^{-1} \cdot (f \cdot (\bar{v}' + \widehat{\beta}' \cdot v') \mod Q) \mod p.$$

As argued above, this $\widehat{\mathbf{Z}}^{(1,0)'}$ and $\widehat{\zeta}^{(1,0)}$ are guaranteed to be included in $\widehat{\mathsf{trans}}^{(1,0)}$, where note that $\widehat{\mathsf{trans}}^{(1,0)}$ is not provided to $\mathsf{Extract_{ss}}$ as input. Since $\mathsf{trans}^{(1,0)}$

and $\widehat{\mathsf{trans}}^{(1,0)}$ are valid and share the same first flow a_1, they also satisfy the same verification equations regarding $\mathbf{w}_1'$ and $\mathbf{w}_2'$ (see Fig. 2). $\mathsf{Extract}_{\mathsf{ss}}$ subtracts these equations to remove $\mathbf{w}_1'$ and $\mathbf{w}_2'$, and obtains the following:

$$(\beta' - \widehat{\beta}') \cdot \mathbf{t}_1 = \mathbf{b}_0\big(\mathbf{Z}^{(1,0)'} - \widehat{\mathbf{Z}}^{(1,0)'}\big) \ (\text{over } R_{q'}),$$

$$(\beta' - \widehat{\beta}') \cdot \mathbf{t}_2 \Delta = \mathbf{b}_1\big(\mathbf{Z}^{(1,0)'} - \widehat{\mathbf{Z}}^{(1,0)'}\big)\Delta + [\zeta^{(1,0)} - \widehat{\zeta}^{(1,0)} \mid 0 \mid \cdots \mid 0] \ (\text{over } R_q).$$

By multiplying Δ^{-1} from both sides in the later equation, $\mathsf{Extract}_{\mathsf{ss}}$ obtains

$$(\beta' - \widehat{\beta}') \cdot \mathbf{t}_2 = \mathbf{b}_1\big(\mathbf{Z}^{(1,0)'} - \widehat{\mathbf{Z}}^{(1,0)'}\big) + (\zeta^{(1,0)} - \widehat{\zeta}^{(1,0)}) \cdot \mathbf{g}.$$

Due to our parameter selection, $(\beta' - \widehat{\beta}')$ is small and is guaranteed to be invertible over R_q. $\mathsf{Extract}_{\mathsf{ss}}$ then checks if $\mathbf{R}' := \big(\mathbf{Z}^{(1,0)'} - \widehat{\mathbf{Z}}^{(1,0)'}\big)/(\beta' - \widehat{\beta}')^{-1}$ consists of polynomials with $\{0, 1, 2\}$-coefficients. If so, $\mathsf{W} := ((\zeta^{(1,0)} - \widehat{\zeta}^{(1,0)}), (\beta' - \widehat{\beta}'), \mathbf{R}')$ is a valid witness for $\mathcal{R}_{\mathsf{gap}}^m$ and thus $\mathsf{Extract}_{\mathsf{ss}}$ outputs W.

We highlight again that if $\mathsf{Extract}_{\mathsf{ss}}$ does not succeed in outputting a valid witness for $\mathcal{R}_{\mathsf{gap}}^m$ in Part (A), then it can only output a solution to the MSIS problem in Parts (B) and (C). $\qquad\square$

We are now ready to finish the proof of Theorem 4.1. The goal of Multi-Extract is to collect the necessary inputs to invoke $\mathsf{Extract}_{\mathsf{ss}}$ defined in Lemma 4.2. Let us informally explain in a bit more detail.

Given a valid proof π^m, Multi-Extract first goes over the challenges in C_{ham} to find another β_t' for which there exists a valid response. Concretely, it decrypts $(\overline{v}' + \beta_t' \cdot v')$ and $(\overline{\mathbf{V}}' + \beta_t' + \mathbf{V}')$ and searches for a pair $(\zeta_t, \mathbf{Z}_t')$ that satisfies $\|\zeta_t\|_2 < B \wedge \|\mathbf{Z}_t'\|_2 < B_{\mathbf{Z}'} \wedge \mathbf{w}_1' = \mathbf{b}_0\mathbf{Z}_t' - \beta_t' \cdot \mathbf{t}_1 \wedge \mathbf{w}_2' = \mathbf{b}_1\mathbf{Z}_t'\Delta + [\zeta_t|0|\cdots|0] - \beta_t' \cdot \mathbf{t}_2\Delta$. If this is satisfied, $\mathsf{resp}_t := \big((\mathbf{Z}_{i,j}, \mathbf{F}_{1,i,j}, \mathbf{F}_{2,i,j})_{(i,j)\in[\tau]\times[\tau']}, \mathbf{Z}_t', \zeta_t, f_1', f_2', \mathbf{F}_1', \mathbf{F}_2'\big)$ is guaranteed to be another valid response where the fourth flow challenge is $\mathbf{c}_{2,t} = (\beta, \beta_t')$. Note that this corresponds to $\widehat{\mathsf{resp}}^{(1,0)}$ and $\widehat{\beta}'$ in Lemma 4.2.

Multi-Extract then goes over *all* the challenges in C_X, which it can do since $|C_X| = 2d = \mathrm{poly}(\lambda)$. Concretely, for all $\beta \in C_X$, it decrypts $(\overline{\mathbf{V}}_{i',j'} + \beta \cdot \mathbf{V}_{i'})$ for all $(i', j') \in [\tau] \times [\tau']$, and checks if it correctly decrypts to some "message" $\mathbf{Z}_{\beta,i',j'}$ such that $\|\mathbf{Z}_{\beta,i',j'}\|_2 < B_{\mathbf{Z}}$. Note that unlike for the above set of challenges in C_{ham}, this check itself does not guarantee that there exists a valid transcript for challenge $\beta \in C_X$. This is because the fact that a valid $\mathbf{Z}_{\beta,i',j'}$ exists does not imply that there exists an associated valid third flow a_2. However, the main observation is that if a valid transcript for challenge $\beta \in C_X$ exists, then $(\overline{\mathbf{V}}_{i',j'} + \beta \cdot \mathbf{V}_{i'})$ must decrypt to $\mathbf{Z}_{\beta,i',j'}$ such that $\|\mathbf{Z}_{\beta,i',j'}\|_2 < B_{\mathbf{Z}}$.

Finally, Multi-Extract is ready to run $\mathsf{Extract}_{\mathsf{ss}}$. It runs through all three pairs of distinct challenges $\big(\beta_{i',j_\eta}^{(\eta,0)}, \beta_{i',j_\eta}^{(\eta,1)}\big)_{\eta\in[3]}$ it collected while going over C_X and executes $\mathsf{Extract}_{\mathsf{ss}}\big(\tau, \mathsf{X}, \big(\beta_{i',j_\eta}^{(\eta,0)}, \beta_{i',j_\eta}^{(\eta,1)}\big)_{\eta\in[3]}, (\beta, \widehat{\beta}')\big)$. We show via Lemmata 4.1 and 4.2 that with non-negligible probability, one of the set of inputs to $\mathsf{Extract}_{\mathsf{ss}}$ must be in the specified form detailed in Lemma 4.2. Moreover, $\mathsf{Extract}_{\mathsf{ss}}$ is only invoked a polynomially number of times. Thus, assuming the MSIS problem is difficult, Multi-Extract extracts a witness in $\mathcal{R}_{\mathsf{gap}}^m$ in polynomial time. $\qquad\square$

4.3   Putting Everything Together

Table 2. Concrete parameters for our scheme.

par.	q	q'	p	Q	τ	τ'	κ	d	k_1	k_2	k_3	k_4	B_c	σ	$\gamma_{DSMR}, \gamma_D, \gamma_{D'}, \gamma_E$
value	$\sim 2^{60}$	$\sim 2^{24}$	$\sim 2^{32}$	$\sim 2^{66}$	6	2	2	2048	3	5	4	19	36	2^{26}	1

Roughly, we consider all the constraints that need to be satisfied by the correctness and security of our blind signature and use the LWE-Estimator from [7] so that every MLWE, MSIS, and DSMR assumptions give at least 128 bits of security. We employ the technique of Bai-Galbraith [12] to reduce the dimension of the signature by 2. We also consider that Gaussians can be encoded in $\log(2\sigma)$ bits by using the encoding of e.g. [46]. The size of the resulting signature is 102.6 KB and we get a first flow message of size 34 MB. However, as explained in the technical overview, we can reduce the first flow message in the classical ROM by removing the Katsumata transform [35] applied to the exact proof of Bootle et al. [17]. With this optimization, the first flow message is greatly reduced to 851 KB (Table 2).

Possible Optimizations. We also mention several possible optimizations. We can first consider using matrices $\mathbf{A}_1, \mathbf{A}_2, \mathbf{B}_1$ instead of $\mathbf{a}_1, \mathbf{a}_2, \mathbf{b}_1$ and lowering the degree d to e.g. 512. This can lower both the signature and first flow message size. This way we would have better granularity when modifying parameters, however we would need a module-NTRU trapdoor on the matrix $\mathbf{A}_1$ which is not constructed in [26] and seems nontrivial to obtain. Another solution would be to additionally prove the sparseness of $\mathbf{R}$ in the multi-proof extractable NIZK, which allows to lower the signature size since we will be able to extract $\mathbf{R}$ with better quality. This is possible by proving statements about the hamming weight of $\mathbf{R}$ but it would make the protocol much more complicated and the size of the first flow message may increase. Using either of these improvements we could lower the signature size to around 50 KB.

Another possible avenue for improvement would be reducing the size of the first flow by considering a better exact zero-knowledge proof. In all likelihood using the same proof as [29] would give the same improvement and bring the size of the first flow down to around 110 KB. However using this zero-knowledge proof is not completely straightforward as extraction is more complicated and the arguments used in Lemma 4.2 might not apply any more, especially when considering extraction in the QROM.

We leave further optimized instantiation of our generic construction as an interesting future work.

Acknowledgements. Shuichi Katsumata was partially supported by JSPS KAK-ENHI Grant Number 22K17892, Japan and JST AIP Acceleration Research JPMJCR22U5, Japan.

References

1. VPN by Google one, explained. https://one.google.com/about/vpn/howitworks
2. Abe, M., Okamoto, T.: Provably secure partially blind signatures. In: Bellare, M. (ed.) CRYPTO 2000. LNCS, vol. 1880, pp. 271–286. Springer, Heidelberg (2000). https://doi.org/10.1007/3-540-44598-6_17
3. Agrawal, S., Boneh, D., Boyen, X.: Efficient lattice (H)IBE in the standard model. In: Gilbert, H. (ed.) EUROCRYPT 2010. LNCS, vol. 6110, pp. 553–572. Springer, Heidelberg (2010). https://doi.org/10.1007/978-3-642-13190-5_28
4. Agrawal, S., Boneh, D., Boyen, X.: Lattice basis delegation in fixed dimension and shorter-ciphertext hierarchical IBE. In: Rabin, T. (ed.) CRYPTO 2010. LNCS, vol. 6223, pp. 98–115. Springer, Heidelberg (2010). https://doi.org/10.1007/978-3-642-14623-7_6
5. Agrawal, S., Kirshanova, E., Stehle, D., Yadav, A.: Can round-optimal lattice-based blind signatures be practical? Cryptology ePrint Archive (2021)
6. Agrawal, S., Kirshanova, E., Stehle, D., Yadav, A.: Practical, round-optimal lattice-based blind signatures. To appear in ACM CCS (2022). https://www.sigsac.org/ccs/CCS2022/program/accepted-papers.html
7. Albrecht, M.R., Player, R., Scott, S.: On the concrete hardness of learning with errors. J. Math. Cryptol. 9(3), 169–203 (2015)
8. Alkeilani Alkadri, N., Harasser, P., Janson, C.: BlindOR: an efficient lattice-based blind signature scheme from OR-proofs. In: Conti, M., Stevens, M., Krenn, S. (eds.) CANS 2021. LNCS, vol. 13099, pp. 95–115. Springer, Cham (2021). https://doi.org/10.1007/978-3-030-92548-2_6
9. Alkeilani Alkadri, N., El Bansarkhani, R., Buchmann, J.: BLAZE: practical lattice-based blind signatures for privacy-preserving applications. In: Bonneau, J., Heninger, N. (eds.) FC 2020. LNCS, vol. 12059, pp. 484–502. Springer, Cham (2020). https://doi.org/10.1007/978-3-030-51280-4_26
10. Alkeilani Alkadri, N., El Bansarkhani, R., Buchmann, J.: On lattice-based interactive protocols: an approach with less or no aborts. In: Liu, J.K., Cui, H. (eds.) ACISP 2020. LNCS, vol. 12248, pp. 41–61. Springer, Cham (2020). https://doi.org/10.1007/978-3-030-55304-3_3
11. Attema, T., Lyubashevsky, V., Seiler, G.: Practical product proofs for lattice commitments. In: Micciancio, D., Ristenpart, T. (eds.) CRYPTO 2020, Part II. LNCS, vol. 12171, pp. 470–499. Springer, Cham (2020). https://doi.org/10.1007/978-3-030-56880-1_17
12. Bai, S., Galbraith, S.D.: An improved compression technique for signatures based on learning with errors. In: Benaloh, J. (ed.) CT-RSA 2014. LNCS, vol. 8366, pp. 28–47. Springer, Cham (2014). https://doi.org/10.1007/978-3-319-04852-9_2
13. Baum, C., Damgård, I., Lyubashevsky, V., Oechsner, S., Peikert, C.: More efficient commitments from structured lattice assumptions. In: Catalano, D., De Prisco, R. (eds.) SCN 2018. LNCS, vol. 11035, pp. 368–385. Springer, Cham (2018). https://doi.org/10.1007/978-3-319-98113-0_20
14. Bellare, M., Neven, G.: Multi-signatures in the plain public-key model and a general forking lemma. In: ACM CCS 2006, pp. 390–399 (2006)
15. Bernhard, D., Fischlin, M., Warinschi, B.: Adaptive proofs of knowledge in the random oracle model. In: Katz, J. (ed.) PKC 2015. LNCS, vol. 9020, pp. 629–649. Springer, Heidelberg (2015). https://doi.org/10.1007/978-3-662-46447-2_28
16. Beullens, W., Dobson, S., Katsumata, S., Lai, Y.F., Pintore, F.: Group signatures and more from isogenies and lattices: generic, simple, and efficient. In: Dunkelman, O., Dziembowski, S. (eds.) EUROCRYPT 2022. LNCS, vol. 13276, pp. 95–126. Springer, Cham (2022). https://doi.org/10.1007/978-3-031-07085-3_4

17. Bootle, J., Lyubashevsky, V., Seiler, G.: Algebraic techniques for short(er) exact lattice-based zero-knowledge proofs. In: Boldyreva, A., Micciancio, D. (eds.) CRYPTO 2019, Part I. LNCS, vol. 11692, pp. 176–202. Springer, Cham (2019). https://doi.org/10.1007/978-3-030-26948-7_7

18. Boyen, X.: Lattice mixing and vanishing trapdoors: a framework for fully secure short signatures and more. In: Nguyen, P.Q., Pointcheval, D. (eds.) PKC 2010. LNCS, vol. 6056, pp. 499–517. Springer, Heidelberg (2010). https://doi.org/10.1007/978-3-642-13013-7_29

19. Brands, S.: Untraceable off-line cash in wallet with observers. In: Stinson, D.R. (ed.) CRYPTO 1993. LNCS, vol. 773, pp. 302–318. Springer, Heidelberg (1994). https://doi.org/10.1007/3-540-48329-2_26

20. Camenisch, J.: Efficient and generalized group signatures. In: Fumy, W. (ed.) EUROCRYPT 1997. LNCS, vol. 1233, pp. 465–479. Springer, Heidelberg (1997). https://doi.org/10.1007/3-540-69053-0_32

21. Camenisch, J., Lysyanskaya, A.: An efficient system for non-transferable anonymous credentials with optional anonymity revocation. In: Pfitzmann, B. (ed.) EUROCRYPT 2001. LNCS, vol. 2045, pp. 93–118. Springer, Heidelberg (2001). https://doi.org/10.1007/3-540-44987-6_7

22. Cash, D., Hofheinz, D., Kiltz, E., Peikert, C.: Bonsai trees, or how to delegate a lattice basis. In: Gilbert, H. (ed.) EUROCRYPT 2010. LNCS, vol. 6110, pp. 523–552. Springer, Heidelberg (2010). https://doi.org/10.1007/978-3-642-13190-5_27

23. Chaum, D.: Blind signatures for untraceable payments. In: Chaum, D., Rivest, R.L., Sherman, A.T. (eds.) Advances in Cryptology, pp. 199–203. Springer, Boston (1983). https://doi.org/10.1007/978-1-4757-0602-4_18

24. Chaum, D.: Elections with unconditionally-secret ballots and disruption equivalent to breaking RSA. In: Barstow, D., et al. (eds.) EUROCRYPT 1988. LNCS, vol. 330, pp. 177–182. Springer, Heidelberg (1988). https://doi.org/10.1007/3-540-45961-8_15

25. Chaum, D., Fiat, A., Naor, M.: Untraceable electronic cash. In: Goldwasser, S. (ed.) CRYPTO 1988. LNCS, vol. 403, pp. 319–327. Springer, New York (1990). https://doi.org/10.1007/0-387-34799-2_25

26. Chuengsatiansup, C., Prest, T., Stehlé, D., Wallet, A., Xagawa, K.: ModFalcon: compact signatures based on module-NTRU lattices. In: ASIACCS 2020, pp. 853–866 (2020)

27. del Pino, R., Lyubashevsky, V., Seiler, G.: Lattice-based group signatures and zero-knowledge proofs of automorphism stability. In: ACM CCS 2018, pp. 574–591 (2018)

28. Ducas, L., et al.: CRYSTALS-dilithium: a lattice-based digital signature scheme. IACR TCHES 1, 238–268 (2018)

29. Esgin, M.F., Nguyen, N.K., Seiler, G.: Practical exact proofs from lattices: new techniques to exploit fully-splitting rings. In: Moriai, S., Wang, H. (eds.) ASIACRYPT 2020, Part II. LNCS, vol. 12492, pp. 259–288. Springer, Cham (2020). https://doi.org/10.1007/978-3-030-64834-3_9

30. Esgin, M.F., Steinfeld, R., Liu, D., Ruj, S.: Efficient hybrid exact/relaxed lattice proofs and applications to rounding and VRFs. Cryptology ePrint Archive (2022)

31. Fischlin, M.: Round-optimal composable blind signatures in the common reference string model. In: Dwork, C. (ed.) CRYPTO 2006. LNCS, vol. 4117, pp. 60–77. Springer, Heidelberg (2006). https://doi.org/10.1007/11818175_4

32. Fujioka, A., Okamoto, T., Ohta, K.: A practical secret voting scheme for large scale elections. In: Seberry, J., Zheng, Y. (eds.) AUSCRYPT 1992. LNCS, vol. 718, pp. 244–251. Springer, Heidelberg (1993). https://doi.org/10.1007/3-540-57220-1_66

33. Garg, S., Rao, V., Sahai, A., Schröder, D., Unruh, D.: Round optimal blind signatures. In: Rogaway, P. (ed.) CRYPTO 2011. LNCS, vol. 6841, pp. 630–648. Springer, Heidelberg (2011). https://doi.org/10.1007/978-3-642-22792-9_36
34. Hauck, E., Kiltz, E., Loss, J., Nguyen, N.K.: Lattice-based blind signatures, revisited. In: Micciancio, D., Ristenpart, T. (eds.) CRYPTO 2020. LNCS, vol. 12171, pp. 500–529. Springer, Cham (2020). https://doi.org/10.1007/978-3-030-56880-1_18
35. Katsumata, S.: A new simple technique to bootstrap various lattice zero-knowledge proofs to QROM secure NIZKs. In: Malkin, T., Peikert, C. (eds.) CRYPTO 2021. LNCS, vol. 12826, pp. 580–610. Springer, Cham (2021). https://doi.org/10.1007/978-3-030-84245-1_20
36. Le, H.Q., Susilo, W., Khuc, T.X., Bui, M.K., Duong, D.H.: A blind signature from module latices. In: Dependable and Secure Computing (DSC), pp. 1–8. IEEE (2019)
37. Lyubashevsky, V.: Fiat-Shamir with aborts: applications to lattice and factoring-based signatures. In: Matsui, M. (ed.) ASIACRYPT 2009. LNCS, vol. 5912, pp. 598–616. Springer, Heidelberg (2009). https://doi.org/10.1007/978-3-642-10366-7_35
38. Lyubashevsky, V.: Lattice signatures without trapdoors. In: Pointcheval, D., Johansson, T. (eds.) EUROCRYPT 2012. LNCS, vol. 7237, pp. 738–755. Springer, Heidelberg (2012). https://doi.org/10.1007/978-3-642-29011-4_43
39. Lyubashevsky, V., Nguyen, N.K., Plancon, M.: Efficient lattice-based blind signatures via Gaussian one-time signatures. In: Hanaoka, G., Shikata, J., Watanabe, Y. (eds.) PKC 2022. LNCS, vol. 13178. Springer, Cham (2022). https://doi.org/10.1007/978-3-030-97131-1_17
40. Lyubashevsky, V., Nguyen, N.K., Plancon, M.: Lattice-based zero-knowledge proofs and applications: shorter, simpler, and more general. In: Dodis, Y., Shrimpton, T. (eds.) CRYPTO 2022, LNCS 13508, pp. xx–yy. Springer, Cham (2022)
41. Lyubashevsky, V., Nguyen, N.K., Seiler, G.: Shorter lattice-based zero-knowledge proofs via one-time commitments. In: Garay, J.A. (ed.) PKC 2021, Part I. LNCS, vol. 12710, pp. 215–241. Springer, Cham (2021). https://doi.org/10.1007/978-3-030-75245-3_9
42. Micciancio, D., Peikert, C.: Trapdoors for lattices: simpler, tighter, faster, smaller. In: Pointcheval, D., Johansson, T. (eds.) EUROCRYPT 2012. LNCS, vol. 7237, pp. 700–718. Springer, Heidelberg (2012). https://doi.org/10.1007/978-3-642-29011-4_41
43. Okamoto, T., Ohta, K.: Universal electronic cash. In: Feigenbaum, J. (ed.) CRYPTO 1991. LNCS, vol. 576, pp. 324–337. Springer, Heidelberg (1992). https://doi.org/10.1007/3-540-46766-1_27
44. Papachristoudis, D., Hristu-Varsakelis, D., Baldimtsi, F., Stephanides, G.: Leakage-resilient lattice-based partially blind signatures. Cryptology ePrint Archive, Report 2019/1452
45. Pointcheval, D., Stern, J.: Security arguments for digital signatures and blind signatures. J. Cryptol. **13**(3), 361–396 (2000)
46. Prest, T., et al.: Falcon: fast-Fourier lattice-based compact signatures over NTRU. Technical report (2018). https://falcon-sign.info/
47. Rückert, M.: Lattice-based blind signatures. In: Abe, M. (ed.) ASIACRYPT 2010. LNCS, vol. 6477, pp. 413–430. Springer, Heidelberg (2010). https://doi.org/10.1007/978-3-642-17373-8_24
48. Schnorr, C.P.: Security of blind discrete log signatures against interactive attacks. In: Qing, S., Okamoto, T., Zhou, J. (eds.) ICICS 2001. LNCS, vol. 2229, pp. 1–12. Springer, Heidelberg (2001). https://doi.org/10.1007/3-540-45600-7_1

49. Shoup, V., Gennaro, R.: Securing threshold cryptosystems against chosen cipher-text attack. In: Nyberg, K. (ed.) EUROCRYPT 1998. LNCS, vol. 1403, pp. 1–16. Springer, Heidelberg (1998). https://doi.org/10.1007/BFb0054113
50. Yi, X., Lam, K.-Y.: A new blind ECDSA scheme for bitcoin transaction anonymity. In: ASIACCS 2019, pp. 613–620 (2019)
51. Zhandry, M.: How to construct quantum random functions. In: 53rd FOCS, pp. 679–687 (2012)

Blockchain

Ofelimos: Combinatorial Optimization via Proof-of-Useful-Work
A Provably Secure Blockchain Protocol

Matthias Fitzi[1], Aggelos Kiayias[1,2], Giorgos Panagiotakos[1(✉)], and Alexander Russell[1,3]

[1] IOHK, Singapore, Singapore
{matthias.fitzi,giorgos.panagiotakos}@iohk.io
[2] University of Edinburgh, Edinburgh, UK
akiayias@inf.ed.ac.uk
[3] University of Connecticut, Storrs, USA
acr@cse.uconn.edu

Abstract. Minimizing the energy cost and carbon footprint of the Bitcoin blockchain and related protocols is one of the most widely identified open questions in the cryptocurrency space. Substituting the proof-of-work (PoW) primitive in Nakamoto's longest-chain protocol with a *proof of useful work* (PoUW) has been long theorized as an ideal solution in many respects but, to this day, the concept still lacks a convincingly secure realization.

In this work we put forth *Ofelimos*, a novel PoUW-based blockchain protocol whose consensus mechanism simultaneously realizes a decentralized optimization-problem solver. Our protocol is built around a novel local search algorithm, which we call Doubly Parallel Local Search (DPLS), that is especially crafted to suit implementation as the PoUW component of our blockchain protocol. We provide a thorough security analysis of our protocol and additionally present metrics that reflect the usefulness of the system. DPLS can be used to implement variants of popular local search algorithms such as WalkSAT that are used for real world combinatorial optimization tasks. In this way, our work paves the way for safely using blockchain systems as generic optimization engines for a variety of hard optimization problems for which a publicly verifiable solution is desired.

Keywords: Blockchain · consensus · proof-of-useful-work · stochastic local search

1 Introduction

Blockchain protocols based on Proof of Work (PoW) capitalize on computational work performed by protocol participants, called miners, to ensure the security of the maintained transaction ledger. In the most prominent Proof-of-Work blockchain designs, the work performed serves no other purpose besides

This work is based upon work supported by the National Science Foundation under Grant No. 1801487.

maintaining security. These protocols also combine permissionless participation with incentives, offering rewards to miners that commit computational effort to the protocol. This has led to an increasing global commitment of energy to systems like Bitcoin as the value of the currency has grown. At the time of this writing, Bitcoin has an annualized energy expenditure on par with many small to medium countries (see, e.g., the Cambridge Bitcoin Electricity Consumption Index, https://cbeci.org).

This trend was identified early on as an important concern in the Bitcoin ecosystem and motivated consideration of two major avenues for potential improvement to the underlying blockchain protocol. The first is aimed at replacing the PoW mechanism with an alternate resource lottery with potentially "greener" characteristics, e.g., proof of stake [14,23,31], proof of space [17,40], proof of space-time [37], and similar mechanisms. A common challenge faced by these approaches is to ensure that the security of the resulting scheme has not been eroded by the change in the underlying primitive (from "work" to something else). The second direction—which, in principle, could entirely ameliorate the issue and is the focus of this work—is to repurpose the invested computational effort towards solving real-world problems. This direction thus posits a proof-of-*useful*-work (PoUW) design approach for blockchain protocols.

Early designs and implementation attempts such as Noocoin [13] and Primecoin [32] highlighted the fundamental issue that would plague future progress towards a satisfactory PoUW system. If the work solved is sufficiently generic, then an attacker may direct the system towards solving problem instances that are easy for them (e.g., due to precomputation or other private advantages "hidden" in the underlying instance-space structure) and hence operate with an advantage in the underlying proof-of-work mechansim, threatening security. At the same time, minimizing the attacker's ability to manipulate the system by adopting more structured "useful" work may render the system's computations useless in practice (e.g., Primecoin [32] and Gapcoin [19] compute sequences of Cunningham primes and gaps between primes respectively—both mathematical objects of dubious usefulness).

1.1   Our Contributions

We propose the first PoUW-based blockchain protocol that is accompanied by a thorough security and usefulness analysis. Central to our construction is a novel general-purpose algorithm for *stochastic local search* called Doubly Parallel Local Search (DPLS). Our key technique for protocol design is to mold the whole blockchain protocol execution into a DPLS engine that demonstrably performs the steps of the algorithm in a publicly verifiable manner. The PoUW operation in our consensus protocol has the miners collectively run DPLS on instances contributed by interested clients. In more detail, our results are the following.

(I) Doubly Parallel Local Search (DPLS). We put forth a new algorithm for stochastic local search. With DPLS we achieve the following two-pronged objective: (i) The structural properties of the algorithm suitably reflect the stochastic dynamics of the underlying permissionless blockchain operation so that a blockchain execution can be viewed as a virtual machine running the algorithm; (ii) Stochastic local search is a powerful, well-studied, and generic algorithmic paradigm for solving computationally hard optimization problems. Thus the DPLS algorithm itself can be evaluated in the context of the broad family of existing stochastic local search algorithm variants and, in particular, assessed with respect to problems of high real-world value.

DPLS is a general-purpose stochastic local search algorithm based on an underlying algorithm M, called the *exploration algorithm*: Given a set of points in the solution space, M searches for a better solution via a local exploration process that requires a modicum of computational effort. (For example, M might call for a fixed number of steps of gradient descent at each input point.) Based on M, DPLS follows a "doubly" parallel search strategy where a number of paths are pursued in parallel, and in each path a number of exploration threads via M are executed; finally, the best one according to a scoring function is selected.

(II) Moderately Hard DAG Computations. To consider the possibility of using a DPLS solver within a proof-of-work setting, it is essential to articulate the conditions under which running the basic exploration algorithm M exhibits *moderate hardness* (MH). This property is the necessary requirement for a computational problem to be applicable in the blockchain setting. What makes the modeling more challenging compared to, say, the case of Bitcoin's PoW algorithm is that we cannot resort to an idealized model (such as the Random Oracle Model) and must express the moderate hardness property in a way that can be suitably utilized in the security arguments of the blockchain protocol.

To capture this and at the same time reflect the parallelizable nature of DPLS, we focus on the DAG-computation abstraction which has been widely used in the modeling of parallel computations (e.g., see [1,39]). In the setting of DPLS the main computational unit is the exploration algorithm M and we are principally interested in expressing the moderate hardness of DAG computations over M. The delicate part of this modeling is to express the advantage ϵ of the adversary over the honest parties as a function of its ability to "grind" the randomness of the DAG computation as well as capitalize on any advantage obtained from observing previously published steps in the computation.

(III) The PoUW-Based Blockchain Protocol. At a high level, our protocol calls for parties to post instances for problems of interest in the ledger, while locking funds denominated in the ledger's native token to incentivize miners to work towards solving them. Maintaining the blockchain translates to performing steps of the DPLS algorithm for the instances in the ledger and being rewarded for that—with foresight, we stress that solving such instances directly (or posting pre-solved instances) will not help an adversary in extending the ledger any faster. Problem posers can keep funding a particular DPLS computation whenever its funds are getting depleted.

The cornerstone of our protocol is its PoUW mechanism that operates in three stages. In the "pre-hash" stage, random strings are repeatedly generated and hashed until one is found that achieves a small hash (as in a standard PoW).

This string will constitute the random seed for the DPLS exploration algorithm M and will be useful for controlling "grinding attacks" in which an adversary attempts to force adoption of a random string that yields a comparatively easy computation. When the exploration stage terminates, a "post-hash" step determines with a single hash query whether the resulting value qualifies as a PoUW. This "sandwiching" of M between two small hashes is essential for security since it forces an adversarial miner to seed the computation with a randomly selected seed and learn that a successful block can be issued only after the exploration step M is complete. However, if we apply this idea naively (e.g., as a drop-in replacement to Bitcoin's PoW algorithm), there are three major disadvantages: first, a number of useful exploration steps will go to waste, since they won't lead to a block; second, adjusting the hardness of block production (which is needed for blockchain security) would impact usefulness (since miners will spend too much effort trying to find small hashes) and, finally, we do not want waste computational cycles by repeating M-computations to verify newly mined blocks.

We resolve these issues with three mechanisms. First, taking advantage of the scoring function, we have the miners publish the best value they have produced based on all their post-hash attempts; in this way, progress in the DPLS computation is not lost. Note that deviating from this strategy may only impact usefulness—the security of the protocol is maintained against any Byzantine deviation. Second, we adopt the 2-for-1 PoW mechanism of [20], which allows for the production of two types of blocks with a single hash attempt: either an "input block", in which case it is inserted in the blockchain as a transaction, or a "ranking block", which extends the blockchain and refers to any number of input blocks. Using this decoupling mechanism, we can keep the steady progress of the DPLS computation and adjust the underlying (ranking) block hardness independently. The crucial property this ensures is that as more miners join the protocol the DPLS computation is sped up proportionally; on the other hand, ranking block production can be kept steady as required for the security of the underlying blockchain protocol. In this way, the more real-world useful problem instances are submitted to the system (as evidenced by the increased funding locked with each one and the platform's native token appreciation), the more computational power will be introduced to the DPLS engine to solve them. Finally, instead of requiring verification to repeat the computations of M, block producers issue a suitable *succinct non-interactive argument of knowledge* (SNARG) (see, e.g., [24]), so that verifier complexity becomes independent of M.

We prove our protocol secure under a standard "honest majority" assumption reminiscent of the Bitcoin protocol analysis, where the distance above $1/2$ depends, among other parameters, on "moderate hardness advantage" ϵ. (We note that even if $\epsilon = 1$, which is to say that we have no moderate hardness guarantees at all, our protocol remains secure with a bound close to $3/4$).

As a final remark, our security treatment must additionally contend with a novel probabilistic challenge. In particular, a fundamental assumption adopted by previous proof-of-work analyses is absent: the guarantee that miners' proof-of-work victories are given by independent Poisson (or "discrete Poisson") processes. In our setting, the process by which miners produce proofs of work is given by a non-trivial Markov chain reflecting the features described above: e.g., pre-hashing, useful work computation, post-hashing, and SNARG computation. Furthermore, adversarial miners are under no obligation to follow the Markov chain; for example, they may restart the process when they choose. (From this perspective, the classical analysis can be viewed as a chain with a single "mining" state with two transitions, one corresponding to a failed mining attempt—which simply carries the chain back to the same mining state—and one corresponding to a successful mining attempt.) This complex mining model even poses significant challenges for the analysis of honest players because honest players' states in the chain may be synchronized by various events (such as the beginning of the protocol or, depending on the details of the algorithm, delivery of a new block). Unfortunately, such synchronization is a direct threat to the production of desirable "uniquely honest" time periods, during which a unique honest miner generates a proof of work. Such uniquely honest time periods are an emblematic ingredient in the consistency of such systems (see, e.g., [30] where this is explored in detail). To manage these correlations in the model, we consider the aggregate Markov chain carried out by (all) the honest players and establish that when the parameters of the chain are under suitable control—essentially, that the "Poisson" parts of the chain "dominate" the other parts of the chain corresponding to useful work and SNARG computation—the chain converges very rapidly to the ideal distribution where each honest participant is in an independent stationary distribution. We then apply the recurrence-time properties of the stationary distribution along with standard tail bounds for independent random variables to bound the events of interest. This is then leveraged to establish the stochastic properties necessary for consistency. We remark that our techniques here are quite general, and could be applied to quite complex "mining chains," so long as they have a sufficiently substantial "Poisson part" (corresponding to standard proof-of-work discovery). In particular, the techniques can be applied to a generic mining problem—even one with very little variance in time to completion—so long as it is followed by a sufficiently difficult proof of work.

(IV) Usefulness Metrics. We devise a two-pronged approach to measuring usefulness. Recall first that our blockchain protocol can be thought as a decentralized DPLS solver. The first usefulness metric asks how good is the blockchain execution as a DPLS engine. This can be done by measuring the ratio per unit of time of the number of steps that the blockchain protocol spends in DPLS computations compared to its total number of steps. We call this metric U_{eng}, as it can be thought to capture the efficiency of the blockchain protocol as an "engine" that runs DPLS. The second metric, denoted U_{alg}, reflects how useful DPLS computations are themselves. For a given instance distribution we define this metric as the ratio between the expected number of steps of the best algorithm for that instance distribution divided by the expected number of steps that DPLS takes. Note that identifying the best algorithm for a problem is typically infeasible based on current state of the art, so in this case the best algorithm can be simply substituted with the best *known* algorithm for the problem at hand.

Combining the above two metrics, we can obtain, as an overall metric of usefulness, the product $U_{eng} \cdot U_{alg}$. The key advantage of our two-pronged approach is that we can completely characterize U_{eng} with protocol analysis, while U_{alg} is an empirical metric that must be assessed in the context of a specific class of problems.

To conclude the discussion on usefulness metrics, we mention that for our protocol it holds that (i) $U_{eng} \leq 1/2$, which stems from the fact that we balance the pre-hash probability of success to require the same effort as the worst-case time complexity of M—this enables us to prove security for any advantage ϵ in the underlying MH assumption; and (ii) U_{eng} will be close to $1/2$ if M's runtime distribution is sufficiently concentrated and the rate at which blocks are produced is sufficiently small compared to the SNARG cost. We note that the $1/2$ bound can be surpassed by taking into account the sensitivity of ϵ and adaptively setting the pre-hash difficulty, however such a direction would be only feasible if we restrict the class of exploration algorithms M to those whose hardness is well understood. Estimating U_{alg} requires some real-world baseline – as an illustrative example we choose Walk-SAT [28,43], a popular local search algorithm for satisfiability problems. Given this choice, U_{alg} would result from comparing how the DPLS implementation fares with respect to running WalkSAT in isolation. Exploring this direction further goes outside the scope of the present paper but we give some insights in the full version of the paper [18]. It is worth noting that the instance distribution would be an important consideration in this analysis; for illustrative purposes in the full version of the paper, we use *Blocks World Planning*, a well known NP-hard problem in AI [26] for which there is an abundance of public data sets. Using WalkSAT as the baseline, we show that a single-thread implementation of DPLS performs reasonably well against WalkSAT, investing about twice as much computational steps, i.e., something that amounts to an estimation of $U_{alg} \approx 1/2$. Similar results are obtained from additional experiments that reflect adversarial deviations and the effect of parallelization.

The above results are evidence for the non-negligible real-world usefulness of our PoUW-based blockchain protocol. We anticipate that investigating further the DPLS blockchain engine as an optimization solver will be an exciting research direction from an algorithmic perspective. There is yet another beneficial dimension of using our blockchain protocol as a DPLS solver: optimization is executed collaboratively in a publicly verifiable manner. Depending on the task, public verifiability has intrinsic usefulness and this can be seen as the price the system pays for the remaining ratio $1 - U_{eng} \cdot U_{alg}$. For instance, optimization tasks such as athletic-competition tournament scheduling or various matching problems (e.g., the allocation of residents to hospitals or radio frequency auctions) can benefit from public verifiability; see the full version of the paper [18] for further discussion and references.

1.2   Related Work

Beyond the early work mentioned above [13,19,32], a number of other works investigated the concept. One line of research considered hybrid constructions where the miner can choose between applying either standard PoW *or* doing some potentially useful computation [11, 38, 45]. Further constructions for PoUW mining were given by Loe et al. [34], Dotan et al. [16], and, closer to our work, Baldominos et al. [7] and Lihu et al. [33], who suggested to base PoUW on stochastic search and machine-learning problems. In all these previous approaches the security of the system was not rigorously analyzed and, in many cases, concrete attacks by e.g., an adversary who directly plants easy instances to solve, are feasible.

In contrast to the above, a formal security approach was adopted by [8] but the published version of the work retracted the "usefulness" dimension of the original paper. Also, their proof-of-work construction is not suited for permissionless ledgers as it does not introduce any variance in puzzle-completion time.

Finally, some alternative approaches to the problem at hand that are worth mentioning in our context are the concept of "merged mining", a technique employed in a number of cryptocurrencies where the mining effort for the blockchain has a dual use as mining Bitcoin and hence it is "useful" in this sense: Permacoin [36] where, via proofs of retrievability, the usefulness dimension is in maintaining a public file store; and useful work enforced via a trusted execution environment [44] where, in contrast to the above solutions, full trust in a specific hardware manufacturer is required.

We stress that, to the best of our knowledge, no prior fully decentralized, PoUW-based blockchain protocol has been published along with a thorough security (or usefulness) analysis.

1.3 Organization of the Paper

In Sect. 2 we describe the computational model and some basic notation. DPLS is presented in Sect. 3. Next, we expand on our notion of moderately hard DAG computations in Sect. 4. In Sect. 5 we present our blockchain protocol, whose security and usefulness we analyze in Sect. 6. Applications and experimental results, as well as some of the code and proofs are presented in the full version of the paper [18].

2 Preliminaries

Notation. For $k \in \mathbb{N}^+$, $[k]$ denotes the set $\{1, \ldots, k\}$. We denote sequences by $(a_i)_{i \in I}$, where I is a countable index set. For a set X, $x \leftarrow X$ denotes sampling an element from X uniformly at random. For a distribution $\mathcal{U}$ over a set X, $x \leftarrow \mathcal{U}$ denotes sampling an element of X according to $\mathcal{U}$. By $\mathcal{U}_m$ we denote the uniform distribution over $\{0, 1\}^m$. We denote that some function f is negligible in λ by $f(\lambda) < negl(\lambda)$. We let λ denote the security parameter.

Security Model. We adopt the computational model of [21], which is a variant of the model presented in [20]. There, the set of parties $\{P_1, \ldots, P_n\}$ running the protocol is fixed and the parties, the environment $\mathcal{Z}$, the adversary $\mathcal{A}$, and the control program $\mathcal{C}$ coordinating the execution are all modeled as IRAMs. The adversary $\mathcal{A}$ is active and can corrupt up to t parties in order to break security.

Communication Model. We follow the communication model used by most previous works [6, 41] that analyze blockchain protocols in the cryptographic setting, where time is discrete and the network is (partially) synchronous. In more detail, the protocol advances in rounds and communication happens through a diffusion functionality. Honest parties can use it to send messages which may be adaptively delayed for up to Δ rounds by the adversary, but are guaranteed to be received by everyone in the network. Communication is not authenticated, in the sense that the functionality does not provide any guarantees regarding the origin of sent messages. Finally, the adversary is rushing and can additionally choose to send its own messages only to a subset of the parties.

Setup. All parties have access to a *common reference string* (CRS), sampled from a known efficiently samplable distribution, which is used to instantiate a succinct non-interactive argument (SNARG) system [24] SNARG $=$ (S, P, V). Note that there are several ways to securely establish a CRS for a SNARG in a permissionless blockchain environment. In particular, assuming the slightly stronger notion of an updatable *structured reference string* (SRS) [25, 35], the construction of [29] allows to obtain a common reference string.

Random Oracle. Parties have access to a random-oracle (RO) functionality [9]. We use both RO and non-RO based moderately hard problems and, in order to argue about security, we need to be able to compare their computational costs. We thus assume that a query to RO takes c_H computational steps both for the honest parties and the adversary.

Concrete Modeling. $\mathcal{A}$ and $\mathcal{Z}$ have a concrete bound of $t \cdot c_H$ steps they can take per round as well as an upper bound θ on the number of messages they can send per round.

3   Doubly Parallel Local Search

One approach to designing a PoUW blockchain for optimization problems is to: (i) first pick your favorite optimization algorithm, and then (ii) try to design a blockchain protocol around it. The disadvantage of such an approach is that any change in the target optimization problem may result in vital changes to the blockchain and consensus system, requiring new security proofs. Here, instead, we adopt a modular approach where we first build a PoUW blockchain based on a generic optimization algorithm, and later, with minimal overhead, instantiate it with the problem-specific parameters. This allows for re-using our blockchain analysis for different instantiations of the optimization algorithm.

We start by giving an overview of DPLS, the generic optimization algorithm that our blockchain protocol is implementing from a client's point of view, i.e., ignoring the internal details of the blockchain algorithm.

3.1 Overview

Clients of our protocol publish on the blockchain the optimization problems that they want miners to solve. Miners, on the other hand, run the Doubly Parallel Local Search (DPLS) algorithm to solve these problems. Solving large optimization problems may require more work than what can be computed by a miner during the mining of a single block. Thus, we design DPLS to be a *distributed algorithm* where the computation result is obtained by multiple state updates – each corresponding to a block –, some of them possibly occurring concurrently. Concurrent updates is the first source of parallelism of DPLS.

In its core, DPLS follows the well-known *stochastic local search* approach: it searches a solution space X by repeatedly exploring the neighborhood of a currently selected point, looking for a neighboring point that promises progress towards an optimal solution. More concretely, based on the description of a problem instance Λ, DPLS gradually builds a directed acyclic graph (DAG) G recording the already explored points in X. A single exploration step then consists of invoking a *generic* exploration algorithm M on G, yielding a new point in X, with the goal of extending G by a point of better quality (computed by a scoring algorithm g_Λ), thereby progressing the exploration. Note that, in a strictly sequential execution, a 'linear' graph G may be sufficient. However, maintaining a DAG of explored points allows for more general flavors of local search where multiple threads are concurrently explored by different parties.

As communication and local pre-computation are important resources in permissionless systems, we cannot afford to publish every exploration step computed by miners. Instead, each miner performs many *randomized* local exploration steps in a batch, publishing only the best one of them. To this end, the exploration algorithm M is parametrized by an *inner state* z that determines the initial state of the search in a batch, e.g., a common starting location in G to focus the batched search, and a randomness seed r ensuring that same-batch steps are independent. Batched search is the second source of parallelism of our doubly parallel algorithm.

Given the above, DPLS is parametrized by the following *problem-specific* sub-algorithms:

- *Initialization* algorithm $\mathsf{Init}(\Lambda)$: A probabilistic algorithm that takes as input an instance description Λ and outputs a DAG G.
- *Focus* algorithm $\mathsf{F}(\Lambda, G)$: A probabilistic algorithm that takes as input Λ, G and outputs an inner-state string z.
- *Exploration* algorithm $M_\Lambda(G, z, r)$: A deterministic algorithm that takes as input a DAG G, an inner state z, and a seed r, and outputs a point $x \in X$.
- *Scoring* algorithm $g_\Lambda(x)$: A deterministic algorithm that takes as input Λ and $x \in X$, and outputs the score $y \in \mathbb{R}$ of x.
- *Termination* algorithm $\mathsf{Finished}(\Lambda, G)$: A deterministic algorithm that takes as input Λ, G and outputs 1 if the algorithm has finished, and 0 otherwise.

3.2 DPLS Modeled in a Blockchain Setting

Problem solving starts by the problem setter posting an instance description Λ together with the output of $\mathsf{Init}(\Lambda)$ in the blockchain, in the form of a special transaction. Miners work on such an instance by running the UPDATE procedure (Algorithm 1), which makes use of the sub-algorithms introduced above. The outputs produced are posted to the blockchain and are in turn used by other parties to produce additional updates. The search algorithm ends when predicate $\mathsf{Finished}(\Lambda, G)$ becomes true.

UPDATE takes as inputs the chosen instance description Λ and the party's current view of the DAG G. The inner state z is generated using algorithm $\mathsf{F}(\Lambda, G)$, while the number of invocations of M in a single batch, denoted by k, is distributed according to the geometric distribution, with the exact parameters of the distribution set by the protocol designer. The sampling of k from the geometric distribution models its integration into the useful-work mining procedure where each computation of M qualifies for block production with probability p_2—the miner must find a block to publish a state update. After k is fixed, that many seeds $(r_i)_{i \in [k]}$ are sampled independently at random, and algorithm $M(G, z, r_i)$ is invoked k times, with the best-scoring result (according to function g) being output by UPDATE.

Algorithm 1. The state update procedure.

---

function UPDATE(Λ, G)

$\quad z \leftarrow \mathsf{F}(\Lambda, G)$ ▷ Compute the inner state

$\quad k \leftarrow Geom(p_2)$ ▷ Sample from geometric

$\quad (r_i)_{i \in [k]} \leftarrow \mathcal{U}_m^k$ ▷ Sample uniformly

$\quad S := \{(z, r_i, x_i) | x_i := M(G, z, r_i), i \in [k]\}$ ▷ Invoke M

$\quad (z, r, x) := \arg\max_{(z,r,x) \in S} g(x)$ ▷ Pick best

$\quad$ **return** (z, r, x)

3.3 An Example

We present an instantiation of DPLS (Init, F, M, g, $\mathsf{Finished}$) for a variant of the classical WalkSAT algorithm [28,43] for the SAT problem.

First, we give a summary of the original WalkSAT algorithm. Starting from some initial configuration, at each step, WalkSAT picks a variable to flip as follows: Given the current configuration, one of the unsatisfied clauses is chosen at random. For each of the variables involved in the clause, a grade is computed which is equal to the number of clauses that are going to be broken (i.e., turn from satisfied to unsatisfied) if the chosen variable is flipped. If there exist variables that have grade 0, then one of them is selected at random and flipped. Otherwise, a variable is selected (and flipped) at random, with probability wp coming from the selected clause, and with probability $1 - wp$ coming from the variables with the best grade. The walk continues until a solution is found, or some other condition is met, e.g., an upper bound on the total number of flips is reached. If no solution is found, the algorithm can be restarted from some other point in the solution space.

In the DPLS variant, the instance description Λ encodes the description of the SAT instance, i.e., the number of variables and the different clauses, with the solution space X being equal to the possible configurations of the SAT variables. Init(Λ), to aid parallelization, outputs a number of different initial configurations in X. In each invocation of UPDATE, miners run function F to pick at random which point/configuration in G to work on and encode this information in z. Given this configuration, exploration algorithm $M(G, z, r)$ is set to run WalkSAT for a fixed number of flips. Note, that the starting configuration is the same for the different runs of M in a single UPDATE invocation, allowing miners to focus their search. On the other hand, the randomness used by the different WalkSAT invocations comes from the respective seeds (r), leading to the exploration of different points in the solution space. To choose the best one among these points, g counts the number of satisfied clauses in the respective ending configurations. Hence, UPDATE outputs the configuration that maximizes g, which is then possibly going to be used by another miner as the starting point of another run of UPDATE. The algorithm terminates after a predefined number of updates have been posted. For the detailed code and the experimental evaluation of the performance of this algorithm, we point the reader to the full version of the paper [18].

3.4 Generality of the Approach

Most well-known stochastic-local-search (SLS) algorithms [27] can be mapped to DPLS as follows: The Init function provides the initial information needed, e.g., a number of different starting locations for parallel search. Given the current location, M is set to explore a single location in its neighborhood and any randomness needed is provided by the seed. Consequently, UPDATE can be interpreted as exploring different points in the neighborhood, and then returning the one that maximizes the scoring function. This point can then serve as the next point in the search. We expect better performance when the total neighborhood size is sufficiently large, such that miners do not explore the same points due to desynchronization and the fact that the points searched are randomly determined. A subclass of SLS algorithms that has this characteristic is Very Large Scale Neighborhood search algorithms [2], where the algorithm (partially) searches a very large neighborhood before making its next step. We provide more evidence about the generality and possible real world applications of DPLS in the full version of the paper [18].

4   Moderately Hard DAG Computations

In DPLS, most of the work is spent running the exploration algorithm M. Hence, it is natural to base security on the moderate hardness of this computation. We next describe in detail the syntax and relevant security properties required for its use in a PoUW protocol.

4.1   Syntax

As explained earlier, an important aspect of DPLS is that state updates are performed in a distributed way, and without much coordination. Based on this observation, we adopt a DAG structure for computations involving M, where each computation corresponds to a vertex on the DAG and depends on multiple previous vertices. Our notion generalizes the iterated computation paradigm [10, 22], where each computation depends on a single vertex.

We note that the parameters of the computation performed will be possibly influenced by the adversary, in the sense that he may try to post a client problem to be solved, only with the purpose of subverting the underlying blockchain protocol. As the security of the blockchain depends on the hardness of individual computations of M, we must guarantee that they remain moderately hard even when parameters are chosen maliciously.

Taking into account these considerations, new vertices of the DAG are generated based on the current view, an inner-state string, and, an unpredictable seed. As explained earlier, the inner-state string allows parties to focus their work in the context of DPLS. On the other hand, the seed randomizes the computation to force the adversary to do work of average-case complexity—in contrast to possibly selecting "cheap" instances to gain an advantage in block production. Next, we formally introduce the notion of a DAG computation.

Definition 1. *(DAG computation/transcript.) A DAG computation is a sequence of instance descriptions $\mathcal{I} = (\Lambda_\lambda)_\lambda$. For every value of the security parameter $\lambda \in \mathbb{N}$, an instance description Λ specifies:*

1. *a finite, non-empty set Z (inner state);*
2. *a finite, non-empty set X (output);*
3. *a deterministic verification algorithm V; and*
4. *a deterministic exploration algorithm M.*

A transcript of a DAG computation Λ corresponds to a labeled DAG G where each vertex in G is labeled with a tuple $(z, r, x) \in Z \times \{0,1\}^\lambda \times X$ (edges have no labels). We say that G is valid if and only if $V(G) = 1$.

Additionally, the following conditions are satisfied:

- *(closure) if G and G' are valid, then $G \cup G'$ is also valid[1];*
- *(correctness) for a valid G and $x \leftarrow M(G, z, r)$, it holds that $G \oplus (z, r, x)$ is valid, where $G \oplus (z, r, x)$ denotes the transcript resulting by adding a vertex with label (z, r, x) to G that is connected to all other vertices.*

We write $\Lambda[Z, X, V, M]$ to indicate that Λ specifies Z, X, V, M as above.

---

[1] Closure ensures that concurrently extending a transcript does not break validity.

We require that the instance descriptions, as well as the elements of the sets Z, X, can be uniquely encoded as bit strings of length polynomial in λ. For simplicity, we will sometimes denote by V_Λ, M_Λ the algorithms corresponding to instance description Λ.

4.2   Moderate Hardness

Next, we introduce a moderate-hardness (MH) notion for DAG computations. Our notion builds on ideas found in [21,22]. On a high level, we require that the time the adversary takes to generate a given number of new vertexes in the DAG, is proportional to their number.

We proceed to describe the security experiment in more detail. Let t be equal to the *worst-case complexity* of M. The adversary has access to three oracles $\mathcal{O}, \mathcal{M}, \mathcal{V}$. Its goal is to compute m new vertices for seeds generated at random from oracle $\mathcal{O}$ in less than $(1 - \epsilon) \cdot mt$ steps, where ϵ reflects the advantage of the adversary compared to M. The adversary is allowed to query oracle $\mathcal{O}$ more than m times, and possibly use oracles $\mathcal{M}$ and $\mathcal{V}$ to simulate new honestly computed vertexes and verify whether a DAG computation is valid, respectively. ϵ is parameterized by the respective rates of queries $q_\mathcal{O}/m, q_\mathcal{M}/m, q_\mathcal{V}/m$ to reflect the possible adversarial advantage. We note, that oracles $\mathcal{M}$ and $\mathcal{V}$ are provided to aid composition;[2] We require that the property holds with overwhelming probability for all m greater than some parameter k.

As we want to build a blockchain that can accommodate solving multiple optimization problems, MH is expressed w.r.t. a family of DAG computations (per security parameter level), each corresponding to a different instantiation of the DPLS algorithm.

Definition 2. *Let $\mathcal{I} = ((\Lambda_{\lambda,i})_i)_\lambda$ be a family of DAG computations. $\mathcal{I}$ is (t, ϵ, k)-Moderately Hard (MH) if for any PPT RAM $\mathcal{A} = (\mathcal{A}_1, \mathcal{A}_2)$, $\lambda \in \mathbb{N}$, and all polynomially large $m \geq k$, it holds that the adversary wins with probability $\mathsf{negl}(\lambda)$ in $\mathrm{Exp}_{\mathcal{A}, \mathcal{I}, \epsilon, t}^{MH}(1^\lambda, m)$*

$$
\left\{
\begin{array}{l}
st \leftarrow \mathcal{A}_1(1^\lambda); ((\Lambda_i, G_i, z_i, r_i, x_i))_{i \in [m]} \leftarrow \mathcal{A}_2^{\mathcal{O}, \mathcal{V}, \mathcal{M}}(st); \\[4pt]
b_1 := \mathsf{Steps}_{\mathcal{A}_2^{\mathcal{O}, \mathcal{M}, \mathcal{V}}}(1^\lambda, st) < (1 - \epsilon(\dfrac{q_\mathcal{O}}{m}, \dfrac{q_\mathcal{V}}{m}, \dfrac{q_\mathcal{M}}{m}))m \cdot t; \\[8pt]
b_2 := \bigwedge_{i=1}^{m} ((G_i, z_i, r_i) \in Q_\mathcal{O} \wedge V_{\Lambda_i}(G_i \oplus (z_i, r_i, x_i)) = 1); \\[4pt]
return\ b_1 \wedge b_2
\end{array}
\right\}
$$

where $q_\mathcal{O}$ queries are made to oracle $\mathcal{O}(\Lambda, G, z) = \{r \leftarrow \{0, 1\}^\lambda; return\ r\}$, $q_\mathcal{V}$ queries are made to oracle

$$
\mathcal{V}(\Lambda, G, z) = \{if\ V_\Lambda(G) = 0,\ then\ return\ 0,\ else\ return\ 1\},
$$

---

[2] In the blockchain setting, the adversary sees blocks generated by other parties, simulated by oracle $\mathcal{M}$, and sends out blocks that other parties may drop or adopt depending on whether they are valid, simulated by oracle $\mathcal{V}$.

and $q_{\mathcal{M}}$ queries are made to oracle

$$\mathcal{M}(\Lambda, G, z) = \left\{ \begin{array}{l} \textit{if } V_\Lambda(G) = 0, \textit{ then return } \bot \\ \textit{else, } r \leftarrow \{0,1\}^\lambda; \textit{ return } (r, M_\Lambda(G, z, r), \mathsf{Steps}_{M_\Lambda}(G, z, r)) \end{array} \right\}.$$

Remark 1. For simplicity, in the MH experiment the adversary ($\mathcal{A}_2$) is given the power to select the DAG transcript it wants to extend (G_i). However we do not want this to be an impediment on its running time in case (a part of) G_i is already defined in the output of $\mathcal{A}_1$; for this reason we will allow $\mathcal{A}_2$ to also determine G_i implicitly by referencing the output of $\mathcal{A}_1$.

Finally, we argue that for any MH DAG computation the speed-up the adversary gets by seeing extra problem instances is bounded. Looking forward, we note that this property will be the cornerstone for the protection of our protocol against grinding attacks. The main idea is that if an attacker $\mathcal{A}$ could get a speed-up on performing DAG computations due to seeing extra problem instances, then we would be able to construct another attacker $\mathcal{A}'$ that could break MH by initially running $\mathcal{A}$ and then performing any remaining "unsolved but queried" DAG computations using M. In the language developed above, extra instances are modeled as extra queries to oracle $\mathcal{O}$, while the adversarial speed-up can be captured by the adversarial advantage difference $\epsilon(1 + a, b, c)$ from $\epsilon(1, b, c)$, where a is the percentage of extra queries. We point to the full version of the paper for the formal proof of the lemma.

Lemma 1. *Let $\mathcal{I}$ be a family of DAG computations that is (t, ϵ, k)-MH. Then, $\mathcal{I}$ is also is (t, ϵ', k)-MH, where for any $a \geq 0, b, c$: $\epsilon'(1 + a, b, c) := \epsilon(1, b, c) + a$*

Remark 2. It is important to note that (t, ϵ, k)-moderate hardness, for reasonable parameters, is not achievable for all families of DAG computations. To illustrate this, consider a family of DAG computations allowing for an instance to be crafted in the following way: a key pair of a trapdoor permutation is generated by the adversary, the public key is embedded in the instance, and the exploration algorithm M is designed such that it implies computing the pre-image of a random nonce. Clearly, such a DAG computation would not be moderately hard in any reasonable way.

Still, moderate hardness seems to be a reasonable assumption for a large class of computations with sufficiently simple exploration and verification algorithms, e.g., for the core randomized search computation of stochastic local search algorithms [27]. The adversary now can still craft problems trying to gain computational advantage in the DAG computation, but the unpredictability of the randomness seed can help to mitigate this effect to a large extent.

Having given an outline of the DPLS optimization algorithm as well as the necessary vocabulary for moderate hardness, we proceed to present Ofelimos, the PoUW blockchain protocol, which builds on the moderate hardness of a generic useful computation to implement both DPLS and a transaction ledger.

5   The PoUW Blockchain Protocol

5.1   Protocol Description

We start, by listing a number of (informal) requirements that any protocol implementing DPLS must satisfy to qualify as a candidate protocol for useful-work mining. We then describe our protocol while motivating the design choices by these requirements. The requirements are motivated from both sides: blockchain security, as well as, efficiency of the DPLS algorithm:

1. Blockchain security:
   (a) No grinding: the adversary cannot gain mining advantage by cherry-picking DPLS exploration steps of low complexity.
   (b) Precomputation resilience: problem instances cannot be adversarially manufactured such that the adversary gains access to faster block production. Computation before seeing the head of the chain to be extended cannot contribute towards computing the respective PoUW.
   (c) Adjustable mining difficulty: The block difficulty can be adjusted to the mining power applied by the network.
2. DPLS efficiency:
   (a) Frequent updates: Results about new points explored are published (relatively) fast.
   (b) Small overhead: The computational overhead of integrating exploration algorithm M into PoUW is small (implying that honest mining performs useful work).

The high-level architecture of the protocol is similar to Bitcoin, i.e., blocks are chained together by referencing each other by hash, and, during each round, a miner selects the longest chain from his view, and tries to extend it by a block. Two modifications are applied: standard PoW is replaced by PoUW, and we apply 2-for-1 PoW [20] in order to accommodate different types of blocks for reasons explained below. See Fig. 1 for further reference.

The core of the mining algorithm consists of applying the exploration algorithm M, constituting the 'useful part' of the PoUW. To defend against precomputation (Requirement 1a), the computation of M is prepended by hashing the candidate block (first $\mathcal{H}$ box in Fig. 1), thereby randomizing the computation to be performed by M. Similarly to Nakamoto consensus, this 'pre-hash' of the block must lie below an initial target T_1, to antagonize grinding for parameters of M that result in lower-than-average computation complexity: resampling new parameters must be more expensive than the worst-case complexity of M.

By Requirement 1c, the mining-success probability must be reduced below the success probability of hashing against T_1—which is fully determined by the computational characteristics of the problem instance and unrelated to mining participation in the network. One possibility to address this issue would be to further lower the target T_1 to make pre-hashing as hard as required for ledger security; however, this would come against a big loss in usefulness, as miners would spend most of their time performing hashing. Instead, we have the miner

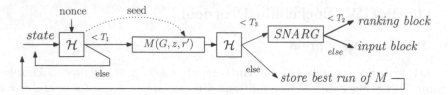

Fig. 1. Diagram of the PoUW mining procedure.

feed the output of M into one *single* round of 'post-hashing' (see second $\mathcal{H}$ box in the figure) that decides, against a threshold T_3, whether the block is eligible for publication. This second threshold adjusts the overall mining difficulty to a level required by the security analysis to guarantee good and secure blockchain characteristics. Note the additional effect of post-hashing to adapt mining difficulty: the miner only learns whether a PoUW attempt is successful *after* executing M, i.e., the computation cannot be cut short to speed up block creation.

A miner loops, many times, the computation sequence of pre-hashing (against T_1), useful work, and one post-hash, until the post-hash of a sequence lies below T_3, allowing for the block to be published. To preserve progress, the best point (by means of scoring algorithm g) from all recent computation sequences is stored for eventual inclusion in a future block to be published. Note that finding a *good* new point is decoupled from mining success, thus helping to establish Requirement 1b. Furthermore, only publishing the best one from a batch of new points, rather than greedily publishing all of them incrementally, helps to accommodate Requirement 2b.

Considering Requirement 2a under Bitcoin parameters, we cannot afford that a miner waits with his update until he mines a block. For this reason, we incorporate 2-for-1 PoW to allow for the publication of different types of blocks, so-called *ranking blocks* which are 'standard' Bitcoin blocks of high difficulty (target T_2), and so-called *input blocks* of low difficulty (target T_3, i.e., hash range $T_2 < h \leq T_3$) which are not part of the chain but are rather handled like transactions to be eventually referenced by a ranking block. A miner now includes his best point explored whenever he hits either type of a block; and by setting the input-block difficulty low enough, the update rate per miner is high enough to distribute progress in the explored points fast, while having no considerable impact on the blockchain characteristics.

A block contains two points explored using M: the 'winner' one that lead to the small post-hash, and the 'best' one that is included to progress the DPLS algorithm. In order to accommodate 2b, we minimize the cost of block verification by having the miner append a SNARG proving correctness of both exploration points contributing to the block, i.e., a SNARG proving membership to the following language: $L = \{((\Lambda, G, z, r', x'), (\Lambda_b, G_b, z_b, r'_b, x'_b))|V_\Lambda(G \oplus (z, r', x')) = 1 \wedge V_{\Lambda_b}(G_b \oplus (z_b, r'_b, x'_b)) = 1\}$, where $G \oplus (z, r', x')$ denotes the graph G extended with vertex (z, r', x') as defined in Sect. 4.

A detailed description of the PoUW procedure is given in Algorithm 2. The mining algorithm is parametrized by the longest blockchain received $\mathcal{C}$, the message to be included in the block m, the problem instance Λ selected by the miner to work on,[3] the related transcript G extracted from $\mathcal{C}$, and the selected inner state z. The pre-hash input includes these parameters, the hash of the previous block s, and a random nonce r; and yields a unique seed r' for M. At this point, all parameters of M, Λ, G, z, and r', are fully determined based on the data initially hashed, thus establishing that each small pre-hash found by the adversary can only be used to perform one matching post-hash attempt. We note that if, in a round, a miner does not have enough steps to finish running the PoUW procedure, e.g., he only manages to find a small pre-hash, he continues the next round from the point it stopped.

Algorithm 2. The PoUW procedure is parameterized by hardness parameters $T_1, T_2, T_3 \in \mathbb{N}$, the SNARG system, hash function $H(\cdot)$, the explore algorithm M, and scoring algorithm g.

1: var $(score_b, \Lambda_b, st_b, com) := (\infty, \bot, \bot, \bot)$ ▷ Best attempt - global variables
2: var $z := \bot$ ▷ Inner state
3:
4: **function** PoUW($\mathcal{C}, m, \Lambda, G$)
5:      $s := H(head(\mathcal{C}))$
6:      **if** $(\Lambda \neq \Lambda_b)$ **then** $z \leftarrow \mathsf{F}(\Lambda, G)$ ▷ Reset inner state
7:      $r \leftarrow \mathcal{U}_\lambda$ ▷ Sample nonce
8:      $h := H(s, m, com, \Lambda, G, z, r)$
9:      **if** $(h < T_1)$ **then**   ▷ Pre-hash
10:          $r' := H(h)$ ▷ Seed
11:          $x' := M_\Lambda(G, z, r')$ ▷ DAG computation
12:          $h' := H(r', x')$
13:          **if** $(h' < T_3)$ **then**   ▷ Post-hash
14:              $st := (s, m, com, \Lambda, G, z, r, x')$
15:              $\pi := \text{SNARG.P}(\Sigma, (st, st_b))$;   ▷ Correctness proof
16:              $B := \langle st, st_b, \pi \rangle$
17:              **if** $(h' < T_2)$ **then** $\mathcal{C} = \mathcal{C}B$ ▷ New ranking block
18:              **else** DIFFUSE($(input, B)$)   ▷ New input block
19:              $(score_b, \Lambda_b, st_b, com) := (\infty, \bot, \bot, \bot)$ ▷ Reset best attempt
20:          **else**
21:              **if** $((\Lambda \neq \Lambda_b)$ or $(g_\Lambda(x') > score_b))$ **then**   ▷ New best found
22:                  $(score_b, \Lambda_b, st_b, com) := (g_\Lambda(x'), \Lambda, st, H(st_b))$
23:      **return** $\mathcal{C}$

Moreover, ranking blocks are also treated as input blocks, and can be included in the payload of other ranking blocks. As in [20], an input block can be included in the payload of different ranking blocks in diverging chains, which ensures that

---

[3] Even if there are no problem instances posted by clients on the blockchain, e.g., during bootstrapping, miners can always generate a MH problem based on the hash of the block they are extending (a fixed-time hash-based PoW ([4,12]) is sufficient for this purpose). This amounts to a 'fall-back' DPLS computation.

all input blocks mined by an honest party will eventually be included in the main chain, and no progress is ever lost. The full pseudo-code of the protocol is presented in the full version of the paper [18].

Remark 3. (SNARG overhead) Note that usefulness is not necessarily substantially impacted by a large SNARG-computation overhead as each state update involves a large number of exploration steps (on average) but SNARGs for only two of the M-computations performed. This average number of exploration steps can thus be raised in a trade-off against the state-update frequency in the system, helping to establish Requirement 2b.

5.2   Deployment Considerations

The following two practical aspects are of special importance when deploying our PoUW blockchain:

Multiple Problem Instances. The system must be able to handle multiple problem instances as the computation of a particular instance will eventually terminate. Also, multiple instances should be able to be computed concurrently to give them fair chances to progress. We achieve this concurrency by running the protocol in epochs, and interleaving different problem instances by assigning exactly one instance to each epoch. As exposed in the full version of the paper, interleaving has an additional advantage: during the epoch, unconfirmed input blocks can be immediately extended in the DAG without risking that the referrer block becomes invalid due to possible non-inclusion of the referenced block in the main chain— thus facilitating fast progress during the time slots allocated to the problem.

Incentive Structure. The participation of miners in the system must be incentivized to guarantee blockchain security and progress in the useful computation. Also, since the miner is free in choosing which one of their state updates to publish in their block, choosing a good solution should be rewarded in order to expedite progress in the useful computation. In the full version, we elaborate on meeting these conditions as well as on guaranteeing reward fairness along the lines of the Fruitchains construction [42].

6   Security Analysis

Next, we formally analyze the security of our protocol. First, we show that— assuming that the underlying DAG computation is moderately hard and that honest parties control the majority of the computational power in the network— our protocol implements a robust transaction ledger. Then, we define and analyze its usefulness rate.

6.1   Ledger Security

Let Π denote our blockchain protocol. The consistency analysis of the longest chain rule appearing in Π involves a number of new challenges, including: (i) an exotic Markov chain governing the mining dynamics and the possibility of "restarts" in this chain generated by the delivery of a new block, perhaps by the adversary, and (ii) basing the hardness of generating new blocks to a problem satisfying the weak moderate hardness notion introduced in Sect. 4. We adapt the language of [5,31] to this setting and then develop the tools necessary for the associated probabilistic analysis. (Our treatment below does not require familiarity with these previous papers.)

For simplicity, in the main body of the paper, we discuss the case *without restarts*, which is to say that the protocol carried out by the honest parties does not restart the mining process when it learns of a longer chain, but rather completes the current computation. Intuitively, restarts *improve* the security properties of the blockchain, as they help ensure that honest parties are mining on current chains. However, the situation is somewhat complicated by the fact that restarts do permit the adversary to correlate the states of the honest parties in the Markov chain. Specifically, note that an adversary holding a chain that exceeds the length of those chains currently held by honest parties may strategically release the chain to honest players—perhaps with detailed knowledge about their current state—so as to achieve some short-term control over the distribution of honest mining successes. Despite such correlations, we show in the full version of the paper that the intuition above is correct: the adversarial advantage achieved by exposing adversarial blocks to honest miners is overshadowed by the fact that such exposures increase the length of the blockchain held by the honest recipient; in the language of the analysis below, such an exposure has an effect just as beneficial as an honest mining victory!

We adopt a discrete time model, dividing time into short "rounds" with duration c_H equal to the time taken to carry out a hash query. We reflect the essential block-generation events of an execution of the protocol with a *characteristic* string: this determines, for each round, the number of adversarial and honest ranking blocks generated. Thus our characteristic strings have the structure $w = w_1, \ldots, w_L$ where each $w_i = (h_i, a_i) \in \mathbb{N}^2$ and h_i and a_i denotes the number of honest and adversarial ranking block discoveries, respectively; here L is the lifetime of the protocol.

Ultimately, our protocol Π determines a blockchain of ranking blocks, which themselves refer to input blocks. Such a structure determines a linear order on the collection of input blocks referenced in the blockchain of ranking blocks (by ordering input blocks referenced in a particular ranking block according to the order of their references in the ranking block). Ultimately, we wish to establish the two fundamental ledger properties: *liveness* and *persistence*.

Persistence with parameter $k \in \mathbb{N}$ Once a node of the system proclaims a certain input block in the *stable* part of its ledger $\mathcal{L}$, the remaining nodes either report the input block in the same position of their ledgers, or report a stable ledger which is a prefix of $\mathcal{L}$. Here the notion of stability is a predicate that is parametrized by a security parameter k; specifically, an input block is declared *stable* if and only if it is in a (ranking) block that is more than k (ranking) blocks deep in the ledger.

Liveness with parameter $u \in \mathbb{N}$. If all honest nodes in the system attempt to include a certain input block then, after the passing of time corresponding to u rounds, all nodes report the input block as stable.

We establish these properties as consequences of three more elementary properties of the blockchain of ranking blocks, originally formulated in [20] (we use a slightly adapted formulation from [15]):

– **Common Prefix (CP); with parameter** $k \in \mathbb{N}$. The chains $\mathcal{C}_1, \mathcal{C}_2$ adopted by two honest parties at the onset of rounds $r_1 \leq r_2$ are such that $\mathcal{C}_1^{\lceil k} \prec \mathcal{C}_2$, where $\mathcal{C}_1^{\lceil k}$ denotes the chain obtained by removing the last k blocks from $\mathcal{C}_1$, and $\prec$ denotes the prefix relation.
– **Existential Chain Quality (ECQ); with parameter** $s \in \mathbb{N}$. Consider the chain $\mathcal{C}$ adopted by an honest party at the onset of a round and any portion of $\mathcal{C}$ spanning s prior rounds; then at least one honestly-generated block appears in this portion.
– **Chain Growth (CG); with parameters** $\tau \in (0, 1]$ **and** $s \in \mathbb{N}$. Consider the chain $\mathcal{C}$ possessed by an honest party at the onset of a round and any portion of $\mathcal{C}$ spanning s contiguous prior rounds; then the number of blocks appearing in this portion of the chain is at least τs. We call τ the *speed coefficient*.

One of the important conclusions of previous work is that these properties (CP, CG, and ECQ) directly imply liveness and persistence and—from an analytic perspective—can be guaranteed merely based on the characteristic string associated with a particular execution. This fact is fairly immediate for CG and ECQ, whereas identification of the properties of the characteristic string that guarantee CP is more delicate.

In the full version of the paper we give a summary of this theory and describe an extension with restarts. Fortunately, it is possible to succinctly reflect the conclusions of this theory as they relate to our needs, which is done below.

To continue, we first introduce two assumptions related to the level of moderate hardness of the underlying DAG-computation family $\mathcal{I}$ used by Π, and the complexity of the SNARG system used.

Assumption 1. *For parameters* $\hat{t}, \hat{\epsilon}, \hat{k}$, *we assume that the DAG computation family* $\mathcal{I}$ *used in* Π *is* $(\hat{t}, \hat{\epsilon}, \hat{k})$-*moderately hard.*

Assumption 2. *For parameters* c_P, c_V, c_S, *we assume that there exists a SNARG system* SNARG *where running the prover (resp., verifier, setup) takes* c_P *(resp.* c_V, c_S*) steps.*

Let $w = w_1, \ldots, w_L$ be a characteristic string, as above. We fix a constant Γ, a time period with the following Γ-*serializing guarantee*: if a ranking block B_2 is generated by an honest party P at least Γ rounds after the honestly-generated ranking block B_1 is diffused, then the full computation supporting B_2 (including the prehash) was carried out while P was aware of B_1. In our setting, Γ can be set to $2 + \Delta + c_P/c_H + \hat{t}/c_H$ (corresponding to the number of rounds taken to produce the prehash (≤ 1), useful work ($\leq \hat{t}/c_H$), post-hash (≤ 1), and SNARG (c_P/c_H) for block B_2 in addition to any network delay). With this in mind, we say that t is a Γ-*isolated uniquely successful round* if the region $w_{t-\Gamma} \ldots w_t \ldots w_{t+\Gamma}$ satisfies $h_t = 1$ and, furthermore, that the sum $\sum h_i = 1$ over this region (recall $w_i = (a_i, h_i)$). Note that a round cannot be isolated if it is not followed by at least Γ symbols. For each t define I_t to be an indicator variable for the event that t is an isolated uniquely successful round.

The basic quantities of interest are given by two conventions for accounting for the balance of adversarial and honest successes.

Definition 3 (The barrier walk; the free walk). *Let* $x = x_1, \ldots, x_n \in \mathbb{N}^*$. *Define the* barrier walk $B(x)$ *by the recursive rule* $B(\epsilon) = 0$ *(for the empty string ϵ) and, for any* $x \in \mathbb{N}^*$ *and* $a \in \mathbb{N}$, $B(xa) = \max(B(x) + a, 0)$. *Likewise, define the* free walk $F(x) = \sum_i x_i$.

Definition 4. *For a characteristic string* $w \in (\mathbb{N}^2)^L$ *and* $0 < t \leq L$, *define the* margin effect $w_t^* = a_t - I_t \in \mathbb{N}$ *(and w^* to be the sequence of elements of $\mathbb{N}$ given by this rule). We then define* $B^*(w) = B(w^*)$ *and* $F^*(w) = F(w^*)$. *Finally, for a characteristic string* $w = xy$ *with* $|x| = \ell$, *we define the* ℓ-isolated margin *of w to be* $\beta_\ell(w) = B(x^*) + F(y^*)$.

The role of ℓ-isolated margin is clarified by the following, which establishes a direct connection to common prefix.

Theorem 1. *Let* $w \in (\mathbb{N}^2)^L$ *be the characteristic string associated with an execution satisfying the Γ-serializing guarantee. Suppose, further, that (i.) the execution satisfies $(k/s, s)$-CG, and (ii.) for any prefix xy of w for which $|y| \geq s$, we have $\beta_{|x|}(xy) < 0$. Then the execution satisfies k-CP.*

This is the major component in the following theorem; as noted, the details of this existing theory are discussed in the full version of the paper.

Theorem 2. *Let* D_Π *be a distribution on characteristic strings of length L (induced by a protocol Π), λ a security parameter, and $\alpha > \beta$ two constants corresponding to the rate of uniquely isolated blocks and the rate of adversarial blocks, respectively. Assume that for a constant $\delta < (\alpha - \beta)/2$, when w is drawn from D_Π, every interval of w of length $\text{poly}(\lambda)$ has at least $\alpha - \delta$ uniquely isolated blocks and no more than $\beta + \delta$ adversarial blocks except with negligible probability. Then, except with negligible probability, the protocol satisfies (i.) CG with $s = \text{poly}(\lambda)$ and constant speed coefficient, (ii.) ECQ with $s = \text{poly}(\lambda)$, and (iii.) CP with parameter $k = \text{poly}(\lambda)$.*

Analysis of the Markov Chain. In light of the description above, we are specifically interested in analyzing the sequence of (i.) adversarial mining successes and (ii.) uniquely isolated honest successes. The analysis is simplified by the fact that the time evolution of the honest parties is independent. We focus on the Markov chain pictured below, showing nodes for "pre-hash", "post-hash", and both "ranking" and "input" block production. It is convenient for us to further decorate our transitions with delays: orange edges are traversed in a single round (or c_H time, corresponding to hash queries), the gray edges are traversed instantaneously, and the blue edges have transition times given by the distribution of useful work (upper bounded by $\hat{t}$) and SNARG times (c_P). (Note that the timing delays indicated in this chain could be implemented with paths of individual states connected by edges with unit delay, so this presentation can be reflected with a standard Markov chain.) While the basic security properties of the protocol depend only on the production of ranking blocks, the dynamics of the Markov chain depends on both ranking and input block production.

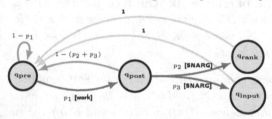

We begin by establishing that—despite the fact that honest parties begin the protocol synchronized (in "pre")—they quickly converge to mutually independent positions in the mining chain. Looking ahead, this mixing argument will be instrumental to establish bounds on uniquely isolated block production.

The Mixing Time; Convergence to Mutual Independence. By a standard coupling argument we get the following:

Lemma 2. *Consider m particles $P_1, \ldots, P_m$ independently evolving on the Markov chain with any fixed initial states. Let $(S_1, \ldots, S_m)$ denote a random variable so that each coordinate is independent and stationary on the chain. Then letting $T = L(1 + (\hat{t} + c_P)/c_H)$,*

$$\|(P_1^T, \ldots, P_m^T) - (S_1, \ldots, S_m)\|_{t.v} \leq m(1 - p_{couple})^L,$$

where $\|X - Y\|_{t.v}$ denotes the distance in total variation between the random variables X and Y. Here $p_{couple} > 0$ is a constant that depends only on $c_P/\hat{t}$.

Proof. We proceed with a standard coupling argument. Consider m particles (parties) $P_1, \ldots, P_m$, initially in the state q_{pre}, that carry out simultaneous, independent evolution according to the dynamics of the chain. We wish to show that the joint distribution of positions of all the particles quickly converges to m independent copies of the stationary distribution. For this purpose, consider m additional particles $R_1, \ldots, R_m$ on the chain, initially distributed independently according to the stationary distribution. We let P_i^t and R_i^t denote the positions of the particles at time t. We give a simple coupling C of the evolution of $P_1^t, \ldots, P_m^t$ with $R_1^t, \ldots, R_m^t$, and apply the standard "coupling lemma" which establishes convergence to the stationary distribution. The coupling C is described, at each time step, by a family of random variables U_i^t; for each

$i \in \{1, \ldots, m\}$, $U_i^t : Q \to Q$ is a function where Q is the set of states of the chain (which is in fact larger than the diagram indicates as a result of implementing the "long" transitions). The "update functions" U_i are chosen so that the full ensemble of entries $(U_i^t(q))$ (over all t, i, and $q \in Q$) are independent and each $U_i(q)$ is distributed according to the defining distribution for the state q. Then P_i and R_i are updated according to the same update: $P_i^{t+1} = U_i(P_i^t)$ and $R_i^{t+1} = U_i(R_i^t)$. Observe that the dynamics of the P_i^t are as promised, each independently evolving according to the chain; the same is true of the R_i^t, which of course continue to be independent and stationary. Observe that if $R_i^t = P_i^t$ at some time t this property will be retained by the coupling in the future (as they are subject to the same update function). Now, consider any time period of length $E = 1 + (\hat{t} + c_{\mathsf{P}})/c_H$ rounds and any pair of particles P_i and Q_i. Observe that both particles must visit the state q_{pre} during this time period (as $\hat{t}$ and c_{P} are upper bounds on the transition times of the blue transitions); it follows that if the first of the two particles to visit q_{pre} remains in that state for the remainder of the E time steps then the two particles must couple (that is, coincide during this time period and forever after). Recalling that we take $T_1 \geq \hat{t}/c_H$, we find that the probability that that first particle remains in q_{pre} when the second one arrives is at least $p_{\mathsf{couple}} := (1 - p_1)^{E/c_H} = (1 - p_1)^{(\hat{t}+c_{\mathsf{P}})/c_H} = [(1 - p_1)^{\hat{t}/c_H}]^{(1+c_{\mathsf{P}}/\hat{t})} \geq [(1 - 1/T_1)^{T_1}]^{(1+c_{\mathsf{P}}/\hat{t})} \geq (1/e - O(1/T_1))^{(1+c_{\mathsf{P}}/\hat{t})}$. Thus p_{couple} is a constant larger than zero (and can be lower bounded as a function of the constant $c_{\mathsf{P}}/\hat{t}$). Note that the events that P_i couples with R_i (for distinct i) during such an epoch are independent, and it follows that after L such epochs the probability that there is a pair (P_i, R_i) that has not coupled is no more than $n(1 - p_{\mathsf{couple}})^L$. By the standard coupling lemma (see, e.g., [3, §12]), after L epochs the distance in total variation between $(P_1, \ldots, P_m)$ and the independent stationary distribution in each coordinate is no more than $m(1 - p_{\mathsf{couple}})^L$, which tends to zero exponentially quickly in L. This proves the lemma.   □

Bounds on the Events of Interest. Consider, as above, the population of particles (players) $P_1, \ldots, P_n$ on the Markov chain. According to an evolution of these particles, given by the random variables P_i^t, we are interested in establishing upper bounds on the rate at which the adversary produces ranking blocks, and a lower bound on the rate at which the honest players produce uniquely isolated blocks.

Lemma 3. *Consider m parties, with arbitrary initial conditions but evolving independently on the Markov chain. Let $S = (\hat{t} + c_{\mathsf{P}})/c_H + 1$ and consider any interval of R rounds, the first of which starts at least S steps after the evolution begins. Then the probability that a particular player generates at least k ranking blocks in this interval is no more than $\binom{R+S}{k}(p_1 p_2)^k \leq (R + S)^k (p_1 p_2)^k$.*

Lemma 4. *Consider m independent parties walking on the Markov chain in the stationary distribution. Let p_{rank}^* denote the stationary probability of q_{rank}, then*

$$\Pr[t \text{ is a uniquely isolated round}] \geq m(1 - (3\Gamma)p_1 p_2)^m p_{rank}^*.$$

In light of Lemma 2, the following is immediate.

Lemma 5. *Consider m players evolving according to the Markov chain, where the players are initially stationary and independent. Let p_{couple} denote the coupling constant of Lemma 2. Consider two rounds $š < s$ for which $|š - s| \geq L(1 + (\hat{t} + c_P)/c_H)$. Let I_s denote the indicator random variable for the event that s is uniquely isolated. Let C denote an arbitrary event depending only on the players trajectories prior to š. Then $|\Pr[I_s|C] - \Pr[I_s]| \leq (1 - p_{couple})^L$.*

Lemma 6. *Consider m players evolving on the Markov chain with any fixed initial states. Let p_{iso} denote the probability that a round is uniquely isolated under the stationary distribution, bounded below by Lemma 4. Fix a parameter $\sigma > 0$ and define $L = \ln(p_{iso}\sigma/2)/\ln(1 - p_{couple})$ and $E = L(1 + (\hat{t} + c_P)/c_H)$. Let $\{R, \ldots, R + S - 1\}$ be a sequence of rounds for which $R \geq E$. Let I_s be the event that the players produce a uniquely isolated block in round s. Then*

$$\Pr\left[\sum_s I_s \leq (1 - \sigma)p_{iso}S\right] \leq E \exp\left(-\frac{(1 - \sigma/2)\sigma^2 p_{iso} \cdot S}{8E}\right).$$

Analysis of the Adversarial Successes. Next, we proceed to bound the rate of adversarial mining successes. Our analysis is going to depend on the level of moderate hardness of the underlying DAG computations family.

By Lemma 1 we argued that the speed-up the adversary gets by each extra queries to oracle $\mathcal{O}$ is bounded. In fact for a single extra query, the lemma tells us that the adversary can speed up its computation by $\hat{t}$ steps. Thus, in order to protect our protocol from grinding attacks, we *set the pre-hash hardness parameter p_1 to $c_H/((1 + \sigma)\hat{t} + 4)$*, where $\sigma \in (0, 1)$ is a parameter associated with the concentration bounds we use later in our analysis. This implies that finding a small pre-hash takes on expectation $c_H/p_1 = (1 + \sigma)\hat{t} + 4 > \hat{t}$ steps, i.e., it is more expensive than running M directly to compute a new PoUW; the extra steps added are related to costs occurring in our reduction later.

To aid our presentation, we define $t' := t + (2n + 4(p_2 + p_3)(nc_P + tc_V)) \cdot p_1/c_H$ to be the increased corruption power the adversary gets, due to fact that our reduction to the MH of $\mathcal{I}$ is not tight, mainly because of the cost of generating and verifying SNARG proofs. With foresight, we let β be an estimation of the rate at which the adversary produces ranking blocks

$$\beta := p_2/\left[(1 - \hat{\epsilon}(1, 2, 2n/t')) \cdot \hat{t} + (1/((1 + \sigma)p_1) + 1) \cdot (c_H - 4p_1)\right].$$

The expected number of steps to find a block, β^{-1}, is basically the number of attempts needed to find a small post-hash $(1/p_2)$, times the number of steps needed to find a small pre-hash (c_H/p_1) plus the time needed to perform the DAG computation $((1 - \hat{\epsilon}) \cdot \hat{t})$. The other constants of the formula are related to our security analysis, i.e., our reduction from an attacker against the blockchain to an attacker against MH. Finally, the parameters $0, 2, 2n/t'$ of $\hat{\epsilon}$ relate to the rate at which the adversary queries oracles $q_{\mathcal{O}}, q_{\mathcal{V}}, q_{\mathcal{M}}$ as explained in Sect. 4.

Table 1. *The parameters of our analysis.*

λ :	security parameter
n :	number of parties
t :	adversarial corruption bound
t' :	amplified adversarial corruption bound
c_H :	"mining" steps each party takes per round
c_P, c_V :	SNARG prover/verifier cost
$\hat{e}, \hat{t}, \hat{k}$:	MH DAG parameters
$T_1, p_1 = T_1/2^\lambda$:	target/success probability of prehash
$T_2, p_2 = T_2/2^\lambda$:	" of ranking block posthash
$T_3, p_3 = \frac{T_3 - T_2}{2^\lambda}$:	" of input block posthash
σ :	concentration-bound parameter
Δ, Γ :	network/serialization worst-case delay
β :	upper bound on ranking-block computation rate
δ_{MH} :	adversarial advantage in DAG computation rate
δ_{Steps} :	honest advantage in number of steps per round
δ_{tot} :	upper bound on the total block generation rate

Let r.v. $Z(S)$ denote the maximum number of distinct blocks computed by the adversary during S, where the pre-hash query for each of these blocks was also issued to the RO during S. We prove in the full version that the adversary cannot mine fresh ranking blocks with rate and probability better than that of breaking the moderate hardness experiment. The main proof idea is to use an adversary that creates blocks fast, to create another adversary that breaks the moderate hardness of $\mathcal{I}$. A summary of our notation is given in Table 1.

Lemma 7. *For any set of consecutive rounds S, where $|S| \geq \hat{k}(1 + \sigma)p_2/(\beta \cdot t'c_H)$, it holds that $Z(S) \geq (1 + \sigma)\beta \cdot t'c_H|S|$ with probability $negl(\lambda)$.*

Putting Everything Together. Next, we show that the probability that a uniquely successful round happens is larger than the expected adversarial mining rate per round. Towards this purpose, our next assumption ensures that the computational steps advantage of honest parties outperforms the moderate hardness advantage of the adversary, while at the same time the rate at which blocks are produced is upper bounded.

Assumption 3. *There exist constants $\delta_{MH}, \delta_{Steps}$ and $\delta_{tot} \in (0, 1)$, such that for sufficiently large $\lambda \in \mathbb{N}$:*
- *$(n - t)(1 - \delta_{Steps}) \geq t'$ (Steps per round gap)*
- *$p_{rank}^* \geq (1 - \delta_{MH})\beta \cdot c_H$ (Moderate hardness gap)*
- *$\delta_{Steps} - \delta_{MH} \geq \delta_{tot}$ (Steps vs. Moderate hardness gap)*
- *$\delta_{tot} > 3\Gamma \cdot \beta c_H(n - t)$ (Bounded block generation rate).*

Based on Assumption 3, we can prove that the rate of uniquely successful rounds is bigger than the rate at which the adversary generates blocks.

Lemma 8. *It holds that $p_{iso} > (1 + \delta_{tot})\beta t'c_H$.*

Together with the appropriate concentration bounds proved in Lemmas 6 and 7, Lemma 8 is sufficient to apply Theorem 2 for Π, which in turn implies that Π satisfies both Persistence and Liveness with overwhelming probability.

Corollary 1. *Given Assumptions 1, 2 and 3, Ofelimos satisfies Persistence and Liveness for $k, u \in poly(\lambda)$, except with negligible probability.*

Finally, in the full version, we argue that under ideal conditions, i.e. optimal MH, small SNARG costs, etc., Ofelimos can tolerate *any dishonest minority*.

A More Detailed Treatment of Useful Work Completion Times. The analysis above calibrates pre-hash hardness as a function of $\hat{t}$, the worst-case completion time of useful work. In certain settings of interest, the time complexity of the useful work task may satisfy a significantly stronger bound with very high probability, in which case this reduced bound can take the place of $\hat{t}$ with only minimal changes to the development above. Specifically, if the time complexity is $\bar{t} < \hat{t}$ except with negligible probability, the value $\bar{t}$ can be uniformly substituted for $\hat{t}$ above with the addition of negligible error terms in the theorems above.

Security Against Multiple Problem Instances. As discussed in Sect. 5.2, our protocol can handle multiple problem instances by interleaving them. Note, that our security analysis extends to this case, since it is agnostic of the level of MH of problem instances. Instead of trying to detect the hardness level of the M computation corresponding to each submitted problem instance, our approach is to keep pre-hash hardness fixed throughout the execution of the protocol, at a level where even if the submitted computation is not MH we still retain some security guarantees.

DPLS Against Adversarial Participation. Executing DPLS in our permissionless PoUW setting potentially implies substantial adversarial participation which can negatively influence the algorithmic performance. In particular, the adversary may not follow Algorithm 1, e.g., by publishing the result of the worst execution of M, instead of the best one.

While the presentation of DPLS is agnostic to adversarial participation, its embedding PoUW protocol is responsible to provide the respective defenses. In the full version of the paper, we present two important quality guarantees of our implementation of DPLS by our PoUW protocol as long as the adversary only controls a minority of the computational power: (i) during any sufficiently large round interval, honest parties contribute new updates at least proportionally to their relative mining power —in particular, the honest parties contribute more updates than the adversary; (ii) the adversary cannot extensively manipulate the score of its updates, as we enforce each update to additionally include the result of a "random" execution of M from the batch (the one that resulted in a small post-hash), which can be used to replace "best" execution if it had worse score in comparison.

Remark 4. (Grinding resistance amplification) As a corollary of our main hardness lemma, we can argue about the amplification of grinding resistance of a MH DAG computation achieved by the following construction: first, the new exploration algorithm tries to find a small pre-hash, which then uses to seed the initial (potentially weakly grinding resistant) DAG computation[4]. Similarly to our PoUW, we set the hardness of finding the pre-hash to be approximately equal to the worst-case complexity of the initial DAG computation. By our lemma, it easily follows that this construction is maximally grinding resistant, i.e., the adversary gains no advantage by seeing extra problem instances, while incurring only a small loss on MH and ensuring that the (potentially useful) initial computation remains a substantial part of the exploration algorithm. In fact, we can do even better in the case where the initial DAG computation enjoys some limited form of grinding resistance, by downgrading the hardness of finding a small pre-hash proportionally to the grinding resistance parameter.

Having argued about the security of Ofelimos as a transaction ledger, we turn our attention to its usefulness as a problem solving system.

6.2   Protocol Usefulness

The goal of any PoUW-based blockchain protocol is to be used to solve some, external to the blockchain, computational problem. We say that such a protocol has a high *usefulness rate* if the total computational work spent to run the blockchain and solve the external problem is not much bigger than just solving the problem with the best possible algorithm (for the setting considered), denoted by A_{best}. We study this rate for our protocol using two metrics. The first metric, U_{eng}, measures the overall ratio of computational steps, performed by honest parties, that the engine directs towards running the DPLS algorithm. Intuitively this metric captures how effective the protocol is as a DPLS engine. We generically define U_{eng} as follows:

$$U_{eng} := \mathbb{E}[\text{DPLS steps per block}]/\mathbb{E}[\text{total steps per block}]$$

Next, we analyze U_{eng} for Ofelimos. First, note that since we set pre-hash hardness based on the worst-case complexity of M, Ofelimos's U_{eng} naturally depends on M's runtime distribution being concentrated close to $\hat{t}$. Fortunately, the core search function of local search algorithms, which M aims to model, usually boils down to iteratively evaluating candidate solutions in a neighborhood, thus making it easy for us to exactly calibrate its runtime, e.g., by counting the number of candidates evaluated. Assuming that this is indeed true, and M's running time is almost always $\hat{t}$, we show that for appropriate protocol parameters Ofelimos has a U_{eng} close to $1/2$, i.e., half of the total work mining a new block goes to running the DPLS engine. The intuition is that as we decrease the probability of finding a new (input or ranking) block, hashing and running M costs dominate the cost of running the SNARG prover. Given now that for our scheme the cost of hashing is approximately equal to the cost of running M, the result is immediate. We formalize this in the next lemma.

---

[4] Our PoUW "collapses" to this construction if we set $p_2 := 1, p_3 := 0$.

Lemma 9. *Assume M has a fixed running time. Then, for any $\rho > \sigma + 4/\hat{t}$, if* $p_2 + p_3 < \frac{(\rho-\sigma)\hat{t}-4}{2 \cdot c_P}$, U_{eng} *is greater than* $\frac{1}{2+\rho}$.

The second metric, U_{alg}, compares the complexity of DPLS to algorithm A_{best}. Note, that for U_{alg} we only take into account the DPLS computation steps and no other steps related to the protocol, e.g., hashing, computing SNARGs.

$$\mathsf{U}_{alg} := \mathbb{E}[\text{total steps of } \mathsf{A}_{best}]/\mathbb{E}[\text{total steps of DPLS}]$$

U_{alg} cannot be studied generically as it depends on the specific external problem solved as well as the computational model we consider. For example, we expect U_{alg} to be much larger when we consider the best algorithm in a distributed setting compared to the best one in the single machine setting. Instead, in the full version of the paper, we showcase how U_{alg} can be estimated experimentally for our WalkSAT DPLS variant.

The two metrics that we introduced clearly separate costs associated with the ledger protocol (hashing and SNARGS) from costs that are induced by the specific algorithm implement. In fact, in the case where blocks are computed using the honest mining algorithm, the product of the two metrics is a good approximation of the usefulness rate.

Remark 5. (Improved U_{eng}) In the analysis of our protocol we did not make any assumptions about the grinding resistance of the underlying DAG computation $\mathcal{I}$. This had the effect of setting the pre-hash hardness (c_H/p_1) to be approximately equal to $\hat{t}$, in turn leading to U_{eng} being less than $1/2$. If $\mathcal{I}$ enjoys some non-trivial level of grinding resistance, we can take advantage of it and downgrade the pre-hash hardness, with the effect of having exactly the same security guarantees but with potentially much less work invested in hashing. In the case where $\mathcal{I}$ is maximally grinding resistant, this leads to U_{eng} being close to 1.

Acknowledgments. We thank Laurent Michel for providing us with valuable information about state-of-the-art stochastic local-search algorithms and their application to real-world problems.

References

1. Aggarwal, A., Chandra, A.K., Snir, M.: Communication complexity of prams. Theor. Comput. Sci. **71**(1), 3–28 (1990)
2. Ahuja, R.K., Ergun, Ö., Orlin, J.B., Punnen, A.P.: A survey of very large-scale neighborhood search techniques. Discret. Appl. Math. **123**(1–3), 75–102 (2002)
3. Aldous, D., Fill, J.A.: Reversible Markov chains and random walks on graphs (2002, Unfinished monograph). http://www.stat.berkeley.edu/~aldous/RWG/book.html
4. Andrychowicz, M., Dziembowski, S.: PoW-based distributed cryptography with no trusted setup. In: Gennaro, R., Robshaw, M. (eds.) CRYPTO 2015. LNCS, vol. 9216, pp. 379–399. Springer, Heidelberg (2015). https://doi.org/10.1007/978-3-662-48000-7_19

5. Badertscher, C., Gazi, P., Kiayias, A., Russell, A., Zikas, V.: Consensus redux: distributed ledgers in the face of adversarial supremacy. IACR Cryptology ePrint Archive, Report 2020/1021 (2020)
6. Badertscher, C., Maurer, U., Tschudi, D., Zikas, V.: Bitcoin as a transaction ledger: a composable treatment. In: Katz, J., Shacham, H. (eds.) CRYPTO 2017. LNCS, vol. 10401, pp. 324–356. Springer, Cham (2017). https://doi.org/10.1007/978-3-319-63688-7_11
7. Baldominos, A., Saez, Y.: Coin. AI: a proof-of-useful-work scheme for blockchain-based distributed deep learning. Entropy **21**(8), 723 (2019)
8. Ball, M., Rosen, A., Sabin, M., Vasudevan, P.N.: Proofs of work from worst-case assumptions. In: Shacham, H., Boldyreva, A. (eds.) CRYPTO 2018. LNCS, vol. 10991, pp. 789–819. Springer, Cham (2018). https://doi.org/10.1007/978-3-319-96884-1_26
9. Bellare, M., Rogaway, P.: Random oracles are practical: a paradigm for designing efficient protocols. In: CCS 1993, Fairfax, Virginia, USA, pp. 62–73 (1993)
10. Boneh, D., Bonneau, J., Bünz, B., Fisch, B.: Verifiable delay functions. In: Shacham, H., Boldyreva, A. (eds.) CRYPTO 2018. LNCS, vol. 10991, pp. 757–788. Springer, Cham (2018). https://doi.org/10.1007/978-3-319-96884-1_25
11. Chatterjee, K., Goharshady, A.K., Pourdamghani, A.: Hybrid mining: exploiting blockchain's computational power for distributed problem solving. In: Proceedings of the 34th ACM/SIGAPP Symposium on Applied Computing (2019)
12. Coelho, F.: An (almost) constant-effort solution-verification proof-of-work protocol based on Merkle trees. Cryptology ePrint Archive, Report 2007/433 (2007)
13. Coventry, A.: Nooshare: a decentralized ledger of shared computational resources (2012). https://web.archive.org/web/20220620105201/. http://web.mit.edu/alex_c/www/nooshare.pdf
14. Daian, P., Pass, R., Shi, E.: Snow white: robustly reconfigurable consensus and applications to provably secure proof of stake. In: Goldberg, I., Moore, T. (eds.) FC 2019. LNCS, vol. 11598, pp. 23–41. Springer, Cham (2019). https://doi.org/10.1007/978-3-030-32101-7_2
15. David, B., Gaži, P., Kiayias, A., Russell, A.: Ouroboros praos: an adaptively-secure, semi-synchronous proof-of-stake blockchain. In: Nielsen, J.B., Rijmen, V. (eds.) EUROCRYPT 2018. LNCS, vol. 10821, pp. 66–98. Springer, Cham (2018). https://doi.org/10.1007/978-3-319-78375-8_3
16. Dotan, M., Tochner, S.: Proofs of useless work-positive and negative results for wasteless mining systems. arXiv preprint arXiv:2007.01046 (2020)
17. Dziembowski, S., Faust, S., Kolmogorov, V., Pietrzak, K.: Proofs of space. In: Gennaro, R., Robshaw, M. (eds.) CRYPTO 2015. LNCS, vol. 9216, pp. 585–605. Springer, Heidelberg (2015). https://doi.org/10.1007/978-3-662-48000-7_29
18. Fitzi, M., Kiayias, A., Panagiotakos, G., Russell, A.: Ofelimos: combinatorial optimization via proof-of-useful-work–a provably secure blockchain protocol. Cryptology ePrint Archive, Paper 2021/1379 (2021)
19. Gapcoin. Gapcoin (2014). https://gapcoin.org/
20. Garay, J., Kiaylas, A., Leonardos, N.: The bitcoin backbone protocol: analysis and applications. In: Oswald, E., Fischlin, M. (eds.) EUROCRYPT 2015. LNCS, vol. 9057, pp. 281–310. Springer, Heidelberg (2015). https://doi.org/10.1007/978-3-662-46803-6_10
21. Garay, J.A., Kiayias, A., Panagiotakos, G.: Consensus from signatures of work. In: Jarecki, S. (ed.) CT-RSA 2020. LNCS, vol. 12006, pp. 319–344. Springer, Cham (2020). https://doi.org/10.1007/978-3-030-40186-3_14

22. Garay, J.A., Kiayias, A., Panagiotakos, G.: Blockchains from non-idealized hash functions. In: Pass, R., Pietrzak, K. (eds.) TCC 2020. LNCS, vol. 12550, pp. 291–321. Springer, Cham (2020). https://doi.org/10.1007/978-3-030-64375-1_11
23. Gilad, Y., Hemo, R., Micali, S., Vlachos, G., Zeldovich, N.: Algorand: scaling byzantine agreements for cryptocurrencies. In: Proceedings of the 26th Symposium on Operating Systems Principles, pp. 51–68 (2017)
24. Groth, J.: On the size of pairing-based non-interactive arguments. In: Fischlin, M., Coron, J.-S. (eds.) EUROCRYPT 2016. LNCS, vol. 9666, pp. 305–326. Springer, Heidelberg (2016). https://doi.org/10.1007/978-3-662-49896-5_11
25. Groth, J., Kohlweiss, M., Maller, M., Meiklejohn, S., Miers, I.: Updatable and universal common reference strings with applications to zk-SNARKs. In: Shacham, H., Boldyreva, A. (eds.) CRYPTO 2018. LNCS, vol. 10993, pp. 698–728. Springer, Cham (2018). https://doi.org/10.1007/978-3-319-96878-0_24
26. Gupta, N., Nau, D.S.: On the complexity of blocks-world planning. Artif. Intell. **56**(2–3), 223–254 (1992)
27. Hoos, H.H., Stützle, T.: Stochastic Local Search: Foundations and Applications. Elsevier, Amsterdam (2004)
28. Kautz, H., Selman, B., McAllester, D.: Walksat in the 2004 SAT competition. In: Proceedings of the International Conference on Theory and Applications of Satisfiability Testing (2004)
29. Kerber, T., Kiayias, A., Kohlweiss, M.: Mining for privacy: how to bootstrap a snarky blockchain. Cryptology ePrint Archive, Report 2020/401 (2020)
30. Kiayias, A., Quader, S., Russell, A.: Consistency of proof-of-stake blockchains with concurrent honest slot leaders. IACR Cryptology ePrint Archive, Report 2020/041 (2020)
31. Kiayias, A., Russell, A., David, B., Oliynykov, R.: Ouroboros: a provably secure proof-of-stake blockchain protocol. In: Katz, J., Shacham, H. (eds.) CRYPTO 2017. LNCS, vol. 10401, pp. 357–388. Springer, Cham (2017). https://doi.org/10.1007/978-3-319-63688-7_12
32. King, S.: Primecoin: cryptocurrency with prime number proof-of-work (2013)
33. Lihu, A., Du, J., Barjaktarevic, I., Gerzanics, P., Harvilla, M.: A proof of useful work for artificial intelligence on the blockchain. arXiv:2001.09244 preprint (2020)
34. Loe, A.F., Quaglia, E.A.: Conquering generals: an NP-hard proof of useful work. In: Proceedings of the 1st Workshop on Cryptocurrencies and Blockchains for Distributed Systems, pp. 54–59 (2018)
35. Maller, M., Bowe, S., Kohlweiss, M., Meiklejohn, S.: Sonic: zero-knowledge snarks from linear-size universal and updatable structured reference strings. In: ACM CCS 2019, London, UK, pp. 2111–2128 (2019)
36. Miller, A., Juels, A., Shi, E., Parno, B., Katz, J.: Permacoin: repurposing bitcoin work for data preservation. In: 2014 IEEE S&P, pp. 475–490. IEEE (2014)
37. Moran, T., Orlov, I.: Simple proofs of space-time and rational proofs of storage. In: Boldyreva, A., Micciancio, D. (eds.) CRYPTO 2019. LNCS, vol. 11692, pp. 381–409. Springer, Cham (2019). https://doi.org/10.1007/978-3-030-26948-7_14
38. Oliver, C.G., Ricottone, A., Philippopoulos, P.: Proposal for a fully decentralized blockchain and proof-of-work algorithm for solving NP-complete problems. arXiv preprint arXiv:1708.09419 (2017)
39. Papadimitriou, C.H., Ullman, J.D.: A communication-time tradeoff. SIAM J. Comput. **16**(4), 639–646 (1987)
40. Park, S., Kwon, A., Fuchsbauer, G., Gaži, P., Alwen, J., Pietrzak, K.: SpaceMint: a cryptocurrency based on proofs of space. In: International Conference on Financial Cryptography and Data Security (2018)

41. Pass, R., Seeman, L., Shelat, A.: Analysis of the blockchain protocol in asynchronous networks. In: Coron, J.-S., Nielsen, J.B. (eds.) EUROCRYPT 2017. LNCS, vol. 10211, pp. 643–673. Springer, Cham (2017). https://doi.org/10.1007/978-3-319-56614-6_22
42. Pass, R., Shi, E.: FruitChains: a fair blockchain. In: Schiller, E.M., Schwarzmann, A.A. (eds.) ACM PODC 2017, Washington, DC, USA, 25–27 July 2017, pp. 315–324. ACM (2017)
43. Selman, B., Kautz, H.A., Cohen, B.: Noise strategies for improving local search. In: Proceedings of the Twelfth National Conference on Artificial Intelligence, AAAI 1994, USA, vol. 1, pp. 337–343 (1994)
44. Zhang, F., Eyal, I., Escriva, R., Juels, A., Van Renesse, R.: REM: resource-efficient mining for blockchains. In: 26th USENIX Security Symposium USENIX Security 2017, pp. 1427–1444 (2017)
45. Zheng, W., Chen, X., Zheng, Z., Luo, X., Cui, J.: AxeChain: a secure and decentralized blockchain for solving easily-verifiable problems. arXiv preprint arXiv:2003.13999 (2020)

Practical Statistically-Sound Proofs of Exponentiation in Any Group

Charlotte Hoffmann[1]([✉])(ID), Pavel Hubáček[2](ID), Chethan Kamath[3],
Karen Klein[4], and Krzysztof Pietrzak[1]

[1] Institute of Science and Technology Austria, Klosterneuburg, Austria
{charlotte.hoffmann,pietrzak}@ist.ac.at
[2] Faculty of Mathematics and Physics, Charles University, Prague, Czech Republic
hubacek@iuuk.mff.cuni.cz
[3] Tel Aviv University, Tel Aviv, Israel
ckamath@protonmail.com
[4] ETH Zurich, Zurich, Switzerland
karen.klein@inf.ethz.ch

Abstract. A proof of exponentiation (PoE) in a group $\mathbb{G}$ of unknown order allows a prover to convince a verifier that a tuple $(x, q, T, y) \in \mathbb{G} \times \mathbb{N} \times \mathbb{N} \times \mathbb{G}$ satisfies $x^{q^T} = y$. This primitive has recently found exciting applications in the constructions of verifiable delay functions and succinct arguments of knowledge. The most practical PoEs only achieve soundness either under computational assumptions, i.e., they are arguments (Wesolowski, Journal of Cryptology 2020), or in groups that come with the promise of not having any small subgroups (Pietrzak, ITCS 2019). The only statistically-sound PoE in *general* groups of unknown order is due to Block et al. (CRYPTO 2021), and can be seen as an elaborate parallel repetition of Pietrzak's PoE: to achieve λ bits of security, say $\lambda = 80$, the number of repetitions required (and thus the blow-up in communication) is as large as λ.

In this work, we propose a statistically-sound PoE for the case where the exponent q is the product of all primes up to some bound B. We show that, in this case, it suffices to run only $\lambda / \log(B)$ parallel instances of Pietrzak's PoE, which reduces the concrete proof-size compared to Block et al. by an order of magnitude. Furthermore, we show that in the known applications where PoEs are used as a building block such structured exponents are viable. Finally, we also discuss batching of our PoE, showing that many proofs (for the same $\mathbb{G}$ and q but different x and T) can be batched by adding only a single element to the proof per additional statement.

Pavel Hubáček was supported by the Grant Agency of the Czech Republic under the grant agreement no. 19-27871X and by the Charles University project UNCE/SCI/004. Chethan Kamath is supported by Azrieli International Postdoctoral Fellowship. Karen Klein was supported in part by ERC CoG grant 724307 and conducted part of this work at Institute of Science and Technology Austria.

Y. Dodis and T. Shrimpton (Eds.): CRYPTO 2022, LNCS 13508, pp. 370–399, 2022.
https://doi.org/10.1007/978-3-031-15979-4_13

1 Introduction

In a proof of exponentiation (PoE) in a group $\mathbb{G}$, a prover $\mathcal{P}$ aims at convincing a verifier $\mathcal{V}$ that a tuple $(x, q, T, y) \in \mathbb{G} \times \mathbb{N} \times \mathbb{N} \times \mathbb{G}$ satisfies $x^{q^T} = y$. Note that such proofs are only of interest if the order $\mathrm{ord}(\mathbb{G})$ of $\mathbb{G}$ is not known: otherwise, one can efficiently compute x^{q^T} by first computing the exponent modulo the group order, i.e., $e = q^T \bmod \mathrm{ord}(\mathbb{G})$, and then computing x^e using a single exponentiation x^e in $\mathbb{G}$.

PoEs in groups of unknown order have found applications for constructing verifiable delay functions (VDFs) [40,50] and as building blocks for time- and space-efficient succinct non-interactive arguments of knowledge (SNARK) [7]. In these applications, the prover and verifier get (x, q, T) and then $\mathcal{P}$ computes x^{q^T} by exponentiating to the power q sequentially[1] T times:

$$x \rightarrow x^q \rightarrow x^{q^2} \rightarrow x^{q^3} \rightarrow \ldots \rightarrow x^{q^T}.$$

In the next step, $\mathcal{P}$ sends y to $\mathcal{V}$ and then they run an interactive protocol where $\mathcal{P}$ convinces $\mathcal{V}$ that $y = x^{q^T}$. The existing protocols are all public-coin and, thus, can be made non-interactive in the random-oracle model using the Fiat-Shamir heuristic [27].

Soundness of PoEs. In the PoEs mentioned above, the prover's computation for the proof is marginal compared to the T exponentiations required to compute y in the first place, but the proofs differ in size. As illustrated in Table 1, in [50] the proof is just one group element, in [40] it is $\log(T)$ elements and in [7] it is $\lambda \log(T)$ elements for a statistical security parameter λ.

On the other hand, [7] is statistically-sound (and the non-interactive proof inherits this security in the random oracle model), while the soundness of [50] relies on a new computational hardness assumption called *adaptive root assumption*. Like with the proof-size, [40] lies in-between the other two protocols also in terms of the assumptions required for its soundness. It relies on the *low order assumption*, which requires that it is hard to find a (non-identity) element with low order in $\mathbb{G}$. This assumption is weaker than the adaptive root assumption [10] and, in groups where no low order elements exist, it holds unconditionally and, thus, the [40] PoE has statistical soundness.

The two concrete groups of unknown order that have been suggested are RSA groups [41] and class groups of imaginary quadratic fields [13]. An RSA group $\mathbb{Z}_N^*$ is defined by a product $N = p \cdot q$ of two large randomly sampled primes p, q. In [40], it was observed that if p, q are chosen to be safe primes[2] then the subgroup of quadratic residues of $\mathbb{Z}_N^*$ has no low order elements and, thus, the PoE is statistically-sound.

---

[1] In VDFs, it is an explicit "sequentiality assumption" that $y = x^{q^T}$ cannot be computed faster (i.e., with fewer sequential computational steps) than as described above, even when using massive parallelism.

[2] A prime p is safe if $(p-1)/2$ is also prime.

While class groups are much less studied than RSA groups, they have one major advantage, explained next. The only known way to sample an RSA group is to first sample p, q and then output $N = p \cdot q$, but this means the sampler knows the factorization and thus the group order $(p-1)(q-1)$. For such groups to be used for VDFs or SNARKs, one thus needs to either employ some trusted party to sample N and truthfully delete p, q, or sample N in an expensive multiparty computation (see, e.g., [17,28] and the references therein). Class groups on the other hand have a "transparent" setup: they can be sampled obliviously in the sense that a random string specifies a group without revealing the order of the group. However, our understanding of non-standard assumptions, like the low-order assumption, is still developing in class groups: in 2020 the authors of [3] showed how to break the low-order assumption in class groups for some classes of prime numbers.

Why Statistical Soundness? Recall that the only statistically-sound PoE in a group with transparent setup is from [7]. There, the PoE is used in a proof of knowledge and, to argue statistical knowledge-soundness of the protocol, the underlying PoE must be statistically-sound.

Also when a PoE is used in VDFs, statistical soundness can be crucial as such VDFs still provide some security even when the group order is revealed. Moreover, in settings where the group order is supposed to be known by some parties, it allows for a much more efficient setup. We discuss those two settings below.

Recall that a VDF has two security properties: the first is the sequentiality, which states that the output $y := x^{q^T}$ cannot be computed faster than by T sequential exponentiations; the second is the soundness of the proof certifying that y is the correct output. If a VDF is statistically-sound then, even in the worst case where an attacker learns the group order (say because the trusted setup failed, or in the case of sampling a weak class group), the attacker will only be able to compute the output fast but it will still not be able to lie about its value. In a design like Chia (chia.net), which combines VDFs with proofs of space to get a secure permissionless blockchain, an attacker that occasionally learns the group order (Chia uses class groups which are sampled freshly every 10 min) has limited impact on the security, but breaking the soundness of the VDF could be potentially devastating.[3]

Statistically-sound VDFs have also been used to construct randomness beacons like in the RandRunner protocol [46]. Their setup is not transparent: every party participating in the protocol realizing the beacon will sample two safe primes which then can be used in Pietrzak's statistically-sound PoE. The fact that these parties know the factorization is actually a feature, as they are occasionally required to use it as a trapdoor to compute and broadcast a VDF output

---

[3] A minor nuisance would be the need to roll back the blockchain once a flawed proof was added and recognized. But an attacker that can forge proofs controls the randomness, and thus can do things like attaching a pre-computed chain to the current one in order to do a double spending attack with only little resources.

and the PoE certifying its correctness fast. To prevent parties from lying, they must provide a zero-knowledge proof that their modulus is the product of two safes primes. Using the statistically-sound PoE from this work, we can avoid this expensive ZK proof and just use any RSA modulus, at the cost of larger PoEs for the individual proofs.

Generally, by using a VDF that is statistically-sound in any group allows us to skip the expensive zero-knowledge proof showing that a group was sampled correctly during setup (i.e., it has no low order elements) for protocols where statistical soundness is required because the party sampling the group knows the group order and, thus, could easily break soundness otherwise. Apart from randomness beacons as RandRunner, a related scenario comes up in the fair multiparty coin-flipping protocol of Freitag et al. [30]. This methodology might also be useful for (non-interactive) timed commitments [11] or encryption [32].

1.1   Our Contribution

As outlined above, Wesolowski's PoE has proofs of size one (group element) under the *adaptive root assumption*, Pietrzak's PoE has proofs of size $\log(T)$ under the weaker *low order assumption*, and the PoE of Block et al. has proofs of size $\log(T) \cdot \lambda$ for a statistical security parameter λ, say $\lambda = 80$. The protocol of Block et al. is the only PoE with statistical soundness in a group with transparent setup.

In this work, we present a new PoE to certify that (x, q, T, y) satisfies $y = x^{q^T}$ with statistical soundness in all groups. Our PoE only works for q of a special form. Namely, q is the product of all primes less than some bound B and, for such q, we get a proof-size $\log(T) \cdot \lambda / \log(B)$, i.e., by a factor $\log(B)$ smaller than in Block et al. [7]. Fortunately for the applications to VDFs or SNARKs discussed above, the choice of q does not really matter: in the SNARKs application [7] one can use any q that is sufficiently large.[4] For VDFs, one typically just sets $q = 2$, so exponentiation means one squaring. Having a more general q we can use square and multiply, so each exponentiation are $\lfloor \log(q) \rfloor$ (not just one) sequential squarings with some multiplications in-between. Note that if q was a power of 2 (which it is not in our case), say 2^k, the initial exponentiation would be of the form $x^{(2^k)^T}$, so one would set the time parameter to $T = T'/k$ in order to get a challenge that takes time T' to compute. Similarly, for our choice of q one sets the time parameter to $T = \lceil T' / \log(q) \rceil$ to get a challenge that takes sequential time T' to compute.

We cannot choose B too large, as a larger B negatively affects the verifier's complexity. As illustrated in Fig. 2, in our most basic protocol, the verifier's complexity is roughly the same as in Block et al. for $B = 521$. For this B, we get the proof down from $\lambda = 80$ to $9 = \lceil 80 / \log(B) \rceil$ elements for each of the $\log(T)$ rounds as illustrated in Fig. 1. In practice, this means that, e.g., for $T = 2^{32}$

---

[4] In [7] many results are stated only for odd choices of q. In Appendix B we show that they also hold for even q.

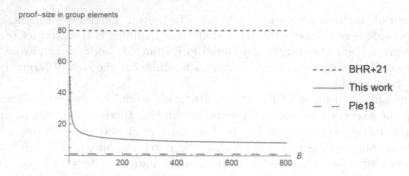

Fig. 1. Number of elements sent by the prover in one round for 80-bit security depending on the bound B. The dotted blue line is the proof-size in [7], the orange graph is the proof-size in our protocol and the dashed green line is the proof-size in [40] (which is one element per round). (Color figure online)

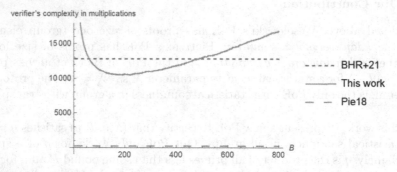

Fig. 2. Number of multiplications of the verifier in one round for 80-bit security depending on the bound B. The dotted blue line is the number of multiplications in [7], the orange graph is the number of multiplications in our protocol and the dashed green line is the verifier's complexity in [40]. In Fig. 4 we dissect the orange curve. (Color figure online)

and a group with elements of size 2048 bits, the proof-size drops from 655 KB to 74 KB.

Basic Protocol and Proof Idea. Our starting point is the following observation on the soundness in Pietrzak's PoE: Pietrzak's protocol proceeds in $\log(T)$ rounds, where each round starts with a claim $x^{q^T} \stackrel{?}{=} y$ and ends with a claim $y' \stackrel{?}{=} x'^{q^{T/2}}$ for a T of half the size. Assume that, at the beginning of a round, we have the wrong claim that $y' \stackrel{?}{=} x^{q^T}$ while $y = x^{q^T}$, where $y' = y \cdot \alpha$ with $\alpha \notin \{1, -1\}$. The soundness of the protocol then depends on the order $\mathrm{ord}(\alpha)$ of α (i.e., $\alpha^{\mathrm{ord}(\alpha)} = 1$). Concretely, if $\mathrm{ord}(\alpha) = p^e$ for some prime power e of p at the beginning of a round (in this introduction, we only consider the special case of a single prime power as it already contains all interesting aspects) then the claim at the end of the round is still wrong with probability $1 - 1/p^e$ (i.e., this round has a soundness error of $1/p^e$). More generally, for any $t \leq e$, we end up with a claim for some $y \cdot \alpha'$ instead of the correct y with probability $1 - 1/p^t$, where $\text{ord}(\alpha') = p^{e'}$ for $e' \geq e - t$.

Note that this means that Pietrzak's protocol is statistically-sound if no low order elements exist. The PoE by Block et al. does not need any assumption about $\text{ord}(\alpha)$, and it achieves statistical soundness even if $\text{ord}(\alpha) = 2$ (while Pietrzak's PoE is only $1/2$ sound for such α) by basically running λ PoEs in parallel. In each round, one starts with λ claims of the form $x^{q^T} \stackrel{?}{=} y$ and, for each claim, the prover provides μ which it claims is the "midpoint" satisfying both $x^{q^{T/2}} \stackrel{?}{=} \mu, \mu^{q^{T/2}} \stackrel{?}{=} y$. At this point, we have 2λ claims, at least one of which is wrong if one of the original claims was wrong. These 2λ claims are then randomly combined into λ claims of the form $x^{q^{T/2}} \stackrel{?}{=} y$. Each of these claims is individually wrong with probability $1/2$ and, thus, at least one of them is wrong with probability $1 - 2^{-\lambda}$. Each round gets the exponent in the claims down from T to $T/2$ and, after $\log(T)$ rounds, we have claims that the verifier can efficiently verify itself with a single exponentiation.

In our protocol, we use a similar strategy as Block et al.: We run ρ PoEs in parallel (where ρ can be smaller than the statistical parameter λ). Unlike Block et al., we require q to be of a special form, in our basic protocol it is the product of all primes less than some bound B. If $\text{ord}(\alpha)$ has a prime divisor $p > B$ then we use the same security argument as above (but with p not 2) to get soundness error $p^{-\rho} \leq B^{-\rho}$, in this case we get soundness $2^{-\lambda}$ as Block et al. with only $\rho \approx \lambda / \log(B)$ instead of λ repetitions. Otherwise, we have $\text{ord}(\alpha) = p^e$ for some $p < B$. If the prime power e is large, concretely $e \geq \log(T)\log(B)$ then we again can basically use the argument above. In each of the $\log(T)$ rounds, the prime power must go down by $\log(B)$ on average, and even for $p = 2$ that only happens with prob $2^{-\log(B)} = 1/B$.

Therefore, we are left with the case $\text{ord}(\alpha) = p^e$ with $e \leq C = \log(T)\log(B)$. To handle this case, we change the statement to be proven from $y \stackrel{?}{=} x^{q^T}$ to $y' \stackrel{?}{=} x^{q^{T-C}}$ and we let the verifier compute the final $y = y'^{q^C}$ itself. Assume that the prover wrongly claims $y'' \stackrel{?}{=} x^{q^{T-C}}$ with $y'' = y' \cdot \alpha$. With α as above, the final exponentiations of the verifier eliminate α. Since now the order p^e of α divides q^C, we have that $\alpha^{q^C} = 1$ and, so,

$$y''^{q^C} = (y' \cdot \alpha)^{q^C} = y'^{q^C} \cdot \alpha^{q^C} = y'^{q^C} = y.$$

Improving the Verifier's Complexity. The basic protocol that we just outlined decreases the number of parallel repetitions, and thus the proof-size in the non-interactive case, by a factor $\log(B)$. But the verifier has to carry out some extra work as it must compute the final exponentiation $(y', q, C) \rightarrow y'^{q^C}$ by itself. This can be quite expensive, especially if we batch many proofs together. In the same group and for the same T, both protocols of Pietrzak and Block et al. can handle many PoEs basically at the price of a single PoE plus a small additive complexity overhead for each proof (this is, in fact, exploited in the SNARKs from [7]). In this work, we show that such batching works even for different values of T. Though, one problem for our new PoE is that, while this batching works also for the first phase of our protocol, the final exponentiation of the verifier cannot be trivially batched and, thus, it must be performed for each statement individually.

We thus further improve the protocol in two ways getting mostly rid of the extra cost for the final exponentiation. The first improvement leverages the observation that, by setting q to be not just the product of all primes $< B$ but taking each prime p with power $\log(B)/\log(p)$, we can already decrease the exponent C for the final exponentiation from $\log(T)\log(B)$ to $\log(T)$. The second improvement comes from the observation that the final exponentiation $(y', q, C) \rightarrow y'^{q^C}$ can be replaced by just another PoE and, using our batching, this statement itself can be just batched together with the original statement. As the exponent ($C = \log(T)$ with the first improvement) is much smaller than T, the final exponentiation now only needs $\log(C) = \log\log(T)$ rounds. Iterating this idea $\log^*(T)$ times (which is at most $5 = \log^*(2^{2^{2^{2^2}}}) = \log^*(2^{65536})$ in practice) we get the number of exponentiations down to 1 with a modest increase (from $\rho \cdot \log(T)$ to $\rho \cdot (\log(T) + \log^*(T))$ group elements) in proof-size. This batching argument only works so conveniently for T of a special form, basically powers of 2: T in the (relevant) range $2^{17} < T < 2^{65536}$ should be of the form $T = 2^t + 2^{16} + 2^4 + 2^2 + 1$. For general T the verifier's cost grows with basically the Hamming weight of $\log(T)$. In Appendix B.1 we analyze the gain in efficiency of the polynomial commitment in [7] when we use this improved version of our PoE as a building block instead of the PoE proposed in [7].

1.2   Additional Related Work

PoE, SNARGs and VDFs. Verifiable Delay Function (VDF), as a cryptographic primitive, was first formalised in [9]. In addition to defining its security requirements, [9] provided theoretical constructions based on incrementally-verifiable computation [48]. Loosely speaking, they used repeated (structured) hashing as their delay function and then relied on succinct non-interactive arguments (SNARGs) to enable efficient verifiability of the result of the repeated hashing. As explained in Sect. 1, (non-interactive) PoE are closely related to VDFs: the practical VDFs of Pietrzak [40] and Wesolowski [50] use repeated squaring in a group of unknown order as their delay function and use a PoE on top to enable efficient, public verifiability of the result of the repeated squaring. The difference between [40] and [50] lies in the way the PoE is implemented: an overview and comparison of these PoE protocols can be found in [10]. Moreover, there is evidence that to construct VDFs over groups, the reliance on the group order being unknown is inherent [37,45], which lends even more importance to PoE protocols from the perspective of efficient VDFs. Finally, PoE have recently been used as a crucial building block in constructing space-efficient general-purpose succinct non-interactive arguments of knowledge (SNARKs) [2,7,14], thus establishing a converse relationship.

Additional Related Work to VDFs. VDFs have also been proposed in other algebraic settings: e.g., the constructions in [16,25,47] are based on supersingular isogenies with the motivation to achieve (some notion of) post-quantum security.[5] In addition to the basic VDFs, refined variants of VDFs have also been explored. For a "continuous" VDF [23], it should be possible (loosely speaking) to take a proof and iterate it to produce a proof for the next iteration of the delay function (instead of having to recompute the proof for the new value from scratch). A "tight" VDF [20] necessitates that the amount of work that is required to generate a proof to be 'comparable' to that required to just compute the function. Finally, we point out that existence of VDFs has implications in complexity theory, in particular to the existence of average-case hardness in complexity classes of total search problems such as **PPAD** [18,23,34].

Timed-Release Cryptography. VDFs fall under the umbrella of timed-release cryptographic primitives [38]. The first of such objects were time-lock puzzles (TLP) [42] and timed commitments [11]. A TLP can be regarded as a delay function that also allows efficient sampling of its output (via a trapdoor). The TLP from [42] uses repeated squaring in RSA group as the delay function, while the output can be efficiently determined using the factorisation of the modulus as trapdoor. Constructions of TLP are scarce – the only other known construction is from [6] and it relies on obfuscation-like assumptions. Prior to VDFs the notion of proofs of sequential work (PoSW) was introduced by Mahmoody, Moran an Vadhan [36]. Like in a VDF, in a PoSW a prover on input some challenge x and time parameter T must perform an (inherently sequential) computation of $\Theta(T)$ steps and provide an efficiently verifiable proof. VDFs are a stronger notion than PoSW as in the latter the proof only certifies that a sequential computation was done, while in a VDF has an additional – for many applications crucial – "uniqueness" property, it certifies that some particular value is the correct output of a deterministic sequential computation. Unlike TLPs, PoSWs can be constructed from random oracles (RO) [35]. The construction from [36] is based on ROs but is not really practical as the prover needs not just T time but also linear in T space to compute the PoSW. A construction using just $\log(T)$ space was given in [19], constructions with extra properties like being that "reversible" [1] or "incremental" [21] were recently proposed. Existing PoSW are quantum secure [8], while as mentioned above, for VDFs post quantum security is largely open. Before practical VDFs were found, the sloth function of Lenstra and Wesolowski [33] was the closest we had to a unique PoSW. The reason sloth was not a unique PoSW was that verification took time linear in the time to compute the output,

---

[5] Note that the delay functions in the RSA group and class groups of imaginary quadratic field lose their sequentiality property in the quantum setting since the order of these groups can be efficiently computed.

but verification is faster by a constant around 1000 (leveraging the difference of squaring and taking roots in groups of *known* order) and can be parallelized.

Repeated Squaring. The use of repeated squaring (a special case of repeated exponentiation) in a group of unknown order as an inherently sequential operation can be traced back to [15,42]. In the algebraic setting of RSA group, there is evidence that speeding up repeated squaring is tantamount to factoring [32,44]. Further support for the sequential hardness of the problem was given in [51] and [49]. In [29] Freitag and Komargodski give a lower bound for the verifier's complexity in interactive proofs for repeated squaring in the generic group model.

Batch Verification. The idea of using batching to reduce the amortized cost per operation has been explored for a host of cryptographic primitives such as, e.g., key agreement [5], signatures [39], and public-key encryption [26]. Closer to our topic, the problem of batching the verification of multiple *exponentiations* in arbitrary groups (not necessary of unknown order) was studied in [4]. They make a heavy use of the random subset and random exponents technique (as pointed out in [43]), which we also do. Building on [4], Rotem [43] recently explored batch-verification of VDFs: as mentioned in Sect. 3, Rotem focused on the verification of statements with the same time parameter, whereas our batching does not have this restriction. We refer the reader to [43] for further related work on batching.

2   Basic Protocol

Block et al. [7] constructed a statistically-sound PoE in any group of unknown order using the PoE from [40] as starting point. To achieve λ bits of security, their construction requires a multiplicative factor of λ in proof-size compared to [40]. Below, we first explain the PoE from [7] in a bit more detail (than Sect. 1.1), and then we explain how our protocol reduces this overhead. For now we just focus on improving the proof-size, but the verifier complexity of our protocol will increase, especially in settings where we batch many proofs – later, in Sect. 3, we will show how to get down the verifier's complexity.

Statistical PoE from [7]. To interactively prove the statement $x^{q^T} \stackrel{?}{=} y$, the prover and verifier first make λ copies of the statement. In every round of the protocol, the original claims are reduced to "smaller" statements by reducing the exponent q^{T_i} to $q^{T_{i+1}} := q^{T_i/2}$ as follows: The i-th round starts with a set of λ statements $\{x_i^{q^{T_i}} \stackrel{?}{=} y_i\}_{i\in[1,\lambda]}$. The prover then sends λ many "midpoints" $\{\mu_i := x_i^{q^{T_i/2}}\}_{i\in[1,\lambda]}$ resulting in 2λ statements of the form $\{u_i^{q^{T_i/2}} \stackrel{?}{=} v_i\}_{i\in[1,2\lambda]}$. To avoid a blow-up in the number of statements in every round, the verifier recombines these 2λ statements by taking a random subset of them and multiplying the statements in the subset together, i.e., obtaining a *single* statement. To ensure soundness, the verifier performs λ many of such recombinations independently and the round ends with λ many new smaller statements. It is easy to see why the recombination step must be performed λ many times: Suppose only one of the 2λ statements is incorrect before the recombination step. Then, with probability $1/2$, the incorrect statement is not chosen among the statements in the random subset used during the recombination step and the resulting new statement is correct. If all new statements are correct, then the verifier falsely outputs accept at the end of the protocol and, therefore, the verifier must perform λ many independent recombinations to ensure λ bit security.

Our Protocol. In this work, we improve the efficiency of the above PoE by introducing the following changes in the protocol:

1. Instead of sampling a subset to construct a new statement, we take each statement to a random exponent in $\{0, 1, \ldots, 2^\kappa - 1\}$, where κ is some small integer, and then multiply them together.
2. We set

$$q := \prod_{\text{prime } p < B} p, \tag{1}$$

   where B is some fixed bound, which can be chosen depending on the application of the PoE.
3. We define a constant C such that the prover gives a proof for the statement $x^{q^{T-C}} \stackrel{?}{=} y'$ (i.e., a C-th root of the original statement) and the verifier computes the final check $(y')^{q^C} = y$ itself.

The above changes allow us to reduce the number of repetitions from λ to $\rho := \lambda/\log(B)$ (for λ bits security). At a first glance, it could seem like the first change is sufficient to avoid the need for λ independent recombinations since the probability that an incorrect statement is part of a new statement is not $1/2$ anymore but seemingly $1/2^\kappa$. Unfortunately, it is not the case that taking κ-bit exponents for the recombination step achieves such a drastic improvement in the bound on the probability of accepting an incorrect statement. Note that the process of raising an incorrect statement to some exponent can also result in a correct statement. This is indeed very likely if an incorrect statement $x^{q^T} \stackrel{?}{=} y$ is "close" to the correct one in the sense that y is the correct result multiplied by a low-order element α. If, for example, this element α is of order two and the statement is raised to an even exponent, say two, the resulting statement $(x^{q^T})^2 \stackrel{?}{=} (y\alpha)^2$ will be a valid one. This observation underlies an attack on [40] that was first described[6] in [10] and it is also the reason why [40] is statistically-sound only in groups that have no elements of small order.

   To circumvent the above attack using low-order elements, we introduce the second and third change in the protocol: instead of the original statement $x^{q^T} \stackrel{?}{=} y$, the (honest) prover only proves the (shorter) modified statement $x^{q^{T-C}} \stackrel{?}{=} y'$,

---

[6] The observation that random batching can be attacked using low-order elements was already made in [12].

where $y' := x^{q^{T-C}}$, and the verifier checks $(y')^{q^C} \overset{?}{=} y$ *by itself* as the final step. Moreover, to ensure that all the low orders are covered, we define q to be the product of all small prime numbers up to a certain bound B as in Eq. (1). Now, a malicious prover that tries to cheat on an original statement by proving a wrong modified statement[7] *will* get caught in the final exponentiation *as long as* the wrong modified statement is "close" to the correct one, where "close" means that the correct result can be multiplied by an element α whose order only has small prime divisors (prime numbers less than B) and the prime divisors have small exponents (integers up to C). To see this, observe that if the modified statement is $x^{q^{T-C}} \overset{?}{=} y'\alpha$ (which is wrong), the final exponentiation with q^C leads to rejection since

$$(\alpha y')^{q^C} = 1 \cdot (x^{q^{T-C}})^{q^C} = x^{q^T} \neq y,$$

where $\alpha^{q^C} = 1$ holds in $\mathbb{G}$ because of our assumption that it has low order. The above changes allow us to restrict to adversaries that try to convince the verifier of statements that are "far" from correct, i.e., where the correct result is multiplied by an element whose order either has a large prime divisor or a divisor which is a small prime number with a large exponent. However, in this case the probability that the protocol ends with only correct statements and the verifier falsely accepts at the end of the protocol is less than $\log(T) \cdot 2^{-\lambda}$ for parameters $C = \log(T)\log(B)$ and $\rho = \lambda/\log(B)$, where ρ takes the role of λ in [7], i.e., it is basically the number of parallel repetitions of Pietrzak's protocol.

We give a formal description of our protocol in Fig. 3. For clarity of exposition[8], we assume that $T = 2^t + C$ for some $t \in \mathbb{N}$. Note that, similarly to [7], the starting instance in our protocol can either contain ρ many different statements with exponent q^T or ρ many copies of the same statement.

2.1   Soundness

We show that our protocol is statistically-sound for arbitrary groups of unknown order. In particular, soundness holds against adversaries that can construct group elements of small order:

Theorem 1. *Let B be any prime number such that $q := \prod_{prime\ p<B} p$ and $\rho \in \mathbb{N}$ be the number of repetitions per round. If we set $C = \log(T)\log(B)$ and let $\kappa \to \infty$, the verifier $\mathcal{V}$ will output* accept *on an incorrect statement $(x, y, T = 2^t + C)$ with probability at most*

$$\frac{t}{B^\rho}.$$

---

[7] If the (malicious) prover does not cheat on the modified statement, the verifier will anyway catch it during the final exponentiation.

[8] The case where $T - C$ is not a power of 2 can be handled by a standard approach similar to [40, Section 3.1].

Instance: (x, T, y), where $x, y \in \mathbb{G}$ and $T \in \mathbb{N}$

Parameters: (determined in the analysis)

1. bound $B \in \mathbb{N}$, which defines the base $q := \prod_{\text{prime } p < B} p$
2. constant for exponentiation $C \in \mathbb{N}$
3. number of parallel repetitions $\rho \in \mathbb{N}$
4. size of individual random coin $\kappa \in \mathbb{N}$

Statement: $x^{q^T} = y$

Protocol: For the ease of exposition, we assume that $T = 2^t + C$. The protocol consists of t rounds described in Item 2 below.

1. The prover sends $y' = x^{q^{T-C}}$ to the verifier, defining the initial ρ instances $\{(x_{0,j}, y_{0,j}, T_0)\}_{j \in [1,\rho]}$, where $T_0 := T - C$ and, for $j \in [1, \rho]$, $x_{0,j} := x$ and $y_{0,j} := y'$.
2. In round $i \in [1, t]$, the prover and verifier engage in the following halving sub-protocol:
   (a) Let $\{(x_{i-1,j}, y_{i-1,j}, T_{i-1} = 2^{t-i+1})\}_{j \in [1,\rho]}$ be the instance from round $i - 1$.
   (b) The prover sends the midpoints $\{\mu_{i,j} := x_{i-1,j}^{q^{T_{i-1}/2}}\}_{j \in [1,\rho]}$ defining 2ρ smaller instances

   $$\{(x_{i-1,j}, \mu_{i,j}, T_i := T_{i-1}/2)\}_{j \in [1,\rho]} \text{ and } \{(\mu_{i,j}, y_{i-1,j}, T_i)\}_{j \in [1,\rho]},$$

   which we denote $\{(u_{i,k}, v_{i,k}, T_i)\}_{k \in [1,2\rho]}$.
   (c) The verifier sends a random challenge $\{r_{i,j,k}\}_{j \in [1,\rho], k \in [1,2\rho]}$ to the prover, where $r_{i,j,k} \leftarrow \{0,1\}^\kappa$ independently for all $j \in [1, \rho]$ and $k \in [1, 2\rho]$.
   (d) They both set $\{(x_{i,j}, y_{i,j}, T_i)\}_{j \in [1,\rho]}$, where

   $$x_{i,j} := \prod_{k \in [1,2\rho]} u_{i,k}^{r_{i,j,k}} \text{ and } y_{i,j} := \prod_{k \in [1,2\rho]} v_{i,k}^{r_{i,j,k}},$$

   and proceed to the next round.
3. The verifier accepts only if $x_{t,j}^q = y_{t,j}$ and $(y')^{q^C} = y$ for all $j \in [1, \rho]$. Otherwise, it rejects.

Fig. 3. Our basic Proof of Exponentiation.

A parameter of our PoE is the bit-size κ of each random element sampled by the verifier. In the statement of Theorem 1, we consider the limit case with κ approaching infinity for the sake of readability. Note that if r is sampled from a randomness space of size 2^κ we have $\Pr[p \text{ divides } r] = 1/p + 1/2^\kappa$. In the limit case $\kappa \to \infty$, the probability is $1/p$. In practice, κ needs to be chosen carefully such that the protocol is still efficient but the probability of the above event is close enough to $1/p$. We discuss this point further in Sect. 2.2.

Before proving Theorem 1, we explain how the order of a group element affects soundness. Let $x^{q^{T-C}} = y'$ but a malicious prover claims that the result is $x^{q^{T-C}} = y'\alpha$. We say that the second statement is α-wrong. Then soundness of the protocol depends on the order of α:

In the execution of the protocol, the prover first sends a midpoint μ, which results in two statements $\mu \overset{?}{=} x^{q^{(T-C)/2}}$ and $\mu^{q^{(T-C)/2}} \overset{?}{=} y'\alpha$. Note that whatever the prover claims to be μ, one of the two statements will be incorrect, so for now we can assume that the prover sends a correct midpoint $\mu = x^{q^{(T-C)/2}}$. We copy each statement ρ many times, raise each copy to a random exponent r_k and then multiply the 2ρ statements together. This results in a new statement that is correct whenever

$$\alpha^{r_1}\alpha^{r_2}\ldots\alpha^{r_\rho} = \alpha^{r_1+r_2+\cdots+r_\rho} = 1.$$

This is the case when $r_1 + r_2 + \cdots + r_\rho \equiv 0 \mod \text{ord}(\alpha)$, which happens with probability $1/\text{ord}(\alpha)$ if we assume that the randomness space is large enough (for more information on the size of the randomness see Sect. 2.2). This means that whenever $\text{ord}(\alpha)$ is large, it is unlikely that the statement is transformed into a correct statement after a single round. However, the order of the element that makes the statement incorrect can also decrease round by round until the statement is transformed into a correct one. To show this, we use the following well-known fact. A proof can be found in any standard textbook on group theory (e.g., [22, Proposition 5]).

Proposition 1. *Let $\mathbb{G}$ be a group, $\alpha \in \mathbb{G}$ a group element and m a positive integer. It holds that*

$$\text{ord}(\alpha^m) = \frac{\text{ord}(\alpha)}{\gcd(\text{ord}(\alpha), m)}.$$

From Proposition 1 we get that $\text{ord}(\alpha^{r_1+r_2+\cdots+r_\rho}) < \text{ord}(\alpha)$ whenever $r_1 + r_2 + \cdots + r_\rho \equiv 0 \mod d$, where d is a divisor of $\text{ord}(\alpha)$. If the order decreases in all of the ρ many new statements obtained this way, the adversary has a better chance to end up with a correct statement in one of the following rounds. We want to bound the probability that after some round of the protocol all of the statements are correct. To this end we need the following Lemma which bounds the probability that recombining a set of $m > \rho$ statements, where at least one statement is wrong, gives ρ correct statements. In the proof of Theorem 1 we always have $m = 2\rho$. Later in Sect. 3 we show how to prove many statements simultaneously so we will use the lemma with different values m.

Lemma 1. *Let $\{(x_i, y_i, T)\}_{i \in [1,m]}$ be a set of m statements such that at least one of the statements is α-wrong for some $\alpha \in \mathbb{G}$. Let $\{(\tilde{x}_j, \tilde{y}_j, T)\}_{j \in [1,\rho]}$ be a set of ρ statements defined as*

$$\tilde{x}_j := \prod_{i \in [1,m]} x_i^{r_{j,i}} \quad and \quad \tilde{y}_j := \prod_{i \in [1,m]} y_i^{r_{j,i}}$$

with independently sampled $r_{j,i} \leftarrow \mathbb{Z}_{2^\kappa}$ uniformly at random for all $i \in [1,m]$ and $j \in [1,\rho]$. Let B be any prime number. If we let $\kappa \to \infty$, the new statements satisfy the following properties with probability at least $1 - (1/B)^\rho$:

1. *If for some prime $p \geq B$ we have $p \mid \mathrm{ord}(\alpha)$, at least one of the instances $\{(\tilde{x}_j, \tilde{y}_j, T)\}_{j \in [1,\rho]}$ is $\tilde{\alpha}$-wrong and $p \mid \mathrm{ord}(\tilde{\alpha})$.*
2. *If for some prime $p < B$ and some integer $e \geq \log(B)$ we have $p^e \mid \mathrm{ord}(\alpha)$, at least one of the instances $\{(\tilde{x}_j, \tilde{y}_j, T)\}_{j \in [1,\rho]}$ is $\tilde{\alpha}$-wrong and $p^{e-\log(B)+1} \mid \mathrm{ord}(\tilde{\alpha})$.*

Proof. Since we want to lower bound the probabilities of the above events, it is sufficient to consider the case where $\mathrm{ord}(\alpha)$ has a single prime divisor. So, we assume $\mathrm{ord}(\alpha) = p^e$ for some prime p and integer e. Using α, we can express the statements $\{(x_i, y_i, T)\}_{i \in [1,m]}$ equivalently in the form $\{(x_i, h_i \alpha^{a_i}, T)\}_{i \in [1,m]}$, where $x_i^{q^T} = h_i$ are the correct results for all $i \in [1,m]$, $a_i \in \mathbb{Z}$ and at least one of the $a_i = 1$. A new statement $(\tilde{x}_j, \tilde{y}_j, T)$ is computed as

$$\tilde{x}_j := \prod_{i \in [1,m]} x_i^{r_{j,i}} \quad and \quad \tilde{y}_j := \prod_{i \in [1,m]} (h_i \alpha^{a_i})^{r_{j,i}}.$$

Let $\tilde{\alpha} := \prod_{i \in [1,m]} \alpha^{a_i \cdot r_{j,i}}$. By Proposition 1, the order of $\tilde{\alpha}$ is

$$\frac{p^e}{\gcd(p^e, \sum_{i=1}^m a_i r_{j,i})} = p^{e-s}$$

for some $s \in \{0, 1, \ldots, e\}$. The probability that $s \geq k$ for any $k \in \{0, 1, \ldots, e\}$ is

$$\Pr[s \geq k] = \Pr\left[\sum_{i=1}^m a_i r_{j,i} \equiv 0 \mod p^k\right] = \frac{1}{p^k}.$$

To obtain the first claim of the lemma, we set $e = 1$ and $p = B$. The probability that the new statement is correct is the probability that $s = 1$, which is $1/B$. Hence, the probability that all of the ρ new instances are correct is $1/B^\rho$.

We obtain the second claim of the lemma by setting $e \geq \log(B)$ and observing that the probability of $s \geq \log(B)$ is $1/p^{\log(B)} \leq 1/2^{\log(B)} = 1/B$. Hence, the probability that this is the case for all ρ statements is at most $1/B^\rho$. $\square$

Proof (of Theorem 1). Assume that the correct result in Step 2 of the protocol is $x^{q^{T-C}} = y'$ but a malicious prover claims that it is $x^{q^{T-C}} = y'\alpha$ (i.e., makes a statement that is α-wrong). Notice that in the case where $\operatorname{ord}(\alpha) \mid q^C$ we have that $(y'\alpha)^{q^C} = (y')^{q^C} = y$ and, hence, the verifier ends up rejecting after Step 3 of the protocol. It follows that an adversary who wants to convince the verifier that the result is not y needs to choose an element α of order not dividing q^C. The adversary wins if all of the ρ statements are correct after t rounds of the protocol. From the discussion above we know that the best option for the adversary is either picking an element of order 2^{C+1} or an element of order p, where p is the smallest prime not dividing q^C. We analyze the two cases separately.

Case 1: Let $\operatorname{ord}(\alpha) = p$. Assume that in round i of the protocol we have ρ many statements $\{(x_{i-1,j}, y_{i-1,j}\alpha^{a_{i-1,j}}, T_{i-1})\}_{j\in[1,\rho]}$ where $a_{i-1,j} \in \mathbb{Z}$ for all $j \in [1, \rho]$. If $a_{i-1,j} \equiv 0 \mod p$, the statement is correct. Otherwise it is wrong and, by Proposition 1 and the primality of p, we know that $\alpha^{a_{i-1,j}}$ has order p. We assume that at least one of the $a_{i-1,j}$ is not divisible by p and we bound the probability that all of the statements are correct in round $i + 1$.

In Step 2 of the protocol, the prover sends midpoints $\mu_{i,j}$ which results in 2ρ statements

$$\{(x_{i-1,j}, \mu_{i,j}, T_i = T_i/2)\}_{j\in[1,\rho]} \text{ and } \{(\mu_{i,j}, y_{i-1,j}\alpha^{a_{i-1,j}}, T_i)\}_{j\in[1,\rho]},$$

which we denote by $\{(u_{i,k}, v_{i,k}\alpha^{b_{i,k}}, T_i)\}_{k\in[1,2\rho]}$. Note that at least one of the $b_{i,k}$ is nonzero modulo p, no matter which elements $\mu_{i,j}$ the prover sends. Hence, the assumption of Lemma 1 is satisfied, so the probability that all of the statements in round $i+1$ are correct is at most $1/B^\rho$. By the union bound, we get that the probability that all statements are correct after t rounds is

$$\frac{t}{B^\rho}.$$

Case 2: Let $\operatorname{ord}(\alpha) = 2^{C+1}$ where $C = t\ell$ for some $\ell \geq \log(B)$. In order to end up with a correct statement after t rounds, the adversary has to decrease the order of the wrong element by a factor of 2^ℓ on average per round. In particular (by an averaging argument) there has to be one round where the order decreases by at least 2^ℓ.

Assume that in round i of the protocol we have ρ statements of the form $\{(x_{i-1,j}, y_{i-1,j}\alpha^{a_{i-1,j}}, T_{i-1})\}_{j\in[1,\rho]}$ where $a_{i-1,j} \in \mathbb{Z}$. Without loss of generality, let $\alpha^{a_{i-1,1}}$ have the largest order of all $\alpha^{a_{i-1,j}}$.

The prover sends midpoints $\mu_{i,j}$ which results in 2ρ statements

$$\{(x_{i-1,j}, \mu_{i,j}, T_i = T_i/2)\}_{j\in[1,\rho]} \text{ and } \{(\mu_{i,j}, y_{i-1,j}\alpha^{a_{i-1,j}}, T_i)\}_{j\in[1,\rho]},$$

which we denote by $\{(u_{i,k}, v_{i,k}\alpha^{b_{i,k}}, T_i)\}_{k\in[1,2\rho]}$.

We note that whatever midpoint the prover sends, the order of the element that makes one of the two statements $\mu_{i,1} \overset{?}{=} x_{i-1,1}^{q^{T_i}}$ and $\mu_{i,1}^{q^{T_i}} \overset{?}{=} y_{i-1,1}\alpha^{a_{i-1,1}}$

incorrect is at least $\mathrm{ord}(\alpha^{a_{i-1,1}})$. To see this, assume that $\mu_{i,1}$ is the correct midpoint but the adversary sends $\mu_{i,1}\beta$ for some group element β. Then the second statement becomes $\mu_{i,1}^{q^{T_i}} \overset{?}{=} y_{i-1,1}\alpha^{a_{i-1,1}}\beta^{-q^{T_i}}$, which is γ-wrong for $\gamma := \alpha^{a_{i-1,1}}\beta^{-q^{T_i}}$. Since $\alpha^{a_{i-1,1}} = \gamma\beta^{q^{T_i}}$ we have that $\mathrm{ord}(\alpha^{a_{i-1,1}})$ divides $\mathrm{lcm}(\mathrm{ord}(\gamma), \mathrm{ord}(\beta^{q^{T_i}}))$. It follows that $\mathrm{ord}(\alpha^{a_{i-1,1}})$ divides either $\mathrm{ord}(\gamma)$ or $\mathrm{ord}(\beta^{q^{T_i}})$ (and hence $\mathrm{ord}(\beta)$) because the order of $\alpha^{a_{i-1,1}}$ is a power of 2.

By Lemma 1, we get that the probability that none of the statements in round $i + 1$ is $\tilde{\alpha}$-wrong, where $\tilde{\alpha}$ is some element with order divisible by $\mathrm{ord}(\alpha^{a_{i-1,1}})/2^{\ell-1}$, is at most $1/B^\rho$. By the union bound, we conclude that the adversary wins after t rounds with probability at most

$$\frac{t}{B^\rho}.$$

Cases 1 and 2 together yield Theorem 1. $\qquad\square$

Corollary 1. *For $C := t\log(B)$ the Fiat-Shamir transform of our PoE yields a sound non-interactive protocol.*

Proof. As we have seen above, a malicious prover is able to convince the verifier of a wrong statement only if there is one round where at least one of the following two events happens depending on which attack is chosen:

- an α-wrong statement where $\mathrm{ord}(\alpha)$ has a prime divisor of size at least B is transformed into a correct one or
- the order of the wrong element decreases by at least $2^{C/t}$.

We know that the probability that the output of a random oracle results in such an event is $(1/B)^\rho$ since by our choice of C we have $1/2^{\rho C/t} = (1/B)^\rho$. By the union bound, the probability that a malicious prover that makes up to Q queries to the random oracle will find such a query is at most $Q \cdot (1/B)^\rho$. $\qquad\square$

2.2 Efficiency

In this section, we analyze the efficiency of the Fiat-Shamir transform of our PoE for proving a statement of the form $x^{q^T} \overset{?}{=} y$ with $T = 2^t + C$.

Randomness Space. In order to keep the cost of exponentiation with random coins low, we need to make the size of the randomness space as small as possible while ensuring that divisibility by B is almost uniformly distributed. For concreteness, we use $\log(B) + 5$ random bits. Then it holds for any prime $p > B$ and $c \in \mathbb{Z}_p$ that

$$\Pr_{r \leftarrow \mathbb{Z}_{2^{\lceil \log(B)\rceil+5}}}[r = c \mod p] < \frac{1}{B} + \frac{1}{B \cdot 2^5} \approx \frac{1.03}{B}.$$

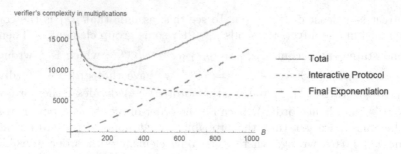

Fig. 4. Number of multiplications of the verifier in one round for 80-bit security depending on the bound B. The orange graph is the total verifier's complexity for one round, the blue dotted graph is the cost of the interactive part of the protocol and the green dashed graph is the cost of the final exponentiation divided by the number of rounds (i.e., we amortize the cost of the final exponentiation over the number of rounds). (Color figure online)

Verifier's Efficiency. The work for the verifier consists of two parts: 1) the interactive part, which is dominated by $t \cdot 4\rho^2$ exponentiations (with exponents of size $\log(B) + 5$) and ρ exponentiations with q, and 2) the final exponentiation with q^C. Each exponentiation with a z-bit exponent via "square and multiply" costs about $1.5z$ multiplications (i.e., z plus the Hamming weight of the exponent), so the small exponentiations have complexity $6t\rho^2(\log(B)+5)$. Additionally, the verifier performs $2t\rho^2$ multiplications to recombine the statements. The exponentiation with q^C takes $C \cdot \log(q)$ multiplications. If we set $C = t \cdot \log(B)$, the total of multiplications performed by the verifier is approximately

$$t \cdot ((6\log(B) + 32)\rho^2 + \log(B) \cdot \log(q)) + \rho \log(q) \approx t \log(B)(6\rho^2 + 2B) + 2\rho B,$$

where we use the upper bound $q \leq 4^B$ of Erdős [24] . As an example, consider an implementation where $t = 32$, $B = 521$, and $\rho = \lceil 80/\log(521)\rceil = 9$. Then we have $\log(q) \approx 703$, so the cost for the verifier is around 426000 multiplications.

In Fig. 4, we plot the complexity of the verifier *in a single round* of the interactive protocol for different values of B. Additionally, we consider the curves for the verifier's complexity of only the interaction with the prover and only the final exponentiation separately. Observe that, for $B < 227$, the total complexity decreases as B increases due to the fact that the number of repetitions $\lambda/\log(B)$ decreases faster than the increasing cost of the final exponentiation with q^C (the latter increases linearly with B). Beyond $B = 227$, it is the other way round and, thus, the total cost increases. Note that $B = 227$ implies $q \approx 2^{287}$. If an application requires either a value q that is much larger than this or PoEs for multiple statements (e.g., in [7], where λ many PoEs are needed in each round), then the final exponentiation of the verifier becomes too expensive. We present two modifications of the protocol that improve this complexity significantly: In Appendix A, we show how to replace $C = \log(T)\log(B)$ with $C = \log(T)$ by

Table 1. Comparison of different PoEs. Verifier's complexity is measured in the number of multiplications and proof-size $|\pi|$ in the number of group elements. We denote by λ the statistical security parameter. [40] is statistically-sound only in groups without elements of small order.

PoE	statistically-sound	Verifier's complexity	$|\pi|$
Our PoE	yes	$(6(\frac{\lambda}{\log(B)})^2 + 2B)\log(B)\log(T) + \frac{2\lambda}{\log(B)}$	$\frac{\lambda}{\log(B)}\log(T)$
[7]	yes	$2\lambda^2\log(T) + 2\lambda\log(q)$	$\lambda\log(T)$
[40]	in some $\mathbb{G}$	$3\lambda\log(T)$	$\log(T)$
[50]	no	$\log(T) + 3\lambda$	1

slightly modifying how we set q. In Sect. 3, we show how to compute the last step interactively without increasing the number of rounds.

Prover's Efficiency. The prover needs to compute x^{q^T} and the midpoints $\mu_{i,j}$. Computing x^{q^T} takes $\log(q) \cdot T$ multiplications. If the prover stores the value $x^{q^{T/2}}$ during that computation, then computing the midpoints takes another $\rho \cdot \log(q) \cdot (T/4 + T/8 + \ldots + 1) \approx \rho \cdot \log(q) \cdot T/2$ multiplications. This number can be significantly reduced by storing a few more elements during the computation of x^{q^T} similarly to [40, Section 6.2]. For sufficiently large values of T, the cost for computing the proof can be made small compared to the cost of the T exponentiations required to compute the output and, moreover, the computation of the proof can be easily be parallelized. For this reason we mostly ignore the prover's complexity in the comparisons.

Communication Complexity. The communication complexity from the prover to the verifier is of interest as it equals the proof-size after using the Fiat-Shamir heuristic. In each of the t rounds, our prover sends ρ many midpoints which are of size $\log N$. If $\log N = 2048$, $t = 32$, and $\rho = 9$ then the communication complexity is approximately 2^{19} bits.

Comparison with Alternative PoEs. In Table 1, we compare our protocol with the proofs of exponentiation from [7,40], and [50]. We list the proof-size and verifier's complexity. Prover's complexity is omitted since the main computation for the prover in all the protocols is dominated by the same factor, i.e., the cost of T sequential exponentiations to compute the output.

We observe that [50] is the most efficient PoE regarding verifier's complexity and proof-size. However, it is not statistically-sound. [40] introduces only a minor increase in overhead, but it has the drawback that it is only statistically-sound in groups with no low-order elements other than the identity. The PoE from [7] and our PoE are both statistically-sound in all groups, while the proof-size of our PoE improves by a factor of $\log(B)$ upon [7] and we compare the communication complexity per round for different values of B in Fig. 1.

The verifier's efficiency of our PoE depends on the choice of the bound B which also determines the size of q. In Fig. 2, we compare the number of multiplications per round for the verifier in both protocols for different choices of B. Additionally to the work in each round, the verifier computes λ many exponentiations with q in the last round of [7] and ρ many exponentiations with q in the last round of our interactive protocol. We see that the verifier's complexity improves for $B \in (59, 499)$, which corresponds to $q \in (2^{71}, 2^{685})$.

It is important to note that this is the verifier's complexity for proving a single statement. The PoE in [7] achieves the same verifier's efficiency for proving λ many different statements with the same exponent simultaneously. Our protocol incurs additional $\log(T) \log(q)$ multiplications for every new statement, since the verifier has to compute the final exponentiation individually for every statement. In Sect. 3, we give a batching protocol that reduces the cost of the final exponentiation to $\log(q)$, which enables us to prove arbitrarily many statements simultaneously without significantly increasing the proof-size and verifier's complexity.

3   Reducing (Verifier-) Complexity by Batching

In this section, we show how to prove arbitrary many statements simultaneously without increasing the number of rounds. This batching protocol serves two purposes:

1. Efficiently proving multiple independent statements. This is needed for example in the polynomial commitment scheme of [7], where in each round λ many statements need to be proven;
2. Reducing the verifier's complexity of the final exponentiation with q^C in our basic protocol. Instead of performing the computation locally, the verifier can request an additional PoE for the statement $(y')^{q^C} = y$ and verify it simultaneously with the original PoE. While now we need to do a final exponentiation for the new statement, the exponent drops from $\log(T)$ to $\log \log(T)$.

In [43] Rotem gives a batching technique for arbitrary PoEs, where the statements have the same exponent. We describe a batching technique for our PoE, where the statements can have different exponents. Furthermore, the protocol can be easily adapted to the PoEs in [40] and [7].

3.1   The Protocol

Assume the prover wants to prove two statements in the same group $\mathbb{G}$:

$$g_1^{q^{2^t + C_1}} \overset{?}{=} h_1 \quad \text{and} \quad g_2^{q^{2^s + C_2}} \overset{?}{=} h_2.$$

The statements can either be independent or one of them is the statement from the final verifier exponentiation of the other. The two statements can be proven simultaneously as follows: First the prover sends the statements

$$g_1^{q^{2^t}} \overset{?}{=} h_1' \quad \text{and} \quad g_2^{q^{2^s}} \overset{?}{=} h_2'.$$

We can assume that $t = \ell + s$ for some $\ell \in \mathbb{N}$. Begin with the proof of the first statement. After executing the protocol for $\ell - 1$ rounds and the prover sending midpoints in round ℓ, we have 2ρ statements of the form

$$u_j^{q^{2^s}} \stackrel{?}{=} v_j$$

for $j \in [2\rho]$. The prover makes this $2\rho + 1$ statements by adding $g_2^{q^{2^s}} \stackrel{?}{=} h_2'$ to these statements. Next the verifier sends $\rho \cdot (2\rho + 1)$ random coins and both parties create ρ new statements similarly to the original protocol. Then they proceed with the PoE protocol. Note that this process neither reduces soundness of the proof of the first statement nor of the second statement since by Lemma 1 we only need one of the statements that are being combined to be incorrect. In the end the verifier checks if $(h_1')^{q^{C_1}} = h_1$ and $(h_2')^{q^{C_2}} = h_2$. This process can be extended to arbitrary-many statements of the form $g_i^{q^{2^r} + C_i} \stackrel{?}{=} h_i$ with the protocol given in Fig. 5. Note that in Step 4 we do not specify whether the verifier checks $(h_i')^{q^C} = h_i$ by carrying out the computation locally or by appending the statement to the instances. This depends on the size of C and on the application.

Remark 1. In the case where the exponents of q are not powers of 2, one can simply divide a statement of the form $x^{q^S} \stackrel{?}{=} y$ for $S \in \mathbb{N}$ into smaller statements as follows: Let $(s_0, s_1, \ldots, s_m)$ be the binary representation of S. Then we have

$$x^{q^S} = x^{q^{\sum s_k \cdot 2^k}} = x^{\prod q^{s_k \cdot 2^k}} = y.$$

This gives at most $m + 1$ smaller statements $x^{q^{s_0}} \stackrel{?}{=} y_1$ and $y_i^{q^{s_i \cdot 2^i}} \stackrel{?}{=} y_{i+1}$ for $i \in [1, m]$ where $y_{m+1} = y$. Again these statements can be proven simultaneously with the batching protocol.

The theorem below follows immediately from the description of the batching protocol and Remark 1.

Theorem 2. *For any $m \in \mathbb{N}$ the statements $\{(g_i, h_i, S_i + C_i)\}_{i \in [1,m]}$ can be proven in at most $1 + \max_i \log(S_i)$ rounds where additionally to one execution of the PoE protocol the following computations need to be performed:*

1. *$\mathcal{P}$ and $\mathcal{V}$ perform*

$$2\rho \sum_{i=1}^m h(S_i)$$

additional exponentiations with exponents of size $\log(B) + 5$. Here $h(S_i)$ denotes the hamming weight of S_i;
2. *$\mathcal{V}$ performs $m - 1$ additional exponentiations with exponents q^{C_i} for $i \in [1, m] \setminus \{\arg\max_i S_i\}$;*

and the communication complexity increases by $m - 1$ group elements.

Instance: $\{(g_i, h_i, 2^{t_i} + C_i)\}_{i \in [1,m]}$ with $g_i, h_i \in \mathbb{G}$ and $t_1 > t_2 > \ldots > t_m \in \mathbb{N}$

Claim: $g_i^{q^{2^{t_i}+C_i}} = h_i$ over $\mathbb{G}$ for all $i \in [1, m]$ and $q \in \mathbb{N}$

Parameters: (determined in the analysis)

1. number of rounds of parallel repetition ρ
2. size of individual random coin κ

Protocol:

1. The prover sends $h_i' := g_i^{q^{2^{t_i}}}$ for all $i \in [1, m]$ to the verifier.
2. Execute Step 2 of the PoE protocol for $(g_1, h_1', 2^{t_1})$ for $t_1 - t_2 - 1$ rounds.
3. In round $i \in [1, m-1]$ of the batching protocol we have ρ instances of the form $\{(x_j, y_j, 2^{t_{i+1}+1})\}_{j \in [1,\rho]}$:
   (a) The prover sends ρ midpoints $\{\mu_j\}_{j \in [1,\rho]}$, which results in 2ρ instances $\{(u_k, v_k, 2^{t_{i+1}})\}_{k \in [1,2\rho]}$
   (b) The prover and verifier append $(g_{j+1}, h_{j+1}', 2^{t_{i+1}})$ to the instances resulting in $2\rho + 1$ instances of the form $\{(\tilde{u}_k, \tilde{v}_k, 2^{t_{i+1}})\}_{k \in [1,2\rho+1]}$.
   (c) The verifier sends the random challenge $\{r_{j,k}\}_{j \in [1,\rho], k \in [1,2\rho+1]}$, where $r_{j,k} \in \{0,1\}^\kappa$.
   (d) They both set $\{(\tilde{x}_j, \tilde{y}_j, 2^{t_{i+1}})\}_{j \in [1,\rho]}$ as the instance for the next execution of the PoE protocol, where

$$\tilde{x}_j := \prod_{k \in [1,2\rho+1]} \tilde{u}_k^{r_{j,k}} \quad \text{and} \quad \tilde{y}_j := \prod_{k \in [1,2\rho+1]} \tilde{v}_k^{r_{j,k}}$$

   (e) If $i < m-1$: Execute Step 2 of the PoE protocol for $t_{i+1} - t_{i+2} - 1$ rounds. Else: Execute Step 2 of the PoE protocol for t_m rounds until the statements are of the form $\{(x_j^*, y_j^*, 1)\}_{j \in [1,\rho]}$.
4. At the end of $m-1$ rounds, the verifier accepts if and only if $(x_j^*)^q = y_j^*$ for all $j \in [1, \rho]$ and $(h_i')^{q^{C_i}} = h_i$ for all $i \in [1, m]$.

Fig. 5. Batching protocol for PoE.

Soundness of the protocol follows immediately from Lemma 1 and Theorem 1 since in the statement of Lemma 1 we consider a set of arbitrary many statements of the form (x_i, y_i, T) in any round. This means that the proof of Theorem 1 also holds when new statements are added during the execution of the protocol.

Theorem 3. *Let B be any prime number such that $q := \prod_{prime\ p < B} p$ and $\rho \in \mathbb{N}$ be the number of repetitions per round. If we set $C = \log(T) \log(B)$ and let $\kappa \to \infty$, the verifier $\mathcal{V}$ will output accept on instance $\{(g_i, h_i, 2^{t_i} + C_i)\}_{i \in [1,m]}$, where $t_1 \geq t_2 \geq \ldots \geq t_m$ and at least one statements is incorrect, with probability at most*

$$\frac{t_1}{B^\rho}.$$

3.2 Improving Verifier's Efficiency

In this section we analyze how the batching protocol reduces the number of multiplications for verifying a statement of the form $x^{q^T} \stackrel{?}{=} y$. In Appendix B.1 we analyze the gain in efficiency of the polynomial commitment in [7] when we use this improved version of our PoE as a building block instead of the PoE proposed in [7].

The first prover message is the value $y' = x^{q^{T-C}}$, where $C \geq \log(T)$. The key idea is that the verifier does not carry out the last exponentiation with q^C but the prover gives an interactive proof of the statement $(y')^{q^C} = y$ (a "smaller" PoE). This reduces the final exponentiation to $(y'')^{q^{C'}} = y$, where y'' is the first prover message in the smaller PoE and $C' \geq \log(C)$ is much smaller than C. This statement can again be proven interactively by an even smaller PoE. In fact, this trick can be applied recursively until the verifier only has to perform a single exponentiation with q in the final step. We make two assumptions in this section:

1. We have $q = \prod_{\text{prime } p < B} p^{\lceil \log(B)/\log(p) \rceil}$ such that the constant C in the PoE protocol is lower bounded only by $\log(T)$ and not $\log(T)\log(B)$. This is the trick we discuss in Appendix A. This assumption is needed to reduce the exponent from q^C to q and should be adopted in practice if one wants to make use of the recursion.
2. Instead of setting C to exactly $\log(T)$, we set $C = 2^{2^{2^2}} + 2^{2^2} + 2^2 + 1$, which will always be larger than $\log(T)$ in practice. This assumption is mainly for the ease of presentation and need not be adopted in practice.

Reducing the Exponent from q^C to $q^{\log(C)}$. We know that exponentiation with q^C takes $C\log(q)$ multiplications. In order to reduce this cost for the verifier, we slightly modify the protocol in the following way: Instead of the verifier performing the last exponentiation locally, the verifier and the prover run the batching protocol with instances

$$\{(x, y, T = T_0 + C), (y', y, C = S_0 + C')\},$$

where $C' = \log(C)$. This modification introduces $3\rho \cdot h(S_0)(\log(B)+5)$ additional multiplications during the interactive part of the protocol (by Theorem 2) *but* reduces the complexity of the final exponentiation to

$$C'\log(q) = \log(C)\log(q) \approx \log\log(T)\log(q).$$

By our special choice of C we have $h(S_0) = 1$ so we can ignore it in the remainder of the section

Applying the Recursion. As we have seen, the exponent q^C can be reduced to $q^{C'}$. Now, the verifier can either perform the final exponentiation with $q^{C'}$ or apply the above procedure recursively until the verifier only has to do a single exponentiation with q in the final step. We denote the number of recursions needed until the exponent is reduced to q by $\log^*(C)$. We have that the entire recursion adds at most $3\log^*(C)\rho \cdot (\log(B)+5)$ multiplications during the interactive part of the protocol but reduces the work of the final exponentiation from $\log(T)\log(q)$ to $\log(q)$.

In Sect. 2.2 we saw that the verifier's complexity without any batching is

$$\log(T) \cdot ((6\log(B) + 32)\rho^2 + \log(q)) + \rho\log(q).$$

Our batching protocol reduces the number of multiplications for verifying the proof of a single statement to approximately

$$\log(T)(6\log(B) + 32)\rho^2 + 3\log^*(C)\rho \cdot (\log(B) + 5) + (\rho + 1)\log(q)$$

and increases the proof-size to $\log^*(C) + \rho\log(T)$ group elements.

Proving Multiple Statements. With this optimization of the cost of verifying a single statement we can now compute the complexity of verifying m statements with our improved protocol. Each additional statement that either has exponent q^T or a smaller power of q adds $\log(q)$ multiplications to compute the final exponentiation, $3\log^*(C)\rho \cdot (\log(B) + 5)$ multiplications during the interactive part and increases the proof-size by at most $\log^*(C)$ elements. We conclude that m many statements can be proven with verifier's complexity

$$\log(T)(6\log(B) + 32)\rho^2 + 3m\log^*(C)\rho \cdot (\log(B) + 5) + (\rho + m)\log(q)$$

and communication complexity $m\log^*(C) + \rho\log(T)$.

A   Improving Verifier's Efficiency

In Fig. 2 we see that for large values of B and q the verifier's complexity increases because the final computation $(y')^{q^C}$ becomes expensive. The cost of this computation is $C \cdot \log(q)$, where so far we have set $C = t\log(B)$. We can reduce this

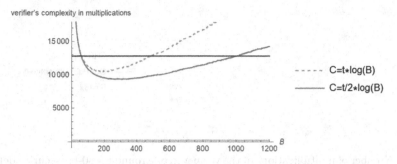

Fig. 6. Number of multiplications of the verifier in one round for 80-bit security depending on the bound B. The blue line is the number of multiplications in [7], the dotted orange graph is the complexity of our protocol with $C = t \log(B)$, the red graph is the complexity in our protocol with $C = t \log(B)/2$ and the green line is the verifier's complexity in [40]. (Color figure online)

number to $C = t \log(B)/2$ by setting q to

$$q = 2^2 \cdot 3^2 \cdot \prod_{3 < p < B} p. \tag{2}$$

It is straightforward to check that this does not affect our soundness bound, but it has a notable effect on verifier's efficiency as shown in Fig. 6.

This approach can be generalized to setting $C = t \log(B)/k$ for any integer $k \leq \log(B)$. To ensure soundness we need to modify q as follows: Let m be the largest prime number such that $m < 2^k$. Then we set

$$q = 2^k \cdot 3^{\lceil k/\log(3) \rceil} \cdot 5^{\lceil k/\log(5) \rceil} \dots m^{\lceil k/\log(m) \rceil} \cdot \prod_{m < p < B} p.$$

In particular, the choice of q that optimizes verifier's efficiency for large values of B is

$$q = \prod_{p < B} p^{\lceil \log(B)/\log(p) \rceil}$$

for which we can set $C = t$. The cost for the verifier with this parameters is shown in Fig. 7. We conclude that the verifier's complexity of our scheme improves upon [7] for values of B from 59 up to 2749, which corresponds to values of q between approximately 2^{71} and $2^{400 \cdot \log(2749)} \approx 2^{3167}$.

B   Application in Polynomial Commitments

In this section we analyse the gain in efficiency when we use our PoE as a building block instead of the one proposed in [7].

In the full version of the paper [31] we provide an overview of the polynomial commitment scheme in [7]. Here we only state the key properties that the PoE should satisfy in order to be applicable in the polynomial commitment scheme.

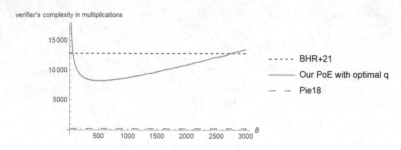

Fig. 7. Number of multiplications of the verifier in one round for 80-bit security depending on the bound B. The dotted blue line is the number of multiplications in [7], the orange graph is the complexity of our protocol with $C = t$ and q as above and the green line is verifier's complexity in [40] (which is 240 multiplications). (Color figure online)

Requirements from the PoE. Note that the use of the PoE in the [7] polynomial commitment is more or less black-box. However, there are two important criteria that it should satisfy.

1. Firstly, the PoE has to satisfy statistical soundness so that the knowledge soundness of the polynomial commitment built upon it can be argued ([7, Lemma 6.4]).[9] Our PoE satisfies statistical soundness.
2. Secondly, the base q used in the PoE protocol is borrowed *from* the polynomial commitment. In order for the polynomial commitment to satisfy its homomorphic properties, [7] set it to be a *large, odd* integer – in particular, they require $q \gg p \cdot 2^n \mathsf{poly}(\lambda)$. This requirement that q be large, as we saw in Sect. 2 is advantageous for our PoE. On the other hand, the requirement that q be odd is in conflict with our trick of choosing an *even* q as in Eq. (1). However, we show in the full version of the paper [31] that the requirement that q be odd is not necessary in [7].

B.1 Efficiency

In this section we analyze the improvement in efficiency of the polynomial commitment scheme in [7] using our PoE, the batching protocol and the optimization in Appendix A. In the polynomial commitment scheme the PoE protocol is used to prove statements of the form $x_i^{q^{2^{n-k-1}}} = y_i$ for every $i \in [\lambda]$ and every $k \in \{0, 1, \ldots, n-1\}$.

Communication Complexity. In [7] the communication complexity of proving λ many statements with the same exponent is $\lambda(n - k - 1)$ group elements. This

---

[9] To be precise, it suffices for the soundness of the PoE to be based on a hardness assumption that is *at most* as strong as the hardness assumption that is used for showing the binding or knowledge soundness of the polynomial commitment.

gives a total PoE proof-size of

$$\lambda \sum_{k=0}^{n-1} (n - k - 1) = \frac{\lambda}{2}(n - 1)n.$$

As we have seen in Sect. 3.2, in our PoE the cost of proving λn statements, in which the largest exponent is q^{n-1}, is

$$\lambda n \log^*(n - 1) + \frac{\lambda}{\log(B)}(n - 1).$$

We conclude that we decrease the proof-size of the polynomial commitment by a factor of approximately $n/(2 \log^*(n - 1))$. This number can be increased to $n/2$ at the cost of a higher verifier complexity. More generally, the number of recursive steps explained in Sect. 3.2 can be used to choose a trade-off between proof-size and verifier efficiency.

Verifier's Efficiency. In [7] the verifier's complexity of proving λ many statements with the same exponent is $2\lambda^2(n - k - 1) + \lambda \log(q)$ multiplications. This gives a total verifier's complexity of

$$2\lambda^2 \sum_{k=0}^{n-1} ((n - k - 1) + \lambda \log(q)) = (\lambda \log(q) + 2\lambda^2(n - 1))n.$$

As we have seen in Sect. 3.2, in our PoE the cost of verifying λn statements, in which the largest exponent is q^{n-1}, is

$$(n - 1)(6 \log(B) + 32)\rho^2 + 3\lambda n \log^*(C)\rho \cdot (\log(B) + 5) + (\rho + \lambda n) \log(q) \approx 15\lambda^2 n + \lambda n \log(q).$$

Since in practice we have $n \approx 32$, we conclude that the verifier's efficiency of the polynomial commitment scheme implemented with our PoE is comparable to that in [7].

References

1. Abusalah, H., Kamath, C., Klein, K., Pietrzak, K., Walter, M.: Reversible proofs of sequential work. In: Ishai, Y., Rijmen, V. (eds.) EUROCRYPT 2019, Part II. LNCS, vol. 11477, pp. 277–291. Springer, Cham (2019). https://doi.org/10.1007/978-3-030-17656-3_10

2. Arun, A., Ganesh, C., Lokam, S., Mopuri, T., Sridhar, S.: Dew: transparent constant-sized zkSNARKs. Cryptology ePrint Archive, Paper 2022/419 (2022). https://eprint.iacr.org/2022/419

3. Belabas, K., Kleinjung, T., Sanso, A., Wesolowski, B.: A note on the low order assumption in class group of an imaginary quadratic number fields. Cryptology ePrint Archive, Paper 2020/1310 (2020). https://eprint.iacr.org/2020/1310

4. Bellare, M., Garay, J.A., Rabin, T.: Fast batch verification for modular exponentiation and digital signatures. In: Nyberg, K. (ed.) EUROCRYPT 1998. LNCS, vol. 1403, pp. 236–250. Springer, Heidelberg (1998). https://doi.org/10.1007/BFb0054130

5. Beller, M.J., Yacobi, Y.: Batch Diffie-Hellman key agreement systems and their application to portable communications. In: Rueppel, R.A. (ed.) EUROCRYPT 1992. LNCS, vol. 658, pp. 208–220. Springer, Heidelberg (1993). https://doi.org/10.1007/3-540-47555-9_19

6. Bitansky, N., Goldwasser, S., Jain, A., Paneth, O., Vaikuntanathan, V., Waters, B.: Time-lock puzzles from randomized encodings. In: Sudan, M. (ed.) Proceedings of the 2016 ACM Conference on Innovations in Theoretical Computer Science, Cambridge, MA, USA, 14–16 January 2016, pp. 345–356. ACM (2016)

7. Block, A.R., Holmgren, J., Rosen, A., Rothblum, R.D., Soni, P.: Time- and space-efficient arguments from groups of unknown order. In: Malkin, T., Peikert, C. (eds.) CRYPTO 2021, Part IV. LNCS, vol. 12828, pp. 123–152. Springer, Cham (2021). https://doi.org/10.1007/978-3-030-84259-8_5

8. Blocki, J., Lee, S., Zhou, S.: On the security of proofs of sequential work in a post-quantum world. In: Tessaro, S. (ed.) 2nd Conference on Information-Theoretic Cryptography, ITC 2021, 23–26 July 2021, Virtual Conference. LIPIcs, vol. 199, pp. 22:1–22:27. Schloss Dagstuhl - Leibniz-Zentrum für Informatik (2021)

9. Boneh, D., Bonneau, J., Bünz, B., Fisch, B.: Verifiable delay functions. In: Shacham, H., Boldyreva, A. (eds.) CRYPTO 2018, Part I. LNCS, vol. 10991, pp. 757–788. Springer, Cham (2018). https://doi.org/10.1007/978-3-319-96884-1_25

10. Boneh, D., Bünz, B., Fisch, B.: A survey of two verifiable delay functions. IACR Cryptology ePrint Archive 2018:712 (2018)

11. Boneh, D., Naor, M.: Timed commitments. In: Bellare, M. (ed.) CRYPTO 2000. LNCS, vol. 1880, pp. 236–254. Springer, Heidelberg (2000). https://doi.org/10.1007/3-540-44598-6_15

12. Boyd, C., Pavlovski, C.: Attacking and repairing batch verification schemes. In: Okamoto, T. (ed.) ASIACRYPT 2000. LNCS, vol. 1976, pp. 58–71. Springer, Heidelberg (2000). https://doi.org/10.1007/3-540-44448-3_5

13. Buchmann, J., Williams, H.C.: A key-exchange system based on imaginary quadratic fields. J. Cryptol. 1(2), 107–118 (1988). https://doi.org/10.1007/BF02351719

14. Bünz, B., Fisch, B., Szepieniec, A.: Transparent SNARKs from DARK compilers. In: Canteaut, A., Ishai, Y. (eds.) EUROCRYPT 2020, Part I. LNCS, vol. 12105, pp. 677–706. Springer, Cham (2020). https://doi.org/10.1007/978-3-030-45721-1_24

15. Cai, J., Lipton, R.J., Sedgewick, R., Yao, A.C.: Towards uncheatable benchmarks. In: 1993 Proceedings of the Eighth Annual Structure in Complexity Theory Conference, pp. 2–11, May 1993

16. Chavez-Saab, J., Henríquez, F.R., Tibouchi, M.: Verifiable isogeny walks: towards an isogeny-based postquantum VDF. Cryptology ePrint Archive, Report 2021/1289 (2021). https://ia.cr/2021/1289

17. Chen, M., et al.: Multiparty generation of an RSA modulus. In: Micciancio, D., Ristenpart, T. (eds.) CRYPTO 2020, Part III. LNCS, vol. 12172, pp. 64–93. Springer, Cham (2020). https://doi.org/10.1007/978-3-030-56877-1_3

18. Choudhuri, A.R., Hubáček, P., Kamath, C., Pietrzak, K., Rosen, A., Rothblum, G.N.: PPAD-hardness via iterated squaring modulo a composite. Cryptology ePrint Archive, Report 2019/667 (2019). https://ia.cr/2019/667

19. Cohen, B., Pietrzak, K.: Simple proofs of sequential work. In: Nielsen, J.B., Rijmen, V. (eds.) EUROCRYPT 2018, Part II. LNCS, vol. 10821, pp. 451–467. Springer, Cham (2018). https://doi.org/10.1007/978-3-319-78375-8_15
20. Döttling, N., Garg, S., Malavolta, G., Vasudevan, P.N.: Tight verifiable delay functions. In: Galdi, C., Kolesnikov, V. (eds.) SCN 2020. LNCS, vol. 12238, pp. 65–84. Springer, Cham (2020). https://doi.org/10.1007/978-3-030-57990-6_4
21. Döttling, N., Lai, R.W.F., Malavolta, G.: Incremental proofs of sequential work. In: Ishai, Y., Rijmen, V. (eds.) EUROCRYPT 2019, Part II. LNCS, vol. 11477, pp. 292–323. Springer, Cham (2019). https://doi.org/10.1007/978-3-030-17656-3_11
22. Dummit, D.S., Foote, R.M.: Abstract Algebra, 3rd edn. Wiley, Hoboken (2003)
23. Ephraim, N., Freitag, C., Komargodski, I., Pass, R.: Continuous verifiable delay functions. In: Canteaut, A., Ishai, Y. (eds.) EUROCRYPT 2020, Part III. LNCS, vol. 12107, pp. 125–154. Springer, Cham (2020). https://doi.org/10.1007/978-3-030-45727-3_5
24. Erdős, P.: Beweis eines satzes von Tschebyschef (on a proof of a theorem of Chebyshev, in German). Acta Litt. Sci. Szeged **5**, 194–198 (1932)
25. De Feo, L., Masson, S., Petit, C., Sanso, A.: Verifiable delay functions from supersingular isogenies and pairings. In: Galbraith, S.D., Moriai, S. (eds.) ASIACRYPT 2019, Part I. LNCS, vol. 11921, pp. 248–277. Springer, Cham (2019). https://doi.org/10.1007/978-3-030-34578-5_10
26. Fiat, A.: Batch RSA. J. Cryptol. **10**(2), 75–88 (1997). https://doi.org/10.1007/s001459900021
27. Fiat, A., Shamir, A.: How to prove yourself: practical solutions to identification and signature problems. In: Odlyzko, A.M. (ed.) CRYPTO 1986. LNCS, vol. 263, pp. 186–194. Springer, Heidelberg (1987). https://doi.org/10.1007/3-540-47721-7_12
28. Frederiksen, T.K., Lindell, Y., Osheter, V., Pinkas, B.: Fast distributed RSA key generation for semi-honest and malicious adversaries. In: Shacham, H., Boldyreva, A. (eds.) CRYPTO 2018, Part II. LNCS, vol. 10992, pp. 331–361. Springer, Cham (2018). https://doi.org/10.1007/978-3-319-96881-0_12
29. Freitag, C., Komargodski, I.: The cost of statistical security in interactive proofs for repeated squaring. Cryptology ePrint Archive, Paper 2022/766 (2022). https://eprint.iacr.org/2022/766
30. Freitag, C., Komargodski, I., Pass, R., Sirkin, N.: Non-malleable time-lock puzzles and applications. In: Nissim, K., Waters, B. (eds.) TCC 2021, Part III. LNCS, vol. 13044, pp. 447–479. Springer, Cham (2021). https://doi.org/10.1007/978-3-030-90456-2_15
31. Hoffmann, C., Hubáček, P., Kamath, C., Klein, K., Pietrzak, K.: Practical statistically-sound proofs of exponentiation in any group. Cryptology ePrint Archive, Report 2022/??? (2022)
32. Katz, J., Loss, J., Xu, J.: On the security of time-lock puzzles and timed commitments. In: Pass, R., Pietrzak, K. (eds.) TCC 2020, Part III. LNCS, vol. 12552, pp. 390–413. Springer, Cham (2020). https://doi.org/10.1007/978-3-030-64381-2_14
33. Lenstra, A.K., Wesolowski, B.: Trustworthy public randomness with sloth, unicorn, and trx. Int. J. Appl. Cryptogr. **3**(4), 330–343 (2017)
34. Lombardi, A., Vaikuntanathan, V.: Fiat-Shamir for repeated squaring with applications to PPAD-hardness and VDFs. In: Micciancio, D., Ristenpart, T. (eds.) CRYPTO 2020, Part III. LNCS, vol. 12172, pp. 632–651. Springer, Cham (2020). https://doi.org/10.1007/978-3-030-56877-1_22
35. Mahmoody, M., Moran, T., Vadhan, S.: Time-lock puzzles in the random oracle model. In: Rogaway, P. (ed.) CRYPTO 2011. LNCS, vol. 6841, pp. 39–50. Springer, Heidelberg (2011). https://doi.org/10.1007/978-3-642-22792-9_3

36. Mahmoody, M., Moran, T., Vadhan, S.P.: Publicly verifiable proofs of sequential work. In: Kleinberg, R.D. (ed.) Innovations in Theoretical Computer Science, ITCS 2013, Berkeley, CA, USA, 9–12 January 2013, pp. 373–388. ACM (2013)

37. Mahmoody, M., Smith, C., Wu, D.J.: Can verifiable delay functions be based on random oracles? In: ICALP. LIPIcs, vol. 168, pp. 83:1–83:17. Schloss Dagstuhl - Leibniz-Zentrum für Informatik (2020)

38. May, T.C.: Timed-release crypto (1994)

39. M'Raïhi, D., Naccache, D.: Batch exponentiation: a fast DLP-based signature generation strategy. In: Gong, L., Stearn, J. (eds.) CCS 1996, Proceedings of the 3rd ACM Conference on Computer and Communications Security, New Delhi, India, 14–16 March 1996, pp. 58–61. ACM (1996)

40. Pietrzak, K.: Simple verifiable delay functions. In: Blum, A. (ed.) 10th Innovations in Theoretical Computer Science Conference, ITCS 2019, San Diego, California, USA, 10–12 January 2019. LIPIcs, vol. 124, pp. 60:1–60:15. Schloss Dagstuhl - Leibniz-Zentrum für Informatik (2019)

41. Rivest, R.L., Shamir, A., Adleman, L.M.: A method for obtaining digital signatures and public-key cryptosystems. Commun. ACM $21(2)$, 120–126 (1978)

42. Rivest, R.L., Shamir, A., Wagner, D.A.: Time-lock puzzles and timed-release crypto. Technical report, Massachusetts Institute of Technology, Cambridge, MA, USA (1996)

43. Rotem, L.: Simple and efficient batch verification techniques for verifiable delay functions. In: Nissim, K., Waters, B. (eds.) TCC 2021, Part III. LNCS, vol. 13044, pp. 382–414. Springer, Cham (2021). https://doi.org/10.1007/978-3-030-90456-2_13

44. Rotem, L., Segev, G.: Generically speeding-up repeated squaring is equivalent to factoring: sharp thresholds for all generic-ring delay functions. In: Micciancio, D., Ristenpart, T. (eds.) CRYPTO 2020, Part III. LNCS, vol. 12172, pp. 481–509. Springer, Cham (2020). https://doi.org/10.1007/978-3-030-56877-1_17

45. Rotem, L., Segev, G., Shahaf, I.: Generic-group delay functions require hidden-order groups. In: Canteaut, A., Ishai, Y. (eds.) EUROCRYPT 2020, Part III. LNCS, vol. 12107, pp. 155–180. Springer, Cham (2020). https://doi.org/10.1007/978-3-030-45727-3_6

46. Schindler, P., Judmayer, A., Hittmeir, M., Stifter, N., Weippl, E.R.: RandRunner: distributed randomness from trapdoor VDFs with strong uniqueness. In: 28th Annual Network and Distributed System Security Symposium, NDSS 2021, Virtually, 21–25 February 2021. The Internet Society (2021)

47. Shani, B.: A note on isogeny-based hybrid verifiable delay functions. Cryptology ePrint Archive, Report 2019/205 (2019). https://ia.cr/2019/205

48. Valiant, P.: Incrementally verifiable computation or proofs of knowledge imply time/space efficiency. In: Canetti, R. (ed.) TCC 2008. LNCS, vol. 4948, pp. 1–18. Springer, Heidelberg (2008). https://doi.org/10.1007/978-3-540-78524-8_1

49. van Baarsen, A., Stevens, M.: On time-lock cryptographic assumptions in abelian hidden-order groups. In: Tibouchi, M., Wang, H. (eds.) ASIACRYPT 2021, Part II. LNCS, vol. 13091, pp. 367–397. Springer, Cham (2021). https://doi.org/10.1007/978-3-030-92075-3_13

50. Wesolowski, B.: Efficient verifiable delay functions. J. Cryptol. **33**, 2113–2147 (2020)
51. Wesolowski, B., Williams, R.: Lower bounds for the depth of modular squaring. Cryptology ePrint Archive, Report 2020/1461 (2020). https://ia.cr/2020/1461

Formalizing Delayed Adaptive Corruptions and the Security of Flooding Networks

Christian Matt[1] , Jesper Buus Nielsen[2] , and Søren Eller Thomsen[2](✉)

[1] Concordium, Zurich, Switzerland
cm@concordium.com
[2] Concordium Blockchain Research Center, Aarhus University, Aarhus, Denmark
{jbn,sethomsen}@cs.au.dk

Abstract. Many decentralized systems rely on flooding protocols for message dissemination. In such a protocol, the sender of a message sends it to a randomly selected set of peers. These peers again send the message to their randomly selected peers, until every network participant has received the message. This type of protocols clearly fail in face of an adaptive adversary who can simply corrupt all peers of the sender and thereby prevent the message from being delivered. Nevertheless, flooding protocols are commonly used within protocols that aim to be cryptographically secure, most notably in blockchain protocols. While it is possible to revert to static corruptions, this gives unsatisfactory security guarantees, especially in the setting of a blockchain that is supposed to run for an extended period of time.

To be able to provide meaningful security guarantees in such settings, we give precise semantics to what we call δ-*delayed adversaries* in the Universal Composability (UC) framework. Such adversaries can adaptively corrupt parties, but there is a delay of time δ from when an adversary decides to corrupt a party until they succeed in overtaking control of the party. Within this model, we formally prove the intuitive result that flooding protocols are secure against δ-delayed adversaries when δ is at least the time it takes to send a message from one peer to another plus the time it takes the recipient to resend the message. To this end, we show how to reduce the adaptive setting with a δ-delayed adversary to a static experiment with an Erdős-Rényi graph. Using the established theory of Erdős-Rényi graphs, we provide upper bounds on the propagation time of the flooding functionality for different neighborhood sizes of the gossip network. More concretely, we show the following for security parameter κ, point-to-point channels with delay at most Δ, and n parties in total, with a sufficiently delayed adversary that can corrupt any constant fraction of the parties: If all parties send to $\Omega(\kappa)$ parties on average, then we can realize a flooding functionality with maximal delay $\mathcal{O}(\Delta \cdot \log(n))$; and if all parties send to $\Omega(\sqrt{\kappa n})$ parties on average, we can realize a flooding functionality with maximal delay $\mathcal{O}(\Delta)$.

Partially funded by The Concordium Foundation; The Danish Independent Research Council under Grant-ID DFF-8021-00366B (BETHE); The Carlsberg Foundation under the Semper Ardens Research Project CF18-112 (BCM).

Y. Dodis and T. Shrimpton (Eds.): CRYPTO 2022, LNCS 13508, pp. 400–430, 2022.
https://doi.org/10.1007/978-3-031-15979-4_14

Keywords: adaptive adversaries · corruption models · universal composability · flooding networks · peer-to-peer networks · blockchain

1   Introduction

1.1   Motivation

In *Nakamoto-style blockchains* (NSBs) such as Bitcoin [35], several parties continuously try to solve cryptographic puzzles. The first party solving the puzzle "wins" the right to create a new block extending the previously longest chain. This block is then distributed to all other parties, who continue solving puzzles to create the next block. Extensive research has shown for different variation of NSBs that security can be guaranteed if a majority of the puzzles are solved by honest parties and if blocks can be propagated fast enough to ensure with high probability that the next winner has learned about the previous block before creating a new block [19, 20, 37, 39].

Since future block creators are unpredictable, these protocols have a high resilience against adaptive corruptions. Intuitively, the only chance to exploit the adaptivity of corruptions is to corrupt a party after learning that it has solved a puzzle and subsequently prevent this party from distributing the created block. An adversary with the power to stop messages from being delivered (or changing the message) by corrupting the sender after sending but before the message is delivered, is often referred to as *strongly adaptive* [1]. On the other hand, if messages from honest senders are guaranteed to be delivered regardless of whether the sender gets corrupted before delivery, the adversary is only *weakly adaptive*, or equivalently, *atomic message send* (AMS) [18] is assumed.

Indeed, several papers [19, 20, 37] have proven the security of Bitcoin's consensus against adaptive corruptions, and Ouroboros Praos [15] has been developed as a proof-of-stake blockchain with resilience against fully adaptive corruptions as one of the main selling points. To achieve this, these papers have to assume atomic message dissemination. In reality, however, NSBs typically use complex peer-to-peer networks to disseminate blocks, in which each party propagates messages to only a small set of other parties (referred to as their neighbors), who will then propagate it to their neighbors and so forth. Even if the point-to-point channels between neighbors allow atomic sends, the overall network will not provide this guarantee because an adaptive adversary can simply corrupt all neighbors of the sender and thereby stop the block from being propagated. Hence, when considering the full protocol, which combines a NSB with a peer-to-peer flooding network, security against fully adaptive corruptions can no longer be guaranteed.

Formalizing Delayed Adaptive Corruptions. To provide meaningful guarantees to blockchain protocols including their peer-to-peer network, we observe that intuitively, one needs to restrict the *corruption speed* of an adversary such that parties in the peer-to-peer network have enough time to pass on the block they receive before being corrupted. Based on this observation, we introduce a precise model for *δ-delayed adversaries* in the Universal Composability framework [7]. Using this model, one can quantify the minimum amount of time δ it takes from when an adversary targets and starts attacking a specific party until this party is actually under adversarial control and prove the security of protocols against such corruptions. This allows us to describe exactly what kind of adversaries different P2P networks and protocols build on top can withstand.

Note that the corruption speed of an adaptive adversary also has a natural translation to reality. For an attacker to succeed in attacking some physical machine it necessarily takes some time from targeting the machine to actually hack into the network (by either physical or digital means) and take over the computer. Denial-of-service attacks are arguably faster to mount, but it still takes nonzero time to target a specific machine.

While unstructured peer-to-peer networks for message dissemination are the main focus of our paper, delayed adversaries have much broader applications and were in fact already used in other works, with varying degree of formality. For example, the original Ouroboros [27], in contrast to its successor Ouroboros Praos [15], which only requires AMS, needs that corruptions are sufficiently delayed. The same is true for Snow White [14], another early proof-of-stake blockchain. Another example is Hybrid Consensus [38], which periodically elects committees using a blockchain and remains secure if corruptions are delayed until the next committee is selected. The same applies to blockchain sharding proposals [29,31,41] in which the members of shards are periodically chosen.

Concrete Analysis of Flooding Networks. As mentioned above, the security of NSBs crucially relies on the assumption that blocks are with high probability propagated to other parties before the next winner creates another new block. If an upper bound on the propagation time is known, the difficulty of the puzzles can be set accordingly to provide this guarantee. Setting the difficulty based on a too optimistic assumption on the delay jeopardizes the security of the system, and setting it based on a too loose upper bound degrades efficiency. Knowing a tight bound on the propagation delay is thus key for the security and efficiency of an NSB.

Even more critical for the security of NSBs are so-called eclipse attacks that prevent some parties from receiving blocks [22,32]. Furthermore, for large-scale distributed systems, the number of neighbors has a significant impact on the required communication. In particular, it is infeasible to simply send the message directly to everybody. In this work, we provide constructions for flooding networks with provable security against eclipse attacks in a well-defined adversarial model and show different trade-offs between the propagation time and neighborhood sizes.

Terminology. In the literature different terminology has been used for the process of disseminating a message to all parties. Common terminology includes "broadcast", "flood" and "multicast". In this paper, we will use the terminology "flood" for this process. Contrary to *byzantine broadcast*, there is no agreement requirement for a flooding network if the sender of a message is dishonest.

1.2 Contributions and Results

Our contributions are twofold:

1. We give precise semantics to δ-*delayed corruptions* (introduced in [38] as δ-agile corruptions) within the UC framework [8]. We define the semantics via corruption shells which allows us to prove how this type of corruptions relate to standard adaptive corruptions.
2. We define a functionality for disseminating information, Flood, that can be used to implement a secure NSB, and that we implement using a flooding protocol against a *slightly delayed* adversary. Importantly, we quantify exactly how much is meant by "slightly" in terms of guarantees provided by the underlying point-to-point channels. We provide two instantiations of our protocol with different efficiency trade-offs.

Below we lay out the specifics of the individual contributions and state our results in more detail.

Precise Model for δ-Delayed Adversaries. We define a δ-delayed adversary as an adversary which uses at least δ time to perform a corruption. We define this notion precisely within the UC framework using the notion of time from [4]. We do so by elaborating on the notion of corruption-shells from [8].

Using the idea of corruption shells, we give semantics to both "normal" byzantine adaptive corruption and δ-delayed corruptions. We capture the semantics of byzantine adaptive corruptions in a corruption-shell, $\mathcal{B}_{\mathsf{Real}}$, for protocols and in a corruption-shell, $\mathcal{B}_{\mathsf{Ideal}}$, for ideal functionalities. Similarly, we capture the semantics of δ-delayed adversaries in a corruption-shell, $\mathcal{D}^{\delta}_{\mathsf{Real}}$, for protocols and in a corruption-shell, $\mathcal{D}^{\delta}_{\mathsf{Ideal}}$, for ideal functionalities. $\mathcal{D}^{\delta}_{\mathsf{Real}}$ and $\mathcal{D}^{\delta}_{\mathsf{Ideal}}$ accepts two inputs: *Precorrupt* and *Corrupt* (both indexed by a specific party). Both shells ensure that at least δ time has passed after receiving *Precorrupt* before reacting upon *Corrupt*. Any *Corrupt* input that is sent prematurely is ignored.

Having defined the semantics for both standard adaptive corruptions and for δ-delayed corruptions using corruption shells, we state basic results relating the two models. We show that a protocol is secure against a standard adaptive adversary *iff* it is secure against a 0-delayed adversary (Theorem 1). Furthermore, we show that if a protocol is secure against a "fast" adversary, then this implies that it is also secure against a "slow" adversary (Theorem 2). Together these results allow constructions proven secure in the standard model of adaptive adversaries to be reused when constructing new protocols secure against a δ-delayed adversary, and to compose protocols that are secure against adversaries with different delays.

Flooding Networks. We define a functionality for flooding messages, $\mathcal{F}^{\Delta}_{\mathsf{Flood}}$. It ensures that all parties learn messages that an honest party has sent or has received within Δ time, and is thereby similar to the flooding functionality assumed in many consensus protocols. We realize our flooding functionality with both a naive protocol, $\pi_{\mathsf{NaiveFlood}}$, where everybody simply sends to everybody, and a more advanced protocol, $\pi_{\mathsf{ERFlood}}(\rho)$, where all parties choose to send to other parties with probability ρ.

In order to realize the flooding functionality, we introduce a functionality for a point-to-point channel $\mathcal{F}^{\sigma,\Delta}_{\mathsf{MessageTransfer}}$. This functionality is also parameterized by a bound for the delivery time Δ, and additionally has a parameter σ describing the time an honest party needs to stay honest after starting to send the message for the delivery guarantee to apply. If $\sigma = 0$ then this corresponds to assuming AMS. On the other hand, if $\sigma \geq \delta$ and we consider δ-delayed adversaries, then this corresponds to not assuming AMS. However, having the time quantified allows us to relate this time to the delay we can tolerate when building more advanced constructions. In particular, we show that π_{ERFlood} using $\mathcal{F}^{\sigma,\Delta}_{\mathsf{MessageTransfer}}$ implements $\mathcal{F}^{\Delta'}_{\mathsf{Flood}}$ against a $(\sigma + \Delta)$-delayed adversary.

In this setting, we provide two different ways to instantiate the probability parameter ρ of π_{ERFlood}, each presenting a different efficiency trade-off. Concretely, let h denote the minimum number of parties that will stay honest throughout the execution of the protocol, let n denote the total number of parties, and let κ be the security parameter. We provide the following two instantiations:

Instantiation 1: Guaranteed delivery within $\Delta' := 2 \cdot \Delta$ for $\rho := \sqrt{\frac{\kappa}{h}}$.
Instantiation 2: Guaranteed delivery within $\Delta' := \Delta \cdot \left(5 \log\left(\frac{n}{2\kappa}\right) + 2\right)$ for $\rho := \frac{\kappa}{h}$.

Both instantiations ensure that the statistical distance between the ideal and the real executions of π_{ERFlood} and $\mathcal{F}^{\Delta'}_{\mathsf{Flood}}$ is negligible in the security parameter. We provide concrete bounds for the statistical distance in Corollary 1. Furthermore, standard probability bounds ensure that each instantiation has a neighborhood of $\mathcal{O}(n \cdot \rho)$ with high probability.

1.3   Techniques

An Erdős-Rényi graph [17] is a graph where each edge appears with an equal and independent probability. Our flooding protocol π_{ERFlood} is strongly inspired by this type of graph. Our main technical contributions are thus concerned with transporting bounds for Erdős-Rényi graphs to the cryptographic setting, especially in presence of adaptive adversaries.

Concrete Bounds for Erdős-Rényi Graphs. The asymptotic behavior of Erdős-Rényi graphs has been thoroughly studied in the literature (for a comprehensive overview see [6]). However, bounds about a graph's behavior when the amount of nodes goes towards infinity is of little use for protocols that are supposed to be run by a finite number of parties. For a protocol imitating the behavior of such graphs, we need concrete bounds when a security parameter is increased. As a technical contribution, we prove such concrete upper-bounds for the diameter of Erdős-Rényi graphs.

Applying Erdős-Rényi Graph Results in the Presence of Adaptive Adversaries. For a flooding protocol as π_{ERFlood}, it is straightforward to apply bounds about the diameter of an Erdős-Rényi to also bound the probability that a message is not delivered in the protocol in presence of a *static* adversary. However, for an adaptive adversary that is capable of preventing certain nodes from connecting to their neighbors, it is by no means this easy. Our main technical contribution is to transfer the bounds on the diameter of an Erdős-Rényi graph to our flooding protocol in presence of an adaptive adversary. We achieve this by relating the protocol execution to 7 random experiments.

First, we relate the protocol execution to a well-defined game between an adversary and an oracle, which returns a graph. The rules of the game is that an adversary can query the oracle to reveal the edges of a node and query the oracle to remove a node from the graph. However, once either an incoming or outgoing edge to a node has been revealed, the adversary can no longer remove this node. This game mimics the powers of a slightly delayed adaptive adversary in the real protocol.

We relate this game to a similar game but with undirected edges, and do a couple of simple gamehops where we show that an adversary does not gain any additional advantage w.r.t. increasing the diameter by stopping this game at an early point nor injecting any additional edges.

As the adversary can only remove nodes for which no information has been revealed, one might be led to believe that the Erdős-Rényi graph results apply for this game. However, the adversary can still dynamically control the size of the graph that is returned. At first, this may seem innocent, but in fact, it is not. Deciding whether or not more nodes are to be included in the graph, can amplify the probability that the returned graph has a high diameter.

Therefore, we relate this game to a new game, which is similar to the other, except that the oracle now at random fixes the size of the graph beforehand. The oracle fixes the size of the graph by making a uniform guess in the range of possible sizes. In case of a correct guess (a guess identical to what the adversary anyway would end up with), the adversary is only left with the choice of which parties to include in the random graph. Finally, we show that this game is equally distributed to a game which specifically embeds an Erdős-Rényi graph of the fixed size. This allows us to apply results bounding diameter of Erdős-Rényi graphs to bound the probability that a message is not delivered timely.

Due to space constraints, many technical details are left out of this version. We refer to the full version of this paper [33] for these.

1.4 Related Work

Hybrid Consensus. Hybrid Consensus [38] is a consensus protocol that uses a blockchain to periodically select committees as subsets of the parties participating in the blockchain protocol, who can subsequently produce blocks more efficiently. Once a committee has been chosen, a fully adaptive adversary can simply corrupt the majority of its members to break the security of the protocol. Hence, the protocol is only secure against corruptions that are delayed until the next committee gets selected.

To prove the security of hybrid consensus, that paper introduces τ-*agile corruptions*, which essentially correspond to the capabilities of our τ-delayed adversaries. While that paper also uses the UC framework, the definitions for the corruption model mostly remain at a high level. For example, their definitions assume there is some notion of time, which does not exist in the original UC formalism. There are also no clear definitions of how the delayed corruptions are precisely embedded in the UC execution model.

In contrast to that, our work provides a precise embedding of the corruption model in the standard UC framework. This allows us to compose protocols formulated in standard UC with protocols proven secure against δ-delayed adversaries. It is thus fair to say that the hybrid consensus paper has introduced the delayed corruption model at an intuitive, semi-formal level, while our work fills in several missing technical details to provide a precise formalization within the UC framework.

Time in UC. [25] models time using a clock functionality that is local to each protocol. This functionality synchronizes the parties by only allowing the adversary to advance time when all parties have reported that they have been activated. As this is a *local* functionality, other ideal functionalities have no access to it, and therefore need to provide their own notion of time which can clutter the final guarantees from the functionality.

[28] takes a similar approach to Katz et al., but changes the clock to be a *global functionality* in GUC [9]. This enables several different protocols to rely on the same notion of time when composed and also solves the problem of time not being available to ideal functionalities. Both functionalities and parties can query the global clock for the current time, and thus inherently makes any protocol modelled with this a synchronous protocol.

A different approach is taken in [4]. They take the standpoint that parties should be oblivious to the passing of time. To allow this they introduce a global functionality, dubbed a *ticker* (written $\bar{\mathcal{G}}_{\text{Ticker}}$), which exposes an interface to learn about the passing of time to functionalities *only*. In particular honest parties are oblivious to the passing of time. This allows time to be modelled without having synchrony as an inherent assumption. The specific timing-assumptions can then be captured by adding an extra ideal functionality which exposes relevant information to the parties.

Contrary to [4,25,28], [10] focuses on modeling and making *real* time available to parties in GUC, and use this to model the expiration of certificates in a public-key infrastructure. In their modeling, a global clock can be advanced by the environment without restrictions. In this work, our protocols do not rely on real-time, but rather on an abstract notion of time used to state assumptions and guarantees about the delivery time of channels and protocols. For the guarantees to be upheld, we rely on restrictions about how time is advanced (namely that all parties have to be activated once each abstract time step) by the environment.

We chose to rely on the modeling of time from [4]. This allows us to model general timing assumptions on the capabilities of the adversary without tying our modeling to a particular assumption on synchrony for actual protocols.

Epidemic and Gossip Protocols. Epidemic algorithms or gossip protocols were first considered for data dissemination by Demers et al. [16], and have been studied extensively since then, see e.g., [5,13,21,23,24,26]. In this line of work, many different protocols have been considered. Some are very closely related to our flooding protocol, where parties simply forward to a random set of parties, and some are more advanced, letting parties keep sending to new random peers until a certain number of recipients replied that they already knew the message. However, this line of work considers only random failures [26] or incomplete network topologies [13,23] and not adaptive corruptions of a malicious adversary. Hence, while some of the protocols are applicable to our setting, their analysis is not. Among other results, [26] showed how random node failures affect the success probability of a flooding process similar to ours. For this setting, they derive connectivity bounds similar to the bounds for logarithmic diameter we present in this work.

Kadcast. Kadcast [40] is a structured peer-to-peer network for blockchains. The paper claims that unstructured networks are inherently inefficient because many superfluous messages are sent to parties who already received the message from other peers. They instead propose a structured network based on Kademlia [34], in which every node has $\mathcal{O}(\log n)$ neighbors and the diameter of the graph is also $\mathcal{O}(\log n)$. Additionally, their protocol includes a parameter for controlling the redundancy and thus the resistance to attacks. Due to the structured nature, the suggested network is, however, not secure against adaptive corruptions of any kind.

The Hidden Graph Model. Chandran et al. [11] consider *communication locality* of multi-party computation (MPC) protocols, which corresponds to the maximal number of parties each honest party needs to interact with. They construct an MPC protocol with poly-logarithmic communication locality that is secure against adaptive corruptions and that runs in a poly-logarithmic number of rounds. Their protocol uses a random communication graph, similar to our flooding protocols. To be secure against adaptive corruptions, they however need to assume that the communication graph between honest parties remains hidden, i.e., they allow honest parties to communicate securely without an adversary learning who is communicating with whom. Furthermore, they only prove very loose bounds on the locality and diameter of the obtained graph by showing that both are poly-logarithmic. In the full version of this work [33], we replicate this result but with concrete bounds.

Message Dissemination Relying on Resource Assumptions. Recently, the problem of disseminating messages assuming a constant fraction of honest resources (computational power, stake, etc.) instead of assuming a constant fraction of honest parties (as assumed in this work) has received attention. Extending on results from this work, [30] provides an efficient flooding protocol relying on a constant fraction of the resources behaving honestly. Their protocols achieve an asymptotic efficiency similar to the protocol presented in this work. [12] presents a block dissemination protocol for the Ouroboros Praos protocol [15] that also relies on the majority of honest stake assumption. By using long-lived connections between parties, they prevent a specific denial-of-service attack possible in the protocol. However, this comes at the cost of allowing a small fraction of honest parties to be eclipsed.

2   Preliminaries

2.1   Notation

We use the infix notation ":=" for assigning a variable a (new) value, the infix notation "≜" to emphasize that a concept is being defined formally for the first time, the infix notation "==" to denote an equality test returning a boolean value, and the infix notation "::" to denote list-extension. In our proofs we will use the acronyms LHS and RHS to refer to respectively the left-hand side and the right-hand side of an equality.

When describing functionalities we let $\mathcal{P}$ be a set of unique party identifiers (PIDs) and will leave out session-identifiers for clarity of presentation. As a convention we use the variable $t \in \mathbb{N}$ to denote the maximal number of parties an adversary can corrupt, use the variable $n := |\mathcal{P}|$ to denote the total number of parties in a protocol (except when we state and prove general results about graphs) and $h := n-t$ to denote the minimal number of honest parties. Whenever we refer to *honest* parties we will refer to parties that have not received any precorrupt or corrupt tokens.

2.2   Universally Composable Security

The UC framework is a general framework for describing and proving cryptographic protocols secure. Its main selling point is that protocols can be described and proven secure in a modular manner while ensuring that the protocol in question remains secure independently of how one may compose the protocol in question with other protocols. We build upon the journal version of UC [8] and refer to this for details about the framework. Below we recap two peculiarities of the framework that are important for our model (Sect. 3).

Corruptions. The UC framework has no built-in semantics for corruption of parties in a protocol. Instead, it is up to each individual protocol description to describe the semantics of corruptions whenever the adversary signals that a specific party should be corrupted. Having no built-in corruption model in UC makes the composition theorem independent of a particular corruption model. This allows several different corruption models to be captured within the framework. Some machinery is however common for many different types of corruptions.

The Corruption Aggregation ITI. The intuition behind UC-security is to translate an attack on the protocol to an attack on the specification (the ideal functionality) and thereby show that an adversary does not gain any capabilities
interacting with an implementation that another adversary did not have interacting with the ideal functionality. That is to show that any attack is not really
an attack as it was already allowed by the specification. This translation between
attacks is what is known as a simulator.

For this intuition to make sense when active corruptions are possible, the
translation between attacks on the protocol and the specification necessarily
needs to be *corruption preserving*. That is, it should not require more corruptions
to attack the ideal functionality than what it takes to attack the real protocol.
In order to ensure this, an additional Interactive Turing Machine Instance (ITI)
called the *corruption aggregation* ITI is run aside the parties in protocol. Whenever a party is corrupted, it registers as corrupted by the corruption aggregation
ITI. The environment can then query the corruption aggregation ITI in order
to get an overview of who is currently corrupted. Similarly, the ideal functionality makes information about who is corrupted available to the environment.
Note that the corruption aggregation ITI is only present for modeling purposes
and thus not present when deploying a protocol. In that way, if the simulator
corrupts differently than the adversary, the environment is immediately able to
distinguish.

Identity Masking Function and PIDs. The UC framework allows for a very fine-
grained control over what knowledge about corruptions is leaked to the environment, by parameterizing the corruptions using an *identity-masking-function*,
which parties will apply to the information that they send to the corruption
aggregation ITI. This can allow an adversary to corrupt only sub-protocols of
a party instead of an entire party. We leave this out of the definitions below
for clarity as we will always consider corruptions of entire parties (known as
PID-wise corruptions within the framework).

Time. There is no built-in notion of time in UC. However, the flexibility of the
framework allows to model a notion of time using an ideal functionality. In this
work we adopt the notion of time presented in TARDIS [4].

In TARDIS time is modelled via a global functionality dubbed a *ticker* (writ-
ten $\bar{\mathcal{G}}_{\text{Ticker}}$). The ticker's job is to keep track of time and enforce that any party
has enough time to perform the actions that it wishes to perform between any
two time-steps. It does so by allowing parties to register by the functionality and
only allows the environment to progress time once it has heard that this is okay
from all registered parties.

Functionalities can query the ticker and get an answer to whether or not time
has passed since the last time they asked the ticker. Importantly, this query can
only be made by functionalities and not parties. That is, this modeling of time
does not tie the protocols to be designed under a specific synchrony assumption,
as parties are oblivious to time. The only way that they can observe the passing

of time is by asking functionalities. This parallels the real world in that we do not have raw access to time, only clocks. The level of information functionalities provide to parties about time is what determines possible assumptions about synchrony.

The complete ticker functionality as described in TARDIS as well as a small note about preventing fast-forwarding is provided in the full version of this work [33].

Ticked?-convention. In the remainder of this paper, we adopt the convention (also used in [4]) that when describing ideal functionalities we omit *Ticked?* queries to $\bar{\mathcal{G}}_{\text{Ticker}}$ from the description. Functionalities are instead assumed to make this query whenever they are activated and in case of a positive answer perform whatever action that is described by **Tick**. We furthermore adopt the convention that for brevity we leave out registration of functionalities and parties by the global ticker. All of the functionalities and protocols we consider will upon initialization as the first thing register by the global ticker.

Global Functionalities within Plain UC. Technically, the ticker functionality in TARDIS is defined within the GUC framework [9]. However, as pointed out in [2], the GUC framework has not been updated since its introduction, even though that it relies on the UC framework which has been revised and updated several times since. Furthermore, [2] points out that several technical subtleties of the composition theorem of GUC are under-specified which at best leaves its correctness unproven. The compatibility with the latest version of UC which we use in this work is thus unclear.

However, [2] introduces machinery to handle "global subroutines", which can be used to model similar global setup assumptions to global functionalities, and extends the composition theorem of UC to cover such "global subroutines" directly within the version of UC also adapted for this work. Additionally, they show how examples of global functionalities that instead can be modelled as global subroutines. One of their examples [2, Section 4.3] of such a transformation is, that they show that [3] that implements a transaction ledger using a global clock (similar to the one from [25]), instead could have been done directly within UC, by modeling the clock as a global subroutine instead of a global functionality. We note that $\bar{\mathcal{G}}_{\text{Ticker}}$ is *regular* (informally, it does not spawn new ITIs) and as all of the protocols considered in this work are $\bar{\mathcal{G}}_{\text{Ticker}}$-*subroutine respecting* (informally, all subroutines except $\bar{\mathcal{G}}_{\text{Ticker}}$ only communicate with ITIs within the session). Therefore, we can use the same approach as [2, Section 4.3] (in particular can adopt the same *identity bound* for the environment to ensure that the ticker works as expected) to keep our modeling within plain UC.

3 Delayed Adversaries Within UC

In this section we describe the semantics of delayed corruptions within the UC framework. First, we introduce the semantics for δ-delayed corruptions via *corruption shells*. Next, we revisit the standard adaptive corruptions using corruption-shells. Finally, we relate the standard notion of adaptive corruptions to a 0-delayed adversary.

We define the notion of a delayed adversary precisely within the UC-model via what we call δ-*delayed corruptions* or a δ-*delayed adversary*. For such an adversary, it takes at least δ time to execute a corruption. The delay can be thought of as either the time it takes to hack into the system or the time it takes to physically orchestrate and attack on the specific property that hosts the system. To capture this within UC we introduce an additional token that an adversary has to use when wanting to corrupt a party. The two corruption tokens that can be passed to a party are the *Precorrupt* token and the *Corrupt* token. When receiving a *Precorrupt* token, the party notes the time it received this token, t, and ignores all *Corrupt* tokens that are received before $t + \delta$. When a *Corrupt* token is received at or after time $t + \delta$, the party becomes corrupted in the usual manner.

Below we give a more precise description of how this corruption model can be captured within the UC framework.

3.1 The δ-Delay Shell

It is tedious and error-prone to include code that models corruption behavior in each protocol description and ideal functionality description. We therefore separate the concern of describing corruption behaviors to that of describing the protocol, by introducing protocol transformers, dubbed *shells*, which extend a protocol that does not handle corruption tokens into one that obeys a particular corruption behavior. In particular we provide the following two shells for δ-delayed corruptions:

$\mathcal{D}^\delta_{\text{Real}}$: This a wrapper around a protocol π. It ensures that the protocol respects δ-delayed corruptions. The wrapper preserves the functionality of π but additionally ensures that corruptions are executed as expected.

$\mathcal{D}^\delta_{\text{Ideal}}$: This is a wrapper around an ideal functionality $\mathcal{F}$. It ensures that the functionality respects δ-delayed corruptions and preserves the functionality of $\mathcal{F}$ but additionally ensures that corruptions are executed as expected.

Both shells intuitively work in the same way: They keep track of when *Precorrupt* tokens are delivered and only accept corruption tokens for a particular party δ time later. Having two different shells is, however, necessary as the protocol shell needs to wrap the individual ITMs actually executing the protocol, whereas the ideal shell needs to wrap only the ITM running the ideal functionality.

Additionally, both shells allow the first message that is sent to a specific party to initialize the precorruption time. The delay shells for real parties ensure to use this initialization option when an inner protocol sends a message to a subroutine for the first time. This ensures that the time of precorruption is inherited when new sub-routines are spawned and thereby induces the natural behavior for PID-wise corruptions, i.e., that any sub-routine can be corrupted no later than the routine that spawned it. The initialized precorruption time is allowed to be negative. This allows the environment to start the protocol in a state where some parties are precorrupted in the past, and hence be able to immediately corrupt these parties at the start of the protocol (similar to letting some parties be statically corrupted).

The shells that wrap the individual party's ITMs do not have access to query the ticker for the time, whereas the ideal shells can do this freely. We solve this by additionally letting the $\mathcal{D}_{\mathsf{Real}}$ spawn a *corruption-clock* (written $\mathcal{F}_{\mathsf{CorruptionClock}}$) which exactly allows the shells to access time. Importantly, this does not reintroduce a global synchrony assumption as our shells prevent the inner protocols from communicating with the corruption clock. The corruption clock is therefore only an artifact of our modeling and will not appear when actually running the protocol.

Functionality $\mathcal{F}_{\mathsf{CorruptionClock}}$

The functionality maintains a counter `Time`. Initially, `Time` := 0.

Time?: When receiving (*Time?*) from a party $p_i \in \mathcal{P}$ it returns (*Time*, `Time`) to p_i.

Tick: It updates `Time` := `Time` + 1.

When describing $\mathcal{D}_{\mathsf{Real}}$ we will leave out calls to $\mathcal{F}_{\mathsf{CorruptionClock}}$ for brevity, but these happens each time the shell uses any notion of time.

We amend the corruption aggregation ITI presented in [8] to also make information about the precorruptions an adversary have used, available to the environment (and similarly the ideal functionalities). This prevents a simulator from using more precorruption tokens or corrupting faster than the real adversary.

Aside from ensuring the protocol corruption delays are respected the $\mathcal{D}_{\mathsf{Ideal}}$ additionally propagates both precorruption and corruption-tokens to the "inner functionality" (the functionality that the shell is a wrapper around). This is done in order to ensure that the simulator appended to the ideal functionalities can actually gain functionality-specific powers when performing a corruption. For example it might be that a certain channel does not need to respect delivery guarantees when the sender gets corrupted (for an example of this see Sect. 4.1).

Below we provide formal descriptions of both shells.

Function $\mathcal{D}_{\mathsf{Real}}^{\delta}(\pi)$

The shell wraps each party $p_i \in \mathcal{P}$ in a small wrapper that maintains a variable $\mathsf{PrecorruptionTime}_i$. Initially, $\mathsf{PrecorruptionTime}_i := \perp$. When receiving precorruptions and corruptions the wrapper has the behavior described below. The wrapper also filters out any communication with $\mathcal{F}_{\mathsf{CorruptionClock}}$ and on all other inputs it simply forwards the inputs/outputs to/from the original protocol.

Initialization: If p_i receives ($Initialize, \tau$) as the first message, then the party updates `PrecorruptionTime`$_i$:= τ and if $\tau \neq \perp$ then also notifies the corruption-aggregation ITI.

Precorruption: If $p_i \in \mathcal{P}$ receives $Precorrupt$ at time τ, then the party first notifies the corruption-aggregation ITI by sending ($Precorrupt, p_i$) to this machine. It then updates `PrecorruptionTime`$_i$:= τ.

Corruption: When p_i receives $Corrupt$ at time τ, then p_i checks if `PrecorruptionTime`$_i$ + $\delta \leq \tau$. If that is not the case the request is ignored. Otherwise the party first notifies the corruption-aggregation ITI by sending ($Corrupt, p_i$) to this machine and then it corrupts p_i by forwarding $Corrupt$ to π. Each time p_i is activated after this it sends its entire local state of the inner protocol to the adversary and furthermore forwards all messages m (assuming that m includes both content and recipient) that are written on the backdoor tape of p_i.

Whenever the shell of p_i detects that the inner protocol sends a message to a new sub-routine for the first time, it sends ($Initialize$, `PrecorruptionTime`$_i$) to the subroutine before forwarding the message of the inner protocol. Furthermore, the shell starts a separate corruption aggregation ITI. It maintains two lists `Precorrupted` and `Corrupted` that initially are both empty. The corruption aggregation ITI has the following behavior:

Precorruption Registration: When receiving a ($Precorrupt, p$) from a party p it sets `Precorrupted` := p :: `Precorrupted`.

Corruption Registration: When receiving a ($Corrupt, p$) from a party p it sets `Corrupted` := p :: `Corrupted`.

Corruption Status: When receiving $CorruptionStatus$ from the environment it queries all sub-functionalities of the protocol for their corruption status and updates the `Precorrupted` and `Corrupted`-lists accordingly. Finally, it sends (`Precorrupted`, `Corrupted`) back to the environment.

Function $\mathcal{D}^{\delta}_{\mathsf{Ideal}}(\mathcal{F})$

The shell wraps the functionality in a wrapper which maintains two lists `Precorrupted` and `Corrupted` that initially are both empty. Furthermore, it has a map `PrecorruptionTimeMap` : $\mathcal{P} \to$ TIME and a counter to keep track of time `Time` which initially is instantiated to be 0. When receiving precorruptions, corruptions and corruption status requests it has the following behavior and on all other inputs/outputs it forwards the inputs to/from $\mathcal{F}$.

Initialization: If the functionality receives ($Initialize, \tau$) at the port belonging to p as the first message for this party, then the party updates `PrecorruptionTimeMap`[p] := τ. If $\tau \neq \perp$ then it also updates

Precorrupted := p :: Precorrupted, and forwards (*Initialize*, τ) to the inner functionality.

Precorruption: When receiving (*Precorrupt*, p) and p is a valid PID of a dummy party then it adds the current time, Time, to PrecorruptionTimeMap[p] := Time and updates Precorrupted := p : : Precorrupted. Furthermore, it propagates (*Precorrupt*, p) to $\mathcal{F}$.

Corruption: When receiving (*Corrupt*, p) where p is a valid PID of a dummy party then the functionality checks if PrecorruptionTimeMap[p] + $\delta \leq$ Time. If that is the case it updates Corrupted := p :: Corrupted and returns to the adversary all the values received from p and output to p so far. From now on inputs from p are ignored but are instead given via the backdoor tape by the adversary. Furthermore, it propagates (*Corrupt*, p) to $\mathcal{F}$.

If the request is send too early, it is ignored.

Inputs: If the functionality receives (*Input*, p, v) from the adversary and $p \in$ Corrupted, then v is forwarded to $\mathcal{F}$ as if it was directly input by p to $\mathcal{F}$.

Corruption Status: When receiving *CorruptionStatus* from the environment it sends (Precorrupted, Corrupted) back to the environment.

Tick: The functionality updates Time := Time + 1.

The additional (*Input*, p, v) command accepted by the ideal shell allows an adversary to input a message v on behalf of party p if p is corrupted. This follows how standard byzantine corruptions are treated and modelled in the UC framework.

We next formally define what it means for a protocol to securely implement a functionality against a δ-delayed adversary, see also Fig. 1 for a graphical depiction.

Definition 1 (UC-security against delayed adversaries). *Let $\delta \in \mathbb{N}$. We say that a protocol π securely implements an ideal functionality $\mathcal{F}$ against a δ-delayed adversary when $\mathcal{D}^\delta_{\mathsf{Real}}(\pi)$ securely implements $\mathcal{D}^\delta_{\mathsf{Ideal}}(\mathcal{F})$ in the usual UC sense [8], i.e., if*

$$\forall \mathcal{A} \; \exists \mathcal{S} \; \forall \mathcal{Z}, \mathrm{EXEC}(\mathcal{Z}, \mathcal{A}, \mathcal{D}^\delta_{\mathsf{Real}}(\pi)) \approx \mathrm{EXEC}(\mathcal{Z}, \mathcal{S}, \mathcal{D}^\delta_{\mathsf{Ideal}}(\mathcal{F}))$$

where $\mathrm{EXEC}(\mathcal{Z}, \cdot, \cdot)$ denotes the random variable describing the binary output of the environment $\mathcal{Z}$, and $\approx$ means that the statistical distance is negligible in the security parameter.

Note that security against a delayed adversary is defined both for functionalities that have special behavior defined for receiving precorruptions and functionalities that do not have any such behavior defined, as the default for protocols/functionalities is to ignore any unrecognized inputs.

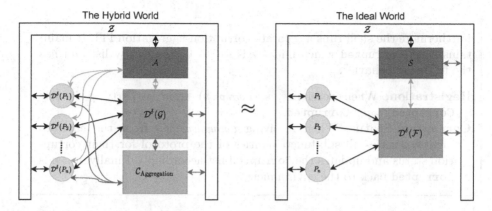

Fig. 1. A depiction of the security statement for a protocol that implements an ideal functionality $\mathcal{F}$ using the functionality $\mathcal{G}$ against a δ-delayed adversary.

3.2 Relating Corruption Models

In this section we relate the notion of a 0-delayed adversary to the standard notion of an adaptive adversary in UC. We further show that any protocol that is secure against a fast adversary is also secure against a slower adversary. These results allow us to reuse cryptographic constructions which are already proven secure modularly when implementing larger constructions.

Byzantine Corruptions and 0-Delayed Corruptions. To showcase the generality of the δ-delayed corruption model, we relate this model to the standard model of adaptive Byzantine corruptions as defined in UC. To be able to precisely quantify how these notions relate, we introduce two Byzantine shells similar to the delay shells. The byzantine-shells are meant to precisely encapsulate the corruption model as presented in [8]. We believe that these are of independent interest as by using these it can be avoided to clutter the protocol and functionality description with a specific corruption model.

Function $\mathcal{B}_{\mathsf{Real}}(\pi)$

The shell adds the following behavior to each party $p_i \in \mathcal{P}$. If any other inputs are received than the ones below, it is the original code of the party that is executed.

Corruption: If $p_i \in \mathcal{P}$ receives *Corrupt* then the party first notifies the corruption-aggregation ITI by sending (*Corrupt*, p_i) to this machine.
Each time p_i is activated after this it sends its entire local state of the inner protocol to the adversary and furthermore forwards all messages m (assuming that m includes both content and recipient) that are written on the backdoor tape of p_i.

Furthermore the shell runs a separate corruption-aggregation ITI. It maintains a list `Corrupted` which initially is set to be the empty list and has the following behavior:

Registration: When receiving a $(Corrupt, p)$ from a party p it sets `Corrupted` $:= p ::$ `Corrupted`.

Corruption Status: When receiving *CorruptionStatus* from the environment it queries all sub-functionalities of the protocol for their corruption status and updates the `Corrupted`-list accordingly. Finally, it sends `Corrupted` back to the environment.

Function $\mathcal{B}_{\mathsf{Ideal}}(\mathcal{F})$

The functionality maintains a list of corrupted parties, `Corrupted`, which initially is set to be the empty list. Upon receiving the following

Corruption: If the functionality receives $(Corrupt, p)$ from the adversary and p is a valid PID of the dummy parties, it updates `Corrupted` $:= p ::$ `Corrupted` and returns to the adversary all the values received from p and output to p so far. From now on inputs from p are ignored but are instead given via the backdoor tape by the adversary. Furthermore it propagates $(Corrupt, p)$ to $\mathcal{F}$.

Inputs: If the functionality receives $(Input, p, v)$ from the adversary and $p \in$ `Corrupted` then v is forwarded to $\mathcal{F}$ as if it was directly input by p to $\mathcal{F}$.

Corruption Status: When receiving *CorruptionStatus* from the environment it sends `Corrupted` back to the environment.

Security against 0-delayed adversary implies security in the standard model and vice versa if the functionality that is implemented ignores precorruption and initialization tokens. We encapsulate this intuition in the theorem below.

Theorem 1. *Let π be a protocol and $\mathcal{F}$ an ideal functionality that ignores precorruptions and initializations. $\mathcal{B}_{\mathsf{Real}}(\pi)$ securely implements $\mathcal{B}_{\mathsf{Ideal}}(\mathcal{F})$ if and only if $\mathcal{D}^0_{\mathsf{Real}}(\pi)$ securely implements $\mathcal{D}^0_{\mathsf{Ideal}}(\mathcal{F})$.*
Formally,

$$\forall \mathcal{A} \ \exists \mathcal{S} \ \forall \mathcal{Z}, \mathrm{EXEC}(\mathcal{Z}, \mathcal{A}, \mathcal{B}_{\mathsf{Real}}(\pi)) \approx \mathrm{EXEC}(\mathcal{Z}, \mathcal{S}, \mathcal{B}_{\mathsf{Ideal}}(\mathcal{F}))$$
$$\iff \forall \mathcal{A}' \ \exists \mathcal{S}' \forall \mathcal{Z}', \mathrm{EXEC}(\mathcal{Z}', \mathcal{A}', \mathcal{D}^0_{\mathsf{Real}}(\pi)) \approx \mathrm{EXEC}(\mathcal{Z}', \mathcal{S}', \mathcal{D}^0_{\mathsf{Ideal}}(\mathcal{F})). \tag{1}$$

Proof (Proof Sketch). We prove the two directions of the implication individually.

"$\implies$": We let $\mathcal{A}'$ be any adversary and construct an adversary $\mathcal{A}$ by wrapping $\mathcal{A}'$ with a shell that forwards all inputs/outputs except precorruptions to/from $\mathcal{A}'$. Whenever $\mathcal{A}$ receives a *Precorrupt* directed to p_i from $\mathcal{A}'$ it forwards (*Precorrupt*, p_i) to the environment instead. We now use the LHS of Eq. (1) to obtain a simulator $\mathcal{S}$ s.t.

$$\forall \mathcal{Z}, \text{EXEC}(\mathcal{Z}, \mathcal{A}, \mathcal{B}_{\text{Real}}(\pi)) \approx \text{EXEC}(\mathcal{Z}, \mathcal{S}, \mathcal{B}_{\text{Ideal}}(\mathcal{F})). \qquad (2)$$

Given $\mathcal{S}$ we construct $\mathcal{S}'$ by running $\mathcal{S}$ inside $\mathcal{S}'$. Each time $\mathcal{S}$ outputs (*Precorrupt*, p_i) to the environment then $\mathcal{S}'$ outputs (*Precorrupt*, p_i) to $\mathcal{D}^0_{\text{Ideal}}(\mathcal{F})$. All other inputs and outputs are forwarded to and from $\mathcal{S}$ directly. Note that precorruptions are ignored by $\mathcal{F}$ and therefore $\mathcal{F}$ does not change its behavior based upon these.

Let us now for the sake of contradiction assume that there exists some environment $\mathcal{Z}'$ that can distinguish against $\mathcal{A}'$ and $\mathcal{S}'$, i.e.,

$$\text{EXEC}(\mathcal{Z}', \mathcal{A}', \mathcal{D}^0_{\text{Real}}(\pi)) \not\approx \text{EXEC}(\mathcal{Z}', \mathcal{S}', \mathcal{D}^0_{\text{Ideal}}(\mathcal{F})) \qquad (3)$$

Let us now show how to construct an environment, $\mathcal{Z}$, that can distinguish for the byzantine setting and thereby contradict Eq. (2).

We build $\mathcal{Z}$ by running $\mathcal{Z}'$ inside, and forward all inputs and outputs to $\mathcal{Z}'$. $\mathcal{Z}$ only deviates from $\mathcal{Z}'$ in the two cases below:

- Whenever a *CorruptionStatus* command is issued by $\mathcal{Z}'$ to the corruption aggregation ITI, we amend the answer with an additional list of precorruptions which we have received from $\mathcal{A}$ so far.
- Whenever a (*Initialize*, τ) command is send to some party it is not forwarded by $\mathcal{Z}$ but instead recorded as a precorruption of this party. This does not change the behavior of the protocol nor the ideal functionality as these are ignored.

In particular, $\mathcal{Z}$ simply forwards the guess on which world it is placed in from $\mathcal{Z}'$.

We observe that

$$\text{EXEC}(\mathcal{Z}, \mathcal{S}, \mathcal{B}_{\text{Ideal}}(\mathcal{F})) \approx \text{EXEC}(\mathcal{Z}', \mathcal{S}', \mathcal{D}^0_{\text{Ideal}}(\mathcal{F})), \qquad (4)$$

and

$$\text{EXEC}(\mathcal{Z}, \mathcal{A}, \mathcal{B}_{\text{Real}}(\pi)) \approx \text{EXEC}(\mathcal{Z}', \mathcal{A}', \mathcal{D}^0_{\text{Real}}(\pi)). \qquad (5)$$

Together with Eq. (3) this contradicts Eq. (2) and thus concludes the case.

"$\Longleftarrow$": The proof of this case mirrors the other case. We are now given $\mathcal{A}$ and construct $\mathcal{A}'$ by sending *Precorrupt*-tokens just before *Corrupt*-tokens. From the RHS of Theorem 1 we get a simulator $\mathcal{S}'$ which we use to construct $\mathcal{S}$ by forwarding everything except *Precorrupt*-tokens. Finally, we assume for the sake of contradiction that there exists a $\mathcal{Z}$ that is able to distinguish, build an environment $\mathcal{Z}'$ using this (removing *Precorrupt*-tokens and initializations), and derive a contradiction similarly to the other case. $\square$

Note that the above theorem allows reusing constructions that are proven secure against a standard adaptive adversary when building complex systems that are to be secure against a 0-delayed adversary.

Lifting Security to Weaker Adversaries. If protocols that are proven secure within different corruption models are composed, it gets hard to identify the final security guarantee that is provided by the composed construction. Intuitively, one would presume that a protocol that is proven secure against an adversary able to do "fast" corruptions is also secure against an adversary only able to do "slow" corruptions. Using precise shells to quantify corruption-speed allows us to capture this intuition in the lemma below.

Theorem 2 (Lifting Security to Slower Corruptions). *Let $\delta, \delta' \in \mathbb{N}$, s.t. $\delta \leq \delta'$, let π be a protocol, and let $\mathcal{F}$ be an ideal functionality. If $\mathcal{D}_{\mathsf{Real}}^{\delta}(\pi)$ securely implements $\mathcal{D}_{\mathsf{Ideal}}^{\delta}(\mathcal{F})$, then $\mathcal{D}_{\mathsf{Real}}^{\delta'}(\pi)$ securely implements $\mathcal{D}_{\mathsf{Ideal}}^{\delta'}(\mathcal{F})$.*

Formally,

$$\forall \mathcal{A}, \exists \mathcal{S}, \forall \mathcal{Z}, \mathrm{EXEC}(\mathcal{Z}, \mathcal{A}, \mathcal{D}_{\mathsf{Real}}^{\delta}(\pi)) \approx \mathrm{EXEC}(\mathcal{Z}, \mathcal{S}, \mathcal{D}_{\mathsf{Ideal}}^{\delta}(\mathcal{F}))$$
$$\Longrightarrow \forall \mathcal{A}', \exists \mathcal{S}', \forall \mathcal{Z}', \mathrm{EXEC}(\mathcal{Z}', \mathcal{A}', \mathcal{D}_{\mathsf{Real}}^{\delta'}(\pi)) \approx \mathrm{EXEC}(\mathcal{Z}', \mathcal{S}', \mathcal{D}_{\mathsf{Ideal}}^{\delta'}(\mathcal{F})). \tag{6}$$

Proof. Let H be the hypothesis (LHS of the implication), and let $\mathcal{A}'$ be an adversary. We define $\mathsf{Filter}(\mathcal{A}, \delta)$ to be a wrapper around an adversary that simply filters out corruption request that are to early w.r.t. δ.

Using H we know that there exists a simulator $\mathcal{S}$ s.t.

$$\forall \mathcal{Z}, \mathrm{EXEC}(\mathcal{Z}, \mathsf{Filter}(\mathcal{A}', \delta'), \mathcal{D}_{\mathsf{Real}}^{\delta}(\pi)) \approx \mathrm{EXEC}(\mathcal{Z}, \mathcal{S}, \mathcal{D}_{\mathsf{Ideal}}^{\delta}(\mathcal{F})). \tag{7}$$

Let us now show,

$$\forall \mathcal{Z}, \mathrm{EXEC}(\mathcal{Z}, \mathsf{Filter}(\mathcal{A}', \delta'), \mathcal{D}_{\mathsf{Real}}^{\delta}(\pi)) \approx \mathrm{EXEC}(\mathcal{Z}, \mathcal{S}, \mathcal{D}_{\mathsf{Ideal}}^{\delta'}(\mathcal{F})). \tag{8}$$

Assume for the sake of contradiction that there exists an environment $\mathcal{Z}$ that is able to distinguish in Eq. (8). We use this to build an environment $\mathcal{Z}'$ which is able to distinguish in Eq. (7) with at least as big an advantage. $\mathcal{Z}'$ works by forwarding everything to and from $\mathcal{Z}$. Except if at any point in time there is a *Precorrupt*-token followed by a *Corrupt* send with strictly less than δ' between them, then $\mathcal{Z}'$ immediately guesses that it is in the ideal case.

As every time that this happens the environment is correct, and every time this does not happen the execution is exactly similar to that of Eq. (7) this implies Eq. (8).

We now define $\mathcal{S}' \triangleq \mathcal{S}$ and let $\mathcal{Z}'$ be any environment. We specialize Eq. (8) with $\mathcal{Z}'$ and obtain

$$\mathrm{EXEC}(\mathcal{Z}', \mathsf{Filter}(\mathcal{A}', \delta'), \mathcal{D}_{\mathsf{Real}}^{\delta}(\pi)) \approx \mathrm{EXEC}(\mathcal{Z}', \mathcal{S}, \mathcal{D}_{\mathsf{Ideal}}^{\delta'}(\mathcal{F})). \tag{9}$$

Furthermore,

$$\mathrm{EXEC}(\mathcal{Z}', \mathsf{Filter}(\mathcal{A}', \delta'), \mathcal{D}_{\mathsf{Real}}^{\delta}(\pi)) \approx \mathrm{EXEC}(\mathcal{Z}', \mathsf{Filter}(\mathcal{A}', \delta'), \mathcal{D}_{\mathsf{Real}}^{\delta'}(\pi)) \tag{10}$$
$$\approx \mathrm{EXEC}(\mathcal{Z}', \mathcal{A}', \mathcal{D}_{\mathsf{Real}}^{\delta'}(\pi)). \tag{11}$$

Equation (10) holds as if early corruptions are ignored, then $\mathcal{D}_{\mathsf{Real}}^{\delta}(\pi)$ and $\mathcal{D}_{\mathsf{Real}}^{\delta'}(\pi)$ are identically distributed. Equation (11) holds as it is not observable by the environment if the corruption is ignored by the filter or the shell. Together Eqs. (9) and (11) finishes the proof. □

Note that if one considered a simpler model with just one corruption token and a subsequent automatic effectuation of the corruption a certain time after such the token was input (instead of a model like ours with separate tokens for precorruptions and corruptions), then Theorem 2 would not hold. The reason is that in such a model a fast adversary would not have the ability to imitate a slow adversary. Hence, in such a model a fast adversary would not be strictly "stronger" than a slow adversary.

Theorems 1 and 2 together imply that any protocol that is secure against a standard adaptive adversary in UC, is also secure against any δ-delayed adversary.

4 Functionalities

In this section we define a time-bounded channel between parties as well as a flooding functionality. The functionalities that we present are:

MessageTransfer: A functionality that allows one party to send messages to another party. This is modeling a point-to-point channel.

Flood: A functionality that allows all honest parties to disseminate to all other parties.

Conventions for Ideal Functionalities. Our functionalities needs to maintain a counter which is incremented each time a tick happens (similarly to what $\mathcal{D}_{\mathsf{Ideal}}$ does). For clarity of presentation, we describe our functionalities without explicitly mentioning this, but instead describe them as having direct access to time. Furthermore, we define the functionalities without specifying the corruption model as we will make use of the shells described in Sect. 3 to make the corruption-model explicit when implementing the functionalities.

Additionally, the behavior of both our functionalities depend on which parties are precorrupted and which parties are corrupted. Therefore they both maintain two sets: Precorrupted and Corrupted which are initially empty. These are updated by the following activation rules which we do not make explicit in the functionalities below for clarity of presentation.

Precorrupt: Upon receiving $(\mathit{Precorrupt}, p_i)$ or an initialization that changes party p_i's status to precorrupted, it sets Precorrupted := Precorrupted $\cup$ $\{p_i\}$.

Corrupt: Upon receiving $(\mathit{Corrupt}, p_i)$ it sets Corrupted := Corrupted $\cup$ $\{p_i\}$.

Furthermore, both of our ideal functionalities are parameterized by a type of messages that can be propagated which we denote MESSAGES.

4.1 MessageTransfer

In this section we present a basic functionality that allows a party to send messages to other parties. This is similar to the point-to-point channel presented in [4], but instead of hardcoding whether we assume AMS (as done in [4]) or not, we introduce an additional parameter which is the time an honest party needs to stay honest for ensuring delivery of the message.

Functionality $\mathcal{F}^{\sigma,\Delta}_{\text{MessageTransfer}}(p_s, p_r)$

The functionality is parameterized by two parties p_s (the sender) and p_r (the receiver), and a time σ which parties needs to stay honest for the delivery guarantee Δ to apply. It maintains a mailbox for p_r, Mailbox : MESSAGES.

Initialize: Initially, Mailbox $:= \varnothing$.

Send: After receiving (Send, m) from p_s it leaks (Leak, p_s, m) to the adversary.

Get Messages: After receiving $(\mathit{GetMessages})$ from p_r it outputs Mailbox to party p_r.

Set Message: After receiving $(\mathit{SetMessage}, m)$ from the adversary, the functionality sets Mailbox $:=$ Mailbox $\cup \{m\}$.

At any time the functionality automatically enforces the following property:

1. Let m be a message that is input for the first time by an honest party $p_s \notin \mathbf{Corrupted}$ at some time τ. If $p_s \notin \mathbf{Corrupted}$ at time $\tau + \sigma$, then by time $\tau + \Delta$ it is ensured that $m \in$ Mailbox.

The property is ensured by the functionality automatically making the minimal possible additional calls with $\mathit{SetMessage}$.

Note that building a construction using $\mathcal{F}^{0,\Delta}_{\text{MessageTransfer}}$ exactly corresponds to assuming AMS whereas assuming $\mathcal{F}^{\sigma,\Delta}_{\text{MessageTransfer}}$ against a δ-delayed adversary with $\delta < \sigma$ corresponds to not assuming AMS.

4.2   Flood

The ideal functionality that we present here provides the guarantees of flooding network, i.e., that all information some honest party knows is disseminated to all other parties within a bounded time.

Functionality $\mathcal{F}^{\Delta}_{\text{Flood}}$

The functionality is parameterized by a set of parties $\mathcal{P}$, and a delivery guarantee Δ.

Furthermore, it keeps track of a set of messages for each party Mailbox : $\mathcal{P} \to$ MESSAGES. These sets contain the messages that each party will receive after fetching.

Initialize: Initially, $\mathbf{Corrupted} := \varnothing$ and Mailbox$[p_i] := \varnothing$ for all $p_i \in \mathcal{P}$.

Send: After receiving (Send, m) from p_i it leaks (Leak, p_i, m) to the adversary.

Get Messages: After receiving (*GetMessages*) from p_i it outputs Mailbox[p_i] to party p_i.

Set Message: After receiving (*SetMessage*, m, p_i) from the adversary, the functionality sets Mailbox[p_i] := Mailbox[p_i] $\cup \{m\}$.

At any time after all parties have been initialized the functionality automatically enforces the following two properties:

1. Let m be a message that is input for the first time to an honest party $p_i \notin$ Precorrupted $\cup$ Corrupted at some time τ. By time $\tau + \Delta$ it is ensured that $\forall p_j \in \mathcal{P} \setminus$ (Corrupted $\cup$ Precorrupted) it holds that $m \in$ Mailbox[p_j].
2. Let m be a message at some time τ is in the mailbox of an honest party $p_i \notin$ Precorrupted $\cup$ Corrupted i.e., $m \in$ Mailbox[p_i]. By time $\tau + \Delta$ it is distributed to all honest mailboxes, i.e., for any party $p_j \in \mathcal{P} \setminus$ (Corrupted $\cup$ Precorrupted) it holds that $m \in$ Mailbox[p_j].

The properties are ensured by the functionality automatically making the minimal possible additional calls with *SetMessage*.

5 Implementations of Flood

In this section we will present the following protocols that implement Flood:

$\pi_{\text{NaiveFlood}}$: Everybody simply sends to everybody.
π_{ERFlood}: Everybody sends to each other party with some fixed probability ρ.

We provide two types of implementations for Flood. A naive approach where everybody sends to everybody and a more efficient one where each party sends to their neighbors with probability ρ. The latter construction allows us to reuse the theoretic foundation of Erdős-Rényi graphs in the distributed systems setting and achieve a variety of properties.

5.1 Naive Flood

We present here a protocol that implements Flood with a message complexity that is quadratic in the number of messages that is input to the system.

The protocol $\pi_{\text{NaiveFlood}}$ works straightforwardly by a peer sending and relaying any non-relayed message to all other parties. As everybody sends to everybody the protocol achieves a very small diameter and resilience against *fairly fast* adaptive adversaries at the cost of a large communication overhead and neighborhood.

Protocol $\pi_{\mathsf{NaiveFlood}}$

Each pair of parties $p_i, p_j \in \mathcal{P}$ has access to a channel $\mathcal{F}^{\sigma,\Delta}_{\mathsf{MessageTransfer}}(p_i, p_j)$. Each party $p_i \in \mathcal{P}$ keeps track of a set of relayed messages $\mathtt{Relayed}_i$.

Initialize: Initially, all parties initialize their channel between them and set $\mathtt{Relayed}_i := \varnothing$.

Send: When p_i receives (Send, m) they now forward inputs (Send, m) to $\mathcal{F}^{\sigma,\Delta}_{\mathsf{MessageTransfer}}(p_i, p_j)$ for all $p_j \in \mathcal{P}$ and set $\mathtt{Relayed}_i := \mathtt{Relayed}_i \cup \{m\}$.

Get Messages: When p_i receives $(\mathit{GetMessages})$ they let M be the union of the messages they achieve by calling $(\mathit{GetMessages})$ to $\mathcal{F}^{\sigma,\Delta}_{\mathsf{MessageTransfer}}(p_i, p_j)$ for all $p_j \in \mathcal{P}$, and outputs M.

Furthermore, once in every activation each honest p_i let M be the union of the messages they achieve by calling $(\mathit{GetMessages})$ to $\mathcal{F}^{\sigma,\Delta}_{\mathsf{MessageTransfer}}(p_i, p_j)$. For any $m \in M \setminus \mathtt{Relayed}_i$, p_i inputs (Send, m) to $\mathcal{F}^{\sigma,\Delta}_{\mathsf{MessageTransfer}}(p_i, p_j)$ for all $p_j \in \mathcal{P}$, and sets $\mathtt{Relayed}_i := \mathtt{Relayed}_i \cup \{m\}$.

An obvious attack on this protocol an adversary might try to perform is to try to corrupt the sender between the time τ that a message is sent and time $\tau + \sigma$ where the delivery guarantee from the underlying $\mathcal{F}^{\sigma,\Delta}_{\mathsf{MessageTransfer}}$ applies. An adversary that succeeds with this can violate both Properties 1 and 2 of $\mathcal{F}^{\Delta}_{\mathsf{Flood}}$. However, σ-delayed adversaries do not have sufficient time to succeed with this as the properties only needs to be upheld for parties that are neither corrupted nor precorrupted when they try to send the message. Below we explicitly[1] prove that against such adversaries the naive protocol actually realizes $\mathcal{F}^{\Delta}_{\mathsf{Flood}}$.

Lemma 1. *Let* $\sigma, \Delta \in \mathbb{N}$. *The protocol* $\pi_{\mathsf{NaiveFlood}}$ *perfectly realizes* $\mathcal{F}^{\Delta}_{\mathsf{Flood}}$ *in the* $\mathcal{F}^{\sigma,\Delta}_{\mathsf{MessageTransfer}}$-*hybrid model against a* σ-*delayed adversary.*

Proof. We construct a simulator $\mathcal{S}$.

1. $\mathcal{S}$ simulates all parties $p_i \in P$ inside it self.
2. When receiving (Leak, p_i, m) from $\mathcal{F}^{\Delta}_{\mathsf{Flood}}$ the simulator inputs (Send, m) to p_i (running inside $\mathcal{S}$).
3. When receiving $(\mathit{SetMessage}, m)$ from the adversary on the port belonging to functionality $\mathcal{F}^{\sigma,\Delta}_{\mathsf{MessageTransfer}}(p_i, p_j)$, $\mathcal{S}$ forwards $(\mathit{SetMessage}, m, p_j)$ to $\mathcal{F}^{\Delta}_{\mathsf{Flood}}$.
4. Whenever $\mathcal{A}$ corrupts some $p_i \in \mathcal{P}$, $\mathcal{S}$ corrupts p_i and sends the simulated internal state to $\mathcal{A}$. From then on the simulated p_i (inside $\mathcal{S}$) follows $\mathcal{A}$'s instructions.

---

[1] In [36, Chapter 3, p. 111], it is shown that it is enough to argue correct realization to achieve secure realization for any protocol which leaks all I/O behavior to the adversary. One may be lead to believe that this result directly applies to $\pi_{\mathsf{NaiveFlood}}$, but as $(\mathit{GetMessages})$ inputs (and corresponding outputs) are hidden from the adversary this is not the case.

5. Whenever the $\bar{\mathcal{G}}_{\text{Ticker}}$ notifies $\mathcal{S}$ about the passing of time, $\mathcal{S}$ ensures to activate $\mathcal{F}_{\text{Flood}}^{\Delta}$.

As protocol, functionality, and simulator are all deterministic it is enough to argue that the I/O behavior of $\mathcal{A}$ interacting with $\pi_{\text{NaiveFlood}}$ is equal to the I/O behavior of $\mathcal{S}$ interacting with $\mathcal{F}_{\text{Flood}}^{\Delta}$ to argue perfect indistinguishability. The send command is invoked at the exact same times in the real execution and in the execution inside $\mathcal{S}$ this produces the exact same behavior. Furthermore, for any send command that is invoked at time τ by an honest party (neither precorrupted nor corrupted) there will be a set-message command within $\tau + \Delta$ for all honest parties in the real protocol as a σ-delayed adversary does not have time to violate the delivery property of the underlying $\mathcal{F}_{\text{MessageTransfer}}^{\sigma,\Delta}(p_i, p_j)$, and therefore Property 1 is upheld. Similarly, the relaying of messages in the real protocol ensure that messages will be delivered by the adversary according to the properties of $\mathcal{F}_{\text{Flood}}^{\Delta}$ in the real protocol (inside $\mathcal{S}$ and therefore also in the ideal) which ensures Property 2.   □

5.2 Efficient Flood

We now present a more efficient version of Flood. The idea is simple: Instead of relaying messages to *all* parties, each party flips a coin for each neighbor that decides if a particular message should be relayed to this party. Compared to the naive implementation of Flood presented in previous section the protocol presented here will have significantly smaller neighborhoods at the cost of larger diameter in the communication graph (the parameter Δ of Flood). Furthermore, the construction is only able to tolerate adversaries that are slightly more delayed than those the naive protocol can tolerate.

The protocol π_{ERFlood} works by letting all parties relay and send messages to a different random subset of parties for each message that is to be sent/relayed. By letting the random subset be large enough we ensure that we establish a connected graph with low diameter for all messages. As the subset of parties each party chooses to send to is random, the protocol achieves quite some robustness against adaptive adversaries, as a slightly delayed adversary cannot predict whom to corrupt in order to eclipse some specific parties.

Protocol $\pi_{\text{ERFlood}}(\rho)$

Each pair of parties $p_i, p_j \in \mathcal{P}$ has access to a channel $\mathcal{F}_{\text{MessageTransfer}}^{\sigma,\Delta}(p_i, p_j)$. Each party $p_i \in \mathcal{P}$ keeps track of a set of relayed messages Relayed_i : Messages.

Initialize: Initially, all parties initialize their channel between them and set $\text{Relayed}_i := \varnothing$.

Send: When p_i receives $(\textit{Send}, m)$, they input $(\textit{Send}, m)$ to $\mathcal{F}_{\text{MessageTransfer}}^{\sigma,\Delta}(p_i, p_j)$ with probability ρ for each party $p_j \in \mathcal{P}$. Finally they set $\text{Relayed}_i := \text{Relayed}_i \cup \{m\}$.

Get Messages: When p_i receives (*GetMessages*) they let M be the union of the messages they achieve by calling (*GetMessages*) to $\mathcal{F}^{\sigma,\Delta}_{\text{MessageTransfer}}(p_i, p_j)$ for all $p_j \in \mathcal{P}$, and outputs M.

Furthermore, once in each activation each honest p_i let M be the union of the messages they achieve by calling (*GetMessages*) to $\mathcal{F}^{\sigma,\Delta}_{\text{MessageTransfer}}(p_i, p_j)$ for all $p_j \in \mathcal{P}$. For any $m \in M \setminus \texttt{Relayed}_i$, p_i inputs (*Send, m*) to $\mathcal{F}^{\sigma,\Delta}_{\text{MessageTransfer}}(p_i, p_j)$ with probability ρ for all $p_j \in \mathcal{P}$, and sets $\texttt{Relayed}_i := \texttt{Relayed}_i \cup \{m\}$.

Depending on the parameter ρ the protocol π_{ERFlood} can achieve a variety of properties. We provide two different instantiations that uses the channel $\mathcal{F}^{\sigma,\Delta}_{\text{MessageTransfer}}$ and all works against a $(\sigma + \Delta)$-delayed adversary. Before going into detail with the actual proof, we provide some intuition for why the protocol is secure against exactly a $(\sigma + \Delta)$-delayed adversary. The main intuition is that such an adversary cannot influence how the communication graph between the parties that are honest are created. If a party decides to send a message at some time τ then the set of parties that receives this message will have completed forwarding the message at time $\tau + \sigma + \Delta$, which is the earliest point on this party can be corrupted based upon this party's role in the specific communication graph. Therefore an adversary cannot make use of the adaptive corruptions to disrupt the propagation of a message.

Each of the instantiations that are presented below provides a trade-off between the diameter of the graph, the average size of the neighborhood and the probability that the graph in fact has these properties. Instantiation 1 ensures a diameter of 2 with a neighborhood of just $\Omega\left(\sqrt{n\kappa}\right)$ and Instantiation 2 ensures a logarithmic diameter with a neighborhood of average size $\Omega\left(\kappa\right)$.

Theorem 3. *Let $\Delta \in \mathbb{N}$ be any delay, let $\sigma \in \mathbb{N}$, let $t < n$ be the maximum number of parties an adversary can corrupt, and let $\kappa \in \mathbb{R}$ be the security parameter. The protocol $\pi_{\text{ERFlood}}(\rho)$ securely implements $\mathcal{F}^{\Delta'}_{\text{Flood}}$ against a $(\sigma + \Delta)$-delayed adversary using $\mathcal{F}^{\sigma,\Delta}_{\text{MessageTransfer}}$. More precisely when r is an upper bound on the number of different messages input (either via Send or via SetMessage), the statistical distance between the real and ideal executions is bounded by the probability p_{bad} for either of the following instantiations:*

1. *Let $\rho := \sqrt{\frac{\kappa}{h}}$ and let $\Delta' := 2\Delta$ then*

$$p_{bad} \leq r \cdot (t+1) \cdot n^2 \cdot e^{-\kappa \cdot \frac{(h-2)}{h}}. \tag{12}$$

2. *Let $\alpha \in \mathbb{R}$, $\gamma, \delta_1, \delta_2 \in [0,1]$, and $\rho := \frac{\kappa}{h}$. Furthermore, let $t_0 := \frac{\log\left(\frac{\gamma n}{(1-\delta_1)\kappa}\right)}{\log((1-\delta_2)\alpha)} + 1$ and $\Delta' := \Delta \cdot (t_0 + 1)$. If*

$$e^{-\kappa\gamma} + \frac{\gamma\alpha}{1-\gamma} \leq 1, \quad \frac{\gamma n}{(1-\delta_1)\kappa} > 1, \quad \text{and} \quad (1-\delta_2) \cdot \alpha > 1, \tag{13}$$

then

$$p_{bad} \leq r \cdot (t+1) \cdot \left(n \cdot \left(e^{-\frac{\delta_1^2 \kappa}{2}} + t_0 e^{-\frac{\delta_2^2 \alpha (1-\delta_1) \kappa}{2}} \right) + e^{-h \cdot (\kappa \gamma^2 - 2)} \right). \quad (14)$$

Proof Sketch. For an adversary we construct a simulator similar to how it is done in the proof of Lemma 1. The only times this is not a perfect simulation is when one of the properties of $\mathcal{F}_{\mathsf{Flood}}^{\Delta'}$ are violated in π_{ERFlood} which will never happen when the environment interacts with $\mathcal{F}_{\mathsf{Flood}}^{\Delta'}$. The main idea of the proof is to argue about the probability that a message m, that is input via either *Send* or *SetMessage*, is not propagated to all parties within Δ' time. We will argue about this via 7 random experiments:

$\mathsf{FloodToER}_1$: An experiment where an adversary interacts with an oracle to learn edges in a directed graph. Only nodes that have an edge to them can have their edges revealed to the adversary but the adversary can inject additional edges in order to be able to reveal more nodes. The adversary has the possibility to remove up to t nodes, but at the point of removal the adversary cannot have learned any edges connecting to the removed node. If at any point there is a cut in the graph the adversary can stop the game.

$\mathsf{FloodToER}_2$: An experiment similar to $\mathsf{FloodToER}_1$ except now the edges are undirected.

$\mathsf{FloodToER}_3$: An experiment similar to $\mathsf{FloodToER}_2$ except the adversary cannot stop the game before all parties have been revealed.

$\mathsf{FloodToER}_4$: An experiment similar to $\mathsf{FloodToER}_3$ except the adversary cannot inject edges between parties.

$\mathsf{FloodToER}_5$: An experiment similar to $\mathsf{FloodToER}_4$ except that the oracle secretly and uniformly predetermines the size of the returned graph, $s \in \{h, \ldots, n\}$. The adversary can however still decide whether or not to remove a particular node given that it does not violate the size that the oracle has determined.

$\mathsf{FloodToER}_6$: An experiment similar to $\mathsf{FloodToER}_5$ except now the oracle also predetermines a Erdős-Rényi graph of the predetermined size and embeds this into the final graph that is returned.

Erdős-Rényi: An experiment that chooses a graph of a certain size and includes each edge independently with probability ρ.

Let $d := \frac{\Delta'}{\Delta}$. We now argue via the following steps:

1. If there is an adversary that prevents timely delivery of m in the real world with some probability, then there exists an adversary that can make $\mathsf{FloodToER}_1$ return a graph where the distance from the sender to some node is larger than d with at least as high a probability.

2. If any adversary can make $\mathsf{FloodToER}_1$ return a graph with a diameter larger than d with probability p, then there exists some adversary that can make $\mathsf{FloodToER}_2$ return a graph where the distance from the sender to some node is larger than d with at least as high a probability.

3. If any adversary can make FloodToER$_2$ return a graph with a diameter larger than d with probability p, then there exists some adversary that can make FloodToER$_3$ return a graph where the distance from the sender to some node is larger than d with at least as high a probability.
4. If any adversary can make FloodToER$_3$ return a graph with a diameter larger than d with probability p, then there exists some adversary that can make FloodToER$_4$ return a graph with a diameter larger than d with at least as high a probability.
5. If any adversary can make the FloodToER$_4$ game return a graph with a diameter larger than d with probability p, then the same adversary can make FloodToER$_5$ return a graph with a diameter larger than d with probability at least $p \cdot (t+1)$.
6. The experiments FloodToER$_5$ and FloodToER$_6$ are distributed identically.
7. The probability that FloodToER$_6$ returns a graph with larger diameter than d must be less than the probability that an Erdős-Rényi graph with the *worst* size has a larger diameter than d.
8. We can now use the Erdős-Rényi graph results to bound the probability that an adversary can prevent the delivery of m in the real world.

We finally do a union bound over the number of different messages that is input to the functionality. The detailed proof can be found in the full version [33]. □

As the results in Theorem 3 are hard to interpret we additionally provide the following corollary which instantiates some of the many constants and makes some simplifying but non-optimal estimates. We emphasize that if one wants to optimize for a particular use-case (i.e., small diameter or very small failure probability) then Theorem 3 can be used to obtain tighter bounds.

Corollary 1. *Let $\Delta \in \mathbb{N}$ be any delay, let $\sigma \in \mathbb{N}$, let $t < n$ be the maximum number of parties an adversary can corrupt, and let $\kappa \in \mathbb{R}$ be the security parameter. The protocol $\pi_{\mathsf{ERFlood}}(\rho)$ securely implements $\mathcal{F}_{\mathsf{Flood}}^{\Delta'}$ against a $(\sigma+\Delta)$-delayed adversary using $\mathcal{F}_{\mathsf{MessageTransfer}}^{\sigma,\Delta}$. More precisely when r is an upper bound on the number of different messages input (either via Send or via SetMessage), the statistical distance between the real and ideal executions is bounded by the probability p_{bad} for either of the following instantiations:*

1. Let $\rho := \sqrt{\frac{\kappa}{h}}$ and let $\Delta' := 2\Delta$ then

$$p_{bad} \leq r \cdot (t+1) \cdot n^2 \cdot e^{-\kappa \cdot \frac{(h-2)}{h}}. \tag{15}$$

2. Let $\rho := \frac{\kappa}{h}$, and $\Delta' := \Delta \cdot (5\log\left(\frac{n}{2\kappa}\right) + 2)$, if $\frac{n}{2\kappa} > 1$ then

$$p_{bad} \leq r \cdot (t+1) \cdot \left(7n\log\left(\frac{n}{2\kappa}\right) e^{-\frac{\kappa}{18}} + e^{-\frac{h(\kappa-18)}{9}}\right). \tag{16}$$

Proof. Instantiation 1 immediately follows from Theorem 3 (Instantiation 1). To derive instantiation Instantiation 2 we again use Theorem 3 (Instantiation 2) and select

$$\delta_1 := \delta_2 := \gamma := \frac{1}{3} \quad \text{and} \quad \alpha := \frac{7}{4}.$$

With these parameters we see that Eq. (13) is fulfilled when $\kappa \geq 1$. Furthermore, we see that

$$
\begin{aligned}
p_{\text{bad}} &\leq r \cdot (t+1) \cdot \left(n \cdot \left(e^{-\frac{\kappa}{18}} + \left(5 \log\left(\frac{n}{2\kappa}\right) + 1 \right) e^{-\frac{7\kappa}{108}} \right) + e^{-\frac{h(\kappa-18)}{9}} \right) \\
&\leq r \cdot (t+1) \cdot \left(7n \log\left(\frac{n}{2\kappa}\right) e^{-\frac{\kappa}{18}} + e^{-\frac{h(\kappa-18)}{9}} \right).
\end{aligned}
\tag{17}
$$

□

The number of neighbors any party will need to send to when they send/relay a message in $\pi_{\text{ERFlood}}(\rho)$ concentrates around $n \cdot \rho$ (this follows from the Chernoff bound and the union bound). Concretely, for Instantiation 1 we get that the number of neighbors is upper-bounded by $\mathcal{O}\left(\sqrt{\kappa n}\right)$ except with a negligible probability, and for Instantiation 2 we get that the number of neighbors is upper-bounded by $\mathcal{O}(\kappa)$ except with a negligible probability.

A Note on Changing from TCP to UDP. Results about Erdős-Rényi graphs can be transferred to a setting without reliable message-transmission. Let us, instead of reliable transmission assume that there is an independent failure probability β for each message that is send via $\mathcal{F}_{\text{MessageTransfer}}$ and ρ is an instantiation of $\pi_{\text{ERFlood}}(\rho)$ that ensures a certain diameter assuming reliable transfer. If we let $\rho' := \frac{\rho}{1-\beta}$ then $\pi_{\text{ERFlood}}(\rho')$ with unreliable transfer is ensured to have the same diameter as $\pi_{\text{ERFlood}}(\rho)$ with reliable transfer. This is because that the probability for a successful propagation from party p_i to p_j will then be $\rho' \cdot (1 - \beta) = \rho$, which ensures that we in this more difficult setting inherent the original results for $\pi_{\text{ERFlood}}(\rho)$.

6 Conclusion and Future Work

We have formally defined the model of δ-delayed adversaries within the UC framework. This has allowed us to precisely characterize and prove the security guarantees of the flooding protocol, π_{ERFlood}. Thereby, we have taken a first step at putting the widely assumed flooding functionalities on firm ground.

Several interesting directions for future work remain. In this work, we have explored a particular type of flooding protocol based upon Erdős-Rényi graphs. However, as discussed earlier, there exist several more complex constructions for different gossip networks in the literature. Analyzing such protocols against δ-delayed corruptions could potentially yield protocols that are even more efficient than what is presented here while also providing a well-understood security guarantee. Another direction could be to optimize for security instead of efficiency. The flooding protocol that we have presented is only secure against adversaries that are delayed by at least $(\sigma+\Delta)$. An interesting question that arises is whether this is inherent for flooding networks, or whether it is possible to implement a flooding network that is secure against a 0-delayed adversary.

Furthermore, this work has considered adaptive but not *mobile* adversaries, which can again uncorrupt parties. For some notion of mobility, it seems that

π_{ERFlood} could be secure even in the presence of such mobile adversaries. Extending the model of δ-delayed adversaries to include some notion of mobility would be useful in order to better understand guarantees of blockchain protocols that are supposed to run for a very long time.

Acknowledgements. We thank Ran Canetti for explaining a subtle detail of the UC framework, Sabine Oechsner for discussions in the initial phase of the project, and the anonymous reviewers of Eurocrypt and Crypto for their feedback.

References

1. Abraham, I., et al.: Communication complexity of Byzantine agreement, revisited. In: PODC, pp. 317–326. ACM (2019)
2. Badertscher, C., Canetti, R., Hesse, J., Tackmann, B., Zikas, V.: Universal composition with global subroutines: capturing global setup within plain UC. In: Pass, R., Pietrzak, K. (eds.) TCC 2020. LNCS, vol. 12552, pp. 1–30. Springer, Cham (2020). https://doi.org/10.1007/978-3-030-64381-2_1
3. Badertscher, C., Maurer, U., Tschudi, D., Zikas, V.: Bitcoin as a transaction ledger: a composable treatment. In: Katz, J., Shacham, H. (eds.) CRYPTO 2017. LNCS, vol. 10401, pp. 324–356. Springer, Cham (2017). https://doi.org/10.1007/978-3-319-63688-7_11
4. Baum, C., David, B., Dowsley, R., Nielsen, J.B., Oechsner, S.: TARDIS: a foundation of time-lock puzzles in UC. In: Canteaut, A., Standaert, F.-X. (eds.) EURO-CRYPT 2021. LNCS, vol. 12698, pp. 429–459. Springer, Cham (2021). https://doi.org/10.1007/978-3-030-77883-5_15
5. Birman, K.P., Hayden, M., Özkasap, Ö., Xiao, Z., Budiu, M., Minsky, Y.: Bimodal multicast. ACM Trans. Comput. Syst. **17**(2), 41–88 (1999). https://doi.org/10.1145/312203.312207
6. Bollobás, B.: Random Graphs. Cambridge Studies in Advanced Mathematics, vol. 73, 2nd edn. Cambridge University Press, Cambridge (2001)
7. Canetti, R.: Universally composable security: a new paradigm for cryptographic protocols. In: Proceedings of 42nd FOCS, Las Vegas, NV, USA, 14–17 October 2001, pp. 136–145. IEEE Computer Society Press (2001). https://doi.org/10.1109/SFCS.2001.959888
8. Canetti, R.: Universally composable security. J. ACM **67**(5), 28:1–28:94 (2020)
9. Canetti, R., Dodis, Y., Pass, R., Walfish, S.: Universally composable security with global setup. In: Vadhan, S.P. (ed.) TCC 2007. LNCS, vol. 4392, pp. 61–85. Springer, Heidelberg (2007). https://doi.org/10.1007/978-3-540-70936-7_4
10. Canetti, R., Hogan, K., Malhotra, A., Varia, M.: A universally composable treatment of network time. In: CSF, pp. 360–375. IEEE Computer Society (2017)
11. Chandran, N., Chongchitmate, W., Garay, J.A., Goldwasser, S., Ostrovsky, R., Zikas, V.: The hidden graph model: communication locality and optimal resiliency with adaptive faults. In: Roughgarden, T. (ed.) ITCS 2015, Rehovot, Israel, 11–13 January 2015, pp. 153–162. ACM (2015). https://doi.org/10.1145/2688073.2688102
12. Coretti, S., Kiayias, A., Moore, C., Russell, A.: The generals' scuttlebutt: Byzantine-resilient gossip protocols. Cryptology ePrint Archive, Report 2022/541 (2022). https://ia.cr/2022/541

13. Crisóstomo, S., Schilcher, U., Bettstetter, C., Barros, J.: Analysis of probabilistic flooding: how do we choose the right coin? In: ICC, pp. 1–6. IEEE (2009)
14. Daian, P., Pass, R., Shi, E.: Snow white: robustly reconfigurable consensus and applications to provably secure proof of stake. In: Goldberg, I., Moore, T. (eds.) FC 2019. LNCS, vol. 11598, pp. 23–41. Springer, Cham (2019). https://doi.org/10.1007/978-3-030-32101-7_2
15. David, B., Gaži, P., Kiayias, A., Russell, A.: Ouroboros praos: an adaptively-secure, semi-synchronous proof-of-stake blockchain. In: Nielsen, J.B., Rijmen, V. (eds.) EUROCRYPT 2018, Part II. LNCS, vol. 10821, pp. 66–98. Springer, Cham (2018). https://doi.org/10.1007/978-3-319-78375-8_3
16. Demers, A.J., et al.: Epidemic algorithms for replicated database maintenance. In: Schneider, F.B. (ed.) 6th ACM PODC, Vancouver, BC, Canada, 10–12 August 1987, pp. 1–12. ACM (1987). https://doi.org/10.1145/41840.41841
17. Erdős, P., Rényi, A.: On the evolution of random graphs. In: Publication of the Mathematical Institute of the Hungarian Academy of Sciences, pp. 17–61 (1960)
18. Garay, J.A., Katz, J., Kumaresan, R., Zhou, H.S.: Adaptively secure broadcast, revisited. In: Gavoille, C., Fraigniaud, P. (eds.) 30th ACM PODC, San Jose, CA, USA, 6–8 June 2011, pp. 179–186. ACM (2011). https://doi.org/10.1145/1993806.1993832
19. Garay, J., Kiayias, A., Leonardos, N.: The bitcoin backbone protocol: analysis and applications. In: Oswald, E., Fischlin, M. (eds.) EUROCRYPT 2015, Part II. LNCS, vol. 9057, pp. 281–310. Springer, Heidelberg (2015). https://doi.org/10.1007/978-3-662-46803-6_10
20. Garay, J., Kiayias, A., Leonardos, N.: The bitcoin backbone protocol with chains of variable difficulty. In: Katz, J., Shacham, H. (eds.) CRYPTO 2017, Part I. LNCS, vol. 10401, pp. 291–323. Springer, Cham (2017). https://doi.org/10.1007/978-3-319-63688-7_10
21. Haas, Z.J., Halpern, J.Y., Li, L.: Gossip-based ad hoc routing. IEEE/ACM Trans. Netw. 14(3), 479–491 (2006). https://doi.org/10.1145/1143396.1143399
22. Heilman, E., Kendler, A., Zohar, A., Goldberg, S.: Eclipse attacks on bitcoin's peer-to-peer network. In: Jung, J., Holz, T. (eds.) USENIX Security 2015, Washington, DC, USA, 12–14 August 2015, pp. 129–144. USENIX Association (2015)
23. Hu, R., Sopena, J., Arantes, L., Sens, P., Demeure, I.M.: Fair comparison of gossip algorithms over large-scale random topologies. In: SRDS, pp. 331–340. IEEE Computer Society (2012)
24. Karp, R.M., Schindelhauer, C., Shenker, S., Vöcking, B.: Randomized rumor spreading. In: 41st FOCS, Redondo Beach, CA, USA, 12–14 November 2000, pp. 565–574. IEEE Computer Society Press (2000). https://doi.org/10.1109/SFCS.2000.892324
25. Katz, J., Maurer, U., Tackmann, B., Zikas, V.: Universally composable synchronous computation. In: Sahai, A. (ed.) TCC 2013. LNCS, vol. 7785, pp. 477–498. Springer, Heidelberg (2013). https://doi.org/10.1007/978-3-642-36594-2_27
26. Kermarrec, A., Massoulié, L., Ganesh, A.J.: Probabilistic reliable dissemination in large-scale systems. IEEE Trans. Parallel Distributed Syst. 14(3), 248–258 (2003)
27. Kiayias, A., Russell, A., David, B., Oliynykov, R.: Ouroboros: a provably secure proof-of-stake blockchain protocol. In: Katz, J., Shacham, H. (eds.) CRYPTO 2017, Part I. LNCS, vol. 10401, pp. 357–388. Springer, Cham (2017). https://doi.org/10.1007/978-3-319-63688-7_12

28. Kiayias, A., Zhou, H.-S., Zikas, V.: Fair and robust multi-party computation using a global transaction ledger. In: Fischlin, M., Coron, J.-S. (eds.) EUROCRYPT 2016. LNCS, vol. 9666, pp. 705–734. Springer, Heidelberg (2016). https://doi.org/10.1007/978-3-662-49896-5_25

29. Kokoris-Kogias, E., Jovanovic, P., Gasser, L., Gailly, N., Syta, E., Ford, B.: OmniLedger: a secure, scale-out, decentralized ledger via sharding. In: 2018 IEEE Symposium on Security and Privacy, San Francisco, CA, USA, 21–23 May 2018, pp. 583–598. IEEE Computer Society Press (2018). https://doi.org/10.1109/SP.2018.000-5

30. Liu-Zhang, C.D., Matt, C., Maurer, U., Rito, G., Thomsen, S.E.: Practical provably secure flooding for blockchains. Cryptology ePrint Archive, Paper 2022/608 (2022). https://eprint.iacr.org/2022/608

31. Luu, L., Narayanan, V., Zheng, C., Baweja, K., Gilbert, S., Saxena, P.: A secure sharding protocol for open blockchains. In: Weippl, E.R., Katzenbeisser, S., Kruegel, C., Myers, A.C., Halevi, S. (eds.) ACM CCS 2016, Vienna, Austria, 24–28 October 2016, pp. 17–30. ACM Press (2016). https://doi.org/10.1145/2976749.2978389

32. Marcus, Y., Heilman, E., Goldberg, S.: Low-resource eclipse attacks on Ethereum's peer-to-peer network. Cryptology ePrint Archive, Report 2018/236 (2018). https://eprint.iacr.org/2018/236

33. Matt, C., Nielsen, J.B., Thomsen, S.E.: Formalizing delayed adaptive corruptions and the security of flooding networks. Cryptology ePrint Archive, Paper 2022/010 (2022). https://eprint.iacr.org/2022/010

34. Maymounkov, P., Mazières, D.: Kademlia: a peer-to-peer information system based on the XOR metric. In: Druschel, P., Kaashoek, F., Rowstron, A. (eds.) IPTPS 2002. LNCS, vol. 2429, pp. 53–65. Springer, Heidelberg (2002). https://doi.org/10.1007/3-540-45748-8_5

35. Nakamoto, S.: Bitcoin: a peer-to-peer electronic cash system (2008)

36. Nielsen, J.B.: On protocol security in the cryptographic model. Ph.D. thesis, Aarhus University (2003)

37. Pass, R., Seeman, L., Shelat, A.: Analysis of the blockchain protocol in asynchronous networks. In: Coron, J.-S., Nielsen, J.B. (eds.) EUROCRYPT 2017, Part II. LNCS, vol. 10211, pp. 643–673. Springer, Cham (2017). https://doi.org/10.1007/978-3-319-56614-6_22

38. Pass, R., Shi, E.: Hybrid consensus: efficient consensus in the permissionless model. In: Richa, A.W. (ed.) 31st International Symposium on Distributed Computing, DISC 2017, Vienna, Austria, 16–20 October 2017. LIPIcs, vol. 91, pp. 39:1–39:16. Schloss Dagstuhl - Leibniz-Zentrum für Informatik (2017). https://doi.org/10.4230/LIPIcs.DISC.2017.39

39. Ren, L.: Analysis of Nakamoto consensus. Cryptology ePrint Archive, Report 2019/943 (2019). https://eprint.iacr.org/2019/943

40. Rohrer, E., Tschorsch, F.: Kadcast: a structured approach to broadcast in blockchain networks. In: Proceedings of the 1st ACM Conference on Advances in Financial Technologies, AFT 2019, Zurich, Switzerland, 21–23 October 2019, pp. 199–213. ACM (2019). https://doi.org/10.1145/3318041.3355469

41. Zamani, M., Movahedi, M., Raykova, M.: RapidChain: scaling blockchain via full sharding. In: Lie, D., Mannan, M., Backes, M., Wang, X. (eds.) ACM CCS 2018, Toronto, ON, Canada, 15–19 October 2018, pp. 931–948. ACM Press (2018). https://doi.org/10.1145/3243734.3243853

Best Paper Awards

Batch Arguments for NP and More from Standard Bilinear Group Assumptions

Brent Waters[1,2] and David J. Wu[1(✉)]

[1] University of Texas at Austin, Austin, TX, USA
dwu4@cs.utexas.edu
[2] NTT Research, Sunnyvale, CA, USA

Abstract. Non-interactive batch arguments for NP provide a way to amortize the cost of NP verification across multiple instances. They enable a prover to convince a verifier of multiple NP statements with communication much smaller than the total witness length and verification time much smaller than individually checking each instance.

In this work, we give the first construction of a non-interactive batch argument for NP from standard assumptions on groups with bilinear maps (specifically, from either the subgroup decision assumption in composite-order groups or from the k-Lin assumption in prime-order groups for any $k \geq 1$). Previously, batch arguments for NP were only known from LWE, or a combination of multiple assumptions, or from non-standard/non-falsifiable assumptions. Moreover, our work introduces a new *direct* approach for batch verification and avoids heavy tools like correlation-intractable hash functions or probabilistically-checkable proofs common to previous approaches.

As corollaries to our main construction, we obtain the first publicly-verifiable non-interactive delegation scheme for RAM programs (i.e., a succinct non-interactive argument (SNARG) for P) with a CRS of sublinear size (in the running time of the RAM program), as well as the first aggregate signature scheme (supporting bounded aggregation) from standard assumptions on bilinear maps.

1 Introduction

Consider the following scenario: a prover has a batch of m NP statements $\mathbf{x}_1, \ldots, \mathbf{x}_m$ and seeks to convince the verifier that all of these statements are true (i.e., convince the verifier that $\mathbf{x}_i \in \mathcal{L}$ for all $i \in [m]$, where $\mathcal{L}$ is the associated NP language). A naïve solution is for the prover to provide the m witnesses $\mathbf{w}_1, \ldots, \mathbf{w}_m$ to the verifier and have the verifier check the NP relation on each pair $(\mathbf{x}_i, \mathbf{w}_i)$. A natural question is whether we could do this more efficiently. Namely, can the prover convince the verifier that $\mathbf{x}_1, \ldots, \mathbf{x}_m \in \mathcal{L}$ with a proof of size $o(m)$—that is, can the size of the proof grow *sublinearly* with the number of instances?

Batch Arguments. The focus of this work is on constructing non-interactive *batch arguments* (BARGs) for NP languages in the common reference string (CRS)

© International Association for Cryptologic Research 2022
Y. Dodis and T. Shrimpton (Eds.): CRYPTO 2022, LNCS 13508, pp. 433–463, 2022.
https://doi.org/10.1007/978-3-031-15979-4_15

model. In this model, a (trusted) setup algorithm samples a common reference string crs that is used to construct and verify proofs. The goal of a BARG is to amortize the cost of NP verification across multiple instances. Specifically, a BARG for NP allows a prover to construct a proof π of m NP statements $\mathbf{x}_1, \ldots, \mathbf{x}_m \in \{0,1\}^n$ where the size of the proof π scales sublinearly with m. We focus on the setting where the proof is *non-interactive* and *publicly verifiable*. The soundness requirement is that no *computationally-bounded* prover can convince the verifier of a tuple $(\mathbf{x}_1, \ldots, \mathbf{x}_m)$ that contains a false instance $\mathbf{x}_i \notin \mathcal{L}$; namely, we focus on batch *argument* systems.

Constructing non-interactive batch arguments for NP is challenging, and until very recently, constructions have either relied on idealized models [Mic95, Gro16, BBHR18, COS20, CHM+20, Set20] or on non-standard [KPY19], and often-times, non-falsifiable cryptographic assumptions [Gro10, BCCT12, DFH12, Lip13, PHGR13, GGPR13, BCI+13, BCPR14, BISW17, BCC+17] (see also Sect. 1.3 for more detail). This state of affairs changed in two very recent and exciting works by Choudhuri et al. In the first work [CJJ21a], they show how to construct a BARG assuming both subexponential hardness of DDH in pairing-free groups and polynomial hardness of QR. Subsequently, they construct a BARG from polynomial hardness of LWE [CJJ21b]. Both works leverage correlation-intractable hash functions [CGH98, CCH+19, PS19, JJ21] to *provably* instantiate the Fiat-Shamir heuristic [FS86].

In this work, we take a *direct* approach for constructing BARGs from bilinear maps, and provide a new instantiation from either polynomial hardness of the k-Lin assumption on prime-order bilinear groups, or from polynomial hardness of the subgroup decision assumption on composite-order bilinear groups. This is the first BARG for NP under standard assumptions over bilinear groups. Moreover, our construction is direct and avoids powerful tools like correlation-intractable hash functions or probabilistically-checkable proofs used in many previous constructions.

Delegation for RAM Programs. A closely related problem is delegation for RAM programs (also known as a succinct non-interactive argument (SNARG) for the class P of polynomial-time deterministic computations). In a delegation scheme for RAM programs, the prover has a RAM program $\mathcal{P}$, an input x, and output y, and its goal is to convince the verifier that $y = \mathcal{P}(x)$. The efficiency requirement is that the length of the proof and the verification time should be sublinear (ideally, polylogarithmic) in the running time of the RAM program. There is a close connection between batch arguments for NP and delegation schemes for RAM programs [BHK17, KPY19, KVZ21, CJJ21b], and several of these works show how to construct a delegation scheme for RAM programs using a batch argument for NP. As a corollary to our main construction, we use our BARG to obtain a non-interactive delegation scheme for RAM programs under the SXDH assumption in asymmetric bilinear groups. The CRS size of our construction is short (i.e., sublinear in the running time of the RAM computation).

Previously, Kalai et al. [KPY19] constructed a delegation scheme for RAM programs with a short CRS from a non-standard, but falsifiable, q-type assumption on bilinear groups, and more recently, González and Zacharakis [GZ21] showed how to construct a delegation scheme with a *long* CRS for arithmetic circuits from a *bilateral* k-Lin assumption in asymmetric bilinear groups.[1] Choudhuri et al. [CJJ21b] showed how to construct a delegation scheme for RAM programs from LWE, and previously, Jawale et al. [JKKZ21] constructed a delegation scheme for bounded-depth circuits also from LWE; both of these schemes also have a short CRS. Recently, Hulett et al. [HJKS22] showed how to construct a SNARG for P from sub-exponential DDH (in *pairing-free* groups) in conjunction with the QR assumption. In the designated-verifier model where a *secret* key is needed to check proofs, Kalai et al. [BHK17] showed how to construct a delegation scheme from any computational private information retrieval scheme.

1.1 Our Contributions

In this work, we introduce a simpler and more direct approach for constructing BARGs using bilinear maps. Our main result is a BARG for NP assuming either the polynomial hardness of k-Lin in asymmetric prime-order pairing groups (for any $k \geq 1$)[2], or alternatively, the subgroup decision assumption in composite-order pairing groups. We capture this in the informal theorem statement below:

Theorem 1.1 (Informal). *Take any constant $\varepsilon > 0$. Under the k-Lin assumption (for any $k \geq 1$) in a prime-order pairing group (alternatively, the subgroup decision assumption in a composite-order pairing group), there exists a publicly-verifiable non-interactive BARG for Boolean circuit satisfiability with proof size* $\mathsf{poly}(\lambda, |C|)$*, verification complexity* $\mathsf{poly}(\lambda, m, n) + \mathsf{poly}(\lambda, |C|)$*, and CRS size* $m^\varepsilon \cdot \mathsf{poly}(\lambda)$*, where λ is a security parameter, $C: \{0,1\}^n \times \{0,1\}^h \to \{0,1\}$ is the Boolean circuit, n is the statement size, and m is the number of instances. The BARG satisfies semi-adaptive soundness (Definition 2.5).*

A New Approach for Batch Verification. In contrast to many recent works (see also Sect. 1.3) on constructing succinct arguments that rely on probabilistically-checkable proofs (PCPs) [KRR13, KRR14, BHK17, CJJ21b, KVZ21] or correlation-intractable hash functions [JKKZ21, CJJ21a, CJJ21b, HJKS22], we take a direct "low-tech" approach in our construction. Our construction follows a "commit-and-prove" strategy and is reminiscent of the classic pairing-based non-interactive proof systems by Groth et al. [GOS06] and Groth and Sahai [GS08]. Essentially, the prover starts by providing a (succinct) commitment to the values associated with each wire in the circuit. The prover commits to m bits for each wire, one for each instance, and we require that the size of the commitment be sublinear in m. Then, for each gate in the circuit, the prover provides a short proof that the committed wire values are consistent with

---

[1] In the bilateral version of the k-Lin assumption, the challenge is encoded in *both* groups rather than one of the groups.

[2] Recall that the case $k = 1$ corresponds to the DDH assumption holding in each base group (i.e., SXDH). The case $k = 2$ corresponds to the DLIN assumption [BBS04, HK07, Sha07].

the gate operation. The succinct commitment scheme to the wire labels can be viewed as a non-hiding version of the vector commitment scheme of Catalano and Fiore [CF13]. The key challenge in the construction is proving consistency of the gate computations given only the *succinct* commitments to the input and output wires of each gate. We give a technical overview of our approach in Sect. 1.2 and the formal description in Sects. 3 and 4.

Application to Delegating RAM Programs. The proof size in Theorem 1.1 is *independent* of the number of instances m, but the verification time contains a component $\mathsf{poly}(\lambda, m, n)$ that scales with m. For general NP languages, some type of linear dependence on the number of instances is inherent since the verification algorithm must at least read the input (of size $m \cdot n$). However, when the statements have a "succinct description," (e.g., they are simply the indices $1, \ldots, m$), and it is unnecessary for the verifier to read the full input, we can reduce the the verification cost down to $\mathsf{poly}(\lambda, \log m, |C|)$. This setting is useful for applications to delegation [CJJ21b, KVZ21]. Our main constructions directly support this setting. Indeed, combining our new pairing-based BARGs with the compiler from Choudhuri et al. [CJJ21b], we also obtain a delegation scheme for RAM programs from the SXDH assumption over pairing groups.

We note here that invoking the compiler from [CJJ21a] additionally requires a "somewhere extractable commitment" scheme (that supports succinct local openings). The pairing-based techniques underlying our BARG construction naturally give rise to a somewhere extractable commitment (in conjunction with a somewhere extractable hash function [HW15, OPWW15]). This is the first construction of a somewhere extractable commitment that supports succinct local openings from standard assumptions over bilinear groups and may be of independent interest. We describe the construction in the full version of this paper [WW22]. We summarize our result on delegation in the following informal theorem:

Theorem 1.2 (Informal). *Take any constant $\varepsilon > 0$. Under the SXDH assumption in a prime-order pairing group, for every polynomial $T = T(\lambda)$, there exists a publicly-verifiable non-interactive delegation scheme for RAM programs with proof size $\mathsf{poly}(\lambda, \log T)$, verification complexity $\mathsf{poly}(\lambda, \log T)$, a verification key of size $\mathsf{poly}(\lambda, \log T)$, and a proving key of size $T^\varepsilon \cdot \mathsf{poly}(\lambda)$. Here, λ is the security parameter and T is the running time of the RAM program. The delegation scheme is adaptively sound.*

Theorem 1.2 gives the first RAM delegation scheme from standard assumptions over bilinear maps with a CRS whose size is *sublinear* in the running time of the computation. Previously constructions of RAM delegation based on pairings either relied on non-standard q-type assumptions [KPY19] or a CRS of size *super-linear* in the running time of the RAM computation [GZ21].

Application to Aggregate Signatures. As a final application, we use our BARG for NP to obtain the first aggregate signature scheme that supports bounded aggregation from standard assumptions over bilinear maps. In an aggregate signature scheme, there is a public algorithm that takes a collection of message-signature pairs $(\mu_1, \sigma_1), \ldots, (\mu_m, \sigma_m)$ under (possibly distinct) verification keys $\mathsf{vk}_1, \ldots, \mathsf{vk}_m$, respectively, and outputs a new signature σ_{agg} on $(\mu_1, \ldots, \mu_m)$ under the joint verification key $(\mathsf{vk}_1, \ldots, \mathsf{vk}_m)$. The requirement is that the size of σ_{agg} scales *sublinearly* with m. A BARG for circuit satisfiability directly yields an aggregate signature scheme via the following straightforward construction. Define the circuit $C(\mathsf{vk}, m, \sigma)$ that takes as input the verification key vk, message μ, and signature σ, and outputs 1 if σ is a valid signature on μ under vk. An aggregate signature on $(\mu_1, \sigma_1, \mathsf{vk}_1), \ldots, (\mu_m, \sigma_m, \mathsf{vk}_m)$ is a BARG proof that $C(\mathsf{vk}_i, \mu_i, \sigma_i) = 1$ for all $i \in [m]$. Succinctness of the BARG ensures that the size of the aggregate signature is sublinear in the number of signatures m. Realizing the above blueprint requires that the underlying BARG satisfy a (weak) form of extractability; the BARGs we construct in this work satisfy this property, and we refer to the full version of this paper [WW22] for the details. We obtain the first aggregate signature scheme supporting (bounded) aggregation from standard pairing assumptions. We summarize the instantiation here and compare with previous approaches in Sect. 1.3:

Corollary 1.3 (Informal). *Under the k-Lin assumption (for any $k \geq 1$) in a prime-order pairing group (alternatively, the subgroup decision assumption in a composite-order pairing group), there exists an aggregate signature scheme that supports bounded aggregation. In particular, for any a priori bounded polynomial $m = m(\lambda)$, aggregating up to $T \leq m$ message-signature pairs $(\mu_1, \sigma_1), \ldots, (\mu_T, \sigma_T)$ under verification keys $\mathsf{vk}_1, \ldots, \mathsf{vk}_T$ yields an aggregate signature σ_{agg} of size $\mathsf{poly}(\lambda)$.*

1.2 Technical Overview

In this work, we focus on constructing BARGs for the language of Boolean circuit satisfiability. Let $C \colon \{0,1\}^n \times \{0,1\}^h \to \{0,1\}$ be a Boolean circuit of size s. A tuple $(C, \mathbf{x}_1, \ldots, \mathbf{x}_m)$ is true if for all $i \in [m]$, there exists a witness $\mathbf{w}_i$ such that $C(\mathbf{x}_i, \mathbf{w}_i) = 1$.

General Blueprint. Our BARG for circuit satisfiability follows a "commit-and-prove" paradigm. To construct a proof π of a statement $(C, \mathbf{x}_1, \ldots, \mathbf{x}_m)$ with associated witnesses $(\mathbf{w}_1, \ldots, \mathbf{w}_m)$, the prover proceeds as follows:

- **Wire commitments:** The prover starts by evaluating $C(\mathbf{x}_i, \mathbf{w}_i)$ for each $i \in [m]$. Let t be the number of wires in circuit C. For each instance $i \in [m]$ and wire $k \in [t]$, we write $w_{i,k} \in \{0,1\}$ to denote the value of wire k in instance i. Then $(w_{1,k}, \ldots, w_{m,k}) \in \{0,1\}^m$ is the vector of assignments to wire k across all m instances. The prover starts by constructing a *vector* commitment U_k to each vector $(w_{1,k}, \ldots, w_{m,k})$. Here, we require the commitment to be succinct: namely, $|U_k| = \mathsf{poly}(\lambda, \log m)$, where λ is a security parameter. The prover additionally constructs a proof V_k that U_k is a commitment to a 0/1 vector (i.e., $w_{i,k} \in \{0,1\}$ for all $i \in [m]$).[3] We similarly require that $|V_k| =$ poly$(\lambda, \log m)$. Both the commitments to the wire assignments $U_1, \ldots, U_k$ and the proofs of valid assignment $V_1, \ldots, V_k$ are included in the BARG proof.

- **Gate satisfiability:** We consider Boolean circuits with fan-in two. Namely, each gate G_ℓ in C can be described by a tuple of $(k_1, k_2, k_3) \in [t]^3$, where k_1, k_2 are the indices for the input wires and k_3 is the index for the output wire. Since NAND gates are universal, we will assume that all of the gates in C are NAND gates.[4] Let s be the number of gates (i.e., the size) of the circuit. For each gate $\ell \in [s]$, the prover constructs a proof W_ℓ that the committed assignments U_{k_3} to the output wire are consistent with the committed assignments U_{k_1}, U_{k_2} to the input wires. For example, if G_ℓ is a NAND gate, U_{k_1} is a commitment to $(w_{1,k_1}, \ldots, w_{m,k_1})$, U_{k_2} is a commitment to $(w_{1,k_2}, \ldots, w_{m,k_2})$, then the prover needs to demonstrate that U_{k_3} is a commitment to $(\mathsf{NAND}(w_{1,k_1}, w_{1,k_2}), \ldots, \mathsf{NAND}(w_{m,k_1}, w_{m,k_2}))$. The size of each proof W_ℓ must also be succinct: $|W_\ell| = $ poly$(\lambda, \log m)$. The prover includes a proof of gate satisfiability W_ℓ for each gate $\ell \in [s]$.

The overall proof is $\pi = \left(\{(U_k, V_k)\}_{k \in [t]}, \{W_\ell\}_{\ell \in [s]}\right)$, and the proof size is $|C| \cdot$ poly$(\lambda, \log m)$, which satisfies the efficiency requirements on the BARG. To verify the proof, the verifier checks the following:

- **Input validity:** Without loss of generality, we associate wires $1, \ldots, n$ with the bits of the statement. The verifier checks that $U_1, \ldots, U_n$ are commitments to the bits of $\mathbf{x}_1, \ldots, \mathbf{x}_m \in \{0,1\}^n$. In our construction, each commitment is a *deterministic* function of the input vector, so the verifier can compute $U_1, \ldots, U_n$ directly from $\mathbf{x}_1, \ldots, \mathbf{x}_m$.
- **Wire validity:** For each $k \in [t]$, the verifier checks that U_k is a commitment to a $0/1$ vector using V_k.
- **Gate consistency:** For each gate $G_\ell = (k_1, k_2, k_3)$, the verifier uses W_ℓ to check that U_{k_1}, U_{k_2}, and U_{k_3} are commitments to a set of valid wire assignments consistent with the gate operation G_ℓ.
- **Output satisfiability:** Let t be the index of the output wire in C. The verifier checks that the commitment to the output wire U_t is a commitment to the all-ones vector (indicating that all m instances accept).

Since the verifier needs to read the statement, the statement validity check runs in time poly(λ, n, m). The remaining checks run in time $|C| \cdot$ poly(λ), which yields the desired verification complexity.

1.2.1   Construction from Composite-Order Pairing Groups

To illustrate the main ideas underlying our construction, we first describe it using symmetric composite-order groups and argue soundness under the subgroup

---

[3] Technically, this is only required for the input wires corresponding to the witness.

[4] Our techniques extend naturally to support binary-valued gates that can compute *arbitrary* quadratic functions of their inputs; see the full version of this paper [WW22].

decision assumption [BGN05]. We believe this construction is conceptually simple and best illustrates the core ideas behind the construction. The approach described here translates to the setting of asymmetric prime-order pairing groups to yield a construction from the k-Lin assumption.

Composite-Order Pairing Groups. A symmetric composite-order pairing group consists of two cyclic groups $\mathbb{G}$ and $\mathbb{G}_T$ of order $N = pq$, where p, q are prime. Let g be a generator of $\mathbb{G}$. By the Chinese Remainder Theorem, we can write $\mathbb{G} \cong \mathbb{G}_p \times \mathbb{G}_q$, where $\mathbb{G}_p$ is a subgroup of order p (generated by $g_p = g^q$) and $\mathbb{G}_q$ is a subgroup of order q (generated by $g_q = g^p$). Additionally, there exists an efficiently-computable, non-degenerate bilinear map $e: \mathbb{G} \times \mathbb{G} \to \mathbb{G}_T$ called the "pairing:" namely, for all $a, b \in \mathbb{Z}_N$, it holds that $e(g^a, g^b) = e(g, g)^{ab}$. Finally, the subgroups $\mathbb{G}_p$ and $\mathbb{G}_q$ are orthogonal: $e(g_p, g_q) = 1$, where 1 denotes the identity element in $\mathbb{G}_T$. In our construction, the real scheme operates entirely in the order-p subgroup $\mathbb{G}_p$ of $\mathbb{G}$; the full group $\mathbb{G}$ only plays a role in the soundness analysis.

Vector Commitments. The first ingredient we need to implement the above blueprint is a vector commitment scheme for vectors of dimension m (m being the number of instances). We start by constructing a common reference string with m group elements $(A_1, \ldots, A_m)$ where each $A_i = g_p^{\alpha_i}$ for some $\alpha_i \xleftarrow{\text{R}} \mathbb{Z}_N$. A commitment to a vector $(w_{1,k}, \ldots, w_{m,k})$ is a subset product of the associated group elements $U_k = \prod_{i \in [m]} A_i^{w_{i,k}} = g_p^{\sum_{i \in [m]} \alpha_i w_{i,k}} \in \mathbb{G}_p$. We note that this is essentially the vector commitment scheme of Catalano and Fiore [CF13] instantiated in $\mathbb{G}_p$, but without randomization (in our setting, we do *not* require a hiding property on the commitments). With this instantiation, the commitment to each wire has size $\mathsf{poly}(\lambda)$, and is independent of m.

Wire Validity Checks. The second ingredient we require is a way for the prover to demonstrate that the committed values satisfy the wire validity and gate consistency relations. We start by describing the wire validity checks. Consider a vector of candidate wire assignments $(w_1, \ldots, w_m)$. The prover needs to convince the verifier that $w_i \in \{0, 1\}$ for all $i \in [m]$, or equivalently, that $w_i^2 = w_i$. Now, a correctly-generated commitment to $(w_1, \ldots, w_m)$ is an encoding of $\sum_{i \in [m]} \alpha_i w_i$ (in the exponent). We can now write

$$\left(\sum_{i \in [m]} \alpha_i \right) \left(\sum_{i \in [m]} \alpha_i w_i \right) = \sum_{i \in [m]} \alpha_i^2 w_i + \sum_{i \neq j} \alpha_i \alpha_j w_j$$

$$\left(\sum_{i \in [m]} \alpha_i w_i \right)^2 = \sum_{i \in [m]} \alpha_i^2 w_i^2 + \sum_{i \neq j} \alpha_i \alpha_j w_i w_j.$$

When $w_i^2 = w_i$, the difference between these two expressions is $\sum_{i \neq j} \alpha_i \alpha_j (1 - w_i) w_j$. Notably, this difference is a linear combination of the products $\alpha_i \alpha_j$ where

$i \neq j$; we refer to these terms as the *cross terms*. Conversely, if $w_i^2 \neq w_i$ for some i, then the difference between the two relations *always* depends on the non-cross-term α_i^2. This suggests the following strategy for proof generation and verification: we publish encodings $B_{i,j} := g_p^{\alpha_i \alpha_j}$ for $i \neq j$ in the CRS to allow the prover to "cancel out" cross terms but *not* the non-cross terms. We also include an encoding $A := \prod_{i \in [m]} A_i = g_p^{\sum_{i \in [m]} \alpha_i}$ that will be used for verification. Specifically, we define the CRS to be

$$\mathsf{crs} = \left(\{ A_i := g_p^{\alpha_i} \}_{i \in [m]}, \ A := \prod_{i \in [m]} A_i = g_p^{\sum_{i \in [m]} \alpha_i}, \ \{ B_{i,j} := g_p^{\alpha_i \alpha_j} \}_{i \neq j} \right). \tag{1.1}$$

Then, the prover can compute the quantity $V = \prod_{i \neq j} B_{i,j}^{(1-w_i)w_j} = g_p^{\sum_{i \neq j} \alpha_i \alpha_j (1-w_i)w_j}$. By the above relations, we see that if $U = g_p^{\sum_{i \in [m]} \alpha_i w_i}$, then

$$e(A, U) = e(U, U)e(g_p, V). \tag{1.2}$$

The analysis above shows that if U is a valid commitment to a binary vector, then the prover can always compute V that satisfies the verification relation. When U is *not* a commitment to a binary vector, we need to argue that the prover cannot craft a proof V that satisfies Eq. (1.2). The intuition is that there will be "non-cross-terms" that cannot be cancelled using the components available to the prover. Formalizing this intuition requires some care and we provide additional details below. We also note here that the size of the CRS (Eq. (1.1)) in our construction scales *quadratically* with the number of instances m. In the following, we will describe a bootstrapping technique to reduce the CRS size to scale with m^ε for any constant $\varepsilon > 0$.

Gate Consistency Checks. The approach we take for wire validity checks readily extends to enable gate consistency checks. We describe our approach for verifying a single NAND gate. To simplify the description, suppose U_1 and U_2 are vector commitments to the input wires $(w_{1,1}, \ldots, w_{m,1})$ and $(w_{1,2}, \ldots, w_{m,2})$, and U_3 is a vector commitment to the output wire $(w_{1,3}, \ldots, w_{m,3})$. The prover wants to show that $w_{i,3} = \mathsf{NAND}(w_{i,1}, w_{i,2})$ for all $i \in [m]$. This is equivalent to checking satisfiability of the *quadratic* relation $w_{i,3} + w_{i,1}w_{i,2} = 1$. In this case, the prover computes the element $W \in \mathbb{G}_p$ such that

$$\frac{e(A, U_3)e(U_1, U_2)}{e(A, A)} = e(g_p, W). \tag{1.3}$$

Suppose U_1, U_2, U_3 are properly-generated commitments. Then, if we consider the exponents for the left-hand side of the verification relation, we have

$$\underbrace{\sum_{i \in [m]} \alpha_i^2 w_{i,3} + \sum_{i \neq j} \alpha_i \alpha_j w_{j,3}}_{e(A, U_3)} + \underbrace{\sum_{i \in [m]} \alpha_i^2 w_{i,1}w_{i,2} + \sum_{i \neq j} \alpha_i \alpha_j w_{i,1}w_{j,2}}_{e(U_1, U_2)} - \underbrace{\sum_{i \in [m]} \alpha_i^2 - \sum_{i \neq j} \alpha_i \alpha_j}_{e(A, A)}.$$

If $w_{i,3} + w_{i,1}w_{i,2} = 1$, then all of the non-cross terms vanish, and we are left with $\sum_{i \neq j} \alpha_i \alpha_j (w_{j,3} + w_{i,1}w_{j,2} - 1)$. The prover can thus set $W = \prod_{i \neq j} B_{i,j}^{w_{j,3} + w_{i,1}w_{j,2} - 1}$

to satisfy the above verification relation. Similar to the case with wire consistency checks, we now have to show that if there exists an $i \in [m]$ where $w_{i,3} + w_{i,1} w_{i,2} \neq 1$, then the prover is *unable* to compute a W that satisfies Eq. (1.3).

Proving Soundness. To argue soundness of our argument system, we take the dual-mode approach from [CJJ21a, CJJ21b].[5] Specifically in this setting, there are two computationally indistinguishable ways to sample the CRS: (1) the normal mode described above; and (2) a trapdoor mode that takes as input an instance index $i^* \in [m]$ and outputs a trapdoor CRS crs*. The requirement is that in trapdoor mode, the scheme is *statistically* sound for instance i^*. Namely, with overwhelming probability over the choice of crs*, there does *not* exist any proof π for $(\mathbf{x}_1, \ldots, \mathbf{x}_m)$ that convinces the verifier when $\mathbf{x}_{i^*}$ is false. However, it is still possible that there exists valid proofs of tuples where $\mathbf{x}_{i^*}$ is true but $\mathbf{x}_i$ is false for some $i \neq i^*$. By a standard hybrid argument, it is easy to see that a BARG with this dual-mode "somewhere statistical soundness" property also satisfies *non-adaptive soundness* (i.e., soundness for statements that are *independent* of the CRS).[6] Achieving the stronger notion of *adaptive* soundness where security holds for statements that depend on the CRS seems challenging and in certain settings, will either require non-black-box techniques or basing security on non-falsifiable assumptions [GW11, BHK17].

Somewhere Statistical Soundness. To argue that our construction above satisfies somewhere statistical soundness, we start by describing the trapdoor CRS. To ensure statistical soundness for index $i^* \in [m]$, we replace the encoding $A_{i^*} = g_p^{\alpha_{i^*}}$ associated with instance i^* with $A_{i^*} \leftarrow g^{\alpha_{i^*}} \in \mathbb{G}$. Critically, A_{i^*} is now in the *full group* rather than the order-p subgroup $\mathbb{G}_p$. The encodings A_i associated with instances $i \neq i^*$ are still sampled from $\mathbb{G}_p$. We can construct the cross terms $B_{i,j}$ in a similar manner as before: the components for $i, j \neq i^*$ are unaffected and we set $B_{i^*,j} = B_{j,i^*} = A_{i^*}^{\alpha_j} \in \mathbb{G}$. The trapdoor CRS is computationally indistinguishable from the normal CRS by the subgroup decision assumption [BGN05]. Consider the wire consistency checks and gate consistency checks:

- **Wire consistency checks.** Let $U \in \mathbb{G}$ be a commitment to a tuple of wire values and $V \in \mathbb{G}$ be the wire consistency proof. We can decompose U as $U = g_p^{\beta_p} g_q^{\beta_q}$ for some $\beta_p \in \mathbb{Z}_p, \beta_q \in \mathbb{Z}_q$. Moreover, by construction, the verification component A is defined to be $A = \prod_{i \in [m]} A_i = g_p^{\sum_{i \in [m]} \alpha_i} g_q^{\alpha_{i^*}}$. Consider now the verification relation from Eq. (1.2). If this relation holds in $\mathbb{G}_T$, it must

---

[5] This is different from the notion of "dual-mode" proof system often encountered in the setting of non-interactive zero-knowledge (NIZK) [GOS06, PS19, LPWW20]. There, the CRS can be sampled in two computationally indistinguishable modes: one mode ensures statistical soundness and the other ensures statistical zero knowledge.

[6] Our construction satisfies the stronger notion of semi-adaptive somewhere soundness [CJJ21b], where the adversary first commits to an index i^*, but is allowed to choose the statements $(\mathbf{x}_1, \ldots, \mathbf{x}_m)$ after seeing the CRS. The adversary wins if the proof is valid but $\mathbf{x}_{i^*}$ is false. This notion is needed for the implications to delegation.

in particular hold in the order-q subgroup of $\mathbb{G}_T$. The key observation is that projecting the relation into the order-q subgroup of $\mathbb{G}_T$ *isolates* instance i^* (since only the encoding A_{i^*} contains components in the order-q subgroup). Moreover, the pairing $e(g_p, V)$ *vanishes* in the order-q subgroup, so the prover has *no control* over the validity check in the order-q subgroup. Now, for Eq. (1.2) to be satisfied, it must be the case that $\alpha_{i^*}\beta_q = \beta_q^2 \bmod q$. Thus, either $\beta_q = 0$ or $\beta_q = \alpha_{i^*}$ and so the wire checks ensure that $U_k = g_p^{\beta_p} g_q^{\xi_k \alpha_{i^*}}$ where $\xi_k \in \{0, 1\}$ for all $k \in [m]$.

- **Gate consistency checks.** Now, consider the gate consistency checks. We again consider the projection of the pairing check into the order-q subgroup. If we project Eq. (1.3) in the order-q subgroup and using the above relations for U_k and A, we obtain the relation

$$\xi_{k_3}\alpha_{i^*}^2 + \xi_{k_1}\xi_{k_2}\alpha_{i^*}^2 - \alpha_{i^*}^2 = 0 \bmod q.$$

If $\alpha_{i^*} \neq 0 \bmod q$, then $\xi_{k_3} + \xi_{k_1}\xi_{k_2} - 1 = 0 \bmod q$. Since $\xi_{k_1}, \xi_{k_2}, \xi_{k_3} \in \{0, 1\}$, this means that $\xi_{k_3} = \mathsf{NAND}(\xi_{k_1}, \xi_{k_2})$.

The above relations show that $(\xi_1, \ldots, \xi_t) \in \{0, 1\}^t$ constitutes a valid assignment to the wires of $C((\xi_1, \ldots, \xi_n), \mathbf{w}^*)$ where $\mathbf{w}^* = (\xi_{n+1}, \ldots, \xi_{n+h})$. Again considering the verification relations in the order-q subgroup, the input validity checks ensure that $\mathbf{x}_{i^*} = (\xi_1, \ldots, \xi_n)$ and the output satisfiability check ensures that $C(\mathbf{x}_{i^*}, \mathbf{w}^*) = \xi_t = 1$. The above argument shows that if all of the validity checks pass, then we can *extract* a witness for instance i^*. Thus, statistical soundness for instance $\mathbf{x}_{i^*}$ holds. In fact, this extraction procedure can be made efficient given a trapdoor (i.e., the factorization of N). We provide the full construction and security analysis in Sect. 3.

1.2.2 The Prime-Order Instantiation, Bootstrapping, and Applications

The BARG construction from symmetric composite-order groups is conceptually simple to describe and illustrates the main ideas behind our construction. We now describe several extensions and generalizations of these ideas.

Instantiation from k-Lin. The ideas underlying the composite-order construction (Sect. 1.2.1 and 3) naturally extend to the setting of asymmetric prime-order groups. Recall that an asymmetric prime-order group consists of two base groups $\mathbb{G}_1$ and $\mathbb{G}_2$, a target group $\mathbb{G}_T$, all of prime order p, and an efficiently-computable, non-degenerate pairing $e \colon \mathbb{G}_1 \times \mathbb{G}_2 \to \mathbb{G}_T$. In this setting, we can base security on the standard k-Lin assumption for any $k \geq 1$. Recall that the case $k = 1$ corresponds to the SXDH assumption (i.e., DDH in $\mathbb{G}_1$ and $\mathbb{G}_2$) and the case $k = 2$ corresponds to the DLIN assumption [BBS04, HK07, Sha07]. The key property we relied on in the soundness analysis of the composite-order construction is the ability to isolate a single instance by *projecting* the verification relations into a suitable subgroup. In the prime-order setting, we can simulate this projection property by considering subspaces of vector spaces [GS08, Fre10]. We refer to Sect. 4 for the full description and security analysis.

Bootstrapping to Reduce CRS Size. The size of the CRS in the above construction scales *quadratically* with the number of instances m (due to the cross terms). However, we can adapt the bootstrapping approach from Kalai et al. [KPY19] reduce the size of the CRS to grow with m^ε (for any constant $\varepsilon > 0$). Soundness of the bootstrapping construction critically relies on the ability to extract the witness for *one* of the instances in the BARG.

The construction is simple. To verify statements $\mathbf{x}_1, \ldots, \mathbf{x}_m$, we consider a two-tiered construction where we group the statements into m/B batches of statements, each containing exactly B statements. We use a BARG (on B instances) to prove that all of the statements in each batch $(\mathbf{x}_{B(i-1)+1}, \ldots, \mathbf{x}_{iB})$ are true. Let π_i be the BARG proof for the ith batch. The prover then shows that it knows accepting proofs $\pi_1, \ldots, \pi_{m/B}$ of each of the m/B batches of statements. Here, it will be critical that the size of the BARG verification circuit for checking π_i be *sublinear* in the batch size B. This is not possible in general since the verification circuit has to read the statement which already has length B. However, when the underlying BARG satisfies a "split verification" property (Definition 2.9), where the verification algorithm decomposes into (1) a circuit-independent preprocessing step that reads the statement and outputs a *succinct* verification key vk; and (2) a fast "online" verification step whose running time is *polylogarithmic* in the number of instances, it suffices to use the BARG to *only* check the online verification step.

Now, if we set $B = \sqrt{m}$ in this framework, both the BARG for checking each batch of B statements as well as the BARG for verifying the $m/B = \sqrt{m}$ batches are BARGs on $\sqrt{m}$ instances. Thus, we can use a BARG on $\sqrt{m}$ instances to construct a BARG on m instances. If we start with a BARG with CRS size m^d, then the two-tiered construction reduces the CRS size to roughly $m^{d/2}$. We can apply this approach recursively (with a constant number of iterations) to reduce the CRS size from $\mathsf{poly}(\lambda, m)$ to $m^\varepsilon \cdot \mathsf{poly}(\lambda)$ for any constant $\varepsilon > 0$. We refer to the full version of this paper [WW22] for the full details.

Application to Delegation. Choudhuri et al. [CJJ21b] showed how to combine a "BARG for index languages" with a somewhere extractable commitment scheme to obtain a delegation scheme for RAM programs. In a BARG for index languages, the statements to the m instances are always fixed to be the binary representation of the integers $1, \ldots, m$. In this setting, the prover and the verifier do *not* need to read the statement anymore, and correspondingly, the verification algorithm is required to run in time $\mathsf{poly}(\lambda, \log m, |C|)$ when checking a circuit C.

Our BARG construction extends naturally to this setting. In the construction described in Sect. 1.2.1 (see also Sect. 3), the verifier starts by computing the commitments $U_1, \ldots, U_n$ to the bits of the statement. This takes time $\mathsf{poly}(\lambda, n, m)$ since the verifier has to minimally read the statement (of length mn). However in the case of an index BARG, the statements are known in *advance*, so the encodings U_i can be computed in advance and included as part of a verification key $\mathsf{vk} = (U_1, \ldots U_n)$ that the verifier uses for verification. Given vk, the statement validity checks can be implemented by simply comparing the precomputed commitments with those provided by the adversary; notably this check is now *independent* of the number of instances. Using the precomputed commitments, we can bring the overall verification cost down to $|C| \cdot \text{poly}(\lambda, \log m)$, which meets the efficiency requirements for an index BARG.

The second ingredient we require to instantiate the Choudhuri et al. [CJJ21b] compiler is a somewhere extractable commitment scheme. Our techniques for constructing BARGs can also be used to directly construct a somewhere extractable commitment scheme (when combined with a somewhere statistically binding hash function [HW15, OPWW15]). We can thus appeal to the compiler of Choudhuri et al. to obtain a delegation scheme for RAM programs from the SXDH assumption in bilinear groups.[7] Similar to the case with BARGs, we first describe a construction with a long CRS where the length of the CRS grows quadratically with the length of the committed message. We then describe a similar kind of bootstrapping technique to obtain a somewhere extractable commitment scheme with a CRS of size sublinear in the message size. We refer to the full version of this paper [WW22] for the full details.

Application to Aggregate Signatures. As described in Sect. 1.1, our BARG construction directly implies an aggregate signature scheme supporting bounded aggregation. We describe this construction in the full version of this paper [WW22].

Generalized BARGs. As previously noted for the case of BARGs for index languages, when the statements are fixed in advance, we can *precompute* commitments to them during setup and include the honestly-generated commitments to their values as part of a verification key. In this case, the verifier can use the precomputed encodings during verification and no longer needs to perform the statement validity checks. In the full version of this paper [WW22], we describe a more generalized view where some of the statement wires are fixed while others can be chosen by the prover. This generalization captures both the standard setting (where all of the statement wires can be chosen by the prover) and the BARG for index languages setting (where all of the statement wires are fixed ahead of time) as special cases.

1.3   Related Work

SNARGs. Batch arguments for NP can be constructed from any succinct non-interactive argument (SNARG) for NP. Existing constructions of SNARGs have either relied on random oracles [Mic95, BBHR18, COS20, CHM+20, Set20], the generic group model [Gro16], or strong non-falsifiable assumptions   [Gro10, BCCT12, DFH12, Lip13, PHGR13, GGPR13, BCI+13, BCPR14,

---

[7] While our BARG scheme can be based on the k-Lin assumption over bilinear groups for any $k \geq 1$, existing constructions of somewhere statistically binding hash functions [OPWW15] rely on the DDH assumption. As such, our current instantiation is based on SXDH. It seems plausible that the DDH-based construction of somewhere statistically binding hash functions can be extended to achieve hardness under the k-Lin assumption, but this is orthogonal to the primary focus of our work.

BISW17, BCC+17]. Indeed, Gentry and Wichs [GW11] showed that no construction of an (adaptively-sound) SNARG for NP can be proven secure via a black-box reduction to a falsifiable assumption [Nao03]. This separation also extends to adaptively-sound BARGs *of knowledge* (i.e., "BARKs") for NP [BHK17]. The only construction of non-adaptively sound SNARGs from falsifiable assumptions is the construction based on indistinguishability obfuscation [SW14]. We note that Lipmaa and Pavlyk [LP21] recently proposed a candidate SNARG from a non-standard, but falsifiable, q-type assumption on bilinear groups. However, we were recently informed [Wic22] that the proof of security was fundamentally flawed and later confirmed this with the authors of [LP21].

Batch Arguments for NP. If we focus specifically on constructions of BARGs for NP, Kalai et al. [KPY19] showed how to construct a BARG for NP from a non-standard, but falsifiable, q-type assumption on bilinear groups. More recently, Choudhuri et al. gave constructions from subexponentially-hard DDH in pairing-free groups in conjunction with polynomial hardness of the QR assumption [CJJ21a], as well as from polynomial hardness of the LWE assumption [CJJ21b]. Both of these constructions leverage correlation-intractable hash functions. The size of the proof in the DDH + QR construction grows with $\sqrt{m}$, where m is the number of instances, while that in the LWE construction scales *polylogarithmically* with the number of instances. Our work provides the first BARG for NP from standard assumptions on bilinear groups (with proof size that is *independent* of the number of instances).

Interactive Schemes. Batch arguments for NP have also been considered in the interactive setting. First, the classic IP = PSPACE theorem [LFKN90, Sha90] implies a interactive *proof* for batch NP verification, albeit with an *inefficient* prover. For interactive proofs with an *efficient* prover, batch verification is known for the class UP of NP languages with *unique* witnesses [RRR16, RRR18, RR20]. If we relax to interactive *arguments*, Brakerski et al. [BHK17] constructed 2-message BARGs for NP from any computational private information retrieval (PIR) scheme.

Delegation Schemes. Many works have focused on constructing delegation schemes for deterministic computations. In the interactive setting, we have succinct *proofs* for both bounded-depth computations [GKR08] and bounded-space computations [RRR16]. In the non-interactive setting, Kalai et al. [KPY19] gave the first construction from a falsifiable (but non-standard) assumption on bilinear groups. Using correlation-intractable hash functions based on LWE, Jawale et al. [JKKZ21] and Choudhuri et al. [CJJ21b] constructed delegation schemes for bounded-depth computations and general polynomial-time computations, respectively. Recently, González and Zacharakis [GZ21] constructed a delegation scheme for arithmetic circuits with a *long* CRS from a *bilateral* (or "split") k-Lin assumption in asymmetric groups. The size of the CRS in their construction is *quadratic* in the circuit size. Our scheme is based on the vanilla SXDH assumption in asymmetric groups and has a CRS whose size is *sublinear* in the running time of the RAM computation (specifically, T^ε for any constant $\varepsilon > 0$, where T is the running time of the RAM computation).

Aggregate Signatures. Aggregate signatures were introduced by Boneh et al. [BGLS03] who also gave an efficient construction using bilinear maps in the random oracle model. In the standard model, constructions of aggregate signatures have typically considered restricted settings such as sequential aggregation [LMRS04, LOS+06] where the aggregate signature is constructed by having each signer *sequentially* "add" its signature to an aggregated signature, or synchronized aggregation [GR06, AGH10, HW18], which assumes that signers have a synchronized clock and aggregation is only allowed on signatures from the same time period (with exactly 1 signature from each signer per time period). Other (standard model) constructions have relied on heavy tools such as multilinear maps [RS09, FHPS13] or indistinguishability obfuscation [HKW15]. Aggregate signatures can also be constructed generically from *adaptively-sound* succinct arguments *of knowledge* (SNARKs), which are only known from non-falsifiable assumptions or idealized models. In the case of bounded aggregation (where there is an *a priori* bound on the number of signatures that can be aggregated), the somewhere extractable BARG by Choudhuri et al. [CJJ21b] can be used to obtain a construction from LWE. Our work provides the first instantiation of an aggregate signature supporting bounded aggregation from standard assumptions over bilinear groups in the plain model.

2   Preliminaries

For a positive integer n, we write $[n]$ to denote the set $\{1, \ldots, n\}$. For a positive integer $p \in \mathbb{N}$, we write $\mathbb{Z}_p$ to denote the ring of integers modulo p. We use bold-face uppercase letters (e.g., $\mathbf{A}$, $\mathbf{B}$ to denote matrices) and bold-face lowercase letters (e.g., $\mathbf{x}$, $\mathbf{w}$) to denote vectors. For a finite set S, we write $x \xleftarrow{\text{R}} S$ to indicate that x is sampled uniformly at random from S. We use non-bold-face letters to denote their components (e.g., $\mathbf{x} = (x_1, \ldots, x_n)$). We write $\mathsf{poly}(\lambda)$ to denote a function that is $O(\lambda^c)$ for some $c \in \mathbb{N}$ and $\mathsf{negl}(\lambda)$ to denote a function that is $o(\lambda^{-c})$ for all $c \in \mathbb{N}$. We say an event E occurs with overwhelming probability if its complement occurs with negligible probability. An algorithm is efficient if it runs in probabilistic polynomial time in its input length. We say that two families of distributions $\mathcal{D}_1 = \{\mathcal{D}_{1,\lambda}\}_{\lambda \in \mathbb{N}}$ and $\mathcal{D}_2 = \{\mathcal{D}_{2,\lambda}\}_{\lambda \in \mathbb{N}}$ are computationally indistinguishable if no efficient algorithm can distinguish them with non-negligible probability. We say they are statistically indistinguishable if the statistical distance between them is bounded by a negligible function.

2.1   Non-Interactive Batch Arguments for NP

In this work, we consider the NP-complete language of Boolean circuit satisfiability. For ease of exposition, we focus on Boolean circuits comprised exclusively of NAND gates in our main construction. In the full version of this paper [WW22], we describe how to generalize the construction to support gates that compute arbitrary quadratic relations over their inputs. This allows us to support both general gates (e.g., AND, OR, XOR) as well as gates with more than two inputs.

For a Boolean circuit $C\colon \{0,1\}^n \times \{0,1\}^h \to \{0,1\}$ with t wires, we associate wires $1, \ldots, n$ with the bits of the statement $x_1, \ldots, x_n$, and wires $n+1, \ldots, n+h$ with the bits of the witness $w_1, \ldots, w_h$, respectively. We associate wire t with the output wire. We measure the size s of C by the number of NAND gates it has. By construction, $t \leq n + h + s$. We now define the (batch) circuit satisfiability language we consider in this work:

Definition 2.1 (Circuit Satisfiability). *We define* $\mathcal{L}_{\mathsf{CSAT}} = \{(C, \mathbf{x}) \mid \exists \mathbf{w} \in \{0,1\}^h : C(\mathbf{x}, \mathbf{w}) = 1\}$ *to be the language of Boolean circuit satisfiability, where* $C\colon \{0,1\}^n \times \{0,1\}^h \to \{0,1\}$ *is a Boolean circuit and* $\mathbf{x} \in \{0,1\}^n$ *is a statement. For a positive integer* $m \in \mathbb{N}$, *we define the* batch circuit satisfiability *language* $\mathcal{L}_{\mathsf{BatchCSAT},m}$ *as follows:*

$$\mathcal{L}_{\mathsf{BatchCSAT},m} = \{(C, \mathbf{x}_1, \ldots, \mathbf{x}_m) \mid \forall i \in [m] : \exists \mathbf{w}_i \in \{0,1\}^h : C(\mathbf{x}_i, \mathbf{w}_i) = 1\},$$

where $C\colon \{0,1\}^n \times \{0,1\}^h \to \{0,1\}$ *is a Boolean circuit and* $\mathbf{x}_1, \ldots, \mathbf{x}_m \in \{0,1\}^n$ *are the instances.*

Definition 2.2 (Batch Argument for Circuit Satisfiability). *A non-interactive batch argument (BARG) for circuit satisfiability is a tuple of three efficient algorithms* $\Pi_{\mathsf{BARG}} = (\mathsf{Setup}, \mathsf{Prove}, \mathsf{Verify})$ *with the following properties:*

- $\mathsf{Setup}(1^\lambda, 1^m, 1^s) \to \mathsf{crs}$*: On input the security parameter* $\lambda \in \mathbb{N}$*, the number of instances* $m \in \mathbb{N}$*, and a bound on the circuit size* $s \in \mathbb{N}$*, the setup algorithm outputs a common reference string* crs*.*
- $\mathsf{Prove}(\mathsf{crs}, C, (\mathbf{x}_1, \ldots, \mathbf{x}_m), (\mathbf{w}_1, \ldots, \mathbf{w}_m)) \to \pi$*: On input the common reference string* crs*, a Boolean circuit* $C\colon \{0,1\}^n \times \{0,1\}^h \to \{0,1\}$*, statements* $\mathbf{x}_1, \ldots, \mathbf{x}_m \in \{0,1\}^n$*, and witnesses* $\mathbf{w}_1, \ldots, \mathbf{w}_m \in \{0,1\}^h$*, the prove algorithm outputs a proof* π*.*
- $\mathsf{Verify}(\mathsf{crs}, C, (\mathbf{x}_1, \ldots, \mathbf{x}_m), \pi) \to b$*: On input the common reference string* crs*, the Boolean circuit* $C\colon \{0,1\}^n \times \{0,1\}^h \to \{0,1\}$*, statements* $\mathbf{x}_1, \ldots, \mathbf{x}_m \in \{0,1\}^n$ *and a proof* π*, the verification algorithm outputs a bit* $b \in \{0,1\}$*.*

Definition 2.3 (Completeness). *A BARG* $\Pi_{\mathsf{BARG}} = (\mathsf{Setup}, \mathsf{Prove}, \mathsf{Verify})$ *is complete if for all* $\lambda, m, s \in \mathbb{N}$*, all Boolean circuits* $C\colon \{0,1\}^n \times \{0,1\}^h \to \{0,1\}$ *of size at most* s*, all statements* $\mathbf{x}_1, \ldots, \mathbf{x}_m \in \{0,1\}^n$*, and all witnesses* $\mathbf{w}_1, \ldots, \mathbf{w}_m \in \{0,1\}^h$ *where* $C(\mathbf{x}_i, \mathbf{w}_i) = 1$ *for all* $i \in [m]$*,*

$$\Pr\left[\mathsf{Verify}(\mathsf{crs}, C, (\mathbf{x}_1, \ldots, \mathbf{x}_m), \pi) = 1 : \begin{array}{l} \mathsf{crs} \leftarrow \mathsf{Setup}(1^\lambda, 1^m, 1^s); \\ \pi \leftarrow \mathsf{Prove}(\mathsf{crs}, C, (\mathbf{x}_1, \ldots, \mathbf{x}_m), (\mathbf{w}_1, \ldots, \mathbf{w}_m)) \end{array}\right] = 1.$$

Definition 2.4 (Soundness). *Let* $\Pi_{\mathsf{BARG}} = (\mathsf{Setup}, \mathsf{Prove}, \mathsf{Verify})$ *be a BARG. We consider two notions of soundness:*

- **Non-adaptive soundness:** *We say that* Π_{BARG} *satisfies non-adaptive soundness if for all polynomials* $m = m(\lambda)$, $s = s(\lambda)$, *and efficient adversary* $\mathcal{A}$, *there exists a negligible function* $\mathsf{negl}(\cdot)$ *such that for all* $\lambda \in \mathbb{N}$, *and every statement* $(C, \mathbf{x}_1, \ldots, \mathbf{x}_m) \notin \mathcal{L}_{\mathsf{BatchCSAT},m}$, *where* $C \colon \{0,1\}^n \times \{0,1\}^h \to \{0,1\}$ *is a Boolean circuit of size at most* $s(\lambda)$ *and* $\mathbf{x}_1, \ldots, \mathbf{x}_n \in \{0,1\}^n$,

$$\Pr\left[\mathsf{Verify}(\mathsf{crs}, C, (\mathbf{x}_1, \ldots, \mathbf{x}_m), \pi) = 1 : \begin{array}{l} \mathsf{crs} \leftarrow \mathsf{Setup}(1^\lambda, 1^m, 1^s); \\ \pi \leftarrow \mathcal{A}(1^\lambda, \mathsf{crs}, C, (\mathbf{x}_1, \ldots, \mathbf{x}_m)) \end{array}\right] = \mathsf{negl}(\lambda).$$

- **Adaptive soundness:** *We say that* Π_{BARG} *is adaptively sound if for every efficient adversary* $\mathcal{A}$ *and every polynomial* $m = m(\lambda)$, $s = s(\lambda)$, *there exists a negligible function of* $\mathsf{negl}(\cdot)$ *such that for all* $\lambda \in \mathbb{N}$,

$$\Pr\left[\begin{array}{c} \mathsf{Verify}(\mathsf{crs}, C, (\mathbf{x}_1, \ldots, \mathbf{x}_m), \pi) = 1 \\ and \\ (C, \mathbf{x}_1, \ldots, \mathbf{x}_m) \notin \mathcal{L}_{\mathsf{BatchCSAT},m} \end{array} : \begin{array}{l} \mathsf{crs} \leftarrow \mathsf{Setup}(1^\lambda, 1^m, 1^s); \\ (C, \mathbf{x}_1, \ldots, \mathbf{x}_m, \pi) \leftarrow \mathcal{A}(1^\lambda, \mathsf{crs}) \end{array}\right] = \mathsf{negl}(\lambda).$$

Definition 2.5 (Semi-Adaptive Somewhere Soundness [CJJ21b]). *A BARG* $\Pi_{\mathsf{BARG}} = (\mathsf{Setup}, \mathsf{Prove}, \mathsf{Verify})$ *satisfies semi-adaptive somewhere soundness if there exists an efficient algorithm* $\mathsf{TrapSetup}$ *with the following properties:*

- $\mathsf{TrapSetup}(1^\lambda, 1^m, 1^s, i^*) \to \mathsf{crs}^*$: *On input the security parameter* $\lambda \in \mathbb{N}$, *the number of instances* $m \in \mathbb{N}$, *the size of the circuit* $s \in \mathbb{N}$, *and an index* $i^* \in [m]$, *the trapdoor setup algorithm outputs a (trapdoor) common reference string* crs^*.

We require $\mathsf{TrapSetup}$ *satisfy the following two properties:*

- **CRS indistinguishability:** *For integers* $m \in \mathbb{N}$, $s \in \mathbb{N}$, *a bit* $b \in \{0,1\}$, *and an adversary* $\mathcal{A}$, *define the CRS indistinguishability experiment* $\mathsf{ExptCRS}_{\mathcal{A}}(\lambda, m, s, b)$ *as follows:*
  1. *Algorithm* $\mathcal{A}(1^\lambda, 1^m, 1^s)$ *outputs an index* $i^* \in [m]$.
  2. *If* $b = 0$, *the challenger gives* $\mathsf{crs} \leftarrow \mathsf{Setup}(1^\lambda, 1^m, 1^s)$ *to* $\mathcal{A}$. *If* $b = 1$, *the challenger gives* $\mathsf{crs}^* \leftarrow \mathsf{TrapSetup}(1^\lambda, 1^m, 1^s, i^*)$ *to* $\mathcal{A}$.
  3. *Algorithm* $\mathcal{A}$ *outputs a bit* $b' \in \{0,1\}$, *which is the output of the experiment.*

  Then, Π_{BARG} *satisfies CRS indistinguishability if for every efficient adversary* $\mathcal{A}$, *every polynomial* $m = m(\lambda)$, $s = s(\lambda)$, *there exists a negligible function* $\mathsf{negl}(\cdot)$ *such that for all* $\lambda \in \mathbb{N}$,

  $$|\Pr[\mathsf{ExptCRS}_{\mathcal{A}}(\lambda, m, s, 0) = 1] - \Pr[\mathsf{ExptCRS}_{\mathcal{A}}(\lambda, m, s, 1) = 1]| = \mathsf{negl}(\lambda).$$

- **Somewhere soundness in trapdoor mode:** *Define the somewhere soundness security game between an adversary* $\mathcal{A}$ *and a challenger as follows:*
  - *Algorithm* $\mathcal{A}(1^\lambda, 1^m, 1^s)$ *outputs an index* $i^* \in [m]$.
  - *The challenger samples* $\mathsf{crs}^* \leftarrow \mathsf{TrapSetup}(1^\lambda, 1^m, 1^s, i^*)$ *and gives* crs^* *to* $\mathcal{A}$.

- Algorithm $\mathcal{A}$ outputs a Boolean circuit $C \colon \{0,1\}^n \times \{0,1\}^h \to \{0,1\}$ of size at most s, statements $\mathbf{x}_1, \ldots, \mathbf{x}_m \in \{0,1\}^n$, and a proof π. The output of the game is $b = 1$ if $\mathsf{Verify}(\mathsf{crs}^*, C, (\mathbf{x}_1, \ldots, \mathbf{x}_m), \pi) = 1$ and $(C, \mathbf{x}_{i^*}) \notin \mathcal{L}_{\mathsf{CSAT}}$. Otherwise, the output is $b = 0$.

Then, Π_{BARG} satisfies somewhere soundness in trapdoor mode if for every adversary $\mathcal{A}$, and every polynomial $m = m(\lambda)$, $s = s(\lambda)$, there exists a negligible function $\mathsf{negl}(\cdot)$ such that for all $\lambda \in \mathbb{N}$, $\Pr[b = 1] = \mathsf{negl}(\lambda)$ in the somewhere soundness security game.

Definition 2.6 (Somewhere Argument of Knowledge [CJJ21b]). A BARG $\Pi_{\mathsf{BARG}} = (\mathsf{Setup}, \mathsf{Prove}, \mathsf{Verify})$ is a somewhere argument of knowledge if there exists a pair of efficient algorithms $(\mathsf{TrapSetup}, \mathsf{Extract})$ with the following properties:

- $\mathsf{TrapSetup}(1^\lambda, 1^m, 1^s, i^*) \to (\mathsf{crs}^*, \mathsf{td})$: On input the security parameter $\lambda \in \mathbb{N}$, the number of instances $m \in \mathbb{N}$, the size of the circuit $s \in \mathbb{N}$, and an index $i^* \in [m]$, the trapdoor setup algorithm outputs a common reference string crs^* and an extraction trapdoor td.
- $\mathsf{Extract}(\mathsf{td}, C, (\mathbf{x}_1, \ldots, \mathbf{x}_m), \pi) \to \mathbf{w}^*$ On input the trapdoor td, statements $\mathbf{x}_1, \ldots, \mathbf{x}_m$, and a proof π, the extraction algorithm outputs a witness $\mathbf{w}^* \in \{0,1\}^h$. The extraction algorithm is deterministic.

We require $(\mathsf{TrapSetup}, \mathsf{Extract})$ to satisfy the following two properties:

- **CRS indistinguishability:** Same as in Definition 2.5.
- **Somewhere extractable in trapdoor mode:** Define the somewhere extractable security game between an adversary $\mathcal{A}$ and a challenger as follows:
  - Algorithm $\mathcal{A}(1^\lambda, 1^m, 1^s)$ outputs an index $i^* \in [m]$.
  - The challenger samples $(\mathsf{crs}^*, \mathsf{td}) \leftarrow \mathsf{TrapSetup}(1^\lambda, 1^m, 1^s, i^*)$ and gives crs^* to $\mathcal{A}$.
  - Algorithm $\mathcal{A}$ outputs a Boolean circuit $C \colon \{0,1\}^n \times \{0,1\}^h \to \{0,1\}$ of size at most s, statements $\mathbf{x}_1, \ldots, \mathbf{x}_m \in \{0,1\}^n$, and a proof π. Let $\mathbf{w}^* \leftarrow \mathsf{Extract}(\mathsf{td}, C, (\mathbf{x}_1, \ldots, \mathbf{w}_m), \pi)$.
  - The output of the game is $b = 1$ if $\mathsf{Verify}(\mathsf{crs}^*, C, (\mathbf{x}_1, \ldots, \mathbf{x}_m), \pi) = 1$ and $C(\mathbf{x}_{i^*}, \mathbf{w}^*) \neq 1$. Otherwise, the output is $b = 0$.

Then Π_{BARG} is somewhere extractable in trapdoor mode if for every adversary $\mathcal{A}$ and every polynomial $m = m(\lambda)$, $s = s(\lambda)$, there exists a negligible function $\mathsf{negl}(\cdot)$ such that $\Pr[b = 1] = \mathsf{negl}(\lambda)$ in the somewhere extractable game.

Remark 2.7 (Soundness Notions). The notion of semi-adaptive somewhere soundness from Defintion 2.5 is stronger than and implies non-adaptive soundness. Somewhere extractability (Defintion 2.6) is a further strengthening of semi-adaptive somewhere soundness.

Definition 2.8 (Succinctness). A BARG $\Pi_{\mathsf{BARG}} = (\mathsf{Setup}, \mathsf{Prove}, \mathsf{Verify})$ is succinct if there exists a fixed polynomial $\mathsf{poly}(\cdot, \cdot, \cdot)$ such that for all $\lambda, m, s \in \mathbb{N}$, all crs in the support of $\mathsf{Setup}(1^\lambda, 1^m, 1^s)$, and all Boolean circuits $C \colon \{0,1\}^n \times \{0,1\}^h \to \{0,1\}$ of size at most s, the following properties hold:

- **Succinct proofs:** *The proof* π *output by* $\mathsf{Prove}(\mathsf{crs}, C, \cdot, \cdot)$ *satisfies* $|\pi| \leq$ $\mathsf{poly}(\lambda, \log m, s)$.
- **Succinct CRS:** $|\mathsf{crs}| \leq \mathsf{poly}(\lambda, m, n) + \mathsf{poly}(\lambda, \log m, s)$.
- **Succinct verification:** *The verification algorithm runs in time* $\mathsf{poly}(\lambda, m, n) + \mathsf{poly}(\lambda, \log m, s)$.

BARGs with Split Verification. Our bootstrapping construction in the full version of this paper [WW22] (for reducing the size of the CRS) will rely on a BARG with a split verification property where the verification algorithm can be decomposed into a input-dependent algorithm that pre-processes the statements into a short verification key together with a fast online verification algorithm that takes the precomputed verification key and checks the proof. A similar property was also considered by Choudhuri et al. [CJJ21b] to realize their RAM delegation construction.

Definition 2.9 (BARG with Split Verification). *A BARG* $\Pi_{\mathsf{BARG}} =$ $(\mathsf{Setup}, \mathsf{Prove}, \mathsf{Verify})$ *supports split verification if there exists a pair of efficient and deterministic algorithms* $(\mathsf{GenVK}, \mathsf{OnlineVerify})$ *with the following properties:*

- $\mathsf{GenVK}(\mathsf{crs}, (\mathbf{x}_1, \ldots, \mathbf{x}_m)) \to \mathsf{vk}$: *On input the common reference string* crs *and statements* $\mathbf{x}_1, \ldots, \mathbf{x}_m \in \{0,1\}^n$, *the verification key generation algorithm outputs a verification key* vk.
- $\mathsf{OnlineVerify}(\mathsf{vk}, C, \pi) \to b$: *On input a verification key* vk, *a Boolean circuit* $C \colon \{0,1\}^n \times \{0,1\}^h \to \{0,1\}$ *and a proof* π, *the verification algorithm outputs a bit* $b \in \{0,1\}$.

Then, we say Π_{BARG} *supports split verification if* $\mathsf{Verify}(\mathsf{crs}, C, (\mathbf{x}_1, \ldots, \mathbf{x}_m), \pi)$ *outputs*

$$\mathsf{OnlineVerify}(\mathsf{GenVK}(\mathsf{crs}, (\mathbf{x}_1, \ldots, \mathbf{x}_m)), C, \pi).$$

We additionally require that there exists a fixed polynomial $\mathsf{poly}(\cdot, \cdot, \cdot)$ *such that for all* $\lambda, m, s \in \mathbb{N}$, *all* crs *in the support of* $\mathsf{Setup}(1^\lambda, 1^m, 1^s)$, *and all Boolean circuits* $C \colon \{0,1\}^n \times \{0,1\}^h \to \{0,1\}$ *of size at most* s, *the following efficiency properties hold (in addition to the properties in Defintion 2.8):*

- **Succinct verification key:** *The verification key generation algorithm* GenVK *runs in time* $\mathsf{poly}(\lambda, m, n)$, *and the size of the* vk *output by* GenVK *satisfies* $|\mathsf{vk}| \leq \mathsf{poly}(\lambda, \log m, n)$.
- **Succinct online verification:** *The algorithm* $\mathsf{OnlineVerify}(\mathsf{vk}, C, \pi)$ *runs in time* $\mathsf{poly}(\lambda, \log m, s)$.

Remark 2.10 (BARGs for Index Languages [CJJ21b]). BARGs for index languages [CJJ21b] ("index BARGs") are a useful building block for constructing delegation schemes for RAM programs. In an index BARG with m instances, the statement to the ith instance is the binary representation of the index i. Since the statements are fixed in an index BARG, they are *not* included in the input to the Prove and Verify algorithms. Moreover, the running time of the verification algorithm Verify on input a verification key vk,[8] a circuit C, and a proof π is required to be $\mathrm{poly}(\lambda, \log m, |C|)$. It is easy to see that any BARG with a split verification procedure can also be used to build an index BARG. Specifically, after the Setup algorithm samples the common reference string crs, it precomputes the (short) verification key vk $\leftarrow$ GenVK(crs, $(1, 2, \ldots, m)$). The verification algorithm Verify then takes as input the precomputed verification key vk, the circuit C, and the proof π, and outputs OnlineVerify(vk, C, π). The succinctness requirements on the split verification procedure implies the succinctness requirement on the index BARG.

3   BARG for NP from Subgroup Decision in Bilinear Groups

In this section, we show how to construct a BARGs from the subgroup decision assumption over symmetric composite-order groups. We refer to Sect. 1.2.1 for a general overview of this construction. We start by recalling the definition of a composite-order pairing group [BGN05] and the subgroup decision assumption.

Definition 3.1 (Composite-Order Bilinear Groups [BGN05]). *A (symmetric) composite-order bilinear group generator is an efficient algorithm* CompGroupGen *that takes as input the security parameter* λ *and outputs a description* $\mathcal{G} = (\mathbb{G}, \mathbb{G}_T, p, q, g, e)$ *of a bilinear group where* p, q *are distinct primes,* $\mathbb{G}$ *and* $\mathbb{G}_T$ *are cyclic groups of order* $N = pq$, *and* $e \colon \mathbb{G} \times \mathbb{G} \to \mathbb{G}_T$ *is a non-degenerate bilinear map (called the "pairing"). We require that the group operation in* $\mathbb{G}$ *and* $\mathbb{G}_T$ *as well as the pairing operation to be efficiently computable.*

Definition 3.2 (Subgroup Decision [BGN05]). *The subgroup decision assumption holds with respect to a composite-order bilinear group generator* CompGroupGen *if for every efficient adversary* $\mathcal{A}$, *there exists a negligible function* $\mathrm{negl}(\cdot)$ *such that for every* $\lambda \in \mathbb{N}$,

$$\left| \Pr[\mathcal{A}((\mathbb{G}, \mathbb{G}_T, N, g_p, e), g^r) = 1] - \Pr[\mathcal{A}((\mathbb{G}, \mathbb{G}_T, N, g_p, e), g_p^r) = 1] \right| = \mathrm{negl}(\lambda),$$

where $(\mathbb{G}, \mathbb{G}_T, p, q, g, e) \leftarrow$ CompGroupGen(1^λ), $N \leftarrow pq$, $g_p \leftarrow g^q$, *and* $r \xleftarrow{\text{R}} \mathbb{Z}_N$.

Construction 3.3 (BARG for NPfrom Subgroup Decision). Take any integer $m \in \mathbb{N}$. We construct a BARG with split verification for the language of circuit satisfiability as follows:

- Setup$(1^\lambda, 1^m, 1^s)$: On input the security parameter λ, the number of instances m, and the bound on the circuit size s, the setup algorithm does the following:
  - Run $(\mathbb{G}, \mathbb{G}_T, p, q, g, e) \leftarrow$ GroupGen(1^λ) and let $N = pq$, $g_p \leftarrow g^q$. In particular, g_p generates a subgroup of order p in $\mathbb{G}$. Let $\mathcal{G} = (\mathbb{G}, \mathbb{G}_T, N, g_p, e)$.

---

[8] Here, we allow the verification algorithm to take in a separate verification key vk, which may be *shorter* than the full common reference string crs. Note that the vk is assumed to be public (i.e., the CRS contains vk and possibly additional components used to construct proofs).

- For each $i \in [m]$, sample $\alpha_i \xleftarrow{\text{R}} \mathbb{Z}_N$. For each $i \in [m]$, let $A_i \leftarrow g_p^{\alpha_i}$. Let $A \leftarrow \prod_{i \in [m]} A_i$.
- For each $i, j \in [m]$ where $i \neq j$, compute $B_{i,j} \leftarrow g_p^{\alpha_i \alpha_j}$.
- Output the common reference string $\mathsf{crs} = \left(\mathcal{G}, A, \{A_i\}_{i \in [m]}, \{B_{i,j}\}_{i \neq j}\right)$.

- Prove$(\mathsf{crs}, C, (\mathbf{x}_1, \ldots, \mathbf{x}_m), (\mathbf{w}_1, \ldots, \mathbf{w}_m))$: On input the common reference string $\mathsf{crs} = \left(\mathcal{G}, A, \{A_i\}_{i \in [m]}, \{B_{i,j}\}_{i \neq j}\right)$, the circuit $C \colon \{0,1\}^n \times \{0,1\}^h \to \{0,1\}$, instances $\mathbf{x}_1, \ldots, \mathbf{x}_m \in \{0,1\}^n$, and witnesses $\mathbf{w}_1, \ldots, \mathbf{w}_m \in \{0,1\}^h$, define t to be the number of wires in C and s to be the number of gates in C. Then, for $i \in [m]$ and $j \in [t]$, let $w_{i,j} \in \{0,1\}$ be the value of wire j in $C(\mathbf{x}_i, \mathbf{w}_i)$. The prover proceeds as follows:
  - **Encoding wire values:** For each $k \in [t]$, let $U_k = \prod_{i \in [m]} A_i^{w_{i,k}}$.
  - **Validity of wire assignments:** For each $k \in [t]$, let $V_k = \prod_{i \neq j} B_{i,j}^{(1 - w_{i,k}) w_{j,k}}$.
  - **Validity of gate computation:** For each NAND gate $G_\ell = (k_1, k_2, k_3) \in [t]^3$ (where $\ell \in [s]$), compute $W_\ell = \prod_{i \neq j} B_{i,j}^{1 - w_{i,k_1} w_{j,k_2} - w_{j,k_3}}$

  Finally, output the proof $\pi = \left(\{U_k, V_k\}_{k \in [t]}, \{W_\ell\}_{\ell \in [s]}\right)$.

- Verify$(\mathsf{crs}, C, (\mathbf{x}_1, \ldots, \mathbf{x}_m), \pi)$: We decompose the verification algorithm into (GenVK, OnlineVerify):
  - GenVK$(\mathsf{crs}, (\mathbf{x}_1, \ldots, \mathbf{x}_m))$: On input the common reference string $\mathsf{crs} = \left(\mathcal{G}, A, \{A_i\}_{i \in [m]}, \{B_{i,j}\}_{i \neq j}\right)$, instances $\mathbf{x}_1, \ldots, \mathbf{x}_m \in \{0,1\}^n$, the verification key generation algorithm computes $U_k^* = \prod_{i \in [m]} A_i^{x_{i,k}}$ for each $k \in [n]$, and outputs the verification key $\mathsf{vk} = (U_1^*, \ldots, U_n^*)$.
  - OnlineVerify(vk, C, π): On input the verification key $\mathsf{vk} = (U_1^*, \ldots, U_n^*)$, a circuit $C \colon \{0,1\}^n \times \{0,1\}^h \to \{0,1\}$ and the proof $\pi = \left(\{U_k, V_k\}_{k \in [t]}, \{W_\ell\}_{\ell \in [s]}\right)$, the verification algorithm checks the following:
    * **Validity of statement:** For each input wire $k \in [n]$, $U_k = U_k^*$.
    * **Validity of wire assignments:** For each $k \in [t]$,

    $$e(A, U_k) = e(g_p, V_k) e(U_k, U_k). \tag{3.1}$$

    Validity of gate computation: For each gate $G_\ell = (k_1, k_2, k_3) \in [t]^3$,

    $$e(A, A) = e(U_{k_1}, U_{k_2}) e(A, U_{k_3}) e(g_p, W_\ell). \tag{3.2}$$

    Output satisfiability: The output encoding U_t satisfies $U_t = A$.

    The algorithm outputs 1 if all checks pass, and outputs 0 otherwise.

  The verification algorithm outputs OnlineVerify(GenVK($\mathsf{crs}, (\mathbf{x}_1, \ldots, \mathbf{x}_m)$), C, π).

Theorem 3.4 (Completeness). *Construction 3.3 is complete.*

Proof Take any circuit $C \colon \{0,1\}^n \times \{0,1\}^h \to \{0,1\}$, instances $\mathbf{x}_1, \ldots, \mathbf{x}_m \in \{0,1\}^n$ and witnesses $\mathbf{w}_1, \ldots, \mathbf{w}_m \in \{0,1\}^h$ such that $C(\mathbf{x}_i, \mathbf{w}_i) = 1$ for all $i \in [m]$. Let $\mathsf{crs} \leftarrow \mathsf{Setup}(1^\lambda, 1^m, 1^s)$ and $\pi \leftarrow \mathsf{Prove}(\mathsf{crs}, (\mathbf{x}_1, \ldots, \mathbf{x}_m), (\mathbf{w}_1, \ldots, \mathbf{w}_m))$. We show that $\mathsf{Verify}(\mathsf{crs}, C, (\mathbf{x}_1, \ldots, \mathbf{x}_m), \pi)$ outputs 1. Consider each of the verification relations:

- **Validity of statement:** By construction of GenVK, $U_k^* = \prod_{i \in [m]} A_i^{x_{i,k}}$ for each $k \in [n]$. By construction of Prove, $U_k = \prod_{i \in [m]} A_i^{w_{i,k}}$. By definition, the first n wires in C coincide with the wires to the statement, so $w_{i,k} = x_{i,k}$ for $k \in [n]$, and $U_k = U_k^*$ for all $k \in [n]$.
- **Validity of wire assignments:** Take any $k \in [t]$. Then $U_k = \prod_{i \in [m]} A_i^{w_{i,k}} = g_p^{\sum_{i \in [m]} \alpha_i w_{i,k}}$. Now,

$$\left(\sum_{i \in [m]} \alpha_i \right) \left(\sum_{j \in [m]} \alpha_j w_{j,k} \right) = \sum_{i \in [m]} \alpha_i^2 w_{i,k} + \sum_{i \neq j} \alpha_i \alpha_j w_{j,k},$$

and

$$\left(\sum_{i \in [m]} \alpha_i w_{i,k} \right) \left(\sum_{j \in [m]} \alpha_j w_{j,k} \right) = \sum_{i \in [m]} \alpha_i^2 w_{i,k} + \sum_{i \neq j} \alpha_i \alpha_j w_{i,k} w_{j,k},$$

using the fact that $w_{i,k} \in \{0,1\}$ so $w_{i,k}^2 = w_{i,k}$. Finally $V_k = \prod_{i \neq j} B_{i,j}^{(1-w_{i,k})w_{j,k}} = g_p^{\sum_{i \neq j} \alpha_i \alpha_j (1-w_{i,k})w_{j,k}}$. Thus, we can write

$$e(g_p, V_k)e(U_k, U_k) = e(g_p, g_p)^{\sum_{i \neq j} \alpha_i \alpha_j (1-w_{i,k})w_{j,k} + \sum_{i \in [m]} \alpha_i^2 w_{i,k} + \sum_{i \neq j} \alpha_i \alpha_j w_{i,k} w_{j,k}}$$
$$= e(g_p, g_p)^{\sum_{i \in [m]} \alpha_i^2 w_{i,k} + \sum_{i \neq j} \alpha_i \alpha_j w_{j,k}}$$
$$= e(A, U_k).$$

- **Validity of gate computation:** Take any gate $G_\ell = (k_1, k_2, k_3) \in [t]^3$. Consider first the exponents for the terms $e(U_{k_1}, U_{k_2})$, $e(A, U_{k_3})$, and $e(A, A)$:

$$\left(\sum_{i \in [m]} \alpha_i w_{i,k_1} \right) \left(\sum_{j \in [m]} \alpha_j w_{j,k_2} \right) = \sum_{i \in [m]} \alpha_i^2 w_{i,k_1} w_{i,k_2} + \sum_{i \neq j} \alpha_i \alpha_j w_{i,k_1} w_{j,k_2}$$

$$\left(\sum_{i \in [m]} \alpha_i \right) \left(\sum_{j \in [m]} \alpha_j w_{j,k_3} \right) = \sum_{i \in [m]} \alpha_i^2 w_{i,k_3} + \sum_{i \neq j} \alpha_i \alpha_j w_{j,k_3}$$

$$\left(\sum_{i \in [m]} \alpha_i \right) \left(\sum_{j \in [m]} \alpha_j \right) = \sum_{i \in [m]} \alpha_i^2 + \sum_{i \neq j} \alpha_i \alpha_j.$$

By definition $w_{i,k_3} = \mathsf{NAND}(w_{i,k_1}, w_{i,k_2})$. This means that for each $i \in [m]$, either $(w_{i,k_1} w_{i,k_2} = 1$ and $w_{i,k_3} = 0)$ or $(w_{i,k_1} w_{i,k_2} = 0$ and $w_{i,k_3} = 1)$. This means that

$$\sum_{i \in [m]} \alpha_i^2 (w_{i,k_1} w_{i,k_2} + w_{i,k_3}) = \sum_{i \in [m]} \alpha_i^2.$$

Combining the above relations in the exponent, we have that

$$
\frac{e(A, A)}{e(U_{k_1}, U_{k_2})e(A, U_{k_3})} = \frac{e(g_p, g_p)^{\sum_{i \in [m]} \alpha_i^2 + \sum_{i \neq j} \alpha_i \alpha_j}}{e(g_p, g_p)^{\sum_{i \in [m]} \alpha_i^2 + \sum_{i \neq j} \alpha_i \alpha_j (w_{i,k_1} w_{j,k_2} + w_{j,k_3})}}
$$

$$
= \prod_{i \neq j} e(g_p, B_{i,j})^{1 - w_{i,k_1} w_{j,k_2} - w_{j,k_3}}
$$

$$
= e(g_p, W_\ell).
$$

- **Output satisfiability:** Since $C(\mathbf{x}_i, \mathbf{w}_i) = 1$, it follows that $w_{i,t} = 1$ for all $i \in [m]$. By definition, $U_t = \prod_{i \in [m]} A_i^{w_{i,t}} = \prod_{i \in [m]} A_i = A$. $\square$

Theorem 3.5 (Somewhere Argument of Knowledge). *Suppose the subgroup decision assumption holds with respect to* CompGroupGen. *Then, Construction 3.3 is a somewhere argument of knowledge.*

Proof We start by defining the trapdoor setup and extraction algorithms:

- TrapSetup$(1^\lambda, 1^m, 1^s, i^*)$: The trapdoor algorithm uses the following procedure (we highlight in green the differences in the common reference string components between TrapSetup and Setup):
  1. Run $(\mathbb{G}, \mathbb{G}_T, p, q, g, e) \leftarrow$ GroupGen(1^λ) and let $N = pq$, $g_p \leftarrow g^q$. Let $\mathcal{G} = (\mathbb{G}, \mathbb{G}_T, N, g_p, e)$.
  2. For each $i \in [m]$, sample $\alpha_i \xleftarrow{\text{R}} \mathbb{Z}_N$. For each $i \neq i^*$, let $A_i \leftarrow g_p^{\alpha_i}$. Let $A_{i^*} \leftarrow g^{\alpha_{i^*}}$. Let $A \leftarrow A_{i^*} \prod_{i \neq i^*} A_i$.
  3. For each $i, j \in [m]$ where $i \neq j$ and $i, j \neq i^*$, compute $B_{i,j} \leftarrow g_p^{\alpha_i \alpha_j}$. Compute $B_{i^*,j} \leftarrow A_{i^*}^{\alpha_j}$ and $B_{i,i^*} \leftarrow A_{i^*}^{\alpha_i}$ for all $i, j \neq i^*$.
  4. Output the common reference string $\mathsf{crs}^* = (\mathcal{G}, A, \{A_i\}_{i \in [m]}, \{B_{i,j}\}_{i \neq j})$ and the trapdoor $\mathsf{td} = g_q \leftarrow g^p$.
- Extract$(\mathsf{td}, C, (\mathbf{x}_1, \ldots, \mathbf{x}_m), \pi)$: On input the trapdoor $\mathsf{td} = g_q$, the Boolean circuit $C: \{0,1\}^n \times \{0,1\}^h \to \{0,1\}$, statements $\mathbf{x}_1, \ldots, \mathbf{x}_m \in \{0,1\}^n$, and the proof $\pi = (\{U_k, V_k\}_{k \in [t]}, \{W_\ell\}_{\ell \in [s]})$, the extraction algorithm sets $w_k^* = 0$ if $e(g_q, U_k) = 1$ and $w_k^* = 1$ otherwise for each $k = n+1, \ldots, n+h$. It outputs $\mathbf{w}^* = (w_{n+1}^*, \ldots, w_{n+h}^*)$.

We now show the CRS indistinguishability and somewhere extractable in trapdoor mode properties.

Lemma 3.6 (CRS Indistinguishability). *If the subgroup decision assumption holds with respect to* CompGroupGen, *then Construction 3.3 satisfies CRS indistinguishability.*

Proof Take any polynomial $m = m(\lambda)$, $s = s(\lambda)$. We proceed via a hybrid argument:

- Hyb_0: This is the real distribution. At the beginning of the security game, the adversary chooses an index $i^* \in [m]$. The challenger then constructs the common reference string by running Setup$(1^\lambda, 1^m, 1^s)$:

- Run $(\mathbb{G}, \mathbb{G}_T, p, q, g, e) \leftarrow \mathsf{GroupGen}(1^\lambda)$ and let $N = pq$, $g_p \leftarrow g^q$. Let $\mathcal{G} = (\mathbb{G}, \mathbb{G}_T, N, g_p, e)$.
- For each $i \in [m]$, sample $\alpha_i \xleftarrow{\text{R}} \mathbb{Z}_N$. For each $i \in [m]$, let $A_i \leftarrow g_p^{\alpha_i}$. Let $A \leftarrow \prod_{i \in [m]} A_i$.
- For each $i, j \in [m]$ where $i \neq j$, compute $B_{i,j} \leftarrow g_p^{\alpha_i \alpha_j}$.
- Output the common reference string $\mathsf{crs} = \left(\mathcal{G}, A, \{A_i\}_{i \in [m]}, \{B_{i,j}\}_{i \neq j}\right)$.

The challenger gives crs to $\mathcal{A}$ and $\mathcal{A}$ outputs a bit $b' \in \{0, 1\}$, which is the output of the experiment.

- Hyb_1: Same as Hyb_0 except the challenger constructs A and $B_{i,j}$ using the procedure from TrapSetup:
  - For each $i \in [m]$, sample $\alpha_i \xleftarrow{\text{R}} \mathbb{Z}_N$. For each $i \in [m]$, let $A_i \leftarrow g_p^{\alpha_i}$. Let $A \leftarrow A_{i^*} \prod_{i \neq i^*} A_i$.
  - For each $i, j \in [m]$ where $i \neq j$ and $i, j \neq i^*$, compute $B_{i,j} \leftarrow g_p^{\alpha_i \alpha_j}$. Compute $B_{i^*,j} \leftarrow A_{i^*}^{\alpha_j}$ and $B_{i,i^*} \leftarrow A_{i^*}^{\alpha_i}$ for all $i, j \neq i^*$.
- Hyb_2: Same as Hyb_1 except the challenger samples $A_{i^*} \leftarrow g^{\alpha_{i^*}}$:
  - For each $i \in [m]$, sample $\alpha_i \xleftarrow{\text{R}} \mathbb{Z}_N$. For each $i \neq i^*$, let $A_i \leftarrow g_p^{\alpha_i}$. Let $A_{i^*} \leftarrow g^{\alpha_{i^*}}$. Let $A \leftarrow A_{i^*} \prod_{i \neq i^*} A_i$.
  - For each $i, j \in [m]$ where $i \neq j$ and $i, j \neq i^*$, compute $B_{i,j} \leftarrow g_p^{\alpha_i \alpha_j}$. Compute $B_{i^*,j} \leftarrow A_{i^*}^{\alpha_j}$ and $B_{i,i^*} \leftarrow A_{i^*}^{\alpha_i}$ for all $i, j \neq i^*$.

In this experiment, crs is distributed according to $\mathsf{TrapSetup}(1^\lambda, 1^m, 1^s, i^*)$.

For an index i, we write $\mathsf{Hyb}_i(\mathcal{A})$ to denote the output of experiment Hyb_i with algorithm $\mathcal{A}$. We show that the output distributions each adjacent pair of experiments are computationally indistinguishable (or identical).

Claim 3.7 For all adversaries $\mathcal{A}$, $\Pr[\mathsf{Hyb}_0(\mathcal{A}) = 1] = \Pr[\mathsf{Hyb}_1(\mathcal{A}) = 1]$.

Proof The difference between Hyb_0 and Hyb_1 is purely syntactic. In Hyb_1, $A_i - A_{i^*} \prod_{i \neq i} A_i = \prod_{i \in [m]} A_i$, which matches the distribution in Hyb_0. Similarly, in Hyb_1,

$$B_{i^*,j} = A_{i^*}^{\alpha_j} = g^{\alpha_{i^*} \alpha_j} \quad \text{and} \quad B_{i,i^*} = A_{i^*}^{\alpha_i} = g^{\alpha_{i^*} \alpha_i},$$

which is precisely the distribution of $B_{i^*,j}$ and B_{i,i^*} in Hyb_0 for all $i, j \neq i^*$. Finally $B_{i,j}$ for $i \neq j$ and $i, j \neq i^*$ are identically distributed in the two experiments.

Claim 3.8 Suppose the subgroup decision assumption holds with respect to GroupGen. Then, for all efficient adversaries $\mathcal{A}$, there exists a negligible function $\mathsf{negl}(\cdot)$ such that for all $\lambda \in \mathbb{N}$, $|\Pr[\mathsf{Hyb}_1(\mathcal{A}) = 1] - \Pr[\mathsf{Hyb}_2(\mathcal{A}) = 1]| = \mathsf{negl}(\lambda)$.

Proof Suppose there exists an efficient adversary $\mathcal{A}$ that distinguishes Hyb_1 and Hyb_2 with non-negligible advantage ε. We use $\mathcal{A}$ to construct an adversary $\mathcal{B}$ for the subgroup decision problem:

1. At the beginning of the game, algorithm $\mathcal{B}$ receives the group description $\mathcal{G} = (\mathbb{G}, \mathbb{G}_T, N, g_p, e)$ and the challenge $Z \in \mathbb{G}$ from the subgroup decision challenger.

2. For $i \neq i^*$, algorithm $\mathcal{B}$ samples $\alpha_i \xleftarrow{\text{R}} \mathbb{Z}_N$ and sets $A_i \leftarrow g_p^{\alpha_i}$. It sets $A_{i^*} \leftarrow Z$ to be the challenge value. Next, it computes $A \leftarrow Z \prod_{i \neq i^*} A_i$. For $i \neq j$ and $i, j \neq i^*$, algorithm $\mathcal{B}$ computes $B_{i,j} \leftarrow g_p^{\alpha_i \alpha_j}$. For $i, j \neq i^*$, it computes $B_{i^*,j} \leftarrow Z^{\alpha_j}$ and $B_{i,i^*} \leftarrow Z^{\alpha_i}$.
3. Algorithm $\mathcal{B}$ gives $\mathsf{crs} = \left(\mathcal{G}, A, \{A_i\}_{i \in [m]}, \{B_{i,j}\}_{i \neq j} \right)$ to $\mathcal{A}$ and outputs whatever $\mathcal{A}$ outputs.

Consider now the two possibilities:

- Suppose $Z = g_p^r$ in the subgroup decision game. Then, $A_{i^*} = g_p^r$ and algorithm $\mathcal{B}$ perfectly simulates the distribution in Hyb_1. In this case, algorithm $\mathcal{B}$ outputs 1 with probability $\Pr[\mathsf{Hyb}_1(\mathcal{A}) = 1]$.
- Suppose $Z = g^r$ in the subgroup decision game. Then, $A_{i^*} = g^r$ and algorithm $\mathcal{B}$ perfectly simulates the distribution in Hyb_2. In this case, algorithm $\mathcal{B}$ outputs 1 with probability $\Pr[\mathsf{Hyb}_2(\mathcal{A}) = 1]$.

The advantage of $\mathcal{B}$ in the subgroup decision game is thus ε.

Combining Claims 3.7 and 3.8, CRS indistinguishability holds.

Lemma 3.9 (Somewhere Extractable in Trapdoor Mode). *Construction 3.3 is somewhere extractable in trapdoor mode.*

Proof Fix polynomials $m = m(\lambda)$ and $s = s(\lambda)$. Let $i^* \leftarrow \mathcal{A}(1^\lambda, 1^m, 1^s)$ and $(\mathsf{crs}^*, \mathsf{td}) \leftarrow \mathsf{TrapSetup}(1^\lambda, 1^m, 1^s, i^*)$. By construction,

$$\mathsf{crs}^* = \left(\mathcal{G}, A, \{A_i\}_{i \in [m]}, \{B_{i,j}\}_{i \neq j} \right) \quad \text{and} \quad \mathsf{td} = g_q,$$

where $\mathcal{G} = (\mathbb{G}, \mathbb{G}_T, N, g_p, e)$. Let $N = pq$ and g be the generator of $\mathbb{G}$ (i.e., $g_p := g^q$ and $g_q := g^p$). Let $\mathbb{G}_p = \langle g_p \rangle$ be the order-p subgroup of $\mathbb{G}$ generated by g_p. Correspondingly, let $\mathbb{G}_q = \langle g_q \rangle$ be the order-q subgroup of $\mathbb{G}$ generated by g_q. By the Chinese Remainder Theorem, $\mathbb{G} \cong \mathbb{G}_p \times \mathbb{G}_q$.

Let $C \colon \{0,1\}^n \times \{0,1\}^h \to \{0,1\}$ be the Boolean circuit, $\mathbf{x}_1, \ldots, \mathbf{x}_m \in \{0,1\}^n$ be the statements, and $\pi = \left(\{U_k, V_k\}_{k \in [t]}, \{W_\ell\}_{\ell \in [s]} \right)$ be the proof the adversary outputs. Suppose $\mathsf{Verify}(\mathsf{crs}^*, (\mathbf{x}_1, \ldots, \mathbf{x}_m), \pi) = 1$. By construction of $\mathsf{TrapSetup}$, we can write $A_{i^*} = g^{\alpha_{i^*}} = g_p^{\alpha_{i^*,p}} g_q^{\alpha_{i^*,q}}$ for some $\alpha_{i^*,p} \in \mathbb{Z}_p$ and $\alpha_{i^*,q} \in \mathbb{Z}_q$. Suppose that $\alpha_{i^*,q} \neq 0$. This holds with overwhelming probability since $\alpha_{i^*} \xleftarrow{\text{R}} \mathbb{Z}_N$. Now the following properties hold:

- For all $k \in [t]$, either $U_k \in \mathbb{G}_p$ or $U_k / g_q^{\alpha_{i^*,q}} \in \mathbb{G}_p$. This follows from the wire validity checks. Specifically, suppose $U_k = g_p^{\beta_p} g_q^{\beta_q}$. We can also write $A = g_p^{\sum_{i \in [m]} \alpha_i} g_q^{\alpha_{i^*,q}}$. Since verification succeeds, it must be the case that

$$e(A, U_k) = e(g_p, V_k) e(U_k, U_k).$$

Consider the projection in the order-q subgroup of $\mathbb{G}_T$. This relation requires that $\alpha_{i^*,q} \cdot \beta_q = \beta_q^2$. This means that either $\beta_q = 0$ (in which case $U_k \in \mathbb{G}_p$) or $\beta_q = \alpha_{i^*,q}$ (in which case $U_k / g_q^{\alpha_{i^*,q}} \in \mathbb{G}_p$).

– For each $k \in [t]$, if $U_k \in \mathbb{G}_p$, then set $\xi_k = 0$. If $U_k / g_q^{\alpha_{i^*,q}} \in \mathbb{G}_p$, then set $\xi_k = 1$. Then, for all gates $G_\ell = (k_1, k_2, k_3) \in [t]^3$ in the circuit, $\xi_{k_3} = \mathsf{NAND}(\xi_{k_1}, \xi_{k_2})$. This follows from the gate validity checks. In particular, if verification succeeds, then Eq. (3.2) holds. From the above analysis, we can write $U_k = g_p^{\beta_{k,p}} g_q^{\xi_k \alpha_{i^*,q}}$ for all $k \in [t]$ and some $\beta_{k,p} \in \mathbb{Z}_p$. Consider the projection of Eq. (3.2) into the order-q subgroup of $\mathbb{G}_T$. This yields the relation

$$\alpha_{i^*,q}^2 = (\xi_{k_1} \alpha_{i^*,q})(\xi_{k_2} \alpha_{i^*,q}) + \alpha_{i^*,q}(\xi_{k_3} \alpha_{i^*,q}) = \alpha_{i^*,q}^2 (\xi_{k_1} \xi_{k_2} + \xi_{k_3}).$$

Since $\alpha_{i^*,q} \neq 0$, this means that $1 = \xi_{k_1} \xi_{k_2} + \xi_{k_3}$, or equivalently, $\xi_{k_3} = 1 - \xi_{k_1} \xi_{k_2} = \mathsf{NAND}(\xi_{k_1}, \xi_{k_2})$.

– Let $\mathbf{x}_{i^*} = (x_{i^*,1}, \ldots, x_{i^*,n})$. For $k \in [n]$, $\xi_k = x_{i^*,k}$.

This follows from the statement validity check. Namely, for $k \in [n]$, the verifier checks that $U_k = A_{i^*}^{x_{i^*,k}} \prod_{i \neq i^*} A_i^{x_{i,k}}$. Since $A_i \in \mathbb{G}_p$ for $i \neq i^*$, it follows that if $x_{i^*,k} = 0$, then $U_k \in \mathbb{G}_p$ (and $\xi_k = 0 = x_{i^*,k}$). Otherwise, if $x_{i^*,k} = 1$, then the component of U_k in $\mathbb{G}_q$ is exactly $g_q^{\alpha_{i^*,q}}$, in which case $\xi_k = 1 = x_{i^*,k}$.

– Finally $\xi_t = 1$. This follows from the output satisfiability check. Namely, the verifier checks that $U_t = A = g_p^{\sum_{i \in [m]} \alpha_i} g_q^{\alpha_{i^*,q}}$. If the verifier accepts, then this relation holds and $\xi_t = 1$.

The above properties show that $\xi_1, \ldots, \xi_t$ is a valid assignment to the wires of C on input $\mathbf{x}_{i^*}$ and witness $\boldsymbol{\xi} = (\xi_{n+1}, \ldots, \xi_{n+h})$. Moreover, $C(\mathbf{x}_{i^*}, \boldsymbol{\xi}) = \xi_t = 1$.

To complete the proof, let $\mathbf{w}^* \leftarrow \mathsf{Extract}(\mathsf{td}, C, (\mathbf{x}_1, \ldots, \mathbf{x}_m), \pi)$. We claim that $\mathbf{w}^* = \boldsymbol{\xi}$. In particular, for $k \in [h]$, if $U_{n+k} \in \mathbb{G}_p$, then $e(g_q, U_k) = 1$ and $w_k^* = 0 = \xi_{n+k}$. Alternatively, if $U_{n+k} / g_p^{\alpha_{i^*,q}} \in \mathbb{G}_p$, then $e(g_q, U_k) = e(g_q, g_q)^{\alpha_{i^*,q}} \neq 1$, so $w_k^* = 1 = \xi_{n+k}$. Thus, with probability $1 - \mathsf{negl}(\lambda)$, either $\mathsf{Verify}(\mathsf{crs}^*, C, (\mathbf{x}_1, \ldots, \mathbf{x}_m), \pi) = 0$ or $C(\mathbf{x}, \mathbf{w}^*) = 1$.

By Lemmas 3.6 and 3.9, Construciton 3.3 is a somewhere argument of knowledge.

Theorem 3.10 (Succinctness). *Construciton 3.3 is succinct and satisfies split verification (Definition 2.9).*

Proof Take any $\lambda, m, s \in \mathbb{N}$ and consider a Boolean circuit $C \colon \{0,1\}^n \times \{0,1\}^h \to \{0,1\}$ of size at most s. Let $t = \mathsf{poly}(s)$ be the number of wires in C. We check each property:

– **Proof size:** A proof π consists of $2t + s$ elements in $\mathbb{G}$, each of which can be represented in $\mathsf{poly}(\lambda)$ bits. Thus, the proof size satisfies $|\pi| = (2t + s) \cdot \mathsf{poly}(\lambda) = \mathsf{poly}(\lambda, s)$.
– **CRS size:** The common reference string crs consists of the group description $\mathcal{G}$, and $m + 1 + m(m-1)/2$ elements in $\mathbb{G}$. Thus, $|\mathsf{crs}| = m^2 \cdot \mathsf{poly}(\lambda)$.
– **Verification key size:** The size of the verification key vk output by GenVK consists of n group elements. Thus, $|\mathsf{vk}| = n \cdot \mathsf{poly}(\lambda)$.
– **Verification key generation time:** The algorithm GenVK performs nm group operations. This takes time $\mathsf{poly}(\lambda, m, n)$.

- **Online verification time:** The running time of the online verification algorithm OnlineVerify is

$$\underbrace{n \cdot \mathsf{poly}(\lambda)}_{\text{statement validity}} + \underbrace{t \cdot \mathsf{poly}(\lambda)}_{\text{wire validity}} + \underbrace{s \cdot \mathsf{poly}(\lambda)}_{\text{gate validity}} + \underbrace{\mathsf{poly}(\lambda)}_{\text{output validity}}$$

$$= \mathsf{poly}(\lambda, s),$$

since $n, t = \mathsf{poly}(s)$. □

Remark 3.11 (Variable Number of Instances). As currently described, the prover and verifier algorithms in Construciton 3.3 takes exactly m instances as input. However, the same scheme can also be used to prove any $T \leq m$ instances (by ignoring components in the CRS). In this case, the proof size is unchanged, and the verification running time (assuming random read access to the CRS) is $\mathsf{poly}(\lambda, n, T) + \mathsf{poly}(\lambda, s)$.

4 BARG for NP from k-Lin in Bilinear Groups

Due to space limitations, we defer our BARG construction from asymmetric prime-order pairing groups (where the k-Lin assumption holds) to the full version of this paper [WW22]. In this setting, the pairing $e \colon \mathbb{G}_1 \times \mathbb{G}_2 \to \mathbb{G}_T$ is an efficiently-computable bilinear map from the base groups $\mathbb{G}_1$ and $\mathbb{G}_2$ to the target group $\mathbb{G}_T$. The construction relies on a similar underlying principle as the construction from symmetric composite-order groups (Construciton 3.3). Here, we summarize the key differences and refer readers to the full version for the complete description and analysis:

- **Randomizing cross-terms in the CRS.** In the symmetric setting, we associated a single encoding A_i with each instance. In the asymmetric setting, we need to encode the instance in *both* $\mathbb{G}_1$ and $\mathbb{G}_2$ in order to apply the pairing consistency checks. Thus, the prover now generates two commitments to the wire labels for each wire, one in $\mathbb{G}_1$ and the other in $\mathbb{G}_2$. This introduces a new challenge when it comes to constructing the *cross-terms* $B_{i,j}$, as it depends on the exponents associated with the encodings in *both* $\mathbb{G}_1$ and $\mathbb{G}_2$. Proving security would seemingly need to rely on a "bilateral" assumption over pairing groups where the assumption gives out elements with correlated exponents in *both* $\mathbb{G}_1$ and $\mathbb{G}_2$. To avoid this and base security on the vanilla k-Lin assumption, we split the cross-terms into two shares, with one share in $\mathbb{G}_1$ and the other in $\mathbb{G}_2$. The extra randomness in the cross terms allows for a simple simulation strategy in the security analysis (see the full version of this paper [WW22]).
- **Simulating projective pairing using outer products.** The key property we relied on in the soundness analysis of the composite-order construction is that the pairing is projecting. Namely, there exists a projection map on $\mathbb{G}$ and $\mathbb{G}_T$ that map into the subgroup of order-q in each respective group; moreover, this projection map *commutes* with the pairing. Then, if a relation like

Eq. (3.1) or Eq. (3.2) holds in the target group, the projected relation formed by projecting the left-hand and right-hand sides into the order-q subgroup also holds. As argued in Lemma 3.9, projecting into the order-q subgroup allows us to isolate a single instance i^*, in which case the verification checks ensure *statistically* soundness for instance i^*. To obtain an analog of projective pairings in the prime order setting, we can replace the subgroups with subspaces of a vector space and define the pairing operation to be an outer (tensor) product of vectors [GS08,Fre10]. As we show in the full version of this paper [WW22], this enables a similar strategy to prove soundness.

5   Extensions and Applications

Bootstrapping to Reduce CRS Size. As mentioned in Sect. 1.2.2, we can leverage a similar type of bootstrapping from the work of Kalai et al. [KPY19] to reduce the size of the CRS in our BARG constructions to grow with m^ε for any $\varepsilon > 0$ and where m is the number of instances. We refer to Sect. 1.2.2 for the overview of this approach and to the full version of this paper [WW22] for the full details.

Application to Delegation. In the full version of this paper [WW22], we show how to use our BARG for NP to obtain a delegation scheme for RAM programs (equivalently, a SNARG for P). Our construction follows the approach from Choudhuri et al. [CJJ21b] of combining a BARG for "index languages" (or more generally, any BARG with the split verification property (Defintion 2.9)) with a somewhere extractable commitment scheme. The BARGs we construct in this work

both satisfy the required split verification property. In the full version of this paper [WW22], we also show how to use our techniques in conjunction with somewhere statistically binding hash functions [HW15] to obtain a somewhere extractable commitment scheme. This suffices to obtain a RAM delegation scheme from the SXDH assumption in asymmetric pairing groups.

Application to Aggregate Signatures. In the full version of this paper [WW22], we describe a simple approach of constructing aggregate signatures that supports bounded aggregation from a BARG for NP. Together with our BARG for NP (from either subgroup decision or k-Lin), we obtain an aggregate signature scheme from the same assumption.

Acknowledgments. B. Waters is supported by NSF CNS-1908611, a Simons Investigator award, and the Packard Foundation Fellowship. D. J. Wu is supported by NSF CNS-1917414, CNS-2045180, a Microsoft Research Faculty Fellowship, and a Google Research Scholar award.

References

[AGH10] Ahn, J.H., Green, M., Hohenberger, S.: Synchronized aggregate signatures: new definitions, constructions and applications. In: ACM CCS (2010)

[BBHR18] Ben-Sasson, E., Bentov, I., Horesh, Y., Riabzev, M.: Scalable, transparent, and post-quantum secure computational integrity. IACR Cryptol. ePrint Arch. **2018**, 1–83 (2018)

[BBS04] Boneh, D., Boyen, X., Shacham, H.: Short group signatures. In: Franklin, M. (ed.) CRYPTO 2004. LNCS, vol. 3152, pp. 41–55. Springer, Heidelberg (2004). https://doi.org/10.1007/978-3-540-28628-8_3

[BCC+17] Bitansky, N., et al.: The hunting of the SNARK. J. Cryptol. **30**(4), 989–1066 (2017)

[BCCT12] Bitansky, N., Canetti, R., Chiesa, A., Tromer, E.: From extractable collision resistance to succinct non-interactive arguments of knowledge, and back again. In: ITCS (2012)

[BCI+13] Bitansky, N., Chiesa, A., Ishai, Y., Paneth, O., Ostrovsky, R.: Succinct non-interactive arguments via linear interactive proofs. In: Sahai, A. (ed.) TCC 2013. LNCS, vol. 7785, pp. 315–333. Springer, Heidelberg (2013). https://doi.org/10.1007/978-3-642-36594-2_18

[BCPR14] Bitansky, N., Canetti, R., Paneth, O., Rosen, A.: On the existence of extractable one-way functions. In: STOC (2014)

[BGLS03] Boneh, D., Gentry, C., Lynn, B., Shacham, H.: Aggregate and verifiably encrypted signatures from bilinear maps. In: Biham, E. (ed.) EUROCRYPT 2003. LNCS, vol. 2656, pp. 416–432. Springer, Heidelberg (2003). https://doi.org/10.1007/3-540-39200-9_26

[BGN05] Boneh, D., Goh, E.-J., Nissim, K.: Evaluating 2-DNF formulas on ciphertexts. In: Kilian, J. (ed.) TCC 2005. LNCS, vol. 3378, pp. 325–341. Springer, Heidelberg (2005). https://doi.org/10.1007/978-3-540-30576-7_18

[BHK17] Brakerski, Z., Holmgren, J., Kalai, Y.T.: Non-interactive delegation and batch NP verification from standard computational assumptions. In: STOC (2017)

[BISW17] Boneh, D., Ishai, Y., Sahai, A., Wu, D.J.: Lattice-based SNARGs and their application to more efficient obfuscation. In: Coron, J.-S., Nielsen, J.B. (eds.) EUROCRYPT 2017. LNCS, vol. 10212, pp. 247–277. Springer, Cham (2017). https://doi.org/10.1007/978-3-319-56617-7_9

[CCH+19] Canetti, R., et al.: Fiat-Shamir: from practice to theory. In: STOC (2019)

[CF13] Catalano, D., Fiore, D.: Vector commitments and their applications. In: Kurosawa, K., Hanaoka, G. (eds.) PKC 2013. LNCS, vol. 7778, pp. 55–72. Springer, Heidelberg (2013). https://doi.org/10.1007/978-3-642-36362-7_5

[CGH98] Canetti, R., Goldreich, O., Halevi, S.: The random oracle methodology, revisited (preliminary version). In: STOC (1998)

[CHM+20] Chiesa, A., Hu, Y., Maller, M., Mishra, P., Vesely, N., Ward, N.: Marlin: preprocessing zkSNARKs with universal and updatable SRS. In: Canteaut, A., Ishai, Y. (eds.) EUROCRYPT 2020. LNCS, vol. 12105, pp. 738–768. Springer, Cham (2020). https://doi.org/10.1007/978-3-030-45721-1_26

[CJJ21a] Choudhuri, A.R., Jain, A., Jin, Z.: Non-interactive batch arguments for NP from standard assumptions. In: Malkin, T., Peikert, C. (eds.) CRYPTO 2021. LNCS, vol. 12828, pp. 394–423. Springer, Cham (2021). https://doi.org/10.1007/978-3-030-84259-8_14

[CJJ21b] Choudhuri, A.R., Jain, A., Jin, Z.: SNARGs for P from LWE. In: FOCS (2021)

[COS20] Chiesa, A., Ojha, D., Spooner, N.: FRACTAL: post-quantum and transparent recursive proofs from holography. In: Canteaut, A., Ishai, Y. (eds.) EUROCRYPT 2020. LNCS, vol. 12105, pp. 769–793. Springer, Cham (2020). https://doi.org/10.1007/978-3-030-45721-1_27

[DFH12] Damgård, I., Faust, S., Hazay, C.: Secure two-party computation with low communication. In: Cramer, R. (ed.) TCC 2012. LNCS, vol. 7194, pp. 54–74. Springer, Heidelberg (2012). https://doi.org/10.1007/978-3-642-28914-9_4

[FHPS13] Freire, E.S.V., Hofheinz, D., Paterson, K.G., Striecks, C.: Programmable hash functions in the multilinear setting. In: Canetti, R., Garay, J.A. (eds.) CRYPTO 2013. LNCS, vol. 8042, pp. 513–530. Springer, Heidelberg (2013). https://doi.org/10.1007/978-3-642-40041-4_28

[Fre10] Freeman, D.M.: Converting pairing-based cryptosystems from composite-order groups to prime-order groups. In: Gilbert, H. (ed.) EUROCRYPT 2010. LNCS, vol. 6110, pp. 44–61. Springer, Heidelberg (2010). https://doi.org/10.1007/978-3-642-13190-5_3

[FS86] Fiat, A., Shamir, A.: How to prove yourself: practical solutions to identification and signature problems. In: Odlyzko, A.M. (ed.) CRYPTO 1986. LNCS, vol. 263, pp. 186–194. Springer, Heidelberg (1987). https://doi.org/10.1007/3-540-47721-7_12

[GGPR13] Gennaro, R., Gentry, C., Parno, B., Raykova, M.: Quadratic span programs and succinct NIZKs without PCPs. In: Johansson, T., Nguyen, P.Q. (eds.) EUROCRYPT 2013. LNCS, vol. 7881, pp. 626–645. Springer, Heidelberg (2013). https://doi.org/10.1007/978-3-642-38348-9_37

[GKR08] Goldwasser, S., Kalai, Y.T., Rothblum, G.N.: Delegating computation: interactive proofs for muggles. In: STOC (2008)

[GOS06] Groth, J., Ostrovsky, R., Sahai, A.: Perfect non-interactive zero knowledge for NP. In: Vaudenay, S. (ed.) EUROCRYPT 2006. LNCS, vol. 4004, pp. 339–358. Springer, Heidelberg (2006). https://doi.org/10.1007/11761679_21

[GR06] Gentry, C., Ramzan, Z.: Identity-based aggregate signatures. In: Yung, M., Dodis, Y., Kiayias, A., Malkin, T. (eds.) PKC 2006. LNCS, vol. 3958, pp. 257–273. Springer, Heidelberg (2006). https://doi.org/10.1007/11745853_17

[Gro10] Groth, J.: Short pairing-based non-interactive zero-knowledge arguments. In: Abe, M. (ed.) ASIACRYPT 2010. LNCS, vol. 6477, pp. 321–340. Springer, Heidelberg (2010). https://doi.org/10.1007/978-3-642-17373-8_19

[Gro16] Groth, J.: On the size of pairing-based non-interactive arguments. In: Fischlin, M., Coron, J.-S. (eds.) EUROCRYPT 2016. LNCS, vol. 9666, pp. 305–326. Springer, Heidelberg (2016). https://doi.org/10.1007/978-3-662-49896-5_11

[GS08] Groth, J., Sahai, A.: Efficient non-interactive proof systems for bilinear groups. In: Smart, N. (ed.) EUROCRYPT 2008. LNCS, vol. 4965, pp. 415–432. Springer, Heidelberg (2008). https://doi.org/10.1007/978-3-540-78967-3_24

[GW11] Gentry, C., Wichs, D.: Separating succinct non-interactive arguments from all falsifiable assumptions. In: STOC (2011)

[GZ21] González, A., Zacharakis, A.: Succinct publicly verifiable computation. In: TCC (2021)

[HJKS22] Hulett, J., Jawale, R., Khurana, D., Srinivasan, A.: SNARGs for P from Sub-exponential DDH and QR. In: Dunkelman, O., Dziembowski, S. (eds.) Advances in Cryptology – EUROCRYPT 2022. EUROCRYPT 2022. Lecture Notes in Computer Science, vol. 13276, pp. 520–549. Springer, Cham (2022). https://doi.org/10.1007/978-3-031-07085-3_18

[HK07] Hofheinz, D., Kiltz, E.: Secure hybrid encryption from weakened key encapsulation. In: Menezes, A. (ed.) CRYPTO 2007. LNCS, vol. 4622, pp. 553–571. Springer, Heidelberg (2007). https://doi.org/10.1007/978-3-540-74143-5_31

[HKW15] Hohenberger, S., Koppula, V., Waters, B.: Universal signature aggregators. In: Oswald, E., Fischlin, M. (eds.) EUROCRYPT 2015. LNCS, vol. 9057, pp. 3–34. Springer, Heidelberg (2015). https://doi.org/10.1007/978-3-662-46803-6_1

[HW15] Hubácek, P., Wichs, D.: On the communication complexity of secure function evaluation with long output. In: ITCS (2015)

[HW18] Hohenberger, S., Waters, B.: Synchronized aggregate signatures from the RSA assumption. In: Nielsen, J.B., Rijmen, V. (eds.) EUROCRYPT 2018. LNCS, vol. 10821, pp. 197–229. Springer, Cham (2018). https://doi.org/10.1007/978-3-319-78375-8_7

[JJ21] Jain, A., Jin, Z.: Non-interactive Zero Knowledge from Sub-exponential DDH. In: Canteaut, A., Standaert, F.-X. (eds.) EUROCRYPT 2021. LNCS, vol. 12696, pp. 3–32. Springer, Cham (2021). https://doi.org/10.1007/978-3-030-77870-5_1

[JKKZ21] Jawale, R., Kalai, Y.T, Khurana, D., Zhang, R.Y.: SNARGs for bounded depth computations and PPAD hardness from sub-exponential LWE. In: STOC (2021)

[KPY19] Kalai, Y.T., Paneth, O., Yang, L.: How to delegate computations publicly. In: STOC (2019)

[KRR13] Kalai, Y.T., Raz, R., Rothblum, R.D.: Delegation for bounded space. In: STOC (2013)

[KRR14] Kalai, Y.T., Raz, R., Rothblum, R.D.: How to delegate computations: the power of no-signaling proofs. In: STOC (2014)

[KVZ21] Kalai, Y.T., Vaikuntanathan, V., Zhang, R.Y.: Somewhere statistical soundness, post-quantum security, and SNARGs. In: Nissim, K., Waters, B. (eds.) TCC 2021. LNCS, vol. 13042, pp. 330–368. Springer, Cham (2021). https://doi.org/10.1007/978-3-030-90459-3_12

[LFKN90] Lund, C., Fortnow, L., Karloff, H.J., Nisan, N.: Algebraic methods for interactive proof systems. In: FOCS (1990)

[Lip13] Lipmaa, H.: Succinct non-interactive zero knowledge arguments from span programs and linear error-correcting codes. In: Sako, K., Sarkar, P. (eds.) ASIACRYPT 2013. LNCS, vol. 8269, pp. 41–60. Springer, Heidelberg (2013). https://doi.org/10.1007/978-3-642-42033-7_3

[LMRS04] Lysyanskaya, A., Micali, S., Reyzin, L., Shacham, H.: Sequential aggregate signatures from trapdoor permutations. In: Cachin, C., Camenisch, J.L. (eds.) EUROCRYPT 2004. LNCS, vol. 3027, pp. 74–90. Springer, Heidelberg (2004). https://doi.org/10.1007/978-3-540-24676-3_5

[LOS+06] Lu, S., Ostrovsky, R., Sahai, A., Shacham, H., Waters, B.: Sequential aggregate signatures and multisignatures without random oracles. In: Vaudenay, S. (ed.) EUROCRYPT 2006. LNCS, vol. 4004, pp. 465–485. Springer, Heidelberg (2006). https://doi.org/10.1007/11761679_28

[LP21] Lipmaa, H., Pavlyk, K.: Gentry-wichs is tight: a falsifiable non-adaptively sound SNARG. In: Tibouchi, M., Wang, H. (eds.) ASIACRYPT 2021. LNCS, vol. 13092, pp. 34–64. Springer, Cham (2021). https://doi.org/10.1007/978-3-030-92078-4_2

[LPWW20] Libert, B., Passelègue, A., Wee, H., Wu, D.J.: New constructions of statistical NIZKs: Dual-Mode DV-NIZKs and more. In: Canteaut, A., Ishai, Y. (eds.) EUROCRYPT 2020. LNCS, vol. 12107, pp. 410–441. Springer, Cham (2020). https://doi.org/10.1007/978-3-030-45727-3_14

[Mic95] Micali, S.: Computationally-sound proofs. In: Proceedings of the Annual European Summer Meeting of the Association of Symbolic Logic (1995)

[Nao03] Naor, M.: On cryptographic assumptions and challenges. In: Boneh, D. (ed.) CRYPTO 2003. LNCS, vol. 2729, pp. 96–109. Springer, Heidelberg (2003). https://doi.org/10.1007/978-3-540-45146-4_6

[OPWW15] Okamoto, T., Pietrzak, K., Waters, B., Wichs, D.: New realizations of somewhere statistically binding hashing and positional accumulators. In: Iwata, T., Cheon, J.H. (eds.) ASIACRYPT 2015. LNCS, vol. 9452, pp. 121–145. Springer, Heidelberg (2015). https://doi.org/10.1007/978-3-662-48797-6_6

[PHGR13] Parno, B., Howell, J., Gentry, C., Raykova, M.: Pinocchio: nearly practical verifiable computation. In: IEEE Symposium on Security and Privacy (2013)

[PS19] Peikert, C., Shiehian, S.: Noninteractive zero knowledge for NP from (plain) learning with errors. In: Boldyreva, A., Micciancio, D. (eds.) CRYPTO 2019. LNCS, vol. 11692, pp. 89–114. Springer, Cham (2019). https://doi.org/10.1007/978-3-030-26948-7_4

[RR20] Rothblum, G.N., Rothblum, R.D.: Batch verification and proofs of proximity with polylog overhead. In: Pass, R., Pietrzak, K. (eds.) TCC 2020. LNCS, vol. 12551, pp. 108–138. Springer, Cham (2020). https://doi.org/10.1007/978-3-030-64378-2_5

[RRR16] Reingold, O., Rothblum, G.N., Rothblum, R.D.: Constant-round interactive proofs for delegating computation. In: STOC (2016)

[RRR18] Reingold, O., Rothblum, G.N., Rothblum, R.D.: Efficient batch verification for UP. In: CCC (2018)

[RS09] Rückert, M., Schröder, D.: Aggregate and verifiably encrypted signatures from multilinear maps without random oracles. In: Park, J.H., Chen, H.-H., Atiquzzaman, M., Lee, C., Kim, T., Yeo, S.-S. (eds.) ISA 2009. LNCS, vol. 5576, pp. 750–759. Springer, Heidelberg (2009). https://doi.org/10.1007/978-3-642-02617-1_76

[Set20] Setty, S.: Spartan: efficient and general-purpose zkSNARKs without trusted setup. In: Micciancio, D., Ristenpart, T. (eds.) CRYPTO 2020. LNCS, vol. 12172, pp. 704–737. Springer, Cham (2020). https://doi.org/10.1007/978-3-030-56877-1_25

[Sha90] Shamir, A.: IP=PSPACE. In: FOCS (1990)

[Sha07] Shacham, H.: A Cramer-Shoup encryption scheme from the linear assumption and from progressively weaker linear variants. IACR Cryptol. ePrint Arch. (2007)

[SW14] Sahai, A., Waters, B.: How to use indistinguishability obfuscation: deniable encryption, and more. In: STOC (2014)

[Wic22] Wichs, D.: Personal communication (2022)

[WW22] Waters, B., Wu, D.J.: Batch arguments for NP and more from standard bilinear group assumptions. IACR Cryptol. ePrint Arch. (2022)

Breaking Rainbow Takes a Weekend on a Laptop

Ward Beullens[✉][iD]

IBM Research, Zurich, Switzerland
wbe@zurich.ibm.com

Abstract. This work introduces new key recovery attacks against the Rainbow signature scheme, which is one of the three finalist signature schemes still in the NIST Post-Quantum Cryptography standardization project. The new attacks outperform previously known attacks for all the parameter sets submitted to NIST and make a key-recovery practical for the SL 1 parameters. Concretely, given a Rainbow public key for the SL 1 parameters of the second-round submission, our attack returns the corresponding secret key after on average 53 h (one weekend) of computation time on a standard laptop.

1 Introduction

The Rainbow signature scheme [7], proposed by Ding and Schmidt in 2005, is one of the oldest and most studied signature schemes in multivariate cryptography. Rainbow is based on the (unbalanced) Oil and Vinegar signature scheme [10,15], which, for properly chosen parameters, has withstood all cryptanalysis since 1999. In the last decade, there has been a renewed interest in multivariate cryptography, because it is believed to resist attacks from quantum adversaries. The goal of this paper is to improve the cryptanalysis of Rainbow, which is an important objective because Rainbow is currently one of three finalist signature schemes in the NIST Post-Quantum Cryptography standardization project.

Related Work. The cryptanalysis of Rainbow and its predecessors was an active area of research for some years in the early 2000s. Attacks from this era include the MinRank attack, HighRank attack, the Billet-Gilbert attack, UOV reconciliation attack, and the Rainbow Band Separation Attack [4,8,9,11,18]. After 2008 the cryptanalysis seemed to have stabilized, until the participation of Rainbow in the NIST PQC project motivated more cryptanalysis. During the second round of the NIST project, Bardet *et al.* proposed a new algorithm for solving the MinRank problem [2]. This drastically improved the efficiency of the

---

Ward Beullens holds Junior Post-Doctoral fellowship 1S95620N from the Research Foundation Flanders (FWO).

Y. Dodis and T. Shrimpton (Eds.): CRYPTO 2022, LNCS 13508, pp. 464–479, 2022.
https://doi.org/10.1007/978-3-031-15979-4_16

MinRank attack, although not enough to threaten the parameters submitted to NIST. A more memory-friendly version of this algorithm was proposed by Baena *et al.* [1]. Perlner and Smith-Tone tightened the analysis of the Rainbow Band Separation attack, showing that the attack was more efficient than previously assumed [16]. This prompted the Rainbow team to increase the parameters slightly for the third round. During the third round, Beullens introduced new attacks [3] which reduced the security level of Rainbow by a factor of 2^{20} for the SL 1 parameters. The Rainbow team argued that despite the new attacks, the Rainbow parameters still meet the NIST requirements [17].

Contributions. This paper introduces two new (partial) key-recovery attacks. Recall that if $\mathcal{P} : \mathbb{F}_q^n \to \mathbb{F}_q^m$ is a Rainbow public key, then the corresponding secret key contains, among some other information, a subspace $O_2 \subset \mathbb{F}_q^n$, such that $\mathcal{P}(O_2) = 0$.

Our attacks are based on the simple observation that for a randomly chosen $\mathbf{x} \in \mathbb{F}_q^n$, the differential

$$D_{\mathbf{x}} : \mathbb{F}_q^n \to \mathbb{F}_q^m : \mathbf{y} \mapsto \mathcal{P}(\mathbf{x} + \mathbf{y}) - \mathcal{P}(\mathbf{x}) - \mathcal{P}(\mathbf{y})$$

(which is a linear map) has a kernel vector in O_2 with probability $\approx 1/q$. Given this observation, we first propose the following simple strategy to find a vector in O_2: Guess a vector $\mathbf{x}$, and try to solve for a vector $\mathbf{o}$ such that

$$\begin{cases} D_{\mathbf{x}}\mathbf{o} = 0 \\ \mathcal{P}(\mathbf{o}) = 0 \end{cases} . \tag{1}$$

If we find such a solution $\mathbf{o}$, then with high probability it is in O_2. If no solution exists, we try again with a different guess for $\mathbf{x}$. In fields of odd characteristic, we find that the quadratic system (1) behaves exactly like a random system. In fields of characteristic 2 (which includes all the parameters submitted to NIST in the second and third rounds), the system has some structure that can be exploited to solve it slightly more efficiently. When a vector in O_2 is found, we can remove the outer layer of the Rainbow public key, which reduces it to a UOV public key with parameters that are too small to be secure. This simple attack is efficient enough to do a key recovery attack in practice for the SL1 parameter set from the second-round submission to the NIST PQC project. For a single guess of $\mathbf{x}$, it takes only 3 h and 32 min to solve system (1), and a guess is good with a probability of approximately $1/15.06$, so on average, a full attack takes $15.06 \cdot 3.53 \approx 53$ h. We estimate that a key recovery for the SL 1 parameter set of the third-round submission requires only a factor 2^8 more effort (see Table 1).

For the parameter sets targeting NIST security levels 3 and 5, we find that the attack can be improved by combining the new technique with the rectangular MinRank attack of Beullens [3]. The combined attack chooses a random $\mathbf{x}$ and essentially restricts $\mathcal{P}$ to the kernel of $D_{\mathbf{x}}$ and runs the rectangular MinRank on this smaller system, which will succeed with a probability of approximately $1/q$. Estimates of the complexities of the simple and combined attacks against the Rainbow parameter sets submitted to NIST are given in Table 1.

Table 1. An overview of the cost of our attacks versus known attacks for the six Rainbow parameter sets submitted to the second round and the finals of the NIST PQC standardization project. Complexities are given as $\log_2$ of the estimated gate count. The complexities of the known attacks are taken from [3]. For the SL I parameters we have a key-recovery attack (marked by *), the other attacks are forgery attacks.

Parameter set		(q, n, m, o_2)	Simple attack	Combined attack	Known attacks
Second round	SL 1	$(16, 96, 64, 32)$	61*	93*	123*
	SL 3	$(256, 140, 72, 36)$	186	131	151
	SL 5	$(256, 188, 96, 48)$	246	164	191
Finals	SL 1	$(16, 100, 64, 32)$	69*	99*	127*
	SL 3	$(256, 148, 80, 48)$	160	157	177
	SL 5	$(256, 196, 100, 64)$	257	206	226

2 Preliminaries

Notation. Let $\mathbb{F}_q$ be the finite field with q elements, and let $\mathcal{P} = \{p_i\}_{i=1}^m$ be a sequence of m multivariate quadratic polynomials in n variables over $\mathbb{F}_q$. We identify $\mathcal{P}$ with the function $\mathcal{P} : \mathbb{F}_q^n \to \mathbb{F}_q^m$ defined as $\mathcal{P}(\mathbf{x}) = \{p_i(\mathbf{x})\}_{i=1}^m$. We define the differential $\mathcal{P}'(\mathbf{x}, \mathbf{y})$ (sometimes called the polar form of $\mathcal{P}$) as $\mathcal{P}'(\mathbf{x}, \mathbf{y}) := \mathcal{P}(\mathbf{x} + \mathbf{y}) - \mathcal{P}(\mathbf{x}) - \mathcal{P}(\mathbf{y}) + \mathcal{P}(0)$. It is easily checked that $\mathcal{P}'(\mathbf{x}, \mathbf{y})$ is symmetric and bilinear.

Solving Multivariate Systems. Our attacks use (in a black-box way) a subroutine that given a homogeneous multivariate quadratic map $\mathcal{P} : \mathbb{F}_q^n \to \mathbb{F}_q^m$, finds a non-zero solution $\mathbf{x}$ such that $\mathcal{P}(\mathbf{x}) = 0$, if such a solution exists. We instantiate this subroutine with the block Wiedemann XL algorithm [5,6,13,14]. This algorithm constructs a large but very sparse system of linear equations and solves it with the block Wiedemann algorithm to take advantage of the sparsity. For the experimental validation of our attacks we used the optimized implementation of Block Wiedemann XL by Cheng, Chou, Niederhagen, and Yang [5]. The cost of this algorithm on an instance with m random homogeneous equations in n variables can be estimated as the cost of

$$3 \binom{n - 1 + D}{D}^2 \binom{n + 1}{2}$$

field multiplications, where D is the *operating degree* of XL, which is chosen to be the smallest integer such that the coefficient of the t^D term in the power series expansion of

$$\frac{(1 - t^2)^m}{(1 - t)^n}$$

is non-positive.

Example 1. Suppose we want to find a solution to a system of 63 homogeneous quadratic equations in 31 variables. We have

$$\frac{(1 - t^2)^{63}}{(1 - t)^{31}} = 1 + 31t + 433t^2 + 3503t^3 + 17081t^4 + 41447t^5 - 44919t^6 + O(t^7),$$

so we can run XL at degree $D = 6$, with an estimated cost of

$$3\binom{31 - 1 + 6}{6}^2 \binom{31 + 1}{2} \approx 2^{52.3}$$

field multiplications.

Solving MinRank Problems. Our attacks will also make use of an algorithm to solve the MinRank problem. An instance of this problem is a list of matrices $L_1, \ldots, L_k \in \mathbb{F}_q^{n \times m}$, and a target rank r. The task is to find a non-zero linear combination of the matrices whose rank is at most r. This NP-hard problem often appears in the cryptanalysis of multivariate and rank metric code-based cryptosystems [8,12], and has therefore been studied relatively well.

Our attacks use the support-minors algorithm of Bardet, Bros, Cabarcas, Gaborit, Perlner, Smith-Tone, Tillich, and Verbel [2]. This algorithm translates the rank condition to a large sparse system of bilinear equations and solves this system using linearization and sparse linear algebra methods. The cost of this algorithm can be estimated as

$$3(k - 1)(r + 1)\binom{m}{r}^2 \binom{k + b - 2}{b}^2$$

field multiplications, where b is the operating degree of the algorithm, which is chosen to be the smallest positive integer such that

$$\binom{m}{r}\binom{K + b - 2}{b} - 1 \leq \sum_{i=1}^{b} (-1)^{i+1} \binom{m}{r + i}\binom{n + i - 1}{i}\binom{K + b - i - 2}{b - i}. \quad (2)$$

It is sometimes beneficial to ignore some columns of the L_i matrices; one can choose to truncate the L_i matrices to their first $m' \leq m$ columns, for some optimal value of m' in the range $[r+1, m]$. It might seem wasteful to not use all the columns, but current MinRank algorithms can unfortunately not always use all the columns efficiently. (Similar to how LWE solving algorithms often cannot make good use of all their LWE samples.)

Example 2. Suppose we are given $k = 92$ matrices with $n = 187$ rows and $m = 96$ columns each, and we know there is a non-zero linear combination of the matrices with rank $r = 48$, which we want to find. Plugging our parameters into inequality (2), we find that can work at degree $b = 1$ as longs as we keep at least 72 columns, we can work at $b = 2$ if we keep at least 68 columns, at $b = 3$ if we keep 65 columns and at $b = 4$ if we keep 63 columns etc. It turns out that we get the most efficient algorithm if we keep $m' = 65$ columns and work at degree $b = 3$. The estimated cost of the algorithm is then

$$3(92 - 1)(48 + 1)\binom{65}{48}^2 \binom{92 + 3 - 2}{3}^2 \approx 2^{149.1}$$

field multiplications.

The Rainbow Trapdoor. We present the Rainbow trapdoor as described by Beullens [3]. A Rainbow instance is parameterized by four parameters:

- q, the size of the finite field,
- n, the number of variables,
- m, the number of equations in the public key, and
- o_2, the dimension of the subspaces $O_2 \subset \mathbb{F}_q^n$ and $W \subset \mathbb{F}_q^m$.

The public key is then a multivariate quadratic map $\mathcal{P} : \mathbb{F}_q^n \to \mathbb{F}_q^m$, and the secret key consists of three linear subspaces O_1, O_2, W, such that (see Fig. 1):

1. $O_2 \subset O_1 \subset \mathbb{F}_q^n$, and $W \subset \mathbb{F}_q^m$,
2. $\dim(O_2) = \dim(W) = o_2$, and $\dim(O_1) = m$,
3. for all $\mathbf{o}_2 \in O_2$ and $\mathbf{x} \in \mathbb{F}_q^n$ we have $\mathcal{P}(\mathbf{o}_2) = 0$ and $\mathcal{P}'(\mathbf{x}, \mathbf{o}_2) \in W$, and
4. for all $\mathbf{o}_1 \in O_1$, we have $\mathcal{P}(\mathbf{o}_1) \in W$.

The key generation algorithm chooses the subspaces $O_2 \subset O_1 \subset \mathbb{F}_q^n$ and $W \subset \mathbb{F}_q^m$ of the correct dimension, and produces a public key $\mathcal{P}$ that is distributed uniformly among all the $\mathcal{P}$ that behave properly on O_2, O_1, W. How to do key generation efficiently, and how to use the trapdoor structure to sample preimages for $\mathcal{P}$ is irrelevant for our attacks, so we refer to [3] for the details. Note that traditionally the Rainbow trapdoor is explained in terms of a *central* multivariate quadratic map $\mathcal{F} : \mathbb{F}_q^n \to \mathbb{F}_q^m$ (sampled from some family of maps for which it is easy to sample preimages), and two random linear maps $S \in GL(\mathbb{F}_q^n)$, $T \in GL(\mathbb{F}_q^m)$. The public key is then $\mathcal{P}(\mathbf{x}) = T \circ \mathcal{F} \circ S(\mathbf{x})$, where the intuition is that the linear maps hide the structure of the system $\mathcal{F}$. Both views are equivalent (see [3]), although arguably the description in terms of the subspaces O_1, O_2 and W conveys the structure of the Rainbow trapdoor better.

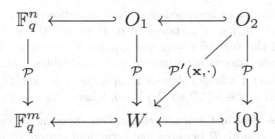

Fig. 1. The structure of a Rainbow public key. The differential $\mathcal{P}'(\mathbf{x}, \cdot)$ maps O_2 to W for every $\mathbf{x} \in \mathbb{F}_q^n$.

3   Simple Attack

Let $(\mathsf{pk} = \mathcal{P}, \mathsf{sk} = (O_2, O_1, W))$ be a Rainbow key pair. For any vector $\mathbf{x} \in \mathbb{F}_q^n$, and any vector $\mathbf{o}_2 \in O_2$, we have by construction (see Sect. 2) that $\mathcal{P}'(\mathbf{x}, \mathbf{o}_2) \in W$. So for any $\mathbf{x}$ we can consider the differential

$$D_{\mathbf{x}} : \mathbb{F}_q^n \to \mathbb{F}_q^m : \mathbf{y} \mapsto \mathcal{P}'(\mathbf{x}, \mathbf{y}),$$

which is a linear map from $\mathbb{F}_q^n$ to $\mathbb{F}_q^m$, that moreover sends O_2 to W. For any fixed non-zero $\mathbf{x}$ the differential $D_{\mathbf{x}}|_{O_2}$ restricted to O_2 is a uniformly random linear map from O_2 to W (over the random bits of the key generation algorithm). Note that $\dim(O_2) = \dim(W) = o_2$, so the probability that $D_{\mathbf{x}}$ has a kernel vector in O_2 is exactly the probability that a random o_2-by-o_2 matrix over $\mathbb{F}_q$ is singular. A matrix is non-singular if the first row is non-zero, and for each $i < o_2$, the $i+1$-th row is not in the span of the first i rows (which happens with probability q^{i-1-o_2}), so the probability of being singular is

$$1 - \prod_{i=0}^{o_2-1} \left(1 - q^{i-o_2}\right),$$

which is close to $1/q$ for sufficiently large q, regardless of o_2. For example, with $q = 16, o_2 = 32$, the probability is approximately $1/15.06$.

Our attack is now to simply pick a random (non-zero) $\mathbf{x}$, hope that the kernel of $D_\mathbf{x}$ intersects O_2 non-trivially, and then try to solve for a vector $\mathbf{o}$ in this intersection. Since $\mathcal{P}(\mathbf{o}) = 0$ for all $\mathbf{o} \in O_2$, we propose to do this by solving the following system

$$
\begin{cases}
D_\mathbf{x}\,\mathbf{o} = 0 \\
\mathcal{P}(\mathbf{o}) = 0
\end{cases}
$$

This system consists of m homogeneous linear equations, and m homogeneous quadratic equations in the n variables of $\mathbf{o}$. If we use the m linear equations to eliminate m of the variables from the quadratic equations, we end up with a system of m homogeneous equations in $n - m$ variables. Concretely, let $B \in \mathbb{F}_q^{n \times (n-m)}$ be a matrix whose columns form a basis for $\ker(D_\mathbf{x})$, then we are looking for a solution $\mathbf{y} \in \mathbb{F}_q^{n-m}$ to $\tilde{\mathcal{P}}(\mathbf{y}) = 0$, where $\tilde{\mathcal{P}}(\mathbf{y}) := \mathcal{P}(B\mathbf{y})$.

Attack in Fields of Odd Characteristic. Our experiments (see Appendix A) show that when q is odd, $\tilde{\mathcal{P}}$ behaves like a random system of m homogeneous quadratic equation in $n - m$ variables in the XL algorithm. The ranks of the XL systems exactly match the ranks of XL systems of systems or random quadratic equations at each operation degree D. In particular, if a solution to $\tilde{\mathcal{P}}(\mathbf{y}) = 0$ exists we can find it with an estimated cost of

$$
3 \binom{n - m - 1 + D}{D}^2 \binom{n - m + 1}{2}
$$

field multiplications, where D is the smallest positive integer such that the t^D coefficient of the power series expansion of $(1 - t^2)^m / (1 - t)^{m-n}$ (see Sect. 2.)

Attack in Fields of Even Characteristic. Our experiments show that for even q, the rank of the XL systems does not match that of random systems, and just applying the XL as in the case of odd characteristic sometimes fails. The reason is that $\mathcal{P}'(\mathbf{x}, \mathbf{x}) = 2\mathcal{P}(\mathbf{x})$ vanishes in characteristic 2, so $\mathbf{x} \in \ker(D_\mathbf{x})$. This means there is a $\tilde{\mathbf{y}} \in \mathbb{F}_q^{n-m}$, known to the attacker, such that $B\tilde{\mathbf{y}} = x$, (recall that the columns of B form a basis for $\ker(D_\mathbf{x})$. For this $\tilde{\mathbf{y}}$ we have that $\tilde{\mathcal{P}}(\tilde{\mathbf{y}} + \mathbf{y}) = \tilde{\mathcal{P}}(\tilde{\mathbf{y}}) + \tilde{\mathcal{P}}(\mathbf{y})$ for all $\mathbf{y} \in \mathbb{F}_q^{n-m}$, which is not something that usually happens for random $\tilde{\mathcal{P}}$.

Luckily for us, this is not a problem for the attack, in fact we can even exploit this property to make the attack slightly more efficient: Recall that we want to find $\mathbf{y}$ such that $\tilde{\mathcal{P}}(\mathbf{y}) = 0$. Let $Y \subset \mathbb{F}_q^{n-m}$ be any subspace of dimension $n-m-1$ that does not contain $\tilde{\mathbf{y}}$, such that $\langle \tilde{\mathbf{y}} \rangle + Y = \mathbb{F}_q^{n-m}$. Then it suffices to find $\mathbf{y}' \in Y$ such that $\tilde{\mathcal{P}}(\mathbf{y}') = \alpha\tilde{\mathcal{P}}(\tilde{\mathbf{y}})$ for some $\alpha \in \mathbb{F}_q$, because then $\mathbf{y} = \sqrt{\alpha}\tilde{\mathbf{y}} + \mathbf{y}'$ is a solution to $\tilde{\mathcal{P}}(\mathbf{y}) = 0$, (recall that every element has a square root in fields of characteristic 2, so $\sqrt{\alpha}$ exists), because

$$
\tilde{\mathcal{P}}(\sqrt{\alpha}\tilde{\mathbf{y}} + \mathbf{y}') = \alpha\tilde{\mathcal{P}}(\tilde{\mathbf{y}}) + \tilde{\mathcal{P}}(\mathbf{y}') = 0.
$$

To find this $\mathbf{y'} \in Y$, we restrict $\tilde{\mathcal{P}}$ to Y, and look for a solution to the $m-1$ homogeneous quadratic equations

$$\hat{\mathcal{P}} := \{\tilde{p}_1 a_i - \tilde{p}_i a_1\}_{i=2}^m,$$

where $\mathbf{a} = \tilde{\mathcal{P}}(\tilde{\mathbf{y}})$, and we assume with loss of generality that $a_1 \neq 0$.

By restricting to Y, we remove the problematic vector $\tilde{\mathbf{y}}$, so it should not be a surprise that our rank experiments show that the new system $\hat{\mathcal{P}}$ behaves like a system of $m-1$ random homogeneous quadratic equations in $n-m-1$ variables (see the rank experiments in Appendix A). Therefore, if a solution exists, we can find it with an estimated cost of

$$3\binom{n-m-2+D}{D}^2 \binom{n-m}{2}$$

field multiplications, where D is the smallest positive integer such that the t^D coefficient of the power series expansion of $(1-t^2)^{m-1}/(1-t)^{m-n-1}$.

Completing the Attack. Once a vector in O_2 is found, the second layer of Rainbow can be removed, and the security of Rainbow is reduced to the security of a smaller UOV system with $m' = m - o_2$ equations in $n' = n - o_2$ variables. See e.g., Section 5.3 of [3]. Given a single vector $\mathbf{o} \in O_2$, one can first compute

$$\langle \mathcal{P}'(\mathbf{o}, \mathbf{e}_1), \ldots, \mathcal{P}'(\mathbf{o}, \mathbf{e}_n) \rangle \subset W,$$

which will with overwhelming probability be an equality. Let V be a change of variables that sends W to the last o_2 coordinates of $\mathbb{F}_q^m$, and split up $V \circ \mathcal{P}$ as

$$V \circ \mathcal{P}(\mathbf{x}) = \begin{cases} \mathcal{P}_1(\mathbf{x}) \\ \mathcal{P}_2(\mathbf{x}) \end{cases}$$

where $\mathcal{P}_1 : \mathbb{F}_q^n \to \mathbb{F}_q^{m-o_2}$ consists of the first $m - o_2$ coordinates of $V \circ \mathcal{P}$ and $\mathcal{P}_2 : \mathbb{F}_q^n \to \mathbb{F}_q^{o_2}$ the remaining o_2 coordinates. Then O_2 can be found as the kernel of the linear map

$$\mathbf{o} \mapsto \begin{pmatrix} \mathcal{P}_1'(\mathbf{e}_1, \mathbf{o}) \\ \cdots \\ \mathcal{P}_1'(\mathbf{e}_n, \mathbf{o}) \end{pmatrix}.$$

The space O_2 sits in this kernel because $\mathcal{P}'(\mathbf{x}, \mathbf{o}) \in W$ for all $\mathbf{x} \in \mathbb{F}_q^n$, and with overwhelming probability, the kernel is exactly equal to O_2.

Now, let U be a change of variables that sends the last o_2 coordinates of $\mathbb{F}_q^n$ to O_2, and let

$$V \circ \mathcal{P} \circ U(\mathbf{x}) = \mathcal{F}(\mathbf{x}) = \begin{cases} \mathcal{F}_1(\mathbf{x}) \\ \mathcal{F}_2(\mathbf{x}), \end{cases}$$

where again, $\mathcal{F}_1$ consists of the first $m - o_2$, and $\mathcal{F}_2$ of the remaining o_2 coordinates of $V \circ \mathcal{P} \circ U$. Then $\mathcal{F}_1$ only depends on the first $n - o_2$ entries of $\mathbf{x}$: Let $\mathbf{y}$ be a vector whose first $n - o_2$ entries are zero, then $U(\mathbf{y}) \in O_2$, so $\mathcal{F}_1(\mathbf{x}+\mathbf{y}) = \mathcal{F}_1(\mathbf{x}) + \mathcal{P}'_1(U(\mathbf{x}), U(\mathbf{y})) + \mathcal{P}(U(\mathbf{y})) = \mathcal{F}_1(\mathbf{x})$. Moreover, $\mathcal{F}_1$ vanishes on $U^{-1}O_1$, because $\mathcal{P}(O_1) \in W$. So, ignoring the last o_2 coordinates, $\mathcal{F}_1$ has the structure of a UOV public key with $n' = n - o_2$ variables and an oil space of dimension $m' = m - o_2$.

Finding preimages for $\mathcal{P}$ is equivalent to finding preimages for $\mathcal{F}$, since they differ by a change of variables known to the attacker. We now show that finding preimages for $\mathcal{F}$ reduces to finding preimages for $\mathcal{F}_1$: Suppose we are given $\mathbf{t} = (\mathbf{t}_1, \mathbf{t}_2)$ and we want to find $\mathbf{x}$ such that $\mathcal{F}_1(\mathbf{x}) = \mathbf{t}_1$ and $\mathcal{F}_2(\mathbf{x}) = \mathbf{t}_2$. We proceed as follows:

1. Find $\mathbf{x}$ such that $\mathcal{F}_1(\mathbf{x}) = \mathbf{t}_1$ with some attack on UOV with parameters $(n', m') = (n - o_2, m - o_2)$,
2. Solve for $\mathbf{o} \in \mathbb{F}_q^n$ whose first $n - o_2$ entries are zero, such that $\mathcal{F}_2(\mathbf{x}+\mathbf{o}) = \mathbf{t}_2$. This is a system of o_2 linear equations in o_2 variables, because $\mathcal{F}_2(\mathbf{x}+\mathbf{o}) = \mathcal{F}_2(\mathbf{x}) + \mathcal{F}'_2(\mathbf{x}, \mathbf{o})$ is linear in $\mathbf{o}$, so this $\mathbf{o}$ can be found efficiently.
3. Output $\mathbf{x} + \mathbf{o}$. Note that $\mathcal{F}_1(\mathbf{x} + \mathbf{o}) = \mathcal{F}_1(\mathbf{x}) = \mathbf{t}_1$ because $\mathcal{F}_1$ only depends on the first $n - o_2$ variables. So $\mathbf{x} + \mathbf{o}$ is really a solution.

Remark 1. This is exactly how the real signing algorithm works, except that a genuine signer has knowledge of O_1, which allows him to do step 1 efficiency.

For the SL 1 parameter sets of the second-round and third-round NIST submissions, $\mathcal{F}_1$ is a UOV map whose parameters are $(n', m') = (64, 32)$ and $(68, 32)$ respectively. In these cases the Kipnis-Shamir attack [11], which runs in time $q^{n'-2m'} \cdot \text{poly}(n')$, can recover O_1 very efficiently, so we have a full key recovery attack. For the SL 3 and 5 parameter set, the UOV instances can resist known key-recovery attacks, so a full key-recovery attack seems out of reach. However, since $m' = m - o_2$ is relatively small, we can still solve $\mathcal{F}_1(\mathbf{x}) = \mathbf{t}_1$ directly, so we can forge signatures without recovering O_1. For the parameters submitted to NIST the cost of solving $\mathcal{F}_1(\mathbf{x}) = \mathbf{t}_1$ with the Wiedemann XL algorithm is lower than the complexity of finding O_2 and W, so the complexity of the forgery attack is dominated by the cost of finding O_2 and W.

Example 3. The SL1 parameter set of the second-round NIST submission is $q = 16, n = 96, m = 64, o_2 = 32$. To find O_2 and W for this parameter set we need to solve systems of $m - 1 = 63$ homogeneous quadratic equations in $n - m - 1 = 31$ variables, so the estimated cost of solving each system is $2^{52.3}$ multiplications (see Example 1). On average we need to try 15.06 systems. If the cost of one $\mathbb{F}_{16}$-multiplication is 36 gates, then we can estimate that the total average gate cost of finding O_2 and W is $2^{52.3} \cdot 15.06 \cdot 36 \approx 2^{61.4}$. After we found O_2 and W, we are left with a UOV public key with $m' = 32$ equations and $n' = 64$ variables. So O_1 can be found in polynomial time with the Kipnis-Shamir attack [11]. The complexity of the attack is dominated by the first step, which has a complexity of $\approx 2^{61.4}$, as reported in Table 1.

4   Combination with Rectangular MinRank Attack

Even though the simple attack from the previous section is very efficient for the NIST SL 1 parameter sets of Rainbow (because $n - m$ is small), we see in Table 1 that for the SL 3 and SL 5 parameter sets, the new attack does not always outperform the rectangular MinRank attack of Beullens [3]. In this section, we first summarize how the rectangular MinRank attack works, and then we show that it can be made more efficient by combining it with our "guess-$D_\mathbf{x}$" technique.

Rectangular MinRank Attack. Let $\mathbf{e}_1, \cdots, \mathbf{e}_n$ be a basis for $\mathbb{F}_q^n$, and let $\mathcal{P}$ be a Rainbow public key. Then we define n rectangular matrices $L_i \in \mathbb{F}_q^{n \times m}$ as

$$L_i := \begin{pmatrix} \mathcal{P}'(\mathbf{e}_1, \mathbf{e}_i) \\ \cdots \\ \mathcal{P}'(\mathbf{e}_n, \mathbf{e}_i) \end{pmatrix},$$

for all i from 1 to n. Let $\mathbf{o} \in \mathbb{F}_q^n$ be a vector, then since $\mathcal{P}'$ is bilinear, we have that

$$\sum_{i=1}^{n} o_i L_i = \begin{pmatrix} \mathcal{P}'(\mathbf{e}_1, \mathbf{o}) \\ \cdots \\ \mathcal{P}'(\mathbf{e}_n, \mathbf{o}), \end{pmatrix}$$

which has rank at most $\dim(W) = o_2$ if $\mathbf{o} \in O_2$, because all the rows of the matrix are in W.

We have n public matrices of dimensions n-by-m, and we know there exist linear combinations of these matrices that have exceptionally low rank $\leq \dim(W)$, so we have an instance of the MinRank problem. We can now use generic MinRank solvers, such as the algorithms by Bardet et al. [2], to find a linear combination $\mathbf{o} \in \mathbb{F}_q^n$, such that $\sum o_i L_i$ has rank at most o_2. If $\mathbf{o}$ is such a solution, then with overwhelming probability $\mathbf{o} \in O_2$.

Note that every $\mathbf{o} \in O_2$ is a solution to the MinRank problem. Therefore, we can discard $o_2 - 1$ of the matrices, and the span of the remaining $n - o_2 + 1$ matrices will still contain a non-zero matrix of low rank. This is useful because reducing the number of matrices in the MinRank problem reduces the cost of finding a solution.

Once a solution $\mathbf{o} \in O_2$ is found, the security of Rainbow is reduced to the security of a small UOV public key, as explained at the end of section Sect. 3.

Remark 2. We have extra information about the solution $\mathbf{o}$ to the MinRank problem, namely that $\mathcal{P}(\mathbf{o}) = 0$. Beullens [3] shows that the MinRank solving algorithm of Bardet *et al.* [2] can be adapted to take advantage of this extra information. This reduces the cost of the attack by a small factor between 2^2 and 2^9 for the Rainbow parameters submitted to NIST.

Combined Attack. The combined attack is straightforward. We choose a random $\mathbf{x} \in \mathbb{F}_q^n$, and then we solve for a vector $\mathbf{o} \in \ker(D_\mathbf{x})$, such that $\sum o_i L_i$ has rank at most o_2. We can use the $D_\mathbf{x}\mathbf{o} = 0$ equations to reduce the number of matrices in the MinRank problem by m. Concretely, let $\mathbf{b}_1, \ldots, \mathbf{b}_{n-m}$ be a basis for $\ker(D_\mathbf{x})$, then we consider the $n - m$ matrices

$$\tilde{L}_i := \sum_{j=1}^n b_{ij} L_j = \begin{pmatrix} \mathcal{P}'(\mathbf{e}_1, \mathbf{b}_i) \\ \cdots \\ \mathcal{P}'(\mathbf{e}_n, \mathbf{b}_i) \end{pmatrix},$$

for all i from 1 to $n - m$. Now $\mathbf{o} = \sum x_i \mathbf{b}_i \in \ker(D_\mathbf{x})$ is a solution to the original MinRank problem if and only if $\mathbf{x}$ is a solution to the new MinRank problem with $n - m$ matrices $\tilde{L}_1, \ldots, \tilde{L}_{n-m}$.

The advantage of this approach is that we now have a MinRank problem with only $n - m$ matrices, which makes finding the solution much easier compared to the original rectangular MinRank attack, where we had $n - o_2 + 1$ matrices. This comes at the cost of having to repeat the attack on average approximately q times, until $\ker(D_\mathbf{x}) \cap O_2 \neq \{0\}$.

Experiments (see Appendix A) reveal that the MinRank instance $\tilde{L}_1, \ldots, \tilde{L}_{n-m}$ does not behave like a random MinRank instance. Upon inspection we see that this is because for all $\tilde{L}_i$, we have

$$\mathbf{x}\tilde{L}_i = \mathcal{P}'(\mathbf{x}, \mathbf{b}_i) = D_\mathbf{x}\mathbf{b}_i = 0.$$

That is, there is a common linear dependency shared by all the $\tilde{L}_i$ matrices. This means that one of the rows is not contributing any information to the MinRank problem. For example, if $x_1 \neq 0$, then the first row of $\sum o_i \tilde{L}_i$ is just a linear combination of the other rows, which means we can safely delete this first row without affecting the rank of $\sum o_i \tilde{L}_i$. After deleting a row from the $\tilde{L}_i$ we get a MinRank problem with $n - m$ matrices of size $(n-1)$-by-m, and for which there exists a solution of rank o_2 if the guess of $D_\mathbf{x}$ was good. Our rank experiments show that this system behaves exactly like a random MinRank instance in fields of odd characteristic. In fields of characteristic two, we occasionally observe some rank defects (see Appendix A). Since the observed defects are small, we believe that the complexity of solving random MinRank instances is a good estimate for the complexity of solving the MinRank instances coming from a Rainbow public key. We leave the investigation of the rank defects and quantifying how much is gained by adding the $\mathcal{P}(\mathbf{o}) = 0$ equations for future work.

Example 4. We estimate the cost of the combined attack against the SL 5 parameter set from the second-round submission to NIST. This parameter set is $q = 256, n = 188, m = 96, o_2 = 48$. This means that after guessing a good $D_{\mathbf{x}}$ (which happens with probability of approximately $1/255$), we get a MinRank instance of $n - m = 92$ matrices with $n - 1 = 187$ rows and $m = 96$ columns, whose span contains a non-zero matrix of rank $o_2 = 48$. Solving this MinRank instance with the algorithm of Bardet *et al.* costs $2^{149.1}$ field multiplications (see Example 2). If the gate cost of a $\mathbb{F}_{256}$-multiplication is 128, then the total expected gate cost of finding O_2 and W is $2^{149.1} \cdot 128 \cdot 255 \approx 2^{164.1}$. Once O_2 and W are known, the security is reduced to the security of a UOV public key $\mathcal{F}_1$ with $m' = 48$ equations and $n' = 140$ variables. A system $\mathcal{F}_1(\mathbf{x}) = \mathbf{t}_1$ can be solved directly with the Wiedemann XL algorithm with an estimated gate cost of $2^{158.6}$, so the total cost of the forgery attack is $2^{158.6} + 2^{164.1} \approx 2^{164.1}$, as reported in Table 1. This is an improvement by a factor 2^{27} over previously known attacks.

5   Experimental Results and Conclusion

To validate our attack and showcase that the attack is efficient enough to be performed in practice, we implemented a Sage script that generates a Rainbow public key, guesses a vector $\mathbf{x} \in \mathbb{F}_q^n$, and constructs (in fields of odd characteristic) the system $\tilde{\mathcal{P}}$ as described in Sect. 3, and writes it to a file in the format readable by the optimized implementation of the block Wiedemann XL algorithm by Cheng, Chou, Niederhagen, and Yang [5]. In fields of characteristic two, the script instead constructs and stores the slightly smaller $\hat{\mathcal{P}}$ system. We then run the block Wiedemann XL algorithm on the stored systems, and find that it indeed finds solutions to $\tilde{\mathcal{P}}(\mathbf{x}) = 0$ (resp. $\hat{\mathcal{P}}(\mathbf{x}) = 0$) if the solutions exist.

The SL 1 parameter set of the second-round Rainbow submission is ($q = 16, n = 96, m = 64, o_2 = 32$). For these parameters solving $\hat{\mathcal{P}}(\mathbf{x}) = 0$ takes three hours and 32 min on a laptop using the 8 cores of an Intel i9-10885H CPU, running at 2.5 GHz. The block Wiedemann XL implementation reports on the rate at which it does $\mathbb{F}_{16}$-multiplications, which fluctuates between 130 and 200 multiplications per cycle. This is consistent with the estimate that solving the system takes $2^{52.3}$ multiplications (Example 1). Solving the system only uses 1 1 GD of memory. Since each guess $\mathbf{x}$ leads to a key recovery with a probability of $1/15.06$, the total expected running time of the attack is $15.06 \cdot 3.53 \approx 53$ h.

We can use the knowledge of the secret key to determine if a guess for $\mathbf{x}$ is good (i.e., if $\ker(D_{\mathbf{x}}) \cap O_2 \neq \{0\}$) without doing the expensive system-solving computation. This allows us to try a large number of guesses and count how often a guess is good. We made 4000 guesses and found that 242 of them are good, which is consistent with the null hypothesis of $1/15.06$ (with a one-sided p-value of 0.085).

We implemented the full attack in a Sage script that makes calls to the optimized system-solving implementation of [5]. This includes a naive Sage implementation of the Kipnis-Shamir attack to break the UOV instance obtained by removing the outer layer of the Rainbow public key. We ran the key recovery attack for the SL1 parameters from the second-round NIST submission. We were somewhat unlucky and it took 20 attempts before we had a success. (The probability of not succeeding in the first 19 attempts is $(14/15)^{19} = 0.27$.) After the first successful WXL step, our script was able to recover the full secret key after $22\,\mathrm{s}$, which is negligible compared to the cost of solving the 20 systems. The sage implementation of our attack and scripts for reproducing the rank experiments of Appendix A are available at

https://github.com/WardBeullens/BreakingRainbow

We can conclude that the cost and success probability of the attack in practice agree very well with what the theory predicts. Moreover, we demonstrated that a key-recovery against the SL 1 parameter set of the second-round submission of Rainbow can be performed in practice by anyone with a decent laptop and some patience (or luck). A key-recovery attack against the SL 1 parameter set of the third-round Rainbow submission is expected to be more costly by only a factor 2^8, so this should be feasible for an attacker with a moderate amount of resources.

In principle, it would be possible to move to larger parameters to protect against the attacks presented in this paper, at the cost of larger key sizes and signature sizes. E.g., the SL 3 parameters of the third-round submission seem to provide enough security for SL 1, but those parameters have signatures and public keys that are larger by a factor 2.5 and 4.4 respectively compared to the SL 1 parameters. However, there seems to be some room for improvement for the attacks in Sect. 4, so more cryptanalysis would be required before we can have confidence in the security of Rainbow. Moreover, the resulting Rainbow signature scheme would be less efficient than the Oil and Vinegar scheme. So there is seemingly no reason to prefer Rainbow over the Oil and Vinegar scheme [15], on which Rainbow is based, and which is older, simpler, and has a strictly smaller attack surface in comparison to Rainbow. (E.g., none of the attacks in this paper seem to apply to the Oil and Vinegar scheme).

A Rank Experiments

Simple Attack. For some rainbow parameter sets over $\mathbb{F}_{31}$ we construct some $\tilde{\mathcal{P}}(\mathbf{x}) = 0$ systems as in our simple attack, and compute the ranks of Macaulay matrices of these systems at various degrees. These ranks are displayed in Table 2. Similarly, for some rainbow parameters over $\mathbb{F}_{16}$, we construct some $\hat{\mathcal{P}}(\mathbf{x}) = 0$ systems, and we displayed the ranks of their Macaulay matrices in Table 3. We observe in both cases that the ranks are identical to the ranks of systems of uniformly random quadratic equations with the same dimensions. I.e., if $\tilde{\mathcal{P}}(\mathbf{x})$ (or $\hat{\mathcal{P}}(\mathbf{x})$) has m equations and n variables, then the rank of its Macaulay matrix at degree D is equal to the coefficient of t^D in the power series expansion of

$$(1 - t)^n (1 - (1 - t^2)^m),$$

if this coefficient is positive. Otherwise, the system has a kernel of dimension 1, which corresponds to the 1-dimensional space of solutions. This is evidence that the $\tilde{\mathcal{P}}(\mathbf{x}) = 0$ and $\hat{\mathcal{P}}(\mathbf{x}) = 0$ systems do not have special properties that make them easier or harder to solve in comparison with random systems.

Combined Attack. Table 4 reports on some of our rank experiments for the combined attack. For some small Rainbow parameter sets, we executed the combined attack from Sect. 4 to derive a MinRank instance with $n - m$ matrices with $n - 1$ rows and m columns (of which we keep m'). Then we constructed the linearized systems as they appear in the MinRank solving algorithm of Bardet *et al.* at several bi-degrees $(b, 1)$, and we compute their ranks. We found that in odd characteristic, the rank of the Macaulay matrices always matches those of random MinRank instances with the same parameters. In contrast, we sometimes observe a small rank defect in characteristic two (they are underlined in the Table 4).

Table 2. The rank and the number of columns of the Macaulay matrices for the $\tilde{\mathcal{P}}(\mathbf{x}) = 0$ system of equations of simple attack over $\mathbb{F}_{31}$. Ranks of the Macaulay matrix of degree D is given in boldface if the system can be solved at that degree.

Rainbow parameters			$\tilde{\mathcal{P}}$ size			Rank of Macaulay matrix at degree D		
n	m	o_2	m	n		$D = 2$	$D = 3$	$D = 4$
30	20	10	20	10	rank	20	200	**714**
					columns	55	220	715
45	30	15	30	15	rank	30	450	**3059**
					columns	120	680	3060
60	40	20	40	20	rank	40	800	7620
					columns	210	1540	8855

Table 3. The rank and the number of columns of the Macaulay matrices for the $\hat{\mathcal{P}}(\mathbf{x}) = 0$ system of equations of simple attack over $\mathbb{F}_{16}$. Ranks of the Macaulay matrix of degree D is given in boldface if the system can be solved at that degree.

Rainbow parameters			$\hat{\mathcal{P}}$ size				Rank of Macaulay matrix at degree D		
n	m	o_2	m	n			$D = 2$	$D = 3$	$D = 4$
30	20	10	19	9	rank		19	**164**	
					columns		45	165	
36	24	12	23	11	rank		23	253	**1000**
					columns		66	286	1001
42	28	14	27	13	rank		27	351	**1819**
					columns		91	455	1820

Table 4. The rank and the number of columns of the Macaulay matrices for the MinRank problems from the combined attack over $\mathbb{F}_{31}$ and $\mathbb{F}_{16}$. Ranks of the Macaulay matrix at bi-degree $(b, 1)$ is given in boldface if the system can be solved at that bi-degree.

Rainbow parameters			MinRank parameters			Rank of Macaulay matrix at bi-degree $(b, 1)$		
n	m	o_2	k	m'		$b = 1$	$b = 2$	$b = 3$
					rank in $\mathbb{F}_{31}$	**279**		
15	10	5	5	8	rank in $\mathbb{F}_{16}$	**279**		
					columns	280		
					rank in $\mathbb{F}_{31}$	98	**314**	
15	10	5	5	7	rank in $\mathbb{F}_{16}$	98	**314**	
					columns	105	315	
					rank in $\mathbb{F}_{31}$	78	533	**1799**
14	6	4	8	6	rank in $\mathbb{F}_{16}$	78	<u>527</u>	**1799**
					columns	120	540	1800

References

1. Baena, J., Briaud, P., Cabarcas, D., Perlner, R., Smith-Tone, D., Verbel, J.: Improving support-minors rank attacks: applications to GeMSS and rainbow. Cryptology ePrint Archive, Report 2021/1677 (2021). https://eprint.iacr.org/2021/1677
2. Bardet, M., et al.: Improvements of algebraic attacks for solving the rank decoding and MinRank problems. In: Moriai, S., Wang, H. (eds.) ASIACRYPT 2020, Part I. LNCS, vol. 12491, pp. 507–536. Springer, Cham (2020). https://doi.org/10.1007/978-3-030-64837-4_17

3. Beullens, W.: Improved cryptanalysis of UOV and rainbow. In: Canteaut, A., Standaert, F.-X. (eds.) EUROCRYPT 2021, Part I. LNCS, vol. 12696, pp. 348–373. Springer, Cham (2021). https://doi.org/10.1007/978-3-030-77870-5_13

4. Billet, O., Gilbert, H.: Cryptanalysis of rainbow. In: De Prisco, R., Yung, M. (eds.) SCN 2006. LNCS, vol. 4116, pp. 336–347. Springer, Heidelberg (2006). https://doi.org/10.1007/11832072_23

5. Cheng, C.-M., Chou, T., Niederhagen, R., Yang, B.-Y.: Solving quadratic equations with XL on parallel architectures. In: Prouff, E., Schaumont, P. (eds.) CHES 2012. LNCS, vol. 7428, pp. 356–373. Springer, Heidelberg (2012). https://doi.org/10.1007/978-3-642-33027-8_21

6. Courtois, N., Klimov, A., Patarin, J., Shamir, A.: Efficient algorithms for solving overdefined systems of multivariate polynomial equations. In: Preneel, B. (ed.) EUROCRYPT 2000. LNCS, vol. 1807, pp. 392–407. Springer, Heidelberg (2000). https://doi.org/10.1007/3-540-45539-6_27

7. Ding, J., Schmidt, D.: Rainbow, a new multivariable polynomial signature scheme. In: Ioannidis, J., Keromytis, A., Yung, M. (eds.) ACNS 2005. LNCS, vol. 3531, pp. 164–175. Springer, Heidelberg (2005). https://doi.org/10.1007/11496137_12

8. Ding, J., Yang, B.-Y., Chen, C.-H.O., Chen, M.-S., Cheng, C.-M.: New differential-algebraic attacks and reparametrization of rainbow. In: Bellovin, S.M., Gennaro, R., Keromytis, A., Yung, M. (eds.) ACNS 2008. LNCS, vol. 5037, pp. 242–257. Springer, Heidelberg (2008). https://doi.org/10.1007/978-3-540-68914-0_15

9. Goubin, L., Courtois, N.T.: Cryptanalysis of the TTM cryptosystem. In: Okamoto, T. (ed.) ASIACRYPT 2000. LNCS, vol. 1976, pp. 44–57. Springer, Heidelberg (2000). https://doi.org/10.1007/3-540-44448-3_4

10. Kipnis, A., Patarin, J., Goubin, L.: Unbalanced oil and vinegar signature schemes. In: Stern, J. (ed.) EUROCRYPT 1999. LNCS, vol. 1592, pp. 206–222. Springer, Heidelberg (1999). https://doi.org/10.1007/3-540-48910-X_15

11. Kipnis, A., Shamir, A.: Cryptanalysis of the oil and vinegar signature scheme. In: Krawczyk, H. (ed.) CRYPTO 1998. LNCS, vol. 1462, pp. 257–266. Springer, Heidelberg (1998). https://doi.org/10.1007/BFb0055733

12. Kipnis, A., Shamir, A.: Cryptanalysis of the HFE public key cryptosystem by relinearization. In: Wiener, M. (ed.) CRYPTO 1999. LNCS, vol. 1666, pp. 19–30. Springer, Heidelberg (1999). https://doi.org/10.1007/3-540-48405-1_2

13. Lazard, D.: Gröbner bases, Gaussian elimination and resolution of systems of algebraic equations. In: van Hulzen, J.A. (ed.) EUROCAL 1983. LNCS, vol. 162, pp. 146–156. Springer, Heidelberg (1983). https://doi.org/10.1007/3-540-12868-9_99

14. Mohamed, W.S.A., Ding, J., Kleinjung, T., Bulygin, S., Buchmann, J.: PWXL: a parallel Wiedemann-XL algorithm for solving polynomial equations over GF(2). In: Conference on Symbolic Computation and Cryptography, p. 89 (2010)

15. Patarin, J.: The oil and vinegar signature scheme. In: Dagstuhl Workshop on Cryptography, September 1997 (1997)

16. Perlner, R., Smith-Tone, D.: Rainbow band separation is better than we thought. Cryptology ePrint Archive, Report 2020/702 (2020). https://eprint.iacr.org/2020/702

17. Response to recent paper by Ward Beullens (2020). https://troll.iis.sinica.edu.tw/by-publ/recent/response-ward.pdf

18. Yang, B.-Y., Chen, J.-M.: Building secure tame-like multivariate public-key cryptosystems: the new TTS. In: Boyd, C., González Nieto, J.M. (eds.) ACISP 2005. LNCS, vol. 3574, pp. 518–531. Springer, Heidelberg (2005). https://doi.org/10.1007/11506157_43

Some Easy Instances of Ideal-SVP and Implications on the Partial Vandermonde Knapsack Problem

Katharina Boudgoust[1(✉)], Erell Gachon[2], and Alice Pellet-Mary[2]

[1] Aarhus University, Aarhus, Denmark
katharina.boudgoust@cs.dk.au
[2] Univ. Bordeaux, CNRS, INRIA, Bordeaux INP, IMB, UMR 5251,
33400 Talence, France
erell.gachon@u-bordeaux.fr, alice.pellet-mary@math.u-bordeaux.fr

Abstract. In this article, we generalize the works of Pan et al. (Eurocrypt'21) and Porter et al. (ArXiv'21) and provide a *simple* condition under which an ideal lattice defines an easy instance of the shortest vector problem. Namely, we show that the more automorphisms stabilize the ideal, the easier it is to find a short vector in it. This observation was already made for prime ideals in Galois fields, and we generalize it to *any* ideal (whose prime factors are not ramified) of *any* number field.

We then provide a cryptographic application of this result by showing that particular instances of the partial Vandermonde knapsack problem, also known as partial Fourier recovery problem, can be solved classically in polynomial time. As a proof of concept, we implemented our attack and managed to solve those particular instances for concrete parameter settings proposed in the literature. For random instances, we can halve the lattice dimension with non-negligible probability.

1 Introduction

Euclidean lattices are mathematical objects that play an important role in many areas of mathematics and computer science. There are several computational problems related to lattices that are proven to be NP-hard, for instance, the problem of finding a shortest vector (SVP) or a set of shortest independent vectors (SIVP) in a given lattice. A standard relaxation consists in solving them only up to some approximation factor $\gamma \geq 1$, denoted γ-S(I)VP. It is commonly conjectured that the problems remain hard to solve for approximation factors that are polynomial in the lattice rank. Their presumed intractability provides a fundamental starting point for the construction of provably secure cryptographic schemes, shown in the seminal works of Ajtai [Ajt96] and Regev [Reg05].

Unfortunately, all cryptographic schemes relying on the hardness of those lattice problems inherently suffer from large keys and slow computation times, being quadratic in the security parameter. In order to improve efficiency, problems on *structured* lattices have been introduced, e.g., [Mic02,LM06,PR06,SSTX09,

© International Association for Cryptologic Research 2022
Y. Dodis and T. Shrimpton (Eds.): CRYPTO 2022, LNCS 13508, pp. 480–509, 2022.
https://doi.org/10.1007/978-3-031-15979-4_17

LPR10,LS15]. The most popular setting is to consider O_K-modules of rank r, where O_K is the ring of integers of some number field K of degree d. By applying the d different field embeddings from K to $\mathbb{C}$, any O_K-module of rank r is mapped to a lattice of rank $d \cdot r$. Those lattices inherit the module structure (i.e., closed with respect to scalar multiplication by ring elements) and are called *module lattices*. If the module rank equals 1, they are called *ideal lattices*.

Many structured lattice assumptions, such as Ring-LWE [SSTX09,LPR10], NTRU [HPS98] or Module-LWE [LS15] can be solved with an SVP solver in module lattices of small rank (≥ 2). This motivates the study of the hardness of SVP in module lattices. To start tackling this problem, many algorithms have focused on the special case of solving SVP in rank-1 modules, that is in ideals. This restricted problem is denoted by Id-SVP. While solving Id-SVP is not known to break any of the three lattice assumptions mentioned above, studying this (potentially easier) problem can be seen as a first step to better understand the hardness behind algebraically structured lattices. Another motivation for studying Id-SVP comes from the fact that the first hardness result for Ring-LWE was a reduction from worst-case Id-SVP [SSTX09,LPR10]. This reduction only provides a lower bound on the hardness of Ring-LWE, and we have today a stronger reduction, from worst-case SVP in modules of rank ≥ 2, for some more restricted regime of parameters of Ring-LWE [AD17]. Still, even if an efficient algorithm for Id-SVP would not have a direct impact on the security of Ring-LWE, it would make the reduction from Id-SVP vacuous, and hence let some interesting regime of Ring-LWE without lower bound security guarantees.

Even though most of the lattice-based cryptographic schemes are not known to reduce to SVP in ideal lattices (but in module lattices of rank ≥ 2), there are a few counter-examples. They can be found among the first constructions of FHE schemes by Gentry [Gen09] or, as we will see below, in the constructions based on the partial Vandermonde knapsack problem [HPS+14] (also known as the partial Fourier recovery problem).

Hardness of Id-SVP. The hardness of Id-SVP has attracted a lot of work in recent years. On the one hand, some works have proven worst-case to average-case reductions for problems in ideal lattices [Gen09,dBDPW20]. They proved that there exist distributions over the set of ideal lattices such that an ideal chosen from this distribution is "as hard as possible". More formally, if one can solve Id-SVP for such random lattices with non-negligible probability, then one can solve Id-SVP in any ideal lattice.

On the other hand, several works have shown weaknesses of Id-SVP for specific choices of ideals or parameters. Cramer et al. [CDPR16] showed that Id-SVP can be solved in quantum polynomial time for *principal* ideals (i.e., ideals generated by a single ring element) of cyclotomic fields, when the generator is sampled from a Gaussian distribution. It is also known that the relaxed variant of Id-SVP with a large approximation factor $\approx 2^{\sqrt{d}}$ can be solved in quantum polynomial time in cyclotomic fields of degree d [CDW21]. In 2021, Pan et al. [PXWC21] showed that, for some prime ideals with a lot of symmetries (in Galois number fields), the Id-SVP problem can be solved classically in polynomial time, with a polynomial approximation factor. This was extended by Porter et al. [PML21, Theorem 3] to a larger class of ideals, whose characterization is harder to state and relies on factoring properties of the ideal, as well as its algebraic norm.

Finally, there is a line of work targeting Id-SVP for all ideals of all number fields, for various approximation factors [PHS19, BR20, BLNR21]. However, the algorithms require an exponential-time pre-processing, and are at the moment no better than lattice reduction algorithms that work on unstructured lattices (e.g. BKZ).

Partial Vandermonde Knapsack. In the late 90's, Hoffman et al. [HKJL+00] patented a method for user identification and digital signatures based on the difficulty of recovering a constrained polynomial from partial information. Afterwards, the partial information was specified as a partial list of the polynomial's Fourier transform resulting in a signature scheme called PASS Sign [HPS+14]. The constraint regarding the polynomial was to choose its coefficients uniformly at random over a bounded set. Lu et al. [LZA18] moved from the Fourier transform (evaluation at all roots of unity) over cyclic rings to the Vandermonde transform (evaluation only at the *primitive* roots of unity) over cyclotomic rings.

The hardness assumption that underlies PASS Sign, as given in [LZA18], is the following. Let q be a prime and let m be an integer such that there exists a primitive m-th root of unity in the quotient ring $\mathbb{Z}_q := \mathbb{Z}/q\mathbb{Z}$. In this case, there exist exactly $d = \phi(m)$ such primitive roots $\{\omega_j\}_{1 \le j \le d}$, where ϕ is Euler's totient function. Further, let $g(X)$ be a polynomial of degree less than d having small integer coefficients. Its Vandermonde transform $\mathbf{V}(g) \in \mathbb{Z}_q^d$ is defined as $g(\omega_j)_{1 \le j \le d} \bmod q$. For a subset $\Omega \subseteq \{1, \ldots, d\}$ of size t, its partial Vandermonde transform $\mathbf{V}_\Omega(g) \in \mathbb{Z}_q^t$ is given by $g(\omega_j)_{j \in \Omega}$. The partial Vandermonde knapsack problem (PV-Knap) asks, given $\mathbf{V}_\Omega(g)$, to recover $g(X)$.[1]

As observed by Boudgoust et al. [BSS22, Bou21], recovering a short polynomial while having access only to a partial list of its Vandermonde transform can be seen as a problem over an ideal lattice. More precisely, in the mathematical setting above, we know that the ideal generated by q in the m-th cyclotomic ring $O_K = \mathbb{Z}[X]/\Phi_m(X)$ completely splits into d prime ideals, where $\Phi_m(X)$ denotes the m-th cyclotomic polynomial.[2] More precisely, it yields $qO_K = \prod_{j=1}^d \mathfrak{p}_j$, where $\mathfrak{p}_j = qO_K + (X - \omega_j)O_K$. Providing the evaluations $g(\omega_j)_{j \in \Omega}$ corresponds to specifying the coset $h := g \bmod I_\Omega$ with respect to the ideal $I_\Omega := \prod_{j \in \Omega} \mathfrak{p}_j$. Hence, PV-Knap essentially requires to recover g (with small coefficients) given h, which yields a problem over ideal lattices.

Contributions. The results of this work can be divided into three different parts. First, we show in Sect. 3 that Id-SVP can be solved efficiently for ideal lattices with a lot of symmetries, generalizing the results of [PXWC21, PML21].

---

[1] In this paper, we only consider regimes where the solution to this problem is unique.

[2] For the sake of simplicity, we focus on cyclotomic fields in the introduction but stress that PV-Knap can be defined over any number field.

We then show in Sect. 4 that there exist *bad* instances of PV-Knap, that are easy to solve using the algorithm above. Last, we present the results of our implemented attacks against different parameter sets and design choices for PV-Knap proposed in the literature (Sect. 5).

Contribution 1. In [PXWC21], the authors identified a class of "bad ideal lattices", i.e., ideal lattices in which Id-SVP can be solved efficiently with a polynomial approximation factor: *prime* ideals in Galois number fields that are above a prime of $\mathbb{Q}$ splitting into many prime factors. This result was later extended to a larger class of ideals (not necessarily prime) in [PML21, Theorem 3]. However, the characterization of the bad ideal lattices of [PML21] is significantly more complex than the one in [PXWC21], and depends on the algebraic norm of the ideal, as well as some hard to compute quantities, related to the ideal's prime decomposition. In this work, we improve upon those results in two ways:

1. we obtain a very simple sufficient condition for an ideal to be a bad ideal;
2. the class of bad ideals that we obtain from this simple condition contains the ones of [PXWC21] and [PML21], while being strictly larger.

We observe that the condition "a prime ideal is above a prime of $\mathbb{Q}$ splitting into many prime factors" from [PXWC21] can be rephrased more simply as a condition on the prime ideal having many symmetries (this observation was also made in [PML21]). By symmetry we mean here that the prime ideal is fixed (as a set) when applying an automorphism of the number field K in which the ideal lives. With this, we are able to generalize the result of [PXWC21] to *any* ideal (modulo a small condition on their algebraic norm) in *any* number field (not necessarily Galois).

Overall, we obtain the following result (informally stated here, see Theorem 3.1 for a formal statement): one can solve Id-SVP in an ideal lattice I in time roughly $\exp(d/n_I)$, where d is the degree of the number field K and n_I is the number of automorphisms of K that fix I as a set (this is an integer between 1 and d). If I has no symmetries, then $n_I = 1$ (I is always fixed by the identity), and we recover the run times of standard lattice reduction algorithms. This result can also be extended to approximation variants of Id-SVP, leading to an algorithm with approximation factor $\gamma \geq 1$ and time roughly $\exp(d/(n_I \cdot \log(\gamma)))$.

Testing whether an ideal I is fixed by an automorphism τ of K can be done efficiently if we have a description of τ and a basis of I. Contrary to previous works, this does not require any knowledge about the factorization of the ideal I. Hence, our characterization of bad ideals can be easily checked and may be useful to cryptographers introducing new assumptions related to ideal lattices.

We note that [PML21] also provides at the bottom of p.14 a simplified condition for their result, which does not require the knowledge of the factorization of I, but still depends on its algebraic norm. This simplified condition however is quite loose, and our simple condition above captures more ideals. This is for instance the case for ideals I of norm $\geq 2^d$ which have many symmetries but whose prime factors have individually very few symmetries: our condition shows that these ideals are bad, whereas the condition of [PML21] does not capture them. Looking ahead, this special family of ideals is exactly the one arising when we transform a PV-Knap instance into an Id-SVP instance.

The fact that Id-SVP is easier to solve in lattices fixed by automorphisms of K is not very surprising. Indeed, we know that an element of K fixed by some automorphisms is actually an element from a subfield of K of smaller dimension. The same holds for ideals: an ideal I fixed by n_I automorphisms can be seen as an ideal in a subfield L of K (this formulation requires some care, it is made formal in Lemma 3.3, which is the main new technical material of this contribution), whose degree is exactly d/n_I (the more automorphisms, the smaller the degree of L). When looking for a short vector in I, one can consider I as an ideal of L instead of K, i.e., a lattice of smaller dimension d/n_I.

Finally, we remark that the results of [PXWC21, PML21] in all Galois fields are only mathematical results characterizing bad ideals and not algorithms. Both works then used this mathematical result to provide an Id-SVP algorithm, but they did so only in cyclotomic number fields. Generalizing the algorithm to other number fields was left as an open problem in [PXWC21, Remark 1]. In this work, we provide both the mathematical result (Theorem 3.2) and the algorithm (Theorem 3.1) for all number fields.

We would like to stress again that our algorithm only solves specific instances of Id-SVP. Hence, it does not have any implications to the hardness of structured problems such as Ring-SIS or Ring-LWE, as their hardness is based on the *worst-case* hardness of Id-SVP, and the reductions are only one-way.

Contribution 2. We now explain how the algorithm above can be used to solve some particular instances of PV-Knap in polynomial time. Recall that PV-Knap asks to recover $g \in O_K$ of small coefficients given $g \bmod I_\Omega$ for the ideal I_Ω. Note that it is easy to find a $g' \in O_K$ of unbounded coefficients such that $g' = g \bmod I_\Omega$. Thus, solving PV-Knap essentially requires to find the (unique) element $h' \in I_\Omega$ that is "close" to g', that is $g' - h' = g$. When interpreting the ideal I_Ω as an ideal lattice, this yields an instance of the bounded distance decoding problem (BDD), as we show in Sect. 4.1. We then argue in Sect. 4.2 that BDD in any ideal I reduces to SVP in its inverse ideal I^{-1}. To do so, we first use Babai's rounding algorithm to reduce BDD in I to SIVP in its dual $I^\vee$. Then, we use that for ideal lattices SIVP reduces to SVP and that we can go from the dual $I^\vee$ to the inverse I^{-1}. All lattice problems are considered with respect to an approximation factor that we specify for general number fields in Lemma 4.1. We provide simplified parameter conditions for power-of-two and prime cyclotomics (Corollary 4.2 and 4.3). We conclude this part by providing in Sect. 4.3 concrete choices of Ω for which we obtain a polynomial time algorithm that solves PV-Knap in I_Ω (using the results from Sect. 3).

Contribution 3. As a third contribution, we implemented the algorithm of Sect. 3 in SageMath and used the observations of Sect. 4 to solve PV-Knap over cyclotomic fields for different choices of Ω. Globally, we tested our attack for two different strategies on how to select Ω. In the first scenario, the set Ω is chosen in an advantageous way (for the attacker) to make the related PV-Knap problem easy. More concretely, we choose Ω so that I_Ω is stable by many automorphisms of the underlying number field K. Our experimental results confirm our asymptotic results from Sect. 4. Applied to different parameter sets that were proposed in the literature [HPS+14, LZA18], we can solve PV-Knap in few minutes or even in few seconds. In the second scenario, we study the case where Ω is chosen at random. For random Ω, the ideal I_Ω is with overwhelming probability not stable by any non-trivial subgroup of the Galois group of K. Thus, one might think that our algorithm won't improve the cryptanalysis of PV-Knap in this case. Perhaps surprisingly, we can still use our algorithm to distinguish PV-Knap instances from random instances with non-negligible probability. The main idea is to forget some of the i's in the set Ω. In general, reducing the size of Ω makes the problem harder, since our target BDD instance lies now in a denser lattice. However, by carefully discarding some elements of Ω, we may hope to obtain a subset Ω' such that $I_{\Omega'}$ is stable by some non-trivial automorphism, hence reducing the dimension of the ideals by some (small) factor. Overall, we observe that for all sets of parameters that we considered, there is a non-negligible probability to sample a random Ω for which one can reduce the dimension of the lattice problem by a factor 2. Finally, we run a full distinguishing attack on the smaller parameter set of [LZA18], which was supposed to provide 128 bits of security. Using the model of [MW18] for bit-security, we show that this set of parameters actually provides at most 87 bits of security against distinguishing attackers. We describe all results of our experiments in more details in Sect. 5.

Implications to Cryptography

Id-SVP *Algorithm.* As explained above, our Id-SVP algorithm only provides improvement compared to standard lattice reduction algorithms if the ideal I is fixed by at least one non-trivial automorphism of K. This is a strong requirement on the ideal, and we expect that random ideals do not usually satisfy this condition (for most of the natural distributions on ideals, such as uniform ideals of norm bounded by some bound B). We note however that choosing ideal lattices with a lot of symmetries may be tempting for cryptographic constructions, as this may lead to faster algorithms. We see our results as a warning to cryptographers: one should not use ideal lattices with symmetries. The exhibition of bad instances of PV-Knap is an illustration of such misuse of ideal lattices.

Summing up, we believe that cryptographers willing to introduce new assumptions based on Id-SVP should follow the following guidelines:

1. check if the scheme can be modified such that the underlying rank increases from 1 to 2 in order to rely on Mod-SVP instead of Id-SVP;
2. if not possible, use random ideals sampled from one of the distributions for which we have a worst-case to average-case reduction [Gen09, dBDPW20];
3. if also not possible, then avoid the known bad ideals: ideals generated by an element sampled from a Gaussian distribution in a cyclotomic number field [CDPR16, CDW21] or ideals fixed by some non-trivial automorphism of the number field (this work);

4. in both cases, do not rely on the hardness of Id-SVP for approximation factors larger than $2^{\sqrt{d}}$ in cyclotomic fields, with d the degree of the number field [CDW21].

PV-Knap *Attacks*. As described above, PV-Knap was first studied in the context of the signature scheme PASS Sign [HPS+14,LZA18]. Its key generation algorithm constructs an instance of PV-Knap (over either cyclic or cyclotomic rings), where the secret key is a ternary polynomial and the public key is given by a partial list of its Fourier/Vandermonde coefficients. Hence, solving the search variant of such PV-Knap instances translates to secret key recovery attacks against PASS Sign. In 2015, Hoffstein and Silverman [HS15] designed a public key encryption scheme called PASS Encrypt whose mathematical building blocks resemble those of PASS Sign. Later, the scheme was slightly modified in order to provide a proof of security with respect to concretely defined hardness assumptions by Boudgoust et al. [BSS22], accessible via one of the author's thesis manuscript [Bou21, Ch. 5+7]. In both variants, the key generation algorithms are the same as for PASS Sign, and thus, solving PV-Knap similarly leads to a secret key recovery attack against PASS Encrypt. Doröz et al. [DHSS20] used PASS Sign to design a signature scheme offering public aggregation of signatures independently issued from different users on different messages, called MMSA(TK). An attacker who is able to recover the secret key of a given "challenge" public key clearly violates the security notion used for aggregate signatures.

We would like to highlight again that our attacks on PV-Knap only impact some specific choices of the set Ω, or decrease the lattice dimension by a factor 2 when Ω is randomly chosen. Hence, they can be prevented by choosing Ω carefully (for instance randomly) and possibly increasing the dimension slightly.

2   Preliminaries

Vectors and matrices are written respectively in bold small letters and bold capital letters. Given a vector $\mathbf{v}$ in $\mathbb{R}^n$ or in $\mathbb{C}^n$, we denote $\|\mathbf{v}\|$ its Euclidean norm (or Hermitian norm if $\mathbf{v}$ has complex coordinates) and $\|\mathbf{v}\|_\infty$ its infinity norm. For a matrix $\mathbf{M}$, we write $\mathbf{M}^T$ for its transposed matrix. By default, we consider matrices with column vectors.

2.1   Number Fields

In this section we recall some definitions and properties about number fields and Galois theory that are used in the article. More information can be found in [Mar77, Chapters 2-4 and Appendix B].

A number field K is a field of the form $K = \mathbb{Q}[X]/f(X)$, where $f(X)$ is irreducible over $\mathbb{Q}$. The degree of K is its dimension as a $\mathbb{Q}$-vector space, which is equal to the degree of f (hence, it is always finite). In this article, K and L

always refer to number fields, with K of degree d. When $L \subseteq K$, we say that K is a field extension of L and write K/L. We let $[K : L]$ denote the degree of the extension, that is the dimension of K as an L-vector space. The degree of a tower of extensions $K/L/M$ is multiplicative, i.e., $[K : M] = [K : L] \cdot [L : M]$.

Canonical Embedding. For a number field K of degree d, we let $\sigma_1, \cdots, \sigma_d$ denote the embeddings of K in $\mathbb{C}$. Using those, we define the canonical embedding of K as $\Sigma_K : K \to \mathbb{C}^d$, where $x \mapsto (\sigma_1(x), \cdots, \sigma_d(x))^T$. The trace $\mathrm{Tr}_K : K \to \mathbb{Q}$ is defined as the sum of the embeddings, i.e., for any $x \in K$, we have $\mathrm{Tr}_K(x) = \sum_{j=1}^d \sigma_j(x)$. Note that if $K/L/\mathbb{Q}$ is a tower of number fields, then any element x of L is also an element of K, and we can consider both $\Sigma_K(x)$ and $\Sigma_L(x)$. These two vectors are related, since we know (see for instance [Mar77, Theorem 50]) that every complex embedding of L extends to exactly $[K : L]$ complex embeddings of K. Hence, the coordinates of $\Sigma_K(x)$ are the same as the ones of $\Sigma_L(x)$, repeated $[K : L]$ times each. From this, we see that

$$\|\Sigma_K(x)\| = \sqrt{[K : L]} \cdot \|\Sigma_L(v)\|. \tag{2.1}$$

Galois Theory. The automorphism group of a field extension K/L, denoted by $\mathrm{Aut}_L(K)$, is the set of all K-automorphisms τ such that $\tau(x) = x$ for all $x \in L$. The number of such automorphisms is always at most the degree of the field extension, that is $|\mathrm{Aut}_L(K)| \leq [K : L]$.

Definition 2.1 (Fixed fields). *Given a field extension K/L and a subgroup H of $\mathrm{Aut}_L(K)$, the fixed field of H is the subfield K_H of K defined by $K_H = \{x \in K \mid \tau(x) = x, \forall \tau \in H\}$. This fields contains L (i.e., we have $K/K_H/L$).*

The extension K/L is said to be Galois if and only if $|\mathrm{Aut}_L(K)| = [K : L]$.[3] In this case, we can also use the notation $\mathrm{Gal}(K/L)$ to refer to the automorphism group $\mathrm{Aut}_L(K)$, and we call it the Galois group of the extension. When the extension K/L is Galois, Galois theory tells us that there is a one to one correspondence between subgroups of the Galois group $\mathrm{Gal}(K/L)$ and subfields of K containing L (see [Mar77, Theorem 55]). This correspondence is given by the maps $H \subseteq \mathrm{Gal}(K/L) \mapsto K_H$ and $L \subset K' \subseteq K \mapsto \mathrm{Aut}_{K'}(K)$.

Lemma 2.2 ([Lan02, Theorem 1.8, Chapter 6]). *Let K/L be an extension (not necessarily Galois). Then, for any subgroup H of $\mathrm{Aut}_L(K)$, the extension K/K_H is Galois and $\mathrm{Gal}(K/K_H) = H$.*

Ring of Integers and Discriminant. For a number field $K = \mathbb{Q}[X]/f(X)$, we write O_K its ring of integer, that is the subset of elements of K that are roots of a monic integer polynomial. It can be shown that O_K is a free $\mathbb{Z}$-module of rank d, where d is the degree of the number field. In other words,

---

[3] This is not the standard definition, see for instance [Mar77, Theorem 52] for a proof that this is an equivalent definition.

there exists a basis $r_1, \ldots, r_d \in O_K$ such that every element in O_K can be uniquely represented as an integer linear combination of those vectors. Often, we assume the knowledge of a short basis $r_1, \ldots, r_d$ of O_K, where the shortness is measured with respect to the canonical embedding Σ_K. To ease notations, we define the constant $C_K^\infty = \max_j \|\Sigma_K(r_j)\|_\infty$, which is used in Sect. 4. It always holds $\mathbb{Z}[X]/f(X) \subseteq O_K$ and for some number fields it also holds $O_K \subseteq \mathbb{Z}[X]/f(X)$ (e.g. for cyclotomic fields, see below). Note that being an integer is a property of the element, that does not depends on the number field. Hence, if K and L are two number fields with $L \subseteq K$, then we have that $O_L = O_K \cap L$.

The (absolute value of the) discriminant of a number field K is defined as $\Delta_K = |\det(\sigma_i(r_j))_{i,j}|^2$, where (r_j) is any basis of O_K. Given a tower of number fields $K/L/\mathbb{Q}$, it holds that $\Delta_K \geq \Delta_L^{[K:L]}$ (cf. [Mar77, Exercise 23]).

Product of Sets. Let X and Y be two subsets of the same field K (so that we can add and multiply their elements). We define the product of X and Y by

$$X \cdot Y = \{\sum_{i=1}^{r} x_i y_i \mid r \geq 0,\, x_i \in X,\, y_i \in Y\}.$$

Note that this product is well defined for any sets X and Y, and not only ideals. This is useful when we consider ideals of subfields, which are not necessarily ideals in the larger field. The product of two sets enjoys commutative and associative properties: $X \cdot Y = Y \cdot X$ and $(X \cdot Y) \cdot Z = X \cdot (Y \cdot Z)$.

Ideals. An integral ideal I of a number field K is a subgroup of O_K such that $I \cdot O_K = I$. A fractional ideal $J \subset O_K$ is a set of the form $J = 1/D \cdot I$, where $D \in \mathbb{Z}_{>0}$ and I is an integral ideal. By default, we use the word "ideal" to refer to fractional ideals, and we specify "integral ideal" when we restrict ourselves to ideals contained in O_K. For $\alpha \in K$, we denote by $\alpha \cdot O_K = \{\alpha \cdot x \mid x \in O_K\}$ the ideal generated by α.

The product of two ideals (using the product of sets defined above) is also an ideal. The set of all non zero ideals forms a group with this product, i.e., for any non-zero ideal I, there exists an ideal I^{-1} such that $I \cdot I^{-1} = O_K$. The norm over K of an integral ideal I is defined as $\mathcal{N}_K(I) = |O_K/I|$, and the norm of a fractional ideal $J = 1/D \cdot I$ (with I integral) is defined as $\mathcal{N}_K(J) = 1/D^d \cdot \mathcal{N}(I)$. The norm function is multiplicative, that is $\mathcal{N}_K(I \cdot J) = \mathcal{N}_K(I) \cdot \mathcal{N}_K(J)$ for every integral ideals I and J of K.

We say that an integral ideal I divides another integral ideal J, denoted by $I | J$, if there exists some integral ideal I' such that $J = I \cdot I'$. This is equivalent to $J \subseteq I$ (see [Mar77, Corollary 3, Theorem 15]).

Proposition 2.3. *Given a tower of number fields $K/L/\mathbb{Q}$, the following holds:*

(1) If I is an integral ideal of K, then $I \cap O_L = I \cap L$ is an integral ideal of L.
(2) If J is an integral ideal of L, then $J \cdot O_K$ is an integral ideal of K.

(3) If J_1, J_2 are integral ideals of L, then $(J_1 \cdot O_K) \cdot (J_2 \cdot O_K) = (J_1 \cdot J_2) \cdot O_K$.
(4) If J is an integral ideal of L, then $\mathcal{N}_K(J \cdot O_K) = \mathcal{N}_L(J)^{[K:L]}$.

We define the dual of an ideal I by $I^\vee = \{x \in K : \mathrm{Tr}_K(xy) \in \mathbb{Z}, \forall y \in I\}$. For any ideal I, its dual and inverse ideal are related to each other via the dual of the corresponding ring of integers, i.e., $I^\vee = I^{-1}O_K^\vee$ (see for instance [Con]). In the case where the ring of integers O_K is of the form $O_K = \mathbb{Z}[X]/f(X)$ for some irreducible polynomial f, we have $O_K^\vee = f'(X)^{-1} \cdot O_K$.

The following definition introduces the notion of decomposition group and decomposition field of an ideal. These notions are usually only defined for prime ideals (see for instance [Mar77, Chapter 4]), but we generalize the terminology to any ideal, since this is needed for the rest of the article.

Definition 2.4. *Let K be a number field and I be an ideal of K. The decomposition group of I is the subgroup H_I of $\mathrm{Aut}_\mathbb{Q}(K)$ defined by $H_I = \{\tau \in \mathrm{Aut}_\mathbb{Q}(K) \mid \tau(I) = I\}$.[4] The decomposition field of I, denoted by K_I, if the fixed field of H_I (cf. Definition 2.1).*

Prime Ideals. A non-zero integral ideal $\mathfrak{p}$ of a number field K is said to be prime if it is maximal, i.e., it is different from O_K and the only ideals that contain it are itself and O_K. Any non-zero integral ideal I in a number field K admits a unique decomposition into prime ideals $I = \prod_{\mathfrak{p} \text{ prime}} \mathfrak{p}^{\alpha_\mathfrak{p}}$, where $\alpha_\mathfrak{p} \geq 0$.

In this article, we are interested in moving prime ideals from a field to a subfield and vice versa. This relates to the terminology of primes lying above or below another prime, as defined in the following lemma.

Lemma 2.5 ([Mar77, **Theorem 19**]). *Let $K/L/\mathbb{Q}$ be a tower of number fields. Let $\mathfrak{p}$ be a prime ideal of K and $\mathfrak{q}$ be a prime ideal of L. The following conditions are equivalent:*

$$(1) \quad \mathfrak{p} \cap L = \mathfrak{q} \qquad and \qquad (2) \quad \mathfrak{p} \mid (\mathfrak{q} \cdot O_K).$$

When these conditions hold, we say that $\mathfrak{p}$ lies above $\mathfrak{q}$, or that $\mathfrak{q}$ lies below $\mathfrak{p}$.

Lemma 2.6 ([Mar77, **Theorem 20**]). *Every prime ideal $\mathfrak{p}$ of K lies above exactly one prime ideal of L. Every prime ideal $\mathfrak{q}$ of L lies below at least one prime ideal of K.*

If $L = \mathbb{Q}$, this lemma implies that any prime ideal $\mathfrak{p}$ of K lies over exactly one rational prime $q \in \mathbb{Z}$. It then holds that $\mathcal{N}_K(\mathfrak{p}) = q^r$ for some $r \in \{1, \cdots, d\}$.

Let $\mathfrak{p}$ be a prime of K and let $\mathfrak{q}$ be the unique prime of L below $\mathfrak{p}$. We say that $\mathfrak{p}$ is ramified in K/L if $\mathfrak{p}^\alpha \mid (\mathfrak{q} \cdot O_K)$ for some exponent $\alpha \geq 2$ (by Lemma 2.5, we know that $\alpha \geq 1$). The largest integer α such that $\mathfrak{p}^\alpha \mid (\mathfrak{q} \cdot O_K)$ is called the ramification index of $\mathfrak{p}$ in K/L. In this article, we are mostly interested in prime ideals that are not ramified. This is the most frequent case, since only a finite number of prime ideals are ramified in K/L (cf. [Mar77, Cor. 3 after Thm. 24]).

---

[4] Note that the equality $\tau(I) = I$ means that the two sets are equal, but it does not mean that all the elements of I are fixed by τ.

Lemma 2.7. *If a prime ideal* $\mathfrak{p}$ *of* K *is unramified in* $K/\mathbb{Q}$, *then it is also unramified in* K/L *for all subfields* L *of* K *containing* $\mathbb{Q}$.

A proof of this lemma is available in the full version [BGP22]. This observation enables us to discard all possible ramified ideals in any subfield of K, by discarding the ones that are ramified in $K/\mathbb{Q}$. Moreover, we know that if a prime $\mathfrak{p}$ is ramified in $K/\mathbb{Q}$, then it is above some $q \in \mathbb{Q}$ that divides Δ_K.

Lemma 2.8 ([Mar77, Thm. 23]). *Let* K/L *be Galois. If* $\mathfrak{p}$ *is a prime ideal of* K *over a prime ideal* $\mathfrak{q}$ *of* L, *then for any* $\tau \in \mathrm{Gal}(K/L)$, *the ideal* $\tau(\mathfrak{p})$ *is also a prime ideal of* K *over* $\mathfrak{q}$. *Conversely, for any two prime ideals* $\mathfrak{p}$ *and* $\mathfrak{p}'$ *of* K *over the same prime* $\mathfrak{q}$ *of* L, *there exists a* $\tau \in \mathrm{Gal}(K/L)$ *such that* $\tau(\mathfrak{p}) = \mathfrak{p}'$.

Cyclotomic Fields. Cyclotomic fields form a special class of number fields. For some integer $m \geq 2$, the m-th cyclotomic field can be described as $K = \mathbb{Q}[X]/\Phi_m(X)$, where its defining polynomial $\Phi_m(X)$ is the m-th cyclotomic polynomial. Its degree equals $\deg(\Phi_m(X)) = \phi(m)$, where $\phi(\cdot)$ is Euler's totient function. If $K = \mathbb{Q}[X]/\Phi_m(X)$ is a cyclotomic field, then $(1, X, \ldots, X^{\phi(m)-1})$ forms a basis of O_K, also called the power basis (cf. [Was82, Theorem 2.6]). In other words, $O_K = \mathbb{Z}[X]/\Phi_m(X)$ and we can set the constant C_K^∞ from above as 1.

All cyclotomic fields are Galois and their Galois group is abelian (cf. [Mar77, Corollary 2, Theorem 3]). The following lemma holds for any finite abelian group. We instantiate it directly with $\mathrm{Gal}(K/\mathbb{Q})$.

Lemma 2.9. *Let* K *be the* m-th *cyclotomic number field. For every* $r \mid \phi(m)$, *there is a subgroup* H *of* $\mathrm{Aut}_{\mathbb{Q}}(K)$ *of cardinality* r.

A proof is available in the full version [BGP22]. The discriminant of the m-th cyclotomic field K is $\Delta_K = \frac{m^{\phi(m)}}{\prod_{p \mid m} p^{\phi(m)/(p-1)}} \leq m^{\phi(m)}$ (cf. [Was82, Prop. 2.7]). For m a power of 2, it simplifies to $\Delta_K = \phi(m)^{\phi(m)}$.

2.2 Lattices

For a lattice L, we denote $\lambda_1(L)$ its first minimum, i.e., $\lambda_1(L) = \min_{v \in L \setminus \{0\}} \|v\|$. The determinant of L is given by $\det(L) = \sqrt{|\det(\mathbf{B}^T \cdot \mathbf{B})|}$ where $\mathbf{B}$ is any basis of L. Minkowski's theorem states that for any lattice L of rank n, it holds that $\lambda_1(L) \leq \sqrt{n} \cdot \det(L)^{1/n}$. We use the notation $\mathrm{Span}_{\mathbb{R}}(L)$ to refer to the real vector space spanned by the vectors of L. Further, we define the dual lattice of L as $L^\vee = \{x \in \mathrm{Span}_{\mathbb{R}}(L) \colon \langle x, y \rangle \in \mathbb{Z} \ \forall \ y \in L\}$. If $\mathbf{B}$ is a basis of L, then $\mathbf{B}^\vee = (\mathbf{B}^T)^{-1}$ is a basis of $L^\vee$. This implies that $\det(L^\vee) = 1/\det(L)$.

Ideal Lattices. When we embed an ideal I of K into $\mathbb{C}^d$ using the canonical embedding, the resulting set $\Sigma_K(I)$ is a lattice of rank d, called an ideal lattice. The determinant of the ideal lattice $\Sigma_K(I)$ is $\det(\Sigma_K(I)) = \mathcal{N}_K(I) \cdot \sqrt{\Delta_K}$. The duality notions of ideals and lattices are closely related. Indeed, it holds that $\Sigma_K(I)^\vee = \overline{\Sigma_K(I^\vee)}$, where $\bar{\cdot}$ denotes the complex conjugation and $\overline{L} := \{\overline{x} \mid x \in L\}$ for any lattice $L \subset \mathbb{C}^d$. From this, we see that

$$\det(\Sigma_K(I^{-1})) = \det(\Sigma_K(I)^\vee) \cdot \Delta_K = \det(\Sigma_K(I^\vee)) \cdot \Delta_K. \qquad (2.2)$$

In the case of ideal lattices, the minimum of a lattice is closely related to the normalized algebraic norm of the ideal

$$\sqrt{d} \cdot \mathcal{N}_K(I)^{1/d} \leq \lambda_1(\Sigma_K(I)) \leq \Delta_K^{1/(2d)} \cdot \sqrt{d} \cdot \mathcal{N}_K(I)^{1/d}, \qquad (2.3)$$

where the first inequality comes from the arithmetic-geometric means inequality applied to a shortest vector of $\Sigma_K(I)$ and the second is Minkowski's theorem.

Algorithmic Problems over Ideal Lattices. In this work, we are interested in three algorithmic problems that we state over ideal lattices: the shortest vector problem (SVP), the shortest independent vector problem (SIVP) and the bounded distance decoding (BDD) problem, all three in their so-called Hermite variant. Whereas in the original formulation those problems are defined with respect to the minimum λ_1 of a lattice L, their Hermite variant phrases them with respect to the determinant $\det(L)$ of the lattice. As we explained above, for ideal lattices both quantities are closely related and only differ by a factor $\Delta_K^{1/(2d)}$ (Eq. 2.3). One of the advantages when working with the Hermite variant is that the quantity $\det(L)$ is easier to compute than the quantity $\lambda_1(L)$. The three problems are defined as follows.

Definition 2.10 (γ-Id-HSVP$_K$). *Let $\gamma \geq 1$ and K be a number field of degree d with ring of integers O_K. The γ-Id-HSVP$_K$ problem asks, given as input an ideal I of O_K, to find a non-zero element $v \in I$ such that*

$$\|\Sigma_K(v)\| \leq \gamma \cdot \det(\Sigma_K(I))^{1/d}.$$

This problem always has a solution as long as $\gamma \geq \sqrt{d}$. There exist in the literature different algorithms for solving Id-HSVP$_K$. One is the BKZ algorithm [SE94], which works for all lattices. The run time of (a variant of) this algorithm was formally studied in [HPS11], achieving the following complexity.

Lemma 2.11 ([HPS11, **Theorem 1**]). *There is a classical probabilistic algorithm that takes as input a basis $\mathbf{B}_L \in \mathbb{Q}^n$ of a lattice L of rank n, a parameter $\gamma \in [\sqrt{n}, 2^n]$, and solves γ-HSVP in L in time $\mathrm{poly}(n, \mathrm{size}(\mathbf{B}_L)) \cdot 2^{O(n \log(n)/\log(\gamma))}$.*

There exist also special algorithms for Id-HSVP, relying on the algebraic properties of the ideals to find short vectors more efficiently. More details about these algorithms may be found in the full version [BGP22] (we don't use them in this article).

Definition 2.12 (γ-Id-HSIVP$_K$). *Let $\gamma \geq 1$ and K be a number field of degree d with ring of integers O_K. The γ-Id-HSIVP$_K$ problem asks, given as input an ideal I of O_K, to output d linearly independent vectors $\mathbf{b}_1, \ldots, \mathbf{b}_d \in \Sigma_K(I)$ such that $\max_j \|\mathbf{b}_j\| \leq \gamma \cdot \det(\Sigma_K(I))^{1/d}$.*

The Hermite variant of the BDD problem over ideal lattices has no official name in the literature yet, we simply call it Hermite Ideal BDD (or Id-HBDD).

Definition 2.13 (worst-case γ-Id-HBDD$_K$). *For $\gamma > 2\Delta_K^{1/2d}/\sqrt{d}$, K a number field of degree d with ring of integers O_K and I an ideal of O_K, the worst-case γ-Id-HBDD$_K$ is the following. Given as input any $\mathbf{t} \in \mathrm{Span}_{\mathbb{R}}(\Sigma_K(I))$ with the promise that $\mathbf{t} = \mathbf{v} + \mathbf{e}$ with $\mathbf{v} \in \Sigma_K(I)$ and $\|\mathbf{e}\| \leq 1/\gamma \cdot \det(\Sigma_K(I))^{1/d}$, the problem asks to output $\mathbf{v}$.*

Note that the constraint $\gamma > 2\Delta_K^{1/2d}/\sqrt{d}$ ensures that there is a unique $\mathbf{v} \in \Sigma_K(I)$ with $\|\mathbf{v} - \mathbf{t}\| \leq 1/\gamma \cdot \det(\Sigma_K(I))^{1/d} \leq 1/2 \cdot \lambda_1(\Sigma_K(I))$, using Eq. 2.3. Hence, the Id-HBDD problem is well defined.[5] The terminology "worst-case" means that we ask an algorithm to be able to solve the problem for all choices of input $\mathbf{t}$ that satisfy the promise.

2.3   Representation and Size of Algebraic Objects

Given a rational number $z = x/y \in \mathbb{Q}$ with x and y coprime integers, we denote by size(z) the quantity $\log_2 |x| + \log_2 |y|$. Up to a bit of sign, this corresponds to the bit-length needed to represent z. For a matrix $\mathbf{M} = (z_{ij})_{i,j}$ over $\mathbb{Q}$, its size($\mathbf{M}$) corresponds to the sum of size(z_{ij}) over all its entries z_{ij}.

Given a number field K of degree d, we often need to assume the knowledge of a basis matrix $\mathbf{B}_K$ of its ring of integers O_K. This basis consists of all the (floating points approximations of the) complex vectors $\Sigma_K(r_i)$, where $(r_i)_i \in O_K^d$ forms a $\mathbb{Z}$-basis of O_K. We use the notation size($\mathbf{B}_K$) = $\max_{i,j}(\log |(\mathbf{B}_K)_{i,j}|)$, where $(\mathbf{B}_K)_{i,j}$ are the coefficients of $\mathbf{B}_K$.

Once the r_i's are fixed, every element x of K can be represented as a rational vector $(x_1, \cdots, x_d)$, such that $x = \sum_i x_i r_i$. This gives us an exact representation for the elements of K, in the basis $(r_i)_i$. Note that an element x is in O_K if and only if the vector $(x_1, \cdots, x_d)$ is in $\mathbb{Z}^d$. For $x \in K$, we let size(x) denote the size of the vector $(x_1, \cdots, x_d) \in \mathbb{Q}^d$, as defined above (note that this depends on the choice of the r_i's, which are assumed to be fixed once and for all).

An ideal I of K is represent by a $\mathbb{Z}$-basis $(b_1, \cdots, b_d) \in K^d$ (i.e., $I = \{\sum_i x_i b_i \mid x_i \in \mathbb{Z}\}$). Every element $b_i \in K$ in the basis is represented by a vector in $\mathbb{Q}^d$, as explained in the previous paragraph. We call basis of I the matrix $\mathbf{B}_I$ whose columns are the vectors corresponding to the b_i's. This is a matrix in $\mathbb{Q}^{d \times d}$ (and in $\mathbb{Z}^{d \times d}$ if I is integral), and we use the notation size($\mathbf{B}_I$) as defined above.

An automorphism $\tau \in \mathrm{Aut}_{\mathbb{Q}}(K)$ is represented by a $d \times d$ matrix $\mathbf{M}_\tau$ whose coefficients are such that $\tau(r_j) = \sum_i (\mathbf{M}_\tau)_{i,j} r_i$ (i.e., the j-th column of $\mathbf{M}_\tau$ corresponds to the coordinates of $\tau(r_j)$ in the basis $(r_i)_i$). Since $\tau(x)$ is an algebraic integer if x is, then $\mathbf{M}_\tau$ has integer coefficients. We let size(τ) denote the size of the integral $d \times d$ matrix $\mathbf{M}_\tau$, as defined above.

---

[5] For arbitrary Euclidean lattices, it is much harder to give concrete conditions which ensure a unique solution for HBDD. This is why we think the definition of this problem only makes sense in the ideal setting.

2.4   The Partial Vandermonde Knapsack Problem

The partial Vandermonde knapsack problem (PV-Knap) was first introduced by Hoffstein et al. [HPS+14][6] and later reformulated over number fields by Lu et al. [LZA18]. As observed by Boudgoust [Bou21, Sec. 5.2], the problem can be phrased as a problem over ideal lattices. We use this formulation in the following. For completeness, we provide an explanation why both, the original and the ideal formulation, are equivalent in the full version [BGP22].

Let K be a number field of degree d with ring of integers O_K. Further, let q be an integer such that the ideal generated by q splits in exactly d different prime ideals, i.e., $qO_K = \prod_{j=1}^{d} \mathfrak{p}_j$, where $\mathfrak{p}_j$ is a prime ideal of norm q. For $t \leq d$, we define $\mathcal{P}_t = \{\Omega \subseteq \{1,\ldots,d\} : |\Omega| = t\}$. For any $\Omega \in \mathcal{P}_t$, we set $I_\Omega := \prod_{j \in \Omega} \mathfrak{p}_j$, yielding an ideal of norm q^t.

Definition 2.14 (PV-Knap). *Let K, O_K, d, q and t be as above. Fix $\Omega \in \mathcal{P}_t$ and let ψ be a distribution over O_K such that $\max_{a \leftarrow \psi} \|\Sigma_K(a)\| \leq B$ for some positive real B fulfilling $2B < \sqrt{d} \cdot q^{t/d}$. Sample $a \leftarrow \psi$. Given $b = a \bmod I_\Omega$, the partial Vandermonde knapsack problem PV-Knap$_{\Omega,\psi}$ asks to find a.*

The constraint $2B < \sqrt{d} \cdot q^{t/d}$ ensures that there is a unique a in the support of ψ such that $b = a \bmod I_\Omega$. By Eq. 2.3, we know that the minimum of $\Sigma_K(I_\Omega)$ with respect to the Euclidean norm is bounded from below by $\sqrt{d} \cdot \mathcal{N}(I_\Omega)^{1/d} = \sqrt{d} \cdot q^{t/d}$. If there were two solutions $a \neq a' \in O_K$ such that $a = a' \bmod I_\Omega$, then the element $a - a'$ would lie in I_Ω and its Euclidean norm with respect to the canonical embedding would be bounded above by $2B < \sqrt{d} \cdot q^{t/d} \leq \lambda_1(\Sigma_K(I_\Omega))$, leading to a contradiction. Hence, the PV-Knap problem is well defined.

We can also define a decision variant of PV-Knap in the natural way. Given Ω and $b + I_\Omega$, one has to decide whether b was defined as in the problem's definition above or if it was sampled uniformly at random.

Whereas in the above definition PV-Knap is defined over O_K, the problem is in some works (e.g. [HPS+14, HS15, DHSS20]) defined over the cyclic ring $\mathbb{Z}[X]/(X^N - 1)$ for some prime integer N. We recall its concrete formulation in the full version [BGP22]. Note that those rings are closely connected to prime cyclotomic number fields as the polynomial $X^N - 1$ factors into two particular irreducible polynomials. More precisely, it yields $X^N - 1 = (X - 1) \cdot \Phi_N(X)$ and thus $\mathbb{Z}[X]/(X^N - 1) \cong \mathbb{Z}[X]/(X - 1) \times \mathbb{Z}[X]/\Phi_N(X)$. Thus, an instance of PV-Knap over the cyclic ring can be formulated as an instance of PV-Knap over the ring of integers of a cyclotomic number field (where the last coefficient of the solution over the cyclic ring can be guessed). Hence, even though the results of Sect. 4 are formulated for number fields, they also apply to the original parameter setting of [HPS+14].

In our definition, the bound B is with respect to the canonical embedding Σ_K, whereas in the former works, it was with respect to the coefficient embedding. In most of the number fields used in lattice-based cryptography, we know how to go from one embedding to another. For instance, for the m-th cyclotomic field we

---

[6] Even though they originally called it the partial Fourier recovery problem.

obtain a bound B in the canonical embedding by multiplying a bound B' in the coefficient embedding by the factor $\sqrt{m}$. A prominent choice in [LZA18, HPS+14] is $B' = 1$, which yields $B = \sqrt{m}$. In the case of power-of-two cyclotomics this bound can be tightened to $B = \sqrt{d}$ where $d = m/2$.

The definition we present doesn't specify how to choose Ω, which we exploit in Sect. 4 when finding *bad* choices of Ω. This follows the same design choice as [HPS+14, HS15, DHSS20]. Other works [LZA18, BSS22, Bou21] decided to sample Ω uniformly at random over the set $\mathcal{P}_t$, which has an important effect on the performance of our attacks as we elaborate later in Sect. 5.

3   Easy Instances of Ideal-SVP

The objective of this section is to prove the following theorem, which gives a simple and sufficient condition under which the Id-HSVP$_K$ problem is easy in an ideal lattice. The condition requires the ideal I to have no ramified prime factors. By Lemma 2.7, this is the case if the ideal's algebraic norm is coprime with the discriminant of K. Hence, the condition can be verified easily, without computing the prime factorization of the ideal.

Theorem 3.1. *Let K be a number field of degree d and I be an integral ideal of K whose prime factors are not ramified in $K/\mathbb{Q}$. There is an algorithm that takes as input a basis $\mathbf{B}_K$ of $\mathcal{O}_K$, a representation G of $\mathrm{Aut}_\mathbb{Q}(K)$, a basis $\mathbf{B}_I$ of I and a parameter $\gamma \geq 2\sqrt{d}$ and solves γ-Id-HSVP$_K$ in I in classical time*

$$\exp\left(O\left(\frac{d \cdot \log(d)}{n_I \cdot \log(\gamma/\sqrt{n_I})}\right)\right) \cdot \mathrm{poly}(\mathrm{size}(\mathbf{B}_I), \mathrm{size}(\mathbf{B}_K), \mathrm{size}(G)),$$

where $n_I := |H_I|$ is the number of K-automorphisms that fix I as a set.

3.1   Reducing the Ideal in a Subfield

In this section, we ignore the representation of the mathematical objects, and concentrate on the following mathematical result. It states that if an ideal is fixed by a sufficiently large group of automorphisms, then one can find a short vector of it by looking for short vectors of its intersection with a subfield of smaller dimension. Hence, we can reduce the dimension of the problem.

Theorem 3.2. *Let K be a number field and I be an integral ideal of K whose prime factors are not ramified in $K/\mathbb{Q}$. Let $K_I \subseteq K$ be the decomposition field of I (see Definition 2.4). We write $d = [K : \mathbb{Q}]$ and $d_I = [K_I : \mathbb{Q}]$, and we let $\gamma \geq 1$.*

Then, any $v \in I \cap K_I$ which is a solution to γ-Id-HSVP$_{K_I}$ in $I \cap K_I$ is also a solution to γ'-Id-HSVP$_K$ in I, where

$$\gamma' = \gamma \cdot \sqrt{d/d_I}.$$

This generalizes Theorem 4 of [PXWC21] to non-prime ideals I, and to number fields that are not necessarily Galois. The latter is easily obtained from the observation that the extension K/K_I is always Galois, even if $K/\mathbb{Q}$ is not (Lemma 2.2). The generalization to non-prime ideals requires more work. The main difficulty of this generalization lies in proving the following lemma.

Lemma 3.3. *Let K/L be a Galois extension of number fields. Let I be an integral ideal of K whose prime factors are not ramified in K/L. If $\sigma(I) = I$ for all $\sigma \in \mathrm{Gal}(K/L)$, then it holds that*

$$I = (I \cap O_L) \cdot O_K.$$

Intuitively, this lemma means that when intersecting the ideal I with the subfield L, one loses no information on I, since it can be recovered simply by multiplying by O_K again. This conveys the intuition that the short vectors of I should also be contained into the intersection $I \cap O_L$.

Proof. Note that the inclusion $I \supseteq (I \cap O_L) \cdot O_K$ always holds, even if I is divisible by ramified primes, or if $\sigma(I) \neq I$ for some $\sigma \in \mathrm{Gal}(K/L)$. However, in the general case, this inclusion is usually not an equality: the set $(I \cap O_L) \cdot O_K$ can be much sparser than I, hence losing information about I. In the rest of this proof, we focus on proving the reverse inclusion $I \subseteq (I \cap O_L) \cdot O_K$.

First, we group the prime factors of I into groups of primes that are all above the same prime in O_L. In other words, we write $I = \prod_{\mathfrak{q} \text{ prime of } O_L} I_q$, where $I_q = \prod_{\mathfrak{p}_i \text{ prime of } O_K \text{above } \mathfrak{q}} \mathfrak{p}_i^{\alpha_i}$.

Let us fix a prime ideal $\mathfrak{q}$ in O_L, which does not ramify in O_K (recall that we required that the prime factors of I are not ramified in K/L). Since $\mathfrak{q}$ does not ramify, we know that $\mathfrak{q} \cdot O_K = \mathfrak{p}_1 \cdots \mathfrak{p}_r$ for some distinct prime ideals $\mathfrak{p}_i$ of O_K.

Next, since K/L is Galois, we know that $\mathrm{Gal}(K/L)$ acts transitively on the $\mathfrak{p}_i$, i.e., for every indices i, j, there is some $\sigma \in \mathrm{Gal}(K/L)$ such that $\sigma(\mathfrak{p}_i) = \mathfrak{p}_j$. Using that $\sigma(I) = I$ for all $\sigma \in \mathrm{Gal}(K/L)$ and that the prime decomposition of an ideal is unique, we conclude that all the $\mathfrak{p}_i$ appear with the same exponent in the prime decomposition of I. Hence, $I_q = \prod_{i=1}^r \mathfrak{p}_i^{\alpha_\mathfrak{q}} = (\mathfrak{q}O_K)^{\alpha_\mathfrak{q}}$, for some $\alpha_\mathfrak{q} \geq 0$.

Summing up, we can write I as a product $I = \prod_i (\mathfrak{q}_i \cdot O_K)^{\alpha_i}$, for some prime ideals $\mathfrak{q}_i$ of O_L and $\alpha_i \geq 1$. We see here that the condition $\sigma(I) = I$ for all $\sigma \in \mathrm{Gal}(K/L)$ (and the fact that I is not divisible by any ramified prime) implies the natural intuition that I is an ideal of O_L, lifted in O_K.

Using this equation, let us now prove that $I \cap O_L = \prod_i \mathfrak{q}_i^{\alpha_i}$. The inclusion $\prod_i \mathfrak{q}_i^{\alpha_i} \subseteq I \cap O_L$ follows from

$$\prod_i \mathfrak{q}_i^{\alpha_i} = \prod_i (\mathfrak{q}_i \cdot O_L)^{\alpha_i} \subseteq \prod_i (\mathfrak{q}_i \cdot O_K)^{\alpha_i} = I.$$

Since $I \cap O_L$ is an ideal of O_L and we have seen that $\prod_i \mathfrak{q}_i^{\alpha_i} \subseteq I \cap O_L$, i.e., $(I \cap O_L) | \prod_i \mathfrak{q}_i^{\alpha_i}$, we know that $(I \cap O_L) = \prod_i \mathfrak{q}_i^{\beta_i}$ for some $\beta_i \leq \alpha_i$. Multiplying this equation by O_K we obtain

$$(I \cap O_L) \cdot O_K = (\prod_i \mathfrak{q}_i^{\beta_i}) \cdot O_K = \prod_i (\mathfrak{q}_i \cdot O_K)^{\beta_i}.$$

We have already seen that $(I \cap O_L) \cdot O_K \subseteq I$. Hence we obtain $\prod_i (\mathfrak{q}_i \cdot O_K)^{\beta_i} \subseteq \prod_i (\mathfrak{q}_i \cdot O_K)^{\alpha_i}$, which holds only if $\beta_i = \alpha_i$ (since $\beta_i \leq \alpha_i$). We then conclude that $(I \cap O_L) = \prod_i \mathfrak{q}_i^{\alpha_i}$ as desired.

Finally, multiplying this equation by O_K, we obtain

$$(I \cap O_L) \cdot O_K = (\prod_i \mathfrak{q}_i^{\alpha_i}) \cdot O_K = \prod_i (\mathfrak{q}_i \cdot O_K)^{\alpha_i} = I,$$

as desired.   □

With this lemma at hand, the proof of Theorem 3.2 follows almost directly the one of Theorem 4 of [PXWC21]. It is available in the full version [BGP22].

3.2   Proof of Theorem 3.1

We are now ready to prove Theorem 3.1. The algorithm to solve Id-HSVP$_K$ in I is described in Algorithm 3.1. It computes the intersection of I with K_I, in order to reduce the dimension of the lattice, solves Id-HSVP$_{K_I}$ in this lattice of smaller dimension, and then uses Theorem 3.2 to claim that the vector it founds is indeed a solution to Id-HSVP$_K$ in I. The proof below shows its correctness, specifies its run time and the size of the objects that are manipulated.

Algorithm 3.1. Solving Id-HSVP$_K$ in an easy ideal I

Input: A basis of O_K, the group of endomorphisms $\mathrm{Aut}_{\mathbb{Q}}(K)$, an ideal I without ramified prime factors, a parameter $\gamma \geq \sqrt{d}$
Output: A solution to γ-Id-HSVP$_K$ in I
1: $H_I = \{\}$
2: **for** $\tau \in \mathrm{Aut}_{\mathbb{Q}}(K)$ **do**
3:      Compute a basis of $\tau(I)$.
4:      **if** $\tau(I) = I$ **then**
5:          Add τ to H_I.
6:      **end if**
7: **end for**
8: Compute a basis of K_I, the subfield of K fixed by H_I.
9: Compute a basis of $J = I \cap K_I$
10: Solve γ'-Id-HSVP$_{K_I}$ in J with $\gamma' = \gamma/\sqrt{|H_I|}$, to obtain an element $x \in J$
11: **return** x

Proof (Proof of Theorem 3.1).

Correctness. Since I has no ramified prime factors, we know from Theorem 3.2 that the element x obtained by solving γ'-Id-HSVP$_{K_I}$ in $I \cap K_I$ is also a solution to $(\gamma' \cdot \sqrt{d/d_I})$-Id-HSVP$_K$ in I. Using the fact that K/K_I is a Galois extension, we know that $|H_I| = |\mathrm{Gal}(K/K_I)| = [K : K_I] = d/d_I$. Hence, by choice of γ', we obtain that $\gamma' \cdot \sqrt{d/d_I} = \gamma$. We conclude that x is indeed a solution to γ-Id-HSVP$_K$ in I as desired.

Run Time. Observe that the for loop of the algorithm runs at most $|\operatorname{Aut}_{\mathbb{Q}}(K)| \leq [K : \mathbb{Q}] = d$ times. At each iteration of the loop, we need to compute a basis of $\tau(I)$. Recall that we know a basis $(x_1, \cdots, x_d)$ of I, where the elements x_i are represented by their integral vector in the known basis $\mathbf{B}_K = (r_1, \cdots, r_d)$ of O_K. Recall that the automorphisms τ of $\operatorname{Aut}_{\mathbb{Q}}(K)$ are linear transforms that are represented by a integral matrices. Hence, to compute a basis of $\tau(I)$, it is sufficient to multiply the matrix corresponding to τ with the basis matrix of I. This is a multiplication of two integral matrices of dimension d, which can be performed in time polynomial in d and in the bit-size of the entry of the two bases. Testing the equality $\tau(I) = I$ can be done by testing whether each vector of the basis of $\tau(I)$ is in the integer span of the basis of I and conversely. This is again polynomial in d and the bit-size of the entries of the two bases.

Let us now consider the computation of a basis of K_I. This is a real subspace of K of dimension $d_I = d/|H_I|$. This subspace is defined by a collection of linear equations $\tau(x) = x$ for all $\tau \in H_I$. Hence, one can compute a basis of this subspace by computing the kernel (over $\mathbb{Q}$) of a matrix with dimension $|H_I| \times d$ and whose coefficients are integers of bit-size polynomial in the input bit-size. This can be done in time polynomial in d and in the bit-size of the coefficients of the matrices corresponding to the automorphisms τ.

Finally, the intersection of a lattice with a rational vector space can be performed in polynomial time (cf. Lemma A.1 in the full version [BGP22]), and so the basis of $J = I \cap K_I$ can be computed efficiently.

Once J is computed, we run an Id-HSVP$_{K_I}$ solver on it. To do so, we use the BKZ algorithm for which we have concrete run time bounds (cf. Lemma 2.11). This algorithm forgets about the ideal structure of the lattice and simply requires as input a basis of the lattice $\Sigma_{K_I}(J)$. In order to obtain such a basis, we can multiply the basis of J (over $(r_1, \cdots, r_d)$) by the matrix $\mathbf{B}_K$ formed by the (known) embeddings $\Sigma_K(r_1), \cdots, \Sigma_K(r_d)$. This gives us a basis of $\Sigma_K(J)$. In order to obtain a basis of $\Sigma_{K_I}(J)$, we then simply remove the multiple coordinates that appear in $\Sigma_K(J)$. These operations can be performed in polynomial time. The BKZ algorithm with parameter γ' then runs in time poly(input size) $\cdot 2^{O(d_I \log(d_I)/\log(\gamma'))}$, since the lattice $\Sigma_{K_I}(J)$ has rank d_I. Note that we used the fact that $\gamma \geq \sqrt{d}$, so that $\gamma' \geq \sqrt{d_I}$ and hence we can indeed apply Lemma 2.11 with parameter γ'. Note also that since $\gamma \geq 2\sqrt{d}$, we have $\gamma' = \gamma/\sqrt{|H_I|} \geq 2$, hence $\log(\gamma')$ is not zero and we can indeed divide by it. $\qquad\square$

4   Easy Instances of Partial Vandermonde Knapsack

In this section, we explain how one can reduce the problem of recovering the secret element of a PV-Knap instance to the problem of finding a short vector in the ideal lattice I_Ω^{-1}, depending on Ω. We conclude the section by remarking that, for some choices of the set Ω, the ideal I_Ω^{-1} is stabilized by a large subgroup of the automorphism group of K, leading to an efficient SVP solver in I_Ω^{-1}, and hence to an efficient attack against PV-Knap (for these specific choices of Ω).

4.1 PV-Knap as an Instance of Ideal Hermite BDD

Recall the definition of the partial Vandermonde knapsack problem (PV-Knap) as introduced in Sect. 2.4 and the definitions of some algorithmic problems over ideal lattices (Id-HSVP, Id-HSIVP, Id-HBDD) as introduced in Sect. 2.2. Let ψ denote a B-bounded distribution over the ring of integers O_K with respect to the canonical embedding and the Euclidean norm, i.e., $\max_{a\leftarrow\psi}\|\Sigma_K(a)\| \le B$. Further, let $b = a \bmod I_\Omega$ be an instance of PV-Knap$_{\Omega,\psi}$. Recall that $I_\Omega = \prod_{j\in\Omega}\mathfrak{p}_j$ where the $\mathfrak{p}_j$ come from the prime ideal factorization of the ideal qO_K and $\Omega \subseteq \{1,\ldots,d\}$ with $|\Omega| = t$. It follows from the definition that this is exactly an instance of γ_1-Id-HBDD$_K$ for the ideal lattice I_Ω, with

$$\gamma_1 = \frac{\det(\Sigma_K(I_\Omega))^{1/d}}{B} = \frac{q^{t/d}\cdot\Delta_K^{1/(2d)}}{B}.$$

4.2 Reduction from Ideal Hermite BDD to Ideal Hermite SVP in the Inverse Ideal

We now show a sequence of reductions that overall reduce Id-HBDD for an ideal I to Id-HSVP in its inverse ideal I^{-1}.

Lemma 4.1. *Let $K = \mathbb{Q}[x]/f(X)$ be a number field of degree d and discriminant Δ_K with $f(X)$ its defining polynomial and let $(r_1,\ldots,r_d)$ be a known basis of O_K. Let $\gamma_1,\gamma_4 > 0$ be such that*

$$\gamma_1 > \gamma_4\cdot 2\Delta_K^{1/d}\cdot C_K^\infty,$$

where $C_K^\infty = \max_j\|\Sigma_K(r_j)\|_\infty$. For any fractional ideal I in K, there is a (deterministic) polynomial-time reduction from γ_1-Id-HBDD$_K$ in I to γ_4-Id-HSVP$_K$ in I^{-1}.

If in addition $O_K = \mathbb{Z}[X]/f(X)$, then the γ_1 can even be as small as

$$\gamma_1 > \gamma_4\cdot 2\Delta_K^{1/d}\cdot\|\Sigma_K(1/f'(X))\|_\infty\cdot C_K^\infty.$$

(Note that this improves upon the previous bound only if $\|\Sigma_K(1/f'(X))\|_\infty < 1$.)

In the case of power-of-two and prime cyclotomics, the parameter conditions simplify to the following.

Corollary 4.2. *Let K be the m-th cyclotomic number field, where m is a power of two, of degree $d = m/2$. There is an efficient reduction from γ_1-Id-HBDD$_K$ in I to γ_4-Id-HSVP$_K$ in I^{-1}, as long as*

$$\gamma_1 > 2\gamma_4.$$

Proof. Using the power basis implies $C_K^\infty = 1$ for all cyclotomic fields and for power-of-two cyclotomics it yields $\Delta_K^{1/d} = d$. Further, $O_K = \mathbb{Z}[X]/f(X)$ with $f(X) = X^d - 1$ and thus $f'(X) = d\cdot X^{d-1}$, completing the proof. $\square$

Corollary 4.3. *Let K be the m-th cyclotomic number field, where $m \geq 2$ is a prime, of degree $d = m - 1$. There is an efficient reduction from γ_1-Id-HBDD$_K$ in I to γ_4-Id-HSVP$_K$ in I^{-1}, as long as*

$$\gamma_1 > 4\gamma_4.$$

Proof. Again, the power basis leads to $C_K^\infty = 1$ and for prime cyclotomics it yields $\sqrt{m} \leq \Delta_K^{1/d} \leq m$. Furthermore, $O_K = \mathbb{Z}[X]/f(X)$ with $f(X) = \frac{X^m - 1}{X - 1}$ and thus $f'(X) = \frac{mX^{m-1} \cdot (X-1) - (X^m - 1)}{(X-1)^2} = \frac{mX^{m-1}}{X-1}$ (since $X^m = 1$ by definition), leading to $\|\Sigma_K(1/f'(X))\|_\infty \leq \frac{2}{m}$ and thus completing the proof.   □

We prove Lemma 4.1 in the following three steps.

Step 1: From Id-HBDD in I to Id-HSIVP in $I^\vee$. This reduction is well-known for BDD and SIVP in their standard formulation and works for any lattice, not only for ideal lattices. It corresponds to solving BDD in a lattice L by using the so-called Babai's rounding algorithm [Bab86], whose performance can be assessed by looking at the size of the vectors of the dual basis of $L^\vee$ (see for instance [CDPR16, Claim 2.1]). For completeness, we detail out how to proceed for the Hermite variant, and quantify the loss in the approximation factor for this variant in the full version [BGP22].

Lemma 4.4 (Id-HBDD to Id-HSIVP). *Let I be a fractional ideal of a number field K of degree d. There is a (deterministic) polynomial-time reduction from γ_1-Id-HBDD$_K$ in I to γ_2-Id-HSIVP$_K$ in $I^\vee$, for any $2\gamma_2 < \gamma_1$.*

Step 2: From Id-HSIVP in $I^\vee$ to Id-HSVP in $I^\vee$. This reduction step is special to ideal lattices, as it uses the fact that in the ideal case one short vector is enough to generate a set of linearly independent short vectors.

Lemma 4.5 (Id-HSIVP to Id-HSVP). *Let I be a fractional ideal of a number field K of degree d. Furthermore, let $r_1, \ldots, r_d \in O_K$ be a known basis of O_K. There is a (deterministic) polynomial-time reduction from γ_2-Id-HSIVP$_K$ in $I^\vee$ to γ_3-Id-HSVP$_K$ in $I^\vee$, where $\gamma_2 = C_K^\infty \cdot \gamma_3$ and $C_K^\infty = \max_j \|\Sigma_K(r_j)\|_\infty$.*

Proof. Assume that we are able to solve γ_3-Id-HSVP$_K$ for the ideal $I^\vee$, i.e., we obtain an element $x \in I^\vee$ of norm $\|\Sigma_K(x)\| \leq \gamma_3 \cdot \det(\Sigma_K(I^\vee))^{1/d}$. Since $I^\vee$ is an ideal and since we know a basis $(r_i)_i$ of O_K, we can transform this single short element into d linearly independent ones: $r_i \cdot x \in I^\vee$, for $i = 1$ to d. These elements satisfy

$$\|\Sigma_K(r_i \cdot x)\| \leq \|\Sigma_K(r_i)\|_\infty \cdot \|\Sigma_K(x)\| \leq C_K^\infty \cdot \gamma_3 \cdot \det(\Sigma_K(I^\vee))^{1/d}.$$

This solves γ_2-HSIVP in $I^\vee$.   □

For a given number field K, the constant C_K^∞ is determined by the quality of a short basis for the ring of integers O_K with respect to the infinity norm that we are able to compute. Note that for cyclotomic fields, we know how to find a basis of infinity norm 1 (the power basis) and thus in this case $\gamma_2 = \gamma_3$.

Step 3: From Id-HSVP in $I^\vee$ to Id-HSVP in I^{-1}. In the last step, we go from the dual to the inverse ideal. This step is motivated from the fact that the shape of I_Ω coming from an instance of PV-Knap is very similar to the shape of its inverse $I_\Omega^{-1} = \frac{1}{q} I_{\Omega^c}$.

Lemma 4.6 (Id-HSVP in $I^\vee$ to Id-HSVP in I^{-1}). *Let I be a fractional ideal of a number field $K = \mathbb{Q}[x]/f(X)$ of degree d and discriminant Δ_K with $f(X)$ its defining polynomial. There is an efficient reduction from γ_3-Id-HSIVP$_K$ in $I^\vee$ to γ_4-Id-HSVP$_K$ in I^{-1}, for any $\gamma_3, \gamma_4 > 0$ such that $\gamma_3 = \gamma_4 \cdot \Delta_K^{1/d}$.*

Furthermore, if $O_K = \mathbb{Z}[X]/f(X)$, the reduction also holds for any $\gamma_3, \gamma_4 > 0$ such that $\gamma_3 = \gamma_4 \cdot \Delta_K^{1/d} \cdot \|\Sigma_K(1/f'(X))\|_\infty$.

Proof. Assume that we are able to solve γ_4-Id-HSVP$_K$ for the ideal I^{-1}, i.e., we obtain an element $x \in I^{-1}$ of norm $\|\Sigma_K(x)\| \le \gamma_4 \cdot \det(\Sigma_K(I^{-1}))^{1/d}$. By the definition of the inverse and dual of I, it yields that $I^{-1} \subseteq I^\vee$ and thus the short vector $\Sigma_K(x)$ is already an element of the ideal lattice $\in \Sigma_K(I^\vee)$. As it yields that $\det(I^{-1}) = \Delta_K \cdot \det(I^\vee)$ (Eq. 2.2), this vector solves $\gamma_4 \cdot \Delta_K$-Id-HSVP$_K$ in $I^\vee$, which proves the first part of the lemma.

Assume now that $O_K = \mathbb{Z}[X]/f(X)$ for some irreducible polynomial $f(X)$. In this specific case, it holds that $I^\vee = I^{-1} \cdot O_K^\vee$ with $O_K^\vee = 1/f'(X) \cdot O_K$. Thus, we can multiply x by the element $1/f'(X)$ and still obtain an element in $I^\vee$. Overall, we obtain a vector $\Sigma_K(x \cdot 1/f'(X))$ whose norm is bounded above by $\gamma_4 \cdot \Delta_K^{1/d} \cdot \|\Sigma_K(1/f'(\zeta))\|_\infty \cdot \det(\Sigma_K(I^\vee))^{1/d}$, which proves the second part of the lemma. □

4.3   Bad Choices of Ω

We now elaborate on how the above results lead to polynomial-time attacks against PV-Knap for some special choices of Ω. In the following, we restrict ourselves to number fields K that are cyclotomic with a conductor m which is either a power of two or a prime integer. These are the number fields used in the literature on PV-Knap, and restricting to these number fields simplifies our attack. Recall that we write $d = \phi(m)$ for the degree of K.

Let q, t, B and $\Omega \in \mathcal{P}_t$ be PV-Knap parameters satisfying $q^{t/d} \ge 8 \cdot B$ (note that this condition is slightly stronger than the condition required in Definition 2.14 of PV-Knap for the problem to be well defined).

Combining Theorem 3.1 and Corollaries 4.2 and 4.3, we obtain a solver for PV-Knap that runs in classical time

$$\exp\left(O\left(\frac{d\log(d)}{|H_{I_\Omega^{-1}}|\log(\gamma_4/|H_{I_\Omega^{-1}}|)}\right)\right) \cdot \text{poly}\,(d, \log q), \tag{4.1}$$

where

$$\gamma_4 = \frac{q^{t/d}\sqrt{d}}{4B} \ge 2\sqrt{d}.$$

The last inequality comes from our lower bound on $q^{t/d}$ and is required to apply Theorem 3.1. Recall that for an ideal I the integer $|H_I|$ denotes the number of K-automorphisms that fix I as a set. By definition all ideals I_Ω are unramified.

In the rest of this section, we show that if $t \geq d/2$, then there are choices of Ω that make $|H_{I_\Omega^{-1}}|$ linear in the degree d of the number field, hence leading to polynomial-time attacks against PV-Knap for this choice of Ω. We also explain how the result degrades for smaller choices of t.

Special Structure of I_Ω. First of all, we observe that an automorphism $\tau \in \mathrm{Aut}_\mathbb{Q}(K)$ fixes a fractional ideal I if and only if it fixes its inverse I^{-1}. Hence, we only focus here on the group of automorphisms H_{I_Ω} fixing I_Ω, instead of $H_{I_\Omega^{-1}}$.

Recall that I_Ω has a special structure, it is equal to $\prod_{i \in \Omega} \mathfrak{p}_i$, where the $\mathfrak{p}_i$'s are all distinct prime ideals above some fully splitting prime q. Recall also that cyclotomic fields are Galois, hence we can apply Lemma 2.8, which implies that

$$\{\mathfrak{p}_i \mid 1 \leq i \leq d\} = \{\tau(\mathfrak{p}_1) \mid \tau \in \mathrm{Aut}_\mathbb{Q}(K)\},$$

where $\mathfrak{p}_1$ is any of the prime ideals above q. Let us fix such a prime ideal $\mathfrak{p}_1$. From the equation above, we know that for any subgroup $H \subseteq \mathrm{Aut}_\mathbb{Q}(K)$, there exists a set $\Omega_H \subset \{1, \ldots, d\}$ with $|\Omega_H| = |H|$ such that

$$\{\tau(\mathfrak{p}_1) \mid \tau \in H\} = \{\mathfrak{p}_i \mid i \in \Omega_H\}.$$

Note that the set Ω_H also depends on the choice of $\mathfrak{p}_1$, but this choice has no impact on our attack, hence we do not mention it in the notation.

By definition of Ω_H, it holds that $I_{\Omega_H} = \prod_{i \in \Omega_H} \mathfrak{p}_i = \prod_{\tau \in H} \tau(\mathfrak{p}_1)$ is fixed by H. The same equation also shows that I_{Ω_H} is not fixed by any strictly larger group of automorphisms containing H.

To conclude, we have a way, given any subgroup H of $\mathrm{Aut}_\mathbb{Q}(K)$, to construct a subset $\Omega_H \in \{1, \cdots, d\}$ such that $|\Omega_H| = |H|$ and $H_{I_{\Omega_H}} = H$.

Subgroups of $\mathrm{Aut}_\mathbb{Q}(K)$ of the Desired Size. Recall that the set Ω of the PV-Knap instance has to have size t. If there exists a subgroup H of $\mathrm{Aut}_\mathbb{Q}(K)$ with size t, then the previous paragraph shows that one can find bad sets Ω of size t with $|H_{I_\Omega}| = t$. This leads to an attack against PV-Knap for those bad sets Ω whose run time is $\exp\left(O\left(\frac{d}{t}\right)\right) \cdot \mathrm{poly}\,(d, \log q)$. It is polynomial if $t = \Omega(d)$, as is usually the case in PV-Knap parameter sets (see for instance Sect. 5).

If there is no subgroup H of $\mathrm{Aut}_\mathbb{Q}(K)$ of size t, one can choose a subgroup H of maximal cardinality, subject to $|H| \leq t$. This provides a set $\Omega' = \Omega_H$ of cardinality $|H| \leq t$ such that $I_{\Omega'}$ is fixed by H. This set Ω' does not have the desired size. However, we observe that one can always transform a PV-Knap instance with respect to Ω into a PV-Knap instance with respect to Ω' for any $\Omega' \subseteq \Omega$. This is done by "forgetting" the value of $a \bmod \mathfrak{p}_i$ for the i's in $\Omega \setminus \Omega'$. Another way to phrase this is to observe that if $\Omega' \subset \Omega$, then I_Ω is a sublattice of $I_{\Omega'}$. Hence, we can view any BDD instance in I_Ω as a BDD instance in $I_{\Omega'}$, provided that the volume of ideal $I_{\Omega'}$ is not too small (so that the BDD instance is still close to a unique point of the ideal $I_{\Omega'}$).

This shows that, even when there are no subgroups H of $\text{Aut}_{\mathbb{Q}}(K)$ with size t, one can find bad sets Ω of size t containing a subset Ω' fixed by some subgroup $H \subseteq \text{Aut}_{\mathbb{Q}}(K)$ of cardinality

$$t_0 = \max(|H| : H \text{ subgroup of } \text{Aut}_{\mathbb{Q}}(K) \text{ and } |H| \leq t).$$

If $q^{t_0/d} \geq 8 \cdot B$, we can solve PV-Knap for Ω in time $\exp\left(O\left(\frac{d}{t_0}\right)\right) \cdot \text{poly}\,(d, \log q)$.

Finally, let us estimate the quantity t_0. We know from Lemma 2.9 that $\text{Aut}_{\mathbb{Q}}(K)$ contains subgroups of any order dividing $\phi(m)$. Hence, one can take

$$t_0 = \max(r : r|\phi(m) \text{ and } r \leq t\}.$$

In the case of power-of-two cyclotomic fields, this means that we always have $t_0 \geq t/2$. Hence, if $t = \Omega(d)$, there always exist bad sets Ω for which the attack runs in polynomial time (provided that $q^{t/(2d)} \geq 8 \cdot B$).

In the case of prime conductors m, we know that $\phi(m) = d$ is odd, hence if $t \geq d/2$, then we have $t_0 \geq d/2$ and there also exist bad sets Ω for which the attack runs in polynomial time.

5   Experimental Results

We implemented the attack described in Sect. 4 in SageMath [The20] to solve easy instances of PV-Knap over cyclotomic fields. The code is available at https://github.com/apelletm/easy-PV-knap.

We tested our attack in two significantly different scenarios. In the first one, the set Ω of the PV-Knap instance is fixed to make the problem easy (i.e., by choosing Ω such that I_Ω is stable by a lot of automorphisms of K, cf. Sect. 4.3). In the second scenario, we consider randomly chosen sets Ω.

Our results show that the easy cases are indeed easy: if Ω is badly chosen, one can solve PV-Knap (in both its search and decision versions) in a few seconds. Perhaps surprisingly, we observe that our attack can also be beneficial for randomly chosen sets Ω, for the decision variant of PV-Knap.

Generation of PV-Knap *Instances.* We decided to generate PV-Knap instances whose parameters are as suggested in [HPS+14] and [LZA18]. These parameters are summarized in Table 1 below. All number fields are cyclotomic, m is the conductor of the cyclotomic field K, d is the degree of K, $t = |\Omega|$ is the size of Ω and q is a rational prime that fully splits in K. The last line of the table contains the security estimates provided in [HPS+14, LZA18] for these parameters.

As explained above, we consider two types of PV-Knap instances. The first type is what we call *worst-case instances*, where we choose the set Ω so that the ideal I_Ω is stable by many automorphisms of the number field K. For this case, the user can choose the size of the subgroup of $\text{Aut}_{\mathbb{Q}}(K)$ fixing I_Ω.

The second type of instances we generate are what we call *random instances*. In this case, the set Ω is sampled uniformly at random among all the subsets of $\{1, \ldots, d\}$ of size t.

Table 1. Parameter sets used for the attack

	LZA 1	LZA 2	HPSSW 1	HPSSW 2	HPSSW 3	HPSSW 4
m	1024	2048	433	577	769	1153
d	512	1024	432	576	768	1152
t	256	512	200	280	386	600
q	65537	65537	775937	743177	1047379	968521
estimated bit security	128	128	$\ll 62$	$\ll 80$	< 100	≤ 130

Regarding historical choices, [LZA18] suggested taking the set Ω uniformly at random, while [HPS+14] seems to assume that Ω can be chosen arbitrarily (and fixed once and for all). Here, we consider all sets of parameters in both regimes where Ω is arbitrary or uniformly chosen.

In both cases, the secret element a and public element b were computed in the same way: we sample $a \in O_K$ uniformly with coefficients in $\{-1, 0, 1\}$ (note that we consider the coefficient embedding of a here, to be consistent with the way PV-Knap instances are described in [HPS+14, LZA18]). We then set $b = a \bmod I_\Omega$.[7]

Worst-Case Instances of Ω. In these experiments, we choose Ω so that I_Ω is stabilized by a large subset of $\mathrm{Aut}_\mathbb{Q}(K)$, as explained in Sect. 4.3. Note that for the HPSSW parameter sets, we do not have subgroups of $\mathrm{Aut}_\mathbb{Q}(K)$ of size exactly t. Hence, we use the technique described above: we take $t_0 = \max(r : r|\phi(m)$ and $r \leq t\}$, a bad set Ω' fixed by a subgroup of order t_0, and run the attack with this set Ω'.

In Table 2 below, we summarize some of the parameters related to the attack. Note that the quantity t_0 is always equal to either $d/2$ or $d/3$, hence we are in a regime where the lattice reduction step can be performed in dimension 2 or 3. Recall that the quantity B is an upper bound on the size of $\|\Sigma_K(a)\|$. In our case, since a has ternary coefficients, this is upper bounded by $\sqrt{d}$.

Recall that our attack from Sect. 4.3 was proven to work when $q^{t_0/d} \geq 8B$. This condition is not always satisfied for our parameter sets, however, we observed that in practice, the attack works for all parameter sets, even when the condition was not satisfied. This is not so surprising since the condition is a sufficient condition for the attack to provably work, but not a necessary one.

For each set of parameters described in Table 1, we performed 20 tests of our search and decision attacks, for an optimal set Ω (optimal for the attack, i.e., containing a subset Ω' fixed by a group of automorphisms of size t_0). The search

---

[7] For the case of HPSSW parameters, the generation of a is slightly different, in order to be consistent with the specifications of [HPS+14]. They consider PV-Knap instances over the cyclic ring $\mathbb{Z}[X]/(X^m - 1)$ instead of O_K. For this specific case, we generate a with ternary coefficients in the ring $\mathbb{Z}[X]/(X^m - 1)$, and then reduce it modulo $\Phi_m(X)$ in order to map it to O_K and continue the attack in O_K, cf. Sect. 2.4.

Table 2. Some quantities related to the attack

	LZA 1	LZA 2	HPSSW 1	HPSSW 2	HPSSW 3	HPSSW 4
t	256	512	200	280	386	600
t_0	256	512	144	192	384	576
$q^{t_0/d}$	256.0	256.0	91.9	90.6	1023.4	984.1
$8 \cdot B$	181.0	256	166.3	192.2	221.8	271.6

and decision attacks both succeeded with probability 1 on all cases. They took
between 5 s for the smallest sets of parameters and 2 min for the largest ones,
on a personal laptop (the timings are for performing the 20 tests, but the short
vector in I_Ω^{-1} is computed only once).

For the large sets of parameters LZA 2 and HPSSW 4, we also tried the
attack with not so optimal sets Ω: we chose Ω so that I_Ω was stable by a subset of $\mathrm{Aut}_\mathbb{Q}(K)$ of size 16, instead of the optimal subsets of size 512 and 576
respectively.[8] This means that the SVP instance we had to solve was in dimension 64 and 72 respectively (instead of dimension 2). Even in this less favorable
scenario, the search attack succeeded with probability 1 over the 20 tests, and
it ran in 2 min and 4 min respectively. Note that recovering the secret a already
solves the decision variant of PV-Knap as well.

Our conclusion is that the easy instances of PV-Knap that we identified are
really easy (solved in less than a few minutes on a personal laptop), even for
number fields of large degree and concrete parameter sets, and even when the
condition $q^{t_0/d} \geq 8B \cdot d^{3/2}$ is not satisfied. Hence, the choice of the set Ω should
absolutely not be given to the attacker.

This worst-case attack can be considered to break (at least partially) the
PV-Knap settings suggested in [HPS+14], since it wasn't specified how the set Ω
should be chosen. For [LZA18], the authors require Ω to be uniformly sampled,
hence the worst-case attack cannot be considered to break their settings.

Random Choices of Ω: Estimating the Cost of Lattice Attacks. We now consider
the cases where the set Ω is chosen uniformly at random among all sets of
size t. In this situation, it is very unlikely that the ideal I_Ω is stable by any
non trivial subgroup of the Galois group. Even for a subgroup of order 2, the
probability that I_Ω is stable by this subgroup is roughly equal to $1/2^t$. Indeed,
let $\tau \in \mathrm{Aut}_\mathbb{Q}(K)$ be an element of order 2 (i.e., $\tau(\tau(x)) = x$ for all x). The
ideal I_Ω is stable by τ if and only if, for every $i \in \Omega$, we have $j \in \Omega$ where j
is such that $\mathfrak{p}_j = \tau(\mathfrak{p}_i)$. Since Ω is chosen uniformly at random, the probability
that $j \in \Omega$ is roughly $1/2$.

Even though I_Ω is very unlikely to be stabilized by a non trivial subgroup
of $\mathrm{Aut}_\mathbb{Q}(K)$, we can still try to apply our attack here. The idea is always the

---

[8] Note that here, we do not reduce the size of Ω below t_0: we take Ω as the union
of multiple sets Ω', each one of size 16 such that $I_{\Omega'}$ is fixed by a subgroup H
of $\mathrm{Aut}_\mathbb{Q}(K)$ of size 16 (the same H for all the Ω').

same: we can forget some of the i's in Ω. As we have already seen, reducing the size of Ω by forgetting some of the i's makes the problem harder, since our target is a BDD instance in a denser lattice, and at some point the solution will not even be unique anymore. On the other hand, by discarding some of the elements of Ω in a carefully chosen way, we may hope to obtain a subset Ω' such that $I_{\Omega'}$ is stable by some non trivial subgroup of $\mathrm{Aut}_{\mathbb{Q}}(K)$.

Our objective is then to reduce Ω to some subset Ω' sufficiently large such that b is still a BDD instance in $I_{\Omega'}$, but with $I_{\Omega'}$ stabilized by a subgroup of $\mathrm{Aut}_{\mathbb{Q}}(K)$ as large as possible. The objective of our experiments in this paragraph was to estimate by how much one can hope to reduce the lattice dimension by using this technique. In other words, what is the largest subset of $\mathrm{Aut}_{\mathbb{Q}}(K)$ that stabilizes a sufficiently large subset Ω' of Ω (so that the problem is still well defined with Ω')?

To estimate this quantity, we proceed in two steps. We first estimate the minimal size of Ω' that we can allow for the distinguishing attack to succeed. This is done experimentally, by estimating the size B of a shortest vector in $qI_{\Omega'}^{-1}$ for Ω' of a given length (note that the volume of $qI_{\Omega'}^{-1}$ is equal to $q^{d-|\Omega'|} \cdot \Delta_K^{1/2}$, which only depends on the size of Ω' and not the actual choice of Ω'). We then compute a short element v of length B and experimentally try to distinguish between $v \cdot a \bmod q$ with a uniformly distributed modulo q and $v \cdot a \bmod q$ with a randomly chosen with ternary coefficients (if v is sufficiently small, we expect that $v \cdot a \bmod q$ has more coefficients $< q/4$ when a is ternary than when a is uniform). This gives us an (experimental) lower bound on the size of Ω' we can take in order to distinguish PV-Knap instances from random elements, with a not too small advantage.

Once this lower bound t_0 on the size of Ω' is computed, we compute the largest subset of $\mathrm{Aut}_{\mathbb{Q}}(K)$ stabilizing a subset Ω' of Ω of size at least t_0. We do that for different random choices of Ω, and compute the probability (over the choice of Ω) that there exists a subset Ω' of Ω of size at least t_0 and such that $I_{\Omega'}$ is stabilized by a subgroup of $\mathrm{Aut}_{\mathbb{Q}}(K)$ of order $1, 2, 3, \ldots$.

We observe that, most of the time, there does not exist a subset Ω' with sufficiently large size and stabilized by a non-trivial subgroup of $\mathrm{Aut}_{\mathbb{Q}}(K)$. In these cases, we cannot use our attack to lower the dimension of the lattices. However, in some cases, we were able to find a sufficiently large set Ω' stabilized by a subgroup of $\mathrm{Aut}_{\mathbb{Q}}(K)$ of order 2. In this case, one can reduce the dimension of the lattice in which to solve SVP by a factor 2. In Table 3 below, we show the empirical probability that Ω contains a large enough subset Ω' stabilized by a subgroup of order k of $\mathrm{Aut}_{\mathbb{Q}}(K)$, for $k = 1$ and $k = 2$ (we never observed a larger k experimentally).

We can see that for all parameter sets, there is a non-negligible probability to sample a random Ω that contains a good subset Ω' allowing to reduce the dimension of the lattice problem by a factor 2. Hence, by sampling many random PV-Knap instance, one can hope to obtain an easier than expected instance in a few trials (between 3 and 2500 trials depending on the parameter sets).

Table 3. Probability to find a good subset Ω' in a random Ω

	LZA 1	LZA 2	HPSSW 1	HPSSW 2	HPSSW 3	HPSSW 4
Subgroup of $\mathrm{Aut}_{\mathbb{Q}}(K)$ of size 1	0.86	0.9996	0.98	0.94	0.55	0.65
Subgroup of $\mathrm{Aut}_{\mathbb{Q}}(K)$ of size 2	0.14	0.0004	0.02	0.06	0.45	0.35

The fact that the probability to find a good subset Ω' increases when the dimension increases in the HPSSW parameter sets might seem surprising at first. We believe that the explanation comes from the choice of t, which is $< d/2$ for HPSSW 1 and HPSSW 2 and is $> d/2$ for HPSSW 3 and HPSSW 4. The larger t, the easier it is to find a not too small subset that has some nice stabilizing properties. We also note that the probability to find a good set Ω seems to vary significantly with the choice of t, and with our estimate of t_0 (the minimal size of Ω' that we can allow). Running the same computation with a different random seed might produce significantly different probabilities. For this reason, the numbers in Table 3 are to be taken as order of magnitudes, and not precise estimates of the success probability.

We conclude that, even when the set Ω is chosen uniformly at random, there is some non-negligible probability that one can reduce the dimension of the lattice in which to solve SVP by a factor 2. This might significantly improve the run time of the attack, since the cost of SVP increases exponentially with the dimension of the lattice. Hence, one should be careful when choosing parameter sets for the PV-Knap problem.

Random Choices of Ω: Full Distinguishing Attack. Finally, we also ran the full distinguishing attack on the parameter set LZA 1, which was supposed to provide 128 bits of security.

We implemented the strategy described above: we sampled 3000 random PV-Knap instances, and kept the one whose set Ω contained the largest subset Ω' stabilized by a subgroup of $\mathrm{Aut}_{\mathbb{Q}}(K)$ of order 2. We then ran BKZ with block size ≤ 50 in the lattice $qI_{\Omega'}^{-1}$ to obtain a sufficiently short element v. This took time roughly 11 h on a personal laptop. We then estimated empirically the probability success of our distinguishing attack given this short element v and random BDD targets b.

We concluded that our short vector v allows us to distinguish uniform targets b from PV-Knap ones with advantage at least 0.0005. We computed this advantage using 10^6 samples, to make sure that the advantage gap we computed was significant (Hoeffding's bound guarantees that our advantage is at least 0.0005, expect with probability at most 0.01). Overall, taking into account the fact that our attack chooses the best Ω among 3000 choices, this means that our distinguishing advantage is at least $3000^{-1} \cdot 0.0005 \geq 2^{-23}$, for a run time of less than 12 h on a personal laptop with a 1.8 GHz processor, hence amounting to $\leq 2^{47}$ bit-operations. It was suggested in [MW18] to define the bit-security of a distinguishing problem as $\log_2(T/\varepsilon^2)$, where ε is the distinguishing advantage of the attacker and T is its time (or, in our case, its number of bit-operations). Our attack hence shows that the parameter set LZA 1 enjoys at most $47 + 2 \cdot 23 = 93$ bits of security, which is significantly smaller than the expected 128 bits of security. We note however that this does not fully invalidate the claim made in [LZA18], since the 128 bit-security is claimed against search attackers, and not distinguishing attackers.

We could also increase the advantage of our attack a bit more, by spending more time on the lattice reduction phase, in order to obtain an even shorter element v. We did so with BKZ with block-size 55 and obtained an attack with advantage roughly $3000^{-1} \cdot 0.0044 \geq 2^{-20}$, for a total time $\leq 20\,\mathrm{h}$. This reduces the security of the parameter set LZA 1 even further to ≤ 87 bits of security (against distinguishing attackers).

This attack shows that the security estimate provided in [LZA18] for the first set of parameters is overestimated for distinguishing attackers, even when the set Ω is chosen uniformly at random. We expect that the other estimates provided in [LZA18] and [HPS+14] might also be overestimated, even though it might not be possible to actually run the full attack in a few hours on a laptop.

Acknowledgments. We are grateful to Amin Sakzad, Damien Stehlé and Ron Steinfeld for helpful discussions. This research was partly funded by the ANR CHARM project (ANR-21-CE94-0003) and further supported by the Danish Independent Research Council under project number 0165-00107B (C3PO).

References

[AD17] Albrecht, M.R., Deo, A.: Large modulus ring-LWE $\geq$ module-LWE. In: Takagi, T., Peyrin, T. (eds.) ASIACRYPT 2017. LNCS, vol. 10624, pp. 267–296. Springer, Cham (2017). https://doi.org/10.1007/978-3-319-70694-8_10

[Ajt96] Ajtai, M.: Generating hard instances of lattice problems (extended abstract). In: STOC, pp. 99–108. ACM (1996)

[Bab86] Babai, L.: On lovász'lattice reduction and the nearest lattice point problem. Combinatorica **6**(1), 1–13 (1986)

[BGP22] Boudgoust, K., Gachon, E., Pellet-Mary, A.: Some easy instances of ideal-SVP and implications on the partial Vandermonde Knapsack problem. Cryptology ePrint Archive, Paper 2022/709 (2022)

[BLNR21] Bernard, O., Lesavourey, A., Nguyen, T.-H., Roux-Langlois, A.: Log-S-unit lattices using explicit stickelberger generators to solve approx ideal-SVP. Cryptology ePrint Archive (2021)

[Bou21] Boudgoust, K.: Theoretical hardness of algebraically structured learning with errors. Ph.D. thesis, Universite Rennes 1 (2021). https://tel.archives-ouvertes.fr/tel-03534254/document

[BR20] Bernard, O., Roux-Langlois, A.: Twisted-PHS: using the product formula to solve approx-SVP in ideal lattices. In: Moriai, S., Wang, H. (eds.) ASIACRYPT 2020. LNCS, vol. 12492, pp. 349–380. Springer, Cham (2020). https://doi.org/10.1007/978-3-030-64834-3_12

[BSS22] Boudgoust, K., Sakzad, A., Steinfeld, R.: Vandermonde meets Regev: public key encryption schemes based on partial Vandermonde problems. Cryptology ePrint Archive, Report 2022/679 (2022)

[CDPR16] Cramer, R., Ducas, L., Peikert, C., Regev, O.: Recovering short generators of principal ideals in cyclotomic rings. In: Fischlin, M., Coron, J.-S. (eds.) EUROCRYPT 2016. LNCS, vol. 9666, pp. 559–585. Springer, Heidelberg (2016). https://doi.org/10.1007/978-3-662-49896-5_20

[CDW21] Cramer, R., Ducas, L., Wesolowski, B.: Mildly short vectors in cyclotomic ideal lattices in quantum polynomial time. J. ACM (JACM) 68(2), 1–26 (2021)

[Con] Conrad, K.: The different ideal. https://kconrad.math.uconn.edu/blurbs/gradnumthy/different.pdf. Accessed 16 Feb 2022

[dBDPW20] de Boer, K., Ducas, L., Pellet-Mary, A., Wesolowski, B.: Random self-reducibility of ideal-SVP via Arakelov random walks. In: Micciancio, D., Ristenpart, T. (eds.) CRYPTO 2020. LNCS, vol. 12171, pp. 243–273. Springer, Cham (2020). https://doi.org/10.1007/978-3-030-56880-1_9

[DHSS20] Doröz, Y., Hoffstein, J., Silverman, J.H., Sunar, B.: MMSAT: a scheme for multimessage multiuser signature aggregation. Cryptology ePrint Archive, Report 2020/520 (2020)

[Gen09] Gentry, C.: A fully homomorphic encryption scheme. Ph.D. thesis, Stanford University (2009). http://crypto.stanford.edu/craig

[HKJL+00] Hoffstein, J., Kaliski, B.S., Jr., Lieman, D.B., Robshaw, M.J.B., Yin, Y.L.: Secure user identification based on constrained polynomials, 13 June 2000. US Patent 6,076,163. Filed 20 October 1997

[HPS98] Hoffstein, J., Pipher, J., Silverman, J.H.: NTRU: a ring-based public key cryptosystem. In: Buhler, J.P. (ed.) ANTS 1998. LNCS, vol. 1423, pp. 267–288. Springer, Heidelberg (1998). https://doi.org/10.1007/BFb0054868

[HPS11] Hanrot, G., Pujol, X., Stehlé, D.: Analyzing blockwise lattice algorithms using dynamical systems. In: Rogaway, P. (ed.) CRYPTO 2011. LNCS, vol. 6841, pp. 447–464. Springer, Heidelberg (2011). https://doi.org/10.1007/978-3-642-22792-9_25

[HPS+14] Hoffstein, J., Pipher, J., Schanck, J.M., Silverman, J.H., Whyte, W.: Practical signatures from the partial Fourier recovery problem. In: Boureanu, I., Owesarski, P., Vaudenay, S. (eds.) ACNS 2014. LNCS, vol. 8479, pp. 476–493. Springer, Cham (2014). https://doi.org/10.1007/978-3-319-07536-5_28

[HS15] Hoffstein, J., Silverman, J.H.: Pass-encrypt: a public key cryptosystem based on partial evaluation of polynomials. Des. Codes Crypt. 77(2), 541–552 (2015)

[Lan02] Lang, S.: Algebra. Springer, Heidelberg (2002). https://doi.org/10.1007/978-1-4613-0041-0

[LM06] Lyubashevsky, V., Micciancio, D.: Generalized compact Knapsacks are collision resistant. In: Bugliesi, M., Preneel, B., Sassone, V., Wegener, I. (eds.) ICALP 2006. LNCS, vol. 4052, pp. 144–155. Springer, Heidelberg (2006). https://doi.org/10.1007/11787006_13

[LPR10] Lyubashevsky, V., Peikert, C., Regev, O.: On ideal lattices and learning with errors over rings. In: Gilbert, H. (ed.) EUROCRYPT 2010. LNCS, vol. 6110, pp. 1–23. Springer, Heidelberg (2010). https://doi.org/10.1007/978-3-642-13190-5_1

[LS15]   Langlois, A., Stehlé, D.: Worst-case to average-case reductions for module lattices. Des. Codes Crypt. **75**(3), 565–599 (2014). https://doi.org/10.1007/s10623-014-9938-4

[LZA18] Lu, X., Zhang, Z., Au, M.H.: Practical signatures from the partial Fourier recovery problem revisited: a provably-secure and Gaussian-distributed construction. In: Susilo, W., Yang, G. (eds.) ACISP 2018. LNCS, vol. 10946, pp. 813–820. Springer, Cham (2018). https://doi.org/10.1007/978-3-319-93638-3_50

[Mar77] Marcus, D.A.: Number Fields, vol. 2. Springer, Heidelberg (1977). https://doi.org/10.1007/978-1-4684-9356-6

[Mic02] Micciancio, D.: Generalized compact knapsacks, cyclic lattices, and efficient one-way functions from worst-case complexity assumptions. In: FOCS, pp. 356–365. IEEE Computer Society (2002)

[MW18]   Micciancio, D., Walter, M.: On the bit security of cryptographic primitives. In: Nielsen, J.B., Rijmen, V. (eds.) EUROCRYPT 2018. LNCS, vol. 10820, pp. 3–28. Springer, Cham (2018). https://doi.org/10.1007/978-3-319-78381-9_1

[PHS19] Pellet-Mary, A., Hanrot, G., Stehlé, D.: Approx-SVP in ideal lattices with pre-processing. In: Ishai, Y., Rijmen, V. (eds.) EUROCRYPT 2019. LNCS, vol. 11477, pp. 685–716. Springer, Cham (2019). https://doi.org/10.1007/978-3-030-17656-3_24

[PML21] Porter, C., Mendelsohn, A., Ling, C.: Subfield algorithms for ideal- and module-SVP based on the decomposition group. arXiv preprint arXiv:2105.03219 (2021)

[PR06]   Peikert, C., Rosen, A.: Efficient collision-resistant hashing from worst-case assumptions on cyclic lattices. In: Halevi, S., Rabin, T. (eds.) TCC 2006. LNCS, vol. 3876, pp. 145–166. Springer, Heidelberg (2006). https://doi.org/10.1007/11681878_8

[PXWC21] Pan, Y., Xu, J., Wadleigh, N., Cheng, Q.: On the ideal shortest vector problem over random rational primes. In: Canteaut, A., Standaert, F.-X. (eds.) EUROCRYPT 2021. LNCS, vol. 12696, pp. 559–583. Springer, Cham (2021). https://doi.org/10.1007/978-3-030-77870-5_20

[Reg05] Regev, O.: On lattices, learning with errors, random linear codes, and cryptography. In: STOC, pp. 84–93. ACM (2005)

[SE94]   Schnorr, C.-P., Euchner, M.: Lattice basis reduction: improved practical algorithms and solving subset sum problems. Math. Program. **66**, 181–199 (1994)

[SSTX09] Stehlé, D., Steinfeld, R., Tanaka, K., Xagawa, K.: Efficient public key encryption based on ideal lattices. In: Matsui, M. (ed.) ASIACRYPT 2009. LNCS, vol. 5912, pp. 617–635. Springer, Heidelberg (2009). https://doi.org/10.1007/978-3-642-10366-7_36

[The20] The Sage Developers. SageMath, the Sage Mathematics Software System (Version 9.0) (2020). https://www.sagemath.org

[Was82] Washington, L.C.: Introduction to Cyclotomic Fields, vol. 83. Springer, Berlin (1982). https://doi.org/10.1007/978-1-4684-0133-2

Coding Theory

On Codes and Learning with Errors over Function Fields

Maxime Bombar[1,2]([⊠]) [iD], Alain Couvreur[1,2][iD],
and Thomas Debris-Alazard[1,2][iD]

[1] LIX, CNRS UMR 7161, École Polytechnique, Institut Polytechnique de Paris,
1 rue Honoré d'Estienne d'Orves, 91120 Palaiseau Cedex, France
[2] Inria Saclay, Palaiseau, France
{maxime.bombar,alain.couvreur,thomas.debris}@inria.fr

Abstract. It is a long standing open problem to find search to decision reductions for structured versions of the decoding problem of linear codes. Such results in the lattice-based setting have been carried out using number fields: Polynomial–LWE, Ring–LWE, Module–LWE and so on. We propose a function field version of the LWE problem. This new framework leads to another point of view on structured codes, *e.g.* quasi-cyclic codes, strengthening the connection between lattice-based and code-based cryptography. In particular, we obtain the first search to decision reduction for structured codes. Following the historical constructions in lattice–based cryptography, we instantiate our construction with function fields analogues of cyclotomic fields, namely *Carlitz* extensions, leading to search to decision reductions on various versions of Ring-LPN, which have applications to secure multiparty computation and to an authentication protocol.

Keywords: Code-based cryptography · Search to decision reductions · LWE · Function fields · Carlitz modules

1 Introduction

Code-Based Cryptography. Error correcting codes are well known to provide quantum resistant cryptographic primitives such as authentication protocols [18,35], signatures [10,13] or encryption schemes such as McEliece [24]. These code-based cryptosystems were built to rely on the following hard problem: finding a close (or far away) codeword to a given word, a task called *decoding*. In the case of random linear codes of length n, which is the standard case, this problem

This work was funded by the French Agence Nationale de la Recherche through ANR JCJC COLA (ANR-21-CE39-0011) and ANR BARRACUDA (ANR-21-CE39-0009-BARRACUDA).

Y. Dodis and T. Shrimpton (Eds.): CRYPTO 2022, LNCS 13508, pp. 513–540, 2022.
https://doi.org/10.1007/978-3-031-15979-4_18

can be expressed as follows. First, we are given a vector space $\mathcal{C}$ (*i.e.* the code) of $\mathbb{F}_q^n$ generated by the rows of some random matrix $\mathbf{G} \in \mathbb{F}_q^{k \times n}$, namely:

$$\mathcal{C} \stackrel{\text{def}}{=} \{\mathbf{mG} \mid \mathbf{m} \in \mathbb{F}_q^k\}. \tag{1}$$

The decoding problem corresponds, given $\mathbf{G}$ (in other words $\mathcal{C}$) and some noisy codeword $\mathbf{mG} + \mathbf{e}$ where the number of non-zero coordinates of $\mathbf{e}$ is equal to t (its Hamming weight is $|\mathbf{e}| = t$), to find the error $\mathbf{e}$ or what amounts to the same, the original codeword $\mathbf{mG}$.

Usually this decoding problem is considered in the regime where the code rate $R \stackrel{\text{def}}{=} \frac{k}{n}$ is fixed, but there are also other interesting parameters for cryptographic applications. For instance, the Learning Parity with Noise problem (LPN) corresponds to the decoding problem where n is the number of samples, k the length of the secret while the error is sampled according to a Bernoulli distribution of fixed rate t/n. As the number of samples in LPN is unlimited, this problem actually corresponds to decoding a random code of rate arbitrarily close to 0.

Despite the promising approach of McEliece, there are two drawbacks if one follows it to design a cryptosystem. First, the public data in McEliece is a representation of a code which has to look like random. Assuming this pseudo-randomness property, the security relies on the hardness of the decoding problem. In that case one needs to publish $\Omega(n^2)$ bits but at the same time, best generic decoding algorithms have a complexity exponential in the number t of errors to correct. Therefore, to reach a security level of 2^λ, the public data are of order $\Theta(\lambda^2)$ if $t = \Theta(n)$ or even worse of the order $\Theta(\lambda^4)$ if $t = \Theta(\sqrt{n})$. On the other hand, in McEliece-like cryptosystems, the owner of the secret key has to know an efficient decoding algorithm for the public code. It turns out that codes for which we know an efficient decoding algorithm are obtained via polynomial evaluations (*e.g.* Goppa codes) or short vectors (*e.g.* MDPC codes). Thus, the owner of the secret key has to hide the peculiar description of the code he publishes. It leads to the fact that in McEliece-like cryptosystems, the security also relies on the difficulty to distinguish the code that is made public from a random one. This is a second assumption to make in addition to the hardness of the decoding problem.

Alekhnovich Cryptosystem. In 2003, Alekhnovich [5] introduced a new approach to design an encryption scheme based on error correcting codes. Unlike McEliece cryptosystem, Alekhnovich truly relies on the hardness of decoding random codes. It starts from a random code $\mathcal{C}$ and proceeds as follows:

- *Key Generation.* Let $\mathbf{e}_{\mathsf{sk}} \in \mathbb{F}_2^n$ of small Hamming weight. The public key is $(\mathcal{C}, \mathbf{c} + \mathbf{e}_{\mathsf{sk}})$ where $\mathbf{c} \in \mathcal{C}$ and the secret key is $\mathbf{e}_{\mathsf{sk}}$.
- *Encryption.* To encrypt one bit $\beta \in \{0, 1\}$ set:
  - $\mathsf{Enc}(1) \stackrel{\text{def}}{=} \mathbf{u}$ where $\mathbf{u} \in \mathbb{F}_2^n$ is a uniformly random vector.
  - $\mathsf{Enc}(0) \stackrel{\text{def}}{=} \mathbf{c}^* + \mathbf{e}$ where $\mathbf{e}$ is of small Hamming weight and $\mathbf{c}^*$ lies in the dual of the code $\mathcal{C}_{\mathsf{pub}}$ spanned by $\mathcal{C}$ and $\mathbf{c} + \mathbf{e}_{\mathsf{sk}}$.

- *Decryption.* The decryption of $\mathsf{Enc}(\beta)$ is $\langle \mathsf{Enc}(\beta), \mathbf{e}_{\mathsf{sk}} \rangle$, where $\langle \cdot, \cdot \rangle$ is the usual inner product on $\mathbb{F}_2^n$.

The correction of this procedure relies on the fact that

$$\langle \mathsf{Enc}(0), \mathbf{e}_{\mathsf{sk}} \rangle = \langle \mathbf{c}^* + \mathbf{e}, \mathbf{e}_{\mathsf{sk}} \rangle = \langle \mathbf{e}, \mathbf{e}_{\mathsf{sk}} \rangle,$$

where we used that $\mathbf{e}_{\mathsf{sk}} \in \mathcal{C}_{\mathsf{pub}}$ while $\mathbf{c}^*$ lies in its dual. Now, this inner product is equal to 0 with overwhelming probability as $\mathbf{e}_{\mathsf{sk}}$ and $\mathbf{e}$ are of small Hamming weight. On the other hand, $\langle \mathsf{Enc}(1), \mathbf{e}_{\mathsf{sk}} \rangle$ is a uniformly random bit.

Therefore, contrary to McEliece cryptosystem, the security of Alekhnovich scheme does not depend on hiding the description of a code:

- *Key security.* Recovering the private key from public data amounts to decoding the random code $\mathcal{C}$.
- *Message security.* Recovering the plaintext from the ciphertext is tantamount to *distinguishing* a noisy codeword from a uniformly random vector.

The message security relies on the *decision* version of the decoding problem. Search and decision versions of the decoding problem are known to be computationally equivalent using Goldreich-Levin theorem [14]. However, Alekhnovich cryptosystem suffers from major drawbacks:

1. Encrypting one bit amounts to sending n bits;
2. The public key size is quadratic in the length of ciphertexts.

While the first issue can easily be addressed, the second flaw needs more work, and as is, Alekhnovich cryptosystem is not practical. However, the approach itself was a major breakthrough in code-based cryptography. It was inspired by the work of Ajtai and Dwork [3] whose cryptosystem is based on solving hard lattice problems. The latter reference from Ajtai and Dwork is also the inspiration of Regev famous Learning With Errors (LWE) problem [30], which is at the origin of an impressive line of work. As Alekhnovich cryptosystem, the original LWE cryptosystem was not practical either and, to address this issue, structured versions were proposed, for instance Polynomial-LWE [34], Ring-LWE [23], Module-LWE [20].

Structured Decoding Problem. In the same fashion, for code–based public key encryptions, it has been proposed to restrict to codes that can be represented more compactly to reduce the key sizes. In McEliece setting, the story begins in 2005 with the results of [15] that suggest to use ℓ–quasi-cyclic codes, *i.e.* codes that are generated by a matrix $\mathbf{G}$ formed out of ℓ blocks:

$$\mathbf{G} = \left(\mathbf{rot}\left(\mathbf{a}^{(1)}\right) \cdots \mathbf{rot}\left(\mathbf{a}^{(\ell)}\right) \right), \tag{2}$$

each block being a circulant matrix, *i.e.* of the form

$$\mathbf{rot(a)} \stackrel{\text{def}}{=} \begin{pmatrix} a_0 & a_1 & \cdots & \cdots & a_{k-1} \\ a_{k-1} & a_0 & \cdots & \cdots & a_{k-2} \\ \vdots & \ddots & \ddots & & \vdots \\ \vdots & & \ddots & \ddots & \vdots \\ a_1 & a_2 & \cdots & a_{k-1} & a_0 \end{pmatrix} \text{ with } \mathbf{a} \in \mathbb{F}_q^k.$$

The key point is that such codes have a large automorphism group G, and instead of publishing a whole basis, one can only publish a generating set for the $\mathbb{F}_q[G]$–module structure of the code. That is to say, a family of vectors whose orbit under the action of G spans the code. For instance, in the case of quasi-cyclic codes (2), one can publish only the first row of the ℓ-circulant generator matrix. It can be argued that the quasi–cyclicity could be used to improve the speed-up of generic decoding, but the best known approach in the generic case uses DOOM [33] which allows to divide the complexity of decoding by $\sqrt{\#G}$, the latter complexity remaining exponential with the same exponent. Hence, one can keep the same security parameter, while the size of the public key can be divided by a factor $O(\#G)$.

This idea leads to very efficient encryption schemes such as BIKE [1], in the McEliece fashion, or HQC [2] which is closer to Ring-LWE. Both proposals use 2-quasi-cyclic codes and have been selected to the third round of NIST competition as alternate candidates. Other structured variants of the decoding problem (referred to as Ring-LPN) were also proposed with applications to authentication [18] or secure MPC [7].

In other words, the security of those cryptosystems now rely on some structured variant of the decoding problem.

A Polynomial Representation. It turns out that a convenient way of seeing ℓ-quasi-cyclic codes, is to represent blocks of their generator matrix as elements of the quotient ring $\mathbb{F}_q[X]/(X^n - 1)$, via the $\mathbb{F}_q$–isomorphism:

$$\begin{cases} \mathbb{F}_q^n & \longrightarrow \mathbb{F}_q[X]/(X^n - 1) \\ \mathbf{a} \stackrel{\text{def}}{=} (a_0, \ldots, a_{n-1}) & \longmapsto \mathbf{a}(X) \stackrel{\text{def}}{=} \sum_{i=0}^{n-1} a_i X^i. \end{cases}$$

A simple computation shows that the product of two elements of $\mathbb{F}_q[X]/(X^n - 1)$ can be represented with the operator $\mathbf{rot}(\cdot)$:

$$\mathbf{u}(X)\mathbf{v}(X) \mod (X^n - 1) = \mathbf{u} \cdot \mathbf{rot}(\mathbf{v}) = \mathbf{v} \cdot \mathbf{rot}(\mathbf{u}) = \mathbf{v}(X)\mathbf{u}(X) \mod (X^n - 1).$$

From now on, $\mathbf{u}$ can denote either a vector of $\mathbb{F}_q^n$ or a polynomial in $\mathbb{F}_q[X]/(X^n - 1)$, and the product of two elements $\mathbf{uv}$ is defined as above.

Consider an ℓ-quasi-cyclic code with a generator matrix $\mathbf{G}$ in ℓ-circulant form. Let $\mathbf{s} \in \mathbb{F}_q^n$ be a secret word of the ambient space and let $\mathbf{e} \in \mathbb{F}_q^{\ell n}$ be an error vector. Under the above map, the noisy codeword $\mathbf{sG} + \mathbf{e}$ is represented by ℓ samples of the form $\mathbf{sa}^{(j)} + \mathbf{e}^{(j)} \in \mathbb{F}_q[X]/(X^n - 1)$ and the decoding problem of ℓ-circulant codes corresponds to recovering the secret $\mathbf{s}$ given ℓ samples. This can be seen as a code analogue of the Ring-LWE problem, with access to a fixed number of samples ℓ. The rate of the code is $\frac{1}{\ell}$, so increasing the number of samples corresponds to decode a code whose rate goes to 0.

A natural generalization would be to consider multiple rows of circulant blocks. In this situation, the generator matrix $\mathbf{G}$ is of the form

$$\mathbf{G} = \begin{pmatrix} \mathbf{rot}(\mathbf{a}^{(1,1)}) & \cdots & \mathbf{rot}(\mathbf{a}^{(1,\ell)}) \\ \vdots & & \vdots \\ \mathbf{rot}(\mathbf{a}^{(m,1)}) & \cdots & \mathbf{rot}(\mathbf{a}^{(m,\ell)}) \end{pmatrix}$$

and a noisy codeword $\mathbf{sG} + \mathbf{e}$ is now represented by ℓ samples of the form

$$\sum_{i=1}^{m} \mathbf{s}_i \mathbf{a}^{(i,j)} + \mathbf{e}_j \in \mathbb{F}_q[X]/(X^n - 1)$$

where $\mathbf{s}$ can be considered as a collection of m secrets $\mathbf{s}_1, \ldots, \mathbf{s}_m$. This would be the code analogue of Module-LWE, with a rank m module and ℓ samples, introduced in [20].

Contrary to structured lattice cryptosystems, up to now, no reduction from the search to the decision version of the structured decoding problem was known. This was pointed out by NIST [4], and was one of the reasons for those code-based cryptosystems to only be considered as alternate candidates for the third round. Actually even before NIST standardization process, this lack of search to decision reduction was already pointed out by the authors of the Ring-LPN based authentication scheme LAPIN [18].

Our Contribution. To handle this lack of search to decision reduction in the code setting, we propose in this article a new generic problem called FF-DP, for *Function Field Decoding Problem*, in the Ring-LWE fashion. One of the key ideas consists in using function fields instead of number fields, the latter being used in the lattice case. This framework enables us to adapt directly the search to decision reduction of [23] in the case of codes. Frequently in the literature on Ring-LWE, the search to decision reduction is instantiated with cyclotomic number fields. In the same spirit we present an instantiation with function fields analogues of cyclotomic fields, namely the so-called *Carlitz extensions*. As we show, this framework is for instance enough to provide a search to decision reduction useful in the context of LAPIN [18] or for a q–ary analogue of Ring-LPN used for secure multiparty computation [7]. If our reduction does not work for every schemes based on structured codes such as HQC, we believe that our work paves the way towards a full reduction.

Remark 1. Note that the use of function fields in coding theory is far from being new. Since the early 80's and the seminal work of Goppa [16], it is well-known that codes called *Algebraic Geometry* (AG) codes can be constructed from algebraic curves or equivalently from function fields and that some of these codes have better asymptotic parameters than random ones [37]. However, the way they are used in the present work is completely different. Indeed, AG codes are a natural generalization of Reed–Solomon codes and, in particular, are codes benefiting from efficient decoding algorithms (see for instance surveys [6,11,19]). In the present article, the approach is somehow orthogonal to the AG codes setting since we use function fields in order to introduce generic problems related to structured codes for which the decoding problem is supposed to be hard.

A Function Field Approach. Lattice-based cryptography has a long standing history of using number fields and their rings of integers to add some structure and reduce the key sizes. Recall that number fields are algebraic extensions of $\mathbb{Q}$ of the form

$$K \overset{\text{def}}{=} \mathbb{Q}[X]/(f(X)),$$

where f is an irreducible polynomial, and the ring of integers $\mathscr{O}_K$ is the integral closure of $\mathbb{Z}$ in K, *i.e.* it is the subring of K composed of elements which are roots of monic polynomials with coefficients in $\mathbb{Z}$. For instance, cyclotomic extensions are of the form $K = \mathbb{Q}(\zeta_m) = \mathbb{Q}[X]/(\varPhi_m(X))$ where ζ_m is a primitive m-th root of unity and $\varPhi_m$ is the m-th cyclotomic polynomial. The ring of cyclotomic integers has a very specific form, namely $\mathscr{O}_K = \mathbb{Z}[\zeta_m]$. One of the most used case is when m is a power of 2. In this case, setting $m = 2n$, we have $\varPhi_m = \varPhi_{2n} = X^n + 1$ and $\mathscr{O}_K = \mathbb{Z}[X]/(X^n + 1)$. Such rings have been widely used since they benefit from a very fast arithmetic thanks to the fast Fourier transform. In the Ring–LWE setting, one reduces all the samples modulo a large prime element $q \in \mathbb{Z}$ called the *modulus* and hence considers the ring $(\mathbb{Z}/q\mathbb{Z})[X]/(X^n + 1)$.

When moving from structured lattices to structured codes, it would be tantalizing to consider the ring $\mathbb{F}_q[X]/(X^n - 1)$ as the analogue of $\mathbb{Z}[X]/(X^n + 1)$. However, if the two rings have a similar expression they have a fundamental difference. Note for instance that the former is finite while the latter is infinite. From a more algebraic point of view, $\mathbb{F}_q[X]/(X^n - 1)$ is said to have *Krull dimension* 0 while $\mathbb{Z}[X]/(X^n + 1)$ has *Krull dimension* 1. In particular, the former has only a finite number of ideals while the latter has infinitely many prime ideals. The main idea of the present article is to lift the decoding problem and to see $\mathbb{F}_q[X]/(X^n - 1)$ as a quotient R/I of some ring R of Krull dimension 1. The ideal I will be the analogue of the *modulus*. This setting can be achieved using so-called *function fields*. It could be argued that the results of this article could have been obtained without introducing function fields. However, we claim that function fields are crucial for at least three reasons:

1. Introducing function fields permits to establish a strong connection between cryptography based on structured lattices involving number fields on the one hand and cryptography based on structured codes on the other hand.
2. Number theory has a rich history with almost one hundred years of development of the theory of function fields. We expect that, as number fields did for structured lattices, function fields will yield a remarkable toolbox to study structured codes and cryptographic questions related to them.

3. A third and more technical evidence is that a crucial part of the search to
decision reduction involves some Galois action. We claim that, even if for a
specific instantiation, this group action could have been described in a pedestrian way on the finite ring $\mathbb{F}_q[X]/(X^n - 1)$, without knowing the context
of function fields, such a group action would really look like "a rabbit pulled
out of a hat". In short, this group action, which is crucial to conclude the
search to decision reduction, cannot appear to be something natural without
considering function fields.

It is well–known for a long time that there is a noticeable analogy between
the theory of number fields and that of function fields. Starting from the ground,
the rings $\mathbb{Z}$ and $\mathbb{F}_q[T]$ share a lot of common features. For instance, they both
have an Euclidean division. Now if one considers their respective fraction fields
$\mathbb{Q}$ and $\mathbb{F}_q(T)$, finite extensions of $\mathbb{Q}$ yield the number fields while finite separable
extensions of $\mathbb{F}_q(T)$ are called *function fields* because they are also the fields
of rational functions on curves over finite fields. Now, a similar arithmetic theory can be developed for both with rings of integers, orders, places and so on.
Both rings of integers are *Dedekind domains*. In particular, every ideal factorizes
uniquely into a product of prime ideals, and the quotient by any non-zero ideal
is always finite. A dictionary summarizing this analogy between number fields
and function fields is represented in Table 1. Note that actually, many properties
that are known for function fields are only conjectures for number fields. The
best example is probably the Riemann hypothesis which has been proved by
Weil in the early 1940s in the function field case.

Table 1. A Number-Function fields analogy

Number fields	Function fields
$\mathbb{Q}$	$\mathbb{F}_q(T)$
$\mathbb{Z}$	$\mathbb{F}_q[T]$
Prime numbers $q \in \mathbb{Z}$	Irreducible polynomials $Q \in \mathbb{F}_q[T]$
$K = \mathbb{Q}[X]/(f(X))$	$K = \mathbb{F}_q(T)[X]/(f(T,X))$
$\mathscr{O}_K$	$\mathscr{O}_K$
$=$ Integral closure of $\mathbb{Z}$	$=$ Integral closure of $\mathbb{F}_q[T]$
Dedekind domain	*Dedekind* domain
characteristic 0	**characteristic > 0**

With this analogy in hand, the idea is to find a nice function field K with
ring of integers $\mathscr{O}_K$ and an irreducible polynomial $Q \in \mathbb{F}_q[T]$, called the *modulus*,
such that $\mathscr{O}_K/Q\mathscr{O}_K = \mathbb{F}_q[X]/(X^n - 1)$. Following the path of [23], we are able

to provide a search to decision reduction for our generic problem FF-DP when two conditions hold:

1. The function field K is Galois.
2. The modulus Q does not ramify in $\mathcal{O}_K$, meaning that the ideal $Q\mathcal{O}_K$ factorizes in product of distinct prime ideals.
3. The distribution of errors is invariant under the action of the Galois group.

This framework is enough to provide a search to decision reduction useful in the context of LAPIN [18] or for a q–ary analogue of Ring–LPN used for secure MPC [7]. It should be emphasized that, in the case of LAPIN, the search to decision reduction requires to adapt the definition of the noise which will remain built by applying independent Bernouilli random variables but with a peculiar choice of $\mathbb{F}_2$–basis of the underlying ring $\mathbb{F}_2[X]/(f(X))$. The chosen basis is a *normal* basis, *i.e.* is globally invariant with respect to the Galois action. This change of basis is very similar to the one performed in lattice based cryptography when, instead of considering the monomial basis $1, X, \ldots, X^{n-1}$ in an order $\mathbb{Z}[X]/(f(X))$, one considers the canonical basis after applying the Minkowski embedding. Indeed, the latter is Galois invariant. We emphasize that, here again, the function field point of view brings in a Galois action which cannot appear when only considering a ring such as $\mathbb{F}_2[X]/(f(X))$. This is another evidence of the need for introducing function fields.

Outline of the Article. The present article is organised as follows. Section 2 recalls the necessary background about function fields (definitions and important properties). In Sect. 3 we present the FF-DP problem (search and decision versions) as well as our main theorem (Theorem 1) which states the search to decision reduction in the function field setting. In Sect. 4 we give a self contain presentation of Carlitz extensions. They will be used to instantiate our search to decision reduction in Sect. 5, which provides our applications.

2   Prerequisites on Function Fields

In this section, we list the minimal basic notions on the arithmetic of function fields that are needed in the sequel. A dictionary drawing the analogies has been given in Table 1. For further references on the arithmetic of function fields, we refer the reader to [32, 36].

Starting from a finite field $\mathbb{F}_q$, a *function field* is a finite extension K of $\mathbb{F}_q(T)$ of degree $n > 0$ of the form

$$K = \mathbb{F}_q(T)[X]/(P(T, X))$$

where $P(T, X) \in \mathbb{F}_q(T)[X]$ is irreducible of degree n. The field $K \cap \overline{\mathbb{F}}_q$ is referred to as *the field of constants* or *constant field* of K, where $\overline{\mathbb{F}}_q$ is the algebraic closure of $\mathbb{F}_q$. In the sequel, we will assume that $\mathbb{F}_q$ is the full field of constants of K, which is equivalent for $P(T, X)$ to be irreducible even regarded as an element of $\overline{\mathbb{F}}_q(T)[X]$ ([36, Cor. 3.6.8]).

Similarly to the number field case, one can define the ring of integers $\mathscr{O}_K$ as the ring of elements of K which are the roots of a monic polynomial in $\mathbb{F}_q[T][X]$. This ring is a *Dedekind domain*. In particular, any ideal $\mathfrak{P}$ has a unique decomposition $\mathfrak{P}_1^{e_1} \cdots \mathfrak{P}_r^{e_r}$ where the $\mathfrak{P}_i$'s are prime ideals.

In the sequel, we frequently focus on the following setting represented in the diagram below: starting from a prime ideal $\mathfrak{p}$ of $\mathbb{F}_q[T]$ (which is nothing but the ideal generated by an irreducible polynomial $Q(T)$ of $\mathbb{F}_q[T]$), we consider the ideal $\mathfrak{P} \stackrel{\text{def}}{=} \mathfrak{p}\mathscr{O}_K$ and its decomposition:

$$\mathfrak{P} = \mathfrak{P}_1^{e_1} \cdots \mathfrak{P}_r^{e_r}.$$

$$
\begin{array}{ccc}
\mathfrak{P} \subset \mathscr{O}_K & \rule{2cm}{0.4pt} & K \\
| & & | \\
\mathfrak{p} \subset \mathbb{F}_q[T] & \rule{2cm}{0.4pt} & \mathbb{F}_q(T)
\end{array}
$$

The prime ideals $\mathfrak{P}_i$'s are said to *lie above* $\mathfrak{p}$. The exponents e_i are referred to as the *ramification indexes*, and the extension is said to be *unramified* at $\mathfrak{P}$ when all the e_i's are equal to 1. Another important constant related to a $\mathfrak{P}_i$ is its *inertia degree*, which is defined as the extension degree $f_i \stackrel{\text{def}}{=} [\mathscr{O}_K/\mathfrak{P}_i : \mathbb{F}_q[T]/\mathfrak{p}]$ (one can prove that $\mathscr{O}_K/\mathfrak{P}_i$ and $\mathbb{F}_q[T]/\mathfrak{p}$ are both finite fields). The Chinese Remainder Theorem (CRT) induces a ring isomorphism between $\mathscr{O}_K/\mathfrak{P}$ and $\prod_{i=1}^r \mathscr{O}_K/\mathfrak{P}_i^{e_i}$. In particular, when the extension is unramified at $\mathfrak{P}$, the quotient $\mathscr{O}_K/\mathfrak{P}$ is a product of finite fields. Finally, a well-known result asserts that

$$n = [K : \mathbb{F}_q(T)] = \sum_{i=1}^r e_i f_i. \tag{3}$$

Finite Galois Extensions. Consider $K/\mathbb{F}_q(T)$ a Galois function field (*i.e.* a function field K which is a Galois extension of $\mathbb{F}_q(T)$), with Galois group $G \stackrel{\text{def}}{=} \text{Gal}(K/\mathbb{F}_q(T))$. Then, G keeps $\mathscr{O}_K$ globally invariant. Furthermore, given $\mathfrak{p}$ a prime ideal of $\mathbb{F}_q[T]$, the group G acts transitively on the set $\{\mathfrak{P}_1, \ldots, \mathfrak{P}_r\}$ of prime ideals of $\mathscr{O}_K$ lying above $\mathfrak{p}$: for any $i \neq j$ there exists $\sigma \in \text{Gal}(K/\mathbb{F}_q(T))$ such that $\sigma(\mathfrak{P}_i) = \mathfrak{P}_j$. In particular, all the ramification indexes e_i (*resp.* the inertia degrees f_i) are equal and denoted by e (*resp.* f) so that $\mathfrak{P} \stackrel{\text{def}}{=} \mathfrak{p}\mathscr{O}_K = (\mathfrak{P}_1 \cdots \mathfrak{P}_r)^e$ and (3) becomes $n = efr$. Another consequence which will be crucial for the applications, is that the action of G on $\mathscr{O}_K$ is well–defined on $\mathscr{O}_K/\mathfrak{P}$ and simply permutes the factors $\mathscr{O}_K/\mathfrak{P}_i^e$. The *decomposition group* of $\mathfrak{P}_i$ over $\mathfrak{p}$ is

$$D_{\mathfrak{P}_i/\mathfrak{p}} \stackrel{\text{def}}{=} \{\sigma \in G \mid \sigma(\mathfrak{P}_i) = \mathfrak{P}_i\}.$$

It has cardinality $e \times f$. In particular, when K is unramified at $\mathfrak{P}$, the ring $\mathscr{O}_K/\mathfrak{P}_i$ is the finite field $\mathbb{F}_{q^f}$ and the action of $D_{\mathfrak{P}_i/\mathfrak{p}}$ on it is the Frobenius automorphism: the reduction modulo $\mathfrak{P}_i$ yields an isomorphism

$$D_{\mathfrak{P}_i/\mathfrak{p}} \simeq \mathrm{Gal}(\mathbb{F}_{q^f}/\mathbb{F}_q). \tag{4}$$

Finally, all the decomposition groups of primes above $\mathfrak{p}$ are conjugate: for any $i \neq j$ there exists $\sigma \in G$ such that $D_{\mathfrak{P}_i/\mathfrak{p}} = \sigma D_{\mathfrak{P}_j/\mathfrak{p}} \sigma^{-1}$.

3   A Function Field Approach for Search to Decision Reductions

Search and Decision Problems. In this section, we introduce a new generic problem that we call FF-DP, which is the analogue of Ring–LWE in the context of function fields. Then, we give our main theorem which states the search-to-decision reduction of FF-DP. Since function fields and number fields share many properties, the present search to decision reduction, will work similarly as in [23].

Consider a function field $K/\mathbb{F}_q(T)$ with constant field $\mathbb{F}_q$ and ring of integers $\mathscr{O}_K$ and let $Q(T) \in \mathbb{F}_q[T]$. Let $\mathfrak{P} \stackrel{\mathrm{def}}{=} Q\mathscr{O}_K$ be the ideal of $\mathscr{O}_K$ generated by Q. Recall that $\mathscr{O}_K/\mathfrak{P}$ is a finite set. FF-DP is parameterized by an element $\mathbf{s} \in \mathscr{O}_K/\mathfrak{P}$ called the *secret* and ψ be a probability distribution over $\mathscr{O}_K/\mathfrak{P}$ called the *error distribution*.

Definition 1 (FF-DP Distribution). *A sample* $(\mathbf{a}, \mathbf{b}) \in \mathscr{O}_K/\mathfrak{P} \times \mathscr{O}_K/\mathfrak{P}$ *is distributed according to the* FF-DP *distribution modulo* $\mathfrak{P}$ *with secret* $\mathbf{s}$ *and error distribution* ψ *if*

- $\mathbf{a}$ *is uniformly distributed over* $\mathscr{O}_K/\mathfrak{P}$,
- $\mathbf{b} = \mathbf{a}\mathbf{s} + \mathbf{e} \in \mathscr{O}_K/\mathfrak{P}$ *where* $\mathbf{e}$ *is distributed according to* ψ.

A sample drawn according to this distribution will be denoted by $(\mathbf{a}, \mathbf{b}) \leftarrow \mathscr{F}_{\mathbf{s},\psi}$.

The aim of the search version of the FF-DP problem is to recover the secret $\mathbf{s}$ given samples drawn from $\mathscr{F}_{\mathbf{s},\psi}$. This is formalized in the following problem.

Definition 2 (FF-DP, Search version). *Let* $\mathbf{s} \in \mathscr{O}_K/\mathfrak{P}$, *and let* ψ *be a probability distribution over* $\mathscr{O}_K/\mathfrak{P}$. *An instance of* FF-DP *problem consists in an oracle giving access to independent samples* $(\mathbf{a}, \mathbf{b}) \leftarrow \mathscr{F}_{\mathbf{s},\psi}$. *The goal is to recover* $\mathbf{s}$.

Remark 2. This problem should be related to structured versions of the decoding problem. Indeed, recall from the discussion in the introduction that, using the polynomial representation, the decoding problem of random quasi-cyclic codes corresponds to recovering a secret polynomial $\mathbf{s}(X) \in \mathbb{F}_q[X]/(X^n - 1)$ given access to samples of the form $\mathbf{a}\mathbf{s} + \mathbf{e} \in \mathbb{F}_q[X]/(X^n - 1)$ where $\mathbf{a}$ is uniformly distributed in $\mathbb{F}_q[X]/(X^n - 1)$. This can be rephrased within the FF-DP framework as follows. Consider the polynomial $f(T, X) \stackrel{\mathrm{def}}{=} X^n + T - 1 \in \mathbb{F}_q(T)[X]$. When n is not divisible by the characteristic of $\mathbb{F}_q$, f is a separable polynomial. Moreover, by Eisenstein criterion f is irreducible. Define the function field K

generated by f, namely the extension $K \stackrel{\text{def}}{=} \mathbb{F}_q(T)[X]/(f(T,X))$. One can prove that $\mathscr{O}_K$ is exactly $\mathbb{F}_q[T][X]/(f(T,X))$. Now, let $\mathfrak{p}$ be the ideal of $\mathbb{F}_q[T]$ defined by the irreducible polynomial T, and let $\mathfrak{P} \stackrel{\text{def}}{=} \mathfrak{p}\mathscr{O}_K = T\mathscr{O}_K$ be the corresponding ideal of $\mathscr{O}_K$. Then the following isomorphisms hold

$$\mathscr{O}_K/\mathfrak{P} \simeq \mathbb{F}_q[T,X]/(T, X^n + T - 1) \simeq \mathbb{F}_q[X]/(X^n - 1).$$

With this particular instantiation, $\mathscr{O}_K/\mathfrak{P}$ is exactly the ambient space from which the samples are defined in the structured versions of the decoding problem. As a consequence, FF-DP is a generalization of structured versions of the decoding problem, when considering arbitrary function fields and ideals.

For cryptographic applications, we are also interested in the *decision* version of this problem. The goal is now to distinguish between the FF-DP distribution and the uniform distribution over $\mathscr{O}_K/\mathfrak{P} \times \mathscr{O}_K/\mathfrak{P}$.

Definition 3 (FF-DP, Decision version). *Let $\mathbf{s}$ be drawn uniformly at random in $\mathscr{O}_K/\mathfrak{P}$ and let ψ be a probability distribution over $\mathscr{O}_K/\mathfrak{P}$. Define $\mathcal{D}_0$ to be the uniform distribution over $\mathscr{O}_K/\mathfrak{P} \times \mathscr{O}_K/\mathfrak{P}$, and $\mathcal{D}_1$ to be the FF-DP distribution with secret $\mathbf{s}$ and error distribution ψ. Furthermore, let b be a uniform element of $\{0,1\}$. Given access to an oracle $\mathcal{O}_b$ providing samples from distribution $\mathcal{D}_b$, the goal of the decision FF-DP is to recover b.*

Remark 3. For some applications, for instance to MPC, it is more convenient to have the secret $\mathbf{s}$ drawn from the error distribution ψ instead of the uniform distribution over $\mathscr{O}_K/\mathfrak{P}$. In the lattice-based setting, this version is sometimes called LWE with *short secret* or LWE in *Hermite normal form*. However, both decision problems are easily proved to be computationally equivalent, see [22, Lemma 3]. The proof applies directly to FF-DP.

A *distinguisher* between two distributions $\mathcal{D}_0$ and $\mathcal{D}_1$ is a probabilistic polynomial time (PPT) algorithm $\mathcal{A}$ that takes as input an oracle $\mathcal{O}_b$ corresponding to a distribution $\mathcal{D}_b$ with $b \in \{0,1\}$ and outputs an element $\mathcal{A}(\mathcal{O}_b) \in \{0,1\}$.

Search to Decision Reduction. We are now ready to present our main theorem.

Theorem 1 (Search to decision reduction for FF-DP). *Let $K/\mathbb{F}_q(T)$ be a Galois function field of degree n with field of constants $\mathbb{F}_q$, and denote by $\mathscr{O}_K$ its ring of integers. Let $Q(T) \in \mathbb{F}_q[T]$ be an irreducible polynomial. Consider the ideal $\mathfrak{P} \stackrel{\text{def}}{=} Q\mathscr{O}_K$. Assume that $\mathfrak{P}$ does not ramify in $\mathscr{O}_K$, and denote by f its inertia degree. Let ψ be a probability distribution over $\mathscr{O}_K/\mathfrak{P}$, closed under the action of $\text{Gal}(K/\mathbb{F}_q(T))$, meaning that if $e \leftarrow \psi$, then for any $\sigma \in \text{Gal}(K/\mathbb{F}_q(T))$, we have $\sigma(e) \leftarrow \psi$. Let $\mathbf{s} \in \mathscr{O}_K/\mathfrak{P}$.*

Suppose that we have an access to $\mathscr{F}_{\mathbf{s},\psi}$ and there exists a distinguisher between the uniform distribution over $\mathscr{O}_K/\mathfrak{P}$ and the FF-DP distribution with uniform secret and error distribution ψ, running in time t and having an advantage

ε. *Then there exists an algorithm that recovers* $\mathbf{s} \in \mathscr{O}_K/\mathfrak{P}$ *(with an overwhelming probability in* n*) in time*

$$O\left(\frac{n^4}{f^3} \times \frac{1}{\varepsilon^2} \times q^{f \deg(Q)} \times t\right).$$

Remark 4. We have assumed implicitly in the statement of the theorem that we have an efficient access to the Galois group of $K/\mathbb{F}_q(T)$ and its action can be computed in polynomial time.

Remark 5. There are many degrees of freedom in the previous statement: choice of the function field K (and on the degree n), choice of the polynomial Q (and on f and $\deg(Q)$). For our instantiations, we will often choose the "modulus" Q to be a linear polynomial ($\deg(Q) = 1$) and K will be a (subfield of) a cyclotomic function field.

Remark 6. Due to the continuity of error distributions used in lattice-based cryptography, a technical tool called the *smoothing parameter* was introduced by Micciancio and Regev in [25]. It characterizes how a Gaussian distribution is close to uniform, both modulo the lattice, and is ubiquitously used in reductions. However, in the function field setting, we do not need to introduce such a tool because the error distribution is discrete and already defined on the quotient $\mathscr{O}_K/\mathfrak{P}$.

Remark 7 (MFF-DP). Instead of considering one secret $\mathbf{s} \in \mathscr{O}_K/\mathfrak{P}$, we could use multiple secrets $(\mathbf{s}_1, \ldots, \mathbf{s}_d) \in (\mathscr{O}_K/\mathfrak{P})^d$. The goal is now to recover the secrets from samples $(\mathbf{a}, \mathbf{b})$ with $\mathbf{a} = (\mathbf{a}_1, \ldots, \mathbf{a}_d)$ uniformly distributed over $(\mathscr{O}_K/\mathfrak{P})^d$ and $\mathbf{b} = \langle \mathbf{a}, \mathbf{s} \rangle + \mathbf{e} = \sum_{i=1}^d \mathbf{a}_i \mathbf{s}_i + \mathbf{e}$ with $\mathbf{e} \leftarrow \psi$. This generalization has been considered in lattice-based cryptography under the terminology Module-LWE [20], because the secret can be thought as an element of $\mathscr{O}_K^d$ which is a free $\mathscr{O}_K$-module or rank d, before a reduction modulo $\mathfrak{P}$ on each component.

Following [20, Sect. 4.3], it is possible to adapt Theorem 1; the search to decision reduction only yielding an overhead of d (the number of secrets). The running time would now be

$$O\left(d \times \frac{n^4}{f^3} \times \frac{1}{\varepsilon^2} \times q^{f \deg(Q)} \times t\right).$$

Sketch of Proof of Theorem 1. The proof of this Theorem is very similar to the one for Ring–LWE and lattices [23]. It uses four steps that we quickly describe. Let $\mathfrak{P} = \mathfrak{P}_1 \ldots \mathfrak{P}_r$, where $r = n/f$, be the factorisation of $\mathfrak{P}$ in prime ideals.

Step 1. Worst to Average Case. In the definition of Problem 3 the secret $\mathbf{s}$ is supposed to be *uniformly* distributed over $\mathscr{O}_K/\mathfrak{P}$, while in the search version the secret is *fixed*. This can easily be addressed, for any sample $(\mathbf{a}, \mathbf{b}) \leftarrow \mathscr{F}_{\mathbf{s},\psi}$ with fixed secret $\mathbf{s}$, it is enough to pick $\mathbf{s}' \leftarrow \mathscr{O}_K/\mathfrak{P}$ and output $(\mathbf{a}, \mathbf{b} + \mathbf{a}\mathbf{s}')$.

Step 2. Hybrid Argument. Sample $(\mathbf{a}, \mathbf{b})$ is said to be distributed according to the hybrid distribution $\mathcal{H}_i$ if it is of the form $(\mathbf{a}', \mathbf{b}' + \mathbf{h})$ where $(\mathbf{a}', \mathbf{b}') \leftarrow \mathscr{F}_{\mathbf{s}, \psi}$ and $\mathbf{h} \in \mathscr{O}_K / \mathfrak{P}$ is uniformly distributed modulo $\mathfrak{P}_j$ for $j \leqslant i$ and $\mathbf{0}$ modulo the other factors. Such an $\mathbf{h}$ can easily be constructed using the Chinese Remainder Theorem. In particular, for $i = 0$, $\mathbf{h}$ is $\mathbf{0}$ modulo all the factors of $\mathfrak{P}$, therefore $\mathbf{h} = \mathbf{0}$ and $\mathcal{H}_0 = \mathscr{F}_{\mathbf{s}, \psi}$. On the other hand, when $i = r$, the element $\mathbf{h}$ is uniformly distributed over $\mathscr{O}_K / \mathfrak{P}$, therefore $\mathcal{H}_r$ is *exactly* the uniform distribution over $\mathscr{O}_K / \mathfrak{P}$.

By a hybrid argument, we can turn a distinguisher $\mathcal{A}$ for FF-DP with advantage ε, into a distinguisher between $(\mathcal{H}_{i_0}, \mathcal{H}_{i_0+1})$ for some i_0 with advantage $\geqslant \varepsilon/r$. Everything is analysed as if we knew this index i_0. In practice we can run $\mathcal{A}$ concurrently with all the r instances.

Step 3. Guess and Search. The idea is to perform an exhaustive search in $\mathscr{O}_K / \mathfrak{P}_{i_0+1}$ and to use $\mathcal{A}$ to recover $\widehat{\mathbf{s}} \stackrel{\text{def}}{=} \mathbf{s} \bmod \mathfrak{P}_{i_0+1}$. Let $\mathbf{g}_{i_0+1} \stackrel{?}{=} \widehat{\mathbf{s}}$ be our guess and set $\mathbf{g} \equiv \mathbf{g}_{i_0+1} \bmod \mathfrak{P}_{i_0+1}$ and $\mathbf{0}$ otherwise. For each sample $(\mathbf{a}, \mathbf{b})$ we compute $\mathbf{a}' \stackrel{\text{def}}{=} \mathbf{a} + \mathbf{v}$ and $\mathbf{b}' \stackrel{\text{def}}{=} \mathbf{b} + \mathbf{h} + \mathbf{v}\mathbf{g} = \mathbf{a}'\mathbf{s} + \mathbf{e} + \mathbf{h}'$ where $\mathbf{h}' = \mathbf{h} + \mathbf{v}(\mathbf{g} - \mathbf{s})$ with $\mathbf{v} \equiv \mathbf{v}_{i_0+1}$ uniform modulo $\mathfrak{P}_{i_0+1}$, and $\mathbf{h}$ uniform modulo the $\mathfrak{P}_j$ for $j \leqslant i_0 + 1$ and $\mathbf{0}$ otherwise. One can verify that,

$$\begin{cases} \mathbf{h}' \equiv \mathbf{h}_j & \bmod \mathfrak{P}_j \text{ for } j \leqslant i_0 \\ \mathbf{h}' \equiv (\mathbf{g}_{i_0+1} - \widehat{\mathbf{s}})\mathbf{v}_{i_0+1} & \bmod \mathfrak{P}_{i_0+1} \\ \mathbf{h}' \equiv \mathbf{0} & \bmod \mathfrak{P}_j \text{ for } j > i_0 + 1. \end{cases}$$

If the guess $\mathbf{g}_{i_0+1}$ is correct, $(\mathbf{a}', \mathbf{b}')$ is distributed according to $\mathcal{H}_{i_0}$. Otherwise, it is distributed according to $\mathcal{H}_{i_0+1}$ because $\mathbf{v}_{i_0+1}$ is uniformly distributed over $\mathscr{O}_K / \mathfrak{P}_{i_0+1}$ which is a field. The distinguisher will succeed with probability $1/2 + \varepsilon/r > 1/2$. It suffices to repeat the procedure $\Theta((r/\varepsilon)^2)$ times, and do a majority voting to know whether the guess $\mathbf{g}_{i_0+1}$ is correct or not. We do that for all the $q^{f \deg(Q)}$ possible guesses.

Step 4. Galois Action. Since $K/\mathbb{F}_q(T)$ is Galois, for any $j \neq i_0$ we take $\sigma \in \mathrm{Gal}(K/\mathbb{F}_q(T))$ such that $\sigma(\mathfrak{P}_j) = \mathfrak{P}_{i_0}$. Now, $(\sigma(\mathbf{a}), \sigma(\mathbf{a})\sigma(\mathbf{s}) + \sigma(\mathbf{e})) \leftarrow \mathscr{F}_{\sigma(\mathbf{s}), \psi}$ because ψ is Galois invariant. The above procedure enables to recover $\sigma(\mathbf{s})$ mod $\mathfrak{P}_{i_0}$. Applying σ^{-1} yields $\mathbf{s}$ mod $\mathfrak{P}_j$. Therefore, we are able to recover $\mathbf{s}$ mod $\mathfrak{P}_j$ for any j. To compute the full secret $\mathbf{s}$ it remains to use the CRT. $\square$

4   Cyclotomic Function Fields and the Carlitz Module

In Sect. 3, we introduced the generic problem FF-DP and noticed that our search to decision reduction needed Galois function fields. In [23], it was proposed to use cyclotomic number fields to instantiate the Ring–LWE problem. Here, we propose to instantiate FF-DP with the function field analogue, namely *Carlitz* extensions. We give a self contained presentation of the theory of Carlitz extensions. The interested reader can refer to [32, ch. 12], [26] and the excellent survey [9] for further reference.

Carlitz extensions are function fields analogues of the cyclotomic extensions of $\mathbb{Q}$. A dictionary summarizing the similarities is given in Table 2. These extensions were discovered by Carlitz in the late 1930s but the analogy was not well known until the work of his student Hayes who studied them in [17] to give an explicit construction of the abelian extensions of the rational function field $\mathbb{F}_q(T)$ and prove an analogue of the usual Kronecker-Webber theorem which states that any abelian extension of $\mathbb{Q}$ is a subfield of cyclotomic number fields. This result was generalized in the following years with the work of Drinfeld and Goss to yield a complete solution to Hilbert twelfth problem in the function field setting. In the number field setting, such an explicit construction is only known for abelian extensions of $\mathbb{Q}$ (cyclotomic extensions) and imaginary quadratic number fields (via the theory of elliptic curves with complex multiplication).

The first idea that comes to mind when one wants to build cyclotomic function fields is to adjoin roots of unity to the field $\mathbb{F}_q(T)$. However, roots of unity are already *algebraic* over $\mathbb{F}_q$. In other words, adding them only yields so–called *extensions of constants*.

Example 1. Let ζ_n be an n–th root of unity in $\overline{\mathbb{F}_q(T)}$. Note that it belongs to some *finite* extension of $\mathbb{F}_q$. Let $\mathbb{F}_{q^m}$ be the extension of $\mathbb{F}_q$ of minimal degree such that $\zeta_n \in \mathbb{F}_{q^m}$ (it can be $\mathbb{F}_q$ itself). Then

$$\mathbb{F}_q(T)[\zeta_n] = \mathbb{F}_{q^m}(T),$$

and the field of constants of $\mathbb{F}_q(T)[\zeta_n]$ is $\mathbb{F}_{q^m}$.

However, in our reduction setting, such extensions will only increase the size of the search space in Step 3. More precisely, if K is an algebraic extension of $\mathbb{F}_q(T)$, the constant field of K is always a subfield of $\mathscr{O}_K/\mathfrak{P}$ for any prime ideal $\mathfrak{P}$ of $\mathscr{O}_K$. But recall that in our search to decision reduction, we need to do an exhaustive search in this quotient $\mathscr{O}_K/\mathfrak{P}$, so we need it to be as small as possible. Henceforth, we cannot afford constant field extensions. For Carlitz extensions, this will be ensured by Theorem 6.

4.1   Roots of Unity and Torsion

As mentioned in the beginning of this section, it is not sufficient to add roots of unity. One has to go deeper into the algebraic structure that is adjoined to $\mathbb{Q}$. Indeed, the set of all m–th roots of unity, denoted by $\mu_m \subset \mathbb{C}$, turns out to be an abelian group under multiplication. Moreover, μ_m is in fact *cyclic*, generated by any *primitive* root of unity.

In commutative algebra, abelian groups are $\mathbb{Z}$–*modules*. Here the action of $\mathbb{Z}$ is given by exponentiation: $n \in \mathbb{Z}$ acts on $\zeta \in \mu_m$ by $n \cdot \zeta \overset{\text{def}}{=} \zeta^n$. This action of $\mathbb{Z}$ can in fact be extended to all $\overline{\mathbb{Q}}^{\times}$. When working with modules over a ring, it is very natural to consider the *torsion elements*, *i.e.* elements of the module that are annihilated by an element of the ring. The torsion elements in the $\mathbb{Z}$–module $\overline{\mathbb{Q}}^{\times}$ are the $\zeta \in \overline{\mathbb{Q}}^{\times}$ such that $\zeta^m = 1$ for some $m > 0$; these are precisely the roots of unity. In other words, the cyclotomic number fields are obtained by adjoining to $\mathbb{Q}$ torsions elements of the $\mathbb{Z}$–module $\overline{\mathbb{Q}}^{\times}$.

Under the analogy summed up in Table 1, replacing $\mathbb{Z}$ by $\mathbb{F}_q[T]$ and $\mathbb{Q}$ by $\mathbb{F}_q(T)$, we would like to consider some $\mathbb{F}_q[T]$–module and adjoin to $\mathbb{F}_q(T)$ the torsion elements. Note that $\mathbb{F}_q[T]$–modules are in particular $\mathbb{F}_q$–vector spaces, hence the action of $\mathbb{F}_q[T]$ should be linear. This new module structure can be defined using so called *Carlitz polynomials*: for each polynomial $M \in \mathbb{F}_q[T]$, we define its Carlitz polynomial $[M](X)$ as a polynomial in X with coefficients in $\mathbb{F}_q[T]$, and $M \in \mathbb{F}_q[T]$ will act on $\alpha \in \overline{\mathbb{F}_q(T)}$ by $M \cdot \alpha \overset{\text{def}}{=} [M](\alpha)$ with $[M](\alpha + \beta) = [M](\alpha) + [M](\beta)$. In other words, $[M](X)$ should be an *additive polynomial*. In positive characteristic this can easily be achieved by considering q–polynomials, *i.e.* polynomials whose monomials are only q–th powers of X, namely of the form

$$P(X) = p_0 X + p_1 X^q + \cdots + p_r X^{q^r}.$$

4.2 Carlitz Polynomials

The definition of Carlitz polynomial will proceed by induction and linearity. Define $[1](X) \overset{\text{def}}{=} X$ and $[T](X) \overset{\text{def}}{=} X^q + TX$. For $n \geqslant 2$, define

$$[T^n](X) \overset{\text{def}}{=} [T]([T^{n-1}](X)) = [T^{n-1}](X)^q + T[T^{n-1}](X).$$

Then, for a polynomial $M = \sum_{i=0}^n a_i T^i \in \mathbb{F}_q[T]$, define $[M](X)$ by forcing $\mathbb{F}_q$–linearity:

$$[M](X) \overset{\text{def}}{=} \sum_{i=0}^n a_i [T^i](X).$$

Example 2. We have,

- $[T^2](X) = [T](X^q + TX) = X^{q^2} + (T^q + T)X^q + T^2 X$
- $[T^2 + T + 1](X) = [T^2](X) + [T](X) + [1](X) = X^{q^2} + (T^q + T + 1)X^q + (T^2 + T + 1)X$.

By construction, Carlitz polynomials are additive polynomials, and $\mathbb{F}_q$–linear. Furthermore, for two polynomials $M, N \in \mathbb{F}_q[T]$, $[MN](X) = [M]([N](X)) = [N]([M](X))$. In particular, Carlitz polynomials commute with each other under composition law, which is not the case in general for q–polynomials.

4.3 Carlitz Module

Endowed with this $\mathbb{F}_q[T]$–module structure, $\overline{\mathbb{F}_q(T)}$ is called the *Carlitz module*.

Definition 4. *For $M \in \mathbb{F}_q[T]$, $M \neq 0$, let $\Lambda_M \overset{\text{def}}{=} \{\lambda \in \overline{\mathbb{F}_q(T)} \mid [M](\lambda) = 0\}$. This is the module of M–torsion of the Carlitz module.*

Example 3. $\Lambda_T = \{\lambda \in \overline{\mathbb{F}_q(T)} \mid \lambda^q + T\lambda = 0\} = \{0\} \cup \{\lambda \mid \lambda^{q-1} = -T\}.$

In the same way that μ_m is an abelian group (*i.e.* a $\mathbb{Z}$–module), note that Λ_M is also a submodule of the Carlitz module: for $\lambda \in \Lambda_M$ and $A \in \mathbb{F}_q[T]$, $[A](\lambda) \in \Lambda_M$. In particular, Λ_M is an $\mathbb{F}_q$–vector space.

Example 4. The module Λ_T defined in Example 3 is an $\mathbb{F}_q$–vector space of dimension 1. In particular, for $\lambda \in \Lambda_T$, and $A \in \mathbb{F}_q[T]$, $[A](\lambda)$ must be a multiple of λ. In fact the Carlitz action of A on λ is through the constant term of A: writing $A = TB + A(0)$ we have

$$[A](\lambda) = [TB + A(0)](\lambda) = [B](\underbrace{[T](\lambda)}_{=0}) + A(0)[1](\lambda) = A(0)\lambda.$$

More generally, even if in general Λ_M is not of dimension 1 over $\mathbb{F}_q$, it is always a *cyclic* $\mathbb{F}_q[T]$–module: as an $\mathbb{F}_q[T]$–module it can be generated by only one element. This is specified in the following theorem.

Theorem 2 ([26, Lemma 3.2.2]). *There exists $\lambda_0 \in \Lambda_M$ such that $\Lambda_M = \{[A](\lambda_0) \mid A \in \mathbb{F}_q[T]/(M)\}$ and the generators of Λ_M are the $[A](\lambda_0)$ for all A prime to M. The choice of a generator yields a non canonical isomorphism $\Lambda_M \simeq \mathbb{F}_q[T]/(M)$ as $\mathbb{F}_q[T]$–modules.*

Remark 8. The previous theorem needs to be related to the cyclotomic case: given the choice of a primitive m–th root of unity, there is a group isomorphism between μ_m and $\mathbb{Z}/m\mathbb{Z}$. Moreover all the m–th roots of unity are of the form ζ^k for $k \in [\![0, m-1]\!]$ and the generators of μ_m are the ζ^k for k prime to m.

4.4 Carlitz Extensions

Recall that the cyclotomic number fields are obtained as extensions of $\mathbb{Q}$ generated by the elements of μ_m. In the similar fashion, for a polynomial $M \in \mathbb{F}_q[T]$, let

$$K_M \overset{\text{def}}{=} \mathbb{F}_q(T)(\Lambda_M) = \mathbb{F}_q(T)(\lambda_M),$$

where λ_M is a generator of Λ_M. One of the most important facts about the cyclotomic number field $\mathbb{Q}(\zeta_m)$ is that it is a finite Galois extension of $\mathbb{Q}$, with Galois group isomorphic to $(\mathbb{Z}/m\mathbb{Z})^\times$. There is an analogue statement for the Carlitz extensions.

Theorem 3 ([26, Th. 3.2.6]). *Let $M \in \mathbb{F}_q[T]$, $M \neq 0$. Then K_M is a finite Galois extension of $\mathbb{F}_q(T)$, with Galois group isomorphic to $(\mathbb{F}_q[T]/(M))^\times$. The isomorphism is given by*

$$\begin{cases} (\mathbb{F}_q[T]/(M))^\times \longrightarrow \mathrm{Gal}(K_M/\mathbb{F}_q(T)) \\ \qquad\quad A \qquad \longmapsto \qquad \sigma_A, \end{cases}$$

where σ_A is completely determined by $\sigma_A(\lambda_M) = [A](\lambda_M).$

Remark 9. In particular, Carlitz extensions are *abelian*.

Another important fact about cyclotomic extensions is the simple description of their ring of integers. Namely, for $K = \mathbb{Q}(\zeta_m)$, we have $\mathscr{O}_K = \mathbb{Z}[\zeta_m] = \mathbb{Z}[X]/(\Phi_m(X))$ where Φ_m denotes the m–th cyclotomic polynomial. This property also holds for Carlitz extensions.

Theorem 4 ([32, Th. 2.9]). *Let $\mathscr{O}_M$ be the integral closure of $\mathbb{F}_q[T]$ in K_M. Then $\mathscr{O}_M = \mathbb{F}_q[T][\lambda_M]$. In particular, let $P(T,X) \in \mathbb{F}_q[T][X]$ be the minimal polynomial of λ_M. Then,*

$$K_M = \mathbb{F}_q(T)[X]/(P(T,X)) \quad and \quad \mathscr{O}_M = \mathbb{F}_q[T][X]/(P(T,X)).$$

Example 5. Reconsider Example 3 and the module $\Lambda_T = \{0\} \cup \{\lambda \mid \lambda^{q-1} = -T\}$. The polynomial $X^{q-1}+T$ is Eisenstein in (T) and therefore is irreducible. Hence,

$$K_T = \mathbb{F}_q(T)[X]/(X^{q-1} + T).$$

Moreover it is Galois, with Galois group $(\mathbb{F}_q[T]/(T))^\times \simeq \mathbb{F}_q^\times$. A non-zero element $a \in \mathbb{F}_q^\times$ will act on $f(T,X) \in K_T$ by

$$a \cdot f(T,X) \overset{\text{def}}{=} f(T,[a](X)) = f(T,aX).$$

The integral closure of $\mathbb{F}_q[T]$ in K_T is

$$\mathscr{O}_T \overset{\text{def}}{=} \mathbb{F}_q[T][X]/(X^{q-1} + T)$$

and

$$\mathscr{O}_T/((T+1)\mathscr{O}_T) = \mathbb{F}_q[T][X]/(T+1, X^{q-1} + T) = \mathbb{F}_q[X]/(X^{q-1} - 1). \quad (5)$$

Finally, the following theorem characterizes the splitting behaviour of primes in Carlitz extensions. A very similar result holds for cyclotomic extensions.

Theorem 5 ([32, Th. 12.10]). *Let $M \in \mathbb{F}_q[T]$, $M \neq 0$, and let $Q \in \mathbb{F}_q[T]$ be a monic, irreducible polynomial. Consider the Carlitz extension K_M and let $\mathscr{O}_M$ denote its ring of integers. Then,*

- *If Q divides M, then $Q\mathscr{O}_M$ is totally ramified.*
- *Otherwise, let f be the smallest integer f such that $Q^f \equiv 1 \mod M$. Then $Q\mathscr{O}_M$ is unramified and has inertia degree f. In particular, Q splits completely if and only if $Q \equiv 1 \mod M$.*

Note that in Ring–LWE, the prime modulus q is often chosen such that $q \equiv 1 \mod m$ so that it splits completely in the cyclotomic extension $\mathbb{Q}(\zeta_m)$.

Example 6. In the previous example, $T+1 \equiv 1 \mod T$ and therefore $(T+1)$ splits completely in $\mathscr{O}_T$. Indeed,

$$\mathscr{O}_T/((T+1)\mathscr{O}_T) = \mathbb{F}_q[X]/(X^{q-1} - 1) = \prod_{\alpha \in \mathbb{F}_q^\times} \mathbb{F}_q[X]/(X - \alpha)$$

is a product of $q-1$ copies of $\mathbb{F}_q$.

It is crucial for the applications that the constant field of K be not too big because, in the search to decision reduction, it determines the search space in Step 3 of the proof of Theorem 1. The following non-trivial theorem gives the field of constants of Carlitz extensions.

Theorem 6 ([32, Cor. of Th. 12.14]). *Let $M \in \mathbb{F}_q[T]$, $M \neq 0$. Then $\mathbb{F}_q$ is the full constant field of K_M.*

The similarities between Carlitz function fields and cyclotomic number fields are summarized in Table 2.

Table 2. Analogies between cyclotomic and Carlitz

$\mathbb{Q}$	$\mathbb{F}_q(T)$
$\mathbb{Z}$	$\mathbb{F}_q[T]$
Prime numbers $q \in \mathbb{Z}$	Irreducible polynomials $Q \in \mathbb{F}_q[T]$
$\mu_m = \langle \zeta \rangle \simeq \mathbb{Z}/m\mathbb{Z}$ (groups)	$\Lambda_M = \langle \lambda \rangle \simeq \mathbb{F}_q[T]/(M)$ (modules)
$d \mid m \Leftrightarrow \mu_d \subset \mu_m$ (subgroups)	$D \mid M \Leftrightarrow \Lambda_D \subset \Lambda_M$ (submodules)
$a \equiv b \mod m \Rightarrow \zeta^a = \zeta^b$	$A \equiv B \mod M \Rightarrow [A](\lambda) = [B](\lambda)$
$K = \mathbb{Q}[\zeta]$	$K = \mathbb{F}_q(T)[\lambda]$
$\mathscr{O}_K = \mathbb{Z}[\zeta]$	$\mathscr{O}_K = \mathbb{F}_q[T][\lambda]$
$\mathrm{Gal}(K/\mathbb{Q}) \simeq (\mathbb{Z}/m\mathbb{Z})^\times$	$\mathrm{Gal}(K/\mathbb{F}_q(T)) \simeq (\mathbb{F}_q[T]/(M))^\times$
Cyclotomic	**Carlitz**

5   Applications

In the current section, we present two applications of our proof techniques. It provides search to decision reductions to generic problems whose hardness assumption has been used to assess the security of some cryptographic designs. The first application concerns Oblivious Linear Evaluation (OLE) which is a crucial primitive for secure multi-party computation. The second one is an authentication protocol called LAPIN. Both designs rely on the hardness of variants of the so-called Learning Parity with Noise (LPN) problem.

5.1   LPN and its Structured Variants

Let us start this subsection by the definitions of the distribution that is involved in the LPN problem.

Definition 5 (Learning Parity with Noise (LPN) distribution). *Let k be a positive integer, $\mathbf{s} \in \mathbb{F}_q^k$ be a uniformly distributed vector and $p \in [0, \frac{1}{2})$. A sample $(\mathbf{a}, b) \in \mathbb{F}_q^k \times \mathbb{F}_q$ is distributed according to the* LPN *distribution with secret $\mathbf{s}$ if*

- $\mathbf{a}$ *is uniformly distributed over $\mathbb{F}_q^k$,*
- $b \overset{def}{=} \langle \mathbf{a}, \mathbf{s} \rangle + e$ *where $\langle \cdot, \cdot \rangle$ denotes the canonical inner product over $\mathbb{F}_q^k$ and e is a q–ary Bernouilli random variable with parameter p, namely $\mathbb{P}(e = 0) = 1 - p$ and $\mathbb{P}(e = a) = \frac{p}{q-1}$ for $a \in \mathbb{F}_q^\times$.*

A sample drawn according to this distribution will be denoted $(\mathbf{a}, \langle \mathbf{a}, \mathbf{s} \rangle + e) \leftarrow \mathcal{D}_{\mathbf{s},p}^{\mathsf{LPN}}$.

Remark 10. This definition is a generalization of the usual LPN distribution defined over $\mathbb{F}_2$. In this situation, the error distribution is a usual Bernouilli: $\mathbb{P}(e = 0) = 1 - p$ and $\mathbb{P}(e = 1) = p$.

Similarly to the LWE problem, structured versions of LPN have been defined ([7,12,18]).

Definition 6 (Ring–LPN distribution). *Fix a positive integer r, a public polynomial $f(X) \in \mathbb{F}_q[X]$ of degree r and $\mathbf{s} \in \mathbb{F}_q[X]/(f(X))$ be a uniformly distributed polynomial. A sample $(\mathbf{a}, \mathbf{b})$ is distributed according to the* RLPN *distribution with secret $\mathbf{s}$ if*

- $\mathbf{a}$ *is drawn uniformly at random over $\mathbb{F}_q[X]/(f(X))$;*
- $\mathbf{b} \overset{def}{=} \mathbf{as} + \mathbf{e}$ *where $\mathbf{e} \overset{def}{=} e_0 + e_1 X + \cdots + e_{r-1}X^{r-1} \in \mathbb{F}_q[X]/(f(X))$ has coefficients e_i's which are independent q–ary Bernouilli random variables with parameter p.*

A sample drawn according to this distribution will be denoted $(\mathbf{a}, \mathbf{as} + \mathbf{e}) \leftarrow \mathcal{D}_{\mathbf{s},p}^{\mathsf{RLPN}}$.

Note that the map

$$\begin{cases} \mathbb{F}_q[X]/(f(X)) \longrightarrow & \mathbb{F}_q[X]/(f(X)) \\ \mathbf{m}(X) \longmapsto & \mathbf{a}(X)\mathbf{m}(X) \mod f(X) \end{cases}$$

can be represented in the canonical basis by an $r \times r$ binary matrix $\mathbf{A}$. Using this point of view, one sample of RLPN can be regarded as r specific samples of LPN.

Search to Decision. Here we present search to decision reductions in two different settings corresponding to two choices of the modulus $f(X)$ in the Ring–LPN problem. Both have been used in the literature for specific applications that are quickly recalled.

A q–ary Version of Ring–LPN with a Totally Split Modulus f. In [7], the authors introduce Ring–LPN over the finite field $\mathbb{F}_q$ and with a modulus f which is totally split, *i.e.* has distinct roots, all living in the ground field $\mathbb{F}_q$.

Motivation: Oblivious Linear Evaluations for secure Multiparty Computation (MPC). A crucial objective in modern secure MPC is to be able to generate efficiently many random pairs $(u, r), (v, s)$ where u, r, v, s are uniformly distributed over $\mathbb{F}_q$ with the correlation $uv = r + s$.

In [7], the authors propose a construction of such pairs $(\mathbf{u}, \mathbf{r}), (\mathbf{v}, \mathbf{s})$ of elements in a ring $\mathscr{R}$, where $\mathscr{R} = \mathbb{F}_q[X]/(f(X))$ such that f is split with simple roots in $\mathbb{F}_q$. Using the Chinese remainder Theorem, one deduces $\deg f$ pairs $(u_i, r_i), (v_i, s_i)$ with $u_i, v_i, r_i, s_i \in \mathbb{F}_q$. The pseudo-randomness of $\mathbf{u}, \mathbf{v}$ rests on the hardness of the Ring–LPN assumption.

Search to Decision Reduction in the [7]-Case. Consider the case of Ring–LPN over $\mathscr{R} = \mathbb{F}_q[X]/(f(X))$, where

$$f(X) \overset{\text{def}}{=} \prod_{a \in \mathbb{F}_q^\times} (X - a) = X^{q-1} - 1.$$

Let us re-introduce the Carlitz function field of Examples 3 and 5, namely

$$K_T = \mathbb{F}_q(T)[X]/(X^{q-1} + T).$$

According to Eq. (5) in Example 5, we have

$$\mathscr{O}_T/(T+1)\mathscr{O}_T \simeq \mathbb{F}_q[X]/(X^{q-1} - 1),$$

which is precisely the ring we consider for the Ring–LPN version of [7]. Therefore, instantiating our FF-DP problem with this function field, modulus $T + 1$, ideal $\mathfrak{P} \overset{\text{def}}{=} (T+1)\mathscr{O}_K$ and applying Theorem 1, we directly obtain the following search to decision reduction.

Theorem 7 (Search to decision reduction for totally-split Ring–LPN). *Let K_T be the Carlitz extension of T–torsion over $\mathbb{F}_q$, and denote by $\mathscr{O}_T$ its ring of integers. Consider the ideal $\mathfrak{P} \overset{\text{def}}{=} (T + 1)\mathscr{O}_{K_T}$. Then $\mathfrak{P}$ splits completely in $q - 1$ factors $\mathfrak{P}_1 \ldots \mathfrak{P}_{q-1}$ and*

$$\mathscr{O}_K/\mathfrak{P} \simeq \prod_{i=1}^{q-1} \mathscr{O}_K/\mathfrak{P}_i \simeq \mathbb{F}_q \times \cdots \times \mathbb{F}_q.$$

Let ψ denote the uniform distribution over polynomials in $\mathbb{F}_q[X]/(X^{q-1} - 1)$ of fixed Hamming weight, or the q-ary Bernouilli distribution. Let $\mathbf{s} \in \mathbb{F}_q[X]/(X^{q-1} - 1)$. Suppose that we have access to $\mathscr{F}_{\mathbf{s},\psi}$ and that there exists a distinguisher between the uniform distribution over $\mathbb{F}_q[X]/(X^{q-1} - 1)$ and $\mathscr{F}_{\mathbf{s},\psi}$ with uniform secret and error distribution ψ, running in time t and having advantage ε.

Then there exists an algorithm that recovers s *with overwhelming probability (in q) in time*

$$O\left(q^5 \times \frac{1}{\varepsilon^2} \times t\right).$$

Proof. The only thing that remains to be proved is that the error distribution is Galois invariant. According to Theorem 3 and Example 5, the Galois group of $K_T/\mathbb{F}_q(T)$ is isomorphic to $(\mathbb{F}_q[T]/(T))^\times \simeq \mathbb{F}_q^\times$. Furthermore, we proved that an element $b \in \mathbb{F}_q^\times$ acts on $f(T,X) \in K_T$ by

$$b \cdot f(T,X) = f(T,[b](X)) = f(T,bX).$$

The Galois action on K_T and $\mathscr{O}_T$ induces an action of $\mathbb{F}_q^\times$ on

$$\mathscr{O}_T/(T+1)\mathscr{O}_T \simeq \mathbb{F}_q[X]/(X^{q-1}-1)$$

by $b \cdot m(X) \overset{\text{def}}{=} m(bX)$. Note that, this operation has no incidence on the Hamming weight of m: it actually *does not change its Hamming support*. Therefore, we easily see here that Galois action keeps the noise distribution invariant.   □

Remark 11. Note that our search to decision reduction could have been performed here without introducing the function field and only considering the ring $\mathbb{F}_q[X]/(X^{q-1}-1)$. Recall that the first ingredient of the reduction is to decompose this ring by the Chinese Remainder Theorem. Here it would give the product $\prod_{a \in \mathbb{F}_q^\times} \mathbb{F}_q[X]/(X-a)$. The final step of the reduction requires the introduction of a group action which induces a permutation of the factors in $\prod_{a \in \mathbb{F}_q^\times} \mathbb{F}_q[X]/(X-a)$. It is precisely what the group action $b \cdot m(X) = m(bX)$ does: it sends the factor $\mathbb{F}_q[X]/(X-a)$ onto $\mathbb{F}_q[X]/(X-b^{-1}a)$. However, introducing this action on the level of $\mathbb{F}_q[X]/(X^{q-1}-1)$ does not look very natural. It turns out that the introduction of function fields permits to interpret this action in terms of a Galois one.

Remark 12. If we replace the Carlitz extension K by some subfield of invariants under the action of a given subgroup of the Galois group, it is possible to extend the result to the case where $f(X) = \prod_{a \in H}(X-a)$ where H is some subgroup of $\mathbb{F}_q^\times$. It is even possible to treat the case where the roots of f form a coset of a given subgroup of $\mathbb{F}_q^\times$.

Ring–LPN with a Modulus f Splitting in Irreducible Polynomials of the Same Degree.

Another cryptographic design whose security rests on the Ring–LPN assumption is an authentication protocol named LAPIN [18]. In the conclusion of their article, the authors mention that

> *"it would be particularly interesting to find out whether there exists an equivalence between the decision and the search versions of the problem similar to the reductions that exist for* LPN *and* Ring–LWE".

For this protocol, the problem is instantiated with the binary field $\mathbb{F}_2$ and with a modulus polynomial f which splits as a product of m distinct irreducible polynomials

$$f(X) = f_1(X) \cdots f_m(X).$$

In this setting and using our techniques, we can provide a search to decision reduction when the f_i's have all the same degree d. Furthermore, for the reduction to run in polynomial time, we need to have $d = O(\log(\deg f))$. Note that the explicit parameters proposed as an example in [18] do not satisfy these assumptions but it would be easy to propose alternative parameters fulfilling them.

In this setting, the Chinese Reminder Theorem entails that

$$\mathbb{F}_2[X]/(f(X)) \simeq \prod_{i=1}^{m} \mathbb{F}_2[X]/(f_i(X)),$$

and the right–hand side is a product of m copies of $\mathbb{F}_{2^d}$. Such a product can be realised as follows. Consider a function field K which is a Galois extension of $\mathbb{F}_2(T)$ with Galois group G and denote by $\mathscr{O}_K$ the integral closure of $\mathbb{F}_2[T]$ in K. Suppose that the ideal (T) of $\mathbb{F}_2[T]$ is unramified in $\mathscr{O}_K$ with inertia degree d. Then $T\mathscr{O}_K$ splits into a product of prime ideals:

$$T\mathscr{O}_K = \mathfrak{P}_1 \cdots \mathfrak{P}_m \quad \text{and} \quad \mathscr{O}_K/T\mathscr{O}_K \simeq \prod_{i=1}^{m} \mathscr{O}_K/\mathfrak{P}_i,$$

where, here again, the right–hand side is a product of m copies of $\mathbb{F}_{2^d}$.

Next, the idea is now to apply Theorem 1 in this setting. However, there is here a difficulty since for our search to decision reduction to hold, the noise should arise from a Galois invariant distribution. Thus, if we want the noise distribution to be Galois invariant we need to have a Galois invariant $\mathbb{F}_2$–basis of the algebra $\mathscr{O}_K/T\mathscr{O}_K$. The first question should be whether such a basis exists. The existence of such a basis can be deduced from deep results of number theory due to Noether [8,27] and asserting the existence of local normal integral bases at non ramified places. Here we give a pedestrian proof resting only on basic facts of number theory.

Proposition 1. *Let $K/\mathbb{F}_q(T)$ be a finite Galois extension of Galois group G and $\mathscr{O}_K$ be the integral closure of $\mathbb{F}_q[T]$ in K. Let $Q \in \mathbb{F}_q[T]$ be an irreducible polynomial such that the corresponding prime ideal is unramified and has inertia degree d. Denote by $\mathfrak{P}_1 \cdots \mathfrak{P}_m$ the decomposition of the ideal $Q\mathscr{O}_K$. Then, G acts on the finite dimensional algebra $\mathscr{O}_K/Q\mathscr{O}_K$ and there exists $\mathbf{x} \in \mathscr{O}_K/Q\mathscr{O}_K$ such that $(\sigma(\mathbf{x}))_{\sigma \in G}$ is an $\mathbb{F}_q$–basis of $\mathscr{O}_K/Q\mathscr{O}_K$.*

Proof. Consider the decomposition group $D_{\mathfrak{P}_1/Q}$. As explained Sect. 2 and in particular in Eq. (4), since $Q\mathscr{O}_K$ is unramified, this decomposition group is isomorphic to $\mathrm{Gal}(\mathscr{O}_K/Q\mathscr{O}_K, \mathbb{F}_q) = \mathrm{Gal}(\mathbb{F}_{q^d}, \mathbb{F}_q)$. This entails in particular that $\#D_{\mathfrak{P}_1/Q} = d$.

According to the Chinese Remainder Theorem,

$$\mathscr{O}_K/Q\mathscr{O}_K \simeq \mathscr{O}_K/\mathfrak{P}_1 \times \cdots \times \mathscr{O}_K/\mathfrak{P}_m.$$

Next, from the Normal basis Theorem (see for instance [21, Thm. 2.35]), there exists $\mathbf{a} \in \mathscr{O}_K/\mathfrak{P}_1$ such that $(\sigma(\mathbf{a}))_{\sigma \in D_{\mathfrak{P}_1/Q}}$ is an $\mathbb{F}_q$–basis of $\mathscr{O}_K/\mathfrak{P}_1$. Now, let

$$\mathbf{b} \stackrel{\text{def}}{=} (\mathbf{a}, 0, \ldots, 0) \in \prod_{i=1}^{m} \mathscr{O}_K/\mathfrak{P}_i \simeq \mathscr{O}_K/Q\mathscr{O}_K.$$

We claim that $(\sigma(\mathbf{b}))_{\sigma \in G}$ is an $\mathbb{F}_q$–basis of $\mathscr{O}_K/Q\mathscr{O}_K$. Indeed, denote by V the $\mathbb{F}_q$–span of $\{\sigma(\mathbf{b}) \mid \sigma \in G\}$ and suppose that V is a proper subspace of $\mathscr{O}_K/Q\mathscr{O}_K$. Then, there exists $i \in [\![1, m]\!]$ such that

$$V \cap \mathscr{O}_K/\mathfrak{P}_i \subsetneq \mathscr{O}_K/\mathfrak{P}_i,$$

where we denote by $\mathscr{O}_K/\mathfrak{P}_i$ the subspace $\{0\} \times \cdots \times \{0\} \times \mathscr{O}_K/\mathfrak{P}_i \times \{0\} \times \cdots \times \{0\}$ of $\prod_i \mathscr{O}_K/\mathfrak{P}_i$.

Since G acts transitively on the $\mathfrak{P}_i$'s, there exists $\sigma_0 \in G$ such that $\sigma_0(\mathfrak{P}_1) = \mathfrak{P}_i$. Then, $\sigma_0(\mathbf{b}) \in V \cap \mathscr{O}_K/\mathfrak{P}_i$ and so does $\sigma\sigma_0(\mathbf{b})$ for any $\sigma \in D_{\mathfrak{P}_i/P}$. Since $V \cap \mathscr{O}_K/\mathfrak{P}_i \subsetneq \mathscr{O}_K/\mathfrak{P}_i$, then $\dim_{\mathbb{F}_q} V < d$ while $\#D_{\mathfrak{P}_i/Q} = d$. Hence, there exist nonzero elements $(\lambda_\sigma)_{\sigma \in D_{\mathfrak{P}_i/Q}} \in \mathbb{F}_q^d$ such that

$$\sum_{\sigma \in D_{\mathfrak{P}_i/Q}} \lambda_\sigma \sigma \sigma_0(\mathbf{b}) = 0. \tag{6}$$

Applying σ_0^{-1} to (6), we get

$$\sum_{\sigma \in D_{\mathfrak{P}_i/Q}} \lambda_\sigma \sigma_0^{-1} \sigma \sigma_0(\mathbf{b}) = 0.$$

As mentioned in Sect. 2, we have $\sigma_0^{-1} D_{\mathfrak{P}_i/Q} \sigma_0 = D_{\mathfrak{P}_1/Q}$ and we deduce that the above sum is in $\mathscr{O}_K/\mathfrak{P}_1$ and, since $\mathbf{a}$ is a generator of a normal basis of $\mathbb{F}_q$, we deduce that the λ_σ's are all zero. A contradiction. $\qquad\square$

The previous proposition asserts the existence of a *normal* $\mathbb{F}_q$–basis of the space $\mathscr{O}_K/Q\mathscr{O}_K$, *i.e.* a Galois invariant basis. For any such basis, $(\mathbf{b}_\sigma)_{\sigma \in G}$ one can define a Galois noise distribution by sampling linear combinations of elements of this basis whose coefficients are independent Bernouilli random variables. Our Ring–LPN distribution is hence defined as pairs $(\mathbf{a}, \mathbf{b}) \in \mathscr{O}_K/Q\mathscr{O}_K \times \mathscr{O}_K/Q\mathscr{O}_K$ such that $\mathbf{a}$ is drawn uniformly at random and $\mathbf{b} = \mathbf{a}s + \mathbf{e}$ where $\mathbf{e}$ is a noise term drawn from the previously described distribution.

Definition 7 (Galois modulus). *Let r and d be positive integers. A polynomial $f(X) \in \mathbb{F}_q[X]$ of degree r is called a Galois modulus of inertia d if there exists a Galois function field $K/\mathbb{F}_q(T)$ and a polynomial $Q(T) \in \mathbb{F}_q[T]$ of degree one such that $\mathbb{F}_q[X]/(f(X)) \simeq \mathscr{O}_K/Q\mathscr{O}_K$ and the ideal $Q\mathscr{O}_K$ has inertia degree d and does not ramify.*

This definition entails that for a polynomial $f(X) \in \mathbb{F}_q[X]$ to be a Galois modulus, it needs to factorize in $\mathbb{F}_q[X]$ as a product of distinct irreducible polynomials of same degree d.

Carlitz extensions permit to easily exhibit many Galois moduli of given inertia d. Indeed, let $M(T) \in \mathbb{F}_q[T]$ be any divisor of $T^d - 1$ which vanishes at least at one primitive d–th root of unity. Set

$$r \stackrel{\text{def}}{=} \frac{\#\left(\mathbb{F}_q[X]/(M(X))\right)^\times}{d}.$$

Then, any polynomial $f(X) \in \mathbb{F}_q[X]$ which is a product of r distinct irreducible polynomials of degree d is a Galois modulus. Indeed, $\mathbb{F}_q[X]/(f(X))$ is isomorphic to a product of r copies of $\mathbb{F}_{2^d}$ and, since the multiplicative order of T modulo $M(T)$ is d, from Theorem 5 so does $\mathscr{O}_M/T\mathscr{O}_M$.

Example 7. The polynomial $f(X) \stackrel{\text{def}}{=} X^{63} + X^7 + 1 \in \mathbb{F}_2[X]$ is a *Galois* modulus of inertia 9. Indeed, let $M(T) \stackrel{\text{def}}{=} T^6 + T^3 + 1$ and consider K_M the Carlitz extension of M–torsion. Denote by $\mathscr{O}_M$ the integral closure of $\mathbb{F}_2[T]$ in $\mathscr{O}_M$. Then $T^9 \equiv 1 \mod M$ and 9 is the smallest integer that has this property. By Theorem 5, the ideal $T\mathscr{O}_M$ splits into 7 ideals $\mathfrak{P}_1, \ldots, \mathfrak{P}_7$ and has inertia 9, and one can prove that $\mathscr{O}_M/(T\mathscr{O}_M) \simeq \mathbb{F}_2[X]/(f(X))$.

Remark 13. The polynomial $f(X)$ of Example 7 is also *lightness-preserving* in the sense of [12, Def 2.22] which can be used to instantiate Ring-LPN.

We are now ready to define a new noise distribution which is Galois invariant for Ring–LPN. We propose to consider it in LAPIN as it enables to apply our search to decision reduction. In the following definition, $\mathcal{B}$ denotes a normal basis whose existence is ensured by Proposition 1. Note that $\mathcal{B}$ need not be exactly the normal basis constructed in the proof of Proposition 1. This is discussed further, after the statement of Theorem 8.

Definition 8 (Normal Ring–LPN distribution). *Let r, d be positive integers, $p \in [0, \frac{1}{2})$ and let $f(X) \in \mathbb{F}_q[X]$ be a Galois modulus of degree r with inertia d. Denote by $\mathcal{B} \stackrel{\text{def}}{=} (\sigma(\mathbf{c})(X))_{\sigma \in G_f}$ the normal basis of $\mathbb{F}_q[X]/(f(X))$ where G_f is the Galois group of the related function field.*

A sample $(\mathbf{a}, \mathbf{b})$ is distributed according to the Normal RLPN distribution relatively to basis $\mathcal{B}$, with secret $\mathbf{s}$ if

- *$\mathbf{a}$ is drawn uniformly at random over $\mathbb{F}_q[X]/(f(X))$;*
- *$\mathbf{b} \stackrel{\text{def}}{=} \mathbf{as} + \mathbf{e}$, where $\mathbf{e}(X) \stackrel{\text{def}}{=} \sum_{\sigma \in G_f} e_\sigma \sigma(\mathbf{c})(X) \in \mathbb{F}_q[X]/(f(X))$ has coefficients e_i's which are independent q–ary Bernouilli random variables with parameter p.*

Theorem 8. *The decision Ring–LPN is equivalent to its search version for the normal Ring–LPN distribution.*

Let us discuss further the choice of the noise distribution and hence that of a Galois-invariant basis. In [18], the authors discuss the case of Ring–LPN when the modulus f splits and mention that in this situation, the Ring–LPN problem reduces to a smaller one by projecting the samples onto a factor $\mathbb{F}_q[X]/(f_i(X))$ of the algebra $\mathbb{F}_q[X]/(f(X))$. The projection onto such a factor, reduces the size of the inputs but increases the rate of the noise.

It should be emphasized that the Galois invariant basis constructed in the proof of Proposition 1 yields a noise which is partially cancelled when applying the projection $\mathscr{O}_K/Q\mathscr{O}_K \to \mathscr{O}_K/\mathfrak{P}_i$, hence, this choice of normal basis might be inaccurate. On the other hand, Proposition 1 is only an existence result and it turns out actually that a random element of $\mathscr{O}_K/Q\mathscr{O}_K$ generates a normal basis with a high probability. Indeed, the existence of such a normal basis can be reformulated as $\mathscr{O}_K/Q\mathscr{O}_K$ is a free $\mathbb{F}_q[G]$–module of rank 1 and a generator $\mathbf{a} \in \mathscr{O}_K/Q\mathscr{O}_K$ is an $\mathbb{F}_q[G]$–basis of $\mathscr{O}_K/Q\mathscr{O}_K$. Now, any other element of $\mathbb{F}_q[G]^\times \mathbf{a}$ is also a generator of a normal basis. Consequently, the probability that a uniformly random element of $\mathscr{O}_K/Q\mathscr{O}_K$ is a generator of a normal basis is

$$\frac{\#\mathbb{F}_q[G]^\times}{\#\mathbb{F}_q[G]}.$$

If for instance, G is cyclic of order N prime to q. Then $X^N - 1$ splits into a product of distinct irreducible factors $u_1 \cdots u_r$ and $\mathbb{F}_q[G] \simeq \mathbb{F}_q[X]/(X^N - 1) \simeq \prod_i \mathbb{F}_q[X]/(u_i(X))$. In this context, the probability that a uniformly random element of $\mathscr{O}_K/Q\mathscr{O}_K$ generates a normal basis is

$$\frac{\prod_{i=1}^r (q^{\deg u_i} - 1)}{q^N}.$$

Conclusion

We introduced a new formalism to study generic problems useful in cryptography based on structured codes. This formalism rests on the introduction of function fields as counterparts of the number fields appearing in cryptography based on structured lattices. Thanks to this new point of view, we succeeded in producing the first search to decision reduction in the spirit of Lyubashevsky, Peikert and Regev's one for Ring-LWE. We emphasize that such reductions were completely absent in cryptography based on structured codes and we expect them to be a first step towards further search to decision reductions.

If one puts into perspective our current assessment with lattice-based cryptography, [23] focuses on cyclotomic number fields, and defines the error distribution to be a Gaussian over $\mathbb{R}^n$ through the Minkowski embedding. Furthermore, the modulus q is chosen to split completely. Then, following this result, [20] uses a "switching modulus" technique in order to relax the arithmetic assumption on the prime modulus, so that it can be arbitrarily chosen. Finally, the search to decision reduction is proved in [31] to hold even when the extension is not Galois, using the Oracle with Hidden Center Problem (OHCP) technique from [28].

Note that this powerful technique has been used recently to provide a search to decision reduction in the context of NTRU [29]. Even though our work does not reflect these recent progresses, we believe, as it was shown by our instantiations, that the introduction of the function field framework paves the way for using these techniques in the code setting in order to get a full reduction applying to cryptosystems such as HQC or BIKE.

References

1. Aguilar Melchor, C., et al.: BIKE. Round 3 Submission to the NIST Post-Quantum Cryptography Call, v. 4.2, September 2021. https://bikesuite.org
2. Aguilar Melchor, C., et al.: HQC. Round 3 Submission to the NIST Post-Quantum Cryptography Call, June 2021. https://pqc-hqc.org/doc/hqc-specification_2021-06-06.pdf
3. Ajtai, M., Dwork, C.: A public-key cryptosystem with worst-case/average-case equivalence. In: Proceedings of the Twenty-Ninth Annual ACM Symposium on the Theory of Computing, El Paso, Texas, USA, 4–6 May 1997, pp. 284–293 (1997). https://doi.org/10.1145/258533.258604, http://doi.acm.org/10.1145/258533.258604
4. Alagic, G., et al.: Status report on the second round of the NIST post-quantum cryptography standardization process (2020)
5. Alekhnovich, M.: More on average case vs approximation complexity. In: Proceedings of the 44th Symposium on Foundations of Computer Science (FOCS 2003), 11–14 October 2003, Cambridge, MA, USA, pp. 298–307. IEEE Computer Society (2003). https://doi.org/10.1109/SFCS.2003.1238204
6. Beelen, P., Høholdt, T.: The decoding of algebraic geometry codes. In: Advances in Algebraic Geometry Codes. Series Coding Theory Cryptology, vol. 5, pp. 49–98. World Scientific Publishing, Hackensack (2008)
7. Boyle, E., Couteau, G., Gilboa, N., Ishai, Y., Kohl, L., Scholl, P.: Efficient pseudorandom correlation generators from ring-LPN. In: Micciancio, D., Ristenpart, T. (eds.) CRYPTO 2020. LNCS, vol. 12171, pp. 387–416. Springer, Cham (2020). https://doi.org/10.1007/978-3-030-56880-1_14
8. Chapman, R.J.: A simple proof of Noether's Theorem. Glasgow Math. J. **38**, 49–51 (1996)
9. Conrad, K.: Carlitz extensions. https://kconrad.math.uconn.edu/blurbs/gradnumthy/carlitz.pdf
10. Courtois, N.T., Finiasz, M., Sendrier, N.: How to achieve a McEliece-based digital signature scheme. In: Boyd, C. (ed.) ASIACRYPT 2001. LNCS, vol. 2248, pp. 157–174. Springer, Heidelberg (2001). https://doi.org/10.1007/3-540-45682-1_10
11. Couvreur, A., Randriambololona, H.: Algebraic geometry codes and some applications, chap. 15, pp. 307–361. CRC Press (2021)
12. Damgård, I., Park, S.: Is public-key encryption based on LPN practical? IACR Cryptol. ePrint Arch., p. 699 (2012). http://eprint.iacr.org/2012/699
13. Debris-Alazard, T., Sendrier, N., Tillich, J.-P.: Wave: a new family of trapdoor one-way preimage sampleable functions based on codes. In: Galbraith, S.D., Moriai, S. (eds.) ASIACRYPT 2019. LNCS, vol. 11921, pp. 21–51. Springer, Cham (2019). https://doi.org/10.1007/978-3-030-34578-5_2
14. Fischer, J.B., Stern, J.: An efficient pseudo-random generator provably as secure as syndrome decoding. In: Maurer, U. (ed.) EUROCRYPT 1996. LNCS, vol. 1070, pp. 245–255. Springer, Heidelberg (1996). https://doi.org/10.1007/3-540-68339-9_22

15. Gaborit, P.: Shorter keys for code based cryptography. In: Proceedings of the 2005 International Workshop on Coding and Cryptography (WCC 2005), Bergen, Norway, pp. 81–91 (2005)

16. Goppa, V.D.: Codes on algebraic curves. Dokl. Akad. Nauk SSSR **259**(6), 1289–1290 (1981). In Russian

17. Hayes, D.R.: Explicit class field theory for rational function fields. Trans. Am. Math. Soc. **189**, 77–91 (1974)

18. Heyse, S., Kiltz, E., Lyubashevsky, V., Paar, C., Pietrzak, K.: Lapin: an efficient authentication protocol based on ring-LPN. In: Canteaut, A. (ed.) FSE 2012. LNCS, vol. 7549, pp. 346–365. Springer, Heidelberg (2012). https://doi.org/10.1007/978-3-642-34047-5_20

19. Høholdt, T., Pellikaan, R.: On the decoding of algebraic-geometric codes. IEEE Trans. Inform. Theory **41**(6), 1589–1614 (1995)

20. Langlois, A., Stehlé, D.: Worst-case to average-case reductions for module lattices. Des. Codes Crypt. **75**(3), 565–599 (2014). https://hal.archives-ouvertes.fr/hal-01240452

21. Lidl, R., Niederreiter, H.: Finite fields. In: Encyclopedia of Mathematics and its Applications, vol. 20, 2nd edn. Cambridge University Press, Cambridge (1997). With a foreword by P. M. Cohn

22. Lyubashevsky, V.: Search to decision reduction for the learning with errors over rings problem. In: ITW, pp. 410–414. IEEE (2011)

23. Lyubashevsky, V., Peikert, C., Regev, O.: On ideal lattices and learning with errors over rings. In: Gilbert, H. (ed.) EUROCRYPT 2010. LNCS, vol. 6110, pp. 1–23. Springer, Heidelberg (2010). https://doi.org/10.1007/978-3-642-13190-5_1

24. McEliece, R.J.: A public-key system based on algebraic coding theory, pp. 114–116. Jet Propulsion Lab (1978). dSN Progress Report 44

25. Micciancio, D., Regev, O.: Worst-case to average-case reductions based on Gaussian measures. In: 45th Annual IEEE Symposium on Foundations of Computer Science, pp. 372–381 (2004). https://doi.org/10.1109/FOCS.2004.72

26. Niederreiter, H., Xing, C.: Rational Points on Curves Over Finite Fields: Theory and Applications, vol. 288. Cambridge University Press, Cambridge (2001)

27. Noether, E.: Normalbasis bei Körpern ohne Höhere Verzweigung. J. Reine Angew. Math. **167**, 147–152 (1932)

28. Peikert, C., Regev, O., Stephens-Davidowitz, N.: Pseudorandomness of ring-LWE for any ring and modulus. In: Proceedings of the 49th Annual ACM SIGACT Symposium on Theory of Computing, pp. 461–473 (2017)

29. Pellet-Mary, A., Stehlé, D.: On the Hardness of the NTRU Problem. In: Tibouchi, M., Wang, H. (eds.) ASIACRYPT 2021. LNCS, vol. 13090, pp. 3–35. Springer, Cham (2021). https://doi.org/10.1007/978-3-030-92062-3_1, https://hal.archives-ouvertes.fr/hal-03348022

30. Regev, O.: On lattices, learning with errors, random linear codes, and cryptography. In: Proceedings of the 37th Annual ACM Symposium on Theory of Computing, Baltimore, MD, USA, 22–24 May 2005, pp. 84–93 (2005). https://doi.org/10.1145/1060590.1060603, http://doi.acm.org/10.1145/1060590.1060603

31. Rosca, M., Stehlé, D., Wallet, A.: On the ring-LWE and polynomial-LWE problems. In: Nielsen, J.B., Rijmen, V. (eds.) EUROCRYPT 2018. LNCS, vol. 10820, pp. 146–173. Springer, Cham (2018). https://doi.org/10.1007/978-3-319-78381-9_6

32. Rosen, M.: Number Theory in Function Fields. Graduate Texts in Mathematics, Springer, New York (2002). https://doi.org/10.1007/978-1-4757-6046-0

33. Sendrier, N.: Decoding one out of many. In: Yang, B.-Y. (ed.) PQCrypto 2011. LNCS, vol. 7071, pp. 51–67. Springer, Heidelberg (2011). https://doi.org/10.1007/978-3-642-25405-5_4

34. Stehlé, D., Steinfeld, R., Tanaka, K., Xagawa, K.: Efficient public key encryption based on ideal lattices. In: Matsui, M. (ed.) ASIACRYPT 2009. LNCS, vol. 5912, pp. 617–635. Springer, Heidelberg (2009). https://doi.org/10.1007/978-3-642-10366-7_36

35. Stern, J.: A new identification scheme based on syndrome decoding. In: Stinson, D.R. (ed.) CRYPTO 1993. LNCS, vol. 773, pp. 13–21. Springer, Heidelberg (1994). https://doi.org/10.1007/3-540-48329-2_2

36. Stichtenoth, H.: Algebraic Function Fields and Codes. Graduate Texts in Mathematics, vol. 254, 2nd edn. Springer, Berlin (2009). https://doi.org/10.1007/978-3-540-76878-4

37. Tsfasman, M.A., Vlăduţ, S.G., Zink, T.: Modular curves, Shimura curves, and Goppa codes, better than Varshamov-Gilbert bound. Math. Nach. 109(1), 21–28 (1982)

Syndrome Decoding in the Head: Shorter Signatures from Zero-Knowledge Proofs

Thibauld Feneuil[1,2]([✉]), Antoine Joux[3], and Matthieu Rivain[1]

[1] CryptoExperts, Paris, France
{thibauld.feneuil,matthieu.rivain}@cryptoexperts.com
[2] Sorbonne Université, CNRS, INRIA, Institut de Mathématiques de Jussieu-Paris
Rive Gauche, Ouragan, Paris, France
[3] CISPA Helmholtz Center for Information Security, Saarbrücken, Germany
joux@cispa.de

Abstract. Zero-knowledge proofs of knowledge are useful tools to design signature schemes. The ongoing effort to build a quantum computer urges the cryptography community to develop new secure cryptographic protocols based on quantum-hard cryptographic problems. One of the few directions is code-based cryptography for which the strongest problem is the *syndrome decoding* (SD) for random linear codes. This problem is known to be NP-hard and the cryptanalysis state of the art has been stable for many years. A zero-knowledge protocol for this problem was pioneered by Stern in 1993. Since its publication, many articles proposed optimizations, implementation, or variants.

In this paper, we introduce a new zero-knowledge proof for the syndrome decoding problem on random linear codes. Instead of using permutations like most of the existing protocols, we rely on the MPC-in-the-head paradigm in which we reduce the task of proving the low Hamming weight of the SD solution to proving some relations between specific polynomials. Specifically, we propose a 5-round zero-knowledge protocol that proves the knowledge of a vector x such that $y = Hx$ and $\text{wt}(x) \leq w$ and which achieves a soundness error closed to $1/N$ for an *arbitrary* N.

While turning this protocol into a signature scheme, we achieve a signature size of 11–12 KB for 128-bit security when relying on the hardness of the SD problem on binary fields. Using larger fields (like $\mathbb{F}_{2^8}$), we can produce fast signatures of around 8 KB. This allows us to outperform Picnic3 and to be competitive with SPHINCS$^+$, both post-quantum signature candidates in the ongoing NIST standardization effort. Moreover, our scheme outperforms all the existing code-based signature schemes for the common "signature size + public key size" metric.

1 Introduction

Zero-knowledge proofs are an important tool for many cryptographic protocols and applications. Such proofs enable a *prover* to prove a statement by interacting with a *verifier* without revealing anything more than the statement itself. Zero-knowledge proofs find application in many contexts. Thanks to the Fiat-Shamir

© International Association for Cryptologic Research 2022
Y. Dodis and T. Shrimpton (Eds.): CRYPTO 2022, LNCS 13508, pp. 541–572, 2022.
https://doi.org/10.1007/978-3-031-15979-4_19

transform [FS87], we can convert such proofs into signature schemes. In this article, we aim to build an efficient code-based signature scheme using this methodology. To do so, we will focus on the *generic decoding* problem, a.k.a. the (computational) *syndrome decoding* (SD) problem: given a matrix $H \in \mathbb{F}_q^{(m-k) \times m}$ and a vector $y \in \mathbb{F}_q^{m-k}$, recover a *small-weight* vector $x \in \mathbb{F}_q^m$ such that $Hx = y$. For random linear codes –*i.e.* for a random matrix H– this problem is known to be NP-hard and widely believed to be robust for practical sets of parameters.

In a pioneering work from three decades ago, Stern proposed a zero-knowledge protocol to prove the knowledge of a syndrome decoding solution [Ste94]. This protocol achieves a *soundness error* of 2/3 which means that a malicious prover can fool the verifier with a 2/3 probability. Although an arbitrary security of $(2/3)^\tau$ can be achieved by repeating the protocol τ times, the induced communication cost for standard security levels (*e.g.* 128 bits) becomes significant, which is partly due to this high soundness error. Since the work of Stern, a few papers have proposed optimizations and implementations of this protocol (see for instance [Vér96, GG07, AGS11, ACBH13]) but the communication cost was still heavy for random linear codes with standard security levels.

In 2007, Ishai, Kushilevitz, Ostrovsky and Sahai proposed a new technique to build zero-knowledge proofs from secure multi-party computation (MPC) protocols, which is known as the *MPC-in-the-Head* (MPCitH) paradigm [IKOS07]. While this construction was mainly considered of theoretical interest at first, it has been increasingly applied to build practical schemes over the last years. In particular, the Picnic post-quantum signature scheme [CDG+20], which is a third-round alternate candidate of the ongoing NIST standardization effort, is based on the MPCitH principle. Recently, new zero-knowledge protocols for the SD problem have been inspired by this principle [GPS22, FJR21, BGKM22]. In particular, these protocols achieve an arbitrary soundness error $1/N$ instead of the 2/3 (or 1/2) of Stern protocol and variants. These protocols result in smaller proof/signature sizes at the cost of computational overheads.

Our Contribution. In this article, we build a new zero-knowledge protocol to prove the knowledge of a syndrome decoding solution using the MPCitH paradigm. We further turn this protocol into an efficient code-based signature scheme.

While proving that $y = Hx$ is communication-free in this paradigm, the hard part consists in proving that x is a small-weight vector. We propose here an efficient way to prove that $\text{wt}(x) \leq w$ through a multi-party computation which is simulated by the prover ("in her head"). The key idea is to prove the equality $x \circ v = 0$ where $\circ$ is the component-wise multiplication and where the coefficients of the vector v are the evaluations of a polynomial Q of degree w. By definition, v has at most w zero coordinates, so the relation $x \circ v = 0$ proves that x has at most w non-zero coordinates (*i.e.* $\text{wt}(x) \leq w$). The roots of the polynomial Q encode the non-zero positions of the vector x. In order to prove the relation $x \circ v = 0$, we use techniques borrowed from the Banquet signature scheme [BdK+21b] with further adaptations. To check that all $x_j \cdot v_j$ are equal to zero, we arrange the input x into a polynomial S, provide a product polynomial $F \cdot P$ as part of the witness, and check that $(F \cdot P)(\cdot)$ indeed equals the product of $S(\cdot)$ and $Q(\cdot)$. This can be done efficiently by only verifying a few products of these polynomials evaluated at some random points. However, instead of revealing the multiplication operands like in [BdK+21b], we rely on the product checking protocol proposed in [LN17,BN20] and its batch version recently introduced in [KZ21].

Let us note that the idea of encoding the non-zero positions in a polynomial to prove a Hamming weight inequality was already used in [DLO+18]. However, the proposed zero-knowledge protocol relies on a linearly homomorphic commitment scheme, and such schemes do not exist yet for post-quantum hardness assumptions.

Thanks to the Fiat-Shamir transform [FS87], we convert our protocol into a signature scheme. Our scheme outperforms all the existing code-based signatures for the "signature size + public key size" metric. When relying on the hardness of the syndrome decoding problem over $\mathbb{F}_{256}$, our scheme is below 10 KB for this metric, which makes it competitive with Picnic3 [KZ20b] and SPHINCS$^+$ [BHK+19]. Compared to other code-based signature schemes (such as Wave [DST19] and Durandal [ABG+19]), our scheme has the significant advantage of relying on a non-structured NP-hard decoding problem which has been widely studied over the last decades.

To provide more flexibility, we introduce a parameter d in the definition of the syndrome decoding problem. The idea is, instead of having a constraint for the global weight of the secret vector x, to split x into d chunks $x := (x_1 \mid \ldots \mid x_d)$ and to have a constraint on the weight of each chunk. By taking $d = 1$, this d-split version is equivalent to the standard syndrome decoding problem. We provide a security reduction from this variant to the standard problem which allows us to compensate the security loss by a slight increase of the parameters. This so-called d-split syndrome decoding problem offers us more flexibility to find better size-performance trade-offs for our signature scheme.

Paper Organization. The paper is organized as follows: In Sect. 2, we introduce the necessary background on the syndrome decoding problem, zero-knowledge proofs, and the MPC-in-the-Head paradigm. We present our protocol in Sect. 3 and the signature scheme obtained through the Fiat-Shamir transform in Sect. 4. To conclude, we provide implementation results and compare our construction with other signature schemes from the state of the art in Sect. 5.

2   Preliminaries

Throughout the paper, $\mathbb{F}$ shall denote a finite field. For any vector $x \in \mathbb{F}^m$, the *Hamming weight* of x, denoted $\mathrm{wt}(x)$, is the number of non-zero coordinates of x. For two vectors $x_1 \in \mathbb{F}^{m_1}$ and $x_2 \in \mathbb{F}^{m_2}$, we denote $(x_1 \mid x_2) \in \mathbb{F}^{m_1+m_2}$ their concatenation. We denote $\circ$ the component-wise multiplication between two vectors. For any $m \in \mathbb{N}^*$, the integer set $\{1, \ldots, m\}$ is denoted $[m]$. For a probability distribution D, the notation $s \leftarrow D$ means that s is sampled from D. For a finite set S, the notation $s \leftarrow S$ means that s is uniformly sampled at random from S. When the set S is clear from the context, we sometimes denote $s \leftarrow \$$ for a uniform random sampling of s from S. For an algorithm $\mathcal{A}$, $out \leftarrow \mathcal{A}(in)$ further means that out is obtained by a call to $\mathcal{A}$ on input in (using uniform random coins whenever $\mathcal{A}$ is probabilistic). Along the paper, probabilistic polynomial time is abbreviated PPT.

A function $\mu : \mathbb{N} \to \mathbb{R}$ is said *negligible* if, for every positive polynomial $p(\cdot)$, there exists an integer $N_p > 0$ such that for every $\lambda > N_p$, we have $|\mu(\lambda)| < 1/p(\lambda)$. When not made explicit, a negligible function in λ is denoted $\mathsf{negl}(\lambda)$ while a polynomial function in λ is denoted $\mathsf{poly}(\lambda)$. We further use the notation $\mathsf{poly}(\lambda_1, \lambda_2, ...)$ for a polynomial function in several variables.

Two distributions $\{D_\lambda\}_\lambda$ and $\{E_\lambda\}_\lambda$ indexed by a security parameter λ are (t, ε)-*indistinguishable* (where t and ε are $\mathbb{N} \to \mathbb{R}$ functions) if, for any algorithm $\mathcal{A}$ running in time at most $t(\lambda)$, we have

$$\left| \Pr[\mathcal{A}(x) = 1 \mid x \leftarrow D_\lambda] - \Pr[\mathcal{A}(x) = 1 \mid x \leftarrow E_\lambda] \right| \leq \varepsilon(\lambda).$$

The two distributions are said

- *computationally indistinguishable* if $\varepsilon \in \mathsf{negl}(\lambda)$ for every $t \in \mathsf{poly}(\lambda)$;
- *statistically indistinguishable* if $\varepsilon \in \mathsf{negl}(\lambda)$ for every (unbounded) t;
- *perfectly indistinguishable* if $\varepsilon = 0$ for every (unbounded) t.

In this paper, we shall use the standard cryptographic notions of secure pseudo-random generator (PRG), tree PRG, collision-resistant hash function, and (hiding and binding) commitment scheme. Those notions are formally defined in the full version [FJR22].

2.1 Syndrome Decoding Problems

Definition 1 (Syndrome Decoding Problem). *Let $\mathbb{F}$ be a finite field. Let m, k and w be positive integers such that $m > k$ and $m > w$. The syndrome decoding problem with parameters $(\mathbb{F}, m, k, w)$ is the following problem:*

Let H, x and y be such that:
1. H is uniformly sampled from $\mathbb{F}^{(m-k) \times m}$,
2. x is uniformly sampled from $\{x \in \mathbb{F}^m : \mathrm{wt}(x) = w\}$,
3. y is defined as $y := Hx$.
From (H, y), find x.

In the following, a pair (H, y) generated as in the above definition is called an *instance* of the syndrome decoding problem for parameters $(\mathbb{F}, m, k, w)$. The syndrome decoding problem is known to be NP-hard. For a weight parameter w lower than the Gilbert-Varshamov radius $\tau_{\mathrm{GV}}(m, k)$, which is defined as:

$$w < \tau_{\mathrm{GV}}(m, k) \quad \Leftrightarrow \quad \sum_{j=0}^{w-1} \binom{m}{j} (q-1)^j < q^{m-k} \quad \text{with} \quad q = |\mathbb{F}|,$$

we know that there exists a unique solution x such that $y = Hx$ with overwhelming probability. Otherwise, an instance has several solutions on average.

There exists two main families of algorithms to solve the syndrome decoding problem: the *information set decoding* (ISD) algorithms and *generalized birthday algorithms* (GBA) [TS16, BBC+19]. To obtain a λ-bit security, the parameters of the syndrome decoding problem are hence chosen in a way to ensure that both kind of algorithms run in time greater than 2^λ.

Instead of working on the standard syndrome decoding problem, we will consider an alternative version that we shall call the *d-split syndrome decoding* problem, where the secret x is split into d chunks of same Hamming weights.

Definition 2 (d-Split Syndrome Decoding Problem). *Let $\mathbb{F}$ be a finite field. Let m, k, w be positive integers such that $m > k$, $m > w$, $d \mid w$ and $d \mid m$. The d-split syndrome decoding problem with parameters $(\mathbb{F}, m, k, w)$ is the following problem:*

Let H, x and y be such that:
1. H is uniformly sampled from $\mathbb{F}^{(m-k) \times m}$,
2. x is uniformly sampled from

$$\left\{ (x_1 \mid \ldots \mid x_d) \in \mathbb{F}^m \ : \ \forall i \in [d], \ x_i \in \mathbb{F}^{m/d}, \ \mathrm{wt}(x_i) = \frac{w}{d} \right\},$$

3. y is defined as $y := Hx$.
From (H, y), find x.

By taking $d = 1$, we get the standard syndrome decoding problem. The following theorem gives a way to estimate the difficulty to solve the d-split syndrome decoding problem.

Theorem 1. *Let $\mathbb{F}$ be a finite field. Let m, k, w be positive integers such that $m > k$, $m > w$, $d \mid w$ and $d \mid m$. Let $\mathcal{A}_d$ be an algorithm which solves a random $(\mathbb{F}, m, k, w)$-instance of the d-split syndrome decoding problem in time t with success probability ε_d. Then there exists an algorithm $\mathcal{A}_1$ which solves a random $(\mathbb{F}, m, k, w)$-instance of the standard syndrome decoding problem in time t with probability ε_1, where*

$$\varepsilon_1 \geq \frac{\binom{m/d}{w/d}^d}{\binom{m}{w}} \cdot \varepsilon_d.$$

Informally, an instance of the standard syndrome decoding problem is an instance of the d-split syndrome decoding problem with probability $\binom{m/d}{w/d}^d / \binom{m}{w}$. Moreover, a standard syndrome decoding instance can be "randomized" and input to the d-split adversary as much as desired. A formal proof of the above theorem is provided in the full version [FJR22].

Let us note that the d-split syndrome decoding problem can be seen as a generalization of the *regular syndrome decoding* problem introduced by [AFS03], for which the ratio w/d is equal to 1.

2.2 Zero-Knowledge Proofs of Knowledge

We will focus on a special kind of two-party protocol called an *interactive proof* which involves a *prover* $\mathcal{P}$ and a *verifier* $\mathcal{V}$. In such a protocol, $\mathcal{P}$ tries to prove a statement to $\mathcal{V}$. The first message sent by $\mathcal{P}$ is called a *commitment*, denoted COM. From this commitment $\mathcal{V}$ produces a first *challenge* CH_1 to which $\mathcal{P}$ answers with a response RSP_1, followed by a next challenge CH_2 from $\mathcal{V}$, and so on. After receiving the last response RSP_n, $\mathcal{V}$ produces a binary output: either 1, meaning that she was convinced by $\mathcal{P}$, or 0 otherwise.

The sequence of exchanged messages is called the *transcript* of the execution, which is denoted

$$\mathrm{View}(\langle \mathcal{P}(in_{\mathcal{P}}), \mathcal{V}(in_{\mathcal{V}}) \rangle) := (\mathrm{COM}, \mathrm{CH}_1, \mathrm{RSP}_1, \dots, \mathrm{CH}_n, \mathrm{RSP}_n)$$

where $in_{\mathcal{P}}$ and $in_{\mathcal{V}}$ respectively denote the prover and verifier inputs. An execution producing an output *out* is further denoted

$$\langle \mathcal{P}(in_{\mathcal{P}}), \mathcal{V}(in_{\mathcal{V}}) \rangle \to out.$$

Definition 3 (Proof of Knowledge). *Let x be a statement of language L in NP, and $W(x)$ the set of witnesses for x such that the following relation holds:*

$$\mathcal{R} = \{(x, w) : x \in L, w \in W(x)\}.$$

A proof of knowledge for relation $\mathcal{R}$ with soundness error ε is a two-party protocol between a prover $\mathcal{P}$ and a verifier $\mathcal{V}$ with the following two properties:

- *(Perfect) Completeness: If $(x, w) \in \mathcal{R}$, then a prover $\mathcal{P}$ who knows a witness w for x succeeds in convincing the verifier $\mathcal{V}$ of his knowledge. More formally:*

$$\Pr[\langle \mathcal{P}(x, w), \mathcal{V}(x) \rangle \to 1] = 1,$$

  i.e. given the interaction between the prover $\mathcal{P}$ and the verifier $\mathcal{V}$, the probability that the verifier is convinced is 1.

- *Soundness: If there exists a PPT prover $\tilde{\mathcal{P}}$ such that*

$$\tilde{\varepsilon} := \Pr[\langle \tilde{\mathcal{P}}(x), \mathcal{V}(x) \rangle \to 1] > \varepsilon,$$

  then there exists an algorithm $\mathcal{E}$ (called an extractor) which, given rewindable black-box access to $\tilde{\mathcal{P}}$, outputs a witness w' for x in time $\mathsf{poly}(\lambda, (\tilde{\varepsilon} - \varepsilon)^{-1})$ with probability at least $1/2$.

Informally, a proof of knowledge has soundness error ε if a prover $\tilde{\mathcal{P}}$ without knowledge of the witness cannot convince the verifier with probability greater than ε assuming that the underlying problem (recovering a witness for the input statement) is hard. Indeed, if a prover $\tilde{\mathcal{P}}$ can succeed with a probability greater than ε, then the existence of the extractor (algorithm $\mathcal{E}$) implies that $\tilde{\mathcal{P}}$ can be used to compute a witness $w' \in W(x)$.

Remark 1. In the present article, we focus on proof of knowledge for a syndrome decoding instance defined by a matrix H and a vector y. The problem parameters m, k and w will be considered to be defined by the security parameter λ. In this context, the syndrome decoding instance (H, y) is the *statement*. A *witness* for this statement is a small-weight vector x such that $y = Hx$.

We now recall the notion of honest-verifier zero-knowledge proof:

Definition 4 (Honest-Verifier Zero-Knowledge Proof). *A proof of knowledge is {computationally, statistically, perfectly} honest-verifier zero-knowledge (HVZK) if there exists a PPT algorithm S (called simulator) whose output distribution is {computationally, statistically, perfectly} indistinguishable from the distribution* $\text{View}(\langle \mathcal{P}(x, w), \mathcal{V}(x) \rangle)$ *obtained with an honest $\mathcal{V}$.*

Informally, the previous definition says a genuine execution of the protocol can be simulated without any knowledge of the witness. In other words, the transcript of an execution between the prover and an honest verifier does not reveal any information about the witness.

2.3 Sharings and Multi-party Computation

In the scope of this article, all the *sharings* are additive. Specifically, an N-sharing of an element $x \in \mathbb{F}^m$ is an N-tuple

$$[\![x]\!] = ([\![x]\!]_1, \ldots, [\![x]\!]_N) \in (\mathbb{F}^m)^N \quad \text{such that} \quad x = \sum_{i=1}^{N} [\![x]\!]_i.$$

Each $[\![x]\!]_i$ is called a *share* of x. For a polynomial $P \in \mathbb{F}[X]$ of degree at most d, we define its sharing $[\![P]\!]$ as a N-tuple of $(\mathbb{F}[X])^N$ such that $P = \sum_{i=1}^{N}[\![P]\!]_i$, where each $[\![P]\!]_i$ is of degree at most d. In particular, a sharing of a degree-d polynomial can be seen as the sharing of the d-tuple of its coefficients.

In the context of multi-party computation (MPC), an N-sharing is usually distributed to N parties, meaning that each party gets one of the N shares. From those shares, the parties can perform distributed computation. Let assume that each party $i \in [N]$ receives the shares $[\![x]\!]_i$, $[\![y]\!]_i$ and $[\![P]\!]_i$ corresponding to shared values $x, y \in \mathbb{F}$ and polynomial $P \in \mathbb{F}[X]$. They can perform the following operations:

- **Addition:** the parties locally compute $[\![x + y]\!]$ by adding their respective shares:
$$\forall i, [\![x + y]\!]_i := [\![x]\!]_i + [\![y]\!]_i.$$
This process is denoted $[\![x + y]\!] = [\![x]\!] + [\![y]\!]$.

- **Addition with a constant:** for a given constant α, the parties locally compute $[\![x + \alpha]\!]$ by doing:
$$\begin{cases} [\![x + \alpha]\!]_1 := [\![x]\!]_1 + \alpha \\ [\![x + \alpha]\!]_i := [\![x]\!]_i \text{ for } i \neq 1 \end{cases}$$
This process is denoted $[\![x + \alpha]\!] = [\![x]\!] + \alpha$.

- **Multiplication by a constant:** for a given constant α, the parties locally compute $[\![\alpha \cdot x]\!]$ by multiplying their respective shares:

$$\forall i, [\![\alpha \cdot x]\!]_i := \alpha \cdot [\![x]\!]_i.$$

  This process is denoted $[\![\alpha \cdot x]\!] = \alpha \cdot [\![x]\!]$.
- **Polynomial evaluation:** for a given r, the parties can locally compute $[\![P(r)]\!]$ by:

$$\forall i, [\![P(r)]\!]_i := [\![P]\!]_i(r) = \sum_{j=0}^{d} [\![P_j]\!]_i \cdot r^j,$$

  where $\{[\![P_j]\!]_i\}_j$ denotes the coefficients of $[\![P]\!]_i$. This process is denoted $[\![P(r)]\!] = [\![P]\!](r)$.

2.4   The MPC-in-the-Head Paradigm

The MPC-in-the-Head (MPCitH) paradigm introduced in [IKOS07] offers a way to build zero-knowledge proofs from secure multi-party computation (MPC) protocols. Let us assume we have an MPC protocol in which N parties $\mathcal{P}_1, \ldots, \mathcal{P}_N$ securely and correctly evaluate a function f on a secret input x with the following properties:

- the secret x is encoded as a sharing $[\![x]\!]$ and each $\mathcal{P}_i$ takes a share $[\![x]\!]_i$ as input;
- the function f outputs ACCEPT or REJECT;
- the views of t parties leak no information about the secret x.

We can use this MPC protocol to build a zero-knowledge proof of knowledge of an x for which $f(x)$ evaluates to ACCEPT. The prover proceeds as follows:

- she builds a random sharing $[\![x]\!]$ of x;
- she simulates locally ("in her head") all the parties of the MPC protocol;
- she sends commitments to each party's view, $i.e.$ party's input share, secret random tape and sent and received messages, to the verifier;
- she sends the output shares $[\![f(x)]\!]$ of the parties, which should correspond to ACCEPT.

Then the verifier randomly chooses t parties and asks the prover to reveal their views. After receiving them, the verifier checks that they are consistent with an honest execution of the MPC protocol and with the commitments. Since only t parties are opened, revealed views leak no information about the secret x, while the random choice of the opened parties makes the cheating probability upper bounded by $(N-t)/N$, thus ensuring the soundness of the zero-knowledge proof.

In this article, we shall only consider the case $t = N-1$, $i.e.$ when the verifier asks to open all the parties except one. We shall further consider that the function f computed by the MPC protocol might be non-deterministic. Specifically, if the protocol takes what we shall call a *good witness* x as input then the protocol returns ACCEPT with probability 1. Otherwise, the protocol shall reject most of the time but might still accept with some *false positive* probability p. To summarize, we consider a setting in which the output of the protocol has a probability distribution of the form described in Table 1.

Table 1. Probability distribution of the output of the MPC protocol

	Output of f	
	ACCEPT	REJECT
x is a good witness	1	0
x is *not* a good witness	p	$1 - p$

While moving to the MPCitH setting, the randomness for f is then provided by the verifier and the "pre-randomness" view of each party (input share, random tape, initial message) must be committed before receiving the randomness from the verifier. If the prover is honest (*i.e.* knows a "good witness" x), it will always convince the verifier. On the other hand, a malicious prover might successfully cheat with probability $1/N$ (by corrupting the computation of one party) or make the MPC protocol produce a false positive with probability p. Thus, the resulting zero-knowledge protocol has a soundness error of

$$1 - \left(1 - \frac{1}{N}\right)(1 - p) = \frac{1}{N} + p - \frac{1}{N} \cdot p.$$

2.5 Multi-party Product Verification

A triple of sharings $(\llbracket a \rrbracket, \llbracket b \rrbracket, \llbracket c \rrbracket)$ of three elements $a, b, c \in \mathbb{F}$ is called a *multiplication triple* (or Beaver triples [Bea92]) if the shared values satisfy $a \cdot b = c$. The ability to check the correctness of a multiplication triple is instrumental in many MPC (in the Head) protocols.

The authors of [LN17, BN20] propose an MPC protocol to verify the correctness of a multiplication triple by "sacrificing" another one. Specifically, given a random triple $(\llbracket a \rrbracket, \llbracket b \rrbracket, \llbracket c \rrbracket)$, the protocol simultaneously verifies the correctness of $(\llbracket x \rrbracket, \llbracket y \rrbracket, \llbracket z \rrbracket)$ and $(\llbracket a \rrbracket, \llbracket b \rrbracket, \llbracket c \rrbracket)$, *i.e.* verifies that $c = a \cdot b$ and $z = x \cdot y$, without revealing any information on (x, y, z) in the following way:

1. The parties get a random $\varepsilon \in \mathbb{F}$ (from the verifier in the MPCitH paradigm),
2. The parties locally set $\llbracket \alpha \rrbracket = \varepsilon \llbracket x \rrbracket + \llbracket a \rrbracket$ and $\llbracket \beta \rrbracket = \llbracket y \rrbracket + \llbracket b \rrbracket$
3. The parties broadcast $\llbracket \alpha \rrbracket$ and $\llbracket \beta \rrbracket$ to obtain α and β.
4. The parties locally set $\llbracket v \rrbracket = \varepsilon \llbracket z \rrbracket - \llbracket c \rrbracket + \alpha \cdot \llbracket b \rrbracket + \beta \cdot \llbracket a \rrbracket - \alpha \cdot \beta$.
5. The parties broadcast $\llbracket v \rrbracket$ to obtain v.
6. The parties output ACCEPT if $v = 0$ and REJECT otherwise.

Observe that if both triples are correct multiplication triples (*i.e.*, $z = xy$ and $c = ab$) then the parties will always accept since

$$v = \varepsilon \cdot z - c + \alpha \cdot b + \beta \cdot a - \alpha \cdot \beta$$
$$= \varepsilon \cdot x \cdot y - a \cdot b + (\varepsilon \cdot x + a) \cdot b + (y + b) \cdot a - (\varepsilon \cdot x + a) \cdot (y + b) = 0$$

In contrast, if one or both triples are incorrect, then the parties will accept with probability at most $1/|\mathbb{F}|$ as shown in Lemma 1.

Lemma 1 ([BN20]). *If $(\llbracket a \rrbracket, \llbracket b \rrbracket, \llbracket c \rrbracket)$ or $(\llbracket x \rrbracket, \llbracket y \rrbracket, \llbracket z \rrbracket)$ is an incorrect multiplication triple then the parties output* ACCEPT *in the sub-protocol above with probability $\frac{1}{|\mathbb{F}|}$.*

The authors of [KZ21] propose a variant of the above protocol to batch the verification of the d multiplication triples $(\llbracket x_j \rrbracket, \llbracket y_j \rrbracket, \llbracket z_j \rrbracket)$ by sacrificing a random *dot-product tuple* $((\llbracket a_j \rrbracket, \llbracket b_j \rrbracket)_{j \in [d]}, \llbracket c \rrbracket)$ verifying $c = \langle a, b \rangle$.

1. The parties gets a random $\varepsilon \in \mathbb{F}^d$ (from the verifier in the MPCitH paradigm),
2. The parties locally set $\llbracket \alpha \rrbracket = \varepsilon \circ \llbracket x \rrbracket + \llbracket a \rrbracket$ and $\llbracket \beta \rrbracket = \llbracket y \rrbracket + \llbracket b \rrbracket$.
3. The parties broadcast $\llbracket \alpha \rrbracket$ and $\llbracket \beta \rrbracket$ to obtain α and β.
4. The parties locally set $\llbracket v \rrbracket = -\llbracket c \rrbracket + \langle \varepsilon, \llbracket z \rrbracket \rangle + \langle \alpha, \llbracket b \rrbracket \rangle + \langle \beta, \llbracket a \rrbracket \rangle - \langle \alpha, \beta \rangle$.
5. The parties broadcast $\llbracket v \rrbracket$ to obtain v.
6. The parties output ACCEPT if $v = 0$ and REJECT otherwise.

Lemma 2 ([KZ21]). *If $(\llbracket x_j \rrbracket, \llbracket y_j \rrbracket, \llbracket z_j \rrbracket)_{j \in [d]}$ contains an incorrect multiplication triple or if $((\llbracket a_j \rrbracket, \llbracket b_j \rrbracket)_{j \in [d]}, \llbracket c \rrbracket)$ form an incorrect dot product, then the parties output* ACCEPT *in the sub-protocol above with probability at most $\frac{1}{|\mathbb{F}|}$.*

This variant requires less communication for c and v, compared to the case where we repeat d times the original protocol. But depending on the context, repeating d times the original protocol might be preferred to lower the false positive probability (*i.e.* $1/|\mathbb{F}|^d$ against $1/|\mathbb{F}|$).

3   A Zero-Knowledge Protocol for Syndrome Decoding

Let us consider an instance (H, y) of the (d-split) syndrome decoding problem, and let us denote x a solution of this instance. We denote $\mathbb{F}_{\text{SD}}$ the field on which the instance is defined.

Without loss of generality, we assume that H is in the standard form, *i.e.* that $H = (H' | I_{m-k})$ for some $H' \in \mathbb{F}_{\text{SD}}^{(m-k) \times k}$. Thus the solution x can be written as $(x_A | x_B)$ such that we have the linear relation

$$y = H' x_A + x_B. \tag{1}$$

This implies that one simply needs to send x_A ($k \cdot \log |\mathbb{F}_{\text{SD}}|$ bits) to reveal the solution of the instance (H, y).

In the following sections, we first build an MPC protocol that takes a sharing of $[\![x_A]\!]$, builds the corresponding $[\![x]\!]$ thanks to Eq. (1), and checks that $[\![x]\!]$ corresponds to a vector with a Hamming weight of at most w/d on each chunk. Since $[\![x]\!]$ would verify $y = Hx$ by construction, this MPC protocol verifies that $[\![x_A]\!]$ corresponds to a solution of the syndrome decoding instance (H, y). Then, in Sect. 3.3, we transform it into a zero-knowledge protocol which proves the knowledge of a solution of the syndrome decoding instance (H, y) thanks to the MPC-in-the-Head paradigm (described in Sect. 2.4).

3.1 Standard Case ($d = 1$)

We first focus on the case where (H, y) is an instance of the standard syndrome decoding problem (*i.e.* we have $d = 1$). We will then show how to extend the protocol to the general case of any d. We consider a field extension $\mathbb{F}_{\text{poly}} \supseteq \mathbb{F}_{\text{SD}}$ such that $|\mathbb{F}_{\text{poly}}| \geq m$ (we recall that m is the length of the secret x, *i.e.* $x \in \mathbb{F}_{\text{SD}}^m$). We denote $\phi : \mathbb{F}_{\text{SD}} \to \mathbb{F}_{\text{poly}}$ the canonical inclusion of $\mathbb{F}_{\text{SD}}$ into $\mathbb{F}_{\text{poly}}$. Let us take a bijection γ between $\{1, \ldots, |\mathbb{F}_{\text{poly}}|\}$ and $\mathbb{F}_{\text{poly}}$. Then, to ease the notation, we denote γ_i for $\gamma(i)$.

The protocol must check that $y = Hx$ and $\text{wt}(x) \leq w$. As explained in the introduction of the section, the input for the MPC protocol will be $[\![x_A]\!]$, then it will build the sharing $[\![x]\!]$ using the linear relation (1). Then we directly have that $y = Hx$. It remains to check that $\text{wt}(x) \leq w$.

To prove that $\text{wt}(x) \leq w$, the prover build the three following polynomials:

- The polynomial $S \in \mathbb{F}_{\text{poly}}[X]$ satisfying

$$\forall i \in [m], \ S(\gamma_i) = \phi(x_i),$$

as well as $\deg S \leq m - 1$. This S is unique and can be computed by interpolation.

- The polynomial $Q \in \mathbb{F}_{\text{poly}}[X]$ defined as

$$Q(X) := \prod_{i \in E} (X - \gamma_i)$$

for some $E \subset [m]$ such that $|E| = w$ and $\{i \in [m] : x_i \neq 0\} \subset E$, implying $\deg Q = w$.

- The polynomial $P \in \mathbb{F}_{\text{poly}}[X]$ defined as

$$P := (Q \cdot S)/F \ \text{ with } \ F(X) := \prod_{i=1}^{m} (X - \gamma_i).$$

We stress some useful properties of these polynomials:

- The polynomial Q is a monic polynomial of degree w. Moreover, for every $i \in [m]$, we have

$$x_i \neq 0 \ \Rightarrow \ i \in E \ \Rightarrow \ Q(\gamma_i) = 0.$$

- The polynomial F divides $Q \cdot S$. Indeed, for every $i \in [m]$, we have

$$(Q \cdot S)(\gamma_i) = 0$$

since $S(\gamma_i) \neq 0 \Rightarrow x_i \neq 0 \Rightarrow Q(\gamma_i) = 0$. The polynomial P is hence well defined.
- The polynomial P has degree $\deg P \leq w - 1$.

If the prover convinces the verifier that there exists two polynomials P (with $\deg P \leq w - 1$) and Q (with $\deg Q = w$) such that $Q \cdot S - P \cdot F = 0$ where S and F are built as described above, then the verifier can deduce the following:

$$\forall i \in [m], \, (Q \cdot S)(\gamma_i) = P(\gamma_i) \cdot F(\gamma_i) = 0$$
$$\Rightarrow \forall i \in [m], \, Q(\gamma_i) = 0 \text{ or } S(\gamma_i) = \phi(x_i) = 0$$

Since Q has at most w roots, the verifier concludes that $\phi(x_i) \neq 0$ in at most w positions. Thus $\mathrm{wt}(x) \leq w$.

We now explain how to prove this statement in the MPCitH paradigm. For this purpose, we describe an MPC protocol, which on input x, P and Q outputs ACCEPT if the above condition is verified and REJECT otherwise, except with a small false positive probability. The parties' inputs are defined as the shares of $[\![x_A]\!]$, $[\![Q]\!]$ and $[\![P]\!]$. Let us recall that a sharing of a polynomial is naturally defined as a sharing of its coefficients (see Sect. 2.3). However, for the sharing of Q, we share all of its coefficients except the leading one. Indeed since Q is monic, its leading coefficient is publicly known and is equal to 1. Moreover, it enables to convince the verifier that Q is of degree *exactly* w, which is important since otherwise, a malicious prover could take Q as the zero polynomial.

From its inputs, the MPC protocol first builds the polynomial S from x_A. Then, to verify $Q \cdot S = P \cdot F$, it evaluates the two sides of the relation on t random points $r_1, \ldots, r_t$ (sampled by the verifier in the MPCitH setting). If the relation is not verified, the probability to observe $Q(r_j) \cdot S(r_j) = P(r_j) \cdot F(r_j)$ for all $j \in [t]$ will be low, which stems from the Schwartz-Zippel Lemma (see the full version [FJR22]). The larger the set from which the evaluation points r_j are sampled, the smaller the false positive probability p. For this reason, we take these evaluation points in a field extension $\mathbb{F}_{\text{points}}$ of $\mathbb{F}_{\text{poly}}$. Such a field extension allows us to have more points and so to detect more efficiently when $Q \cdot S \neq P \cdot F$. In practice, given an evaluation point r_j, the parties of the MPC protocol verify the relations $Q(r_j) \cdot S(r_j) = (P \cdot F)(r_j)$ by sacrificing multiplication triples as described in Sect. 2.5. To proceed, the prover must previously build t multiplication triples $([\![a_j]\!], [\![b_j]\!], [\![c_j]\!])$ for random elements $a_j, b_j, c_j \in \mathbb{F}_{\text{points}}$ satisfying $a_j \cdot b_j = c_j$ for $j \in [t]$ and include them to the parties' inputs (each party getting its corresponding share from $[\![a_j]\!]$, $[\![b_j]\!]$ and $[\![c_j]\!]$).

The MPC protocol runs as follows:

1. The parties sample t random points $r_1, \ldots, r_t$ of $\mathbb{F}_{\text{points}}$.

2. The parties locally compute $[\![x]\!]$ from $[\![x_A]\!]$ using Eq. (1).
3. The parties locally compute $[\![S(r_j)]\!]$, $[\![Q(r_j)]\!]$ and $[\![(F \cdot P)(r_j)]\!]$ for all $j \in [t]$. Let us remark that $[\![S(r_j)]\!]$ can be computed from $[\![x]\!]$ by the parties without any interaction thanks to the linearity of Lagrange interpolation formula:

$$[\![S(r_j)]\!] = \sum_{i \in [m]} [\![x_i]\!] \prod_{\ell \in [m], \ell \neq i} \frac{r_j - \gamma_\ell}{\gamma_i - \gamma_\ell} \,.$$

On the other hand $[\![(F \cdot P)(r_j)]\!]$ is computed as $F(r_j) \cdot [\![P(r_j)]\!]$ since F is publicly known.
4. For every $j \in [t]$, the parties run an MPC verification of the multiplication triple $([\![S(r_j)]\!], [\![Q(r_j)]\!], [\![(F \cdot P)(r_j)]\!])$ by sacrificing the triple $([\![a_j]\!], [\![b_j]\!], [\![c_j]\!])$:
   – The parties sample a random $\varepsilon_j \in \mathbb{F}_{\text{points}}$.
   – The parties locally set

$$[\![\alpha_j]\!] = \varepsilon_j \cdot [\![Q(r_j)]\!] + [\![a_j]\!] \text{ and } [\![\beta_j]\!] = [\![S(r_j)]\!] + [\![b_j]\!].$$

   – The parties broadcast $[\![\alpha_j]\!]$ and $[\![\beta_j]\!]$ to obtain α_j and β_j.
   – The parties locally set

$$[\![v_j]\!] = \varepsilon_j \cdot [\![(F \cdot P)(r_j)]\!] - [\![c_j]\!] + \alpha_j \cdot [\![b_j]\!] + \beta_j \cdot [\![a_j]\!] - \alpha_j \cdot \beta_j \,.$$

   – The parties broadcast $[\![v_j]\!]$ to obtain v_j.
5. The parties output ACCEPT if $v = 0$ and REJECT otherwise.

Note that we do not need to specify how the random values r_j's and ε_j's are sampled by the parties since they will be provided as challenges from the verifier while turning to the zero-knowledge setting.

The above MPC protocol computes a non-deterministic function f which takes x, Q and P (and t multiplication triples) as input and which outputs ACCEPT or REJECT. The randomness of this function comes from the random evaluations points $r_1, \ldots, r_t$ and from the random challenges $\varepsilon_1, \ldots, \varepsilon_t$ used by the product checking protocol. Whenever x indeed satisfies $\mathrm{wt}(x) \leq w$ and the polynomials P and Q are genuinely computed as described above, the protocol outputs ACCEPT with probability one. Whenever the protocol input is not of this form, the protocol shall output REJECT except with a small false positive probability p. In other words, the output of the above protocol follows the distribution depicted in Table 1 where a good witness here means an x of weight at most w and polynomials P and Q which are correctly built.

Let us make explicit the false positive probability p. We shall denote $\Delta := |\mathbb{F}_{\text{points}}|$. Whenever the protocol input is not a good witness, i.e. $\mathrm{wt}(x) > w$, P or Q are not correctly built, we have $Q \cdot S \neq F \cdot P$. In the above protocol, both sides of the relation are evaluated in t random points. The probability to have the equality for i evaluation points among the t points is at most

$$\frac{\max_{\ell \leq m+w-1} \left\{ \binom{\ell}{i} \binom{\Delta - \ell}{t - i} \right\}}{\binom{\Delta}{t}}$$

since $Q \cdot S - F \cdot P$ is a polynomial of degree at most $m + w - 1$. This holds from a simple extension of the Schwartz-Zippel Lemma that we provide in the full version [FJR22]. When this event occurs, the probability to obtain ACCEPT as output is

$$\left(\frac{1}{\Delta}\right)^{t-i},$$

which corresponds to the probability to get the $t - i$ false positives in the verification of multiplication triples (for the $t - i$ remaining evaluation points r_j for which $Q(r_j) \cdot S(r_j) \neq F(r_j) \cdot P(r_j)$). Thus, the global false positive probability p satisfies

$$p \leq \sum_{i=0}^{t} \frac{\max_{\ell \leq m+w-1}\left\{\binom{\ell}{i}\binom{\Delta-\ell}{t-i}\right\}}{\binom{\Delta}{t}} \left(\frac{1}{\Delta}\right)^{t-i}. \tag{2}$$

3.2   General Case (any d)

Let us now assume that (H, y) is an instance of a d-split syndrome decoding problem for some $d \geq 1$. We can easily adapt our protocol in that case. Instead of having a unique polynomial Q of degree w, we will have d polynomials $Q_1, \ldots, Q_d$ of degree exactly w/d to prove the weight bound $\mathrm{wt}(x_j) \leq w/d$ for each chunk x_j of the SD solution. We then have d polynomials S_j (of degree $m/d - 1$) and d polynomials P_j (of degree $w/d - 1$) satisfying the d relations $Q_j \cdot S_j = F \cdot P_j$ with $F := \prod_{j=1}^{m/d}(X - \gamma_j)$. To prove those d relations we evaluate each of them on t random points $r_1, \ldots, r_t$. We stress that the same t random points can be used for each chunk, *i.e.* for every $j \in [d]$.

A malicious prover might try to cheat on a single relation (*i.e.* on a single chunk of the SD solution), in such a way that there exists $j_0 \in [d]$ with

$$\begin{cases} Q_{j_0} \cdot S_{j_0} \neq F \cdot P_{j_0}, \\ \forall j \neq j_0, \ Q_j \cdot S_j = F \cdot P_j. \end{cases}$$

So for a given point r, we use the dot-product checking of [KZ21] (described in Sect. 2.5) to check all the equalities $Q_j(r) \cdot S_j(r) = F(r) \cdot P_j(r)$ at once. This saves communication without impacting the soundness error compared to independent checks of the d relations.

Whenever the input $x, \{P_j\}, \{Q_j\}$ is not a good witness (*i.e.* whenever one x_j has a weight greater than w/d or one polynomial P_j or Q_j is not correctly built), at least one of the relations $Q_j \cdot S_j = F \cdot P_j$ is not verified. Since $Q_j \cdot S_j - F \cdot P_j$ is a polynomial of degree at most $(m + w)/d - 1$, the global false positive probability for the d-split variant becomes

$$p \leq \sum_{i=0}^{t} \frac{\max_{\ell \leq (m+w)/d-1}\left\{\binom{\ell}{i}\binom{\Delta-\ell}{t-i}\right\}}{\binom{\Delta}{t}} \left(\frac{1}{\Delta}\right)^{t-i} \tag{3}$$

with $\Delta := |\mathbb{F}_{\text{points}}|$. (This upper bound is equivalent to (2) where the max degree $m + w - 1$ is replaced by $(m + w)/d - 1$.)

The constraint on the size of $\mathbb{F}_{poly}$ now becomes

$$|\mathbb{F}_{poly}| \geq \frac{m}{d}$$

since we only need w/d points for the interpolation of the polynomials $S_1, \ldots S_d$. Thus using the d-split version allows us to use smaller fields for $\mathbb{F}_{poly}$ and $\mathbb{F}_{points}$.

Let us note that in practice the new communication is not smaller than before, but rather equivalent or higher, since we need to use bigger syndrome decoding instances to compensate the security loss of the d-split version. The main benefit to introduce the d-split version is to work on polynomials of smaller degree and/or on specific fields which provides better performance trade-offs (see Sect. 4.5).

3.3 Description of the Protocol

We now give the formal description of our zero-knowledge protocol (general case) in Protocol 1. For the sake of clarity in the protocol description, we denote $\boldsymbol{Q}$ the tuple of polynomials $(Q_1, \ldots, Q_d)$. Same for the polynomials $\boldsymbol{P}$ and $\boldsymbol{S}$. The additions, substractions and polynomial evaluations of these tuples are component-wise defined. For example, for a point $r \in \mathbb{F}_{points}$, $\boldsymbol{Q}(r)$ means $(Q_1(r), \ldots, Q_d(r))$. We also use this bold notation for $\boldsymbol{a}_j, \boldsymbol{b}_j, \boldsymbol{\alpha}_j, \boldsymbol{\beta}_j$ and $\boldsymbol{\varepsilon}_j$ which shall represent vectors of $\mathbb{F}_{points}^d$. Let us recall that $\circ$ denotes the component-wise multiplication. In the scope of this protocol, the polynomial F is defined as $F(X) := \prod_{i=1}^{m/d}(X - \gamma_i)$ with $\mathbb{F}_{poly} = \{\gamma_1, \gamma_2, \ldots\}$.

3.4 Security Proofs

The following theorems state the completeness, zero-knowledge and soundness of Protocol 1. The proofs of Theorems 3 and 4 are provided in the full version [FJR22].

Theorem 2 (Completeness). *Protocol 1 is perfectly complete, i.e. a prover $\mathcal{P}$ who knows a solution x to the syndrome decoding instance (H, y) and who follows the steps of the protocol always succeeds in convincing the verifier $\mathcal{V}$.*

Proof. For any sampling of the random coins of $\mathcal{P}$ and $\mathcal{V}$, if the computation described in Protocol 1 is genuinely performed then all the checks of $\mathcal{V}$ pass. $\square$

Theorem 3 (Honest-Verifier Zero-Knowledge). *Let the PRG used in Protocol 1 be (t, ε_{PRG})-secure and the commitment scheme Com be (t, ε_{Com})-hiding. There exists an efficient simulator $\mathcal{S}$ which, given random challenge i^* outputs a transcript which is $(t, \varepsilon_{PRG} + \varepsilon_{Com})$-indistinguishable from a real transcript of Protocol 1.*

Theorem 4 (Soundness). *Suppose that there is an efficient prover $\tilde{\mathcal{P}}$ that, on input (H, y), convinces the honest verifier $\mathcal{V}$ on input H, y to accept with probability*

$$\tilde{\varepsilon} := \Pr[\langle \tilde{\mathcal{P}}, \mathcal{V}\rangle(H, y) \to 1] > \varepsilon$$

Inputs: Both parties have $H = (H'|I_{m-k}) \in \mathbb{F}_{\mathrm{SD}}^{(m-k)\times m}$ and $y \in \mathbb{F}_{\mathrm{SD}}^{m-k}$, the prover also holds $x := (x_1 \mid x_2 \mid \ldots \mid x_d) \in \mathbb{F}_{\mathrm{SD}}^m$ such that $y = Hx$ and $\mathrm{wt}(x_j) \le w$ for $j \in [d]$.

Round 1: The prover computes the proof witness: for all chunk $j \in [d]$,

1. Choose a set $E_j \subset [\frac{m}{d}]$ s.t. $|E_j| = \frac{w}{d}$ and $\{\ell : (x_j)_\ell \ne 0\} \subset E_j$.
2. Compute $Q_j(X) = \prod_{\ell \in E_j}(X - \gamma_\ell) \in \mathbb{F}_{\mathrm{poly}}[X]$.
3. Compute $S_j(X) \in \mathbb{F}_{\mathrm{poly}}[X]$ by interpolation $s.t.$ $\deg S_j \le \frac{m}{d} - 1$ and $\forall \ell \in [\frac{m}{d}], S_j(\gamma_\ell) = (x_j)_\ell$.
4. Compute $P_j(X) = S_j(X)Q_j(X)/F(X) \in \mathbb{F}_{\mathrm{poly}}[X]$.

Then, the prover prepares the inputs for the multi-party computation as follows:

1. Sample a root seed: $\mathsf{seed} \xleftarrow{\$} \{0,1\}^\lambda$.
2. Compute parties' seeds and commitment randomness $(\mathsf{seed}_i, \rho_i)_{i \in [N]}$ with $\mathrm{TreePRG}(\mathsf{seed})$.
3. For each party $i \in \{1, \ldots, N\}$,
   - $[\![a_j]\!]_i, [\![b_j]\!]_i \leftarrow \mathrm{PRG}(\mathsf{seed}_i)$, for each $j \in [t]$
   - If $i \ne N$,
     - $\{[\![c_j]\!]_i\}_{j \in [t]}, [\![x_A]\!]_i, [\![Q]\!]_i, [\![P]\!]_i \leftarrow \mathrm{PRG}(\mathsf{seed}_i)$
     - $\mathsf{state}_i = \mathsf{seed}_i$
   - Else,
     - $[\![x_A]\!]_N = x_A - \sum_{\ell \ne N}[\![x_A]\!]_\ell$.
     - $[\![Q]\!]_N = Q - \sum_{\ell \ne N}[\![Q]\!]_\ell$.
     - $[\![P]\!]_N = P - \sum_{\ell \ne N}[\![P]\!]_\ell$.
     - $[\![c_j]\!]_N = \langle a_j, b_j \rangle - \sum_{\ell \ne N}[\![c_j]\!]_\ell$, for each $j \in [t]$
     - $\mathsf{aux} = ([\![x_A]\!]_N, [\![Q]\!]_N, [\![P]\!]_N, \{[\![c_j]\!]_N\}_{j \in [t]})$
     - $\mathsf{state}_N = \mathsf{seed}_N \,\|\, \mathsf{aux}$
   - Commit the party's state: $\mathsf{com}_i = \mathrm{Com}(\mathsf{state}_i; \rho_i)$.

The prover builds $h = \mathrm{Hash}(\mathsf{com}_1, \ldots, \mathsf{com}_N)$ and sends it to the verifier.

Round 2: The verifier uniformly samples, for each $j \in [t]$, an evaluation point $r_j \leftarrow \mathbb{F}_{\mathrm{points}}$ and a vector $\varepsilon_j \leftarrow \mathbb{F}_{\mathrm{points}}^d$, and sends them to the prover.

Round 3: The prover simulates the MPC protocol:

1. The parties locally set $[\![x_B]\!] = y - H'[\![x_A]\!]$.
2. The parties locally compute $[\![S]\!]$ by interpolation using $[\![x]\!] := ([\![x_A]\!] \mid [\![x_B]\!])$.
3. Then for all $j \in [t]$,
   - The parties locally compute $[\![S(r_j)]\!]$, $[\![Q(r_j)]\!]$ and $[\![P(r_j)]\!]$.
   - They locally set $[\![\alpha_j]\!] = \varepsilon_j \circ [\![Q(r_j)]\!] + [\![a_j]\!]$.
   - They locally set $[\![\beta_j]\!] = [\![S(r_j)]\!] + [\![b_j]\!]$.
   - The parties open $[\![\alpha_j]\!]$ and $[\![\beta_j]\!]$ to get α_j and β_j.
   - The parties locally set

$$[\![v_j]\!] = -[\![c_j]\!] + \langle \varepsilon_j, F(r_j) \cdot [\![P(r_j)]\!]\rangle + \langle \alpha_j, [\![b_j]\!]\rangle + \langle \beta_j, [\![a_j]\!]\rangle - \langle \alpha_j, \beta_j \rangle \,.$$

The prover builds $h' = \mathrm{Hash}([\![\alpha_1]\!], [\![\beta_1]\!], [\![v_1]\!], \ldots, [\![\alpha_t]\!], [\![\beta_t]\!], [\![v_t]\!])$ and sends it to the verifier.

Round 4: The verifier uniformly samples $i^* \leftarrow [N]$ and sends it to the prover.

Round 5: The prover sends $(\mathsf{state}_i, \rho_i)_{i \ne i^*}$, com_{i^*}, $\{[\![\alpha_j]\!]_{i^*}\}_{j \in [t]}$ and $\{[\![\beta_j]\!]_{i^*}\}_{j \in [t]}$.

Verification: The verifier accepts iff all the following checks succeed:

1. For each $i \ne i^*$, she computes all the commitments to the parties' states: $\mathsf{com}_i = \mathrm{Com}(\mathsf{state}_i; \rho_i)$. Then she checks that $h \overset{?}{=} \mathrm{Hash}(\mathsf{com}_1, \ldots, \mathsf{com}_N)$.
2. Using $\{\mathsf{state}_i\}_{i \ne i^*}$, she simulates all the parties except for i^*. From the recomputed shares, she checks that $h' \overset{?}{=} \mathrm{Hash}([\![\alpha_1]\!], [\![\beta_1]\!], [\![v_1]\!], \ldots, [\![\alpha_t]\!], [\![\beta_t]\!], [\![v_t]\!])$ where $[\![v_j]\!]_{i^*} := -\sum_{i \ne i^*}[\![v_j]\!]_i$.

Protocol 1: Zero-knowledge proof for syndrome decoding.

where the soundness error ε is equal to

$$p + \frac{1}{N} - p \cdot \frac{1}{N}$$

with p defined in Eq. (3). Then, there exists an efficient probabilistic extraction algorithm $\mathcal{E}$ that, given rewindable black-box access to $\tilde{\mathcal{P}}$, produces with either a witness x such that $y = Hx$ and $\mathrm{wt}(x) \leq w$, or a commitment collision, by making an average number of calls to $\tilde{\mathcal{P}}$ which is upper bounded by

$$\frac{4}{\tilde{\varepsilon} - \varepsilon} \cdot \left(1 + \tilde{\varepsilon} \cdot \frac{2 \cdot \ln(2)}{\tilde{\varepsilon} - \varepsilon}\right).$$

By adapting the parameters t and Δ, we can produce a protocol with soundness error arbitrarily close to $1/N$.

3.5 Performance

In the following analysis, we exclude the challenges from the communication cost since they are of very moderate impact (and do not count whenever making the protocol non-interactive). The communication then consists into

- $\textsc{Com} := h$,
- $\textsc{Res}_1 := h'$ and
- $\textsc{Res}_2 := \left((\mathsf{state}_i, \rho_i)_{i \neq i^*}, \mathsf{com}_{i^*}, \{[\![\alpha_j]\!]_{i^*}\}_{j \in [t]}, \{[\![\beta_j]\!]_{i^*}\}_{j \in [t]}\right).$

For $i \neq N$, state_i simply consists in a seed of λ bits. For $i = N$, state_i contains

- a seed of λ bits,
- the share $[\![x_A]\!]_N$ of a plaintext,
- the shares $[\![Q]\!]_N$ and $[\![P]\!]_N$ which are $2 \cdot d$ polynomials of degree $w/d - 1$,
- and the shares $\{[\![c_j]\!]_N\}_{j \in [t]}$ of t points of $\mathbb{F}_{\mathrm{points}}$.

Let us recall that seeds are sampled using a tree PRG. Instead of sending the $N - 1$ seeds and commitment randomness of $(\mathsf{state}_i, \rho_i)_{i \neq i^*}$, we can instead send the sibling path from $(\mathsf{state}_{i^*}, \rho_{i^*})$ to the tree root, it costs at most $\lambda \cdot \log_2(N)$ bits (we need to reveal $\log_2(N)$ nodes of the tree). Moreover com_{i^*} is a commitment of 2λ bits, and $\{[\![\alpha_j]\!]_{i^*}\}_{j \in [t]}, \{[\![\beta_j]\!]_{i^*}\}_{j \in [t]}$ are elements of $\mathbb{F}_{\mathrm{points}}$. The communication cost (in bits) of the protocol is then

$$\textsc{Size} = 4\lambda + \underbrace{k \cdot \log_2 |\mathbb{F}_{\mathrm{SD}}|}_{[\![x_A]\!]_N} + \underbrace{(2 \cdot w) \cdot \log_2 |\mathbb{F}_{\mathrm{poly}}|}_{[\![Q]\!]_N, [\![P]\!]_N}$$

$$+ \underbrace{(2 \cdot d + 1) \cdot t \cdot \log_2 |\mathbb{F}_{\mathrm{points}}|}_{\{[\![\alpha_j]\!]_{i^*}, [\![\beta_j]\!]_{i^*}, [\![c_j]\!]_N\}_{j \in [t]}} + \underbrace{\lambda \cdot \log_2(N)}_{(\mathsf{seed}_i)_{i \neq i^*}} + \underbrace{2\lambda}_{\mathsf{com}_{i^*}}$$

As usual, to achieve a targeted soundness error $2^{-\lambda}$, we can perform τ parallel repetitions of the protocol such that $\varepsilon^\tau \leq 2^{-\lambda}$. And instead of sending τ values for h and h', we can merge them together to send a single h and a single h'. The communication cost (in bits) of the protocol with τ repetitions is

$$\text{SIZE} = 4\lambda + \tau \cdot \Big(k \cdot \log_2 |\mathbb{F}_{\text{SD}}| + (2 \cdot w) \cdot \log_2 |\mathbb{F}_{\text{poly}}|$$

$$+ (2 \cdot d + 1) \cdot t \cdot \log_2 |\mathbb{F}_{\text{points}}| + \lambda \cdot \log_2(N) + 2\lambda \Big)$$

and the obtained soundness error is

$$\left(p + \frac{1}{n} - p \cdot \frac{1}{n} \right)^{\tau}.$$

3.6 Comparison

We compare our new protocol with existing zero-knowledge protocols for syndrome decoding (or equivalently for *message decoding*). We compare these protocols on two SD instances of 128-bit security:

– Instance 1 [FJR21]: Syndrome Decoding on $\mathbb{F}_2$ with parameters

$$(m, k, w) = (1280, 640, 132);$$

– Instance 2 [CVE11]: Syndrome Decoding on $\mathbb{F}_{2^8}$ with parameters

$$(m, k, w) = (208, 104, 78).$$

The comparison for a soundness error of 2^{-128} is given in the Table 2. For our protocol, we provide two instantiations for each syndrome decoding instance to give the reader an idea of the obtained performance while changing the number of parties. The first instantiation called "short" corresponds to an instantiation which provides small communication cost. The second one called "fast" corresponds to an instantiation with faster computation but higher communication cost. The used parameters $(N, \tau, |\mathbb{F}_{\text{poly}}|, |\mathbb{F}_{\text{points}}|, t)$ for our scheme are

– Instance 1:
  Short: $(256, 16, 2^{11}, 2^{22}, 2) \Rightarrow \varepsilon^{\tau} = 2^{-128.0}$
  Fast: $(32, 26, 2^{11}, 2^{22}, 1) \Rightarrow \varepsilon^{\tau} = 2^{-129.6}$
– Instance 2:
  Short: $(256, 16, 2^8, 2^{24}, 2) \Rightarrow \varepsilon^{\tau} = 2^{-128.0}$
  Fast: $(32, 26, 2^8, 2^{24}, 1) \Rightarrow \varepsilon^{\tau} = 2^{-130.0}$

We can remark that all the previous protocols prove an equality for the Hamming weight by relying on isometries (*i.e.* permutations if $\mathbb{F}_{\text{SD}} = \mathbb{F}_2$). On our side, we only prove the inequality $\text{wt}(w) \leq w$. We stress that both versions (equality or inequality) can be merely equivalent for some SD parameters. Indeed, if w is chosen sufficiently below the Gilbert-Varshamov bound and if we know there exists an SD solution x of Hamming weight w, then proving the knowledge of a solution x' with $\text{wt}(x') \leq w$ amounts to proving the knowledge of x with overwhelming probability.

Table 2. Comparison of our protocol with state-of-the-art zero-knowledge protocols for syndrome decoding. The formulae for the communication costs of the different protocols and the used parameters are detailed in the full version [FJR22].

Name Protocol	Year	Instance 1	Instance 2	Proved statement
[Ste94]	1993	37.4 KB	46.1 KB	$y = Hx$, $\text{wt}(x) = w$
[Vér96]	1997	31.7 KB	38.7 KB	*message decoding*
[CVE11]	2010	-	37.4 KB	$y = Hx$, $\text{wt}(x) = w$
[AGS11]	2011	24.8 KB	-	$y = Hx$, $\text{wt}(x) = w$
[GPS22] (short)	2021	-	15.2 KB	$y = Hx$, $\text{wt}(x) = w$
[GPS22] (fast)	2021	-	19.9 KB	$y = Hx$, $\text{wt}(x) = w$
[FJR21] (short)	2021	12.9 KB	15.6 KB	$y = Hx$, $\text{wt}(x) = w$
[FJR21] (fast)	2021	20.0 KB	24.7 KB	$y = Hx$, $\text{wt}(x) = w$
Our scheme (short)	2022	9.7 KB	6.9 KB	$y = Hx$, $\text{wt}(x) \leq w$
Our scheme (fast)	2022	14.4 KB	9.7 KB	$y = Hx$, $\text{wt}(x) \leq w$

4   The Signature Scheme

A signature scheme is a triplet of PPT algorithms (KeyGen, Sign, Verif). On input 1^λ for security level λ, KeyGen outputs a pair (pk, sk) where $pk \in \{0, 1\}^{\text{poly}(\lambda)}$ is a public key and $sk \in \{0, 1\}^{\text{poly}(\lambda)}$ is a private key (a.k.a. secret key). On input a secret key sk and a message $m \in \{0, 1\}^*$, Sign produces a signature $s \in \{0, 1\}^{\text{poly}(\lambda)}$. Verif is a deterministic algorithm which, on input a public key pk, a signature s and a message m, outputs 1 if s is a valid signature for m under pk (meaning that it is a possible output $s \leftarrow \text{Sign}(sk, m)$ for the corresponding sk) and it outputs 0 otherwise. The standard security property for a signature scheme is the *existential unforgeability* against chosen message attacks: an adversary $\mathcal{A}$ given pk and a oracle access to $\text{Sign}(sk, \cdot)$ should not be able to produce a pair (s, m) satisfying $\text{Verif}(pk, s, m) = 1$ (for a message m which was not queried to the signing oracle).

In this section, we show how to turn our 5-round HVZK protocol into a signature scheme using the Fiat-Shamir transform [FS87, AABN02]. After explaining the transformation, we give the description of the signature scheme and then provide a security proof in the random oracle model (ROM).

4.1   Transformation into a Non-interactive Scheme

To transform our protocol into a non-interactive scheme, we apply the multi-round variant of the Fiat-Shamir transform [FS87] (see *e.g.* [EDV+12, CHR+16]). Concretely, we compute the challenge CH_1 and CH_2 as

$$h_1 = \text{Hash}_1(m, \text{salt}, h)$$
$$\text{CH}_1 \leftarrow \text{PRG}(h_1)$$

and

$$h_2 = \text{Hash}_2(m, \text{salt}, h, h')$$
$$\text{CH}_2 \leftarrow \text{PRG}(h_2)$$

where m is the input message, where Hash_1 and Hash_2 are some hash functions (that shall be modeled as random oracles) and where h and h' are the Round 1 and Round 3 hash commitments merged for the τ repetitions. We introduce a value salt called *salt* which is sampled from $\{0,1\}^{2\lambda}$ at the beginning of the signing process. This value is then used for each commitment to the parties' states. Without it, the security of the signature would be at most $2^{\lambda/2}$ because of the seed collisions between several signatures. Moreover, since the signature security relies on the random oracle model, we can safely replace the commitment scheme Com of the Protocol 1 by a single hash function Hash_0.

The security of the obtained scheme is lower than the soundness error of Protocol 1. Indeed, in [KZ20a], Kales and Zaverucha describe a forgery attack against signature schemes obtained by applying the Fiat-Shamir transform to 5-round protocols. Adapting this attack to our context yields a forgery cost of

$$\text{cost}_{\text{forge}} := \min_{\tau_1, \tau_2 : \tau_1 + \tau_2 = \tau} \left\{ \frac{1}{\sum_{i=\tau_1}^{\tau} \binom{\tau}{i} p^i (1-p)^{\tau-i}} + N^{\tau_2} \right\} \quad (4)$$

with p defined in Eq. (3). This is substantially lower than the target forgery cost of $1/\varepsilon$, for ε being the soundness error of Protocol 1 (see Theorem 4). We therefore need to adapt the parameters to fill this gap.

4.2 Description of the Signature Scheme

In our signature scheme, the key generation algorithm randomly samples a syndrome decoding instance (H, y) of the syndrome decoding problem with solution x (*i.e.* $y = Hx$) with security parameter λ. In order to make the key pair compact, the matrix H is pseudorandomly generated from a λ-bit seed. Specifically, a call to the KeyGen algorithm outputs a pair $(pk, sk) := ((\text{seed}_H, y), \text{mseed})$ generated as follows:

1. $\text{mseed} \leftarrow \{0,1\}^{\lambda}$
2. $(\text{seed}_H, x) \leftarrow \text{PRG}(\text{mseed})$ where x is sampled in $\{x \in \mathbb{F}_2^m \mid \text{wt}(x) = w\}$
3. $H \leftarrow \text{PRG}(\text{seed}_H)$
4. $y = Hx$; $pk = (\text{seed}_H, y)$; $sk = \text{mseed}$

For the sake of simplicity, we omit the re-generation of H and x from the seeds in the algorithms below and assume $pk = (H, y)$ and $sk = (H, y, x)$.

Given a secret key $sk = (H, y, x)$ and a message $m \in \{0,1\}^*$, the algorithm Sign proceeds as described in Fig. 1. And given a public key $pk = (H, y)$, a signature σ and a message $m \in \{0,1\}^*$, the algorithm Verif proceeds as described in Fig. 2. For the sake of clarity, as for the protocol description in Sect. 3.3, we use the bold notation to represent a tuple of d polynomials or of d points.

4.3 Signature Properties

We now state the security of our signature scheme in the following theorem. The proof is provided in the full version [FJR22].

Inputs: A secret key $sk = (H, y, x)$ and a message $m \in \{0, 1\}^*$.

Sample a random salt $\mathsf{salt} \leftarrow \{0, 1\}^{2\lambda}$.

Phase 1.0: Building of the proof witness. For all chunk $j \in [d]$,

1. Compute $Q_j(X) = \prod_{\ell \in E_j}(X - \gamma_\ell) \in \mathbb{F}_{\mathrm{poly}}[X]$ where $E_j = \{\ell : (x_j)_\ell \neq 0\}$.
2. Compute $S_j(X) \in \mathbb{F}_{\mathrm{poly}}[X]$ by interpolation $s.t.$ $\deg S_j \leq \frac{m}{d} - 1$ and $\forall \ell \in [\frac{m}{d}], S_j(\gamma_\ell) = (x_j)_\ell$.
3. Compute $P_j(X) = S_j(X)Q_j(X)/F(X) \in \mathbb{F}_{\mathrm{poly}}[X]$.

Phase 1.1: Preparation of the MPC-in-the-Head inputs. For each iteration $e \in [\tau]$,

1. Sample a root seed: $\mathsf{seed}^{[e]} \xleftarrow{\$} \{0, 1\}^\lambda$.
2. Compute parties' seeds $\mathsf{seed}_1^{[e]}, \ldots, \mathsf{seed}_N^{[e]}$ with $\mathsf{TreePRG}(\mathsf{salt}, \mathsf{seed})$.
3. For each party $i \in \{1, \ldots, N\}$,
   - $[\![a_j^{[e]}]\!]_i, [\![b_j^{[e]}]\!]_i \leftarrow \mathsf{PRG}(\mathsf{salt}, \mathsf{seed}_i^{[e]})$, for each $j \in [t]$
   - If $i \neq N$,
     - $\{[\![c_j^{[e]}]\!]_i\}_{j \in [t]}, [\![x_A^{[e]}]\!]_i, [\![Q^{[e]}]\!]_i, [\![P^{[e]}]\!]_i \leftarrow \mathsf{PRG}(\mathsf{salt}, \mathsf{seed}_i^{[e]})$
     - $\mathsf{state}_i^{[e]} = \mathsf{seed}_i^{[e]}$
   - Else,
     - $[\![x_A^{[e]}]\!]_N = x_A - \sum_{j \neq N}[\![x_A^{[e]}]\!]_j$
     - $[\![Q^{[e]}]\!]_N = Q - \sum_{\ell \neq N}[\![Q^{[e]}]\!]_\ell$
     - $[\![P^{[e]}]\!]_N = P - \sum_{\ell \neq N}[\![P^{[e]}]\!]_\ell$
     - $[\![c_j^{[e]}]\!]_N = \langle a_j^{[e]}, b_j^{[e]}\rangle - \sum_{\ell \neq N}[\![c_j^{[e]}]\!]_\ell$, for each $j \in [t]$
     - $\mathsf{aux}^{[e]} = ([\![x_A^{[e]}]\!]_N, [\![Q^{[e]}]\!]_N, [\![P^{[e]}]\!]_N, \{[\![c_j^{[e]}]\!]_N\}_{j \in [t]})$
     - $\mathsf{state}_N^{[e]} = \mathsf{seed}_N^{[e]} \| \mathsf{aux}^{[e]}$
   - Compute $\mathsf{com}_i^{[e]} = \mathsf{Hash}_0(\mathsf{salt}, e, i, \mathsf{state}_i^{[e]})$.

Phase 2: First challenge (randomness for the MPC protocol).

1. Compute $h_1 = \mathsf{Hash}_1(m, \mathsf{salt}, \mathsf{com}_1^{[1]}, \mathsf{com}_2^{[1]}, \ldots, \mathsf{com}_{N-1}^{[\tau]}, \mathsf{com}_N^{[\tau]})$.
2. Extend hash $\{r_j^{[e]}, \varepsilon_j^{[e]}\}_{e \in [\tau], j \in [t]} \leftarrow \mathsf{PRG}(h_1)$ where $r_j^{[e]} \in \mathbb{F}_{\mathrm{points}}$ and $\varepsilon_j^{[e]} \in \mathbb{F}_{\mathrm{points}}^d$.

Phase 3: Simulation of the MPC protocol. For each iteration $e \in [\tau]$,

1. The parties locally set $[\![x_B^{[e]}]\!] = y - H'[\![x_A^{[e]}]\!]$.
2. Then for all $j \in [t]$,
   The parties locally compute $[\![S^{[e]}]\!]$ by interpolation using $[\![x^{[e]}]\!] := ([\![x_A^{[e]}]\!] \mid [\![x_B^{[e]}]\!])$.
   - They locally compute $[\![S^{[e]}(r_j^{[e]})]\!]$, $[\![Q^{[e]}(r_j^{[e]})]\!]$ and $[\![P^{[e]}(r_j^{[e]})]\!]$.
   - They locally set $[\![\alpha_j^{[e]}]\!] = \varepsilon_j^{[e]} \circ [\![Q^{[e]}(r_j^{[e]})]\!] + [\![a_j^{[e]}]\!]$.
   - They locally set $[\![\beta_j^{[e]}]\!] = [\![S^{[e]}(r_j^{[e]})]\!] + [\![b_j^{[e]}]\!]$.
   - The parties open $[\![\alpha_j^{[e]}]\!]$ and $[\![\beta_j^{[e]}]\!]$ to get $\alpha_j^{[e]}$ and $\beta_j^{[e]}$.
   - The parties locally set

$$[\![v_j^{[e]}]\!] = -[\![c_j^{[e]}]\!] + \langle \varepsilon_j^{[e]}, F(r_j^{[e]}) \cdot [\![P^{[e]}(r_j^{[e]})]\!]\rangle + \langle \alpha_j^{[e]}, [\![b_j^{[e]}]\!]\rangle + \langle \beta_j^{[e]}, [\![a_j^{[e]}]\!]\rangle - \langle \alpha_j^{[e]}, \beta_j^{[e]}\rangle .$$

Phase 4: Second challenge (parties to be opened).

1. Compute $h_2 = \mathsf{Hash}_2(m, \mathsf{salt}, h_1, \{[\![\alpha_j^{[e]}]\!], [\![\beta_j^{[e]}]\!], [\![v_j^{[e]}]\!]\}_{j \in [t], e \in [\tau]})$.
2. Expand hash $\{i^{*[e]}\}_{e \in [\tau]} \leftarrow \mathsf{PRG}(h_2)$ where $i^{*[e]} \in [N]$.

Phase 5: Building of the signature. Output the signature σ built as

$$\mathsf{salt} \mid h_1 \mid h_2 \mid \left((\mathsf{state}_i^{[u]})_{i \neq i^{*[e]}} \mid \mathsf{com}_{i^{*[e]}}^{[e]} \mid \{[\![\alpha_j^{[e]}]\!]_{i^{*[e]}}\}_{j \in [t]} \mid \{[\![\beta_j^{[e]}]\!]_{i^{*[e]}}\}_{j \in [t]}\right)_{e \in [\tau]} .$$

Fig. 1. Code-based signature scheme - Signing algorithm.

Inputs: A public key $pk = (H, y)$, a signature σ and a message $m \in \{0, 1\}^*$.

1. Parse the signature σ as

$$\mathsf{salt} \mid h_1 \mid h_2 \mid \left(\left(\mathsf{state}_i^{[e]}\right)_{i \neq i^*[e]} \mid \mathsf{com}_{i^*[e]}^{[e]} \mid \{[\![\alpha^{[e]}{}_j]\!]_{i^*[e]}\}_{j \in [t]} \mid \{[\![\beta^{[e]}{}_j]\!]_{i^*[e]}\}_{j \in [t]}\right)_{e \in [\tau]} .$$

2. Extend hash $\{r_j^{[e]}, \varepsilon_j^{[e]}\}_{e \in [\tau], j \in [t]} \leftarrow \mathrm{PRG}(h_1)$ where $r_j^{[e]} \in \mathbb{F}_{\mathrm{points}}$ and $\varepsilon_j^{[e]} \in \mathbb{F}_{\mathrm{points}}^d$.
3. Extend hash $\{i^*[e]\}_{e \in [\tau]} \leftarrow \mathrm{PRG}(h_2)$ where $i^*[e] \in [N]$.
4. For each iteration $e \in [\tau]$,
   - For each $i \neq i^*[e]$, computes $\mathsf{com}_i^{[e]} = \mathrm{Hash}_0(\mathsf{salt}, e, i, \mathsf{state}_i^{[e]})$.
   - Using $\{\mathsf{state}_i^{[e]}\}_{i \neq i^*[e]}$, simulate all the parties except for $i^*[e]$ as in the Phase 3 of the signing algorithm and get $[\![\alpha_1]\!], \ldots, [\![\alpha_t]\!], [\![\beta_1]\!], \ldots, [\![\beta_t]\!], [\![v]\!]$ for all parties except for $i^*[e]$.
   - Compute $[\![v_j^{[e]}]\!]_{i^*[e]} := -\sum_{i \neq i^*[e]} [\![v_j^{[e]}]\!]_i$ for all $j \in [t]$.
5. Compute $h_1' = \mathrm{Hash}_1(m, \mathsf{com}_1^{[1]}, \mathsf{com}_2^{[1]}, \ldots, \mathsf{com}_{N-1}^{[\tau]}, \mathsf{com}_N^{[\tau]})$.
6. Compute $h_2' = \mathrm{Hash}_2(m, \{[\![\alpha_j^{[e]}]\!], [\![\beta_j^{[e]}]\!], [\![v_j^{[e]}]\!]\}_{j \in [t], e \in [\tau]})$.
7. Output ACCEPT iff $h_1' \stackrel{?}{=} h_1$ and $h_2' \stackrel{?}{=} h_2$.

Fig. 2. Code-based signature scheme - Verification algorithm.

Theorem 5. *Suppose the PRG used is (t, ε_{PRG})-secure and any adversary running in time t has at most an advantage ε_{SD} against the underlying d-split syndrome decoding problem. Model $\mathrm{Hash}_0, \mathrm{Hash}_1$ and Hash_2 as random oracles where $\mathrm{Hash}_0, \mathrm{Hash}_1$ and Hash_2 have 2λ-bit output length. Then chosen-message adversary against the signature scheme depicted in Fig. 1, running in time t, making q_s signing queries, and making q_0, q_1, q_2 queries, respectively, to the random oracles, succeeds in outputting a valid forgery with probability*

$$\Pr[\mathrm{Forge}] \leq \frac{(q_0 + \tau N q_s)^2}{2 \cdot 2^{2\lambda}} + \frac{q_s(q_s + q_0 + q_1 + q_2)}{2^{2\lambda}} + q_s \cdot \tau \cdot \varepsilon_{PRG} + \varepsilon_{SD} + q_2 \cdot \varepsilon^\tau,$$

where $\varepsilon = p + \frac{1}{N} - p \cdot \frac{1}{N}$ and p defined in Eq. (3).

4.4 Parameters

In what follows, we propose three parameter sets which achieve a security level of 128 bits for the signature:

- the first one shall rely on the hardness to solve the SD problem on $\mathbb{F}_2$;
- the second one shall also rely on the hardness to solve the SD problem on $\mathbb{F}_2$, but we shall use a d-split version to get polynomials over a chosen field, concretely $\mathbb{F}_{256}$;
- the last one shall rely on the hardness to solve the SD problem on $\mathbb{F}_{256}$.

Choice of the SD Parameters. Let us first describe how we estimate the security level of a syndrome decoding instance for a random linear code over $\mathbb{F}_2$. The best *practical* attack for our parameters is the algorithm of May, Meurer and

Thomae [MMT11]. As argued in [FJR21], we can lower bound the cost of this attack by only considering the cost of its topmost recursion step:

$$\frac{\binom{m}{w}}{\binom{k+\ell}{p}\binom{m-k-\ell}{w-p}} \cdot \left(L + \frac{L^2}{2^{\ell-p}}\right) \quad \text{with} \quad L := \frac{\binom{k+\ell}{p/2}}{2^p}.$$

As usual in ISD algorithm we need to optimize for the parameters ℓ (a number of rows) and p (a partial Hamming weight). Since we only account for the cost of the topmost level in the algorithm, this yields a slightly conservative estimate for the security level. We use this estimate to choose the parameters of our scheme.

Given these considerations, we suggest the following concrete parameters:

- Variant 1: standard binary syndrome decoding problem. We propose the parameters

$$(q, m, k, w, d) = (2, 1280, 640, 132, 1)$$

which achieve a security level of 128 bits according to the above formula.
- Variant 2: d-split binary syndrome syndrome decoding problem, where d is taken to have $m/d \leq 256$ so that $\mathbb{F}_{\text{poly}} = \mathbb{F}_{256}$. We propose the parameters

$$(q, m, k, w, d) = (2, 1536, 888, 120, 6)$$

which achieve a security of 129 bits. Indeed, the standard SD problem with the same parameters (but $d = 1$) has a security of 145 bits and we know, thanks to the Theorem 2, that there is a security loss of at most 16 bits while switching to $d = 6$. Let us stress that this choice is conservative since the current state of the art does not contain attacks filling the gap of this reduction. Our aim here was to build a practical signature scheme with conservative security, but searching for more aggressive parameters for the d-split syndrome decoding problem would be an interesting direction for future research.
- Variant 3: syndrome decoding instance defined over $\mathbb{F}_{256}$. The cryptanalysis of the syndrome decoding problem on a field which is larger than $\mathbb{F}_2$ has been less studied. Previous articles [CVE11, GPS22] propose parameters sets for syndrome decoding instances over $\mathbb{F}_{2^8}$ where the code length m is between 200 and 210. In our case, we choose $m = 256$ in such a way that the polynomial degree is equal to the field size. Besides being more conservative, this choice has the advantage of easing the use of a Fast Fourier Transform. We propose the following parameters[1] for this variant:

$$(q, m, k, w, d) = (256, 256, 128, 80, 1).$$

Choice of the MPC Parameters. For each variant, we suggest in Table 3 a parameter set for the MPC protocol.

---

[1] More cryptanalysis of the SD problem over $\mathbb{F}_{256}$ would be welcome to get more confidence in the choice of the parameters. Such research is out of the scope of present article.

Table 3. SD and MPC parameters.

Scheme	SD Parameters					MPC Parameters			
	q	m	k	w	d	$|\mathbb{F}_{\text{poly}}|$	$|\mathbb{F}_{\text{points}}|$	t	p
Variant 1	2	1280	640	132	1	2^{11}	2^{22}	6	$\approx 2^{-69}$
Variant 2	2	1536	888	120	6	2^{8}	2^{24}	5	$\approx 2^{-79}$
Variant 3	2^{8}	256	128	80	1	2^{8}	2^{24}	5	$\approx 2^{-78}$

To have a short signature, we take the smallest possible field $\mathbb{F}_{\text{poly}}$ since a signature transcript includes polynomials on that field. As explained in Sect. 3, $\mathbb{F}_{\text{poly}}$ must be a field extension of $\mathbb{F}_{\text{SD}}$ which verifies the relation $|\mathbb{F}_{\text{poly}}| \geq m/d$. Then, it remains to choose $|\mathbb{F}_{\text{points}}|$ and t. These parameters are chosen to make the false positive probability p is negligible compared to $1/N$ such that the optimal forgery strategy of an attacker is to take $\tau_1 = 1$ in the Eq. (4). As a result, we just need to increase the number of iterations τ by one compared to the interactive protocol.

4.5 Implementation and Performances

For each repetition in the computation of each party, d polynomial interpolations are involved. Indeed, from $[\![x]\!]$, the parties must compute

$$[\![S_\ell]\!](X) = \sum_{i=1}^{m/d} [\![x_{\frac{m}{d}\ell+i}]\!] \cdot \prod_{j=1, j\neq i}^{m/d} \frac{X - w_j}{w_i - w_j}$$

for all $\ell \in [d]$. Then, the parties must evaluate $[\![S_\ell]\!]$ in t random evaluation points sampled by the verifier, for all $\ell \in [d]$. The natural way to implement that is to compute the coefficients of all the polynomials $\{[\![S_\ell]\!]\}_\ell$ from $[\![x]\!]$, then to evaluate these polynomials t times. However this implies that the signer must realize $\tau \cdot N \cdot d$ interpolations. Instead, the signer can compute the vector $u(r)$ defined as

$$u(r) = \left(\prod_{j=1, j\neq i}^{m/d} \frac{r - w_j}{w_i - w_j} \right)_{1 \leq i \leq \frac{m}{d}}$$

for each evaluation point r, and then use these vectors in the computation of all the parties as

$$[\![S_\ell(r)]\!] = \langle [\![x_\ell]\!], u(r) \rangle$$

where $[\![x_\ell]\!]$ is the ℓth chunk of $[\![x]\!]$. By proceeding this way, the number of (transposed) interpolations done by the signer is of $\tau \cdot t$.

To reduce the computational cost of the interpolations, we can make use of a Fast Fourier Transform (FFT). We are working on field extensions of $\mathbb{F}_2$, so we can use the Additive FFT independently introduced by Wang-Zhu in 1988 [WZ88] and by Cantor in 1989 [Can89], which was further improved in [vzGG03,GM10]. Although such additive FFT exists for any extension of $\mathbb{F}_2$, the algorithms are simpler for a field of size $2^{(2^i)}$ for some i, which is why we define $\mathbb{F}_{poly}$ as $\mathbb{F}_{256}$. On such a field $\mathbb{F}$, we indeed have an efficient additive FFT using $\frac{1}{2}|\mathbb{F}|\log_2|\mathbb{F}|$ multiplications to evaluate a polynomial (of degree lower than $|\mathbb{F}|$) in $|\mathbb{F}|$ points.

We implemented the signature scheme in C. In our implementation, the pseudo-randomness is generated using AES in counter mode and the hash function is instantiated with SHAKE. We benchmarked our scheme on a 3.8 GHz Intel Core i7 CPU with support of AVX2 and AES instructions. All the reported timings were measured on this CPU while disabling Intel Turbo Boost.

Remark 2. Another motivation for using $\mathbb{F}_{poly} = \mathbb{F}_{256}$ is that some Intel processors have dedicated instructions for $\mathbb{F}_{256}$ arithmetic. We therefore expect substantial speed-ups for the instances of our signature scheme using $\mathbb{F}_{poly} = \mathbb{F}_{256}$ on these processors. Optimizing and benchmarking such implementations is left for future research.

We instantiate two trade-offs per variant: the first one lowering communication cost to produce short signatures, and the second one lowering computational cost to get a fast signature computation. We obtain the parameters and sizes described in Table 4. We provide the measured computational performances of our signature implementation in Table 5.

Table 4. Parameters (N, τ) with the achieved communication costs (in bytes).

λ	Scheme	Aim	Parameters		|pk|	|sk|	Signature	
			N	τ			|sgn| (max)	|sgn| (avg, std)
128	Variant 1	Fast	32	27	96	16	16 422	16 006, 446
128		Short	256	17	96	16	11 193	11 160, 127
128	Variant 2	Fast	32	27	97	16	17 866	17 406, 494
128		Short	256	17	97	16	12 102	12 066, 141
128	Variant 3	Fast	32	27	144	16	12 115	11 835, 302
128		Short	256	17	144	16	8 481	8 459, 86

Future Investigations. We tried to optimize the implementation using some algorithmic tricks, but we did not yet investigate the possible software optimizations like vectorization or bitslicing. Although the variants 1 and 2 are more conservative because they rely on the hardness of the binary syndrome decoding problem, variant 3 is more promising in terms of signature size and computation time. While we have investigated parameter sets where $\mathbb{F}_{SD}$ is a field extension of $\mathbb{F}_2$, more cryptanalysis for the SD problem on those fields as well as on non-binary fields would be welcome. An interesting idea would be to instantiate

Table 5. Benchmarks of our signature implementation. Timings are averaged over 10 000 measurements. The CPU clock cycles have been measured using SUPERCOP (https://bench.cr.yp.to/supercop.html).

λ	Variant	Aim	Keygen	Sign	Verify
128	Variant 1	Fast		n/a[†]	
128		Short			
128	Variant 2	Fast	0.03 ms 114 162 cycles	13.4 ms 52 463 114 cycles	12.7 ms 50 306 845 cycles
128		Short	0.03 ms 113 852 cycles	64.2 ms 251 099 099 cycles	60.7 ms 243 055 474 cycles
128	Variant 3	Fast	0.01 ms 49 181 cycles	6.4 ms 25 253 580 cycles	5.9 ms 23 816 143 cycles
128		Short	0.01 ms 49 057 cycles	29.5 ms 114 226 505 cycles	27.1 ms 108 541 768 cycles

[†] *We only have a proof of concept implementation with irrelevant timings.*

our scheme with a prime field $\mathbb{F}_{SD}$ for which the Number-Theoretic Transform (NTT) is defined. If $\mathbb{F}_{SD}$ is large enough, we could then take the same field for $\mathbb{F}_{poly}$ than $\mathbb{F}_{SD}$ and we would have fast polynomial interpolations and simpler multiplication operations.

5   Comparison

In this section, we compare our scheme to different code-based and post-quantum signature schemes from the literature.

5.1   Comparison with Other Code-Based Signature Schemes

In the state of the art, there exist two approaches to build signatures. On one hand, there is the hash-and-sign paradigm which relies on the existence of a (code-based) trapdoor permutation. Wave [DST19] is a code-based signature scheme in this paradigm. Such schemes are often more vulnerable to structural attacks. On the other hand, further signature schemes are constructed by applying the Fiat-Shamir transform to (zero-knowledge) identification schemes, which can rely on weaker assumptions (and typically the SD for random linear codes). Historically such schemes, like the famous Stern protocol, give rise to large signatures because of the high soundness error of the underlying identification scheme (2/3 or 1/2). To avoid this issue, a solution consists in relying on different code-based problems. For instance, LESS is a recent scheme which security relies on the hardness of the Linear Code Equivalence problem [BMPS20, BBPS21]. Another direction is to find a way to adapt the Schnorr-Lyubashevsky approach to code-based cryptography. Durandal is a recent scheme following this approach [ABG+19]. More recently, some works [GPS22, FJR21, BGKM22] have obtained better soundness by relying on the MPC-in-the-Head principle. The proposed schemes achieve small signature sizes at the cost of slower computation. Depending on the setting, they can produce signatures with different trade-offs between the signature size and the computational cost. The current work follows this approach while achieving better trade-offs than any of these previous works.

Table 6. Comparison of our scheme with signatures from the literature (128-bit security). The sizes are in bytes and the timings are in milliseconds. Reported timings are from the original publications: Wave has been benchmarked on a 3.5 Ghz Intel Xeon E3-1240 v5, Durandal on a 2.8 Ghz Intel Core i5-7440HQ, while [FJR21] and our scheme on a 3.8 GHz Intel Core i7.

Scheme Name	Year	|sgn|	|pk|	t_{sgn}	t_{verif}	Assumption
Wave	2019	2.07 K	3.2 M	300	-	SD over $\mathbb{F}_3$ (large weight) $(U, U + V)$-codes indisting.
Durandal - I	2018	3.97 K	14.9 K	4	5	Rank SD over $\mathbb{F}_{2^m}$
Durandal - II	2018	4.90 K	18.2 K	5	6	Rank SD over $\mathbb{F}_{2^m}$
LESS-FM - I	2020	15.2 K	9.77 K	-	-	Linear Code Equivalence
LESS-FM - II	2020	5.25 K	206 K	-	-	Perm. Code Equivalence
LESS-FM - III	2020	10.39 K	11.57 K	-	-	Perm. Code Equivalence
[GPS22]-256	2021	24.0 K	0.11 K	-	-	SD over $\mathbb{F}_{256}$
[GPS22]-1024	2021	19.8 K	0.12 K	-	-	SD over $\mathbb{F}_{1024}$
[FJR21] (fast)	2021	22.6 K	0.09 K	13	12	SD over $\mathbb{F}_2$
[FJR21] (short)	2021	16.0 K	0.09 K	62	57	SD over $\mathbb{F}_2$
[BGKM22] - Sig1	2022	23.7 K	0.1 K	-	-	SD over $\mathbb{F}_2$
[BGKM22] - Sig2	2022	20.6 K	0.2 K	-	-	(QC)SD over $\mathbb{F}_2$
Our scheme - Var1f	2022	15.6 K	0.09 K	-	-	SD over $\mathbb{F}_2$
Our scheme - Var1s	2022	10.9 K	0.09 K	-	-	SD over $\mathbb{F}_2$
Our scheme - Var2f	2022	17.0 K	0.09 K	13	13	SD over $\mathbb{F}_2$
Our scheme - Var2s	2022	11.8 K	0.09 K	64	61	SD over $\mathbb{F}_2$
Our scheme - Var3f	2022	11.5 K	0.14 K	6	6	SD over $\mathbb{F}_{256}$
Our scheme - Var3s	2022	8.26 K	0.14 K	30	27	SD over $\mathbb{F}_{256}$

Table 6 compares the performances of our scheme with the current code-based signature state of the art, for the 128-bit security level.[2] We observe that our scheme outperforms all the existing code-based signatures for the $|\mathsf{sgn}| + |\mathsf{pk}|$ metric. Depending on the parameters, it can even produce signatures such that $|\mathsf{sgn}| + |\mathsf{pk}|$ is below the symbolic cap of 10 KB. Regardless of the key size, Wave still achieves the shortest signatures. In terms of security, our scheme has the advantage of relying on the hardness of one of the oldest problems of the code-based cryptography, namely the syndrome decoding for random linear codes in Hamming weight metric.

---

[2] We did not include "Sig 3" from [BGKM22] since it is similar to [FJR21] with slight differences (*message decoding* setting) which do not improve the scheme.

5.2   Comparison with Other Post-Quantum Signature Schemes

Finally, we compare in Table 7 our construction with other signature schemes aiming at post-quantum security. First of all, let us note that the lattice-based signature schemes (such as Dilithium [BDK+21a] and Falcon [FHK+20]) are currently the most efficient post-quantum signature schemes. They achieve small signature size and efficient running time. However, the goal of our construction is to propose a signature scheme based on an alternative problem for the sake of diversity of security assumptions. All the others schemes have very short public keys and secret keys (less than 150 bytes for 128-bit security), which is hence not a point for comparison. Depending on the chosen parameters, our scheme can be competitive with Picnic3 [KZ20b] and the recently proposed "Picnic4" [KZ21] which also rely on the MPC-in-the-Head paradigm. Like Picnic4, it can produce signatures with a size of around 8 KB. However, our scheme is arguably more conservative in terms of security since Picnic is based on the hardness of inverting LowMC [ARS+15], a cipher with unconventional design choices, while our scheme is based on the hardness of the syndrome decoding problem on linear codes, which has a long cryptanalysis history and is believed to be very robust. Banquet [BdK+21b] is a signature scheme for which the security is based on the

Table 7. Comparison of our scheme with signatures from the literature. The sizes are in bytes and the timings are in milliseconds. Reported timings for Falcon have been benchmarked on a 2.3 Ghz Intel Core i5-8259U in [FHK+20], and timings for Dilithium and our scheme have been benchmarked on a 3.8 Ghz Intel Core i7. The benchmarks of the other schemes have been realized on a Intel Xeon W-2133 CPU at 3.60 GHz, the values for SPHINCS+ and Banquet have been extracted from [BdK+21b] while the values for Picnic3 have been extracted from its original publication [KZ20b].

Scheme Name	|sgn|	|pk|	t_{sgn}	t_{verif}
Dilithium2	2.4 K	1.3 K	0.065	0.024
Falcon-512	0.65 K	0.88 K	0.168	0.036
SPHINCS+-128f	16.7 K	0.03 K	14	1.7
SPHINCS+-128s	7.7 K	0.03 K	239	0.7
Picnic3	12.3 K	0.03 K	5.2	4.0
Picnic4	7.8 K	0.03 K	≈ 20	≈ 20
Banquet (fast)	19.3 K	0.03 K	6	5
Banquet (short)	13.0 K	0.03 K	44	40
Our scheme - Var1f	15.6 K	0.09 K	-	-
Our scheme - Var1s	10.9 K	0.09 K	-	-
Our scheme - Var2f	17.0 K	0.09 K	13	13
Our scheme - Var2s	11.8 K	0.09 K	64	61
Our scheme - Var3f	11.5 K	0.14 K	6	6
Our scheme - Var3s	8.3 K	0.14 K	30	27

hardness of inverting AES (instead of LowMC), which can also be argued to be a conservative choice. Our scheme over $\mathbb{F}_2$ is competitive with Banquet: slightly shorter and slightly slower (but the timing could be optimized). On the other hand, our scheme on $\mathbb{F}_{256}$ clearly outperforms Banquet. Our scheme can also be competitive with SPHINCS$^+$ [BHK+19] depending on the exact criteria. For similar signature sizes, our signature computation is significantly faster while our signature verification is significantly slower than those of SPHINCS$^+$.

Acknowledgements. This work has been supported by the European Union's H2020 Programme under grant agreement number ERC-669891.

References

[AABN02] Abdalla, M., An, J.H., Bellare, M., Namprempre, C.: From identification to signatures via the Fiat-Shamir transform: minimizing assumptions for security and forward-security. In: Knudsen, L.R. (ed.) EUROCRYPT 2002. LNCS, vol. 2332, pp. 418–433. Springer, Heidelberg (2002). https://doi.org/10.1007/3-540-46035-7_28

[ABG+19] Aragon, N., Blazy, O., Gaborit, P., Hauteville, A., Zémor, G.: Durandal: a rank metric based signature scheme. In: Ishai, Y., Rijmen, V. (eds.) EUROCRYPT 2019, Part III. LNCS, vol. 11478, pp. 728–758. Springer, Cham (2019). https://doi.org/10.1007/978-3-030-17659-4_25

[ACBH13] El Yousfi Alaoui, S.M., Cayrel, P.-L., El Bansarkhani, R., Hoffmann, G.: Code-based identification and signature schemes in software. In: Cuzzocrea, A., Kittl, C., Simos, D.E., Weippl, E., Xu, L. (eds.) CD-ARES 2013. LNCS, vol. 8128, pp. 122–136. Springer, Heidelberg (2013). https://doi.org/10.1007/978-3-642-40588-4_9

[AFS03] Augot, D., Finiasz, M., Sendrier, N.: A fast provably secure cryptographic hash function. Cryptology ePrint Archive, Report 2003/230 (2003). https://eprint.iacr.org/2003/230

[AGS11] Aguilar, C., Gaborit, P., Schrek, J.: A new zero-knowledge code based identification scheme with reduced communication. In: 2011 IEEE Information Theory Workshop, pp. 648–652 (2011)

[ARS+15] Albrecht, M.R., Rechberger, C., Schneider, T., Tiessen, T., Zohner, M.: Ciphers for MPC and FHE. In: Oswald, E., Fischlin, M. (eds.) EUROCRYPT 2015, Part I. LNCS, vol. 9056, pp. 430–454. Springer, Heidelberg (2015). https://doi.org/10.1007/978-3-662-46800-5_17

[BBC+19] Baldi, M., Barenghi, A., Chiaraluce, F., Pelosi, G., Santini, P.: A finite regime analysis of information set decoding algorithms. Algorithms 12(10), 209 (2019)

[BBPS21] Barenghi, A., Biasse, J.-F., Persichetti, E., Santini, P.: LESS-FM: fine-tuning signatures from the code equivalence problem. In: Choon, J.H., Tillich, J.-P. (eds.) PQCrypto 2021 2021. LNCS, vol. 12841, pp. 23–43. Springer, Cham (2021). https://doi.org/10.1007/978-3-030-81293-5_2

[BDK+21a] Bai, S., et al.: Crypstals-dilithium - algorithm specifications and supporting documentation. Version 3.1, 8 February 2021 (2021). https://pq-crystals.org/dilithium/data/dilithium-specification-round3-20210208.pdf

[BdK+21b] Baum, C., de Saint Guilhem, C.D., Kales, D., Orsini, E., Scholl, P., Zaverucha, G.: Banquet: short and fast signatures from AES. In: Garay, J.A. (ed.) PKC 2021, Part I. LNCS, vol. 12710, pp. 266–297. Springer, Cham (2021). https://doi.org/10.1007/978-3-030-75245-3_11

[Bea92] Beaver, D.: Efficient multiparty protocols using circuit randomization. In: Feigenbaum, J. (ed.) CRYPTO 1991. LNCS, vol. 576, pp. 420–432. Springer, Heidelberg (1992). https://doi.org/10.1007/3-540-46766-1_34

[BGKM22] Bidoux, L., Gaborit, P., Kulkarni, M., Mateu, V.: Code-based signatures from new proofs of knowledge for the syndrome decoding problem (2022)

[BHK+19] Bernstein, D.J., Hülsing, A., Kölbl, S., Niederhagen, R., Rijneveld, J., Schwabe, P.: The SPHINCS$^+$ signature framework. In: Cavallaro, L., Kinder, J., Wang, X., Katz, J. (eds.) ACM CCS 2019, pp. 2129–2146. ACM Press, November 2019

[BMPS20] Biasse, J.-F., Micheli, G., Persichetti, E., Santini, P.: LESS is more: code-based signatures without syndromes. In: Nitaj, A., Youssef, A. (eds.) AFRICACRYPT 2020. LNCS, vol. 12174, pp. 45–65. Springer, Cham (2020). https://doi.org/10.1007/978-3-030-51938-4_3

[BN20] Baum, C., Nof, A.: Concretely-efficient zero-knowledge arguments for arithmetic circuits and their application to lattice-based cryptography. In: Kiayias, A., Kohlweiss, M., Wallden, P., Zikas, V. (eds.) PKC 2020, Part I. LNCS, vol. 12110, pp. 495–526. Springer, Cham (2020). https://doi.org/10.1007/978-3-030-45374-9_17

[Can89] Cantor, D.G.: On arithmetical algorithms over finite fields. J. Combin. Theory Ser. A **50**, 285–300 (1989)

[CDG+20] Chase, M., et al.: The picnic signature scheme - design document. Version 2.2, 14 April 2020 (2020). https://raw.githubusercontent.com/microsoft/Picnic/master/spec/design-v2.2.pdf

[CHR+16] Chen, M.-S., Hülsing, A., Rijneveld, J., Samardjiska, S., Schwabe, P.: From 5-pass $\mathcal{MQ}$-based identification to $\mathcal{MQ}$-based signatures. In: Cheon, J.H., Takagi, T. (eds.) ASIACRYPT 2016, Part II. LNCS, vol. 10032, pp. 135–165. Springer, Heidelberg (2016). https://doi.org/10.1007/978-3-662-53890-6_5

[CVE11] Cayrel, P.-L., Véron, P., El Yousfi Alaoui, S.M.: A zero-knowledge identification scheme based on the Q-ary syndrome decoding problem. In: Biryukov, A., Gong, G., Stinson, D.R. (eds.) SAC 2010. LNCS, vol. 6544, pp. 171–186. Springer, Heidelberg (2011). https://doi.org/10.1007/978-3-642-19574-7_12

[DLO+18] Damgård, I., Luo, J., Oechsner, S., Scholl, P., Simkin, M.: Compact zero-knowledge proofs of small hamming weight. In: Abdalla, M., Dahab, R. (eds.) PKC 2018, Part II. LNCS, vol. 10770, pp. 530–560. Springer, Cham (2018). https://doi.org/10.1007/978-3-319-76581-5_18

[DST19] Debris-Alazard, T., Sendrier, N., Tillich, J.-P.: Wave: a new family of trapdoor one-way preimage sampleable functions based on codes. In: Galbraith, S.D., Moriai, S. (eds.) ASIACRYPT 2019, Part I. LNCS, vol. 11921, pp. 21–51. Springer, Cham (2019). https://doi.org/10.1007/978-3-030-34578-5_2

[EDV+12] El Yousfi Alaoui, S.M., Dagdelen, Ö., Véron, P., Galindo, D., Cayrel, P.-L.: Extended security arguments for signature schemes. In: Mitrokotsa, A., Vaudenay, S. (eds.) AFRICACRYPT 2012. LNCS, vol. 7374, pp. 19–34. Springer, Heidelberg (2012). https://doi.org/10.1007/978-3-642-31410-0_2

[FHK+20] Fouque, P.-A., et al.: Falcon: fast-fourier lattice-based compact signatures over NTRU. Version 1.2, 1 October 2020 (2020). https://falcon-sign.info/falcon.pdf

[FJR21]   Feneuil, T., Joux, A., Rivain, M.: Shared permutation for syndrome decoding: new zero-knowledge protocol and code-based signature. Cryptology ePrint Archive, Report 2021/1576 (2021). https://eprint.iacr.org/2021/1576

[FJR22]   Feneuil, T., Joux, A., Rivain, M.: Syndrome decoding in the head: shorter signatures from zero-knowledge proofs. Cryptology ePrint Archive, Report 2022/188 (2022). https://eprint.iacr.org/2022/188

[FS87]   Fiat, A., Shamir, A.: How to prove yourself: practical solutions to identification and signature problems. In: Odlyzko, A.M. (ed.) CRYPTO 1986. LNCS, vol. 263, pp. 186–194. Springer, Heidelberg (1987). https://doi.org/10.1007/3-540-47721-7_12

[GG07]   Gaborit, P., Girault, M.: Lightweight code-based identification and signature. In: IEEE International Symposium on Information Theory, ISIT 2007, Nice, France, 24–29 June 2007, pp. 191–195. IEEE (2007)

[GM10]   Gao, S., Mateer, T.: Additive fast fourier transforms over finite fields. IEEE Trans. Inf. Theory **56**(12), 6265–6272 (2010)

[GPS22]   Gueron, S., Persichetti, E., Santini, P.: Designing a practical code-based signature scheme from zero-knowledge proofs with trusted setup. Cryptography **6**(1), 5 (2022)

[IKOS07] Ishai, Y., Kushilevitz, E., Ostrovsky, R., Sahai, A.: Zero-knowledge from secure multiparty computation. In: Johnson, D.S., Feige, U. (eds.) 39th ACM STOC, pp. 21–30. ACM Press, June 2007

[KZ20a]   Kales, D., Zaverucha, G.: An attack on some signature schemes constructed from five-pass identification schemes. In: Krenn, S., Shulman, H., Vaudenay, S. (eds.) CANS 2020. LNCS, vol. 12579, pp. 3–22. Springer, Cham (2020). https://doi.org/10.1007/978-3-030-65411-5_1

[KZ20b]   Kales, D., Zaverucha, G.: Improving the performance of the Picnic signature scheme. IACR TCHES **2020**(4), 154–188 (2020). https://tches.iacr.org/index.php/TCHES/article/view/8680

[KZ21]   Kales, D., Zaverucha, G.: Efficient lifting for shorter zero-knowledge proofs and post-quantum signatures. Preliminary Draft, 29 October 2021 (2021). https://groups.google.com/a/list.nist.gov/g/pqc-forum/c/vLyUa_NFUsY/m/gNSnuhmxBQAJ

[LN17]   Lindell, Y., Nof, A.: A framework for constructing fast MPC over arithmetic circuits with malicious adversaries and an honest-majority. In: Thuraisingham, B.M., Evans, D., Malkin, T., Xu, D. (eds.) ACM CCS 2017, pp. 259–276. ACM Press, October/November 2017

[MMT11]   May, A., Meurer, A., Thomae, E.: Decoding random linear codes in $\tilde{\mathcal{O}}(2^{0.054n})$. In: Lee, D.H., Wang, X. (eds.) ASIACRYPT 2011. LNCS, vol. 7073, pp. 107–124. Springer, Heidelberg (2011). https://doi.org/10.1007/978-3-642-25385-0_6

[Ste94]   Stern, J.: A new identification scheme based on syndrome decoding. In: Stinson, D.R. (ed.) CRYPTO 1993. LNCS, vol. 773, pp. 13–21. Springer, Heidelberg (1994). https://doi.org/10.1007/3-540-48329-2_2

[TS16]   Canto Torres, R., Sendrier, N.: Analysis of information set decoding for a sub-linear error weight. In: Takagi, T. (ed.) PQCrypto 2016. LNCS, vol. 9606, pp. 144–161. Springer, Cham (2016). https://doi.org/10.1007/978-3-319-29360-8_10

[Vér96] Véron, P.: Improved identification schemes based on error-correcting codes. Appl. Algebra Eng. Commun. Comput. **8**(1), 57–69 (1996)

[vzGG03] von zur Gathen, J., Gerhard, J.: Modern Computer Algebra. Cambridge University Press, Cambridge (2003)

[WZ88] Wang, Y., Zhu, X.: A fast algorithm for the Fourier transform over finite fields and its VLSI implementation. IEEE J. Sel. Areas Commun. **6**(3), 572–577 (1988)

Beyond the Csiszár-Korner Bound: Best-Possible Wiretap Coding via Obfuscation

Yuval Ishai[1], Alexis Korb[2(✉)], Paul Lou[2], and Amit Sahai[2]

[1] Technion, Haifa, Israel
yuvali@cs.technion.ac.il
[2] UCLA, Los Angeles, USA
{alexiskorb,pslou,sahai}@cs.ucla.edu

Abstract. A *wiretap coding scheme* (Wyner, Bell Syst. Tech. J. 1975) enables Alice to reliably communicate a message m to an honest Bob by sending an encoding c over a noisy channel ChB, while at the same time hiding m from Eve who receives c over another noisy channel ChE.

Wiretap coding is clearly impossible when ChB is a *degraded* version of ChE, in the sense that the output of ChB can be simulated using only the output of ChE. A classic work of Csiszár and Korner (IEEE Trans. Inf. Theory, 1978) shows that the converse does not hold. This follows from their full characterization of the channel pairs (ChB, ChE) that enable information-theoretic wiretap coding.

In this work, we show that in fact the converse *does* hold when considering *computational security*; that is, wiretap coding against a computationally bounded Eve is possible *if and only if* ChB is not a degraded version of ChE. Our construction assumes the existence of virtual black-box (VBB) obfuscation of specific classes of "evasive" functions that generalize fuzzy point functions, and can be heuristically instantiated using indistinguishability obfuscation. Finally, our solution has the appealing feature of being *universal* in the sense that Alice's algorithm depends only on ChB and not on ChE.

1 Introduction

The wiretap channel, first introduced by Wyner [26], captures a unidirectional communication setting in which Alice transmits an encoding of a message across two discrete memoryless channels: a main channel (Bob's channel) for the intended receiver Bob and an eavesdropping channel (Eve's channel) for an adversarial receiver Eve. Two conditions are desired: correctness and security. Informally, correctness guarantees that Bob can decode the message with overwhelming probability, and security requires that Eve learn essentially nothing about the message. The wiretap coding problem is then to find a (randomized) encoding algorithm that satisfies both conditions. The wiretap coding question represents a basic and fundamental question regarding secure transmission over

---

The full version of this paper can be found at https://eprint.iacr.org/2022/343.pdf.

Y. Dodis and T. Shrimpton (Eds.): CRYPTO 2022, LNCS 13508, pp. 573–602, 2022.
https://doi.org/10.1007/978-3-031-15979-4_20

noisy channels, and indeed Wyner's work has been incredibly influential: Google Scholar reports that the literature citing [26] surpasses 7000 papers, and Wyner's work is considered *the* foundational work on using noisy channels for cryptography. Much of the interest in this question comes from its relevance to physical layer security, a large area of research that exploits physical properties of communication channels to enhance communication security through coding and signal processing. See, e.g., [24] for a survey.

The classic work of Csiszár and Korner [10] completely characterized the pairs of channels for which wiretap coding is possible information theoretically. Roughly speaking, their work defined a notion of one channel being *less noisy* than the other (see Definition 8), and they proved that wiretap coding is possible information theoretically if and only if Eve's channel is *not* less noisy than Bob's channel.

To illustrate this, let's consider a specific case: suppose that Bob's channel is a binary symmetric channel, flipping each bit that Alice sends with probability $p = 0.1$; at the same time, suppose Eve's channel is a binary erasure channel, erasing each bit that Alice sends (i.e., replacing it with $\perp$) with probability ϵ. Then, it turns out [23] that Eve's channel is not less noisy than Bob's channel if and only if $\epsilon > 0.36 = 4p(1 - p)$, and thus by [10], information-theoretic wiretap coding is only possible under this condition.

A New Feasibility Result for Wiretap Coding. In cryptography, we often take for granted that assuming adversaries to be computationally bounded should lead to improved feasibility results. Indeed, we have seen this many times especially in the early history of cryptography: from re-usable secret keys for encryption [6,27] to the feasibility of secure multi-party computation with a dishonest majority [14]. However, despite the popularity of Wyner's work, no improvement over [10] in terms of feasibility against computationally bounded adversaries has been obtained in *over 40 years*.

Nevertheless, in this work, we ask: is it possible to obtain new feasibility results for wiretap coding for computationally bounded eavesdroppers?

Taking a fresh look at this scenario, we observe that if $\epsilon \leq 0.2 = 2p$, then wiretap coding is completely impossible: If $\epsilon \leq 0.2 = 2p$, then Eve can simulate Bob's channel. For example, if $\epsilon = 0.2 = 2p$, then Eve can assign each $\perp$ that she receives a uniform value in $\{0, 1\}$, and this would exactly yield a binary symmetric channel with flip probability $p = 0.1$, thus exactly simulating the distribution received by Bob. Since wiretap coding is non-interactive, if Bob can recover the message with high probability, then so can Eve, violating security. Indeed, whenever Eve can efficiently simulate Bob's channel, we say that Bob's channel is a *degraded* version of Eve's channel [9]. When this is true, wiretap coding is clearly impossible, even for efficient eavesdroppers Eve.

In our main result, we show that assuming secure program obfuscation for simple specific classes of functionalities (as we describe in more detail below), the above limitation presents the *only* obstacle to feasibility of wiretap coding against computationally bounded eavesdroppers. In particular, for the scenario described above, we show that wiretap coding is possible whenever $\epsilon > 0.2 = 2p$, even though [10,23] showed that information-theoretic wiretap coding is impossible for $\epsilon < 0.36 = 4p(1 - p)$. More generally, we show that wiretap coding is possible whenever Bob's channel is *not* a degraded version of Eve's channel. We now describe our results in more detail.

1.1 Our Contributions

Let ChB represent Bob's channel, and let ChE represent Eve's channel. Observe that the input alphabets for the channels ChB and ChE must be identical; we will denote this input alphabet by $\mathcal{X}$, and consider 1-bit messages for simplicity.[1]

We first consider an oracle-based model in which a wiretap coding scheme consists of two algorithms:

- $\mathrm{Enc}(1^\lambda, m)$: The (randomized) encoder takes as input a security parameter λ and a message bit $m \in \{0, 1\}$. The output of Enc consists of: (1) a string $c \in \mathcal{X}^*$, and (2) a circuit describing a function f. The string c is transmitted over channels ChB and ChE to Bob and Eve respectively. However, both Bob and Eve are granted oracle access to f.
- $\mathrm{Dec}^f(y)$: The deterministic decoder is a polynomial-time oracle algorithm with oracle access to f. Dec^f takes as input the string y received by Bob over his channel.

We obtain our main result in two steps. In our first and primary step, we prove:

Theorem 1 (Informal). *For any pair of discrete memoryless channels* (ChB, ChE) *where* ChB *is not a degraded version of* ChE, *there exist PPT encoding and decoding algorithms* $(\mathrm{Enc}, \mathrm{Dec}^{(\cdot)})$ *which achieve:*

- *Correctness: For all messages* $m \in \{0, 1\}$,

$$\Pr[\mathrm{Dec}^f(1^\lambda, \mathsf{ChB}(c)) = m \mid (f, c) \leftarrow \mathrm{Enc}(1^\lambda, m)] \geq 1 - \mathsf{negl}(\lambda)$$

- *Security: For all computationally unbounded adversaries* $\mathcal{A}^{(\cdot)}$ *that are allowed to make polynomially many queries to their oracle,*

$$\Pr[\mathcal{A}^{f_b}(1^\lambda, \mathsf{ChE}(c_b)) = b \mid (f_b, c_b) \leftarrow \mathrm{Enc}(1^\lambda, b)] \leq \frac{1}{2} + \mathsf{negl}(\lambda)$$

where b *is uniformly distributed over* $\{0, 1\}$.

Theorem 1 can be viewed as an unconditional construction using an *ideal obfuscation* of the oracle f. Our use of obfuscation in this context was inspired by the recent work of Agrawal et al. [1], which used ideal obfuscation to obtain a new feasibility result for secure computation using unidirectional communication over noisy channels (see Sect. 1.2 for comparison and more related work).

---

[1] In the computational setting, any wiretap coding scheme for 1-bit messages can be bootstrapped into one that encodes long messages with rate achieving the capacity of ChB via the use of a standard hybrid encryption technique (see the full version for more details).

In our second step, we show how to bootstrap from Theorem 1 to obtain wire-tap coding in the plain model secure against computationally bounded adversaries, via a suitable form of cryptographic program obfuscation.

More concretely, we use the notion of virtual black-box (VBB) obfuscation for *evasive circuits* [3], for a specific class of evasive circuits that we call generalized fuzzy point functions, and with a very simple kind of auxiliary information that corresponds to the message that Eve receives when Alice transmits a uniformly random message across Eve's channel (see Sect. 7 for details). Using this kind of obfuscation, we obtain the following result in the plain model:

Theorem 2 (Informal). *Assume that $\mathcal{O}$ is a secure evasive function obfuscation scheme for the class of generalized fuzzy point functions. Then, for any pair of discrete memoryless channels* (ChB, ChE) *where* ChB *is not a degraded version of* ChE, *there exist PPT encoding and decoding algorithms* (Enc, Dec) *which achieve:*

– **Correctness:** *For all messages* $m \in \{0, 1\}$,

$$\Pr[\mathsf{Dec}(1^\lambda, \mathcal{O}(f), \mathsf{ChB}(c)) = m \mid (f, c) \leftarrow \mathsf{Enc}(1^\lambda, m)] \geq 1 - \mathsf{negl}(\lambda)$$

– **Security:** *For all computationally bounded adversaries* $\mathcal{A}$,

$$\Pr[\mathcal{A}(1^\lambda, \mathcal{O}(f_b), \mathsf{ChE}(c_b)) = b \mid (f_b, c_b) \leftarrow \mathsf{Enc}(1^\lambda, b)] \leq \frac{1}{2} + \mathsf{negl}(\lambda)$$

where b is uniformly distributed over $\{0, 1\}$.

Note that since $\mathcal{O}(f)$ can be made public to both Bob and Eve, it can be communicated by using a standard encoding scheme for ChB, with no security requirements.

On Instantiating Obfuscation. We conjecture that indistinguishability obfuscation (iO) provides a secure realization of the obfuscation needed in our wiretap coding scheme. The recent work of [18] provides a construction of iO from well-studied hardness assumptions, and thus gives a conservative and explicit candidate realization. We provide several arguments in favor of our conjecture (see Sect. 7 for details regarding all the points below):

– First, we stress that VBB obfuscation for *evasive* circuit families is not known to be subject to any impossibility results, under any hardness assumptions, even wildly speculative ones. This is because the notion of evasiveness that we consider is *statistical* in the following sense: even a computationally unbounded Eve, that can make any polynomially bounded number of queries to our oracle, cannot find an input z to the oracle f such that $f(z) = 1$. This property rules out all known techniques for proving impossibility of obfuscation that we are aware of (c.f. [4, 15]). But in fact, our situation is even further away from impossibility results because we obfuscate simple distributions of evasive functions that generalize random fuzzy point functions and only need to leak simple auxiliary information about the obfuscated function.

- Furthermore, in fact, the work of [2] gives a construction of VBB obfuscation for evasive circuits from multilinear maps, which is designed to be immune to all known attacks on multilinear map candidates, and has never been successfully attacked.
- Finally, indistinguishability obfuscation is a "best-possible obfuscation" [17], and therefore, roughly speaking, if *any* way exists to securely realize the ideal oracle in our construction to achieve wiretap coding, then using iO must also yield secure wiretap coding.

Optimal-Rate Wiretap Coding. We stress that the problem of achieving asymptotically optimal *rate* follows almost immediately from our solution to the feasibility question above. This is because the feasibility solution can be used to transmit a secret key, and then the encrypted message can be transmitted using any reliable coding scheme to Bob. The security of encryption will ensure that even if Eve learns the ciphertext, because she is guaranteed not to learn the encryption key due to our solution to the feasibility problem above, the (computationally bounded) Eve cannot learn anything about the message. Using standard Rate 1 symmetric key encryption, therefore, we achieve asymptotic wiretap coding rate equal to the capacity of Bob's channel, regardless of the quality of Eve's channel.

Universal Wiretap Coding. An appealing feature of our solution to the wiretap problem is that it gives a *universal* encoding, meaning that (Enc, Dec) depend only on the main channel ChB and not on the eavesdropper's channel ChE. This is not possible in the information-theoretic regime.

1.2 Related Works

Our work was inspired by the recent work of Agrawal et al. [1], who proposed a similar obfuscation-based approach for establishing a feasibility result for secure *computation* over unidirectional noisy channels. In contrast to our work, the use of ideal obfuscation in [1] applies to more complex functions that are not even "evasive" in the standard sense. We stress that beyond inspiration and a common use of obfuscation, there is no other technical overlap between [1] and our work.

Another closely related line of work studies the notion of fuzzy extractors, introduced by Dodis et al. [11]. A fuzzy extractor can be used to encode a message m in a way that: (1) any message m' which is "close" to m (with respect to some metric) can be used to decode m, and (2) if m has sufficiently high min-entropy, its encoding hides m. The possibility of constructing strong forms of computational fuzzy extractors from strong forms of fuzzy point function obfuscation was discussed by Canetti et al. [7] and Fuller et al. [12]. The wiretap coding problem can be loosely cast as a variant of fuzzy extractors where the metric is induced by the main channel ChB and security should hold with respect to a specific entropic source defined by the eavesdropper's channel ChE. The latter relaxation makes the notion of obfuscation we need qualitatively weaker.

Various extensions to the wiretap setting have been studied in the information theoretic setting, and we discuss a very limited subset here that relate most closely to our work. Further generalizations were made by Liang et al.'s [21] introduction of the compound wiretap channel, in which there are finitely many honest receiver and finitely many eavesdroppers, modeling a transmitter's uncertainty about the receiver's channel and the eavesdropper's channel. The upper and lower bounds on secrecy capacity of the compound wiretap channel suggest the impossibility of positive rate universal encodings. Maurer [22] showed that a public channel and *interaction* between the transmitter and honest receiver circumvent the necessity of ChE being not less noisy than ChB for security. We stress that the focus of our paper is the non-interactive case, without any feedback channels. Nair [23] studied information-theoretic relationships between BSC and BEC channels.

Bellare et al. [5] introduced stronger security notions for wiretap coding than the notions that existed within the information theoretic community. In particular, they introduced an information theoretic notion of semantic security, which we also achieve in our work. They also provided an efficient information-theoretic encoding and decoding scheme for many channels that achieves correctness, semantic security, and rate achieving the Csiszár-Korner bound. Previously, most works on wiretap coding had only proven the existence of wiretap encoding and decoding schemes, and not provided explicit constructions.

Finally, the wiretap problem we study is also related to other fuzzy cryptographic primitives, including fuzzy vaults [19] and fuzzy commitments [20]. However, our work is technically incomparable because they use different definitions of noise and study security in different regimes. In both cases, the achieved parameters are not optimal (certainly not in a computational setting), whereas our construction achieves the best possible parameters.

2   Technical Overview

In the wiretap setting, we consider two discrete memoryless channels (DMCs): ChB : $\mathcal{X} \to \mathcal{Y}$ from Alice to the intended receiver Bob, and ChE : $\mathcal{X} \to \mathcal{Z}$ from Alice to an eavesdropper Eve. Alice's goal is to transmit an encoding of a message $m \in \mathcal{M} = \{0,1\}$ across both channels so that Bob can decode m with high probability and Eve learns negligible information about m. Our goal is to build an encoder and a decoder that satisfies these requirements.

Definition 1 (Discrete Memoryless Channel (DMC)). *We define a discrete memoryless channel (DMC)* ChW : $\mathcal{X} \to \mathcal{Y}$ *to be a randomized function from input alphabet* $\mathcal{X}$ *to output alphabet* $\mathcal{Y}$.
We associate ChW *with its stochastic matrix* $P_W = [p_W(y|x)]_{x \in \mathcal{X}, y \in \mathcal{Y}}$.

Warmup: The $\mathsf{BSC}_{0.1}$-$\mathsf{BEC}_{0.3}$ *Wiretap Setting.* We first consider a simple example. Consider a wiretap setting in which Alice has a $\mathsf{BSC}_{0.1}$ between her and Bob and a $\mathsf{BEC}_{0.3}$ between her and Eve. Alice wishes to send $m \in \{0,1\}$ to Bob, but not to Eve. First observe that on a uniform random input distribution, Eve's information about the input is greater than Bob's information. Indeed, Eve's $\mathsf{BEC}_{0.3}$ channel has greater capacity than Bob's $\mathsf{BSC}_{0.1}$ channel. In fact, it can be proven [10,23] that in the information theoretic setting with these channel parameters, then there does not exist any encoding scheme that Alice can use to encode her message so that Bob can decode with high probability but Eve cannot.

Acknowledging this obstacle, how can we favor Bob's decoding probability and disadvantage Eve in the computational setting? A simple observation is that on a uniform random input $r \in \{0,1\}^n$ to the channels, then Bob's output distribution is different from Eve's output distribution. Indeed, for large enough n, Bob's $BSC_{0.1}$'s output r_B should contain approximately 10% bit flips relative to r, whereas Eve's $BEC_{0.3}$ output r_E should contain approximately 30% erasures.

Now, suppose Bob and Eve both had access to an oracle that outputs m on binary inputs containing approximately 10% bit flips relative to r and outputs $\perp$ on all other inputs. Then, Bob can decode m by simply sending his received output r_B to the oracle. However, in order to learn m, Eve must be able to guess a $\widehat{r}_B$ that has 10% bit flips relative to r. It is simple to observe that Eve's best strategy for guessing such an $\widehat{r}_B$ is to generate it from her channel output r_E by replacing each erasure in r_E with a uniformly random bit. But observe that with high probability this $\widehat{r}_B$ will contain roughly 15% bit flips relatives to r. Thus, with high probability, Eve cannot generate a $\widehat{r}_B$ with only 10% bit flips, so she cannot learn m.

This motivates our use of the ideal obfuscation model in which Alice, in addition to specifying a string r to send across both channels can also specify an oracle f which is perfectly transmitted to Bob and Eve who get bounded access to the oracle. In this model, we can achieve secure wiretap coding schemes. To encode $m \in \{0,1\}$, Alice picks a random string r that will be sent across both channels and specifies the oracle mentioned above which is perfectly transmitted to Bob and Eve. By the above argument, this encoding satisfies both correctness and security.

Handling all Non-degraded Channels. Now, consider the case where Bob's channel ChB $: \mathcal{X} \to \mathcal{Y}$ and Eve's channel ChE $: \mathcal{X} \to \mathcal{Z}$ are arbitrary channels with the same input domain $\mathcal{X}$ with the sole restriction that ChB is not a degradation of ChE. We first build intuition about channel degradation.

Definition 2 (Channel Degradation). *We say that channel* ChB *is a degradation of channel* ChE *if there exists a channel* ChS *such that*

$$\mathsf{ChB} = \mathsf{ChS} \circ \mathsf{ChE}$$

where $\circ$ denotes channel concatenation, that is $(\mathsf{ChS} \circ \mathsf{ChE})(x) = \mathsf{ChS}(\mathsf{ChE}(x))$.

Observe that if ChB is a degradation of ChE, then secure wiretap coding schemes are impossible even in the computational setting since then there exists a ChS such that ChB = ChS ∘ ChE, which means Eve can simulate Bob's output by running her channel output through ChS and thus learn as much information as Bob learns.

On the other hand, if ChB is not a degradation of ChE, then this means that for every channel ChS, there exists an $x^* \in \mathcal{X}$ and $y^* \in \mathcal{Y}$ such that

$$|p_B(y^* \mid x^*) - p_{E \cdot S}(y^* \mid x^*)| > 0$$

where $p_B(y^* \mid x^*) = \Pr[\mathsf{ChB}(x^*) = y^*]$ and $p_{E \cdot S}(y^* \mid x^*) = \Pr[\mathsf{ChS}(\mathsf{ChE}(x^*)) = y^*]$. In fact, by using properties of continuity and compactness, we can prove that there is a constant $d > 0$ such that for every ChS, there exists an $x^* \in \mathcal{X}$ and $y^* \in \mathcal{Y}$ such that

$$|p_B(y^* \mid x^*) - p_{E \cdot S}(y^* \mid x^*)| \geq d$$

Now, define the following notation.

Definition 3. *Let $\mathcal{X}$ and $\mathcal{Y}$ be any two discrete finite sets and let $n \in \mathbb{N}$. For $r \in \mathcal{X}^n$ and $s \in \mathcal{Y}^n$ and for any $x \in \mathcal{X}$ and $y \in \mathcal{Y}$, we define the fraction of x's in r that are y's in s to be*

$$\mathrm{RATIO}_{x \to y}(r, s) = \frac{|\{i \in [n] : r_i = x, s_i = y\}|}{|\{i \in [n] : r_i = x\}|}.$$

If $|i \in [n] : r_i = x| = 0$, then we define $\mathrm{RATIO}_{x \to y}(r, s) = 0$.

Fix any $\mathsf{ChS} : \mathcal{Z} \to \mathcal{Y}$ and let x^* and y^* be defined as above. Consider sending a uniform random string $r \in \mathcal{X}^n$ through ChB and $\mathsf{ChS} \circ \mathsf{ChE}$. By a Chernoff bound, we expect that with high probability, $\mathrm{RATIO}_{x^* \to y^*}(r, \mathsf{ChB}(r))$ should be close to $p_B(y^* \mid x^*)$ and $\mathrm{RATIO}_{x^* \to y^*}(r, \mathsf{ChS}(\mathsf{ChE}(r)))$ should be close to $p_{E \cdot S}(y^* \mid x^*)$. But since $p_{E \cdot S}(y^* \mid x^*)$ and $p_B(y^* \mid x^*)$ differ by a constant, we expect $\mathrm{RATIO}_{x^* \to y^*}(r, \mathsf{ChS}(\mathsf{ChE}(r)))$ to differ by a constant from $p_B(y^* \mid x^*)$ with high probability.

Thus, $\mathrm{RATIO}_{x^* \to y^*}$ forms a distinguisher between ChB and $\mathsf{ChS} \circ \mathsf{ChE}$. Therefore, we can define the following function which outputs m with high probability on an input sampled from $\mathsf{ChB}(r)$ and outputs m with negligible probability on an input sampled from $\mathsf{ChS}(\mathsf{ChE}(r))$ for any channel ChS.[2]

$h_{m,r,\mathsf{ChB},n}(r_B)$:

If for all $x \in \mathcal{X}$ and $y \in \mathcal{Y}$, $|\mathrm{RATIO}_{x \to y}(r, r_B) - p_B(y \mid x)| \leq n^{-\frac{1}{3}}$, output m.

Else, output $\perp$.

In fact, since we are considering the ratios of all pairs $(x, y) \in \mathcal{X} \times \mathcal{Y}$, the same observation holds for the following function that considers only one-sided bounds.

---

[2] A slight caveat is that this holds only when r contains sufficiently many of each $x \in \mathcal{X}$, but this occurs with overwhelming probability over the choice of r.

$f_{m,r,\mathsf{ChB},n}(r_B)$:

  If for all $x \in \mathcal{X}$ and $y \in \mathcal{Y}$, $\mathrm{RATIO}_{x \to y}(r, r_B) \leq p_B(y \mid x) + n^{-\frac{1}{3}}$, output m.
  Else, output $\perp$.

Construction Overview. We now describe our coding scheme for wiretap channel $(\mathsf{ChB}, \mathsf{ChE})$. Our encoder $\mathsf{Enc}_{\mathsf{ChB}}$ takes a security parameter 1^λ and a message $m \in \mathcal{M}$ and outputs a description of a circuit computing some function f and a string $r \in \mathcal{X}^n$. Our decoder $\mathsf{Dec}^{(\cdot)}$ takes as input a security parameter 1^λ and a string $r_B \in \mathcal{Y}^n$ and outputs some message in $\mathcal{M}$. The string r is sent across both channels, and both Bob and Eve obtain bounded oracle access to f.

$\mathsf{Enc}_{\mathsf{ChB}}(1^\lambda, m)$:

1. Let $n = \lambda$
2. Sample $r \leftarrow \mathcal{X}^n$.
3. Define $f_{m,r,\mathsf{ChB},n} : \mathcal{Y}^n \to \{\mathcal{M}, \perp\}$ where

   $f_{m,r,\mathsf{ChB},n}(r_B)$:
     If for all $x \in \mathcal{X}$ and $y \in \mathcal{Y}$, $\mathrm{RATIO}_{x \to y}(r, r_B) \leq p_B(y \mid x) + n^{-\frac{1}{3}}$, output m.
     Here, $p_B(y \mid x) = \Pr[\mathsf{ChB}(x) = y]$.
     Else, output $\perp$.

4. Output $(f_{m,r,\mathsf{ChB},n}, r)$.

$\mathsf{Dec}^f_{\mathsf{ChB}}(1^\lambda, r_B)$:

1. Output $f(r_B)$.

For convenience, we define R to be a uniform random input over $\mathcal{X}^n$, $R_E = \mathsf{ChE}(R)$, and $R_B = \mathsf{ChB}(R)$.

Correctness holds since Bob can decode with high probability since $f_{m,r,\mathsf{ChB},n}$ on $\mathsf{ChB}(r)$ will output m with high probability.

Security Overview. Now consider security. Intuitively, since r is independent of the message bit b, then Eve should only be able to learn b if she can generate a guess $\widehat{r}_B$ such that $f_{b,r,\mathsf{ChB},n}(\widehat{r}_B) = b$. Consider a strategy g that given input $r_E \leftarrow \mathsf{ChE}(r)$ from Eve's channel seeks to produce an output $\widehat{r}_B$ that maximizes the probability that $f_{b,r,\mathsf{ChB},n}(\widehat{r}_B) = f_{b,r,\mathsf{ChB},n}(g(r_E)) = b$. We say that g wins if this occurs and b is output.

If strategy g is to send Eve's channel output r_E through some discrete memoryless channel ChS (i.e. $g(r_E) = \mathsf{ChS}(r_E)$), then by our previous discussion on non-degraded channels, there exists some $x^* \in \mathcal{X}$ and $y^* \in \mathcal{Y}$ such that with high probability, $\text{RATIO}_{x^* \to y^*}(r, g(\mathsf{ChE}(r)))$ differs from $p_B(y^* \mid x^*)$ by at least a constant. Thus, such a g would only win with negligible probability.

However, Eve can choose any arbitrary strategy g. Nevertheless, we can still prove that any strategy g has only a negligible chance of winning. To do so, we show through a series of hybrids that any strategy g is only polynomially better than a strategy EVE_3, where EVE_3's strategy is to apply a DMC independently to each symbol of r_E. Then, we can use the non-degraded condition to show that EVE_3's probability of success on a single query to the oracle is negligible, and thus that any g's probability of success on a single query to the oracle is negligible. This hybrid argument is the main technical argument in our work, and it is summarized below.

The Hybrid Argument: Proving g has a Negligible Chance of Winning. We first observe that an arbitrary strategy g cannot perform better than an optimal strategy g^* defined as follows:

Definition 4. *For any m, we say that a strategy $g^* : \mathcal{Z}^n \to \mathcal{Y}^n$ for guessing $\widehat{r}_B$ is optimal if*

$$g^* = \arg\max_g \left(\Pr_{R, \mathsf{ChE}}[f_{m, R, \mathsf{ChB}, n}(g(R_E)) = m] \right).$$

Now, consider any deterministic optimal strategy. (Observe that there always exists an optimal g^* that is deterministic since g^* can arbitrarily break ties in the maximum).

Our first step is to simplify our function g^* by a symmetrization argument. We observe that our definition of evaluation function $f_{m, r, \mathsf{ChB}, n}$ on input $\widehat{r}_B$ considers only the mapping ratios $\text{RATIO}_{x \to y}(r, \widehat{r}_B)$ for all $x \in \mathcal{X}, y \in \mathcal{Y}$ from r to $\widehat{r}_B$. An immediate consequence of this recollection is that the probability of success for Eve when the input string is r and the guessed string is $\widehat{r}_B = g^*(r_E)$ is permutation-invariant. That is, for every permutation $\pi \in S_n$, the probability of succeeding on $\widehat{r}_B$ when the input string is r is equivalent to the probability of succeeding on $\pi(\widehat{r}_B)$ when the input string is $\pi(r)$ because

$$\text{RATIO}_{x \to y}(r, \widehat{r}_B) = \text{RATIO}_{x \to y}(\pi(r), \pi(\widehat{r}_B)).$$

Thus, since r is uniformly random, then we have $\Pr[R = \pi(r)] = \Pr[R = r]$, so morally an optimal g^*'s success probability on r_E and $\pi(r_E)$ should be the same. This is formally seen by a symmetrization argument regarding the equivalence relation we define below.

Definition 5. *For $r_E \in \mathcal{Z}^n$, we define the weight of r_E as*

$$\mathsf{wt}(r_E) = (N_{z_1}(r_E), \ldots, N_{z_{|\mathcal{Z}|}}(r_E))$$

where $\mathcal{Z} = \{z_1, \ldots, z_{|\mathcal{Z}|}\}$ and $N_{z_i}(r_E) = |i \in [n] \mid r_{Ei} = z_i|$. We define an equivalence relation EQWT on $\mathcal{Z}^n \times \mathcal{Z}^n$ by

$$\begin{aligned} \text{EQWT} &= \{(r_E, r_E') \in \mathcal{Z}^n \times \mathcal{Z}^n \mid \mathsf{wt}(r_E) = \mathsf{wt}(r_E')\} \\ &= \{(r_E, r_E') \in \mathcal{Z}^n \times \mathcal{Z}^n \mid \exists \pi \in S_n, \, r_E = \pi(r_E')\}. \end{aligned}$$

Let $r_{Ew,0}$ denote the lexicographically first vector in the equivalence class $\{r_E \in \mathcal{Z}^n \mid \mathrm{wt}(r_E) = w\}$.

Then since g^* performs equally well on all permutations of r_E, we can create a new optimal deterministic strategy EVE_0 which behaves in a structured manner on all strings r_E from the same equivalence class. Importantly, EVE_0 has the nice property that for any permutation π, then $\pi(\mathrm{EVE}_0(r_E)) = \mathrm{EVE}_0(\pi(r_E))$.

$\mathrm{EVE}_0(r_E)$:
Given optimal deterministic strategy g^*.

1. Let $w = \mathrm{wt}(r_E)$. Let $r_{Ew,0}$ be the lexicographically first vector in $\mathcal{Z}^n$ of weight w.
2. Let permutation $\sigma \in S_n$ be such that $\sigma(r_{Ew,0}) = r_E$.
3. Output $\widehat{r}_B = \sigma(g^*(\sigma^{-1}(r_E))) = \sigma(g^*(r_{Ew,0}))$.

Now, consider a probabilistic EVE_1 that on input $r_E \in \mathcal{Z}^n$ deviates slightly from the deterministic EVE_0. For any $z \in \mathcal{Z}$, $y \in \mathcal{Y}$, and input $r_E \in \mathcal{Z}^n$, observe that EVE_0 will map some deterministically chosen subset of size $k_{z,y}$ of the y's in r_E to be a z in $\widehat{r}_B$. Instead, we will have EVE_1 map a random subset of size $k_{z,y}$ of the y's in r_E to be a z in $\widehat{r}_B$. By a similar symmetrization argument and the construction of EVE_0, then EVE_1's probability of success is equal to that of EVE_0.

$\mathrm{EVE}_1(r_E)$:

1. For each $y \in \mathcal{Y}$ and $z \in \mathcal{Z}$, compute $k_{z,y} = N_z(r_E) \cdot \mathrm{RATIO}_{z \to y}(r_E, \mathrm{EVE}_0(r_E))$.
2. Start with $S = [n]$.
   For each $y \in \mathcal{Y}$ and $z \in \mathcal{Z}$
   (a) Pick a random set $S_{z,y} \subset S \cap \{i \in [n] \mid r_{E,i} = z\}$ such that $|S_{z,y}| = k_{z,y}$.
   (b) Set $\widehat{r}_{B,i} = y$ for all $i \in S_{z,y}$.
   (c) Set $S = S \backslash S_{z,y}$.
3. Output $\widehat{r}_B$.

Now, we relax the necessity of requiring that exactly $k_{z,y}$ of the z's in r_E map to y's in $\widehat{r}_B$. This relaxation is done by defining a set of stochastic matrices that model a DMC. In particular, we use the probabilistic strategy of EVE_1 to define a set of DMCs Ch_{r_E} where $p_{r_E}(z \mid y) = \mathrm{RATIO}_{z \to y}(r_E, \mathrm{EVE}_1(r_E))$ (which is also equal to $\mathrm{RATIO}_{z \to y}(r_{Ew,0}, \mathrm{EVE}_0(r_{Ew,0}))$) by definition of EVE_1). We then define a new strategy EVE_2 which on input r_E applies the corresponding channel Ch_{r_E} on each symbol of r_E to get $\widehat{r}_B$. Then EVE_2 acts identically to EVE_1 whenever each of the ratios $\mathrm{RATIO}_{z \to y}(r_E, \mathrm{EVE}_2(r_E))$ hit their expected value. We prove that this happens with probability at least $\frac{1}{\mathrm{poly}(n)}$, so therefore, EVE_2 wins at least inverse polynomially as often as EVE_1.

$\text{EVE}_2(r_E)$:

1. Define a channel Ch_{r_E} from $\mathcal{Z}$ to $\mathcal{Y}$ by stochastic matrix

$$P_{r_E} = [p_{r_E}(y \mid z)]_{z \in \mathcal{Z}, y \in \mathcal{Y}} = [\text{RATIO}_{z \to y}(r_E, \text{EVE}_0(r_E))]_{z \in \mathcal{Z}, y \in \mathcal{Y}}$$

2. For $i \in [n]$, set $\widehat{r}_{Bi} = \mathsf{Ch}_{r_E}(r_{Ei})$.
3. Output $\widehat{r}_B$.

Although EVE_2's strategy is to apply a channel Ch_{r_E} to each symbol of her input r_E, the choice of channel she applies is dependent on which r_E she received. However, it turns out that there are only polynomially many possible channels that EVE_2 may construct. In particular, the set of channels that EVE_2 can construct is in bijective correspondence with the equivalence classes EQWT. To see this, observe that for any permutation π, $\mathsf{Ch}_{r_E} = \mathsf{Ch}_{\pi(r_E)}$ because $\text{EVE}_0(\pi(r_E)) = \pi(\text{EVE}_0(r_E))$. Thus, the total number of possible channels that EVE_2 may apply to r_E is bounded by the number of equivalence classes of EQWT, which is polynomial in size. We define Ch_w to be equal to Ch_{r_E} for any r_E of weight w.

Thus, instead of having EVE_2 choose a channel based on r_E's weight, we define a new strategy that randomly selects the channel before seeing r_E. In particular, we construct an EVE_3 which in addition to getting input r_E also gets an independently chosen random input w that defines which channel Ch_w that EVE_3 should apply to r_E.

$\text{EVE}_3(w, r_E)$:

1. Let $r_{Ew,0} \in \mathcal{Z}^n$ be the lexicographically first vector in $\mathcal{Z}^n$ of weight w.
2. Define a channel Ch_w from $\mathcal{Z}$ to $\mathcal{Y}$ by stochastic matrix

$$P_w = [p_w(y \mid z)]_{z \in \mathcal{Z}, y \in \mathcal{Y}} = [\text{RATIO}_{z \to y}(r_{Ew,0}, \text{EVE}_0(r_{Ew,0}))]_{z \in \mathcal{Z}, y \in \mathcal{Y}}$$

3. For $i \in [n]$, set $\widehat{r}_{Bi} = \mathsf{Ch}_w(r_{Ei})$.
4. Output $\widehat{r}_B$.

Now, if the randomly chosen w equals $\mathsf{wt}(r_E)$, then EVE_3 acts identically to EVE_2. But since there are only polynomially many weight vectors, an independently chosen random w equals $\mathsf{wt}(r_E)$ with probability $\frac{1}{\text{poly}(n)}$. Thus, the probability that EVE_3 succeeds given a random w is only polynomially worse than the probability that EVE_2 succeeds.

However, for any weight w, it is now the case that EVE_3 applies an input-independent channel to each symbol of r_E. Thus, we can now apply the non-degraded condition to prove that EVE_3's probability of success is negligible for any input weight w. This then implies that any arbitrary strategy g has a negligible probability of winning.

3   Preliminaries

Throughout, we will use λ to denote a security parameter.

Notation

- We say that a function $f(\lambda)$ is negligible in λ if $f(\lambda) = \lambda^{-\omega(1)}$, and we denote it by $f(\lambda) = \mathsf{negl}(\lambda)$.
- We say that a function $g(\lambda)$ is polynomial in λ if $g(\lambda) = p(\lambda)$ for some fixed polynomial p, and we denote it by $g(\lambda) = \mathsf{poly}(\lambda)$.
- For $n \in \mathbb{N}$, we use $[n]$ to denote $\{1, \ldots, n\}$.
- If R is a random variable, then $r \leftarrow R$ denotes sampling r from R. If T is a set, then $i \leftarrow T$ denotes sampling i uniformly at random from T.
- Let S_n denote the symmetric group on n letters.

Definition 6 (Max Norm of a Matrix). *Let A by any $n \times m$ matrix. We define the max norm to be the maximal magnitude of any entry and denote it with*

$$\|A\|_{\max} = \max_{i,j} |A_{i,j}|.$$

Remark 1. As a reminder, computationally bounded adversaries are described as non-uniform polynomial-time throughout the paper but can be equivalently given as a family of polynomial-size circuits.

Definition 7 (Discrete Memoryless Channel (DMC)). *We define a discrete memoryless channel (DMC) $\mathsf{ChW} : \mathcal{X} \to \mathcal{Y}$ to be a randomized function from input alphabet $\mathcal{X}$ to output alphabet $\mathcal{Y}$.*
We associate ChW with its stochastic matrix

$$P_W = [p_W(y|x)]_{x \in \mathcal{X}, y \in \mathcal{Y}}$$

For $x \in \mathcal{X}$, we use $\mathsf{ChW}(x)$ to denote a random variable over $\mathcal{Y}$ such that for $y \in \mathcal{Y}$,

$$\Pr[\mathsf{ChW}(x) = y] = p_W(y|x)$$

For $n \in \mathbb{N}$ and $r = (r_1, \ldots, r_n) \in \mathcal{X}^n$, we define

$$\mathsf{ChW}(r) = \mathsf{ChW}(r_1) \ldots \mathsf{ChW}(r_n)$$

Whenever we discuss channels in the context of efficient algorithms, we assume all channels have finite description size with constant alphabet size and rational probabilities.

Notation. If ChE is a channel, we may use $\Pr_{\mathsf{ChE}}$ to denote the probability over the randomness of ChE. Similarly, if f is a randomized function, we may use $\Pr_f$ to denote the probability over the randomness of f.

Less Noisy and Channel Degradation

Definition 8 (Less Noisy, [10]). *Channel* ChE *is less noisy than channel* ChB *if for every Markov chain* $V \to X \to YZ$ *such that* $p_{Y|X}(y|x)$ *corresponds to* ChB *and* $p_{Z|X}(z|x)$ *correspond to* ChE *then*

$$I(V;Z) \geq I(V;Y).$$

Definition 9 (Channel Degradation, [9]). *We say that channel* ChB *is a degradation of channel* ChE *if there exists a channel* ChS *such that*

$$\text{ChB} = \text{ChS} \circ \text{ChE}$$

where $\circ$ *denotes channel concatenation, that is* $(\text{ChS} \circ \text{ChE})(x) = \text{ChS}(\text{ChE}(x))$.

Definition 10 (Channel Degradation Equivalent Definition). *Equivalently, we say that channel* ChB $: \mathcal{X} \to \mathcal{Y}$ *is a degradation of channel* ChE $: \mathcal{X} \to \mathcal{Z}$ *if there exists a stochastic matrix* $P_S = [p_S(y \mid z)]_{z \in \mathcal{Z}, y \in \mathcal{Y}}$ *such that*

$$P_B = P_E \cdot P_S$$

where $P_B = [p_B(y \mid x)]_{x \in \mathcal{X}, y \in \mathcal{Y}}$ *is the stochastic matrix of* ChB *and* $P_E = [p_E(z \mid x)]_{x \in \mathcal{X}, z \in \mathcal{Z}}$ *is the stochastic matrix of* ChE.

Remark 2 (Notions of Degradation). The notion of degradation defined above is sometimes referred to as *stochastic* degradation. There is also a notion of *physical* degradation. (See [25] for further discussion.) However, the difference between these notions is irrelevant in the current context.

Provided in the full version, we obtain the following Lemma:

Lemma 1. *If channel* ChB *is not a degradation of channel* ChE, *then there exists a constant* $d > 0$ *such that for all stochastic matrices* $P_S = [p_S(y \mid z)]_{z \in \mathcal{Z}, y \in \mathcal{Y}}$,

$$\|P_B - P_E \cdot P_S\|_{\max} \geq d$$

where $P_B = [p_B(y \mid x)]_{x \in \mathcal{X}, y \in \mathcal{Y}}$ *is the stochastic matrix of* ChB *and* $P_E = [p_E(z \mid x)]_{x \in \mathcal{X}, z \in \mathcal{Z}}$ *is the stochastic matrix of* ChE.

Proof. We defer the proof to the full version.

4   Wiretap Channels

A wiretap channel [10, 26] is defined by two discrete memoryless channels (ChB, ChE) with the same input domain $\mathcal{X}$ where ChB $: \mathcal{X} \to \mathcal{Y}$ is the main channel and ChE $: \mathcal{X} \to \mathcal{Z}$ is the eavesdropper channel. We characterize ChB by its stochastic matrix $P_B = [p_B(y \mid x)]_{x \in \mathcal{X}, y \in \mathcal{Y}}$ and ChE by its stochastic matrix $P_E = [p_E(z \mid x)]_{x \in \mathcal{X}, z \in \mathcal{Z}}$. Throughout, we will use $\mathcal{X}, \mathcal{Y}, \mathcal{Z}$ to denote respectively the input alphabet of ChB and ChE, the output alphabet of ChB, and the output alphabet of ChE. We use $\mathcal{M}$ to denote the message space.

Definition 11 (Wiretap Coding Scheme: Syntax). *A wiretap coding scheme Π for wiretap channel* $(\mathsf{ChB}, \mathsf{ChE})$ *and message space $\mathcal{M}$ is a pair of algorithms* $(\mathsf{Enc}, \mathsf{Dec})$*. Enc is a randomized encoding algorithm that takes as input a security parameter 1^λ, a message $m \in \mathcal{M}$, and outputs a finite length encoding in $\mathcal{X}^n$ where $n = n(\lambda)$. Dec is a deterministic decoding algorithm that takes as input a security parameter 1^λ, and a string from $\mathcal{Y}^n$ and outputs a message in $\mathcal{M}$.*

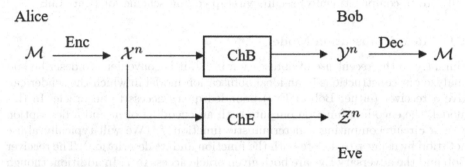

A wiretap coding scheme satisfies correctness if Bob can decode the output of ChB on an encoding of a message. Security holds if Eve when given the output of ChE on the encoding of the message cannot learn the message. Similarly to [5][3], we use the standard notion of semantic security [16]. For simplicity, we only consider the case when $\mathcal{M} = \{0, 1\}$. However, we can easily generalize our definition to consider larger families of message spaces. (See the full version).

Definition 12 (Statistically Secure Wiretap Coding Scheme). *A wiretap coding scheme $\Pi = (\mathsf{Enc}, \mathsf{Dec})$ is a statistically secure wiretap coding scheme for wiretap channel $(\mathsf{ChB}, \mathsf{ChE})$ and message space $\mathcal{M} = \{0, 1\}$ if there exist negligible functions $\epsilon(\lambda), \mu(\lambda)$ such that*

- *Correctness: For all messages $m \in \{0, 1\}$,*

$$\Pr[\mathsf{Dec}(1^\lambda, \mathsf{ChB}(\mathsf{Enc}(1^\lambda, m))) = m] \geq 1 - \epsilon(\lambda)$$

- *Security: For all adversaries $\mathcal{A}$,*

$$\Pr[\mathcal{A}(1^\lambda, \mathsf{ChE}(\mathsf{Enc}(1^\lambda, b))) = b] \leq \frac{1}{2} + \mu(\lambda)$$

where b is uniformly distributed over $\{0, 1\}$.

We may similarly refer to a finite scheme Π_0 (with a fixed λ) as being ϵ_0-correct and μ_0-secure.

---

[3] Our security definition corresponds to requiring the distinguishing advantage Adv^{ds} of [5] to be negligible. [5] define a separate notion for semantic security, but prove that the two definitions are equivalent.

Definition 13 (Computationally Secure Wiretap Coding Scheme).
$\Pi = (\text{Enc}, \text{Dec})$ *is a computationally secure wiretap coding scheme if* Enc *and* Dec *are PPT algorithms, and if it satisfies the above definition except that we only require security against non-uniform polynomial-time adversaries* $\mathcal{A}$.

Notation. We say that a wiretap channel (ChB, ChE) admits a statistically (resp. computationally) secure wiretap coding scheme if there exists a statistically (resp. computationally) secure wiretap coding scheme for (ChB, ChE).

4.1   Ideal Obfuscation Model

Similarly to the recent use of obfuscation in [1], it is convenient to describe and analyze our constructions in an ideal obfuscation model in which the sender can give a receiver (either Bob or Eve) bounded query access to an oracle. In this model, the encoding function outputs both an encoding of m and a description $\hat{f}$ of a circuit computing a deterministic function f. (We will typically abuse notation by using f to denote both the function and its description). The receiver Bob and the adversary Eve are both given oracle access to f. In addition, though we require Eve to only make polynomially many queries to the oracle f, we allow Eve to be otherwise unbounded by default (see Remark 3 below for a relaxed definition variant). We will later consider the question of instantiating the ideal obfuscation primitive in the plain model under concrete cryptographic assumptions (see Sect. 7).

Definition 14 (Wiretap Coding Scheme in the Ideal Obfuscation Model: Syntax). *A wiretap coding scheme Π for wiretap channel (ChB, ChE) and message space $\mathcal{M}$ in the ideal obfuscation model is a pair of algorithms $(\text{Enc}, \text{Dec}^{(\cdot)})$.* Enc *is a randomized encoding algorithm that takes as input a security parameter 1^λ and a message $m \in \mathcal{M}$, and outputs a finite length encoding in $\mathcal{X}^n$ where $n = n(\lambda)$ and a description $\hat{f}$ of a circuit computing some deterministic function f.* $\text{Dec}^{(\cdot)}$ *is a deterministic decoding algorithm with polynomially bounded access to an oracle. It takes as input a security parameter 1^λ, a string from $\mathcal{Y}^n$, and outputs a message in $\mathcal{M}$.*

Definition 15 (Bounded Query Secure Wiretap Coding Scheme in the Ideal Obfuscation Model). *A wiretap coding scheme $\Pi = (\text{Enc}, \text{Dec}^{(\cdot)})$ is a bounded query secure wiretap coding scheme in the ideal obfuscation model for wiretap channel (ChB, ChE) and message space $\mathcal{M} = \{0, 1\}$ if* Enc *and* $\text{Dec}^{(\cdot)}$ *are PPT algorithms which satisfy*

- **Correctness:** *For all messages $m \in \{0, 1\}$,*
$$\Pr[\text{Dec}^f(1^\lambda, \text{ChB}(c)) = m \mid (f, c) \leftarrow \text{Enc}(1^\lambda, m)] \geq 1 - \text{negl}(\lambda)$$

- **Security:** *For every polynomial query bound $q(\lambda)$ and (computationally unbounded) adversary $\mathcal{A}^{(\cdot)}$ that makes at most $q(\lambda)$ queries to its oracle f,*

$$\Pr[\mathcal{A}^{f_b}(1^\lambda, \text{ChE}(c_b)) = b \mid (f_b, c_b) \leftarrow \text{Enc}(1^\lambda, b)] \leq \frac{1}{2} + \text{negl}(\lambda)$$

where b is uniformly distributed over $\{0, 1\}$.

We will prove the following characterization of the wiretap feasibility region in the information theoretic setting:

Theorem 3. ChE *is not less noisy than* ChB *if and only if there exists a statistically secure wiretap coding scheme for* (ChB, ChE).[4]

Proof. We defer the proof to the full version.

Remark 3 (Computationally bounded adversaries). Definition 15 only bounds the number of queries made by $\mathcal{A}$ but does not otherwise bound its computational complexity. This makes our main feasibility results stronger. One may also consider a relaxed variant of the definition in which $\mathcal{A}$ is computationally bounded, as in Definition 13.

5   Constructing Bounded Query Secure Wiretap Coding Schemes in the Ideal Obfuscation Model

We consider the setting of a (ChB, ChE) wiretap channel where the main channel ChB : $\mathcal{X} \to \mathcal{Y}$ is not a degradation of the eavesdropping channel ChE : $\mathcal{X} \to \mathcal{Z}$. For the entirety of this section, we will characterize ChB by its stochastic matrix $P_B = [p_B(y \mid x)]_{x \in \mathcal{X}, y \in \mathcal{Y}}$ and channel ChE by its stochastic matrix $P_E = [p_E(z \mid x)]_{x \in \mathcal{X}, z \in \mathcal{Z}}$. We let $\mathcal{M} = \{0, 1\}$.

Let λ be a security parameter, and let $n = \lambda$. Our encoding of a message $m \in \mathcal{M}$ will specify a codeword and an oracle. The codeword will be a random string $r \in \mathcal{X}^n$ which will be sent across the two channels. We define R to be a uniform random variable over $\mathcal{X}^n$, $R_B := \mathsf{ChB}(R)$, and $R_E := \mathsf{ChE}(R)$. The oracle, which is transmitted perfectly to both parties, will output the message m if it receives an input which is "typical" for R_B conditioned on $R = r$ (notationally $R_{B|R=r}$) and will output $\bot$ otherwise. We will define typicality in terms of the expected number of x's in r that should turn into y's in $R_{B|R=r}$ for each pair $(x, y) \in \mathcal{X} \times \mathcal{Y}$ as specified by Bob's channel probability matrix P_B. The receiver Bob should be able to recover m simply by sending his received value of R_B to the oracle. Thus, the decoder will simply output the value of the oracle on its input. Security holds if the eavesdropper Eve cannot create a "typical" channel value for $R_{B|R=r}$ given only $R_{E|R=r}$. To specify this more formally, we first define the following:

Definition 16. *Let* $\mathcal{X}$ *be any discrete finite set and* $n \in \mathbb{N}$. *For any* $r \in \mathcal{X}^n$ *and* $x \in \mathcal{X}$, *we define the number of* x's *in* r *to be*

$$N_x(r) = |\{i \in [n] : r_i = x\}|$$

---

[4] This is also true with respect to statistically secure wiretap coding schemes over larger message spaces (see the full version).

Definition 17. *Let $\mathcal{X}$ and $\mathcal{Y}$ be any two discrete finite sets and $n \in \mathbb{N}$. For $r \in \mathcal{X}^n$ and $s \in \mathcal{Y}^n$ and for any $x \in \mathcal{X}$ and $y \in \mathcal{Y}$, we define the fraction of x's in r that are y's in s to be*

$$\text{RATIO}_{x \to y}(r, s) = \frac{|\{i \in [n] : r_i = x, s_i = y\}|}{N_x(r)}.$$

If $N_x(r) = 0$, then we define $\text{RATIO}_{x \to y}(r, s) = 0$.

We now describe our wiretap encoder-decoder pair $(\text{Enc}_{\mathsf{ChB}}, \text{Dec}_{\mathsf{ChB}})$ for main channel ChB.

$\text{Enc}_{\mathsf{ChB}}(1^\lambda, m)$:

1. Let $n = \lambda$
2. Sample $r \leftarrow \mathcal{X}^n$.
3. Define $f_{m,r,\mathsf{ChB},n} : \mathcal{Y}^n \to \{\mathcal{M}, \bot\}$ where

> $f_{m,r,\mathsf{ChB},n}(r_B)$:
> If for all $x \in \mathcal{X}$ and $y \in \mathcal{Y}$, $\text{RATIO}_{x \to y}(r, r_B) \le p_B(y \mid x) + n^{-\frac{1}{3}}$, output m.
> Else, output $\bot$.

4. Output $(f_{m,r,\mathsf{ChB},n}, r)$.

$\text{Dec}^f_{\mathsf{ChB}}(1^\lambda, r_B)$:

1. Output $f(r_B)$.

We then prove that our coding scheme gives us both correctness and security.

Theorem 4. *If $(\mathsf{ChB}, \mathsf{ChE})$ is a wiretap channel where ChB is not a degradation of ChE, then $(\text{Enc}_{\mathsf{ChB}}, \text{Dec}^{(\cdot)}_{\mathsf{ChB}})$ achieves*

- **Correctness:** *For all messages $m \in \{0, 1\}$,*

$$\Pr[\text{Dec}^{f_{m,r,\mathsf{ChB},n}}_{\mathsf{ChB}}(1^\lambda, \mathsf{ChB}(r)) = m \mid (f_{m,r,\mathsf{ChB},n}, r) \leftarrow \text{Enc}_{\mathsf{ChB}}(1^\lambda, m)] \ge 1 - \text{negl}(\lambda)$$

- **Security:** *For every polynomial query bound $q(\lambda)$ and (computationally unbounded) adversary $\mathcal{A}^{(\cdot)}$ that makes at most $q(\lambda)$ queries to its oracle,*

$$\Pr[\mathcal{A}^{f_{b,r,\mathsf{ChB},n}}(1^\lambda, \mathsf{ChE}(r)) = b \mid (f_{b,r,\mathsf{ChB},n}, r) \leftarrow \text{Enc}_{\mathsf{ChB}}(1^\lambda, b)] \le \frac{1}{2} + \text{negl}(\lambda)$$

where b is uniformly distributed over $\{0, 1\}$.

Proof. Correctness follows by a simple Chernoff bound which we defer to the full version. Security follows by Theorem 7 which are proven below.

Since $\mathsf{Enc}_{\mathsf{ChB}}$ and $\mathsf{Dec}_{\mathsf{ChB}}^{(\cdot)}$ are PPT, we get the following corollary.

Corollary 1. *If* $(\mathsf{ChB}, \mathsf{ChE})$ *is a wiretap channel where* ChB *is not a degradation of* ChE, *then* $(\mathsf{Enc}_{\mathsf{ChB}}, \mathsf{Dec}_{\mathsf{ChB}}^{(\cdot)})$ *is a bounded query secure wiretap coding scheme in the ideal obfuscation model.*

Remark 4. Theorem 4 and Corollary 1 hold even if we modify $f_{m,r,\mathsf{ChB},n}$ to have binary output domain by outputting 0 in place of $\perp$. Correctness still holds since the probability that the decoder using the original function outputs $\perp$ is negligible, so changing $\perp$ to 0 results in at most a negligible change in correctness. For security, observe that by outputting 0 instead of $\perp$, Eve gets strictly less information as she cannot tell whether an observed 0 from the oracle is an indicator of failure to receive the message bit or is the message bit itself.

5.1 Security

Overview. In our security game, the adversary receives $R_E = \mathsf{ChE}(R)$ and oracle access to $f_{b,R,\mathsf{ChB},n}$ for a random $b \in \{0,1\}$ and tries to guess b. Intuitively, since R is independent of b, if for all $b \in \{0,1\}$, an adversary is unable to generate an input $\widehat{r}_B$ such that $f_{b,r,\mathsf{ChB},n}(\widehat{r}_B) \neq \perp$, then the adversary should be unable to learn anything about b. Thus, we will first attempt to show this.

To simplify our proof, we define the following function $h_{r,\mathsf{ChB},n}$ which on input r_B outputs 1 if all of the ratios $\mathrm{RATIO}_{x \to y}(r, r_B)$ are sufficiently close to the channel probabilities $p_B(y \mid x)$ and 0 otherwise.

Definition 18. *Let* $r \in \mathcal{X}^n$ *and* $r_B \in \mathcal{Y}^n$. *Define* $h_{r,\mathsf{ChB},n} : \mathcal{Y}^n \to \{0,1\}$ *as*

> $h_{r,\mathsf{ChB},n}(r_B)$:
>
> If for all $x \in \mathcal{X}$ and $y \in \mathcal{Y}$, $|\mathrm{RATIO}_{x \to y}(r, r_B) - p_B(y \mid x)| \leq |\mathcal{Y}| \cdot n^{-\frac{1}{3}}$,
> output 1.
> Else, output 0.

We will first show that for any arbitrary strategy g that an adversary applies to R_E,

$$\Pr[h_{R,\mathsf{ChB},n}(g(R_E)) = 1] \leq \mathsf{negl}(\lambda).$$

We will then prove that this implies that for any arbitrary strategy g that an adversary applies to R_E,

$$\Pr[f_{m,R,\mathsf{ChB},n}(g(R_E)) \neq \perp] \leq \mathsf{negl}(\lambda).$$

Then we will prove that this implies security.

To prove the first step, we will need to rely on the fact that ChB is not a degradation of ChE. This means that for all channels ChS, then $\mathsf{ChB} \neq \mathsf{ChS} \circ \mathsf{ChE}$. Thus, if Eve's strategy g was to apply a DMC channel ChS to each symbol of R_E, then the distribution of $g(R_E) = \mathsf{ChS}(\mathsf{ChE}(R))$ should differ from the distribution of $\mathsf{ChB}(R)$, and therefore result in $h_{R,\mathsf{ChB},n}(g(R_E)) = 0$ with high probability.

However, Eve may instead choose any arbitrary strategy g. Thus, to prove our result, we will show through a series of hybrids $g, \mathrm{EVE}_0, \mathrm{EVE}_1, \mathrm{EVE}_2, \mathrm{EVE}_3$ that strategy g is only polynomially better that strategy EVE_3, where EVE_3's strategy is to apply a DMC independently to each symbol of R_E. Then, we can use the not-degraded condition to show that EVE_3's probability of success is negligible. We refer further intuition to the Technical Overview.

We will first assume that Eve's arbitrary strategy g is optimal, defined below:

Definition 19. *We say that a strategy* $g^* : \mathcal{Z}^n \to \mathcal{Y}^n$ *for guessing* $\widehat{r}_B$ *is optimal if*

$$g^* = \arg\max_g \left(\Pr_{R,\mathsf{ChE}}[h_{R,\mathsf{ChB},n}(g(R_E)) = 1] \right).$$

Remark 5. By definition, for any optimal strategy g^*,

$$g^*(r_E) = \max_{\widehat{r}_B} \left(\Pr_{R,\mathsf{ChE}}[h_{R,\mathsf{ChB},n}(\widehat{r}_B) = 1 \mid R_E = r_E] \right)$$

Observe that there may be multiple possible optimal strategies g^* which achieve the same maximal probability of success. Furthermore, since g^* may arbitrarily break ties for the maximum, then there always exists an optimal strategy which is deterministic.

We also define a notion of weight.

Definition 20. *For* $r_E \in \mathcal{Z}^n$, *we define the weight of* r_E *as*

$$\mathsf{wt}(r_E) = (N_{z_1}(r_E), \dots, N_{z_{|\mathcal{Z}|}}(r_E))$$

where $\mathcal{Z} = \{z_1, \dots, z_{|\mathcal{Z}|}\}$. *We define an equivalence relation* EQWT *on* $\mathcal{Z}^n \times \mathcal{Z}^n$ *by*

$$\mathrm{EQWT} = \{(r_E, r_E') \in \mathcal{Z}^n \times \mathcal{Z}^n \mid \mathsf{wt}(r_E) = \mathsf{wt}(r_E')\}$$
$$= \{(r_E, r_E') \in \mathcal{Z}^n \times \mathcal{Z}^n \mid \exists \pi \in S_n, \; r_E = \pi(r_E')\}.$$

We define the lexicographically first element in the equivalence class to be the canonical representative of the class.

Definition 21. *Let* $r_{Ew,0}$ *denote the lexicographically first vector in the equivalence class* $\{r_E \in \mathcal{Z}^n \mid \mathsf{wt}(r_E) = w\}$.

Applying Symmetry. Let g^* be any optimal deterministic strategy. We will first construct a new optimal strategy EVE_0 that has the property that for all $r_E \in \mathcal{Z}^n$ and all permutations π, $\mathrm{EVE}_0(\pi(r_E)) = \pi(\mathrm{EVE}_0(r_E))$.

First, we prove a fact about symmetry.

Lemma 2. *For all* $\widehat{r}_B \in \mathcal{Y}^n, r_E \in \mathcal{Z}^n, \pi \in S_n,$

$$\Pr_{R,\mathsf{ChE}}[h_{R,\mathsf{ChB},n}(\widehat{r}_B) = 1 \mid R_E = r_E] = \Pr_{R,\mathsf{ChE}}[h_{R,\mathsf{ChB},n}(\pi(\widehat{r}_B)) = 1 \mid R_E = \pi(r_E)]$$

Proof. We defer the proof to the full version.

Now, we can prove that any optimal deterministic strategy $g^* : \mathcal{X}^n \to \mathcal{Y}^n$ does equally well on all permutations of received string r_E.

Lemma 3. *For all* $r_E \in \mathcal{Z}^n, \pi \in S_n,$ *and for any optimal deterministic strategy* $g^* : \mathcal{X}^n \to \mathcal{Y}^n,$

$$\Pr_{R,\mathsf{ChE}}[h_{R,\mathsf{ChB},n}(g^*(R_E)) \mid R_E = r_E] = \Pr_{R,\mathsf{ChE}}[h_{R,\mathsf{ChB},n}(g^*(R_E)) \mid R_E = \pi(r_E)]$$

Proof. We defer the proof to the full version.

Although g^* has the same probability of success on all permutations of a given string r_E, g^* may still behave rather differently on each permutation. To deal with this, we construct a new optimal strategy EVE_0 that acts in a structured manner on each permutation of r_E so that $\mathrm{EVE}_0(\pi(r_E)) = \pi(\mathrm{EVE}_0(r_E))$ for all $\pi \in S_n$.

We define EVE_0 from g^* as follows:

$\mathrm{EVE}_0(r_E)$:
Given optimal deterministic strategy g^*.

1. Let $w = \mathsf{wt}(r_E)$. Let $r_{Ew,0}$ be the lexicographically first vector in $\mathcal{Z}^n$ of weight w.
2. Let permutation $\sigma \in S_n$ be such that $\sigma(r_{Ew,0}) = r_E$.
3. Output $\widehat{r}_B = \sigma(g^*(\sigma^{-1}(r_E))) = \sigma(g^*(r_{Ew,0}))$.

Remark 6. For any weight w and any permutation $\tau \in S_n$, $\mathrm{EVE}_0(\tau(r_{Ew,0})) = \tau(g^*(r_{Ew,0}))$ In particular, $\mathrm{EVE}_0(r_{Ew,0}) = g^*(r_{Ew,0})$.

Lemma 4. *If* $g^* : \mathcal{Z}^n \to \mathcal{Y}^n$ *is an optimal deterministic strategy, then* $\mathrm{EVE}_0 :$ $\mathcal{Z}^n \to \mathcal{Y}^n$ *is an optimal strategy. Moreover, for any* $r_E \in \mathcal{Z}^n$ *and* $\pi \in S_n,$ $\mathrm{EVE}_0(\pi(r_E)) = \pi(\mathrm{EVE}_0(r_E))$.

Proof. We defer the proof to the full version.

Randomized Locations. Consider a probabilistic EVE_1 that on input $r_E \in \mathcal{Z}^n$ deviates slightly from the deterministic EVE_0. For any $z \in \mathcal{Z}$, $y \in \mathcal{Y}$, and input $r_E \in \mathcal{Z}^n$, EVE_0 maps some deterministically chosen subset of size $k_{z,y}$ of the y's in r_E to be a z in $\widehat{r}_B$. Instead, EVE_1, will map a random subset of size $k_{z,y}$ of the y's in r_E to be a z in $\widehat{r}_B$.

More formally, we define EVE_1 as follows.

$\text{EVE}_1(r_E)$:

1. $\forall y \in \mathcal{Y}, z \in \mathcal{Z}$, compute $k_{z,y} = N_z(r_E) \cdot \text{RATIO}_{z \to y}(r_E, \text{EVE}_0(r_E))$.
2. Start with $S = [n]$.
   For each $y \in \mathcal{Y}$ and $z \in \mathcal{Z}$
   (a) Pick a random set $S_{z,y} \subset S \cap \{i \in [n] \mid r_{E,i} = z\}$ such that $|S_{z,y}| = k_{z,y}$.
   (b) Set $\widehat{r}_{B,i} = y$ for all $i \in S_{z,y}$.
   (c) Set $S = S \backslash S_{z,y}$.
3. Output $\widehat{r}_B$.

Remark 7. Observe that for any fixed randomness e of EVE_1 and any $r_E \in \mathcal{Z}^n$, then there exists a permutation $\pi_e \in S_n$ such that $\text{EVE}_1(r_E; e) = \pi_e(\text{EVE}_0(r_E))$ where $\pi_e(r_E) = r_E$.

We show that such a probabilistic EVE_1 has the same success probability as EVE_0.

Lemma 5.

$$\Pr_{R, \text{ChE}, \text{EVE}_1}[h_{R, \text{ChB}, n}(\text{EVE}_1(R_E)) = 1] = \Pr_{R, \text{ChE}}[h_{R, \text{ChB}, n}(\text{EVE}_0(R_E)) = 1]$$

Proof. We defer the proof to the full version.

Stochastic Matrix Strategy. Consider a probabilistic EVE_2 that on input $r_E \in \mathcal{Z}^n$ defines a new channel Ch_{r_E} from $\mathcal{Z}$ to $\mathcal{Y}$ such that $p_{r_E}(z \mid y) = \text{RATIO}_{z \to y}(r_E, \text{EVE}_0(r_E))$ and applies this channel to each symbol of r_E to get $\widehat{r}_B$.

$\text{EVE}_2(r_E)$:

1. Define a channel Ch_{r_E} from $\mathcal{Z}$ to $\mathcal{Y}$ by stochastic matrix

   $$P_{r_E} = [p_{r_E}(y \mid z)]_{z \in \mathcal{Z}, y \in \mathcal{Y}} = [\text{RATIO}_{z \to y}(r_E, \text{EVE}_0(r_E))]_{z \in \mathcal{Z}, y \in \mathcal{Y}}$$

2. For $i \in [n]$, set $\widehat{r}_{Bi} = \text{Ch}_{r_E}(r_{Ei})$.
3. Output $\widehat{r}_B$.

We will now prove that EVE_2 cannot perform much worse than EVE_1. In particular, we will prove that for an overwhelming fraction of $r_E \in \mathcal{Z}^n$, then with probability at least $\frac{1}{\text{poly}(n)}$, $\text{EVE}_2(r_E)$ will produce an output that is distributed identically to the distribution of $\text{EVE}_1(r_E)$.

Definition 22.
Let $\text{GOOD}_E = \{r_E \in \mathcal{Z}^n \mid \forall z \in \mathcal{Z}, N_z(r_E) \geq \frac{n}{2|\mathcal{X}|} \cdot \max_{x \in \mathcal{X}}(p_E(z|x))\} \subset \mathcal{Z}^n$.
Observe that for all $r_E \in \text{GOOD}_E$ *and* $z \in \mathcal{Z}$, *then* $N_z(r_E) = \Theta(n)$.

Lemma 6. $\Pr_{R,\mathsf{ChE}}[r_E \in \mathrm{GOOD}_E] \geq 1 - \mathsf{negl}(\lambda)$

Proof. We defer the proof to the full version.

Lemma 7. *For all* $r_E \in \mathrm{GOOD}_E$, *there exists a polynomial* $p(n) = O\left(n^{|\mathcal{Z}||\mathcal{Y}|/2}\right)$ *such that*

$$\Pr_{R,\mathsf{ChE},\mathrm{EVE}_2}[h_{R,\mathsf{ChB},n}(\mathrm{EVE}_2(R_E)) = 1 \mid R_E = r_E]$$

$$\geq \frac{1}{p(n)} \cdot \Pr_{R,\mathsf{ChE},\mathrm{EVE}_1}[h_{R,\mathsf{ChB},n}(\mathrm{EVE}_1(R_E)) = 1 \mid R_E = r_E]$$

Proof. We defer the proof to the full version.

Corollary 2. *There exists a polynomial* $p(n) = O\left(n^{|\mathcal{Z}||\mathcal{Y}|/2}\right)$ *such that*

$$p(n) \cdot \Pr_{R,\mathsf{ChE},\mathrm{EVE}_2}[h_{R,\mathsf{ChB},n}(\mathrm{EVE}_2(R_E)) = 1] + \mathsf{negl}(\lambda) \geq \Pr_{R,\mathsf{ChE},\mathrm{EVE}_1}[h_{R,\mathsf{ChB},n}(\mathrm{EVE}_1(R_E)) = 1]$$

Proof. We defer the proof to the full version.

Input-Independent Strategy. Now, although EVE_2's strategy is to apply a channel Ch_{r_E} to each symbol of her input r_E, the choice of channel she applies is dependent on which r_E she received. To remove this dependence, we construct an EVE_3 who in addition to getting input r_E also gets an independent random input w that defines which channel Ch_w that EVE_3 should apply to r_E. More formally,

---

$\mathrm{EVE}_3(w, r_E)$:

1. Let $r_{Ew,0} \in \mathcal{Z}^n$ be the lexicographically first vector of weight w.
2. Define a channel Ch_w from $\mathcal{Z}$ to $\mathcal{Y}$ by stochastic matrix

$$P_w = [p_w(y \mid z)]_{z \in \mathcal{Z}, y \in \mathcal{Y}} = [\mathrm{RATIO}_{z \to y}(r_{Ew,0}, \mathrm{EVE}_0(r_{Ew,0}))]_{z \in \mathcal{Z}, y \in \mathcal{Y}}$$

3. For $i \in [n]$, set $\widehat{r}_{Bi} = \mathsf{Ch}_w(r_{Ei})$.
4. Output $\widehat{r}_B$.

Notation

- Let $\mathcal{W}_n = \{w = (w_1, \ldots, w_{|\mathcal{Z}|}) \mid \sum_{i=1}^{|\mathcal{Z}|}(w_i) = n\} = \{w \in \mathbb{N}^n \mid w = \mathsf{wt}(r_E)$ for some $r_E \in \mathcal{Z}^n\}$ be the set of all weight vectors of $\mathcal{Z}^n$.
- Note that $|\mathcal{W}_n| = \binom{n+|\mathcal{Z}|-1}{|\mathcal{Z}|-1} = \mathsf{poly}(n)$.
- Let W be a random variable uniformly distributed over $\mathcal{W}_n$.

Now, we will show that $\mathrm{EVE}_3(\mathsf{wt}(r_E), r_E)$ has the same behavior as $\mathrm{EVE}_2(r_E)$.

Lemma 8. *For all weights $w \in \mathcal{W}_n$ and all $r_E \in \mathcal{Z}^n$ such that $\mathsf{wt}(r_E) = w$, then $\mathsf{Ch}_w = \mathsf{Ch}_{r_E}$ where Ch_w is defined as in EVE_3 and Ch_{r_E} is defined as in EVE_2.*

Proof. We defer the proof to the full version.

Corollary 3. *For any $r_E \in \mathcal{Z}^n$, the distribution of $\mathrm{EVE}_3(\mathsf{wt}(r_E), r_E)$ is the same as the distribution of $\mathrm{EVE}_2(r_E)$.*

Proof. This follows directly from Lemma 8 by definition of EVE_2 and EVE_3.

We claim that given a uniformly randomly chosen weight vector w, EVE_3's probability of success is not much worse than EVE_2's probability of success. This follows since there are only polynomially many possible weight vectors, so with some inverse polynomially probability, the randomly chosen weight w for EVE_3 will be equal to $\mathsf{wt}(r_E)$ and thus EVE_3 will act identically to EVE_2.

Lemma 9.

$$\Pr_{R,\mathsf{ChE},\mathrm{EVE}_3,W}[h_{R,\mathsf{ChB},n}(\mathrm{EVE}_3(W, R_E)) = 1] \geq \frac{1}{q(n)} \cdot \Pr_{R,\mathsf{ChE},\mathrm{EVE}_2}[h_{R,\mathsf{ChB},n}(\mathrm{EVE}_2(R_E)) = 1]$$

where $q(n) = \binom{n+|\mathcal{Z}|-1}{|\mathcal{Z}|-1} = |\mathcal{W}_n| = \mathsf{poly}(n)$.

Proof. We defer the proof to the full version.

Finally, we prove that EVE_3 only succeeds with negligible probability. This step crucially requires that the main channel ChB is not a degradation of Eve's channel ChE.

Lemma 10.

$$\Pr_{R,\mathsf{ChE},\mathrm{EVE}_3,W}[h_{R,\mathsf{ChB},n}(\mathrm{EVE}_3(W, R_E)) = 1] \leq \mathsf{negl}(\lambda)$$

Proof. We defer the proof to the full version.

Putting it Together

Theorem 5. *For all randomized functions $g : \mathcal{Z}^n \to \mathcal{Y}^n$,*

$$\Pr_{R,\mathsf{ChE},g}[h_{R,\mathsf{ChB},n}(g(R_E)) = 1] \leq \mathsf{negl}(\lambda)$$

Proof. By Lemma 4, EVE_0 is an optimal strategy so

$$\Pr_{R,\mathsf{ChE},g}[h_{R,\mathsf{ChB},n}(g(R_E)) = 1] \leq \Pr_{R,\mathsf{ChE}}[h_{R,\mathsf{ChB},n}(\mathrm{EVE}_0(R_E)) = 1]$$

Then, by Lemma 5, Corollary 2, Lemma 9, and Lemma 10 for some polynomials $p(n), q(n) = \mathsf{poly}(n)$,

$$\Pr_{R,\mathsf{ChE}}[h_{R,\mathsf{ChB},n}(\mathsf{Eve_0}(R_E)) = 1] = \Pr_{R,\mathsf{ChE},\mathsf{Eve_1}}[h_{R,\mathsf{ChB},n}(\mathsf{Eve_1}(R_E)) = 1]$$

$$\leq p(n) \cdot \Pr_{R,\mathsf{ChE},\mathsf{Eve_2}}[h_{R,\mathsf{ChB},n}(\mathsf{Eve_2}(R_E)) = 1] + \mathsf{negl}(\lambda)$$

$$\leq p(n) \cdot q(n) \cdot \Pr_{R,\mathsf{ChE},\mathsf{Eve_3},W}[h_{R,\mathsf{ChB},n}(\mathsf{Eve_3}(W, R_E)) = 1]$$
$$+ \mathsf{negl}(\lambda)$$

$$\leq p(n) \cdot q(n) \cdot \mathsf{negl}(\lambda) + \mathsf{negl}(\lambda)$$

$$\leq \mathsf{negl}(\lambda)$$

We now show that this implies that any strategy g can only cause $f_{m,R,\mathsf{ChB},n}$ to output m with negligible probability. This follows from the lemma below:

Lemma 11. *For any* $r \in \mathcal{X}^n$ *and* $\widehat{r}_B \in \mathcal{Y}^n$,

$$\forall x \in \mathcal{X}, y \in \mathcal{Y}, \text{ } \mathrm{RATIO}_{x \to y}(r, \widehat{r}_B) \leq p_B(y|x) + n^{-\frac{1}{3}},$$

implies

$$\forall x \in \mathcal{X}, y \in \mathcal{Y}, |\mathrm{RATIO}_{x \to y}(r, \widehat{r}_B) - p_B(y|x)| \leq |\mathcal{Y}| \cdot n^{-\frac{1}{3}}$$

Proof. We defer the proof to the full version.

Therefore, we obtain

Theorem 6. *For all randomized functions* $g : \mathcal{Z}^n \to \mathcal{Y}^n$ *and any message* $m \in \{0,1\}$,

$$\Pr_{R,\mathsf{ChE},g}[f_{m,R,\mathsf{ChB},n}(g(R_E)) \neq \bot] \leq \mathsf{negl}(\lambda)$$

Proof. We defer the proof to the full version.

We now prove full security.

Theorem 7. *For every polynomial query bound* $q(\lambda)$ *and (computationally unbounded) adversary* $\mathcal{A}^{(\cdot)}$ *that makes at most* $q(\lambda)$ *queries to its oracle,*

$$\Pr[\mathcal{A}^{f_{b,r,\mathsf{ChB},n}}(1^\lambda, \mathsf{ChE}(r)) = b \mid (f_{b,r,\mathsf{ChB},n}, r) \leftarrow \mathsf{Enc}_{\mathsf{ChB}}(1^\lambda, b)] \leq \frac{1}{2} + \mathsf{negl}(\lambda)$$

where b *is uniformly distributed over* $\{0,1\}$.

Proof. We defer the proof to the full version.

6   Universal Coding Schemes

A universal coding scheme for a main channel ChB is a wiretap coding scheme that allows decoding for Bob but is secure against any eavesdropping channel ChE from some set $\mathcal{E}$.

Definition 23 (Secure $(ChB, \mathcal{E})$-universal coding scheme). *A statistically secure (resp. computationally secure, resp. bounded query secure in the ideal obfuscation model) $(ChB, \mathcal{E})$-universal coding scheme for channel ChB, a class of eavesdropping channels $\mathcal{E}$, and message space $\mathcal{M}$ is a wiretap coding scheme (Enc, Dec) that is a statistically secure (resp. computationally secure, resp. bounded query secure in the ideal obfuscation model) wiretap coding scheme for all wiretap channels in the set $\{(ChB, ChE) \mid ChE \in \mathcal{E}\}$ and for message space $\mathcal{M}$.*

We observe that for any channel ChB, our wiretap coding scheme $(\mathrm{Enc}_{ChB}, \mathrm{Dec}_{ChB})$ in the ideal oracle model gives us a universal coding scheme against all eavesdropping channels for which secure wiretap coding schemes are possible. Recall, that if ChB is a degradation of ChE, then no secure wiretap coding scheme is possible since the adversary can simulate anything that ChB produces.

Theorem 8. *Let ChB be any channel and let*

$$\mathsf{Not\text{-}Degraded}(ChB) = \{ChE \mid ChB \text{ is not a degradation of } ChE\}.$$

Then, $(\mathrm{Enc}_{ChB}, \mathrm{Dec}_{ChB}^{(\cdot)})$ is a bounded query secure $(ChB, \mathsf{Not\text{-}Degraded}(ChB))$ wiretap coding scheme in the ideal oracle model.

Proof. The proof follows by Corollary 1 and the observation that $(\mathrm{Enc}_{ChB}, \mathrm{Dec}_{ChB}^{(\cdot)})$ only depend on ChB.

In contrast, in the information theoretic setting, there exist channels ChB for which there is no positive rate universal coding schemes against all channels ChE that are not less noisy than ChB.

We defer further discussion on this to the full version.

7   Instantiating the Oracle via Obfuscation

7.1   Obfuscation Definitions

We now give obfuscation definitions that suffice for building computationally secure wiretap coding schemes. Crucially, we will use the fact that the function classes we are obfuscating are *statistically evasive* – that is, even given the information that Eve receives over her channel, it is infeasible for (even a computationally unbounded) Eve to find even one input that causes the function to output anything but 0. We formalize this notion now.

Definition 24 (Statistically Evasive Circuit Collection with Auxiliary Input). *A statistically evasive circuit collection with auxiliary input $(\mathscr{F}, \mathscr{G})$ is defined by*

- a collection $\mathscr{F} = \{\mathcal{C}_\lambda\}_{\lambda \in \mathbb{N}}$ of circuits such that each $C \in \mathcal{C}_\lambda$ maps λ input bits to a single output bit and has size $\mathsf{poly}(\lambda)$
- a collection $\mathscr{G}$ of pairs (D, Aux) where D is a PPT sampler that takes as input the security parameter 1^λ and output circuits from $\mathcal{C}_\lambda$, and Aux is a PPT auxiliary input generator that takes as input the security parameter 1^λ and a circuit in $\mathcal{C}_\lambda$ and outputs an auxiliary input

such that for every computationally unbounded oracle machine $\mathcal{A}^{(\cdot)}$ that is limited to polynomially many queries to the oracle, and for every $(D, \mathsf{Aux}) \in \mathscr{G}$, there exists a negligible function μ such that for every $\lambda \in \mathbb{N}$,

$$\Pr_{C \leftarrow D(1^\lambda)} \left[C \left(\mathcal{A}^C \left(1^\lambda, \mathsf{Aux}(1^\lambda, C) \right) \right) = 1 \right] \leq \mu(\lambda).$$

Obfuscation for evasive functions has been studied in several works, most relevantly for us in [2,3]. We stress that while there are impossibility results for several definitions of obfuscation, there are no impossibility results known for obfuscation of statistically evasive circuits with auxiliary input. Indeed, this is for good reason: all known impossibilities for obfuscating circuits involve either: *(i)* providing (computationally hiding) obfuscations as auxiliary input [15], which is ruled out in the statistically evasive case; or *(ii)* "feeding an obfuscated circuit to itself" [4] which requires a non-evasive circuit family. Beyond merely avoiding impossibilities, both the circuit families that we are obfuscating and the auxiliary inputs we are considering are quite natural, and there are multiple natural avenues for instantiating our obfuscation using previous work.

In particular, we consider essentially Definition 2.3 from [2], which is itself a generalization of the standard average-case VBB definition of obfuscation [4], but extended to consider auxiliary input. The work of [2] gives a construction achieving this definition for evasive functions based on multilinear map candidates [8,13], that remain secure even in light of all known attacks on multilinear map candidates (when instantiated with sufficiently large security parameters). Below, we also comment that the recent construction of indistinguishability obfuscation from well-studied assumptions [18] also gives a plausible candidate for obfuscating our oracle.

Here, our definition slightly extends the average-case VBB definition given in [2] only in that we consider security with respect to a class of possibly randomized auxiliary input generators as opposed to a single deterministic auxiliary input generator. The proof of security in [2] is oblivious to this change. We also restrict our notion of obfuscation to statistically evasive circuits collections with auxiliary input.

Definition 25 (Average-Case Virtual Black Box Obfuscation for Statistically Evasive Circuit Collections with Auxiliary Input). *Consider a statistically evasive circuit collection with auxiliary input, $(\mathscr{F}, \mathscr{G})$ where $\mathscr{F} = \{\mathcal{C}_\lambda\}_{\lambda \in \mathbb{N}}$ and $\mathscr{G}$ are defined as in Definition 24. A uniform PPT algorithm Obf is an average-case virtual black box obfuscator for $(\mathscr{F}, \mathscr{G})$ if there exist negligible functions ϵ and μ such that*

- **Correctness:** *For all* $\lambda \in \mathbb{N}$, *every circuit* $C \in \mathcal{C}_\lambda$, *and every input* y *to* C,

$$\Pr\left[\mathsf{Obf}(1^\lambda, C)(y) \neq C(y)\right] \leq \epsilon(\lambda)$$

- **$\mathscr{G}$-VBB Security:** *For all non-uniform polynomial time adversaries* $\mathcal{A}$, *there exists a non-uniform polynomial time oracle algorithm* $\mathsf{Sim}^{(\cdot)}$ *such that for all* $\lambda \in \mathbb{N}$ *and for every* $(D, \mathsf{Aux}) \in \mathscr{G}$,

$$\Big| \Pr_{C \leftarrow D(1^\lambda)}[\mathcal{A}(1^\lambda, \mathsf{Obf}(1^\lambda, C), \mathsf{Aux}(1^\lambda, C)) = 1]$$
$$- \Pr_{C \leftarrow D(1^\lambda)}[\mathsf{Sim}^C(1^\lambda, 1^{|C|}, \mathsf{Aux}(1^\lambda, C)) = 1] \Big| \leq \mu(\lambda)$$

7.2   Fuzzy Point Function Obfuscation for the BSC-BEC Case

As a warm-up we consider fuzzy point function obfuscation which suffices when the main channel is a BSC_p channel and Eve's channel is a BEC_ϵ channel such that $\epsilon > 2p$. Notably this fuzzy point function solution uses only Hamming distance. Therefore this solution is based on a standard definition of fuzzy point functions.

We defer this section to the full version.

7.3   Generalized Fuzzy Point Function Obfuscation

In general wiretap settings, a fuzzy point function obfuscation does not suffice to produce secure wiretap coding schemes. Thus, we define a generalization of fuzzy point functions that do suffice.

We defer this section to the full version.

7.4   Construction from $i\mathcal{O}$

Finally, we remark that if there exists a uniformly bounded average case virtual black box with auxiliary input obfuscator, then $i\mathcal{O}$ (indistinguishability obfuscation) also implies secure wiretap coding schemes for $(\mathsf{ChB}, \mathsf{ChE})$ wiretap channels where ChB is not a degradation of ChE. We use the definition of indistinguishability obfuscation ($i\mathcal{O}$) defined in [18].

Following the discussion on $i\mathcal{O}$ in [1], we note that $i\mathcal{O}$ is a "best-possible" obfuscation [17]. More specifically, if there exists some instantiation of the ideal obfuscation that gives a secure computational wiretap coding scheme, then replacing that instantiation with $i\mathcal{O}$ should preserve the security properties. However, in our setting, the adversary is given additional auxiliary information that may depend on the obfuscated circuit. Despite this auxiliary information, we show in the full version that $i\mathcal{O}$ still behaves as a best possible obfuscation.

Acknowledgements. Y. Ishai was supported in part by ERC Project NTSC (742754), BSF grant 2018393, and ISF grant 2774/20. This research was supported in part from a Simons Investigator Award, DARPA SIEVE award, NTT Research, NSF Frontier Award 1413955, BSF grant 2012378, a Xerox Faculty Research Award, a Google Faculty Research Award, and an Okawa Foundation Research Grant. This material is based upon work supported by the Defense Advanced Research Projects Agency through Award HR00112020024. We would also like to thank Mark Zhandry for his useful comments.

References

1. Agrawal, S., et al.: Secure computation from one-way noisy communication, or: anti-correlation via anti-concentration. In: Malkin, T., Peikert, C. (eds.) CRYPTO 2021. LNCS, vol. 12826, pp. 124–154. Springer, Cham (2021). https://doi.org/10.1007/978-3-030-84245-1_5
2. Badrinarayanan, S., Miles, E., Sahai, A., Zhandry, M.: Post-zeroizing obfuscation: new mathematical tools, and the case of evasive circuits. In: Fischlin, M., Coron, J.-S. (eds.) EUROCRYPT 2016, Part II. LNCS, vol. 9666, pp. 764–791. Springer, Heidelberg (2016). https://doi.org/10.1007/978-3-662-49896-5_27
3. Barak, B., Bitansky, N., Canetti, R., Kalai, Y.T., Paneth, O., Sahai, A.: Obfuscation for evasive functions. In: Lindell, Y. (ed.) TCC 2014. LNCS, vol. 8349, pp. 26–51. Springer, Heidelberg (2014). https://doi.org/10.1007/978-3-642-54242-8_2
4. Barak, B., et al.: On the (im)possibility of obfuscating programs. In: Kilian, J. (ed.) CRYPTO 2001. LNCS, vol. 2139, pp. 1–18. Springer, Heidelberg (2001). https://doi.org/10.1007/3-540-44647-8_1
5. Bellare, M., Tessaro, S., Vardy, A.: Semantic security for the wiretap channel. In: Safavi-Naini, R., Canetti, R. (eds.) CRYPTO 2012. LNCS, vol. 7417, pp. 294–311. Springer, Heidelberg (2012). https://doi.org/10.1007/978-3-642-32009-5_18
6. Blum, M., Micali, S.: How to generate cryptographically strong sequences of pseudorandom bits. SIAM J. Comput. **13**(4), 850–864 (1984)
7. Canetti, R., Fuller, B., Paneth, O., Reyzin, L., Smith, A.D.: Reusable fuzzy extractors for low-entropy distributions. J. Cryptol. **34**(1), 2 (2021). Earlier version in Eurcrypt 2016
8. Coron, J.S., Lepoint, T., Tibouchi, M.: Practical multilinear maps over the integers. In: Canetti, R., Garay, J.A. (eds.) CRYPTO 2013. LNCS, vol. 8042, pp. 476–493. Springer, Heidelberg (2013). https://doi.org/10.1007/978-3-642-40041-4_26
9. Cover, T.: Broadcast channels. IEEE Trans. Inf. Theory **18**(1), 2–14 (1972)
10. Csiszár, I., Korner, J.: Broadcast channels with confidential messages. IEEE Trans. Inf. Theory **24**(3), 339–348 (1978)
11. Dodis, Y., Ostrovsky, R., Reyzin, L., Smith, A.D.: Fuzzy extractors: how to generate strong keys from biometrics and other noisy data. SIAM J. Comput. **38**(1), 97–139 (2008)
12. Fuller, B., Meng, X., Reyzin, L.: Computational fuzzy extractors. Inf. Comput. **275**, 104602 (2020). Earlier version in Asiacrypt 2013
13. Garg, S., Gentry, C., Halevi, S.: Candidate multilinear maps from ideal lattices. In: Johansson, T., Nguyen, P.Q. (eds.) EUROCRYPT 2013. LNCS, vol. 7881, pp. 1–17. Springer, Heidelberg (2013). https://doi.org/10.1007/978-3-642-38348-9_1
14. Goldreich, O., Micali, S., Wigderson, A.: How to play any mental game or a completeness theorem for protocols with honest majority. In: Aho, A. (ed.) 19th Annual ACM Symposium on Theory of Computing, pp. 218–229. ACM Press, New York City, 25–27 May 1987

15. Goldwasser, S., Kalai, Y.T.: On the impossibility of obfuscation with auxiliary input. In: 46th Annual Symposium on Foundations of Computer Science, pp. 553–562. IEEE Computer Society Press, Pittsburgh, 23–25 October 2005

16. Goldwasser, S., Micali, S.: Probabilistic encryption. J. Comput. Syst. Sci. **28**(2), 270–299 (1984)

17. Goldwasser, S., Rothblum, G.N.: On best-possible obfuscation. In: Vadhan, S.P. (ed.) TCC 2007. LNCS, vol. 4392, pp. 194–213. Springer, Heidelberg (2007). https://doi.org/10.1007/978-3-540-70936-7_11

18. Jain, A., Lin, H., Sahai, A.: Indistinguishability obfuscation from well-founded assumptions. In: Proceedings of the 53rd Annual ACM SIGACT Symposium on Theory of Computing, pp. 60–73 (2021)

19. Juels, A., Sudan, M.: A fuzzy vault scheme. Des. Codes Crypt. **38**(2), 237–257 (2006)

20. Juels, A., Wattenberg, M.: A fuzzy commitment scheme. In: Motiwalla, J., Tsudik, G. (eds.) ACM CCS 1999: 6th Conference on Computer and Communications Security, pp. 28–36. ACM Press, Singapore, 1–4 November 1999

21. Liang, Y., Kramer, G., Poor, H.V.: Compound wiretap channels. EURASIP J. Wirel. Commun. Netw. **2009**, 1–12 (2009)

22. Maurer, U.: Secret key agreement by public discussion from common information. IEEE Trans. Inf. Theory **39**(3), 733–742 (1993)

23. Nair, C.: Capacity regions of two new classes of two-receiver broadcast channels. IEEE Trans. Inf. Theory **56**(9), 4207–4214 (2010)

24. Poor, H.V., Schaefer, R.F.: Wireless physical layer security. Proc. Natl. Acad. Sci. **114**(1), 19–26 (2017). https://www.pnas.org/content/114/1/19

25. Thomas, M., Joy, A.T.: Elements of Information Theory. Wiley-Interscience, Hoboken (2006)

26. Wyner, A.D.: The wire-tap channel. Bell Syst. Tech. J. **54**(8), 1355–1387 (1975)

27. Yao, A.C.: Theory and application of trapdoor functions. In: 23rd Annual Symposium on Foundations of Computer Science (SFCS 1982), pp. 80–91. IEEE (1982)

Correlated Pseudorandomness from Expand-Accumulate Codes

Elette Boyle[1,2], Geoffroy Couteau[3], Niv Gilboa[4], Yuval Ishai[5], Lisa Kohl[6], Nicolas Resch[6], and Peter Scholl[7(✉)]

[1] IDC Herzliya, Herzliya, Israel
[2] NTT Research, Sunnyvale, USA
[3] IRIF, Paris, France
[4] Ben-Gurion University, Beersheba, Israel
[5] Technion, Haifa, Israel
[6] Cryptology Group, CWI Amsterdam, Amsterdam, The Netherlands
[7] Aarhus University, Aarhus, Denmark
peter.scholl@cs.au.dk

Abstract. A pseudorandom correlation generator (PCG) is a recent tool for securely generating useful sources of correlated randomness, such as random oblivious transfers (OT) and vector oblivious linear evaluations (VOLE), with low communication cost.

We introduce a simple new design for PCGs based on so-called *expand-accumulate* codes, which first apply a sparse random expander graph to replicate each message entry, and then accumulate the entries by computing the sum of each prefix. Our design offers the following advantages compared to state-of-the-art PCG constructions:

- Competitive concrete efficiency backed by provable security against relevant classes of attacks;
- An offline-online mode that combines near-optimal cache-friendliness with simple parallelization;
- Concretely efficient extensions to pseudorandom correlation *functions*, which enable incremental generation of new correlation instances on demand, and to new kinds of correlated randomness that include circuit-dependent correlations.

To further improve the concrete computational cost, we propose a method for speeding up a full-domain evaluation of a puncturable pseudorandom function (PPRF). This is independently motivated by other cryptographic applications of PPRFs.

1 Introduction

Correlated secret randomness is a powerful and ubiquitous resource for cryptographic applications. In the context of secure multiparty computation (MPC) with a dishonest majority, simple sources of correlated randomness can serve as a "one-time pad" for lightweight, concretely efficient protocols [Bea91]. As a classical example, consider the case of a random *oblivious transfer* (OT) correlation,

© International Association for Cryptologic Research 2022
Y. Dodis and T. Shrimpton (Eds.): CRYPTO 2022, LNCS 13508, pp. 603–633, 2022.
https://doi.org/10.1007/978-3-031-15979-4_21

in which Alice and Bob receive (s_0, s_1) and (b, s_b) respectively, where s_0, s_1, b are random bits. Given $2n$ independent instances of this simple OT correlation, Alice and Bob can evaluate any Boolean circuit with n gates (excluding XOR and NOT gates) on their inputs, with perfect semi-honest security, by each sending 2 bits and performing a small constant number of Boolean operations per gate.

The usefulness of correlated randomness for MPC gave rise to the following popular two-phase approach. First, the parties run an input-independent *preprocessing protocol* for secure distributed generation of correlated randomness. This correlated randomness is then consumed by an *online protocol* that performs a secure computation on the inputs. Traditional approaches for implementing the preprocessing protocol (e.g., [IKNP03, DPSZ12, KPR18]) have an $\Omega(n)$ communication cost that usually forms the main efficiency bottleneck of the entire protocol.

This situation changed in a recent line of work, initiated in [BCG+17, BCGI18, BCG+19b], that suggested a new approach. At the heart of the new approach is the following simple observation: by settling for generating a *pseudorandom* correlation, which is indistinguishable from the ideal target correlation even from the point of view of insiders, the offline communication can be sublinear in n while retaining the asymptotic and concrete efficiency advantages of the online protocol.

This approach was implemented through the notion of a *pseudorandom correlation generator* (PCG) [BCGI18, BCG+19b]. A PCG enables two or more parties to *locally* stretch short correlated seeds into long pseudorandom strings that emulate a specified ideal target correlation, such as n instances of the OT correlation. This was recently extended to the notion of a *pseudorandom correlation function* (PCF) [BCG+20b], which essentially emulates random access to exponentially many PCG outputs, analogously to the way a standard pseudorandom function (PRF) extends a standard pseudorandom generator (PRG).

Generating Pseudorandom Correlations: A Template. To construct these primitives, a general template was put forth in [BCGI18], and further refined in subsequent works. At a high level, the template combines two key ingredients: a method to generate a *sparse* version of the target correlation, and a carefully chosen linear code where the syndrome decoding problem is conjectured to be intractable. To give a concrete example, let us focus on the *vector oblivious linear evaluation* (VOLE) correlation, which is in a sense a minimal step above simple linear correlations. The correlation distributes $(\vec{u}, \vec{v})$ to Alice and $(\Delta, \vec{w})$ to Bob; here, $\vec{u}, \vec{v}, \vec{w}$ are length-n vectors over a finite field $\mathbb{F}$ and $\Delta \in \mathbb{F}$ is a scalar, all chosen at random subject to satisfying the correlation $\vec{w} = \Delta \cdot \vec{u} + \vec{v}$. Among other applications [DIO20, BMRS21, YSWW21, RS21b], VOLE is an appealing target correlation because (a simple variant of) VOLE can be locally converted into n pseudorandom instances of OT correlation using a suitable hash function [IKNP03, BCG+19b].

For the first ingredient, there is a simple construction that allows generating (from short seeds) pairs $(\vec{u}, \vec{v})$ and $(\Delta, \vec{w})$ as above, but where $\vec{u}$ is a random *unit* vector. This uses a *puncturable pseudorandom function* (PPRF), a type of PRF where some keys can be restricted to hide the PRF value at a fixed point.

A bit more concretely, $\vec{v}$ and $\vec{w}$ will be generated by evaluating the PRF on its entire domain; the missing value will be at the only position i where $u_i \neq 0$, and the party with the punctured key will fill it using a share of $\mathsf{PRF}_K(i) + \Delta \cdot u_i$. Such a PPRF can be efficiently constructed from any length-doubling PRG [GGM86, KPTZ13, BW13, BGI14]. With a t-fold repetition of this process (keeping Δ the same across all instances), after locally summing their expanded vectors, the parties obtain the target correlation, where $\vec{u}$ is t-sparse. As long as t remains small, the seed size is small as well.

The aim of the second ingredient is to transform this sparse correlation into a *pseudorandom* correlation. To this end, the parties multiply their vectors with a public compressing matrix H, obtaining $(H \cdot \vec{u}, H \cdot \vec{v})$ and $(\Delta, H \cdot \vec{w})$. When H is random, $H \cdot \vec{u}$ is pseudorandom: this is exactly the dual variant of the *learning parity with noise* (LPN) assumption [BFKL94, IPS09]. However, computing $H \cdot \vec{v}$ (or $H \cdot \vec{w}$) takes time $\Omega(n^2)$. When n is in the millions, as in typical MPC applications, this is clearly infeasible. A better approach is to sample H from a distribution such that (1) $H \cdot \vec{u}$ is still plausibly pseudorandom, and yet (2) the mapping $\vec{v} \mapsto H \cdot \vec{v}$ can be computed efficiently, ideally in time $\tilde{O}(n)$ or even $O(n)$.

The Quest for the Right Code. In essence, all previous works in this area [BCGI18, BCG+19b, BCG+19a, SGRR19, BCG+20b, YWL+20, BCG+20a, CRR21] have built upon this template, sometimes for more general classes of correlations [BCG+20b], sometimes to achieve the more flexible notion of PCF [BCG+20a], or trying to strike the best balance between security and efficiency [BCGI18, BCG+19a, CRR21]. At the heart of all these works is, every time, a careful choice of which linear code to use. In [BCGI18, BCG+19a], it is suggested that relying on LDPC codes or on quasi-cyclic codes provides a reasonable balance between security (since the underlying LPN assumptions are well studied [Ale03, ABB+20]) and efficiency. In contrast, [CRR21] advocates a more aggressive choice, building a new concrete linear code, highly optimized for correlated randomness generation, guided by heuristic considerations and extensive computer simulations. Taking a different route, [BCG+20a] shows how a newly defined family of *variable density* linear codes allows generating a virtually unbounded amount of correlated randomness on demand, and [BCG+20b] generates more general correlations using an LPN variant over polynomial rings.

These works demonstrate that with a careful choice of code, silent preprocessing can have an extremely high throughput [CRR21] (as fast as generating tens of millions of pseudorandom oblivious transfers per second on one core of a standard laptop with low communication costs), broad expressiveness [BCG+20b] (handling richer correlations which are crucial in some advanced MPC protocols [ANO+21, RS21a]), and advantageous flexibility [BCG+20a] (generating any amount of correlated randomness on demand). Nonetheless, on most aspects, this area of research is in its infancy. Some important correlations remain frustratingly out of reach, such as circuit-dependent correlations (used e.g. in [DNNR17, HOSS18, WRK17b, Cou19, BGI19]), or authenticated multiplication triples over $\mathbb{F}_2$ (used in [HSS17, WRK17a]). The current fastest construction [CRR21] lacks any clear theoretical security analysis, but constructions built on firmer grounds are an order of magnitude slower. Finally, the PCFs of [BCG+20a] are only realistically usable in a regime of parameters where they lack any security analysis.

The quest for constructions with clear, rigorous security arguments *and* very high concrete efficiency remains largely open; its fulfilment, we believe, is a promising path towards making MPC truly efficient on a large scale.

1.1 Our Contributions

In this work, we push forward the study of efficient generation of correlated randomness, significantly improving over the state of the art on several fronts. Our main contributions are threefold.

Expand-Accumulate Codes. We put forth a new simple family of linear codes, called *expand-accumulate codes* (EA codes), which are related to the well-studied class of repeat-accumulate codes [DJM98]. To encode a message with an EA code, a sparse degree-ℓ expander is first applied to the input, effectively replicating each message entry a small number of times; the result is then *accumulated* by computing the sum of all prefixes. We demonstrate that such an EA code is a particularly appealing choice of linear code in the context of generating correlated pseudorandomness, which uniquely combines multiple attractive features: firm security foundations, extremely high concrete efficiency, and a high level of *parallelization* and *cache-friendliness*. Furthermore, the special structure of EA codes allows us to obtain several advanced constructions, including PCFs (with better efficiency and security foundations compared to [BCG+20a]), and the first practical PCGs for useful correlations such as circuit-dependent correlations. In more detail:

1. We formally prove that the (dual-)LPN assumption for EA codes, denoted EA-LPN, cannot be broken by a large class of attacks, which captures in particular all relevant known attacks on LPN. Our analysis comes with concrete, usable security bounds for realistic parameters. In contrast, previous works either only achieved provable bounds in a purely asymptotic sense [BCG+20a] (with poor concrete efficiency), or heuristically extrapolated plausible parameters through computer simulations on small instances [CRR21].
2. We also derive sets of more aggressive parameters through heuristics and simulations to obtain apple-to-apple efficiency comparisons with the work of [CRR21]. We show that EA codes are highly competitive with the code of [CRR21], while having a much simpler structure (hence simpler to implement and more amenable to analysis).
3. When implemented in an "offline-online" mode, PCGs built from EA-LPN are *highly parallelizable*, allowing for simultaneously achieving low latency and high throughput. This stands in stark contrast with essentially *all* previous constructions, including the recent high-throughput construction from [CRR21].[1]

---

[1] A notable exception is the "primal" PCG construction of [BCGI18], which is also parallelizable. However, this PCG is limited to quadratic stretch; in practice, this makes it less efficient than other alternatives, even when using the bootstrapping approach from [YWL+20].

Hence, over multicore architectures, we expect our new PCG to outperform all alternatives by a large margin.

4. We obtain the first practical PCG constructions for different kinds of useful correlations including circuit-dependent correlations (which show up in communication-efficient MPC protocols [DNNR17, HOSS18, WRK17b, Cou19, BGI19] and in constant-round MPC protocols based on garbled circuits [WRK17b]). Generating n bits of correlations with our construction requires $O(n \log^2 n)$ work. In contrast, the only known previous approaches either use LPN but incur a prohibitive $\Omega(n^2)$ cost [BCG+19b] or require expensive high-end cryptographic primitives, such as multi-key threshold FHE [DHRW16, BCG+19b].

5. Finally, we construct a pseudorandom correlation *function* from the EA-LPN assumption, the first such construction to be both concretely efficient and standing on firm security arguments. The only other practically feasible constructions of PCFs are the variable-density construction of [BCG+20a] (which is much slower, even for aggressive parameters, and only has asymptotic security guarantees) and the recent construction of [OSY21] (which relies on the standard DCR assumption, but is also slower, is restricted to OT and VOLE correlations – our construction can handle other useful correlations – and is not post-quantum – our construction plausibly is).

Offline-Online Pseudorandom Correlation Generators. PCGs allow one to expand, in a "silent" fashion (*i.e.* without any communication), short seeds into long sources of correlated pseudorandomness. This silent expansion largely dominates the overall computational cost of the entire protocol: in the online phase, the computation amounts to a few cheap xor operations per gate, and the limiting factor is communication. Even with a very high bandwidth, the latency of multi-round protocols can form a bottleneck. This implies that, in many settings, some idle computation time is wasted during the online phase. We put forth a new notion of PCG, called *offline-online* PCG, which seeks to push the vast majority of the offline work back to the online phase, but in an incremental fashion that minimizes latency.

In more detail, most of the computational slowdown in the silent expansion of modern PCGs is incurred by cache misses. Indeed, most of the efficiency improvements of the PCG of [CRR21] come precisely from heuristically building a cache-friendly linear code. However, constructing such cache-friendly codes with firm security foundations remains elusive. Moreover, the cache-friendliness of the construction from [CRR21] comes at the expense of a fully sequential silent expansion. Instead, we suggest a new approach: using EA codes, cache misses are bound to occur because of their expander-based structure; however, it is relatively easy to push all these cache misses to the online phase, where they will happen during idle moments (caused by bandwidth limitations or latency). Concretely, EA codes achieve the following:

- In the offline phase, the *sparse version* of the correlation is generated using a PPRF; this amounts to computing a few hundred binary trees of hashes (*a* la GGM), which is highly parallelizable and cache-friendly. In the literature, this is typically referred to as the *full evaluation* part, because it amounts to evaluating several PRRFs on their entire domain.

- Still in the offline phase, an *accumulation step* is performed, which converts a vector $(x_1, x_2, \cdots, x_N)$ in an accumulated vector $(x_1, x_1 \oplus x_2, \cdots, \bigoplus_{i=1}^{N} x_i)$. This can be done with $N - 1$ `xors` of short strings in one pass, which is extremely fast and cache-friendly; furthermore, this accumulation is easy to parallelize with a simple two-pass algorithm while still retaining cache-friendliness.

- At the end of the offline phase, a length-N vector $\vec{y}$ of short strings is stored, where N is a small constant factor times the target amount n of correlations (concretely, $N \approx 5 \cdot n$ in our instantiations). Eventually, to generate an instance of the target correlation, one must retrieve ℓ random entries of $\vec{y}$, and `xor` them, where the *output locality* parameter ℓ corresponds to the degree of the graph defining the EA code. This is where cache misses can occur; however, this step is still highly parallelizable, and these random accesses can easily be arranged to fill exactly the idle computation time of the online phase. Concretely, for conservative parameters fully within the bound of our theoretical analysis, ℓ can be set to about 40 when producing $n \geq 2^{20}$ correlations; using more aggressive parameters, setting ℓ as low as 7 seems to nonetheless provide a sufficient security level according to our experiments.

Our estimates suggest that relying on offline-online PCGs instead of standard PCGs will likely lead to significant improvements in MPC protocols. The offline part of our EA-based offline-online PCGs is insanely fast – we estimate of the order of 100ms to generate the offline material for 10 million random OTs on a single core of a standard laptop, a runtime which can be sped up by almost a factor of k when k processors are available, even with a few dozen processors.

Further Speedups in the Offline Phase. Up to this point, we discussed the application of a new family of linear codes to speed up PCGs and achieve new advanced constructions. We now turn our attention to the other main component of a PCG: the *full evaluation* procedure, which boils down to evaluating several PPRFs on their entire domain. Concretely, using the GGM PPRF [GGM86, KPTZ13, BW13, BGI14], generating a length-N vector with this procedure requires $2N$ calls to a hash function along the leaves of a full binary tree. We obtain new PPRF constructions that aim to reduce the total number of calls to the underlying hash function. Our main construction reduces the number of calls to $1.5N$; we prove its security in the random oracle model. We also put forth a candidate construction with the same $1.5N$ cost in the ideal cipher model (supporting an implementation based on standard block ciphers such as AES), but leave its security analysis open. We describe several additional optimizations; in particular:

- We show that, by "flattening the GGM tree," the number of calls can be further reduced, at the cost of sightly increasing the seed size (and seed distribution cost). Concretely, we can reduce the total number of calls to $1.17N$, only increasing the seed size and seed distribution time by a factor of 1.5

(this is a desirable tradeoff, since these costs vanish when N increases, and are typically marginal with standard parameters).
- We show that, in the specific context of generating OT correlations, the cost can be further reduced to N (without the flattening optimization) or $0.67N$ (with flattening) calls to the hash function.

We note that these contributions are of a very different nature compared to our previous constructions, and add to the growing body of work on the analysis in idealized models of symmetric primitives for MPC applications [GKWY20, CT21]. Since full evaluations of PPRFs have many applications beyond PCGs, to problems such as zero-knowledge proofs [KKW18, CDG+20, KZ20, FS21], circuit garbling [HK21], secure shuffling [CGP20] and private information retrieval [MZR+13], these results are also of independent interest.

1.2 Technical Overview

We now survey the technical tools that we use to achieve our results.

EA *Codes.* A generator matrix H for an EA code is of the form $H = BA$, where $B \in \mathbb{F}_2^{n \times N}$ is a matrix with sparse rows, and $A \in \mathbb{F}_2^{N \times N}$ is the accumulator matrix, that is, $\vec{x}^\mathsf{T} A = (x_1, x_1 + x_2, \ldots, x_1 + \cdots + x_N)$. We propose the EA-LPN-assumption which states that samples of the form $H\vec{e}$, where $\vec{e} \in \mathbb{F}_2^N$ is a random sparse vector, are computationally indistinguishable from uniform.

In order to provide evidence for the EA-LPN-assumption, we show that it is not susceptible to *linear tests*. While this class of tests is very large, they all boil down to the same general strategy: given the vector $\vec{b}$ (which is either uniformly random or $H\vec{e}$ with $\vec{e}$ sparse), one looks at the matrix H, chooses some nonzero vector $\vec{x} \in \mathbb{F}_2^n$, and then checks if the dot product $\vec{x}^\mathsf{T} \cdot \vec{b}$ is biased towards 0. If $\vec{x}^\mathsf{T} H$ and $\vec{e}$ are both sufficiently dense then we can rule out the possibility that $\vec{x}^\mathsf{T} \cdot (H\vec{e}) = (\vec{x}^\mathsf{T} H) \cdot \vec{e}$ has noticeable bias. As we would like to keep $\vec{e}$ as sparse as possible, we need to show that for every nonzero vector $\vec{x} \in \mathbb{F}_2^n$, $\vec{x}^\mathsf{T} H$ has large weight. In other words, we need to show that the code generated by H has good minimum distance.

We now briefly outline how we show that a random EA code has good minimum distance. It is convenient for us to assume that the coordinates of B are all sampled independently as Bernoulli random variables with probability p. Writing $(y_1, \ldots, y_N) := \vec{x}^\mathsf{T} H = \vec{x}^\mathsf{T}(BA)$ we can view the sequence of $y_1, \ldots, y_N$ as an N-step random walk (over the randomness of B) on a Markov chain with state space $\{0, 1\}$, where the transition probabilities are governed by the Hamming weight $\mathcal{HW}(\vec{x})$. Furthermore the *spectral gap* of this Markov chain is easily computable, allowing us to apply an *expander Hoeffding bound* which tells us that the random walk $y_1, \ldots, y_N$ is unlikely to spend too much time on the 0 state; equivalently, it is unlikely that $\mathcal{HW}(\vec{y}^\mathsf{T}) = \mathcal{HW}(\vec{x}^\mathsf{T} H)$ is too small. By taking a union bound over all nonzero vectors $\vec{x} \in \mathbb{F}_2^n$ and doing a case-analysis based on $\mathcal{HW}(\vec{x})$, we can show that so long as $p = \Omega(\log N/N)$, except with probability $1 - 1/\mathsf{poly}(N)$ the code has minimum distance $\Omega(N)$. If one desires negligible in N failure probability this can also be obtained by slightly increasing p: e.g., $p = \Omega(\log^2 N/N)$ suffices to guarantee $n^{-O(\log N)}$ failure probability. Further, we can show that this analysis is (asymptotically) tight.

Offline-Online PCGs from EA Codes. We introduce the notion of offline-online PCGs, where an offline and online key are generated. Each party σ uses its offline key to generate a local offline string Y_σ from which it can later use its online key to generate a (vector of) samples from the target correlation. We call the length of Y_σ the *storage cost*, and the number of entries that must be read from Y_σ to generate a single sample the *output locality*.

Recall that the goal of VOLE is to obtain correlations $((\vec{u}, \vec{v}), (\Delta, \vec{w}))$, where $\vec{u}, \vec{v}, \vec{w}$ are length-n vectors over a finite field $\mathbb{F}$ and $\Delta \in \mathbb{F}$ is a scalar, all chosen at random subject to satisfying the correlation $\vec{w} = \Delta \cdot \vec{u} + \vec{v}$. Using PPRFs, during the offline phase the parties expand their keys to obtain strings $\vec{w}', \vec{u}', \vec{v}' \in \mathbb{F}^N$, where $\vec{u}'$ is a sparse, EA-LPN noise vector and $\vec{w}', \vec{v}'$ are pseudorandom conditioned on satisfying $\vec{w}' = \Delta \cdot \vec{u}' + \vec{v}'$. Further, the parties already perform the accumulation step and output $\vec{u}^{\text{off}} = A \cdot \vec{u}'$ and $\vec{v}^{\text{off}} = A \cdot \vec{v}'$, and $\vec{w}^{\text{out}} = A \cdot \vec{w}'$ and Δ, respectively. In the online phase, the parties can then recover a tuple $((u_i, v_i), (\Delta, w_i))$ by checking only an expected number of $p \cdot N$ of the offline strings, resulting in an online locality of $p \cdot N$. We can thereby obtain offline-online PCGs with highly parallelizable and cache-friendly offline phase, and online phase with low locality (recall that we can choose p as low as $p = c \cdot \log N/N$, thereby resulting in $\ell = c \cdot \log N$).

PCFs from EA Codes. We have already described a general recipe for using compressing matrices H for which the LPN assumption plausibly holds to construct PCGs; indeed, we even sketched an offline-online PCG. However, in order to use EA codes to obtain PCFs, more care is required. Recall that a PCF must behave in an incremental fashion, using the short correlated seeds to provide as many pseudorandom instances of the target correlation as required. The main challenge is that to obtain a PCF we need to set N to be superpolynomial in the security parameter, and thus computing matrix-vector products of the form $A \cdot \vec{e}$ is too expensive. Fortunately, we can avoid the need to explicitly compute $A \cdot \vec{e}$ by appealing to *distributed comparison functions* (DCFs). DCFs, which can be constructed with PRGs as is the case for distributed point functions [BGI16, BCG+21], allow one to efficiently share a comparison function $f_{<\alpha}^\beta : [N] \to \mathbb{F}$ which maps every $x < \alpha$ to β and every $x \geq \alpha$ to 0. When the noise $\vec{e}$ has a *regular* structure (i.e., it consists of N/t unit vectors concatenated together) one can naturally view $A \cdot \vec{e}$ (after permuting the coordinates) as a concatenation of comparison functions. We furthermore observe that for constructing PCFs for VOLE and OT we can use a *relaxed* version of a DCF, denoted RDCF, as we only require α to be hidden from one of the two parties.

In the following we give a high-level overview of our RDCF construction. For simplicity we assume we want to share a comparison function with range $(\{0, 1\}^\lambda, \oplus)$, although our construction generalizes to arbitrary abelian groups $(\mathbb{G}, +)$. Our construction follows the spirit of the DCF construction of [BCG+21],

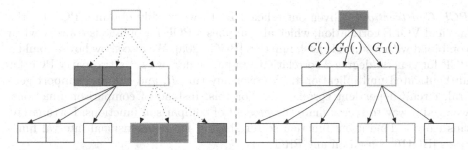

Fig. 1. Pictorial representation of our relaxed DCF construction. In our example the path $\alpha = 10 \in \{0,1\}^2$ is marked in blue, the box marked in red corresponds to box where β is added, and the boxes filled in gray correspond to the key of P_0 (in knowledge of α) and P_1, respectively. (Color figure online)

but one party knowing α allows for significant savings. We build on PRGs $G_0, G_1, C \colon \{0,1\}^\lambda \to \{0,1\}^\lambda$ such that the concatenation of the three is a secure PRG. In Fig. 1 we give a pictorial representation of the relaxed DCF construction, which we explain in the following.

To evaluate the RDCF on an input x, one traverses the tree and adds up all "C" values on the path from the root to the corresponding leaf and finally adds the "G" value of this leaf. The idea is that P_0 will add β (blinded by a "C" value) to the output, if and only if it leaves the path defined by α to the *left* (which happens if and only if $x < \alpha$). For concreteness, say one wants to evaluate the RDCF in Fig. 1 on input $x = 00$. Then, both parties add the first box on the second level (the first "C" value, marked in red), the first box on the third level (the second "C" value) and the second box on the third level (the "G" value of the leaf), which P_1 can both derive from its key. The corresponding output shares add up to β as required, since β is added to the first "C" value held by P_0. Further, β remains hidden from P_0 by the pseudorandomness of the PRG C.

One of our improvements compared to the DCF construction of [BCG+21] is that we observe that we only need "C" values on the left children, since only there the β value has to be hidden potentially. This leads to shorter keys and savings on the number of PRG evaluations.

Overall, comparing with the standard DCF construction of [BCG+21] where each key is of size $2 \log N(\lambda + \log |\mathbb{F}|)$, in our RDCF one of the party's keys is only of size λ, and the other is roughly half the size of [BCG+21]. Further, our construction reduces the number of calls to AES (when using this to implement a PRG) by 25% on average.

Additionally, we show that in the setting where a full evaluation is feasible (i.e., where one is interested in an iterative PCG rather than a full-fledged PCF), the keys of our RDCF can be distributed in 2-PC with a simple, 2-round protocol based on 2-round OT following the techniques of [Ds17, BCG+19a], whereas the corresponding distributed setup protocol for the DCF construction of [BCG+21] would require $\log N$ rounds.

PCF Constructions. Given our relaxed DCF, we readily obtain a PCF for the subfield VOLE correlation, which also implies a PCF for oblivious transfer when combined with a suitable hash function [BCG+20a]. We also show how to build a PCF for general degree-2 correlations: in particular, we get a two-party PCF for authenticated multiplication triples over any ring R, and can also support general, circuit-dependent correlations. For this, instead of comparison functions, we need a way to secret share the *product* of comparison functions. Fortunately, this can be done using function secret sharing for 2-dimensional interval functions [BGI16], based on any PRG.

We show that our EA-LPN-based PCFs can obtain good concrete efficiency. With conservative parameter choices, which our simulated experiments show resist linear attacks, our PCF for VOLE has comparable key size to the most aggressive variant of the PCF from [BCG+20a] (which did not have any provable security analysis), while we need around an order of magnitude less computation. For our degree-2 PCFs, to get good concrete efficiency we need to rely on more aggressive EA-LPN parameters with a lower noise weight. With this, our PCFs for VOLE/OT have key sizes of under 1MB, and takes only a few thousand PRG evaluations to compute each output. Our PCF for general degree-2 correlations (including multiplication triples, matrix triples and circuit-dependent correlations) has key sizes of around 200MB, and requires 2–3M PRG evaluations per output. The degree-2 PCF from [BCG+20a] does not come close to this level of efficiency, since it is not compatible with the most efficient variant of LPN they use.

Speeding Up the Offline Phase. The final task that we set for ourselves is to improve the runtime of the offline phase for PCGs, where the offline phase requires evaluating several punctured PRFs (PPRFs) on their entire domain, a functionality called FullEval. As alluded to earlier we apply the GGM construction to obtain a PPRF from a hash function. The standard way to do this is as follows: given hash functions H_0, H_1 (which can be modeled as random oracles (RO)) one generates the GGM tree corresponding to secret key k, that is, the depth m binary tree where the root is labeled by k and the left and right child of a node labeled by x are labeled by $H_0(x)$ and $H_1(x)$, respectively. To puncture a key at a point $\alpha \in \{0,1\}^m$ one gives the values of the nodes of the *co-path*, *i.e.*, the siblings of each node appearing on the path indexed by α.

To save on the calls to the hash function we consider the following definition: given an RO H we define $H_0(x) = H(x)$ and $H_1(x) = H(x) \oplus x$. Note that this clearly fails to give a PPRF, as given $H(x)$ and $H(x) \oplus x$ one can recover x and thereby distinguish the value at the punctured point from random. Nonetheless, we can show that the resulting construction yields a weaker primitive that we call a *strong unpredictable punctured function* (strong UPF), which informally means that given a key punctured at a point α one essentially cannot predict the value at α any better than by randomly guessing. While this primitive is weaker, we note that it already suffices for some applications (such as PCGs for OT), reducing the number of necessary calls to the random oracle for a full evaluation by half. If one subsequently hashes the right child at the leaves, we can further show that this does yield a genuine PPRF. In this way, we require only $1.5N$

calls to the hash function for a FullEval, whereas the standard GGM approach requires $2N$ calls, providing us with a 25% cost reduction.

To prove the construction yields a strong UPF, we observe that the punctured key can be equivalently sampled by choosing random values for the co-path and then programming the random oracle so as to be consistent with these choices. Assuming there are no collisions, such a punctured key is then independent of the value of the function at α, so the only way for an adversary to learn the value at α is if it happens to query H at one of m values on the path that it does not see.

To increase our savings, we consider k-ary trees for $k > 2$, which informally corresponds to "flattening" the GGM tree. This does incur a $(k-1)\log_2 k$ factor increase in the size of the punctured key; however, with the standard GGM construction of a PPRF the number of calls to the hash function in an invocation of FullEval now drops to $(1 + 1/(k-1))N$. By combining this with the first optimization, when $k = 3$ we can decrease the number of calls to H to $1.33N$, and when $k = 4$ to $1.17N$.

Lastly, given the current hardware support of AES, we also put forward a candidate construction of a weaker notion of UPF given an ideal invertible permutation. Recall that the standard strategy to construct a hard-to-invert function from an invertible permutation is via the Davies-Meyer construction, where H is defined as $H(k) := P(k) \oplus k$ for an invertible permutation P. Unfortunately, instantiating H this way clearly breaks down with our previous construction, as $H_1(k)$ would become equal to $P(k)$, and hence be invertible. Instead, the idea of the construction is to set $H_0(k) := H(k) \oplus k$ and $H_1(k) := H(k) + k \bmod 2^\lambda$. While on first glance one might seem easy to predict given the other, we show that this is not the case, thereby giving some evidence that the corresponding candidate indeed achieves unpredictability. We cannot hope to achieve the same strong notion of unpredictability as we do with our random oracle construction though, since $H(k) \oplus k$ does in general leak some information about $H_1(k) := H(k) + k \bmod 2^\lambda$. Still, by subsequently hashing the right child at all leaves standard unpredictability would be sufficient to obtain a true PPRF, thereby yielding a 25% cost reduction for PPRF constructions implemented with fixed-key AES. We leave the full analysis of the construction to future work.

1.3   Roadmap

We start by giving preliminaries in Sect. 2. In Sect. 3 we present EA codes and provide a security analysis of EA-LPN. In Sect. 4 we provide new constructions of PCFs based on the EA-LPN assumption. Finally, in Sect. 5, we give a brief overview of optimizations for the offline costs of PCG constructions. For a formal definition of offline-online PCGs and a construction of offline-online PCGs for subfield VOLE from EA codes, we refer to the full version of this paper.

2   Preliminaries

For preliminaries on bias and Markov chains we refer to the full version of this paper.

2.1   Learning Parity with Noise and LPN-Friendly Codes

We define the LPN assumption over a ring $\mathcal{R}$ with dimension n, number of samples N, w.r.t. a code generation algorithm $\mathbf{C}$, and a noise distribution $\mathcal{D}$:

Definition 1 (Dual LPN). *Let $\mathcal{D}(\mathcal{R}) = \{\mathcal{D}_{n,N}(\mathcal{R})\}_{n,N\in\mathbb{N}}$ denote a family of efficiently sampleable distributions over a ring $\mathcal{R}$, such that for any $n, N \in \mathbb{N}$, $\mathsf{Im}(\mathcal{D}_{n,N}(\mathcal{R})) \subseteq \mathcal{R}^N$. Let $\mathbf{C}$ be a probabilistic code generation algorithm such that $\mathbf{C}(n, N, \mathcal{R})$ outputs a matrix $H \in \mathcal{R}^{n\times N}$. For dimension $n = n(\lambda)$, number of samples (or block length) $N = N(\lambda)$, and ring $\mathcal{R} = \mathcal{R}(\lambda)$, the (dual) $(\mathcal{D}, \mathbf{C}, \mathcal{R})$-LPN$(n, N)$ assumption states that*

$$\{(H, \vec{b}) \mid H \xleftarrow{\$} \mathbf{C}(n, N, \mathcal{R}), \vec{e} \xleftarrow{\$} \mathcal{D}_{n,N}(\mathcal{R}), \vec{b} \leftarrow H \cdot \vec{s}\}$$
$$\stackrel{c}{\approx} \{(H, \vec{b}) \mid H \xleftarrow{\$} \mathbf{C}(n, N, \mathcal{R}), \vec{b} \xleftarrow{\$} \mathcal{R}^N\}.$$

Note that the generator matrix H sampled from $\mathbf{C}$ is used in the reverse direction compared to encoding: a codeword is a vector $\vec{x} \cdot H$, where $\vec{x} \in \mathcal{R}^{1\times n}$, while the assumption is about vectors of the form $H \cdot \vec{e}$ for $\vec{e} \in \mathcal{R}^N$. The dual LPN assumption is also called the *syndrome decoding assumption* in the code-based cryptography literature; in this case, H is typically seen as the *parity-check matrix* of a code generated by a matrix G such that $H \cdot G = 0$. The dual LPN assumption as written above is equivalent to the (perhaps more common) *primal* LPN assumption with respect to G (a matrix $G \in \mathcal{R}^{N\times N-n}$ such that $H \cdot G = 0$), which states that $G \cdot \vec{s} + \vec{e}$ is indistinguishable from random, where $\vec{s} \xleftarrow{\$} \mathcal{R}^{N-n}$ and $\vec{e} \xleftarrow{\$} \mathcal{D}_{n,N}(\mathcal{R})$; the equivalence follows from the fact that $H \cdot (G \cdot \vec{s} + \vec{e}) = H \cdot \vec{e}$.

We say that a family of codes sampled by a code generation algorithm $\mathbf{C}$ is *LPN-friendly* when instantiating the general LPN assumption with these codes leads to a secure flavor of the assumption for standard noise distributions. Of course, when we call a code "LPN-friendly", this implicitly means "plausibly LPN-friendly in light of known cryptanalysis of LPN".

Examples of Noise Distributions. Several choices of noise distribution are common in the literature. Fix for example $\mathcal{R} = \mathbb{F}_2$ (all the distributions below generalize to other structures) and a parameter t which governs the average density of nonzero entry in a random noise vector. Then the following choices are standard:

- Bernoulli noise: the noise vector $\vec{e}$ is sampled from $\mathsf{Ber}^N_{t/N}(\mathbb{F}_2)$. This is the most common choice in theory papers.
- Exact noise: the noise vector $\vec{e}$ is a uniformly random weight-t vector from $\mathbb{F}_2^N$; let us denote $\mathsf{HW}^N_t(\mathbb{F}_2)$ this distribution. This is the most common choice in concrete LPN-based constructions.
- Regular noise: the noise vector $\vec{e}$ is a concatenation of t random unit vectors from $\mathbb{F}_2^{N/t}$; let us denote $\mathsf{Reg}^N_t(\mathbb{F}_2)$ this distribution. This is a very natural choice in the construction of pseudorandom correlation generators as it significantly improves efficiency [BCGI18, BCG+19b, BCG+19a] without harming security.

Examples of LPN-Friendly Codes. Over the years, many codes have been conjectured to be LPN friendly. Common choices include setting H to be a uniformly random matrix over $\mathbb{F}_2$ (this is the standard LPN assumption), the generating matrix of an LDPC code [Ale03] (often called the "Alekhnovich assumption"), a quasi-cyclic code (used in several recent submissions to the NIST postquantum competition [ABB+17, AMBD+18, MAB+18] and in previous works on pseudorandom correlation generators, such as [BCG+19a]), Toeplitz matrices [GRS08, LM13] and many more. All these variants of LPN generalize naturally to larger fields (and LPN is typically believed to be at least as hard, if not harder, over larger fields).

When designing new LPN-based primitives, different choices of code lead to different performance profiles. Established codes, such as those listed above, have the advantage of having been analyzed by experts for years or decades; however, it might happen in some applications that all established codes lead to poor performance. Plausibly secure but yet-unstudied codes could yield considerable performance improvements. In light of this, we require a heuristic to select plausibly LPN-friendly codes. Such a heuristic has been implicit in the literature for some time, and was put forth explicitly in recent works [BCG+20a, CRR21].

From Large Minimum Distance to LPN-Friendliness. The core observation is that essentially all known attacks (attacks based on Gaussian elimination and the BKW algorithm [BKW00, Lyu05, LF06, EKM17] and variants based on covering codes [ZJW16, BV16, BTV16, GJL20], information set decoding attacks [Pra62, Ste88, FS09, BLP11, MMT11, BJMM12, MO15, EKM17, BM18], statistical decoding attacks [AJ01, FKI06, Ove06, DAT17], generalized birthday attacks [Wag02, Kir11], linearization attacks [BM97, Saa07], attacks based on finding low weight code vectors [Zic17], or on finding correlations with low-degree polynomials [ABG+14, BR17]) fit in a common framework of *linear tests* which corresponds, roughly, to attacks where an adversary tries to detect a bias in the LPN samples by computing a linear function of these samples. (The choice of the linear function itself can depend arbitrarily on the code matrix.) Then, it is relatively easy to show that for any noise distribution $\mathcal{D}$ whose nonzero entries "hit any large subset" with high enough probability, the LPN assumption with respect to a code generator $\mathbf{C}$ and $\mathcal{D}$ provably resists (exponentially) all linear tests as long as a random code from $\mathbf{C}$ has high minimum distance with good probability. This is formalized below.

Definition 2 (Security against Linear Tests). *Let $\mathcal{R}$ be a ring, and let $\mathcal{D} = \{\mathcal{D}_{n,N}\}_{n,N \in \mathbb{N}}$ denote a family of noise distributions over $\mathcal{R}^N$. Let $\mathbf{C}$ be a probabilistic code generation algorithm such that $\mathbf{C}(n, N)$ outputs a matrix $H \in \mathcal{R}^{n \times N}$. Let $\varepsilon, \eta : \mathbb{N} \mapsto [0,1]$ be two functions. We say that the $(\mathcal{D}, \mathbf{C}, \mathcal{R})$-LPN$(n, N)$ is (ε, η)-secure against linear tests if for any (possibly inefficient) adversary $\mathcal{A}$ which, on input H outputs a nonzero $\vec{v} \in \mathcal{R}^n$, it holds that*

$$\Pr[H \xleftarrow{\$} \mathbf{C}(n, N), \vec{v} \xleftarrow{\$} \mathcal{A}(H) \; : \; \mathsf{bias}_{\vec{v}}(\mathcal{D}_H) \geq \varepsilon(\lambda)] \leq \eta(\lambda),$$

where $\mathcal{D}_H$ denotes the distribution induced by sampling $\vec{e} \leftarrow \mathcal{D}_{n,N}$, and outputting the LPN samples $H \cdot \vec{e}$.

The *minimum distance* of a matrix H, denoted $\mathsf{d}(H)$, is the minimum weight of a vector in its row-span. Then, we have the following straightforward lemma:

Lemma 3. *Let $\mathcal{D} = \{\mathcal{D}_{n,N}\}_{n,N \in \mathbb{N}}$ denote a family of noise distributions over $\mathcal{R}^N$. Let $\mathbf{C}$ be a probabilistic code generation algorithm. Then for any $d \in \mathbb{N}$, the $(\mathcal{D}, \mathbf{C}, \mathcal{R})$-LPN$(n, N)$ assumption is (ε_d, η_d)-secure against linear tests, where*

$$\varepsilon_d = \max_{\mathsf{HW}(\vec{v})>d} \mathsf{bias}_{\vec{v}}(\mathcal{D}_{n,N}), \qquad and \qquad \eta_d = \Pr_{H \xleftarrow{\$} \mathbf{C}(n,N)} [\mathsf{d}(H) \geq d].$$

For example, using a Bernoulli noise distribution of error rate t/N, for any $\vec{v}$ of weight at least d, it holds that $\mathsf{bias}_{\vec{v}}(\mathsf{Ber}_{t/N}^n(\mathbb{F}_2)) = (1 - 2t/N)^d/2 < e^{-2td/N}$; that is, if the relative distance d/N of the code is a constant (*i.e.* the code is a good code), the bias will decrease exponentially with t. Similar calculations show that for any $\vec{v}$ of weight at least d, $\mathsf{bias}_{\vec{v}}(\mathsf{Reg}_t^N) \leq (1 - 2(d/t)/(N/t))^t < e^{-2td/N}$.

When the Minimum Distance Heuristic Fails. From the above, one can be tempted to conjecture that any good code, say, together with Bernoulli noise, is LPN-friendly. However, this is known to fail in at least three situations:

1. When the code is strongly algebraic. For example, Reed-Solomon codes, which have a strong algebraic structure, have high minimum distance, but can be decoded efficiently with the Berlekamp-Massey algorithm, hence they do not lead to a secure LPN instance (and indeed, Berlekamp-Massey does not fit in the linear test framework).
2. When the noise is structured (which is the case e.g. for regular noise) and the adversary can see enough samples. This opens the door to algebraic attacks such as the Arora-Ge attack [AG11]. However, this typically requires a large number of samples: for example, using regular noise, one needs $N = \Omega((N - n)^2)$ for the attack to apply. In contrast, all our instances will have $N = O(N - n)$.
3. When $\mathcal{R}$ has a subring, one can always project onto the subring before performing a linear attack; this technically does not directly fit in the linear test framework. When analyzing security against linear test, one must therefore account for all subrings the attacker could first project the problem onto. In polynomial rings, the reducible case of cyclotomics is discussed in [BCG+20b]. In integer rings like $\mathbb{Z}_{2^k}$, one weakness is that projecting onto $\mathbb{Z}_2$ can make error values become zero with probability $1/2$ [LWYY22], reducing the effective noise rate. To fix this, [LWYY22] propose an alternative noise distribution that is provably as secure as LPN over $\mathbb{F}_2$, but with k times the noise rate. Alternatively, a plausible fix without increasing the noise rate is to choose error values to be invertible, which ensures they are non-zero in all subrings.

The above three scenarios are the only exceptions we are aware of. Hence the following natural rule of thumb: if a code is combinatorial in nature (it is not a strongly algebraic code, such as Reed-Solomon or Reed-Müller), and if the code rate is not too close to 1 (e.g. code rate $1/2$, i.e. $n = N/2$), then being a good code makes it a plausible LPN-friendly candidate.

2.2 Puncturable Pseudorandom Functions

Pseudorandom functions (PRF), introduced in [GGM86], are keyed functions which are indistinguishable from truly random functions. A *puncturable pseudorandom function* (PPRF) is a PRF F such that given an input x, and a PRF key k, one can generate a *punctured* key, denoted $k\{x\}$, which allows evaluating F at every point except for x, and does not reveal any information about the value $F.\mathsf{Eval}(k, x)$. PPRFs have been introduced in [KPTZ13,BW13,BGI14].

Definition 4 (t-Puncturable Pseudorandom Function). *A puncturable pseudorandom function (PPRF) with key space $\mathcal{K}$, domain $\mathcal{X}$, and range $\mathcal{Y}$, is a pseudorandom function F with an additional punctured key space $\mathcal{K}_p$ and three probabilistic polynomial-time algorithms $(F.\mathsf{KeyGen}, F.\mathsf{Puncture}, F.\mathsf{Eval})$ such that*

- *$F.\mathsf{KeyGen}(1^\lambda)$ outputs a random key $K \in \mathcal{K}$,*
- *$F.\mathsf{Puncture}(K, \{S\})$, on input a ley $K \in \mathcal{K}$, and a subset $S \subset \mathcal{X}$ of size t, outputs a punctured key $K\{S\} \in \mathcal{K}_p$,*
- *$F.\mathsf{Eval}(K\{S\}, x)$, on input a key $K\{S\}$ punctured at all points in S, and a point x, outputs $F(K, x)$ if $x \notin S$, and $\perp$ otherwise,*

The security requirement is that for any set S, given a punctured key $K\{S\}$, the values $(F(K, x))_{x \in S}$ are pseudorandom.

In the full version of this paper, we recall the PPRF construction based on any length-doubling pseudorandom generator from [KPTZ13,BW13,BGI14].

2.3 Pseudorandom Correlation Generators and Functions

For a full definition of pseudorandom correlation generators and function, we refer to [BCG+19b] and [BCG+20a], or to the full version of this paper. In the following we only provide a sketch of the definitions.

Correlation. We say a PPT algorithm $\mathcal{Y}$ is a *correlation*, if $\mathcal{Y}$ on input 1^λ outputs a pair of strings $(y_0, y_1) \in \{0, 1\}^{\tau_0} \times \{0, 1\}^{\tau_1}$ where $\tau_0(\lambda), \tau_1(\lambda) \in \mathsf{poly}(\lambda)$ describe the output lengths.

The security definition of PCGs requires the target correlation to satisfy a technical requirement, which roughly says that it is possible to efficiently sample from the conditional distribution of y_0 given y_1 and vice versa. More precisely, we require the existence of a PPT algorithm $\mathsf{RSample}$ that on input (σ, y_σ) outputs $y_{1-\sigma}$, such that the distributions $\{(y_\sigma, y_{1-\sigma}) \mid (y_0, y_1) \leftarrow \mathcal{Y}(1^\lambda)\}$ and $\{(y_\sigma, y'_{1-\sigma}) \mid (y_0, y_1) \leftarrow \mathcal{Y}(1^\lambda), y'_{1-\sigma} \leftarrow \mathsf{RSample}(\sigma, y_\sigma)\}$ are statistically close. We call such a correlation generator *reverse-sampleable*.

By $\mathcal{Y}^n$ we define the algorithm outputting n instance according to $\mathcal{Y}$. We refer to such an algorithm also as *correlation generator*. Further, we extend RSample to input vectors R_σ of the form $R_\sigma = (y_\sigma^1, \ldots, y_\sigma^n)$ by applying RSample componentwise.

Pseudorandom Correlation Generator. If $\mathcal{Y}$ is a reverse-sampleable correlation generator, then a *pseudorandom correlation generator (PCG)* for $\mathcal{Y}$ with stretch n is a tuple of PPT algorithms (PCG.Gen, PCG.Expand), such that the following holds

- PCG.Gen(1^λ) outputs a pair of seeds (k_0, k_1);
- PCG.Expand(σ, k_σ) on input of $\sigma \in \{0,1\}$ and a seed k_σ, deterministically outputs a bit string $R_\sigma \in (\{0,1\}^{\tau_\sigma})^n$.
- **Correctness.** The correlation obtained via:

$$\{(R_0, R_1) \mid (k_0, k_1) \xleftarrow{\$} \text{PCG.Gen}(1^\lambda), (R_\sigma \leftarrow \text{PCG.Expand}(\sigma, k_\sigma))_{\sigma=0,1}\}$$

is computationally indistinguishable from $\mathcal{Y}^n(1^\lambda)$.
- **Security.** For any $\sigma \in \{0,1\}$, the following two distributions are computationally indistinguishable:

$$\{(k_{1-\sigma}, R_\sigma) \mid (k_0, k_1) \xleftarrow{\$} \text{PCG.Gen}(1^\lambda), R_\sigma \leftarrow \text{PCG.Expand}(\sigma, k_\sigma)\} \text{ and}$$

$$\{(k_{1-\sigma}, R_\sigma) \mid (k_0, k_1) \xleftarrow{\$} \text{PCG.Gen}(1^\lambda), R_{1-\sigma} \leftarrow \text{PCG.Expand}(\sigma, k_{1-\sigma}),$$
$$R_\sigma \xleftarrow{\$} \text{RSample}(\sigma, R_{1-\sigma})\}$$

where RSample is the reverse sampling algorithm for correlation $\mathcal{C}$.

Examples of Correlations. A random OT correlation is a pair $(y_0, y_1) \in \{0,1\}^2 \times \{0,1\}^2$, where $y_0 = (u, v)$ for two random bits u, v, and $y_1 = (b, u \cdot b \oplus v)$ for a random bit b. OT correlations is perhaps the most common and fundamental type of correlation in secure computation (though many others – such as Beaver triples, authenticated Beaver triples, or function-dependent correlations – are also standard).

It is known that, to generate n pseudorandom OT correlations, it suffices to generate the following simpler correlation: Alice gets a (pseudo)random pair of length-n vectors $(\vec{u}, \vec{v})$, where $\vec{u} \xleftarrow{\$} \mathbb{F}_2^n$ and $\vec{v} \in \mathbb{F}_{2\lambda}^n$, and Bob gets $x \xleftarrow{\$} \mathbb{F}_{2\lambda}$ and $\vec{w} \leftarrow x \cdot \vec{u} + \vec{v}$. This correlation (known as the *subfield vector-OLE* correlation) can be locally converted by Alice and Bob into n pseudorandom OT correlations using a correlation-robust hash function; see [BCG+19b] for details.

For a general template to construct PCGs for VOLE from PPRFs and LPN-friendly codes, we refer to [BCG+19b], or the full version of this paper.

Pseudorandom Correlation Function. If $\mathcal{Y}$ is a reverse-sampleable correlation generator, then a *pseudorandom correlation function (PCF)* for $\mathcal{Y}$ with input length $\nu = \nu(\lambda) \in \mathbb{N}$ is a tuple of PPT algorithms (PCF.Gen, PCF.Eval) with the following syntax:

- PCF.Gen(1^λ) outputs a pair of keys (k_0, k_1);
- PCF.Eval(σ, k_σ, x) on input of $\sigma \in \{0, 1\}$, a key k_σ and an input $x \in \{0, 1\}^\nu$, deterministically outputs a tuple $(y_0, y_1) \in \{0, 1\}^{\tau_0} \times \{0, 1\}^{\tau_1}$.

Correctness and security are defined similarly to a PCG, except that instead of obtaining the complete (potentially exponential-sized) output the adversary gets to query the output string an arbitary polynomial number of times, to obtain a tuple $(x, \text{Eval}(\sigma, k_\sigma, x))$ (or the according reverse-sampled correlation) for x sampled uniformly at random.

3   Expand-Accumulate Codes

In this section we introduce expand-accumulate codes, which are defined by the product $H = BA$ for a sparse expanding matrix B and the accumulator matrix A. We conjecture that the LPN problem is hard to solve for this matrix ensemble and provide theoretical evidence for this conjecture by demonstrating that it resists linear attacks.

3.1   Expand-Accumulate Codes, and the EA-LPN Assumption

First, we formally define the accumulator matrix.

Definition 5 (Accumulator Matrix). *For a positive integer N and ring $\mathcal{R}$, the* accumulator matrix $A \in \mathcal{R}^{N \times N}$ *is the matrix with 1's on and below the main diagonal, and 0's elsewhere.*

In particular, if $A\vec{x} = \vec{y}$ with $\vec{x}, \vec{y} \in \mathcal{R}^N$, we have the following relations:

$$y_i = \sum_{j=1}^{i} x_j \; \forall i \in [N] \qquad\qquad y_i := x_i + y_{i-1} \; \forall 2 \leq i \leq N . \qquad (1)$$

Note in particular that (1) guarantees that the vector-matrix product $A\vec{x}$ can be computed with only $N - 1$ (sequential) ring addition operations. In particular, when $\mathcal{R}$ is the binary field $\mathbb{F}_2$, this requires just $N - 1$ xor operations. Furthermore, this can be computed even more efficiently in *parallel*, which is a major benefit of our construction; please see the full version for more details. We now formally introduce *expand-accumulate* (EA) codes, which underline our main constructions of offline-online PCGs.[2]

Definition 6 (Expand-Accumulate (EA) codes). *Let $n, N \in \mathbb{N}$ with $n \leq N$ and let $\mathcal{R}$ be a ring. For a desired density $p \in (0, 1)$, a generator matrix for an expand-accumulate (EA) code is sampled as follows:*

---

[2] These codes are heavily inspired by *repeat-accumulate* codes; the full version elaborates further on this point.

– *Sample row vectors* $\vec{r}_1^{\mathsf{T}}, \vec{r}_2^{\mathsf{T}}, \ldots, \vec{r}_n^{\mathsf{T}} \xleftarrow{\$} \mathsf{Ber}_p^N(\mathcal{R})$ *independently and put*

$$B = \begin{bmatrix} \underline{\quad\vec{r}_1^{\mathsf{T}}\quad} \\ \underline{\quad\vec{r}_2^{\mathsf{T}}\quad} \\ \vdots \quad \vdots \quad \vdots \\ \underline{\quad\vec{r}_n^{\mathsf{T}}\quad} \end{bmatrix}.$$

– *Output the matrix-matrix product* BA, *where* $A \in \mathcal{R}^{N \times N}$ *is the accumulator matrix.*

We use $\mathsf{EA}(n, N, p, \mathcal{R})$ to denote a code sampled from this distribution, and the sampling of the corresponding generator matrix is denoted $H \xleftarrow{\$} \mathsf{EAGen}(n, N, p, \mathcal{R})$. When the ring $\mathcal{R}$ is omitted it is assumed $\mathcal{R} = \mathbb{F}_2$.

Remark 7. While it is more standard in the coding-theoretic literature to use G for a generator matrix of a code, as we are interested in the *dual* LPN assumption connected to a code, we actually view H as the parity-check matrix for the code for which the EA code is the dual. Thus, as H is the standard notation for a parity-check matrix, we have chosen to use this notation for the generator matrix of an EA code.

3.2   The EA-LPN Assumption and Security Analysis

In this work, we provide a new (dual) LPN-type assumption connected to EA codes which we term EA-LPN. It is obtained by specializing Definition 1 to the case where the code generation algorithm samples $H \xleftarrow{\$} \mathsf{EAGen}$. For the noise distribution $\mathcal{D}(\mathcal{R})$, we can consider Bernoulli noise $\mathsf{Ber}_{t/N}^N(\mathcal{R})$, exact noise $\mathsf{HW}_t^N(\mathcal{R})$, and regular noise $\mathsf{Reg}_t^N(\mathcal{R})$.

Definition 8 (EA-LPN Assumption).   *Let* $\mathcal{D}(\mathcal{R}) = \{\mathcal{D}_N(\mathcal{R})\}_{N \in \mathbb{N}}$ *denote a family of efficiently sampleable distributions over* $\mathcal{R}$, *such that for any* $N \in \mathbb{N}$, $\mathsf{Im}(\mathcal{D}_N(\mathcal{R})) \subseteq \mathcal{R}^N$. *For a dimension* $n = n(\lambda)$, *number of samples* $N = N(\lambda)$, *ring* $\mathcal{R} = \mathcal{R}(\lambda)$ *and parameter* $p = p(\lambda) \in (0, 1)$ *the* $(\mathcal{D}, \mathcal{R})$-$\mathsf{EA\text{-}LPN}(n(\lambda), N(\lambda), p(\lambda))$ *assumption states that*

$$\{(H, \vec{b}) \mid H \xleftarrow{\$} \mathsf{EAGen}(n, N, p, \mathcal{R}), \vec{e} \xleftarrow{\$} \mathcal{D}_N(\mathcal{R}), \vec{b} \leftarrow H \cdot \vec{e}\}$$
$$\stackrel{c}{\approx} \{(H, \vec{b}) \mid H \xleftarrow{\$} \mathsf{EAGen}(n, N, p, \mathcal{R}), \vec{b} \xleftarrow{\$} \mathcal{R}^N\}.$$

In order to provide evidence for the EA-LPN-assumption, we will show that it is secure against linear tests (Definition 2), at least when $\mathcal{R} = \mathbb{F}_2$. To do this, recalling Lemma 3, it suffices to show that $\mathsf{d}(H)$ is large (with high probability). The technical core of our proof is the following bound on the probability that a message vector $\vec{x} \in \mathbb{F}_2^n$ of weight r is mapped to a codeword of weight $\leq \delta N$.

Lemma 9. *Let* $n, N \in \mathbb{N}$ *with* $n \leq N$ *and put* $R = \frac{n}{N}$. *Fix* $p \in (0, 1/2)$ *and* $\delta > 0$, *and put* $\beta = 1/2 - \delta$. *Let* $r \in \mathbb{N}$ *and let* $\vec{x} \in \mathbb{F}_2^n$ *be a vector of weight* r. *Define* $\xi_r = (1 - 2p)^r$. *Then,*

$$\Pr\left[\mathcal{HW}(\vec{x}^{\mathsf{T}} H) \leq \delta N \mid H \xleftarrow{\$} \mathsf{EAGen}(n, N, p)\right] \leq 2 \exp\left(-2\frac{1 - \xi_r}{1 + \xi_r} N \beta^2\right).$$

To prove this lemma, we imagine revealing the coordinates of the random vector $\vec{x}^\intercal H$ one at a time, and observe that this can be viewed as a random walk on a Markov chain with state space $\{0, 1\}$ and second eigenvalue ξ_r. We can then apply an Expander Hoeffding bound to guarantee that such a random walk is unlikely to spend too much time on the 0 state, which is equivalent to saying that the random vector $\vec{x}^\intercal H$ does not have too small weight. For space reasons, the proof is deferred to the full version of this paper.

We now state the main theorem of this section.

Theorem 10. *Let* $n, N \in \mathbb{N}$ *with* $n \leq N$ *and put* $R = \frac{n}{N}$, *which we assume to be a constant. Let* $C > 0$ *and set* $p = \frac{C \ln N}{N} \in (0, 1/2)$. *Fix* $\delta \in (0, 1/2)$ *and put* $\beta = 1/2 - \delta$. *Assume the following relation holds:*

$$R < \min\left\{\frac{2}{\ln 2} \cdot \frac{1 - e^{-1}}{1 + e^{-1}} \cdot \beta^2, \frac{2}{e}\right\} \tag{2}$$

Then, assuming N *is sufficiently large we have*

$$\Pr\left[\mathsf{d}(H) \geq \delta N \mid H \xleftarrow{\$} \mathsf{EAGen}(n, N, p)\right] \geq 1 - 2\sum_{r=1}^{n}\binom{n}{r}\exp\left(-2\frac{1 - \xi_r}{1 + \xi_r}N\beta^2\right) \tag{3}$$

$$\geq 1 - 2RN^{-2\beta^2 C + 2}.$$

Informally, the conclusion is that when $p = \Theta(\log N / N)$ a constant rate EA code will have distance $\Omega(N)$ with probability $1 - 1/\mathsf{poly}(N)$. If one would like the failure probability to be negligible in N this can still be achieved by increasing p: for example, if $p = \Theta(\log^2 N / N)$ the failure probability is $N^{-O(\log N)}$. The proof is again deferred to the full version.

3.3   Discussion

In our investigation of EA codes we considered many variants and studied plausibly secure concrete parameter choices. For space reasons, many of these details are necessarily deferred to the full version. In this section, we summarize our main findings.

Different Expanding Matrices. Rather than sampling each row of B according to the Bernoulli distribution, one could naturally try the exact distribution $\mathsf{HW}_\ell^N(\mathbb{F}_2)$, or even the regular distribution $\mathsf{Reg}_\ell^N(\mathbb{F}_2)$. Unfortunately, these matrices are not as amenable to analysis. Nonetheless, after running some computer simulations we are willing to conjecture that they should behave relatively similarly: once $\ell = \Omega(\log N)$ we can hope to have constant rate and relative distance.

Arbitrary Rings. We also consider the minimum distance of EA codes over arbitrary rings. Guided by computer simulations, we are willing to conjecture that the minimum distance should only increase as the ring size increases, thereby implying that its resilience to linear attacks only increases. However, we caution that for rings like $\mathbb{F}_{2^k}$ "modular reduction/projection" attacks allow one to work modulo 2 and, e.g., recover the coordinates bit-by-bit (this attack is outside the scope of the linear tests framework). Thus, the general conclusion is that the security one obtains for the EA-LPN assumption should only increase as the characteristic of the ring increases.

Pseudodistance. By showing that H has large distance, we can rule out any linear test. However, we are only concerned with *efficient* linear tests, *i.e.*, tests that can efficiently find the attack vector from the matrix H. So long as δ and R satisfy $\delta < (1 - R)/2$ (this rules out the standard *information set decoding* attack) we conjecture that it is infeasible to find $\vec{x}$ for which $\mathcal{HW}(\vec{x}^{\mathsf{T}} H) \leq \delta N$ when $p = \Omega(\log N/N)$ is sufficiently large.

Rejection Sampling. Our analysis suggests that when an EA code fails to have good minimum distance it is often for the simple reason that the generator matrix H already has a low weight row. Thus, we propose testing the matrix after it is sampled to verify that indeed all the rows have large weight, and we heuristically argue that this leads to significant savings in the failure probability.

Density of B. From a theoretical standpoint, we can unfortunately show that the condition that $p = \Omega(\log N/N)$ is necessary. However, from a concrete standpoint we believe it is reasonable to choose the density of B much smaller. We elaborate upon this further in the following section.

3.4   Concrete Parameter Choices

Conservative Parameters. In this section, we consider relatively conservative parameter choices, and compute the failure probability as given by (3). That is, instead of computing the probability that $d(H) \leq \delta N$ for $H \leftarrow \mathsf{EA}(n, N, p)$ as $2RN^{-2C\beta^2 + 2}$ (where, as in the theorem statement, $\beta = 1/2 - \delta$, $R = n/N$ and $p = \frac{C \ln N}{N}$) we endeavour to numerically compute the bound

$$2 \sum_{r=1}^{n} \binom{n}{r} \exp\left(-2\frac{1 - \xi_r}{1 + \xi_r} N\beta^2\right),$$

where as before $\xi_r = (1 - 2p)^r$. For our applications we would like $n = 2^{20}$, 2^{25} and 2^{30}. It is reasonable to choose $R = 0.2$, implying $N = 5 \cdot n$. Our results are summarized in Fig. 2.

For context, we recall Lemma 3 which translates minimum distance into security against linear tests. It says that if $H \xleftarrow{\$} \mathsf{EAGen}(n, N, p)$ has minimum

	$C = 3$			$C = 2.5$			$C = 2.3$		
δ \ n	2^{20}	2^{25}	2^{30}	2^{20}	2^{25}	2^{30}	2^{20}	2^{25}	2^{30}
0.005	0.000317	0.0000686	0.0000148	0.0133	0.00645	0.00312	0.0599	0.0401	0.0268
0.02	0.00120	0.000347	0.000100	0.0410	0.0253	0.0156	0.174	0.147	0.124
0.05	0.0157	0.00794	0.00402						

Fig. 2. In this table, we list the (extrapolated) analytical upper bounds on the failure probabilities for various parameter choices. The rate is set to $1/5$, i.e., $N = 5n$. If the cell is empty it is because the extrapolated value exceeds 1.

distance δN with probability at least $\eta(\lambda)$ and the error vector $\vec{e} \in \mathbb{F}_2^N$ has (expected) weight t (e.g., $\vec{e} \xleftarrow{\$} \mathsf{Ber}_{t/N}^N(\mathbb{F}_2)$, $\mathsf{HW}_{t/N}^N(\mathbb{F}_2)$ or $\mathsf{Reg}_t^N(\mathbb{F}_2)$), then if we want $(2^{-\lambda}, \eta(\lambda))$-security against linear tests we require $e^{-2t\delta} \leq 2^{-\lambda}$, i.e., $t \geq \frac{(\ln 2) \cdot \lambda}{2\delta}$.

Looking at Fig. 2, for $n = 2^{30}$ and $N = 5n$, if $t = 664$ then we have $t > \frac{(\ln 2) \cdot 98}{2 \cdot 0.05}$, which implies that $H \xleftarrow{\$} \mathsf{EAGen}\left(n, N, \frac{3\ln N}{N}\right)$ is $(2^{-98 - \log_2 5}, 0.00402)$-secure[3] against linear tests. Decreasing C, if $H \xleftarrow{\$} \mathsf{EAGen}\left(n, N, \frac{2.3 \ln N}{N}\right)$ then so long as $t \geq 1658$ it is $(2^{-98 - \log_2 5}, 0.124)$-secure against linear tests.

For all of the extrapolated values in Fig. 2, we provide the necessary number of noisy coordinates for 128 bits of security against linear tests.

Density of B, Concretely. However, when it comes to concrete parameter choices, it is reasonable to be more aggressive. Our intuition, which is guided by the proof of Theorem 10, tells us that if there is to be a low-weight vector in an EA code, then it is likely obtained as the encoding of a low-weight message. In particular, if an EA code has distance d it is probably because $H \xleftarrow{\$} \mathsf{EAGen}$ has a row of weight d. Furthermore, while there could very well be lower weight vectors in the EA codes, we do not see an easy means to *find* these vectors. Recalling the discussion of the notion of *pseudodistance*, this already implies that the construction could be secure against *efficient* linear attacks.

Being aggressive, we consider $\ell = 7, 9, 11$, and then empirically estimate the minimum (relative) weight of a row of an EA matrix $H \xleftarrow{\$} \mathsf{EAGenReg}(n, 5 \cdot n, \ell)^4$ for $n = 2^{20}, 2^{25}, 2^{30}$. For $\ell = 7, 9, 11$, we endeavour to empirically estimate the minimum row weight of a matrix $H \xleftarrow{\$} \mathsf{EAGenReg}(n, 5 \cdot n, \ell)$ (see Footnote 4).

These experiments embolden us to make the following sort of conjecture: given a matrix $H \xleftarrow{\$} \mathsf{EAGenReg}(2^{30}, 5 \cdot 2^{30}, 7)$, we expect it to be hard to find a vector in the row-span of H with relative weight less than 0.02, even though

---

[3] Note that as computing a dot-product requires $5 \cdot 2^{30}$ time, this is sufficient for 128 bits of security.

[4] The regular distribution appears to us to be the most reasonable in practice; however, other distributions appear to behave similarly.

δ \ n	2^{20}	2^{25}	2^{30}
0.005	7326	6979	6632
0.02	1832	1745	1658
0.05	732	698	664

(a) Value of t required for $128 - \log_2 N$-bit security against linear tests. The failure probability for different values of C is found in Fig. 2.

n \ ℓ	7	9	11
2^{20}	0.0613	0.0923	0.121
2^{25}	0.0370	0.0624	0.0879
2^{30}	0.0223	0.0422	0.06391

(b) The (extrapolated, empirical) average minimum row-weight for H sampled as $H \leftarrow \mathsf{EAGenReg}(n, 5n, \ell)$.

we expect there to exist (many) such vectors. We leave testing of the validity of this assumption as an interesting challenge for future work.

Relation to Silver. [CRR21] also introduced a new code family, called Silver. However, their security analysis is purely based on computer simulation. Concretely, the authors of [CRR21] sampled random choices of code parameters, and sampled many instances of the code for small value of n. Then, they approximated the minimum distance for each sample by encoding low-weight vectors, and estimated the variance from the distance distribution. From that, they extrapolated a lower bound on the minimum distance for multiple small values of n, which they further extrapolated, from the curve of these lower bounds, to larger values of n. In the end, they picked the parameters that led to the best extrapolations.

We applied a relatively similar heuristic, by using computer simulations to approximate the minimum distance of our code for small values of n, and extrapolating its behavior for large values of n, with the purpose of enabling an apple-to-apple comparison with Silver. We observed that, already when setting the number of ones per row of B to only 7 and using $t \approx 5000$ noisy coordinates, we achieve heuristic security guarantees roughly on par with Silver. Note that the choice of increasing t to lower the row-weight of B is well motivated, since it vanishes when n grows and only influences the seed size, which is $\Omega(t\lambda \log n)$.

4 Pseudorandom Correlated Functions from Expand-Accumulate Codes

In this section, we give a high-level summary of the ideas behind the PCF for subfield-VOLE. For more details on how to obtain PCFs for subfield VOLE, OT and general degree-two correlations over a ring under (variants of) the EA-LPN assumption, we refer to the full version of this paper.

Fix an extension field $\mathbb{F}$ of $\mathbb{F}_2$; we target PCF for the (subfield) VOLE correlation over $\mathbb{F}$. That is, PCF.Gen outputs a pair (k_0, k_1) of correlated keys such that for any input x, writing $(u, v) \leftarrow \mathsf{PCF.Eval}(0, k_0, x)$ and $w \leftarrow \mathsf{PCF.Eval}(1, k_1, x)$, it always holds that $w = \Delta \cdot u + v$, where $\Delta \in \mathbb{F}$ is the same accross all evaluations, $(v, w) \in \mathbb{F}^2$, and $u \in \mathbb{F}_2$. We refer to the full version for a reminder of the formal definition of the security properties of a PCF. As for PCGs, one can use a correlation-robust hash function to turn a PCF for subfield-VOLE over $\mathbb{F} = \mathbb{F}_{2^\lambda}$ (where λ is a security parameter) into a PCF for the (one out of two) oblivious transfer correlation over $\mathbb{F}$.

The main difference between an offline-online PCG and a PCF is that the latter must operate in a fully incremental fashion: given the short correlated keys, the parties should be able to obtain pseudorandom instances of the target correlation on demand, without having to stretch the entire pseudorandom correlation. At a high level, our PCF construction proceeds as follows: given the two keys k_0, k_1, the parties will be able to locally retrieve (in time logarithmic in N) additive shares (over $\mathbb{F}$) of any given position in the vector $\Delta \cdot A \cdot \vec{e}$, where $\Delta \in \mathbb{F}$ is a scalar known to P_1, $\vec{e}$ is a sparse noise vector (over $\mathbb{F}_2$) known to P_0, and A is the accumulator matrix of Definition 5.

Suppose we manage to achieve the above. Then, a random input x to the PCF is parsed by both players as defining a random row B_x of the sparse matrix B; that is, x is the randomness used to sample a row B_x from $\mathsf{Ber}_p^N(\mathbb{F}_2)$. Let ℓ be the number of ones in the sampled row; with the parameters of our analysis, $\ell = O(\log N)$ with overwhelming probability. Let $\vec{e}' = A \cdot \vec{e}$ denote the accumulated noise vector. To evaluate PCF.Eval on x, the parties compute shares of $\Delta \cdot e_i'$ for all ℓ positions i corresponding to non-zero entries in B_x, and locally sum their shares. This procedure takes total time $O(\ell \log N) = O(\log^2 N)$, polylogarithmic in N: we can therefore set N to be exponential in the security parameter λ to allow for an exponential stretch. Defining $u_i \leftarrow B \cdot e_i'$ and $(-v_i, w_i)$ to be the shares computed this way, it is easy to check that the relation $\Delta \cdot u_i + v_i = w_i$ holds, and that u_i is indeed pseudorandom under the EA-LPN assumption.

It remains to find a way to locally construct these shares of $\Delta \cdot e_i'$. Here, observe that we cannot use anymore a puncturable pseudorandom function as in our construction of offline-online PCG: the accumulation step, while very efficient and parallelizable, runs in time *linear in N*. For a PCF, however, N is necessarily superpolynomial, since a PCF allows to stretch (on demand) an arbitrary polynomial amount of correlated pseudorandomness. Fortunately, we can sidestep this unaffordable accumulation step by relying on a primitive known as a *distributed comparison function* (DCF), of which very efficient instantiations (from any one-way function) were recently proposed in [BGI19, BCG+21]. For subfield VOLE, it's enough to use a weaker form of distributed comparison function, where one party knows part of the function, which we show can be constructed more efficiently.

5   Optimizing Offline Cost

Up to now, focus has been placed on optimizing the *online* portion of the offline-online PCG constructions, corresponding to the choice and analysis of advantageous linear codes. In this section, we turn attention to the *offline* portion of our construction, consisting of two primary components:

1. Evaluating several punctured PRFs (PPRFs) on their entire domain (a functionality called FullEval), and

2. Performing an *accumulation* step, which converts a vector $(x_1, \cdots, x_N)$ to an accumulated vector $(x_1, x_1 \oplus x_2, \cdots, \bigoplus_{i=1}^{N} x_i)$.

Recall that with respect to the general template of PCG construction, the combination of the accumulation step and the online process in our construction jointly play the role of applying a compressing linear map $\vec{x} \mapsto H \cdot \vec{x}$ as dictated by the selected linear code.

We remark that all previous works in this line (of constructing PCGs from the linear code plus PPRF template) focused almost exclusively on optimizing this $\vec{x} \mapsto H \cdot \vec{x}$ step, which was for a long time the dominant cost of the construction. We now instead focus on reducing the cost of the FullEval (and accumulation) component. Our motivations are threefold:

1. First, in the recent work of [CRR21], the cost of the mapping is reduced so significantly that, according to their evaluation, the cost of FullEval now accounts for about half of the total computation. Reducing the cost of FullEval has therefore an important impact on the total runtime.
2. Second, using our new notion of offline-online PCGs and instantiating them with expand-accumulate codes, the offline part boils down solely to a FullEval computation and an accumulation. The cost of accumulate is exceptionally small, and dominated by the cost of FullEval (by several orders of magnitude). Hence, reducing the cost of FullEval directly translate to reducing the cost of the offline PCG expansion, by the same factor.
3. Eventually, PCGs are not the sole target: other cryptographic primitives also sometimes rely on the FullEval algorithm of a PPRF. Reducing the cost of FullEval directly translates to improvements for these primitives.

The high-level intuition of our main results in this section correspond to the observation that for PCG construction, in fact a PPRF is a *stronger* tool than necessary. In doing so, we put forth and explore a weaker notion with the aim of improved efficiency.

In the following we give an overview of our results. For details, we refer to the full version of this paper.

Overview of the Results. First, we give high-level optimizations for the offline operations. This includes procedures for parallelizing the accumulation step, as well as methods for improving the computation cost of FullEval for GGM-type constructions such as PPRF in exchange for increased key size, by "flattening" the depth of the GGM tree.

Next, we introduce a relaxed version of PPRF, a *(strong) unpredictable punctured function* (UPF). We provide constructions of (strong) UPFs in the random oracle (RO) model (ROM) that require half the number of RO calls for FullEval as compared with the standard RO-based PPRF construction. Given the current existence of hardware support for AES, we additionally provide a conjectured construction given access to the Random Invertible Permutation Model (RIPM).

We further explore conversions from UPF to the (stronger) standard notion of PPRF in the random oracle model, beginning with a generic compiler that simply applies the random oracle to each UPF output. For our specific RO-based UPF construction of the previous subsection, we show that this same goal can be achieved by applying the RO to only half of the UPF outputs. In turn, this provides a construction of standard PPRF in the RO model in which FullEval on a domain of size N requires only $1.5N$ calls to the random oracle.

Finally, we prove that for some PCG constructions, strong UPFs already suffice in the place of PPRFs. In particular, this holds for the PCG constructions of subfield VOLE and Silent OT. In these applications, we can thus replace the PPRF by our RO-based strong UPF, in which FullEval on a domain of size N requires only N calls to the random oracle, in comparison to $2N$ when based on PPRF.

Applications and Bottom Line. Using the baseline GGM PPRF with domain size N, the cost of FullEval (i.e., evaluating the entire binary tree with N leaves) boils down to $2N$ calls to the underlying primitives (in concrete instantiations, this can translate to $2N$ evaluations of fixed-key AES). To reduce this cost, we suggest to replace the GGM PPRF by our proposed PPRF construction. Concretely, computing all leaves of the UPF requires exactly N calls to the underlying primitive (modeled either as a random oracle or as a random invertible permutation) in each of our two constructions. Converting the UPF to a PPRF requires further hashing half of the leaves, leading to a total cost of $1.5N$ calls to the underlying primitive. This is a 25% cost reduction compared to the GGM PPRF approach.

The "tree-flattening" optimizations translate to a 41.5% reduction of the FullEval time, hence of the entire offline time of our offline-online PCG construction. Since FullEval also amounts to roughly 50% of the cost of the full PCG expansion in [CRR21], plugging our new constructions should directly translate to a reduction of the total cost by about 20% (which is quite significant given how fast the construction already is).

As mentioned, for certain PCG constructions, such as Silent OT, these numbers jump already to 50% cost reduction of FullEval, corresponding to roughly 25% reduction in the overall cost of full PCG expansion.

These results also have further implications beyond PCGs. The FullEval algorithm of PPRFs and related primitives is also used in some zero-knowledge applications, typically in the MPC-in-the-head paradigm. Some examples include Picnic [KKW18, CDG+20] and its variants [KZ20], the signature schemes of [Beu20], or the zero-knowledge proof of [FS21]. FullEval is also used in some constructions of private information retrieval, such as [MZR+13]; the list is not exhaustive. In all these applications, replacing FullEval by our improved variant leads to computational savings (the amount of which depends on how dominant the cost of FullEval is in each application).

Acknowledgements. E. Boyle supported by AFOSR Award FA9550-21-1-0046, a Google Research Award, and ERC Project HSS (852952). G. Couteau supported by the ANR SCENE. N. Gilboa supported by ISF grant 2951/20, ERC grant 876110, and a grant by the BGU Cyber Center. Y. Ishai supported by ERC Project NTSC (742754), BSF grant 2018393, and ISF grant 2774/20. L. Kohl is funded by NWO Gravitation project QSC. N. Resch is supported by ERC H2020 grant No.74079 (ALGSTRONGCRYPTO). P. Scholl is supported by the Danish Independent Research Council under project number 0165-00107B (C3PO) and an Aarhus University Research Foundation starting grant.

References

[ABB+17]   Aragon, N., et al.: Bike: bit flipping key encapsulation (2017)

[ABB+20]   Aragon, N., et al.: BIKE. Technical report, National Institute of Standards and Technology (2020). https://csrc.nist.gov/projects/post-quantum-cryptography/round-3-submissions

[ABG+14]   Akavia, A., Bogdanov, A., Guo, S., Kamath, A., Rosen, A.: Candidate weak pseudorandom functions in AC^0 MOD_2. In: ITCS 2014, January 2014

[AG11]   Arora, S., Ge, R.: New algorithms for learning in presence of errors. In: Aceto, L., Henzinger, M., Sgall, J. (eds.) ICALP 2011. LNCS, vol. 6755, pp. 403–415. Springer, Heidelberg (2011). https://doi.org/10.1007/978-3-642-22006-7_34

[AJ01]   Jabri, A.A.: A statistical decoding algorithm for general linear block codes. In: Honary, B. (ed.) Cryptography and Coding 2001. LNCS, vol. 2260, pp. 1–8. Springer, Heidelberg (2001). https://doi.org/10.1007/3-540-45325-3_1

[Ale03]   Alekhnovich, M.: More on average case vs approximation complexity. In: 44th FOCS, October 2003

[AMBD+18]   Aguilar-Melchor, C., Blazy, O., Deneuville, J.-C., Gaborit, P., Zémor, G.: Efficient encryption from random quasi-cyclic codes. IEEE Trans. Inf. Theory **64**(5), 3927–3943 (2018)

[ANO+21]   Abram, D., Nof, A., Orlandi, C., Scholl, P., Shlomovits, O.: Low-bandwidth threshold ECDSA via pseudorandom correlation generators. Cryptology ePrint Archive, Report 2021/1587 (2021). https://eprint.iacr.org/2021/1587

[BCG+17]   Boyle, E., Couteau, G., Gilboa, N., Ishai, Y., Orrù, M.: Homomorphic secret sharing: optimizations and applications. In: ACM CCS 2017, October/November 2017

[BCG+19a]   Boyle, E., et al.: Efficient two-round OT extension and silent non-interactive secure computation. In: ACM CCS 2019, November 2019

[BCG+19b]   Boyle, E., Couteau, G., Gilboa, N., Ishai, Y., Kohl, L., Scholl, P.: Efficient pseudorandom correlation generators: silent OT extension and more. In: Boldyreva, A., Micciancio, D. (eds.) CRYPTO 2019, Part III. LNCS, vol. 11694, pp. 489–518. Springer, Cham (2019). https://doi.org/10.1007/978-3-030-26954-8_16

[BCG+20a]   Boyle, E., Couteau, G., Gilboa, N., Ishai, Y., Kohl, L., Scholl, P.: Correlated pseudorandom functions from variable-density LPN. In: 61st FOCS, November 2020

[BCG+20b]   Boyle, E., Couteau, G., Gilboa, N., Ishai, Y., Kohl, L., Scholl, P.: Efficient pseudorandom correlation generators from ring-LPN. In: Micciancio, D., Ristenpart, T. (eds.) CRYPTO 2020, Part II. LNCS, vol. 12171, pp. 387–416. Springer, Cham (2020). https://doi.org/10.1007/978-3-030-56880-1_14

[BCG+21] Boyle, E., et al.: Function secret sharing for mixed-mode and fixed-point secure computation. In: Canteaut, A., Standaert, F.-X. (eds.) EURO-CRYPT 2021, Part II. LNCS, vol. 12697, pp. 871–900. Springer, Cham (2021). https://doi.org/10.1007/978-3-030-77886-6_30

[BCGI18] Boyle, E., Couteau, G., Gilboa, N., Ishai, Y.: Compressing vector OLE. In: ACM CCS 2018, October 2018

[Bea91] Beaver, D.: Efficient multiparty protocols using circuit randomization. In: Feigenbaum, J. (ed.) CRYPTO 1991. LNCS, vol. 576, pp. 420–432. Springer, Heidelberg (1992). https://doi.org/10.1007/3-540-46766-1_34

[Beu20] Beullens, W.: Sigma protocols for MQ, PKP and SIS, and fishy signature schemes. In: Canteaut, A., Ishai, Y. (eds.) EUROCRYPT 2020, Part III. LNCS, vol. 12107, pp. 183–211. Springer, Cham (2020). https://doi.org/10.1007/978-3-030-45727-3_7

[BFKL94] Blum, A., Furst, M., Kearns, M., Lipton, R.J.: Cryptographic primitives based on hard learning problems. In: Stinson, D.R. (ed.) CRYPTO 1993. LNCS, vol. 773, pp. 278–291. Springer, Heidelberg (1994). https://doi.org/10.1007/3-540-48329-2_24

[BGI14] Boyle, E., Goldwasser, S., Ivan, I.: Functional signatures and pseudorandom functions. In: Krawczyk, H. (ed.) PKC 2014. LNCS, vol. 8383, pp. 501–519. Springer, Heidelberg (2014). https://doi.org/10.1007/978-3-642-54631-0_29

[BGI16] Boyle, E., Gilboa, N., Ishai, Y.: Function secret sharing: improvements and extensions. In: ACM CCS 2016, October 2016

[BGI19] Boyle, E., Gilboa, N., Ishai, Y.: Secure computation with preprocessing via function secret sharing. In: Hofheinz, D., Rosen, A. (eds.) TCC 2019, Part I. LNCS, vol. 11891, pp. 341–371. Springer, Cham (2019). https://doi.org/10.1007/978-3-030-36030-6_14

[BJMM12] Becker, A., Joux, A., May, A., Meurer, A.: Decoding random binary linear codes in $2^{n/20}$: how 1+1=0 improves information set decoding. In: Pointcheval, D., Johansson, T. (eds.) EUROCRYPT 2012. LNCS, vol. 7237, pp. 520–536. Springer, Heidelberg (2012). https://doi.org/10.1007/978-3-642-29011-4_31

[BKW00] Blum, A., Kalai, A., Wasserman, H.: Noise-tolerant learning, the parity problem, and the statistical query model. In: 32nd ACM STOC, May 2000

[BLP11] Bernstein, D.J., Lange, T., Peters, C.: Smaller decoding exponents: ball-collision decoding. In: Rogaway, P. (ed.) CRYPTO 2011. LNCS, vol. 6841, pp. 743–760. Springer, Heidelberg (2011). https://doi.org/10.1007/978-3-642-22792-9_42

[BM97] Bellare, M., Micciancio, D.: A new paradigm for collision-free hashing: incrementality at reduced cost. In: Fumy, W. (ed.) EUROCRYPT 1997. LNCS, vol. 1233, pp. 163–192. Springer, Heidelberg (1997). https://doi.org/10.1007/3-540-69053-0_13

[BM18] Both, L., May, A.: Decoding linear codes with high error rate and its impact for LPN security. In: Lange, T., Steinwandt, R. (eds.) PQCrypto 2018. LNCS, vol. 10786, pp. 25–46. Springer, Cham (2018). https://doi.org/10.1007/978-3-319-79063-3_2

[BMRS21] Baum, C., Malozemoff, A.J., Rosen, M.B., Scholl, P.: Mac'n'Cheese: zero-knowledge proofs for boolean and arithmetic circuits with nested disjunctions. In: Malkin, T., Peikert, C. (eds.) CRYPTO 2021, Part IV. LNCS, vol. 12828, pp. 92–122. Springer, Cham (2021). https://doi.org/10.1007/978-3-030-84259-8_4

[BR17]   Bogdanov, A., Rosen, A.: Pseudorandom functions: three decades later. Cryptology ePrint Archive, Report 2017/652 (2017). https://eprint.iacr.org/2017/652

[BTV16]   Bogos, S., Tramer, F., Vaudenay, S.: On solving LPN using BKW and variants. Cryptogr. Commun. 8(3), 331–369 (2016)

[BV16]   Bogos, S., Vaudenay, S.: Optimization of LPN solving algorithms. In: Cheon, J.H., Takagi, T. (eds.) ASIACRYPT 2016, Part I. LNCS, vol. 10031, pp. 703–728. Springer, Heidelberg (2016). https://doi.org/10.1007/978-3-662-53887-6_26

[BW13]   Boneh, D., Waters, B.: Constrained pseudorandom functions and their applications. In: Sako, K., Sarkar, P. (eds.) ASIACRYPT 2013, Part II. LNCS, vol. 8270, pp. 280–300. Springer, Heidelberg (2013). https://doi.org/10.1007/978-3-642-42045-0_15

[CDG+20] Chase, M., et al.: The picnic signature scheme (2020)

[CGP20]   Chase, M., Ghosh, E., Poburinnaya, O.: Secret-shared shuffle. In: Moriai, S., Wang, H. (eds.) ASIACRYPT 2020, Part III. LNCS, vol. 12493, pp. 342–372. Springer, Cham (2020). https://doi.org/10.1007/978-3-030-64840-4_12

[Cou19]   Couteau, G.: A note on the communication complexity of multiparty computation in the correlated randomness model. In: Ishai, Y., Rijmen, V. (eds.) EUROCRYPT 2019, Part II. LNCS, vol. 11477, pp. 473–503. Springer, Cham (2019). https://doi.org/10.1007/978-3-030-17656-3_17

[CRR21]   Couteau, G., Rindal, P., Raghuraman, S.: Silver: silent VOLE and oblivious transfer from hardness of decoding structured LDPC codes. In: Malkin, T., Peikert, C. (eds.) CRYPTO 2021, Part III. LNCS, vol. 12827, pp. 502–534. Springer, Cham (2021). https://doi.org/10.1007/978-3-030-84252-9_17

[CT21]   Chen, Y.L., Tessaro, S.: Better security-efficiency trade-offs in permutation-based two-party computation. In: Tibouchi, M., Wang, H. (eds.) ASIACRYPT 2021. LNCS, vol. 13091, pp. 275–304. Springer, Cham (2021). https://doi.org/10.1007/978-3-030-92075-3_10

[DAT17]   Debris-Alazard, T., Tillich, J.-P.: Statistical decoding. In: 2017 IEEE International Symposium on Information Theory (ISIT), pp. 1798–1802. IEEE (2017)

[DHRW16] Dodis, Y., Halevi, S., Rothblum, R.D., Wichs, D.: Spooky encryption and its applications. In: Robshaw, M., Katz, J. (eds.) CRYPTO 2016, Part III. LNCS, vol. 9816, pp. 93–122. Springer, Heidelberg (2016). https://doi.org/10.1007/978-3-662-53015-3_4

[DIO20]   Dittmer, S., Ishai, Y., Ostrovsky, R.: Line-point zero knowledge and its applications. Cryptology ePrint Archive, Report 2020/1446 (2020). https://eprint.iacr.org/2020/1446

[DJM98]   Divsalar, D., Jin, H., McEliece, R.J.: Coding theorems for "turbo-like" codes. In: Proceedings of the Annual Allerton Conference on Communication Control and Computing, vol. 36, pp. 201–210. University of Illinois (1998)

[DNNR17]   Damgård, I., Nielsen, J.B., Nielsen, M., Ranellucci, S.: The TinyTable protocol for 2-party secure computation, or: gate-scrambling revisited. In: Katz, J., Shacham, H. (eds.) CRYPTO 2017, Part I. LNCS, vol. 10401, pp. 167–187. Springer, Cham (2017). https://doi.org/10.1007/978-3-319-63688-7_6

[DPSZ12]   Damgård, I., Pastro, V., Smart, N., Zakarias, S.: Multiparty computation from somewhat homomorphic encryption. In: Safavi-Naini, R., Canetti, R. (eds.) CRYPTO 2012. LNCS, vol. 7417, pp. 643–662. Springer, Heidelberg (2012). https://doi.org/10.1007/978-3-642-32009-5_38

[Ds17]   Doerner, J., Shelat, A.: Scaling ORAM for secure computation. In: ACM CCS 2017, October/November 2017

[EKM17]   Esser, A., Kübler, R., May, A.: LPN decoded. In: Katz, J., Shacham, H. (eds.) CRYPTO 2017, Part II. LNCS, vol. 10402, pp. 486–514. Springer, Cham (2017). https://doi.org/10.1007/978-3-319-63715-0_17

[FKI06]   Fossorier, M.P.C., Kobara, K., Imai, H.: Modeling bit flipping decoding based on nonorthogonal check sums with application to iterative decoding attack of McEliece cryptosystem. IEEE Trans. Inf. Theory 53(1), 402–411 (2006)

[FS09]   Finiasz, M., Sendrier, N.: Security bounds for the design of code-based cryptosystems. In: Matsui, M. (ed.) ASIACRYPT 2009. LNCS, vol. 5912, pp. 88–105. Springer, Heidelberg (2009). https://doi.org/10.1007/978-3-642-10366-7_6

[FS21]   Fleischhacker, N., Simkin, M.: On publicly-accountable zero-knowledge and small shuffle arguments. In: Garay, J.A. (ed.) PKC 2021, Part II. LNCS, vol. 12711, pp. 618–648. Springer, Cham (2021). https://doi.org/10.1007/978-3-030-75248-4_22

[GGM86]   Goldreich, O., Goldwasser, S., Micali, S.: How to construct random functions. J. ACM 33(4), 792–807 (1986)

[GJL20]   Guo, Q., Johansson, T., Löndahl, C.: Solving LPN using covering codes. J. Cryptol. 33(1), 1–33 (2020)

[GKWY20]   Guo, C., Katz, J., Wang, X., Yu, Y.: Efficient and secure multiparty computation from fixed-key block ciphers. In: 2020 IEEE Symposium on Security and Privacy, May 2020

[GRS08]   Gilbert, H., Robshaw, M.J.B., Seurin, Y.: Good variants of HB$^+$ are hard to find. In: Tsudik, G. (ed.) FC 2008. LNCS, vol. 5143, pp. 156–170. Springer, Heidelberg (2008). https://doi.org/10.1007/978-3-540-85230-8_12

[HK21]   Heath, D., Kolesnikov, V.: One hot garbling. In: Kim, Y., Kim, J., Vigna, G., Shi, E. (eds.) CCS 2021: 2021 ACM SIGSAC Conference on Computer and Communications Security, pp. 574–593. ACM (2021)

[HOSS18]   Hazay, C., Orsini, E., Scholl, P., Soria-Vazquez, E.: Concretely efficient large-scale MPC with active security (or, TinyKeys for TinyOT). In: Peyrin, T., Galbraith, S. (eds.) ASIACRYPT 2018, Part III. LNCS, vol. 11274, pp. 86–117. Springer, Cham (2018). https://doi.org/10.1007/978-3-030-03332-3_4

[HSS17]   Hazay, C., Scholl, P., Soria-Vazquez, E.: Low cost constant round MPC combining BMR and oblivious transfer. In: Takagi, T., Peyrin, T. (eds.) ASIACRYPT 2017, Part I. LNCS, vol. 10624, pp. 598–628. Springer, Cham (2017). https://doi.org/10.1007/978-3-319-70694-8_21

[IKNP03] Ishai, Y., Kilian, J., Nissim, K., Petrank, E.: Extending oblivious transfers efficiently. In: Boneh, D. (ed.) CRYPTO 2003. LNCS, vol. 2729, pp. 145–161. Springer, Heidelberg (2003). https://doi.org/10.1007/978-3-540-45146-4_9

[IPS09] Ishai, Y., Prabhakaran, M., Sahai, A.: Secure arithmetic computation with no honest majority. In: Reingold, O. (ed.) TCC 2009. LNCS, vol. 5444, pp. 294–314. Springer, Heidelberg (2009). https://doi.org/10.1007/978-3-642-00457-5_18

[Kir11] Kirchner, P.: Improved generalized birthday attack. Cryptology ePrint Archive, Report 2011/377 (2011). https://eprint.iacr.org/2011/377

[KKW18] Katz, J., Kolesnikov, V., Wang, X.: Improved non-interactive zero knowledge with applications to post-quantum signatures. In: ACM CCS 2018, October 2018

[KPR18] Keller, M., Pastro, V., Rotaru, D.: Overdrive: making SPDZ great again. In: Nielsen, J.B., Rijmen, V. (eds.) EUROCRYPT 2018, Part III. LNCS, vol. 10822, pp. 158–189. Springer, Cham (2018). https://doi.org/10.1007/978-3-319-78372-7_6

[KPTZ13] Kiayias, A., Papadopoulos, S., Triandopoulos, N., Zacharias, T.: Delegatable pseudorandom functions and applications. In: ACM CCS 2013, November 2013

[KZ20] Kales, D., Zaverucha, G.: Improving the performance of the picnic signature scheme. IACR Trans. Cryptogr. Hardware Embed. Syst. 154–188 (2020)

[LF06] Levieil, É., Fouque, P.-A.: An improved LPN algorithm. In: De Prisco, R., Yung, M. (eds.) SCN 2006. LNCS, vol. 4116, pp. 348–359. Springer, Heidelberg (2006). https://doi.org/10.1007/11832072_24

[LM13] Lyubashevsky, V., Masny, D.: Man-in-the-middle secure authentication schemes from LPN and weak PRFs. In: Canetti, R., Garay, J.A. (eds.) CRYPTO 2013, Part II. LNCS, vol. 8043, pp. 308–325. Springer, Heidelberg (2013). https://doi.org/10.1007/978-3-642-40084-1_18

[LWYY22] Liu, H., Wang, X., Yang, K., Yu, Y.: The hardness of LPN over any integer ring and field for PCG applications. Cryptology ePrint Archive, Paper 2022/712 (2022). https://eprint.iacr.org/2022/712

[Lyu05] Lyubashevsky, V.: The parity problem in the presence of noise, decoding random linear codes, and the subset sum problem. In: Chekuri, C., Jansen, K., Rolim, J.D.P., Trevisan, L. (eds.) APPROX/RANDOM - 2005. LNCS, vol. 3624, pp. 378–389. Springer, Heidelberg (2005). https://doi.org/10.1007/11538462_32

[MAB+18] Melchor, C.A., et al.: Hamming quasi-cyclic (HQC). NIST PQC Round 2, 4–13 (2018)

[MMT11] May, A., Meurer, A., Thomae, E.: Decoding random linear codes in $\tilde{O}(2^{0.054n})$. In: Lee, D.H., Wang, X. (eds.) ASIACRYPT 2011. LNCS, vol. 7073, pp. 107–124. Springer, Heidelberg (2011). https://doi.org/10.1007/978-3-642-25385-0_6

[MO15] May, A., Ozerov, I.: On computing nearest neighbors with applications to decoding of binary linear codes. In: Oswald, E., Fischlin, M. (eds.) EUROCRYPT 2015, Part I. LNCS, vol. 9056, pp. 203–228. Springer, Heidelberg (2015). https://doi.org/10.1007/978-3-662-46800-5_9

[MZR+13] Ma, Y., et al.: Incremental offline/online PIR. J. Clin. Investig. **123**(1) (2013)

[OSY21] Orlandi, C., Scholl, P., Yakoubov, S.: The rise of paillier: homomorphic secret sharing and public-key silent OT. In: Canteaut, A., Standaert, F.-X. (eds.) EUROCRYPT 2021, Part I. LNCS, vol. 12696, pp. 678–708. Springer, Cham (2021). https://doi.org/10.1007/978-3-030-77870-5_24

[Ove06] Overbeck, R.: Statistical decoding revisited. In: Batten, L.M., Safavi-Naini, R. (eds.) ACISP 2006. LNCS, vol. 4058, pp. 283–294. Springer, Heidelberg (2006). https://doi.org/10.1007/11780656_24

[Pra62] Prange, E.: The use of information sets in decoding cyclic codes. IRE Trans. Inf. Theory **8**(5), 5–9 (1962)

[RS21a] Rachuri, R., Scholl, P.: Le mans: dynamic and fluid MPC for dishonest majority. Cryptology ePrint Archive, Report 2021/1579 (2021). https://eprint.iacr.org/2021/1579

[RS21b] Rindal, P., Schoppmann, P.: VOLE-PSI: fast OPRF and circuit-PSI from vector-OLE. In: Canteaut, A., Standaert, F.-X. (eds.) EUROCRYPT 2021, Part II. LNCS, vol. 12697, pp. 901–930. Springer, Cham (2021). https://doi.org/10.1007/978-3-030-77886-6_31

[Saa07] Saarinen, M.-J.O.: Linearization attacks against syndrome based hashes. In: Srinathan, K., Rangan, C.P., Yung, M. (eds.) INDOCRYPT 2007. LNCS, vol. 4859, pp. 1–9. Springer, Heidelberg (2007). https://doi.org/10.1007/978-3-540-77026-8_1

[SGRR19] Schoppmann, P., Gascón, A., Reichert, L., Raykova, M.: Distributed vector-OLE: improved constructions and implementation. In: ACM CCS 2019, November 2019

[Ste88] Stern, J.: A method for finding codewords of small weight. In: Cohen, G., Wolfmann, J. (eds.) Coding Theory 1988. LNCS, vol. 388, pp. 106–113. Springer, Heidelberg (1989). https://doi.org/10.1007/BFb0019850

[Wag02] Wagner, D.: A generalized birthday problem. In: Yung, M. (ed.) CRYPTO 2002. LNCS, vol. 2442, pp. 288–304. Springer, Heidelberg (2002). https://doi.org/10.1007/3-540-45708-9_19

[WRK17a] Wang, X., Ranellucci, S., Katz, J.: Authenticated garbling and efficient maliciously secure two-party computation. In: ACM CCS 2017, October/November 2017

[WRK17b] Wang, X., Ranellucci, S., Katz, J.: Global-scale secure multiparty computation. In: ACM CCS 2017, October/November 2017

[YSWW21] Yang, K., Sarkar, P., Weng, C., Wang, X.: QuickSilver: efficient and affordable zero-knowledge proofs for circuits and polynomials over any field. Cryptology ePrint Archive, Report 2021/076 (2021). https://eprint.iacr.org/2021/076

[YWL+20] Yang, K., Weng, C., Lan, X., Zhang, J., Wang, X.: Ferret: fast extension for correlated OT with small communication. In: ACM CCS 2020, November 2020

[Zic17] Zichron, L.: Locally computable arithmetic pseudorandom generators. Master's thesis, School of Electrical Engineering, Tel Aviv University (2017)

[ZJW16] Zhang, B., Jiao, L., Wang, M.: Faster algorithms for solving LPN. In: Fischlin, M., Coron, J.-S. (eds.) EUROCRYPT 2016. LNCS, vol. 9665, pp. 168–195. Springer, Heidelberg (2016). https://doi.org/10.1007/978-3-662-49890-3_7

Public Key Cryptography

Public-Key Watermarking Schemes
for Pseudorandom Functions

Rupeng Yang[1,2(✉)], Zuoxia Yu[1,2], Man Ho Au[1], and Willy Susilo[2]

[1] Department of Computer Science, The University of Hong Kong, Hong Kong, China
orbbyrp@gmail.com , allenau@cs.hku.hk
[2] Institute of Cybersecurity and Cryptology, School of Computing and Information
Technology, University of Wollongong, Wollongong, NSW, Australia
wsusilo@uow.edu.au

Abstract. A software watermarking scheme can embed a message into
a program while preserving its functionality. The embedded message can
be extracted later by an extraction algorithm, and no one could remove it
without significantly changing the functionality of the program. A watermarking scheme is public key if neither the marking procedure nor the
extraction procedure needs a watermarking secret key. Prior constructions of watermarking schemes mainly focus on watermarking pseudorandom functions (PRFs), and the major open problem in this direction is
to construct a public-key watermarkable PRF.

In this work, we solve the open problem via constructing public-key
watermarkable PRFs with different trade-offs from various assumptions,
ranging from standard lattice assumptions to the existence of indistinguishability obfuscation. To achieve the results, we first construct watermarking schemes in a weaker model, where the extraction algorithm is
provided with a "hint" about the watermarked PRF key. Then we upgrade
the constructions to standard watermarking schemes using a robust unobfuscatable PRF. We also provide the first construction of robust unobfuscatable PRF in this work, which is of independent interest.

1 Introduction

A software watermarking scheme allows one to embed a message into a program
without significantly changing its functionality. Moreover, any attempt to remove
the embedded message would destroy the functionality of the watermarked program. Watermarking schemes have many real-world applications, including ownership protection, traitor tracing, etc., and recently, it is also applied in new
applications such as quantum copy-protection [ALL+21,KNY21].

The theoretical study of software watermarking is initiated by Barak et al.
[BGI+01] and Hopper et al. [HMW07], where formal definitions are presented.
They also explore the (im)possibility to achieve certain definitions of watermark-
ing and study connections between different definitions. However, neither of them

Y. Dodis and T. Shrimpton (Eds.): CRYPTO 2022, LNCS 13508, pp. 637–667, 2022.
https://doi.org/10.1007/978-3-031-15979-4_22

provides a concrete construction. It is notoriously hard to construct watermarking schemes with provable security, and early constructions [NSS99,YF11,Nis13] are only proven secure against restricted adversaries, which are not allowed to change the format of the watermarked object.

Cohen et al. [CHN+16] propose the first watermarking scheme with provable security against arbitrary removal strategies. They also show that it is impossible to watermark learnable functions. A natural class of non-learnable functions are the cryptographic ones, such as pseudorandom function (PRF). Therefore, Cohen et al. and subsequent works mainly study watermarking for cryptographic functionalities, with a primary focus on watermarkable PRFs, which can be applied to construct watermarking schemes for various primitives in minicrypt and has many real-world applications as discussed in [CHN+16]. In this work, we also consider watermarking schemes for PRFs.

Watermarking PRFs. A watermarkable PRF is a PRF family F with two additional algorithms, namely, the marking algorithm and the extraction algorithm. The marking algorithm takes as input the mark key, a message, and a PRF key k, and outputs a watermarked circuit, which approximately evaluates $F_k(\cdot)$. The extraction algorithm extracts the embedded message from a watermarked circuit with an extraction key. Its main security property is unremovability, which requires that given a watermarked circuit C^* for a random PRF key (namely, the challenge key), the adversary is not able to produce a circuit that agrees with C^* on almost all inputs, yet the extraction algorithm fails to extract the original message from it. The mark key and the extraction key are generated when setting up the scheme, and a watermarking scheme is *public key* if both the mark key and the extraction key can be made public. Also, a secret-key watermarking scheme has *public extraction* (resp. *public marking*) if it is secure against an adversary with the extraction key (resp. *mark key*).

The first construction of watermarkable PRF is presented by Cohen et al. in [CHN+16]. The construction is based on an indistinguishability obfuscation (iO) and has public extraction. Then in [YAL+19], Yang et al. improve Cohen et al.'s scheme to further achieve collusion resistant security, where the adversary is allowed to view multiple watermarked circuits for the challenge key. However, in both constructions, the mark key should be kept private.

In another line of work, Boneh et al. [BLW17] propose a new approach that builds watermarkable PRF from variants of constrained PRFs [BW13,KPTZ13, BGI14]. The scheme in [BLW17] is still instantiated from iO. Then in [KW17], Kim and Wu present the first watermarkable PRF from standard assumptions. Later, in [PS18,PS20], Peikert and Shiehian also instantiate the construction in [BLW17] from standard lattice assumptions. However, these schemes need a secret key in both the marking algorithm and the extraction algorithm.

Subsequent works explore how to construct watermarkable PRF with stronger security from standard assumptions. In [QWZ18,KW19], watermarkable PRFs that have public marking are constructed. The schemes also achieve security with extraction queries, where the adversary can learn extraction results of its generated circuits. However, they do not have standard pseudorandomness against an adversary with the extraction key. Recently, in [YAYX20], Yang et al. upgrade previous watermarkable PRFs from standard assumptions to further achieve collusion resistance. Nonetheless, none of these schemes support public extraction.

Motivation. There are no candidate constructions of public-key watermarkable PRFs in the literature. Even worse, in previous secret-key watermarkable PRFs, the watermarking authority, who holds the secret key, can remove the watermark embedded in any watermarked circuit. This is a severe threat to all users. In contrast, in a public-key watermarking scheme, no one has this privilege since the scheme does not have such secret key. Therefore, no trust assumption is needed in a public-key watermarking scheme and it can provide a much better security guarantee in practice. This raises the following natural question:

Can we construct public-key watermarkable PRFs?

There are a few technical barriers towards this goal. First, existing approaches for achieving public marking [QWZ18,KW19] will lead to a watermarkable PRF that is only pseudorandom against adversaries without the extraction key of the scheme, and one can compromise its pseudorandomness using the extraction key. This relaxed pseudorandomness is acceptable in the secret extraction setting since the extraction key is held by an authority. However, there is no authority for a public-key watermarking scheme. Thus, if we combine previous ideas for obtaining public marking and that for obtaining public extraction, we will get a public-key watermarkable "PRF" without pseudorandomness.

Moreover, known techniques for constructing watermarkable PRFs with public extraction rely on iO. Despite recent breakthrough [JLS21] that constructs indistinguishability obfuscations from well-founded assumptions, the construction is not post-quantum secure. Thus, new ideas that construct watermarkable PRFs with public extraction from standard lattice assumptions are desired.

Our Results. In this work, we affirmatively answer the above question and present constructions of public-key watermarking schemes for PRFs. To overcome the technical issues, we introduce a new framework that constructs watermarkable PRFs from an *unobfuscatable PRF* [BGI+01] with *robust learnability* [BP13] and a new primitive called *hinting watermarkable PRF*, which relaxes a standard watermarking scheme by allowing its extraction algorithm to use an extra "hint" about the watermarked PRF key. We remark that via our framework, we can obtain (public-key) watermarkable PRFs with standard pseudorandomness from (public-key) hinting watermarkable PRFs with relaxed pseudorandomness, and this solves the first technical issue described above. We then construct public-key hinting watermarkable PRFs from either standard lattice assumptions or iO, with different trade-offs that will be discussed below. To obtain the lattice based constructions, we introduce some new techniques for achieving public extraction from standard lattice assumptions. Besides, we construct the first unobfuscatable PRF with robust learnability in this work. The new framework, notion and constructions may find further applications.[1]

---

[1] For example, we can apply our new framework to upgrade the watermarking schemes in [QWZ18,KW19] to achieve full pseudorandomness, by viewing them as (secret-key) hinting watermarkable PRFs. This solves an open problem in these two works.

Table 1. Properties achieved by existing watermarkable PRFs. For the parameter ϵ, the term "$\approx \frac{1}{2}$" denotes that $\epsilon = \frac{1}{2} - \frac{1}{poly}$, the term "negl" denotes that ϵ can be any negligible function, the term "1/exp" denotes that ϵ is equal to a concrete value that is exponentially-small, and the term "$\approx \frac{1}{6}$" denotes that $\epsilon = \frac{1}{6} - \frac{1}{poly}$. We use "CR" to denote collusion resistant unremovability. We consider pseudorandomness against an adversary with the mark key and the extraction key (even for a secret-key watermarking scheme). We use "UK" to denote pseudorandomness of PRF evaluations using unmarked keys and use "MK" to denote pseudorandomness of PRF evaluations using marked keys.

	Message Embedding	Public Marking	Public Extraction	Unremovability		Pseudorandomness		Assumptions
				ϵ	CR	UK	MK	
[CHN+16]	✓	✗	✓	$\approx \frac{1}{2}$	✗	✓	✗	Lattice+iO
[BLW17]	✓	✗	✗	negl	✗	✓	✗	Lattice+iO
[YAL+19]	✓	✗	✓	negl	✓	✓	✗	Lattice+iO
[KW17]	✓	✗	✗	negl	✗	✓	✗	Lattice
[QWZ18]	✓	✓	✗	$\approx \frac{1}{2}$	✗	✗	✗	Lattice
[KW19]	✓	✓	✗	$\approx \frac{1}{2}$	✗	✓‡	✗	Lattice
[YAYX20]	✓	✗	✗	negl	✓	✓	✗	Lattice
	✓	✓	✗	$\approx \frac{1}{2}$	✓	✓‡	✗	Lattice
	✗	✓	✓	negl	-	✓	✓	Lattice
	✓	✓	✓	1/exp	✓	✓	✓	Lattice
This Work	✗	✓	✓	$\approx \frac{1}{6}$	-	✓	✓	Lattice+FHE
	✓	✓	✓	negl	✗	✓	✓	Lattice+iO
	✓	✓	✓	$\approx \frac{1}{6}$	✗	✓	✓	Lattice+FHE+iO

‡: A weaker T-restricted pseudorandomness (see [KW19]) is achieved.

By instantiating our constructions, we obtain public-key watermarkable PRFs from different assumptions. We consider three types of assumptions in this work, namely, standard lattice assumptions, the assumption that the GSW encryption scheme [GSW13] is circular secure[2], and the existence of iO. The three assumptions are denoted as "Lattice", "FHE", and "iO" respectively. Also, we consider constructions in either the *mark-embedding* setting, where a program is either marked or unmarked, or the *message-embedding* setting, where a marked program is embedded with a message. Besides, we use ϵ to denote the fraction of inputs of the watermarked circuits that can be modified by the adversary when defining unremovability. More precisely, let λ be the security parameter, we have:

- From **Lattice**, we construct a public-key watermarkable PRF in the mark-embedding setting, where $\epsilon = negl(\lambda)$, i.e., the scheme guarantees that an adversary cannot remove the mark in a watermarked circuit if it modifies the circuit on a negligible fraction of inputs.
- From **Lattice**, we construct a public-key watermarkable PRF in the message-embedding setting. The scheme also has collusion resistant security. A caveat of this construction is that it only has exponentially-small ϵ, i.e., the adversary can modify the watermarked circuit on at most $M = 2^n/2^{poly(\lambda)}$ inputs, where n is the input length. Nonetheless, we still have $M = 2^{poly(\lambda)}$.

---

[2] Formal definition for this assumption can be found in the full version.

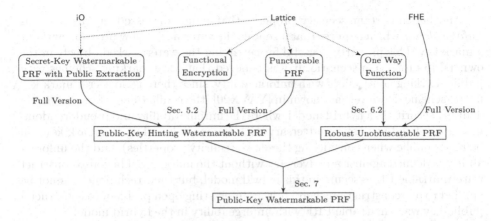

Fig. 1. The roadmap for constructing public-key watermarkable PRFs from concrete assumptions. The dotted lines denote results from previous work.

- From Lattice and FHE, we construct a public-key mark-embedding watermarkable PRF with $\epsilon = 1/6 - 1/poly(\lambda)$.
- From Lattice and iO, we construct a public-key message-embedding watermarkable PRF with $\epsilon = negl(\lambda)$.
- From Lattice, FHE and iO, we construct a public-key message-embedding watermarkable PRF with $\epsilon = 1/6 - 1/poly(\lambda)$.

Features of our constructions, together with comparison with previous watermarkable PRFs are presented in Table 1. Also, we illustrate how to instantiate our public-key watermarkable PRFs from concrete assumptions in Fig. 1.

We stress that all public-key watermarkable PRFs constructed in this work have pseudorandomness for marked keys, i.e., no one could distinguish outputs of a watermarked PRF key and outputs of a random function. This property is not achieved in previous watermarkable PRFs with public extraction. This is because in these constructions, an adversary with an extraction key can extract meaningful information via oracle access to the marked key. In our construction, we circumvent this barrier by using a white-box extraction algorithm, where the algorithm must view the code of the marked key. We refer the reader to [Zha21] for a more detailed discussion on the notion of white-box tracing/extraction.

Open Problems. We initiate the study of public-key watermarkable PRFs in this work. We give mark-embedding constructions from lattice and message-embedding constructions from iO. We also construct a lattice based message-embedding scheme, but it restricts the parameter $\epsilon = 1/2^{poly(\lambda)}$. This is smaller than the parameter ϵ in previous works, which is either a constant number or restricted by any (rather than a concrete) negligible function. The main open problem is therefore to construct a message-embedding public-key watermarkable PRF with larger ϵ from standard lattice assumptions. Besides, in our mark-embedding constructions and iO based constructions, we need additionally assume circular security of the GSW scheme to achieve a constant ϵ. It will be interesting to obtain constant ϵ without such additional assumptions.

Another important security property that is not discussed in this paper is *unforgeability*, which requires that no one could watermark a new program without a mark key. This property is useful for certifying the watermarked objects in the ownership protection scenario. It was believed that watermarking schemes with public marking contradicts with unforgeability, since there is no secret mark key in the scheme. However, as shown in [YAYX20], the conflict can be overcome via defining security in a hybrid model, where the unremovability and pseudorandomness are defined against an adversary with the mark key (i.e., the mark key can be made public when considering these two security properties), and the unforgeability is defined against an adversary without the mark key. They also construct watermarkable PRFs secure in this hybrid model, but their techniques cannot be applied to our constructions here. It is an interesting open problem to construct a public-key watermarkable PRF with unforgeability in the hybrid model.

2   Technical Overview

In this section, we provide a technical overview of our constructions of public-key watermarkable PRFs. We first consider a relaxed notion of watermarking, where each PRF key is associated with a "hint" that can be used to help extract messages. We call it hinting watermarking and in Sect. 2.1, we explain our main ideas for constructing public-key hinting watermarkable PRFs. Then in Sect. 2.2, we show how to upgrade a public-key hinting watermarkable PRF to a standard public-key watermarkable PRF by using an unobfuscatable PRF with "robust learnability". Existing constructions of unobfuscatable PRFs [BGI+01] do not have robust learnability and in Sect. 2.3, we describe how to achieve it.

2.1   Constructing Public-Key Hinting Watermarkable PRFs

The syntax of a hinting watermarkable PRF is identical to a standard watermarkable PRF except that each of its PRF keys is associated with a hint and the hint is used in the extraction algorithm to help extract messages. We assume that the extraction algorithm always uses the correct hint when defining the security of a hinting watermarking scheme, i.e., given a (modified) watermarked PRF key, the hint associated with the PRF key will be employed in the extraction algorithm. Besides, we require its security to hold against an adversary that has the hint associated with the challenge key, yet we only need its pseudorandomness to hold against an adversary without the hint. Next, we describe how to construct public-key hinting watermarkable PRFs.

Construction from Indistinguishability Obfuscation. We first present a general construction of public-key hinting watermarkable PRF from a watermarkable PRF F with secret marking and public extraction. Our main strategy is to generate a fresh mark key/extraction key pair for each PRF key. In this way, there are no global mark keys that should be kept secret. In addition, we set the hint for a PRF key as its extraction key and this allows the extraction key to be used in the extraction algorithm.

In more detail, the PRF key of the public-key hinting watermarkable PRF is $K = (mk, k)$ and the associated hint is $\mathtt{hint} = ek$, where (mk, ek) is a mark key/extraction key pair of F and k is a PRF key of F. Given the PRF key $K = (mk, k)$ and an input x, the evaluation algorithm of the new scheme runs the evaluation algorithm of F on input (k, x), and given $K = (mk, k)$ and a message msg, the marking algorithm of the new scheme runs the marking algorithm of F on input (mk, k, msg). Besides, given a circuit C and a hint $\mathtt{hint} = ek$, the extraction algorithm runs the extraction algorithm of F on input (ek, C). Security of the constructed public-key hinting watermarkable PRF comes from the assumption that the correct hint is always used and the fact that F is unremovable even if ek is public.

Now, if we instantiate this general construction from previous watermarkable PRFs with public extraction [CHN+16], we obtain public-key hinting watermarkable PRFs from iO. Next, we propose constructions from cryptographic primitives that can be instantiated from standard lattice assumptions, including puncturable PRF, functional encryption, etc.

Mark-Embedding Public-Key Hinting Watermarking from Lattices. First, we consider mark-embedding public-key hinting watermarkable PRFs.

The Starting Point. The starting point of our construction is a watermarking scheme with public marking and *secret extraction* presented in [QWZ18]. The scheme is built on a puncturable PRF [SW14] and a public key encryption (PKE). A puncturable PRF F is a family of PRF that allows one to derive a punctured key k_{x^*} from a PRF key k, where $\mathsf{F}_{k_{x^*}}(\cdot)$ and $\mathsf{F}_k(\cdot)$ evaluate identically on almost all inputs except at the "punctured" point x^*. Its security requires that given the punctured key k_{x^*}, $\mathsf{F}_k(x^*)$ is still pseudorandom.

Here, we slightly modify the scheme and describe it as a hinting watermarking scheme. Its extraction key is a secret key of the PKE scheme. Also, the PRF key $K = k$ is a key of the puncturable PRF F, and the hint is $\mathtt{hint} = (x^*, ct^*)$, where x^* is a random input of F and ct^* is an encryption of $y^* = \mathsf{F}_k(x^*)$. Given a PRF key $K = k$ and an input x, the evaluation algorithm outputs $\mathsf{F}_k(x)$. Also, on input a PRF key $K = k$, the marking algorithm punctures k on x^* and generates a circuit C s.t. $\mathsf{C}(x) = \mathsf{F}_{k_{x^*}}(x)$. To test if a circuit C is watermarked, the extraction algorithm first recovers y^* by decrypting ct^* in the hint and outputs "marked" iff C is punctured (i.e., $\mathsf{C}(x^*) \neq y^*$).

By security of the puncturable PRF and the PKE scheme, y^* is hidden from an adversary given a watermarked circuit and the hint. Thus, the adversary cannot create a circuit that outputs y^* on input x^* and security of the scheme follows. However, when the extraction key, which is the secret key of the underlying PKE scheme, is made public, the adversary will be able to recover y^* from ct^* and thus compromise security of the scheme.

On Achieving Public Extraction. We solve the problem by designing an extraction algorithm that tests if output of a circuit equals to a given value without knowing the target value. This is achieved by using an injective one way function

f. More precisely, in our new scheme, there are no extraction keys and the ciphertext ct^* in the hint is replaced with $z^* = f(y^*)$ (i.e., $\mathtt{hint} = (x^*, z^*)$), where $y^* = \mathsf{F}_k(x^*)$. For a PRF key $K = k$, the evaluation algorithm still outputs $\mathsf{F}_k(x)$ on input x and the marked version of K is still a circuit C s.t. $\mathsf{C}(x) = \mathsf{F}_{k_{x^*}}(x)$. Besides, to test if a circuit C is watermarked, the extraction algorithm outputs "marked" iff $z^* \neq f(\mathsf{C}(x^*))$.

The new extraction algorithm actually tests if $\mathsf{C}(x^*)$ is not equal to y^*. Also, security of the one way function plus security of the puncturable PRF guarantee that the adversary cannot learn y^* from a watermarked circuit and the hint. Thus, it is not able to produce a circuit that outputs y^* on input x^*. Therefore, our new construction achieves security in the public extraction setting and thus is a secure public-key hinting watermarkable PRF.

Message-Embedding Public-Key Hinting Watermarking from Lattices. Next, we show how to construct public-key hinting watermarkable PRFs with message embedding from lattices. The construction relies on a functional encryption (FE) scheme [BSW11,O'N10] and is inspired by the construction of watermarkable PKE scheme presented in [GKM+19]. In a nutshell, an FE scheme is a PKE scheme that associates each secret key sk_f with a function f, where the secret keys can be derived from a master secret key. Besides, by using the secret key sk_f to decrypt a ciphertext that encrypts a plaintext m, one can obtain $f(m)$, but nothing else.

From FE to Publicly Verifiable Puncturing. We can use the FE scheme to realize a puncturable "PRF" that supports public verifiability of punctured keys. More precisely, we set the normal PRF key as a secret key sk_{f_ε} of FE, where $f_\varepsilon(t\|\mu) = \mu$. Also, we puncture the key on (inputs that encrypts) plaintexts with prefix t^* by generating a key $sk_{f_{t^*}}$, where $f_{t^*}(t\|\mu) = \mu$ if $t \neq t^*$ and $f_{t^*}(t\|\mu) = 0$ if $t = t^*$. To evaluate the PRF (with either a normal PRF key or a punctured key), the evaluation algorithm just decrypts the input with the secret key. Note that the normal PRF key and the punctured key function identically on an input if it encrypts a plaintext with prefix $t \neq t^*$. In addition, given a punctured key, one could not learn any information about μ from punctured inputs that encrypt $t^*\|\mu$, due to security of the FE scheme. Finally, given the master public key, one can publicly check if a key is punctured on plaintexts with prefix t^* by sampling a random μ, encrypting $t^*\|\mu$, and checking if its decryption is not equal to μ.

From Publicly Verifiable Puncturing to Public-Key Hinting Watermarking. The FE-based puncturable "PRF" with public verifiability implies a public-key hinting watermarkable "PRF" with mark embedding immediately. In particular, the PRF key of the scheme is $K = (msk, sk_{f_\varepsilon})$, where msk is a master secret key of FE and sk_{f_ε} is a secret key derived from msk. The hint for K is the master public key mpk for msk. Given an input x, the evaluation algorithm decrypts x with sk_{f_ε} and outputs the decryption result. The marking algorithm punctures sk_{f_ε} on a public random string t^* and outputs a circuit that decrypts inputs with the punctured key. Given a circuit C, the extraction algorithm outputs "marked" iff the circuit is punctured on plaintexts with prefix t^*. The extraction algorithm can be run publicly with the hint mpk since the underlying puncturable PRF is publicly verifiable. Also, security of the hinting watermarking scheme follows from security of the puncturable PRF directly.

On Supporting Message Embedding. Based on this, we construct hinting watermarking scheme with message embedding by employing the message embedding technique introduced in [GKM+19, YAL+19]. To support this, we define $g_\varepsilon(ind\|t\|\mu) = \mu$ and define

$$g_{msg,t^*}(ind\|t\|\mu) = \begin{cases} 0 & \text{If } t = t^* \wedge ind \geq msg \\ \mu & \text{Otherwise} \end{cases}$$

In the message-embedding construction, the PRF key is $K = (msk, sk_{g_\varepsilon})$ and the hint is still the corresponding master public key. The evaluation algorithm decrypts the input with sk_{g_ε}, and to embed a message msg into a PRF key, the marking algorithm generates a circuit that decrypts with the secret key $sk_{g_{msg,t^*}}$. Then, to extract the embedded message from a circuit C, the extraction algorithm will test if the circuit is punctured on prefix $ind\|t^*$ for all possible[3] ind and output msg if it is not punctured on prefix $(msg - 1)\|t^*$, but is punctured on prefix $msg\|t^*$.

Now, given a watermarked circuit embedded with a message msg^*, the adversary cannot modify the embedded message since by security of the FE scheme:

1. The adversary cannot distinguish a ciphertext encrypting $ind\|t^*\|\mu$ from a ciphertext that encrypts a random plaintext if $ind < msg^*$. As the adversary is not allowed to change the functionality of the watermarked circuit too much, it cannot puncture on these ciphertexts.
2. The adversary cannot learn μ from a ciphertext encrypting $ind\|t^*\|\mu$ if $ind \geq msg^*$, thus it cannot "unpuncture" the watermarked circuit on these punctured points.

Similarly, we can show that the construction is collusion resistant if the underlying FE is collusion resistant.

On Achieving Pseudorandomness. The above construction actually does not have pseudorandomness. We solve the problem by using a PKE scheme with pseudorandom ciphertexts and a PRF F. In more detail, we add a secret key k of F in both the normal PRF key and the marked keys. Then the evaluation algorithm (resp. the marked circuit) will encrypt the output of the evaluation algorithm (resp. the marked circuit) of previous construction with the PKE scheme, where the encryption randomness is $F_k(x)$. Note that we can put the secret key of the PKE scheme into the hint and thus the extraction algorithm can still test if a given circuit is punctured on plaintexts with a specific prefix. Thus, security of the scheme still holds. In addition, its pseudorandomness is guaranteed by the (ciphertext) pseudorandomness of the underlying PRF and PKE scheme.

On Instantiating the FE Scheme. In above discussion, we implicitly assume that all ciphertexts in the ciphertext space of the FE scheme (i.e., the input space of

---

[3] Here, we assume that the message space of the hinting watermarking scheme is of polynomial-size, and this restriction can be removed if we use the jump finding technique introduced in [BCP14, NWZ16].

the hinting watermarkable PRF) can be output by the encryption algorithm. However, to the best of our knowledge, existing FE schemes from standard assumptions [GVW12, GKP+13, AR17, AV19] do not satisfy this property. Even worse, in all of these schemes, the ratio between the number of honestly encrypted ciphertexts and the size of the ciphertext space is exponentially-small. Thus, we have to carefully deal with those "invalid" ciphertexts, which are not output by the encryption algorithm, in the ciphertext space.

First, to ensure that the functionality of a PRF key will not change significantly after watermarking, we need to guarantee that both the normal PRF key and the watermarked PRF key, which use different secret keys of the FE scheme, evaluate identically on input an invalid ciphertext. We achieve this by requiring the FE scheme to have a special correctness, namely, given any secret key and any invalid ciphertext, the decryption result is always a decryption failure symbol $\perp$. We construct FE scheme with this correctness property from any FE scheme with perfect correctness and statistically sound non-interactive zero-knowledge (NIZK) proofs.

Besides, since the ratio ρ between the number of valid ciphertexts and the number of all possible ciphertexts is exponentially-small, the adversary can damage the evaluation on all valid ciphertexts and thus remove the embedded message even if it can only modify the watermarked circuit on a negligible fraction of inputs. We circumvent this problem by requiring that the adversary has to submit a circuit that agrees with the watermarked circuit on a $(1-\rho\cdot(1-1/poly(\lambda)))$ fraction of inputs. Note that even with this restriction, the adversary can still modify the watermarked circuit on exponentially-many inputs.

Remark 2.1. Our FE based construction only allows the adversary to modify the watermarked circuit on an exponentially-small fraction of inputs. Actually, a simple construction from any PRF also satisfies this weak security requirement. In particular, the marking algorithm replaces the PRF outputs with the embedded message if the input has prefix 0^λ, and the extraction algorithm runs the watermarked circuit on random inputs with prefix 0^λ and outputs the majority of the evaluation results. In this construction, the marking algorithm changes the PRF on $1/2^\lambda$ fraction of inputs, and an adversary can remove the watermark only if it changes the watermarked circuit on about $1/2^{\lambda+1}$ fraction of inputs. However, the scheme is less preferable for the following two reasons:

- In this construction, the adversary can remove the watermark by merely changing the circuit on half of the points modified by the marking algorithm. In contrast, the marking algorithm in our construction only changes the output on a negligible fraction of valid ciphertext, and the adversary has to change the outputs on nearly all valid ciphertexts to remove the watermark.
- Our construction will have a good parameter if we use an FE scheme with dense valid ciphertexts in its ciphertext space, but it seems impossible to improve the parameter of the simple construction described above.

We also would like to stress that our goal is to explore the possibility of building full-fledged public-key watermarkable PRFs from standard assumptions rather than constructing a watermarking scheme with weak security guarantee. We demonstrate that the goal is achievable, but our solution has some restrictions. The restrictions can be removed via either using a better FE scheme or improving the proposed construction. We believe our result would inspire future works that completely solve the problem.

2.2 From Public-Key Hinting Watermarkable PRFs to Public-Key Watermarkable PRFs

Next, we discuss how to transform a public-key hinting watermarkable PRF to a public-key watermarkable PRF. Note that a hinting watermarking scheme is already a standard watermarking scheme except that its extraction algorithm needs the correct hint for the given watermarked key. Thus, the main problem here is how to send the correct hint to the extraction algorithm.

To complete this task, we use an unobfuscatable PRF with robust learnability. In a nutshell, in an unobfuscatable PRF UF, each secret key uk_s is embedded with a secret information s. The function $\mathsf{UF}_{uk_s}(\cdot)$ is still pseudorandom if the adversary is only given oracle accesses to it. In addition, one can learn the secret information s given any circuit that implements the function. An unobfuscatable PRF has robust learnability if the secret information s can be learned from any circuit that *approximately* implements $\mathsf{UF}_{uk_s}(\cdot)$, i.e., the circuit may differ from the function on a small fraction of inputs.

Given a public-key hinting watermarkable PRF HF and an unobfuscatable PRF UF, we can construct a public-key watermarkable PRF as follows. The PRF key of the new scheme includes the PRF key k of HF and the PRF key uk_{hint} of UF, where hint is the hint for k and is embedded into uk_{hint} as the secret information. Given an input x, the evaluation algorithm outputs $(\mathsf{HF}_k(x), \mathsf{UF}_{uk_{\mathsf{hint}}}(x))$. To embed a message msg into the PRF key, the marking algorithm first generates k_{msg} by embedding msg to k and then outputs a circuit C s.t. $C(x) = (\mathsf{HF}_{k_{msg}}(x), \mathsf{UF}_{uk_{\mathsf{hint}}}(x))$. Finally, given a circuit C, the extraction algorithm first recovers hint from the second part of the circuit and then extracts the message from the first part of the circuit with hint.

Robust learnability of UF ensures that the extracted hint is correct, thus, security of the new scheme comes from the security of the underlying hinting watermarking scheme directly. The above construction also has pseudorandomness for unmarked keys due to the pseudorandomness of the underlying schemes, but it would not have pseudorandomness for marked keys if the underlying hinting watermarkable PRF does not have this property (recall that we do not require it when defining hinting watermarkable PRFs).

On Achieving Pseudorandomness for Marked Keys. We solve this issue by additionally using a PRF F to mask outputs of HF in both the evaluation algorithm and the marked circuit. The key k' of F is also embedded into the PRF key of UF and this allows the extraction algorithm to obtain k' and use it to unmask outputs of HF. In this way, security of the scheme is preserved. Besides, pseudorandomness of UF guarantees that k' is hidden to an adversary that can only access the marked key in a black-box manner. Then by the pseudorandomness of F and UF, the outputs of the marked key are also pseudorandom.

2.3   Constructing Robust Unobfuscatable PRFs

It remains to show how to construct an unobfuscatable PRF with robust learnability, which is a PRF family UF that allows one to learn the secret information s embedded in a PRF key k_s from any circuit that agrees with $UF_{k_s}(\cdot)$ on a large fraction of inputs. We first review existing constructions of unobfuscatable functions and explain why they do not lead to a robust unobfuscatable PRF.

The first constructions of unobfuscatable (pseudorandom) functions are presented by Barak et al. in [BGI+01]. Their unobfuscatable PRF also supports learnability from a circuit that approximates the PRF, but it does not allow the circuit to modify the PRF evaluation on particular inputs with a high probability. In contrast, we require that the secret information can be learned from a circuit that may modify the PRF evaluation on any input with probability 1 as long as the fraction of modified inputs is small. Then, in [BP13], Bitansky and Paneth construct an unobfuscatable function with robust learnability. However, the extraction algorithm of the scheme needs a verification key and it should be included in all outputs of the function. Therefore, the scheme cannot be pseudorandom. Recently, Zhandry [Zha21] constructs a robust unobfuscatable function for decryption functionality from an unobfuscatable function without robust learnability and a public-key traitor tracing scheme. It seems that the idea also works for the PRF setting, but this needs a public-key watermarkable PRF, which does not have a candidate construction yet[4].

Next, we describe our constructions of unobfuscatable PRFs with robust learnability. The constructions are inspired by techniques provided in [BGI+01,BP13]. In particular, both our construction and the construction of robust unobfuscatable function given in [BP13] can be viewed as random-self-reducible versions of the non-robust unobfuscatable functions constructed in [BGI+01]. However, as discussed above, the main techniques in [BP13] contradict the requirement of pseudorandomness, and we introduce some new ideas to overcome the difficulties.

Construction from Fully Homomorphic Encryption. The construction needs two PRFs F and F'. Besides, it relies on a special fully homomorphic encryption (FHE) scheme with the following properties[5]:

1. One can homomorphically evaluate a circuit over a ciphertext and rerandomize a ciphertext, without using the public key of the FHE scheme.
2. The ciphertext of the FHE scheme should be pseudorandom.
3. Even given the secret key of the FHE scheme, no one could distinguish a rerandomized ciphertext that encrypts a random plaintext from a random string in the ciphertext space.

The PRF key of the constructed robust unobfuscatable PRF UF is $K = (\alpha, \beta, k, k', pk, sk, s)$, where α, β are random strings, k and k' are PRF keys of F and F' respectively, (pk, sk) is a key pair of the FHE scheme, and s is the secret

---

[4] Recall that the main goal of this work is to construct the first public-key watermarkable PRF.

[5] We show how to construct the desired FHE scheme later in this section.

information. Then, given an input $X = (ind, x, ct)$, the PRF is defined as follows:

$$\mathsf{UF}_K(X) = \begin{cases} \mathsf{Enc}(pk, \alpha; \mathsf{F}'_{k'}(X)) & \text{If ind} = 0; \\ \mathsf{F}_k(x \| ct) & \text{If ind} = 1; \\ \mathsf{F}_k(x \oplus \alpha \| ct) \oplus \beta & \text{If ind} = 2; \\ \mathsf{F}_k(x \oplus \mathsf{Dec}(sk, ct) \oplus \beta \| ct) \oplus s & \text{If ind} = 3. \end{cases}$$

where Enc and Dec are the encryption algorithm and the decryption algorithm of the underlying FHE scheme respectively.

Robust Learnability of the Construction. We first explain why the above construction has robust learnability. For simplicity, we assume that the extractor is given a circuit C that agrees with $\mathsf{UF}_K(\cdot)$ on all but negligible fraction of inputs.

The extractor first gets an encryption of α via computing $ct^*_\alpha = \mathsf{C}(0 \| x_1 \| ct_1)$, where x_1 and ct_1 are random strings. As C and $\mathsf{UF}_K(\cdot)$ agree on all but negligible fraction of inputs, we have $ct^*_\alpha = \mathsf{UF}_K(0 \| x_1 \| ct_1) = \mathsf{Enc}(pk, \alpha; \mathsf{F}'_{k'}(0 \| x_1 \| ct_1))$ with all but negligible probability, i.e., ct^*_α should be an encryption of α.

Then, the extractor obtains an encryption of β as follows. It first computes $y_2 = \mathsf{C}(1 \| x_2 \| ct_2)$, where x_2 and ct_2 are random strings. Similar, we have $y_2 = \mathsf{F}_k(x_2 \| ct_2)$ with all but negligible probability. Next, it runs a circuit $\mathsf{P}(\cdot)$ on ct^*_α to obtain ct^*_β, where for any string a, $\mathsf{P}(a) = \mathsf{C}(2 \| x_2 \oplus a \| ct_2) \oplus y_2$. Again, with all but negligible probability, we have $\mathsf{C}(2 \| x_2 \oplus \alpha \| ct_2) = \mathsf{UF}_K(2 \| x_2 \oplus \alpha \| ct_2) = \mathsf{F}_k(x_2 \| ct_2) \oplus \beta$, which implies $\mathsf{P}(\alpha) = \beta$, i.e., ct^*_β is an encryption of β.

Now, with ct^*_α and ct^*_β, the extractor is ready to learn the secret information. It first samples a random γ and computes ct^*_3 as a rerandomized encryption of $\beta \oplus \gamma$. Then it computes $y_3 = \mathsf{C}(3 \| x_3 \| ct^*_3)$, where x_3 is a random string. Note that ct^*_3 is also random due to Property 3 of the special FHE scheme and the fact that γ is a random string. Thus we have $y_3 = \mathsf{UF}_K(3 \| x_3 \| ct^*_3) = \mathsf{F}_k(x_3 \oplus \gamma \| ct^*_3) \oplus s$ with all but negligible probability. Next, the extractor computes $y'_3 = \mathsf{C}(1 \| x_3 \oplus \gamma \| ct^*_3)$ and recovers $\bar{s} = y_3 \oplus y'_3$. As x_3 is a random string, γ is still hidden given $x_3 \oplus \gamma$, thus $x_3 \oplus \gamma \| ct^*_3$ is indistinguishable from a random string and with all but negligible probability, we have $y'_3 = \mathsf{UF}_K(1 \| x_3 \oplus \gamma \| ct^*_3) = \mathsf{F}_k(x_3 \oplus \gamma \| ct^*_3)$, which implies that $\bar{s} = s$. Therefore, the extractor can succeed in recovering s from the circuit C with all but negligible probability.

Remark 2.2. The above construction also supports learnability from a circuit that deviates from $\mathsf{UF}_K(\cdot)$ on a constant fraction of inputs. To achieve this, the extractor needs to produce multiple test points in each step and choose the majorities. In more detail, let N be a suitable polynomial. The extractor first produces N ciphertexts ct^*_α via running the circuit C on N independent inputs (x_1, ct_1). Then for each ct^*_α, it produces N ciphertexts ct^*_β and for each pair $(ct^*_\alpha, ct^*_\beta)$, it computes N results $\bar{s}$. The extractor sets the extraction outputs as the majority-of-majorities-of-majorities. More precisely, for each pair $(ct^*_\alpha, ct^*_\beta)$, it chooses the extracted result for this pair as the majority of all N results $\bar{s}$ produced for this pair. It also chooses the extracted result for each ct^*_α as the majority of all N results for the N pairs $(ct^*_\alpha, ct^*_\beta)$. Finally, it outputs the majority of all N results for the N ciphertexts ct^*_α.

In above extraction procedure, inputs (excluding the index ind) to the circuit C are all random since they are composed of either random strings or rerandomized ciphertexts encrypting random plaintexts, which are random due to Property 3 of the special FHE scheme. Thus, if the fraction of inputs that C differs with $UF_K(\cdot)$ is a small constant δ, the majority result at each step should be the correct secret information. In particular, the extraction result will be correct if

$$\Pr[C(0\|x_1\|ct_1) = UF_K(0\|x_1\|ct_1)] > 1/2$$
$$\Pr[C(1\|x_2\|ct_2) = UF_K(1\|x_2\|ct_2) \wedge C(2\|x_2 \oplus \alpha\|ct_2) = UF_K(2\|x_2 \oplus \alpha\|ct_2)] > 1/2$$
$$\Pr[C(1\|x_3 \oplus \gamma\|ct_3^*) = UF_K(1\|x_3 \oplus \gamma\|ct_3^*) \wedge C(3\|x_3\|ct_3^*) = UF_K(3\|x_3\|ct_3^*)] > 1/2$$

for random $x_1\|ct_1$, $x_2\|ct_2$, and $x_3\|ct_3^*$, and all three inequalities can be satisfied if $\delta < 1/8$. Besides, the constant δ can be improved to be about $\frac{1}{6}$ if we slightly modify the above construction. Please see the full version for more details.

Pseudorandomness of the Construction. Next, we explain why UF is pseudorandom. We assume w.l.o.g. that all queries submitted by the adversary are distinct.

First, suppose that there are no collisions in the inputs to $F_k(\cdot)$ when answering queries from the adversary, then outputs of $F_k(\cdot)$ would be indistinguishable from strings sampled uniformly and independently from its output space, i.e., outputs of $UF_K(ind\|x\|ct)$ will be pseudorandom if $ind \in \{1, 2, 3\}$. This also implies that the adversary cannot learn any information about sk. Then by ciphertext pseudorandomness of the FHE scheme, outputs of $UF_K(ind\|x\|ct)$ will also be pseudorandom if $ind = 0$. To summarize, the adversary cannot distinguish UF from a random function if there are no collisions in the inputs to $F_k(\cdot)$.

Next, we show why the collisions do not occur. In a nutshell, this is because to make a collision, the adversary must have the knowledge of α, β, or encryption of β, and none of them can be obtained via black-box accesses to $UF_K(\cdot)$. In more detail, assume that there are no collisions in the first q queries to the oracle, then responses of these q queries would be indistinguishable from random strings, which contain no information. Thus, the adversary also cannot make a collision in the $(q+1)$-th query. There is no collision if the adversary only makes one oracle query, then by the above statement, the adversary cannot make any collision when querying $UF_K(\cdot)$. Therefore, the pseudorandomness follows.

Construction from One Way Function. Next, we show how to construct robust unobfuscatable PRFs without using FHE. More precisely, the new construction only relies on a standard secret-key encryption scheme with some specific properties, which can be instantiated from any one way function.

Following [BGI+01,BP13], we remove the dependency on homomorphic encryption via performing the homomorphic operations by $UF_K(\cdot)$. In particular, given an input $X = (ind, x, ct)$, the new PRF proceeds identically as in the construction from FHE if $ind \in \{0, 1, 2, 3\}$. In addition, if $ind = 4$, it decrypts the ciphertext ct, performs the specified homomorphic operation over the decrypted bits and outputs an encryption of the evaluation result, where the randomness is derived from $F'_{k'}(X)$.

The extractor can use this additional functionality of UF to evaluate P gate by gate. Thus, it can still succeed in extracting the secret information from a circuit C that approximates $\mathsf{UF}_K(\cdot)$ even if the underlying encryption scheme does not support homomorphic evaluation over encrypted data.[6]

Constructing Special Fully Homomorphic Encryption. We finally show how to construct the special FHE needed. Our starting point is the GSW homomorphic encryption scheme presented in [GSW13]. In a nutshell, the secret key of the scheme is a random vector $s \in \mathbb{Z}_q^n$. Its public key contains a matrix

$$A = \begin{pmatrix} B \\ s^\mathsf{T} B + e^\mathsf{T} \end{pmatrix} \mod q$$

and a ciphertext ct_{sk}^*, where B is a random matrix in $\mathbb{Z}_q^{n \times m}$, e is a "short" vector in $\mathbb{Z}^m$ and ct_{sk}^* is an encryption of the secret key s. The ciphertext that encrypts a bit μ is defined as[7]

$$C = \mu \cdot G + A \cdot R \mod q$$

where R is a random binary matrix and G is the standard powers-of-two gadget matrix [MP12]. Besides, to rerandomize a ciphertext C, the rerandomization algorithm adds the ciphertext with an encryption of 0. Next, we describe how to adapt the construction to achieve the three properties needed.

Achieving Property 1 and Property 2. In the evaluation algorithm of the GSW scheme, the ciphertext ct_{sk}^* should be used to perform the bootstrapping procedure. Also, the rerandomization algorithm needs the matrix A to generate an encryption of 0. Both variables are contained in the public key and thus the first property, which requires that the evaluation algorithm and the rerandomization algorithm can be performed without using the public key, is not satisfied.

We solve the problem by putting randomized versions of both variables into the ciphertext of the scheme. In particular, the new ciphertext is (ct_μ, ct_{sk}, ct_0), where ct_μ is an encryption of the message, ct_{sk} is generated by reramdomizing ct_{sk}^* and ct_0 is a fresh encryption of 0. Then we can use ct_{sk} and ct_0 instead of ct_{sk}^* and A when running the evaluation algorithm and the rerandomization algorithm, and Property 1 follows. In addition, as the new ciphertext consists of ciphertexts of the original scheme, the ciphertext pseudorandomness of the modified scheme (i.e., Property 2) comes from that of the original scheme, which can be guaranteed by the circular-secure learning with errors (LWE) assumption.

There is one subtle issue when employing this scheme in the construction of unobfuscatable PRF. That is the extractor can obtain ct_0 only from output of the circuit, which may deviate the PRF evaluation on a $1/6$ fraction of inputs, and the obtained ct_0 may not be pseudorandom (e.g., the circuit could rejects to output ct_0 if its first 3 bits are 000). As a result, the output distribution of the rerandomization algorithm may also be changed. We fix the issue by

---

[6] We notice that however, the trick presented in Remark 2.2 does not work in this setting as it will require the extractor to produce $N^{O(|\mathsf{C}|)}$ test points, which is exponential in the size of the circuit C. Thus, the construction only supports learnability from a circuit that deviates from $\mathsf{UF}_K(\cdot)$ on a negligible fraction of inputs.

[7] Here, we change the format of the ciphertext of the original GSW scheme slightly.

including multiple ct_0 in each ciphertext and use a random subset sum of them in the rerandomization algorithm. The selection of the subset provides additional entropy and we can show that the result is pseudorandom by using the leftover hash lemma and the fact that A is pseudorandom.

Achieving Property 3. The third property of the special FHE scheme requires that a rerandomized ciphertext of a random plaintext should look uniform even given the secret key of the FHE scheme. Here we relax this property and only require that one can transform a rerandomized ciphertext of the FHE scheme into a ciphertext with this strong uniformity. The transformed ciphertext is still decryptable, but does not have to support homomorphic evaluation over it. Note that this relaxed property is sufficient in our construction of unobfuscatable PRF.

Given a ciphertext $CT = (C, ct_{sk}, ct_0)$, where C encrypts a bit μ, we first transform it as:

$$c = \begin{pmatrix} \mathbf{0} \\ \mu \cdot \frac{q+1}{2} \end{pmatrix} + Ar \mod q$$

where r is a short vector in $\mathbb{Z}_q^m$. We can obtain c via summing some columns of C. In addition, to decrypt the ciphertext, one can first compute

$$(-s^\mathsf{T}, 1) \cdot c = \mu \cdot \frac{q+1}{2} + e^\mathsf{T} \cdot r \mod q \tag{1}$$

where e is the short error term in A. Then the decryption result will be 1 if Eq. (1) is close to $\frac{q+1}{2}$ and it will be 0 if Eq. (1) is close to 0.

However, the above transformed ciphertext can be distinguished from a random vector given s due to the following decryption attack. Given a ciphertext c, which is either a transformed ciphertext or a random vector, the distinguisher with the secret key s first computes Eq. (1). It will get a number that is close to $\frac{q+1}{2}$ or 0 if c is a transformed ciphertext and it will get a random number in $\mathbb{Z}_q$ if c is a random vector. Thus, it could distinguish these two cases.

We prevent the attack via adding a number $z \xleftarrow{\$} [0, \frac{q-1}{2}]$ to the last element of the transformed ciphertext and require that q is much larger than the error term $e^\mathsf{T} \cdot r$. One will get $\mu \cdot \frac{q+1}{2} + e^\mathsf{T} \cdot r + z$ via computing Eq. (1) on a transformed ciphertext that encrypts μ, and this will be a random number in $[\mu \cdot \frac{q+1}{2}, \mu \cdot \frac{q+1}{2} + \frac{q-1}{2}]$ due to the smudging lemma [AJLA+12], which states that a small error (i.e., $e^\mathsf{T} \cdot r$) can be smudged out by a large error (i.e., z). The encrypted message can still be recovered from c via computing Eq. (1) and checking if the result exceeds $\frac{q-1}{2}$. Besides, if c is a transformed ciphertext that encrypts a random bit, then Eq. (1) would also be a random number in $\mathbb{Z}_q$ and thus the distinguisher cannot distinguish it from a random vector.

3   Notations

We write $negl(\cdot)$ to denote a negligible function and write $poly(\cdot)$ to denote a polynomial. For integers $a \leq b$, we write $[a, b]$ to denote all integers from a to b. Let s be a string, we use $|s|$ to denote the length of s. For integers $a \leq |s|$,

$s[a]$ denotes the a-th character of s and for integers $a \leq b \leq |s|$, $s[a:b]$ denotes the substring $(s[a], s[a+1], \ldots, s[b])$. Let S be a finite set, we use $|S|$ to denote the size of S, and use $s \xleftarrow{\$} S$ to denote sampling an element s uniformly from set S. Let $\mathcal{D}$ be a distribution, we use $d \leftarrow \mathcal{D}$ to denote sampling d according to $\mathcal{D}$. Following the syntax in [BLW17], for a circuit family C indexed by a few, say m, constants, we write $C[c_1, \ldots, c_m]$ to denote a circuit with constants $c_1, \ldots, c_m$. We use $\bar{\wedge}$ to denote the NAND gate and suppose that all circuits are composed exclusively by NAND gates unless otherwise specified. We provide more background knowledge and recall definitions of cryptographic primitives employed in this work in the full version.

4   Definition of Public-Key Watermarkable PRFs

In this section, we provide the definition of public-key watermarkable PRFs, which is adapted from definitions of watermarkable PRFs in previous works [CHN+16, BLW17, KW17, QWZ18, KW19, YAL+19, YAYX20]. More precisely, a public-key watermarkable PRF with key space $\mathcal{K}$, input space $\mathcal{X}$, output space $\mathcal{Y}$, and message space $\mathcal{M}$ consists of the following algorithms:

- $\mathtt{Setup}(1^\lambda) \to PP$: On input the security parameter 1^λ, the setup algorithm outputs the public parameter PP.
- $\mathtt{KeyGen}(PP) \to k$: On input the public parameter PP, the key generation algorithm outputs a PRF key $k \in \mathcal{K}$.
- $\mathtt{Eval}(PP, k, x) \to y$: On input the public parameter PP, a PRF key $k \in \mathcal{K}$, and an input $x \in \mathcal{X}$, the evaluation algorithm outputs an output $y \in \mathcal{Y}$.
- $\mathtt{Mark}(PP, k, msg) \to C$: On input the public parameter PP, a PRF key $k \in \mathcal{K}$, and a message $msg \in \mathcal{M}$, the marking algorithm outputs a marked circuit $C : \mathcal{X} \to \mathcal{Y}$.
- $\mathtt{Extract}(PP, C) \to msg$: On input the public parameter PP and a circuit C, the extraction algorithm outputs a message $msg \in \mathcal{M} \cup \{\bot\}$, where $\bot$ denotes that the circuit is unmarked.

Correctness. The correctness of a watermarking scheme includes three properties. The functionality preserving property requires that the watermarked key can roughly preserve the functionality of the original key.

Definition 4.1 (Functionality Preserving). *For any* $msg \in \mathcal{M}$*, let* $PP \leftarrow$ $\mathtt{Setup}(1^\lambda)$*,* $k \leftarrow \mathtt{KeyGen}(PP)$*,* $C \leftarrow \mathtt{Mark}(PP, k, msg)$*,* $x \xleftarrow{\$} \mathcal{X}$*, then we have* $\Pr[C(x) \neq \mathtt{Eval}(PP, k, x)] \leq negl(\lambda)$*.*

The extraction correctness requires that the extraction algorithm can extract the correct message from an honestly-watermarked key and will obtain the "unmarked" symbol when extracting an unmarked key.

Definition 4.2 (Extraction Correctness). *For any* $msg \in \mathcal{M}$*, let* $PP \leftarrow$ $\mathtt{Setup}(1^\lambda)$*,* $k \leftarrow \mathtt{KeyGen}(PP)$*, and* $C \leftarrow \mathtt{Mark}(PP, k, msg)$*, then we have*

$$\Pr[\mathtt{Extract}(PP, C) \neq msg] \leq negl(\lambda)$$

$$\Pr[\mathtt{Extract}(PP, \mathtt{Eval}(PP, k, \cdot)) \neq \bot] \leq negl(\lambda)$$

The meaningfulness property requires that most circuits are unmarked, which rules out the trivial construction that regards all circuits as marked.

Definition 4.3 (Watermarking Meaningfulness). *For any circuit* $C\colon \mathcal{X} \to \mathcal{Y}$, *let* $PP \leftarrow \mathtt{Setup}(1^\lambda)$, *then we have* $\Pr[\mathtt{Extract}(PP, C) \neq \perp] \le negl(\lambda)$.

Pseudorandomness. Our definition of pseudorandomness is twofold, including pseudorandomness for unmarked keys and that for marked keys. The properties require that given oracle access to an unmarked PRF key (or a marked key), the adversary cannot distinguish it from a random function.

Definition 4.4 (Pseudorandomness for Unmarked Keys). *Let* $PP \leftarrow \mathtt{Setup}(1^\lambda)$, $k \leftarrow \mathtt{KeyGen}(PP)$, *and* f *be a random function from* $\mathcal{X}$ *to* $\mathcal{Y}$. *Also, let* $\mathcal{O}_0(\cdot)$ *be an oracle that takes as input a string* $x \in \mathcal{X}$ *and returns* $\mathtt{Eval}(PP, k, x)$, *and let* $\mathcal{O}_1(\cdot)$ *be an oracle that takes as input a string* $x \in \mathcal{X}$ *and returns* $f(x)$. *Then for all probabilistic polynomial-time (PPT) adversary* $\mathcal{A}$, *we have:*

$$| \Pr[\mathcal{A}^{\mathcal{O}_0(\cdot)}(PP) = 1] - \Pr[\mathcal{A}^{\mathcal{O}_1(\cdot)}(PP) = 1] |\le negl(\lambda)$$

Definition 4.5 (Pseudorandomness for Marked Keys). *For any PPT adversary* $\mathcal{A} = (\mathcal{A}_1, \mathcal{A}_2)$, *let* $PP \leftarrow \mathtt{Setup}(1^\lambda)$ *and* $k \leftarrow \mathtt{KeyGen}(PP)$. *Also, let* $(msg, state) \leftarrow \mathcal{A}_1(PP)$, $C \leftarrow \mathtt{Mark}(PP, k, msg)$, *and* f *be a random function from* $\mathcal{X}$ *to* $\mathcal{Y}$. *Let* $\mathcal{O}_0(\cdot)$ *be an oracle that takes as input a string* $x \in \mathcal{X}$ *and returns* $C(x)$, *and let* $\mathcal{O}_1(\cdot)$ *be an oracle that takes as input a string* $x \in \mathcal{X}$ *and returns* $f(x)$. *Then we have:*

$$| \Pr[\mathcal{A}_2^{\mathcal{O}_0(\cdot)}(state) = 1] - \Pr[\mathcal{A}_2^{\mathcal{O}_1(\cdot)}(state) = 1] |\le negl(\lambda)$$

Unremovability. This is the main security requirement for a watermarking scheme, which requires that the adversary cannot remove or modify the messages embedded in a random PRF key without significantly changing its functionality.

Definition 4.6 (Q-Bounded ϵ-Unremovability). *A watermarkable PRF is* Q-*bounded* ϵ-*unremovable if for all PPT and* ϵ-*unremoving-admissible adversaries* $\mathcal{A}$, *we have* $\Pr[\mathtt{ExptUR}_{\mathcal{A},Q}(\lambda) = 1] \le negl(\lambda)$, *where we define the experiment* $\mathtt{ExptUR}$ *as follows:*

1. *The challenger samples* $PP \leftarrow \mathtt{Setup}(1^\lambda)$ *and* $k^* \leftarrow \mathtt{KeyGen}(PP)$.
2. *Then, it returns* PP *to* $\mathcal{A}$ *and answers* $\mathcal{A}$'s *challenge oracle queries. Here,* $\mathcal{A}$ *is only allowed to query the challenge oracle for at most* Q *times.*
   - *Challenge Oracle. On input a message* $msg \in \mathcal{M}$, *the challenge oracle returns a circuit* $C^* \leftarrow \mathtt{Mark}(PP, k^*, msg)$ *to the adversary.*
3. *Finally,* $\mathcal{A}$ *submits a circuit* $\tilde{C}$ *and the experiment outputs 1 iff* $\mathtt{Extract}(PP, \tilde{C}) \notin \mathcal{Q}^*$. *Here, we use* $\mathcal{Q}^*$ *to denote all messages submitted to the challenge oracle and use* $\mathcal{R}^*$ *to denote all circuits returned by the challenge oracle.*

We say that an adversary $\mathcal{A}$ *is* ϵ-*unremoving-admissible if there exists circuit* $C^* \in \mathcal{R}^*$ *that* $|\{x \in \mathcal{X} : C^*(x) \neq \tilde{C}(x)\}| \le \epsilon \cdot |\mathcal{X}|$.

Remark 4.1. We can also define $negl(\lambda)$-unremovability for a watermarkable PRF, which is identical to the definition of ϵ-unremovability for concrete ϵ, except that $\mathcal{A}$ should be $negl(\lambda)$-unremoving-admissible, i.e., there exists circuit $C^* \in \mathcal{R}^*$ that $|\{x \in \mathcal{X} : C^*(x) \neq \tilde{C}(x)\}| \le negl(\lambda) \cdot |\mathcal{X}|$.

5 Public-Key Hinting Watermarkable PRFs

We define and construct public-key hinting watermarkable PRFs in this section. We provide its formal definition in Sect. 5.1. Then in Sect. 5.2, we construct it from functional encryption schemes. We provide more constructions with different properties in the full version.

5.1 The Definition

The definition of public-key hinting watermarkable PRF is similar to the definition of standard public-key watermarkable PRFs given in Sect. 4 except that its key generation algorithm will generate a *"hint"* together with the PRF key, which can be used later in the extraction algorithm. More precisely, a public-key hinting watermarkable PRF with key space $\mathcal{K}$, input space $\mathcal{X}$, output space $\mathcal{Y}$, and message space $\mathcal{M}$ consists of the following algorithms:

- $\mathtt{Setup}(1^\lambda) \to PP$: On input the security parameter 1^λ, the setup algorithm outputs the public parameter PP.
- $\mathtt{KeyGen}(PP) \to (k, \mathtt{hint})$: On input the public parameter PP, the key generation algorithm outputs a PRF key $k \in \mathcal{K}$ and a hint $\mathtt{hint}$.
- $\mathtt{Eval}(PP, k, x) \to y$: On input the public parameter PP, a PRF key $k \in \mathcal{K}$, and an input $x \in \mathcal{X}$, the evaluation algorithm outputs an output $y \in \mathcal{Y}$.
- $\mathtt{Mark}(PP, k, msg) \to \mathtt{C}$: On input the public parameter PP, a PRF key $k \in \mathcal{K}$, and a message $msg \in \mathcal{M}$, the marking algorithm outputs a marked circuit $\mathtt{C} : \mathcal{X} \to \mathcal{Y}$.
- $\mathtt{Extract}(PP, \mathtt{C}, \mathtt{hint}) \to msg$: On input the public parameter PP, a circuit $\mathtt{C}$, and a hint $\mathtt{hint}$, the extraction algorithm outputs a message $msg \in \mathcal{M} \cup \{\bot\}$, where $\bot$ denotes that the circuit is unmarked.

Correctness. The correctness of a public-key hinting watermarkable PRF also requires the following three properties. Here for the extraction correctness, we require that the *correct hint* is used.

- **Functionality Preserving.** For any $msg \in \mathcal{M}$, let $PP \leftarrow \mathtt{Setup}(1^\lambda)$, $(k, \mathtt{hint}) \leftarrow \mathtt{KeyGen}(PP)$, $\mathtt{C} \leftarrow \mathtt{Mark}(PP, k, msg)$, $x \xleftarrow{\$} \mathcal{X}$, then we have $\Pr[\mathtt{C}(x) \neq \mathtt{Eval}(PP, k, x)] \leq negl(\lambda)$.
- **Extraction Correctness.** For any $msg \in \mathcal{M}$, let $PP \leftarrow \mathtt{Setup}(1^\lambda)$, $(k, \mathtt{hint}) \leftarrow \mathtt{KeyGen}(PP)$, and $\mathtt{C} \leftarrow \mathtt{Mark}(PP, k, msg)$, then we have

$$\Pr[\mathtt{Extract}(PP, \mathtt{C}, \mathtt{hint}) \neq msg] \leq negl(\lambda)$$

$$\Pr[\mathtt{Extract}(PP, \mathtt{Eval}(PP, k, \cdot), \mathtt{hint}) \neq \bot] \leq negl(\lambda)$$

- **Watermarking Meaningfulness.** For any circuit $\mathtt{C} : \mathcal{X} \to \mathcal{Y}$ and any $\mathtt{hint}$, let $PP \leftarrow \mathtt{Setup}(1^\lambda)$, then we have $\Pr[\mathtt{Extract}(PP, \mathtt{C}, \mathtt{hint}) \neq \bot] \leq negl(\lambda)$.

Pseudorandomness. The pseudorandomness property requires that the evaluation of the PRF with an unmarked key should be pseudorandom. Here, the adversary is *not* allowed to access the hint associated with the PRF key.

Definition 5.1 (Pseudorandomness). *Let* $PP \leftarrow \mathtt{Setup}(1^\lambda)$, $(k, \mathtt{hint}) \leftarrow$ *$\mathtt{KeyGen}(PP)$, and f be a random function from $\mathcal{X}$ to $\mathcal{Y}$. Also, let $\mathcal{O}_0(\cdot)$ be an oracle that takes as input a string $x \in \mathcal{X}$ and returns $\mathtt{Eval}(PP, k, x)$, and let $\mathcal{O}_1(\cdot)$ be an oracle that takes as input a string $x \in \mathcal{X}$ and returns $f(x)$. Then for all PPT adversary $\mathcal{A}$, we have:*

$$| \Pr[\mathcal{A}^{\mathcal{O}_0(\cdot)}(PP) = 1] - \Pr[\mathcal{A}^{\mathcal{O}_1(\cdot)}(PP) = 1] | \leq negl(\lambda)$$

Unremovability. The unremovability property also requires that an adversary cannot remove or modify the message embedded in a watermarked PRF key while keeping its functionality. Here, we allow the adversary to learn the *hint* associated with the PRF key. Also, we require that the *correct hint* should be used when extracting the circuit submitted by the adversary.

Definition 5.2 (Q-Bounded ϵ-Unremovability). *A hinting watermarkable PRF is Q-bounded ϵ-unremovable if for all PPT and ϵ-unremoving-admissible adversaries $\mathcal{A}$, we have $\Pr[\mathtt{ExptUR}_{\mathcal{A},Q}(\lambda) = 1] \leq negl(\lambda)$, where we define the experiment $\mathtt{ExptUR}$ as follows:*

1. *The challenger samples $PP \leftarrow \mathtt{Setup}(1^\lambda)$ and $(k^*, \mathtt{hint}^*) \leftarrow \mathtt{KeyGen}(PP)$.*
2. *Then, it returns $(PP, \mathtt{hint}^*)$ to $\mathcal{A}$ and answers $\mathcal{A}$'s challenge oracle queries. Here, $\mathcal{A}$ is only allowed to query the challenge oracle for at most Q times.*
   - *$\boldsymbol{\mathit{Challenge\ Oracle}}$. On input a message $msg \in \mathcal{M}$, the challenge oracle returns a circuit $C^* \leftarrow \mathtt{Mark}(PP, k^*, msg)$ to the adversary.*
3. *Finally, $\mathcal{A}$ submits a circuit $\tilde{C}$ and the experiment outputs 1 iff $\mathtt{Extract}(PP, \tilde{C}, \mathtt{hint}^*) \notin \mathcal{Q}^*$. Here, we use $\mathcal{Q}^*$ to denote all messages submitted to the challenge oracle and use $\mathcal{R}^*$ to denote all circuits returned by the challenge oracle.*

We say that an adversary $\mathcal{A}$ is ϵ-unremoving-admissible if there exists circuit $C^* \in \mathcal{R}^*$ that $|\{x \in \mathcal{X} : C^*(x) \neq \tilde{C}(x)\}| \leq \epsilon \cdot |\mathcal{X}|.$[8]

5.2 The Construction

Let λ be the security parameter. Let n, m, κ, Q be positive integers that are polynomial in λ. Let ρ, θ be real values in $(0, 1)$ s.t. $1/\theta$ is polynomial in λ. Let $\varphi = \theta/(5 + (\kappa - 1)Q)$. Let $T = \lambda/\varphi^2$. Let $\epsilon = \rho \cdot (1 - \theta)$.

Also, for any $(msg, t^*) \in [0, 2^\kappa - 1] \times \{0, 1\}^\lambda$, we define the following functions from $[0, 2^\kappa - 1] \times \{0, 1\}^\lambda \times \{0, 1\}^\lambda$ to $\{0, 1\}^\lambda$:

$$f_\perp(ind\|t\|\mu) = \mu$$

$$f_{msg,t^*}(ind\|t\|\mu) = \begin{cases} 0^\lambda & \text{If } t = t^* \wedge ind \geq msg \\ \mu & \text{Otherwise} \end{cases}$$

Our construction is built on the following building blocks:

---

[8] Similar to a standard watermarkable PRF, we can define $negl(\lambda)$-unremovability, which requires that $\exists C^* \in \mathcal{R}^*$ s.t. $|\{x \in \mathcal{X} : C^*(x) \neq \tilde{C}(x)\}| \leq negl(\lambda) \cdot |\mathcal{X}|$.

- An FE scheme $\mathsf{FE} = (\mathsf{FE.Setup}, \mathsf{FE.KeyGen}, \mathsf{FE.Enc}, \mathsf{FE.Dec})$ with message space $\{0,1\}^{\kappa+2\lambda}$, ciphertext space $\{0,1\}^n$ and density ρ.[9] In addition, we assume w.l.o.g. that $\mathsf{FE.Dec}$ is a deterministic algorithm.
- A PKE scheme $\mathsf{PKE} = (\mathsf{PKE.KeyGen}, \mathsf{PKE.Enc}, \mathsf{PKE.Dec})$ with message space $\{0,1\}^\lambda$ and ciphertext space $\{0,1\}^m$. Also, we use $\mathcal{R}_{\mathsf{PKE.Enc}}$ to denote the randomness space for the algorithm $\mathsf{PKE.Enc}$.
- A PRF $\mathsf{F} = (\mathsf{F.KeyGen}, \mathsf{F.Eval})$ with input space $\{0,1\}^n$ and output space $\mathcal{R}_{\mathsf{PKE.Enc}}$.

We construct the public-key hinting watermarkable PRF $\mathsf{HWF} = (\mathsf{Setup}, \mathsf{KeyGen}, \mathsf{Eval}, \mathsf{Mark}, \mathsf{Extract})$, which has input space $\{0,1\}^n$, output space $\{0,1\}^m$ and message space $\{0,1\}^\kappa \setminus \{0^\kappa\} = [1, 2^\kappa - 1]$ as follows:

- Setup. On input the security parameter 1^λ, the setup algorithm samples $w \xleftarrow{\$} \{0,1\}^\lambda$, $t^* \xleftarrow{\$} \{0,1\}^\lambda$, and outputs the public parameter $PP = (w, t^*)$.
- KeyGen. On input the public parameter $PP = (w, t^*)$, the key generation algorithm computes
  1. $(mpk, msk) \leftarrow \mathsf{FE.Setup}(1^\lambda)$.
  2. $(pk, sk) \leftarrow \mathsf{PKE.KeyGen}(1^\lambda)$.
  3. $k \leftarrow \mathsf{F.KeyGen}(1^\lambda)$.
  4. $fsk \leftarrow \mathsf{FE.KeyGen}(mpk, msk, f_\perp)$.
  and outputs the PRF key $K = (mpk, msk, pk, k, fsk)$ and the hint $\mathsf{hint} = (mpk, sk, w)$.
- Eval. On input the public parameter $PP = (w, t^*)$, the PRF key $K = (mpk, msk, pk, k, fsk)$, and an input $x \in \{0,1\}^n$, the evaluation algorithm outputs $\mathsf{M}[mpk, fsk, pk, k](x)$, where M is defined in Fig. 2.
- Mark. On input the public parameter $PP = (w, t^*)$, the PRF key $K = (mpk, msk, pk, k, fsk)$, and a message $msg \in [1, 2^\kappa - 1]$, the marking algorithm computes $fsk_{msg} \leftarrow \mathsf{FE.KeyGen}(mpk, msk, f_{msg,t^*})$ and outputs the circuit $\mathsf{M}[mpk, fsk_{msg}, pk, k]$, where M is defined in Fig. 2.
- Extract. On input the public parameter $PP = (w, t^*)$, a circuit C, and a hint $\mathsf{hint} = (\overline{mpk}, \overline{sk}, \overline{w})$, the extraction algorithm output $\perp$ if $\overline{w} \neq w$. Otherwise, it runs the jump finding algorithm Trace (described in Fig. 3) to extract messages from C, where the Test algorithm is also defined in Fig. 3. More precisely, it proceeds as follow:
  1. Set the constant for the algorithm Test as $(\mathsf{C}, \overline{mpk}, \overline{sk}, t^*)$.
  2. $p_0 = \mathsf{Test}(0)$.
  3. $p_{2^\kappa - 1} = \mathsf{Test}(2^\kappa - 1)$.
  4. $\mathcal{M} \leftarrow \mathsf{Trace}(0, 2^\kappa - 1, p_0, p_{2^\kappa - 1})$. Here, the extraction algorithm will abort and output $\perp$ if the Test algorithm has been invoked for more than $Q \cdot (\kappa + 1)$ times in the Trace algorithm.
  5. If $\mathcal{M} = \emptyset$, output $\perp$.
  6. $msg \xleftarrow{\$} \mathcal{M}$.
  7. Output msg.

---

[9] We use density to denote the fraction of honestly generated ciphertexts in the ciphertext space. Its formal definition is given in the full version.

> **M**
>
> **Constant:** mpk, fsk, pk, k
>
> **Input:** x
>
> 1. $\mu = \mathsf{FE.Dec}(mpk, fsk, x)$.
> 2. If $\mu = \perp$, set $\mu = 0^\lambda$.
> 3. Output $y = \mathsf{PKE.Enc}(pk, \mu; \mathsf{F.Eval}(k, x))$.

Fig. 2. The circuit M.

Trace	Test
Input: ind_1, ind_2, p_1, p_2	**Constant:** E, mpk, sk, t^*
1. $\Delta = \|p_1 - p_2\|$.	**Input:** ind
2. If $\Delta \leq \varphi$:	1. $Acc = 0$
Return $\emptyset$.	2. For $i \in [1, T]$:
3. If $ind_2 - ind_1 = 1$:	(a) Sample $\mu \xleftarrow{\$} \{0,1\}^\lambda$.
Return $\{ind_2\}$.	(b) $x \leftarrow \mathsf{FE.Enc}(mpk, ind\|t^*\|\mu)$.
4. $ind_3 = \lfloor \frac{ind_1 + ind_2}{2} \rfloor$.	(c) $y = \mathsf{E}(x)$.
5. $p_3 = \mathsf{Test}(ind_3)$.	(d) $\bar{\mu} = \mathsf{PKE.Dec}(sk, y)$.
6. **Return** $\mathsf{Trace}(ind_1, ind_3, p_1, p_3) \cup$	(e) If $\mu = \bar{\mu}$: $Acc = Acc + 1$.
$\mathsf{Trace}(ind_3, ind_2, p_3, p_2)$.	3. Return $\frac{Acc}{T}$.

Fig. 3. The algorithms Trace and Test.

Theorem 5.1. *If* FE *is a secure functional encryption scheme with Q-adaptive indistinguishability and strong correctness[10], PKE is a secure PKE scheme with ciphertext pseudorandomness, and F is a secure PRF, then HWF is a secure public-key hinting watermarkable PRF with Q-bounded ϵ-unremovability.*

We present proof of Theorem 5.1 in the full version.

6 Robust Unobfuscatable PRFs

In this section, we define and construct robust unobfuscatable PRFs. We first give its formal definition in Sect. 6.1. Then in Sect. 6.2, we construct it from one way function. We provide the construction from FHE in the full version.

6.1 The Definition

We give definition of robust unobfuscatable PRFs in this section, which follows definitions in previous works [BGI+01, BP13, Zha21] with slight modifications. More precisely, an unobfuscatable PRF with input space $\mathcal{X}$, output space $\mathcal{Y}$, and message space $\mathcal{M}$ consists of the following algorithms:

---

[10] The strong correctness requires that the decryption will always output $\perp$ given an invalid ciphertext and will always output the correct result given a valid ciphertext. Please see the full version for a formal definition.

- $\texttt{Setup}(1^\lambda) \to PP$: On input the security parameter 1^λ, the setup algorithm outputs the public parameter PP.
- $\texttt{KeyGen}(PP, msg) \to K$: On input the public parameter PP and a message $msg \in \mathcal{M}$, the key generation algorithm outputs a PRF key K.
- $\texttt{Eval}(PP, K, x) \to y$: On input the public parameter PP, a PRF key K, and an input $x \in \mathcal{X}$, the evaluation algorithm outputs an output $y \in \mathcal{Y}$.
- $\texttt{Extract}(PP, \mathsf{C}) \to msg$: On input the public parameter PP and a circuit C, the extraction algorithm outputs a message $msg \in \mathcal{M} \cup \{\bot\}$, where $\bot$ denotes that the extraction fails.

Correctness. Its correctness requires that the extraction algorithms can always output the correct message given an honestly generated secret key.

Definition 6.1 (Correctness). *For any $msg \in \mathcal{M}$, let $PP \leftarrow \texttt{Setup}(1^\lambda)$ and $K \leftarrow \texttt{KeyGen}(PP, msg)$, then we have $\Pr[\texttt{Extract}(PP, \texttt{Eval}(PP, K, \cdot)) \neq msg] = 0$.*

Pseudorandomness. Its black-box pseudorandomness requires that outputs of the evaluation algorithm are indistinguishable from outputs of a random function if the adversary is only given oracle access to the evaluation algorithm.

Definition 6.2 (Black-Box Pseudorandomness). *For any PPT adversary $\mathcal{A} = (\mathcal{A}_1, \mathcal{A}_2)$, let $PP \leftarrow \texttt{Setup}(1^\lambda)$. Also, let $(msg, state) \leftarrow \mathcal{A}_1(PP)$, $K \leftarrow \texttt{KeyGen}(PP, msg)$, and f be a random function from $\mathcal{X}$ to $\mathcal{Y}$. Let $\mathcal{O}_0(\cdot)$ be an oracle that takes as input a string $x \in \mathcal{X}$ and returns $\texttt{Eval}(PP, K, x)$, and let $\mathcal{O}_1(\cdot)$ be an oracle that takes as input a string $x \in \mathcal{X}$ and returns $f(x)$. We have*

$$| \Pr[\mathcal{A}_2^{\mathcal{O}_0(\cdot)}(state) = 1] - \Pr[\mathcal{A}_2^{\mathcal{O}_1(\cdot)}(state) = 1] | \leq negl(\lambda)$$

Learnability. Its robust non-black-box learnability requires that one can learn the message from a circuit that approximately evaluates the PRF. In particular, for any function $\epsilon \in [0, 1]$, we define ϵ-robust learnability as follows.

Definition 6.3 (ϵ-Robust Learnability). *For all PPT and ϵ-admissible adversaries $\mathcal{A} = (\mathcal{A}_1, \mathcal{A}_2)$, we have*

$$\Pr \left[\begin{array}{l} PP \leftarrow \texttt{Setup}(1^\lambda); \\ (msg, state) \leftarrow \mathcal{A}_1(PP); \\ K \leftarrow \texttt{KeyGen}(PP, msg); \quad : \quad \overline{msg} \neq msg \\ \mathsf{C} \leftarrow \mathcal{A}_2(K, state); \\ \overline{msg} \leftarrow \texttt{Extract}(PP, \mathsf{C}); \end{array} \right] \leq negl(\lambda)$$

Here, we say that an adversary $\mathcal{A}$ is ϵ-admissible if $|\{x \in \mathcal{X} : \mathsf{C}(x) \neq \texttt{Eval}(PP, K, x)\}| \leq \epsilon \cdot |\mathcal{X}|$.[11]

---

[11] Similar to a (hinting) watermarkable PRF, we can define $negl(\lambda)$-robust learnability, which requires that $|\{x \in \mathcal{X} : \mathsf{C}(x) \neq \texttt{Eval}(PP, K, x)\}| \leq negl(\lambda) \cdot |\mathcal{X}|$.

6.2   The Construction

Let λ be the security parameter. Let $n_0 = 3$, $n_1 = (\lambda + 2) \cdot \lambda$, $n_2 = 2(\lambda + 1)$, $n_3 = \lambda + 1$, $n_4 = \lambda$, $n_5 = \lambda \cdot (\lambda + 1)$. Let $n = n_0 + n_1 + n_2 + n_3 + n_4 + n_5$. Let m be a positive integer that is polynomial in λ s.t. $m \geq \lambda \cdot (\lambda + 1)$.

Our construction is built on the following building blocks, all of which can be constructed from one way functions:

- A PRF $\mathsf{F}_{enc} = (\mathsf{F}_{enc}.\mathsf{KeyGen}, \mathsf{F}_{enc}.\mathsf{Eval})$ with input space $\{0,1\}^\lambda$ and output space $\{0,1\}$.
- An invoker randomizable PRF $\mathsf{F}_{IR} = (\mathsf{F}_{IR}.\mathsf{KeyGen}, \mathsf{F}_{IR}.\mathsf{Eval})$ with input space $\{0,1\}^{n-n_1} \times \{0,1\}^{n_1}$ and output space $\{0,1\}^{n_1}$.
- A PRF $\mathsf{F}_{mask} = (\mathsf{F}_{mask}.\mathsf{KeyGen}, \mathsf{F}_{mask}.\mathsf{Eval})$ with input space $\{0,1\}^{n-n_0}$ and output space $\{0,1\}^m$.
- A PRF $\mathsf{F}_{pad} = (\mathsf{F}_{pad}.\mathsf{KeyGen}, \mathsf{F}_{pad}.\mathsf{Eval})$ with input space $\{0,1\}^n$ and output space $\{0,1\}^m$.

We construct the robust unobfuscatable PRF $\mathsf{UOF} = (\mathsf{Setup}, \mathsf{KeyGen}, \mathsf{Eval}, \mathsf{Extract})$, which has input space $\{0,1\}^n$, output space $\{0,1\}^m$, and message space $\{0,1\}^m$ as follows:

- **Setup.** There is no need to set the public parameter in this construction and the setup algorithm outputs $PP = 1^\lambda$ on input the security parameter 1^λ.
- **KeyGen.** On input the security parameter 1^λ and the message msg, the key generation algorithm samples $\alpha \xleftarrow{\$} \{0,1\}^\lambda$ and $\beta \xleftarrow{\$} \{0,1\}^\lambda$. Then it generates PRF keys $k_{enc} \leftarrow \mathsf{F}_{enc}.\mathsf{KeyGen}(1^\lambda)$, $k_{IR} \leftarrow \mathsf{F}_{IR}.\mathsf{KeyGen}(1^\lambda)$, $k_{mask} \leftarrow \mathsf{F}_{mask}.\mathsf{KeyGen}(1^\lambda)$, and $k_{pad} \leftarrow \mathsf{F}_{pad}.\mathsf{KeyGen}(1^\lambda)$. Finally, it outputs the PRF key
$$K = (\alpha, \beta, k_{enc}, k_{IR}, k_{mask}, k_{pad}, msg)$$
- **Eval.** On input the secret key $K = (\alpha, \beta, k_{enc}, k_{IR}, k_{mask}, k_{pad}, msg)$ and an input $x \in \{0,1\}^n$, the evaluation algorithm first parses $x = (u_0, u_1, u_2, u_3, u_4, u_5) \in \{0,1\}^{n_0} \times \{0,1\}^{n_1} \times \{0,1\}^{n_2} \times \{0,1\}^{n_3} \times \{0,1\}^{n_4} \times \{0,1\}^{n_5}$. Then it sets $w = (u_0, u_2, u_3, u_4, u_5)$ and computes $(r_1, r_2, \ldots, r_{\lambda+2}) = \mathsf{F}_{IR}.\mathsf{Eval}(k_{IR}, w, u_1)$, where $r_i \in \{0,1\}^\lambda$ for $i \in [1, \lambda + 2]$. Next, it deals with the following cases:
  - If $u_0 = 0$:
    1. For $i \in [1, \lambda]$:
       (a) $ct_i = r_i \| \mathsf{F}_{enc}.\mathsf{Eval}(k_{enc}, r_i) \oplus \alpha[i]$.
    2. $y_{pad} = \mathsf{F}_{pad}.\mathsf{Eval}(k_{pad}, x)[1 : m - \lambda \cdot (\lambda + 1)]$.
    3. Output $ct_1 \| \ldots \| ct_\lambda \| y_{pad}$.
  - If $u_0 = 1$:
    1. Parse $u_2 = (\bar{r}_1, \bar{c}_1, \bar{r}_2, \bar{c}_2) \in \{0,1\}^\lambda \times \{0,1\} \times \{0,1\}^\lambda \times \{0,1\}$.
    2. $\mu_1 = \mathsf{F}_{enc}.\mathsf{Eval}(k_{enc}, \bar{r}_1) \oplus \bar{c}_1$.
    3. $\mu_2 = \mathsf{F}_{enc}.\mathsf{Eval}(k_{enc}, \bar{r}_2) \oplus \bar{c}_2$.
    4. $\mu = \mu_1 \bar{\wedge} \mu_2$.

   5. $ct = r_{\lambda+1} \| F_{enc}.\text{Eval}(k_{enc}, r_{\lambda+1}) \oplus \mu$.
   6. $y_{pad} = F_{pad}.\text{Eval}(k_{pad}, x)[1 : m - (\lambda + 1)]$.
   7. Output $ct \| y_{pad}$.

– If $u_0 = 2$:
   1. Parse $u_3 = (\bar{r}, \bar{c}) \in \{0,1\}^\lambda \times \{0,1\}$.
   2. $\mu = F_{enc}.\text{Eval}(k_{enc}, \bar{r}) \oplus \bar{c}$.
   3. $ct = r_{\lambda+2} \| F_{enc}.\text{Eval}(k_{enc}, r_{\lambda+2}) \oplus \mu$.
   4. $y_{pad} = F_{pad}.\text{Eval}(k_{pad}, x)[1 : m - (\lambda + 1)]$.
   5. Output $ct \| y_{pad}$.

– If $u_0 = 3$:
   1. $z = (u_1, u_2, u_3, u_4, u_5)$.
   2. $y_{mask} = F_{mask}.\text{Eval}(k_{mask}, z)$.
   3. Output y_{mask}.

– If $u_0 = 4$:
   1. $u_4' = u_4 \oplus \alpha$.
   2. $z = (u_1, u_2, u_3, u_4', u_5)$.
   3. $y_{mask} = F_{mask}.\text{Eval}(k_{mask}, z)$.
   4. Output $(\beta \| 0^{m-\lambda}) \oplus y_{mask}$.

– If $u_0 = 5$:
   1. Parse $u_5 = (\bar{r}_i, \bar{c}_i)_{i \in [1,\lambda]} \in (\{0,1\}^\lambda \times \{0,1\})^\lambda$.
   2. For $i \in [1, \lambda]$:
     (a) $\mu_i = F_{enc}.\text{Eval}(k_{enc}, \bar{r}_i) \oplus \bar{c}_i$.
   3. $\nu = \mu_1 \| \ldots \| \mu_\lambda$.
   4. $u_4' = u_4 \oplus \nu \oplus \beta$.
   5. $z = (u_1, u_2, u_3, u_4', u_5)$.
   6. $y_{mask} = F_{mask}.\text{Eval}(k_{mask}, z)$.
   7. Output $msg \oplus y_{mask}$.

– If $u_0 = 6$ or $u_0 = 7$:
   1. $y_{pad} = F_{pad}.\text{Eval}(k_{pad}, x)$.
   2. Output y_{pad}.

- **Extract.** On input a circuit C, the extraction algorithm first obtains $ct_1, \ldots, ct_\lambda$ as follows:

$$x_0' \xleftarrow{\$} \{0,1\}^{n-n_0}, \quad x_0 = 000 \| x_0', \quad y_0 = \text{C}(x_0)$$
$$(ct_1, \ldots, ct_\lambda) = y_0[1 : \lambda \cdot (\lambda + 1)]$$

Then it computes:

$$x_1' \xleftarrow{\$} \{0,1\}^{n-n_0}, \quad x_1 = 011 \| x_1', \quad y_1 = \text{C}(x_1)$$

and samples $\gamma \xleftarrow{\$} \{0,1\}^\lambda$. Let $P = \bar{P}[x_1', \text{C}, y_1, \gamma]$, where $\bar{P}$ is defined in Fig. 4. Let $|P|$ be the number of wires for the circuit P and label each wire of P with a number in $[1, |P|]$, where each wire has a larger label than its children. We can label the input wires as $1, \ldots, \lambda$. Also, we can label the output wires as $|P| - \lambda + 1, \ldots, |P|$, where the i-th output wire is labeled with $|P| - \lambda + i$. Next, the extraction algorithm proceeds as follows for $j \in [\lambda + 1, |P|]$, where j_L and j_R are the labels of the children of the wire labelled with j:

1. $u_1^{(j)} \xleftarrow{\$} \{0,1\}^{n_1}$.
2. $(u_3^{(j)}, u_4^{(j)}, u_5^{(j)}) \xleftarrow{\$} \{0,1\}^{n_3} \times \{0,1\}^{n_4} \times \{0,1\}^{n_5}$.
3. If $j_L \neq j_R$:
   (a) $u_2^{(j)} = (ct_{j_L}, ct_{j_R})$.
4. If $j_L = j_R$:
   (a) $(\bar{u}_1^{(j)}, \bar{u}_2^{(j)}) \xleftarrow{\$} \{0,1\}^{n_1} \times \{0,1\}^{n_2}$.
   (b) $(\bar{u}_4^{(j)}, \bar{u}_5^{(j)}) \xleftarrow{\$} \{0,1\}^{n_4} \times \{0,1\}^{n_5}$.
   (c) $\bar{u}_3^{(j)} = ct_{j_L}$.
   (d) $\bar{u}_0^{(j)} = 010$.
   (e) $\bar{x}_{2,j} = \bar{u}_0^{(j)} \| \bar{u}_1^{(j)} \| \bar{u}_2^{(j)} \| \bar{u}_3^{(j)} \| \bar{u}_4^{(j)} \| \bar{u}_5^{(j)}$.
   (f) $\bar{y}_{2,j} = \mathsf{C}(\bar{x}_{2,j})$.
   (g) $\bar{ct}_{j_L} = \bar{y}_{2,j}[1 : \lambda + 1]$.
   (h) $u_2^{(j)} = (ct_{j_L}, \bar{ct}_{j_L})$.
5. $u_0^{(j)} = 001$.
6. $x_{2,j} = u_0^{(j)} \| u_1^{(j)} \| u_2^{(j)} \| u_3^{(j)} \| u_4^{(j)} \| u_5^{(j)}$.
7. $y_{2,j} = \mathsf{C}(x_{2,j})$.
8. $ct_j = y_{2,j}[1 : \lambda + 1]$.

After obtaining $ct_{|\mathsf{P}|-\lambda+1}, \ldots, ct_{|\mathsf{P}|}$, the extraction algorithm finally extracts the message as follows:

1. $(u_1, u_2, u_3, u_4) \xleftarrow{\$} \{0,1\}^{n_1} \times \{0,1\}^{n_2} \times \{0,1\}^{n_3} \times \{0,1\}^{n_4}$.
2. $u_5 = (ct_{|\mathsf{P}|-\lambda+1}, \ldots, ct_{|\mathsf{P}|})$.
3. $u_0 = 101$.
4. $x_3 = u_0 \| u_1 \| u_2 \| u_3 \| u_4 \| u_5$.
5. $y_3 = \mathsf{C}(x_3)$.
6. $\tilde{u}_0 = 011$.
7. $\tilde{u}_4 = u_4 \oplus \gamma$.
8. $\tilde{x}_3 = \tilde{u}_0 \| u_1 \| u_2 \| u_3 \| \tilde{u}_4 \| u_5$.
9. $\tilde{y}_3 = \mathsf{C}(\tilde{x}_3)$.
10. $msg = \tilde{y}_3 \oplus y_3$.

Finally, it outputs msg.

Theorem 6.1. *If* $\mathsf{F}_{enc}, \mathsf{F}_{mask}, \mathsf{F}_{pad}$ *are secure PRFs and* F_{IR} *is a secure invoker randomizable PRF, then* UOF *is a secure robust unobfuscatable PRF family with* $negl(\lambda)$-*robust learnability.*

We present proof of Theorem 6.1 in the full version.

7   Construction of Public-Key Watermarkable PRFs

Now, we present the general construction of public-key watermarkable PRFs from public-key hinting watermarkable PRFs and robust unobfuscatable PRFs.

$$\bar{P}$$

Constant: x_1', C, y_1, γ

Input: a

1. Parse $x_1' = (u_1, u_2, u_3, u_4, u_5) \in \{0,1\}^{n_1} \times \{0,1\}^{n_2} \times \{0,1\}^{n_3} \times \{0,1\}^{n_4} \times \{0,1\}^{n_5}$.
2. $\tilde{u}_0 = 100$.
3. $\tilde{u}_4 = u_4 \oplus a$.
4. $\tilde{x}_1 = \tilde{u}_0 \| u_1 \| u_2 \| u_3 \| \tilde{u}_4 \| u_5$.
5. $\tilde{y}_1 = C(\tilde{x}_1)$.
6. $b = (\tilde{y}_1 \oplus y_1)[1 : \lambda]$.
7. Output $b \oplus \gamma$.

Fig. 4. The circuit $\bar{P}$.

Let λ be the security parameter. Let $n, m, m_1, m_2, \kappa, l, l_1, l_2, Q$ be positive integers that are polynomial in λ and satisfy $m = m_1 + m_2$ and $l = l_1 + l_2$. Let $\epsilon_1, \epsilon_2, \epsilon$ be real values in $(0,1)$ s.t. $\epsilon = min(\epsilon_1, \epsilon_2)$.[12]

Our construction is built on the following building blocks:

- A public-key hinting watermarkable PRF HWF = (HWF.Setup, HWF.KeyGen, HWF.Eval, HWF.Mark, HWF.Extract) with input space $\{0,1\}^n$, output space $\{0,1\}^{m_1}$, and message space $\{0,1\}^\kappa$. Also, we use l_1 to denote the length of the hint of HWF (i.e., each hint can be represented by a string in $\{0,1\}^{l_1}$).
- A robust unobfuscatable PRF UOF = (UOF.Setup, UOF.KeyGen, UOF.Eval, UOF.Extract) with input space $\{0,1\}^n$, output space $\{0,1\}^{m_2}$, and message space $\{0,1\}^l$.
- A PRF F = (F.KeyGen, F.Eval) with key space $\{0,1\}^{l_2}$, input space $\{0,1\}^n$ and output space $\{0,1\}^{m_1}$.

We construct the public-key watermarkable PRF WPRF = (Setup, KeyGen, Eval, Mark, Extract), which has input space $\{0,1\}^n$, output space $\{0,1\}^m$ and message space $\{0,1\}^\kappa$ as follows:

- **Setup.** On input the security parameter 1^λ, the setup algorithm samples $pp_{hw} \leftarrow$ HWF.Setup(1^λ) and $pp_{uo} \leftarrow$ UOF.Setup(1^λ). Then it outputs the public parameter $PP = (pp_{hw}, pp_{uo})$.
- **KeyGen.** On input the public parameter $PP = (pp_{hw}, pp_{uo})$, the key generation algorithm first generates $(k_{hw}, \text{hint}) \leftarrow$ HWF.KeyGen(pp_{hw}), $k_f \leftarrow$ F.KeyGen(1^λ), and $k_{uo} \leftarrow$ UOF.KeyGen$(pp_{uo}, \text{hint} \| k_f)$. Then, it outputs the PRF key $K = (k_{hw}, k_f, k_{uo})$.
- **Eval.** On input the public parameter $PP = (pp_{hw}, pp_{uo})$, the PRF key $K = (k_{hw}, k_f, k_{uo})$, and an input $x \in \{0,1\}^n$, the evaluation algorithm proceeds as follows:
  1. $y_{hw} = $ HWF.Eval(pp_{hw}, k_{hw}, x).
  2. $y_f = $ F.Eval(k_f, x).

---

[12] Here, $\epsilon_1, \epsilon_2, \epsilon$ can be the negligible function $negl(\lambda)$ instead of a concrete value.

3. $y_{uo} = \mathsf{UOF.Eval}(pp_{uo}, k_{uo}, x)$.
4. Outputs $y = (y_{hw} \oplus y_f, y_{uo})$.

- **Mark.** On input the public parameter $PP = (pp_{hw}, pp_{uo})$, the PRF key $K = (k_{hw}, k_f, k_{uo})$, and a message $msg \in \{0,1\}^{\kappa}$, the marking algorithm computes $\mathsf{C}_{hw} \leftarrow \mathsf{HWF.Mark}(pp_{hw}, k_{hw}, msg)$. Then it outputs a circuit $\mathsf{C} : \{0,1\}^n \rightarrow \{0,1\}^m$ s.t. for any $x \in \{0,1\}^n$:

$$\mathsf{C}(x) = (\mathsf{C}_{hw}(x) \oplus \mathsf{F.Eval}(k_f, x), \mathsf{UOF.Eval}(pp_{uo}, k_{uo}, x))$$

- **Extract.** On input the public parameter $PP = (pp_{hw}, pp_{uo})$, and a circuit C, the extraction algorithm proceeds as follow:
  1. Set C_{uo} as a circuit that for any $x \in \{0,1\}^n$, $\mathsf{C}_{uo}(x) = \mathsf{C}(x)[m_1 + 1 : m]$.
  2. $(\mathsf{hint}, k_f) \leftarrow \mathsf{UOF.Extract}(pp_{uo}, \mathsf{C}_{uo})$.
  3. If $(\mathsf{hint}, k_f) =\perp$: output $\perp$.
  4. Set C_{hw} as a circuit that for any $x \in \{0,1\}^n$, $\mathsf{C}_{hw}(x) = \mathsf{C}(x)[1 : m_1] \oplus \mathsf{F.Eval}(k_f, x)$.
  5. Output $msg \leftarrow \mathsf{HWF.Extract}(pp_{hw}, \mathsf{C}_{hw}, \mathsf{hint})$.

Theorem 7.1. *If* HWF *is a secure public-key hinting watermarkable PRF with Q-bounded ϵ_1-unremovability,* UOF *is a secure robust unobfuscatable PRF with ϵ_2-robust learnability, and* F *is a secure PRF, then* WPRF *is a secure public-key watermarkable PRF with Q-bounded ϵ-unremovability.*

We present proof of Theorem 7.1 in the full version.

Acknowledgement. We appreciate the anonymous reviewers for their valuable comments. Part of this work is supported by the National Science Foundation China (Project No. 61972332), the Innovation Technology Fund (Project No. ITS/224/20FP), the Hong Kong Research Grant Council (Project No. 17201421), and HKU Seed Fund (grant number: 201909185070). Willy Susilo is partially supported by the Australian Research Council Discovery Projects DP200100144 and DP220100003.

References

[AJLA+12] Asharov, G., Jain, A., López-Alt, A., Tromer, E., Vaikuntanathan, V., Wichs, D.: Multiparty computation with low communication, computation and interaction via threshold FHE. In: Pointcheval, D., Johansson, T. (eds.) EUROCRYPT 2012. LNCS, vol. 7237, pp. 483–501. Springer, Heidelberg (2012). https://doi.org/10.1007/978-3-642-29011-4_29

[ALL+21] Aaronson, S., Liu, J., Liu, Q., Zhandry, M., Zhang, R.: New approaches for quantum copy-protection. In: Malkin, T., Peikert, C. (eds.) CRYPTO 2021. LNCS, vol. 12825, pp. 526–555. Springer, Cham (2021). https://doi.org/10.1007/978-3-030-84242-0_19

[AR17] Agrawal, S., Rosen, A.: Functional encryption for bounded collusions, revisited. In: Kalai, Y., Reyzin, L. (eds.) TCC 2017. LNCS, vol. 10677, pp. 173–205. Springer, Cham (2017). https://doi.org/10.1007/978-3-319-70500-2_7

[AV19] Ananth, P., Vaikuntanathan, V.: Optimal bounded-collusion secure functional encryption. In: Hofheinz, D., Rosen, A. (eds.) TCC 2019. LNCS, vol. 11891, pp. 174–198. Springer, Cham (2019). https://doi.org/10.1007/978-3-030-36030-6_8

[BCP14] Boyle, E., Chung, K.-M., Pass, R.: On extractability obfuscation. In: Lindell, Y. (ed.) TCC 2014. LNCS, vol. 8349, pp. 52–73. Springer, Heidelberg (2014). https://doi.org/10.1007/978-3-642-54242-8_3

[BGI+01] Barak, B., et al.: On the (im)possibility of obfuscating programs. In: Kilian, J. (ed.) CRYPTO 2001. LNCS, vol. 2139, pp. 1–18. Springer, Heidelberg (2001). https://doi.org/10.1007/3-540-44647-8_1

[BGI14] Boyle, E., Goldwasser, S., Ivan, I.: Functional signatures and pseudorandom functions. In: Krawczyk, H. (ed.) PKC 2014. LNCS, vol. 8383, pp. 501–519. Springer, Heidelberg (2014). https://doi.org/10.1007/978-3-642-54631-0_29

[BLW17] Boneh, D., Lewi, K., Wu, D.J.: Constraining pseudorandom functions privately. In: Fehr, S. (ed.) PKC 2017. LNCS, vol. 10175, pp. 494–524. Springer, Heidelberg (2017). https://doi.org/10.1007/978-3-662-54388-7_17

[BP13] Bitansky, N., Paneth, O.: On the impossibility of approximate obfuscation and applications to resettable cryptography. In: STOC, pp. 241–250 (2013)

[BSW11] Boneh, D., Sahai, A., Waters, B.: Functional encryption: definitions and challenges. In: Ishai, Y. (ed.) TCC 2011. LNCS, vol. 6597, pp. 253–273. Springer, Heidelberg (2011). https://doi.org/10.1007/978-3-642-19571-6_16

[BW13] Boneh, D., Waters, B.: Constrained pseudorandom functions and their applications. In: Sako, K., Sarkar, P. (eds.) ASIACRYPT 2013. LNCS, vol. 8270, pp. 280–300. Springer, Heidelberg (2013). https://doi.org/10.1007/978-3-642-42045-0_15

[CHN+16] Cohen, A., Holmgren, J., Nishimaki, R., Vaikuntanathan, V., Wichs, D.: Watermarking cryptographic capabilities. In: STOC, pp. 1115–1127 (2016)

[GKM+19] Goyal, R., Kim, S., Manohar, N., Waters, B., Wu, D.J.: Watermarking public-key cryptographic primitives. In: Boldyreva, A., Micciancio, D. (eds.) CRYPTO 2019. LNCS, vol. 11694, pp. 367–398. Springer, Cham (2019). https://doi.org/10.1007/978-3-030-26954-8_12

[GKP+13] Goldwasser, S., Kalai, Y., Popa, R.A., Vaikuntanathan, V., Zeldovich, N.: Reusable garbled circuits and succinct functional encryption. In: STOC, pp. 555–564 (2013)

[GSW13] Gentry, C., Sahai, A., Waters, B.: Homomorphic encryption from learning with errors: conceptually-simpler, asymptotically-faster, attribute-based. In: Canetti, R., Garay, J.A. (eds.) CRYPTO 2013. LNCS, vol. 8042, pp. 75–92. Springer, Heidelberg (2013). https://doi.org/10.1007/978-3-642-40041-4_5

[GVW12] Gorbunov, S., Vaikuntanathan, V., Wee, H.: Functional encryption with bounded collusions via multi-party computation. In: Safavi-Naini, R., Canetti, R. (eds.) CRYPTO 2012. LNCS, vol. 7417, pp. 162–179. Springer, Heidelberg (2012). https://doi.org/10.1007/978-3-642-32009-5_11

[HMW07] Hopper, N., Molnar, D., Wagner, D.: From weak to strong watermarking. In: Vadhan, S.P. (ed.) TCC 2007. LNCS, vol. 4392, pp. 362–382. Springer, Heidelberg (2007). https://doi.org/10.1007/978-3-540-70936-7_20

[JLS21] Jain, A., Lin, H., Sahai., A.: Indistinguishability obfuscation from well-founded assumptions. In: STOC, pp. 60–73 (2021)

[KNY21] Kitagawa, F., Nishimaki, R., Yamakawa, T.: Secure software leasing from standard assumptions. In: Nissim, K., Waters, B. (eds.) TCC 2021. LNCS, vol. 13042, pp. 31–61. Springer, Cham (2021). https://doi.org/10.1007/978-3-030-90459-3_2

[KPTZ13] Kiayias, A., Papadopoulos, S., Triandopoulos, N., Zacharias, T.: Delegatable pseudorandom functions and applications. In: CCS, pp. 669–684. ACM (2013)

[KW17] Kim, S., Wu, D.J.: Watermarking cryptographic functionalities from standard lattice assumptions. In: Katz, J., Shacham, H. (eds.) CRYPTO 2017. LNCS, vol. 10401, pp. 503–536. Springer, Cham (2017). https://doi.org/10.1007/978-3-319-63688-7_17

[KW19] Kim, S., Wu, D.J.: Watermarking PRFs from lattices: stronger security via extractable PRFs. In: Boldyreva, A., Micciancio, D. (eds.) CRYPTO 2019. LNCS, vol. 11694, pp. 335–366. Springer, Cham (2019). https://doi.org/10.1007/978-3-030-26954-8_11

[MP12] Micciancio, D., Peikert, C.: Trapdoors for lattices: simpler, tighter, faster, smaller. In: Pointcheval, D., Johansson, T. (eds.) EUROCRYPT 2012. LNCS, vol. 7237, pp. 700–718. Springer, Heidelberg (2012). https://doi.org/10.1007/978-3-642-29011-4_41

[Nis13] Nishimaki, R.: How to watermark cryptographic functions. In: Johansson, T., Nguyen, P.Q. (eds.) EUROCRYPT 2013. LNCS, vol. 7881, pp. 111–125. Springer, Heidelberg (2013). https://doi.org/10.1007/978-3-642-38348-9_7

[NSS99] Naccache, D., Shamir, A., Stern, J.P.: How to copyright a function? In: Imai, H., Zheng, Y. (eds.) PKC 1999. LNCS, vol. 1560, pp. 188–196. Springer, Heidelberg (1999). https://doi.org/10.1007/3-540-49162-7_14

[NWZ16] Nishimaki, R., Wichs, D., Zhandry, M.: Anonymous traitor tracing: how to embed arbitrary information in a key. In: Fischlin, M., Coron, J.-S. (eds.) EUROCRYPT 2016. LNCS, vol. 9666, pp. 388–419. Springer, Heidelberg (2016). https://doi.org/10.1007/978-3-662-49896-5_14

[O'N10] O'Neill, A.: Definitional issues in functional encryption. Cryptology ePrint Archive, Report 2010/556 (2010). https://ia.cr/2010/556

[PS18] Peikert, C., Shiehian, S.: Privately constraining and programming PRFs, the LWE way. In: Abdalla, M., Dahab, R. (eds.) PKC 2018. LNCS, vol. 10770, pp. 675–701. Springer, Cham (2018). https://doi.org/10.1007/978-3-319-76581-5_23

[PS20] Peikert, C., Shiehian, S.: Constraining and watermarking PRFs from milder assumptions. In: Kiayias, A., Kohlweiss, M., Wallden, P., Zikas, V. (eds.) PKC 2020. LNCS, vol. 12110, pp. 431–461. Springer, Cham (2020). https://doi.org/10.1007/978-3-030-45374-9_15

[QWZ18] Quach, W., Wichs, D., Zirdelis, G.: Watermarking PRFs under standard assumptions: public marking and security with extraction queries. In: Beimel, A., Dziembowski, S. (eds.) TCC 2018. LNCS, vol. 11240, pp. 669–698. Springer, Cham (2018). https://doi.org/10.1007/978-3-030-03810-6_24

[SW14] Sahai, A., Waters, B.: How to use indistinguishability obfuscation: deniable encryption, and more. In: STOC, pp. 475–484 (2014)

[YAL+19] Yang, R., Au, M.H., Lai, J., Xu, Q., Yu, Z.: Collusion resistant watermarking schemes for cryptographic functionalities. In: Galbraith, S.D., Moriai, S. (eds.) ASIACRYPT 2019. LNCS, vol. 11921, pp. 371–398. Springer, Cham (2019). https://doi.org/10.1007/978-3-030-34578-5_14

[YAYX20] Yang, R., Au, M.H., Yu, Z., Xu, Q.: Collusion resistant watermarkable PRFs from standard assumptions. In: Micciancio, D., Ristenpart, T. (eds.) CRYPTO 2020. LNCS, vol. 12170, pp. 590–620. Springer, Cham (2020). https://doi.org/10.1007/978-3-030-56784-2_20

[YF11] Yoshida, M., Fujiwara, T.: Toward digital watermarking for cryptographic data. IEICE Trans. Fundam. Electron. Commun. Comput. Sci. **94**(1), 270–272 (2011)

[Zha21] Zhandry, M.: White box traitor tracing. In: Malkin, T., Peikert, C. (eds.) CRYPTO 2021. LNCS, vol. 12828, pp. 303–333. Springer, Cham (2021). https://doi.org/10.1007/978-3-030-84259-8_11

CHIP and CRISP:
Protecting All Parties Against Compromise Through Identity-Binding PAKEs

Cas Cremers[1] , Moni Naor[2], Shahar Paz[3], and Eyal Ronen[3(✉)]

[1] CISPA Helmholtz Center for Information Security, Saarbrücken, Germany
cremers@cispa.de
[2] Faculty of Mathematics and Computer Science, Weizmann Institute of Science, Rehovot, Israel
moni.naor@weizmann.ac.il
[3] School of Computer Science, Tel Aviv University, Tel Aviv, Israel
{shaharps,eyal.ronen}@cs.tau.ac.il

Abstract. Recent advances in password-based authenticated key exchange (PAKE) protocols can offer stronger security guarantees for globally deployed security protocols. Notably, the OPAQUE protocol [Eurocrypt2018] realizes Strong Asymmetric PAKE (saPAKE), strengthening the protection offered by aPAKE to compromised servers: after compromising an saPAKE server, the adversary still has to perform a full brute-force search to recover any passwords or impersonate users. However, (s)aPAKEs do not protect client storage, and can only be applied in the so-called *asymmetric* setting, in which some parties, such as servers, do not communicate with each other using the protocol.

Nonetheless, passwords are also widely used in *symmetric* settings, where a group of parties share a password and can all communicate (e.g., Wi-Fi with client devices, routers, and mesh nodes; or industrial IoT scenarios). In these settings, the (s)aPAKE techniques cannot be applied, and the state-of-the-art still involves handling plaintext passwords.

In this work, we propose the notions of *(strong) identity-binding PAKEs* that improve this situation: they protect against compromise of *any* party, and can also be applied in the symmetric setting. We propose counterparts to state-of-the-art security notions from the asymmetric setting in the UC model, and construct protocols that provably realize them. Our constructions bind the local storage of all parties to abstract identities, building on ideas from identity-based key exchange, but without requiring a third party.

Our first protocol, CHIP, generalizes the security of aPAKE protocols to all parties, forcing the adversary to perform a brute-force search to recover passwords or impersonate others. Our second protocol, CRISP, additionally renders any adversarial pre-computation useless, thereby offering saPAKE-like guarantees for all parties, instead of only the server.

We evaluate prototype implementations of our protocols and show that even though they offer stronger security for real-world use cases, their performance is in line with, or even better than, state-of-the-art protocols.

Keywords: Password authentication · PAKE · Symmetric PAKE · Compromise Resilience · Key Compromise Impersonation

© International Association for Cryptologic Research 2022
Y. Dodis and T. Shrimpton (Eds.): CRYPTO 2022, LNCS 13508, pp. 668–698, 2022.
https://doi.org/10.1007/978-3-031-15979-4_23

1   Introduction

Passwords are arguably the most widely deployed authentication method today, and are used in a vast range of applications from authentication on the internet (e.g., email and bank servers), wireless network encryption (e.g., Wi-Fi, Smart Homes, Industry 4.0), and enterprise network authentication (e.g., Kerberos [27], EAP-pwd [21]). Early password-based protocols allowed adversaries to verify password guesses offline against observed network traffic. To remedy this, Password Authenticated Key Exchange (PAKE) protocols were proposed, as first studied by Bellovin and Merritt [3]. PAKEs allow parties to negotiate a strong secret key based only on a shared and possibly low-entropy password, do not leak any information about the password to passive adversaries, and allow only an inevitable online password guess attack.

The traditional PAKE threat model does not include compromise of the local storage – notably, most PAKEs work in a way that requires the plaintext password to be available at both parties, including SPAKE-2 and WPA3's DragonFly/SAE. This implies that non-interactive parties such as servers, IoT devices, and wireless access points, need to store the password in plaintext. Compromising the database of these parties directly reveals the password. In the client-server model, this means that a server compromise allows the adversary to impersonate as the client or server towards either, or perform a MiTM attack. Moreover, because clients often re-use passwords across services, this enables credential stuffing.

To partially mitigate this threat, Bellovin and Merritt [4] proposed so-called asymmetric PAKEs (also known as aPAKEs, Augmented PAKEs, or V(erifier)-PAKEs) that make this much harder: the clients still need to provide the password in plaintext, but the verifying servers now only need to provide, and thus store, information that (a) is derived from the password using a one-way function, yet (b) allows establishing a shared key with a party that knows the password. Thus, compromising an aPAKE server does not allow the adversary to impersonate the client, and forces it to perform a brute-force attempt to extract the password.

1.1   Identity-Binding PAKEs (iPAKE)

aPAKE protocols still have substantial limitations: they only protect the server, and perhaps more importantly, cannot be applied to settings that do not fall into the client-server model, e.g., where a password can be shared among group members that can communicate with all other members. Prime examples of such *symmetric* settings are found in wireless networking and IoT settings. For example, the globally deployed IEEE 802.11 Wi-Fi standard includes the WPA protocol, which uses network passwords to enable devices to automatically connect to routers, extenders, and mesh network nodes; crucially, all parties can automatically communicate with each other using the network password without any user input. This led the Wi-Fi alliance to base their latest WPA3 protocol [31] on a symmetric PAKE for mesh networks called Simultaneous Authentication of Equals (SAE) [20].

In such settings, asymmetric PAKEs cannot be applied, because protecting two parties using known aPAKE-server methods stops them from being able to communicate with each other: by construction, aPAKE's servers can only authenticate themselves to clients, not to other servers. Furthermore, because parties in common symmetric group settings operate without user input, they need to store the password in plaintext. E.g., Wi-Fi passwords are stored in plaintext on users' devices.

Hence, despite the many advances made over the years, all state-of-the-art PAKEs in the symmetric setting offer substantially weaker protection and no containment: compromising any party allows impersonation of any other party in the group, thus compromising the entire group.

In this work we address this gap by initiating the study and construction of so-called *identity-binding* PAKEs (iPAKE). We provide a UC-security definition that is the symmetric counterpart to aPAKE. We instantiate iPAKE with CHIP, a novel compiler from any PAKE to iPAKE. We leverage ideas from Identity-Based Key-Exchange to introduce abstract identities for each party, and effectively bind the locally stored password-derived data to these identities, while retaining the required key agreement functionality. Unlike Identity-Based Key-Exchange, we do not require a third party: instead, each party locally simulates the Key Distribution Center during the password file generation. Identities can be arbitrary bit strings, and could also encode functions or roles instead of the party's name, e.g., "server", "router", or "fire brigade chief", "Elon's third iPhone". Binding the locally stored password-derived data to identities is useful for many purposes, such as preventing reflection attacks, revocation of compromised or disposed of devices, network segmentation (i.e., which nodes may interact), permissions (e.g., prevent guest devices from configuring an access point), and authentic audit logs that allow anomaly detection and reliable retroactive damage assessment.

1.2 Strong Identity-Binding PAKEs (siPAKE)

In 2018, Jarecki, Krawczyk, and Xu [23] strengthened the aPAKE notion by additionally requiring that an adversary gains no benefits from any pre-computations performed before a server compromise, thereby forcing it to do a full brute-force attack after the compromise. They named this notion *strong* asymmetric PAKE (saPAKE), and proposed the OPAQUE protocol to meet it. This has been widely regarded as a major step forward, and has led the Internet Engineering Task Force (IETF) to work towards standardizing OPAQUE and its use for TLS 1.3's password-based logins [7].

To provide similar protection against pre-computations, we strengthen iPAKE to *strong identity-binding* PAKEs (siPAKE), and provide a UC-security definition that is the symmetric counterpart to saPAKE. We instantiate siPAKE with CRISP, a novel compiler from any PAKE to siPAKE, that extends the protection provided by state-of-the-art saPAKE protocols [9,23] to all parties.

We prove the correctness of both of our constructions, provide open source prototype implementations, and evaluate their efficiency.

1.3   Contributions

1. We initiate the study of *identity-binding PAKEs*, which offer additional security guarantees compared to their corresponding state-of-the-art aPAKE relatives. In particular:
   - Identity-binding PAKEs offer containment against compromise of any party, instead of only a specific subset such as servers.
   - Unlike aPAKEs, iPAKEs are symmetric and allow all parties to communicate with each other, and can therefore also be applied to settings such as IEEE 802.11's WPA (Wi-Fi).
2. We define the ideal functionality $\mathcal{F}_{\text{iPAKE}}$ for **identity-binding PAKE (iPAKE)** in the UC model, and construct the **CHIP** compiler that turns any symmetric PAKE into an iPAKE. CHIP offers aPAKE-like guarantees for all parties: the compromise of any party does not allow the adversary to impersonate another unless they perform a brute-force attack. We prove that CHIP is secure in the Programmable Random Oracle Model (ROM) under the Strong Diffie-Hellman assumption.
3. We define the ideal functionality $\mathcal{F}_{\text{siPAKE}}$ for **strong identity-binding PAKE (siPAKE)** in the UC model, and construct the **CRISP** compiler that turns any symmetric PAKE into an siPAKE. CRISP offers saPAKE/OPAQUE-like guarantees for *all* parties: to impersonate any other party after a compromise, the adversary's brute-force attack additionally cannot utilize any pre-computation in a useful manner. CRISP is based on a bilinear group with pairing and "Hash-to-Group", and we prove it secure in the Generic Group with Random Oracle Model (GGM+ROM).
4. We implemented prototypes of both our protocols. While our protocols offer substantial security benefits over existing state-of-the-art PAKEs for the symmetric setting, a performance benchmark (Sect. 8.4) that shows their performance is in line with, or even better than, state-of-the-art protocols.

Table 1 summarizes the different security notions and example protocols.

Prototype Implementations. We provide open source implementations of both protocols at https://github.com/shapaz/CRISP.

1.4   Structure of the Paper

We give background on the formalization of PAKEs in Sect. 2. We discuss various methods for compromise resilience in Sect. 3. In Sect. 4 we describe the notation and UC building blocks we use. We present our new ideal functionalities for iPAKE and siPAKE in Sect. 5. We introduce the CHIP compiler in Sect. 6 and the CRISP compiler in Sect. 7. In Sect. 8 we analyze the computational cost of running our protocols and the cost of the inevitable brute-force attack. We also propose several optimization to the protocol as well as performance benchmarks. We conclude and present open problems in Sect. 9.

We provide full proofs and more in the full version of our paper [15].

Table 1. PAKE notions, example protocols, and security guarantees. ○ denotes the property is not provided; ◐ denotes that the property only holds for servers, and can *only* be applied to the asymmetric setting; and ● denotes that it is provided for all parties.

Security notion		Example protocol		Post-compromise impersonation resistance	Secure against pre-computation
PAKE	[13]	CPace	[19]	○	○
aPAKE	[17]	AuCPace	[19]	◐	○
iPAKE	(Section 4)	**CHIP**	(Section 6)	●	○
saPAKE	[23]	OPAQUE	[23]	◐	◐
siPAKE	(Section 4)	**CRISP**	(Section 7)	●	●

2   Related Work on Formalizing PAKE

Bellare, Pointcheval, and Rogaway [2] were the first to formalize the notion of PAKE. Canetti, Halevi, Katz, Lindell, and MacKenzie [13] formalized PAKE in the Universal Composability (UC) framework [11]. Their ideal functionality $\mathcal{F}_{\mathrm{PAKE}}$ (originally denoted $\mathcal{F}_{\mathrm{pwKE}}$) trades each party's password with a randomly chosen key for the session, only allowing the adversary an online attack where a single guess may be made to some party's password.

Asymmetric PAKE (aPAKE) protocols (a.k.a. Augmented PAKEs or Verifier PAKEs) were formalized by Boyko, MacKenzie, and Patel [8]. They address the problem of password compromise from long term storage by introducing *asymmetry*, separating parties into "clients" and "servers". While clients supply their passwords on every session, servers use a "password file" generated in a setup phase. To prevent servers from impersonating clients, it should be "hard" to directly extract the password from such a file. However, since we assume that the password domain is small, an attacker can run an *offline dictionary attack*, testing every possible password against the file until one is accepted. The best one can hope for is that password extraction time will be linear in the dictionary's size. Gentry, MacKenzie, and Ramzan [17] formalized an ideal functionality $\mathcal{F}_{\mathrm{aPAKE}}$ in the UC framework, and presented a generic compiler from $\mathcal{F}_{\mathrm{PAKE}}$ to $\mathcal{F}_{\mathrm{aPAKE}}$.

The notion of Strong Asymmetric PAKE $\mathcal{F}_{\mathrm{saPAKE}}$ by Jarecki, Krawczyk, and Xu [23] addresses an issue with the original $\mathcal{F}_{\mathrm{aPAKE}}$, that allowed a pre-computation attack: password guesses could have been submitted before a server compromise. Most of the computational work could have been done prior to the actual compromise of the password file, allowing "instantaneous" password recovery upon compromise. For example, the attacker can pre-compute the hash value for all passwords in a given dictionary in advance. When a server is compromised at a later point, the adversary can find the pre-image for the compromised hash value, retrieving the password immediately.

In summary, while (s)aPAKE protect against server compromise in the asymmetric setting, prior works did not address party compromise in the symmetric setting or client compromise (in the asymmetric setting).

3   Methods and Limitations for Compromise Resilience

In compromise resilience of PAKE protocols, we consider two main parameters:

1. The computational cost of a brute-force attack to recover the original password, using the information stored on the device in the offline phase (i.e., in the password file).
2. The possibility of performing a trade-off between the pre-computation cost (performed before the compromise of the device) and the computation cost (performed after the compromise).

We assume the adversary holds a password dictionary that contains the right password, and a brute-force attack's computational cost is proportional to the size of that dictionary. Being a "machine-in-the-middle", our adversary may alter messages and exploit information sent in the online phase of the protocol, and might target multiple passwords used by different users.

We note that in practice, passwords are used across many types of devices. Some of these devices are directly controlled by (human) users, such as phones or laptops, which either don't store the password (e.g., user remembers) or store it protected by another interactive security mechanism (e.g., biometrics, password, PIN), thereby making the compromise of the password file harder. However, a large proportion of devices that share the same password have no such user interaction, such as internet routers, TVs, IoT devices, and drones; and compromising them thus can lead to revealing the unprotected password file.

We survey known methods for achieving various levels of compromise resilience and also give examples for systems using them:

1. **Plaintext password:** The password is stored as-is in the password file. No computation is required for password recovery. This is the case for the WPA3 protocol in Wi-Fi [31], and the client-side for aPAKEs.
2. **Hashed password:** A one-way function of the password is stored in the password file. This option is only beneficial when using a high entropy password chosen from a password space that is too large to pre-compute. Otherwise, an adversary might hash every possible password and prepare a reverse lookup table from hash value to plain password, allowing password recovery in $O(1)$ time. This can be done once, amortizing the cost of the pre-computation over multiple password recoveries.
3. **Hashed password with public identifiers:** A one-way function of the password and some public identifiers of the connection is computed and stored in the password file. For example, the public identifiers can be derived from the SSID (network name) in Wi-Fi or a combination of the server and user names. In this case, pre-computation is still possible, but amortization is prevented, since the pre-computation does not apply for different public identifiers. This protection is offered by some aPAKE protocols [19] and by our novel iPAKE protocol.

4. **Hashed password with public "salt":** A one-way function of the password and a randomly generated value ("salt") is computed and stored in the password file. The "salt" is sent in the clear, as part of the PAKE protocol. As in the previous case, pre-computation before a compromise is possible, but only after the adversary eavesdrops to a PAKE protocol of the target device and learns the "salt". This is the case for the server side in some aPAKE protocols [19,32].
5. **Hashed password with *secret* "salt":** In this case, the random "salt" is kept secret, which requires more intricate mechanisms than with the public salt, since it is no longer possible to send the salt in the clear. This approach prevents any pre-computation, and yields a level of protection that is offered by saPAKE for the servers in the asymmetric setting, and by our novel siPAKE protocol for all parties in any setting. The only remaining attack left for the adversary is a brute-force post-compromise attack, which is inevitable, as we show below.

Inevitable Generic Post-compromise Brute-Force Attack

Post-compromise brute-force dictionary attacks are inevitable for any PAKE protocol. In the following attack, we assume that the correct password is in the dictionary and exploit the property that PAKE protocols fail to agree on a key when the participants have different passwords. The attack works by simulating a normal protocol run, where one party uses the compromised data, and the peer uses the password guess:

1. Retrieve a password file FILE from a compromised device.
2. For every password guess π' in the dictionary:
   (a) Derive password file FILE' according to the protocol specification's setup phase for the peer, using π'.
   (b) Use FILE and FILE' to simulate both parties in a normal run of the PAKE protocol.
   (c) If the simulated parties negotiate the same key, π' is the correct password for the compromised device.

The cost of each password guess in the black-box attack is the cost of deriving the password file from a password and running the protocol for both parties. This generic attack provides an upper bound to the cost of the brute-force attack on any PAKE protocol. To increase the cost of the generic attack, we must also increase the computational cost of either password file derivation or running the online phase of the protocol. Note that the password file derivation can be done in pre-computation.

4   Notation and UC Building Blocks

In this section, we first introduce some notational convention and recall the symmetric PAKE functionality. We then introduce modelling of the random oracle model and the generic group model.

Notation and Conventions. Our notational conventions inherit from the PAKE and UC settings:

π	a password
id	some party's abstract identifier
$\mathcal{P}$	a party interacting in either real or ideal world
κ	a security parameter
q	a large prime number $q \geq 2^\kappa$
$\mathbb{Z}_q$	the field of integers modulo q, $\mathbb{Z}_q^* = \mathbb{Z}_q \backslash \{0\}$
x	an element of $\mathbb{Z}_q$
F	a polynomial in $\mathbb{Z}_q[X]$
X	a formal variable in a polynomial (indeterminate)
$\mathbb{G}$	a cyclic group of order q
$[x]_{\mathbb{G}}$	a member of group $\mathbb{G}$, identified by the exponent x of some public generator $g \in \mathbb{G}$: $[x]_{\mathbb{G}} = g^x$
$\{0,1\}^n$	the set of binary strings of length n
$\{0,1\}^*$	the set of binary strings of any length
$x \xleftarrow{R} S$	sampling x from uniform distribution over set S
$x_{\in S}$	restriction: x must be an element of S
H	a hash function
$\hat{H}$	a hash-to-group function

Similar to existing asymmetric PAKE constructions analyzed in the UC framework, we use two levels of sessions:

sid	identifies a static session, e.g., a group of parties communicating using the same shared password. (E.g., when instantiated in the Wi-Fi setting, this could be the Wi-Fi network identifier)
$ssid$	identifies a particular online exchange, i.e., a sub-session.

Symmetric PAKE Functionality. In Fig. 1 we restate the symmetric PAKE functionality $\mathcal{F}_{\text{PAKE}}$ from Canetti et al. [13] (denoted $\mathcal{F}_{\text{pwKE}}$ there), incorporating the fix recommended by Abdalla et al. [1]. In our presentation of $\mathcal{F}_{\text{PAKE}}$, we explicitly record keys handed to parties in FRESH sessions using $\langle \text{KEY}, \ldots \rangle$ records, which we will later use in our protocol proofs.

Whenever an ideal functionality is required to retrieve some record ("Retrieve $\langle \text{RECORD}, \ldots \rangle$") but it cannot be found, the functionality is said to implicitly ignore the query.

4.1   UC Modelling of Random Oracle and Generic Group

The necessity of non-black-box assumptions for proving compromise resilience in the UC framework has been previously observed (see [17,23] and [9]). Hesse [22] proved that UC-realization of aPAKE is impossible under non-programmable ROM. In this work we rely on programmable ROM for proving CHIP and on Generic Group Model for CRISP.

We model ROM in UC by allowing parties in the real world to access an ideal functionality $\mathcal{F}_{\text{RO}}$, depicted in Fig. 2. Invocations of hash functions in the protocol are modelled as queries to $\mathcal{F}_{\text{RO}}$. The functionality acts as an oracle, answering fresh queries with independent random values, but consistent results

---

Functionality $\mathcal{F}_{\text{PAKE}}$, with security parameter κ, interacting with parties $\{\mathcal{P}_i\}_{i=1}^n$ and an adversary $\mathcal{S}$.

Upon $(\text{NEWSESSION}, sid, \mathcal{P}_j, \pi_i)$ **from** $\mathcal{P}_i$:
- Send $(\text{NEWSESSION}, sid, \mathcal{P}_i, \mathcal{P}_j)$ to $\mathcal{S}$
- If there is no record $\langle \text{SESSION}, \mathcal{P}_i, \mathcal{P}_j, \cdot, \cdot \rangle$:
  - ▷ record $\langle \text{SESSION}, \mathcal{P}_i, \mathcal{P}_j, \pi_i \rangle$ and mark it FRESH

Upon $(\text{TESTPWD}, sid, \mathcal{P}_i, \pi')$ **from** $\mathcal{S}$:
- Retrieve $\langle \text{SESSION}, \mathcal{P}_i, \mathcal{P}_j, \pi_i \rangle$ marked FRESH
- If $\pi_i = \pi'$: mark the session COMPROMISED and return "correct guess" to $\mathcal{S}$
- otherwise: mark the session INTERRUPTED and return "wrong guess" to $\mathcal{S}$

Upon $(\text{NEWKEY}, sid, \mathcal{P}_i, K'_{\in\{0,1\}^\kappa})$ **from** $\mathcal{S}$:
- Retrieve $\langle \text{SESSION}, \mathcal{P}_i, \mathcal{P}_j, \pi_i \rangle$ not marked COMPLETED
- If it is marked COMPROMISED: $K_i \leftarrow K'$
- else if it is marked FRESH and there is a record $\langle \text{KEY}, \mathcal{P}_j, \pi_j, K_j \rangle$ with $\pi_i = \pi_j$: $K_i \leftarrow K_j$
- otherwise: pick $K_i \xleftarrow{\text{R}} \{0,1\}^\kappa$
- If the session is marked FRESH: record $\langle \text{KEY}, \mathcal{P}_i, \pi_i, K_i \rangle$
- Mark the session COMPLETED and send $\langle sid, K_i \rangle$ to $\mathcal{P}_i$

Fig. 1. Symmetric PAKE functionality $\mathcal{F}_{\text{PAKE}}$ from [13] with the fix recommended by [1] and minor presentational modifications to simplify comparison.

Functionality $\mathcal{F}_{\text{RO}}$, parametrized by domain D and range E, interacting with parties $\{\mathcal{P}_i\}_{i=1}^n$ and adversary $\mathcal{S}$.

Upon $(\text{HASH}, sid, s_{\in D})$ **from** $\mathcal{P} \in \{\mathcal{P}_i\}_{i=1}^n \cup \{\mathcal{S}\}$:

- If there is no record $\langle \text{HASH}, s, h \rangle$:
  - ▷ Pick $h \xleftarrow{\text{R}} E$ and record $\langle \text{HASH}, s, h \rangle$
- Return h to $\mathcal{P}$.

Fig. 2. Random Oracle functionality $\mathcal{F}_{\text{RO}}$

to repeated queries. The model is *programmable*, meaning that the simulator is able to view hash queries and program their results. The model is also *local*, meaning that every session has a separate independent $\mathcal{F}_{\text{RO}}$ machine. However, every HASH query is parametrized by a unique sid, effectively separating the hash domain. Consequently, a single global random oracle in the real world suffices to handle queries from multiple sessions.

The Generic Group Model (GGM), introduced by [30], allows proving properties of algorithms, assuming the only permitted operations on group elements are the group operation and comparison. Hence a "generic group element" has no meaningful representation. Algorithms in GGM operate on encodings of elements, and may consult a group oracle which computes the group operation for two valid encodings, returning the encoded result. The group oracle declines queries for encodings not returned by some previous query.

Functionality $\mathcal{F}_{GG}$, parametrized by group order q, encoding set $\mathbb{E}$ ($|\mathbb{E}| \geq q$) and generator $g \in \mathbb{E}$, interacting with parties $\{\mathcal{P}_i\}_{i=1}^n$ and adversary $\mathcal{S}$.

Initially, $S = \{1\}$, $[1]_G = g$ and $[x]_G$ is undefined for any other $x \in \mathbb{Z}_q$. Whenever $\mathcal{F}_{GG}$ references an undefined $[x]_G$, set $[x]_G \xleftarrow{R} \mathbb{E} \backslash S$ and insert $[x]_G$ to S.

Upon $(\text{MULDIV}, sid, [x_1]_G, [x_2]_G, s_{\in\{0,1\}})$ **from** $\mathcal{P} \in \{\mathcal{P}_i\}_{i=1}^n \cup \{\mathcal{S}\}$:
  ○ $x \leftarrow x_1 + (-1)^s x_2 \mod q$
  ○ Return $[x]_G$ to $\mathcal{P}$

Fig. 3. Generic Group functionality $\mathcal{F}_{GG}$

Any cyclic group $\mathbb{G}$ of prime-order q with generator g can be viewed as $\{[x]_G \mid x \in \mathbb{Z}_q\}$ with group operations $[x]_G \odot [y]_G = [x+y]_G$ and $[x]_G \oslash [y]_G = [x-y]_G$, unit element $[0]_G$ and generator $[1]_G$, using some encoding function $[\cdot]_G$: $x \mapsto g^x$. In GGM we consider encoding functions carrying no further information about the group, e.g., encodings using random bit-strings or numbers in the range $\{0, \ldots, q-1\}$. This is in contrast to concrete groups which might have a meaningful encoding.

In order to prove CRISP's security under Universal Composition, we need to formalize GGM in terms of an ideal functionality $\mathcal{F}_{GG}$. Figure 3 shows the basic GGM functionality $\mathcal{F}_{GG}$, which answers group operation queries (multiply/divide) on encoded elements. As with $\mathcal{F}_{RO}$, functionality $\mathcal{F}_{GG}$ is both programmable and local. Unlike ROM, where local independent oracles can be created from a single global one, the same is not trivial with generic groups. The full version [15] deals with group reuse across instances of CRISP.

For simplicity one can think of the set of encoding $\mathbb{E} = \mathbb{Z}_q$, so each exponent $x \in \mathbb{Z}_q$ is encoded as $[x]_G = \xi \in \mathbb{Z}_q$, resulting in the encoding function being a random permutation over $\mathbb{Z}_q$, ensuring no information about oracle usage is disclosed between parties.

Note that although the group order q might be (exponentially) large, $\mathcal{F}_{GG}$ maps at most one new element per query. Also note the mapping is injective.

A bilinear group is a triplet of cyclic groups $\mathbb{G}_1, \mathbb{G}_2, \mathbb{G}_T$ of prime order q, with an efficiently computable bilinear map $\hat{e}: \mathbb{G}_1 \times \mathbb{G}_2 \rightarrow \mathbb{G}_T$ satisfying the following requirements:

- **Bilinearity:** $\hat{e}(g_1^x, g_2^y) = \hat{e}(g_1, g_2)^{xy}$ for all $x, y \in \mathbb{Z}_q$.
- **Non-degeneracy:** $\hat{e}(g_1, g_2) \neq 1_T$.

where g_1, g_2 are generators for $\mathbb{G}_1, \mathbb{G}_2$ respectively. We also consider an efficiently computable isomorphism $\psi: \mathbb{G}_2 \rightarrow \mathbb{G}_1$ satisfying $\psi(g_2) = g_1$.

A hash to group, also referred to as Hash2Curve, is an efficiently computable hash function, modelled as random oracle, whose range is a group. For the bilinear setting, we consider the range $\mathbb{G}_2$.

In order to represent groups with pairing and hash into group, we suggest a modified functionality $\mathcal{F}_{GGP}$, depicted in Fig. 4, similar to the extension of GGM to bilinear groups by [6]. $\mathcal{F}_{GGP}$ can be queried MULDIV for each of $\mathbb{G}_1$, $\mathbb{G}_2$ and $\mathbb{G}_T$, and maintains separate encoding maps for each group. It introduces three

---

Functionality $\mathcal{F}_{\text{GGP}}$, parametrized by group order q, encoding sets $\mathbb{E}_1, \mathbb{E}_2, \mathbb{E}_T$ ($|\mathbb{E}_j| \geq q$ for $j \in \{1, 2, T\}$) and generators $g_1 \in \mathbb{E}_1$, $g_2 \in \mathbb{E}_2$, interacting with parties $\{\mathcal{P}_i\}_{i=1}^n$ and adversary $\mathcal{S}$. Let $\mathfrak{P} = \{\mathcal{P}_i\}_{i=1}^n \cup \{\mathcal{S}\}$.

Initially, $S_1 = S_2 = \{1\}$, $S_T = \varnothing$, $[1]_{\mathbb{G}_1} = g_1$, $[1]_{\mathbb{G}_2} = g_2$ and $[x]_{\mathbb{G}_j}$ is undefined for any other $x \in \mathbb{Z}_q$ $j \in \{1, 2, T\}$. Whenever $\mathcal{F}_{\text{GGP}}$ references an undefined $[x]_{\mathbb{G}_j}$, set $[x]_{\mathbb{G}_j} \xleftarrow{\text{R}} \mathbb{E} \backslash S_j$ and insert $[x]_{\mathbb{G}_j}$ to S_j.

Upon $(\text{MULDIV}, sid, j_{\in \{1,2,T\}}, [x_1]_{\mathbb{G}_j}, [x_2]_{\mathbb{G}_j}, s_{\in \{0,1\}})$ **from** $\mathcal{P} \in \mathfrak{P}$:
  ○ Return $[x \leftarrow x_1 + (-1)^s x_2 \mod q]_{\mathbb{G}_j}$ to $\mathcal{P}$

Upon $(\text{PAIRING}, sid, [x_1]_{\mathbb{G}_1}, [x_2]_{\mathbb{G}_2})$ **from** $\mathcal{P} \in \mathfrak{P}$:
  ○ Return $[x_T \leftarrow x_1 \cdot x_2 \mod q]_{\mathbb{G}_T}$ to $\mathcal{P}$

Upon $(\text{ISOMORPHISM}, sid, j_{\in \{1,2\}}, [x]_{\mathbb{G}_j})$ **from** $\mathcal{S}$:
  ○ Return $[x]_{\mathbb{G}_{3-j}}$ to $\mathcal{P}$

Upon (HASH, sid, s) **from** $\mathcal{P} \in \mathfrak{P}$:
  ○ If there is no record $\langle \text{HASH}, s, [x]_{\mathbb{G}_2} \rangle$:
    ▷ pick $x \xleftarrow{\text{R}} \mathbb{Z}_q^*$ and record $\langle \text{HASH}, s, [x]_{\mathbb{G}_2} \rangle$
  ○ Return $[x]_{\mathbb{G}_2}$ to $\mathcal{P}$

Fig. 4. Generic Group with Pairing and Hash-to-Group functionality $\mathcal{F}_{\text{GGP}}$

new queries: (a) PAIRING to compute the bilinear pairing $\hat{e}$: $([x_1]_{\mathbb{G}_1}, [x_2]_{\mathbb{G}_2}) \mapsto [x_1 \cdot x_2]_{\mathbb{G}_T}$; (b) ISOMORPHISM to compute an isomorphism ψ, ψ^{-1} between $\mathbb{G}_2$ and $\mathbb{G}_1$: $[x]_{\mathbb{G}_1} \mapsto [x]_{\mathbb{G}_1}$, $[x]_{\mathbb{G}_1} \mapsto [x]_{\mathbb{G}_2}$; and (c) HASH which is a random oracle into $\mathbb{G}_2$: for each freshly queried string $s \in \{0, 1\}^*$ it picks a random exponent $x \xleftarrow{\text{R}} \mathbb{Z}_q^*$, then returns its encoding $[x]_{\mathbb{G}_2}$.

We note that there are groups for which only ψ is efficiently computable but ψ^{-1} is not, or even ψ itself is inefficient. However, CRISP does not require these ISOMORPHISM queries and they can be omitted for such groups. We state that equipping the adversary with ISOMORPHISM queries guarantees security even when such isomorphism is found.

5   (Strong) Identity-Binding PAKE Functionality

In Fig. 5 we present the Identity-binding PAKE functionality $\mathcal{F}_{\text{iPAKE}}$ and the Strong Identity-binding PAKE functionality $\mathcal{F}_{\text{siPAKE}}$. Essentially, they preserve the symmetry of $\mathcal{F}_{\text{PAKE}}$ while adopting the notion of password files and party compromise from the Asymmetric PAKE functionality $\mathcal{F}_{\text{aPAKE}}$ of [17] and Strong Asymmetric PAKE functionality $\mathcal{F}_{\text{saPAKE}}$ of [23] (found in the full version [15].

Informally speaking, our threat model includes the online adversary from traditional PAKEs. Additionally, we consider adversaries that may compromise parties in order to impersonate as other parties, e.g., compromise an IoT device to impersonate as the router or server. The strong form additionally considers adversaries that can perform large amounts of precomputation.

Compared to the asymmetric functionalities, our main addition is the notion of abstract identities (id_i) assigned by the environment to parties, and reported

Functionalities $\mathcal{F}_{\text{iPAKE}}$ and $\mathcal{F}_{\text{siPAKE}}$, with security parameter κ, interacting with parties $\{\mathcal{P}_i\}_{i=1}^n$ and adversary $\mathcal{S}$.

Upon (STOREPWDFILE, sid, id_i, π_i) **from** $\mathcal{P}_i$:
  ○ If there is no record $\langle \text{FILE}, \mathcal{P}_i, \cdot, \cdot \rangle$:
    ▷ record $\langle \text{FILE}, \mathcal{P}_i, \text{id}_i, \pi_i \rangle$ and mark it UNCOMPROMISED

Upon (STEALPWDFILE, sid, $\mathcal{P}_i$) **from** $\mathcal{S}$:
  ○ If there is a record $\langle \text{FILE}, \mathcal{P}_i, \text{id}_i, \pi_i \rangle$:
    ▷ $\pi \leftarrow \begin{cases} \pi_i & \text{if there is a record } \langle \text{OFFLINE}, \mathcal{P}_i, \pi_i \rangle \\ \bot & \text{otherwise} \end{cases}$
    ▷ mark the file COMPROMISED and return ("password file stolen", id_i, π) to $\mathcal{S}$
  ○ otherwise: return "no password file" to $\mathcal{S}$

Upon (OFFLINETESTPWD, sid, $\mathcal{P}_i$, π') **from** $\mathcal{S}$:
  ○ Retrieve $\langle \text{FILE}, \mathcal{P}_i, \text{id}_i, \pi_i \rangle$
  ○ If it is marked COMPROMISED:
    ▷ return "correct guess" to $\mathcal{S}$ if $\pi_i = \pi'$, and "wrong guess" otherwise
  ○ otherwise: Record $\langle \text{OFFLINE}, \mathcal{P}_i, \pi' \rangle$

Upon (OFFLINECOMPAREPWD, sid, $\mathcal{P}_i$, $\mathcal{P}_j$) **from** $\mathcal{S}$:
  ○ Retrieve $\langle \text{FILE}, \mathcal{P}_i, \text{id}_i, \pi_i \rangle$ and $\langle \text{FILE}, \mathcal{P}_j, \text{id}_j, \pi_j \rangle$ both marked COMPROMISED
  ○ Return "passwords match" to $\mathcal{S}$ if $\pi_i = \pi_j$, and "passwords differ" otherwise

Upon (NEWSESSION, sid, $ssid$, $\mathcal{P}_j$) **from** $\mathcal{P}_i$:
  ○ Retrieve $\langle \text{FILE}, \mathcal{P}_i, \text{id}_i, \pi_i \rangle$ and send (NEWSESSION, $ssid$, $\mathcal{P}_i$, $\mathcal{P}_j$, id_i) to $\mathcal{S}$
  ○ If there is no record $\langle \text{SESSION}, ssid, \mathcal{P}_i, \mathcal{P}_j, \cdot \rangle$:
    ▷ record $\langle \text{SESSION}, ssid, \mathcal{P}_i, \mathcal{P}_j, \pi_i \rangle$ and mark it FRESH

Upon (ONLINETESTPWD, sid, $ssid$, $\mathcal{P}_i$, π') **from** $\mathcal{S}$:
  ○ Retrieve $\langle \text{SESSION}, ssid, \mathcal{P}_i, \mathcal{P}_j, \pi_i \rangle$ marked FRESH or COMPROMISED
  ○ If $\pi_i = \pi'$: record $\langle \text{IMP}, ssid, \mathcal{P}_i, \star \rangle$
  ○ If $\pi_i = \pi'$: mark the session COMPROMISED and return "correct guess" to $\mathcal{S}$
  ○ otherwise: mark the session INTERRUPTED and return "wrong guess" to $\mathcal{S}$

Upon (IMPERSONATE, sid, $ssid$, $\mathcal{P}_i$, $\mathcal{P}_k$) **from** $\mathcal{S}$:
  ○ Retrieve $\langle \text{SESSION}, ssid, \mathcal{P}_i, \mathcal{P}_j, \pi_i \rangle$ marked FRESH or COMPROMISED
  ○ Retrieve $\langle \text{FILE}, \mathcal{P}_k, \text{id}_k, \pi_k \rangle$ marked COMPROMISED
  ○ If $\pi_i = \pi_k$: record $\langle \text{IMP}, ssid, \mathcal{P}_i, \text{id}_k \rangle$
  ○ If $\pi_i = \pi_k$: mark the session COMPROMISED and return "correct guess" to $\mathcal{S}$
  ○ otherwise: mark the session INTERRUPTED and return "wrong guess" to $\mathcal{S}$

Upon (NEWKEY, sid, $ssid$, $\mathcal{P}_i$, id', $K'_{\in\{0,1\}^\kappa}$) **from** $\mathcal{S}$:
  ○ Retrieve $\langle \text{SESSION}, ssid, \mathcal{P}_i, \mathcal{P}_j, \pi_i \rangle$ not marked COMPLETED and $\langle \text{FILE}, \mathcal{P}_j, \text{id}_j, \pi_j \rangle$
  ○ Ignore the query if either the session is marked FRESH and $\text{id}' \neq \text{id}_j$, or it is COMPROMISED and $\langle \text{IMP}, ssid, \mathcal{P}_i, \text{id} \rangle$ is not recorded for both $\text{id} \in \{\text{id}', \star\}$
  ○ If the session is marked COMPROMISED: $K_i \leftarrow K'$
  ○ else if it is marked FRESH and there is a record $\langle \text{KEY}, ssid, \mathcal{P}_j, \pi_j, K_j \rangle$ with $\pi_i = \pi_j$: $K_i \leftarrow K_j$
  ○ otherwise: pick $K_i \xleftarrow{\text{R}} \{0,1\}^\kappa$
  ○ If the session is marked FRESH: record $\langle \text{KEY}, ssid, \mathcal{P}_i, \pi_i, K_i \rangle$
  ○ Mark the session COMPLETED and send $\langle ssid, \text{id}', K_i \rangle$ to $\mathcal{P}_i$

Fig. 5. Functionality $\mathcal{F}_{\text{iPAKE}}$ is defined by the full text (including grey text), and $\mathcal{F}_{\text{siPAKE}}$ is defined by the text excluding grey text.

to participating parties as output alongside the session key. Without them, a single party compromise would allow the adversary to compromise any sub-session by impersonating any other party or perform a MiTM attack. Having the functionality inform a party of its peer identity prevents such attacks.

For symmetry, we restored the notation of parties as $\{\mathcal{P}_i\}_{i=1}^n$: All parties invoke STOREPWDFILE before starting a session and all use the password file instead of providing a password when starting a session; USRSESSION query was eliminated, and SVRSESSION was renamed NEWSESSION as in $\mathcal{F}_{\text{PAKE}}$. We also parametrized queries on $\mathcal{P}_i$ and $\mathcal{P}_j$ where $\mathcal{F}_{\text{aPAKE}}$ and $\mathcal{F}_{\text{saPAKE}}$ omitted them, since in the symmetric setting those queries may be applied to several parties, e.g., STEALPWDFILE applying to any party. On the other hand, we omit $\mathcal{P}_j$ from STOREPWDFILE; in our setting a password file is derived for each party independently, and is not bound to specific peers.

Our functionalities introduce a new query OFFLINECOMPAREPWD, allowing the adversary to test whether two stolen password files correspond to the same password. In the real world, such attack is always possible by an adversary simulating the protocol for those parties, and comparing the resulting keys. We argue that in most real-world settings, all parties of the same session use the same password (e.g., devices connecting to the same Wi-Fi network), and hence such a query is both inevitable and non-beneficial for the adversary.

Notice the four types of records used by the functionalities:

1. $\langle \text{FILE}, \mathcal{P}_i, \text{id}_i, \pi_i \rangle$ records represent password files created for each party $\mathcal{P}_i$, and are derived from its password π_i and identity id_i. Similar type of records exist in $\mathcal{F}_{\text{PAKE}}$ and $\mathcal{F}_{\text{saPAKE}}$ (without identities) only for the server.
2. $\langle \text{SESSION}, ssid, \mathcal{P}_i, \mathcal{P}_j, \text{id}_i, \pi_i \rangle$ records represent party $\mathcal{P}_i$'s view of a sub-session with identifier $ssid$ between $\mathcal{P}_i$ and $\mathcal{P}_j$. Similar type of records exist in $\mathcal{F}_{\text{aPAKE}}$ and $\mathcal{F}_{\text{saPAKE}}$, without identities.
3. $\langle \text{KEY}, ssid, \mathcal{P}_i, \pi_i, K_i \rangle$ records represent sub-session keys K_i created for party $\mathcal{P}_i$ participating in sub-session $ssid$ with password π_i, and whose session was not compromised or interrupted. These records were implicitly required in prior UC PAKE works [13,17,23], and appear here explicitly for clarity.
4. $\langle \text{IMP}, ssid, \mathcal{P}_i, \text{id}' \rangle$ records represent "permissions" for the adversary to set the peer identity observed by party $\mathcal{P}_i$ in sub-session $ssid$ to id'. They are created when the adversary invokes one of the online attack queries ONLINETEST-PWD or IMPERSONATE. The functionalities reject NEWKEY queries with non-permitted id'. When $\text{id}' = \star$ this record acts as a "wild card", permitting the adversary to select any identity.

Additionally, $\mathcal{F}_{\text{iPAKE}}$ inherits from $\mathcal{F}_{\text{aPAKE}}$ the following record type:

5. $\langle \text{OFFLINE}, \mathcal{P}_i, \pi' \rangle$ records represent an offline-guess π' for party $\mathcal{P}_i$'s password, submitted by $\mathcal{S}$ before compromising $\mathcal{P}_i$. If $\mathcal{P}_i$ is later compromised, $\mathcal{S}$ will instantly learn if the guess was successful, i.e., $\pi' = \pi_i$.

Identity verification is implicit. When no attack is carried out by the adversary, both parties report each other's real identities. However, when the adversary succeeds in an online attack, it is allowed to change the reported identities.

A successful ONLINETESTPWD query allows the adversary to specify any identity, while a successful IMPERSONATE query limits the choice to the impersonated party's real identity only. If any of the attacks fails, we still allow the adversary to control the reported identity, at the cost of causing each party to output an independent random key. Therefore, in the absence of a successful online attack, matching session keys indicate the reported identities are correct.

To simplify our UC simulator, we additionally allow both ONLINETESTPWD and IMPERSONATE queries against the same session, as long as they succeed[1]. This is achieved by accepting them on COMPROMISED sessions, not only FRESH. Note that this permits at most one failed attempt per session, which has no impact on security.

The $\mathcal{F}_{iPAKE}$ functionality is weaker than $\mathcal{F}_{siPAKE}$ in the sense that it permits pre-computation of OFFLINETESTPWD queries prior to party compromise. It is therefore only of interest when permitting more efficient constructions than its strong counterpart. Indeed, we present the more efficient CHIP protocol (Sect. 6) realizing $\mathcal{F}_{iPAKE}$ in ROM using any cyclic group, while CRISP (Sect. 7) requires bilinear groups for realizing $\mathcal{F}_{siPAKE}$ in GGM.

Comparison to (s)aPAKE. The symmetric functionalities $\mathcal{F}_{iPAKE}$ and $\mathcal{F}_{siPAKE}$ offer security guarantees beyond their asymmetric counterparts: given a $\mathcal{F}_{iPAKE}$ (respectively, $\mathcal{F}_{siPAKE}$) functionality, it is trivial to realize the $\mathcal{F}_{aPAKE}$ (respectively, $\mathcal{F}_{saPAKE}$) functionality. The client party U will be assigned identity "client" and will simply compute its password file on each session, when receiving USRSESSION query from the environment. The server party S will be identified as "server" and will have to verify its peer identity is "client". Nevertheless, we are not aware of any direct extension of $\mathcal{F}_{aPAKE}/\mathcal{F}_{saPAKE}$ to $\mathcal{F}_{iPAKE}/\mathcal{F}_{siPAKE}$.

Sessions and Identifiers. The distinction between a "static" session (identified by sid) and an "online" sub-session (identified by $ssid$) was inherited from $\mathcal{F}_{aPAKE}$ and $\mathcal{F}_{saPAKE}$.

A static session represents a set of parties which are expected to communicate with each other, such as devices connected to the same Wi-Fi network (sid can be the network name). Normally, all such parties are configured with the same password. Otherwise, only parties with matching passwords will be able to derive a shared key. Since sid is selected locally, it is possible to have two unrelated networks configured with the same identifier (e.g., two home networks named "Miller"). As long as their passwords differ, there will not be any real impact on security; password files created for one network are unusable for the other.

An online sub-session is a specific run of the protocol between two parties of a static session. $ssid$ is given as external input to the protocol in order to uniquely identify message flows within a sub-session among parties of the same static session. In many cases the transport layer's communication identifiers (e.g.,

---

[1] In fact, our relaxed functionality now allows for a stronger adversary that can submit as many such queries as it chooses. However, the first failed query interrupts the session, thus preventing subsequent queries. On the other hand, after a successful attack, the adversary has already compromised the session.

TCP/IP 5-tuple) suffice. If necessary, an additional communication round can be used to negotiate unique *ssid* (as in [19]).

6   The CHIP iPAKE Protocol

6.1   Design Motivation

When extending the protection of traditional PAKE to consider party compromise attacks, one might think of a trivial solution: simply store the hash of the password, and use this hash value in the PAKE, instead of the plain password. While this solves the problem of leaking the password upon party compromise, it does not protect from impersonation. Since hash values are not bound to any identity, a hash value stolen from a compromised party $\mathcal{P}_i$ can be used to impersonate any non-compromised party $\mathcal{P}_j$ towards anyone. This is known as a Key Compromise Impersonation (KCI) attack.

To protect against KCI attacks we need to bind those hash values to identities. However, KCI resistance is not trivial to achieve. For instance, if parties were to concatenate their identity to the password as input to a hash function: $h_i \leftarrow H(\mathsf{id}_i, \pi)$, there would be no simple means for party $\mathcal{P}_i$ knowing h_i (but no longer π) to derive a shared key with another party $\mathcal{P}_j$ that only holds h_j.

One family of protocols that provides KCI resistance by design is Identity-Based Key-Exchange (IB-KE), introduced by Günther [18]. Unfortunately, IB-KE protocols require a trusted third party called Key Distribution Centre (KDC). The KDC is responsible for delivering identity-bound key material to other parties in a setup phase. In our setting, there is no trusted third party, only a password that is shared between the parties. To remove the KDC requirement, we modify the IB-KE protocol by allowing each party to *locally simulate the operation of the KDC*. To achieve this, we use the password hash as the KDC's secret data. This ensures that all parties with the same password are simulating "the same" KDC, i.e., using the same KDC secrets to derive password files.

Unfortunately, this construction might still be vulnerable to offline password guessing. Since an IB-KE protocol assumes the KDC secret to have high entropy, IB-KE protocols might send information that is dependent on this value. For instance, a certificate signed by the KDC secret key might be sent in the clear. With the KDC secrets being derived deterministically from a low entropy password, a passive eavesdropper might capture such a message then start an offline brute-force attack to find the correct password.

We solve this by considering IB-KE protocols with message flows independent from the KDC secrets. Specifically, we chose the Identity-Based Key-Agreement (IB-KA) protocol by Fiore and Gennaro [16]. IB-KA requires a single simultaneous communication round, is proven secure in the Canetti-Krawczyk model [12] under the strong Diffie-Hellman assumption, and provides weak Forward Secrecy (wFS) and KCI resistance.

A final issue with the construction is that the output key of IB-KA depends on the KDC secret. Recall that Forward Secrecy (ephemeral key secrecy after long-term keys are compromised) in IB-KA is not perfect but weak (i.e., only holds against passive adversaries), therefore an active adversary can modify the

Public Parameters: Cyclic group $\mathbb{G}$ of prime order $q \geq 2^\kappa$ with generator $g \in \mathbb{G}$, a PAKE protocol realizing $\mathcal{F}_{\text{PAKE}}$, hash functions $H_1, H_2: \{0,1\}^* \rightarrow \mathbb{Z}_q^*$, and κ a security parameter. Note that here sid is explicitly concatenated to the input of H_1, H_2 invocations for domain separation.

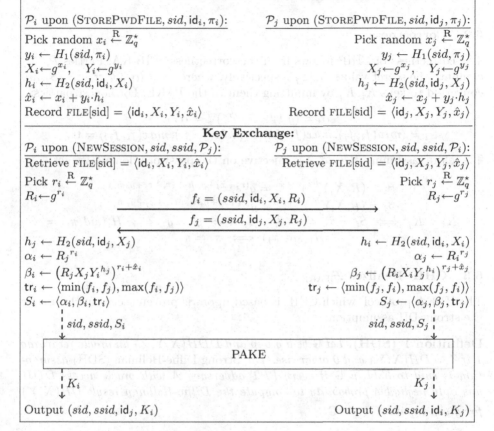

Password File Generation:

$\mathcal{P}_i$ upon $(\text{StorePwdFile}, sid, \mathsf{id}_i, \pi_i)$: $\qquad$ $\mathcal{P}_j$ upon $(\text{StorePwdFile}, sid, \mathsf{id}_j, \pi_j)$:

Pick random $x_i \xleftarrow{\text{R}} \mathbb{Z}_q^*$ $\qquad\qquad\qquad$ Pick random $x_j \xleftarrow{\text{R}} \mathbb{Z}_q^*$

$y_i \leftarrow H_1(sid, \pi_i)$ $\qquad\qquad\qquad\qquad\qquad$ $y_j \leftarrow H_1(sid, \pi_j)$

$X_i \leftarrow g^{x_i}, \quad Y_i \leftarrow g^{y_i}$ $\qquad\qquad\qquad$ $X_j \leftarrow g^{x_j}, \quad Y_j \leftarrow g^{y_j}$

$h_i \leftarrow H_2(sid, \mathsf{id}_i, X_i)$ $\qquad\qquad\qquad$ $h_j \leftarrow H_2(sid, \mathsf{id}_j, X_j)$

$\hat{x}_i \leftarrow x_i + y_i \cdot h_i$ $\qquad\qquad\qquad\qquad$ $\hat{x}_j \leftarrow x_j + y_j \cdot h_j$

Record FILE[sid] $= \langle \mathsf{id}_i, X_i, Y_i, \hat{x}_i \rangle$ $\qquad$ Record FILE[sid] $= \langle \mathsf{id}_j, X_j, Y_j, \hat{x}_j \rangle$

Key Exchange:

$\mathcal{P}_i$ upon $(\text{NewSession}, sid, ssid, \mathcal{P}_j)$: $\qquad$ $\mathcal{P}_j$ upon $(\text{NewSession}, sid, ssid, \mathcal{P}_i)$:

Retrieve FILE[sid] $= \langle \mathsf{id}_i, X_i, Y_i, \hat{x}_i \rangle$ $\qquad$ Retrieve FILE[sid] $= \langle \mathsf{id}_j, X_j, Y_j, \hat{x}_j \rangle$

Pick $r_i \xleftarrow{\text{R}} \mathbb{Z}_q^*$ $\qquad\qquad\qquad\qquad\qquad$ Pick $r_j \xleftarrow{\text{R}} \mathbb{Z}_q^*$

$R_i \leftarrow g^{r_i}$ $\qquad\qquad$ $f_i = (ssid, \mathsf{id}_i, X_i, R_i)$ $\qquad\qquad$ $R_j \leftarrow g^{r_j}$

$\qquad\qquad\qquad\qquad f_j = (ssid, \mathsf{id}_j, X_j, R_j)$

$h_j \leftarrow H_2(sid, \mathsf{id}_j, X_j)$ $\qquad\qquad\qquad\qquad$ $h_i \leftarrow H_2(sid, \mathsf{id}_i, X_i)$

$\alpha_i \leftarrow R_j{}^{r_i}$ $\qquad\qquad\qquad\qquad\qquad\qquad$ $\alpha_j \leftarrow R_i{}^{r_j}$

$\beta_i \leftarrow \left(R_j X_j Y_i{}^{h_j}\right)^{r_i + \hat{x}_i}$ $\qquad\qquad\qquad$ $\beta_j \leftarrow \left(R_i X_i Y_j{}^{h_i}\right)^{r_j + \hat{x}_j}$

$\mathsf{tr}_i \leftarrow \langle \min(f_i, f_j), \max(f_i, f_j) \rangle$ $\qquad$ $\mathsf{tr}_j \leftarrow \langle \min(f_j, f_i), \max(f_j, f_i) \rangle$

$S_i \leftarrow \langle \alpha_i, \beta_i, \mathsf{tr}_i \rangle$ $\qquad\qquad\qquad\qquad$ $S_j \leftarrow \langle \alpha_j, \beta_j, \mathsf{tr}_j \rangle$

$sid, ssid, S_i$ $\qquad\qquad\qquad\qquad\qquad\qquad$ $sid, ssid, S_j$

PAKE

K_i $\qquad\qquad\qquad\qquad\qquad\qquad\qquad\qquad$ K_j

Output $(sid, ssid, \mathsf{id}_j, K_i)$ $\qquad\qquad\qquad$ Output $(sid, ssid, \mathsf{id}_i, K_j)$

Fig. 6. CHIP protocol

incoming flow to party $\mathcal{P}_i$, then offline derive the resulting key from every possible password guess π'. Any subsequent usage of the key, e.g. for data authentication, would allow the adversary to test the password guesses and extract the correct session key. We resolve this by using the IB-KA output key as input to a symmetric PAKE, along with the transcript of the IB-KA.

Figure 6 depicts CHIP, which transforms any PAKE into an iPAKE using the modified IB-KA protocol [16], with the following changes:

- **KDC Simulation:** Instead of using a real KDC, each party $\mathcal{P}_i$ simulates the KDC's setup phase during its password file generation. This is achieved by replacing the KDC's randomly generated private value y_i with the hash of $\mathcal{P}_i$'s password $H_1(sid, \pi_i)$.

- **PAKE Integration:** We use the output of IB-KA (α_i, β_i) alongside the IB-KA transcript (tr_i) as input to a PAKE instance. The output from this PAKE, K_i, is the resulting session key.

6.2 Correctness

The correctness of CHIP follows from the correctness of IB-KA. Parties $\mathcal{P}_i$, $\mathcal{P}_j$ compute the secret values S_i, S_j respectively, where $S_i = \langle \alpha_i, \beta_i, \text{tr}_i \rangle$. S_i, S_j are converted to keys K_i, K_j by inputting them to the PAKE. For honest parties:

$$\alpha_i = (g^{r_i})^{r_j} = (g^{r_j})^{r_i} = \alpha_j$$
$$\text{tr}_i = \langle min(f_i, f_j), max(f_j, f_i) \rangle = \langle min(f_j, f_i), max(f_i, f_j) \rangle = \text{tr}_j$$

Therefore, assuming $H_1(sid, \cdot)$ is injective on the password domain we get:

$$\beta_i = (R_j X_j Y_i^{h_j})^{r_i + \hat{x}_i} = g^{(r_j + x_j + y_i \cdot h_j) \cdot (r_i + x_i + y_i \cdot h_i)}$$
$$\beta_j = (R_i X_i Y_j^{h_i})^{r_j + \hat{x}_j} = g^{(r_i + x_i + y_j \cdot h_i) \cdot (r_j + x_j + y_j \cdot h_j)}$$
$$K_i = K_j \iff S_i = S_j \iff \beta_i = \beta_j \iff y_i = y_j \iff H_1(sid, \pi_i) = H_1(sid, \pi_j) \iff \pi_i = \pi_j$$

6.3 CHIP Realizes $\mathcal{F}_{\text{iPAKE}}$

The IB-KA protocol, which CHIP is based upon, is proven secure in [16] under the strong DH assumption:

Definition 1 (SDH). *Let $\mathbb{G}$ be a group and $DDH(X, Y, Z)$ an oracle returning 1 if $Z = DH(X, Y)$ and 0 otherwise. The Strong Diffie-Hellman (SDH) assumption is said to hold in $\mathbb{G}$ if every PPT adversary $\mathcal{A}$ with oracle access DDH has only negligible probability to compute the Diffie-Hellman result $DH(X, Y)$ for given inputs $X, Y \xleftarrow{R} \mathbb{G}$.*

The following theorem (proven in full version of the paper [15] states the security of CHIP as an iPAKE protocol in the UC framework.

Theorem 1. *If the SDH assumption holds in $\mathbb{G}$, then the CHIP protocol in Fig. 6 UC-realizes $\mathcal{F}_{\text{iPAKE}}$ in the $(\mathcal{F}_{\text{PAKE}}, \mathcal{F}_{\text{RO}})$-hybrid world.*

Proof Technique Intuition

To prove that CHIP UC-realizes $\mathcal{F}_{\text{iPAKE}}$ we need to show how CHIP can be simulated using $\mathcal{F}_{\text{iPAKE}}$. Here we provide some intuition for key aspects of our simulation and proof.

Simulation of Message Flows. One of the properties of IB-KA is that its flows are independent of the KDC secrets, which in our setting translates to being independent of the passwords. This has the side-effect of allowing us to easily simulate message flows.

Simulating Password Files. When a password hash is requested we employ the programmability of our ROM to set the hash value in correspondence with previously stolen password files. We use OFFLINECOMPAREPWD to ensure consistency of generated hash values across parties with the same password. If a party is compromised after the hash is computed, we take advantage of OFFLINETESTPWD executed during HASH simulation to reveal the correct password of the party to be compromised, then simulate a password file with the known hash.

Simulating TestPwd. To extract a password guess from the environment's TESTPWD input we consider all possible password hash values: If a previous $H_1(\pi')$ query outputs a value satisfying $\mathcal{Z}$'s input, we mount an ONLINETESTPWD against $\mathcal{F}_{\mathsf{iPAKE}}$ with π'; If a previously compromised password file contained a hash value satisfying the input, then we IMPERSONATE that compromised party. It is possible that $\mathcal{Z}$'s guess was incorrect, in which case our attacks will also fail.

Preserving KCI-Resistance. We state that despite simulating the KDC using a hash of a password, we preserve the KCI resistance property of IB-KE, as long as the password remains secret. That is, modelling the hash function applied to the password as a random oracle, the adversary has no access to the random value $H(\pi)$ until it queries the oracle with the correct password. Thus, the local generation of a password file under our modification is equivalent to a KDC generating key files, while $H(\pi)$ is not queried by the adversary.

6.4   The Cost of Brute-Force Attack on CHIP

We note that in our proof, H_1 corresponds to OFFLINETESTPWD or the cost of a single password guess. Therefore, to increase the cost of a brute-force attack, it is advised to choose a computationally costly hash function (see Sect. 8.1).

CHIP is vulnerable to pre-computation. CHIP's password files include the (unsalted) hash value $Y = g^y = g^{H_1(sid,\pi)}$. While extracting the password from a compromised file requires a brute-force attack, this property enables pre-computation: if the adversary prepares a mapping $Y_{\pi'} \mapsto \pi'$ for each password guess π' in advance for a specific sid, it can discover the correct password immediately after compromising a party. Our next protocol mitigates this.

7   The CRISP siPAKE Protocol

7.1   Protocol Description

CRISP is a compiler that transforms any PAKE into a compromise resilient, identity-binding, and symmetric PAKE. CRISP (defined in Fig. 7) is composed of the following phases:

1. **Public Parameters Generation:** In this phase, public parameters common to all parties are generated from a security parameter κ. These parameters include the bilinear groups $\mathbb{G}_1$, $\mathbb{G}_2$, $\mathbb{G}_T$ with hash to group functions $\hat{H}_1$, $\hat{H}_2$, and the PAKE protocol to be used.
2. **Password File Derivation:** In this phase, the user enters a password π_i and an identifier id_i for a party $\mathcal{P}_i$ (e.g., some device such as a personal computer, smartphone, server or access point). The party selects an independent and uniform random salt, and then derives and stores the password file.

Public Parameters: Cyclic groups $\mathbb{G}_1, \mathbb{G}_2, \mathbb{G}_T$ of prime order $q \geq 2^\kappa$ with generator $g_2 \in \mathbb{G}_2$, bilinear pairing $\hat{e}: \mathbb{G}_1 \times \mathbb{G}_2 \to \mathbb{G}_T$, a PAKE protocol realizing $\mathcal{F}_{\text{PAKE}}$, hash functions $\hat{H}_1, \hat{H}_2: \{0,1\}^* \to \mathbb{G}_2$ and κ a security parameter. Note that here sid is explicitly concatenated to the input of $\hat{H}_1, \hat{H}_2$ invocations for domain separation.

Password File Derivation (offline)

$\mathcal{P}_i$ upon $(\text{StorePwdFile}, sid, \text{id}_i, \pi_i)$:

Pick random salt $x_i \xleftarrow{\text{R}} \mathbb{Z}_q^*$
$A_i \leftarrow g_1^{x_i}$
$B_i \leftarrow \hat{H}_1(sid, \pi_i)^{x_i}, \quad C_i \leftarrow \hat{H}_2(sid, \text{id}_i)^{x_i}$
Record $\text{File}[sid] = \langle \text{id}_i, A_i, B_i, C_i \rangle$

$\mathcal{P}_j$ upon $(\text{StorePwdFile}, sid, \text{id}_j, \pi_j)$:

Pick random salt $x_j \xleftarrow{\text{R}} \mathbb{Z}_q^*$
$A_j \leftarrow g_1^{x_j}$
$B_j \leftarrow \hat{H}_1(sid, \pi_j)^{x_j}, \quad C_j \leftarrow \hat{H}_2(sid, \text{id}_j)^{x_j}$
Record $\text{File}[sid] = \langle \text{id}_j, A_j, B_j, C_j \rangle$

Key Exchange

$\mathcal{P}_i$ upon $(\text{NewSession}, sid, ssid, \mathcal{P}_j)$:
Retrieve $\text{File}[sid] = \langle \text{id}_i, A_i, B_i, C_i \rangle$
Pick random exponent $r_i \xleftarrow{\text{R}} \mathbb{Z}_q^*$
$\tilde{A}_i \leftarrow A_i^{r_i}, \quad \tilde{B}_i \leftarrow B_i^{r_i}, \quad \tilde{C}_i \leftarrow C_i^{r_i}$

$\mathcal{P}_j$ upon $(\text{NewSession}, sid, ssid, \mathcal{P}_i)$:
Retrieve $\text{File}[sid] = \langle \text{id}_j, A_j, B_j, C_j \rangle$
Pick random exponent $r_j \xleftarrow{\text{R}} \mathbb{Z}_q^*$
$\tilde{A}_j \leftarrow A_j^{r_j}, \quad \tilde{B}_j \leftarrow B_j^{r_j}, \quad \tilde{C}_j \leftarrow C_j^{r_j}$

$(ssid, \text{id}_i, \tilde{A}_i, \tilde{C}_i) \longrightarrow$

$\longleftarrow (ssid, \text{id}_j, \tilde{A}_j, \tilde{C}_j)$

Ignore if $\tilde{A}_j = 1_{\mathbb{G}_1}$ or $\tilde{A}_j \notin \mathbb{G}_1$
or $\hat{e}(g_1, \tilde{C}_j) \neq \hat{e}(\tilde{A}_j, \hat{H}_2(sid, \text{id}_j))$
$S_i \leftarrow \hat{e}(\tilde{A}_j, \tilde{B}_i)$

Ignore if $\tilde{A}_i = 1_{\mathbb{G}_1}$ or $\tilde{A}_i \notin \mathbb{G}_1$
or $\hat{e}(g_1, \tilde{C}_i) \neq \hat{e}(\tilde{A}_i, \hat{H}_2(sid, \text{id}_i))$
$S_j \leftarrow \hat{e}(\tilde{A}_i, \tilde{B}_j)$

$sid, ssid, S_i$ $sid, ssid, S_j$

PAKE

K_i K_j

Output $(sid, ssid, \text{id}_j, K_i)$ Output $(sid, ssid, \text{id}_i, K_j)$

Fig. 7. CRISP protocol

3. **Key Exchange:** In this phase, two parties, $\mathcal{P}_i$ and $\mathcal{P}_j$ engage in a sub-session to derive a shared key. This phase consists of three stages:
   (a) *Blinding.* Values from the password file are raised to the power of a randomly selected exponent. This stage can be performed once and re-used across sub-sessions (see Sect. 8.3).
   (b) *Secret Exchange.* Using a single communication round (two messages), each party computes a secret value. These values depend on the generating party's password, and both parties' salt and blinding exponents.
   (c) *PAKE.* Both parties engage in a PAKE where they input their secret values as passwords to receive secure cryptographic keys.

The hash-to-group functions ($\hat{H}_1$ and $\hat{H}_2$) can be realized by $\mathcal{F}_{\text{GGP}}$'s Hash queries using domain separation with different prefixes: $\hat{H}_1(sid, \pi)$ will query Hash using $s = 1 \| \pi$, and $\hat{H}_2(sid, \text{id})$ will use $s = 2 \| \text{id}$.

We provide intuition by explaining the necessity of several components.

Bilinear Pairing. To protect against pre-computation attacks the password file cannot contain neither the plain password, nor its unsalted hash. Nevertheless, the classical salted hash method (e.g., $H(\pi, x)$ for a random salt x) guarantees pre-computation resistance, but cannot be used to derive a shared key across parties with independent salts, because the hashes have no structure to link them with each other, in the absence of the password during the online key exchange. Storing $\langle x, Y \rangle$ for a random x and $Y = g^{H(\pi) \cdot x}$ is also vulnerable to pre-computation of a map $M \colon g^{H(\pi')} \mapsto \pi'$, then finding the password π immediately with $M[Y^{1/x}]$.

In search of a construct that is both resilient to pre-computation and has some algebraic structure we considered $\langle X, Y \rangle$ for $X = g_1^x$, $Y = g_2^{H(\pi) \cdot x}$ and random x. This utilizes the oracle hashing scheme [10] $\langle X, X^{H(v)} \rangle$, which implies pre-computation resistance. The parties can then compute a shared value using bilinear pairing:

$$\hat{e}(X_i, Y_j) = \hat{e}(g_1^{x_i}, g_2^{H(\pi) \cdot x_j}) = \hat{e}(g_1, g_2)^{H(\pi) \cdot x_i \cdot x_j} = \hat{e}(g_1^{x_j}, g_2^{H(\pi) \cdot x_i}) = \hat{e}(X_j, Y_i)$$

Hash-to-Group. Although the $\langle X, Y \rangle$ construct from last paragraph satisfies pre-computation resistance, it has inherent asymmetry in the computation cost: while honest parties are required to run bilinear pairing to derive a shared key, an adversary that has stolen a password file can test passwords offline with a cost of one exponentiation per password guess. This is accomplished by pre-computing $h[\pi'] = H(\pi')$, then after compromising a party testing whether $X^{h[\pi']} \stackrel{?}{=} \psi(Y)$ for each password guess π'.[2]

The similar approach selected for CRISP is $\langle X, Y \rangle$ for $X = g_1^x$, $Y = \hat{H}(\pi)^x$ and x generated at random, using a hash-to-group function $\hat{H}$. This ensures that the exponent e for $g_2^e = \hat{H}(\pi)$ is kept hidden, even from those who possess the password. Thus, the adversary is required to compute a bilinear pairing per password guess post compromise.

Blinding. The blinding stage perfectly hides the salt x_i (information theoretically) in the first message transmitted from $\mathcal{P}_i$, since $\langle \tilde{A}_i, \tilde{C}_i \rangle = \langle g_1^{\tilde{x}_i}, \hat{H}_2(sid, \mathrm{id}_i)^{\tilde{x}_i} \rangle$ for $\tilde{x}_i = x_i r_i$ which is a random element of $\mathbb{Z}_q^\star$. Blinding is required because transmitting the raw A_i value allows $\mathcal{A}$ to mount a pre-computation attack. $\mathcal{A}$ may compute the inverse map $B_{\pi'} \mapsto \pi'$ for any password guess π':

$$B_{\pi'} = \hat{e}(A_i, \hat{H}_1(sid, \pi')) = \hat{e}(g_1, \hat{H}_1(sid, \pi'))^{x_i}$$

Then after compromising $\mathcal{P}_i$, use the map to lookup:

$$\hat{e}(y_1, B_i) = \hat{e}(g_1, \hat{H}_1(sid, \pi_i)^{x_i}) = \hat{e}(g_1, \hat{H}_1(sid, \pi_i))^{x_i},$$

finding the correct $\pi' = \pi_i$ instantly. A similar attack would have also been possible if the values $\tilde{B}_i = B_i^{r_i}$ or r_i were disclosed to $\mathcal{A}$ upon compromise.

---

[2] Even without ψ, $\mathcal{A}$ can compute $X_T = \hat{e}(X, g_2)$ and $Y_T = \hat{e}(g_1, Y)$ with just two pairings, then test each password guess π' using a single exponentiation: $X_T^{h[\pi']} \stackrel{?}{=} Y_T$.

Symmetric PAKE. The final key K_i should be derived from the secret S_i using a PAKE and not some deterministic key derivation function. The reason is the lack of perfect forward secrecy in the first message exchange, as explained for CHIP in Sect. 6.1. Concretely, consider the following attack:

Adversary $\mathcal{A}$ modifies the flow from $\mathcal{P}_j$ to $\mathcal{P}_i$ into $\tilde{A}'_j = g_1^{x'_j}$, $\tilde{C}'_j = \hat{H}_2(sid, \mathsf{id}_j)^{x'_j}$ using some arbirarily chosen exponent x'_j. $\mathcal{A}$ can now use $\tilde{A}_i$ (sent by an honest party $\mathcal{P}_i$) to compute the value $S[\pi'] = \hat{e}(\tilde{A}_i, \hat{H}_1(sid, \pi')^{x'_j})$ for any password guess π'. $\mathcal{A}$ can now derive a guess for the resulting key K' and test this key against encrypted messages sent by P_i. A correct key implies the password guess was right. This can be repeated for multiple guesses without engaging in additional online exchanges.

Generic Group Model. As discussed in Sect. 4.1 we require a non-black-box assumption to prove pre-computation resilience, and "count" the number of operations required for an offline brute-force attack. Similarly to [9], we use GGM to bind each offline guess to a group operation. In our case, we bind it to the computationally expensive operation of pairing. This is explained in more detail in Sect. 7.4. CRISP is proven in *local* GGM. The full version [15] discuss how we can modify the functionality to allow the reuse of a single generic group for all CRISP instances. It also discusses the limitation on composing CRISP with other protocols sharing the same group (e.g., same bilinear curve).

7.2   Correctness

Honest parties $\mathcal{P}_i$, $\mathcal{P}_j$ compute the secrets S_i, S_j respectively, which are used as inputs to $\mathcal{F}_{\mathsf{PAKE}}$ to get K_i, K_j. Assuming $\hat{H}_1(sid, \cdot)$ is injective on the password domain we get:

$$S_i = \hat{e}(\tilde{A}_j, \tilde{B}_i) = \hat{e}(g_1^{x_j r_j}, \hat{H}_1(sid, \pi_i)^{x_i r_i}) = \hat{e}(g_1, \hat{H}_1(sid, \pi_i))^{x_i r_i \cdot x_j r_j}$$
$$S_j = \hat{e}(\tilde{A}_i, \tilde{B}_j) = \hat{e}(g_1^{x_i r_i}, \hat{H}_1(sid, \pi_j)^{x_j r_j}) = \hat{e}(g_1, \hat{H}_1(sid, \pi_j))^{x_j r_j \cdot x_i r_i}$$
$$K_i = K_j \iff S_i = S_j \iff \hat{H}_1(sid, \pi_i) = \hat{H}_1(sid, \pi_j) \iff \pi_i = \pi_j$$

7.3   CRISP Realizes $\mathcal{F}_{\mathsf{siPAKE}}$

Theorem 2. *Protocol CRISP as depicted in Fig. 7 UC-realizes $\mathcal{F}_{\mathsf{siPAKE}}$ in the $(\mathcal{F}_{\mathsf{PAKE}}, \mathcal{F}_{\mathsf{GGP}})$-hybrid world.*

We give the full proof in the full version [15] and describe the high-level strategy below. In the UC proof, we omit sid from $\hat{H}_1$ and $\hat{H}_2$ for the sake of brevity.

We prove CRISP's UC-security by providing an ideal-world adversary $\mathcal{S}$, that simulates a real-world adversary $\mathcal{A}$ against CRISP, while only having access to the ideal functionality $\mathcal{F}_{\mathsf{siPAKE}}$. We show the real and ideal worlds in Fig. 8.

The main challenge for $\mathcal{S}$ is the unknown passwords assigned to parties by $\mathcal{Z}$. To overcome this, $\mathcal{S}$ simulates the real-world $\hat{H}_1(\pi_i) = [y_{\pi_i}]_{\mathbb{G}_2}$ using a formal variable (indeterminate) Z_i in the ideal-world: $\hat{H}_1^*(\pi_i) = [\mathsf{Z}_i]_{\mathbb{G}_2}$. Wherever the real world uses group encodings of exponents, $\mathcal{S}$ simulates them using encodings of polynomials with these formal variables: $[F]_{\mathbb{G}_j}$ for polynomial F.

This simulation technique, using formal variables for unknown values, is very common in GGM proofs. It "works" because $\mathcal{Z}$ is only able to detect equality

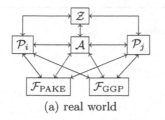 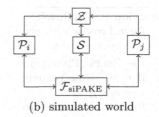

(a) real world   (b) simulated world

Fig. 8. Depiction of real world running protocol CRISP with adversary $\mathcal{A}$ versus simulated world running the ideal protocol for $\mathcal{F}_{\mathsf{siPAKE}}$ with adversary $\mathcal{S}$.

of group elements, and group operations produce only linear combinations of the exponents. Two formally distinct polynomials $F_1 \neq F_2$ in the ideal world would only represent the same value in the real world in the case of a collision on some unknown value: $F_1(x) = F_2(x)$. Since these unknown values are uniformly selected over a large domain and the polynomials have low degrees, the probability of collisions is negligible.

To simulate several unknown values, we use these variables:

1. $\mathbf{X}_i$ represents party $\mathcal{P}_i$'s salt x_i.
2. $\mathbf{Y}_\pi$ represents the unknown exponent y_π s.t. $\hat{H}_1(\pi) = g_2^{y_\pi}$, for any password π.
3. $\mathbf{I}_{\mathsf{id}}$ represents the unknown exponent ι_{id} s.t. $\hat{H}_2(\mathsf{id}) = g_2^{\iota_{\mathsf{id}}}$.
4. $\mathbf{R}_{i,ssid}$ represents party $\mathcal{P}_i$'s blinding value r_i in sub-session $ssid$.
5. $\mathbf{Z}_i$ is an alias for $\mathbf{Y}_{\pi_i}$, where π_i is party $\mathcal{P}_i$'s password.

Note that some variables are created "on the fly" during the simulation. For example, upon every fresh $\hat{H}_1(\pi)$ query $\mathcal{S}$ creates a new variable $\mathbf{Y}_\pi$.

Using these variables, $\mathcal{S}$ simulates the following:

- **Hash queries:** $\hat{H}_1(\pi) = [\mathbf{Y}_\pi]_{\mathbb{G}_2}$ and $\hat{H}_2(\mathsf{id}) = [\mathbf{I}_{\mathsf{id}}]_{\mathbb{G}_2}$.
- **Group operations:** $[F_1]_{\mathbb{G}_j} \odot [F_2]_{\mathbb{G}_j} = [F_1{+}F_2]_{\mathbb{G}_j}$, $[F_1]_{\mathbb{G}_j} \oslash [F_2]_{\mathbb{G}_j} = [F_1{-}F_2]_{\mathbb{G}_j}$, $\hat{e}([F_1]_{\mathbb{G}_1}, [F_2]_{\mathbb{G}_2}) = [F_1{\cdot}F_2]_{\mathbb{G}_T}$, $\psi([F]_{\mathbb{G}_2}) = [F]_{\mathbb{G}_1}$ and $\psi^{-1}([F]_{\mathbb{G}_1}) = [F]_{\mathbb{G}_2}$.
- $\mathcal{P}_i$'s **password file:** $\langle \mathsf{id}_i, [\mathbf{X}_i]_{\mathbb{G}_1}, [\mathbf{X}_i\mathbf{Z}_i]_{\mathbb{G}_2}, [\mathbf{X}_i\mathbf{I}_{\mathsf{id}_i}]_{\mathbb{G}_2} \rangle$.
- **First message from** $\mathcal{P}_i$: $(ssid, \mathsf{id}_i, [\mathbf{X}_i\mathbf{R}_{i,ssid}]_{\mathbb{G}_1}, [\mathbf{X}_i\mathbf{R}_{i,ssid}\mathbf{I}_{\mathsf{id}_i}]_{\mathbb{G}_2})$.

Variable Aliasing. Note that $\mathcal{S}$ uses both $\mathbf{Y}_\pi$ and $\mathbf{Z}_i$ variables: $\mathbf{Y}_\pi$ are used for simulating an evaluation of $\hat{H}_1(\pi)$, while $\mathbf{Z}_i$ are used for simulating $\mathcal{P}_i$'s password file. Since $\mathbf{Y}_{\pi_i}$ and $\mathbf{Z}_i$ are distinct variables that might represent the same value in the real world, the simulation seems flawed. For instance, $\mathcal{Z}$ might ask $\mathcal{A}$ to compromise a party $\mathcal{P}_i$ and then evaluate $\hat{e}(g_1, B_i) = \hat{e}(g_1, \hat{H}_1(\pi_i)^{x_i})$ and $\hat{e}(A_i, \hat{H}_1(\pi')) = \hat{e}(g_1^{x_i}, \hat{H}_1(\pi'))$. With overwhelming probability, these encodings will be equal if and only if $\mathcal{Z}$ chose $\pi_i = \pi'$, since collisions in $\hat{H}_1$ only occur with negligible probability. Yet because of using the alias $\mathbf{Z}_i$, $\mathcal{S}$ would generate $\hat{e}(g_1, B_i) = \hat{e}([1]_{\mathbb{G}_1}, [\mathbf{X}_i\mathbf{Z}_i]) = [\mathbf{X}_i\mathbf{Z}_i]_{\mathbb{G}_T}$ and $\hat{e}(A_i, \hat{H}_1(\pi')) = \hat{e}([\mathbf{X}_i]_{\mathbb{G}_1}, [\mathbf{Y}_{\pi'}]_{\mathbb{G}_2}) = [\mathbf{X}_i\mathbf{Y}_{\pi'}]_{\mathbb{G}_T}$ which are always different encodings.

Nevertheless, $\mathcal{S}$ is able to detect possible aliasing collisions: when two distinct polynomials, whose group encodings were sent to the environment $\mathcal{Z}$, become

---

1: **function** INSERTROW(v)
2:     **for all** row w with pivot column j in M **do**
3:         $v \leftarrow v - v[j] \cdot w$
4:     $j \leftarrow$ SELECTPIVOT(v)
5:     **if** $v = \vec{0}$ **then return**
6:     $v \leftarrow v/v[j]$
7:     **for all** row w in M **do**
8:         $w \leftarrow w - w[j] \cdot v$
9:     Insert row v with pivot column j to M

10: **function** SELECTPIVOT(v)
11:     sent $\leftarrow$ **false**
12:     **for all** compromised party $\mathcal{P}_i$ with identifier id_i **do**
13:         **for all** passwords π' that were queried by $\hat{H}_1(\pi')$ **do**
14:             $j_1 \leftarrow$ index of monomial $\mathrm{X}_i \mathrm{Y}_{\pi'}$
15:             $j_2 \leftarrow$ index of monomial $\mathrm{X}_i \mathrm{Y}_{\pi'} \mathrm{I}_{\mathrm{id}_i}$
16:             **if** $v[j_1] \neq 0$ **or** $v[j_2] \neq 0$ **then**
17:                 Send (OFFLINETESTPWD, $sid, \mathcal{P}_i, \pi'$) to $\mathcal{F}_{\mathsf{siPAKE}}$
18:                 sent $\leftarrow$ **true**
19:                 **if** $\mathcal{F}_{\mathsf{siPAKE}}$ returned "wrong guess" **then**
20:                     **return** $\begin{cases} j_1 & \textbf{if } v[j_1] \neq 0 \\ j_2 & \textbf{otherwise} \end{cases}$
21:             Substitute variable Z_i with $\mathrm{Y}_{\pi'}$ in all polynomials
22:             Merge corresponding columns of M, v
23:     **if** some party $\mathcal{P}_i$ has been compromised **and** sent = **false then**
24:         Send (OFFLINETESTPWD, $sid, \mathcal{P}_i, \perp$) to $\mathcal{F}_{\mathsf{siPAKE}}$
25:     **if** $v \neq \vec{0}$ **then return** arbitrary column j having $v[j] \neq 0$

Algorithm 1: $\mathcal{S}$'s row reduction algorithm, using OFFLINETESTPWD queries

equal under substitution of Z_i with $\mathrm{Y}_{\pi'}$ (for some previously evaluated $\hat{H}_1(\pi')$), $\mathcal{S}$ knows there will be a collision if $\pi_i = \pi'$. This condition can be tested by $\mathcal{S}$ using OFFLINETESTPWD queries, for a compromised party $\mathcal{P}_i$. When $\mathcal{F}_{\mathsf{siPAKE}}$ replies "correct guess" to such query, $\mathcal{S}$ substitutes $\mathrm{Y}_{\pi'}$ for Z_i in all its data sets.

While we could have identified collisions across all $\mathcal{F}_{\mathsf{GGP}}$ queries, we chose to limit OFFLINETESTPWD to only pairing evaluations (PAIRING simulation), for better modelling of pre-computation resilience (see Sect. 7.4). This implies that $\mathcal{S}$ needs to predict possible future collisions when simulating a pairing. This prediction is achieved by the polynomial matrix explained below.

Polynomial Matrix. Throughout the simulation $\mathcal{S}$ maintains a matrix M whose rows correspond to polynomials in $\mathbb{G}_T$, and its columns to possible terms. A polynomial is represented in M by its coefficients stored in the appropriate columns. For example, if columns 1 to 3 correspond to terms X_i, $\mathrm{X}_i \mathrm{Z}_i$ and $\mathrm{X}_i \mathrm{Y}_{\pi'}$ respectively, then polynomial $F = 2\mathrm{X}_i \mathrm{Z}_i - 3\mathrm{X}_i \mathrm{Y}_{\pi'}$ will be represented in M by a row $(0, 2, -3)$.

Matrix M is extended during the simulation: when a new variable is introduced (e.g., when $\mathcal{A}$ issues a HASH query) new columns are added; and when a new polynomial is created in $\mathbb{G}_T$ by a PAIRING query, another row is added to M, but using a row-reduction algorithm (see Algorithm 1) so the matrix is always kept in reduced row-echelon form. Note that when polynomials are created due to MULDIV operations in $\mathbb{G}_T$, $\mathcal{S}$ does not extend the table, as the created polynomial is by definition a linear combination of others, so it would have been eliminated by the row-reduction algorithm. It is therefore clear that all polynomials created by $\mathcal{S}$ in $\mathbb{G}_T$ are linear combinations of the matrix rows seen as polynomials.

When invoked by $\mathcal{A}$ to compute a pairing $\hat{e}([F_1]_{\mathbb{G}_1}, [F_2]_{\mathbb{G}_2})$, $\mathcal{S}$ first computes the product polynomial $F_T = F_1 \cdot F_2$, converts it to a coefficient vector V then applies the first step of row-reduction; that is, a linear combination of M's rows is added to V so to zero V's entries already selected as pivots for these rows. $\mathcal{S}$ then scans V for a non-zero entry corresponding to a term $X_i Y_{\pi'}$ (or $X_i I_{\mathsf{id}_i} Y_{\pi'}$) for some compromised party $\mathcal{P}_i$ and a password guess π', where password guesses are taken from $\mathcal{A}$'s $\hat{H}_1(\pi')$ queries. If such non-zero entry exists in V, $\mathcal{S}$ sends OFFLINETESTPWD query to $\mathcal{F}_{\mathsf{siPAKE}}$ testing whether party $\mathcal{P}_i$ was assigned password π' (i.e., $\pi_i = \pi'$). If the guess failed, $\mathcal{S}$ chooses this as the pivot entry. Otherwise, $\mathcal{S}$ merges the variable Z_i with $Y_{\pi'}$, and repeats the process until some test fails or no more entries of the specified form are non-zero in V. If $V \neq 0$ and no pivot is selected, arbitrary non-zero entry is selected. $\mathcal{S}$ then applies the second step of row-reduction; that is $\mathcal{S}$ uses V to zero the entries of the selected pivot entry in other rows, and insert V as a new row to M. Finally, $\mathcal{S}$ proceeds as usual for group operations, choosing the encoding $[F_T]_{\mathbb{G}_T}$ using the original F_T, possibly merging some variables.

This completes the proof sketch; for further details we refer the full version [15].

7.4 Cost of Offline Brute-Force Attack on CRISP

In the full version of the paper [15] we provide a lower bound for the cost of offline brute-force attack. This is usually achieved by binding the offline tests OFFLINETESTPWD with some real-world work. For instance, [23] requires OPRF query for each tested password, while [9] shows linear relation between the number of offline tests and Generic Group operations. We bind each ideal-world OFFLINETESTPWD query with a bilinear pairing computed (after a compromise). In Sect. 8.2 we explain why binding to bilinear pairing is favorable compare to other group operations.

7.5 Primum Non Nocere - Breakdown Resilience of CRISP

Our CRISP compiler is based on pairing-friendly group and UC-realizes $\mathcal{F}_{\mathsf{siPAKE}}$ assuming the Generic Group Model with pairing. However, we can show that CRISP preserves several important properties even when the *pairing-friendly* group's security is completely broken (e.g., discrete log is easy).

Unconditional PAKE Security. First we consider the underlying symmetric PAKE's original properties. To show this, we are only concerned with the additional actions added before invoking the PAKE. Recall that the message added

Table 2. Comparison of costly operations in CRISP and CHIP

		CHIP	CRISP
Password file derivation		$2H + 2E$	$2\hat{H} + 3E$
Key exchange:	Blinding	$1E$	$3E$
	Identity check	0	$1\hat{H} + 2P$
	Key generation	$1H + 3E + \text{PAKE}$	$1P + \text{PAKE}$

by CRISP for party $\mathcal{P}_i$ is:

$$\text{id}_i, \tilde{A}_i, \tilde{C}_i = \text{id}_i, (g_1^{x_i})^{r_i}, (\hat{H}_2(sid, \text{id}_i)^{x_i})^{r_i},$$

where r_i and x_i are random values. This message is thus completely independent of the password and does not leak any information about it. Also, we recall from Sect. 7.2 that the inputs to $\mathcal{F}_{\text{PAKE}}$ S_i, S_j are equal if and only if the passwords are equal (only assuming $\hat{H}_1$ is injective on the password domain). Thus, unless a party is compromised, the underlying PAKE properties (leaking no information of the password and allowing a single online guess) are preserved by CRISP.

GGM-Free Password File Security. Recall that CRISP's password file for party $\mathcal{P}_i$ takes the following form: $\langle \text{FILE}, \text{id}_i, A_i, B_i, C_i, \rangle$ where only B_i is derived from the password π_i as $B_i = \hat{H}_1(\pi_i)^{x_i}$ with a random salt x_i. Hash-to-Group functions usually consist of a composition of a "conventional" hash function H with a Map-to-Group function F: $\hat{H}_i(s) \leftarrow F(H_i(s))$. Therefore, the password file is derived from a "conventionally hashed" password $H_1(\pi_i)$ rather than the plain password. Thus, modelling H_1 as RO, to mount a brute-force attack against a compromised password file, the adversary has to evaluate H_1 on the each guess π', regardless of group properties.

For example, with discrete log capabilities, the adversary can extract the salt x_i from $A_i = g_1^{x_i}$. Assuming F^{-1} is efficiently computable, they can extract:

$$F^{-1}(B_i^{1/x_i}) = F^{-1}(\hat{H}_1(\pi_i)^{x_i/x_i}) = F^{-1}(F(H_1(\pi_i))) = H_1(\pi_i)$$

However, a conventional hash computation is still required to test each password guess: $H_1(\pi') \stackrel{?}{=} H_1(\pi_i)$. Note that hash evaluation of guesses can be precomputed. GGM is only used to prove that some work per guess (specifically, bilinear pairing) is required from the attacker post-compromise.

8   Computational Cost

The computational costs for CHIP and CRISP are summarized in Table 2 in terms of costly operations. In the table, we use H, $\hat{H}$, E, and P to denote Hash, Hash-to-Group, Exponentiation, and Pairing costs, respectively, and PAKE denotes the additional cost of the underlying PAKE used. We ignore the cost of group multiplications.

8.1   Password Hardening for Pre-compromise

Common password hardening techniques (e.g., PBKDF2 [26], Argon2 [5], and scrypt [28]) are used in the process of deriving a key from a password to increase the cost of brute-force attacks. As mentioned in Sect. 3 both CHIP and CRISP protocols can use those techniques to increase the cost of the pre-compromise computation phase of the attack (pre-computation). In CHIP, we can use any of those hardening techniques to implement the hash function denoted as H_1. Similarly, in CRISP, we can use those techniques as the first step in implementing the Hash-to-Group function denoted as $\hat{H}_1$. As those functions are only called once in the password file derivation phase, we can increase their cost without increasing the cost of the online phase of the protocol.

8.2   Password Hardening for Post-compromise

In addition to the cost of the pre-compromise phase, the CRISP protocol also requires the attacker to perform a post-compromise phase. The offline test post-compromise cost mentioned above is taken from the lower bound proved in Sect. 7.4. This is also an upper bound for CRISP, since having compromised a password file, an adversary can check for any password guess π' if:

$$\hat{e}(g_1, B_i) \overset{?}{=} \hat{e}(A_i, \hat{H}_1(sid, \pi'))$$

The left-hand side can be computed once and re-used for different guesses. The right-hand side must be computed per-password, but the invocation of $\hat{H}_1$ can be done prior to the compromise.

We stress that a pairing operation is preferred over exponentiation when considering the cost of an offline test. While the latter can be significantly amortized (e.g., by using a window implementation), to the best of our knowledge, only 37% speed-up can be achieved for pairing with a fixed point [14]. Moreover, pairing requires more memory than a simple point multiplication and is harder to accelerate using GPUs [29].

In OPAQUE [23], the difficulty of offline tests was increased by iterative hashing (password hardening). CRISP cannot benefit from this approach for post-compromise hardening, because the design does not allow the salt inside the hash. However, by using larger group sizes, we can increase the cost of each pairing and slow down offline tests. Although coarse-grained, this allows some trade-off between compromise resilience and computational complexity of CRISP.

8.3   CRISP Optimization

We can optimize the CRISP protocol in several ways to reduce the added computational cost and latency.

Identity Verification. A substantial part of the added computational cost of the protocol is the identity verification that requires two pairing operations. We propose two options to optimize this cost:

1. Reducing latency – The verification does not affect the derived key or the subsequent messages. This implies we can continue with the protocol by sending the next message and postpone the verification for later, while we wait for

Table 3. Online performance comparison and proven security notions for PAKEs.

	CPace	SAE	CHIP	OPAQUE	CRISP
CPU time (ms)	0.2	>1.3	0.6	0.6	4.1
Communication rounds	1	2	2	2	2
Security notion	PAKE	none	iPAKE	saPAKE	siPAKE

the other party to respond. The total computational cost remains the same, but the latency (or running time) of the protocol is reduced.

2. Verification delegation – Any party that receives the protocol messages, can verify the identity appearing in it (verification is only based on the identity and blinded values). We consider the following scenario, where we have a broadcast network with many low-end devices, such as IoT devices, and one or more high-end devices, such as a controller or bridge. The bridge can perform the identity verification for all protocols in the network, and alert the user if any verification fails.

Number of Messages. CRISP requires two additional messages compared to the underlying PAKE. We can trivially reduce this to one additional message. The first message remains the same, but after receiving it, the other party can already derive the shared secret S_i and prepare the first PAKE message. Consequently, CRISP's second message can be combined with the first PAKE message, resulting in a single additional message, and again reducing the total latency of the protocol. As any PAKE protocol requires at least two simultaneous messages [25], we can implement CRISP using only three sequential messages. The same optimization applies to CHIP.

8.4 Performance Benchmark

We provide open source implementations for CHIP and CRISP. In both we rely on CPace [19] as the underlying symmetric PAKE. CHIP was implemented on top of Ristretto255 curve from the libsodium library (v1.0.18). CRISP uses the pairing friendly curve BLS12-381 from the MCL library (v1.22). Both curves are assumed to provide 128-bit of security strength. The source code is available at https://github.com/shapaz/CRISP.

In Table 3 we compare the online performance of CHIP and CRISP with those of other popular PAKE protocols, running on an i7-4790 processor. CPace and OPAQUE [23] were chosen by IETF CFRG as symmetric and asymmetric PAKEs (respectively) for usage with TLS 1.3, and are considered to be very efficient. SAE [20] is the underlying symmetric PAKE of Wi-Fi's WPA-3 and is designed to be supported by low-resource embedded devices. For measurements, our code implements both CPace and OPAQUE over Ristretto255. For SAE we used the official hostapd/wpa_supplicant. Note that although Wi-Fi's SAE was designed to be a PAKE, its security was never proven.

9   Conclusions and Discussion

In this paper, we formalized the novel notions of iPAKE and siPAKE, that bring compromise resilience to all parties, and can also be applied in the symmetric setting. We presented CHIP, which we proved to UC-realize $\mathcal{F}_{iPAKE}$ under ROM. We also introduced CRISP, which we proved to realize $\mathcal{F}_{siPAKE}$ under GGM+ROM. Moreover, we have shown that each offline password guess for CRISP requires a computational cost equivalent to one pairing operation. Finally, we showed our protocols are practical and efficient.

Deploying (s)iPAKE. Deploying (s)iPAKEs in practice could be done by, e.g., using CRISP or CHIP inside a Wi-Fi handshake, and choosing roles and device names ("Phone: Elon's third iPhone") as the identities, and requiring consistency between the reported identity and the identity in the handshake. A compromise of the phone would afterwards only allow the adversary to impersonate as this device identity, which would enable manual detection (e.g., a lost phone appearing as an access point) and facilitate allow/deny listing. Other application examples include IoT settings, where one could link role identities to capabilities, e.g., the window cannot instruct the garage door to open.

Comparison of CRISP and CHIP. CHIP and CRISP both provide Password Authenticated Key Exchange with compromise resilience, and allow fine-grained password hardening by selecting computationally hard hash functions (Sect. 8.1). Parties running CHIP or CRISP only evaluate those hash functions once in the offline setup phase, which means that computationally costly variants can be chosen.

However, while CHIP realizes $\mathcal{F}_{iPAKE}$ providing "Hashed password with public identifiers" level of compromise resilience (Sect. 3), CRISP realizes $\mathcal{F}_{siPAKE}$, providing the more secure "Hashed password with secret salt" level. Thus, CRISP requires the adversary to pay an additional coarse-grained cost after party compromise (Sect. 8.2). CRISP's pre-computation resistance comes at a cost: CHIP is faster, requires standard assumptions, and can be implemented with simple group operations; CRISP, on the other hand, requires bilinear pairing and *local* GGM, and cannot be trivially composed with other protocols that share the same group.

Going forward with the concept of identity-binding PAKEs, we identify several remaining open problems:

Two Message Protocol. In Sect. 8.3, we showed how our protocols require only three messages. As shown in [25], PAKE can be realized with only two messages. It is an open problem to either prove a lower bound of three messages or to implement a two message iPAKE or siPAKE protocol. To the best of our knowledge, there are no two message (s)aPAKE protocols. Jutla and Roy [24] propose a one-round aPAKE, but it seems that they require an additional message from the server before the protocol [23].

Optimal Bound on the Cost of Brute-Force Attack. In Sect. 3 we showed a black-box post-compromise brute-force attack on any PAKE protocol. The computational cost of the attack is *two* runs (i.e., for both parties) of the PAKE protocol for each offline password guess. However, to the best of our knowledge, brute-forcing current PAKE implementations requires a computational cost equivalent to only *one* run of the protocol. It remains an open problem to find a more efficient black-box attack or to implement a more resilient PAKE.

Fine-Grained Password Hardening. While both CHIP and CRISP allow for fine-grained password hardening, CRISP additionally provides coarse-grained post-compromise password hardening by enlarging the group (e.g., curves of larger size). Allowing fine-grained hardening (e.g., iterative hashing) while preserving pre-computation resistance for all parties remains an open problem.

Acknowledgement. We thank Nir Bitansky, Ran Canetti, Ben Fisch, Hugo Krawczyk, and Eylon Yogev for many helpful discussions and insightful ideas.

The second author is supported in part by grants from the Israel Science Foundation (no. 2686/20) and by the Simons Foundation Collaboration on the Theory of Algorithmic Fairness. Incumbent of the Judith Kleeman Professorial Chair. The fourth author is supported in part by Len Blavatnik and the Blavatnik Family foundation, the Blavatnik ICRC, and Robert Bosch Technologies Israel Ltd. Member of the Check Point Institute for Information Security.

References

1. Abdalla, M., Haase, B., Hesse, J.: Security analysis of CPace. In: Tibouchi, M., Wang, H. (eds.) ASIACRYPT 2021. LNCS, vol. 13093, pp. 711–741. Springer, Cham (2021). https://doi.org/10.1007/978-3-030-92068-5_24
2. Bellare, M., Pointcheval, D., Rogaway, P.: Authenticated key exchange secure against dictionary attacks. In: Preneel, B. (ed.) EUROCRYPT 2000. LNCS, vol. 1807, pp. 139–155. Springer, Heidelberg (2000). https://doi.org/10.1007/3-540-45539-6_11
3. Bellovin, S.M., Merritt, M.: Encrypted key exchange: password-based protocols secure against dictionary attacks. In: IEEE Symposium on Security and Privacy (1992)
4. Bellovin, S.M., Merritt, M.: Augmented encrypted key exchange: a password-based protocol secure against dictionary attacks and password file compromise. In: ACM CCS (1993)
5. Biryukov, A., Dinu, D., Khovratovich, D.: Argon2: new generation of memory-hard functions for password hashing and other applications. In: EuroS&P. IEEE (2016)
6. Boneh, D., Boyen, X.: Short signatures without random oracles. In: Cachin, C., Camenisch, J.L. (eds.) EUROCRYPT 2004. LNCS, vol. 3027, pp. 56–73. Springer, Heidelberg (2004). https://doi.org/10.1007/978-3-540-24676-3_4
7. Bourdrez, D., Krawczyk, H., Lewi, K., Wood, C.A.: The OPAQUE asymmetric PAKE protocol. Internet-Draft draft-irtf-cfrg-opaque-08, Internet Engineering Task Force, March 2022. https://datatracker.ietf.org/doc/html/draft-irtf-cfrg-opaque-08
8. Boyko, V., MacKenzie, P.D., Patel, S.: Provably secure password-authenticated key exchange using Diffie-Hellman. In: Preneel, B. (ed.) EUROCRYPT 2000. LNCS, vol. 1807, pp. 156–171. Springer, Heidelberg (2000). https://doi.org/10.1007/3-540-45539-6_12

9. Bradley, T., Jarecki, S., Xu, J.: Strong asymmetric PAKE based on trapdoor CKEM. In: Boldyreva, A., Micciancio, D. (eds.) CRYPTO 2019. LNCS, vol. 11694, pp. 798–825. Springer, Cham (2019). https://doi.org/10.1007/978-3-030-26954-8_26

10. Canetti, R.: Towards realizing random oracles: hash functions that hide all partial information. In: Kaliski, B.S. (ed.) CRYPTO 1997. LNCS, vol. 1294, pp. 455–469. Springer, Heidelberg (1997). https://doi.org/10.1007/BFb0052255

11. Canetti, R.: Universally composable security: a new paradigm for cryptographic protocols. In: FOCS (2001)

12. Canetti, R., Krawczyk, H.: Analysis of key-exchange protocols and their use for building secure channels. In: Pfitzmann, B. (ed.) EUROCRYPT 2001. LNCS, vol. 2045, pp. 453–474. Springer, Heidelberg (2001). https://doi.org/10.1007/3-540-44987-6_28

13. Canetti, R., Halevi, S., Katz, J., Lindell, Y., MacKenzie, P.D.: Universally composable password-based key exchange. In: Cramer, R. (ed.) EUROCRYPT 2005. LNCS, vol. 3494, pp. 404–421. Springer, Heidelberg (2005). https://doi.org/10.1007/11426639_24

14. Costello, C., Stebila, D.: Fixed argument pairings. In: Abdalla, M., Barreto, P.S.L.M. (eds.) LATINCRYPT 2010. LNCS, vol. 6212, pp. 92–108. Springer, Heidelberg (2010). https://doi.org/10.1007/978-3-642-14712-8_6

15. Cremers, C., Naor, M., Paz, S., Ronen, E.: CHIP and CRISP: protecting all parties against compromise through identity-binding PAKEs. Cryptology ePrint Archive (2020). https://eprint.iacr.org/2020/529

16. Fiore, D., Gennaro, R.: Identity-based key exchange protocols without pairings. Trans. Comput. Sci. **10**, 42–77 (2010)

17. Gentry, C., MacKenzie, P.D., Ramzan, Z.: A method for making password-based key exchange resilient to server compromise. In: Dwork, C. (ed.) CRYPTO 2006. LNCS, vol. 4117, pp. 142–159. Springer, Heidelberg (2006). https://doi.org/10.1007/11818175_9

18. Günther, C.G.: An identity-based key-exchange protocol. In: Quisquater, J.-J., Vandewalle, J. (eds.) EUROCRYPT 1989. LNCS, vol. 434, pp. 29–37. Springer, Heidelberg (1990). https://doi.org/10.1007/3-540-46885-4_5

19. Haase, B., Labrique, B.: AuCPace: efficient verifier-based PAKE protocol tailored for the IIoT. IACR Trans. Cryptogr. Hardw. Embed. Syst. (2019)

20. Harkins, D.: Simultaneous authentication of equals: a secure, password-based key exchange for mesh networks. In: 2008 Second International Conference on Sensor Technologies and Applications (2008)

21. Harkins, D., Zorn, G.: Extensible authentication protocol (EAP) Authentication using only a password. RFC 5931, August 2010

22. Hesse, J.: Separating symmetric and asymmetric password-authenticated key exchange. In: Galdi, C., Kolesnikov, V. (eds.) SCN 2020. LNCS, vol. 12238, pp. 579–599. Springer, Cham (2020). https://doi.org/10.1007/978-3-030-57990-6_29

23. Jarecki, S., Krawczyk, H., Xu, J.: OPAQUE: an asymmetric PAKE protocol secure against pre-computation attacks. In: Nielsen, J.B., Rijmen, V. (eds.) EUROCRYPT 2018. LNCS, vol. 10822, pp. 456–486. Springer, Cham (2018). https://doi.org/10.1007/978-3-319-78372-7_15

24. Jutla, C.S., Roy, A.: Smooth NIZK arguments. In: Beimel, A., Dziembowski, S. (eds.) TCC 2018. LNCS, vol. 11239, pp. 235–262. Springer, Cham (2018). https://doi.org/10.1007/978-3-030-03807-6_9

25. Katz, J., Vaikuntanathan, V.: Round-optimal password-based authenticated key exchange. In: Ishai, Y. (ed.) TCC 2011. LNCS, vol. 6597, pp. 293–310. Springer, Heidelberg (2011). https://doi.org/10.1007/978-3-642-19571-6_18
26. Moriarty, K., Kaliski, B., Rusch, A.: PKCS #5: password-based cryptography specification version 2.1. RFC 8018, January 2017
27. Neuman, C., Yu, T., Hartman, S., Raeburn, K.: The kerberos network authentication service (V5). RFC 4120, July 2005
28. Percival, C., Josefsson, S.: The scrypt password-based key derivation function. RFC 7914, August 2016
29. Pu, S., Liu, J.-C.: EAGL: an elliptic curve arithmetic GPU-based library for bilinear pairing. In: Cao, Z., Zhang, F. (eds.) Pairing 2013. LNCS, vol. 8365, pp. 1–19. Springer, Cham (2014). https://doi.org/10.1007/978-3-319-04873-4_1
30. Shoup, V.: Lower bounds for discrete logarithms and related problems. In: Fumy, W. (ed.) EUROCRYPT 1997. LNCS, vol. 1233, pp. 256–266. Springer, Heidelberg (1997). https://doi.org/10.1007/3-540-69053-0_18
31. Wi-Fi Alliance. WPA3 specification version 1.0, April 2018. https://www.wi-fi.org/file/wpa3-specification-v10. Accessed 6 Apr 2019
32. Wu, T.D.: The secure remote password protocol. In: NDSS. The Internet Society (1998)

Password-Authenticated Key Exchange from Group Actions

Michel Abdalla[1,2] , Thorsten Eisenhofer[3], Eike Kiltz[3] ,
Sabrina Kunzweiler[3] , and Doreen Riepel[3(✉)]

[1] DFINITY, Zürich, Switzerland
[2] DIENS, École normale supérieure, CNRS, PSL University, Paris, France
michel.abdalla@ens.fr
[3] Ruhr-Universität Bochum, Bochum, Germany
{thorsten.eisenhofer,eike.kiltz,sabrina.kunzweiler,doreen.riepel}@rub.de

Abstract. We present two provably secure password-authenticated key exchange (PAKE) protocols based on a commutative group action. To date the most important instantiation of isogeny-based group actions is given by CSIDH. To model the properties more accurately, we extend the framework of cryptographic group actions (Alamati et al., ASIACRYPT 2020) by the ability of computing the quadratic twist of an elliptic curve. This property is always present in the CSIDH setting and turns out to be crucial in the security analysis of our PAKE protocols.

Despite the resemblance, the translation of Diffie-Hellman based PAKE protocols to group actions either does not work with known techniques or is insecure ("How not to create an isogeny-based PAKE", Azarderakhsh et al., ACNS 2020). We overcome the difficulties mentioned in previous work by using a "bit-by-bit" approach, where each password bit is considered separately.

Our first protocol X-GA-PAKE$_\ell$ can be executed in a single round. Both parties need to send two set elements for each password bit in order to prevent offline dictionary attacks. The second protocol Com-GA-PAKE$_\ell$ requires only one set element per password bit, but one party has to send a commitment on its message first. We also discuss different optimizations that can be used to reduce the computational cost. We provide comprehensive security proofs for our base protocols and deduce security for the optimized versions.

Keywords: Password-authenticated key exchange · group actions · CSIDH

1 Introduction

Password-authenticated key exchange (PAKE) enables two parties to securely establish a joint session key assuming that they only share a low-entropy secret known as the password. This reflects that passwords are often represented in short human-readable formats and are chosen from a small set of possible values, often referred to as dictionary.

© International Association for Cryptologic Research 2022
Y. Dodis and T. Shrimpton (Eds.): CRYPTO 2022, LNCS 13508, pp. 699–728, 2022.
https://doi.org/10.1007/978-3-031-15979-4_24

Since the introduction of PAKE by Bellovin and Merritt [8], many PAKE protocols have been proposed, including SPEKE [20], SPAKE2 [4], J-PAKE [19] and CPace [18]. In particular over the last few years, the design and construction of PAKE protocols has attracted increasing attention, as the Crypto Forum Research Group (CFRG) which is part of the Internet Research Task Force (IETF) started a selection process to decide which PAKE protocols should be used in IETF protocols. Recently, CPace was selected as the recommended protocol for symmetric PAKE, where both parties share the same password.

Different models have been used to formally prove security of PAKE protocols, like indistinguishability-based models or the universal composability framework. In general, a PAKE protocol should resist offline and online dictionary attacks. On the one hand an adversary should not be able to perform an exhaustive search of the password offline. On the other hand, an active adversary should only be able to try a small number of passwords in one protocol execution. Furthermore, forward security ensures that session keys are still secure, even if the password is leaked at a later point in time. The same should hold if session keys are disclosed, which should not affect security of other session keys.

CSIDH and Group Actions. The PAKE protocols mentioned above are mostly based on a Diffie-Hellman key exchange in a prime order group. A promising post-quantum replacement is isogeny-based key exchange. The different isogeny-based protocols can be divided into two groups. On the one hand there are constructions based on commutative group actions on a set of elliptic curves. The first proposals by Couveignes [12], and Stolbunov and Rostovtsev [27] suggested to use the action of the class group $cl(\mathcal{O})$ on the set of $\mathbb{F}_q$-isomorphism classes of *ordinary* elliptic curves with endomorphism ring $\mathcal{O}$. In 2018, Castryck et al. showed that this idea can also be adapted to the class group action on the set of $\mathbb{F}_p$-isomorphism classes of *supersingular* elliptic curves [11]. The resulting scheme is called CSIDH and constitutes the first practical key exchange scheme based on class group actions.

In [12], Couveignes introduces *hard homogeneous spaces* - an abstract framework for group actions that models isogeny-based assumptions. This framework has been further refined by Alamati et al. in [5]. Using the abstract setting of *cryptographic group actions* the authors develop several new cryptographic primitives that can be instantiated with CSIDH. On the other hand there is the Supersingular Isogeny Diffie-Hellman (SIDH) protocol suggested by Jao and De Feo in 2011 [21]. Here, the set of $\mathbb{F}_{p^2}$-isomorphism classes of *supersingular* elliptic curves is considered. The endomorphism ring of a supersingular elliptic curve over $\mathbb{F}_{p^2}$ is non-commutative, hence protocols based on SIDH do not fall into the group action framework.

We now recall the framework of (restricted) effective group actions introduced in [5]. Throughout, $\mathcal{G}$ denotes a finite commutative group and $\mathcal{X}$ a set. We assume that $\mathcal{G}$ acts regularly on $\mathcal{X}$ via the operator $\star : \mathcal{G} \times \mathcal{X} \to \mathcal{X}$. Regularity guarantees that for any $x, y \in \mathcal{X}$ there exists precisely one group element $g \in \mathcal{G}$ satisfying

$y = g \star x$. Broadly speaking, we are interested in group actions, where evaluation is easy, but the "discrete logarithm problem" is hard. Expressed differently:

– Given $x \in \mathcal{X}$ and $g \in \mathcal{G}$, one can efficiently compute the set element $y = g \star x$.
– Given $x, y \in \mathcal{X}$, it is hard to find the element $g \in \mathcal{G}$ satisfying $y = g \star x$.

These properties facilitate the definition of a Diffie-Hellman key exchange. Let x be some fixed set element. Alice chooses a secret $g_A \in \mathcal{G}$ and publishes $y_A = g_A \star x$. Similarly Bob chooses $g_B \in \mathcal{G}$ and publishes $y_B = g_B \star x$. They can both compute the shared secret $y_{AB} = g_A \star y_B = g_B \star y_A$. The group action computational Diffie-Hellman problem (GA-CDH) then states that given y_A and y_B, it is hard to compute y_{AB}. We refer to Sect. 3 for more precise definitions.

Contributions and Technical Details. Our main contributions are the two PAKE protocols X-GA-PAKE$_\ell$ and Com-GA-PAKE$_\ell$ based on commutative group actions. These are the first two provably secure PAKE protocols that are directly constructed from isogenies.

GROUP ACTIONS WITH TWISTS. To date the most important instantiation of isogeny-based group actions is given by CSIDH. To model this situation more accurately, we suggest an enhancement of the framework which includes the ability of computing the quadratic twist of an elliptic curve efficiently. This property is inherent to CSIDH (cf. [11]) and it turns out to be crucial in the security analysis of our PAKE protocols. On the one hand, twisting allows us to construct an offline dictionary attack against our first natural PAKE attempt GA-PAKE$_\ell$. Notably, this first protocol is secure for group actions where twisting is not possible efficiently. On the other hand, twists play an important role in various security reductions applied to prove the security of our new protocols X-GA-PAKE$_\ell$ and Com-GA-PAKE$_\ell$. Interestingly, this is also the case when twists are not part of any of the two problems involved in the reduction.

FIRST ATTEMPT: GA-PAKE$_\ell$. Our two secure PAKE protocols are modifications of GA-PAKE$_\ell$. In order to illustrate the main idea behind the protocols, we describe GA-PAKE$_\ell$ in more detail here. The protocol (Fig. 1) can be seen as an adaption of the simple password exponential key exchange protocol SPEKE [20] to the group action setting. In SPEKE the password is used to hash to a generator of the group. Then the user and the server establish a session key following the Diffie-Hellman key exchange. Directly translating this protocol to the group action setting requires to hash the password to a random set element $x \in \mathcal{X}$. For isogeny-based group actions, this is still an open problem, hence (at the moment) a straight-forward translation of SPEKE is not possible (see also [6, §4.1]). In GA-PAKE$_\ell$ we map the password to an ℓ-tuple of elements in $\mathcal{X}$ instead of hashing to one element. More precisely, two elements crs $= (x_0, x_1) \in \mathcal{X}^2$ are fixed by a trusted party and a password pw $= (b_1, \ldots, b_\ell) \in \{0,1\}^\ell$ is mapped to the tuple $(x_{b_1}, \cdots, x_{b_\ell}) \in \mathcal{X}^\ell$. Then a Diffie-Hellman key exchange is performed with basis x_{b_i} for each $i \in [\ell]$. This means the user generates ℓ random group elements $u_1, \ldots, u_\ell$ and computes the elements $x_1^{\mathsf{U}} = u_1 \star x_{b_1}, \ldots, x_\ell^{\mathsf{U}} = u_\ell \star x_{b_\ell}$ which it sends to the server. Similarly, the server generates ℓ random group elements $s_1, \ldots, s_\ell$ and computes $x_1^{\mathsf{S}} = s_1 \star x_{b_1}, \ldots, x_\ell^{\mathsf{S}} = s_\ell \star x_{b_\ell}$ which it sends

User U		**Server S**
	$\mathsf{crs} := (x_0, x_1) \in \mathcal{X}^2$,	
	$\mathsf{pw} := (b_1, ..., b_\ell) \in \{0,1\}^\ell$	
$(u_1, ..., u_\ell) \xleftarrow{\$} \mathcal{G}^\ell$		$(s_1, ..., s_\ell) \xleftarrow{\$} \mathcal{G}^\ell$
for $i \in [\ell]$		**for** $i \in [\ell]$
$x_i^{\mathsf{U}} := u_i \star x_{b_i}$	$\xrightarrow{x_1^{\mathsf{U}}, ..., x_\ell^{\mathsf{U}}}$	$x_i^{\mathsf{S}} := s_i \star x_{b_i}$
	$\xleftarrow{x_1^{\mathsf{S}}, ..., x_\ell^{\mathsf{S}}}$	
for $i \in [\ell]$		**for** $i \in [\ell]$
$z_i := u_i \star x_i^{\mathsf{S}}$		$z_i := s_i \star x_i^{\mathsf{U}}$
	$K := \mathsf{H}(\mathsf{U}, \mathsf{S}, x_1^{\mathsf{U}}, ..., x_\ell^{\mathsf{U}}, x_1^{\mathsf{S}}, ..., x_\ell^{\mathsf{S}}, \mathsf{pw}, z_1, ..., z_\ell)$	

Fig. 1. First Attempt: Protocol $\mathsf{GA\text{-}PAKE}_\ell$.

to the user. Note that the messages may be sent simultaneously in one round. Then both parties compute $z_i = u_i \star x_i^{\mathsf{S}} = s_i \star x_i^{\mathsf{U}}$ for each $i \in [\ell]$. Finally the session key K is computed as $K = \mathsf{H}(\mathsf{U}, \mathsf{S}, x_1^{\mathsf{U}}, ..., x_\ell^{\mathsf{U}}, x_1^{\mathsf{S}}, ..., x_\ell^{\mathsf{S}}, \mathsf{pw}, z_1, ..., z_\ell)$, where $\mathsf{H} : \{0,1\}^* \to \mathcal{K}$ is a hash function into the key space $\mathcal{K}$.

In Sect. 5, we present an offline dictionary attack against $\mathsf{GA\text{-}PAKE}_\ell$ for group actions with twists. This attack is not captured by the abstract group action framework defined in [5] which underlines the necessity of our suggested enhancement of the framework. Roughly speaking, the attack uses the fact that an attacker can choose its message in dependence on the other party's message. Using twists, it can then achieve that certain terms in the key derivation cancel out and the session key no longer depends on the other party's input.

Secure PAKE: $\mathsf{X\text{-}GA\text{-}PAKE}_\ell$ and $\mathsf{Com\text{-}GA\text{-}PAKE}_\ell$. The protocol $\mathsf{X\text{-}GA\text{-}PAKE}_\ell$ is a modified version of $\mathsf{GA\text{-}PAKE}_\ell$. Here security is achieved by doubling the message length in the first round of the protocol and tripling it in the key derivation. Intuitively the additional parts of the message can be viewed as an additional challenge for the key derivation that inhibits an attacker from choosing its message depending on the other party's message. The security of the protocol relies on a new computational assumption, $\mathsf{SqInv\text{-}GA\text{-}StCDH}$, in which the adversary needs to compute the square and the inverse of its input at the same time (cf. Definition 7, Theorem 1).

The protocol $\mathsf{Com\text{-}GA\text{-}PAKE}_\ell$ is a modification of $\mathsf{GA\text{-}PAKE}_\ell$ as well. In order to achieve security against offline dictionary attacks, the protocol requires that the server sends a commitment before receiving the first message from the user. This prevents that any party chooses its message depending on the other party's message. We reduce the security of the protocol to the hardness of standard security assumptions in the isogeny-based setting (Theorem 2). An overview of our results is provided in Fig. 2.

Optimizations. Both $\mathsf{X\text{-}GA\text{-}PAKE}_\ell$ and $\mathsf{Com\text{-}GA\text{-}PAKE}_\ell$ require to compute multiple group action evaluations. In the last section, we discuss two

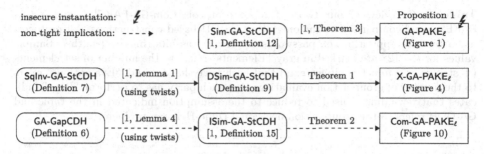

insecure instantiation: ⚡
non-tight implication: ----►

Fig. 2. Overview of our security implications between assumptions (round boxes) and schemes (square boxes). Note that there exists an attack against protocol GA-PAKE$_\ell$ using twists which makes it insecure for CSIDH. Our two main protocols X-GA-PAKE$_\ell$ and Com-GA-PAKE$_\ell$ are proven secure under protocol-specific assumptions, but we also give reductions to simpler assumptions making use of the twisting property. Solid arrows denote tight reductions, dashed arrows non-tight reductions.

optimizations that can be used to reduce the number of evaluations and show that these do not affect the security of the protocols. The first makes a tradeoff between the size of the public parameters (the common reference string crs) and the number of elements that have to be sent as well as the group actions that have to be performed. The second optimization relies on the possibility to compute twists efficiently, which is yet another advantage of adding this property to the framework and which allows to decrease the size of the public parameters by a factor of 2. We denote the final optimizations by Com-GA-PAKE$_{\ell,N}^t$ and X-GA-PAKE$_{\ell,N}^t$, where N is a parameter for the crs size. If N equals 1, we omit it. An overview and example of the parameter choice is provided in Table 1.

Difficulties in Constructing PAKE from Isogenies. Terada and Yoneyama [30] proposed isogeny-based PAKE based on the EKE approach. The basic idea is that the parties perform an SIDH or CSIDH key exchange where the messages are encrypted with the password. However, as shown in [6], these protocols are not only vulnerable to offline dictionary attacks, but a modified version is even vulnerable to man-in-the-middle attacks. The main reason for the insecurity is that the elliptic curves used in the key exchange and encrypted with the password are distinguishable from random bitstrings. An exhaustive search over all passwords just requires to check if the decrypted message is a valid curve.

Another proposal based on SIDH was made by Taraskin et al. [29]. In this protocol the password is used to obfuscate the auxiliary points that are exchanged during an SIDH key exchange. While their obfuscation method prevents a certain type of offline dictionary attack, the authors were not able to provide a security proof for their protocol. The same is true for a symmetric variant of the protocol proposed by Soukharev and Hess [28]. Until now these are the only PAKE protocol based on isogenies which are not broken.

As noted in [6], other popular Diffie-Hellman constructions may also not be directly translated into the isogeny setting. The main reason is that hashing into

Table 1. Overview of our two optimized protocols Com-GA-PAKE$_{\ell,N}^t$ and X-GA-PAKE$_{\ell,N}^t$ and comparison to the only other CSIDH-based constructions. All protocols use a bit-wise approach, i.e., passwords are treated as bitstrings of length ℓ. Sample values for $\ell = 128$ are marked in gray. "Elements" refers to the number of set elements (+ strings or symmetric ciphertexts) that each party has to send. "Evaluations" refers to the number of group action evaluations that each party has to perform. "Rew." indicates that rewinding is used to reduce to the assumption indicated in the table and GA-DDH refers to the group action decisional Diffie-Hellman problem.

Protocol	$|crs|$	Elements	Evaluations	Rounds	Assumption	Rew.	ROM
X-GA-PAKE$_{\ell,N}^t$	2^{N-1}	$2\ell/N$	$5\ell/N$	1	SqInv-GA-StCDH	no	yes
$\hookrightarrow (\ell, N) = (128, 8)$	128	32	80				
Com-GA-PAKE$_{\ell,N}^t$	2^{N-1}	ℓ/N (+1)	$2\ell/N$	3	Sq-GA-GapCDH	yes	yes
$\hookrightarrow (\ell, N) = (128, 8)$	128	16 (+1)	32				
OT-based$_\ell$ [10,24]	1	3ℓ (+6ℓ)	11ℓ	4	GA-CDH	yes	yes
$\hookrightarrow \ell = 128$	1	384 (+768)	1408				
OT-based$_\ell$ [5,10,25]	4	$> \ell^2$	$> \ell^2$	3	GA-DDH + CCA PKE	no	no
$\hookrightarrow \ell = 128$	4	$> 16,000$	$> 16,000$				

the set of supersingular elliptic curves is still an open problem. This approach is for example used in SPEKE. (However, we show how to non-trivially translate the idea.) Also the approach of J-PAKE seems difficult as in this scheme different public keys are combined to obtain certain "mixed" public keys. In isogeny-based protocols, the public keys are elliptic curves and there is no natural ring structure on the set of elliptic curves that would allow to combine two elliptic curves.

In the following, we elaborate known generic constructions of PAKE from hash proof systems (HPS) and oblivious transfer (OT). We explain that the only known isogeny-based HPS is not suitable for generic constructions. On the other hand, the isogeny-based OT protocols from the literature are suited for generic constructions. However, we show that the resulting PAKE protocols are less efficient than our new proposals.

Using the framework of cryptographic group actions, Alamati et al. construct a universal hash proof system [5, §4.1]. In general, it is known how to build CCA-secure encryption [13] and also PAKE from hash proof systems [17]. However, the details here are less clear. The hashing key consists of multiple elements linear in the size of the universality parameter. The reason being that we can only make use of one group operation provided by the group action. This also needs to be considered when constructing an encryption scheme. In order to construct PAKE, the framework by Gennaro and Lindell and follow-up works require a hash proof system for the language of ciphertexts of a public-key encryption scheme, which seems to be hard to construct given only the operation of the group action. The HPS in [5] is only based on a DDH-like assumption.

It is well known that PAKE can also be generically constructed from OT [10]. One construction uses a UC-secure OT protocol and the other one a statistically receiver-private OT protocol. In both, the password is interpreted as a bit string and for each bit, the user and server run the oblivious transfer protocol for randomly chosen messages which will be used to derive the session key. In the following, we apply the construction to two existing OT protocols.

– Alamati et al. propose a two-message statistically *sender*-private OT, however we can construct a similar receiver-private OT protocol based on their dual-mode public-key encryption scheme and the transformation given in [25]. The resulting OT protocol already uses a "bit-by-bit" approach, hence the resulting PAKE will have communication and computation complexity quadratic in the parameter ℓ.
– Recently, Lai et al. proposed a new very efficient CSIDH-based OT protocol using twists and the random oracle model [24]. However, in order to achieve active security the protocol needs four rounds.[1] Additionally applying the generic PAKE compiler results in a protocol with complexity linear in ℓ.

The efficiency of the generic constructions is compared to our new protocols in Table 1. While the computational cost of our protocols Com-GA-PAKE$_{\ell,N}$ and X-GA-PAKE$_{\ell,N}$ is also linear in ℓ, the cost is considerably lower for concrete instantiations. Moreover, our scheme X-GA-PAKE$_{\ell,N}$ is the only one-round protocol, where both parties send simultaneous flows.

Open Problems and Future Work. Until now, protocols based on CSIDH or group actions that use search problems together with the random oracle model do not consider quantum access to the ROM [16,22–24,31]. Since PAKE proofs are already complex, we also did not prove security in the QROM. Although no reprogramming of the random oracle is necessary, the main difficulty in the QROM is to simulate the real session keys using the decision oracle. We leave this as future work. We believe that we can easily allow quantum access to the additional random oracle that is used in Com-GA-PAKE$_\ell$ to commit on the message. In this case, the output is transferred classically in the first message flow such that extraction is possible using recently developed techniques [15].

As [24], we use rewinding to reduce the interactive assumption underlying Com-GA-PAKE$_\ell$ to a standard assumption. An interesting open question is whether current techniques enabling quantum rewinding are applicable here.

Outline. Section 3 sets the framework for our paper. We introduce (restricted) effective group actions with twists and define the computational assumptions underlying the security of our protocols. In Sect. 4, we give some background on the security model that is used in the subsequent sections. In Sect. 5 we present our first attempt for a PAKE protocol, GA-PAKE$_\ell$, and explain its security gap. Section 6 contains a thorough analysis of our new secure protocol X-GA-PAKE$_\ell$. In Sect. 7 we present the protocol Com-GA-PAKE$_\ell$ and sketch the security proof. Finally, we discuss possible optimizations of the protocols in Sect. 8.

---

[1] The original (three-round) version of this protocol was later found to have a (fixable) bug, cf. https://iacr.org/submit/files/slides/2021/eurocrypt/eurocrypt2021/20/slides.pdf.

2   Preliminaries

For integers m, n where $m < n$, $[m, n]$ denotes the set $\{m, m+1, ..., n\}$. For $m = 1$, we simply write $[n]$. For a set S, $s \xleftarrow{\$} S$ denotes that s is sampled uniformly and independently at random from S. $y \leftarrow \mathcal{A}(x_1, x_2, ...)$ denotes that on input $x_1, x_2, ...$ the probabilistic algorithm $\mathcal{A}$ returns y. $\mathcal{A}^O$ denotes that algorithm $\mathcal{A}$ has access to oracle O. An adversary is a probabilistic algorithm. We will use code-based games, where $\Pr[\mathsf{G} \Rightarrow 1]$ denotes the probability that the final output of game G is 1.

3   (Restricted) Effective Group Actions (with Twists)

In this section we recall the definition of (restricted) effective group actions from [5], which provides an abstract framework to build cryptographic primitives relying on isogeny-based assumptions such as CSIDH. Moreover, we suggest an enhancement of this framework, by introducing (restricted) effective group actions with twists. This addition is essential for the security analysis of our new PAKE protocols.

Definition 1 (Group Action). *Let $(\mathcal{G}, \cdot)$ be a group with identity element $id \in \mathcal{G}$, and $\mathcal{X}$ a set. A map*

$$\star : \mathcal{G} \times \mathcal{X} \rightarrow \mathcal{X}$$

is a group action if it satisfies the following properties:

1. *Identity: $id \star x = x$ for all $x \in \mathcal{X}$.*
2. *Compatibility: $(g \cdot h) \star x = g \star (h \star x)$ for all $g, h \in \mathcal{G}$ and $x \in \mathcal{X}$.*

Remark 1. Throughout this paper, we only consider group actions, where $\mathcal{G}$ is commutative. Moreover we assume that the group action is regular. This means that for any $x, y \in \mathcal{X}$ there exists precisely one $g \in \mathcal{G}$ satisfying $y = g \star x$.

Definition 2 (Effective Group Action). *Let $(\mathcal{G}, \mathcal{X}, \star)$ be a group action satisfying the following properties:*

1. *The group $\mathcal{G}$ is finite and there exist efficient (PPT) algorithms for membership and equality testing, (random) sampling, group operation and inversion.*
2. *The set $\mathcal{X}$ is finite and there exist efficient algorithms for membership testing and to compute a unique representation.*
3. *There exists a distinguished element $\tilde{x} \in \mathcal{X}$ with known representation.*
4. *There exists an efficient algorithm to evaluate the group action, i.e. to compute $g \star x$ given g and x.*

Then we call $\tilde{x} \in \mathcal{X}$ the origin and $(\mathcal{G}, \mathcal{X}, \star, \tilde{x})$ an effective group action (EGA).

In practice, the requirements from the definition of EGA are often too strong. Therefore we will consider the weaker notion of restricted effective group actions.

Definition 3 (Restricted Effective Group Action). *Let $(\mathcal{G}, \mathcal{X}, \star)$ be a group action and let $\boldsymbol{g} = (g_1, ..., g_n)$ be a generating set for $\mathcal{G}$. Assume that the following properties are satisfied:*

1. *The group $\mathcal{G}$ is finite and $n = poly(\log(\#\mathcal{G}))$.*
2. *The set $\mathcal{X}$ is finite and there exist efficient algorithms for membership testing and to compute a unique representation.*
3. *There exists a distinguished element $\tilde{x} \in \mathcal{X}$ with known representation.*
4. *There exists an efficient algorithm that given $g_i \in \boldsymbol{g}$ and $x \in \mathcal{X}$, outputs $g_i \star x$ and $g_i^{-1} \star x$.*

Then we call $(\mathcal{G}, \mathcal{X}, \star, \tilde{x})$ a restricted effective group action (REGA).

3.1 Isogeny-Based REGAs

An important instantiation of REGAs is provided by isogeny-based group actions. We will focus on the CSIDH setting and present a refined definition of REGAs tailored to this situation.

Let p be a large prime of the form $p = 4 \cdot \ell_1 \cdots \ell_n - 1$, where the ℓ_i are small distinct odd primes. Fix the elliptic curve $E_0 : y^2 = x^3 + x$ over $\mathbb{F}_p$. The curve E_0 is supersingular and its $\mathbb{F}_p$-rational endomorphism ring is $\mathcal{O} = \mathbb{Z}[\pi]$, where π is the Frobenius endomorphism. Let $\mathcal{E}\ell\ell_p(\mathcal{O})$ be the set of elliptic curves defined over $\mathbb{F}_p$, with endomorphism ring $\mathcal{O}$. The ideal class group $cl(\mathcal{O})$ acts on the set $\mathcal{E}\ell\ell_p(\mathcal{O})$, i.e., there is a map

$$\star : cl(\mathcal{O}) \times \mathcal{E}\ell\ell_p(\mathcal{O}) \to \mathcal{E}\ell\ell_p(\mathcal{O})$$
$$([\mathfrak{a}], E) \mapsto [\mathfrak{a}] \star E,$$

satisfying the properties from Definition 1 [11, Theorem 7]. Moreover the analysis in [11] readily shows that $(cl(\mathcal{O}), \mathcal{E}\ell\ell_p(\mathcal{O}), \star, E_0)$ is indeed a REGA.

Elliptic curves in $\mathcal{E}\ell\ell_p(\mathcal{O})$ admit equations of the form $F_A : y^2 = x^3 + Ax^2 + x$, which allows to represent them by their Montgomery coefficient $A \in \mathbb{F}_p$. An intrinsic property of the CSIDH group action which is not covered by Definition 3, is the following. For any curve $E_A = [\mathfrak{a}] \star E_0 \in \mathcal{E}\ell\ell_p(\mathcal{O})$, its quadratic twist is easily computed as $(E_A)^t = E_{-A}$ and satisfies the property $(E_A)^t = [\mathfrak{a}]^{-1} \star E_0$.

Definition 4 ((Restricted) Effective Group Action with Twists). *We say that a (R)EGA $(\mathcal{G}, \mathcal{X}, \star, \tilde{x})$ is a (Restricted) Effective Group Action with Twists ((R)EGAT) if there exists an efficient algorithm that given $x = g \star \tilde{x} \in \mathcal{X}$ computes $x^t = g^{-1} \star \tilde{x}$.*

As noted in [11, §10], this property contrasts with the classical group-based setting. It has already been used for the design of new cryptographic primitives based on CSIDH such as the signature scheme CSIFiSh [9] and the OT protocol in [24]. Moreover, it is important to consider twists in the security analysis of schemes based on group actions. In Sect. 5 we use twists to construct an attack on the protocol GA-PAKE$_\ell$ showing that it cannot be securely instantiated with the CSIDH group action. On the other hand, we prove that GA-PAKE$_\ell$ is secure when instantiated with a group action without efficient twisting. The proof for that is given in the full version [1, Appendix C].

3.2   Computational Assumptions

For cryptographic applications, we are interested in (restricted) effective group actions that are equipped with the following hardness properties:

- Given $(x, y) \in \mathcal{X}^2$, it is hard to find $g \in \mathcal{G}$ such that $y = g \star x$.
- Given $(x, y_0, y_1) \in \mathcal{X}^3$, it is hard to find $z = (g_0 \cdot g_1) \star x$, where $g_0, g_1 \in \mathcal{G}$ are such that $y_0 = g_0 \star x$ and $y_1 = g_1 \star x$.

In [5] such group actions are called cryptographic group actions, and in [12] they are called hard homogeneous spaces.

The two hardness assumptions are the natural generalizations of the discrete logarithm assumption and the Diffie-Hellman assumption in the traditional group based setting. In analogy to this setting, we introduce the notation

$$\mathsf{GA\text{-}CDH}_x(y_0, y_1) = g_0 \star y_1, \quad \text{where } g_0 \in \mathcal{G} \text{ such that } y_0 = g_0 \star x$$

and define the decision oracle

$$\mathsf{GA\text{-}DDH}_x(y_0, y_1, z) = \begin{cases} 1 & \text{if } \mathsf{GA\text{-}CDH}_x(y_0, y_1) = z, \\ 0 & \text{otherwise.} \end{cases}$$

For both, GA-CDH and GA-DDH, we omit the index x if $x = \tilde{x}$, i.e., we set $\mathsf{GA\text{-}CDH}_{\tilde{x}}(y_0, y_1) = \mathsf{GA\text{-}CDH}(y_0, y_1)$ and equivalently for $\mathsf{GA\text{-}DDH}_{\tilde{x}}(y_0, y_1, z)$.

We now introduce three computational problems GA-StCDH, GA-GapCDH, SqInv-GA-StCDH (Definitions 5 to 7). The security of our PAKE protocols relies on the hardness of these problems.

The first two problems are variants of the standard Diffie-Hellman problem, where an adversary is either given access to some fixed-basis decision oracles (indicated by the prefix *strong*) or to a general decision oracle (indicated by the prefix *gap*). Note that these problems were already defined and used in previous work [16,22,23,31]. Since the problem from Definition 7 has not been studied in any previous work, we provide evidence for its hardness in Remark 3.

Definition 5 (Group Action Strong Computational Diffie-Hellman Problem (GA-StCDH)). *On input* $(g \star \tilde{x}, h \star \tilde{x}) \in \mathcal{X}^2$, *the* GA-StCDH *problem requires to compute the set element* $(g \cdot h) \star \tilde{x}$. *To an effective group action* XXX $\in \{$EGA, REGA, EGAT, REGAT$\}$, *we associate the advantage function of an adversary* $\mathcal{A}$ *as*

$$\mathsf{Adv}_{\mathsf{XXX}}^{\mathsf{GA\text{-}StCDH}}(\mathcal{A}) := \Pr[\mathcal{A}^{\mathsf{GA\text{-}DDH}(g \star \tilde{x}, \cdot, \cdot)}(g \star \tilde{x}, h \star \tilde{x}) \Rightarrow (g \cdot h) \star \tilde{x}],$$

where $(g, h) \xleftarrow{\$} \mathcal{G}^2$ *and* $\mathcal{A}$ *has access to decision oracle* $\mathsf{GA\text{-}DDH}(g \star \tilde{x}, \cdot, \cdot)$.

Definition 6 (Group Action Gap Computational Diffie-Hellman Problem (GA-GapCDH)). *On input* $(g \star \tilde{x}, h \star \tilde{x}) \in \mathcal{X}^2$, *the* GA-GapCDH *problem requires to compute the set element* $(g \cdot h) \star \tilde{x}$. *To an effective group action* XXX $\in \{$EGA, REGA, EGAT, REGAT$\}$, *we associate the advantage function of an adversary* $\mathcal{A}$ *as*

$$\mathsf{Adv}_{\mathsf{XXX}}^{\mathsf{GA\text{-}GapCDH}}(\mathcal{A}) := \Pr[\mathcal{A}^{\mathsf{GA\text{-}DDH}_*}(g \star \tilde{x}, h \star \tilde{x}) \Rightarrow (g \cdot h) \star \tilde{x}],$$

where $(g, h) \xleftarrow{\$} \mathcal{G}^2$ *and* $\mathcal{A}$ *has access to a general decision oracle* $\mathsf{GA\text{-}DDH}_*$.

Remark 2. A group action where the group action computational Diffie-Hellman problem (without any decision oracle) is hard, is the same as a weak unpredictable group action as defined by Alamati et al. [5]. Further details are given in the full version [1, Appendix A]. Also note that the ability to compute the twist of a set element does not help in solving these problems. Hence, all results based on these problems remain true for (R)EGAT.

Definition 7 (Square-Inverse GA-StCDH (SqInv-GA-StCDH)). *On input* $x = g \star \tilde{x}$, *the* SqInv-GA-StCDH *problem requires to find a tuple* $(y, y_0, y_1) \in \mathcal{X}^3$ *such that* $y_0 = g^2 \star y$ *and* $y_1 = g^{-1} \star y$. *For a group action* XXX $\in$ {EGA, REGA, EGAT, REGAT}, *we define the advantage function of* $\mathcal{A}$ *as*

$$\mathsf{Adv}_{\mathsf{XXX}}^{\mathsf{SqInv\text{-}GA\text{-}StCDH}}(\mathcal{A}) := \Pr\left[\begin{array}{c} y_0 = \mathsf{GA\text{-}CDH}_{x^t}(x, y) \\ y_1 = \mathsf{GA\text{-}CDH}(x^t, y) \end{array} \middle| \begin{array}{c} g \xleftarrow{\$} \mathcal{G} \\ x = g \star \tilde{x} \\ (y, y_0, y_1) \leftarrow \mathcal{A}^O(x) \end{array} \right],$$

where $O = \{\mathsf{GA\text{-}DDH}_{x^t}(x, \cdot, \cdot), \mathsf{GA\text{-}DDH}(x, \cdot, \cdot)\}$.

Remark 3. Intuitively SqInv-GA-StCDH is hard if we assume that the adversary can only use the group and twist operation. To go into more detail, $\mathcal{A}$ can choose y only based on known elements, that is either based on $\tilde{x}$, its input x or x^t.

If $\mathcal{A}$ chooses $y = \alpha \star \tilde{x}$ for some $\alpha \in \mathcal{G}$, then it can easily compute $y_1 = \alpha \star x^t$, but not $y_0 = \alpha g^2 \star \tilde{x}$. If $\mathcal{A}$ chooses $y = \alpha \star x$, then computing $y_1 = \alpha \star \tilde{x}$ is trivial, but computing $y_0 = \alpha g^3 \star \tilde{x}$ is hard. If $\mathcal{A}$ chooses $y = \alpha \star x^t$, then computing $y_0 = \alpha \star x$ is trivial, but computing $y_1 = \alpha g^{-2} \star \tilde{x}$ is hard.

4   Password Authenticated Key Exchange

Password-authenticated key exchange (PAKE) allows two parties, typically referred to as the user and the server, to establish a shared session key with the help of a short secret, known as a password, which can be drawn from a small set of possible values. To prove security of a PAKE protocol, we use the indistinguishability-based model by Bellare, Pointcheval and Rogaway [7] and its extension to multiple test queries by Abdalla, Fouque and Pointcheval [2].

The name spaces for users $\mathcal{U}$ and servers $\mathcal{S}$ are assumed to be disjoint. Each pair of user and server $(\mathsf{U}, \mathsf{S}) \in \mathcal{U} \times \mathcal{S}$ holds a shared password $\mathsf{pw}_{\mathsf{US}}$. A party P denotes either a user or server. Each party P has multiple instances π_P^i and each instance has its own state. We denote the session key space by $\mathcal{K}$. Passwords are bit strings of length ℓ and we define the password space as $\mathcal{PW} \subsetneq \{0,1\}^\ell$.

Instance State. The state of an instance π_P^i is a tuple $(\mathsf{e}, \mathsf{tr}, K, \mathsf{acc})$ where

- e stores the (secret) ephemeral values chosen by the party in that instance.
  tr stores the trace of that instance, i.e., the user and server name involved in the protocol execution and the messages sent and received by that instance.
- K is the accepted session key.
- acc is a Boolean flag that indicates whether the instance has accepted the session key. As long as the instance did not receive the last message, acc $= \bot$.

To access individual components of the state, we write $\pi_\mathsf{P}^t.\{\mathsf{e}, \mathsf{tr}, K, \mathsf{acc}\}$.

Partnering. Partnering is defined via matching conversations. In particular, a user instance $\pi_U^{t_0}$ and a server instance $\pi_S^{t_1}$ are partnered iff

$$\pi_U^{t_0}.\mathrm{acc} = \pi_S^{t_1}.\mathrm{acc} = \mathbf{true} \quad \mathbf{and} \quad \pi_U^{t_0}.\mathrm{tr} = \pi_S^{t_1}.\mathrm{tr}.$$

Two user instances are never partnered, neither are two server instances. We define a partner predicate $\mathsf{Partner}(\pi_{P_0}^{t_0}, \pi_{P_1}^{t_1})$ which outputs 1 if the two instances $\pi_{P_0}^{t_0}$ and $\pi_{P_1}^{t_1}$ are partnered and 0 otherwise.

Security Experiment. The security experiment is played between a challenger and an adversary $\mathcal{A}$. The challenger draws a random challenge bit β and creates the public parameters. Then it outputs the public parameters to $\mathcal{A}$. Now $\mathcal{A}$ has access to the following oracles:

- EXECUTE(U, t_0, S, t_1): one complete protocol execution between user instance $\pi_U^{t_0}$ and server instance $\pi_S^{t_1}$. This query models security against passive adversaries.
- SENDINIT, SENDRESP, SENDTERMINIT, SENDTERMRESP: send oracles to model security against active adversaries. SENDTERMRESP is only available for three-message protocols.
- CORRUPT(U, S): outputs the shared password pw_{US} of U and S.
- REVEAL(P, t): outputs the session key of instance π_P^t.
- TEST(P, t): challenge query. Depending on the challenge bit β, the experiment outputs either the session key of instance π_P^t or a uniformly random key. By $\pi_P^t.\mathrm{test} = \mathbf{true}$, we mark an instance as tested.

We denote the experiment by $\mathsf{Exp_{PAKE}}$. The pseudocode is given in G_0 in Fig. 5, instantiated with our first PAKE protocol.

Freshness. During the game, we register if a query is allowed to prevent trivial wins. Therefore, we define a freshness predicate $\mathsf{Fresh}(P, i)$. An instance π_P^t is fresh iff

1. π_P^t accepted.
2. π_P^t was not queried to TEST or REVEAL before.
3. At least one of the following conditions holds:
   3.1 π_P^t accepted during a query to EXECUTE.
   3.2 There exists more than one partner instance.
   3.3 A unique fresh partner instance exists.
   3.4 No partner exists and CORRUPT was not queried.

Definition 8 (Security of PAKE). *We define the security experiment, partnering and freshness conditions as above. The advantage of an adversary $\mathcal{A}$ against a password authenticated key exchange protocol PAKE in $\mathsf{Exp_{PAKE}}$ is defined as*

$$\mathsf{Adv_{PAKE}}(\mathcal{A}) := \left| \Pr[\mathsf{Exp_{PAKE}} \Rightarrow 1] - \frac{1}{2} \right|.$$

A PAKE is considered secure if the best the adversary can do is to perform an online dictionary attack. More concretely, this means that the advantage of the adversary should be negligibly close to $q_s/|\mathcal{PW}|$ when passwords are drawn uniformly and independently from $\mathcal{PW}$, where q_s is the number of send queries made by the adversary.

Note that this definition captures weak forward secrecy. In the full version of our paper, we give an extended security definition capturing also perfect forward secrecy, as well as proofs for our protocols [1, Appendix F].

5 First Attempt: Protocol GA-PAKE$_\ell$

The GA-PAKE$_\ell$ protocol was already introduced in the introduction (Sect. 1). We refer to Fig. 1 for a description of the protocol. In contrast to the two PAKE protocols from Sects. 6 and 7, GA-PAKE$_\ell$ is not secure for EGATs, i.e., if it is possible to compute twists of set elements efficiently. In particular it should not be instantiated with the CSIDH-group action. However, it is instructive to examine its security and it serves as a good motivation for the design of the two secure PAKE protocols X-GA-PAKE$_\ell$ and Com-GA-PAKE$_\ell$.

In this section we present an offline dictionary attack against GA-PAKE$_\ell$ for (R)EGAT. However, if twisting is hard, then we can prove security of GA-PAKE$_\ell$ based on a hardness assumption that is similar to the simultaneous Diffie-Hellman problem which was introduced to the security of TBPEKE and CPace [3,26]. The proof for GA-PAKE$_\ell$ is given in the full version [1, Appendix C].

Proposition 1. *For EGATs, the protocol GA-PAKE$_\ell$ is vulnerable to offline dictionary attacks.*

Proof. We construct an adversary $\mathcal{A}$ that takes the role of the server. The attack is summarized in Fig. 3. After receiving x^U, the adversary computes

$$x_i^S = \tilde{s}_i \star (x_i^U)^t = \tilde{s}_i \star (u_i \star x_{b_i})^t = (\tilde{s}_i \cdot u_i^{-1}) \star x_{b_i}^t = (\tilde{s}_i \cdot u_i^{-1} \cdot g_{b_i}^{-1}) \star \tilde{x}$$

for each $i \in [\ell]$ and sends $x_1^S, \ldots, x_\ell^S$ to the user. Then the user computes $z_i = u_i \star x_i^S = (\tilde{s}_i \cdot g_{b_i}^{-1}) \star \tilde{x} = \tilde{s}_i \star x_{b_i}^t$. For each $i \in [\ell]$, the adversary $\mathcal{A}$ can now compute z_i for both possibilities $b_i = 0$ and $b_i = 1$. This allows him to compute K for all possible passwords $\mathsf{pw} \in \mathcal{PW} \subsetneq \{0,1\}^\ell$ (being offline). $\square$

This offline attack can easily be used to win the security experiment with high probability. $\mathcal{A}$ only needs to issue two send queries. It chooses any user U, initiates a session and computes its message $x_1^S, \ldots, x_\ell^S$ as described in Fig. 3. It reveals the corresponding session key and starts its offline attack by brute forcing all $\mathsf{pw} \in \mathcal{PW}$ until it finds a match for a candidate pw^*. Now $\mathcal{A}$ issues its second send query. This time it computes the message following the protocol using pw^* and derives a key K^*. It issues a test query and gets K_β. If $K^* = K_\beta$, then it outputs 0, otherwise it outputs 1. In case there is more than one password

$$\boxed{\begin{array}{ll}
\textbf{User U} & \textbf{Adversary } \mathcal{A} \\[2pt]
\multicolumn{2}{c}{\mathsf{crs} := (x_0, x_1) \in \mathcal{X}^2,} \\
\multicolumn{2}{c}{\mathsf{pw} := (b_1, ..., b_\ell) \in \{0,1\}^\ell} \\[4pt]
(u_1, ..., u_\ell) \xleftarrow{\$} \mathcal{G}^\ell & (\tilde{s}_1, ..., \tilde{s}_\ell) \xleftarrow{\$} \mathcal{G}^\ell \\
\textbf{for } i \in [\ell] & \textbf{for } i \in [\ell] \\
x_i^{\mathsf{U}} := u_i \star x_{b_i} & x_i^{\mathsf{S}} := \tilde{s}_i \star (x_i^{\mathsf{U}})^t \\
\textbf{for } i \in [\ell] & \textbf{for } i \in [\ell] \\
z_i := u_i \star x_i^{\mathsf{S}} & z_i := \tilde{s}_i \star x_0^t \text{ for } b_i = 0 \\
& z_i := \tilde{s}_i \star x_1^t \text{ for } b_i = 1 \\[4pt]
\multicolumn{2}{c}{K := \mathsf{H}(\mathsf{U}, \mathsf{S}, x_1^{\mathsf{U}}, ..., x_\ell^{\mathsf{U}}, x_1^{\mathsf{S}}, ..., x_\ell^{\mathsf{S}}, \mathsf{pw}, z_1, ..., z_\ell)}
\end{array}}$$

with arrows: $x^{\mathsf{U}} = (x_1^{\mathsf{U}}, ..., x_\ell^{\mathsf{U}})$ sent right, $x^{\mathsf{S}} = (x_1^{\mathsf{S}}, ..., x_\ell^{\mathsf{S}})$ sent left.

Fig. 3. Attack against GA-PAKE$_\ell$ using twists.

candidate, i.e., two inputs to H lead to the same K^*, then $\mathcal{A}$ can issue another send and reveal query to rule out false positives. In the end, it can still happen that $\beta = 1$ and $K^* = K$, but this event only occurs with probability $1/|\mathcal{K}|$.

Corollary 1. *For any adversary $\mathcal{A}$ against* GA-PAKE$_\ell$ *instantiated with an EGAT, we have* $\Pr[\mathsf{Exp}_{\mathsf{GA\text{-}PAKE}_\ell} \Rightarrow 1] = 1 - \frac{1}{|\mathcal{K}|}$.

6   X-GA-PAKE$_\ell$: One-Round PAKE from Group Actions

In the previous section we showed that GA-PAKE$_\ell$ is insecure when instantiated with an EGAT. Here, we present the modification X-GA-PAKE$_\ell$, which impedes the offline dictionary attack presented in that section. Broadly speaking, the idea is to double the message size of both parties in the first flow. In the second flow it is then necessary to compute certain "cross products" which is only possible if the previous message has been honestly generated. The letter X in X-GA-PAKE$_\ell$ stands for cross product.

By means of these modifications, the protocol X-GA-PAKE$_\ell$ is provably secure for EGATs. We show that its security can be reduced to the hardness of the computational problems GA-StCDH and SqInv-GA-StCDH (Theorem 1).

The setup for X-GA-PAKE$_\ell$ is the same as for GA-PAKE$_\ell$. The $\mathsf{crs} = (x_0, x_1)$ comprises two elements of the set $\mathcal{X}$, and the shared password is a bit string $(b_1, \ldots, b_\ell)$ of length ℓ. In the first flow of the protocol the user generates $2 \cdot \ell$ random group elements, $u_1, \ldots, u_\ell$ and $\hat{u}_1, \ldots, \hat{u}_\ell$. Using these elements it computes the set elements $x_i^{\mathsf{U}} = u_i \star x_{b_i}$ and $\hat{x}_i^{\mathsf{U}} = \hat{u}_i \star x_{b_i}$ for each $i \in [\ell]$ and sends these to the server. Simultaneously, the server generates the random group elements $s_1, \ldots, s_\ell$ and $\hat{s}_1, \ldots, \hat{s}_\ell$, which it uses to compute the set elements $x_i^{\mathsf{S}} = s_i \star x_{b_i}$ and $\hat{x}_i^{\mathsf{S}} = \hat{s}_i \star x_{b_i}$ for each $i \in [\ell]$ and sends these to the user. Upon receiving the set elements from the other party, both the server and the user compute

$$z_{i,1} = u_i \star x_i^{\mathsf{S}} = s_i \star x_i^{\mathsf{U}}, \quad z_{i,2} = \hat{u}_i \star x_i^{\mathsf{S}} = s_i \star \hat{x}_i^{\mathsf{U}}, \quad z_{i,3} = u_i \star \hat{x}_i^{\mathsf{S}} = \hat{s}_i \star x_i^{\mathsf{U}},$$

$$\boxed{\begin{array}{ll}
\textbf{User U} & \textbf{Server S} \\
\multicolumn{2}{c}{\mathsf{crs} := (x_0, x_1) \in \mathcal{X}^2,} \\
\multicolumn{2}{c}{\mathsf{pw} := (b_1, ..., b_\ell) \in \{0,1\}^\ell} \\
\end{array}}$$

Fig. 4. PAKE protocol X-GA-PAKE$_\ell$ from group actions.

for each $i \in [\ell]$. Finally, these elements are used to compute the session key K. The protocol is sketched in Fig. 4.

We now prove the security of X-GA-PAKE$_\ell$ for EGATs.

Theorem 1 (Security of X-GA-PAKE$_\ell$). *For any adversary $\mathcal{A}$ against X-GA-PAKE$_\ell$ that issues at most q_e execute queries and q_s send queries and where H is modeled as a random oracle, there exist an adversary $\mathcal{B}_1$ against GA-StCDH and an adversary $\mathcal{B}_2$ against Sqlnv-GA-StCDH such that*

$$\mathsf{Adv}_{\text{X-GA-PAKE}_\ell}(\mathcal{A}) \le \mathsf{Adv}_{\mathsf{EGAT}}^{\mathsf{GA\text{-}StCDH}}(\mathcal{B}_1) + \mathsf{Adv}_{\mathsf{EGAT}}^{\mathsf{Sqlnv\text{-}GA\text{-}StCDH}}(\mathcal{B}_2) + \frac{q_s}{|\mathcal{PW}|} + \frac{(q_s + q_e)^2}{|\mathcal{G}|^{2\ell}}.$$

Before proving Theorem 1, we will introduce a new computational assumption which is tailored to the protocol.

Definition 9 (Double Simultaneous GA-StCDH (DSim-GA-StCDH)). *On input $(x_0, x_1, w_0, w_1) = (g_0 \star \tilde{x}, g_1 \star \tilde{x}, h_0 \star \tilde{x}, h_1 \star \tilde{x}) \in \mathcal{X}^4$, the DSim-GA-StCDH problem requires to find a tuple $(y, y_0, y_1, y_2, y_3) \in \mathcal{X}^5$ such that*

$$(y_0, y_1, y_2, y_3) = (g_0^{-1} \cdot h_0 \star y, \ g_0^{-1} \cdot h_1 \star y, \ g_1^{-1} \cdot h_0 \star y, \ g_1^{-1} \cdot h_1 \star y).$$

For a group action $\mathsf{XXX} \in \{\mathsf{EGA}, \mathsf{REGA}, \mathsf{EGAT}, \mathsf{REGAT}\}$, we define the advantage function of an adversary $\mathcal{A}$ as

$$\mathsf{Adv}_{\mathsf{XXX}}^{\mathsf{DSim\text{-}GA\text{-}StCDH}}(\mathcal{A}) := \Pr\left[\begin{array}{l|l}
y_0 = \mathsf{GA\text{-}CDH}_{x_0}(w_0, y) & (g_0, g_1, h_0, h_1) \xleftarrow{\$} \mathcal{G}^4 \\
y_1 = \mathsf{GA\text{-}CDH}_{x_0}(w_1, y) & (x_0, x_1) = (y_0 \star \tilde{x}, y_1 \star \tilde{x}) \\
y_2 = \mathsf{GA\text{-}CDH}_{x_1}(w_0, y) & (w_0, w_1) = (h_0 \star \tilde{x}, h_1 \star \tilde{x}) \\
y_3 = \mathsf{GA\text{-}CDH}_{x_1}(w_1, y) & (y, y_0, y_1, y_2, y_3) \leftarrow \mathcal{A}^{\mathsf{O}}(x_0, x_1, w_0, w_1)
\end{array}\right],$$

where $\mathsf{O} = \{\mathsf{GA\text{-}DDH}_{x_j}(w_i, \cdot, \cdot)\}_{i,j \in \{0,1\}}$.

Remark 4. Note that DSim-GA-StCDH may be viewed as the doubled version of the Sim-GA-StCDH problem defined in the full version of the paper [1, Definition

12]. The latter is an assumption underlying the security of GA-PAKE$_\ell$ and (in the notation of the above problem) it only requires to find the tuple (y, y_0, y_2). For a group action with twists, this admits the trivial solution $(y, y_0, y_2) = (w_0^t, x_0^t, x_1^t)$. Such a trivial solution is inhibited by requiring to find y_1 and y_3 as well.

The DSim-GA-StCDH problem is implied by SqInv-GA-StCDH, more precisely

$$\mathsf{Adv}_{\mathsf{EGAT}}^{\mathsf{DSim\text{-}GA\text{-}StCDH}}(\mathcal{A}) \leq \mathsf{Adv}_{\mathsf{EGAT}}^{\mathsf{SqInv\text{-}GA\text{-}StCDH}}(\mathcal{B}). \tag{1}$$

A proof of this implication is given in the full version [1, Lemma 1].

Proof (of Theorem 1). Let $\mathcal{A}$ be an adversary against X-GA-PAKE$_\ell$. Consider the games in Figs. 5, 7, 8.

GAME G_0. This is the original game, hence

$$\mathsf{Adv}_{\mathsf{X\text{-}GA\text{-}PAKE}_\ell}(\mathcal{A}) \leq |\Pr[\mathsf{G}_0 \Rightarrow 1] - 1/2|.$$

GAME G_1. In game G_1, we raise flag $\mathbf{bad}_{\mathrm{coll}}$ whenever a server instance computes the same trace as any other accepted instance (line 69) or a user instance computes the same trace as any other accepted user instance (line 84). In this case, SENDRESP or SENDTERMINIT return $\bot$. We do the same if a trace that is computed in an EXECUTE query collides with one of a previously accepted instance (line 28). Due to the difference lemma,

$$|\Pr[\mathsf{G}_1 \Rightarrow 1] - \Pr[\mathsf{G}_0 \Rightarrow 1]| \leq \Pr[\mathbf{bad}_{\mathrm{coll}}].$$

Note that when $\mathbf{bad}_{\mathrm{coll}}$ is not raised, each instance is unique and has at most one partner. In order to bound $\mathbf{bad}_{\mathrm{coll}}$, recall that the trace of an oracle π_P^t consists of $(\mathsf{U}, \mathsf{S}, x^\mathsf{U} = (x_1^\mathsf{U}, ..., x_\ell^\mathsf{U}), \hat{x}^\mathsf{U} = (\hat{x}_1^\mathsf{U}, ...\hat{x}_\ell^\mathsf{U}), x^\mathsf{S} = (x_1^\mathsf{S}, ..., x_\ell^\mathsf{S}), \hat{x}^\mathsf{S} = (\hat{x}_1^\mathsf{S}, ..., \hat{x}_\ell^\mathsf{S}))$, where at least one of the message pairs $(x^\mathsf{U}, \hat{x}^\mathsf{U})$ or $(x^\mathsf{S}, \hat{x}^\mathsf{S})$ was chosen by the game. Thus, $\mathbf{bad}_{\mathrm{coll}}$ can only happen if all those $2 \cdot \ell$ set elements collide with all $2 \cdot \ell$ set elements of another instance. The probability that this happens for two (fixed) sessions is $|\mathcal{G}|^{-2\ell}$, hence the union bound over q_e and q_s sessions yields

$$|\Pr[\mathsf{G}_1 \Rightarrow 1] - \Pr[\mathsf{G}_0 \Rightarrow 1]| \leq \Pr[\mathbf{bad}_{\mathrm{coll}}] \leq \binom{q_e + q_s}{2} \cdot \frac{1}{|\mathcal{G}|^{2\ell}} \leq \frac{(q_e + q_s)^2}{|\mathcal{G}|^{2\ell}}.$$

GAME G_2. In game G_2, we make the freshness explicit. To each oracle π_P^t, we assign an additional variable $\pi_\mathsf{P}^t.\mathrm{fr}$ which is updated during the game. In particular, all instances used in execute queries are marked as fresh (line 34).

An instance is fresh if the password was not corrupted yet (lines 72, 89). Otherwise, it is not fresh (lines 74, 91). For user instances we also check if there exists a fresh partner (line 87). If $\mathcal{A}$ issues a CORRUPT query later, the freshness variable will also be updated (line 103). When the session key of an instance is revealed, this instance and its potential partner instance are marked as not fresh (line 41). On a query to test, the game then only checks the freshness variable (line 44). These are only a conceptual changes, hence

$$\Pr[\mathsf{G}_2 \Rightarrow 1] = \Pr[\mathsf{G}_1 \Rightarrow 1].$$

GAMES G_0-G_4

```
00 (g_0, g_1) ←$ G²
01 (x_0, x_1) := (g_0 ⋆ x̃, g_1 ⋆ x̃)
02 (C, T) := (∅, ∅)
03 bad_coll := false
04 β ←$ {0, 1}
05 for (U, S) ∈ U × S
06    pw_US ←$ PW
07 β' ← A^O(x_0, x_1)
08 return [[β = β']]
```

EXECUTE(U, t_0, S, t_1)
```
09 if π_U^{t_0} ≠ ⊥ or π_S^{t_1} ≠ ⊥
10    return ⊥
11 (b_1, ..., b_ℓ) := pw_US                                    //G_0-G_3
12 u := (u_1, ..., u_ℓ) ←$ G^ℓ
13 û := (û_1, ..., û_ℓ) ←$ G^ℓ
14 s := (s_1, ..., s_ℓ) ←$ G^ℓ
15 ŝ := (ŝ_1, ..., ŝ_ℓ) ←$ G^ℓ
16 x^U := (x_1^U, ..., x_ℓ^U) := (u_1 ⋆ x_{b_1}, ..., u_ℓ ⋆ x_{b_ℓ})   //G_0-G_3
17 x̂^U := (x̂_1^U, ..., x̂_ℓ^U) := (û_1 ⋆ x_{b_1}, ..., û_ℓ ⋆ x_{b_ℓ})   //G_0-G_3
18 x^S := (x_1^S, ..., x_ℓ^S) := (s_1 ⋆ x_{b_1}, ..., s_ℓ ⋆ x_{b_ℓ})   //G_0-G_3
19 x̂^S := (x̂_1^S, ..., x̂_ℓ^S) := (ŝ_1 ⋆ x_{b_1}, ..., ŝ_ℓ ⋆ x_{b_ℓ})   //G_0-G_0
20 for i ∈ [ℓ] :                                              //G_0-G_3
21    z_i := (z_{i,1}, z_{i,2}, z_{i,3}) := (u_i ⋆ x_i^S, û_i ⋆ x_i^S, u_i ⋆ x̂_i^S)  //G_0-G_3
22 z := (z_1, ..., z_ℓ)                                       //G_0-G_3
23 x^U := (x_1^U, ..., x_ℓ^U) := (u_1 ⋆ x̃, ..., u_ℓ ⋆ x̃)       //G_4
24 x̂^U := (x̂_1^U, ..., x̂_ℓ^U) := (û_1 ⋆ x̃, ..., û_ℓ ⋆ x̃)       //G_4
25 x^S := (x_1^S, ..., x_ℓ^S) := (s_1 ⋆ x̃, ..., s_ℓ ⋆ x̃)       //G_4
26 x̂^S := (x̂_1^S, ..., x̂_ℓ^S) := (ŝ_1 ⋆ x̃, ..., ŝ_ℓ ⋆ x̃)       //G_4
27 if ∃P ∈ U ∪ S, t' s.t. π_P^{t'}.tr = (U, S, x^U, x̂^U, x^S, x̂^S)  //G_1-G_4
28    bad_coll := true                                        //G_1-G_4
29    return ⊥                                                //G_1-G_4
30 K := H(U, S, x^U, x̂^U, x^S, x̂^S, pw_US, z)                  //G_0-G_2
31 K ←$ K                                                     //G_3-G_4
32 π_U^{t_0} := ((u, û), (U, S, x^U, x̂^U, x^S, x̂^S), K, true)
33 π_S^{t_1} := ((s, ŝ), (U, S, x^U, x̂^U, x^S, x̂^S), K, true)
34 (π_U^{t_0}.fr, π_S^{t_1}.fr) := (true, true)               //G_2-G_4
35 return (U, x^U, x̂^U, S, x^S, x̂^S)
```

REVEAL(P, t)
```
36 if π_P^t.acc ≠ true or π_P^t.test = true
37    return ⊥
38 if ∃P' ∈ U ∪ S, t' s.t. Partner(π_P^t, π_{P'}^{t'}) = 1
      and π_{P'}^t.test = true
39    return ⊥
40 ∀(P', t') s.t. π_{P'}^{t'}.tr = π_P^t.tr                    //G_2-G_4
41    π_{P'}^t.fr := false                                     //G_2-G_4
42 return π_P^t.K
```

TEST(P, t)
```
43 if Fresh(π_P^t) = false return ⊥                          //G_0-G_1
44 if π_P^t.fr = false return ⊥                              //G_2-G_4
45 K_0^* := REVEAL(P, t)
46 if K_0^* = ⊥ return ⊥
47 K_1^* ←$ K
48 π_P^t.test := true
49 return K_β^*
```

H(U, S, x^U, $x̂^U$, x^S, $x̂^S$, pw, z)
```
50 if T[U, S, x^U, x̂^U, x^S, x̂^S, pw, z] = K ≠ ⊥
51    return K
52 T[U, S, x^U, x̂^U, x^S, x̂^S, pw, Z] ←$ K
53 return T[U, S, x^U, x̂^U, x^S, x̂^S, pw, z]
```

SENDINIT(U, t, S)
```
54 if π_U^t ≠ ⊥ return ⊥
55 (b_1, ..., b_ℓ) := pw_US
56 u := (u_1, ..., u_ℓ) ←$ G^ℓ
57 û := (û_1, ..., û_ℓ) ←$ G^ℓ
58 x^U := (x_1^U, ..., x_ℓ^U) := (u_1 ⋆ x_{b_1}, ..., u_ℓ ⋆ x_{b_ℓ})
59 x̂^U := (x̂_1^U, ..., x̂_ℓ^U) := (û_1 ⋆ x_{b_1}, ..., û_ℓ ⋆ x_{b_ℓ})
60 π_U^t := ((u, û), (U, S, x^U, x̂^U, ⊥, ⊥), ⊥, ⊥)
61 π_U^t.fr := false                                         //G_2-G_4
62 return (U, x^U, x̂^U)
```

SENDRESP(S, t, U, x^U, $x̂^U$)
```
63 if π_S^t ≠ ⊥ return ⊥
64 (b_1, ..., b_ℓ) := pw_US
65 (s_1, ..., s_ℓ) ←$ G^ℓ
66 x^S := (x_1^S, ..., x_ℓ^S) := (s_1 ⋆ x_{b_1}, ..., s_ℓ ⋆ x_{b_ℓ})
67 x̂^S := (x̂_1^S, ..., x̂_ℓ^S) := (ŝ_1 ⋆ x_{b_1}, ..., ŝ_ℓ ⋆ x_{b_ℓ})
68 if ∃P ∈ U ∪ S, t' s.t. π_P^{t'}.tr = (U, S, x^U, x̂^U, x^S, x̂^S)  //G_1-G_4
69    bad_coll := true                                        //G_1-G_4
70    return ⊥                                                //G_1-G_4
71 if (U, S) ∉ C                                              //G_2-G_4
72    π_S^t.fr := true                                         //G_2-G_4
73 else                                                       //G_2-G_4
74    π_S^t.fr := false                                        //G_2-G_4
75 for i ∈ [ℓ] :
76    z_i := (z_{i,1}, z_{i,2}, z_{i,3}) := (s_i ⋆ x_i^U, s ⋆ x̂_i^U, ŝ_i ⋆ x_i^U)
77 z := (z_1, ..., z_ℓ)
78 K := H(U, S, x^U, x̂^U, x^S, x̂^S, pw_US, z)
79 π_S^t := ((s, ŝ), (U, S, x^U, x̂^U, x^S, x̂^S), K, true)
80 return (S, x^S, x̂^S)
```

SENDTERMINIT(U, t, S, x^S, $x̂^S$)
```
81 if π_U^t ≠ ((u, û), (U, S, x^U, x̂^U, ⊥, ⊥), ⊥, ⊥)
82    return ⊥
83 if ∃P ∈ U, t' s.t. π_P^{t'}.tr = (U, S, x^U, x̂^U, x^S, x̂^S)  //G_1-G_4
84    bad_coll := true                                        //G_1-G_4
85    return ⊥                                                //G_1-G_4
86 if ∃t' s.t. π_S^{t'}.tr = (U, S, x^U, x̂^U, x^S, x̂^S)
      and π_S^{t'}.fr = true                                  //G_2-G_4
87    π_U^t.fr := true                                         //G_2-G_4
88 else if (U, S) ∉ C                                         //G_2-G_4
89    π_U^t.fr := true                                         //G_2-G_4
90 else                                                       //G_2-G_4
91    π_U^t.fr := false                                        //G_2-G_4
92 for i ∈ [ℓ] :
93    z_i := (z_{i,1}, z_{i,2}, z_{i,3}) := (u_i ⋆ x_i^S, û_i ⋆ x_i^S, u_i ⋆ x̂_i^S)
94 z := (z_1, ..., z_ℓ)
95 K := H(U, S, x^U, x̂^U, x^S, x̂^S, pw_US, z)
96 π_U^t := ((u, û), (U, S, x^U, x̂^U, x^S, x̂^S), K, true)
97 return true
```

CORRUPT(U, S)
```
98 if (U, S) ∈ C return ⊥
99 for P ∈ {U, S}
100    if ∃t s.t. π_P^t.test = true
         and ∄P' ∈ U ∪ S, t' s.t. Partner(π_P^t, π_{P'}^{t'}) = 1
101       return ⊥
102    ∀π_P^t : if ∄P' ∈ U ∪ S, t' s.t. Partner(π_P^t, π_{P'}^{t'}) = 1  //G_2-G_4
103       π_P^t.fr := false                                   //G_2-G_4
104 C := C ∪ {(U, S)}
105 return pw_US
```

Fig. 5. Games G_0-G_4 for the proof of Theorem 1. A has access to oracles O := {EXECUTE, SENDINIT, SENDRESP, SENDTERMINIT, REVEAL, CORRUPT, TEST, H}.

$\mathcal{B}_1^{\text{GA-DDH}(x,\cdot,\cdot)}(x,y)$

00 $(g_0, g_1) \stackrel{\$}{\leftarrow} \mathcal{G}^2$
01 $(x_0, x_1) := (g_0 \star \tilde{x}, g_1 \star \tilde{x})$
02 $(\mathcal{C}, T, T_e) := (\emptyset, \emptyset, \emptyset)$
03 $\text{bad}_{\text{coll}} := \text{false}$
04 $\beta \stackrel{\$}{\leftarrow} \{0,1\}$
05 for $(U, S) \in \mathcal{U} \times \mathcal{S}$
06 $\quad \text{pw}_{US} \stackrel{\$}{\leftarrow} \mathcal{PW}$
07 $\beta' \leftarrow \mathcal{A}^O(x_0, x_1)$
08 Stop.

$H(U, S, x^U, x^S, \text{pw}, z)$

09 if $\exists (u, \hat{u}, \hat{s})$
   s.t. $(U, S, x^U, \hat{x}^U, x^S, \hat{x}^S, \text{pw}, u, \hat{u}, s, \hat{s}) \in T_e$
10 $\quad (b_1, ..., b_\ell) := \text{pw}$
11 $\quad$ for $i \in [\ell]$
12 $\qquad (z_{i,1}, z_{i,2}, z_{i,3}) := z_i$
13 $\qquad$ if GA-DDH$(x, x_i^S, (u_i^{-1} \cdot g_{b_i}) \star z_{i,1}) = 1$
14 $\qquad\quad$ Stop with $(u_i^{-1} \cdot s_i^{-1} \cdot g_{b_i}) \star z_{i,1}$
15 $\qquad$ if GA-DDH$(x, x_i^S, (\hat{u}_i^{-1} \cdot g_{b_i}) \star z_{i,2}) = 1$
16 $\qquad\quad$ Stop with $(\hat{u}_i^{-1} \cdot s_i^{-1} \cdot g_{b_i}) \star z_{i,2}$
17 $\qquad$ if GA-DDH$(x, x_i^S, (u_i^{-1} \cdot g_{b_i}) \star z_{i,3}) = 1$
18 $\qquad\quad$ Stop with $(u_i^{-1} \cdot \hat{s}_i^{-1} \cdot g_{b_i}) \star z_{i,3}$
19 if $T[U, S, x^U, \hat{x}^U, x^S, \hat{x}^S, \text{pw}, z] = K \neq \bot$
20 $\quad$ return K
21 $T[U, S, x^U, \hat{x}^U, x^S, \hat{x}^S, \text{pw}, z] \stackrel{\$}{\leftarrow} \mathcal{K}$
22 return $T[U, S, x^U, \hat{x}^U, x^S, \hat{x}^S, \text{pw}, z]$

EXECUTE(U, t_0, S, t_1)

23 if $\pi_U^{t_0} \neq \bot$ or $\pi_S^{t_1} \neq \bot$
24 $\quad$ return $\bot$
25 $(b_1, ..., b_\ell) := \text{pw}_{US}$
26 $u := (u_1, ..., u_\ell) \stackrel{\$}{\leftarrow} \mathcal{G}^\ell$
27 $\hat{u} := (\hat{u}_1, ..., \hat{u}_\ell) \stackrel{\$}{\leftarrow} \mathcal{G}^\ell$
28 $s := (s_1, ..., s_\ell) \stackrel{\$}{\leftarrow} \mathcal{G}^\ell$
29 $\hat{s} := (\hat{s}_1, ..., \hat{s}_\ell) \stackrel{\$}{\leftarrow} \mathcal{G}^\ell$
30 $x^U := (x_1^U, ..., x_\ell^U) := (u_1 \star x, ..., u_\ell \star x)$
31 $\hat{x}^U := (\hat{x}_1^U, ..., \hat{x}_\ell^U) := (\hat{u}_1 \star x, ..., \hat{u}_\ell \star x)$
32 $x^S := (x_1^S, ..., x_\ell^S) := (s_1 \star y, ..., s_\ell \star y)$
33 $\hat{x}^S := (\hat{x}_1^S, ..., \hat{x}_\ell^S) := (\hat{s}_1 \star y, ..., \hat{s}_\ell \star y)$
34 if $\exists P \in \mathcal{U} \cup \mathcal{S}, t'$ s.t. $\pi_P^{t'}.\text{tr} = (U, S, x^U, \hat{x}^U, x^S, \hat{x}^S)$
35 $\quad \text{bad}_{\text{coll}} := \text{true}$
36 $\quad$ return $\bot$
37 $\forall z$ s.t. $(U, S, x^U, \hat{x}^U, x^S, \hat{x}^S, \text{pw}_{US}, z) \in T$
38 $\quad$ for $i \in [\ell]$
39 $\qquad (z_{i,1}, z_{i,2}, z_{i,3}) := z_i$
40 $\qquad$ if GA-DDH$(x, x_i^S, (u_i^{-1} \cdot g_{b_i}) \star z_{i,1}) = 1$
41 $\qquad\quad$ Stop with $(u_i^{-1} \cdot s_i^{-1} \cdot g_{b_i}) \star z_{i,1}$
42 $\qquad$ if GA-DDH$(x, x_i^S, (\hat{u}_i^{-1} \cdot g_{b_i}) \star z_{i,2}) = 1$
43 $\qquad\quad$ Stop with $(\hat{u}_i^{-1} \cdot s_i^{-1} \cdot g_{b_i}) \star z_{i,2}$
44 $\qquad$ if GA-DDH$(x, x_i^S, (u_i^{-1} \cdot g_{b_i}) \star z_{i,3}) = 1$
45 $\qquad\quad$ Stop with $(u_i^{-1} \cdot \hat{s}_i^{-1} \cdot g_{b_i}) \star z_{i,3}$
46 $T_e := T_e \cup \{U, S, x^U, \hat{x}^U, x^S, \hat{x}^S, \text{pw}_{US}, u, \hat{u}, s, \hat{s}\}$
47 $K \stackrel{\$}{\leftarrow} \mathcal{K}$
48 $\pi_U^{t_0} := ((u, \hat{u}), (U, S, x^U, \hat{x}^U, x^S, \hat{x}^S), K, \text{true})$
49 $\pi_S^{t_1} := ((s, \hat{s}), (U, S, x^U, \hat{x}^U, x^S, \hat{x}^S), K, \text{true})$
50 $(\pi_U^{t_0}.\text{fr}, \pi_S^{t_1}.\text{fr}) := (\text{true}, \text{true})$
51 return $(U, x^U, \hat{x}^U, S, x^S, \hat{x}^S)$

Fig. 6. Adversary $\mathcal{B}_1$ against GA-StCDH for the proof of Theorem 1. $\mathcal{A}$ has access to oracles $O := \{\text{EXECUTE}, \text{SENDINIT}, \text{SENDRESP}, \text{SENDTERMINIT}, \text{REVEAL}, \text{CORRUPT}, \text{TEST}, H\}$. Oracles SENDINIT, SENDRESP, SENDTERMINIT, REVEAL, CORRUPT and TEST are defined as in G_2. Lines written in blue show how $\mathcal{B}_1$ simulates the game. (Color figure online)

GAME G_3. In game G_3, we choose random keys for instances queried to EXECUTE. We construct adversary $\mathcal{B}_1$ against GA-StCDH in Fig. 6 and show that

$$|\Pr[G_3 \Rightarrow 1] - \Pr[G_2 \Rightarrow 1]| \leq \text{Adv}_{\text{EGAT}}^{\text{GA-StCDH}}(\mathcal{B}_1).$$

Adversary $\mathcal{B}_1$ inputs a GA-StCDH challenge $(x, y) = (g \star \tilde{x}, h \star \tilde{x})$ and has access to a decision oracle GA-DDH$(x, \cdot, \cdot)$. First, it generates the crs elements (x_0, x_1) as in game G_3 and then runs adversary $\mathcal{A}$. Queries to EXECUTE are simulated as follows: It chooses random group elements $u_i, \hat{u}_i$ and $s_i, \hat{s}_i$ for user and server instances and $i \in [\ell]$, but instead of using (x_0, x_1) to compute the set elements, $\mathcal{B}_1$ uses x for the user instance and y for the server instance, independent of the password bits b_i (lines 30 to 33). We can rewrite this as

$$x_i^U = u_i \star x = (u_i \cdot g) \star \tilde{x} = (u_i \cdot g \cdot g_{b_i} \cdot g_{b_i}^{-1}) \star \tilde{x} = \underbrace{(u_i \cdot g \cdot g_{b_i}^{-1})}_{u_i'} \star x_{b_i},$$

where u_i' is the group element that the user actually needs in order to compute the session key. In the same way, $\hat{u}_i' = \hat{u}_i \cdot g \cdot g_{b_i}^{-1}$, $s_i' = s_i \cdot h \cdot g_{b_i}^{-1}$ and $\hat{s}_i' = \hat{s}_i \cdot h \cdot g_{b_i}^{-1}$.

Note that $z_i = (z_{i,1}, z_{i,2}, z_{i,3})$ is implicitly set to

$$z_{i,1} = (u_i' \cdot s_i') \star x_{b_i} = u_i \cdot g \cdot s_i \cdot h \cdot g_{b_i}^{-1} \star \tilde{x},$$

$$z_{i,2} = (\hat{u}_i' \cdot s_i') \star x_{b_i} = \hat{u}_i \cdot g \cdot s_i \cdot h \cdot g_{b_i}^{-1} \star \tilde{x},$$

$$z_{i,3} = (u_i' \cdot \hat{s}_i') \star x_{b_i} = u_i \cdot g \cdot \hat{s}_i \cdot h \cdot g_{b_i}^{-1} \star \tilde{x}.$$

Before choosing a random session key, we check if there has been a query to the random oracle H that matches the session key (line 37–45). We iterate over the entries in T, where U, S, x^U, $\hat{x}^U$, x^S, $\hat{x}^S$ and pw_{US} match, and check if one of the entries in z is correct. Note that we can use the following equivalences:

$$GA\text{-}CDH_{x_{b_i}}(x_i^U, x_i^S) = z_{i,1} \quad \Leftrightarrow \quad GA\text{-}CDH(x, x_i^S) = (u_i^{-1} \cdot g_{b_i}) \star z_{i,1},$$

$$GA\text{-}CDH_{x_{b_i}}(\hat{x}_i^U, x_i^S) = z_{i,2} \quad \Leftrightarrow \quad GA\text{-}CDH(x, x_i^S) = (\hat{u}_i^{-1} \cdot g_{b_i}) \star z_{i,2},$$

$$GA\text{-}CDH_{x_{b_i}}(x_i^U, \hat{x}_i^S) = z_{i,3} \quad \Leftrightarrow \quad GA\text{-}CDH(x, \hat{x}_i^S) = (u_i^{-1} \cdot g_{b_i}) \star z_{i,3},$$

which allows us to use the restricted decision oracle $GA\text{-}DDH(x, \cdot, \cdot)$. If one of $z_{i,1}, z_{i,2}, z_{i,3}$ is correct, $\mathcal{B}_1$ aborts and outputs the solution $(g \cdot h) \star \tilde{x}$ which is respectively given by $(u_i^{-1} \cdot s_i^{-1} \cdot g_{b_i}) \star z_{i,1}$, $(\hat{u}_i^{-1} \cdot s_i^{-1} \cdot g_{b_i}) \star z_{i,2}$ or $(u_i^{-1} \cdot \hat{s}_i^{-1} \cdot g_{b_i}) \star z_{i,3}$.

Otherwise, we store the values $u_i, \hat{u}_i$ and $s_i, \hat{s}_i$ in list T_e together with the trace and the password (line 46) and choose a session key uniformly at random. We need list T_e to identify relevant queries to H. In particular, if the trace and password appear in a query, we retrieve the values $u_i, \hat{u}_i$ and $s_i, \hat{s}_i$ to check whether the provided z_i are correct. We do this in the same way as described above using the decision oracle (lines 09–18). If the oracle returns 1 for any $z_{i,j}$, $\mathcal{B}_1$ aborts and outputs the solution for $(g \cdot h) \star \tilde{x}$ which is respectively given by $(u_i^{-1} \cdot s_i^{-1} \cdot g_{b_i}) \star z_{i,1}$, $(\hat{u}_i^{-1} \cdot s_i^{-1} \cdot g_{b_i}) \star z_{i,2}$ or $(u_i^{-1} \cdot \hat{s}_i^{-1} \cdot g_{b_i}) \star z_{i,3}$.

GAME G_4. In game G_4, we remove the password from execute queries. In particular, we do not compute $x^U, \hat{x}^U, x^S, \hat{x}^S$ to the basis x_{b_i}, but simply use $\tilde{x}$. Note that the values have the same distribution as in the previous game. Also, the group elements $u, \hat{u}, s$ and $\hat{s}$ are not used to derive the key. Hence, this change is not observable by $\mathcal{A}$ and

$$\Pr[G_4 \Rightarrow 1] = \Pr[G_3 \Rightarrow 1].$$

GAME G_5. G_5 is given in Fig. 7. In this game we want to replace the session keys by random for all fresh instances in oracles SENDRESP and SENDTERMINIT (lines 62, 83). Therefore, we introduce an additional independent random oracle T_s which maps only the trace of an instance to a key (lines 63, 84). We keep partner instances consistent, i.e., in case the adversary queries SENDTERMINIT for a user instance and there exists a fresh partner instance, then we retrieve the corresponding key from T_s and also assign it to this instance (line 78). For all instances that are not fresh, we simply compute the correct key using random oracle H (lines 66–69, 87–90). If a session is fresh and there is an inconsistency between T and T_s, we raise flag **bad**. This happens in the following cases:

– a server instance is about to compute the session key, the password was not
  corrupted, but there already exists an entry in T with the correct password
  and z (lines 60–61).
– a user instance is about to compute the session key, there exists no partner
  instance and the password was not corrupted, but there already exists an
  entry in T with the correct password and z (lines 81–82).
– the random oracle is queried on some trace that appears in T_s together with
  the correct password and z (lines 36–47). At this point, we also check if
  the password was corrupted in the meantime and if this is the case and the
  adversary issues the correct query, we output the key stored in T_s (line 46)
  as this instance cannot be tested. This case corresponds to perfect forward
  secrecy which we cover in the full version of the paper [1, Appendix E].

When **bad** is not raised, there is no difference between G_4 and G_5. Hence,

$$|\Pr[G_5 \Rightarrow 1] - \Pr[G_4 \Rightarrow 1]| \leq \Pr[G_5 \Rightarrow \mathbf{bad}].$$

GAME G_6. G_6 is given in Fig. 8. In this game we remove the password from
send queries and generate passwords as late as possible, that is either when the
adversary issues a corrupt query (line 21) or after it has stopped with output β'
(line 07). In SENDINIT and SENDRESP we still choose group elements $u_i, \hat{u}_i, s_i$
and $\hat{s}_i$ uniformly at random, but now compute $x_i^U, \hat{x}_i^U, x_i^S$ and $\hat{x}_i^S$ using the origin
element (lines 26, 27, 51 and 52). Thus, depending on which password is chosen
afterwards, we implicitly set

$$x_i^U = u_i \cdot \tilde{x} = (u_i \cdot g_0^{-1}) \star x_0 = (u_i \cdot g_1^{-1}) \star x_1$$

and analogously for $\hat{x}_i^U, x_i^S$ and $\hat{x}_i^S$. For all instances that are not fresh, we have
to compute the real session key using $z_i = (s_i \cdot g_{b_i}^{-1} \star x_i^U, s_i \cdot g_{b_i}^{-1} \star \hat{x}_i^U, \hat{s}_i \cdot g_{b_i}^{-1} \star x_i^U)$
(line 70) or $z_i = (u_i \cdot g_{b_i}^{-1} \star x_i^S, \hat{u}_i \cdot g_{b_i}^{-1} \star x_i^S, u_i \cdot g_{b_i}^{-1} \star \hat{x}_i^S)$ (line 97). Note that the
password is already defined for these instances.

Recall that event **bad** in game G_5 is raised whenever there is an inconsistency
in the random oracle queries and the keys of fresh instances. In this game, we
split event **bad** into two different events:

– **bad**$_{pw}$ captures the event that there exists more than one valid entry in T
  for the same trace of a fresh instance, but different passwords.
– **bad**$_{guess}$ happens only if **bad**$_{pw}$ does not happen and is raised if there exists
  a valid entry in T for the trace of a fresh instance and the correct password,
  where the password was not corrupted when the query to H was made.

To identify the different events, we introduce a new set T_{bad}. For all fresh
instances in SENDRESP and SENDTERMINIT, we now iterate over all entries
in T that contain the corresponding trace. We check if the given password and
z are valid for this trace by computing the real values z' in the same way as for
non-fresh instances. If $z = z'$, we add this entry to the set T_{bad} (lines 57–63, 84–
90). We essentially do the same when the random oracle H is queried on a trace

GAME G_5

```
00  (g_0, g_1) ←$ G²
01  (x_0, x_1) := (g_0 ⋆ x̃, g_1 ⋆ x̃)
02  (C, T, T_s) := (∅, ∅, ∅)
03  bad := false
04  β ←$ {0, 1}
05  for (U, S) ∈ U × S
06    pw_US ←$ PW
07  β' ← A^O(x_0, x_1)
08  return [[β = β']]
```

EXECUTE(U, t_0, S, t_1)

```
09  if π_U^{t_0} ≠ ⊥ or π_S^{t_1} ≠ ⊥: return ⊥
10  u := (u_1, ..., u_ℓ) ←$ G^ℓ
11  û := (û_1, ..., û_ℓ) ←$ G^ℓ
12  s := (s_1, ..., s_ℓ) ←$ G^ℓ
13  ŝ := (ŝ_1, ..., ŝ_ℓ) ←$ G^ℓ
14  x^U := (x_1^U, ..., x_ℓ^U) := (u_1 ⋆ x̃, ..., u_ℓ ⋆ x̃)
15  x̂^U := (x̂_1^U, ..., x̂_ℓ^U) := (û_1 ⋆ x̃, ..., û_ℓ ⋆ x̃)
16  x^S := (x_1^S, ..., x_ℓ^S) := (s_1 ⋆ x̃, ..., s_ℓ ⋆ x̃)
17  x̂^S := (x̂_1^S, ..., x̂_ℓ^S) := (ŝ_1 ⋆ x̃, ..., ŝ_ℓ ⋆ x̃)
18  if ∃P ∈ U ∪ S, t' s.t. π_P^{t'}.tr = (U, S, x^U, x̂^U, x^S, x̂^S)
19    return ⊥
20  K ←$ K
21  π_U^{t_0} := ((u, û), (U, S, x^U, x̂^U, x^S, x̂^S), K, true)
22  π_S^{t_1} := ((s, ŝ), (U, S, x^U, x̂^U, x^S, x̂^S), K, true)
23  (π_U^{t_0}.fr, π_S^{t_1}.fr) := (true, true)
24  return (U, x^U, x̂^U, S, x^S, x̂^S)
```

SENDINIT(U, t, S)

```
25  if π_U^t ≠ ⊥ return ⊥
26  (b_1, ..., b_ℓ) := pw_US
27  u := (u_1, ..., u_ℓ) ←$ G^ℓ
28  û := (û_1, ..., û_ℓ) ←$ G^ℓ
29  x^U := (x_1^U, ..., x_ℓ^U) := (u_1 ⋆ x_{b_1}, ..., u_ℓ ⋆ x_{b_ℓ})
30  x̂^U := (x̂_1^U, ..., x̂_ℓ^U) := (û_1 ⋆ x_{b_1}, ..., û_ℓ ⋆ x_{b_ℓ})
31  π_U^t := ((u, û), (U, S, x^U, x̂^U, ⊥, ⊥), ⊥, ⊥)
32  π_U^t.fr := false
33  return (U, x^U, x̂^U)
```

H$(U, S, x^U, x̂^U, x^S, x̂^S, pw, z)$

```
34  if T[U, S, x^U, x̂^U, x^S, x̂^S, pw, z] = K ≠ ⊥
35    return K
36  if (U, S, x^U, x̂^U, x^S, x̂^S) ∈ T_s and pw = pw_US
37    if T_s[U, S, x^U, x̂^U, x^S, x̂^S] = (U, (u, û), K)
38      for i ∈ [ℓ]
39        z_i' := (u_i ⋆ x_i^S, û_i ⋆ x_i^S, u_i ⋆ x̂_i^S)
40      z' := (z_1', ..., z_ℓ')
41    if T_s[U, S, x^U, x̂^U, x^S, x̂^S] = (S, (s, ŝ), K)
42      for i ∈ [ℓ]
43        z_i' := (s_i ⋆ x_i^U, s_i ⋆ x̂_i^U, ŝ_i ⋆ x_i^U)
44      z' := (z_1', ..., z_ℓ')
45    if z = z'
46      if (U, S) ∈ C: return K
47      if (U, S) ∉ C: bad := true
48  T[U, S, x^U, x̂^U, x^S, x̂^S, pw, z] := K
49  return T[U, S, x^U, x̂^U, x^S, x̂^S, pw, z]
```

SENDRESP$(S, t, U, x^U, x̂^U)$

```
50  if π_S^t ≠ ⊥ return ⊥
51  (b_1, ..., b_ℓ) := pw_US
52  s := (s_1, ..., s_ℓ) ←$ G^ℓ
53  ŝ := (ŝ_1, ..., ŝ_ℓ) ←$ G^ℓ
54  x^S := (x_1^S, ..., x_ℓ^S) := (s_1 ⋆ x_{b_1}, ..., s_ℓ ⋆ x_{b_ℓ})
55  x̂^S := (x̂_1^S, ..., x̂_ℓ^S) := (ŝ_1 ⋆ x_{b_1}, ..., ŝ_ℓ ⋆ x_{b_ℓ})
56  if ∃P ∈ U ∪ S, t' s.t. π_P^{t'}.tr = (U, S, x^U, x̂^U, x^S, x̂^S)
57    return ⊥
58  if (U, S) ∉ C
59    π_S^t.fr := true
60    if ∃z s.t. (U, S, x^U, x̂^U, x^S, x̂^S, pw_US, z) ∈ T
      and z_i = (s_i ⋆ x_i^U, s_i ⋆ x̂_i^U, ŝ_i ⋆ x_i^U) ∀i ∈ [ℓ]
61      bad := true
62      K ←$ K
63      T_s[U, S, x^U, x̂^U, x^S, x̂^S] := (S, (s, ŝ), K)
64    else
65      π_S^t.fr := false
66      for i ∈ [ℓ]
67        z_i := (s_i ⋆ x_i^U, s_i ⋆ x̂_i^U, ŝ_i ⋆ x_i^U)
68      z := (z_1, ..., z_ℓ)
69      K := H(U, S, x^U, x̂^U, x^S, x̂^S, pw_US, z)
70    π_S^t := ((s, ŝ), (U, S, x^U, x̂^U, x^S, x̂^S), K, true)
71    return (S, x^S, x̂^S)
```

SENDTERMINIT$(U, t, S, x^S, x̂^S)$

```
72  if π_U^t ≠ ((u, û), (U, S, x^U, x̂^U, ⊥, ⊥), ⊥, ⊥)
73    return ⊥
74  if ∃P ∈ U, t' s.t. π_P^{t'}.tr = (U, S, x^U, x̂^U, x^S, x̂^S)
75    return ⊥
76  if ∃t' s.t. π_S^{t'}.tr = (U, S, x^U, x̂^U, x^S, x̂^S)
    and π_S^{t'}.fr = true
77    π_U^t.fr := true
78    (S, (s, ŝ), K) := T_s[U, S, x^U, x̂^U, x^S, x̂^S]
79  else if (U, S) ∉ C
80    π_U^t.fr := true
81    if ∃z s.t. (U, S, x^U, x̂^U, x^S, x̂^S, pw_US, z) ∈ T
      and z_i = (u_i ⋆ x_i^S, û_i ⋆ x_i^S, u_i ⋆ x̂_i^S) ∀i ∈ [ℓ]
82      bad := true
83      K ←$ K
84      T_s[U, S, x^U, x̂^U, x^S, x̂^S] := (U, (u, û), K)
85    else
86      π_U^t.fr := false
87      for i ∈ [ℓ]
88        z_i := (u_i ⋆ x_i^S, û_i ⋆ x_i^S, u_i ⋆ x̂_i^S)
89      z := (z_1, ..., z_ℓ)
90      K := H(U, S, x^U, x̂^U, x^S, x̂^S, pw_US, z)
91    π_U^t := ((u, û), (U, S, x^U, x̂^U, x^S, x̂^S), K, true)
92  return true
```

Fig. 7. Game G_5 for the proof of Theorem 1. A has access to oracles $O := \{$EXECUTE, SENDINIT, SENDRESP, SENDTERMINIT, REVEAL, CORRUPT, TEST, H$\}$. REVEAL, TEST and CORRUPT are defined as in Figure 5. Differences to G_4 are highlighted in blue. (Color figure online)

that appears in T_s. Here, the adversary specifies the password and we check if z is valid for that password using the $u_i, û_i$ stored in T_s for user instances and $s_i, ŝ_i$ for server instances. If z is valid and the instance is still fresh, we add the query

```
GAME G_6                                              SENDRESP(S, t, U, x^U, x̂^U)
00 (g_0, g_1) ←$ G^2                                  48 if π_S^t ≠ ⊥ return ⊥
01 (x_0, x_1) := (g_0 ⋆ x̃, g_1 ⋆ x̃)                   49 s := (s_1, ..., s_ℓ) ←$ G^ℓ
02 (C, T, T_s, T_bad) := (∅, ∅, ∅, ∅)                 50 ŝ := (ŝ_1, ..., ŝ_ℓ) ←$ G^ℓ
03 (bad_guess, bad_pw) := (false, false)              51 x^S := (x_1^S, ..., x_ℓ^S) := (s_1 ⋆ x̃, ..., s_ℓ ⋆ x̃)
04 β ←$ {0,1}                                          52 x̂^S := (x̂_1^S, ..., x̂_ℓ^S) := (ŝ_1 ⋆ x̃, ..., ŝ_ℓ ⋆ x̃)
05 β' ← A^O(x_0, x_1)                                  53 if ∃P ∈ U ∪ S, t' s.t. π_P^{t'}.tr = (U, S, x^U, x̂^U, x^S, x̂^S)
06 for (U, S) ∈ U × S \ C                              54    return ⊥
07   pw_US ←$ PW                                        55 if (U, S) ∉ C
08   if ∃pw, pw', (U, S, x^U, x̂^U, x^S, x̂^S, z, z')   56   π_S^t.fr := true
      s.t. (U, S, x^U, x̂^U, x^S, x̂^S, pw, z) ∈ T_bad  57   ∀pw, z s.t. (U, S, x^U, x̂^U, x^S, x̂^S, pw, z) ∈ T
      and (U, S, x^U, x̂^U, x^S, x̂^S, pw', z') ∈ T_bad 58     (b_1, ..., b_ℓ) := pw
09     bad_pw := true                                  59     for i ∈ [ℓ]
10   else                                              60       z_i' := (s_i · g_{b_i}^{-1} ⋆ x_i^U, s_i · g_{b_i}^{-1} ⋆ x̂_i^U, ŝ_i · g_{b_i}^{-1} ⋆ x_i^U)
11     if ∃U, S, x^U, x̂^U, x^S, x̂^S, z                61     z' := (z_1', ..., z_ℓ')
        s.t. (U, S, x^U, x̂^U, x^S, x̂^S, pw_US, z) ∈ T_bad 62  if z = z'
12       bad_guess := true                             63       T_bad := T_bad ∪ {(U, S, x^U, x̂^U, x^S, x̂^S, pw, z)}
13 return [[β = β']]                                   64   K ←$ K
                                                       65   T_s[U, S, x^U, x̂^U, x^S, x̂^S] := (S, (s, ŝ), K)
CORRUPT(U, S)                                          66 else
14 if (U, S) ∈ C return ⊥                              67   π_S^t.fr := false
15 for P ∈ {U, S}                                      68   (b_1, ..., b_ℓ) := pw_US
16   if ∃t s.t. π_P^t.test = true                      69   for i ∈ [ℓ]
      and ∄P' ∈ U ∪ S, t' s.t. Partner(π_P^t, π_P'^{t'}) = 1  70     z_i := (s_i · g_{b_i}^{-1} ⋆ x_i^U, s_i · g_{b_i}^{-1} ⋆ x̂_i^U, ŝ_i · g_{b_i}^{-1} ⋆ x_i^U)
17     return ⊥                                        71   z := (z_1, ..., z_ℓ)
18   ∀π_P^t : if ∄P' ∈ U ∪ S, t' s.t. Partner(π_P^t, π_P'^{t'}) = 1  72   K := H(U, S, x^U, x̂^U, x^S, x̂^S, pw_US, z)
19     π_P^t.fr = false                                73 π_S^t := ((s, ŝ), (U, S, x^U, x̂^U, x^S, x̂^S), K, true)
20 C := C ∪ {(U, S)}                                   74 return (S, x^S, x̂^S)
21 pw_US ←$ PW
22 return pw_US                                        SENDTERMINIT(U, t, S, x^S, x̂^S)
                                                       75 if π_U^t ≠ ((u, û), (U, S, x^U, x̂^U, ⊥, ⊥), ⊥, ⊥)
SENDINIT(U, t, S)                                      76    return ⊥
23 if π_U^t ≠ ⊥ return ⊥                               77 if ∃P ∈ U, t' s.t. π_P^{t'}.tr = (U, S, x^U, x̂^U, x^S, x̂^S)
24 u := (u_1, ..., u_ℓ) ←$ G^ℓ                         78    return ⊥
25 û := (û_1, ..., û_ℓ) ←$ G^ℓ                         79 if ∃t' s.t. π_S^{t'}.tr = (U, S, x^U, x̂^U, x^S, x̂^S)
26 x^U := (x_1^U, ..., x_ℓ^U) := (u_1 ⋆ x̃, ..., u_ℓ ⋆ x̃)    and π_S^{t'}.fr = true
27 x̂^U := (x̂_1^U, ..., x̂_ℓ^U) := (û_1 ⋆ x̃, ..., û_ℓ ⋆ x̃)  80   π_U^t.fr := true
28 π_U^t := ((u, û), (U, S, x^U, x̂^U, ⊥, ⊥), ⊥, ⊥)    81   (S, (s, ŝ), K) := T_s[U, S, x^U, x̂^U, x^S, x̂^S]
29 π_U^t.fr := ⊥                                       82 else if (U, S) ∉ C
30 return (U, x^U, x̂^U)                                83   π_U^t.fr := true
                                                       84   ∀pw, z s.t. (U, S, x^U, x̂^U, x^S, x̂^S, pw, z) ∈ T
H(U, S, x^U, x̂^U, x^S, x̂^S, pw, z)                    85     (b_1, ..., b_ℓ) := pw
31 if T[U, S, x^U, x̂^U, x^S, x̂^S, pw, z] = K ≠ ⊥      86     for i ∈ [ℓ]
32    return K                                         87       z_i' := (u_i · g_{b_i}^{-1} ⋆ x_i^S, û_i · g_{b_i}^{-1} ⋆ x_i^S, u_i · g_{b_i}^{-1} ⋆ x̂_i^S)
33 if (U, S, x^U, x̂^U, x^S, x̂^S) ∈ T_s               88     z' := (z_1', ..., z_ℓ')
34   (b_1, ..., b_ℓ) := pw                             89     if z = z'
35   if T_s[U, S, x^U, x̂^U, x^S, x̂^S] = (U, (u, û), K) 90       T_bad := T_bad ∪ {(U, S, x^U, x̂^U, x^S, x̂^S, pw, z)}
36     for i ∈ [ℓ]                                     91   K ←$ K
37       z_i' := (u_i · g_{b_i}^{-1} ⋆ x_i^S, û_i · g_{b_i}^{-1} ⋆ x_i^S, u_i · g_{b_i}^{-1} ⋆ x̂_i^S)  92   T_s[U, S, x^U, x̂^U, x^S, x̂^S] := (U, (u, û), K)
38     z' := (z_1', ..., z_ℓ')                         93 else
39   if T_s[U, S, x^U, x̂^U, x^S, x̂^S] = (S, (s, ŝ), K) 94   π_U^t.fr := false
40     for i ∈ [ℓ]                                     95   (b_1, ..., b_ℓ) := pw_US
41       z_i' := (s_i · g_{b_i}^{-1} ⋆ x_i^U, s_i · g_{b_i}^{-1} ⋆ x̂_i^U, ŝ_i · g_{b_i}^{-1} ⋆ x_i^U)  96   for i ∈ [ℓ]
42     z' := (z_1', ..., z_ℓ')                         97     z_i := (u_i · g_{b_i}^{-1} ⋆ x_i^S, û_i · g_{b_i}^{-1} ⋆ x_i^S, u_i · g_{b_i}^{-1} ⋆ x̂_i^S)
43   if z = z'                                         98   z := (z_1, ..., z_ℓ)
44     if (U, S) ∈ C and pw = pw_US: return K          99   K := H(U, S, x^U, x̂^U, x^S, x̂^S, pw_US, z)
45     if (U, S) ∉ C: T_bad := T_bad ∪ {U, S, x^U, x̂^U, x^S, x̂^S, pw, z}  100 π_U^t := ((u_1, ..., u_ℓ), (U, S, x^U, x̂^U, x^S, x̂^S), K, true)
46 T[U, S, x^U, x̂^U, x^S, x̂^S, pw, z] ←$ K            101 return true
47 return T[U, S, x^U, x̂^U, x^S, x̂^S, pw, z]
```

Fig. 8. Game G_6 for the proof of Theorem 1. $\mathcal{A}$ has access to oracles $O := \{$EXECUTE, SENDINIT, SENDRESP, SENDTERMINIT, REVEAL, CORRUPT, TEST, H$\}$. Oracles REVEAL and TEST are defined as in game G_4 in Figure 5. Oracle EXECUTE is defined as in Figure 7. Differences to G_5 are highlighted in blue. (Color figure online)

to T_{bad} (lines 33–45). In case the password was corrupted in the meantime, we output the key stored in T_s as introduced in the previous game.

After the adversary terminates, we check T_{bad} whether event $\mathbf{bad}_{\mathsf{pw}}$ (line 09) or event $\mathbf{bad}_{\mathsf{guess}}$ (line 12) occurred. We will bound these events below. First note that whenever $\mathbf{bad}$ is raised in G_5, then either flag $\mathbf{bad}_{\mathsf{guess}}$ or $\mathbf{bad}_{\mathsf{pw}}$ is raised in G_6, thus

$$\Pr[\mathsf{G}_5 \Rightarrow \mathbf{bad}] \leq \Pr[\mathsf{G}_6 \Rightarrow \mathbf{bad}_{\mathsf{pw}}] + \Pr[\mathsf{G}_6 \Rightarrow \mathbf{bad}_{\mathsf{guess}}].$$

Finally, we bound the probabilities of the two events. We start with $\mathbf{bad}_{\mathsf{pw}}$. In Fig. 9, we construct adversary $\mathcal{B}_2$ against DSim-GA-StCDH that simulates G_6.

We show that when $\mathbf{bad}_{\mathsf{pw}}$ occurs, then $\mathcal{B}_2$ can solve DSim-GA-StCDH. Hence,

$$\Pr[\mathsf{G}_6 \Rightarrow \mathbf{bad}_{\mathsf{pw}}] \leq \mathsf{Adv}_{\mathsf{EGA}}^{\mathsf{DSim\text{-}GA\text{-}StCDH}}(\mathcal{B}_2).$$

Adversary $\mathcal{B}_2$ inputs (x_0, x_1, w_0, w_1), where $x_0 = g_0 \star \tilde{x}$, $x_1 = g_1 \star \tilde{x}$, $w_0 = h_0 \star \tilde{x}$ and $w_1 = h_1 \star \tilde{x}$ for group elements $g_0, g_1, h_0, h_1 \in \mathcal{G}$ chosen uniformly at random. Adversary $\mathcal{B}_2$ also has access to decision oracles $\mathsf{GA\text{-}DDH}_{x_j}(w_i, \cdot, \cdot)$ for $(i, j) \in \{0,1\}^2$. It runs adversary $\mathcal{A}$ on (x_0, x_1). Queries to SENDINIT are simulated as follows: $\mathcal{B}_2$ chooses group elements u_i and $\hat{u}_i$ uniformly at random and sets

$$x_i^{\mathsf{U}} = u_i \star w_0 = (u_i \cdot h_0 \cdot g_0^{-1}) \star x_0 = (u_i \cdot h_0 \cdot g_1^{-1}) \star x_1,$$
$$\hat{x}_i^{\mathsf{U}} = \hat{u}_i \star w_1 = (\hat{u}_i \cdot h_1 \cdot g_0^{-1}) \star x_0 = (\hat{u}_i \cdot h_1 \cdot g_1^{-1}) \star x_1.$$

The simulation of x_i^{S} and $\hat{x}_i^{\mathsf{S}}$ in SENDRESP is done in the same way, choosing random s_i and $\hat{s}_i$. In case the server instance is fresh, we must check if there already exists an entry in T that causes an inconsistency. As in G_6, we iterate over all pw, z, in T that contain the trace of this instance. In particular, we must check whether

$$z_{i,1} = \mathsf{GA\text{-}CDH}_{x_{b_i}}(x_i^{\mathsf{U}}, x_i^{\mathsf{S}}) \quad \Leftrightarrow \quad \mathsf{GA\text{-}CDH}_{x_{b_i}}(w_0, x_i^{\mathsf{U}}) = s_i^{-1} \star z_{i,1},$$
$$z_{i,2} = \mathsf{GA\text{-}CDH}_{x_{b_i}}(\hat{x}_i^{\mathsf{U}}, x_i^{\mathsf{S}}) \quad \Leftrightarrow \quad \mathsf{GA\text{-}CDH}_{x_{b_i}}(w_0, \hat{x}_i^{\mathsf{U}}) = s_i^{-1} \star z_{i,2},$$
$$z_{i,3} = \mathsf{GA\text{-}CDH}_{x_{b_i}}(x_i^{\mathsf{U}}, \hat{x}_i^{\mathsf{S}}) \quad \Leftrightarrow \quad \mathsf{GA\text{-}CDH}_{x_{b_i}}(w_1, x_i^{\mathsf{U}}) = \hat{s}_i^{-1} \star z_{i,3},$$

which can be done with the decision oracles $\mathsf{GA\text{-}DDH}_{x_{b_i}}(w_j, \cdot, \cdot)$. If all z_i are valid, then we add this entry to T_{bad} (lines 56–59).

If the instance is not fresh, then we have to compute the correct key. We check list T for a valid entry z as explained above and if it exists, we assign this value to the session key (line 66). Otherwise, we choose a random key and add a special entry to T, which instead of z contains the secret group elements s_i and $\hat{s}_i$ (line 69) so that we can patch the random oracle later. SENDTERMINIT is simulated analogously, using the secret group elements u_i and $\hat{u}_i$.

Now we look at the random oracle queries. If the trace is contained in set T_{s} which means the corresponding instance was fresh when the send query was issued, we check if z is valid using the GA-DDH oracle. We do this as described above, depending on whether it is a user or a server instance (lines 25, 31). In case z is valid, we first check if the instance is still fresh (i.e., the password was not corrupted in the meantime) and if this is the case, we add the query to T_{bad}

$\mathcal{B}_2^{\{\text{GA-DDH}_{x_j}(w_{i,\cdot,\cdot})\}_{i,j\in\{0,1\}}}(x_0, x_1, w_0, w_1)$

```
00  (C, T, T_s, T_bad) := (∅, ∅, ∅, ∅)
01  β ←$ {0,1}
02  β' ← A^O(x_0, x_1)
03  for (U,S) ∈ U × S \ C
04      pw_US ←$ PW
05      if ∃pw, pw', (U, S, x^U, x̂^U, x^S, x̂^S, z, z')
            s.t. (U, S, x^U, x̂^U, x^S, x̂^S, pw, z) ∈ T_bad
            and (U, S, x^U, x̂^U, x^S, x̂^S, pw, z') ∈ T_bad
06          (b_1, ..., b_ℓ) := pw
07          (b'_1, ..., b'_ℓ) := pw'
08          Find first index i such that b_i ≠ b'_i
09          W.l.o.g. let b_i = 0, b'_i = 1
10          if T_s[U, S, x^U, x̂^U, x^S, x̂^S] = (U, (u, û), K)
11              Stop with (x^S_i, u_i^{-1} ⋆ z_{i,1}, û_i^{-1} ⋆ z_{i,2}, u_i^{-1} ⋆ z'_{i,1}, û_i^{-1} ⋆ z'_{i,2})
12          if T_s[U, S, x^U, x̂^U, x^S, x̂^S] = (S, (s, ŝ), K)
13              Stop with (x^U_i, s_i^{-1} ⋆ z_{i,1}, ŝ_i^{-1} ⋆ z_{i,3}, s_i^{-1} ⋆ z'_{i,1}, ŝ_i^{-1} ⋆ z'_{i,3})
```

```
SendInit(U, t, S)
14  if π_U^t ≠ ⊥ return ⊥
15  u := u_1, ..., u_ℓ ←$ G^ℓ
16  û := (û_1, ..., û_ℓ) ←$ G^ℓ
17  x^U := (x^U_1, ..., x^U_ℓ) := (u_1 ⋆ w_0, ..., u_ℓ ⋆ w_0)
18  x̂^U := (x̂^U_1, ..., x̂^U_ℓ) := (û_1 ⋆ w_1, ..., û_ℓ ⋆ w_1)
19  π_U^t := ((u, û), (U, S, x^U, x̂^U, ⊥, ⊥), ⊥, ⊥)
20  return (U, x^U, x̂^U)
```

```
H(U, S, x^U, x̂^U, x^S, x̂^S, pw, z)
21  if T[U, S, x^U, x̂^U, x^S, x̂^S, pw, z] = K ≠ ⊥
22      return K
23  if (U, S, x^U, x̂^U, x^S, x̂^S) ∈ T_s
24      (b_1, ..., b_ℓ) := pw
25      if T_s[U, S, x^U, x̂^U, x^S, x̂^S] = (U, (u, û), K)
26          if GA-DDH_{x_{b_i}}(w_0, x^S_i, u_i^{-1} ⋆ z_{i,1}) = 1 ∀i ∈ [ℓ]
                and GA-DDH_{x_{b_i}}(w_1, x̂^S_i, û_i^{-1} ⋆ z_{i,2}) = 1 ∀i ∈ [ℓ]
                and GA-DDH_{x_{b_i}}(w_0, x̂^S_i, u_i^{-1} ⋆ z_{i,3}) = 1 ∀i ∈ [ℓ]
27              if (U,S) ∉ C
28                  T_bad := T_bad ∪ {(U, S, x^U, x̂^U, x^S, x̂^S, pw, z)}
29              if (U,S) ∈ C and pw = pw_US
30                  return K
31      if T_s[U, S, x^U, x̂^U, x^S, x̂^S] = (S, (s, ŝ), K)
32          if GA-DDH_{x_{b_i}}(w_0, x^U_i, s_i^{-1} ⋆ z_{i,1}) = 1 ∀i ∈ [ℓ]
                and GA-DDH_{x_{b_i}}(w_0, x̂^U_i, s_i^{-1} ⋆ z_{i,2}) = 1 ∀i ∈ [ℓ]
                and GA-DDH_{x_{b_i}}(w_1, x̂^U_i, ŝ_i^{-1} ⋆ z_{i,3}) = 1 ∀i ∈ [ℓ]
33              if (U,S) ∉ C
34                  T_bad := T_bad ∪ {(U, S, x^U, x̂^U, x^S, x̂^S, pw, z)}
35              if (U,S) ∈ C and pw = pw_US
36                  return K
37  if ∃(u, û) s.t. (U, S, x^U, x̂^U, x^S, x̂^S, pw, (u, û)) ∈ T
38      (b_1, ..., b_ℓ) := pw
39      if GA-DDH_{x_{b_i}}(w_0, x^S_i, u_i^{-1} ⋆ z_{i,1}) = 1 ∀i ∈ [ℓ]
            and GA-DDH_{x_{b_i}}(w_1, x̂^S_i, û_i^{-1} ⋆ z_{i,2}) = 1 ∀i ∈ [ℓ]
            and GA-DDH_{x_{b_i}}(w_0, x̂^S_i, u_i^{-1} ⋆ z_{i,3}) = 1 ∀i ∈ [ℓ]
40          return T[U, S, x^U, x̂^U, x^S, x̂^S, pw, (u, û)]
41  else if ∃(s, ŝ) s.t. (U, S, x^U, x̂^U, x^S, x̂^S, pw, (s, ŝ)) ∈ T
42      (b_1, ..., b_ℓ) := pw
43      if GA-DDH_{x_{b_i}}(w_0, x^U_i, s_i^{-1} ⋆ z_{i,1}) = 1 ∀i ∈ [ℓ]
            and GA-DDH_{x_{b_i}}(w_0, x̂^U_i, s_i^{-1} ⋆ z_{i,2}) = 1 ∀i ∈ [ℓ]
            and GA-DDH_{x_{b_i}}(w_1, x̂^U_i, ŝ_i^{-1} ⋆ z_{i,3}) = 1 ∀i ∈ [ℓ]
44          return T[U, S, x^U, x̂^U, x^S, x̂^S, pw, (s, ŝ)]
45  T[U, S, x^U, x̂^U, x^S, x̂^S, pw, z] ←$ K
46  return T[U, S, x^U, x̂^U, x^S, x̂^S, pw, z]
```

```
SendResp(S, t, U, x^U)
47  if π_S^t ≠ ⊥ return ⊥
48  s := (s_1, ..., s_ℓ) ←$ G^ℓ
49  ŝ := (ŝ_1, ..., ŝ_ℓ) ←$ G^ℓ
50  x^S := (x^S_1, ..., x^S_ℓ) := (s_1 ⋆ w_0, ..., s_ℓ ⋆ w_0)
51  x̂^S := (x̂^S_1, ..., x̂^S_ℓ) := (ŝ_1 ⋆ w_1, ..., ŝ_ℓ ⋆ w_1)
52  if ∃P ∈ U ∪ S, t' s.t. π_P^{t'}.tr = (U, S, x^U, x̂^U, x^S, x̂^S)
53      return ⊥
54  if (U,S) ∉ C
55      π_S^t.fr := true
56      ∀pw, z s.t. (U, S, x^U, x̂^U, x^S, x̂^S, pw, z) ∈ T
57          (b_1, ..., b_ℓ) := pw
58          if GA-DDH_{x_{b_i}}(w_0, x^U_i, s_i^{-1} ⋆ z_{i,1}) = 1 ∀i ∈ [ℓ]
                and GA-DDH_{x_{b_i}}(w_0, x̂^U_i, s_i^{-1} ⋆ z_{i,2}) = 1 ∀i ∈ [ℓ]
                and GA-DDH_{x_{b_i}}(w_1, x̂^U_i, ŝ_i^{-1} ⋆ z_{i,3}) = 1 ∀i ∈ [ℓ]
59              T_bad := T_bad ∪ {(U, S, x^U, x̂^U, x^S, x̂^S, pw, z)}
60      K ←$ K
61      T_s[U, S, x^U, x̂^U, x^S, x̂^S] := (S, (s, ŝ), K)
62  else
63      π_S^t.fr := false
64      (b_1, ..., b_ℓ) := pw_US
65      if ∃z s.t. (U, S, x^U, x̂^U, x^S, x̂^S, pw_US, z) ∈ T
            and GA-DDH_{x_{b_i}}(w_0, x^U_i, s_i^{-1} ⋆ z_{i,1}) = 1 ∀i ∈ [ℓ]
            and GA-DDH_{x_{b_i}}(w_0, x̂^U_i, s_i^{-1} ⋆ z_{i,2}) = 1 ∀i ∈ [ℓ]
            and GA-DDH_{x_{b_i}}(w_1, x̂^U_i, ŝ_i^{-1} ⋆ z_{i,3}) = 1 ∀i ∈ [ℓ]
66          K := T[U, S, x^U, x̂^U, x^S, x̂^S, pw_US, z]
67      else
68          K ←$ K
69          T[U, S, x^U, x̂^U, x^S, x̂^S, pw_US, (s, ŝ)] := K
70      π_S^t := ((s, ŝ), (U, S, x^U, x̂^U, x^S, x̂^S), K, true)
71  return (S, x^S, x̂^S)
```

```
SendTermInit(U, t, S, x^S, x̂^S)
72  if π_U^t ≠ ((u, û), (U, S, x^U, x̂^U, ⊥, ⊥), ⊥, ⊥) return ⊥
73  if ∃P ∈ U, t' s.t. π_P^{t'}.tr = (U, S, x^U, x̂^U, x^S, x̂^S) return ⊥
74  if ∃t' s.t. π_S^{t'}.tr = (U, S, x^U, x̂^U, x^S, x̂^S) and π_S^{t'}.fr = true
75      π_U^t.fr := true
76      (S, (s, ŝ), K) := T_s[U, S, x^U, x̂^U, x^S, x̂^S]
77  else if (U,S) ∉ C
78      π_U^t.fr := true
79      ∀pw, z s.t. (U, S, x^U, x̂^U, x^S, x̂^S, pw, z) ∈ T
80          (b_1, ..., b_ℓ) := pw
81          if GA-DDH_{x_{b_i}}(w_0, x^S_i, u_i^{-1} ⋆ z_{i,1}) = 1 ∀i ∈ [ℓ]
                and GA-DDH_{x_{b_i}}(w_1, x̂^S_i, û_i^{-1} ⋆ z_{i,2}) = 1 ∀i ∈ [ℓ]
                and GA-DDH_{x_{b_i}}(w_0, x̂^S_i, u_i^{-1} ⋆ z_{i,3}) = 1 ∀i ∈ [ℓ]
82              T_bad := T_bad ∪ {(U, S, x^U, x̂^U, x^S, x̂^S, pw, z)}
83      K ←$ K
84      T_s[U, S, x^U, x̂^U, x^S, x̂^S] := (U, (u, û), K)
85  else
86      π_U^t.fr := false
87      (b_1, ..., b_ℓ) := pw_US
88      if ∃z s.t. (U, S, x^U, x̂^U, x^S, x̂^S, pw_US, z) ∈ T
            and GA-DDH_{x_{b_i}}(w_0, x^S_i, u_i^{-1} ⋆ z_{i,1}) = 1 ∀i ∈ [ℓ]
            and GA-DDH_{x_{b_i}}(w_1, x̂^S_i, û_i^{-1} ⋆ z_{i,2}) = 1 ∀i ∈ [ℓ]
            and GA-DDH_{x_{b_i}}(w_0, x̂^S_i, u_i^{-1} ⋆ z_{i,3}) = 1 ∀i ∈ [ℓ]
89          K := T[U, S, x^U, x̂^U, x^S, x̂^S, pw_US, z]
90      else
91          K ←$ K
92          T[U, S, x^U, x̂^U, x^S, x̂^S, pw_US, (u, û)] := K
93      π_U^t := ((u, û), (U, S, x^U, x̂^U, x^S, x̂^S), K, true)
94  return true
```

Fig. 9. Adversary $\mathcal{B}_2$ against DSim-GA-StCDH for the proof of Theorem 1. $\mathcal{A}$ has access to oracles $O := \{$Execute, SendInit, SendResp, SendTermInit, Reveal, Corrupt, Test, H$\}$. Oracles Execute, Reveal, Corrupt and Test are defined as in G_6. Lines written in blue show how $\mathcal{B}_2$ simulates the game. (Color figure online)

(lines 28, 34). Otherwise, if the password was corrupted and is specified in the query, we return the session key stored in T_s (lines 30, 36).

Next, we check if the query matches a special entry in T that was added in SENDRESP or SENDTERMINIT for a non-fresh instance, which means we have to output the same key that was chosen before. Again, we can use the GA-DDH oracle and differentiate between user and server instances (lines 37–44).

After $\mathcal{A}$ terminates with output β', $\mathcal{B}_2$ chooses the passwords which have not been generated in a CORRUPT query yet. If $\mathbf{bad_{pw}}$ occurred (lines 05–13), then there must be two entries in T_{bad} for the same trace and different passwords $\mathsf{pw} \neq \mathsf{pw}'$ along with values z and z'. Let i be the first index where the two passwords differ, i.e., $b_i \neq b_i'$. Without loss of generality assume that $b_i = 0$ and $b_i' = 1$, otherwise swap pw, z and pw', z'. If the entries in T_{bad} are those of a user instance, we retrieve the secret group elements $u, \hat{u}_i$ from T_{s}.

Recall that the DSim-GA-StCDH problem requires to compute $y_0 = \mathsf{GA\text{-}CDH}_{x_0}(w_0, y)$, $y_1 = \mathsf{GA\text{-}CDH}_{x_0}(w_1, y)$, $y_2 = \mathsf{GA\text{-}CDH}_{x_1}(w_0, y)$ and $y_3 = \mathsf{GA\text{-}CDH}_{x_1}(w_1, y)$, where y can be chosen by the adversary. $\mathcal{B}_2$ sets $y = x_i^{\mathsf{S}}$, and outputs y and

$$y_0 = u_i^{-1} \star z_{i,1} = \mathsf{GA\text{-}CDH}_{x_0}(u_i^{-1} \star x_i^{\mathsf{U}}, x_i^{\mathsf{S}}) = \mathsf{GA\text{-}CDH}_{x_0}(w_0, x_i^{\mathsf{S}}),$$
$$y_1 = \hat{u}_i^{-1} \star z_{i,2} = \mathsf{GA\text{-}CDH}_{x_0}(\hat{u}_i^{-1} \star \hat{x}_i^{\mathsf{U}}, x_i^{\mathsf{S}}) = \mathsf{GA\text{-}CDH}_{x_0}(w_1, x_i^{\mathsf{S}}),$$
$$y_2 = u_i^{-1} \star z_{i,1}' = \mathsf{GA\text{-}CDH}_{x_1}(u_i^{-1} \star x_i^{\mathsf{U}}, x_i^{\mathsf{S}}) = \mathsf{GA\text{-}CDH}_{x_1}(w_0, x_i^{\mathsf{S}}),$$
$$y_3 = \hat{u}_i^{-1} \star z_{i,2}' = \mathsf{GA\text{-}CDH}_{x_1}(\hat{u}_i^{-1} \star \hat{x}_i^{\mathsf{U}}, x_i^{\mathsf{S}}) = \mathsf{GA\text{-}CDH}_{x_1}(w_1, x_i^{\mathsf{S}}).$$

If the instance is a server instance, $\mathcal{B}_2$ outputs $(y, y_0, y_1, y_2, y_3) = (x_i^{\mathsf{U}}, s_i^{-1} \star z_{i,1}, \hat{s}_i^{-1} \star z_{i,3}, s_i^{-1} \star z_{i,1}', \hat{s}_i^{-1} \star z_{i,3}')$. This concludes the analysis of $\mathbf{bad_{pw}}$.

Next, we analyze event $\mathbf{bad_{guess}}$. Recall that $\mathbf{bad_{guess}}$ happens only if $\mathbf{bad_{pw}}$ does not happen. Hence, for each instance there is at most one entry in T_{bad} and the size of T_{bad} is at most q_s. As all entries were added before the corresponding password was sampled, the probability is bounded by

$$\Pr[\mathsf{G}_6 \Rightarrow \mathbf{bad_{guess}}] \leq \frac{q_s}{|\mathcal{PW}|}.$$

Finally, note that if none of the bad events happens in G_6, all session keys output by TEST are uniformly random and the adversary can only guess β. Hence, $\Pr[\mathsf{G}_6 \Rightarrow 1] = \frac{1}{2}$. Collecting the probabilities and using Eq. 1 yields the bound in Theorem 1. $\qquad\square$

7   Com-GA-PAKE$_\ell$: Three-Round PAKE from Group Actions

In this section we present a second modification of GA-PAKE$_\ell$, which can be securely instantiated with an EGAT. The protocol Com-GA-PAKE$_\ell$ extends GA-PAKE$_\ell$ by a commitment that has to be sent before sending the actual messages. This ensures that the server cannot choose the set elements depending on the message it receives from the user which was the crucial step in the attack against GA-PAKE$_\ell$. In the second round, the user sends its message to the server and only after receiving that message, the server sends its message to the user. The protocol is sketched in Fig. 10 and its security is established in Theorem 2. While this protocol adds two rounds to the original protocol, the total computational cost is lower than for X-GA-PAKE$_\ell$.

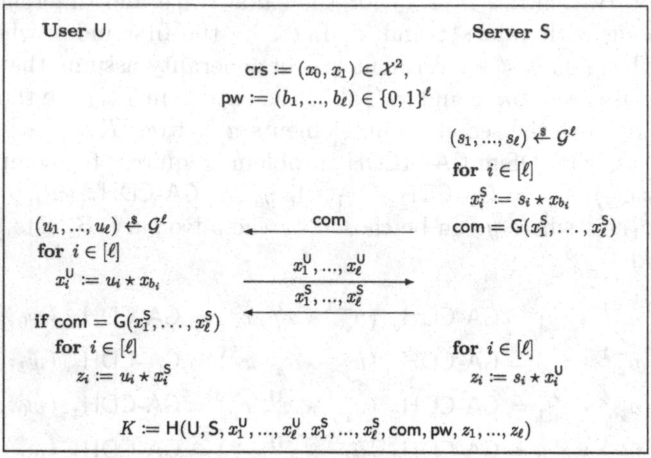

Fig. 10. PAKE protocol Com-GA-PAKE$_\ell$ from group actions.

Theorem 2 (Security of Com-GA-PAKE$_\ell$). *For any adversary $\mathcal{A}$ against* Com-GA-PAKE$_\ell$ *that issues at most q_e execute queries, q_s send queries and at most q_G and q_H queries to random oracles G and H, there exist an adversary $\mathcal{B}_1$ against* GA-StCDH *and an adversary $\mathcal{B}_2$ against* GA-GapCDH *such that*

$$\mathsf{Adv}_{\mathsf{Com\text{-}GA\text{-}PAKE}_\ell}(\mathcal{A}) \leq \mathsf{Adv}_{\mathsf{EGAT}}^{\mathsf{GA\text{-}StCDH}}(\mathcal{B}_1) + q_s\ell \cdot \sqrt{\mathsf{Adv}_{\mathsf{EGAT}}^{\mathsf{GA\text{-}GapCDH}}(\mathcal{B}_2)} + \frac{(q_s + q_e)^2}{|\mathcal{G}|^\ell}$$

$$+ \frac{q_G q_s}{|\mathcal{G}|^\ell} + \frac{2 \cdot (q_G + q_s + q_e)^2}{2^\lambda} + \frac{q_s}{|\mathcal{PW}|},$$

where λ is the output length of G in bits.

The proof is similar to the one of Theorem 1 so we will only sketch it here. The full proof is given in the long version of the paper [1, Appendix E].

Proof (Sketch). After ensuring that all traces are unique, we need to deal with the commitment and in particular collisions. First, we require that there are never two inputs to the random oracle G that return the same commitment. This is to ensure that the adversary cannot open a commitment to a different value, which might depend on previous messages.

Second, we need to ensure that after the adversary has seen a commitment, it does not query G on the input, which is the hiding property of the commitment.

What we actually do here is that we choose a random commitment in the first round. Only later we choose the input and patch the random oracle accordingly.

Now we can replace the session keys of instances which are used in execute queries. Here, the freshness condition allows the adversary to corrupt the password. However, as both x^S and x^U are generated by the experiment, the only chance to notice this change is to solve the GA-StCDH problem, where the decision oracle is required to simulate instances correctly.

In order to replace the session keys of fresh instances which are used in send queries, we make the key independent of the password. The session key of a fresh instance is now defined by the trace of that instance. The only issue that may arise here is an inconsistency between the session key that is derived using the trace and the session key that is derived using the random oracle H. Whenever such an inconsistency occurs, we differentiate between two cases:

- There exists more than one valid entry in T_H for the same trace of a fresh instance, but different passwords.
- There exists a valid entry in T_H for the trace of a fresh instance and the correct password, where the password was not corrupted when the query to H was made.

Finally, we bound the probabilities of the two cases. Similar to Theorem 1, we will define a new computational problem that reflects exactly the interaction in the protocol. We show that this problem is implied by GA-GapCDH using the reset lemma. The general idea is that the adversary can always compute the session key for one password guess, but not for a second one. After excluding this, we choose the actual password, which is possible because session keys are computed independently of the password. Thus, looking at one fixed instance, the probability that the adversary guessed the password correctly is $1/|\mathcal{PW}|$. □

8   Variants of the PAKE Protocols

Both protocols X-GA-PAKE$_\ell$ and Com-GA-PAKE$_\ell$ require that the user and the server generate multiple random group elements and evaluate their action on certain set elements. In this section we present two optimizations that allow us to reduce the number of random group elements and the number of evaluations.

8.1   Increasing the Number of Public Parameters

In X-GA-PAKE$_\ell$ and Com-GA-PAKE$_\ell$ the common reference string is set to crs := $(x_0, x_1) \in \mathcal{X}^2$. Increasing the number of public parameters allows to reduce the number of group action evaluations in the execution of the protocol. The idea is similar to the optimizations deployed to speed up the CSIDH-based signatures schemes SeaSign [14] and CSI-FiSh [9]. We refer to Table 1 in the introduction for an overview and example of the parameter choice.

We explain the changes on the basis of protocol X-GA-PAKE$_\ell$. The variant of Com-GA-PAKE$_\ell$ is similar and is provided in the full version of the paper

[1, Appendix E], together with a security analysis for both variants. For some positive integer N dividing ℓ, we set

$$\mathsf{crs} := (x_0, \ldots, x_{2^N-1}) \in \mathcal{X}^{2^N} \quad \text{and} \quad \mathsf{pw} = (b_1, \ldots, b_{\ell/N}) \in \{0, \ldots, 2^N - 1\}^{\ell/N}.$$

Note that as before, the password is a bitstring of length ℓ, but it is divided into ℓ/N blocks of length N. In particular x_{b_i} refers to one of the 2^N different set elements in the crs. The general outline of the protocol does not change. The only difference is that in the first step both the server and the user only generate $2 \cdot \ell/N$ random group elements (instead of $2 \cdot \ell$). Hence they only need to perform $2 \cdot \ell/N$ group action evaluations in the first round and $3 \cdot \ell/N$ evaluations in the session key derivation. We write X-GA-PAKE$_{\ell,N}$ for this variant of the protocol.

8.2   Using Twists in the Setup

Both X-GA-PAKE$_\ell$ and Com-GA-PAKE$_\ell$ require that some trusted party generates two random set elements $\mathsf{crs} = (x_0, x_1)$. Here, we shortly discuss the setup where x_1 is replaced by the twist of x_0, i.e. $\mathsf{crs} := (x_0, x_0^t)$.

This simplification is particularly helpful when applied to one of the variants from the previous subsection. These modified versions require to generate 2^N random set elements for the crs. Using twists it suffices to generate 2^{N-1} elements $(x_0, \ldots, x_{2^{N-1}-1}) \in \mathcal{X}^{2^{N-1}}$ and setting $x_{i+2^{N-1}} = x_i^t$ for each $i \in [0, 2^{N-1} - 1]$.

The security of X-GA-PAKE$_\ell^t$ and Com-GA-PAKE$_\ell^t$ (the twisted versions of the protocols) is discussed in the full version [1, Appendices D, E].

Acknowledgments. Thorsten Eisenhofer, Eike Kiltz, Sabrina Kunzweiler and Doreen Riepel were supported by the DFG under Germany's Excellence Strategy - EXC 2092 CASA - 390781972.

References

1. Abdalla, M., Eisenhofer, T., Kiltz, E., Kunzweiler, S., Riepel, D.: Password-authenticated key exchange from group actions. Cryptology ePrint Archive, Report 2022/770 (2022). https://eprint.iacr.org/2022/770
2. Abdalla, M., Fouque, P.-A., Pointcheval, D.: Password-based authenticated key exchange in the three-party setting. In: Vaudenay, S. (ed.) PKC 2005. LNCS, vol. 3386, pp. 65–84. Springer, Heidelberg (2005). https://doi.org/10.1007/978-3-540-30580-4_6
3. Abdalla, M., Haase, B., Hesse, J.: Security analysis of CPace. Cryptology ePrint Archive, Report 2021/114 (2021). https://eprint.iacr.org/2021/114
4. Abdalla, M., Pointcheval, D.: Simple password-based encrypted key exchange protocols. In: Menezes, A. (ed.) CT-RSA 2005. LNCS, vol. 3376, pp. 191–208. Springer, Heidelberg (2005). https://doi.org/10.1007/978-3-540-30574-3_14
5. Alamati, N., De Feo, L., Montgomery, H., Patranabis, S.: Cryptographic group actions and applications. In: Moriai, S., Wang, H. (eds.) ASIACRYPT 2020, Part II. LNCS, vol. 12492, pp. 411–439. Springer, Cham (2020). https://doi.org/10.1007/978-3-030-64834-3_14

6. Azarderakhsh, R., Jao, D., Koziel, B., LeGrow, J.T., Soukharev, V., Taraskin, O.: How not to create an isogeny-based PAKE. In: Conti, M., Zhou, J., Casalicchio, E., Spognardi, A. (eds.) ACNS 2020, Part I. LNCS, vol. 12146, pp. 169–186. Springer, Cham (2020). https://doi.org/10.1007/978-3-030-57808-4_9

7. Bellare, M., Pointcheval, D., Rogaway, P.: Authenticated key exchange secure against dictionary attacks. In: Preneel, B. (ed.) EUROCRYPT 2000. LNCS, vol. 1807, pp. 139–155. Springer, Heidelberg (2000). https://doi.org/10.1007/3-540-45539-6_11

8. Bellovin, S.M., Merritt, M.: Encrypted key exchange: password-based protocols secure against dictionary attacks. In: 1992 IEEE Symposium on Security and Privacy, pp. 72–84. IEEE Computer Society Press, May 1992. https://doi.org/10.1109/RISP.1992.213269

9. Beullens, W., Kleinjung, T., Vercauteren, F.: CSI-FiSh: efficient isogeny based signatures through class group computations. In: Galbraith, S.D., Moriai, S. (eds.) ASIACRYPT 2019, Part I. LNCS, vol. 11921, pp. 227–247. Springer, Cham (2019). https://doi.org/10.1007/978-3-030-34578-5_9

10. Canetti, R., Dachman-Soled, D., Vaikuntanathan, V., Wee, H.: Efficient password authenticated key exchange via oblivious transfer. In: Fischlin, M., Buchmann, J., Manulis, M. (eds.) PKC 2012. LNCS, vol. 7293, pp. 449–466. Springer, Heidelberg (2012). https://doi.org/10.1007/978-3-642-30057-8_27

11. Castryck, W., Lange, T., Martindale, C., Panny, L., Renes, J.: CSIDH: an efficient post-quantum commutative group action. In: Peyrin, T., Galbraith, S. (eds.) ASIACRYPT 2018, Part III. LNCS, vol. 11274, pp. 395–427. Springer, Cham (2018). https://doi.org/10.1007/978-3-030-03332-3_15

12. Couveignes, J.M.: Hard homogeneous spaces. Cryptology ePrint Archive, Report 2006/291 (2006). https://eprint.iacr.org/2006/291

13. Cramer, R., Shoup, V.: Universal hash proofs and a paradigm for adaptive chosen ciphertext secure public-key encryption. In: Knudsen, L.R. (ed.) EUROCRYPT 2002. LNCS, vol. 2332, pp. 45–64. Springer, Heidelberg (2002). https://doi.org/10.1007/3-540-46035-7_4

14. De Feo, L., Galbraith, S.D.: SeaSign: compact isogeny signatures from class group actions. In: Ishai, Y., Rijmen, V. (eds.) EUROCRYPT 2019, Part III. LNCS, vol. 11478, pp. 759–789. Springer, Cham (2019). https://doi.org/10.1007/978-3-030-17659-4_26

15. Don, J., Fehr, S., Majenz, C., Schaffner, C.: Online-extractability in the quantum random-oracle model. Cryptology ePrint Archive, Report 2021/280 (2021). https://eprint.iacr.org/2021/280

16. Fujioka, A., Takashima, K., Yoneyama, K.: One-round authenticated group key exchange from isogenies. In: Steinfeld, R., Yuen, T.H. (eds.) ProvSec 2019. LNCS, vol. 11821, pp. 330–338. Springer, Cham (2019). https://doi.org/10.1007/978-3-030-31919-9_20

17. Gennaro, R., Lindell, Y.: A framework for password-based authenticated key exchange. In: Biham, E. (ed.) EUROCRYPT 2003. LNCS, vol. 2656, pp. 524–543. Springer, Heidelberg (2003). https://doi.org/10.1007/3-540-39200-9_33 . https://eprint.iacr.org/2003/032.ps.gz

18. Haase, B., Labrique, B.: AuCPace: efficient verifier-based PAKE protocol tailored for the IIoT. IACR TCHES 2019(2), 1–48 (2019). https://doi.org/10.13154/tches.v2019.i2.1-48. https://tches.iacr.org/index.php/TCHES/article/view/7384

19. Hao, F., Ryan, P.: J-PAKE: authenticated key exchange without PKI. Cryptology ePrint Archive, Report 2010/190 (2010). https://eprint.iacr.org/2010/190

20. Jablon, D.P.: Strong password-only authenticated key exchange. ACM SIGCOMM Comput. Commun. Rev. **26**(5), 5–26 (1996)
21. Jao, D., De Feo, L.: Towards quantum-resistant cryptosystems from supersingular elliptic curve isogenies. In: Yang, B.-Y. (ed.) PQCrypto 2011. LNCS, vol. 7071, pp. 19–34. Springer, Heidelberg (2011). https://doi.org/10.1007/978-3-642-25405-5_2
22. Kawashima, T., Takashima, K., Aikawa, Y., Takagi, T.: An efficient authenticated key exchange from random self-reducibility on CSIDH. In: Hong, D. (ed.) ICISC 2020. LNCS, vol. 12593, pp. 58–84. Springer, Cham (2021). https://doi.org/10.1007/978-3-030-68890-5_4
23. de Kock, B., Gjøsteen, K., Veroni, M.: Practical isogeny-based key-exchange with optimal tightness. In: Dunkelman, O., Jacobson, Jr., M.J., O'Flynn, C. (eds.) SAC 2020. LNCS, vol. 12804, pp. 451–479. Springer, Cham (2021). https://doi.org/10.1007/978-3-030-81652-0_18
24. Lai, Y.-F., Galbraith, S.D., Delpech de Saint Guilhem, C.: Compact, efficient and UC-secure isogeny-based oblivious transfer. In: Canteaut, A., Standaert, F.-X. (eds.) EUROCRYPT 2021, Part I. LNCS, vol. 12696, pp. 213–241. Springer, Cham (2021). https://doi.org/10.1007/978-3-030-77870-5_8
25. Peikert, C., Vaikuntanathan, V., Waters, B.: A framework for efficient and composable oblivious transfer. In: Wagner, D. (ed.) CRYPTO 2008. LNCS, vol. 5157, pp. 554–571. Springer, Heidelberg (2008). https://doi.org/10.1007/978-3-540-85174-5_31
26. Pointcheval, D., Wang, G.: VTBPEKE: verifier-based two-basis password exponential key exchange. In: Karri, R., Sinanoglu, O., Sadeghi, A.R., Yi, X. (eds.) ASIACCS 2017, pp. 301–312. ACM Press, April 2017
27. Rostovtsev, A., Stolbunov, A.: Public-key cryptosystem based on isogenies. Cryptology ePrint Archive, Report 2006/145 (2006). https://eprint.iacr.org/2006/145
28. Soukharev, V., Hess, B.: PQDH: a quantum-safe replacement for Diffie-Hellman based on SIDH. Cryptology ePrint Archive, Report 2019/730 (2019). https://eprint.iacr.org/2019/730
29. Taraskin, O., Soukharev, V., Jao, D., LeGrow, J.: An isogeny-based password-authenticated key establishment protocol. Cryptology ePrint Archive, Report 2018/886 (2018). https://eprint.iacr.org/2018/886
30. Terada, S., Yoneyama, K.: Password-based authenticated key exchange from standard isogeny assumptions. In: Steinfeld, R., Yuen, T.H. (eds.) ProvSec 2019. LNCS, vol. 11821, pp. 41–56. Springer, Cham (2019). https://doi.org/10.1007/978-3-030-31919-9_3
31. Yoneyama, K.: Post-quantum variants of ISO/IEC standards: compact chosen ciphertext secure key encapsulation mechanism from isogeny. In: Proceedings of the 5th ACM Workshop on Security Standardisation Research Workshop, SSR 2019, pp. 13–21. Association for Computing Machinery, New York (2019). https://doi.org/10.1145/3338500.3360336

Efficient NIZKs and Signatures from Commit-and-Open Protocols in the QROM

Jelle Don[1]([⊠]), Serge Fehr[1,2], Christian Majenz[1,4], and Christian Schaffner[3,4]

[1] Centrum Wiskunde and Informatica (CWI), Amsterdam, Netherlands
{jelle.don,serge.fehr,christian.majenz}@cwi.nl
[2] Mathematical Institute, Leiden University, Leiden, Netherlands
[3] Informatics Institute, University of Amsterdam, Amsterdam, Netherlands
c.schaffner@uva.nl
[4] QuSoft, Amsterdam, Netherlands

Abstract. Commit-and-open Σ-protocols are a popular class of protocols for constructing non-interactive zero-knowledge arguments and digital-signature schemes via the Fiat-Shamir transformation. Instantiated with hash-based commitments, the resulting non-interactive schemes enjoy tight online-extractability in the random oracle model. Online extractability improves the tightness of security proofs for the resulting digital-signature schemes by avoiding lossy rewinding or forking-lemma based extraction.

In this work, we prove tight online extractability in the quantum random oracle model (QROM), showing that the construction supports post-quantum security. First, we consider the default case where committing is done by element-wise hashing. In a second part, we extend our result to Merkle-tree based commitments. Our results yield a significant improvement of the provable post-quantum security of the digital-signature scheme Picnic.

Our analysis makes use of a recent framework by Chung et al. [CFHL21] for analysing quantum algorithms in the QROM using purely classical reasoning. Therefore, our results can to a large extent be understood and verified without prior knowledge of quantum information science.

1 Introduction

Some interactive proofs come with amazing properties like *zero-knowledge* which intuitively allows a prover to convince a verifier that she knows the witness to an NP-statement without giving away information about this witness. Such zero-knowledge proofs of knowledge are some of the most fascinating objects in cryptography, and possibly in all of theoretical computer science. One might suspect that their "magic" is due to the prover and verifier running an *interactive* protocol with each other, and that this interaction causes the verifier to be convinced. Surprisingly, if the interactive proof is of suitable form, e.g. a Σ-protocol (i.e. a

Full version available at https://eprint.iacr.org/2022/270.

3-round public-coin protocol), the Fiat-Shamir transformation [FS87] provides a natural way to remove the interaction from such protocols while preserving (most of) the security properties, resulting in *non-interactive zero-knowledge* proofs (NIZKs). The idea is to compute the challenge c as a hash $c = H(a)$ of the first message, rather than letting the verifier choose c. If the original Σ-protocol has additional soundness properties, the resulting NIZK after the Fiat-Shamir transformation is ideally suited to construct a *digital-signature scheme*, simply by hashing the message m to be signed together with the first message a in order to obtain the challenge c. The candidates Picnic [CDG+17] and Dilithium [DKL+18] in the ongoing NIST post-quantum cryptography competition follow this design paradigm.

This intuitive preservation of security properties under the Fiat-Shamir transformation can be formalized in the random-oracle model (ROM), where the hash function H is treated as a uniformly random function, and the security reduction gets *enhanced access* to anybody who queries the random oracle, by seeing which values are queried, and by possibly returning (random-looking) outputs. While this situation is conveniently easy to handle in a non-quantum world, complications arise in the context of post-quantum security. When studying the security of these non-quantum protocols against attackers equipped with large-enough quantum computers, it is natural to assume that such attackers have access to the public description of the employed hash function, and can therefore compute it in superposition on their quantum computers. Therefore, the proper notion of post-quantum security for random oracles is the *quantum-accessible random-oracle model (QROM)* as introduced in [BDF+11]. Due to the difficulty of recording adversarial random-oracle queries in superposition (also referred to as the *recording barrier*), establishing post-quantum security in the QROM has turned out to be quite a bit more difficult compared to the regular ROM.

Previous results in [DFMS19] (and concurrently in [LZ19b]) establish that for any interactive Σ-protocol Π that is a proof of knowledge, the non-interactive $FS[\Pi]$ is a proof of knowledge in the QROM. [DFM20] simplified the technical proof and extended these results to multi-round interactive proofs. However, the most desirable property from such a proof of knowledge is *online extractability* Indeed, online extractability avoids *rewinding*, which typically causes a significant loss in the security reduction and has other disadvantages (see later for a comparison). Thus, online extractability allows for the tightest security reductions.

Chailloux was the first to aim for showing online extractability of the Fiat-Shamir transformation in the QROM when considering the relevant class of *commit-and-open* (C&O) Σ-protocols and modelling the hash function used for the commitments (and for computing the challenge) as a random oracle. Indeed, the Fiat-Shamir transformation of such C&O Σ-protocols are known to be online extractable in the classical ROM (see e.g. discussion in [Fis05]). In a first attempt [Cha19], Chailloux tried to lift the argument to the quantum setting by means of Zhandry's compressed-oracle technique [Zha19], which offers a powerful approach for re-establishing ROM results in the QROM, that has been successful in many instances. Unfortunately, this first attempt contained a subtle flaw, which turned out to be unfixable, and despite changing the technical approach, the latest version of this work still contains an open gap in the proof, which is put as an assumption in [Cha21].[1]

In a recent article [DFMS21], online extractability of *interactive* C&O Σ-protocols Π in the QROM is established ; the result applies as soon as Π stisfies some liberal notion of *special soundness*, which is typically satisfied . As pointed out in Appendix E of [DFMS21], one can use previous results from [DFMS19, LZ19b, DFM20] to reduce the extractability of the resulting non-interactive protocol FS[Π] to the extractability of the interactive protocol Π. However, the resulting extraction error scales as $O(\varepsilon/q^2)$ which results in a prohibitive loss for digital-signature schemes (see Table 1), leaving open the main question originally posed by Chailloux:

How to establish tight security reductions of the Fiat-Shamir transformation for commit-and-open Σ-protocols in the QROM?

As the technical quantum details of Zhandry's compressed-oracle technique are rather complicated and only accessible for experts, a recent article by Chung, Fehr, Huang and Liao [CFHL21] establish a framework that allows researchers without extensive quantum knowledge to still deploy the compressed-oracle technique (in certain cases), basically by reasoning about classical quantities only. In short, the punchline of [CFHL21] is that, if applicable, one can prove *quantum* query complexity lower bounds (think of collision finding, for instance) by means of the following recipe, which is an abstraction of the technique developed in a line of works started by Zhandry [Zha19, LZ19a, CGLQ20, HM21]. First, one considers the corresponding *classical* query complexity problem, analyzing it by simulating the random oracle using lazy sampling and showing that the database, which keeps track of the oracle queries and the responses, is unlikely to satisfy a certain property (e.g. to contain a collision) after a bounded number of queries. Then, one lifts the analysis to the quantum setting by plugging key observations from the classical analysis into generic theorems provided by the [CFHL21] framework. A similar framework, using slightly different language (and limited to sequential queries) was given in [CMS19].

1.1 Our Contributions

In this work, we slightly extend the framework from [CFHL21], and use it to establish strong and tight security statements for a large, popular class of

---

[1] Informally, quoting from [Cha21], the considered Assumption 2 is that the random oracle can be replaced with a random function of a particular form *"without harming too much the studied scheme"*. More formally, the security loss caused by the considered replacement is assumed to remain bounded by a given function of the number of oracle queries. This assumption is rather ad-hoc and non-standard in that it is very much tailored to the scheme and its proof. Furthermore, even though Assumption 2 is an assumption that could potentially be proven in future work , it is hard to judge whether proving the assumption is actually any easier than proving the security of the considered scheme *directly*, avoiding Assumption 2—as a matter of fact, in this work we show that the latter is feasible, while Assumption 2 remains open.

non-interactive zero-knowledge proofs and digital signature schemes. In broad strokes, our contributions are threefold.

Online Extractability for a Class of NIZKs in the QROM. We prove online extractability of the Fiat-Shamir transformation in the QROM for (a large class of) C&O Σ-protocols. This solves the problem considered and attacked by Chailloux. In more detail, we prove that if the considered C&O Σ-protocol satisfies some very liberal notion of special soundness , then the resulting NIZK is a proof of knowledge with online extractability in the QROM, i.e., when the hash function used for the commitments and the FS transformation is modeled as a quantum-accessible random oracle. Our security reduction is tight: Whenever a prover outputs a valid proof, the online-extractor succeeds, except with a small probability accounting for collision and preimage attacks on the involved hash functions. For previous reductions, the guaranteed extraction success probability was at least by a factor of q^2 smaller than the succes probability of the prover subjected to extraction (see Table 1). This is our main technical contribution, see Theorem 4.2. Our result also applies to a variant of the Fiat-Shamir transformation where a digital signature scheme (DSS) is constructed. It thereby, for the first time, enables a multiplicatively tight security reduction for, e.g., DSS based on the MPC-in-the-head paradigm [IKOS07], like Picnic [CDG+17], Banquet [BdSGK+21] and Rainier [DKR+21], in the QROM.

A More Efficient Unruh Transformation. When a Σ-protocol does not have the mentioned C&O structure, a non-interactive proof of knowledge with online extractability in the QROM can be obtained using the Unruh transformation [Unr15]. For technical reasons, the original Unruh transformation requires the hash function to be *length preserving*, which may result in large commitments, and thus large NIZKs and digital signature schemes. In the full version, we revisit this transformation and show, by a rather direct application of our main result above, that the online extractability of the Unruh transform still holds when using a *compressing* hash function. The crucial observation is that the Unruh transformation can be viewed as the composition of a "pre-Unruh" transformation, which makes use of hash-based commitments and results in a C&O protocol, and the Fiat-Shamir transformation. By applying our security reduction, we then obtain the tight online extractability without requiring the hash function to be length preserving.

More Efficient NIZKs via Merkle Tree Based Commitments. In real-world constructions based on C&O protocols, like e.g., the Picnic digital signature scheme, commitments and their openings are responsible for a significant fraction of the signature/proof size. For certain parameters, this cost can be reduced by using a collective commitment mechanism based on Merkle trees. This was observed in passing, e.g. in [Fis05], and is exploited in the most recent versions of Picnic. We formalize Merkle-tree-based C&O protocols and extend our main result to NIZKs constructed from them (see Theorem 5.2). Applications include a security reduction of Picnic 3, the newest version of the Picnic digital signature scheme, that is significantly tighter than existing ones: An adversary against the Picnic 3 signature scheme in the QROM with success probability ε can now be used to break the underlying hard problem with probability ε, up to some additive error terms, while previous reductions yielded at most ε^5/q^{10}, where q is the number of random oracle queries. We outline this reduction in Sect. 5.3.

We compare our reductions in detail to existing techniques in Table 1.

Table 1. Comparison of the losses of different reductions for the construction of a NIZK proof of knowledge (NIZK-PoK) from a special-sound (Merkle tree based) C&O protocol with constant challenge space size C using r-fold parallel repetition and the Fiat-Shamir transformation. "OE" stands for online extraction, 2-s for special sound-ness, UF-NMA for plain unforgeability and DSS for digital signature scheme. If the content of a cell in row "security property A $\Rightarrow$ security property B" is $f(\varepsilon)$, this means that an adversary breaking property B with probability ε yields an adversary break-ing property A with probabilty $f(\varepsilon)$. Grey text indicates results that do not apply to Merkle-tree-based C&O protocols like the one used to construct the digital signa-ture schemes Picnic 2 [KZ20] and Picnic 3 [CDG+19b]. The additive error terms are $g(q,r,n) = C^{-r} + O(rq2^{-n/2}) + O(q^3 2^{-n})$ and $h(q,r,n) = O(q^3 2^{-n}) + O(q^2 C^{-r})$, where n is the output length of the random oracles, and q is the number of adversarial (quantum) queries to the random oracle. Finally, we note that the constants hidden by the big-O in $h(q,r,n)$ are reasonable, see Theorems 4.2 and 5.2.

	2-s$\Rightarrow$PoK	PoK$\overset{FS}{\Rightarrow}$NIZK-PoK, PoK$\overset{FS}{\Rightarrow}$UF-NMA DSS	2-s$\overset{FS}{\Rightarrow}$NIZK-PoK, 2-s$\overset{FS}{\Rightarrow}$UF-NMA DSS
Unruh rewinding [Unr12] + generic FS [DFMS19]	$O(\varepsilon^3)$	$O(\varepsilon/q^2)$	$O(\varepsilon^3/q^6)$
Σ-protocol OE [DFMS21] + generic FS [DFMS19]	$\varepsilon - g(q,r,n)$	$O(\varepsilon/q^2)$	$O(\varepsilon/q^2) - g(q,r,n)$
this work: NIZK OE	–	–	$\varepsilon - h(q,r,n)$

1.2 Technical Overview

Our starting point is the fact that the compressed-oracle technique can be seen as a variant of the classical lazy-sampling technique that is applicable in the QROM. Namely, to some extent and informally described here, the compressed-oracle technique gives access to a database that contains the hash values that the adversary $\mathcal{A}$, who has interacted with the random oracle (RO), may know. In particular, up to a small error, for any claimed-to-be hash value y output by $\mathcal{A}$, one can find its preimage x by inspecting the database (and one can safely conclude that $\mathcal{A}$ does not know a preimage of y if there is none in the database). Recalling that a C&O Σ-protocol Π is an interactive proof where the first message consists of hash-based commitments, and exploiting that typically some sort of special soundness property ensures that knowing sufficiently many preimages of these commitments/hashes allows one to efficiently compute a witness, constructing an online extractor for the Fiat-Shamir transformation $FS[\Pi]$ then appears straightforward: The extractor $\mathcal{E}$ simply runs the (possibly dishonest) prover P^*, answering RO queries using the compressed oracle. Once P^* has finished and outputs a proof, $\mathcal{E}$ measures the compressed-oracle database and classically reads off any preimages of the commitments in the proof. Finally, $\mathcal{E}$ run the special soundness extractor that computes a witness from the obtained preimages . It is, however, not obvious that the database contains the preimages of the commitments that are *not* opened in the proof, or that these preimages are correctly formed. Intuitively this should be the case: the RO used for the Fiat-Shamir transformation replaces interaction in that it forces the prover to chose a full set of commitments *before* knowing which ones need to be opened. The crux lies in replacing this intuition by a rigorous proof .

The main insight leading to our proof is that the event that needs to be controlled, namely that *the prover succeeds yet the extractor fails*, can be translated into a property SUC (as in "adversarial SUCcess") of the compressed-oracle database, which needs to be satisfied for the event to hold. It is somewhat of a peculiar property though. The database properties that have led to query complexity lower bounds in prior work, e.g. for (multi-)collision finding [LZ19a, HM21, CFHL21] and similar problems [Zha19, CGLQ20, BLZ21], require the database to contain some particular input-output pairs (e.g. pairs that collide), while the database property SUC additionally *forbids* certain input-output pairs to be contained.

Indeed, the framework from [CFHL21] is almost expressive enough to treat our problem. So, after a mild extension, we can apply it to prove that it is hard for any query algorithm to cause the compressed-oracle database to have property SUC. Analyzing the relevant classical statistical properties of SUC is somewhat tedious but can be done (see the proof of Lemma 5.1). The resulting bound on the probability for the database to satisfy SUC then gives us a bound on the probability of the event that the prover succeeds in producing a valid proof while at the same time fooling the extractor.

Whenever it is advantageous for communication complexity, a Merkle tree can be used to collectively commit to all required messages in a C&O protocol. This collective commitment is one of the optimizations that improve the performance of, e.g. Picnic 2 [KZ20] over Picnic [CDG+17]. As the above-described argument for the extractability of C&O protocols already analyses iterated hashing (the hash-based commitments are hashed to compute the challenge), it generalizes to Merkle-tree-based C&O protocols without too much effort. We present this generalization in Sect. 5, and obtain similar bounds (see Theorem 5.2).

1.3   Additional Related Work

Besides the already mentioned work above, we note that Chiesa, Manohar and Spooner [CMS19] consider and prove security of various SNARG constructions, while we consider the Fiat-Shamir transformation of C&O protocols with a form of special soundness. Similar in to [CFHL21], they also provide some tools for deducing security of certain oracle games against quantum attacks by bounding a natural classical variant of the game.

2   Preliminaries

Our main technical proofs reliy on the recently introduced framework by Chung, Fehr, Huang, and Liao [CFHL21] for proving query complexity bounds in the QROM. This framework exploits Zhandry's compressed-oracle technique but abstracts away all the quantum aspects, so that the reasoning becomes purely classical. We give here an introduction to a simplified, and slightly adjusted version that does not consider parallel queries. We start with recalling (a particular view on) the compressed oracle. Along the way, we also give an improved version of Zhandry's central lemma for the compressed oracle.

Before getting into this, we fix the following standard notation. For any positive integer $\ell > 0$, we set $[\ell] := \{1, 2, \ldots, \ell\}$, and we let $2^{[\ell]}$ denote the power set of $[\ell]$, i.e., the set of all subsets of $[\ell]$.

Finally, for any finite non-empty set $\mathcal{Z}$, $\mathbb{C}[\mathcal{Z}]$ denotes the Hilbert space $\mathbb{C}^{|\mathcal{Z}|}$ together with a basis $\{|z\rangle\}$ labeled by the elements $z \in \mathcal{Z}$.

2.1   The Compressed Oracle — Seen as Quantum Lazy Sampling

With the goal to analyze oracle algorithms that interact with a RO $H : \mathcal{X} \to \mathcal{Y}$, consider the set $\mathfrak{D}$ of all functions $D : \mathcal{X} \to \mathcal{Y} \cup \{\bot\}$, where $\bot$ is a special symbol. Such a function is referred to as a *database*. Later, we will fix $\mathcal{X} = \{0,1\}^{\leq B}$ and $\mathcal{Y} = \{0,1\}^n$. For $D \in \mathfrak{D}$, $x \in \mathcal{X}$ and $y \in \mathcal{Y} \cup \{\bot\}$, $D[x \mapsto y]$ denotes the database that maps x to y and otherwise coincides with D, i.e., $D[x \mapsto y](x) = y$ and $D[x \mapsto y](\bar{x}) = D(\bar{x})$ for all $\bar{x} \in \mathcal{X} \setminus \{x\}$.

Following the exposition of [CFHL21], the compressed-oracle technique is a quantum analogue of the classical lazy-sampling technique, commonly used to analyze algorithms in the classical ROM. In the classical lazy-sampling technique, the (simulated) RO starts off with the empty database, i.e., with $D_0 = \bot$, which maps any $x \in \mathcal{X}$ to $\bot$. Then, recursively, upon a query x, the current database D_i is updated to $D_{i+1} := D_i$ if $D_i(x) \neq \bot$, and to $D_{i+1} := D_i[x \mapsto y]$ for a randomly chosen $y \in \mathcal{Y}$ otherwise. This construction ensures that $|\{x \mid D_i(x) \neq \bot\}| \leq i$; after i queries thus, using standard sparse-encoding techniques, the database D_i can be efficiently represented and updated.

In the compressed-oracle quantum analogue of this lazy-sampling technique, the (simulated) RO also starts off with the empty database, but now considered as a quantum state $|\bot\rangle$ in the $|\mathfrak{D}|$-dimensional state space $\mathbb{C}[\mathfrak{D}]$, and after i queries the state of the compressed oracle is then supported by databases $|D_i\rangle$ for which $|\{x \mid D_i(x) = \bot\}| \leq i$.[2] Here, the update is given by a unitary operator

---

[2] This means that the density operator that describes the state of the compressed oracle has its support contained in the span of these $|D_i\rangle$.

cO acting on $\mathbb{C}[\mathcal{X}] \otimes \mathbb{C}[\mathcal{Y}] \otimes \mathbb{C}[\mathfrak{D}]$, i.e., on the query register, the response register, and the state of the compressed oracle. With respect to the computational basis $\{|x\rangle\}$ of $\mathbb{C}[\mathcal{X}]$ and the Fourier basis $\{|\hat{y}\rangle\}$ of $\mathbb{C}[\mathcal{Y}]$, cO is a *control* unitary, i.e., of the form $\mathsf{cO} = \sum_{x,\hat{y}} |x\rangle\langle x| \otimes |\hat{y}\rangle\langle \hat{y}| \otimes \mathsf{cO}_{x,\hat{y}}$, where $\mathsf{cO}_{x,\hat{y}}$ is a unitary on $\mathbb{C}[\mathcal{Y} \cup \{\bot\}]$, which in the above expression is understood to act on the register that carries the value of the database at the point x. More formally, $\mathsf{cO}_{x,\hat{y}}$ acts on register R_x when identifying $\mathbb{C}[\mathfrak{D}]$ with $\bigotimes_{x \in \mathcal{X}} \mathbb{C}[\mathcal{Y} \cup \{\bot\}]$ by means of the isomorphism $|D\rangle \mapsto \bigotimes_{x \in \mathcal{X}} |D(x)\rangle_{R_x}$. We refer to Lemma 4.3 in the full version of [CFHL21] for the full specification of $\mathsf{cO}_{x,\hat{y}}$.

The compressed oracle is tightly related to the *purified* oracle, which initiates its internal state with a uniform superposition $\sum_h |H\rangle \in \mathbb{C}[\mathfrak{D}]$ of all functions $H : \mathcal{X} \to \mathcal{Y}$, and then answers queries "in superposition". Indeed, at any point in time during the interaction with an oracle quantum algorithm $\mathcal{A}$, the joint state of $\mathcal{A}$ and the compressed oracle coincides with the joint state of $\mathcal{A}$ and the purified oracle after "compressing" the latter.[3] Formally, identifying $\mathbb{C}[\mathfrak{D}]$ with $\bigotimes_{x \in \mathcal{X}} \mathbb{C}[\mathcal{Y} \cup \{\bot\}]$ again, the compression of the state of the purified oracle works by applying the unitary Comp to each register R_x, where

$$\mathsf{Comp} : |y\rangle \mapsto (|y\rangle + (|\bot\rangle - |\hat{0}\rangle))/\sqrt{|\mathcal{Y}|}$$

for any $y \in \mathcal{Y}$, and $\mathsf{Comp} : |\bot\rangle \mapsto |\hat{0}\rangle$. Here, $|\hat{0}\rangle$ is the $\hat{0}$-vector from the Fourier basis $\{|\hat{y}\rangle\}$ of $\mathbb{C}[\mathcal{Y}]$.

Similarly to the classical case, by exploiting a quantum version of the sparse-encoding technique, both the internal state of the compressed oracle and the evolution cO can be efficiently computed. Furthermore, for any classical function $f : \mathfrak{D} \to \mathcal{T}$ that can be efficiently computed when given the sparse representation of $D \in \mathfrak{D}$, the corresponding quantum measurement given by the projections $P_t = \sum_{D : f(D)=t} |D\rangle\langle D|$ can be efficiently performed when given the sparse representation of the internal state of the compressed oracle. In particular, in Lemma 2.1 below, the condition $\mathbf{y} = D(\mathbf{x})$ for given $\mathbf{x}$ and $\mathbf{y}$ can be efficiently checked by a measurement. See Appendix A in (the full version of) [CFHL21], or Appendix B in [DFMS21] for more details on this technique.

In the classical lazy-sampling technique, if at the end of the execution of an oracle algorithm $\mathcal{A}$, having made q queries to the (lazy-sampled) RO, the database D_q is such that, say, $D_q(x) \neq 0$ for any $x \in \mathcal{X}$, then $\mathcal{A}$'s output is unlikely to be a 0-preimage, i.e., an x that is hashed to 0 upon one more query. $\mathcal{A}$'s best chance is to output an x that he has not queried yet, and thus $D_q(x) = \bot$, and then he has a $1/|\mathcal{Y}|$-chance that $D_{q+1}(x) := D_q[x \mapsto y](x) = 0$, given that y is randomly chosen. Something similar holds in the quantum setting, with some adjustments. The general statement is given by the following result by Zhandry.

Lemma 2.1 (Lemma 5 in [Zha19]). *Let $R \subseteq \mathcal{X}^\ell \times \mathcal{Y}^\ell \times \mathcal{Z}$ be a relation, and let $\mathcal{A}$ be an oracle quantum algorithm that outputs $\mathbf{x} \in \mathcal{X}^\ell$, $\mathbf{y} \in \mathcal{Y}^\ell$ and $z \in \mathcal{Z}$.*

---

[3] The terminology is somewhat misleading here; the actual compression takes place when invoking the sparse encoding (see below).

Furthermore, let

$$p = p(\mathcal{A}) := \Pr[\mathbf{y} = H(\mathbf{x}) \wedge (\mathbf{x}, \mathbf{y}, z) \in R]$$

be the considered probability when $\mathcal{A}$ has interacted with the standard RO, initialized with a uniformly random function H, and let

$$p' = p'(\mathcal{A}) := \Pr[\mathbf{y} = D(\mathbf{x}) \wedge (\mathbf{x}, \mathbf{y}, z) \in R]$$

be the considered probability when $\mathcal{A}$ has interacted with the compressed oracle instead and D is obtained by measuring its internal state (in the basis $\{|D\rangle\}_{D \in \mathfrak{D}}$). Then

$$\sqrt{p} \leq \sqrt{p'} + \sqrt{\ell/|\mathcal{Y}|}.$$

In Sect. 2.3 we give an alternative (and in typical cases tighter) such relation between the success probability of an algorithm interacting with the actual RO, and probabilities obtained by inspecting the compressed oracle instead.

2.2   The Quantum Transition Capacity and Its Relevance

The above discussion shows that, in order to bound the success probability p of an oracle algorithm $\mathcal{A}$, it is sufficient to bound p'', the probability of the database D, obtained by measuring the internal state of the compressed oracle after the interaction with $\mathcal{A}$, satisfying a certain property (e.g., the property of there existing an x such that $D(x) = 0$).

To facilitate that latter, Chung et al. [CFHL21] introduced a framework that, in certain cases, allows to bound this alternative figure of merit by means of purely classical reasoning. We briefly recall here some of the core elements of this framework, which are relevant to us. Note that [CFHL21] considers the parallel-query model, where in each of the q (sequential) interactions with the RO, a q-query oracle algorithm $\mathcal{A}$ can make k queries simultaneously in parallel. Here, we consider the (more) standard model of one query per interaction, i.e., setting $k = 1$. On the other hand, we state and prove a slight generalization of Theorem 5.16 in [CFHL21] (when restricted to $k = 1$).

A subset $\mathsf{P} \subseteq \mathfrak{D}$ is called a *database property*. We say that $D \in \mathfrak{D}$ *satisfies* P if $D \in \mathsf{P}$, and the complement of P is denoted $\neg\mathsf{P} = \mathfrak{D} \setminus \mathsf{P}$. For such a database property P, [CFHL21] defines $[\![\bot \overset{q}{\Longrightarrow} \mathsf{P}]\!]$ as the square-root of the maximal probability of D satisfying P when D is obtained by measuring the internal state of the compressed oracle after the interaction with $\mathcal{A}$, maximized over all oracle quantum algorithms $\mathcal{A}$ with query complexity q, i.e., in short

$$[\![\bot \overset{q}{\Longrightarrow} \mathsf{P}]\!] := \max_{\mathcal{A}} \sqrt{\Pr[D \in \mathsf{P}]}. \tag{1}$$

In the context of Lemma 2.1 for the case $\mathcal{Z} = \emptyset$, we can define the database property $\mathsf{P}^R := \{D \in \mathfrak{D} \mid \exists \mathbf{x} \in \mathcal{X}^\ell : (\mathbf{x}, D(\mathbf{x})) \in R\}$ induced by R, and thus bound

$$p'(\mathcal{A}) \leq \Pr[(\mathbf{x}, D(\mathbf{x})) \in R] \leq \Pr[D \in \mathsf{P}^R] \leq [\![\bot \overset{q}{\Longrightarrow} \mathsf{P}^R]\!]^2 \tag{2}$$

for any oracle quantum algorithm $\mathcal{A}$ with query complexity q.

Furthermore, Lemma 5.6 in [CFHL21] shows that for any target database property P and for any sequence $P_0, P_1, \ldots, P_q$ with $\neg P_0 = \{\bot\}$ and $P_q = P$,

$$\llbracket \bot \overset{q}{\Longrightarrow} P \rrbracket \leq \sum_{s=1}^{q} \llbracket \neg P_{s-1} \to P_s \rrbracket, \tag{3}$$

where, for any database properties P and P', the definition of the *quantum transition capacity* $\llbracket P \to P' \rrbracket$ is recalled in the full version.

The nice aspect of the framework of [CFHL21] is that it provides means to manipulate and bound quantum transition capacities using purely classical reasoning, i.e., without the need to understand and work with the definition. Indeed, for instance Theorem 2.2 below, which is a variant of Theorem 5.17 in (the full version of) [CFHL21], shows how to bound $\llbracket P \to P' \rrbracket$ by means of a certain classical probability; furthermore, to facilitate the application of such theorems, [CFHL21] showed that the quantum transition capacity satisfies several natural manipulation rules, like $\llbracket P \to P' \rrbracket = \llbracket P' \to P \rrbracket$ (i.e., it is symmetric), and

$$\llbracket P \cap Q \to P' \rrbracket \leq \min\{\llbracket P \to P' \rrbracket, \llbracket Q \to P' \rrbracket\} \qquad \text{and}$$
$$\min\{\llbracket P \to P' \rrbracket, \llbracket P \to Q' \rrbracket\} \leq \llbracket P \to P' \cup Q' \rrbracket \leq \llbracket P \to P' \rrbracket + \llbracket P \to Q' \rrbracket, \tag{4}$$

which allow to decompose complicated capacities into simpler ones. Therefore, by means of the above series of inequalities with p from Lemma 2.1 on the left hand side, it is possible (in certain cases) to bound the success probability of any oracle quantum algorithm $\mathcal{A}$ in the QROM by means of the following recipe: (1) Choose suitable transitions $P_{s-1} \to P_s$, (2) decompose the capacities $\llbracket \neg P_{s-1} \to P_s \rrbracket$ into simpler ones using manipulation rules as above, and (3) bound the simplified capacities by certain classical probabilities, exploiting results like Theorem 2.2.

In order to state and later use Theorem 2.2, we need to introduce the following additional concepts. As explained above, there is no need to actually spell out the definition of the quantum transition capacity in order to use Theorem 2.2; for completeness, and since it is needed for the proof of Theorem 2.2, we provide it in the full version (where we also give the proof of Theorem 2.2).

For any database $D \in \mathfrak{D}$ and any $x \in \mathcal{X}$, $D|^x := \{D[x \mapsto y] \mid y \in \mathcal{Y} \cup \{\bot\}\}$ denotes the set of all databases that coincide with D outside of x. Furthermore, for a database property P,

$$P|_{D|^x} := \{y \in \mathcal{Y} \cup \{\bot\} \mid D[x \mapsto y] \in P\} \subseteq \mathcal{Y} \cup \{\bot\}$$

denotes the set of values y for which $D[x \mapsto y]$ satisfies P.

The following is a variation of Theorem 5.17 in (the full version of) [CFHL21], obtained by restricting k to 1. On the other hand, we exploit and include some symmetry that is not explicit in the original statement. The proof, given in the full version, is a small adjustment to the original proof.

Theorem 2.2. *Let* P *and* P' *be database properties with trivial intersection, i.e.,* $\mathsf{P} \cap \mathsf{P}' = \emptyset$, *and for every* $D \in \mathfrak{D}$ *and* $x \in \mathcal{X}$ *let*

$$\mathsf{L}^{x,D} := \begin{cases} \mathsf{P}|_{D|^x} & \textit{if } \bot \in \mathsf{P}'|_{D|^x} \\ \mathsf{P}'|_{D|^x} & \textit{if } \bot \in \mathsf{P}|_{D|^x}, \end{cases}$$

with $\mathsf{L}^{x,D}$ *being either of the two if* $\bot \notin \mathsf{P}|_{D|^x} \cup \mathsf{P}'|_{D|^x}$.[4] *Then*

$$[\![\mathsf{P} \to \mathsf{P}']\!] \leq \max_{x,D} \sqrt{10 P[U \in \mathsf{L}^{x,D}]},$$

where U *is uniform over* $\mathcal{Y}$, *and the maximization can be restricted to* $D \in \mathfrak{D}$ *and* $x \in \mathcal{X}$ *for which both* $\mathsf{P}|_{D|^x}$ *and* $\mathsf{P}'|_{D|^x}$ *are non-empty.*

Remark 2.3. Both, $\mathsf{P}|_{D|^x}$ and $\mathsf{P}'|_{D|^x}$, and thus also $\mathsf{L}^{x,D}$, do not depend on the value of $D(x)$, only on the values of D outside of x.

2.3 An Improved Variant of Zhandry's Lemma

We show here an alternative to Zhandry's lemma (Lemma 2.1), which offers a better bound in typical applications. To start with, note that Lemma 2.1 considers an algorithm $\mathcal{A}$ that not only outputs $\mathbf{x} = (x_1, \ldots, x_\ell)$ but also $\mathbf{y} = (y_1, \ldots, y_\ell)$, where the latter is supposed to be the point-wise hash of $\mathbf{x}$; indeed, this is what is being checked in the definition of the probability p, along with $(\mathbf{x}, \mathbf{y}, z) \in R$. This requirement is somewhat unnatural, in that an algorithm $\mathcal{A}$ for, say, finding a collision, i.e., $x_1 \neq x_2$ with $H(x_1) = H(x_2)$, does *not* necessarily output the (supposed to be equal) hashes $y_1 = H(x_1)$ and $y_2 = H(x_2)$. Of course, this is no problem since one can easily transform such an algorithm $\mathcal{A}$ that does not output the hashes into one that does, simply by making a few more (classical) queries to the RO at the end of the execution, and then one can apply Lemma 2.1 to this tweaked algorithm $\tilde{\mathcal{A}}$.

We show below that if we anyway consider this tweaked algorithm $\tilde{\mathcal{A}}$, which is *promised* to query the RO to obtain and then output the hashes of $\mathbf{x} = (x_1, \ldots, x_\ell)$, then we can actually improve the bound and avoid the square-roots in Lemma 2.1. On top, the proof is much simpler than Zhandry's proof for his lemma. At the core is the following lemma; Corollary 2.5 then puts it in a form that is comparable to Lemma 2.1 and shows the improvement.

Lemma 2.4. *Let* $\mathcal{A}$ *be an oracle quantum algorithm that outputs* $\mathbf{x} = (x_1, \ldots, x_\ell) \in \mathcal{X}^\ell$ *and* $z \in \mathcal{Z}$. *Let* $\tilde{\mathcal{A}}$ *be the oracle quantum algorithm that runs* $\mathcal{A}$, *makes* ℓ *classical queries on the outputs* x_i *to obtain* $\mathbf{y} = H(\mathbf{x})$, *and then outputs* $(\mathbf{x}, \mathbf{y}, z)$. *When* $\tilde{\mathcal{A}}$ *interacts with the compressed oracle instead, and at the end* D *is obtained by measuring the internal state of the compressed oracle, then, conditioned on* $\tilde{\mathcal{A}}$'*s output* $(\mathbf{x}, \mathbf{y}, z)$,

$$\Pr[\mathbf{y} = D(\mathbf{x}) | (\mathbf{x}, \mathbf{y}, z)] \geq 1 - \frac{2\ell}{|\mathcal{Y}|}.$$

---

[4] By the disjointness requirement, $\bot$ cannot be contained in both.

Proof. Consider first $\tilde{\mathcal{A}}$ interacting with the *purified* (yet uncompressed) oracle. Conditioned on $\tilde{\mathcal{A}}$'s output $(\mathbf{x}, \mathbf{y}, z)$, the state of the oracle is then supported by $|H\rangle$ with $H(x_i) = y_i$ for all $i \in \{1, \ldots, \ell\}$, i.e., the registers labeled by $x_1, \ldots, x_\ell$ are in state $|y_1\rangle \cdots |y_\ell\rangle$. Given that the compressed oracle is obtained by applying Comp to all the registers, we thus have that

$$\Pr[y_i = y_i' | (\mathbf{x}, \mathbf{y}, z)] = \left|\langle y_i | \mathsf{Comp} | y_i \rangle\right|^2 = \left|\langle y_i | \left(|y_i\rangle + \frac{1}{\sqrt{|\mathcal{Y}|}}(|\bot\rangle - |\hat{0}\rangle)\right)\right|^2$$

$$= \left|1 - \frac{1}{\sqrt{|\mathcal{Y}|}}\langle y_i | \hat{0}\rangle\right|^2 = \left|1 - \frac{1}{|\mathcal{Y}|}\right|^2 \geq 1 - \frac{2}{|\mathcal{Y}|}.$$

Applying union bound concludes the claim. $\qquad\qquad\qquad\qquad\qquad\qquad\square$

The following corollary of Lemma 2.4 is put in a form that can be nicely compared with Lemma 2.1, understanding that typically Lemma 2.1 is applied to $\tilde{\mathcal{A}}$.

Corollary 2.5. *Let $R \subseteq \mathcal{X}^\ell \times \mathcal{Y}^\ell \times \mathcal{Z}$ be a relation. Let $\mathcal{A}$ be an oracle quantum algorithm that outputs $\mathbf{x} \in \mathcal{X}^\ell$ and $z \in \mathcal{Z}$, and let $\tilde{\mathcal{A}}$ be as in Lemma 2.4. Let*

$$p_\circ(\mathcal{A}) := \Pr[(\mathbf{x}, H(\mathbf{x}), z) \in R]$$

be the considered probability when $\mathcal{A}$ has interacted with the RO. Furthermore, let $p(\tilde{\mathcal{A}})$ and $p'(\tilde{\mathcal{A}})$ be defined as in Lemma 2.1 (but now for $\tilde{\mathcal{A}}$). Then

$$p_\circ(\mathcal{A}) = p(\tilde{\mathcal{A}}) \leq p'(\tilde{\mathcal{A}}) + \frac{2\ell}{|\mathcal{Y}|}.$$

In the full version, we show yet another corollary of Lemma 2.4, where $\tilde{\mathcal{A}}$ may make a more involved computation on $\mathbf{x}$, possibly calling H adaptively.

3   Some Background on (Non-)Interactive Proofs

Throughout this and later sections, we consider a hash function $H : \mathcal{X} \to \mathcal{Y}$, to be modeled as a RO then. For concreteness and simplicity, we assume that all relevant variables are encoded as bit strings, and that we can therefore choose $H : \{0,1\}^{\leq B} \to \{0,1\}^n$ for sufficiently large B and n.[5]

Let $\{\mathcal{I}_\lambda\}_{\lambda \in \mathbb{N}}$ and $\{\mathcal{W}_\lambda\}_{\lambda \in \mathbb{N}}$ be two families of sets, with the members being labeled by the security parameter $\lambda \in \mathbb{N}$. Let $R_\lambda \subseteq \mathcal{I}_\lambda \times \mathcal{W}_\lambda$ be a relation that is polynomial-time computable in λ. $w \in \mathcal{W}_\lambda$ is called a *witness* for $inst \in \mathcal{I}_\lambda$ if $R_\lambda(inst, w)$, and L_λ is the language $L_\lambda = \{inst \in \mathcal{I}_\lambda \mid \exists w \in \mathcal{W}_\lambda : R_\lambda(inst, w)\}$.

Below, we recall some concepts in the context of interactive and non-interactive proofs for such families $\{R_\lambda\}_{\lambda \in \mathbb{N}}$ of relations. We start by discussing the aspired security definition for non-interactive proofs.

---

[5] B and n may depend on the security parameter $\lambda \in \mathbb{N}$. We will then assume that B and n can be computed from λ in polynomial time (in λ).

3.1 Non-interactive Proofs and Online Extractability

An *non-interactive proof in the random-oracle model* for a family $\{R_\lambda\}_{\lambda \in \mathbb{N}}$ of relations consists of a pair $(\mathcal{P}, \mathcal{V})$ of oracle algorithms, referred to as *prover* and *verifier*, both making queries to the RO $H : \mathcal{X} \to \mathcal{Y}$. The prover $\mathcal{P}$ takes as input $\lambda \in \mathbb{N}$ and an instance *inst* $\in L_\lambda$ and outputs a *proof* $\pi \in \Pi_\lambda$, and $\mathcal{V}$ takes as input $\lambda \in \mathbb{N}$ and a pair *(inst, π)* $\in \mathcal{I}_\lambda \times \Pi_\lambda$ and outputs a Boolean value, 0 or 1, or accept or reject. The verifier $\mathcal{V}$ is required to run in time polynomial in λ, while, *per-se*, $\mathcal{P}$ may have unbounded running time.[6]

By default, we require correctness and soundness, i.e., that for any $\lambda \in \mathbb{N}$ and any *inst* $\in L_\lambda$ the probability $\Pr\left[\mathcal{V}^H(\lambda, \textit{inst}, \pi) : \pi \leftarrow \mathcal{P}^H(\lambda, \textit{inst})\right]$ is close to 1, while for any $\lambda \in \mathbb{N}$ and any oracle quantum algorithm $\mathcal{P}^*$ with bounded query complexity the probability $\Pr\left[\textit{inst} \notin L_\lambda \wedge \mathcal{V}^H(\lambda, \textit{inst}, \pi) : (\textit{inst}, \pi) \leftarrow \mathcal{P}^{*H}(\lambda)\right]$ is close to vanishing. The fact that the instance *inst*, for which $\mathcal{P}^*$ tries to forge a proof, is not given as input to $\mathcal{P}^*$ but is instead chosen by $\mathcal{P}^*$ is referred to as $\mathcal{P}^*$ being *adaptive*.

We now move towards defining *online extractability* (for adaptive $\mathcal{P}^*$). For that purpose, let $\mathcal{P}^*$ be a dishonest prover as above, except that it potentially outputs some additional auxiliary (possibly quantum) output Z next to *(inst, π)*. We then consider an interactive algorithm $\mathcal{E}$, called *online extractor*, which takes $\lambda \in \mathbb{N}$ as input and simulates the answers to the oracle queries in the execution of $\mathcal{V}^H \circ \mathcal{P}^{*H}(\lambda)$, which we define to run *(inst, π, Z)* $\leftarrow \mathcal{P}^{*H}(\lambda)$ followed by $v \leftarrow \mathcal{V}^H(\lambda, \textit{inst}, \pi)$; furthermore, at the end, $\mathcal{E}$ outputs $w \in \mathcal{W}_\lambda$. We denote the execution of $\mathcal{V}^H \circ \mathcal{P}^{*H}(\lambda)$ with the calls to H simulated by $\mathcal{E}$, and considering $\mathcal{E}$'s final output w as well, as *(inst, π, Z; v; w)* $\leftarrow \mathcal{V}^{\mathcal{E}} \circ \mathcal{P}^{*\mathcal{E}}(\lambda)$.

Definition 3.1. *A non-interactive proof in the (quantum-accessible) RO model (QROM) for $\{R_\lambda\}_{\lambda \in \mathbb{N}}$ is a* proof of knowledge with online extractability (PoK-OE) *against adaptive adversaries if there exists an* online extractor $\mathcal{E}$, *and functions ε_{sim} (the* simulation error*) and ε_{ex} (the* extraction error*), with the following properties. For any $\lambda \in \mathbb{N}$ and for any dishonest prover $\mathcal{P}^*$ with query complexity q,*

$$\delta\left([(\textit{inst}, \pi, Z, v)]_{\mathcal{V}^H \circ \mathcal{P}^{*H}(\lambda)}, [(\textit{inst}, \pi, Z, v)]_{\mathcal{V}^{\mathcal{E}} \circ \mathcal{P}^{*\mathcal{E}}(\lambda)}\right) \leq \varepsilon_{\text{sim}}(\lambda, q, n) \qquad and$$

$$\Pr\left[v = \texttt{accept} \wedge (\textit{inst}, w) \notin R : (\textit{inst}, \pi, Z; v; w) \leftarrow \mathcal{V}^{\mathcal{E}} \circ \mathcal{P}^{*\mathcal{E}}(\lambda)\right] \leq \varepsilon_{\text{ex}}(\lambda, q, n).$$

Furthermore, the runtime of $\mathcal{E}$ is polynomial in $\lambda + q + n$, and $\varepsilon_{\text{sim}}(\lambda, q, n)$ and $\varepsilon_{\text{ex}}(\lambda, q, n)$ are negligible in λ whenever q and n are polynomial in λ.

Remark 3.2. In the classical definition of a proof of knowledge, the extractor $\mathcal{E}$ interacts with $\mathcal{P}^*$ only, and the verifier $\mathcal{V}$ is not explicitly involved, but would typically be run by $\mathcal{E}$. Here, in the context of online extractability, it is necessary to explicitly go through the verification procedure, which also makes oracle queries, to determine whether a proof is valid, i.e., for the event $v = \texttt{accept}$ to be well defined.

---

[6] Alternatively, one may consider a witness w for *inst* to be given as additional input to $\mathcal{P}$, and then ask $\mathcal{P}$ to be polynomial-time as well.

3.2   (Commit-and-Open) Σ-Protocols

A Σ-*protocol* is a 3-round public-coin interactive proof $(\mathcal{P}, \mathcal{V})$ for a relation $R_\lambda \subseteq \mathcal{I}_\lambda \times \mathcal{W}_\lambda$, indexed by the security parameter. From now on, we leave any dependencies on the security parameter implicit. We therefore simply write R etc. By definition, a Σ-protocol has the following communication pattern. In the first round, $\mathcal{P}$ sends a *first message* a; in the second round, $\mathcal{V}$ sends a random *challenge* $c \in \mathcal{C}$; and in the third round, $\mathcal{P}$ sends a *response* z. By a slight abuse of notation, we sometimes write $\mathcal{V}(\mathit{inst}, a, c, z)$ for the predicate that determines whether $\mathcal{V}$ accepts the transcript (a, c, z) on input inst.

For the purpose of this work, a *commit-and-open* Σ-protocol, or *C&O Σ-protocol* or *C&O protocol* for short, is a Σ-protocol $\Pi = (\mathcal{P}, \mathcal{V})$ of a special form, involving a hash function H that is modeled as a RO.[7] Concretely, in a C&O protocol, the transcript (a, c, z) is of the following form. The first message a consists of *commitments* $y_1, \ldots, y_\ell$, computed as $y_i = H(m_i)$ for *messages* $m_1, \ldots, m_\ell \in \mathcal{M}$, and possibly an additional string $a_\circ$.[8] The challenge c is picked uniformly at random from the challenge space $\mathcal{C} \subseteq 2^{[\ell]}$, which is set to be a subset of $2^{[\ell]}$. Finally, the response z is given by $\mathbf{m}_c = (m_i)_{i \in c}$. Eventually, $\mathcal{V}$ accepts if and only if $H(m_i) = y_i$ for all $i \in c$ and some given predicate $V(\mathit{inst}, c, \mathbf{m}_c, a_\circ)$ is satisfied.

For the above to be meaningful, we obviously need that $\mathcal{M} \subseteq \mathcal{X}$, i.e., the bit size of the possible m_i's are upper bounded by B. Furthermore, the parameter n determines the hardness of finding a collision in H (in the random oracle model), and thus the level of binding the commitments provide.

Remark 3.3. Looking ahead, we may also consider a generalization of the above notion of a C&O protocol, where the first message is parsed as a *single* commitment y of the ℓ messages $m_1, \ldots, m_\ell$ and where this commitment is computed by means of an arbitrary "multi-message" commitment scheme involving H, which has the property that any subset of $m_1, \ldots, m_\ell$ can be opened without revealing the remaining m_i's. The above component-wise hashing is then one particular instantiation, but alternatively one can for instance also compute y by means of a Merkle tree (see Sect. 5.1), and then open individual m_i's by revealing the corresponding authentication paths. We stress that the concepts discussed below: the notions of $\mathfrak{S}$-soundness and $\mathfrak{S}$-soundness* and the probability $p_{triv}^{\mathfrak{S}}$, do not depend on the choice of commitment scheme, and thus remain unaffected when considering such a *Merkle-tree-based C&O* protocol. To emphasize the default choice of the commitment scheme, which is element-wise hashing, we sometimes also speak of an *ordinary* C&O protocol.

---

[7] One could also refer to Σ-protocols that use non-hash-based commitments, and/or are analyzed in the standard model, as *C&O protocols*, but this is not the scope here.

[8] Note that $m_i \in \mathcal{M}$ may consist of the actual "message" (computed by the prover using the witness w), possibly concatenated with randomness.

3.3 $\mathfrak{S}$-soundness of C&O Σ-Protocols

We briefly recall the notion of $\mathfrak{S}$-soundness and $\mathfrak{S}$-soundness* for C&O protocols, as considered in [DFMS21], which offers a convenient general notion of special soundness, or more generally k-soundness for C&O protocols. A similar notion of $\mathfrak{S}$-soundness naturally exists for plain Σ-protocols, i.e., Σ-protocols in the plain model. For completeness, we formalize the latter in the full version.

Here and below, given a C&O protocol Π with challenge space $\mathcal{C} \subseteq 2^{[\ell]}$, we let $\mathfrak{S} \subseteq 2^{\mathcal{C}}$ be an arbitrary non-empty, monotone increasing set of subsets $S \subseteq \mathcal{C}$, where the monotonicity means that $S \in \mathfrak{S} \wedge S \subseteq S' \Rightarrow S' \in \mathfrak{S}$. We then also set $\mathfrak{S}_{\min} := \{S \in \mathfrak{S} \mid S_\circ \subsetneq S \Rightarrow S_\circ \notin \mathfrak{S}\}$ to be the minimal sets in $\mathfrak{S}$.

For simplicity, the reader can consider $\mathfrak{S} = \mathfrak{T}_k := \{S \subseteq \mathcal{C} \mid |S| \geq k\}$ for some threshold k, and thus $\mathfrak{S}_{\min} = \{S \subseteq \mathcal{C} \mid |S| = k\}$. This then corresponds to the notion of k-soundness for C&O protocols, which in turn means that the witness can be computed from valid responses to k (or more) distinct challenges for a given first message $y_1, \ldots, y_\ell$, assuming the messages $m_1, \ldots, m_\ell$ to be uniquely determined by their commitments.

Definition 3.4 ([DFMS21] Def. 5.1). *A C&O protocol Π is $\mathfrak{S}$-sound if there exists an efficient deterministic algorithm $\mathcal{E}_{\mathfrak{S}}(\textsf{inst}, m_1, \ldots, m_\ell, a_\circ, S)$ that takes as input an instance $\textsf{inst} \in \mathcal{I}$, messages $m_1, \ldots, m_\ell \in \mathcal{M} \cup \{\bot\}$, a string $a_\circ$, and a set $S \in \mathfrak{S}_{\min}$, and outputs a witness for $\textsf{inst}$ if $V(\textsf{inst}, c, \mathbf{m}_c, a_\circ)$ for all $c \in S$.*[9]

A slightly stronger condition than $\mathfrak{S}$-*soundness* is the following variant, which differs in that the extractor needs to work as soon as there *exists* a set S as specified, without the extractor being given S as input. We refer to [DFMS21] for a more detailed discussion of this aspect. As explained there, whether S is given or not often makes no (big) difference.

For instance, when $\mathfrak{S}_{\min}$ consists of a polynomial number of sets S then the extractor can do a brute-force search to find S, and so $\mathfrak{S}$-soundness* is then implied by $\mathfrak{S}$-soundness. Also, the r-fold parallel repetition of a $\mathfrak{S}$-sound protocol, which by default is a $\mathfrak{S}^{\vee r}$-sound protocol (see [DFMS21]), is automatically $\mathfrak{S}^\vee$-sound* if $\mathfrak{S}_{\min}$ is polynomial in size: the extractor can then do a brute-force search in every repeated instance.

Definition 3.5 ([DFMS21] Def. 5.2). *A C&O protocol Π is $\mathfrak{S}$-sound* if there exists an efficient deterministic algorithm $\mathcal{E}^*_{\mathfrak{S}}(\textsf{inst}, m_1, \ldots, m_\ell, a_\circ)$ that takes as input an instance $\textsf{inst} \in \mathcal{I}$ and strings $m_1, \ldots, m_\ell \in \mathcal{M} \cup \{\bot\}$ and $a_\circ$, and it outputs a witness for $\textsf{inst}$ if there exists $S \in \mathfrak{S}$ such that $V(\textsf{inst}, c, \mathbf{m}_c, a_\circ)$ for all $c \in S$.*

As in [DFMS21], we define

$$p^{\mathfrak{S}}_{triv} := \frac{1}{|\mathcal{C}|} \max_{\hat{S} \notin \mathfrak{S}} |\hat{S}|, \tag{5}$$

---

[9] The restriction for S to be in $\mathfrak{S}_{\min}$, rather than in $\mathfrak{S}$, is to avoid an exponentially sized input while asking $\mathcal{E}_{\mathfrak{S}}$ to be efficient.

capturing the "trivial" attack of picking a set $\hat{S} = \{\hat{c}_1, \ldots, \hat{c}_m\} \notin \mathfrak{S}$ of challenges $\hat{c}_i \in \mathcal{C}$ and then prepare $\hat{\mathbf{m}} = (\hat{m}_1, \ldots, \hat{m}_\ell)$ and a_o in such a way that $V(inst, c, \hat{\mathbf{m}}_c, a_o)$ holds if $c \in \hat{S}$. After committing to $\hat{m}_1, \ldots, \hat{m}_\ell$, the prover can successfully answer to challenges $c \in \hat{S}$.

3.4   The Fiat-Shamir Transformation of (C&O) Σ-Protocols

The Fiat-Shamir (FS) transformation [FS87] turns arbitrary Σ-protocols into non-interactive proofs in the random oracle model by setting the challenge $c \in \mathcal{C}$ to be the hash of the instance and the first message a. For this transformation to work smoothly, it is typically assumed that $|\mathcal{C}|$ is a power of 2 and its elements are represented as bit strings of size $\log|\mathcal{C}|$, so that one can indeed set c to be (the first $\log|\mathcal{C}|$ bits of) the hash $H(inst, a)$. The assumption on $|\mathcal{C}|$ is essentially without loss of generality (WLOG), since one can always reduce the size of $|\mathcal{C}|$ to the next lower power of 2, at the cost of losing at most 1 bit of security. However, for a C&O Σ-protocol, where a challenge space $\mathcal{C}$ is a (typically strict) subset of $2^{[\ell]}$, there is not necessarily a natural way to represent $c \in \mathcal{C}$ as a bitstring of size $\log|\mathcal{C}|$. Therefore, we will make it explicit that the challenge-set $c \in \mathcal{C} \subset 2^{[\ell]}$ is computed from the "raw randomness" $H(inst, y_1, \ldots, y_\ell, a_o)$ in a deterministic way as $c = \gamma \circ H(inst, y_1, \ldots, y_\ell, a_o)$ for an appropriate function $\gamma : \mathcal{Y} \to \mathcal{C}$, mapping a uniformly random hash in $\mathcal{Y}$ to a random challenge-set in $\mathcal{C}$. Obviously, for $H(inst, y_1, \ldots, y_\ell, a_o)$ to be defined, in addition to $\mathcal{M} \subseteq \mathcal{X}$ we also need that $\mathcal{I} \times \mathcal{Y}^\ell \subseteq \mathcal{X}$, which again just means that B needs to be large enough. We write $\mathsf{FS}[\Pi]$ for the FS transformation of a (C&O) Σ-protocol Π.

Remark 3.6. Additionally, we need that n is sufficiently large, so that there is a sufficient amount of randomness in the hash value $H(inst, y_1, \ldots, y_\ell)$ in order to be mapped to a random $c \in \mathcal{C}$. The canonical choice for γ is then the function that the *interactive* verifier applies to his local randomness to compute the random challenge $c \in \mathcal{C}$. To simplify the exposition, we assume that n is indeed sufficiently large. Otherwise, one can simply set $\mathcal{Y} := \{0,1\}^{n'}$ instead, for sufficiently large n', and then let y_i be $H(m_i)$ *truncated* to the original number n of bits again. This truncation has no effect on our results.

Remark 3.7. We assume WLOG that the two kinds of inputs to H, i.e., m_i and $(inst, y_1, \ldots, y_\ell, a_o)$, are differently formatted, e.g., bit strings of different respective sizes or prefixes (this is referred to as *domain separation*). In other words, we assume that $\mathcal{M}$ and $\mathcal{I} \times \mathcal{Y}^\ell$ are disjoint.

Remark 3.8. When considering the adaptive security of a FS transformation $\mathsf{FS}[\Pi]$ of a C&O protocol Π for a relation R, the additional string a_o, which may be part of the first message a of the original protocol Π, may WLOG be considered to be part of the instance *inst* instead.

Indeed, any dishonest prover $\mathcal{P}^*$ against $\mathsf{FS}[\Pi]$, which (by Definition 3.1) outputs an instance *inst* and a proof $\pi = (a_o, y_1, \ldots y_\ell)$, can alternatively be parsed as a dishonest prover that outputs an instance $inst' = (inst, a_o)$ and a proof $\pi' = (y_1, \ldots y_\ell)$. Thus, $\mathcal{P}^*$ can be parsed as a dishonest prover against

FS[Π'], where the C&O protocol Π' works as Π, except that a_o is considered as part of the instance, rather than as part of the first message, and thus Π' is a C&O protocol for the relation $((inst, a_o), w) \in R' :\Leftrightarrow (inst, w) \in R$.[10] Therefore, security (in the sense of Definition 3.1) for FS[Π'] implies that of FS[Π].

4 Online Extractability of the FS-Transformation: The Case of Ordinary C&O Protocols

We now consider the FS transformation FS[Π] of an ordinary C&O protocol Π. Our goal is to show that FS[Π] admits online extraction. We note that by exploiting Remark 3.8, we may assume WLOG that the first message of Π consists of the commitments $y_1, \ldots, y_\ell$ only, and no additional string a_o. In Sect. 5, we then consider the case of Merkle-tree-based C&O protocols.

Our analysis of FS[Π] uses the framework of Chung et al. [CFHL21], discussed and outlined in Sect. 2. Thus, at the core of our analysis is a bound on a certain quantum transition capacity. This is treated in the upcoming subsection.

4.1 Technical Preface

We first introduce a couple of elementary database properties (related to Collisions and the SiZe of the database) that will be useful for us:

$$\mathsf{CL} := \{D \mid \exists x \neq x' : D(x) = D(x') \neq \bot\} \quad \text{and} \quad \mathsf{SZ}_{\leq s} := \{D \mid \#\{z \mid D(z) \neq \bot\} \leq s\}.$$

Next, for an instance $inst \in \mathcal{I}$, we want to specify the database property that captures a cheating prover that succeeds in producing an accepting proof while fooling the extractor. For the purpose of specifying this database property, we introduce the following notation. For a given database $D \in \mathfrak{D}$ and for a commitment $y \in \mathcal{Y}$, we define $D^{-1}(y)$ to be the smallest $x \in \mathcal{X}$ with $D(x) = y$, with the convention that $D^{-1}(y) := \bot$ if there is no such x, as well as $D^{-1}(\bot) := \bot$. By removing collisions, we ensure that there is at most one such x; thus, taking the smallest one in case of multiple choices is not important but only for well-definedness. The database property of interest can now be defined as

$$\mathsf{SUC} := \left\{ D \;\middle|\; \begin{array}{c} \exists \mathbf{y} \in \mathcal{Y}^\ell \text{ and } inst \in \mathcal{I} \text{ so that } \mathbf{m} := D^{-1}(\mathbf{y}) \text{ satisfies} \\ V(inst, c, \mathbf{m}_c) \text{ for } c := \gamma \circ D(inst, \mathbf{y}) \text{ and } (inst, \mathcal{E}^*(inst, \mathbf{m})) \notin R \end{array} \right\}. \tag{6}$$

Informally, assuming no collisions (i.e., restricting to $D \notin \mathsf{CL}$), the database property SUC captures whether a database D admits a *valid* proof $\pi = (\mathbf{y}, \mathbf{m}_c)$ for an instance $inst$ for which the (canonical) extractor, which first computes $\mathbf{m}$ by inverting D and then runs $\mathcal{E}^*$, *fails* to produce a witness.

---

[10] We do not specify the local computation of the honest prover $\mathcal{P}'$ in $\Pi' = (\mathcal{P}', \mathcal{V}')$, i.e., how to act when a_o is part of the input, and in general it might not be efficient, but this is fine since we are interested in the security against dishonest provers.

Our (first) goal is to show that $[\![\perp \overset{q}{\Longrightarrow} \mathsf{SUC} \cup \mathsf{CL}]\!]$ is small, capturing that it is unlikely that after q queries the compressed database contains collisions or admits a valid proof upon which the extractor fails. Indeed, we show the following, where p^{G}_{triv} is the trivial cheating probability of Π as defined in (5).

Lemma 4.1. $[\![\perp \overset{q}{\Longrightarrow} \mathsf{SUC} \cup \mathsf{CL}]\!] \leq 2eq^{3/2}2^{-n/2} + q\sqrt{10 \max\left(q\ell \cdot 2^{-n}, p^{\mathsf{G}}_{triv}\right)}.$

We begin with an outline of the proof. In a first step, by using (3) and union-bound-like properties of the transition capacity, and additionally exploiting a bound from [CFHL21] to control the transition capacity of CL, we reduce the problem to bounding the quantum transition capacity $[\![\mathsf{SZ}_{\leq s} \backslash \mathsf{SUC} \rightarrow \mathsf{SUC}]\!]$ for $s < q$. Informally, this capacity is a measure of the "likelihood" — but then in a *quantum*-sense — that a database $D \in \mathfrak{D}$ that is bounded in size and not in SUC turns into a database D' that *is* in SUC, when D is updated to $D' = D[x \mapsto U]$ with U uniformly random in $\mathcal{Y}$, for any fixed x.

We emphasize that the state of the compressed oracle at any point is a *superposition* of databases, and a query is made up of a *superposition* of inputs; nevertheless, due to Theorem 2.2, the above classical intuition is actually very close to what needs to be shown to rigorously bound the considered quantum transition capacity. Formally, as will become clear in the proof below, we need to show that for any database $D \in \mathsf{SZ}_{\leq s} \backslash \mathsf{SUC}$ and for any $x \in \mathcal{X}$ with $D(x) = \perp$, the probability that $D[x \mapsto U] \in \mathsf{SUC}$ is small. Below, this probability is bounded in the *Case 2* and *Case 3* parts of the proof, where the two cases distinguish between x being a "commit query" or a "challenge query".

Informally, for D with $D(x) = \perp$, if x is a "commit query" then assigning a value to $D(x)$ can only turn $D \notin \mathsf{SUC}$ into $D[x \mapsto u] \in \mathsf{SUC}$, if u is a coordinate of some $\mathbf{y} \in \mathcal{Y}^\ell$ for which $D(inst, \mathbf{y}) \neq \perp$ for some $inst$. Indeed, otherwise, $D[x \mapsto u]$ does not contribute to a valid proof π that did not exist before. Thus, given the bound $s < q$ on the size of D, this happens with probability at most $q\ell/2^n$ for a random u. Similarly, if x is a "challenge query", i.e. of the form $x = (inst, \mathbf{y})$, then assigning a value u to $D(x)$ can only make a difference if $V(inst, c, \mathbf{m}_c)$ is satisfied for $c = \gamma(u)$ and $\mathbf{m} = D^{-1}(\mathbf{y})$, while $\mathcal{E}^*(inst, \mathbf{m})$ is not a witness for $inst$. However, for a random u, this is bounded by p^{G}_{triv}.

But then, on top of the above, due to the quantum nature of the quantum transition capacity,[11] Theorem 2.2 requires to also show the "reverse", i.e., that for any $D \in \mathsf{SUC}$ and for any $x \in \mathcal{X}$ with $D(x) \neq \perp$, the probability that $D[x \mapsto U] \in \mathsf{SZ}_{\leq s} \backslash \mathsf{SUC}$ is small; this is analyzed in *Case 1* below.

Thus, by exploiting the framework of [CFHL21], the core of the reasoning is purely classical, very closely mimicking how one would have to reason the classical setting with a classical RO. Due to the rather complex definition of SUC, the formal argument in each case is still somewhat cumbersome.

---

[11] At the core, this is related to the reversibility of quantum computing and the resulting ability to "uncompute" a query.

Proof. We first observe that, by (3) (which is Lemma 5.6 in [CFHL21]) and basic properties of the quantum transition capacity as in (4),

$$\llbracket \bot \overset{q}{\Longrightarrow} \mathsf{SUC} \cup \mathsf{CL} \rrbracket \leq \sum_{s=0}^{q-1} \llbracket \mathsf{SZ}_{\leq s} \backslash \mathsf{SUC} \backslash \mathsf{CL} \to \mathsf{SUC} \cup \mathsf{CL} \cup \neg \mathsf{SZ}_{\leq s+1} \rrbracket$$

$$\leq \sum_{s=0}^{q-1} \left(\llbracket \mathsf{SZ}_{\leq s} \to \neg \mathsf{SZ}_{\leq s+1} \rrbracket + \llbracket \mathsf{SZ}_{\leq s} \backslash \mathsf{CL} \to \mathsf{CL} \rrbracket + \llbracket \mathsf{SZ}_{\leq s} \backslash \mathsf{SUC} \to \mathsf{SUC} \rrbracket \right). \quad (7)$$

The first term, $\llbracket \mathsf{SZ}_{\leq s} \to \neg \mathsf{SZ}_{\leq s+1} \rrbracket$, vanishes, while the second term was shown to be bounded as

$$\llbracket \mathsf{SZ}_{\leq s} \backslash \mathsf{CL} \to \mathsf{CL} \rrbracket \leq 2e\sqrt{(s+1)/|\mathcal{Y}|} \leq 2e\sqrt{q/2^n} \quad (8)$$

in Example 5.28 in [CFHL21]. Thus, it remains to control the third term, which we will do by means of Theorem 2.2 with $\mathsf{P} := \mathsf{SZ}_{\leq s} \backslash \mathsf{SUC}$ and $\mathsf{P}' := \mathsf{SUC}$.

To this end, we consider arbitrary but fixed $D \in \mathfrak{D}$ and input $x \in \mathcal{X}$. By Remark 2.3, we may assume that $D(x) = \bot$. Furthermore, for $\mathsf{P}|_{D|^x}$ to be non-empty, it must be that $D \in \mathsf{SZ}_{\leq s}$, i.e., D is bounded in size. We now distinguish between the following cases for the considered D and x.

Case 1: $D \in \mathsf{SUC}$. In particular, $\bot \in \mathsf{SUC}|_{D|^x} = \mathsf{P}'_{D|^x}$. So, Theorem 2.2 instructs us to set $\mathsf{L} := \mathsf{P}_{D|^x}$, where we leave the dependency of L on D and x implicit to simplify notation. Given that $D \in \mathsf{SUC}$, we can consider *inst* and $\mathbf{y}$ as promised by the definition of SUC in (6), i.e., such that $V(inst, c, \mathbf{m}_c)$ and $(inst, \mathcal{E}^*(inst, \mathbf{m})) \notin R$ for

$$c := \gamma \circ D(inst, \mathbf{y}) \quad \text{and} \quad m_i := D^{-1}(y_i),$$

where it is understood that $\mathbf{m} = (m_1, \ldots, m_\ell)$. Recall that $D(x) = \bot$; thus, by definition of the m_i's, it must be that $x \neq m_i$ for all i, and the fact that $V(inst, c, \mathbf{m}_c)$ is satisfied for c as defined implies that $x \neq (inst, \mathbf{y})$. Furthermore,

$$u \in \mathsf{L} \iff D[x \mapsto u] \in \mathsf{P} \implies D[x \mapsto u] \notin \mathsf{SUC} \implies u \in \{y_1, \ldots, y_\ell\},$$

where the last implication is easiest seen by contraposition: Assume that $u \notin \{y_1, \ldots, y_\ell\}$. Then, also recalling that $x \neq m_i$, we have that $m_i = D^{-1}(y_i) = D[x \mapsto u]^{-1}(y_i)$. But also $c = \gamma \circ D(inst, \mathbf{y}) = \gamma \circ D[x \mapsto u](inst, \mathbf{y})$. Together, this implies that the defining property of SUC is also satisfied for $D[x \mapsto u]$, i.e., $D[x \mapsto u] \in \mathsf{SUC}$, as was to be shown. Thus, we can bound

$$P[U \in \mathsf{L}] \leq P[U \in \{y_1, \ldots, y_\ell\}] \leq \frac{\ell}{|\mathcal{Y}|}. \quad (9)$$

Case 2: $D \notin \mathsf{SUC}$, and x is a "commit query", i.e., $x = m \in \mathcal{M}$. In particular, $\bot \notin \mathsf{P}'|_{D|^x}$ (by the assumption that $D(x) = \bot$) and so in light of Theorem 2.2 we may choose $\mathsf{L} := \mathsf{P}'|_{D|^x}$. We then have

$$u \in \mathsf{L} \iff D[x \mapsto u] \in \mathsf{P}' = \mathsf{SUC} \implies \exists \, inst, \mathbf{y}, i : D(inst, \mathbf{y}) \neq \bot \wedge u = y_i. \quad (10)$$

The last implication can be seen as follows. By definition of SUC, the assumption $D[x \mapsto u] \in$ SUC implies the existence of $inst$ and $\mathbf{y} = (y_1, \ldots, y_\ell)$ with $V(inst, c, \mathbf{m}_c)$ and $(inst, \mathcal{E}^*(inst, \mathbf{m})) \notin R$ for

$$c := \gamma \circ D[x \mapsto u](inst, \mathbf{y}) = \gamma \circ D(inst, \mathbf{y}) \quad \text{and} \quad m_i := D[x \mapsto u]^{-1}(y_i),$$

where the equality in the definition of c exploits that x is not a "challenge" query. With the goal to reach a contradiction, assume that $u \neq y_i$ for all i. This assumption implies that $D[x \mapsto u](x) = u \neq y_i$. But also $D(x) = \bot \neq y_i$, and hence for all $\xi \in \mathcal{X}$ and $i \in \{1, \ldots, \ell\}$: $D(\xi) = y_i \Leftrightarrow D[x \mapsto u](\xi) = y_i$. Therefore, $m_i = D[x \mapsto u]^{-1}(y_i) = D^{-1}(y_i)$ for all i, and the above then implies that $D \in$ SUC, a contradiction. Thus, there exists i for which $u = y_i$; furthermore, $D(inst, \mathbf{y}) \neq \bot$ given that $V(inst, u, \mathbf{m}_c)$ is satisfied for $c = \gamma \circ D(inst, \mathbf{y})$. This shows the claimed implication. Thus, we can bound

$$P[U \in \mathsf{L}] \leq P[\exists\, inst, \mathbf{y}, i : D(inst, \mathbf{y}) \neq \bot \wedge u = y_i] \leq s\ell/|\mathcal{Y}| \leq q\ell/|\mathcal{Y}|. \quad (11)$$

Case 3: $D \notin$ SUC, and x is a "challenge query", i.e., $x = (inst, \mathbf{y}) \in \mathcal{I} \times \mathcal{Y}^\ell$. Set $\mathbf{m} = (m_1, \ldots, m_\ell)$ for $m_i := D^{-1}(y_i)$. Again, we have that $\bot \notin \mathsf{SUC}|_{D|^x} = \mathsf{P}'_{D|^x}$, and so by Theorem 2.2 we may set $\mathsf{L} := \mathsf{P}'_{D|^x}$. Here, we can argue that

$$u \in \mathsf{L} \Longleftrightarrow D[x \mapsto u] \in \mathsf{P}' = \mathsf{SUC} \Longrightarrow V(inst, u, \mathbf{m}_{\gamma(u)}) \wedge (inst, \mathcal{E}^*(inst, \mathbf{m})) \notin R,$$

where the final implication can be seen as follows. By definition of SUC, the assumption $D[x \mapsto u] \in$ SUC implies the existence of $inst'$ and $\mathbf{y}' = (y_1', \ldots, y_\ell')$ with $V(inst', u, \mathbf{m}_c')$ and $\mathcal{E}^*(inst', \mathbf{m}') \neq w$ for

$$c := \gamma \circ D[x \mapsto u](inst', \mathbf{y}') \quad \text{and} \quad m_i' := D[x \mapsto u]^{-1}(y_i') = D^{-1}(y_i'),$$

where the very last equality exploits that x is not a "commit" query. With the goal to come to a contradiction, assume that $(inst', \mathbf{y}') \neq (inst, \mathbf{y}) = x$. Then, $c = \gamma \circ D[x \mapsto u](inst', \mathbf{y}') = \gamma \circ D(inst', \mathbf{y}')$, and the above then implies that $D \in$ SUC, a contradiction. Thus, $(inst', \mathbf{y}') = (inst, \mathbf{y}) = x$. In particular, $\mathbf{m}' = \mathbf{m}$ and $c = \gamma \circ D[x \mapsto u](inst', \mathbf{y}') = \gamma \circ D[x \mapsto u](x) = \gamma(u)$. Hence, the claimed implication holds.

Thus, we can bound

$$P[U \in \mathsf{L}] \leq P[V(inst, \gamma(U), \mathbf{m}_{\gamma(U)}) \wedge \mathcal{E}^*(inst, \mathbf{m}) \neq w]$$
$$\leq P[V(inst, \gamma(U), \mathbf{m}_{\gamma(U)}) \wedge S := \{c \mid V(inst, c, \mathbf{m}_c)\} \notin \mathfrak{S}]$$
$$\leq P[\gamma(U) \in S := \{c \mid V(inst, c, \mathbf{m}_c)\} \notin \mathfrak{S}] \leq \max_{S \notin \mathfrak{S}} P[\gamma(U) \in S] \leq p_{triv}^{\mathfrak{S}}. \quad (12)$$

By Theorem 2.2, we now get

$$[\![\mathsf{SZ}_{\leq s} \backslash \mathsf{SUC} \backslash \mathsf{CL} \to \mathsf{SUC}]\!] \leq \max_{x, D} \sqrt{10 P[U \in \mathsf{L}^{x,D}]}$$

$$\leq \sqrt{10}\sqrt{\max(\ell/|\mathcal{Y}|, q\ell/|\mathcal{Y}|, p_{triv}^{\mathfrak{S}})} \leq \sqrt{10}\sqrt{\max(q\ell \cdot 2^{-n}, p_{triv}^{\mathfrak{S}})},$$

where we have used Eqs. (9), (11) and (12) in the second inequality. Combining with Eqs. (8) and (7) yields the desired bound.   □

4.2 Online Extractability of the Fiat-Shamir Transformation

We are now ready to state and proof the claimed online-extractability result for the FS transformation of (ordinary) C&O protocols.

Theorem 4.2. *Let Π be a $\mathfrak{S}$-sound* ordinary C&O protocol with challenge space $\mathcal{C}_\lambda$ and $\ell = \ell(\lambda)$ commitments, and set $\kappa = \kappa(\lambda) := \max_{c \in \mathcal{C}_\lambda} |c|$. Then, FS$[\Pi]$ is a PoK-OE in the QROM (as in Definition 3.1), with $\varepsilon_{\text{sim}}(\lambda, q, n) = 0$ and*

$$\varepsilon_{\text{ex}}(\lambda, q, n) \leq 2(\kappa + 1) \cdot 2^{-n} + \left(2eq^{3/2}2^{-n/2} + q\sqrt{10 \max \left(q\ell \cdot 2^{-n}, p^{\mathfrak{S}}_{triv} \right)} \right)^2$$

$$\leq (22\ell + 60)q^3 2^{-n} + 20q^2 p^{\mathfrak{S}}_{triv} \,.$$

The runtime of the extractor is dominated by running the compressed oracle, which has complexity $O(q^2) \cdot poly(n, B)$, and running $\mathcal{E}^*$.

We note that the above bound on ε_{ex} is asymptotically tight, except for the factor ℓ. Indeed, the binding property of the hash-based commitment can be invalidated by means of a collision finding attack, which succeeds with probability $\Omega(q^3/2^n)$. Furthermore the trivial soundness attack, which potentially applies to a $\mathfrak{S}$-sound* C&O protocol Π, can be complemented with a Grover search, yielding an attack against FS$[\Pi]$ that succeeds with probability $\Omega(q^2 p^{\mathfrak{S}}_{triv})$. The non-tightness by a factor of ℓ is very mild in most cases. In particular, the number of commitments ℓ is polynomial in λ and thus in n. For the most common case of a parallel repetition of a protocol with a constant number of commitments, using a hash function with output length linear in λ (e.g. $n = 3\lambda$) results in $\ell = O(n) = O(\lambda)$.

Proof. We consider an arbitrary but fixed $\lambda \in \mathbb{N}$. For simplicity, we assume that $|c|$ is the same for all $c \in \mathcal{C}_\lambda$, and thus equal to $\kappa = \kappa(\lambda)$. If it is not, we could always make the prover output a couple of dummy outputs m_i to match the upper bound on $|c|$. Let $\mathcal{P}^*$ be a dishonest prover that, after making q queries to a RO H, outputs $(inst, \pi) = (inst, \mathbf{y}, \mathbf{m}_\circ)$ plus some (possibly quantum) auxiliary output Z. In the experiment $\mathcal{V}^{\mathcal{E}} \circ \mathcal{P}^{*\mathcal{E}}(\lambda)$, our extractor $\mathcal{E}$ works as follows while simulating all queries to H (by $\mathcal{P}^*$ and $\mathcal{V}$) with the compressed oracle:

1. Run $\mathcal{P}^*(\lambda)$ to obtain $(inst, \pi, Z)$ where $\pi = (\mathbf{y}, \mathbf{m}_\circ)$ with $\mathbf{m}_\circ = (m_1, \dots, m_\kappa)$.
2. Run $\mathcal{V}(\lambda, inst, \pi)$ to obtain v. In detail: obtain $h_0 := H(inst, \mathbf{y})$ and $h_j := H(m_j)$ for $j \in \{1, \dots, \kappa\}$, and set $v := \mathsf{accept}$ if and only if the pair consisting of $\mathbf{x} = ((inst, \mathbf{y}), m_1, \dots, m_\kappa)$ and $\mathbf{h} = (h_0, h_1, \dots, h_\kappa)$ satisfies the relation $\tilde{R}$, defined to hold if and only if

$$(h_1, \dots, h_\kappa) = \mathbf{y}_c \quad \wedge \quad V(inst, c, \mathbf{m}_\circ) \quad \text{where} \quad c := \gamma(h_0) \,.$$

3. Measure the internal state of the compressed oracle to obtain D.
4. Run $\mathcal{E}^*(inst, \mathbf{m})$ on input $inst$ and $\mathbf{m} := D^{-1}(\mathbf{y})$ to obtain w.

Note that in the views of both $\mathcal{P}^*$ and $\mathcal{V}$, the interaction with H and the interaction with $\mathcal{E}$ differ only in that their oracle queries are answered by a compressed oracle instead of a real random-oracle in the latter case. This simulation is perfect and therefore $\varepsilon_{\mathsf{sim}}(\lambda, q, n) = 0$.

Considering $\mathcal{P}^*$ as the algorithm $\mathcal{A}$ in Lemma 2.4, the additional classical oracle queries that $\mathcal{V}$ performs in $\mathcal{V} \circ \mathcal{P}^*$ then match up with the algorithm $\tilde{\mathcal{A}}$, with $h_0, \ldots, h_\kappa$ here playing the role of $y_1, \ldots, y_\ell$ in Lemma 2.4. Thus,

$$\Pr[\mathbf{h} \neq D(\mathbf{x})] \leq 2(\kappa(\lambda) + 1) \cdot 2^{-n}.$$

Therefore, we can bound the figure of merit $\varepsilon_{\mathsf{ex}}$ as

$$\begin{aligned}
\varepsilon_{\mathsf{ex}}(\lambda, q, n) &= \Pr[v = \mathsf{accept} \wedge (inst, w) \notin R] \\
&= \Pr[(\mathbf{x}, \mathbf{h}) \in \tilde{R} \wedge (inst, w) \notin R] \\
&\leq \Pr[(\mathbf{x}, D(\mathbf{x})) \in \tilde{R} \wedge (inst, w) \notin R] + 2(\kappa(\lambda) + 1) \cdot 2^{-n} \\
&\leq \Pr[(\mathbf{x}, D(\mathbf{x})) \in \tilde{R} \wedge (inst, w) \notin R \,|\, D \notin \mathsf{SUC} \cup \mathsf{CL}] \\
&\quad + \Pr[D \in \mathsf{SUC} \cup \mathsf{CL}] + 2(\kappa(\lambda) + 1) \cdot 2^{-n}.
\end{aligned}$$

Using the definition of $\tilde{R}$, understanding that $c := \gamma \circ D(inst, \mathbf{y})$, we can write the first term as

$$\begin{aligned}
\Pr[D(\mathbf{m}_o) &= \mathbf{y}_c \wedge V(\lambda, inst, c, \mathbf{m}_o) \wedge (inst, w) \notin R \,|\, D \notin \mathsf{SUC} \cup \mathsf{CL}] \\
&\leq \Pr[V(\lambda, inst, c, \mathbf{m}_c) \text{ for } \mathbf{m} := D^{-1}(\mathbf{y}) \wedge (inst, w) \notin R \,|\, D \notin \mathsf{SUC} \cup \mathsf{CL}] \\
&\leq \Pr[D \in \mathsf{SUC} \,|\, D \notin \mathsf{SUC} \cup \mathsf{CL}] = 0,
\end{aligned}$$

where the first equality exploits that $D(m) = y$ iff $m = D^{-1}(y)$ for $D \notin \mathsf{CL}$. We may thus conclude that

$$\begin{aligned}
\varepsilon_{\mathsf{ex}}(\lambda, q, n) &\leq (2\kappa(\lambda) + 1) \cdot 2^{-n} + \Pr[D \in \mathsf{SUC} \cup \mathsf{CL}] \\
&\leq (2\kappa(\lambda) + 1) \cdot 2^{-n} + [\![\bot \overset{q}{\Longrightarrow} \mathsf{SUC} \cup \mathsf{CL}]\!]^2,
\end{aligned}$$

using Eq. (1) in the last inequality. The bound now follows from Lemma 4.1. $\square$

5 Online Extractability of the FS-Transformation: The Case of Merkle-tree-based C&O Protocols

For an ordinary C&O protocol with reasonable concrete security (e.g., 128 bits), the number of commitments ℓ might be considerable. In this case, the communication complexity of the protocol (and thus the size of the non-interactive proof system, or digital-signature scheme, obtained via the FS transformation) can be reduced by using a *Merkle tree* to collectively commit to the ℓ strings m_i. Such a construction is mentioned in [Fis05], and it is used in the construction of the digital-signature schemes Picnic2 and Picnic3 [KKW18, KZ20, CDG+19a]. The Merkle-tree-based C&O mechanism shrinks the commitment information from

$\ell \cdot n$ to n, at the expense of increasing the cost of opening $|c|$ values m_i by an additive term of about $\lesssim |c| \cdot n \cdot \log \ell$.

The cost of opening can, in fact, be slightly reduced again, by streamlining the opening information. When opening several leaves of a Merkle tree, the authentication paths overlap, so opening requires a number of hash values less than h per leaf, where h is the height of the tree. This overlap was observed and exploited in the octopus authentication algorithm which constitutes one of the optimizations of the stateless hash-based signature scheme gravity-SPHINCS [AE18], as well as in Picnic2 and Picnic3 [KZ20]. In the following section, we formalize tree-based collective commitment schemes with "octopus" opening.

5.1   Merkle-Tree-Based C&O Protocols

In line with Remark 3.3, we can consider C&O protocols with a different choice of commitment scheme, compared to the default choice of committing by element-wise hashing. Here, we discuss a particular choice of an alternative commitment scheme, which gives rise to more efficient C&O protocols in certain cases when ℓ is large. Informally, we consider C&O protocols where $m_1, \ldots, m_\ell$ is committed to by using a *Merkle tree*, and individual m_i's are opened by announcing the corresponding authentication paths.

To make this more formal, we introduce the following notation (see the full version for a formal discussion, and see Fig. 1 for an example). For simplicity, we assume that ℓ is a power of 2. We write $\mathsf{MTree}_H(\mathbf{m})$ for the Merkle tree of messages $\mathbf{m} = (m_1, \ldots, m_\ell)$ computed using hash function H; more formally, the (labels of the) vertices in the Merkle tree are recursively computed as $l_v(\mathbf{m}) := H\big(l_{v\|0}(\mathbf{m})\|l_{v\|1}(\mathbf{m})\big)$, with the leaves being the hashes of the m_i's. $\mathsf{MRoot}_H(\mathbf{m})$ then denotes the root of the Merkle tree. Furthermore, for $c \subseteq [\ell]$, we write $\mathsf{MAuth}_H(c, \mathbf{m})$ for the union of the authentication paths for all messages m_i with $i \subset c$, and the *octopus* $\mathsf{MOcto}_H(c, \mathbf{m})$ denotes all the vertices needed to compute all the authentication paths in $\mathsf{MAuth}_H(c, \mathbf{m})$, but excluding the hashes of the actual messages m_i with $i \in c$ (see Fig. 1).

A *Merkle-tree-based C&O* protocol is now defined to be a variation of a C&O protocol, as hinted at in Remark 3.3, where the first message of the protocol, i.e., the commitment of $\mathbf{m} = (m_1, \ldots, m_\ell)$, is computed as $y = \mathsf{MRoot}_H(\mathbf{m})$, and the response z for challenge-set c then consists of the messages $\mathbf{m}_c = (m_i)_{i \in c}$ together with $O = \mathsf{MOcto}_H(c, \mathbf{m})$. The verifier $\mathcal{V}$ then accepts if and only if $\mathbf{m}_c$ and O "hash down to" y and the predicate $V(\lambda, inst, c, \mathbf{m}_c, a)$ is satisfied. More formally, the former means that $\mathcal{V}$ computes $\mathsf{MAuth}_H(c, \mathbf{m})$ from $O \cup \{(\mathsf{lf}(i), H(m_i)) \mid i \in c\}$ in the obvious way, and then checks whether $l_\emptyset(\mathbf{m}) = y$. This verification is denoted by $OctoVerify^H(c, y, \mathbf{m}_c, O)$.

Looking ahead, we may also consider a variation where the verifier resamples the challenge c if the resulting octopus is bigger than a given bound. Formally, this means that the challenge space of the Merkle-tree-based C&O protocol is restricted to those challenges $c \in [\ell]$ for which $\mathsf{Octo}(c)$ is not too large.

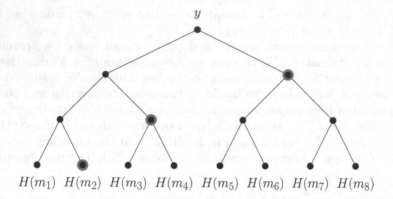

Fig. 1. The Merkle tree $\mathsf{MTree}_H(\mathbf{m})$ for $\mathbf{m} = (m_1, \ldots, m_8)$ with $\mathsf{MRoot}_H(\mathbf{m}) = y$. The yellow vertices mark the octopus $\mathsf{MOcto}_H(\{1\}, \mathbf{m})$, which is revealed (along with m_1) when opening the commitment y to m_1. (Color figure online)

5.2   Online Extractability of the Fiat-Shamir Transformation

The analysis in Sect. 4 can be generalized to the case of FS-transformed Merkle-tree-based C&O protocols. To that end, we generalize the notation from that section as follows. Let Π be a Merkle-tree-based C&O protocol with number of messages to be committed equal to $\ell = 2^h$ where h is the height of the commitment Merkle tree.[12]

For a given database $D \in \mathfrak{D}$, recall from Sect. 4 the definition of D^{-1}; applied to a tuple $\mathbf{y} = (y_1, \ldots, y_\ell) \in \mathcal{Y}^\ell$ of commitments, D^{-1} attempts to recover the corresponding committed messages $m_1, \ldots, m_\ell$. Here, in a similar spirit but now considering the Merkle-tree commitment, MRoot_D^{-1} attempts to recover the committed messages from the root label of the Merkle tree.

In more detail, for a commitment $y \in \mathcal{Y} = \{0,1\}^n$ we reverse engineer the Merkle tree in the obvious way; namely, accepting a small clash in notation with the labeling function $l_v(\mathbf{m})$ defined for a tuple $\mathbf{m} \in \mathcal{M}^\ell$, we set the root label $l_\emptyset(y) := y$, and recursively define

$$\left(l_{v\|0}(y), l_{v\|1}(y)\right) := \mathsf{split} \circ D^{-1}\left(l_v(y)\right) \in \mathcal{Y} \times \mathcal{Y}$$

for $\emptyset \neq v \in \{0,1\}^{\leq h}$, where split maps any $2n$-bit string, parsed as $y_1\|y_2$ with $y_1, y_2 \in \{0,1\}^n$, to the pair (y_1, y_2) of n-bit strings, while it maps anything else to $(\bot, \bot)$. Then, accepting a small clash in notation again, we set

$$\mathsf{MTree}_D(y) := \{l_v(y) \mid v \in \{0,1\}^{\leq h}\},$$

and finally, with $\mathrm{lf}(i)$ denoting the i-th leaf in the tree,

$$\mathsf{MRoot}_D^{-1}(y) := \left(D^{-1}\left(l_{\mathrm{lf}(1)}(y)\right), \ldots, D^{-1}\left(l_{\mathrm{lf}(\ell)}(y)\right)\right).$$

---

[12] As in the previous section we assume that ℓ is a power of 2 for ease of exposition.

Following the strategy we used in Sect. 4, we define the database property

$$\mathsf{SUC} := \left\{ D \;\middle|\; \begin{array}{l} \exists y \in \mathcal{Y} \text{ and } \mathit{inst} \in \mathcal{I} \text{ so that } \mathbf{m} := \mathsf{MRoot}_D^{-1}(y) \text{ satisfies} \\ V(\mathit{inst}, c, \mathbf{m}_c) \text{ for } c := \gamma \circ D(\mathit{inst}, y) \text{ and } (\mathit{inst}, \mathcal{E}^*(\mathit{inst}, \mathbf{m})) \notin R \end{array} \right\},$$

and our first goal is to show that $[\![\bot \overset{q}{\Longrightarrow} \mathsf{SUC} \cup \mathsf{CL}]\!]$ is small.

Lemma 5.1. $[\![\bot \overset{q}{\Longrightarrow} \mathsf{SUC} \cup \mathsf{CL}]\!] \leq 2eq^{3/2}2^{-n/2} + q\sqrt{10 \max\left(q\ell \cdot 2^{-n+1}, p_{triv}^{\mathfrak{S}}\right)}.$

The proof works exactly as the proof of Lemma 4.1, accounting for some syntactic differences due to the Merkle tree commitment. In particular, where in Case 1 and 2 of the proof of Lemma 4.1 we have to exclude U from falling on one of the hash values $y_1, \ldots, y_\ell$ in order to keep the $\mathbf{m}$ that was constructed from the database intact, we now have a similar restriction for U, but with respect to the whole tree $\mathsf{MTree}_D(y)$. The full proof can be found in the full version.

Similarly to Theorem 4.2, we now obtain the following.

Theorem 5.2. *Let Π be an $\mathfrak{S}$-sound* Merkle-tree-based C&O protocol with challenge space $\mathcal{C}_\lambda$. Then $\mathsf{FS}[\Pi]$ is a PoK-OE in the QROM (as in Definition 3.1), with $\varepsilon_{\mathsf{sim}}(\lambda, q, n) = 0$ and*

$$\varepsilon_{\mathsf{ex}}(\lambda, q, n) \leq 2(\kappa \log \ell + 1) \cdot 2^{-n} + \left(2eq^{3/2}2^{-n/2} + q\sqrt{10 \max\left(q\ell \cdot 2^{-n+1}, p_{triv}^{\mathfrak{S}}\right)}\right)^2$$

$$\leq (22\ell \log \ell + 60) q^3 2^{-n} + 20q^2 p_{triv}^{\mathfrak{S}}$$

where $\kappa = \kappa(\lambda) := \max_{c \in \mathcal{C}_\lambda} |c|$ and ℓ is the number of leaves of the Merkle-tree-based commitment. The running time of the extractor is dominated by running the compressed oracle, which has complexity $O(q^2) \cdot \mathrm{poly}(n, B)$, and by computing $\mathsf{MRoot}_D^{-1}(y)$ and running $\mathcal{E}^*$.

Here again the proof follows exactly the outline of its counterpart from Sect. 4.2, with some minor alterations to cope with the formalism of a Merkle-tree based C&O Σ-protocol. The difference in the bound is simply due to the difference between Lemmas 4.1 and 5.1. We refer to the full version for the full proof.

5.3 Discussion: Application to Picnic, and Limiting the Proof Size

Application to Picnic. A prominent use case of C&O protocols is the construction of digital signature schemes via the FS transformation. An important example is Picnic [CDG+17] currently under consideration as an alternate candidate in the NIST standardization process for post-quantum cryptographic schemes [NIS]. On a high level, the design of Picnic can be described as follows. A C&O Σ-protocol is constructed using the MPC-in-the-head paradigm [IKOS07]. Then, the FS transformation is applied in the usual way to obtain a digital signature scheme. There are three evolutions of Picnic: Picnic-FS, Picnic

2 and Picnic 3.[13] Picnic-FS uses plain hash-based commitments, while Picnic 2 and Picnic 3 use a Merkle-tree-based collective commitment.

All three evolutions enjoy provable post-quantum security when the hash function used for the FS transformation is modeled as a (quantum-accessible) RO. The best reduction applying to all of them proceeds as follows. First, Unruh's rewinding lemma [Unr12] is used to construct a knowledge extractor for the underlying Σ-protocol based on an appropriate $\mathfrak{S}$-soundness notion. Then, the *generic* QROM reduction for the FS transformation from [DFMS19] is used to construct a knowledge extractor for the signature scheme in the QROM from the extractor for the Σ-protocol. Finally, the technique from [GHHM21] is used for simulating the chosen-message oracle to reduce breaking NMA (no-message attack) security to breaking CMA (chosen-message attack) security. This final step connects to the previous one because for the signature scheme the witness extracted from an NMA attacker is the secret key.

The first two steps, i.e. Unruh's rewinding and [DFMS19], are not tight: The former loses at least a fifth power in the Picnic case, and the latter a factor of q^2, where q is the number of RO queries. This means that an NMA attacker with success probability ϵ can be used to break the underlying hard problem with probability $\Omega(\epsilon^5/q^{10})$ (or worse, depending on the Picnic variant).

For Picnic-FS (only), when in addition modeling the hash function used for the commitments as a RO, Unruh's rewinding can be replaced with tight online extraction from [DFMS21]. The remaining loss due to the FS reduction is of order ϵ/q^2, up to some additive terms accounting for search and collision finding in the RO, a sizable improvement over the above but still not tight.

By analyzing the FS transformation of a C&O protocol (with or without Merkle tree commitments) directly, our results provide a tight alternative to the above lossy reductions. Using Theorems 4.2 (for Picnic-FS) and 5.2 (for Picnic 2 and Picnic 3) we can avoid all multiplicative/power losses in the reduction for NMA security. An NMA attacker with success probability ϵ can thus be used to break the underlying hard problem with probability $\Omega(\epsilon)$, up to unavoidable additive terms due to search and collision finding in the RO.

An Observation About Octopus Opening Sizes. Depending on the parameters of the C&O protocol, the octopus opening information, $\mathsf{MOcto}(c, \mathbf{m})$ can be much smaller than the concatenation of the individual authentication paths. On the other hand, it is also *variable in size* (namely dependent on the choice of the challenge c), and the variance can be significant (see e.g. the computations for gravity SPHINCS in [AE18]). In the context of a digital signature scheme constructed via the FS transformation of a Merkle-tree-based C&O protocol, like, e.g., Picnic 2 and Picnic 3, this leads to the undesirable property of a variable signature size, where signatures can be quite a bit larger in the worst case than on average. This might, e.g., lead to problems when looking for a drop-in replacement for quantum-broken digital signature schemes for use in a larger protocol, where signatures need to be stored in a data field of fixed size.

---

[13] There is also a version using the Unruh transformation.

One option to mitigate this situation is to cut off the tail of the octopus size distribution, i.e. to restrict the challenge space of the Merkle-tree-based C&O protocol to challenges whose octopus is not larger than some bound. This can be done before applying the FS transformation, e.g. using rejection sampling. In that way, one obtains a digital signature scheme with significantly reduced worst case signature size, at the expense of a tiny security loss.

Acknowledgements. JD was funded by ERC-ADG project 740972 (ALGSTRONG-CRYPTO). CM was funded by a NWO VENI grant (Project No. VI.Veni.192.159). CS was supported by a NWO VIDI grant (Project No. 639.022.519).

References

[AE18] Aumasson, J.-P., Endignoux, G.: Improving stateless hash-based signatures. In: Smart, N.P. (ed.) CT-RSA 2018. LNCS, vol. 10808, pp. 219–242. Springer, Cham (2018). https://doi.org/10.1007/978-3-319-76953-0_12

[BDF+11] Boneh, D., Dagdelen, Ö., Fischlin, M., Lehmann, A., Schaffner, C., Zhandry, M.: Random oracles in a quantum world. In: Lee, D.H., Wang, X. (eds.) ASIACRYPT 2011. LNCS, vol. 7073, pp. 41–69. Springer, Heidelberg (2011). https://doi.org/10.1007/978-3-642-25385-0_3

[BdSGK+21] Baum, C., de Saint Guilhem, C.D., Kales, D., Orsini, E., Scholl, P., Zaverucha, G.: Banquet: short and fast signatures from AES. In: Garay, J.A. (ed.) PKC 2021. LNCS, vol. 12710, pp. 266–297. Springer, Cham (2021). https://doi.org/10.1007/978-3-030-75245-3_11

[BLZ21] Blocki, J., Lee, S., Zhou, S.: On the security of proofs of sequential work in a post-quantum world (2021)

[CDG+17] Chase, M., et al.: Post-quantum zero-knowledge and signatures from symmetric-key primitives. In: Proceedings of the 2017 ACM SIGSAC Conference on Computer and Communications Security, CCS 2017, pp. 1825–1842. ACM, New York (2017)

[CDG+19a] Chase, M., et al.: The picnic signature scheme. In: Submission to NIST Post-Quantum Cryptography project (2019)

[CDG+19b] Chase, M., et al.: Picnic (2019). https://www.microsoft.com/en-us/research/project/picnic/, Accessed 9 Apr 2019

[CFHL21] Chung, K.-M., Fehr, S., Huang, Y.-H., Liao, T.-N.: On the compressed-oracle technique, and post-quantum security of proofs of sequential work. In: Canteaut, A., Standaert, F.-X. (eds.) EUROCRYPT 2021. LNCS, vol. 12697, pp. 598–629. Springer, Cham (2021). https://doi.org/10.1007/978-3-030-77886-6_21

[CGLQ20] Chung, K.M., Guo, S., Liu, Q., Qian, L.: Tight quantum time-space tradeoffs for function inversion. In: 2020 IEEE 61st Annual Symposium on Foundations of Computer Science (FOCS), pp. 673–684 (2020)

[Cha19] Chailloux, A.: Tight quantum security of the Fiat-Shamir transform for commit-and-open identification schemes with applications to post-quantum signature schemes. Cryptology ePrint Archive, Report 2019/699, version 1 July 2019 (2019). https://eprint.iacr.org/2019/699/20190701:091436

[Cha21] Chailloux, A.: Tight quantum security of the Fiat-Shamir transform for commit-and-open identification schemes with applications to post-quantum signature schemes. Cryptology ePrint Archive, Report 2019/699, version 16 March 2021 (2021). https://eprint.iacr.org/2019/699/20210316:124850

[CMS19] Chiesa, A., Manohar, P., Spooner, N.: Succinct arguments in the quantum random oracle model. In: Hofheinz, D., Rosen, A. (eds.) TCC 2019. LNCS, vol. 11892, pp. 1–29. Springer, Cham (2019). https://doi.org/10.1007/978-3-030-36033-7_1

[DFM20] Don, J., Fehr, S., Majenz, C.: The measure-and-reprogram technique 2.0: multi-round fiat-shamir and more. In: Micciancio, D., Ristenpart, T. (eds.) CRYPTO 2020. LNCS, vol. 12172, pp. 602–631. Springer, Cham (2020). https://doi.org/10.1007/978-3-030-56877-1_21

[DFMS19] Don, J., Fehr, S., Majenz, C., Schaffner, C.: Security of the fiat-shamir transformation in the quantum random-oracle model. In: Boldyreva, A., Micciancio, D. (eds.) CRYPTO 2019. LNCS, vol. 11693, pp. 356–383. Springer, Cham (2019). https://doi.org/10.1007/978-3-030-26951-7_13

[DFMS21] Don, J., Fehr, S., Majenz, C., Schaffner, C.: Online-extractability in the quantum random-oracle model. Cryptology ePrint Archive, Report 2021/280 (2021). https://eprint.iacr.org/2021/280

[DKL+18] Ducas, L., et al.: Crystals-dilithium: a lattice-based digital signature scheme. IACR Trans. Cryptographic Hardware Embed. Syst. **2018**(1), 238–268 (2018)

[DKR+21] Dobraunig, C., Kales, D., Rechberger, C., Schofnegger, M., Zaverucha, G.: Shorter signatures based on tailor-made minimalist symmetric-key crypto. Cryptology ePrint Archive, Report 2021/692 (2021). https://ia.cr/2021/692

[Fis05] Fischlin, M.: Communication-efficient non-interactive proofs of knowledge with online extractors. In: Shoup, V. (ed.) CRYPTO 2005. LNCS, vol. 3621, pp. 152–168. Springer, Heidelberg (2005). https://doi.org/10.1007/11535218_10

[FS87] Fiat, A., Shamir, A.: How to prove yourself: practical solutions to identification and signature problems. In: Odlyzko, A.M. (ed.) CRYPTO 1986. LNCS, vol. 263, pp. 186–194. Springer, Heidelberg (1987). https://doi.org/10.1007/3-540-47721-7_12

[GHHM21] Grilo, A.B., Hövelmanns, K., Hülsing, A., Majenz, C.: Tight adaptive reprogramming in the QROM. In: Tibouchi, M., Wang, H. (eds.) ASIACRYPT 2021. LNCS, vol. 13090, pp. 637–667. Springer, Cham (2021). https://doi.org/10.1007/978-3-030-92062-3_22

[HM21] Hamoudi, Y., Magniez, F.: Quantum time-space tradeoff for finding multiple collision pairs. In: Hsieh, M.-H. (ed.) 16th Conference on the Theory of Quantum Computation, Communication and Cryptography (TQC 2021), vol. 197 of Leibniz International Proceedings in Informatics (LIPIcs), pp. 1:1–1:21. Schloss Dagstuhl - Leibniz-Zentrum für Informatik, Dagstuhl (2021)

[IKOS07] Ishai, Y., Kushilevitz, E., Ostrovsky, R., Sahai, A.: Zero-knowledge from secure multiparty computation. In: Proceedings of the Thirty-Ninth Annual ACM Symposium on Theory of Computing, STOC 2007, pp. 21–30. Association for Computing Machinery, New York (2007)

[KKW18] Katz, J., Kolesnikov, V., Wang, X.: Improved non-interactive zero knowledge with applications to post-quantum signatures. In: Proceedings of the 2018 ACM SIGSAC Conference on Computer and Communications Security, CCS 2018, pp. 525–537. Association for Computing Machinery, New York (2018)

[KZ20] Kales, D., Zaverucha, G.: Improving the performance of the picnic signature scheme. IACR Trans. Cryptographic Hardware Embed. Syst., 154–188 (2020)

[LZ19a] Liu, Q., Zhandry, M.: On finding quantum multi-collisions. In: Ishai, Y., Rijmen, V. (eds.) EUROCRYPT 2019. LNCS, vol. 11478, pp. 189–218. Springer, Cham (2019). https://doi.org/10.1007/978-3-030-17659-4_7

[LZ19b] Liu, Q., Zhandry, M.: Revisiting post-quantum fiat-shamir. In: Boldyreva, A., Micciancio, D. (eds.) CRYPTO 2019. LNCS, vol. 11693, pp. 326–355. Springer, Cham (2019). https://doi.org/10.1007/978-3-030-26951-7_12

[NIS] Nist post-quantum cryptography standardization. https://csrc.nist.gov/projects/post-quantum-cryptography/round-1-submissions

[Unr12] Unruh, D.: Quantum proofs of knowledge. In: Pointcheval, D., Johansson, T. (eds.) EUROCRYPT 2012. LNCS, vol. 7237, pp. 135–152. Springer, Heidelberg (2012). https://doi.org/10.1007/978-3-642-29011-4_10

[Unr15] Unruh, D.: Non-interactive zero-knowledge proofs in the quantum random oracle model. In: Oswald, E., Fischlin, M. (eds.) EUROCRYPT 2015. LNCS, vol. 9057, pp. 755–784. Springer, Heidelberg (2015). https://doi.org/10.1007/978-3-662-46803-6_25

[Zha19] Zhandry, M.: How to record quantum queries, and applications to quantum indifferentiability. In: Boldyreva, A., Micciancio, D. (eds.) CRYPTO 2019. LNCS, vol. 11693, pp. 239–268. Springer, Cham (2019). https://doi.org/10.1007/978-3-030-26951-7_9

Signatures

Locally Verifiable Signature and Key Aggregation

Rishab Goyal$^{(\boxtimes)}$ and Vinod Vaikuntanathan

MIT, Cambridge, MA, USA
goyal@utexas.edu, vinodv@mit.edu

Abstract. Aggregate signatures (Boneh, Gentry, Lynn, Shacham, Eurocrypt 2003) enable compressing a set of N signatures on N different messages into a short aggregate signature. This reduces the space complexity of storing the signatures from linear in N to a fixed constant (that depends only on the security parameter). However, verifying the aggregate signature requires access to all N messages, resulting in the complexity of verification being at least $\Omega(N)$.

In this work, we introduce the notion of *locally verifiable* aggregate signatures that enable *efficient verification*: given a short aggregate signature σ (corresponding to a set $\mathcal{M}$ of N messages), the verifier can check whether a particular message m is in the set, in time independent of N. Verification does *not* require knowledge of the entire set $\mathcal{M}$. We demonstrate many natural applications of locally verifiable aggregate signature schemes: in the context of certificate transparency logs; in blockchains; and for redacting signatures, even when all the original signatures are produced by a single user.

We provide two constructions of single-signer locally verifiable aggregate signatures, the first based on the RSA assumption and the second on the bilinear Diffie-Hellman inversion assumption, both in the random oracle model.

As an additional contribution, we introduce the notion of compressing cryptographic keys in identity-based encryption (IBE) schemes, show applications of this notion, and construct an IBE scheme where the secret keys for N identities can be compressed into a single aggregate key, which can then be used to decrypt ciphertexts sent to any of the N identities.

1 Introduction

The notion of aggregate signatures, introduced by Boneh, Gentry, Lynn, and Shacham [BGLS03a], enables the compression of several signatures σ_i of messages m_i with respect to public keys vk_i, into a single, short signature $\hat{\sigma}$ which

R. Goyal—Research supported by grants listed under the second author.
V. Vaikuntanathan—Research supported in part by NSF CNS Award #1718161, an IBM-MIT grant, and by the Defense Advanced Research Projects Agency (DARPA) under Contract No. HR00112020023. Any opinions, findings and conclusions or recommendations expressed in this material are those of the author(s) and do not necessarily reflect the views of the United States Government or DARPA.

© International Association for Cryptologic Research 2022
Y. Dodis and T. Shrimpton (Eds.): CRYPTO 2022, LNCS 13508, pp. 761–791, 2022.
https://doi.org/10.1007/978-3-031-15979-4_26

authenticates the entire tuple of messages with respect to the tuple of public keys. While the original motivation for aggregate signatures was the compression of certificate chains and the aggregation of signatures in secure BGP, the notion has found a great deal of practical interest recently in the context of blockchains [Gor18].

While the aggregate signatures are short, verifying them requires access to *all* the messages. In many practical scenarios, as we describe below, the verifier is merely interested in checking if $\widehat{\sigma}$ is an aggregated signature of *some* set that contains a particular message m. It may be infeasible or undesirable to download the entire list of messages, and perform a verification computation whose runtime scales with the number of messages N. This leads us to the central question that motivates this work: *Can we construct* locally verifiable *aggregate signatures?*

Locality in access and computation is a central theme in computer science, in areas ranging from coding theory [Yek12] to proof systems [Sud09] to sub-linear algorithms [Gol17]. Thus, the question of local verifiability is both practically motivated, and also conceptually very natural.

1.1 Locally Verifiable Aggregate Signatures

Our first contribution is a definition of the notion of *locally verifiable aggregate signatures*, which turns out to require some care.

A natural formalization asks for two algorithms: an aggregation algorithm Aggregate, that takes a set of tuples $\{(m_i, \mathsf{vk}_i, \sigma_i)\}_{i=1}^N$ and produces a short aggregate signature $\widehat{\sigma}$ of size, say, $\mathsf{poly}(\lambda)$ bits and a local verification algorithm LocalAggVerify, that takes the aggregate signature $\widehat{\sigma}$, a public key vk, and a message m, and outputs accept or reject. It seems natural to require that LocalAggVerify runs in time independent of N, and accepts $(m, \mathsf{vk}, \widehat{\sigma})$ if and only if $(m, \mathsf{vk}) \in \{(m_i, \mathsf{vk}_i)\}_{i=1}^N$.

It is not hard to see that this notion is *impossible* to achieve, even in the *single-signer setting* where all signatures are produced w.r.t. a single public key vk, due to a simple incompressibility argument. Indeed, such a pair of algorithms can be used to recover all the messages given just the aggregate signature, violating incompressibility. In more detail, assume that the messages are of the form (i, b_i) where $b_i \in \{0, 1\}$ is a bit. To recover all the bits b_i given $\widehat{\sigma}$, one simply runs the LocalAggVerify algorithm with both $(i, 0)$ and $(i, 1)$ for every i.

In this work, we define the notion of locally verifiable aggregate signatures, overcoming the above incompressibility barrier. We focus on the single-signer setting, and show several applications of our notion.

Our Definition. To circumvent the incompressibility barrier, we include a hint generation algorithm LocalOpen that computes a short hint to aid local verification. Formally, in addition to the key generation, signing, and verification algorithms, a locally verifiable aggregate signature scheme consists of three additional algorithms. For the sake of concreteness, the reader should imagine three types of parties: signers who run KeyGen and Sign, storage servers (or aggregators) who run Aggregate and LocalOpen, and verifiers who run Verify and LocalAggVerify.

Aggregate is the (single-signer) signature aggregation algorithm which takes as input a sequence of pairs (m_i, σ_i) under a public key vk and produces an aggregate signature $\widehat{\sigma}$;

LocalOpen is the hint generator (also called the opening algorithm) that takes as input the aggregate signature $\widehat{\sigma}$ and the set of messages $\mathbf{m} = \{m_i\}_{i=1}^{N}$, and a target message $m \in \mathbf{m}$, and produces a *short hint* h;

(crucially, LocalOpen does *not* have access to the original signatures σ_i as they have been *forgotten* at this point).

LocalAggVerify is the local verification algorithm that verifies the aggregate signature $\widehat{\sigma}$ and the short hint h for a message m.

(importantly, the run-time of LocalAggVerify is independent of N).

The first thing to note is that our formalization circumvents the incompressibility barrier as local verification uses a message-dependent hint, and the hint generation depends on the set of all messages $\mathbf{m}$ (and not just the target message). Secondly, we will shortly describe how our definition fits into several practical applications of aggregate signatures.

For security, we propose an enhanced unforgeability property which protects from both a *malicious* aggregator and a *malicious* hint generator. It is defined against an adversary who obtains signatures for a set $\mathbf{m}$ and tries to produce a "fake" aggregate signature and a "fake" hint that makes the aggregate verifier accept a message $m \notin \mathbf{m}$. For more details, we refer the reader to Sect. 3.1.

How to Use Locally Verifiable Aggregate Signatures in Applications.
Local verifiability is an extremely desirable feature as it leads to many applications in certificate transparency logs and blockchains, generic implications to signature redactability, and provides a robust time-space tradeoff that can smoothly interpolate between aggregate signatures and plain signatures.

CERTIFICATE TRANSPARENCY LOGS. Certificate transparency (CT) [BLK13] is an internet security standard that creates public logs which record all certificates issued by certificate authorities (CAs). The log is audited periodically to identify mistakenly or maliciously issued certificates. A user's browser receives a certificate σ from a website, say on the message (domain-name,IP), and checks whether the entry exists in the CT log before proceeding to accept the connection. (This simplified description is sufficient for our purposes; however, for more details on how CT logs work, we refer the reader to [CTg]).

Aggregate signatures can *ease the burden of storage* on the CT log. Without aggregate signatures, the CT log has to store all the signatures (certificates) explicitly. With aggregate signatures, the CT log can store a short aggregate signature together with an arbitrary compressed data structure that compactly stores the list of messages (namely, domain names and IP addresses). However, even if the user's browser stores or downloads an aggregate signature, the only way to verify whether a particular entry exists in the log is to download all entries. Locally verifiable aggregate signatures allow the CT log to compress the certificates into a short aggregate signature while allowing the user to verify the existence of an entry by downloading just a few additional kilobytes (in the form of a short hint) and performing a fast computation (using the LocalAggVerify algorithm). Furthermore, our enhanced unforgeability property guarantees that this is secure against even a malicious CT log who may try to convince the user that a message $m \in \mathbf{m}$ when it isn't.

We note that *even single-signer* locally verifiable aggregate signatures are a meaningful solution in this scenario given that the certificate authorities number in the *hundreds* while the certificates generated number in the *billions*. The hints need not be explicitly stored, and can be computed on-the-fly by the CT log enabling natural forms of space-time tradeoffs and caching mechanisms (for the hints) for frequently accessed websites. Jumping ahead, we note that one of our constructions (in particular, the RSA-based construction) has the surprising additional feature of being able to *reconstruct* the original signature of any particular message $m \in \mathbf{m}$ given only the aggregate signature and the set of messages $\mathbf{m}$—this could come in handy during the auditing of the CT log.

BLOCKCHAINS. Another application scenario arises in the context of blockchains where a user or an organization wants to aggregate the signatures on the set of all transactions *originating from a single payer*, and later wishes to quickly and with little communication convince a third party (e.g. an auditor) of the existence of a particular transaction. Again, the above problem can be elegantly solved by using locally verifiable aggregate signatures as the user/organization can compute the short hint to prove the existence of the appropriate transaction.

We note that local verification implicitly provides a useful privacy feature. The user/organization can prove knowledge of a single transaction without revealing the remaining transactions. This follows from the succinctness requirements, as neither the aggregate signature nor the hint grow with the number of transactions; thus, the signature and the hint jointly cannot leak too much information about the other transactions. In addition, some of our constructions satisfy properties such as *dynamic aggregation* which could be very useful in this scenario.

TIME-SPACE TRADEOFFS FROM LOCAL VERIFIABILITY. Consider a server that stores a collection of N messages $\{m_i\}_{i=1}^N$ along with signatures $\{\sigma_i\}_{i=1}^N$, and several possible clients who wish to download single messages and check that they indeed belong to the collection. While this can be solved by using vanilla signatures, the server must dedicate large space for storing all N signatures. Traditional aggregate signatures can handle the server space issue, but they incur (huge) linear runtime cost for each individual client. As summarized in Table 1, the run-time for individual clients can be lowered to $O(1)$ by using locally verifiable aggregate signatures.

We can also obtain a smooth time-space tradeoff that interpolates between locally verifiable aggregate signatures and vanilla signatures. For example, the server could split the collection of N messages into blocks of length L and aggregate each block of L signatures, reducing the server run-time to $O(L)$ at

Table 1. Time-Space Tradeoffs with Locally Verifiable (L.V.) Aggregate Signatures.

Type of Signatures	Server space (for signatures)	Server time	Per-client space (for signatures)	Per-client time
Vanilla Signatures	$O(N)$	$O(1)$	$O(1)$	$O(1)$
Aggregate Signatures	$O(1)$	$O(1)$	$O(1)$	$O(N)$
L.V. Aggregate	$O(1)$	$O(N)$	$O(1)$	$O(1)$
Hybrid (with L_2 batch and $L_1 L_2$ block size)	$O\left(\dfrac{N}{L_1 L_2}\right)$	$O(L_1)$	$O(1)$	$O(L_2)$

the cost of increasing the server storage to $O(N/L)$. This mechanism can be further generalized to obtain a three-way time-space tradeoff that interpolates between vanilla signatures, aggregate signatures, and locally verifiable aggregate signatures. In this hybrid mode of local verification, the signer signs blocks of L_2 messages by hashing the block first and then signing it. The server stores N messages by splitting them into $N/(L_1 L_2)$ super-blocks, each of which contains L_1 blocks, where each block, in turn, contains L_2 messages (as above). The server aggregates the L_1 (locally verifiable aggregate) signatures in each super-block and stores them. The server thus stores $N/L_1 L_2$ signatures. To access a message, the client retrieves an entire block containing the message, spending $O(L_2)$ time. To answer the client query, the server runs in time $O(L_1)$ to generate the hint corresponding to the hash of the block queried by the client. In short, the new notion of local verification provides a *robust time-space tradeoff* for the parties involved.

Given that most data in the real world is compressible, locally verifiable aggregate signatures give the server the ability to fully leverage compression and reduce the *total* storage (including the messages) and communication to sublinear in N. This is possible neither with vanilla signatures (where one cannot compress the signatures) nor with regular aggregate signatures (where a client cannot avoid downloading all messages). Although the hint generation is expensive, it is done once by the (potentially untrusted) server as opposed to imposing a heavy verification cost per client as in regular aggregate signatures. Furthermore, the hints for the most frequently accessed messages can be cached for better performance. In a nutshell, locally verifiable aggregate signatures open up a rich space of tradeoffs in storage, communication and verification of signatures.

REDACTABLE SIGNATURES. Redactable signature schemes [JMSW02, SBZ01] allow a signature holder to publicly censor parts of a signed document such that the corresponding signature σ can be efficiently updated without the secret signing key, and the updated signature can still be verified given only the redacted document. These signatures have many real-world applications in privacy-preserving authentication as they can be used to sanitize digital signatures. (See [DPSS15, DKS16] for a detailed overview).

Locally verifiable aggregate signatures provide a fresh approach to redactability and sanitization. Briefly, using a locally verifiable aggregate signature, we can sign the large sensitive document in three steps: first, split the document into small message blocks; second, sign the message blocks individually, together with their index; and third, aggregate these individual signatures and output the aggregated signature as the final signature for the full document. To verify the full (unredacted) document, one could use the regular verification algorithm that takes the entire document as input. For redaction, the redacting party can generate short hints for each of the unredacted portions of the document, and include these as part of the redacted signature. Note that the redacted signature can be verified by running local verification. At a very informal level, since the redacted signature is shorter than the total number of message blocks, this seems to guarantee some form of privacy.

While this general outline is problematic for several reasons: first, the redacted signatures are long; and secondly, the above argument does not guarantee true privacy, namely that the signature on the redacted document does not reveal *any* information about the redacted messages. However, it turns out that our RSA-based construction and a slight modification of our pairing-based construction give a complete solution to the problem, ensuring privacy of the original (unredacted) message, enabling multi-hop redaction as well as constant-size redacted signatures, improving on the construction in [JMSW02]. We refer the reader to Sect. 2 for more details.

1.2 Locally Verifiable Aggregate Signatures: Our Results

Our main result constructs a single-signer locally verifiable aggregate signature scheme secure under the strong RSA assumption [BP97].

Theorem 1.1 (Informal). *Assuming strong RSA, there is a locally verifiable aggregate signature scheme. In the random oracle model, it is fully secure; and in the standard model, it is statically secure.*

Our second result shows a weaker scheme under the bilinear Diffie-Hellman inversion (BDHI) assumption [MSK02,BB04a,BB04b]. The scheme requires a long common reference string (CRS) of size equal to the number of aggregated messages. The verifier, however, only needs access to a fixed constant size portion of the CRS and is, therefore, still efficient.

Theorem 1.2 (Informal). *Under the BDHI assumption, there is a locally verifiable aggregate signature scheme in the long CRS model. With random oracles, the scheme is fully secure; and in the standard model, it is statically secure.*

Finally, we show an initial feasibility result for a *multi-signer* locally verifiable aggregate signatures using the machinery of succinct non-interactive arguments of knowledge (SNARKs). We note that single-signer aggregate signature schemes, without locality, have several (folklore) instantiations based on the RSA assumption, the SIS assumption, and so on. This is in contrast to the multi-signer setting where bilinear maps seem to dominate. Our work generalizes single-signer aggregate signatures in a different direction, requiring locality, and exposing a new, challenging, and practically motivated facet of the problem.

1.3   Compressing Cryptographic Keys

As an independently interesting contribution, we introduce a novel generalization of signature aggregation to the setting of compressing the keys in identity-based and, more generally, attribute-based encryption schemes (IBE, ABE). This enables the decryption key holders to compress multiple keys into a short key such that the aggregated key can be used to decrypt all ciphertexts that any of individual (unaggregated) decryption keys are authorized to decrypt. Since one of the main motivations behind designing advanced encryption systems is to have the ability to generate separate keys for different users, thus it might feel counterintuitive to study compression of keys. However, there are two main reasons to study aggregation in encryption systems.

First, this immediately can be used to reduce storage space in many simple applications. For example, consider the classical application of using IBE to delegate access over time. In particular, there is a user who has an IBE master secret key msk, and generates temporary keys sk_{date} for other devices (such as mobile phones) that are more easily stolen. The messages encrypted are tagged with different dates, so the temporary keys can decrypt only the corresponding ciphertexts. *Aggregatable IBE* allows to compress any subset of these temporary keys into one short key that can decrypt ciphertexts encrypted to any of underlying dates. While one could use heavyweight tools (such as ABE) to solve this problem, our observation is that IBE constructions with such great aggregation properties can lead to a simpler and relatively lightweight solution. This directly leads to the second (and broader) reason for studying aggregatable encryption systems which is that they can enable simpler solutions to problems that otherwise needed more advanced objects. We also provide a simple construction for an aggregatable IBE scheme from the BDHI assumption.

Theorem 1.3 (Informal). *Under the BDHI assumption, there is an aggregatable IBE scheme in the random oracle model.*

1.4   Other Related Work

The concept of aggregate signatures was first put forth by Boneh, Gentry, Lynn, and Shacham [BGLS03a] to allow a third party to compress an arbitrary group of signatures into a short aggregated signature that jointly authenticates all the compressed signatures. Aggregate signatures are related to, but significantly different from, multisignatures [IN83, Oka88, OO99, MOR01, Bol03] which were introduced in 1983 [IN83], but received a formal treatment much later by Ohta and Okamoto [Oka88, OO99] and Micali, Ohta, and Reyzin [MOR01]. They differ in terms of functionality and applications since in multisignatures, a set of users all sign the same message and the result is a single signature; while aggregate signatures are used to compress a group of signatures, where each signature might be signing a distinct message. In addition to the differing functionalities, multisignatures can have the group of signers or verifiers cooperate interactively, while aggregate signatures are more commonly studied in non-interactive settings.

Variants of aggregate signatures have been studied in the sequential [LMRS04] and synchronized [GR06] settings. In the sequential mode of aggregation, the signers are required to interact either by signing in a sequential chain; while in the synchronized setting, the signing algorithm takes as input a (time) period t, and the security of the scheme is conditioned on a signer signing at most once for each period t.

Numerous works have constructed (single- and multi-signer) aggregate signatures from pairing based assumptions [BGLS03a, BGLS03b, Bol03, GR06, LOS+06, BNN07, BGOY07, MT07, RS09, AGH10], factoring based assumptions [LMRS04, BN07, Nev08, BJ10, FLS12, LLY13a, LLY13b, BGR14, BMP16, HW18], and multilinear maps (and obfuscation) [FHPS13, HSW13, HKW15].

Another concept, loosely related to the notion of single-signer aggregate signatures, is that of batch verification which has been very well studied since the foundational work of Fiat [Fia89]. The main motivation behind batch verification of signatures (generated by a single signer) is to improve the concrete performance of the verifier checking a large sequence of messages. Thus, batch verification of signatures is not designed to produce a shorter aggregated signature which is our main goal.

2   Technical Overview

In this technical overview, we describe our RSA-based construction of locally verifiable aggregate signature in detail (proving Theorem 1.1), and briefly describe our pairing-based construction which uses similar high-level ideas but different algebraic tricks. At the end of the technical overview, we also discuss a SNARK-based construction of multi-signer locally verifiable aggregate signatures.

RSA-Based Locally Verifiable Aggregate Signature. Our starting point is the classical RSA-based single-signer[1] aggregate signature scheme where the signature of a message m with respect to an RSA public key (N, e) is $\sigma = H(m)^d$ (mod N), where $ed = 1$ (mod $\varphi(N)$) and H is a hash function modeled as a random oracle in the security analysis. Given L message-signature pairs $\{(m_i, \sigma_i)\}_{i=1}^{L}$, the aggregate signature is simply their product $\widehat{\sigma} = \prod_{i=1}^{L} \sigma_i$ (mod N). Verification proceeds by checking that

$$\widehat{\sigma}^e = \prod_{i=1}^{L} H(m_i) \pmod{N}.$$

Unfortunately, it is completely unclear how to "locally" verify a single message m_i given $\widehat{\sigma}$ and some hint h_i related to the message vector $\mathbf{m}$. Concretely, deducing how to even define the message-dependent hint is unclear. One may attempt

---

[1] Incidentally, we mention that the problem of constructing a *multi-signer* aggregate signature scheme from RSA has been a long-standing open problem, although constructions of relaxed variants such as sequential or synchronized (multi-signer) aggregate signature schemes based on RSA exist [LMRS04, HW18].

to define the hint h_i to be the product of all hash values $H(m_j)$ for $j \neq i$, and let the local verifier check that $\widehat{\sigma}^e = h_i \cdot H(m_i)$. However, a malicious hint generator can easily fool the verifier: the hint is adversarially generated and the verifier has no mechanism to check that the hint is well-formed without recomputing it which, in turn, seems to require the verifier to know all the underlying messages, in direct conflict with the requirement of local verification. In a nutshell, the accumulator-style aggregation and the presence of a random oracle seems to make local verification challenging.

To avoid this issue, we look at other RSA-based signature schemes [GMR88, DN94, CD96, GHR99, CS00, Fis03] for adding local verifiability. While this seems like a plausible approach, it quickly gets stuck at a much earlier point. Namely, for all these schemes, the notion of single-signer aggregation has not even been studied (to the best of our knowledge). A closer inspection shows that, unlike the classical RSA-based signature scheme, most of these schemes do not support aggregation. A notable exception is the Gennaro, Halevi, and Rabin [GHR99] scheme which works as follows. Suppose H is a collision-resistant function that maps messages into large (λ-bit) *prime* numbers. The signature of a message m is $\sigma = g^{1/H(m)} \pmod{N}$ where $g \in \mathbb{Z}_N^*$ is random and (N, g) is in the public key. Letting e_{m_i} denote $H(m_i)$ and $\sigma_i = g^{1/e_{m_i}} \pmod{N}$ denote the signature of m_i, the aggregation algorithm can simply compute $\widehat{\sigma} = \prod_i \sigma_i \pmod{N}$ as the aggregated signature. Regular (non-local) verification can be performed by the following equation:

$$(\widehat{\sigma})^{\Pi_i e_{m_i}} \stackrel{?}{=} \prod_i g^{\Pi_{j \neq i} e_{m_j}} \pmod{N}.$$

A correctly generated aggregate signature passes the check because

$$(\widehat{\sigma})^{\Pi_i e_{m_i}} = \left(\prod_i \sigma_i\right)^{\Pi_i e_{m_i}} = \prod_i g^{\Pi_{j \neq i} e_{m_j}} \pmod{N}. \tag{1}$$

We now show that the aggregate signatures $\widehat{\sigma}$ can also be *locally verified* w.r.t a message $m_j \in \mathbf{m}$ (the latter being the set of all messages whose signatures have been aggregated into $\widehat{\sigma}$) without knowing $\mathbf{m}$ but given only a short verification hint that depends on $\mathbf{m}$ and $\widehat{\sigma}$. Our first idea is to generate the following two whole numbers as the hint:

$$e_{\mathbf{m} \backslash m_j} = \prod_{i \neq j} e_{m_i}, \quad f_j = \sum_{i \neq j} \prod_{k \notin \{i,j\}} e_{m_k}.$$

Our key observation is the following equation (which is exactly the same as Eq. 1 except it uses a different exponent for $\widehat{\sigma}$)

$$(\widehat{\sigma})^{e_{\mathbf{m} \backslash m_j}} = g^{f_j} \cdot g^{e_{\mathbf{m} \backslash m_j}/e_{m_j}} \pmod{N}. \tag{2}$$

This can be translated into the following verification equation:

$$\left((\widehat{\sigma})^{e_{\mathbf{m} \backslash m_j}}/g^{f_j}\right)^{e_{m_j}} \stackrel{?}{=} g^{e_{\mathbf{m} \backslash m_j}} \pmod{N}. \tag{3}$$

Since e_{m_j} can be computed from just the target message m_j, releasing $e_{\mathbf{m} \backslash m_j}$ and f_j as the hint enables local verification of the aggregate signature $\hat{\sigma}$ via the above equation. It can also be proven secure in the presence of malicious hint generators as long as the local verification algorithm also checks that the numbers $e_{\mathbf{m} \backslash m_j}$ and e_{m_j} are co-prime (that is, $\gcd(e_{\mathbf{m} \backslash m_j}, e_{m_j}) = 1$).)

At a first glance, the above scheme seems to solve the problem of locally verifiable single-signer aggregate signatures from RSA; however, unfortunately, this is not the case. The hints $e_{\mathbf{m} \backslash m_j}$ and f_j have to be computed modulo $\phi(N)$, but the hint generator does not (and must not) know $\phi(N)$. The only way out seems to be to compute them over the integers which again does not work as they could be large $O(L)$-bit numbers, which is decidedly not short. These together seem like an unfortunate limitation to obtaining local verifiability. Luckily, this conundrum can be resolved in a rather simple, yet elegant, way using the surprising power of Shamir's trick [Sha84].

Our central observation is that the hint generator can completely *re-compute* the (unique) signature of *every* message in the set, starting from just the aggregate signature $\hat{\sigma}$. In more detail, the hint generator first computes

$$z_j := (\hat{\sigma})^{e_{\mathbf{m} \backslash m_j}} / g^{f_j} := g^{e_{\mathbf{m} \backslash m_j} / e_{m_j}} \pmod{N}.$$

Note that $e_{\mathbf{m} \backslash m_j}$ and e_{m_j} are co-prime, thus there exist efficiently computable integers α and β such that $\alpha \cdot e_{\mathbf{m} \backslash m_j} + \beta \cdot e_{m_j} = 1$. The hint generator next *re*-computes the signature $g^{1/e_{m_j}}$ of m_j as

$$g^{1/e_{m_j}} = g^{(\alpha \cdot e_{\mathbf{m} \backslash m_j} + \beta \cdot e_{m_j})/e_{m_j}} = (g^{e_{\mathbf{m} \backslash m_j}/e_{m_j}})^{\alpha} \cdot g^{\beta} = z_j^{\alpha} \cdot g^{\beta} \pmod{N}.$$

It then outputs $g^{1/e_{m_j}}$ as the hint, and the local verification algorithm simply checks it by running the plain (non-aggregated) verification algorithm interpreting the hint as a signature on the message m_j. (In fact, the local verification algorithm is independent of the aggregated signature $\hat{\sigma}$, and only needs the hint for verification. A detailed discussion is provided in Sect. 4.2).

This summarizes our RSA-based locally verifiable aggregate signature scheme, and the final remaining detail is to figure out how the function H is selected. To that end, we present two choices—the first is to let H employ a prime sequence generator based on a random oracle, which gives us a scheme that is fully secure in the random oracle model; and the second is to employ a technique similar to Micali, Rabin, and Vadhan [MRV99] (who used a t-wise independent hash function, but we use PRFs; see Sect. 4.1 for more details) to instantiate the scheme in the standard model. We point out that we could prove our standard model instantiation to be statically secure (in the sense that the adversary must query all messages before it sees the verification key). We leave the problem of constructing a fully secure scheme without random oracles as an interesting open problem.

In addition to the surprising (in our mind) property of allowing exact *re-computation* of individual signatures from aggregate signatures, our RSA-based scheme satisfies several additional properties such as support for multi-hop aggregation as well as unordered sequential aggregation. We also point out that the aforementioned exact re-computation property of our aggregate signatures is very useful for obtaining a redactable signature scheme which has constant-size redacted as well as unredacted signatures. In a nutshell, the redaction algorithm can first compute the individual signatures of all message blocks whose signature it wants to release, and can aggregate them again to create a shorter signature.

Pairing-Based Locally Verifiable Aggregation. Our pairing-based signature scheme relies on similar core ideas, but very different details due to differing algebraic structures.

Our starting point is to translate the above process of RSA-based signature generation to bilinear maps as follows. Recall the signature of a message m is computed as $\sigma = g^{1/H(m)}$, where H is a collision-resistant function that maps messages into large *prime* numbers and the inverse in the exponent, $1/H(m)$, is computed using the factorization of the RSA modulus. To port this over to bilinear maps, we substitute $H(m)$ with $\alpha + m$, where α is a secret exponent from the master key. Basically, the signature is set as $\sigma = g^{1/(\alpha+m)}$, where g is a random public source group generator. The signature verification performs a bilinear pairing to check that $e(\sigma, g^\alpha g^m) = e(g, g)$, where g^α is part of the public key as well.

Coincidentally, this is exactly the weakly secure short signature scheme of Boneh and Boyen (BB) [BB04b, §4.3], and can be visualized as a bilinear analog of the RSA-based Gennaro-Halevi-Rabin scheme. Unfortunately, the BB scheme is also not known to be aggregatable, and while there exist pairing-based (multi-signer) aggregate signature schemes [BGLS03a], they are algebraically similar to the classical RSA-based schemes, thus do not appear to support local verifiability.

Our first main observation is that the BB scheme can actually be shown to be a single-signer aggregatable scheme. Although the signature aggregation is not as simple as multiplying the signatures (as in the RSA setting), we observe that, by Lagrange's inverse polynomial interpolation technique, we can aggregate a sequence of signatures $\sigma_i = g^{1/(\alpha+m_i)}$ into $\widehat{\sigma} = g^{\prod_i 1/(\alpha+m_i)}$. Simply put, Lagrange's inverse polynomial interpolation allows the following computation without the knowledge of the secret exponent α:

$$\prod_{i=1}^{L} \frac{1}{\alpha + m_i} = \frac{\gamma_1}{\alpha + m_1} + \cdots + \frac{\gamma_L}{\alpha + m_L},$$

where the coefficients γ_i can be publicly computed given only the sequence of messages $\{m_i\}_{i=1}^{L}$. Thus, the aggregate signature $\widehat{\sigma}$ can be computed as

$$\widehat{\sigma} = \prod_{i=1}^{L} \sigma_i^{\gamma_i}.$$

In a different context of attribute-based encryption (ABE), this idea was used by Delerablée, Paillier, and Pointcheval [DPP07,DP08], except that they employed Newton's iterative algorithm instead of Lagrange's technique. More details about aggregating the group elements is provided in detail later in Sect. 5.

Note that while the above allows aggregation of signatures, for regular (non-local) verification, the verifier requires higher degree monomials of the secret exponent α. Concretely, the aggregate verifier symbolically evaluates the polynomial $\prod_{i=1}^{L}(X + m_i)$ to simplify it as $\sum_{i=0}^{L} \delta_i X^i$, and using bilinear maps it can verify the aggregate signature as $e(\widehat{\sigma}, \prod_i (g^{\alpha^i})^{\delta_i}) = e(g, g)$, but this needs the monomials g^{α^i} as part of the public key. This is precisely why our pairing-based scheme requires a long CRS/public key.

Unlike the [BGLS03a] aggregate signature scheme, we can show that this scheme is locally verifiable. Our main observation here is that the non-local verification algorithm works in two phases. First, it pre-processes the public key, given only the set of messages, to compute $\prod_i (g^{\alpha^i})^{\delta_i} = g^{\prod_i (\alpha+m_i)}$ in the source group; second, it uses the bilinear map to pair this with the aggregate signature $\widehat{\sigma}$ and compare with $e(g, g)$. We note that the first step in the verification is inefficient, but a hint generator can speed it up for any target message m_j by generating the following two group elements as part of the short hint:

$$h_1 = g^{\prod_{i \neq j}(\alpha+m_i)}, \quad h_2 = g^{\alpha \prod_{i \neq j}(\alpha+m_i)} = h_1^{\alpha}.$$

Note that both h_1 and h_2 can also be publicly computed given only the public key, and set of messages contained in the aggregated signature. (This follows from the same symbolic execution of appropriate polynomials).

And, given the hints h_1, h_2, a verifier can locally verify the aggregate signature as

$$e(\widehat{\sigma}, h_1^{m_j} h_2) = e(g, g).$$

However, the above verification check alone is insufficient as a malicious hint generator can very easily fool the verifier. To address malicious hint generators, we also include a simple well-formedness check of the hint as follows:

$$e(g^{\alpha}, h_1) = e(g, h_2).$$

Putting these ideas together, we construct the pairing-based locally verification single-signer aggregate signature scheme in the long CRS setting. We prove this to be statically secure in the standard model, and adaptively secure in the random oracle model by replacing $\alpha + m$ terms with $\alpha + H(m)$. For more details, see Sect. 5. We leave the problems of reducing the CRS size and removing the random oracle an interesting open problems.

We also note that while the above construction needs a long CRS, it satisfies a very interesting property, namely that the hint generation algorithm is *fully public*, and does not even depend on the aggregate signature. Such fully public hint generation will be useful in applications where the hint generator is unaware of the underlying aggregate signature, or the user wants to generate the hint even before the aggregate signature has been generated or made available.

Lastly, our aggregatable IBE scheme builds on the above ideas. For details, we refer the reader to the full version of this paper [GV22].

Multi-signer Scheme from SNARKs. In the "folklore" construction of aggregate signatures from succinct non-interactive arguments of knowledge (SNARKs), the aggregation algorithm simply proves, w.r.t. a sequence of verification key-message pairs $\{(\mathsf{vk}_i, m_i)\}_i$, that it knows a sequence of signatures $(\sigma_1, \ldots, \sigma_N)$ such that σ_i is an accepting signature for (vk_i, m_i). This results in short (aggregate) signatures and fast verification, while also ensuring that from an accepting proof, the extractor can extract an accepting signature for every verification key-message pair.

This outline can be extended in a simple way to give us a locally verifiable aggregate signature. To generate the short hint, the hint generator creates another SNARK proof, w.r.t. a target key-message pair (vk, m), that proves knowledge of a sequence of key-message pairs $\{(\mathsf{vk}_i, m_i)\}_i$ and an aggregate signature $\hat{\sigma}$ such that (vk, m) is one of the tuples in the sequence, and $\hat{\sigma}$ is an accepting signature for that sequence of key-message pairs. Clearly, the hint generator has the witness (i.e., sequence of key-message pairs and an accepting aggregated signature) available, thus by correctness and efficiency of SNARKs we get that the resulting proof is short and efficiently verifiable. The enhanced local unforgeability of the resulting construction follows from the extractability of SNARKs and the unforgeability of the underlying (plain) aggregate signature scheme.

We note that the above sketch serves as a proof of concept of the feasibility of locally verifiable aggregate signatures in the *multi-signer* setting. However, a direct construction is more interesting and desirable for several reasons. First, conceptually, SNARKs seem too big of a hammer to construct aggregate signatures. Secondly, in practice, SNARKs have a high concrete performance overhead, while direct constructions based on number theory are much more efficient (this is akin to why number-theoretic accumulators and plain aggregate signatures are used in practice as opposed to Merkle trees and SNARK-based plain aggregate signatures). Finally, SNARKs suffer from impossibility results in the plain model [GW11], and are often constructed in the random oracle model or from knowledge-type assumptions, while locally verifiable aggregate signatures can potentially be built from fully standard assumptions in the plain model. Our single-signer constructions demonstrate this in the static security model; we believe that adaptive security is achievable without random oracles, but leave it as a fascinating open problem. Yet another fascinating open problem is to construct a multi-signer locally verifiable aggregate signature scheme.

Notation. We will let PPT denote probabilistic polynomial-time. We denote the set of all positive integers up to n as $[n] := \{1, \ldots, n\}$. Also, we use $[0, n]$ to denote the set of all non-negative integers up to n, i.e. $[0, n] := \{0\} \cup [n]$. Throughout this paper, unless specified, all polynomials we consider are positive polynomials. For any finite set S, $x \leftarrow S$ denotes a uniformly random element x from the set S. Similarly, for any distribution $\mathcal{D}$, $x \leftarrow \mathcal{D}$ denotes an element x drawn from distribution $\mathcal{D}$. The distribution $\mathcal{D}^n$ is used to represent a distribution over vectors of n components, where each component is drawn independently from the distribution $\mathcal{D}$.

3   Aggregate Cryptosystems with Local Properties

In this section, we recall the notion of single-signer aggregate signatures, and introduce the concept of local verification for aggregate signatures. Due to space constraints, we defer the definitions of locally verifiable aggregate signatures in the multi-signer setting and that of aggregate identity-based encryption to the full version [GV22].

3.1   Aggregate Signatures

The notion of aggregate signatures as introduced by Boneh, Gentry, Lynn and Shacham [BGLS03a] is simply a regular signature scheme that comes with two poly-time algorithms Aggregate and AggVerify, where Aggregate is used to aggregate an arbitrary polynomial number of message-signature pairs $\{(m_i, \sigma_i)\}_i$ generated using verification keys $\{vk_i\}_i$, into a shorter aggregate signature $\widehat{\sigma}$, and AggVerify can be used to verify such aggregate signatures with respect to the sequence of messages $(m_1, \ldots, m_\ell)$ and the verification keys $(vk_1, \ldots, vk_\ell)$.

An aggregate signature scheme is said to be a single-signer aggregate signature scheme if the aggregation algorithm requires all the verification keys $\{vk_i\}_i$ to be the same. Below we define it formally.

Syntax. A single-signer aggregate signature scheme $\mathcal{S}$ for message space $\mathcal{M}$ consists of the following polynomial time algorithms:

Setup(1^λ) $\rightarrow$ (vk, sk). The setup algorithm, on input the security parameter λ, outputs a pair of signing and verification keys (vk, sk).

Sign(sk, m) $\rightarrow \sigma$. The signing algorithm takes as input a signing key sk and a message $m \in \mathcal{M}$, and computes a signature σ.

Verify(vk, m, σ) $\rightarrow$ 0/1. The verification algorithm takes as input a verification key vk, a message $m \in \mathcal{M}$, and a signature σ. It outputs a bit to signal whether the signature is valid or not.

Aggregate (vk, $\{(m_i, \sigma_i)\}_i$) $\rightarrow \widehat{\sigma}/\bot$. The signature aggregation algorithm takes as input a verification key vk, a sequence of tuples, each containing a message m_i and signature σ_i, and it outputs either an aggregated signature $\widehat{\sigma}$ or a special abort symbol $\bot$.

AggVerify (vk, $\{m_i\}_i$, $\widehat{\sigma}$) $\rightarrow$ 0/1. The aggregate verify algorithm takes as input a verification key vk, a sequence of messages m_i, and it outputs a bit to signal whether the aggregated signature $\widehat{\sigma}$ is valid or not.

Correctness and Compactness. An aggregate signature scheme is said to be correct and compact if for all $\lambda, \ell \in \mathbb{N}$, every verification-signing key pair (vk, sk) $\leftarrow$ Setup(1^λ), messages m_i for $i \in [\ell]$, and every signature $\sigma_i \leftarrow$ Sign(sk, m_i) for $i \in [\ell]$, the following holds:

Correctness of signing. For all $i \in [\ell]$, Verify(vk, m_i, σ_i) = 1.

Correctness of aggregation. If $\widehat{\sigma} = \mathsf{Aggregate}\,(\mathsf{vk}, \{(m_i, \sigma_i)\}_i)$, then

$$\mathsf{AggVerify}\,(\mathsf{vk}, \{m_i\}_i, \widehat{\sigma}) = 1.$$

Compactness of aggregation. $|\widehat{\sigma}| \leq \mathsf{poly}(\lambda)$. That is, the size of an aggregated signature is a fixed polynomial in the security parameter λ, independent of the number of aggregations ℓ.

Security. Next, we recall the security notion for regular signatures as well as for the setting of aggregate signatures.

Definition 3.1 (Unforgeability). *A signature scheme* $(\mathsf{Setup}, \mathsf{Sign}, \mathsf{Verify})$ *is said to be a secure signature scheme if for every admissible PPT attacker* $\mathcal{A}$, *there exists a negligible function* $\mathsf{negl}(\cdot)$ *such that for all* $\lambda \in \mathbb{N}$, *the following holds*

$$\Pr\left[\mathsf{Verify}(\mathsf{vk}, m^*, \sigma^*) = 1 : \begin{array}{l} (\mathsf{vk}, \mathsf{sk}) \leftarrow \mathsf{Setup}(1^\lambda) \\ (m^*, \sigma^*) \leftarrow \mathcal{A}^{\mathsf{Sign}(\mathsf{sk}, \cdot)}(1^\lambda, \mathsf{vk}) \end{array}\right] \leq \mathsf{negl}(\lambda),$$

and $\mathcal{A}$ *is admissible as long as it did not query* m^* *to the* Sign *oracle.*

Definition 3.2 (Static Unforgeability). *We say the signature scheme is statically secure if the adversary in the above game is confined to make all of its message queries* $\{m_i\}_{i \in [q]}$ *and declare the challenge message* m^* *at the beginning of the game (defined in Definition 3.1) before it receives the verification key* vk.

Definition 3.3 (Aggregated Unforgeability). *A single-signer aggregate signature scheme* $(\mathsf{Setup}, \mathsf{Sign}, \mathsf{Verify}, \mathsf{Aggregate}, \mathsf{AggVerify})$ *is said to be a secure aggregate signature scheme if for every admissible PPT attacker* $\mathcal{A}$, *there exists a negligible function* $\mathsf{negl}(\cdot)$ *such that for all* $\lambda \in \mathbb{N}$, *the following holds*

$$\Pr\left[\begin{array}{l} \mathsf{AggVerify}\,(\mathsf{vk}, \{m_i^*\}_{i \in [\ell]}, \widehat{\sigma}^*) = 1 : \\ (\mathsf{vk}, \mathsf{sk}) \leftarrow \mathsf{Setup}(1^\lambda); (\{m_i^*\}_{i \in [\ell]}, \widehat{\sigma}^*) \leftarrow \mathcal{A}^{\mathsf{Sign}(\mathsf{sk}, \cdot)}(1^\lambda, \mathsf{vk}) \end{array}\right] \leq \mathsf{negl}(\lambda),$$

where $\mathcal{A}$ *is admissible if there exists* $i \in [\ell]$ *such that* m_i^* *was not queried by* $\mathcal{A}$ *to the* $\mathsf{Sign}(\mathsf{sk}, \cdot)$ *oracle.*

Definition 3.4 (Static Aggregated Unforgeability). *We say the aggregate signature scheme is statically secure if the adversary in the above game is confined to make all of its message queries* $\{m_i\}_{i \in [q]}$ *and declare the challenge messages* $\{m_i^*\}_{i \in [\ell]}$ *at the beginning of the game (defined in Definition 3.3) before it receives the verification key* vk.

Our definition of static security is identical to the weak-CMA security for plain signatures as defined by Boneh and Boyen [BB04b]. In addition to the above security properties, there are a number of other interesting properties such as unique signatures, multi-hop aggregation etc. that have been considered in the literature; we defer their description to the full version [GV22]. Our aggregate signature schemes satisfy most of these properties.

Locally Verifiable Aggregate Signatures. In this work, we introduce the notion of local openings for aggregate signatures that enable faster local verification. As described above, in existing aggregate signatures the verification algorithm for an aggregate signature takes as input the entire sequence of messages $(m_1, \ldots, m_\ell)$ aggregated inside signature $\widehat{\sigma}$. Thus, the run-time of verification scales *polynomially* with the number of messages ℓ.

Aggregate signatures with local opening enable efficient verifiability, where the local verification algorithm takes as input only the message m that has to be verified against the claimed aggregated signature $\widehat{\sigma}$, instead of all ℓ messages. However, without any other modifications to the syntax of the aggregate signatures, the notion of local verifiability is impossible to achieve (as discussed in the introduction). In order to make the notion feasible, we introduce an auxiliary local opening generator that generates some auxiliary information specific to the message m being locally verified, and this algorithm does not require any of the input signatures $\{\sigma_i\}_i$ that were aggregated, but the final aggregated signature $\widehat{\sigma}$. Below we define the algorithms formally.

LocalOpen$(\widehat{\sigma}, \mathsf{vk}, \{m_i\}_{i \in [\ell]}, j \in [\ell]) \to \mathsf{aux}_j$. The local opening algorithm takes as input an aggregated signature $\widehat{\sigma}$, a verification key vk, a sequence of messages m_i for $i \in [\ell]$, and an index $j \in [\ell]$. It outputs auxiliary information aux_j corresponding to the message m_i.

LocalAggVerify$(\widehat{\sigma}, \mathsf{vk}, m, \mathsf{aux}) \to 0/1$. The local aggregate verification algorithm takes as input an aggregated signature $\widehat{\sigma}$, a verification key vk, a message m, and auxiliary information aux. It outputs a bit to signal whether the aggregate signature $\widehat{\sigma}$ contains a signature for message m under verification key vk, or not.

Correctness and Compactness of Local Opening. An aggregate signature scheme with local openings is said to be correct and compact if for all $\lambda, \ell \in \mathbb{N}$, every verification-signing key pair $(\mathsf{vk}, \mathsf{sk}) \leftarrow \mathsf{Setup}(1^\lambda)$, messages m_i for $i \in [\ell]$, and every signature $\sigma_i \leftarrow \mathsf{Sign}(\mathsf{sk}, m_i)$ for $i \in [\ell]$, the following holds:

Correctness of local opening. For all $k \in [\ell]$, we have

$$\mathsf{LocalAggVerify}\,(\widehat{\sigma}, \mathsf{vk}, m_k, \mathsf{LocalOpen}(\widehat{\sigma}, \mathsf{vk}, \{m_i\}_i, k)) = 1.$$

Compactness of opening. $|\mathsf{aux}| \leq \mathsf{poly}(\lambda)$. That is, the size of the auxiliary opening information is a fixed polynomial in the security parameter λ, independent of the number of aggregations ℓ.

Security Against Adversarial Openings. Now we define the security notion for aggregate signatures with local openings.

Definition 3.5 (Aggregated Unforgeability with Adversarial Opening).
A locally-verifiable aggregate signature scheme (Setup, Sign, Verify, Aggregate, AggVerify, LocalOpen, LocalAggVerify) *is said to be a secure aggregate signature scheme against adversarial openings if for every admissible PPT attacker $\mathcal{A}$,*

there exists a negligible function negl($\cdot$) *such that for all* $\lambda \in \mathbb{N}$, *the following holds*

$$\Pr \left[\begin{array}{l} \mathsf{LocalAggVerify}(\widehat{\sigma}^*, \mathsf{vk}, m^*, \mathsf{aux}^*) = 1 : \\ (\mathsf{vk}, \mathsf{sk}) \leftarrow \mathsf{Setup}(1^\lambda); (\widehat{\sigma}^*, \mathsf{aux}^*, m^*) \leftarrow \mathcal{A}^{\mathsf{Sign}(\mathsf{sk},\cdot)}(1^\lambda, \mathsf{vk}) \end{array} \right] \leq \mathsf{negl}(\lambda),$$

where $\mathcal{A}$ *is admissible if* m^* *was not queried by* $\mathcal{A}$ *to the* $\mathsf{Sign}(\mathsf{sk}, \cdot)$ *oracle.*

Definition 3.6 (Static Aggregate Unforgeability with Adversarial Opening). *We say the locally-verifiable aggregate signature scheme is statically secure against adversarial openings if the adversary in the above game is confined to make all of its message queries* $\{m_i\}_{i \in [q]}$ *and declare the challenge message* m^* *at the beginning of the game (defined in Definition 3.5) before it receives the verification key* vk.

Fully Public Openings for Aggregate Signatures. We additionally consider the setting where the local opening algorithm does not need an aggregate signature to provide an opening w.r.t., but only the sequence of messages.

Remark 3.1 (Fully Public Openings). An aggregate signature scheme is said to have fully local public openings if the algorithm $\mathsf{LocalOpen}$ has the following syntax—$\mathsf{LocalOpen}(\mathsf{vk}, \{m_i\}_{i \in [\ell]}, j \in [\ell]) \rightarrow \mathsf{aux}_j$. That is, $\mathsf{LocalOpen}$ is oblivious to the aggregated signature.

Remark 3.2 (Optimal Compactness and Efficiency). In our definitions, we consider the size of the aggregate signatures, auxiliary opening information, running time of the local verifier to be independent of the number of aggregations. However, one could also consider schemes where the compactness and efficiency of the scheme grows poly-logarithmically with the number of aggregations, as for most applications poly-logarithmically dependence can be asymptotically captured within the polynomial dependence on the security parameter.

4   RSA-Based Locally Verifiable Aggregate Signatures

In this section, we provide a locally verifiable single-signer aggregate signature scheme based on the hardness of RSA. Our scheme satisfies a number of interesting properties, and relies on an efficient deterministic non-colliding prime sequence enumeration.

4.1   Deterministic Prime Sequence Enumeration

Here we are interested in an efficient injective mapping from the message space $(\mathcal{M}_\lambda = \{0,1\}^\lambda)$ to the set of $(\lambda+1)$-bit prime numbers. Such injective mappings were constructed by Cachin, Micali, and Stadler [CMS99] by relying on $2\lambda^2$-wise independent hash functions, (randomized) primality testing [SS77, Rab80], and prime density theorems [DlVP97]. The idea is to enumerate over a fixed length

($\approx 2\lambda^2$) sequence of $(\lambda + 1)$-bit numbers for each message in the message space, and select the lexicographically first prime number in that sequence (where the sequence is decided by the hash function). Since the hash function is pairwise independent, by relying on prime number density theorems, one gets that with all but negligible probability, such prime numbers for each message exist in the $2\lambda^2$ length sequence.

In this work, we rely on a similar prime sequence enumeration technique, but we slightly adapt it as it leads to different security proofs of our aggregate signature construction. Concretely, we rely on deterministic primality testing [AKS04] to avoid keeping random coins as part of the setup[2], and also replace the hash function with a PRF-based hash function in one instantiation (which results in static security of our signature scheme), and with a Random Oracle [BR93] in the second instantiation (which results in full security of our signature scheme). Additionally, we make the sampling process to be expected polynomial time instead as we consider exponential length sequences for the prime search. The sampling time could be done in worst-case polynomial time by relying on well-known prime gap conjectures.

Prime Sequence Enumerator via Pseudorandom Functions. Let PRF = (PRF.Setup, PRF.Eval) be a secure PRF that outputs λ bits of output. Below, we describe our prime sequence enumerator based on PRFs. A (fully secure) prime sequence enumerator in the random oracle model (ROM) is described in the full version [GV22].

$\mathsf{PrimeSeq}^{\mathsf{PRF}}(1^\lambda) \to$ samp. It samples a PRF key $K \leftarrow \mathsf{PRF.Setup}(1^\lambda, 1^{2\lambda})$, and sets samp $= K$.
$\mathsf{PrimeSamp}^{\mathsf{PRF}}(\mathsf{samp} = K, m) \to e_m$. It proceeds as follows:
  1. Set count $:= 0$, flag $:=$ false.
  2. While flag $=$ false:
     (a) Let $y := \mathsf{PRF.Eval}(K, m \| \mathsf{count})$ where $m \| \mathsf{count}$ is interpreted as a 2λ length bit string.
     (b) Run PrimalityTest to check if $2^\lambda + y$ is a prime. If it is a prime, set flag $:=$ true and $e_m := 2^\lambda + y$. Otherwise, set count $:=$ count $+ 1$.
  Output e_m.

Theorem 4.1 (Efficient and Statically Secure Enumeration via PRFs).
If PRF *is a secure pseudorandom function, then* $(\mathsf{PrimeSeq}^{\mathsf{PRF}}, \mathsf{PrimeSamp}^{\mathsf{PRF}})$ *satisfies the following properties:*

---

[2] We point out that *we use deterministic primality testing only for the ease of exposition*, and this is not necessary as our scheme is secure even if we rely on efficient randomized primality testing. Such an approach was already outlined in [MRV99] where the idea is to generate a sequence of random coins as part of the setup, and use those random coins to run the randomized primality test deterministically on all those random coins. The proof relies on the fact that, with all but negligible probability over the choice of random coins sampled during setup, randomized primality test will fail on at least one random coins for a non-prime.

Efficient Sampling. *For every* $\lambda \in \mathbb{N}$, $m \in \{0,1\}^\lambda$, *the prime sampling algorithm* $\mathsf{PrimeSamp}^{\mathsf{PRF}}$ *runs in expected polynomial time, where the probability is taken over the coins of setup algorithm* $\mathsf{PrimeSeq}^{\mathsf{PRF}}$.

Statically Secure Non-Colliding Prime Enumeration. *For any PPT adversary* $\mathcal{A}$, *there exists a negligible function* $\mathsf{negl}(\cdot)$, *such that for all* $\lambda \in \mathbb{N}$, *we have that*

$$\Pr\left[\begin{array}{c} \exists i \neq j \in [Q] \ s.t. \\ e_i = e_j \wedge m_i \neq m_j \end{array} : \begin{array}{c} \{m_i\}_{i \in [Q]} \leftarrow \mathcal{A}(1^\lambda) \\ \mathsf{samp} \leftarrow \mathsf{PrimeSeq}^{\mathsf{PRF}}(1^\lambda) \\ \{e_i = \mathsf{PrimeSamp}^{\mathsf{PRF}}(\mathsf{samp}, m_i)\}_i \end{array}\right] \leq \mathsf{negl}(\lambda).$$

Proof. The proof follows from [CMS99] which relied on $2\lambda^2$-wise independent hash function instead of a PRF as we do above. Also, as in [MRV99], we force the enumerator to output truly $(\lambda + 1)$-bit primes by fixing the leading bit to be 1 (i.e., adding 2^λ to the randomly sampled number). Now by relying on the pseudorandomness property of the underlying PRFs, we get the desired properties for a sequence of polynomial but "a-priori unbounded" number of messages. Since PRFs are poly-wise independent functions by pseudorandomness for any arbitrary polynomial poly, thus the theorem follows. Note that here the PRF key is being released as part of the public sampling parameters, and despite that fact we are relying on PRF security for security of our samplers. Briefly, this is due to the fact that an attacker in the static non-colliding prime enumeration is required to commit all its messages at the beginning of the game, and the public sampling parameters (i.e., the PRF key) is sampled after the messages are committed by the adversary. Therefore, we do not need to supply the attacker the PRF key, and can simply check whether the non-colliding property failed by querying the PRF oracle. $\qquad\square$

Shamir's Trick. Our construction makes use of the following classical lemma due to Shamir [Sha83] whose proof is provided for completeness.

Lemma 4.1. *Given* $x, y \in \mathbb{Z}_N$ *together with* $a, b \in \mathbb{Z}$ *such that* $x^a = y^b \pmod{N}$ *and* $\gcd(a, b) = 1$, *there is an efficient algorithm for computing* $z \in \mathbb{Z}_N$ *such that* $z^a = y \pmod{N}$.

Proof. Let $\alpha, \beta \in \mathbb{Z}$ be integers such that $\alpha a + \beta b = 1$. Then, $z = y^\alpha x^\beta$ is the desired number as $z^a = y^{\alpha a} x^{\beta a} = y^{\alpha a} y^{\beta b} = y^{\alpha a + \beta b} = y \pmod{N}$. $\qquad\square$

4.2   Construction

Below we provide our construction of single-signer aggregate signatures with λ-bit messages.

$\mathsf{Setup}(1^\lambda) \to (\mathsf{vk}, \mathsf{sk})$. The setup algorithm generates an RSA modulus $N = pq$, where p, q are random primes of $\lambda/2$ bits each. Next, it chooses a random element $g \leftarrow \mathbb{Z}_N^*$, and samples the public parameters for prime sequence enumeration as $\mathsf{samp} \leftarrow \mathsf{PrimeSeq}(1^\lambda)$. It sets the key pair as $\mathsf{vk} = (N, \mathsf{samp}, g)$ and $\mathsf{sk} = (p, q, \mathsf{samp}, g)$.

Sign(sk, m) → σ. It parses sk as above, and computes the prime number e_m = PrimeSamp(samp, m). It computes the signature as $g^{e_m^{-1}}$ (mod N) using p and q from the secret key and computing e_m^{-1} (mod $\phi(N)$).

Verify(vk, m, σ). It parses vk as above, and computes the prime number e_m = PrimeSamp(samp, m). It checks whether σ^{e_m} (mod N) = g. If the check succeeds, then it outputs 1 to signal that the signature is valid, otherwise it outputs 0.

Aggregate (vk, $\{(m_i, \sigma_i)\}_i$) → $\widehat{\sigma}/\bot$. The signature aggregation algorithm first verifies all the input signatures σ_i, and outputs $\bot$ if any of these verifications fail. Otherwise, it computes the aggregated signature as

$$\widehat{\sigma} = \prod_i \sigma_i \ (\text{mod } N).$$

AggVerify (vk, $\{m_i\}_{i \in [\ell]}$, $\widehat{\sigma}$). The signature verification algorithm parses the verification key as above, and computes the sequence of primes corresponding to the messages as e_{m_i} = PrimeSamp(samp, m_i) for all $i \in [\ell]$ where ℓ is the number of aggregated messages. It then checks whether the following is true or not:

$$\widehat{\sigma}^{\prod_i e_{m_i}} = \prod_i g^{\prod_{j \neq i} e_{m_j}} \ (\text{mod } N).$$

If the check succeeds, then it outputs 1 to signal that the aggregated signature is valid, otherwise it outputs 0.

LocalOpen($\widehat{\sigma}$, vk, $\{m_i\}_{i \in [\ell]}$, $j \in [\ell]$) → aux_j. It parses vk as above, and computes the sequence of prime numbers corresponding to the messages as e_{m_i} = PrimeSamp(samp, m_i) for all $i \in [\ell]$. It then computes the following terms:

$$e_{\mathbf{m} \backslash m_j} = \prod_{i \neq j} e_{m_i}, \quad f_j = \sum_{i \neq j} \prod_{k \neq \{i,j\}} e_{m_k}.$$

Note that since vk contains only N and not $\phi(N)$, thus the algorithm computes the above as large integers without performing any modular reductions. It then computes the following:

$$x = \widehat{\sigma}^{e_{\mathbf{m} \backslash m_j}} / g^{f_j} \ (\text{mod } N).$$

And, it checks that $\gcd(e_{\mathbf{m} \backslash m_j}, e_{m_j}) = 1$. If the check fails, it outputs $\bot$, otherwise using Shamir's trick (Lemma 4.1), it computes aux_j as

$$\text{aux}_j = \text{Shamir}(x, y = g, a = e_{m_j}, b = e_{\mathbf{m} \backslash m_j}).$$

LocalAggVerify($\widehat{\sigma}$, vk, m, aux). The local verification algorithm simply runs the unaggregated verification and outputs Verify(vk, m, σ = aux). That is, it interprets aux as the original signature on m, ignores $\widehat{\sigma}$, and verifies aux as a signature for m.

Basically, the aggregate signature scheme has the special property that the local opening algorithm is able to recover the signature for message under consideration from the aggregated signature, therefore the local opening for a message is simply its signature. Hence, the above local verification algorithm only needs to check that the opening information aux is a valid signature for m, and no extra checks are needed for the aggregated signature $\hat{\sigma}$.[3]

In addition to the above algorithms, we want to point out that the scheme supports *unordered* sequential signing as well as multi-hop aggregation. Below we describe our sequential signing and verification algorithms:

SeqAggSign $(\mathsf{sk}, m', \{m_i\}_i, \hat{\sigma}) \to \hat{\sigma}'$. The sequential signing algorithm first verifies the input aggregated signature $\hat{\sigma}$, and outputs $\bot$ if the verification fails. Otherwise, it computes the prime $e_{m'}$ as $e_{m'} = \mathsf{PrimeSamp}(\mathsf{samp}, m')$, and computes the new aggregated signature as $\hat{\sigma}^{e_{m'}^{-1}} \pmod{N}$ since it knows $\phi(N)$.

SeqAggVerify $(\mathsf{vk}, \{m_i\}_{i \in [\ell]}, \hat{\sigma})$. The sequential aggregated verification algorithm parses the verification key as above, and computes the sequence of primes corresponding to the messages as $e_{m_i} = \mathsf{PrimeSamp}(\mathsf{samp}, m_i)$ for all $i \in [\ell]$ where ℓ is the number of aggregated messages. It then checks whether the following is true or not:

$$\hat{\sigma}^{\prod_i e_{m_i}} = g \pmod{N}.$$

If the check succeeds, then it outputs 1 to signal that the aggregated signature is valid, otherwise it outputs 0.

4.3   Correctness, Compactness, and More Properties

Correctness of Signing. This follows directly from the fact that PrimeSamp is a deterministic prime number sampler, and that $\left(g^{e_m^{-1}}\right)^{e_m} = g \pmod{N}$ for every m and $e_m = \mathsf{PrimeSamp}(\mathsf{samp}, m)$.

Correctness of Aggregation. Consider any sequence of messages $m_1, \ldots, m_\ell$, and corresponding signatures $\sigma_i = g^{e_{m_i}^{-1}}$ for $i \in [\ell]$ where $e_{m_i} = \mathsf{PrimeSamp}(\mathsf{samp}, m_i)$. We know that aggregating these signatures is done as $\hat{\sigma} = \prod_i \sigma_i \pmod{N}$. And, the aggregated verification checks the following:

$$\hat{\sigma}^{\prod_i e_{m_i}} = \prod_i g^{\prod_{j \neq i} e_{m_j}} \pmod{N}.$$

---

[3] We point out that this does not contradict our unforgeability property with adversarial openings. Since, irrespective of whether the adversary is maliciously aggregating signature or generating hints in a malicious way, the adversary is never allowed to make a sign query for the message associated with a forged signature. While it seems like since local verifier is independent of the aggregate signature $\hat{\sigma}$, thus a verifier might supply any arbitrary string and still pass local verification. The point is in order for the local verification to accept, it must be provided with a valid signature (as a hint), thus an attacker can not forge by supplying only malformed aggregated signatures $\hat{\sigma}$.

Now to verify that the above check succeeds for honestly computed and aggregated signatures, let us simplify the left side term $\widehat{\sigma}^{\prod_i e_{m_i}}$.

$$\widehat{\sigma}^{\prod_i e_{m_i}} = \left(\prod_j \sigma_j \right)^{\prod_i e_{m_i}} = \left(\prod_j g^{e_{m_j}^{-1}} \right)^{\prod_i e_{m_i}}.$$

Now since we have that $\left(g^{e_{m_j}^{-1}} \right)^{\prod_i e_{m_i}} = g^{\prod_{j \neq i} e_{m_j}} \pmod{N}$, the correctness of aggregated verification follows.

Compactness of Aggregation. The size of an aggregated signature is same as that of an *unaggregated* signature, which simply is a number between 0 and N.

Unique Signatues. Note that the above signature scheme is a unique signature scheme. This follows from the fact that the prime number enumeration samples $(\lambda + 1)$-bit primes, and since all factors of $\phi(N)$ are primes less than $\lambda/2$-bits, thus $e_m^{-1} \pmod{\phi(N)}$ is uniquely and well defined. Thus, the inversion operation $g^{e_m^{-1}} \pmod{N}$ is an injective mapping.

Multi-hop, Unordered and Interleavable Aggregation. We would like to point out that the above construction is a multi-hop aggregate signature scheme as well as the sequential signing and non-sequential aggregation can be arbitrarily interleaved. The multi-hop property follows directly from inspection since the aggregation algorithm is an unordered product of the corresponding signatures. And, since the product operation is independent of the sequence of multiplication, thus the aggregated verification does not depend on the order of aggregation, but only the needs the unordered sequence of aggregated messages. Lastly, we could also interleave the sequential and non-sequential signature aggregation algorithm, and the corresponding verification would need to be appropriately modified and altered.

4.4   Security

Static (Aggregated) Unforgeability. We show that if we instantiate the prime sequence enumeration based on PRFs in our above aggregate signature construction, then the resulting scheme satisfies static unforgeability. Formally, we prove the following.

Theorem 4.2 (Static Unforgeability). *If the Strong RSA assumption holds, and* (PrimeSeq, PrimeSamp) *is instantiated based on secure PRFs (as described in Sect. 4.1), then the aggregate signature scheme described above satisfies static unforgeability, static aggregated unforgeability, and static aggregated unforgeability with adversarial openings (Definition 3.2, 3.4 and 3.6).*

Full (Aggregated) Unforgeability in ROM. Next, we show that if we instantiate the prime sequence enumeration in the ROM, then the above aggregate signature construction satisfies full unforgeability. Formally, we prove the following.

Theorem 4.3 (Full Unforgeability). *If the RSA assumption with large exponents holds, and* (PrimeSeq, PrimeSamp) *is instantiated in the ROM (as described in Sect. 4.1), then the aggregate signature scheme described above satisfies (full) unforgeability, aggregated unforgeability, and aggregated unforgeability with adversarial openings (Definition 3.1, 3.3 and 3.5).*

Due to space constraints, the proofs are delegated to the full version [GV22].

5   Pairing-Based Locally Verifiable Aggregate Signatures

In this section, we provide a locally verifiable single-signer aggregate signature scheme with *fully public* local openings based on the hardness of Diffie-Hellman Inversion problem. Our scheme satisfies a number of interesting properties that we discuss later, however it supports only bounded single-hop aggregation.

Injective Message Hashing. Similar to our RSA based construction, we are interested in an injective mapping from the message space $(\mathcal{M}_\lambda = \{0,1\}^\lambda)$ to the prime field $\mathbb{Z}_p$ for $p > 2^\lambda$. We consider two simple such mappings (HGen, H) that lead to static and full adaptive security for our final construction respectively.

Identity Map. The hash setup $\mathsf{HGen}^\mathcal{I}$ is simply the empty algorithm that outputs $\mathsf{hk} = \epsilon$, and $\mathsf{H}^\mathcal{I}(\epsilon, m) = m$ where output m is interpreted as a field element of $\mathbb{Z}_p$.

RO Map. Let $\mathcal{H} = \{\mathcal{H}_\lambda\}_\lambda$ be a family of hash functions where each $h \in \mathcal{H}_\lambda$ takes λ bits as input, and outputs λ-bits of output. The hash setup $\mathsf{HGen}^\mathcal{H}$ simply samples a hash function $h \in \mathcal{H}_\lambda$ and outputs $\mathsf{hk} = h$, and $\mathsf{H}^\mathcal{H}(\mathsf{hk} = h, m) = h(m)$ where output $h(m)$ is interpreted as a field element of $\mathbb{Z}_p$. Clearly, if h is modeled as a random oracle, then so is the resulting mapping.

Aggregating Inverse Exponents. Our aggregate signature scheme relies on the "key accumulation" algorithm of Delerablée, Paillier, and Pointcheval [DPP07, DP08]. We refer to the algorithm as the DPP algorithm which takes as input a sequence of group elements $\{g^{\frac{r}{\gamma + x_i}}, x_i\}_{i \in [\ell]}$, and outputs $g^{\frac{r}{\prod_{i \in [\ell]}(\gamma + x_i)}}$. However, as discussed in the introduction, we can rely on the alternate and more efficient Lagrange's inverse polynomial interpolation technique for a simpler aggregation algorithm. The idea behind our more efficient accumulation algorithm is as follows. By Lagrange's polynomial interpolation formula we know that for a degree-ℓ polynomial passing through points (x_i, y_i) for $i \in [\ell]$, the corresponding polynomial $p(x)$ can be written as follows

$$p(x) = \sum_{j \in [\ell]} y_j L_j(x), \qquad \text{where } L_j(x) = \frac{\prod_{i \neq j}(x - x_i)}{\prod_{i \neq j}(x_j - x_i)}.$$

Now if we set $y_i = 1$ for all $i \in [\ell]$. That is, $p(x_i) = 1$ for all i. Then, by inspection, we know that $p(x) = \prod_i (x - x_i) + 1$ is an identity. Thus, by using the above Lagrange's polynomial interpolation equation, we get that

$$\prod_i (x - x_i) + 1 = \sum_{j \in [\ell]} \frac{\prod_{i \neq j}(x - x_i)}{\prod_{i \neq j}(x_j - x_i)}.$$

Dividing both sides by $\prod_i (x - x_i)$ we get that

$$1 + \frac{1}{\prod_i (x - x_i)} = \sum_{i \in [\ell]} \frac{\Delta_i}{x - x_i}, \qquad \text{where } \Delta_i = \frac{1}{\prod_{j \neq i}(x_i - x_j)}.$$

Since Δ_i can be publicly computed given the list $x_1, \ldots, x_\ell$, thus the aggregation algorithm for group elements follows.

5.1   Construction

Below we provide our construction for single-signer aggregate signatures with λ-bit messages. Since we are in the single-signer setting, thus we no longer need to introduce the CRS algorithm as part of its description.

$\mathsf{Setup}(1^\lambda, 1^B) \to (\mathsf{vk}^{(\mathsf{local})}, \mathsf{vk}, \mathsf{sk})$. The setup algorithm takes as input the security parameter, λ, as well as the upper bound on number of aggregations, B. It samples the bilinear group parameters $\Pi = (p, \mathbb{G}, \mathbb{G}_T, g, e(\cdot, \cdot)) \leftarrow \mathsf{Gen}(1^\lambda)$, and samples a random exponent $\alpha \leftarrow \mathbb{Z}_p^*$. It also samples the public parameters for message hashing as $\mathsf{hk} \leftarrow \mathsf{HGen}(1^\lambda)$. It sets the key pair as $\mathsf{vk} = (\Pi, \mathsf{hk}, \{g^{\alpha^i}\}_{i \in [B]})$ and $\mathsf{sk} = (\Pi, \mathsf{hk}, \alpha)$. It also sets the local verification key $\mathsf{vk}^{(\mathsf{local})}$ as $\mathsf{vk}^{(\mathsf{local})} = (\Pi, \mathsf{hk}, g^\alpha)$.

   NOTE. We would like to point out that the setup algorithm for aggregate signatures typically outputs only a verification-signing key pair. However, here also introduce a *local* verification key that is entirely contained inside the full verification key, but it serves as a shorter key for the local verification algorithm to use. Simply put, here we consider bounded aggregate signatures with local verification, and to make the notion of local verification interesting in the bounded aggregation setting, we introduce a local verification key whose size is independent of the aggregation bound B thereby enabling the local verification algorithm to be independent of the number of aggregations. One could have instead defined local verification algorithm to have RAM access over the full verification key, and require the worst case run-time of the local verification to not grow with the number of underlying aggregations whenever the local verification is modeled as a RAM.

$\mathsf{Sign}(\mathsf{sk}, m) \to \sigma$. It parses sk as above, and hashes the message as $h_m = \mathsf{H}(\mathsf{hk}, m)$. It computes the signature as $g^{(\alpha + h_m)^{-1}}$ which can be computed efficiently since it knows α.[4]

---

[4] For simplicity, we ignore the possibility that $\alpha + h_m = 0$ as that could be easily handled as a special case by outputting the identity group element, but keeping it as part of the scheme description makes it cumbersome.

Verify(vk, m, σ). It parses vk as above, and computes the message hash as $h_m = \mathsf{H}(\mathsf{hk}, m)$. It checks whether $e(\sigma, g^\alpha g^{h_m}) = e(g, g)$ where g^α is taken from the verification key vk.[5] If the check succeeds, then it outputs 1 to signal that the signature is valid, otherwise it outputs 0.

Aggregate ($\mathsf{vk}, \{(m_i, \sigma_i)\}_i$) $\rightarrow \widehat{\sigma}/\bot$. The signature aggregation algorithm first verifies all the input signatures σ_i, and outputs $\bot$ if any of these verifications fail. Otherwise, it computes the aggregated signature as

$$\widehat{\sigma} = \mathsf{DPP}(\{\sigma_i, x_i\}_i),$$

where $x_i = \mathsf{H}(\mathsf{hk}, m_i)$.

AggVerify ($\mathsf{vk}, \{m_i\}_{i \in [\ell]}, \widehat{\sigma}$). The signature verification algorithm parses the verification key as above, and computes the sequence of hashed messages as $x_i = \mathsf{H}(\mathsf{hk}, m_i)$ for all $i \in [\ell]$ where ℓ is the number of aggregated messages. It then computes the following polynomial P symbolically to obtain the coefficients $\{\beta_i \in \mathbb{Z}_p\}_{i \in [\ell]}$:

$$P_{\{x_i\}_{i \in [\ell]}}(y) = \prod_{i \in [\ell]} (y + x_i) = \sum_{i=0}^{\ell} \beta_i y^i \pmod{p}. \tag{4}$$

It then checks that $\ell \leq B$ and whether the following is true or not:

$$e(\widehat{\sigma}, \prod_{i=0}^{\ell} (g^{\alpha^i})^{\beta_i}) = e(g, g),$$

where g^{α^i} are taken from the verification key vk. If the check succeeds, then it outputs 1 to signal that the aggregated signature is valid, otherwise it outputs 0.

LocalOpen($\mathsf{vk}, \{m_i\}_{i \in [\ell]}, j \in [\ell]$) $\rightarrow \mathsf{aux}_j$. It parses vk as above, computes the sequence of hash messages as $x_i = \mathsf{H}(\mathsf{hk}, m_i)$ for all $i \in [\ell] \backslash \{j\}$, and computes the coefficients $\{\widetilde{\beta}_i \in \mathbb{Z}_p\}_{i \in [\ell-1]}$, similar to that in Eq. (4) except it removes $(y + x_j)$ from the list of monomials. Concretely, it computes

$$P_{\{x_i\}_{i \in [\ell] \backslash \{j\}}}(y) = \prod_{i \in [\ell] \backslash \{j\}} (y + x_i) = \sum_{i=0}^{\ell-1} \widetilde{\beta}_i y^i \pmod{p}. \tag{5}$$

It then outputs the auxiliary opening information $\mathsf{aux}_j = (\mathsf{aux}_{j,1}, \mathsf{aux}_{j,2})$ where $\mathsf{aux}_{j,1}, \mathsf{aux}_{j,2}$ are computed as

$$\mathsf{aux}_{j,1} = \prod_{i=0}^{\ell-1} (g^{\alpha^i})^{\widetilde{\beta}_i}, \qquad \mathsf{aux}_{j,2} - \prod_{i=0}^{\ell-1} (y^{\alpha^{i+1}})^{\widetilde{\beta}_i},$$

where g^{α^i} are taken from the verification key vk.

---

[5] Note that the verification algorithm does not the entire verification key, but the local portion of verification key would be sufficient.

LocalAggVerify$(\widehat{\sigma}, \mathsf{vk}^{(\mathsf{local})}, m, \mathsf{aux})$. The local verification algorithm parses the local verification key $\mathsf{vk}^{(\mathsf{local})}$ as above, and auxiliary opening $\mathsf{aux} = (\mathsf{aux}_1, \mathsf{aux}_2)$, and computes the message hash as $h_m = \mathsf{H}(\mathsf{hk}, m)$. It checks the following two conditions:

$$e(\widehat{\sigma}, \mathsf{aux}_1{}^{h_m}\mathsf{aux}_2) = e(g, g)$$
$$e(g^\alpha, \mathsf{aux}_1) = e(g, \mathsf{aux}_2)$$

where g^α is taken from the local verification key vk. If both the check succeed, then it outputs 1 to signal that the signature is valid, otherwise it outputs 0. NOTE. As we pointed out before, instead of defining the local verification key, we could provide the local verifier RAM access to the full verification key, and since it only needs to extract g^α from the full verification key, thus the verification will be efficient even with that formalization.

In addition to the above algorithms, we want to point out that the scheme supports *unordered* sequential signing on top of single-hop aggregation. Below we describe our sequential signing and verification algorithms:

SeqAggSign $(\mathsf{sk}, m', \{m_i\}_i, \widehat{\sigma}) \rightarrow \widehat{\sigma}'$. The sequential signing algorithm first verifies the input aggregated signature $\widehat{\sigma}$, and outputs $\perp$ if the verification fails. Otherwise, it hashes the message as $h_{m'} = \mathsf{H}(\mathsf{hk}, m')$, and computes the new aggregated signature as $\widehat{\sigma}^{(\alpha+h_{m'})^{-1}}$ since it knows α.

SeqAggVerify $(\mathsf{vk}, \{m_i\}_{i\in[\ell]}, \widehat{\sigma})$. The sequential verification algorithm runs the (non-sequential) aggregated verification and outputs AggVerify$(\mathsf{vk}, \{m_i\}_i, \widehat{\sigma})$. That is, it interprets $\widehat{\sigma}$ as a non-sequential aggregated signature on $\{m_i\}_{i\in[\ell]}$, and verifies $\widehat{\sigma}$.

5.2 Correctness, Compactness, and More

Correctness of Signing. This follows from the fact that $e(g^{(\alpha+h_m)^{-1}}, g^\alpha g^{h_m}) = e(g, g)$ where $h_m = \mathsf{H}(\mathsf{hk}, m)$.

Correctness of Aggregation. Consider any sequence of messages $m_1, \ldots, m_\ell$, and corresponding signatures $\sigma_i = g^{(\alpha+h_{m_i})^{-1}}$ for $i \in [\ell]$ where $h_{m_i} = \mathsf{H}(\mathsf{hk}, m_i)$. We know that aggregating these signatures is done as $\widehat{\sigma} = \mathsf{DPP}(\{\sigma_i, h_{m_i}\}_i)$. Now by the correctness of the key accumulation algorithm of [DPP07, DP08], we have that $\widehat{\sigma} = g^{\Pi_i(\alpha+h_{m_i})^{-1}}$. And, the aggregated verification checks the following:

$$e\left(\widehat{\sigma}, \prod_{i=0}^{\ell}(g^{\alpha^i})^{\beta_i}\right) = e(g, g),$$

where β_i's are such that $\sum_{i=0}^{\ell}\beta_i y^i = \prod_{i\in[\ell]}(y + h_{m_i}) \pmod{p}$. Thus, we have that

$$\prod_{i=0}^{\ell}(g^{\alpha^i})^{\beta_i} = g^{\sum_{i=0}^{\ell}\alpha^i\beta_i} = g^{\Pi_{i\in[\ell]}(\alpha+h_{m_i})}.$$

Therefore, for honestly computed and aggregated signatures, the above check succeeds and correctness follows.

Compactness of Aggregation. The size of an aggregated signature is same as that of an *unaggregated* signature, which simply is a source group element (i.e., $\hat{\sigma} \in \mathbb{G}$).

Unique Signatures. Note that the above signature scheme is a unique signature scheme. This follows from the fact that the message hashing is a deterministic function, and if $e(\sigma, g^{\alpha}g^{h_m}) = e(g, g)$, then it must be that $\sigma = g^{(\alpha+h_m)^{-1}}$ which can be uniquely computed since $\mathbb{G}$ is a prime order source group.

Single-Hop, Unordered Sequential Aggregation with Fully Public Local Openings. We would like to point out that the above construction is a single-hop aggregate signature scheme. And, since the product operation is independent of the sequence of multiplication, thus the aggregated verification does not depend on the order of aggregation, but only the needs the unordered sequence of aggregated messages. Here the sequential signing can be performed arbitrarily on top of an aggregated signature.

Lastly, an interesting feature of these signatures is that they provide fully public local openings, and the LocalOpen algorithm does not need an aggregated signature as an extra input.

5.3 Security

Static (Aggregated) Unforgeability. We show that if we instantiate the message hashing as the identity map in our above aggregate signature construction, then the resulting scheme satisfies static unforgeability. Formally, we prove the following.

Theorem 5.1 (Static Unforgeability). *If the Diffie-Hellman inversion assumption holds, and* (HGen, H) *is an identity hash, then the aggregate signature scheme described above satisfies static unforgeability, and static aggregated unforgeability (Definition 3.2 and 3.4).*

Also, if the bilinear Diffie-Hellman inversion assumption holds, and (HGen, H) *is an identity hash, then the aggregate signature scheme described above also satisfies static aggregated unforgeability with adversarial openings (Definition 3.6).*

Full (Aggregated) Unforgeability in ROM. Next, we show that if we instantiate the message hashing in the ROM, then the above aggregate signature construction satisfies full unforgeability. Formally, we prove the following.

Theorem 5.2 (Full Unforgeability). *If the Diffie-Hellman inversion assumption holds, and* (HGen, H) *is instantiated in the ROM, then the aggregate signature scheme described above satisfies (full) unforgeability, and aggregated unforgeability (Definition 3.1 and 3.3).*

Also, if the bilinear Diffie-Hellman Inversion assumption holds, and (HGen, H) *is instantiated in the ROM, then the aggregate signature scheme described above also satisfies (full) aggregated unforgeability with adversarial openings (Definition 3.5).*

Due to space constraints, the proofs are deferred to the full version [GV22].

References

[AGH10] Ahn, J.H., Green, M., Hohenberger, S.: Synchronized aggregate signatures: new definitions, constructions and applications. In: CCS (2010)

[AKS04] Agrawal, M., Kayal, N., Saxena, N.: PRIMES is in P. Ann. Math. **160**(2), 781–793 (2004)

[BB04a] Boneh, D., Boyen, X.: Secure identity based encryption without random oracles. In: Franklin, M. (ed.) CRYPTO 2004. LNCS, vol. 3152, pp. 443–459. Springer, Heidelberg (2004). https://doi.org/10.1007/978-3-540-28628-8_27

[BB04b] Boneh, D., Boyen, X.: Short signatures without random oracles. In: Cachin, C., Camenisch, J.L. (eds.) EUROCRYPT 2004. LNCS, vol. 3027, pp. 56–73. Springer, Heidelberg (2004). https://doi.org/10.1007/978-3-540-24676-3_4

[BGLS03a] Boneh, D., Gentry, C., Lynn, B., Shacham, H.: Aggregate and verifiably encrypted signatures from bilinear maps. In: Biham, E. (ed.) EUROCRYPT 2003. LNCS, vol. 2656, pp. 416–432. Springer, Heidelberg (2003). https://doi.org/10.1007/3-540-39200-9_26

[BGLS03b] Boneh, D., Gentry, C., Lynn, B., Shacham, H.: I. A survey of two signature aggregation techniques. CryptoBytes (2003)

[BGOY07] Boldyreva, A., Gentry, C., O'Neill, A., Yum, D.H.: Ordered multisignatures and identity-based sequential aggregate signatures, with applications to secure routing. In: CCS (2007)

[BGR14] Brogle, K., Goldberg, S., Reyzin, L.: Sequential aggregate signatures with lazy verification from trapdoor permutations. Inf. Comput. **239**, 356–376 (2014)

[BJ10] Bagherzandi, A., Jarecki, S.: Identity-based aggregate and multi-signature schemes based on RSA. In: Nguyen, P.Q., Pointcheval, D. (eds.) PKC 2010. LNCS, vol. 6056, pp. 480–498. Springer, Heidelberg (2010). https://doi.org/10.1007/978-3-642-13013-7_28

[BLK13] Langley, A., Laurie, B., Kasper, E.: Certificate transparency (2013). https://datatracker.ietf.org/doc/html/rfc6962

[BMP16] El Bansarkhani, R., Mohamed, M.S.E., Petzoldt, A.: MQSAS - a multivariate sequential aggregate signature scheme. In: Bishop, M., Nascimento, A.C.A. (eds.) ISC 2016. LNCS, vol. 9866, pp. 426–439. Springer, Cham (2016). https://doi.org/10.1007/978-3-319-45871-7_25

[BN07] Bellare, M., Neven, G.: Identity-based multi-signatures from RSA. In: Abe, M. (ed.) CT-RSA 2007. LNCS, vol. 4377, pp. 145–162. Springer, Heidelberg (2006). https://doi.org/10.1007/11967668_10

[BNN07] Bellare, M., Namprempre, C., Neven, G.: Unrestricted aggregate signatures. In: Arge, L., Cachin, C., Jurdziński, T., Tarlecki, A. (eds.) ICALP 2007. LNCS, vol. 4596, pp. 411–422. Springer, Heidelberg (2007). https://doi.org/10.1007/978-3-540-73420-8_37

[Bol03] Boldyreva, A.: Threshold signatures, multisignatures and blind signatures based on the gap-Diffie-Hellman-group signature scheme. In: Desmedt, Y.G. (ed.) PKC 2003. LNCS, vol. 2567, pp. 31–46. Springer, Heidelberg (2003). https://doi.org/10.1007/3-540-36288-6_3

[BP97] Barić, N., Pfitzmann, B.: Collision-free accumulators and fail-stop signature schemes without trees. In: Fumy, W. (ed.) EUROCRYPT 1997. LNCS, vol. 1233, pp. 480–494. Springer, Heidelberg (1997). https://doi.org/10.1007/3-540-69053-0_33

[BR93] Bellare, M., Rogaway, P.: Random oracles are practical: a paradigm for designing efficient protocols. In: CCS (1993)

[CD96] Cramer, R., Damgård, I.: New generation of secure and practical RSA-based signatures. In: Koblitz, N. (ed.) CRYPTO 1996. LNCS, vol. 1109, pp. 173–185. Springer, Heidelberg (1996). https://doi.org/10.1007/3-540-68697-5_14

[CMS99] Cachin, C., Micali, S., Stadler, M.: Computationally private information retrieval with polylogarithmic communication. In: Stern, J. (ed.) EUROCRYPT 1999. LNCS, vol. 1592, pp. 402–414. Springer, Heidelberg (1999). https://doi.org/10.1007/3-540-48910-X_28

[CS00] Cramer, R., Shoup, V.: Signature schemes based on the strong RSA assumption. TISSEC 3(3), 161–185 (2000)

[CTg] Certificate transparency project. https://certificate.transparency.dev/

[DKS16] Derler, D., Krenn, S., Slamanig, D.: Signer-anonymous designated-verifier redactable signatures for cloud-based data sharing. In: Foresti, S., Persiano, G. (eds.) CANS 2016. LNCS, vol. 10052, pp. 211–227. Springer, Cham (2016). https://doi.org/10.1007/978-3-319-48965-0_13

[DlVP97] De la Vallée Poussin, C.-J.: Recherches analytiques sur la théorie des nombres premiers. Hayez, Imprimeur de l'Académie royale de Belgique (1897)

[DN94] Dwork, C., Naor, M.: An efficient existentially unforgeable signature scheme and its applications. In: Desmedt, Y.G. (ed.) CRYPTO 1994. LNCS, vol. 839, pp. 234–246. Springer, Heidelberg (1994). https://doi.org/10.1007/3-540-48658-5_23

[DP08] Delerablée, C., Pointcheval, D.: Dynamic threshold public-key encryption. In: Wagner, D. (ed.) CRYPTO 2008. LNCS, vol. 5157, pp. 317–334. Springer, Heidelberg (2008). https://doi.org/10.1007/978-3-540-85174-5_18

[DPP07] Delerablée, C., Paillier, P., Pointcheval, D.: Fully collusion secure dynamic broadcast encryption with constant-size ciphertexts or decryption keys. In: Takagi, T., Okamoto, E., Okamoto, T., Okamoto, T. (eds.) Pairing 2007. LNCS, vol. 4575, pp. 39–59. Springer, Heidelberg (2007). https://doi.org/10.1007/978-3-540-73489-5_4

[DPSS15] Derler, D., Pöhls, H.C., Samelin, K., Slamanig, D.: A general framework for redactable signatures and new constructions. In: Kwon, S., Yun, A. (eds.) ICISC 2015. LNCS, vol. 9558, pp. 3–19. Springer, Cham (2016). https://doi.org/10.1007/978-3-319-30840-1_1

[FHPS13] Freire, E.S.V., Hofheinz, D., Paterson, K.G., Striecks, C.: Programmable hash functions in the multilinear setting. In: Canetti, R., Garay, J.A. (eds.) CRYPTO 2013, Part I. LNCS, vol. 8042, pp. 513–530. Springer, Heidelberg (2013). https://doi.org/10.1007/978-3-642-40041-4_28

[Fia89] Fiat, A.: Batch RSA. In: Brassard, G. (ed.) CRYPTO 1989. LNCS, vol. 435, pp. 175–185. Springer, New York (1990). https://doi.org/10.1007/0-387-34805-0_17

[Fis03] Fischlin, M.: The Cramer-Shoup strong-RSA signature scheme revisited. In: Desmedt, Y.G. (ed.) PKC 2003. LNCS, vol. 2567, pp. 116–129. Springer, Heidelberg (2003). https://doi.org/10.1007/3-540-36288-6_9

[FLS12] Fischlin, M., Lehmann, A., Schröder, D.: History-free sequential aggregate signatures. In: Visconti, I., De Prisco, R. (eds.) SCN 2012. LNCS, vol. 7485, pp. 113–130. Springer, Heidelberg (2012). https://doi.org/10.1007/978-3-642-32928-9_7

[GHR99] Gennaro, R., Halevi, S., Rabin, T.: Secure hash-and-sign signatures without the random oracle. In: Stern, J. (ed.) EUROCRYPT 1999. LNCS, vol. 1592, pp. 123–139. Springer, Heidelberg (1999). https://doi.org/10.1007/3-540-48910-X_9

[GMR88] Goldwasser, S., Micali, S., Rivest, R.L.: A digital signature scheme secure against adaptive chosen-message attacks. SIAM J. Comput. 17(2), 281–308 (1988)

[Gol17] Goldreich, O.: Introduction to Property Testing. Cambridge University Press, Cambridge (2017)

[Gor18] Gorbunov, S.: How not to use aggregate signatures in your blockchain (2018)

[GR06] Gentry, C., Ramzan, Z.: Identity-based aggregate signatures. In: Yung, M., Dodis, Y., Kiayias, A., Malkin, T. (eds.) PKC 2006. LNCS, vol. 3958, pp. 257–273. Springer, Heidelberg (2006). https://doi.org/10.1007/11745853_17

[GV22] Goyal, R., Vaikuntanathan, V.: Locally verifiable signature and key aggregation. Cryptology ePrint Archive, Paper 2022/179 (2022). https://eprint.iacr.org/2022/179

[GW11] Gentry, C., Wichs, D.: Separating succinct non-interactive arguments from all falsifiable assumptions. In: STOC (2011)

[HKW15] Hohenberger, S., Koppula, V., Waters, B.: Universal signature aggregators. In: Oswald, E., Fischlin, M. (eds.) EUROCRYPT 2015, Part II. LNCS, vol. 9057, pp. 3–34. Springer, Heidelberg (2015). https://doi.org/10.1007/978-3-662-46803-6_1

[HSW13] Hohenberger, S., Sahai, A., Waters, B.: Full domain hash from (leveled) multilinear maps and identity-based aggregate signatures. In: Canetti, R., Garay, J.A. (eds.) CRYPTO 2013, Part I. LNCS, vol. 8042, pp. 494–512. Springer, Heidelberg (2013). https://doi.org/10.1007/978-3-642-40041-4_27

[HW18] Hohenberger, S., Waters, B.: Synchronized aggregate signatures from the RSA assumption. In: Nielsen, J.B., Rijmen, V. (eds.) EUROCRYPT 2018, Part II. LNCS, vol. 10821, pp. 197–229. Springer, Cham (2018). https://doi.org/10.1007/978-3-319-78375-8_7

[IN83] Itakura, K., Nakamura, K.: A public-key cryptosystem suitable for digital multisignatures. NEC J. Res. Dev. 71, 1–8 (1983)

[JMSW02] Johnson, R., Molnar, D., Song, D., Wagner, D.: Homomorphic signature schemes. In: Preneel, B. (ed.) CT-RSA 2002. LNCS, vol. 2271, pp. 244–262. Springer, Heidelberg (2002). https://doi.org/10.1007/3-540-45760-7_17

[LLY13a] Lee, K., Lee, D.H., Yung, M.: Sequential aggregate signatures made shorter. In: Jacobson, M., Locasto, M., Mohassel, P., Safavi-Naini, R. (eds.) ACNS 2013. LNCS, vol. 7954, pp. 202–217. Springer, Heidelberg (2013). https://doi.org/10.1007/978-3-642-38980-1_13

[LLY13b] Lee, K., Lee, D.H., Yung, M.: Sequential aggregate signatures with short public keys: design, analysis and implementation studies. In: Kurosawa, K., Hanaoka, G. (eds.) PKC 2013. LNCS, vol. 7778, pp. 423–442. Springer, Heidelberg (2013). https://doi.org/10.1007/978-3-642-36362-7_26

[LMRS04] Lysyanskaya, A., Micali, S., Reyzin, L., Shacham, H.: Sequential aggregate signatures from trapdoor permutations. In: Cachin, C., Camenisch, J.L. (eds.) EUROCRYPT 2004. LNCS, vol. 3027, pp. 74–90. Springer, Heidelberg (2004). https://doi.org/10.1007/978-3-540-24676-3_5

[LOS+06] Lu, S., Ostrovsky, R., Sahai, A., Shacham, H., Waters, B.: Sequential aggregate signatures and multisignatures without random oracles. In: Vaudenay, S. (ed.) EUROCRYPT 2006. LNCS, vol. 4004, pp. 465–485. Springer, Heidelberg (2006). https://doi.org/10.1007/11761679_28

[MOR01] Micali, S., Ohta, K., Reyzin, L.: Accountable-subgroup multisignatures. In: CCS (2001)

[MRV99] Micali, S., Rabin, M., Vadhan, S.: Verifiable random functions. In: FOCS (1999)

[MSK02] Mitsunari, S., Sakai, R., Kasahara, M.: A new traitor tracing. IEICE Trans. Fundam. Electron. Commun. Comput. Sci. 85(2), 481–484 (2002)

[MT07] Ma, D., Tsudik, G.: Forward-secure sequential aggregate authentication. In: SP (2007)

[Nev08] Neven, G.: Efficient sequential aggregate signed data. In: Smart, N. (ed.) EUROCRYPT 2008. LNCS, vol. 4965, pp. 52–69. Springer, Heidelberg (2008). https://doi.org/10.1007/978-3-540-78967-3_4

[Oka88] Okamoto, T.: A digital multisignature scheme using bijective public-key cryptosystems. TOCS 6(4), 432–441 (1988)

[OO99] Ohta, K., Okamoto, T.: Multi-signature schemes secure against active insider attacks. IEICE Trans. Fundam. Electron. Commun. Comput. Sci. 82(1), 21–31 (1999)

[Rab80] Rabin, M.O.: Probabilistic algorithm for testing primality. J. Number Theory 12(1), 128–138 (1980)

[RS09] Rückert, M., Schröder, D.: Aggregate and verifiably encrypted signatures from multilinear maps without random oracles. In: Park, J.H., Chen, H.-H., Atiquzzaman, M., Lee, C., Kim, T., Yeo, S.-S. (eds.) ISA 2009. LNCS, vol. 5576, pp. 750–759. Springer, Heidelberg (2009). https://doi.org/10.1007/978-3-642-02617-1_76

[SBZ01] Steinfeld, R., Bull, L., Zheng, Y.: Content extraction signatures. In: Kim, K. (ed.) ICISC 2001. LNCS, vol. 2288, pp. 285–304. Springer, Heidelberg (2002). https://doi.org/10.1007/3-540-45861-1_22

[Sha83] Shamir, A.: On the generation of cryptographically strong pseudorandom sequences. ACM Trans. Comput. Syst. 1(1), 38–44 (1983)

[Sha84] Shamir, A.: Identity-based cryptosystems and signature schemes. In: Blakley, G.R., Chaum, D. (eds.) CRYPTO 1984. LNCS, vol. 196, pp. 47–53. Springer, Heidelberg (1985). https://doi.org/10.1007/3-540-39568-7_5

[SS77] Solovay, R., Strassen, V.: A fast Monte-Carlo test for primality. SIAM J. Comput. 6(1), 84–85 (1977)

[Sud09] Sudan, M.: Probabilistically checkable proofs. Commun. ACM 52(3), 76–84 (2009)

[Yek12] Yekhanin, S.: Locally decodable codes. Found. Trends Theor. Comput. Sci. 6(3), 139–255 (2012)

Multimodal Private Signatures

Khoa Nguyen$^{(\boxtimes)}$ iD, Fuchun Guo iD, Willy Susilo iD, and Guomin Yang iD

Institute of Cybersecurity and Cryptology,
School of Computing and Information Technology,
University of Wollongong, Northfields Avenue, Wollongong, NSW 2522, Australia
{khoa,fuchun,wsusilo,gyang}@uow.edu.au

Abstract. We introduce Multimodal Private Signature (MPS) - an anonymous signature system that offers a novel accountability feature: it allows a designated opening authority to learn *some partial information* op about the signer's identity id, and nothing beyond. Such partial information can flexibly be defined as op = id (as in group signatures), or as op = $\mathbf{0}$ (like in ring signatures), or more generally, as op = $G_j(\mathsf{id})$, where $G_j(\cdot)$ is a certain disclosing function. Importantly, the value of op is known in advance by the signer, and hence, the latter can decide whether she/he wants to disclose that piece of information. The concept of MPS significantly generalizes the notion of tracing in traditional anonymity-oriented signature primitives, and can enable various new and appealing privacy-preserving applications.

We formalize the definitions and security requirements for MPS. We next present a generic construction to demonstrate the feasibility of designing MPS in a modular manner and from commonly used cryptographic building blocks (ordinary signatures, public-key encryption and NIZKs). We also provide an efficient construction in the standard model based on pairings, and a lattice-based construction in the random oracle model.

Keywords: new models · anonymous authentications · accountability · fine-grained information disclosure · modular constructions · zero-knowledge · lattices · pairings

1 Introduction

Privacy is a fundamental human right and is an interdisciplinary area of study [53]. In the digital era, where most of our daily communications are done over computer networks, the problem of privacy protection has become increasingly important and challenging. On the other hand, the development of information technology and cryptography also brings new technical solutions for privacy protection. Since the 1980s [16], various privacy-preserving cryptographic protocols have been proposed for this purpose. This essential area gets a lot of traction not only because of growing practical demands, but also due to its great theoretical interests. Indeed, designing these advanced systems is highly challenging, as they typically require

© International Association for Cryptologic Research 2022
Y. Dodis and T. Shrimpton (Eds.): CRYPTO 2022, LNCS 13508, pp. 792–822, 2022.
https://doi.org/10.1007/978-3-031-15979-4_27

not only basic algorithms but also non-trivial and specially-developed tools such as ledge proofs [27] - a beautiful tool allowing to prove the truth of given statements without revealing any additional information.

While privacy-sensitive users want to protect their anonymity as much as possible, excessive privacy could be abused for illegal or inappropriate activities. Hence, from the system authorities' viewpoint, all users who carry out problematic activities should be kept accountable. Thus, there is an uneasy "privacy vs accountability" tension corresponding to the incentives of users and authorities. In privacy-preserving cryptosystems focusing on anonymity that had been proposed before the year 2021, either the users are granted absolute anonymity and can never be traced [3,44,50], or there exists an authority who can break users' privacy without their consent [17,18,24,36]. In other words, these systems always lean rigidly, either in favour of the users or of the authorities. A breakthrough in tackling the "privacy vs accountability" tension was recently put forward in [42], which introduced Bifurcated Anonymous Signatures (BiAS) - a novel primitive in which whether the signer of a given signature can have absolute anonymity or can be traced is made context-dependent and is known to the signer at the time of signature generation. As a result, tracing can only be done with users' consent on the one hand, and no traceable signature can escape being traced on the other hand. This primitive provides a reasonably fair setting for both authorities and users and seems to have offered a satisfying resolution for the discussed tension.

However, a crucial disadvantage of BiAS and of previous proposals is that accountability is realized via a total tracing procedure, during which all the personal identifying information of the traced users must be disclosed to the authorities. This level of accountability is indeed a serious violation of users' privacy. Note that, while privacy is a complicated notion that has differed throughout history [53], in its purest sense, it can be defined as the right of an individual to control which information about herself or himself can be disclosed [45]. Furthermore, in many real-life situations, it is not necessarily the authorities' highest priority to perform a total tracing. For instance, the authorities could only be interested in learning whether an anonymous user is over 18 years old, or works in a given organization, or lives in a particular area, or has been fully vaccinated against COVID-19, or has an annual income exceeding certain threshold. In the following, let us discuss several concrete examples.

Consider the scenario where an anonymous financial transaction (such as the privacy-preserving cryptocurrency Monero [47]) with a hidden amount of money is used to conduct online transactions. When an amount less than $100 is transferred, then the transaction will be anonymous to everyone, including the authority. However, when an amount between $100 and $1,000 is transferred, the authority will be able to evaluate partial information about the sender, namely which country the sender originated from. When an amount between $1,000 and $10,000 is transferred, then the authority will be able to identify the country and the organization where the transfer originated from. When an amount larger than $10,000 is transferred, then the identity of the individual from the organization in that specific country will be identified. In other words, depending on the underlying transaction amounts, the authority can learn different pieces of information about the sender. There are four different levels of information disclosure in the above scenario.

A more simplistic scenario can be related to an IP address, which is of the form of w.x.y.z. When a small transaction is issued, then the authority will not be able to learn any information about the address. However, when a medium range of transactions is issued, then the authority will be able to compute w.x.*.*, which denote the range of IP addresses within an organization. Finally, then a large transaction is issued, then the full IP address can be identified.

As another example, imagine the situation where a data broker company quietly sells people's personal information to others. While this activity is illegitimate, especially with the introduction of GDPR (General Data Protection Regulation), this kind of activity remains happening in the wild. Suppose a whistleblower who works in the data broker company, wants to "leak" this information to the authority. The purpose is to allow the authority to trace the data broker company while protecting the whistleblower's identity. Therefore, it is essential that the whistleblower can still sell the data from the data broker correctly. Those data eventually will trigger the authority to find some partial identity information from the whistleblower, which points to the data broker company.

Unfortunately, all existing cryptographic methods fail to offer such type of balance between privacy and accountability, i.e., a setting in which authorities can only learn the piece of partial information about the user that the latter would like to disclose - and nothing else. Providing such fine-grained accountable privacy is a highly important and desirable research goal, and addressing it would likely require truly innovative technical ideas and approaches.

OUR CONTRIBUTIONS. We put forward the concept of "Multimodal Private Signatures" (MPS), which provides a novel approach for private information disclosure in anonymity-oriented authentication systems. In an MPS scheme, registered users can generate signatures that remain anonymous to the public, but can be opened by the authority to some partial information op on the identity of the signer. Such partial information can flexibly be defined as op = id (as in group signatures), or as op = $\mathbf{0}$ (like in ring signatures), or more generally, as op = $G(\mathsf{id})$, where $G(\cdot)$ is certain "disclosing function". Importantly, the value of op is known in advance by the signer, and hence, the latter can decide whether she/he wants to disclose that piece of information.

In group signature, the disclosing function $G(\cdot)$ is basically the identity function, and in BiAS, $G(\cdot)$ is an all-or-nothing function. However, as mentioned in the examples motivating MPS, a set of more flexible and fine-grained disclosing functions are demanded to balance privacy and accountability in different applications. In MPS, this is achieved via two steps: first, we introduce a signing function F that determines whether a message M is valid (e.g., the transaction amount is below the limit set by the monetary authority), and if so, the critical level j of M; secondly, we define a family of disclosing functions $\mathcal{G} = \{G_j(\cdot)\}$ that discloses the appropriate level of identity information (i.e., $G_j(\mathsf{id})$) to the opening authority based on the critical level of M. It is worth noting that, for privacy purposes, we also want to hide the critical level j, meaning M could be a transformation of the real "message", which we call the witness w of M. Looking ahead, in the pairing-based and lattice-based constructions presented in this paper, we use $M = \mathsf{COM}(w)$ where $\mathsf{COM}(\cdot)$ denotes a secure commitment scheme. Clearly, the privacy against the opening authority in MPS is more intricate than that in other traceable anonymous signatures. Specifically, we require that the opening authority learns only $G_j(\mathsf{id})$ from a valid signature but nothing else.

More formally, an MPS system is associated with a collection of signing functions $\mathcal{F}$ and a collection of disclosing functions $\{G_1, \ldots, G_K\}$. When user id would like to sign a message M with respect to signing function $F \in \mathcal{F}$, it computes $j = F(M, w, \mathsf{id}) \in [0, K]$, where w is a "witness" - a context-dependent piece of information available to the user (that intuitively explains why $F(M, w, \mathsf{id}) = j$). The value of j governs the signability of (M, w, id) as well as the accountability of the resulting signature. Specifically, if $j = 0$, then id is not allowed to sign. Otherwise, then id should be able to obtain a valid signature that can be opened by the authority to the value $G_j(\mathsf{id})$.

The concept of MPS could enable various appealing applications that previously have not been considered or realized. Apart from the examples we discussed above, let us provide a few more illustrating scenarios.

In the context of anonymous surveys, one may implement an MPS system allowing the survey conductor to learn some specific piece of information (e.g., age, gender, location) about participants who provided answers that meet certain conditions (with the participant's consensus). As for private access to buildings or to online systems, the administrator may also use an MPS system so that to gain certain statistics about the characteristics or activities of the anonymous visitors. From another perspective, the signers may also use MPS to purposely send some information to the authorities, e.g., for claiming the financial incentives of releasing the signed messages.

Let us consider another hypothetical scenario concerning paper submissions and reviews for a conference. An MPS system can help to keep both the authors and the reviewers anonymous to the PC chair, yet allowing the latter to check for CoI (Conflict of Interest). To this end, when submitting a paper, the author signs the paper together with a commitment c to her identity id. The chair can set up the system so that he can open the author's affiliation z based on the signature. If the paper is later accepted, the author can open c to reveal id and claim authorship. Meanwhile, PC members can anonymously post comments on the paper, yet disclose their affiliation z' to the chair. The latter hence can oversee if a CoI has occurred. Moreover, if a PC member would like to post a negative comment on the paper, such as "I previously reviewed this paper and the authors did not take my comments into account.", then it should be backed up with a legitimate witness w. Such a setting therefore can provide a much higher level of privacy protection than contemporary conference management systems.

Having convinced ourselves that MPS is a highly interesting concept, we come to the next steps: formal definitions and technical constructions for MPS.

Formalizations of MPS. To formalize MPS, we follow the setting of dynamic group signatures [5,33], that was also employed in [42]. Namely, an MPS scheme is a tuple of algorithms (**Setup**, ⟨**Join; Issue**⟩, **Sign**, **Verify**, **Open**). The main differences here is that MPS additionally relies on signing functions $F \in \mathcal{F}$ to control signability of (M, w, id) and disclosing functions $G_1, \ldots, G_K$ to realize partial information disclosure. Correctness ensures that as long as $j = F(M, w, \text{id}) \neq 0$ where id is a joined user, then the resulting signature Σ should be accepted by the verification algorithm and should be opened to $G_j(\text{id})$. Regarding security, we demand two major requirements: privacy and unforgeability. For each of these notions, we consider two types of adversary.

Regarding privacy, the first type of adversary can corrupt everyone in the system, except the opening authority. This adversary acts like the CCA2-anonymity adversary in group signatures. It is given the secret key of the group manager (GM) - who is in charge of user enrolments, as well as signing keys of all users. It is not allowed to corrupt the opening authority (OA), but it can adaptively query the opening oracle. Roughly speaking, we require that it should be infeasible for this adversary to learn any information about the signer id beyond the fact that M is signable for id. The second type of privacy adversary is even stronger, as it is even allowed to corrupt the OA. For this adversary, we require that no additional information beyond $G_j(\text{id})$ can be learned. (Note that the OA can always learn $G_j(\text{id})$).

As for unforgeability, we would like to capture several requirements. First, it should be infeasible for signer with identifier id to generate a valid signature Σ associated with (M, F) if $F(M, w, \text{id}) = 0$. Second, it should also be infeasible to "mislead" the signature opening: if **Open** outputs op, then we expect that there exists a registered id whose valid signing key was used by the signer as well as a witness w such that $\text{op} = G_{F(M,w,\text{id})}(\text{id})$. Third, we demand that, no one, even a coalition of a corrupted GM and a corrupted OA, can issue signatures on behalf of honest user id. Note that the last two requirements resemble the notions of full-traceability and non-frameability in dynamic group signatures [5,33].

However, formally defining unforgeability for MPS is a considerably nontrivial task. The main reason is that the original algorithms in the system do not provide a rigorous mechanism to determine whether a tuple $(M^\star, F^\star, \Sigma^\star)$ forms a valid forgery. In particular, invoking **Open** only provides us with a value op, which does not allow us to answer crucial questions such as: (i) Is message $M^\star$ actually signable with respect to $F^\star$ and some id? (ii) Is this the case that $\text{op} = G_{F(M^\star, w', \text{id}')}(\text{id}')$ for some (id', w')? Therefore, for definitional purposes, we would need to introduce certain auxiliary algorithms, namely, **SimSetup** and **Extract**, that allow us to extract additional information, e.g., some identity id' and some witness w', so that we can meaningfully explain whether and how a forgery has occurred. We note that, previous works such as [3,42] also had to overcome similar situations.

Generic Constructions. Next, to demonstrate the feasibility of building MPS based on standard assumptions and in a modular manner, we provide a generic construction. The construction makes use of common cryptographic tools including ordinary signatures, public-key encryption, and non-interactive zero-knowledge (NIZK) proofs/arguments with two (indistinguishable) modes: a hiding mode with statistical zero-knowledge, and a binding mode with statistical soundness and extractability. At a high level, the construction follows the classical sign-then-encrypt-then-prove paradigm that is typically used for building group signatures [4,17]. The main difference here is that we do not encrypt the signer's identity id (as in group signatures) or "id or 0" (as in BiAS [42]). Instead, we let the signer encrypt the function value $\mathsf{op} = G_j(\mathsf{id})$ and prove the well-formedness of the resulting ciphertext - which includes proving knowledge of (id, w) such that $\mathsf{op} = G_{F(M,w,\mathsf{id})}(\mathsf{id})$ is contained in the ciphertext. While such involved statements can be proved in zero-knowledge using well-known NIZK systems for NP such as [29,49], the resulting proofs/arguments would likely have sizes depending on the sizes of the circuits computing functions $F, G_1, \ldots, G_K$.

Theoretically speaking, the dependency of the proof size (and hence, of the signature size) can potentially be reduced by using advanced techniques such as fully-homomorphic encryption (FHE) [25,42], for which the main idea is to compute over encrypted data so that to (publicly) obtain a ciphertext that will decrypt to $G_{F(M,w,\mathsf{id})}(\mathsf{id})$. Nevertheless, using FHEs in that manner would require significant computation costs and/or a large number of initial ciphertexts, and could end up being less efficient than the usual sign-then-encrypt-then-prove approach. We also investigate the potential of efficiently constructing MPS based on functional encryption (FE) [7], since the idea that decryption reveals a function of id is closely related to the spirit of FE. However, we have been unable to progress in this direction: the main obstacle is to ensure that only $G_j(\mathsf{id})$ can be revealed via opening. For instance, giving the opening authority all the decryption keys corresponding to $(G_1, \ldots, G_K)$ would not work well, as the authority may additionally learn the index j. We therefore stick with the usual design approach, and leave efficient FHE-based and FE-based constructions of MPS as appealing open questions.

Our sign-then-encrypt-then-prove construction can also have efficiency advantage when we instantiate the system with concrete signing and disclosing functions, the correct evaluations of which can be efficiently proved in zero-knowledge. As illustrations, we provide a relatively efficient pairing-based construction in the standard model, as well as a lattice-based scheme in the random oracle model (ROM) that potentially enjoys post-quantum security. To be more specific, in both instantiations, we consider $\mathcal{G}$ to be a family of linear transformation functions on id, which are sufficient for many of the motivating applications.

Pairing-Based Constructions in the Standard Model. We present an instantiation of the generic construction under pairing groups. The core components of the construction include the Groth-Sahai proof system [30], a structure-preserving signature (SPS) scheme [35], the Boneh-Boyen (BB) signature [6] and a tag-based PKE [34].

We can apply the aforementioned tools to construct efficient group signatures without random oracles, as shown in [28]. The main challenge to construct an MPS is handling the disclosed identity information $G_j(\text{id})$. Different from group signature, we need to ensure not only the encrypted $G_j(\text{id})$ matches the real id but also the disclosing function $G_j(\cdot)$ is the correct function to be applied.

In our construction, we consider a message $M \in \mathbb{G}_1$ being signed to be a Pedersen commitment [48] for some value $v \in \mathbb{Z}_p$. The disclosing function to be applied when signing a message depends on the value of v. For simplicity, in our instantiation, we consider 4 possible ranges $[A_{j-1}, A_j)$ ($1 \leq j \leq 4$), and for each range, we define a disclosing function $G_j(\text{id})$. When generating a signature on M, the signer needs to compute a ciphertext ct of $G_j(\text{id})$ under the OA's public key opk and then prove that

$$M = \text{COM}(v) \wedge A_{j-1} \leq v < A_j \wedge \text{ct} = \text{Enc}(\text{opk}, G_j(\text{id})).$$

To ensure the correct extraction of $G_j(\text{id})$, we need to extract the value v from the NIZK proof. However, the Groth-Sahai proof does not support the extraction of a random value in $\mathbb{Z}_p$. To address this issue, we convert the above statement by utilizing the homomorphic property of the Pedersen commitment. Instead of proving $A_j \leq v < A_{j+1}$, we let the signer represent the value committed in M/g^{A_j}, i.e., $v - A_j$, as a k-bit binary number, so that each bit can be extracted. In addition, to extract the specific range, among all the possible ranges, the value v actually falls in, we add two additional bits and express the proof statement in the form of an OR-statement, where the additional bits point to the real statement being proved.

Lattice-Based Constructions. While it is feasible to instantiate MPS in the standard model via the lattice-based NIZK techniques of Peikert and Shiehian [49], such a construction would expectedly be extremely inefficient. Here, our goal is to build more efficient constructions in the ROM, where we can employ concrete techniques for obtaining interactive ZK arguments for lattice-based relations, and then remove interaction via the Fiat-Shamir transformation [22].

Similar to our pairing-based construction, here we consider the setting with 1 signing function F and 4 disclosing functions. We also let message M be a commitment to witness w and define $j = F(M, w) \in [0, 4]$ based on integer ranges. We consider 4 disclosing functions, and for each $j \in [1, 4]$ define G_j as a linear endomorphism over $\mathbb{Z}_2^k$. Specifically, let $\mathbf{G}_1, \mathbf{G}_2, \mathbf{G}_3, \mathbf{G}_4 \in \mathbb{Z}_2^{k \times k}$ be public matrices, then let $G_j(\text{id}) := \mathbf{G}_j \cdot \text{id}$. This definition is quite general and expressive, in the sense that it captures many natural ways to disclose partial information about id. For instance, we can set $\mathbf{G}_1 = \mathbf{0}^{k \times k}$ and $\mathbf{G}_4 = \mathbf{I}_k$, so that $G_1(\text{id}) = \mathbf{0}$ (i.e., non-traceable case) and $G_4(\text{id}) = \text{id}$ (i.e., fully traceable case). We can also easily define $\mathbf{G}_2, \mathbf{G}_3$ so that $G_2(\text{id}), G_3(\text{id})$ each reveals a specific subset of coordinates of id.

Our construction is proven secure under the Learning With Errors (LWE) and the Short Integer Solutions (SIS) assumptions. The construction employs the following lattice-based building blocks: (i) the KTX SIS-based commitment scheme [31]; (ii) the SIS-based signature scheme from [37], which admits efficient zero-knowledge arguments of knowledge of a valid message-signature pair; (iii) an LWE-based CCA2-secure PKE scheme obtained from the GPV IBE [26] and the CHK transformation [14]; (iv) a SIS-based one-way function [1]; and (v) an interactive statistical ZK argument system that can handle relatively sophisticated linear and quadratic relations with respect to two moduli ($q_1 = 2$ and $q_2 > 2$) and that is compatible with the signature scheme from [37]. Indeed, we need to prove in ZK that a plaintext $\mathbf{y}$, encrypted under the GPV IBE scheme, is exactly the value $G_j(\mathsf{id})$, which is the major technical difficulty in our design process. To this end, we adapt the Stern-like [52] framework from [40] and then, employ several dedicated techniques to capture the relation $\mathbf{y} = G_j(\mathsf{id})$ by equations modulo 2, that are compatible with the framework. We note that, there are more efficient systems, such as [9, 20, 21, 55], however, they are not known to be applicable to the two-moduli setting here.

RELATED WORK. There has been a vast body of work on anonymity-oriented signature systems. One of the most prominent examples is group signature [17], in which registered users are allowed to anonymously sign any message, but are fully traceable by the opening authority. Group signature thus can be viewed as a special case of MPS with a single disclosing function $G(\mathsf{id}) = \mathsf{id}$. Ring signature [50], another well-known primitive, provides anonymity with no tracing, yet can also be seen as an MPS system with $G(\mathsf{id}) = \mathbf{0}$. Accountable ring signature [8, 54] offers either the ring-signature functionality or the group-signature functionality, but the two modes are separated and distinguishable. Bifurcated anonymous signature (BiAS) [42], a recently proposed concept, simultaneously provide both "ring-signature mode" and "group-signature mode", as well as indistinguishability between the two modes. BiAS is therefore a special case of MPS, with two disclosing functions $G_1(\mathsf{id}) = \mathbf{0}$ and $G_2(\mathsf{id}) = \mathsf{id}$ (but no signing functions).

There have also been various attempts to increase the privacy of signers against the opening authorities in group signatures, such as traceable signatures [32], group signatures with message-dependent opening [51], accountable tracing signatures [36] or threshold group signatures [11]. In the reverse direction are proposals that aim to increase signers' accountability, such as traceable ring signatures [23], e-cash-related primitives [12, 13] and traceable attribute-based signatures [19]. However, in all these systems, the disclosing functions, once activated, would reveal the full identity, i.e., $G(\mathsf{id}) = \mathsf{id}$.

Attribute-based signature [44] and predicate signature [2, 46] provide fine-grained controls on "who can sign", while policy-based signature [3] and functional signature [10] govern "which messages can be signed". These controls of signability can also be viewed as instances of MPS's signing functions $F(M, w, \mathsf{id})$ (with restricted function range $\{0, 1\}$, rather than $[0, K]$).

As a summary, MPS does capture the appealing features of the primitives listed above, and does further generalize and empower them in several dimensions. In particular, the attractive generalization from all-or-nothing tracing of signer's identity to fine-grained disclosure of signer's partial information could have a great impact in this research area.

At a high level, our conception of MPS based on group signature somewhat resembles the revolutionizing conception of functional encryption [7] over ordinary PKE, in the sense that the decrypting/opening procedure can only reveal a function of the plaintext/identity, rather than the whole plaintext/identity. However, from a more technical perspective, there could be some crucial difference: while it is known how to build group signatures from PKE in a modular manner, the connection between MPS and functional encryption is still unclear.

ORGANIZATION. The rest of the paper is organized as follows. In Sect. 2, we provide our definitions of MPS, describe its syntax and formalize the security requirements. Then, in Sect. 3, we give a generic construction of MPS satisfying our model, based on commonly used cryptographic primitives. A pairing-based instantiation is then presented in Sect. 4. A lattice-based construction then follows in Sect. 5. We finally list several interesting open questions in Sect. 6.

Due to space restrictions, the reminders on the cryptographic building blocks employed in our constructions and most of the security analyses have to be deferred to the full version.

2   Multimodal Private Signatures

2.1   Syntax

Let $\lambda \in \mathbb{N}$ be a security parameter. Any Multimodal Private Signature system is associated with natural numbers $N, K \in \mathsf{poly}(\lambda)$; a message space $\mathcal{M}$; a witness space $\mathcal{W}$; an identity space $\mathcal{ID}$; an opening space $\mathcal{OP}$; together with a collection $\mathcal{F}$ of N signing functions and a collection of K disclosing functions $\mathcal{G} = \{G_1, \ldots, G_K\}$, where

$$F : \mathcal{M} \times \mathcal{W} \times \mathcal{ID} \to [0, K], \; \forall F \in \mathcal{F}; \qquad G_j : \mathcal{ID} \to \mathcal{OP}, \; \forall j \in [1, K].$$

The parties involving in an MPS system are similar to those of dynamic group signatures [5,33], namely, a trusted authority (TA), a group manager (GM), an opening authority (OA), signers and verifiers. The job of TA consists of setting up the system, announcing the public parameters and providing a secret key for each of GM and OA. Eligible signers are enrolled to the system via an interactive protocol with GM - who records the registration information into a table. A registered signer with personal identifiable information $\mathsf{id} \in \mathcal{ID}$ can issue a signature Σ on a message $M \in \mathcal{M}$ and with respect to function $F \in \mathcal{F}$, if the signer possesses a witness $w \in \mathcal{W}$ such that $j = F(M, w, \mathsf{id}) \neq 0$, i.e., $j \in [1, K]$. Here, the witness w is a context-dependent string that (intuitively) serves as an evidence for the signability of id on M and w.r.t F, and how w comes into the signer's possession is outside of the model (see also discussions in [3,42]). A legitimate signature Σ should be publicly verifiable by any verifier, and could be opened by OA - who would then learn the value of $G_j(\mathsf{id}) \in \mathcal{OP}$.

Formally, an MPS scheme associated with $(N, K, \mathcal{M}, \mathcal{W}, \mathcal{ID}, \mathcal{OP}, \mathcal{F}, \mathcal{G})$ is a tuple of polynomial-time algorithms (**Setup**, ⟨**Join**; **Issue**⟩, **Sign**, **Verify**, **Open**), defined as follows.

Setup(λ) $\to$ (pp, msk, osk, **reg**). On input security parameter λ, this probabilistic algorithm generates public parameters pp, a secret key msk for the Group Manager (GM) and a secret key osk for the Opening Authority (OA). It also initializes a registration table **reg** := $\emptyset$.

$\langle$**Join**(pp); **Issue**(pp, msk, **reg**)$\rangle$. This is an interactive protocol run by a user who wishes to become a group member and the GM. If it completes successfully, then:

- Algorithm **Join** outputs user's signing key $\mathsf{sk_{id}}$ = (id, $\mathsf{sec_{id}}$, $\mathsf{cert_{id}}$), where id $\in \mathcal{ID}$ is a unique identifier, $\mathsf{sec_{id}}$ is a membership secret (that is known only by the user), and $\mathsf{cert_{id}}$ is a membership certificate.
- Algorithm **Issue** stores the transcript of the protocol in the registration table **reg** := **reg** $\cup$ $\mathsf{trans_{id}}$.

Sign(pp, $\mathsf{sk_{id}}$, M, w, F) $\to \Sigma/\bot$. Given pp, signing key $\mathsf{sk_{id}}$ = (id, $\mathsf{sec_{id}}$, $\mathsf{cert_{id}}$), message $M \in \mathcal{M}$, witness $w \in \mathcal{W}$, and a signing function $F \in \mathcal{F}$, this probabilistic algorithm outputs a signature Σ or a symbol $\bot$ indicating failure.

Verify(pp, M, F, Σ) $\to 1/0$. This deterministic algorithm checks the validity of the signature Σ on message $M \in \mathcal{M}$ with respect to signing function $F \in \mathcal{F}$. It outputs a bit indicating the validity or invalidity of Σ.

Open(pp, osk, Σ, M, F) $\to$ op/$\bot$. This algorithm takes as inputs the public parameters pp, the OA's secret key osk, a signature Σ on message $M \in \mathcal{M}$ with respect to signing function $F \in \mathcal{F}$. It outputs either an opening result op $\in \mathcal{OP}$ or symbol $\bot$ to indicate failure.

2.2 Correctness and Security

The requirements that any Multimodal Private Signature system should satisfy are *correctness*, *privacy* and *unforgeability*.

CORRECTNESS. Correctness of MPS guarantees that honest signers can join the group, and when $j = F(M, w, \mathsf{id}) \neq 0$, signer id should be able to issue an accepted signature Σ on message M and with respect to signing function F, and that Σ should be opened to the value $G_j(\mathsf{id})$. More formally, correctness of MPS is defined as follows.

Definition 1 (Correctness). *An MPS system associated with $(N, K, \mathcal{M}, \mathcal{W}, \mathcal{ID}, \mathcal{OP}, \mathcal{F}, \mathcal{G})$, where $\mathcal{G} = \{G_1, \ldots, G_K\}$, is called* correct, *if for all $\lambda \in \mathbb{N}$, all (pp, msk, osk, **reg**) $\leftarrow$ **Setup**(λ), the following conditions hold with overwhelming probability in λ.*

1. *If$\langle$**Join**(pp); **Issue**(pp, msk, **reg**)$\rangle$ is run by two honest parties, then it completes successfully, and the signer obtains $\mathsf{sk_{id}}$ = (id, $\mathsf{sec_{id}}$, $\mathsf{cert_{id}}$).*
2. *If $M \in \mathcal{M}$, $F \in \mathcal{F}$, id $\in \mathcal{ID}$, $w \subset \mathcal{W}$ and if $j = F(M, w, \mathsf{id}) \in [1, K]$, then algorithm **Sign**(pp, $\mathsf{sk_{id}}$, M, w, F) does not fail and*

$$\textbf{Verify}\big(\text{pp}, M, F, \textbf{Sign}(\text{pp}, \text{sk}_{\text{id}}, M, w, F)\big) = 1$$
$$\textbf{Open}\big(\text{pp}, \text{osk}, \textbf{Sign}(\text{pp}, \text{sk}_{\text{id}}, M, w, F), M, F\big) = G_j(\text{id}).$$

SECURITY. We require two main security properties for MPS, namely, privacy and unforgeability. Informally, these properties capture the following intuitions.

Privacy roughly ensures that each party in the system can only learn the piece of signer's information which the signer intends to disclose. Given a valid signature $\Sigma \leftarrow \textbf{Sign}(\text{pp}, \text{sk}_{\text{id}}, M, w, F)$, it should be infeasible for everyone - excluding the OA - to learn anything about the signer's private information, apart from the fact that M is signable, i.e., $j = F(M, w, \text{id}) \neq 0$. Furthermore, even the OA should be able to additionally learn only the value $G_j(\text{id})$, and should remain oblivious about j and id.

Unforgeability captures several requirements. First, it should be infeasible for signer with identifier id to generate a valid signature Σ associated with (M, F) if $F(M, w, \text{id}) = 0$. Second, it should also be infeasible to "mislead" the signature opening: if $\textbf{Open}(\text{pp}, \text{osk}, \Sigma, M, F)$ outputs $\text{op} \in \mathcal{OP}$, then we expect that there exist a registered id whose valid signing key was used by the signer as well as a witness $w \in \mathcal{W}$ such that $\text{op} = G_{F(M, w, \text{id})}(\text{id})$. Third, we demand that, without the knowledge of membership secret sec_{id}, no one, even a coalition of corrupted GM and OA, can issue signatures on behalf of honest user id. Note that the last two requirements resemble the notions of full-traceability and non-frameability in dynamic group signatures [5,33].

For each of the above security properties, we therefore will consider two types of adversaries, whose goals and powers are related but different from each other. For formalization, we will follow the definitional approach used by Libert et al. [42], which was first put forward by Kiayias and Yung [33].

We will consider experiments in which the adversary interacts with a stateful interface $\mathcal{I}$ that maintains the following variables:

- $\text{state}_{\mathcal{I}}$: is a data structure representing the state of the interface as the adversary invokes the various oracles available in the attack games. It is initialized as $\text{state}_{\mathcal{I}} = (\text{pp}, \text{msk}, \text{osk}, \textbf{reg})$, where **reg** is initially empty and later will store all transcripts of $\langle \textbf{Join}; \textbf{Issue} \rangle$.
- SIGS: is a database of honestly generated signatures created by the signing oracle. Each entry consists of a tuple $(\Sigma, \text{id}, M, w, F)$ indicating that signature Σ was returned in response to a signing query involving identity id, message M, witness w and signing function F.
- HUL: is an initially empty list of honest users introduced in the system by the adversary acting as a dishonest GM. For these users, the adversary obtains the transcript of $\langle \textbf{Join}; \textbf{Issue} \rangle$ but not the user's membership secret.
- CUL: is an initially empty list of corrupted users that are introduced by the adversary in the system in an execution of the join protocol.

In attack games, adversaries are granted access to the following oracles:

- $\mathcal{O}_{\text{CU}}$: allows the adversary to introduce users under its control in the group. A $\langle \textbf{Join}; \textbf{Issue} \rangle$ protocol is run, in which the adversary plays the role of the prospective user. If the protocol successfully completes, a new user id is added to CUL and the protocol transcript trans_{id} is added to **reg**.

- $\mathcal{O}_{\text{HU}}$: allows the adversary, acting as a corrupted GM, to introduce new honest group members of its choice. A ⟨**Join**; **Issue**⟩ protocol is run, in which the adversary plays the role of the GM. If the protocol successfully completes, a new user id is added to HUL and protocol transcript trans_{id} is added to **reg**. The interface stores the membership certificate cert_{id} and the membership secret sec_{id} in a *private* part of $\text{state}_{\mathcal{I}}$.

- $\mathcal{O}_{\text{sig}}$: given a tuple (M, w, F) and an identifier id, the interface returns $\perp$ if $F(M, w, \text{id}) = 0$ or if $\text{id} \notin \text{HUL}$. Otherwise, the private area of $\text{state}_{\mathcal{I}}$ must contain a certificate cert_{id} and a membership secret sec_{id}. The interface outputs a signature Σ on behalf of user id and also updates $\text{SIGS} \leftarrow \text{SIGS} \| (\Sigma, \text{id}, M, w, F)$.

- $\mathcal{O}_{\text{open}}$: when this oracle is invoked on input of a valid triple (M, Σ, F), the interface runs algorithm Open using osk. When S is a set of tuples of the form (M, Σ, F), $\mathcal{O}_{\text{open}}^{\neg S}$ denotes a restricted oracle that only applies the opening algorithm to tuples (M, Σ, F) which are not in S.

- $\mathcal{O}_{\text{read}}$ and $\mathcal{O}_{\text{write}}$: are used by the adversary to read and write the content of **reg**. At each invocation, $\mathcal{O}_{\text{read}}$ outputs the current records in **reg**. Meanwhile, $\mathcal{O}_{\text{write}}$ enables the adversary to modify **reg** as long as the table remains well-formed.

PRIVACY. We say that an MPS scheme is private if it satisfies **computational privacy** against Type-1-Adversary and **computational/statistical privacy** against Type-2-Adversary.

Privacy Against Type-1 Adversary. This captures the power of the CCA2-anonymity adversary in group signatures [4,5,33]. The adversary is allowed to corrupt the GM, corrupt all users, and is allowed to make queries to various oracles, including adaptive queries to the opening oracle.

In the challenge phase, adversary returns a function $F^\star \in \mathcal{F}$, a message $M^\star \in \mathcal{M}$, together with two valid signing keys $\text{sk}_{\text{id}_0} = (\text{id}_0, \text{sec}_{\text{id}_0}, \text{cert}_{\text{id}_0})$, $\text{sk}_{\text{id}_1} = (\text{id}_1, \text{sec}_{\text{id}_1}, \text{cert}_{\text{id}_1})$, as well as witnesses $w_0, w_1 \in \mathcal{W}$. Here, by "valid signing keys", we mean that the keys have been formed correctly via certain legitimate executions of ⟨**Join**; **Issue**⟩, initiated by the adversary. Furthermore, for the challenge to be meaningful, $(M^\star, F^\star)$ should be signable by both id_0 and id_1, i.e.,

$$\left(j_0 = F^\star(M^\star, w_0, \text{id}_0) \neq 0\right) \;\wedge\; \left(j_1 = F^\star(M^\star, w_1, \text{id}_1) \neq 0\right).$$

Receiving a challenge signature $\Sigma^\star \leftarrow \text{Sign}(\text{pp}, \text{sk}_{\text{id}_b}, M^\star, w_b, F^\star)$, where $b \xleftarrow{\$} \{0, 1\}$, the adversary can continue making non-trivial opening queries, i.e., those that do not involve $(M^\star, \Sigma^\star, F^\star)$. Eventually, it outputs a guess $b' \in \{0, 1\}$ and wins if the guess is correct with non-negligible advantage.

Privacy Against Type-2 Adversary. This strong adversary can potentially be computationally unbounded and can corrupt everyone in the system: GM, all users and even OA. It is also allowed to make unrestricted queries to all available oracles. Privacy against this adversary roughly demands that, apart from the opening result $G_j(\mathsf{id})$ (and, obviously, the fact that the underlying message-function pair is signable by id), the adversary can learn no additional information about j or id.

In the challenge phase, when adversary returns $(F^\star, M^\star, \mathsf{sk}_{\mathsf{id}_0}, w_0, \mathsf{sk}_{\mathsf{id}_1}, w_1)$, we additionally require that $G_{j_0}(\mathsf{id}_0) = G_{j_1}(\mathsf{id}_1)$, namely, the opening information corresponding to both choices of the challenger must be the same. This restriction is necessary (as the adversary knows osk) and also sufficient to capture the requirement that signature opening only reveals $G_j(\mathsf{id})$.

---

1 $(\mathsf{pp}, \mathsf{msk}, \mathsf{osk}, \mathbf{reg} = \emptyset) \leftarrow \mathbf{Setup}(\lambda)$.

2 $\boxed{(F^\star, M^\star, \mathsf{sk}_{\mathsf{id}_0}, w_0, \mathsf{sk}_{\mathsf{id}_1}, w_1) \leftarrow \mathcal{A}^{\mathcal{O}_{\mathsf{read}}, \mathcal{O}_{\mathsf{write}}, \mathcal{O}_{\mathsf{CU}}, \mathcal{O}_{\mathsf{HU}}, \mathcal{O}_{\mathsf{sig}}, \mathcal{O}_{\mathsf{open}}}(\mathsf{pp}, \mathsf{msk})}$.

3 $(F^\star, M^\star, \mathsf{sk}_{\mathsf{id}_0}, w_0, \mathsf{sk}_{\mathsf{id}_1}, w_1) \leftarrow \mathcal{A}^{\mathcal{O}_{\mathsf{read}}, \mathcal{O}_{\mathsf{write}}, \mathcal{O}_{\mathsf{CU}}, \mathcal{O}_{\mathsf{HU}}, \mathcal{O}_{\mathsf{sig}}, \mathcal{O}_{\mathsf{open}}}(\mathsf{pp}, \mathsf{msk}, \mathsf{osk})$.

4 If $F^\star \notin \mathcal{F}$, or $M^\star \notin \mathcal{M}$, or $\mathsf{sk}_{\mathsf{id}_0}$ is not valid, or $\mathsf{sk}_{\mathsf{id}_1}$ is not valid, return 0.

5 If $j_0 = F^\star(M^\star, w_0, \mathsf{id}_0) = 0$ or $j_1 = F^\star(M^\star, w_1, \mathsf{id}_1) = 0$, return 0.

6 If $G_{j_0}(\mathsf{id}_0) \neq G_{j_1}(\mathsf{id}_1)$, return 0.

7 $b \xleftarrow{\$} \{0,1\}; \qquad \Sigma^\star \leftarrow \mathbf{Sign}(\mathsf{pp}, \mathsf{sk}_{\mathsf{id}_b}, M^\star, w_b, F^\star)$.

8 $\boxed{b' \leftarrow \mathcal{A}^{\mathcal{O}_{\mathsf{read}}, \mathcal{O}_{\mathsf{write}}, \mathcal{O}_{\mathsf{CU}}, \mathcal{O}_{\mathsf{HU}}, \mathcal{O}_{\mathsf{sig}}, \mathcal{O}_{\mathsf{open}}^{\neg(M^\star, \Sigma^\star, F^\star)}}(\Sigma^\star)}$.

9 $b' \leftarrow \mathcal{A}^{\mathcal{O}_{\mathsf{read}}, \mathcal{O}_{\mathsf{write}}, \mathcal{O}_{\mathsf{CU}}, \mathcal{O}_{\mathsf{HU}}, \mathcal{O}_{\mathsf{sig}}, \mathcal{O}_{\mathsf{open}}}(\Sigma^\star)$.

10 Return $(b' = b)$.

Fig. 1. Experiment $\mathbf{Exp}_{\mathcal{A}}^{\mathsf{privacy}-1}(\lambda)$ (*resp.*, $\mathbf{Exp}_{\mathcal{A}}^{\mathsf{privacy}-2}(\lambda)$) excluding the dotted (*resp.*, solid) boxes.

The respective experiments, $\mathbf{Exp}_{\mathcal{A}}^{\mathsf{privacy}-1}(\lambda)$ and $\mathbf{Exp}_{\mathcal{A}}^{\mathsf{privacy}-2}(\lambda)$, are described in Fig. 1. We hence come to the following formal definition of privacy for MPS.

Definition 2 (Privacy). *An MPS system associated with* $(N, K, \mathcal{M}, \mathcal{W}, \mathcal{ID}, \mathcal{OP}, \mathcal{F}, \mathcal{G})$ *is called private if the following conditions hold.*

1. *Computational privacy against Type-1 adversary: For any PPT adversary $\mathcal{A}$, one has*

$$\mathbf{Adv}_{\mathcal{A}}^{\mathsf{privacy}-1}(\lambda) := \left| \Pr[\mathbf{Exp}_{\mathcal{A}}^{\mathsf{privacy}-1}(\lambda) = 1] - 1/2 \right| \in \mathsf{negl}(\lambda).$$

2. *Statistical (resp., computational) privacy against Type-2 adversary: For any adversary $\mathcal{A}$ (resp., any PPT adversary $\mathcal{A}$), one has*

$$\mathbf{Adv}_{\mathcal{A}}^{\mathsf{privacy}-2}(\lambda) := \left| \Pr[\mathbf{Exp}_{\mathcal{A}}^{\mathsf{privacy}-2}(\lambda) = 1] - 1/2 \right| \in \mathsf{negl}(\lambda).$$

UNFORGEABILITY. Defining unforgeability for MPS is a considerably non-trivial task. The main reason is that the original algorithms in the system do not provide a rigorous mechanism to determine whether a tuple $(M^\star, F^\star, \Sigma^\star)$ forms a valid forgery. Therefore, for definitional purposes, we would need to introduce certain auxiliary algorithms that allow us to extract additional information, e.g., some identity id' and some witness w', so that we can meaningfully explain whether and how a forgery has occurred.

To that end, we assume the existence of the following two auxiliary algorithms, namely, **SimSetup** and **Extract**.

SimSetup(λ) Given the security parameter λ, this algorithm generates simulated $(\mathsf{pp}, \mathsf{msk}, \mathsf{osk}, \mathbf{reg})$, together with an extraction trapdoor τ_{ext}.

Extract$(\tau_{\mathsf{ext}}, (\mathsf{pp}, \Sigma, M, F))$ Given trapdoor τ_{ext}, a *valid* signature Σ on message M and with respect to signing function F, i.e., **Verify**$(\mathsf{pp}, M, F, \Sigma) = 1$, this extraction algorithm returns a pair $\zeta = (\mathsf{id}', w') \in \mathcal{ID} \times \mathcal{W}$.

Naturally, we demand that the outputs of **SimSetup** and **Setup** are indistinguishable to the adversary. Next, we require that (id', w') outputted by **Extract** is compatible with the value op outputted by **Open**. Specifically, w' should be a valid witness for the signability of identity id' w.r.t. $(M^\star, F^\star)$, i.e., $j' = F(M^\star, w', \mathsf{id}') \neq 0$, and, furthermore, $G_{j'}(\mathsf{id}')$ should coincide with op. Formally, we define *extractability* as a "supporting" security property for unforgeability. The definition uses experiment $\mathbf{Exp}_{\mathcal{A}}^{\mathsf{extract}}(\lambda)$ described in Fig. 2.

Definition 3 (Extractability). *An MPS system with auxiliary algorithms **SimSetup**, **Extract** is called* extractable *if the following conditions hold.*

1. *The distribution of simulated $(\mathsf{pp}, \mathsf{msk}, \mathsf{osk}, \mathbf{reg}) \leftarrow \mathbf{SimSetup}(\lambda)$ is computationally close to the distribution of a real output of **Setup**.*
2. *For any PPT adversary $\mathcal{A}$ involving in the experiment of Fig. 2, the advantage $\mathbf{Adv}_{\mathcal{A}}^{\mathsf{extract}}(\lambda) := \Pr\left[\mathbf{Exp}_{\mathcal{A}}^{\mathsf{extract}}(\lambda) = 1\right]$ is negligible in λ.*

---

1 $((\mathsf{pp}, \mathsf{msk}, \mathsf{osk}, \mathbf{reg} = \emptyset), \tau_{\mathsf{ext}}) \leftarrow \mathbf{SimSetup}(\lambda)$.

2 $(F, M, \Sigma) \leftarrow \mathcal{A}^{\mathcal{O}_{\mathsf{read}}, \mathcal{O}_{\mathsf{write}}, \mathcal{O}_{\mathsf{CU}}, \mathcal{O}_{\mathsf{HU}}, \mathcal{O}_{\mathsf{sig}}, \mathcal{O}_{\mathsf{open}}}(\mathsf{pp}, \mathsf{msk}, \mathsf{osk})$,

3 If $F \notin \mathcal{F}$, or $M \notin \mathcal{M}$, or **Verify**$(\mathsf{pp}, M, F, \Sigma) = 0$, return 0.

4 $(\mathsf{id}', w') \leftarrow \mathbf{Extract}(\tau_{ext}, (\mathsf{pp}, \Sigma, M, F)); \quad j' = F(M, w', \mathsf{id}');$

5 If $j' = 0$, return 1.

6 $\mathsf{op} \leftarrow \mathbf{Open}(\mathsf{pp}, \mathsf{osk}, \Sigma, M, F);$

7 If $G_{j'}(\mathsf{id}') \neq \mathsf{op}$, return 1.

8 Return 0.

Fig. 2. Experiment $\mathbf{Exp}_{\mathcal{A}}^{\mathsf{extract}}(\lambda)$.

Now, we are ready for the definitions of unforgeability. An MPS scheme is said to satisfy unforgeability if it is extractable and has computational security against Type-1-Forger and Type-2-Forger.

1   $((\mathsf{pp}, \mathsf{msk}, \mathsf{osk}, \mathbf{reg} = \emptyset), \tau_{ext}) \leftarrow \mathbf{SimSetup}(\lambda).$

2   $\boxed{(M^\star, F^\star, \Sigma^\star) \leftarrow \mathcal{A}^{\mathcal{O}_{\mathsf{read}}, \mathcal{O}_{\mathsf{write}}, \mathcal{O}_{\mathsf{CU}}, \mathcal{O}_{\mathsf{HU}}, \mathcal{O}_{\mathsf{sig}}, \mathcal{O}_{\mathsf{open}}}(\mathsf{pp}, \mathsf{osk}).}$

3   $\overline{(M^\star, F^\star, \Sigma^\star) \leftarrow \mathcal{A}^{\mathcal{O}_{\mathsf{read}}, \mathcal{O}_{\mathsf{write}}, \mathcal{O}_{\mathsf{CU}}, \mathcal{O}_{\mathsf{HU}}, \mathcal{O}_{\mathsf{sig}}, \mathcal{O}_{\mathsf{open}}}(\mathsf{pp}, \mathsf{osk}, \mathsf{msk}).}$

4   If $F^\star \notin \mathcal{F}$, or $M^\star \notin \mathcal{M}$, or $\mathbf{Verify}(\mathsf{pp}, M^\star, F^\star, \Sigma^\star) = 0$, return 0.

5   $(\mathsf{id}', \cdot) \leftarrow \mathbf{Extract}(\tau_{ext}, (\mathsf{pp}, \Sigma^\star, M^\star, F^\star)).$

6   If $(\Sigma^\star, \mathsf{id}', M^\star, \cdot, F^\star) \in \mathsf{SIGS}$, return 0.

7   $\boxed{\text{If } \mathsf{id}' \notin \mathsf{CUL}, \text{ return } 1.}$

8   $\overline{\text{If } \mathsf{id}' \in \mathsf{HUL}, \text{ return } 1.}$

9   Return 0.

Fig. 3. Experiment $\mathbf{Exp}_{\mathcal{A}}^{\mathsf{unforge}-1}(\lambda)$ (*resp.*, $\mathbf{Exp}_{\mathcal{A}}^{\mathsf{unforge}-2}(\lambda)$) excluding the dotted (*resp.*, solid) boxes.

- Type-1-Forger roughly captures the traceability adversary in group signatures. It can fully corrupt the OA, corrupt a number of users and can make various oracle queries. Its goal is to output a valid forgery $(\Sigma^\star, M^\star, F^\star)$ such that the extraction points to some identity id' which it has not previously corrupted.
- Type-2-Forger is similar to the non-frameability adversary in group signatures, whose goal is to point the opening/extraction to an innocent user. The adversary can corrupt everyone else in the system, i.e., GM, OA and all other users. It succeeds if it can output a valid forgery that is extracted to some honest identity id'.

In Fig. 3, we formalize the respective security experiments, i.e., $\mathbf{Exp}_{\mathcal{A}}^{\mathsf{unforge}-1}(\lambda)$ and $\mathbf{Exp}_{\mathcal{A}}^{\mathsf{unforge}-2}(\lambda)$). The formal definition of unforgeability follows.

Definition 4 (Unforgeability). *An MPS system associated is called unforgeable if it satisfies extractability, and for any PPT adversary $\mathcal{A}$, one has*

$$\mathbf{Adv}_{\mathcal{A}}^{\mathsf{unforge}-1}(\lambda) := \Pr[\mathbf{Exp}_{\mathcal{A}}^{\mathsf{unforge}-1}(\lambda) = 1] \in \mathsf{negl}(\lambda);$$
$$\mathbf{Adv}_{\mathcal{A}}^{\mathsf{unforge}-2}(\lambda) := \Pr[\mathbf{Exp}_{\mathcal{A}}^{\mathsf{unforge}-2}(\lambda) = 1] \in \mathsf{negl}(\lambda).$$

3   Generic Constructions

In this section, we present a generic construction of MPS for arbitrary signing functions F's and arbitrary disclosing functions $G_1, \ldots, G_K$. The construction satisfies the correctness and security properties defined in Sect. 2, and employs cryptographic building blocks that are commonly used for designing advanced privacy-preserving primitives: ordinary (one-time) signatures, public-key encryption and non-interactive zero-knowledge (NIZK) proofs/arguments for some NP-relations. For the latter ingredient, we additionally require the dual-mode property, i.e., we will use a NIZK system that operates in two modes: hiding mode (for the real scheme and simulation) and binding mode (for simulated setup and extraction).

Our construction can serve as a proof of feasibility of designing MPS based on standard assumptions and in a modular manner. In particular, it can be realized in the standard model from pairings and from lattices, using the techniques for obtaining NIZKs for NP by Groth-Ostrovsky-Sahai [29] and by Peikert-Shiehian [49], respectively.

At a high level, the construction follows the classical sign-then-encrypt-then-prove paradigm. The main difference here is that we do not encrypt the signer's identity id (as in group signatures) or "id or 0" (as in BiAS [42]). Instead, we let the signer encrypt the function value $\mathsf{op} = G_j(\mathsf{id})$ and prove the well-formedness of the resulting ciphertext - which includes proving knowledge of (id, w) such that $\mathsf{op} = G_{F(M,w,\mathsf{id})}(\mathsf{id})$ is contained in the ciphertext. While such involved statements can be proved in zero-knowledge using well-known NIZK systems for NP such as [29,49], the resulting proofs/arguments would likely have sizes depending on the sizes of the circuits computing functions $F, G_1, \ldots, G_K$.

Our construction can also have efficiency advantage when we instantiate the system with *concrete* signing and disclosing functions, the correct evaluations of which can be efficiently proved in zero-knowledge. As illustrations, we will later present relatively efficient pairing-based and lattice-based constructions of MPS for some specific functions $F, G_1, \ldots, G_K$, in Sect. 4 and Sect. 5, respectively.

In the following, we will give a technical overview of our generic construction in Sect. 3.1, then describe it in detail in Sect. 3.2 and provide its analyses in Sect. 3.3.

3.1   Technical Overview

The construction employs the following technical building blocks.

- A secure digital signature scheme $\mathcal{S} = (\mathsf{S.Kg}, \mathsf{S.Sign}, \mathsf{S.Ver})$;
- A secure one-time signature scheme $\mathcal{OTS} = (\mathsf{O.Kg}, \mathsf{O.Sign}, \mathsf{O.Ver})$;
- A secure public-key encryption scheme $\mathcal{E} = (\mathsf{E.Kg}, \mathsf{E.Enc}, \mathsf{E.Dec})$;
- A dual-mode NIZK argument system $\mathcal{NIZK} = (\mathsf{ZK.Setup}, \mathsf{ZK.ExtSetup}, \mathsf{ZK.Prove}, \mathsf{ZK.Ver}, \mathsf{ZK.Sim}, \mathsf{ZK.Extr})$ for the NP-relation $\mathcal{R}$ defined below.

The main ideas underlying the construction are as follows. The GM is associated with a signing-verification key-pair $(\mathsf{msk}, \mathsf{mpk})$ for $\mathcal{S}$, while the OA is associated with a decryption-encryption key-pair $(\mathsf{osk}, \mathsf{opk})$ for $\mathcal{E}$. When joining, a perspective user generates a signature key-pair $(\mathsf{sec_{id}}, \mathsf{upk})$, sends upk together with its personal identifiable information id to GM. The latter certifies $(\mathsf{id} \parallel \mathsf{upk})$ in the form of a signature $\mathsf{cert_{id}}$. When signing, the signer first generates a one-time signature key-pair (otk, ovk), uses its secret key $\mathsf{sec_{id}}$ to certify ovk as signature s. Then it evaluates $j = F(M, w, \mathsf{id})$ and encrypts $G_j(\mathsf{id})$ under opk with randomness r, obtaining ciphertext $\mathbf{c}$. The signer then generates a NIZK argument π for the relation $\mathcal{R}$ defined as follows

$$\mathcal{R} := \Big\{\ (\mathsf{mpk}, \mathsf{opk}, \mathbf{c}, M, F, ovk), (\mathsf{id}, \mathsf{upk}, \mathsf{cert}_{\mathsf{id}}, s, w, j, r) :$$
$$(\mathsf{S.Ver}(\mathsf{upk}, ovk, s) = 1) \wedge (\mathsf{S.Ver}(\mathsf{mpk}, (\mathsf{id} \parallel \mathsf{upk}), \mathsf{cert}_{\mathsf{id}}) = 1) \wedge$$
$$(F(M, w, \mathsf{id}) = j) \wedge (j \in [1, K]) \wedge (\mathbf{c} = \mathsf{E.Enc}(\mathsf{opk}, G_j(\mathsf{id}); r)) \Big\}.$$

Next, the signer uses otk to one-time sign $(M, F, \mathbf{c}, \pi)$ as sig, and outputs the final signature as $\Sigma = (ovk, \mathbf{c}, \pi, sig)$. Verification of Σ basically consists of verifying sig and π. Meanwhile, opening of Σ is done via decrypting $\mathbf{c}$ with key osk.

Roughly speaking, the correctness of the obtained MPS scheme is based on the correctness/completeness of the underlying building blocks. Privacy is achieved as long as $\mathcal{E}$ is IND-CCA2 secure and $\mathcal{NIZK}$ has the ZK property. Meanwhile, unforgeability is based on the soundness of $\mathcal{NIZK}$, the unforgeability of $\mathcal{S}$ and the strong unforgeability of $\mathcal{OTS}$.

3.2   Description

Let $\lambda \in \mathbb{N}$ be a security parameter. Our generic construction of an MPS system associated with $(N, K, \mathcal{M}, \mathcal{W}, \mathcal{ID}, \mathcal{OP}, \mathcal{F}, \mathcal{G})$ works as follows.

Setup$(\lambda) \rightarrow (\mathsf{pp}, \mathsf{msk}, \mathsf{osk}, \mathbf{reg})$. On input security parameter λ, this probabilistic algorithm performs the following steps:
   1. Run $\mathsf{S.Kg}(\lambda)$ to obtain a signing-verification key-pair $(\mathsf{msk}, \mathsf{mpk})$.
   2. Run $\mathsf{E.Kg}(\lambda)$ to obtain an decryption-encryption key-pair $(\mathsf{osk}, \mathsf{opk})$.
   3. Run $\mathsf{ZK.Setup}(\lambda)$ to obtain a common reference string crs (and a simulation trapdoor τ_{sim} - which is discarded) for the NIZK system.
   Then, it sets $\mathsf{pp} := (\mathsf{crs}, \mathsf{mpk}, \mathsf{opk})$, GM's secret key as msk and OA's secret key as osk, and initializes $\mathbf{reg} := \emptyset$.

$\langle \mathbf{Join}(\mathsf{pp}); \mathbf{Issue}(\mathsf{pp}, \mathsf{msk}, \mathbf{reg}) \rangle$. A user with personal identifiable information id, who would like to join the group, interacts with the GM as follows.
   1. User runs $\mathsf{S.Kg}(\lambda)$ to obtain a signing-verification key-pair $(\mathsf{usk}, \mathsf{upk})$. Then it generates $sig_{\mathsf{id}} \leftarrow \mathsf{S.Sign}(\mathsf{usk}, (\mathsf{id} \| \mathsf{upk}))$, and sends $(\mathsf{id}, \mathsf{upk}, sig_{\mathsf{id}})$ to GM.
   2. GM verifies that $\mathsf{S.Ver}(\mathsf{upk}, (\mathsf{id} \| \mathsf{upk}), sig_{\mathsf{id}}) = 1$, and checks that id has not been registered in table $\mathbf{reg}$. If any of these conditions does not hold, GM aborts. Otherwise, GM issues a signature $\sigma_{\mathsf{id}} \leftarrow \mathsf{S.Sign}(\mathsf{msk}, (\mathsf{id} \| \mathsf{upk}))$, sends σ_{id} to the user, sets $\mathsf{trans}_{\mathsf{id}} := (\mathsf{id}, \mathsf{upk}, sig_{\mathsf{id}}, \sigma_{\mathsf{id}})$ and updates the registration table $\mathbf{reg} := \mathbf{reg} \cup \mathsf{trans}_{\mathsf{id}}$.
   3. The user verifies that $\mathsf{S.Ver}(\mathsf{mpk}, \mathsf{id} \| \mathsf{upk}, \sigma_{\mathsf{id}}) = 1$, and aborts if it is not the case. Otherwise, user sets $\mathsf{sk}_{\mathsf{id}} = (\mathsf{id}, \mathsf{sec}_{\mathsf{id}}, \mathsf{cert}_{\mathsf{id}})$, where $\mathsf{sec}_{\mathsf{id}} = \mathsf{usk}$ and $\mathsf{cert}_{\mathsf{id}} = (\sigma_{\mathsf{id}}, \mathsf{upk})$.

$\mathbf{Sign}(\mathsf{pp}, \mathsf{sk}_{\mathsf{id}}, M, w, F) \rightarrow \Sigma/\bot$. Let $\mathsf{sk}_{\mathsf{id}} = (\mathsf{id}, \mathsf{sec}_{\mathsf{id}}, \mathsf{cert}_{\mathsf{id}})$, where $\mathsf{sec}_{\mathsf{id}} = \mathsf{usk}$ and $\mathsf{cert}_{\mathsf{id}} = (\sigma_{\mathsf{id}}, \mathsf{upk})$. The signing algorithm then proceeds as follows.

1. Compute $j = F(M, w, \mathsf{id}) \in [0, K]$. Return $\bot$ if $j = 0$.
2. Generate a one-time signature key-pair $(otk, ovk) \leftarrow \mathsf{O.Kg}(\lambda)$.
3. Use usk to certify ovk as signature $s \leftarrow \mathsf{S.Sign}(\mathsf{usk}, ovk)$.
4. Encrypt $G_j(\mathsf{id})$ under public key opk as $\mathbf{c} = \mathsf{E.Enc}(\mathsf{opk}, G_j(\mathsf{id}); r)$, where r is the encryption randomness.
5. Generate an NIZK proof

$$\pi \leftarrow \mathsf{ZK.Prove}\Big(\mathsf{crs}, \big((\mathsf{mpk}, \mathsf{opk}, \mathbf{c}, M, F, ovk), (\mathsf{id}, \mathsf{upk}, \mathsf{cert}_{\mathsf{id}}, s, w, j, r)\big)\Big)$$

to prove that $\big((\mathsf{mpk}, \mathsf{opk}, \mathbf{c}, M, F, ovk), (\mathsf{id}, \mathsf{cert}_{\mathsf{id}}, s, w, j, r)\big) \in \mathcal{R}$, where $\mathcal{R}$ is the NP-relation defined above.
6. Use otk to issue a one-time signature $sig \leftarrow \mathsf{O.Sign}(otk, (M, F, \mathbf{c}, \pi))$.
7. Return the signature $\Sigma := (ovk, \mathbf{c}, \pi, sig)$.

Verify$(\mathsf{pp}, M, F, \Sigma) \rightarrow 0/1$. Given a purported signature $\Sigma = (ovk, \mathbf{c}, \pi, sig)$ on message M and with respect to signing function F, the verification algorithm proceeds as follows.
1. If $\mathsf{O.Ver}(ovk, (M, F, \mathbf{c}, \pi), sig) = 0$, then return 0.
2. If $\mathsf{ZK.Ver}\big(\mathsf{crs}, (\mathsf{mpk}, \mathsf{opk}, \mathbf{c}, M, F, ovk), \pi\big) = 0$, then return 0.
3. Return 1.

Open$(\mathsf{pp}, \mathsf{osk}, \Sigma, M, F)$. Given $\Sigma = (ovk, \mathbf{c}, \pi, sig)$, the opening algorithm proceeds as follows.
1. Use osk to decrypt $\mathbf{c}$ and obtain $z \leftarrow \mathsf{E.Dec}(\mathsf{osk}, \mathbf{c}) \in \mathcal{OP} \cup \{\bot\}$.
2. Return $\bot$ if $z = \bot$. Otherwise, return $\mathsf{op} = z \in \mathcal{OP}$.

AUXILIARY ALGORITHMS. Let us describe the auxiliary algorithms **SimSetup** and **Extract** associated with the above MPS system, which are required by the security model and are helpful for the security analyses.

SimSetup(λ). This algorithm is almost the same as the real setup algorithm presented above. The only difference is that, at Step 3, instead of generating $\mathsf{crs} \leftarrow \mathsf{ZK.Setup}(\lambda)$, one runs $\mathsf{ZK.ExtSetup}(\lambda)$ to obtain a common reference string crs together with an extraction trapdoor τ_{ext}. The simulated public parameters are then set as $\mathsf{pp} = (\mathsf{crs}, \mathsf{mpk}, \mathsf{opk})$.

Extract$\big(\tau_{\mathsf{ext}}, (\mathsf{pp}, \Sigma, M, F)\big)$. Given the extraction trapdoor τ_{ext}, a *valid* signature $\Sigma = (ovk, \mathbf{c}, \pi, sig)$ on message M and with respect to signing function F, this algorithm runs $\mathsf{ZK.Extr}(\mathsf{crs}, \tau_{\mathsf{ext}}, \pi)$ to obtain a witness $(\mathsf{id}', \mathsf{cert}'_{\mathsf{id}}, s', w', j', r')$ for the relation $\mathcal{R}$. It then outputs $\zeta = (\mathsf{id}', w')$.

3.3 Analyses

Theorem 1 states that the correctness and security properties of the presented MPS system can be based on the completeness/correctness and security features of the employed cryptographic building blocks.

Theorem 1. *Assume that $\mathcal{S}$ is an unforgeable signature scheme under adaptive chosen-message attacks, $\mathcal{OTS}$ is a strongly unforgeable one-time signature scheme, $\mathcal{E}$ is an IND-CCA2-secure public-key encryption scheme and $\mathcal{NIZK}$ is a dual-model non-interactive zero-knowledge argument system for relation $\mathcal{R}$. Then, the described MPS system satisfies correctness, privacy and unforgeability.*

We prove Theorem 1 via Lemma 1–6. The proofs of Lemma 2–6 are provided in the full version.

Lemma 1 (Correctness). *If $\mathcal{S}$, $\mathcal{OTS}$ and $\mathcal{E}$ are correct, and $\mathcal{NIZK}$ is complete, then the presented MPS scheme satisfies correctness.*

Proof. The proof is straightforward. It follows from the correctness of $\mathcal{S}$ that

$$\mathsf{S.Ver}(\mathsf{upk}, \mathsf{id}, \mathsf{S.Sign}(\mathsf{usk}, \mathsf{id})) = 1, \quad \mathsf{S.Ver}(\mathsf{mpk}, \mathsf{id}, \mathsf{S.Sign}(\mathsf{msk}, \mathsf{id})) = 1.$$

Hence, an honest signer should be able to enrol in the group and obtain a legitimate signing key $\mathsf{sk_{id}} = (\mathsf{id}, \mathsf{sec_{id}}, \mathsf{cert_{id}})$.

Next, thanks to the correctness of $\mathcal{S}$ as well as the completeness of $\mathcal{NIZK}$, the signer should be able to obtain a valid witness $(\mathsf{id}, \mathsf{cert_{id}}, s, w, j, r)$ for the relation $\mathcal{R}$, and proof π should be accepted by $\mathsf{ZK.Ver}$. Furthermore, one-time signature *sig* should pass the verification algorithm $\mathsf{O.Ver}$. Therefore, as long as $j = F(M, w, \mathsf{id}) \neq 0$, one should have $\mathbf{Verify}(\mathsf{pp}, M, F, \Sigma) = 1$.

Finally, the correctness of $\mathcal{E}$ guarantees that $\mathsf{E.Dec}(\mathsf{osk}, \mathsf{E.Enc}(\mathsf{opk}, G_j(\mathsf{id}), r)))$ returns $G_j(\mathsf{id})$, and so does $\mathbf{Open}(\mathsf{pp}, \mathsf{osk}, \Sigma, M, F)$.   □

Lemma 2 (Type-1 Privacy). *The described MPS system satisfies computational privacy against Type-1 adversary if (i) $\mathcal{E}$ has IND-CCA2 security; (ii) $\mathcal{NIZK}$ has (computational/statistical) zero-knowledge property.*

Lemma 3 (Type-2 Privacy). *The described MPS system satisfies statistical (resp. computational) privacy against Type-2 adversary if $\mathcal{NIZK}$ has statistical (resp. computational) zero-knowledge property.*

Lemma 4 (Extractability). *The described MPS scheme is extractable if $\mathcal{NIZK}$ has CRS indistinguishability and extractability in the binding mode, and if $\mathcal{E}$ is correct.*

Lemma 5 (Type-1 Unforgeability). *The described MPS system satisfies unforgeability against Type-1 forger if (i) the conditions of Lemma 4 hold; (ii) $\mathcal{S}$ is unforgeable under chosen-message attacks; (iii) $\mathcal{OTS}$ is a strongly unforgeable one-time signature; (iv) $\mathcal{NIZK}$ is computationally sound.*

Lemma 6 (Type-2 Unforgeability). *The described MPS system satisfies unforgeability against Type-2 forger if (i) the conditions of Lemma 4 hold; (ii) $\mathcal{S}$ is unforgeable under chosen-message attacks; (iii) $\mathcal{OTS}$ is a strongly unforgeable one-time signature; (iv) $\mathcal{NIZK}$ is computationally sound.*

4   A Construction from Pairings

4.1   Notations and Parameters

Let $(\hat{e} : \mathbb{G}_1 \times \mathbb{G}_1 \to \mathbb{G}_T)$ denote a non-degenerate bilinear map over pairing groups $\mathbb{G}_1$ and $\mathbb{G}_T$ of prime order p and $\mathbb{G}_1^* := \mathbb{G}_1\backslash\{1\}$. Let g, h be random generators of $\mathbb{G}_1$. Our construction assumes the following parameter spaces:

- an identity space $\mathcal{ID} = (\mathbb{G}_1^*)^2$ where each user identity is encoded as $\mathrm{id} = (\mathrm{id}_1, \mathrm{id}_2) \in (\mathbb{G}_1^*)^2$;
- a user public key space $\mathcal{UPK} = \mathbb{G}_1^*$;
- a message space $\mathcal{M} = \mathbb{G}_1$ for the signers where each $M \in \mathcal{M}$ is a Pedersen commitment for an integer value $w_1 \in \mathbb{Z}_p$ with randomness $w_2 \in \mathbb{Z}_p$;
- a witness space $\mathcal{W} = \mathbb{Z}_p^2$ where a witness $w = (w_1, w_2)$ for $M \in \mathcal{M}$ consists of the opening for M;
- a function index space $\mathcal{J} = [1, 4]$;
- the valid ranges of w_1, denoted by $[A_{i-1}, A_i)$ for $(1 \le i \le 4)$;
- a signing function F defined as

$$
F(M, w = (w_1, w_2)) := \begin{cases}
1 & \text{iff } (M = g^{w_1} h^{w_2} \wedge A_0 \le w_1 < A_1) \\
2 & \text{iff } (M = g^{w_1} h^{w_2} \wedge A_1 \le w_1 < A_2) \\
3 & \text{iff } (M = g^{w_1} h^{w_2} \wedge A_2 \le w_1 < A_3) \\
4 & \text{iff } (M = g^{w_1} h^{w_2} \wedge A_3 \le w_1 < A_4) \\
0 & \text{otherwise}
\end{cases}
$$

- an opening space $\mathcal{OP} = \mathbb{G}_1^2$;
- a family of disclosing functions $\mathcal{G} = \{G_j : (\mathbb{G}_1^*)^2 \to \mathbb{G}_1^2\}$ $(j \in [1, 4])$ such that for an identity $\mathrm{id} = (\mathrm{id}_1, \mathrm{id}_2) \in (\mathbb{G}_1^*)^2$

$$
G_1(\mathrm{id}) = (1_{\mathbb{G}_1}, 1_{\mathbb{G}_1}), G_2(\mathrm{id}) = (1_{\mathbb{G}_1}, \mathrm{id}_2), G_3(\mathrm{id}) = (\mathrm{id}_1, 1_{\mathbb{G}_1}), G_4(\mathrm{id}) = (\mathrm{id}_1, \mathrm{id}_2).
$$

4.2   Technical Overview

In our pairing-based MPS, a message $M \in \mathbb{G}_1$ is in the form of a Pedersen commitment [48], i.e., $M = g^v h^r$ where v represents a value (e.g., a transaction amount) and r is the randomness. The construction follows the same paradigm as the generic construction, but we change/adapt some of the building blocks by following the design of an efficient group signature scheme by Groth [28], which makes the construction more efficient. Specifically, we apply the following tools in our construction:

- The structure-preserving digital signature scheme by Kiltz et al. [35] $\mathcal{SPS} = (\mathsf{SPS.Kg}, \mathsf{SPS.Sign}, \mathsf{SPS.Ver})$ with message space $\mathcal{ID} \times \mathcal{UPK} = (\mathbb{G}_1^*)^3$ and signature space $\mathbb{G}_1^{10}$.

- The (weak) Boneh-Boyen (BB) digital signature scheme [6] $\mathcal{BBS} = $ (BBS.Kg, BBS.Sign, BBS.Ver) with public key space $\mathcal{UPK} = \mathbb{G}_1^*$ and signature space $\mathbb{G}_1^*$.
- The Pedersen commitment scheme [48] $\mathcal{CM} = $ (CM.Setup, CM.Cmt, CM.Open, CM.Ver) with witness space $\mathcal{W} = \mathbb{Z}_p^2$ and commitment space $\mathbb{G}_1$.
- The tag-based PKE by Kiltz [34] $\mathcal{E} = $ (E.Kg, E.Enc, E.Ver, E.Dec) with message space $\mathbb{G}_1$ and ciphertext space $\mathbb{G}_1^5$. Note that E.Ver allows public verification of a ciphertext w.r.t. an encryption tag.
- The DLIN-based instantiation of the Groth-Sahai proof system [30] $\mathcal{GS} = $ (GS.Setup, GS.Prove, GS.Ver, GS.SimSetup, GS.SimProve, GS.Extract) which includes two DLIN-based commitment schemes $\mathcal{GSCM}_i = $ (GSCM$_i$.Cmt, GSCM$_i$. Open, GSCM$_i$.Ver) $i \in \{1, 2\}$ for committing elements in $\mathbb{G}_1$ and $\mathbb{Z}_p$, respectively. Both commitments use $\mathsf{crs}_{\mathsf{GS}} \leftarrow $ GS.Setup(λ) as the commitment key.
- A strongly unforgeable one-time digital signature scheme $\mathcal{OTS} = $ (O.Kg, O.Sign, O.Ver).

In the center of our construction is the Groth-Sahai Proof system [30] that enables efficient non-interactive proofs for statements expressed in the forms of pairing product equations, multi-exponentiation equations and quadratic equations. To be compatible with Groth-Sahai proof, we adopt a Structure Preserving Signature [35] for the issuing of cert$_{\mathsf{id}}$ w.r.t. (id, upk) for a signer. To sign a message, the signer randomly generates a one-time key pair (ovk, otk), certifies ovk using usk, and employs the Groth-Sahai Proof system to prove that there is a valid certification chain mpk $\rightarrow$ upk $\rightarrow ovk$, without revealing id, upk or cert$_{\mathsf{id}}$. The one-time key is used to generate the final signature. However, since the Groth-Sahai Proof system does not have NIZK for general pairing product equations, we replace the NIZK proof by NIWI proof, as in [28].

Proving $G_j(\mathsf{id})$. The main difference between our construction and [28] is in dealing with the disclosed identity information $G_j(\mathsf{id})$. In [28], the disclosing function is the identity function, i.e., $G(\mathsf{id}) = \mathsf{id}$, so the opening authority OA's secret key is the same as the extraction key for the Groth-Sahai proof system in the binding mode. In MPS, we need to separate OA's secret key from the extraction key as even the OA should not learn more than $G_j(\mathsf{id})$. Moreover, we need to ensure extractability, meaning that the correct identity information $G_j(\mathsf{id})$ is encrypted by the signer and $j = F(M, w) \in [1, 4]$ is correctly computed based on the witness w of the message M.

The Groth-Sahai Proof system allows perfect extraction of committed group elements in $\mathbb{G}_1$, but not arbitrary elements in $\mathbb{Z}_p$. To achieve extractability in MPS, we need to ensure the correct extraction of not only $G_j(\mathsf{id})$ but also $j = F(M, w)$ where $w \in \mathbb{Z}_p$. Meanwhile, we observe that if a committed value in $\mathbb{Z}_p$ is a binary value, then we can also perfectly extract it from the commitment. This motivates us to convert the witness w into binary form, and prove in zero-knowledge that $j = F(M, w)$.

To do so, we first observe that the Pedersen commitment is homomorphic. Hence, to prove that the witness v of a message $M = g^v h^r$ falls in a range, say $[A_i, A_{i+1})$ where $A_{i+1} - A_i = 2^k$, we only need to prove that M/g^{A_i} is a correct commitment for $v - A_i \in [0, 2^k)$. To do so, we follow the standard range proof approach by converting $v - A_i$ into a k-bit binary string and proving that each position has a binary value. We then employ additional bits (2 bits in our concrete instantiation in this paper) to specify which range, among all the possible ranges, the value v actually falls in. This is achieved by expressing the proof statement in the form of an OR-proof, where the additional bits point to the real statement being proved.

As a result, we convert the NIZK proof for $G_j(\mathsf{id})$ into a collection of multi-exponentiation equations in $\mathbb{G}_1$ and quadratic equations (for binary values) in $\mathbb{Z}_p$, which can be proved using the Groth-Sahai Proof system while achieving extractability.

It is worth noting that the above approach allows us to support a larger identity space, e.g., $\mathsf{id} \in (\mathbb{G}_1^*)^n$, accompanied with a variety of disclosing functions.

Due to the space limit, the details are presented in the full version.

5 A Construction from Lattices

In this section, we present a concrete construction of MPS which is proven secure under lattice-based assumptions in the random oracle model (ROM).

Let integers $n, m, q, k = 3n\lceil \log q \rceil, L$ and $0 < A_1 < A_2 < A_3 < 2^L - 1$ be the system parameters. Let $(\mathbf{C}_1, \mathbf{C}_2) \in \mathbb{Z}_q^{n \times L} \times \mathbb{Z}_q^{n \times m}$ be a commitment key for the KTX commitment scheme [31], which is statistically hiding and computationally binding under the SIS assumption.

Similar to the pairing-based construction presented in Sect. 4, this lattice-based scheme is also associated with $N = 1$ signing function F and $K = 4$ disclosing functions $G_1, \ldots, G_4$, and also consider the setting where $\mathbf{m} = \mathsf{com}(\mathbf{w}_1, \mathbf{w}_2)$, with $\mathbf{m}$ is a message to be signed, and $\mathbf{w} = (\mathbf{w}_1, \mathbf{w}_2)$ is a witness.

Let $\mathcal{M} = \mathbb{Z}_q^n, \mathcal{W} = \{0,1\}^L \times \{0,1\}^m, \mathcal{ID} = \mathcal{OP} = \{0,1\}^k$. Define the signing function $F : \mathcal{M} \times \mathcal{W} \to [0, 4]$ as follows.

$$F(\mathbf{m}, \mathbf{w}) := \begin{cases} 0 & \text{if } \mathbf{m} \neq \mathbf{C}_1 \cdot \mathbf{w}_1 + \mathbf{C}_2 \cdot \mathbf{w}_2 \bmod q, \text{ else} \\ 1 & \text{if } (0 \leq W_1 < A_1), \text{ else} \\ 2 & \text{if } (A_1 \leq W_1 < A_2), \text{ else} \\ 3 & \text{if } (A_2 \leq W_1 < A_3), \text{ else} \\ 4 & \text{if } (A_3 \leq W_1 \leq 2^L - 1), \end{cases}$$

where $W_1 = \mathsf{int}(\mathbf{w}_1)$ - the integer in $[0, 2^L - 1]$ whose binary representation is $\mathbf{w}_1$.

Disclosing Functions. For each $j \in [1, 4]$ define G_j as a linear endomorphism over $\mathbb{Z}_2^k$. Specifically, let $\mathbf{G}_1, \mathbf{G}_2, \mathbf{G}_3, \mathbf{G}_4 \in \mathbb{Z}_2^{k \times k}$ be public matrices, then let

$$G_j(\mathsf{id}) = \mathbf{G}_j \cdot \mathsf{id}.$$

The definition is quite general and expressive, in the sense that it captures many natural ways to disclose partial information about id. For instance, we can set $\mathbf{G}_1 = \mathbf{0}^{k \times k}$ and $\mathbf{G}_4 = \mathbf{I}_k$, so that $G_1(\mathsf{id}) = \mathbf{0}$ (i.e., non-traceable case) and $G_4(\mathsf{id}) = \mathsf{id}$ (i.e., fully traceable case). We can also easily define $\mathbf{G}_2, \mathbf{G}_3$ so that $G_2(\mathsf{id}), G_3(\mathsf{id})$ each reveals a specific subset of coordinates of id.

5.1   Technical Overview

While it is feasible to instantiate MPS in the standard model via the lattice-based NIZK techniques of Peikert and Shiehian [49], such a construction would expectedly be extremely inefficient. Here, our goal is to build more efficient constructions in the ROM, where we can employ concrete techniques for obtaining interactive ZK arguments for lattice-based relations, and then remove interaction via the Fiat-Shamir transformation [22].

Regarding lattice-based building blocks, apart from the KTX SIS-based commitment scheme [31] which we mentioned above, we employ the following ingredients:

- The SIS-based signature scheme from [37], which admits efficient zero-knowledge arguments of knowledge of a valid message-signature pair. This signature scheme will be used by the GM to issue users' certificates.
- An LWE-based CCA2-secure PKE scheme obtained from the GPV IBE [26] and the CHK transformation [14]. This encryption scheme will be used to encrypt $G_j(\mathsf{id})$, and ciphertexts will be decryptable by the OA.
- A SIS-based one-way function [1]. In the ROM, since the NIZK argument π included in Σ can be viewed as a signature of knowledge [15] of the signer's membership secret $\mathsf{sec}_{\mathsf{id}}$, we can slightly depart from the generic construction of Sect. 3, by equipping users with a one-way function rather than an ordinary signature scheme.
- We also need a statistical ZK argument system that can handle relatively sophisticated linear and quadratic relations with respect to two moduli ($q_1 = 2$ and $q_2 > 2$) and that is compatible with the signature scheme from [37]. To this end, we choose to employ the Stern-like [52] framework from [40].

Proving in ZK that $\mathbf{y} = G_j(\mathsf{id})$. The major technical difficulty that we have to overcome is to prove in ZK that a plaintext $\mathbf{y}$, encrypted under the GPV IBE scheme, is exactly the value $G_j(\mathsf{id})$. To this end, we first would need to show that the index $j = F(\mathbf{m}, \mathbf{w}) \in [1, 4]$ is computed correctly. Our techniques are as follows.

We first "extract" the position of $W_1 = \mathsf{int}(\mathbf{w}_1) \in [0, 2^L - 1]$ relative to A_1, A_2, A_3 by defining bits $b_1, b_2, b_3 \in \{0, 1\}$ such that

$$
\begin{aligned}
0 \le W_1 < A_1 &\iff (b_1, b_2, b_3) = (0, 0, 0) \iff (1 - b_1)(1 - b_2)(1 - b_3) = 1; \\
A_1 \le W_1 < A_2 &\iff (b_1, b_2, b_3) = (1, 0, 0) \iff b_1(1 - b_2)(1 - b_3) = 1; \\
A_2 \le W_1 < A_3 &\iff (b_1, b_2, b_3) = (1, 1, 0) \iff b_1 b_2(1 - b_3) = 1; \\
A_3 \le W_1 < 2^L - 1 &\iff (b_1, b_2, b_3) = (1, 1, 1) \iff b_1 b_2 b_3 = 1.
\end{aligned}
$$

This can be realized by viewing inequalities under the lens of integer additions, in the following way. Suppose that there exist (non-negative) L-bit integers $Y_0, Y_1, Z_0, Z_1, T_0, T_1$ and bits b_1, b_2, b_3 such that:

$$W_1 + (1 - b_1) \cdot Y_1 + (1 - b_1) = A_1 + b_1 \cdot Y_0,$$
$$W_1 + (1 - b_2) \cdot Z_1 + (1 - b_2) = A_2 + b_2 \cdot Z_0, \qquad (1)$$
$$W_1 + (1 - b_3) \cdot T_1 + (1 - b_3) = A_3 + b_3 \cdot Y_0.$$

Observe that, when $b_1 = 0$, we have $W_1 + Y_1 + 1 = A_1$, implying that $W_1 < A_1$ since $Y_1 \geq 0$. On the other hand, if $b_1 = 1$, we have $W_1 = A_1 + Y_0$, and as $Y_0 \geq 0$, we can deduce that $W_1 \geq A_1$. In other words, b_1 captures the predicate $(W_1 \geq A_1)$. Similarly, we have $b_2 = (W_1 \geq A_2)$ and $b_3 = (W_1 \geq A_3)$.

Next, let us consider bits $f_0, f_1 \in \{0, 1\}$ such that

$$\mathbf{y} = G_j(\mathsf{id}) = \mathbf{G}_j \cdot \mathsf{id} = (1 - f_0)(1 - f_1) \cdot \mathbf{G}_1 \cdot \mathsf{id} + (1 - f_0)f_1 \cdot \mathbf{G}_2 \cdot \mathsf{id}$$
$$+ f_0 \cdot (1 - f_1) \cdot \mathbf{G}_3 \cdot \mathsf{id} + f_0 \cdot f_1 \cdot \mathbf{G}_4 \cdot \mathsf{id} \mod 2. \quad (2)$$

In other words, f_0, f_1 are such that $j = 1, 2, 3, 4$ if and only if $(f_0, f_1) = (0, 0), (0, 1), (1, 0), (1, 1)$, respectively.

Now, observe that f_0, f_1 and b_1, b_2, b_3 are connected via the following equation:

$$(f_0, f_1) = (1 - b_1)(1 - b_2)(1 - b_3) \cdot (0, 0) + b_1(1 - b_2)(1 - b_3) \cdot (0, 1)$$
$$+ b_1 b_2 (1 - b_3) \cdot (1, 0) + b_1 b_2 b_3 \cdot (1, 1) \mod 2. \quad (3)$$

As a summary of the above ideas, we have reduced the problem of proving that $\mathbf{y} = G_j(\mathsf{id})$ to the equivalent problem of proving knowledge of bits b_1, b_2, b_3, f_0, f_1 and L-bit integers $Y_0, Y_1, Z_0, Z_1, T_0, T_1$ satisfying equations in (1), (2) and (3).

We note that equations in (1) can be proved in zero-knowledge using the techniques from [41], which, in a nutshell, translate integer additions into binary adders with carries, and hence obtain a system of equations modulo 2. Combining with equations in (2) and (3), we can obtain an equation of the form

$$\mathbf{M}_2 \cdot \mathbf{p}_2 = \mathbf{u}_2 \mod 2, \qquad (4)$$

where matrix $\mathbf{M}_2$ and vector $\mathbf{u}_2$ are public, and $\mathbf{p}_2$ is a binary vector that encodes all the information of vector id, bits b_1, b_2, b_3, f_0, f_1 and integers $Y_0, Y_1, Z_0, Z_1, T_0, T_1$.

The Main ZK Argument System. Our construction will make use of a ZK argument system that allows to prove knowledge of a tuple $(\mathsf{id}, \mathbf{z}, \mathbf{x}, \mathsf{cert}_{\mathsf{id}} = (\tau, \mathbf{v}, \mathbf{s}), \mathbf{w} = (\mathbf{w}_1, \mathbf{w}_2), \mathbf{y}, (\mathbf{r}, \mathbf{e}_1, \mathbf{e}_2))$ satisfying the following conditions:

(i) $(\mathbf{z}, \mathbf{x})$ is a preimage-image pair of a SIS-based one-way function;

(ii) $\mathsf{cert}_{\mathsf{id}} = (\tau, \mathbf{v}, \mathbf{s})$ is a signature on message $(\mathsf{id}\|\mathbf{x})$, with respect to the signature scheme from [37];

(iii) A GPV IBE ciphertext is a correct encryption of plaintext $\mathbf{y}$, with randomness $(\mathbf{r}, \mathbf{e}_1, \mathbf{e}_2)$;

(iv) $\mathbf{m}$ is a KTX commitment of $\mathbf{w}_1$ with randomness $\mathbf{w}_2$;

(v) $\mathbf{y} = \mathbf{G}_j(\mathrm{id})$, where $j = F(\mathbf{m}, \mathbf{w}) \in [1, 4]$.

Recall that item (v) can be handled using the ideas we discussed above. As for (i), (ii), (iii), (iv) we can use the techniques from [37,43] to obtain a vector $\mathbf{p}_1$ that has coordinates in $\{-1, 0, 1\}$ and that encodes the information of $(\mathbf{z}, \mathbf{x}, \tau, \mathbf{v}, \mathbf{s}, \mathrm{id}, \mathbf{r}, \mathbf{e}_1, \mathbf{e}_2, \mathbf{w}_1, \mathbf{w}_2)$, and that satisfies an equation of the form

$$\mathbf{M}_1 \cdot \mathbf{p}_1 = \mathbf{u}_1 \mod q, \tag{5}$$

where matrix $\mathbf{M}_1$ and vector $\mathbf{u}_1$ are public.

Now, our task is to prove that Eqs. (4) and (5) hold for the constructed vectors $\mathbf{p}_1$ and $\mathbf{p}_2$, both of which contain encoded information of id. To this end, we can employ dedicated Stern-like permuting techniques [38,39] to reduce the underlying relation to an instance of the abstract relation considered in [40]. (An adaptation of [40], where there are two moduli $q_1 = q$ and $q_2 = 2$, is presented in detail in the full version.) As a result, we can obtain a statistical ZK argument of knowledge for the considered relation.

5.2   Description of the Scheme

The scheme can be seen as an extension of the dynamic GS from [37]. The scheme works with lattice parameter $n \in \mathcal{O}(\lambda)$, parameter $\ell = \mathcal{O}(\log n)$, prime modulus $q = \widetilde{\mathcal{O}}(n^4)$, dimensions $m = 2n\lceil \log q \rceil$, $k = 3n\lceil \log q \rceil$, $L = \mathcal{O}(n)$, Gaussian parameter $\sigma = \Omega(\sqrt{n \log q} \log n)$ and infinity norm bounds $\beta = \sigma\omega(\log m)$. Let $\mathrm{bin}(\cdot)$ be a function mapping vectors over $\mathbb{Z}_q$ to their binary representations.

The main ZK protocol of the scheme is for the relation $\mathcal{R}_{\mathsf{Imps}}$, defined below.

Definition 5. *Define*

$$\mathcal{R}_{\mathsf{Imps}} = \Big\{ \ \big((\mathbf{A}, \{\mathbf{A}_j\}_{j=0}^{\ell}, \mathbf{D}, \mathbf{D}_0, \mathbf{D}_1, \mathbf{u}, \mathbf{F}, \mathbf{C}_1, \mathbf{C}_2, \mathbf{m}, \{\mathbf{G}_j\}_{j=1}^4, \mathbf{B}, \mathbf{G}, \mathbf{c}_1, \mathbf{c}_2),$$
$$(\mathrm{id}, \mathbf{z}, \mathbf{x}, \mathsf{cert}_{\mathrm{id}} = (\tau, \mathbf{v}, \mathbf{s}), \mathbf{w} = (\mathbf{w}_1, \mathbf{w}_2), \mathbf{y}, (\mathbf{r}, \mathbf{e}_1, \mathbf{e}_2))\big) \Big\}$$

as a relation, where

- $\mathbf{A}, \mathbf{A}_0, \mathbf{A}_1, \ldots, \mathbf{A}_{\ell}, \mathbf{D}, \mathbf{B}, \mathbf{F}, \mathbf{C}_2 \in \mathbb{Z}_q^{n \times m}$, $\mathbf{D}_0, \mathbf{D}_1 \in \mathbb{Z}_q^{2n \times 2m}$, $\mathbf{C}_1 \in \mathbb{Z}_q^{n \times L}$, $\mathbf{G} \in \mathbb{Z}_q^{n \times k}$, $\mathbf{u} \in \mathbb{Z}_q^n$, $\mathbf{c}_1 \in \mathbb{Z}_q^m$, $\mathbf{c}_2 \in \mathbb{Z}_q^k$, $\mathbf{G}_1, \ldots, \mathbf{G}_4 \in \mathbb{Z}_2^{k \times k}$.
- $\mathrm{id}, \mathbf{y} \in \{0,1\}^k$, $\mathbf{z} \in \{0,1\}^m$, $\mathbf{x} \in \{0,1\}^{n\lceil \log q \rceil}$, $\tau \in \{0,1\}^{\ell}$, $\mathbf{v}, \mathbf{s} \in [-\beta, \beta]^{2m}$, $\mathbf{w}_1 \in \{0,1\}^L$, $\mathbf{w}_2 \in \{0,1\}^m$, $\mathbf{r} \in [-B, B]^n$, $\mathbf{e}_1 \in [-B, B]^m$, $\mathbf{e}_2 \in [-B, B]^k$.
- $\mathbf{x} = \mathrm{bin}(\mathbf{F} \cdot \mathbf{z} \mod q)$.
- $[\mathbf{A} \mid \mathbf{A}_0 + \sum_{j=1}^{\ell} \tau_j \cdot \mathbf{A}_j] \cdot \mathbf{v} = \mathbf{u} + \mathbf{D} \cdot \mathrm{bin}(\mathbf{D}_0 \cdot \mathbf{s} + \mathbf{D}_1 \cdot (\mathrm{id} \| \mathbf{x})) \mod q$.
- $\mathbf{c}_1 = \mathbf{B}^\top \cdot \mathbf{r} + \mathbf{e}_1 \mod q$, $\mathbf{c}_2 = \mathbf{G}^\top \cdot \mathbf{r} + \mathbf{e}_2 + \lfloor q/2 \rfloor \cdot \mathbf{y} \mod q$.
- $\mathbf{m} = \mathbf{C}_1 \cdot \mathbf{w}_1 + \mathbf{C}_2 \cdot \mathbf{w}_2 \mod q$.
- $\mathbf{y} = G_j(\mathrm{id})$.

Using the techniques discussed above, we can obtain a statistical ZK argument for $\mathcal{R}_{\mathsf{lmps}}$. The protocol, has soundness error $2/3$. It is repeated $\kappa = \mathcal{O}(\lambda)$ times in parallel to make the error negligibly small, and then made non-interactive via the Fiat-Shamir heuristic. Our lattice-based MPS scheme works as follows.

Setup$(\lambda) \to (\mathsf{pp}, \mathsf{msk}, \mathsf{osk}, \mathbf{reg})$. This algorithm performs the following steps.

1. Generate verification key

$$(\mathbf{A}, \mathbf{A}_0, \mathbf{A}_1, \ldots, \mathbf{A}_\ell, \mathbf{D}, \mathbf{D}_0, \mathbf{D}_1, \mathbf{u}) \in (\mathbb{Z}_q^{n \times m})^{\ell+3} \times (\mathbb{Z}_q^{2n \times 2m})^2 \times \mathbb{Z}_q^n$$

and signing key $\mathbf{T_A}$ for the signature scheme from [37].
2. Generate master public key $\mathbf{B} \in \mathbb{Z}_q^{n \times m}$ and master secret key $\mathbf{T_B}$ for the GPV IBE scheme [26].
3. Choose uniformly random matrices $\mathbf{F} \in \mathbb{Z}_q^{n \times m}$, and $\mathbf{C}_1 \in \mathbb{Z}_q^{n \times \ell}$, $\mathbf{C}_2 \in \mathbb{Z}_q^{n \times m}$. Looking ahead, $\mathbf{F}$ will define a SIS-based one-way function, while $(\mathbf{C}_1, \mathbf{C}_2)$ will serve as a KTX commitment key for L-bit messages.
4. Let χ be a B-bounded distribution.
5. Choose a one-time signature scheme $\mathcal{OTS} = (\mathsf{O.Kg}, \mathsf{O.Sign}, \mathsf{O.Ver})$.
6. Choose hash functions $H_{FS} : \{0,1\}^* \to \{1,2,3\}^\kappa$ and $H_{GPV} : \{0,1\}^* \to \mathbb{Z}_q^{n \times k}$ that will be modeled as random oracles.

Output $\mathsf{msk} = \mathbf{T_A}$, $\mathsf{osk} = \mathbf{T_B}$, $\mathbf{reg} = \emptyset$ and

$$\mathsf{pp} = (\mathbf{A}, \mathbf{A}_0, \mathbf{A}_1, \ldots, \mathbf{A}_\ell, \mathbf{D}, \mathbf{D}_0, \mathbf{D}_1, \mathbf{u}, \mathbf{B}, \mathbf{F}, \mathbf{C}_1, \mathbf{C}_2, \mathbf{F}, \chi, \mathcal{OTS}, H_{FS}, H_{GPV}).$$

$\langle\mathbf{Join}(\mathsf{pp}); \mathbf{Issue}(\mathsf{pp}, \mathsf{msk} = \mathbf{T_A}, \mathbf{reg})\rangle$. A prospective user with identity $\mathsf{id} \in \mathbb{Z}_q^k$ interacts with the GM as follows.

1. User selects $\mathbf{z} \xleftarrow{\$} \{0,1\}^m$, computes $\mathbf{x} = \mathsf{bin}(\mathbf{F} \cdot \mathbf{z}) \in \{0,1\}^{n\lceil \log q \rceil}$. User then signs $(\mathsf{id}\|\mathbf{x}) \in \{0,1\}^{2m}$ using an ordinary signature and sends $(\mathsf{id}\|\mathbf{x})$ together with the signature sig_{id} to the GM.
2. GM verifies sig_{id} and then certifies $(\mathsf{id}\|\mathbf{x})$ using $\mathbf{T_A}$. The certificate has the form $\mathsf{cert}_{\mathsf{id}} = (\tau, \mathbf{v}, \mathbf{s}) \in \{0,1\}^\ell \times [-\beta, \beta]^{2m} \times [-\beta, \beta]^{2m}$, satisfying

$$\left[\mathbf{A} \mid \mathbf{A}_0 + \sum_{j=1}^{\ell} \tau_j \cdot \mathbf{A}_j\right] \cdot \mathbf{v} = \mathbf{u} + \mathbf{D} \cdot \mathsf{bin}(\mathbf{D}_0 \cdot \mathbf{s} + \mathbf{D}_1 \cdot (\mathsf{id}\|\mathbf{x})) \bmod q. \quad (6)$$

3. User id verifies the validity of $\mathsf{cert}_{\mathsf{id}}$ and outputs $\mathsf{sk}_{\mathsf{id}} = (\mathsf{id}, \mathsf{sec}_{\mathsf{id}}, \mathsf{cert}_{\mathsf{id}})$, where $\mathsf{sec}_{\mathsf{id}} = \mathbf{z}$.
4. GM computes $\mathsf{trans}_{\mathsf{id}} = (\mathsf{id}, \mathbf{x}, sig_{\mathsf{id}}, \mathsf{cert}_{\mathsf{id}})$ and updates the registration table $\mathbf{reg} := \mathbf{reg} \cup \mathsf{trans}_{\mathsf{id}}$.

Sign$(\mathsf{pp}, \mathsf{sk}_{\mathsf{id}}, \mathbf{m}, \mathbf{w} = (\mathbf{w}_1, \mathbf{w}_2), F)$. Given pp, signing key $\mathsf{sk}_{\mathsf{id}} = (\mathsf{id}, \mathsf{sec}_{\mathsf{id}}, \mathsf{cert}_{\mathsf{id}})$, message $\mathbf{m} \in \mathcal{M}$, witness $w \in \mathcal{W}$, and signing function F, this algorithm performs the following steps.

1. Check that $F(\mathbf{m}, \mathbf{w}, \mathsf{id}) \neq 0$, i.e., $\mathbf{w}_1 \in \{0,1\}^L$, $\mathbf{w}_2 \in \{0,1\}^m$ and $\mathbf{m} = \mathbf{C}_1 \cdot \mathbf{w}_1 + \mathbf{C}_2 \cdot \mathbf{w}_2 \bmod q$. Return $\bot$ if this is not the case.

2. Determine the value of $j = F(\mathbf{m}, \mathbf{w}, \mathsf{id}) \in [1, 4]$. Let $\mathbf{y} = G_j(\mathsf{id}) \in \{0, 1\}^k$.
3. Generate a key-pair $(otk, ovk) \leftarrow \mathsf{O.Kg}(\lambda)$ and encrypt $\mathbf{y}$ with respect to "identity" ovk as follows. Let $\mathbf{G} = H_{GPV}(ovk) \in \mathbb{Z}_q^{n \times k}$. Sample $\mathbf{r} \leftarrow \chi^n$, $\mathbf{e}_1 \leftarrow \chi^m$, $\mathbf{e}_2 \leftarrow \chi^k$, then compute the ciphertext

$$(\mathbf{c}_1 = \mathbf{B}^\top \cdot \mathbf{r} + \mathbf{e}_1, \quad \mathbf{c}_2 = \mathbf{G}^\top \cdot \mathbf{r} + \mathbf{e}_2 + \lfloor q/2 \rfloor \cdot \mathbf{y}) \in \mathbb{Z}_q^m \times \mathbb{Z}_q^k.$$

4. Using witness $(\mathsf{id}, \mathbf{z}, \mathbf{x}, \mathsf{cert}_{\mathsf{id}} = (\tau, \mathbf{v}, \mathbf{s}), \mathbf{w} = (\mathbf{w}_1, \mathbf{w}_2), \mathbf{y}, (\mathbf{r}, \mathbf{e}_1, \mathbf{e}_2))$, generate a NIZKAoK π for the relation $\mathcal{R}_{\mathsf{lmps}}$ (Definition 5). This is done by repeating κ times an interactive ZK argument of knowledge for $\mathcal{R}_{\mathsf{lmps}}$, and made non-interactive as a triple $\pi = (\{\mathrm{CMT}_j\}_{j \in [\kappa]}, \mathrm{CH}, \{\mathrm{RSP}_j\}_{j \in [\kappa]})$, where $\mathrm{CH} = H_{FS}(\mathbf{m}, ovk, \mathbf{c}_1, \mathbf{c}_2, \{\mathrm{CMT}_j\}_{j \in [\kappa]}) \in \{1, 2, 3\}^\kappa$.
5. Compute a one-time signature $sig \leftarrow \mathsf{O.Sign}(otk, (\mathbf{m}, F, \mathbf{c}_1, \mathbf{c}_2, \pi))$.

Output the signature

$$\Sigma = (ovk, \mathbf{c}_1, \mathbf{c}_2, \pi, sig). \tag{7}$$

Verify$(\mathsf{pp}, \mathbf{m}, F, \Sigma)$. This algorithm parses Σ as in (7), and returns 1 if:
1. $\mathsf{O.Ver}(ovk, (\mathbf{m}, F, \mathbf{c}_1, \mathbf{c}_2, \pi), sig) = 1$;
2. π is a valid NIZKAoK for $\mathcal{R}_{\mathsf{lmps}}$.

Open$(\mathsf{pp}, \mathsf{osk} = \mathbf{T_B}, \Sigma, \mathbf{m}, F)$. This algorithm proceeds as follows.
1. Compute $\mathbf{G} = H_{GPV}(ovk) \in \mathbb{Z}_q^{n \times k}$, then using $\mathbf{T_B}$ to sample a small-norm matrix $\mathbf{E}_{ovk}$ such that $\mathbf{B} \cdot \mathbf{E}_{ovk} = \mathbf{G} \bmod q$.
2. Using $\mathbf{E}_{ovk}$ to decrypt $(\mathbf{c}_1, \mathbf{c}_2)$ (by computing $\lfloor (\mathbf{c}_2 - \mathbf{E}_{ovk}^\top \cdot \mathbf{c}_1)/(q/2) \rceil$), so that to obtain $\mathbf{y} \in \{0, 1\}^k$. Output $\perp$ if the decryption fails.
3. Output $\mathsf{op} = \mathbf{y}$.

5.3 Analyses of the Scheme

EFFICIENCY. Let us analyze the asymptotic efficiency of the proposed scheme. The size of pp is dominated by that of the verification key of the signature scheme from [37] and has bit-size $\mathcal{O}(\ell m n \log q) = \widetilde{\mathcal{O}}(\lambda^2)$. A signing key $\mathsf{sk}_{\mathsf{id}}$ consists of a few small-norm vectors and has bit-size $\mathcal{O}(m \log q \log \beta) = \widetilde{\mathcal{O}}(\lambda)$. The size of each signature Σ is dominated by that of the NIZKAoK π, which is roughly $\kappa = \mathcal{O}(\lambda)$ times the bit-size of the underlying witness $(\mathsf{id}, \mathbf{z}, \mathbf{x}, \mathsf{cert}_{\mathsf{id}} = (\tau, \mathbf{v}, \mathbf{s}), \mathbf{w} = (\mathbf{w}_1, \mathbf{w}_2), \mathbf{y}, (\mathbf{r}, \mathbf{e}_1, \mathbf{e}_2))$. Overall, Σ has bit-size $\widetilde{\mathcal{O}}(\lambda^2)$.

CORRECTNESS. The correctness of the described MPS scheme follows directly from the correctness of the signature scheme from [37], the correctness of the GPV IBE scheme [26] and the perfect completeness of the employed Stern-like argument system [40, 52].

SECURITY. The security of the scheme can be proven in the ROM, under the SIS and the LWE assumptions.

Theorem 2. *In the random oracle model, the described MPS system satisfies privacy and unforgeability if (i) the* SIS *and* LWE *assumptions hold; (ii)* $\mathcal{OTS}$ *is a strongly unforgeable one-time signature; (iii) The employed argument system is a statistically ZKAoK.*

Due to space restriction, the proof of Theorem 2 is deferred to the full version.

6   Open Questions

As the first work that proposes the brand-new concept of Multimodal Private Signatures, we do not expect to provide a thorough study of this primitive. We leave several fascinating open questions for future investigations:

1. Constructing practically usable MPS schemes with expressive signing and disclosing functions;
2. Studying theoretical connections between MPS and other advanced primitives like functional encryption and fully-homomorphic encryption;
3. Designing efficient MPS schemes with post-quantum security;
4. Equipping MPS with additional functionalities such as verifiable opening and/or user revocation.

Acknowledgements. We would like to thank Dung Duong for helpful discussions. We would also like to thank the anonymous reviewers of CRYPTO 2022 for valuable suggestions. F. Guo, W. Susilo and G. Yang are partially supported by the Australian Research Council Discovery Projects DP200100144 and DP220100003.

References

1. Ajtai, M.: Generating hard instances of lattice problems (extended abstract). In: STOC 1996, pp. 99–108. ACM (1996)
2. Attrapadung, N., Hanaoka, G., Yamada, S.: Conversions among several classes of predicate encryption and applications to ABE with various compactness tradeoffs. In: Iwata, T., Cheon, J.H. (eds.) ASIACRYPT 2015, Part I. LNCS, vol. 9452, pp. 575–601. Springer, Heidelberg (2015). https://doi.org/10.1007/978-3-662-48797-6_24
3. Bellare, M., Fuchsbauer, G.: Policy-based signatures. In: Krawczyk, H. (ed.) PKC 2014. LNCS, vol. 8383, pp. 520–537. Springer, Heidelberg (2014). https://doi.org/10.1007/978-3-642-54631-0_30
4. Bellare, M., Micciancio, D., Warinschi, B.: Foundations of group signatures: formal definitions, simplified requirements, and a construction based on general assumptions. In: Biham, E. (ed.) EUROCRYPT 2003. LNCS, vol. 2656, pp. 614–629. Springer, Heidelberg (2003). https://doi.org/10.1007/3-540-39200-9_38
5. Bellare, M., Shi, H., Zhang, C.: Foundations of group signatures: the case of dynamic groups. In: Menezes, A. (ed.) CT-RSA 2005. LNCS, vol. 3376, pp. 136–153. Springer, Heidelberg (2005). https://doi.org/10.1007/978-3-540-30574-3_11
6. Boneh, D., Boyen, X.: Short signatures without random oracles. In: Cachin, C., Camenisch, J.L. (eds.) EUROCRYPT 2004. LNCS, vol. 3027, pp. 56–73. Springer, Heidelberg (2004). https://doi.org/10.1007/978-3-540-24676-3_4
7. Boneh, D., Sahai, A., Waters, B.: Functional encryption: a new vision for public-key cryptography. Commun. ACM 55(11), 56–64 (2012)
8. Bootle, J., Cerulli, A., Chaidos, P., Ghadafi, E., Groth, J., Petit, C.: Short accountable ring signatures based on DDH. In: Pernul, G., Ryan, P.Y.A., Weippl, E. (eds.) ESORICS 2015, Part I. LNCS, vol. 9326, pp. 243–265. Springer, Cham (2015). https://doi.org/10.1007/978-3-319-24174-6_13

9. Bootle, J., Lyubashevsky, V., Seiler, G.: Algebraic techniques for short(er) exact lattice-based zero-knowledge proofs. In: Boldyreva, A., Micciancio, D. (eds.) CRYPTO 2019, Part I. LNCS, vol. 11692, pp. 176–202. Springer, Cham (2019). https://doi.org/10.1007/978-3-030-26948-7_7

10. Boyle, E., Goldwasser, S., Ivan, I.: Functional signatures and pseudorandom functions. In: Krawczyk, H. (ed.) PKC 2014. LNCS, vol. 8383, pp. 501–519. Springer, Heidelberg (2014). https://doi.org/10.1007/978-3-642-54631-0_29

11. Camenisch, J., Drijvers, M., Lehmann, A., Neven, G., Towa, P.: Short threshold dynamic group signatures. In: Galdi, C., Kolesnikov, V. (eds.) SCN 2020. LNCS, vol. 12238, pp. 401–423. Springer, Cham (2020). https://doi.org/10.1007/978-3-030-57990-6_20

12. Camenisch, J., Hohenberger, S., Lysyanskaya, A.: Compact E-cash. In: Cramer, R. (ed.) EUROCRYPT 2005. LNCS, vol. 3494, pp. 302–321. Springer, Heidelberg (2005). https://doi.org/10.1007/11426639_18

13. Camenisch, J., Hohenberger, S., Lysyanskaya, A.: Balancing accountability and privacy using E-cash (extended abstract). In: De Prisco, R., Yung, M. (eds.) SCN 2006. LNCS, vol. 4116, pp. 141–155. Springer, Heidelberg (2006). https://doi.org/10.1007/11832072_10

14. Canetti, R., Halevi, S., Katz, J.: Chosen-ciphertext security from identity-based encryption. In: Cachin, C., Camenisch, J.L. (eds.) EUROCRYPT 2004. LNCS, vol. 3027, pp. 207–222. Springer, Heidelberg (2004). https://doi.org/10.1007/978-3-540-24676-3_13

15. Chase, M., Lysyanskaya, A.: On signatures of knowledge. In: Dwork, C. (ed.) CRYPTO 2006. LNCS, vol. 4117, pp. 78–96. Springer, Heidelberg (2006). https://doi.org/10.1007/11818175_5

16. Chaum, D.: Security without identification: transactions system to make big brother obsolete. Commun. ACM **28**(10), 1030–1044 (1985)

17. Chaum, D., van Heyst, E.: Group signatures. In: Davies, D.W. (ed.) EUROCRYPT 1991. LNCS, vol. 547, pp. 257–265. Springer, Heidelberg (1991). https://doi.org/10.1007/3-540-46416-6_22

18. Diaz, J., Lehmann, A.: Group signatures with user-controlled and sequential linkability. In: Garay, J.A. (ed.) PKC 2021, Part I. LNCS, vol. 12710, pp. 360–388. Springer, Cham (2021). https://doi.org/10.1007/978-3-030-75245-3_14

19. El Kaafarani, A., Ghadafi, E., Khader, D.: Decentralized traceable attribute-based signatures. In: Benaloh, J. (ed.) CT-RSA 2014. LNCS, vol. 8366, pp. 327–348. Springer, Cham (2014). https://doi.org/10.1007/978-3-319-04852-9_17

20. Esgin, M.F., Nguyen, N.K., Seiler, G.: Practical exact proofs from lattices: new techniques to exploit fully-splitting rings. In: Moriai, S., Wang, H. (eds.) ASIACRYPT 2020, Part II. LNCS, vol. 12492, pp. 259–288. Springer, Cham (2020). https://doi.org/10.1007/978-3-030-64834-3_9

21. Esgin, M.F., Steinfeld, R., Liu, J.K., Liu, D.: Lattice-based zero-knowledge proofs: new techniques for shorter and faster constructions and applications. In: Boldyreva, A., Micciancio, D. (eds.) CRYPTO 2019, Part I. LNCS, vol. 11692, pp. 115–146. Springer, Cham (2019). https://doi.org/10.1007/978-3-030-26948-7_5

22. Fiat, A., Shamir, A.: How to prove yourself: practical solutions to identification and signature problems. In: Odlyzko, A.M. (ed.) CRYPTO 1986. LNCS, vol. 263, pp. 186–194. Springer, Heidelberg (1987). https://doi.org/10.1007/3-540-47721-7_12

23. Fujisaki, E., Suzuki, K.: Traceable ring signature. In: Okamoto, T., Wang, X. (eds.) PKC 2007. LNCS, vol. 4450, pp. 181–200. Springer, Heidelberg (2007). https://doi.org/10.1007/978-3-540-71677-8_13

24. Garms, L., Lehmann, A.: Group signatures with selective linkability. In: Lin, D., Sako, K. (eds.) PKC 2019, Part I. LNCS, vol. 11442, pp. 190–220. Springer, Cham (2019). https://doi.org/10.1007/978-3-030-17253-4_7

25. Gentry, C., Groth, J., Ishai, Y., Peikert, C., Sahai, A., Smith, A.D.: Using fully homomorphic hybrid encryption to minimize non-interactive zero-knowledge proofs. J. Cryptol. **28**(4), 820–843 (2015). https://doi.org/10.1007/s00145-014-9184-y

26. Gentry, C., Peikert, C., Vaikuntanathan, V.: Trapdoors for hard lattices and new cryptographic constructions. In: STOC 2008. ACM (2008)

27. Goldwasser, S., Micali, S., Rackoff, C.: The knowledge complexity of interactive proof-systems. In: STOC 1985, pp. 291–304. ACM (1985)

28. Groth, J.: Fully anonymous group signatures without random oracles. In: Kurosawa, K. (ed.) ASIACRYPT 2007. LNCS, vol. 4833, pp. 164–180. Springer, Heidelberg (2007). https://doi.org/10.1007/978-3-540-76900-2_10

29. Groth, J., Ostrovsky, R., Sahai, A.: Perfect non-interactive zero knowledge for NP. In: Vaudenay, S. (ed.) EUROCRYPT 2006. LNCS, vol. 4004, pp. 339–358. Springer, Heidelberg (2006). https://doi.org/10.1007/11761679_21

30. Groth, J., Sahai, A.: Efficient non-interactive proof systems for bilinear groups. In: Smart, N. (ed.) EUROCRYPT 2008. LNCS, vol. 4965, pp. 415–432. Springer, Heidelberg (2008). https://doi.org/10.1007/978-3-540-78967-3_24

31. Kawachi, A., Tanaka, K., Xagawa, K.: Concurrently secure identification schemes based on the worst-case hardness of lattice problems. In: Pieprzyk, J. (ed.) ASIACRYPT 2008. LNCS, vol. 5350, pp. 372–389. Springer, Heidelberg (2008). https://doi.org/10.1007/978-3-540-89255-7_23

32. Kiayias, A., Tsiounis, Y., Yung, M.: Traceable signatures. In: Cachin, C., Camenisch, J.L. (eds.) EUROCRYPT 2004. LNCS, vol. 3027, pp. 571–589. Springer, Heidelberg (2004). https://doi.org/10.1007/978-3-540-24676-3_34

33. Kiayias, A., Yung, M.: Secure scalable group signature with dynamic joins and separable authorities. Int. J. Secur. Netw. **1**(1/2), 24–45 (2006)

34. Kiltz, E.: Chosen-ciphertext security from tag-based encryption. In: Halevi, S., Rabin, T. (eds.) TCC 2006. LNCS, vol. 3876, pp. 581–600. Springer, Heidelberg (2006). https://doi.org/10.1007/11681878_30

35. Kiltz, E., Pan, J., Wee, H.: Structure-preserving signatures from standard assumptions, revisited. In: Gennaro, R., Robshaw, M. (eds.) CRYPTO 2015, Part II. LNCS, vol. 9216, pp. 275–295. Springer, Heidelberg (2015). https://doi.org/10.1007/978-3-662-48000-7_14

36. Kohlweiss, M., Miers, I.: Accountable metadata-hiding escrow: a group signature case study. In: PoPETs (2015)

37. Libert, B., Ling, S., Mouhartem, F., Nguyen, K., Wang, H.: Signature schemes with efficient protocols and dynamic group signatures from lattice assumptions. In: Cheon, J.H., Takagi, T. (eds.) ASIACRYPT 2016, Part II. LNCS, vol. 10032, pp. 373–403. Springer, Heidelberg (2016). https://doi.org/10.1007/978-3-662-53890-6_13

38. Libert, B., Ling, S., Mouhartem, F., Nguyen, K., Wang, H.: Zero-knowledge arguments for matrix-vector relations and lattice-based group encryption. In: Cheon, J.H., Takagi, T. (eds.) ASIACRYPT 2016, Part II. LNCS, vol. 10032, pp. 101–131. Springer, Heidelberg (2016). https://doi.org/10.1007/978-3-662-53890-6_4

39. Libert, B., Ling, S., Nguyen, K., Wang, H.: Zero-knowledge arguments for lattice-based accumulators: logarithmic-size ring signatures and group signatures without trapdoors. In: Fischlin, M., Coron, J.-S. (eds.) EUROCRYPT 2016, Part II. LNCS, vol. 9666, pp. 1–31. Springer, Heidelberg (2016). https://doi.org/10.1007/978-3-662-49896-5_1

40. Libert, B., Ling, S., Nguyen, K., Wang, H.: Zero-knowledge arguments for lattice-based PRFs and applications to E-cash. In: Takagi, T., Peyrin, T. (eds.) ASIACRYPT 2017, Part III. LNCS, vol. 10626, pp. 304–335. Springer, Cham (2017). https://doi.org/10.1007/978-3-319-70700-6_11

41. Libert, B., Ling, S., Nguyen, K., Wang, H.: Lattice-based zero-knowledge arguments for integer relations. In: Shacham, H., Boldyreva, A. (eds.) CRYPTO 2018, Part II. LNCS, vol. 10992, pp. 700–732. Springer, Cham (2018). https://doi.org/10.1007/978-3-319-96881-0_24

42. Libert, B., Nguyen, K., Peters, T., Yung, M.: Bifurcated signatures: folding the accountability vs. anonymity dilemma into a single private signing scheme. In: Canteaut, A., Standaert, F.-X. (eds.) EUROCRYPT 2021, Part III. LNCS, vol. 12698, pp. 521–552. Springer, Cham (2021). https://doi.org/10.1007/978-3-030-77883-5_18

43. Ling, S., Nguyen, K., Stehlé, D., Wang, H.: Improved zero-knowledge proofs of knowledge for the ISIS problem, and applications. In: Kurosawa, K., Hanaoka, G. (eds.) PKC 2013. LNCS, vol. 7778, pp. 107–124. Springer, Heidelberg (2013). https://doi.org/10.1007/978-3-642-36362-7_8

44. Maji, H.K., Prabhakaran, M., Rosulek, M.: Attribute-based signatures. In: Kiayias, A. (ed.) CT-RSA 2011. LNCS, vol. 6558, pp. 376–392. Springer, Heidelberg (2011). https://doi.org/10.1007/978-3-642-19074-2_24

45. Masur, P.K.: Situational Privacy and Self-Disclosure: Communication Processes in Online Environments. Springer, Cham (2019). https://doi.org/10.1007/978-3-319-78884-5

46. Nandi, M., Pandit, T.: Predicate signatures from pair encodings via dual system proof technique. J. Math. Cryptol. 13(3–4), 197–228 (2019)

47. Noether, S.: Ring signature confidential transactions for Monero. IACR Cryptology ePrint Archive 2015/1098 (2015)

48. Pedersen, T.P.: Non-interactive and information-theoretic secure verifiable secret sharing. In: Feigenbaum, J. (ed.) CRYPTO 1991. LNCS, vol. 576, pp. 129–140. Springer, Heidelberg (1992). https://doi.org/10.1007/3-540-46766-1_9

49. Peikert, C., Shiehian, S.: Noninteractive zero knowledge for NP from (plain) learning with errors. In: Boldyreva, A., Micciancio, D. (eds.) CRYPTO 2019, Part I. LNCS, vol. 11692, pp. 89–114. Springer, Cham (2019). https://doi.org/10.1007/978-3-030-26948-7_4

50. Rivest, R.L., Shamir, A., Tauman, Y.: How to leak a secret. In: Boyd, C. (ed.) ASIACRYPT 2001. LNCS, vol. 2248, pp. 552–565. Springer, Heidelberg (2001). https://doi.org/10.1007/3-540-45682-1_32

51. Sakai, Y., Emura, K., Hanaoka, G., Kawai, Y., Matsuda, T., Omote, K.: Group signatures with message-dependent opening. In: Abdalla, M., Lange, T. (eds.) Pairing 2012. LNCS, vol. 7708, pp. 270–294. Springer, Heidelberg (2013). https://doi.org/10.1007/978-3-642-36334-4_18

52. Stern, J.: A new paradigm for public key identification. IEEE Trans. Inf. Theory 42(6), 1757–1768 (1996)

53. van der Sloot, B., de Groot, A. (eds.): The Handbook of Privacy Studies: An Interdisciplinary Introduction. Amsterdam University Press, Amsterdam (2018)

54. Xu, S., Yung, M.: Accountable ring signatures: a smart card approach. In: Quisquater, J.-J., Paradinas, P., Deswarte, Y., El Kalam, A.A. (eds.) CARDIS 2004. IIFIP, vol. 153, pp. 271–286. Springer, Boston, MA (2004). https://doi.org/10.1007/1-4020-8147-2_18

55. Yang, R., Au, M.H., Zhang, Z., Xu, Q., Yu, Z., Whyte, W.: Efficient lattice-based zero-knowledge arguments with standard soundness: construction and applications. In: Boldyreva, A., Micciancio, D. (eds.) CRYPTO 2019, Part I. LNCS, vol. 11692, pp. 147–175. Springer, Cham (2019). https://doi.org/10.1007/978-3-030-26948-7_6

Author Index

Printed in the United States
by Baker & Taylor Publisher Services

Printed in the United States
by Baker & Taylor Publisher Services